DEVELOPMENTS IN

THEORETICAL AND APPLIED MECHANICS

VOLUME 5

DEVELOPMENTS IN

THEORETICAL AND

APPLIED MECHANICS

Volume 5

Proceedings of the Fifth Southeastern Conference on
Theoretical and Applied Mechanics

*Sponsored by North Carolina State and
Duke Universities*

*Held in
Raleigh-Durham, North Carolina, April 16-17, 1970*

Edited by

GROVER L. ROGERS

Co-Edited by

S. C. KRANC   E. G. HENNEKE
Florida State University

Executive Chairman

P. H. McDONALD, JR.
North Carolina State University

The University of North Carolina Press

Chapel Hill

Manufactured in the United States of America
ISBN 0-8078-1180-7
Library of Congress Catalog Card Number 63-1602

CONTENTS

INVITED LECTURE

BIOMECHANICS

DYNAMICS OF PLATES

WAVE PROPAGATION

PLATES

FOREWORD

Southeastern Conference on Theoretical and Applied Mechanics was organized in 1962 by the Founders, W. L. Greenstreet, R. N. Maxwell, C. H. Parr, C. E. Stoneking, W. A. Shaw, and W. F. Swinson, to stimulate interest in Mechanics in the Southeast by providing an outlet for technical papers on the results of scientific and engineering research of both applied and theoretical nature, and by encouraging informal exchange of ideas in the field of mechanics.

The various sessions of each of the several biennial Conferences have served to fulfill in part the aspirations of the Founders, and it has been the true desire of each of the host institutions that the meetings themselves have, in addition, been pleasant and profitable to those in attendance. But of course the full realization of the potential of the Conference is only achieved in the publication of the Proceedings, and the Founders again displayed their wisdom in setting forth the following policy in the By-Laws.

> "The purpose of publication and the guiding principle in the choice of publication arrangements is the widest possible circulation of the papers presented at the Conference session."

The four preceding SECTAMS have served to establish a high order of quality in terms of papers submitted, papers accepted and presented, and papers published, as well as interesting meetings. Each Conference has displayed its own uniqueness, and yet each has, in its own way, held to the central heritage of its reason for being.

It is the sincere wish of those responsible for Fifth SECTAM that it will have measured up to these expectations of Founders, authors, and attendees, and that there may be many others who will profit also by these Proceedings.

We wish to record our appreciation to those who have contributed so much to our effort: to the Founders for their vision and continuing support; the Past Chairmen for their legacy; Dean R. E. Fadum for financial assistance and institutional cooperation; Editorial Committee members for their labors and superior judgment; Reviewers for their willingness to serve; Session Chairmen for their judiciousness; the

Executive Committee for its cooperation. Much gratitude is due to Messrs. M. E. Starnes, H. M. Eckerlin, C. Akkoç, B. H. Garcia, M. H. Clayton, R. A. Douglas, J. B. Miller, E. D. Gurley and C. M. Chang, and in addition to Mrs. Mia Vesiç, Mrs. Virginia McDonald, and Mrs. Nancy Stout.

Our very special thanks are owed to Professors E. G. Henneke and S. C. Kranc for a superior performance, and to Professor J. F. Wilson for things shared only by Co-Chairmen.

We trust that our appreciation of the contributions of our friend Dean Grover L. Rogers is noted in the dedication of this volume to his memory.

North Carolina State University
Raleigh, North Carolina

P. H. McDonald, Jr.
Executive Chairman

PREFACE

The Fifth Southeastern Conference on Theoretical and Applied Mechanics was held April 16 and 17, 1970, at North Carolina State University at Raleigh, and Duke University at Durham, North Carolina. The Executive Committee was composed of

P. H. McDonald, Executive Chairman
North Carolina State University

J. F. Wilson, Co-Chairman
Duke University

J. E. Griffith, Vice-Chairman
University of South Florida

E. D. Gurley, Secretary
North Carolina State University

G. L. Rogers, Editorial Chairman
Florida State University

E. H. Harris
Tulane University

J. D. Waugh
University of South Carolina

D. Frederick
Virginia Polytechnic Institute

Members of the Editorial Committee were:

Grover L. Rogers, Chairman
Florida State University

Helmut F. Bauer
Georgia Institute of Technology

Daniel Frederick
Virginia Polytechnic Institute

Barry I. Hyman
George Washington University

Norman C. Small
University of South Florida

Forty-four papers were presented, including two invited lectures. There were over 200 registrants participating in the conference.

The program follows.

THURSDAY, APRIL 16, 1970 MORNING SESSION

VISCOUS FLOWS

J. Parker Lamb, Chairman
University of Texas

"Application of Boundary Layer Concepts to Turbulent Lubrication Theory of Bearings and Seals"
William T. Snyder, University of Tennessee Space Institute
William K. Stair, University of Tennessee

"Damping Characteristics of a Liquid Squeeze Film"
Takeya Yabe, Japan
Phillip K. Davis, Southern Illinois University

"Laminar Flow in an Annulus with Porous Outer Wall"
M. S. Tsai
Colorado State University
H. L. Weissberg
University of Tennessee

"Unsteady Spherical Couette Flow"
Phillip R. Smith and Michel Charles
New Mexico State University

SANDWICH MATERIAL

N. C. Small, Chairman
University of South Florida

"Symmetrical and Antisymmetrical Wrinkling"
I. K. Ebcioglu and S. J. Kim
University of Florida

"Theory of Micropolar Sandwich Plates"
M. Cengiz Dokmeci
Cornell University

"A Sandwiched Layer of Dissimilar Material Weakened by Cracklike Imperfection"
P. D. Hilton and G. C. Sih
Lehigh University

"Internal Buckling of a Laminated Medium"
J. Kiusalaas and W. Jaunzemis
Pennsylvania State University

DYNAMICS

Helmut Bauer, Chairman
Georgia Institute of Technology

"A Theoretical and Experimental Investigation of Impact Loads in Stranded Steel Cables during Longitudinal Excitation"
Jacques F. Goeller, U. S. Naval Ordnunce Laboratory
Patricio A. Laura, Catholic University of America

"Some Properties Pertaining to the Stability of Circulatory Systems"
I. C. Jong
University of Arkansas

"Numerical Solution of the Mean First-Passage-Time for the Snap-Through of Shells"
H. N. Pi, S. T. Ariaratnam, and W. C. Lennox
University of Waterloo

"Fluid Oscillations in a Partially-Filled Cylindrical Tank with a Spring-Supported Elastic Floor"
Julius Siekmann and Shih-chih Chang
Georgia Institute of Technology

THURSDAY, APRIL 16, 1970 AFTERNOON SESSIONS

Invited Lecture: "Cancer: An Unstable Biodynamic Field"
Okan Gurel
IBM New York Scientific Center

BIOMECHANICS

E. F. Byars, Chairman
West Virginia University

"Forced Axisymmetric Response of Fluid-Filled Spherical Shells"
Y. C. Lee and S. H. Advani
West Virginia University

"Oscillatory Flow of a Viscous Fluid in a Flexible Walled Two-Dimensional Channel"
M. Varner and B. Ross
University of South Florida

"Cylindrical Bones as Anisotropic Poroelastic Members Subjected to Hydrostatic Pressure"
J. L. Nowinski
University of Delaware

DYNAMICS OF PLATES

A. Vesiç, Chairman
Duke University

"Impact Waves in Elastic Plates"
William F. Hartman
Johns Hopkins University

"The Effect of an Elastic Edge Restraint on the Forced Vibration of a Rectangular Plate"
F. D. Henry and M. Egle
University of Oklahoma

"The Dynamic Characteristics of Clamped Rectangular Plates of Orthotropic Material"
James E. Ashton
General Dynamics

WAVE PROPAGATION

M. Stippes, Chairman
University of Illinois

"A Study of Thermoelastic Waves by the Method of Characteristics"
A. A. Lopez and H. W. Lord
Michigan Technological University

"Wave Propagation in Two Joined Elastic Quarter-Spaces"
L. M. Brock and
J. D. Achenbach
Northwestern University

"Propagation and Attenuation of Harmonic Waves in a Viscoelastic Circular Cylinder"
J. L. Lai
B. F. Goodrich Company
T. R. Tauchert and
E. H. Dowell
Princeton University

FRIDAY, APRIL 17, 1970 MORNING SESSIONS

PLATES

D. L. Dean, Chairman
North Carolina State University

"Infinite Plate with a Supported Reinforced Circular Hole"
R. Amon and O. E. Widera
University of Illinois

"On the Contact of Axisymmetric Plates of Variable Thickness"
M. B. McGrath and
F. Essenburg
University of Colorado

"Elastic Stability of Folded Plate Structures"
S. E. Swartz and
S. A. Guralnick
Kansas State University

"Application of Conformal Transformation to Variational Method-Buckling Loads of Polygonal Plates"
James C. M. Yu
Auburn University

CONTINUUM MECHANICS

Daniel Frederick, Chairman
Virginia Polytechnic Institute

"A Non-Linear Integral-Type Theory of Inelasticity for Transversely Isotropic Materials"
Robert D. Snyder and T. L. Ho
West Virginia University
Alvin Strauss
University of Kentucky

"On the Role of Density Gradients in the Continuum Theory of Mixtures"
G. A. Ramirez and S. T. Wu
University of Alabama

"Dynamic Response of Viscoelastic Fluid Lines"
Wen-Jei Yang
University of Michigan

"On the Numerical Solution of a Class of Non-Linear Problems in Dynamic Coupled Thermoelasticity"
J. T. Oden and J. Poe
University of Alabama

BARS

Furman W. Barton, Chairman
University of Virginia

"Stability of Parametrically Excited Vibrations of an Elastic Rod"
Edward C. Haight, MITRE Corp.
Wilton W. King
Georgia Institute of Technology

"Nonstationary Parametric Response of a Non-Linear Column"
R. M. Evan-Iwanowski and
W. F. Sanford
Syracuse University
T. Kehagioglou, IBM, New York

"A Comparison of Initial Velocities for Dynamic Instability of a Shallow Arch"
C. H. Popelar
Ohio State University
G. M. Abraham
Bell Telephone Laboratories, Inc.

"Axial-Symmetric Deformations of a Rubber-Like Cylinder Under Initial Stress"
C. T. Sun
Iowa State University

Invited Lecture: "Some Problems in Astroelasticity"
Yi-Yuan Yu
General Electric Company

FRIDAY, APRIL 17, 1970 AFTERNOON SESSIONS

FLUID DYNAMICS

T. S. Chang, Chairman
North Carolina State University

"A Note on Flow Over a Flat Plate"
Arsev H. Eraslan
University of Tennessee
John A. Benek, University of Tennessee Space Institute

"A Comparison of the Solutions of Prandtl's and Navier-Stokes Equations in a Superposed Fluctuating Flow"
Z. U. A. Warsi
Mississippi State University

"On the Intrinsic Representation of Flows with Lamb Surfaces"
S. L. Passman
U. S. Naval Academy

MATERIAL BEHAVIOR

W. L. Greenstreet, Chairman
Oak Ridge National Laboratory

"Effect of Fiber End, Fiber Orientation and Spacing in Composite Materials"
Hui Pih and David R. Sutliff
University of Tennessee

"On Strain Energy and Constitutive Relations for Alkali Metals"
J. Eftis, G. M. Arkilic and D. C. MacDonald
George Washington University

"Viscoelastic Analysis of Graphite under Neutron Irradiation and Temperature Distribution"
Shih-Jung Chang, C. E. Pugh and S. E. Moore, Oak Ridge National Laboratory

SHELLS

B. I. Hyman, Chairman
George Washington University

"On the Transient Response of a Closed Spherical Shell to a Local Radial Impulse"
Ali E. Engin
University of Michigan

"On the Accuracy and Application of the Point Matching Method for Shallow Shells"
Arthur W. Leissa and
Abdel S. Kadi
Ohio State University

"A Proof of the Accuracy of a Set of Simplified Buckling Equations for Circular Cylindrical Elastic Shells"
D. A. Danielson and
J. G. Simmonds
University of Virginia

REVIEWERS FOR FIFTH SECTAM

O. R. Ainsworth	University of Alabama
T. Ariman	University of Notre Dame
Ozer A. Arnas	Robert College (Turkey)
Cecil D. Bailey	Ohio State University
Allen R. Barbin	Auburn University
W. L. Bingham	North Carolina State University
Paul J. Blatz	North American Rockwell
P. A. Blythe	Lehigh University
Arthur P. Boresi	University of Illinois
H. F. Brinson	Virginia Polytechnic Institute
Ed F. Byars	West Virginia University
J. P. Callahan	Oak Ridge National Laboratory
H. H. Calvit	University of Texas
C. H. Chang	University of Alabama
Shih-Jung Chang	Oak Ridge National Laboratory
W. H. Chu	Southwest Research Institute
M. H. Clayton	North Carolina State University
J. M. Corum	Oak Ridge National Laboratory
F. R. E. Crossley	University of Massachusetts
J. W. Dally	Illinois Institute of Technology
R. T. Davis	Virginia Polytechnic Institute
Samuel DeLeeuw	University of Mississippi
O. Dillon	University of Kentucky
J. Dundurs	Northwestern University
J. Dvorak	Duke University
A. J. Edmondson	University of Tennessee
Richard T. Eppink	University of Virginia
Arsev H. Eraslan	University of Tennessee
R. M. Evan-Iwanowski	Syracuse University
David C. Feng	University of Colorado
W. B. Fichter	NASA - Langley
Bert H. Garcia	North Carolina State University
W. Goldsmith	University of California
D. L. Guell	University of Missouri
Edward Huag	University of Iowa
James L. Hill	University of Texas
W. H. Hoppmann, II	University of South Carolina
Henry F. Hrubecky	Tulane University
William C. L. Hu	University of California
Ronald L. Huston	University of Cincinnati
Peter F. Jordan	Martin Marietta Corporation
Daniel D. Kana	Southwest Research Institute
W. W. King	Georgia Institute of Technology
Ray Kinslow	Tennessee Technological University
William L. Ko	Southwest Research Institute
R. H. Lance	Cornell University
L. H. N. Lee	University of Notre Dame
D. C. Leigh	University of Kentucky
A. W. Leissa	Ohio State University
Chi-Wen Lin	Westinghouse Electric Corporation
Y. K. Lin	University of Illinois
U. S. Lindholm	Southwest Research Institute

K. C. Liu	Oak Ridge National Laboratory
Robert R. Long	Johns Hopkins University
Lawrence R. Mack	University of Texas
A. W. Marris	Georgia Institute of Technology
K. G. McConnell	Iowa State University
Robert E. Miller	University of Illinois
Bruce J. Muga	Duke University
T. Mura	National Bureau of Standards
R. E. Nickell	Bell Telephone Laboratories
J. L. Nowinski	University of Delaware
E. T. Onat	Yale University
S. I. Pai	University of Maryland
Fred N. Peebles	University of Tennessee
Aris Phillips	Yale University
Daniel Post	Photolastic, Inc.
C. E. Pugh	Oak Ridge National Laboratory
M. E. Raville	Georgia Institute of Technology
Joe W. Reece	Auburn University
E. Reissner	Massachusetts Institute of Technology
M. K. Richardson	Clemson University
William F. Riley	Iowa State University
B. E. Ross	University of South Florida
Vireschwar Sahai	Tennessee Technological University
W. Schnell	Lehrstuhl für Mechanik (Germany)
W. N. Sharpe	Michigan State University
J. Siekmann	Georgia Institute of Technology
R. L. Sierakowski	University of Florida
George C. Sih	Lehigh University
Robert D. Snyder	University of West Virginia
W. T. Snyder	University of Tennessee Space Institute
J. Somerset	Syracuse University
F. Y. Sorrell	North Carolina State University
Kenneth A. Stead	University of Mississippi
K. K. Stevens	Ohio State University
M. Stippes	University of Illinois
C. E. Stoneking	Georgia Institute of Technology
C. E. Taylor	University of Illinois
J. F. Thorpe	University of Cincinnati
K. N. Tong	Syracuse University
John R. Uldrick	U. S. Naval Academy
K. C. Valanis	University of Iowa
Milton Van Dyke	Stanford University
James Ting-Shun Wang	Georgia Institute of Technology
George R. Webb	Tulane University
Frank M. White	University of Rhode Island
J. F. Wilson	Duke University
Don J. Wood	University of Kentucky
James H. Woodward	University of Alabama
Hsiang-Yueh Yeh	Prairie View A & M College
C. S. Yih	University of Michigan
Yi-Yuan Yu	General Electric Company

The response by authors and registrants to the Conference was most gratifying. Unfortunately, we could not accept many good papers which were submitted to the Conference because of size limitations, and would like to take this opportunity to thank all those authors for their interest.

We express our appreciation to the editorial committee and the many able reviewers for their assistance and advice, and to Dr. P. H. McDonald and the members of the executive committee for their help and cooperation. A special word of thanks is due to Mrs. Frances Tavolieri, our devoted secretary, for her long hours of service.

We have dedicated this volume to the editor, Grover L. Rogers, who worked unstintingly to plan the editorial work of the conference. His untimely death on June 29, 1970, left all of us with a feeling of great loss.

Florida State University
Tallahassee, Florida

S. C. Kranc
E. G. Henneke
Co-Editors

I N M E M O R I A M

GROVER L. ROGERS

Editor and Editorial Chairman
Fifth Southeastern Conference on
Theoretical and Applied Mechanics

Dean of The School of Engineering Science
Florida State University

V I S C O U S   F L O W S

APPLICATION OF BOUNDARY LAYER CONCEPTS TO TURBULENT LUBRICATION THEORY OF BEARINGS AND SEALS

William T. Snyder
The University of Tennessee Space Institute

William K. Stair
The University of Tennessee

ABSTRACT

As part of a long range effort to contribute to the development of a viable theory of turbulent lubrication of bearings and seals, the linear slider bearing is analyzed for turbulent flow including inertia effects. The governing equations are the boundary layer equations and are integrated numerically by using an implicit finite difference approximation. Numerical results are obtained for the load capacity, friction power loss, and location of maximum pressure. It is concluded that the concepts and methods of analysis of boundary layer theory are applicable to the theory of turbulent lubrication of bearings and seals.

LIST OF NOTATIONS

A(m,n)	Finite difference equation coefficient, Eq. (16)
B(m,n)	Finite difference equation coefficient, Eq. (17)
C	Empirical mixing length constant, Eq. (6)
$\bar{C}$	Dimensionless mixing length constant, Eq. (7)
C(m,n)	Finite difference equation coefficient, Eq. (18)
FPL	Friction power loss, Eq. (28)
$\overline{FPL}$	Dimensionless friction power loss, Eq. (29)
G(m,n)	Finite difference equation coefficient, Eq. (19)
h	Film thickness, Figure 1
$\bar{h}$	Dimensionless film thickness, Eq. (7)

h_1, h_2	Maximum and minimum film thickness, Figure 1
ℓ	Mixing length, Eq. (6)
LO	Load capacity, Eq. (26)
$\overline{LO}$	Dimensionless load capacity, Eq. (27)
m,n	Nodal point identification, Figure 2
P	Pressure
$\bar{P}$	Dimensionless pressure, $P/\rho U^2$
Re	Reynolds number, $\rho UL/\mu$
Re*	Reduced Reynolds number, $(\rho U h_1/\mu)(h_1/x_1-x_2)$
TR	Thickness ratio, h_2/h_1
u	x-velocity component
$\bar{u}$	Dimensionless x-velocity component, Eq. (7)
U	Slider surface velocity
v	y-velocity component
$\bar{v}$	Dimensionless y-velocity component, Eq. (7)
x	Space coordinate parallel to slider motion
$\bar{x}$	Dimensionless x-coordinate, Eq. (7)
x_1, x_2	Coordinates of ends of bearing, Figure 1
y	Space coordinate across film
$\bar{y}$	Dimensionless y-coordinate, Eq. (7)
α	Slider surface inclination, Figure 1
$\Delta\bar{x}, \Delta\bar{y}$	Finite difference increments, Figure 2
ρ	Density
μ	Viscosity

INTRODUCTION

In a recent review paper, Kulinski and Ostrach [1] presented a critical evaluation of the status of the theory of high speed fluid film lubrication. The term "high speed fluid film lubrication" refers to operating conditions of high speed and/or low viscosity such that turbulence and inertia must be included in the analysis. As indicated by the above authors, a viable theory of turbulent lubrication is not available at the present time.

Most of the efforts made to develop a theory of turbulent lubrication have been based on an extension of the equations of motion of classical lubrication theory to include the turbulent stresses.

Classical lubrication theory neglects the inertia terms in the equations of motion. A number of theoretical analyses of turbulent lubrication have been published [2-9] for both the slider bearing and journal bearing geometries. Sneck [10] considered the effect of turbulent flow on the performance of the face seal, a geometry of particular interest as a later extension of the present study. All of these analyses are similar in that they neglect the inertia terms, differing only in the assumptions made concerning the variation of the turbulent stress across the film.

It is pointed out by an order of magnitude analysis in Ref. [1] that it is incorrect to neglect the inertia terms in the equations of motion for turbulent lubrication. The reason for this is clear from a physical point of view. The presence of turbulence in a flow results from the fact that the viscous stresses are not sufficiently large to damp small disturbances in the flow. Thus turbulence is a large Reynolds number phenomenon, and if the Reynolds number in a lubricant film is large enough to result in turbulence, then it is large enough for the inertia terms to become important.

Most of the analyses cited above treat the turbulent shear stress by some version of the Prandtl mixing length theory, differing primarily in the degree of sophistication used to describe the variation of the mixing length across the fluid film. The limitation of the mixing length theory to describe turbulent shear flows has been known for some time. In a mixing length model, convection and diffusion of turbulent kinetic energy are neglected resulting in a limitation which is inherent in the mixing length model and cannot be circumvented by using more sophisticated descriptions of the mixing length. In recent years newer theories of turbulent shear flow have been developed [11, 12] which include the convection and diffusion of turbulent kinetic energy. To date these newer turbulent theories have not been applied to lubrication problems.

Another aspect of turbulent lubrication theory which has not been resolved satisfactorily is the question of stability, i.e., the conditions under which a high speed lubricant film is likely to undergo transition from laminar to turbulent flow. For the journal bearing geometry, the prediction of the onset of turbulence has been based on the classical instability analysis of G. I. Taylor [13] for circumferential flow between rotating, concentric cylinders. As pointed out in Ref. [1], Taylor's analysis was for the prediction of the onset of a secondary vortex flow regime and not turbulence. In any event, the analysis of Taylor was for a concentric geometry, and the analysis should be extended to the eccentric case, the geometry encountered in a journal bearing configuration. Efforts along this line have been made by Di Prima [14, 15] and Kulinski and Ostrach [16].

In initiating the present study of turbulent lubrication, two aspects of turbulent lubrication theory were identified in which it was felt that additional effort is needed.

1) Any theory of turbulent lubrication must include the inertia terms as indicated by the order of magnitude analysis of Ref. [1]. The inclusion of the inertia terms becomes feasible by utilizing a high speed digital computer and the numerical techniques which have been developed and successfully applied in solving the boundary layer equations in recent years.

2) The basic physical limitation of the mixing length theory of turbulence must be recognized and improved. This limitation arises from the neglect of convection and diffusion of turbulent kinetic energy, effects which are likely to be important in high speed, high shear rate bearing and seal films. The newer theories of turbulent shear flows, particularly those developed by Bradshaw et al. [11] and Kovasznay et al. [12] should be incorporated into a theory of turbulent lubrication.

In the present investigation, an effort is made to extend the current status of turbulent lubrication theory by application of concepts and numerical techniques of modern boundary layer theory. The geometry considered in the present study is the infinite slider bearing (no side leakage) which is chosen for convenience and to allow the emphasis to be placed on the physical aspects of the problem. The performance of face seals and viscoseals with turbulence and inertia effects is of particular interest, and the present work will be extended in the future to include these geometries.

Governing Equations for the Linear Slider Bearing

The geometry of the linear slider bearing is shown in Figure 1. The linear geometry is chosen for convenience since it is well known that

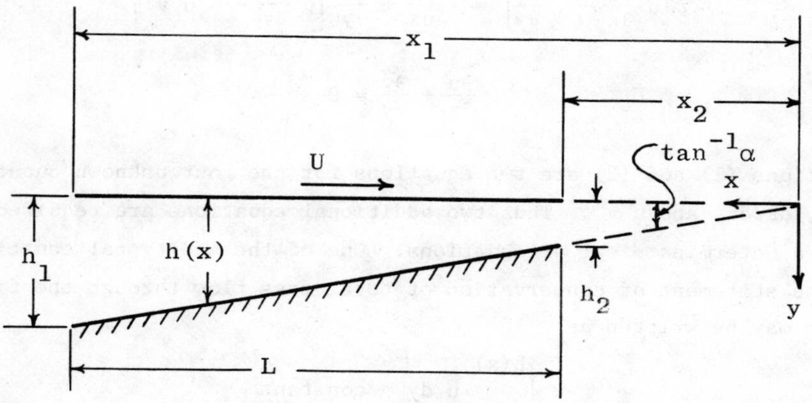

Fig. 1. Linear Slider Bearing Geometry.

the load capacity of a slider bearing depends primarily on the ratio of maximum to minimum film thickness and is only slightly dependent on the shape of the film [17]. The large Reynolds number limit or boundary layer form of the equations of motion will be assumed to be valid in describing the hydrodynamics of the film.

The governing equations, in dimensional form are

$$\rho\left(u\frac{\partial u}{\partial x} + v\frac{\partial u}{\partial y}\right) = -\frac{dP}{dx} + \frac{\partial}{\partial y}\left[\mu\frac{\partial u}{\partial y} - \rho\,\overline{u'v'}\right] \tag{1}$$

$$\frac{\partial u}{\partial x} + \frac{\partial v}{\partial y} = 0 \tag{2}$$

Equations (1) and (2) are two equations for the four unknown quantities u, v, dP/dx, and $\overline{u'v'}$. Thus two additional equations are required to give a determinate set of equations. One of the additional equations is the statement of conservation of total mass flow through the film which may be written as

$$\int_0^{h(x)} u\,dy = \text{constant} \tag{3}$$

Differentiating Eq. (3) and applying the Leibnitz rule for differentiating an integral with a variable limit gives the equivalent form

$$\int_0^{h(x)} \frac{\partial u}{\partial x}\,dy = 0 \tag{4}$$

Equation (4) is more convenient to apply in a numerical treatment than Eq. (3).

The remaining equation to be supplied is the modeling of the Reynolds stress, $-\rho\,\overline{u'v'}$: By modeling is meant the making of a suitable assumption which relates the Reynolds stress to the mean flow. The most widely used model for describing the Reynolds stress is the Prandtl mixing length model. In this model, the relation between the Reynolds stress and the mean flow is

$$-\rho\,\overline{u'v'} = \rho\ell^2\left|\frac{\partial u}{\partial y}\right|\frac{\partial u}{\partial y} \tag{5}$$

where ℓ is the mixing length, a function of y. Prandtl assumed that ℓ varies linearly with distance from the wall in a turbulent boundary layer. Since the Reynolds stress must vanish at a solid boundary, ℓ must be zero at a solid boundary. Chou and Saibel [4] assumed an ℓ variation for the slider bearing of the form

$$\rho\ell^2 = C^2 y(h - y) \tag{6}$$

where C is a constant the value of which must be determined from experiment. Since the emphasis in the present investigation is on the development of numerical techniques for applying the turbulent boundary layer equations to turbulent lubrication, the above mixing length model will be assumed for convenience. Future extensions of the present investigation are planned using different turbulent models.

For the slider bearing geometry it is convenient to define dimensionless quantities as follows.

$$\bar{u} = -\frac{u}{U}, \quad \bar{v} = \left(\frac{1 - \frac{h_2}{h_1}}{\alpha}\right)\frac{v}{U}, \quad \bar{x} = \frac{x - x_1}{x_2 - x_1}, \quad \bar{y} = \frac{y}{h(x)}$$

$$\bar{P} = \frac{P}{\rho U^2}, \quad \bar{h}(\bar{x}) = \frac{h(x)}{h_1} = 1 - \left(1 - \frac{h_2}{h_1}\right)\bar{x}, \quad \bar{C} = \frac{C^2 U h_1}{\mu} \tag{7}$$

The dimensionless equations then become

$$\bar{u}\frac{\partial\bar{u}}{\partial\bar{x}} + \frac{\bar{y}}{\bar{h}}\left(1 - \frac{h_2}{h_1}\right)\bar{u}\frac{\partial\bar{u}}{\partial\bar{y}} + \frac{\bar{v}}{\bar{h}}\frac{\partial\bar{u}}{\partial\bar{y}} = -\frac{d\bar{P}}{d\bar{x}} + \frac{1}{Re^*\bar{h}^2}\frac{\partial^2\bar{u}}{\partial\bar{y}^2}$$

$$+ \frac{\bar{C}}{Re^*\bar{h}}\frac{\partial}{\partial\bar{y}}\left[\bar{y}(1 - \bar{y})\left|\frac{\partial\bar{u}}{\partial\bar{y}}\right|\frac{\partial\bar{u}}{\partial\bar{y}}\right] \tag{8}$$

$$\frac{\partial\bar{u}}{\partial\bar{x}} + \frac{\bar{y}}{\bar{h}}\left(1 - \frac{h_2}{h_1}\right)\frac{\partial\bar{u}}{\partial\bar{y}} + \frac{1}{\bar{h}}\frac{\partial\bar{v}}{\partial\bar{y}} = 0 \tag{9}$$

$$\int_0^1 \left[\frac{\partial\bar{u}}{\partial\bar{x}} + \frac{\bar{y}}{\bar{h}}\left(1 - \frac{h_2}{h_1}\right)\frac{\partial\bar{u}}{\partial\bar{y}}\right]d\bar{y} = 0 \tag{10}$$

where

$$Re^* = \left(\frac{\rho U h_1}{\mu}\right)\left(\frac{h_1}{x_1 - x_2}\right)$$

is the reduced Reynolds number.

Equations (8), (9), and (10) are three equations for the three unknowns $\bar{u}$, $\bar{v}$, and $d\bar{P}/d\bar{x}$. An equivalent equation for determining $d\bar{P}/d\bar{x}$ can be obtained instead of Eq. (10) by integrating the equation of motion across the channel with the result

$$\frac{d\bar{P}}{d\bar{x}} = \frac{1}{Re^{*}\bar{h}^2}\left[\frac{\partial\bar{u}}{\partial\bar{y}}\Big)_{\bar{y}=1} - \frac{\partial\bar{u}}{\partial\bar{y}}\Big)_{\bar{y}=0}\right] - \int_0^1 \frac{\partial\bar{u}^2}{\partial\bar{x}}\,d\bar{y} + \frac{1}{\bar{h}}\left(1 - \frac{h_2}{h_1}\right)\int_0^1 \bar{u}^2\,d\bar{y} \tag{11}$$

Equation (11) was found by experience to be a more convenient equation for calculating the pressure gradient at each $\bar{x}$ location where velocity profiles were calculated.

Solution by Finite Difference Method

Finite Difference Form of Equations / The dimensionless equations describing the linear slider bearing for turbulent flow including inertia are given by Eqs. (8)-(11). Because of the strongly nonlinear character of the equation of motion, the only feasible approach to obtaining a solution is a numerical approach. In the present analysis, an implicit finite difference approach is used.

The film region is transformed into a rectangular region in the dimensionless $(\bar{x},\bar{y})$ space where $\bar{x}$ and $\bar{y}$ are defined by Eq. (7). The ranges of variation of the two independent variables are $0 \leq \bar{x} \leq 1$ and $0 \leq \bar{y} \leq 1$. The rectangular region is covered with a set of grid lines as shown in Figure 2. The velocity profile and pressure gradient are considered to be known at column (n) and it is desired to calculate the velocity profile and pressure gradient at column n+1. A central difference formula is used for the $\bar{y}$ derivatives and a backward difference formula for the $\bar{x}$ derivatives with the finite difference equations evaluated at nodal point (m, n+1).

The $\bar{y}$ derivative of the absolute value of a function is required also since $\left|\frac{\partial\bar{u}}{\partial\bar{y}}\right|$ appears in Eq. (8). Noting that $|f| = \sqrt{f^2}$, we may write

$$\frac{\partial|f|}{\partial\bar{y}} = \frac{\partial\sqrt{f^2}}{\partial\bar{y}} = \frac{f}{|f|}\frac{\partial f}{\partial\bar{y}} \tag{12}$$

The derivatives appearing in the turbulent term of Eq. (8) may be manipulated by the chain rule of partial differentiation as follows.

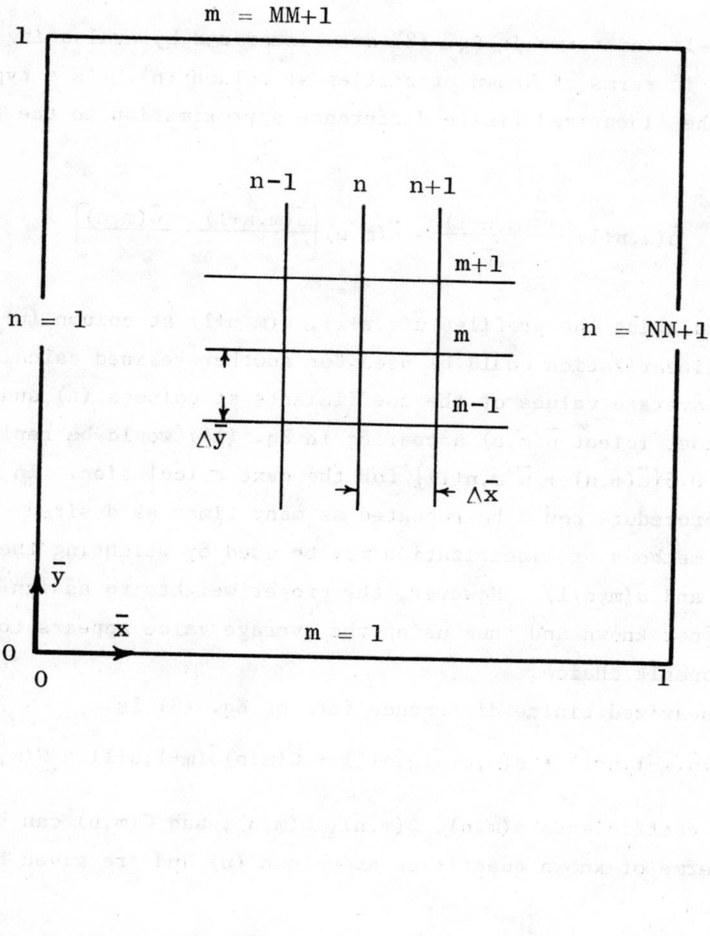

Fig. 2. Finite Difference Grid Geometry.

$$\frac{\partial}{\partial \bar{y}}\left[\bar{y}(1-\bar{y})\left|\frac{\partial \bar{u}}{\partial \bar{y}}\right|\frac{\partial \bar{u}}{\partial \bar{y}}\right] = (1-2\bar{y})\left|\frac{\partial \bar{u}}{\partial \bar{y}}\right|\frac{\partial \bar{u}}{\partial \bar{y}}$$

$$+\ \bar{y}(1-\bar{y})\left[\left|\frac{\partial \bar{u}}{\partial \bar{y}}\right|\frac{\partial^2 \bar{u}}{\partial \bar{y}^2} + \frac{\partial \bar{u}}{\partial \bar{y}}\frac{\partial}{\partial \bar{y}}\left|\frac{\partial \bar{u}}{\partial \bar{y}}\right|\right]$$

$$= \left|\frac{\partial \bar{u}}{\partial \bar{y}}\right|\left[(1-2\bar{y})\frac{\partial \bar{u}}{\partial \bar{y}} + 2\bar{y}(1-\bar{y})\frac{\partial^2 \bar{u}}{\partial \bar{y}^2}\right] \tag{13}$$

The non-linear terms in Eq. (8) are linearized by evaluating the coefficients in terms of known properties at column (n). As a typical example, the linearized finite difference approximation to the term $\bar{u}\frac{\partial \bar{u}}{\partial \bar{x}}$ is

$$\bar{u}(m,n+1)\ \frac{\partial \bar{u}(m,n+1)}{\partial \bar{x}} = \bar{u}(m,n)\left[\frac{\bar{u}(m,n+1) - \bar{u}(m,n)}{\Delta \bar{x}}\right] \tag{14}$$

After calculating the profiles $\bar{u}(m,n+1)$, $\bar{v}(m,n+1)$ at column (n+1), an improved linearization could be used for another refined calculation by using the average values of the coefficients at columns (n) and (n+1). Thus the coefficient $\bar{u}(m,n)$ appearing in Eq. (14) would be replaced by the value $0.5\left(\bar{u}(m,n) + \bar{u}(m,n+1)\right)$ for the next calculation. In principle this procedure could be repeated as many times as desired. More elaborate methods of linearization may be used by weighting the values of $\bar{u}(m,n)$ and $\bar{u}(m,n+1)$. However, the proper weights to assign the two values is not known and thus using the average value appears to be the most reasonable choice.

The linearized finite difference form of Eq. (8) is

$$A(m,n)\bar{u}(m-1,n+1) + B(m,n)\bar{u}(m,n+1) + C(m,n)\bar{u}(m+1,n+1) = G(m,n) \tag{15}$$

where the coefficients A(m,n), B(m,n), C(m,n), and G(m,n) can be evaluated in terms of known quantities at column (n) and are given by the expressions

$$A(m,n) = (1-TR)\frac{\bar{y}\bar{u}(m,n)}{2\bar{h}\Delta\bar{y}} + \frac{\bar{v}(m,n)}{2\bar{h}\Delta\bar{y}} + \frac{1}{Re^*\bar{h}^2\Delta\bar{y}^2}$$

$$-\ \frac{\bar{C}}{Re^*\bar{h}}\left[\frac{1-2\bar{y}}{2\Delta\bar{y}} - \frac{2\bar{y}(1-\bar{y})}{\Delta\bar{y}^2}\right]\left|\frac{\bar{u}(m+1,n) - \bar{u}(m-1,n)}{2\Delta\bar{y}}\right| \tag{16}$$

$$B(m,n) = -\frac{\bar{u}(m,n)}{\Delta\bar{x}} - \frac{2}{Re^*\bar{h}^2\Delta\bar{y}^2}$$

$$-\frac{\bar{C}}{Re^*\bar{h}}\left[\frac{4\bar{y}(1-\bar{y})}{\Delta\bar{y}^2}\right]\left|\frac{\bar{u}(m+1,n) - \bar{u}(m-1,n)}{2\Delta\bar{y}}\right| \tag{17}$$

$$C(m,n) = -(1 - TR)\frac{\overline{\bar{y}\bar{u}}(m,n)}{2\bar{h}\Delta\bar{y}} - \frac{\bar{v}(m,n)}{2\bar{h}\Delta\bar{y}} + \frac{1}{Re^*\bar{h}^2\Delta\bar{y}^2}$$

$$+\frac{\bar{C}}{Re^*\bar{h}}\left[\frac{1-2\bar{y}}{2\Delta\bar{y}} + \frac{2\bar{y}(1-\bar{y})}{\Delta\bar{y}^2}\right]\left|\frac{\bar{u}(m+1,n) - \bar{u}(m-1,n)}{2\Delta\bar{y}}\right| \tag{18}$$

$$G(m,n) = \frac{d\bar{P}(n)}{d\bar{x}} - \frac{[\bar{u}(m,n)]^2}{\Delta\bar{x}} \tag{19}$$

It should be noted that the pressure gradient at column (n) is used in the equation of motion to solve for velocity profiles at column (n+1). After the velocity profiles have been calculated at column (n+1), the pressure gradient $d\bar{P}(n+1)/d\bar{x}$ is then determined by a method to be discussed later. Improved values of the profiles at column (n+1) could be obtained by using the average value of $d\bar{P}/d\bar{x}$ at column (n+1) and column (n), the same procedure discussed earlier for improving the linearization of the coefficients A(m,n), B(m,n), C(m,n) by using the average of the velocities at columns (n) and (n+1).

If the film region $0 \le \bar{y} \le 1$ is divided into M strips (M+1 mesh lines including both boundaries), Eq. (15) represents a set of linear algebraic equations to be solved simultaneously for the M-1 unknown values of velocity $\bar{u}(m,n+1)$, $2 \le m \le M$. The coefficient matrix of the unknowns is tridiagonal, a fact that avoids the necessity of inverting a large matrix. A recurrence relation can be developed which involves only algebraic operations at each step of the calculation.

After the velocities $\bar{u}(m,n+1)$ have been calculated and stored at column n+1, the transverse velocity component $\bar{v}(m,n+1)$ is determined from the continuity equation in integral form

$$\bar{v}(\bar{y}) = -\bar{h}\int_0^{\bar{y}} \frac{\partial\bar{u}}{\partial\bar{x}}\, d\bar{y}' - (1-TR)\left[\overline{\bar{y}\bar{u}} - \int_0^{\bar{y}} \bar{u}d\bar{y}'\right] \tag{20}$$

Evaluation of the Pressure Gradient / The pressure gradient at column (n+1) can be evaluated by integrating the equation of motion across the channel. Multiplying Eq. (9), the continuity equation, by $\bar{u}$ and adding the result to Eq. (8), the equation of motion, gives

$$\frac{\partial \bar{u}^2}{\partial \bar{x}} + \frac{\bar{y}}{\bar{h}}(1-TR)\frac{\partial \bar{u}^2}{\partial \bar{y}} + \frac{1}{\bar{h}}\frac{\partial \bar{u}\bar{v}}{\partial \bar{y}} = -\frac{d\bar{P}}{d\bar{x}} + \frac{1}{Re^*\bar{h}^2}\frac{\partial^2 \bar{u}}{\partial \bar{y}}$$

$$+ \frac{\bar{C}}{Re^*\bar{h}}\frac{\partial}{\partial \bar{y}}\left[\bar{y}(1-\bar{y})\left|\frac{\partial \bar{u}}{\partial \bar{y}}\right|\frac{\partial \bar{u}}{\partial \bar{y}}\right] \tag{21}$$

Integrating Eq. (21) from $\bar{y} = 0$ to $\bar{y} = 1$ and utilizing the boundary conditions $\bar{u}(\bar{y} = 0) = 1$, $\bar{u}(\bar{y} = 1) = 0$, $\bar{v}(\bar{y} = 0) = 0$, $\bar{v}(\bar{y} = 1) = 0$ gives

$$\frac{d\bar{P}}{d\bar{x}} = \frac{1}{Re^*\bar{h}^2}\left[\frac{\partial \bar{u}(\bar{y}=1)}{\partial \bar{y}} - \frac{\partial \bar{u}(\bar{y}=0)}{\partial \bar{y}}\right] - \int_0^1 \frac{\partial \bar{u}^2}{\partial \bar{x}}\, d\bar{y} + \frac{1}{\bar{h}}(1-TR)\int_0^1 \bar{u}^2 d\bar{y} \tag{21}$$

The integrals in Eq. (21) are evaluated numerically based on the velocity and velocity gradients at column (n+1). The velocity gradients at $\bar{y} = 0$ and $\bar{y} = 1$ may be evaluated by using Lagrange's interpolation formula (19). Using the four point interpolation formula gives

$$\frac{\partial \bar{u}(\bar{y}=0)}{\partial \bar{y}} = \frac{1}{\Delta \bar{y}}\left[-\frac{11}{6} + 3\bar{u}(2) - \frac{3}{2}\bar{u}(3) + \frac{1}{3}\bar{u}(4)\right] \tag{22}$$

$$\frac{\partial \bar{u}(\bar{y}=1)}{\partial \bar{y}} = \frac{1}{\Delta \bar{y}}\left[-3\bar{u}(M) + \frac{3}{2}\bar{u}(M-1) - \frac{1}{3}\bar{u}(M-2)\right] \tag{23}$$

With the pressure gradient and velocity components now known at column (n+1), the coefficients A(m,n+1), B(m,n+1), C(m,n+1), G(m,n+1) defined by Eqs. (16)-(19) may be recalculated based on the new values and the calculation procedure repeated to calculate new values of velocity and the pressure gradient at column (n+2). Continuing in this manner, the velocity profiles and pressure gradient may be calculated at discrete stations over the entire dimensionless bearing length $0 \leq x \leq 1$.

Initial Conditions for Numerical Calculations / To initiate the calculations, the pressure gradient, $d\bar{P}/d\bar{x}$ and velocity profiles for $\bar{u}$ and $\bar{v}$ must be specified at the inlet to the bearing, $\bar{x} = 0$. In the present study, the assumed initial velocity profiles were

$$\bar{u}(\bar{x}=0,\bar{y}) = (1-\bar{y}) - \frac{Re^*\bar{h}^2}{2}\,\bar{y}(1-\bar{y})\,\frac{d\bar{P}(\bar{x}=0)}{d\bar{x}}$$

$$\bar{v}(\bar{x}=0,\bar{y}) = 0 \tag{24}$$

The assumed initial $\bar{u}$ profile is seen to be the profile corresponding to laminar flow in the absence of inertia. The initial pressure gradient appearing in Eq. (24) will not be the same as the laminar, inertialess pressure gradient since the presence of the inertia terms and the turbulent term will influence the pressure gradient.

The correct value of the initial pressure gradient with inertia and turbulent terms present is not known a priori and must be determined by iteration such that the pressure boundary conditions $\bar{P}(\bar{x}=0) = 0$ and $\bar{P}(\bar{x}=1) = 0$ are satisfied. The pressure boundary conditions are equivalent to the condition

$$\int_0^1 \frac{d\bar{P}}{d\bar{x}}\,d\bar{x} = 0 \tag{25}$$

It was found by experience that the value of the integral in Eq. (25) is a monotonic increasing function of the assumed initial pressure gradient $\frac{d\bar{P}}{d\bar{x}}(\bar{x}=0)$.

Thus an iteration scheme was developed to suitably adjust $\frac{d\bar{P}}{d\bar{x}}(\bar{x}=0)$ until Eq. (25) is satisfied. As a first guess, the pressure gradient corresponding to laminar flow without inertia with $\bar{h} = 1$, was used. The calculations were then carried out over the entire bearing length $0 \le \bar{x} \le 1$ and Eq. (25) checked. If this equation was not satisfied, the initial pressure gradient was adjusted (increased if the integral of Eq. (25) was negative and decreased if the integral was positive) and the calculations repeated. A linear interpolation procedure was developed based on the value of the integral $\int_o^1 \frac{d\bar{P}}{d\bar{x}}\,d\bar{x}$ for two successive calculations, and convergence was generally obtained with 3 or 4 iterations.

Numerical Results

The numerical results obtained for a reduced Reynolds number $Re^* = 10$ are shown in Figures 3-5. The thickness ratio range covered is $0.5 \le$ $TR \le 0.8$ and four values of the dimensionless mixing length constant

$\bar{C}$ = 0, 10, 100, 1000 were used. The case $\bar{C}$ = 0 thus corresponds to laminar flow including inertia.

The load capacity of the bearing is given by the expression

$$LO = \int_{x_2}^{x_1} P\ dx \tag{26}$$

which may be written in dimensionless form as

$$\overline{LO} = \frac{LO}{\rho U^2 (x_1 - x_2)} = \int_0^1 \bar{P}(\bar{x})d\bar{x} \tag{27}$$

The friction power loss is given by the expression

$$FPL = -U \int_{x_2}^{x_1} \mu \left.\frac{\partial u}{\partial y}\right)_{y=0} dx \tag{28}$$

or in dimensionless form

$$\overline{FPL} = \frac{FPL}{\rho U^3 h_1} = -\frac{1}{Re^*} \int_0^1 \frac{1}{\bar{h}(\bar{x})} \left.\frac{\partial \bar{u}}{\partial \bar{y}}\right)_{\bar{y}=0} d\bar{x} \tag{29}$$

Figure 3 shows the dimensionless load capacity defined by Eq. (27), as a function of TR with $\bar{C}$ as a parameter. Shown also is the load capacity curve for laminar flow neglecting inertia. Increasing the turbulence level as manifested by increasing $\bar{C}$ results in a significant increase in load capacity.

The data of Figure 3 are replotted in Figure 4 as the ratio of load capacity including inertia and turbulence to the load capacity for laminar flow neglecting inertia. The curve $\bar{C}$ = 0 shows the influence of inertia only on increasing load capacity. In the absence of turbulence, corresponding to $\bar{C}$ = 0, the influence of inertia becomes relatively more important as TR decreases. The combined effects of turbulence and inertia, however, become relatively more important with increasing TR. For Re* = 10, the $\bar{C}$ = 0 curve shows that at TR = 0.8, the load capacity including inertia is about 14% larger than for laminar flow neglecting inertia, and about 34% larger at TR = 0.5.

Figure 5 shows the dimensionless friction power loss, defined by Eq. (29) as a function of TR with $\bar{C}$ as parameter. Both the effects of

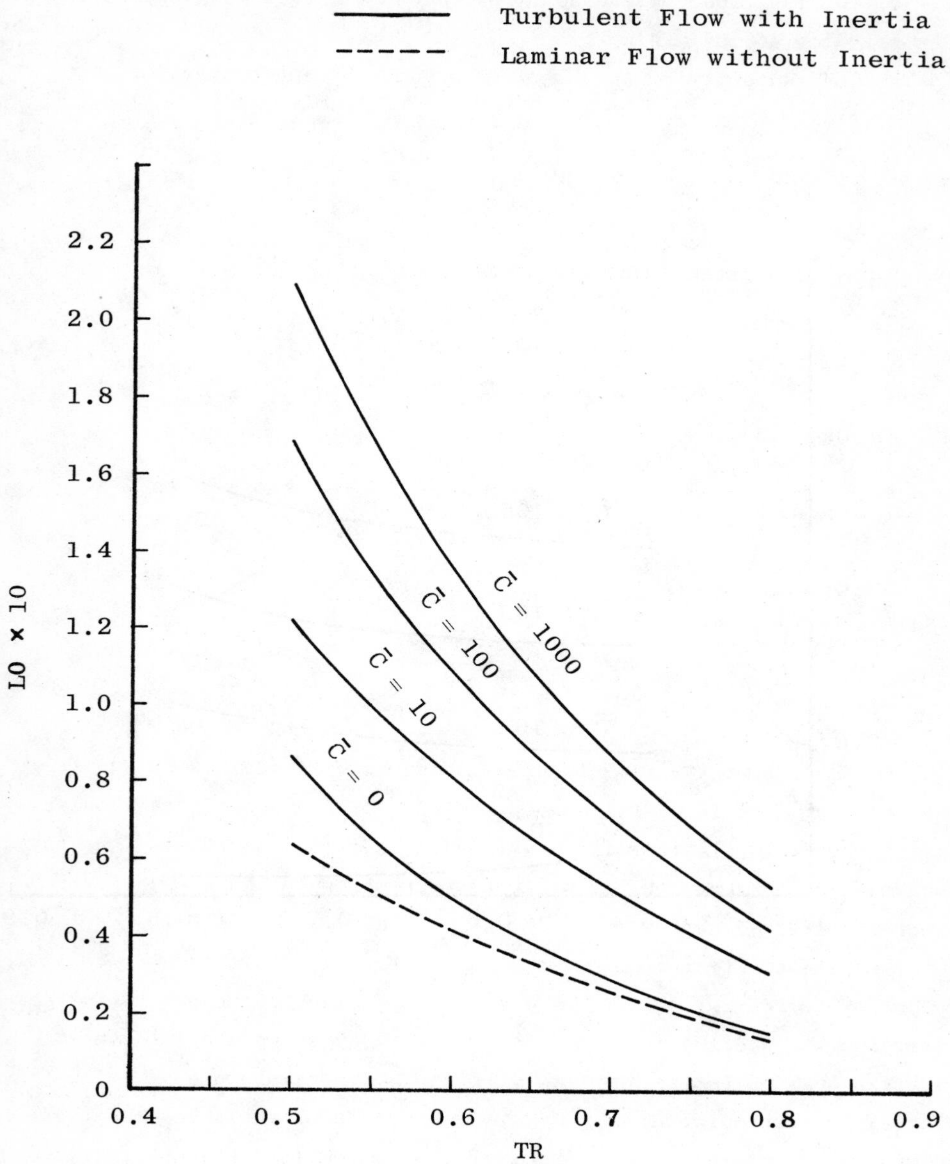

Fig. 3. Dimensionless Load Capacity for Re* = 10.

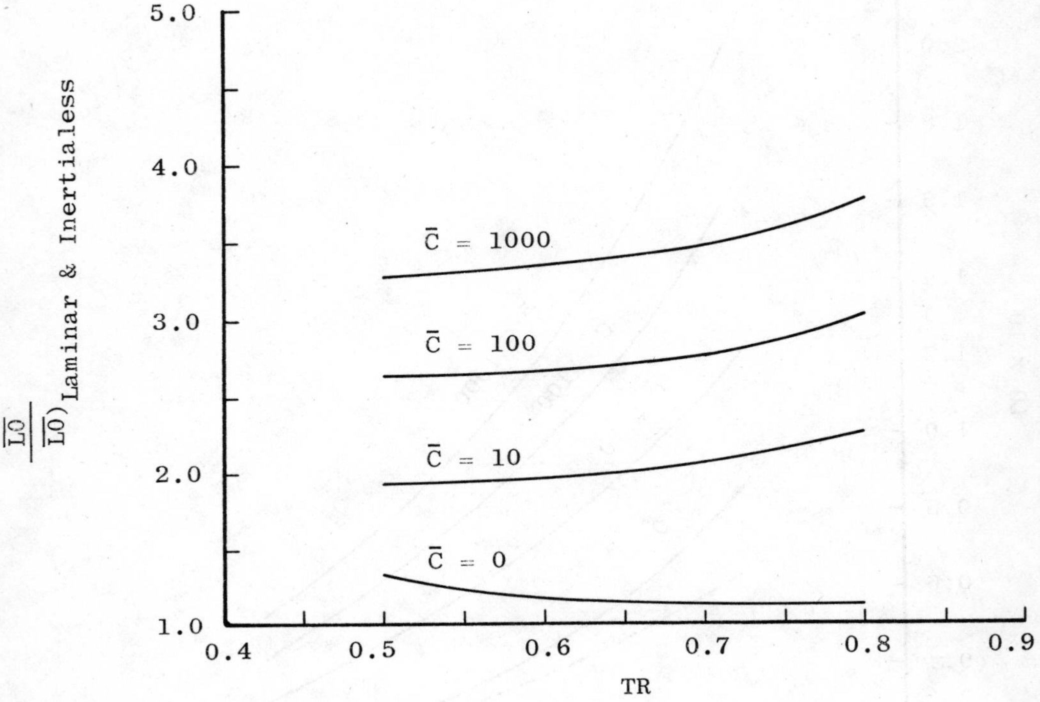

Fig. 4. Ratio of Load Capacity Including Inertia and Turbulence to Load Capacity for Laminar Flow without Inertia for Re* = 10.

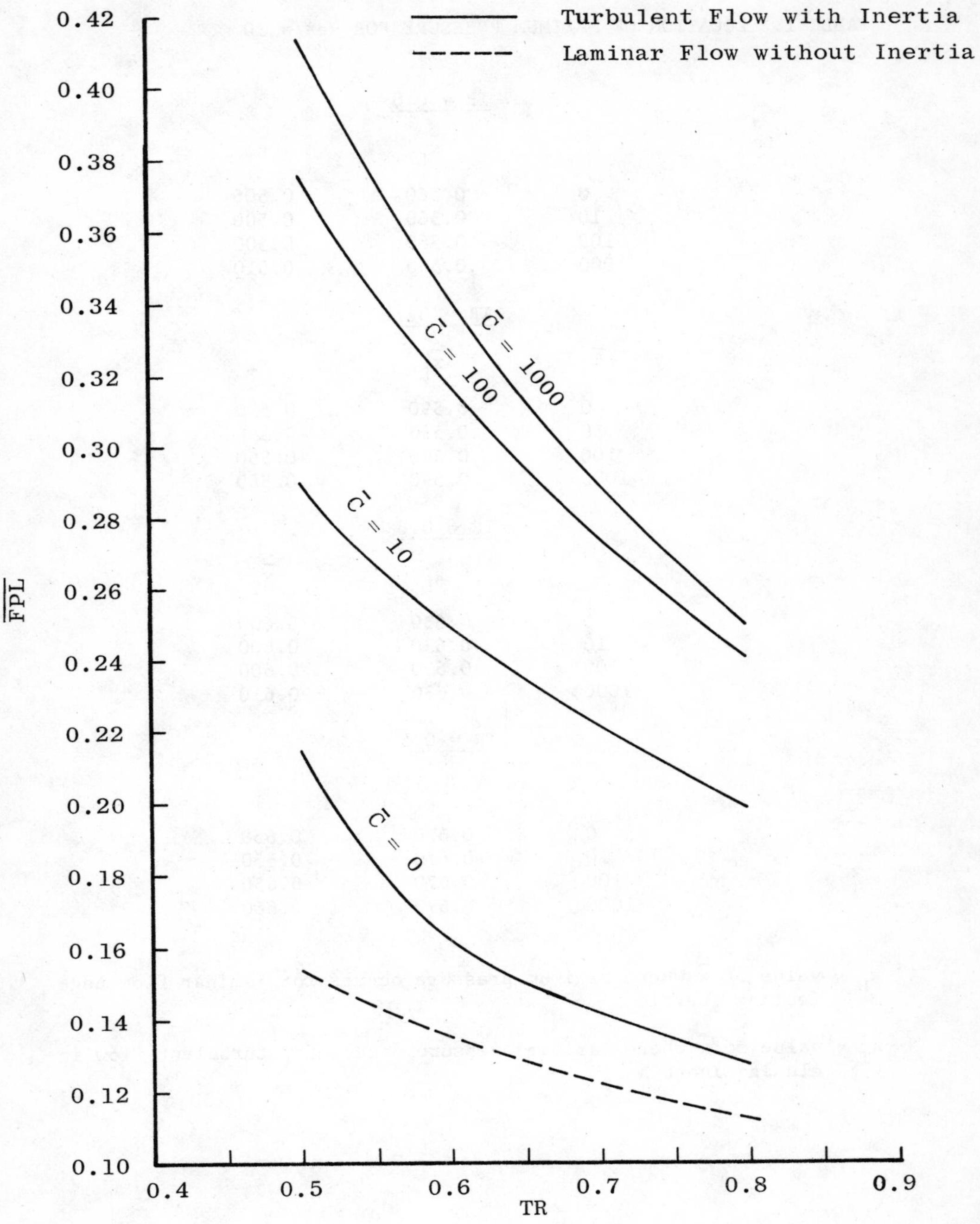

Fig. 5. Dimensionless Friction Power Loss for Re* = 10.

TABLE 1. LOCATION OF MAXIMUM PRESSURE FOR Re* = 10

TR = 0.8

$\bar{C}$	$\bar{x}_L$	$\bar{x}_T$
0	0.560	0.506
10	0.560	0.500
100	0.560	0.500
1000	0.560	0.510

TR = 0.7

$\bar{C}$	$\bar{x}_L$	$\bar{x}_T$
0	0.590	0.550
10	0.590	0.550
100	0.590	0.550
1000	0.590	0.560

TR = 0.6

$\bar{C}$	$\bar{x}_L$	$\bar{x}_T$
0	0.630	0.600
10	0.630	0.600
100	0.630	0.600
1000	0.630	0.610

TR = 0.5

$\bar{C}$	$\bar{x}_L$	$\bar{x}_T$
0	0.670	0.650
10	0.670	0.650
100	0.670	0.650
1000	0.670	0.660

$\bar{x}_L$ - value of $\bar{x}$ where maximum pressure occurs for laminar flow neglecting inertia

$\bar{x}_T$ - value of $\bar{x}$ where maximum pressure occurs for turbulent flow including inertia

inertia and turbulence increase the friction power loss. An increase in friction power loss would be expected to accompany an increase in load capacity since the basic physical mechanism involved in a lubricant film is the balance between the pressure gradient and the viscous stress. This balance is modified by the inclusion of the inertia terms, but an increase in load capacity implies an increase in pressure gradient in certain portions of the film which must be balanced by an increase in viscous stress.

Table 1 shows the influence of turbulence and inertia on the location of maximum pressure. Decreasing the film thickness ratio, TR, moves the point of maximum pressure toward the bearing exit. However, inertia and turbulence shift the maximum pressure toward the bearing inlet. This shift is primarily due to the inertia effect and is only slightly modified by the turbulence at the highest level of turbulence.

CONCLUSIONS

The numerical integration of the turbulent boundary layer equations has been shown to be a promising technique for analyzing the hydrodynamic flow in thin films of bearings and seals. The present investigation was limited to the linear slider bearing because of its geometric simplicity to allow the emphasis to be placed on the physical aspects of the problem. Also, the present analysis was limited to a mixing length model of the turbulent Reynolds stress.

Based on the experience obtained from the present investigation, the analysis will next be extended to the face seal and viscoseal geometries. Additionally other turbulent models besides the mixing length model will be considered.

ADKNOWLEDGMENT

The work reported herein was supported by Project THEMIS under Office of Naval Research Contract No. N00014-68-A-0144.

REFERENCES

1. Kulinski, E. S. and Ostrach, S., "A Critical Evaluation of the Status and Trends in High Speed Fluid Film Lubrication," NASA CR-1058.

2. Tao, L. N., "A Theory of Lubrication in Short Journal Bearing with Turbulent Flow," Trans. ASME, Vol. 80, pp. 1734-1740, 1958.

3. Constantinescu, V. N., "On Turbulent Lubrication," Inst. Mech. Engrs., Vol. 173, pp. 881-900, 1959.

4. Chou, Y. T. and Saibel, E., "The Effect of Turbulence on Slider Bearing Lubrication," Jour. Appl. Mech., Vol. 26, pp. 122-126, 1959.

5. Constantinescu, V. N., "Analysis of Bearings Operating in Turbulent Regime," Jour. Basic Engr., pp. 139-151, 1962.

6. Sternlicht, B. et al., "Analysis of Plane Cylindrical Journal Bearings in Turbulent Regimes," ASME Paper 63-LUB-11.

7. Reynolds, A. L., "Analysis of Turbulent Bearing Films," Jour. Mech. Eng. Science, Vol. 5, pp. 258-272, 1963.

8. Ng, C. W., "Fluid Dynamics Foundation of Turbulent Lubrication Theory," ASLE Paper 64-AM-332.

9. Burton, R. A., "Turbulent Film Bearings Under Small Displacements," ASLE Paper 64-AM-331.

10. Sneck, H. J., "The Effects of Geometry and Inertia on Face Seal Performance," ASME Paper No. 67-WA/Lub-16.

11. Bradshaw, P., Ferriss, D. H. and Atwell, N. P., "Calculation of Boundary Layer Development Using the Turbulent Energy Equation," J. Fluid Mech., Vol. 28, Part 3, pp. 593-616, 1967.

12. Nee, Victor W., Kovasznay, Leslie S. G., "Simple Phenomenological Theory of Turbulent Shear Flows," Physics of Fluids, Vol. 2, No. 3, pp. 473-484, 1969.

13. Taylor, G. I., "Stability of Viscous Liquid Contained Between Two Rotating Cylinders," Phil. Trans. Royal Soc., Series A, Vol. 223, pp. 289-343, 1923.

14. Di Prima, R. C., "A Note on the Stability of Flow in Loaded Journal Bearings," ASLE Trans., Vol. 6, pp. 249-253, 1963.

15. Di Prima, R. C., "Viscous Flow Between Rotating Concentric Cylinders with a Circumferential Pressure Gradient at Speeds above Critical," ASLE Trans., Vol. 7, 1964.

16. Kulinski, E. S. and Ostrach, S., "Journal Bearing Velocity Profiles for Small Eccentricity and Moderate Modified Reynolds Numbers," Jour. Appl. Mech., Vol. 34, No. 1, pp. 16-22, 1967.

17. Pinkus, O. and Sternlicht, B., Theory of Hydrodynamic Lubrication, McGraw-Hill, p. 59, 1961.

18. Agarwal, U. and Torda, T. P., "Numerical Investigation of Unsteady Laminar Incompressible Co-Axial Boundary Layer Flows," NASA CR-908.

19. Kelly, Louis G., Handbook of Numerical Methods and Applications, Addison Wesley Pub. Co., Inc., p. 43, 1967.

DAMPING CHARACTERISTICS OF A LIQUID SQUEEZE FILM

Takeya Yabe
Tokyo, Japan

Philip K. Davis
Southern Illinois University

ABSTRACT

"Liquid squeeze film" is used herein to designate a liquid film located between two nearly parallel plane surfaces in relative normal motion which are always closely spaced compared to the dimensions describing the area of the two like surfaces. It was found that if the motion is slow enough (≃ 3 cps or less), the fluid inertia can be neglected and the resulting fluid flow conforms to Reynold's lubrication theory. However, most vibration problems are inherently of a more dynamic nature and in such problems the fluid inertia must be included unless the solid mass undergoing oscillatory motion is quite large compared to the mass of liquid undergoing motion.

Experiments were also carried out to determine how the damping factor of a liquid squeeze film varies with film viscosity, film thickness, amplitude, and frequency under free vibration of a single-degree-of-freedom system. The data are compared to computer solutions of the non-linear differential equation of a motion (using both the Reynolds theory and a theory that includes fluid inertia). With other variables held constant, the damping factor was found to (1) decrease as the plate spacing is increased, (2) decrease as the viscosity is decreased, and (3) increase as the initial spacing is decreased.

LIST OF NOTATIONS

A   Constant of integration

B	Constant of integration
D	Damping coefficient
D_c	Critical damping coefficient
F	Force
h(t)	Plate spacing
h_o	Initial plate spacing
k	Spring modulus
m	Mass of the oscillating plate
N	Cycle number
p	Total pressure
p_d	Dynamic pressure
p_s	Static pressure
r_o	Plate radius
r	Coordinate
t	Time
$V(t) = \frac{dh}{dt}$	Velocity of oscillating plate
V_r	Fluid velocity in r-direction
V_z	Fluid velocity in z-direction
W	Weight of oscillating mass
X(t)	Plate displacement
X_1	Amplitude of first cycle
X_2	Amplitude of second cycle
X_I	Initial displacement of oscillating plate
δ	Damping factor (logarithmic decrement)
δ_T	Total logarithmic decrement
δ_L	Logarithmic decrement due to energy losses without liquid film
ζ	D/D_c
μ	Viscosity
ν	Kinematic viscosity
ρ	Mass density of the liquid
τ	Period of oscillation
W_n	Natural frequency of the system

INTRODUCTION

Liquid squeeze film is the designation commonly given to a liquid film located between two nearly parallel plane surfaces in relative normal motion which are always closely spaced compared to the dimensions describing the area of the two like surfaces. The fluid movement which results from the approach or separation of the surfaces is called "squeezing flow." If the surfaces are in relative oscillatory motion, the fluid will dissipate energy and damp the motion. If the squeezing motion is slow enough that the fluid inertia can be neglected, the resulting fluid flow conforms to Reynolds' [1] theory. However, most vibration problems are inherently of a dynamic nature so one would not expect the Reynolds theory to be valid in oscillatory squeezing flows except in flow resulting from very slow oscillations.

A literature search has shown that little is known about the damping characteristics of a liquid squeeze film under dynamic conditions. It was suggested by Sommer [2] that a liquid squeeze film might serve well as a damping agent in practical problems in which high damping is required and the space for damping is limited. Sommer points out that the nonlinear effects of liquid squeeze film damping must be taken into consideration since squeeze film damping is nonlinear even when the Reynolds theory is used. The importance of the nonlinear terms in the liquid squeeze film equations was mentioned previously by Jackson [3], but was not discussed in detail. Jackson and Kuzma [4] obtained approximate solutions to the equations including fluid inertia in squeezing flow motion. Ishizawa [5] obtained an exact solution to the complete equations in a "multifold" series form. However, attention was not focused on the liquid squeeze film damping characteristics and no experiments involving oscillatory motion were performed.

The research reported herein is concerned in part with the experimental investigation of the damping characteristics of a liquid squeeze film under oscillating dynamic conditions. How do the damping characteristics vary with viscosity, mean film thickness, amplitude, and frequency under free vibration of a single-degree-of-freedom system? How much do the solutions to the nonlinear governing differential equations differ when using (1) the Reynolds theory and (2) the results of Jackson, Kuzma and Ishizawa for the damping, and how much do these results differ from actual experimental data? In order to answer these

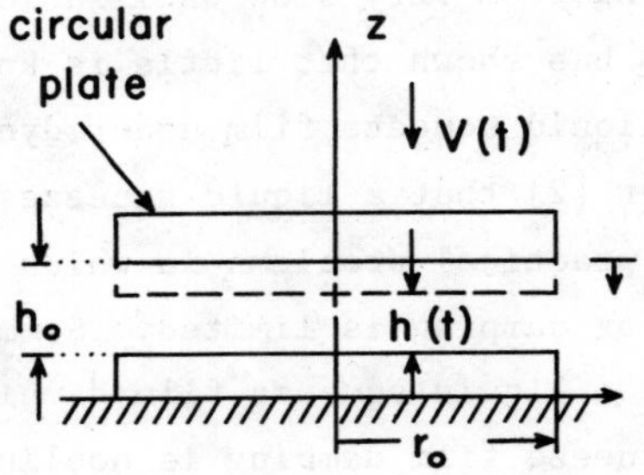

Fig. 1. Reference Diagram.

questions, computer solutions to the nonlinear differential equations of motion were obtained and experimental data were taken in the frequency range of from 3 to 12 cycles per second.

Theoretical Considerations

A simplified diagram of the liquid squeeze film system is shown in Fig. 1. h_o is the initial spacing between the plates, h(t) is the gap width as a function of time and x(t) is the displacement of the upper plate as a function of time such that $h(t) = h_o - x(t)$. The velocity of the fluid in the θ-direction is zero because the problem is axisymmetric for the cylindrical coordinates with no motion to induce a swirl velocity. The Navier-Stokes equations for the liquid squeeze film in which the fluid inertia can be neglected reduce to[1]

$$\frac{\partial p_d}{\partial r} = \mu \frac{\partial^2 V_r}{\partial z^2} \tag{1}$$

and

$$\frac{\partial p_d}{\partial z} = \mu \frac{\partial^2 V_z}{\partial z^2} \tag{2}$$

The continuity equation in cylindrical coordinates simplifies to

$$\frac{1}{r}\frac{\partial (rV_r)}{\partial r} + \frac{\partial V_z}{\partial z} = 0 \tag{3}$$

Reynolds [1] assumed that

$$\frac{\partial p_d}{\partial z} = 0 \tag{4}$$

for quasi-static squeeze film motion.

The pressure field of the liquid squeeze film is obtained by integrating Eqs. (1) and (2) along with Eq. (4) and the appropriate boundary conditions. The resulting pressure is given by

$$p_d = \frac{3\mu V}{h^3}(r_o^2 - r^2) \tag{5}$$

where p_d is the dynamic pressure, $V = \frac{dh}{dt}$ is the normal velocity of the upper plate, and μ is the viscosity of the liquid.

---

1. $p = p_d + p_s$ where p is the total pressure, p_d is the dynamic pressure, and p_s is the static pressure.

The damping coefficient is defined as

$$D = \frac{F}{V} \tag{6}$$

where the fluid pressure force F acting on the plate is obtained by integrating Eq. (5) over the surface of the top plate. Thus the damping coefficient for the circular surfaces of radius r_o corresponding to a squeeze film in which the fluid inertia is neglected (Reynolds theory), is

$$D = \frac{3\pi\mu r_o^4}{2h^3} \tag{7}$$

The governing differential equation which describes the single-degree-of-freedom motion x(t) of a spring-mass system with damping is

$$m\frac{d^2x}{dt^2} + D\frac{dx}{dt} + kx = 0 \tag{8}$$

where m is the mass of the vibrating plate (upper), D represents the damping coefficient, and k is the spring modulus. Substituting Eq. (7) into Eq. (8) gives

$$m\frac{d^2x}{dt^2} + \frac{3\pi\mu r_o^4}{2(h_o-x)^3}\frac{dx}{dt} + kx = 0 \tag{9}$$

where $(h_o-x) = h$. Even though the damping factor is based on the Reynolds theory, Eq. (9) is nonlinear since the damping coefficient is a function of the displacement x for a given μ, h_o, and r_o. However, if x is small compared to h_o (i.e., $h \simeq h_o$), then D is approximately constant. If D is assumed to be constant, the equation becomes

$$m\frac{d^2x}{dt^2} + \frac{3\pi\mu r_o^4}{2h_o^3}\frac{dx}{dt} + kx = 0 \tag{10}$$

The well-known general solution to Eq. (10) is

$$x(t) = e^{-\frac{D}{2m}t}\left[A\cos\left(\sqrt{\frac{k}{m} - \frac{D^2}{4m^2}}\right)t + B\sin\left(\sqrt{\frac{k}{m} - \frac{D^2}{4m^2}}\right)t\right] \tag{11}$$

The rate of decay of the oscillating motion governed by Eq. (10) is commonly expressed mathematically by means of the logarithmic decrement δ; δ is defined as

$$\delta = \ln\left(\frac{x_1}{x_2}\right) = \ln\left(\frac{e^{-\zeta\omega_n t_1}}{e^{-\zeta\omega_n (t_1+\tau)}}\right) = \ln\left(\frac{1}{e^{-\zeta\omega_n \tau}}\right)$$

or $$\delta = \zeta\omega_n\tau \tag{12}$$

where $$\zeta = \frac{D}{D_c} \tag{13}$$

$$\omega_n = \frac{D_c}{2m} = \sqrt{\frac{k}{m}} \tag{14}$$

and $$\tau = \frac{2\pi}{\omega_n\sqrt{1 - \zeta^2}} \tag{15}$$

x_1, x_2, and τ are defined in Fig. 2, D_c represents the critical damping coefficient and ω_n is the natural circular frequency of the spring-mass system. Substituting Eqs. (13) and (15) into Eq. (12), δ may be expressed as

$$\delta = \frac{\pi}{\sqrt{\frac{mk}{D^2} - \frac{1}{4}}} \tag{16}$$

This expression for the logarithmic decrement was used to calculate a theoretical value for the damped spring-mass oscillation.

For experimental data, it is common to use an average logarithmic decrement to evaluate the actual damped motion expressed by

$$\delta = \frac{1}{N} \ln\left(\frac{x_n}{x_{n+N}}\right)$$

where x_n is the amplitude of cycle n, x_{n+N} is the amplitude of cycle n + N in which N is the number of cycles between cycle n and cycle n + N.

The energy losses attributed to the spring-mass system alone such as internal energy dissipation, joint losses of the spring system, and external losses were subtracted from the total measured decrement so that a value could be obtained representing the energy dissipation in the squeezing film alone. The resulting decrement is expressed as

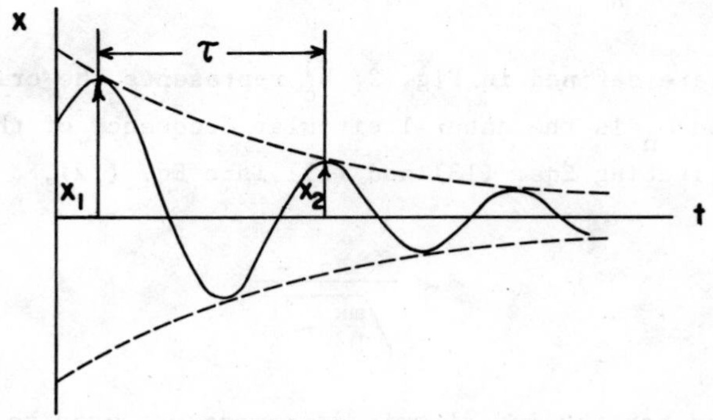

Fig. 2. x(t) vs. t for Damped Oscillation Motion.

$$\delta = \delta_T - \delta_L \tag{18}$$

where δ represents the actual logarithmic decrement due to the squeeze film,

δ_T represents the total logarithmic decrement,

and δ_L represents the logarithmic decrement of the system due to energy losses without a liquid film.

Thus the data were first taken with a liquid squeeze film and then without it in order to get the logarithmic decrement δ_T and δ_L respectively. These logarithmic decrements were evaluated using Eq. (17) for N = 3 and the actual (experimental) squeeze film logarithmic decrement was obtained by Eq. (18).

The computer solution of Eq. (9) was accomplished by means of a finite difference method using a time increment of 0.001 second. Jackson [3], Kuzma [4], and Ishizawa [5] obtained approximate solutions to the squeeze film equations with inertia terms included. The squeeze film force F given by Jackson [3], for example, is

$$F = \frac{\pi r_o^4}{4}\left\{\frac{6\mu}{h^3}\frac{dh}{dt} - \rho\left[\frac{48}{70h^2}\left(\frac{dh}{dt}\right)^2 - \frac{3}{5h}\frac{d^2h}{dt^2}\right]\right\} \tag{19}$$

Kuzma and Ishizawa obtained the same terms $\left(\frac{3\pi\mu r_o^4}{2h^3}\frac{dh}{dt}, \frac{3\pi\rho r_o^4}{20h}\frac{d^2h}{dt^2}\right)$ in the expression for F but the coefficient for the term $\frac{\pi\rho r_o^4}{h^2}\left(\frac{dh}{dt}\right)^2$ is different in each solution (Ishizawa's solution has additional terms of higher order). To give an indication of the effect of additional fluid inertia terms in the problem, Eq. (19), with the term involving $\left(\frac{dh}{dt}\right)^2$ deleted, was used to obtain

$$\left[m + \frac{3\pi\rho r_o^4}{20(h_o - x)}\right]\frac{d^2x}{dt^2} + \frac{3\pi\mu r_o^4}{2(h_o - x)^3}\frac{dx}{dt} + kx = 0 \tag{20}$$

Equation (20) was solved on the computer by means of the same finite difference technique used to obtain a solution to Eq. (9).

Experimental Apparatus

A simplified diagram of the apparatus and a photograph of the system are shown in Figures 3 and 4, respectively. Figure 5 is a close-up

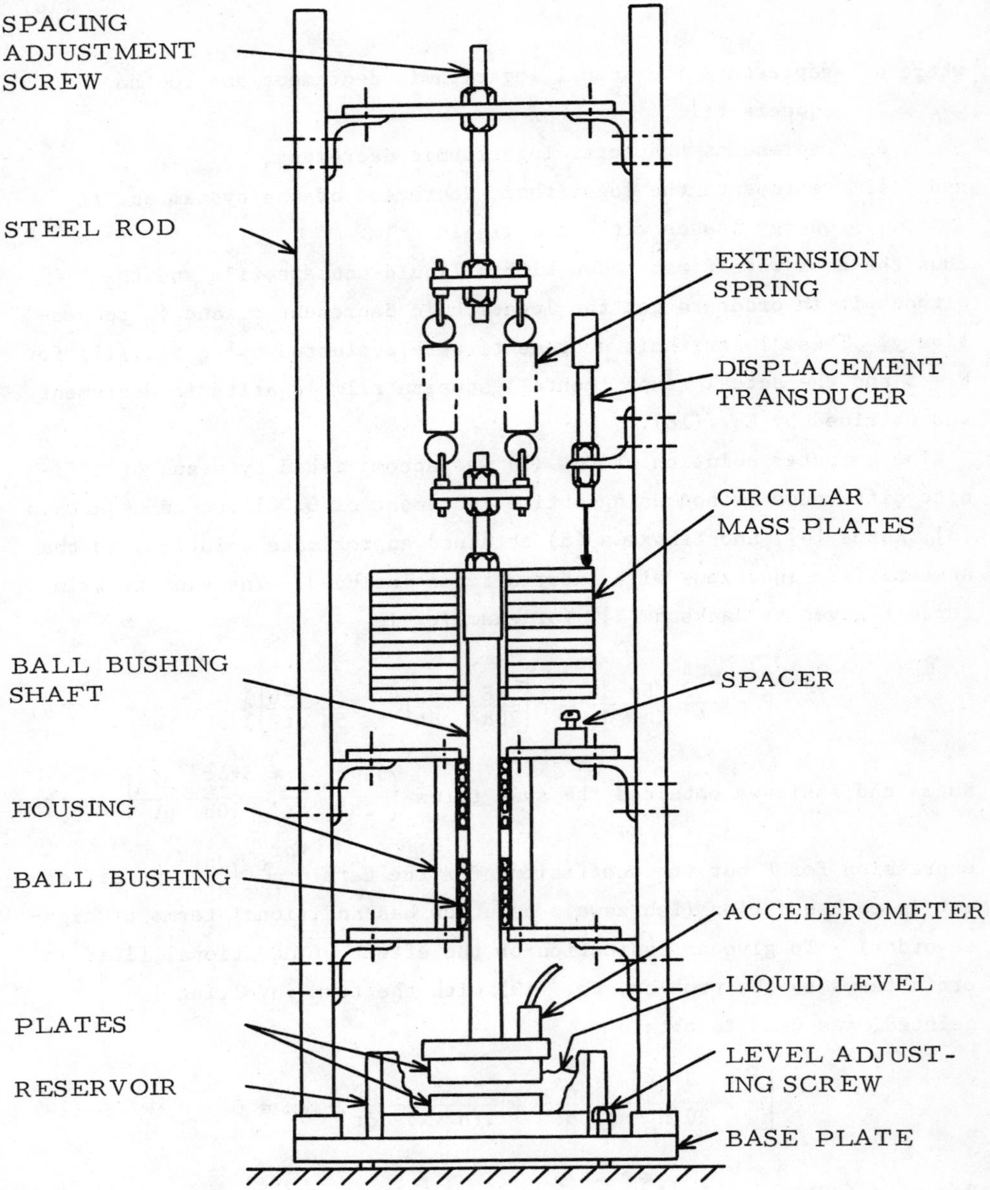

Fig. 3. Diagram of Apparatus.

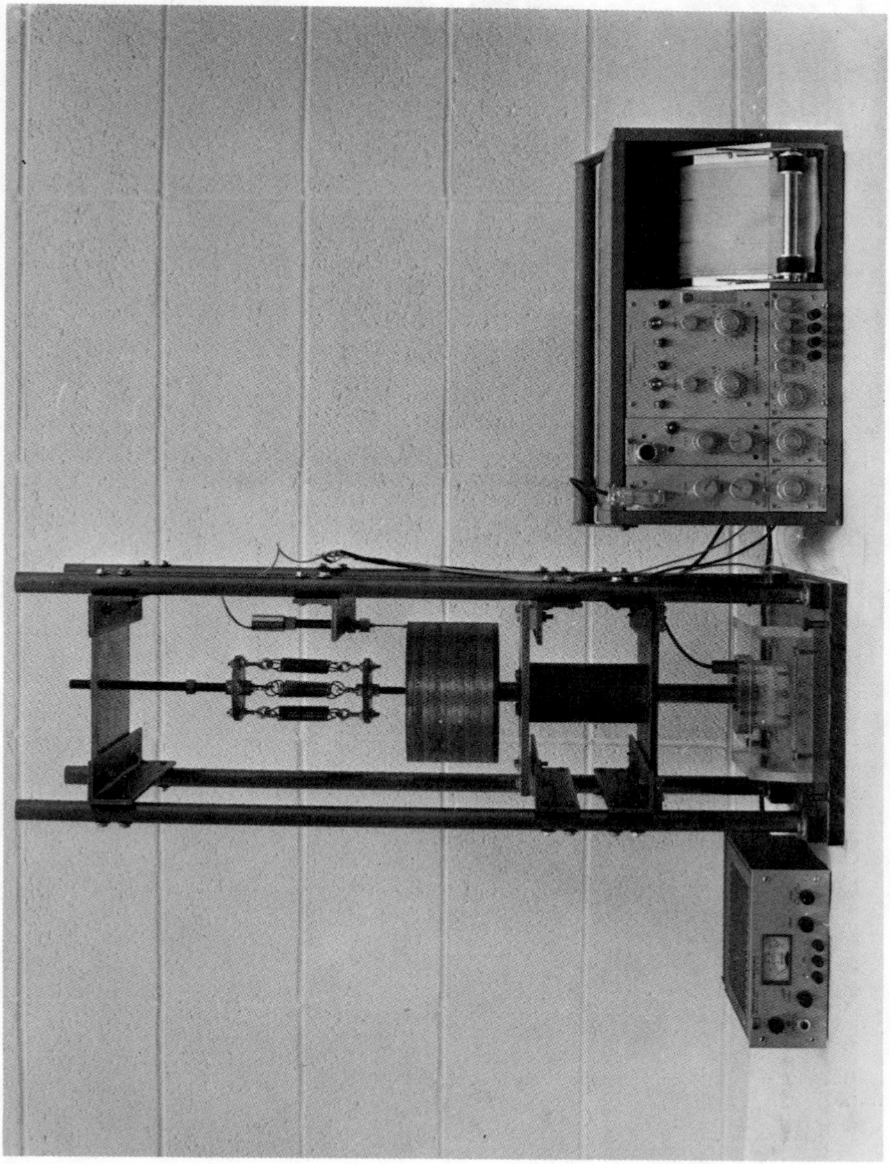

Fig. 4. Experimental Apparatus and Equipment.

Fig. 5. Spring-Mass System (Above).

Fig. 6. Plates and Reservoir (Below).

photograph of the spring-mass system and Figure 6 is a picture of the plates and reservoir. A liquid film was placed between two circular Plexiglas plates which were 0.88 in. in thickness and 3.5 in. in diameter. The surfaces in direct contact with the liquid were the original surfaces of the Plexiglas plates (roughness = 2μ in. r.m.s.). The two plates were parallel to within 0.0005 inch over the surfaces. The 7.5 in. square reservoir was filled to a depth of 2.75 in. The reservoir walls were made out of clear Plexiglas for visualization purposes.

A piezoelectric accelerometer was attached to the upper plate and a displacement transducer was mounted above the mass-plate (see Figure 3); these transducers were used to measure respectively the acceleration and the displacement of the upper plate. The output signals from the transducers were fed into the amplifiers and recorded by the two channel Beckman strip chart recorder shown in Figure 4.

The liquids used in the experiments were silicon oils. Silicon oils were chosen because they are nearly colorless and their viscosity variation with the small temperature changes observed in the laboratory is negligible.

Procedure

A silicon oil with the desired viscosity was added to the reservoir until it extended 1/4 in. (in all the experiments) above the bottom surface of the upper plate; no significant change in damping was noted upon varying this from 3/16 to 3/8 in. The lower surface of the upper plate always remained submerged in the liquid during the oscillating motion. Fine threaded adjustable screws were placed at the corner of the base plate so that the system could be leveled by means of a circular level (see Fig. 3). The reservoir was mounted on the steel base plate. The two Plexiglas plates were carefully adjusted for parallelism and coinciding axes.

The desired initial spacing h_o was achieved by using a spacer whose thickness was measured by means of a micrometer. The spacer was placed between the moving and stationary plate. The spring-mass system was then positioned by the spacing adjustment screw at the top of the apparatus; this was the equilibrium position for the spring-mass system having the initial spacing h_o. The spacer used for determining h_o was removed and replaced by another preset spacer (h_1) used to obtain an initial displacement X_1. The initial displacement ($X_1 = h_o - h_1$) was achieved by first pulling the mass-plates down until the lower plate contacted the spacer and then the mass-plates were abruptly released in order to start the oscillating motion. The acceleration and displacement of the oscillating plate were measured by means of electronic transducers and a strip chart recorder.

The extension springs were adjusted to obtain the same initial tension in each spring. The spring constant was measured by measuring the system displacement due to a known weight with a micrometer. The following two different combinations of springs were used to obtain different frequencies of free oscillating motion: (a) the mass-plate (weight) was attached under the extension springs as shown in Fig. 7(a), when the ratio (w/k) of the weight of the mass to the spring constant was close to 1, i.e., if the springs were initially extended approximately 1 in. then free oscillatory motion could be obtained when a displacement was given to the spring-mass system and (b) the mass-plate was attached between the upper extension springs applying initial tension when the ratio (w/k) was small. When the ratio (w/k) is small, the springs cannot be initially extended so that free oscillation can not be started even if an initial displacement is given to the system. Therefore the initial tension was given to the springs in order to attain at least 0.5 in. displacement for the spring-mass system. The simple diagrams of case (a) and (b) are shown in Fig. 7.

Results

The logarithmic decrement δ, which describes the damping, was found to depend upon the plate spacing h_o, liquid viscosity μ, initial displacement X_1, and frequency.

The experimental logarithmic decrement δ was evaluated by using the recorded displacement curve and Eq. (17) for N = 3. When the duration of oscillating motion was shorter than 3 cycles, N was chosen less than 3 (such conditions were obtained with large viscosity liquids and close spacing). The theoretical δ for Eq. (9) and (20) was evaluated in the same way as it was for the experiments taking N = 3 except for one condition (N was 2 at μ = 150 centipoise, h_o = 3/32 in.). Figure 8 shows how the experimental and theoretical δ's were evaluated.

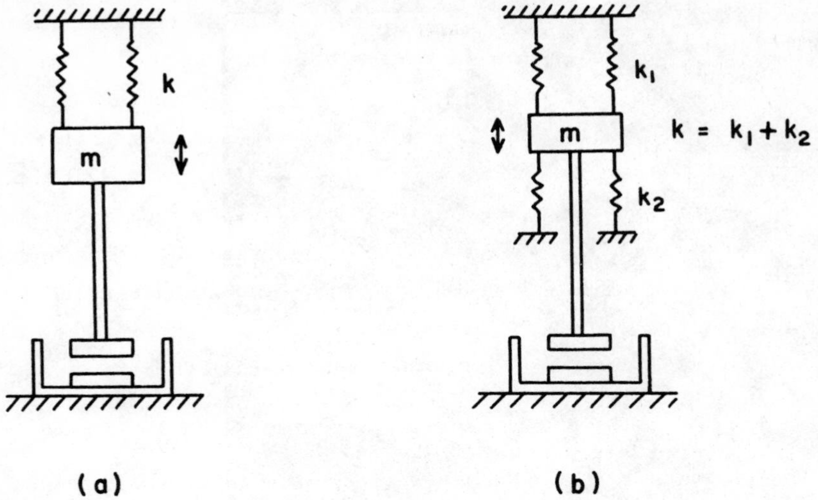

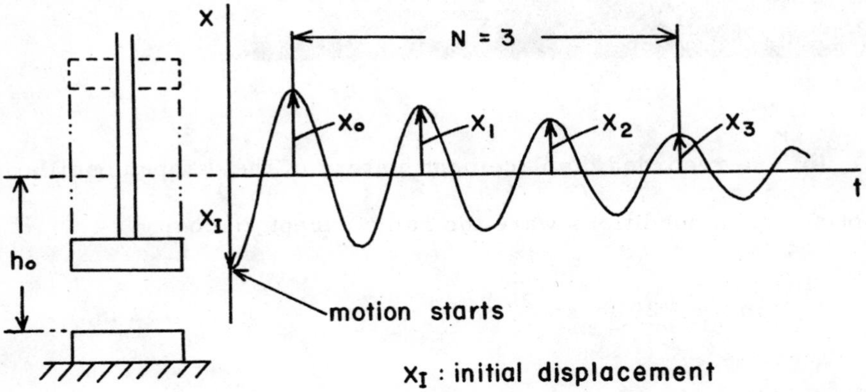

$$\delta = \frac{1}{N} \ln \frac{X_0}{X_N}$$

Fig. 7. Combinations of Springs. (Above)

Fig. 8. Evaluations of δ for the Finite Difference Solutions of Equations (9) and (20) and Experiments. (Below)

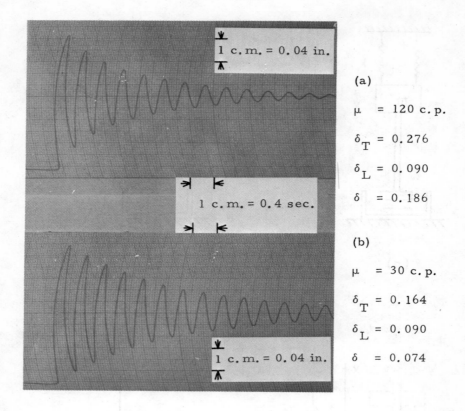

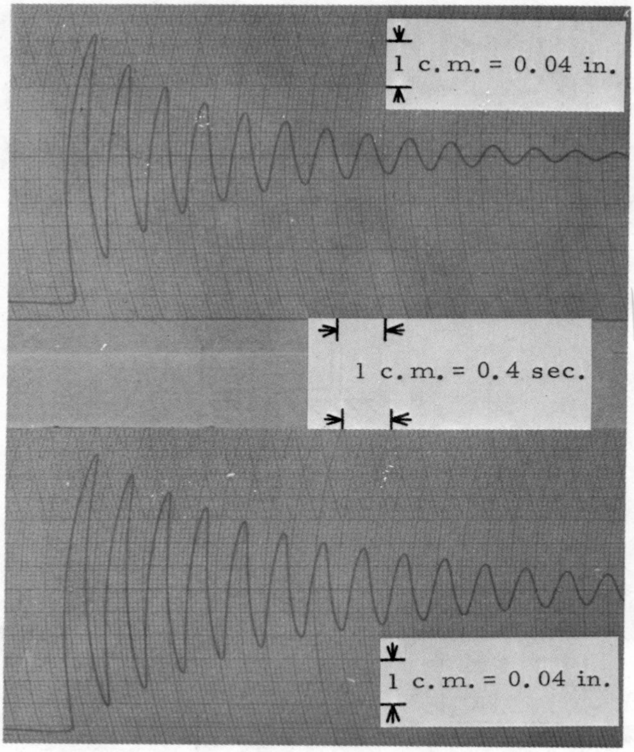

(a)

μ = 120 c.p.

δ_T = 0.276

δ_L = 0.090

δ = 0.186

(b)

μ = 30 c.p.

δ_T = 0.164

δ_L = 0.090

δ = 0.074

(a), (b) are recorded displacement history of the damped oscillating motion. The conditions were the same except viscosity.

m = o.129 lb-sec^2/in $\qquad$ h_o = 6/32 in.

k = 46.2 lb/in $\qquad$ X_I = 4/32 in.

Fig. 9. Samples of Recorded Displacement History.

The value of the properties of the silicon oils and the physical constants of the system are listed in Tables I and II respectively. Figure 9 is presented to show samples of the recorded displacement history of the oscillating motion of the plate taken with the strip chart recorder.

The data are presented graphically in Figs. 10 through 18. Figures 10 to 13 and Figs. 14 to 16 show δ vs. $\frac{h_o}{r_o}$ and $\frac{\mu}{\rho r_o^2}\sqrt{m/k}$ respectively. δ vs. $\frac{X_1}{h_o}$ and δ vs. frequency are presented in Figs. 17 and 18 respectively. The logarithmic decrements evaluated from a finite difference solution of each of the nonlinear differential Eqs. (9) and (20) and from the solution (using Eq. (16)) of the linearized differential equation are presented in each graph.

Discussion

a) Damping Factor as a Function of Plate Spacing / The damping coefficient of the liquid squeeze film based on Reynolds' theory is given as

$$D = \frac{3\pi\mu r_o^4}{2h^3} \tag{7}$$

When Eq. (7) is applied to the differential equation of a damped spring-mass system, i.e., Eq. (8), the differential equation becomes

$$m\frac{d^2h}{dt^2} + \frac{3\pi\mu r_o^4}{2h^3}\frac{dh}{dt} + k(h - h_o) = 0 \tag{21}$$

Since D varies inversely with the cube of the spacing h, it is a nonlinear function of h for a given viscosity and plate radius. Figures 10, 11, and 12 show that the solutions to (10) and (21) give logarithmic decrements which vary nearly as $C\,e^{n(h_o/r_o)}$ where n is the slope of the straight line. The upper theoretical curve for each viscosity was obtained by solving the nonlinear differential Eq. (21) using the finite difference method and the lower theoretical curve represents the solution of the linearized differential Eq. (10) in which D is taken to be constant during the oscillatory motion of the mass m. Hence the difference between the logarithmic decrement δ for the two theoretical curves shows clearly that the nonlinear effects of squeeze film damping may be appreciable, and that the effect becomes more pronounced with increasing plate spacing and with decreasing viscosity.

TABLE I. SILICON OIL PROPERTIES (72°F)

μ centipoise	ρ $\frac{\text{slugs}}{\text{ft}^3}$	ν $\frac{\text{ft}^2}{\text{sec}}$
30	1.82	3.44×10^{-4}
50	1.84	5.67×10^{-4}
70	1.85	7.91×10^{-4}
100	1.86	11.3×10^{-4}
120	1.86	13.5×10^{-4}
150	1.86	16.8×10^{-4}

TABLE II. CONDITIONS OF THE SYSTEM

held const. / variable	r_o in.	m $\frac{\text{lb-sec}^2}{\text{in}}$	k $\frac{\text{lb}}{\text{in}}$	frequency $\frac{\text{cycles}}{\text{sec}}$	h_o in.	X_I in.	μ centipoise
h_o	1.75	0.129	46.2	3.0		$h_o/2$	30-150
μ	1.75	0.129	46.2	3.0	3/32-6/32	$h_o/2$	
X_I	1.75	0.129	46.2	3.0	6/32		30-150
frequency	1.75	0.0505	19.7		6/32	3/32	
	1.75	0.0318	31.4		6/32	3/32	30 70
	1.75	0.0198	50.3		6/32	3/32	120
	1.75	0.0128	78.0		6/32	3/32	

As expected, the experimental results agree with the solution to Eq. (21) better than that of the linearized Eq. (10). However, it should be kept in mind that even Eq. (21) does not take into account the fluid inertia.

The oscillating motion with $h_o = 3/32$ in. decays more quickly than that with $h_o = 6/32$ in. since the damping coefficient increases rapidly as $h \to 0$. The spacing h between two plates approaches the equilibrium position h_o more quickly for the closely spaced plates than for the

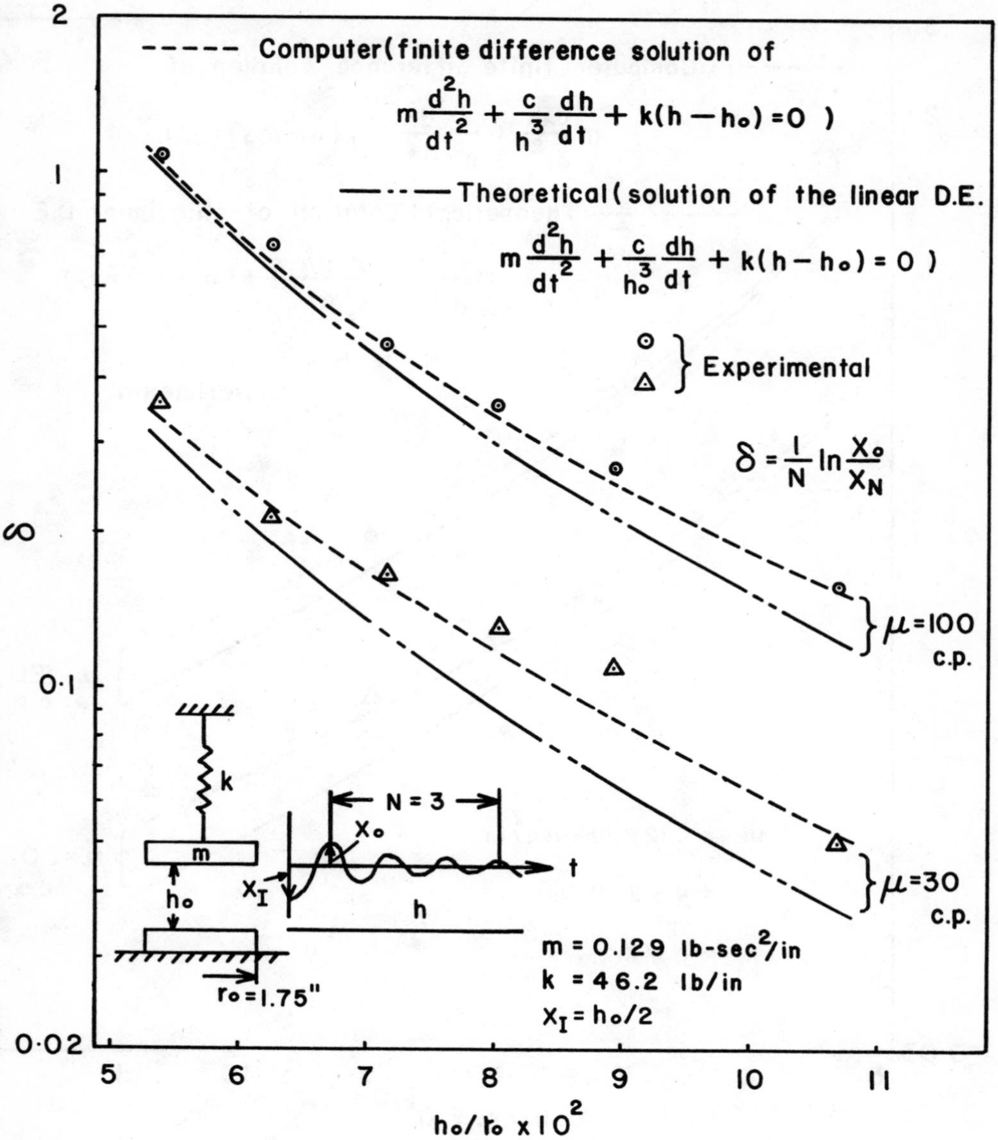

Fig. 10. Damping Factor Versus Plate Spacing for μ = 30 and 100 centi-poise.

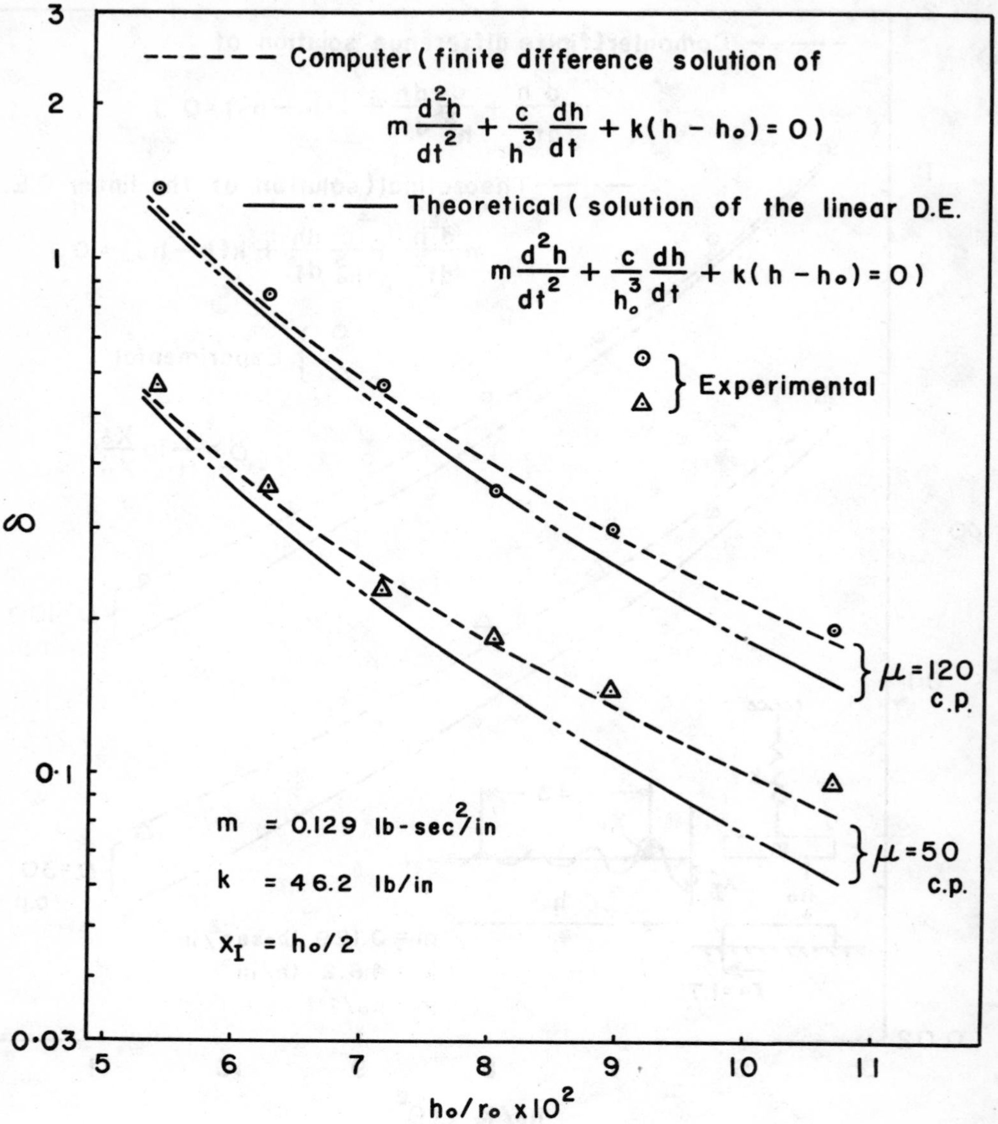

Fig. 11. Damping Factor Versus Plate Spacing for μ = 50 and 120 centi-poise.

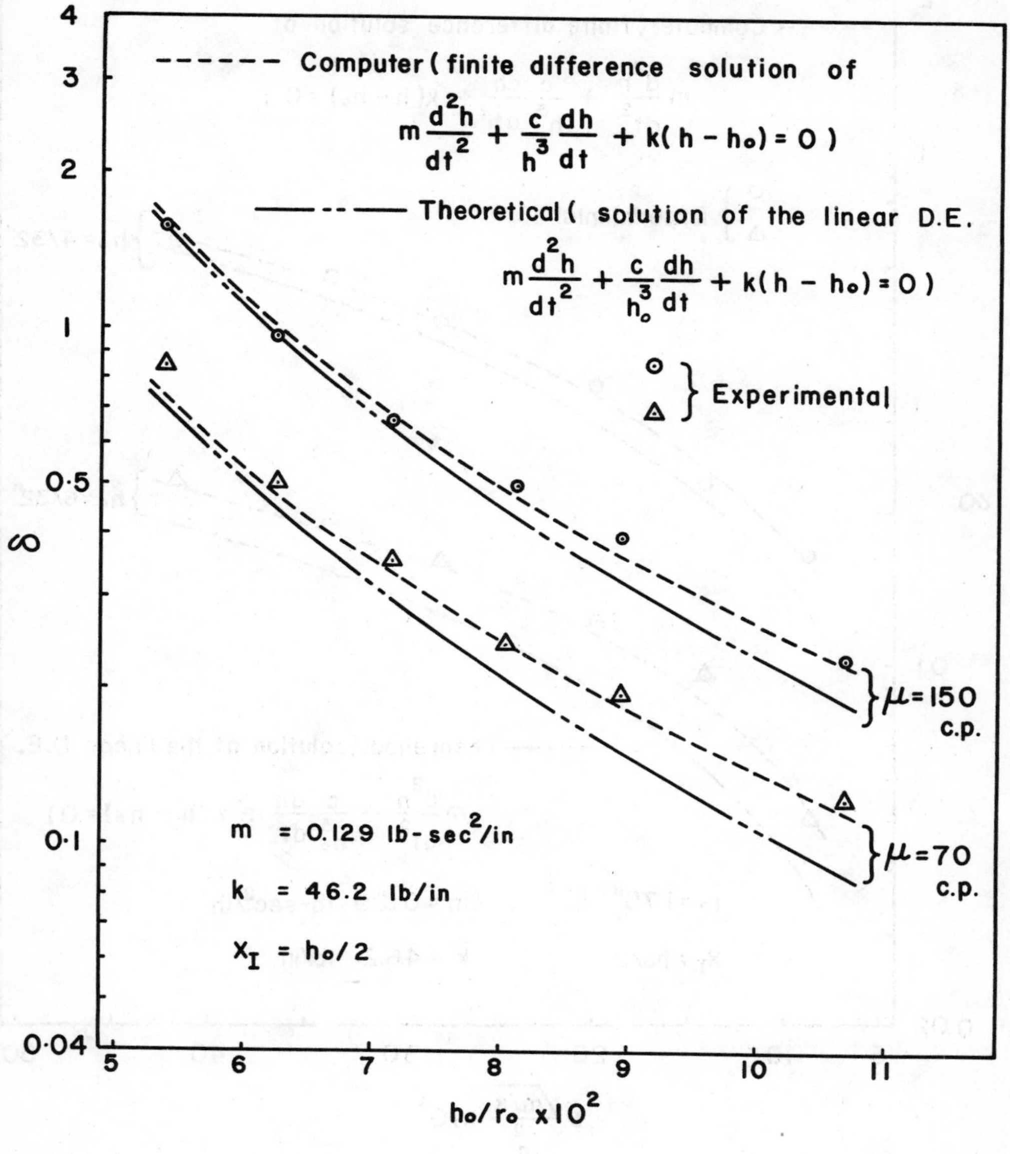

Fig. 12. Damping Factor Versus Plate Spacing for μ = 70 and 150 centi-poise.

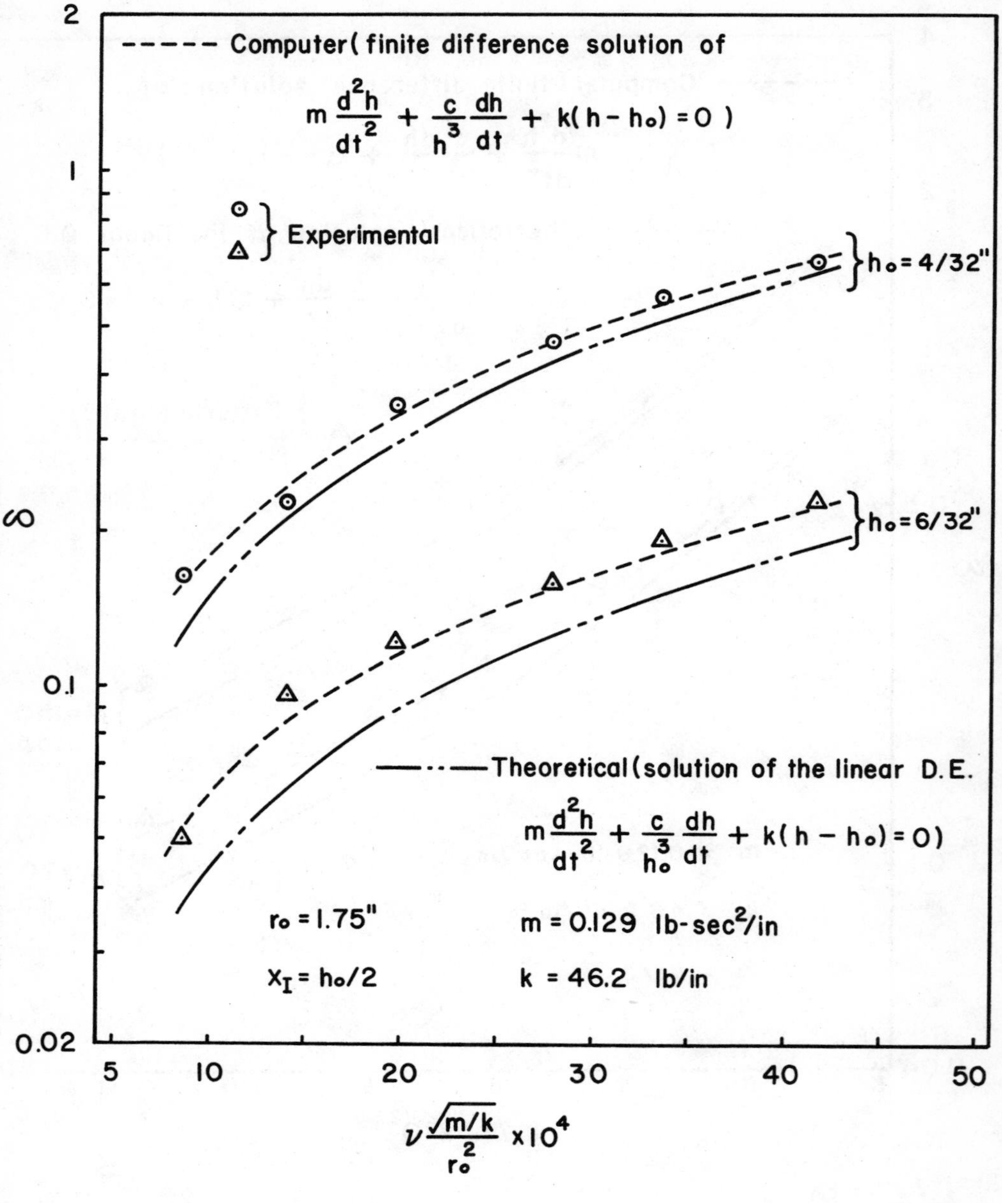

Fig. 13. Damping Factor Versus Viscosity for h_o = 4/32" and 6/32".

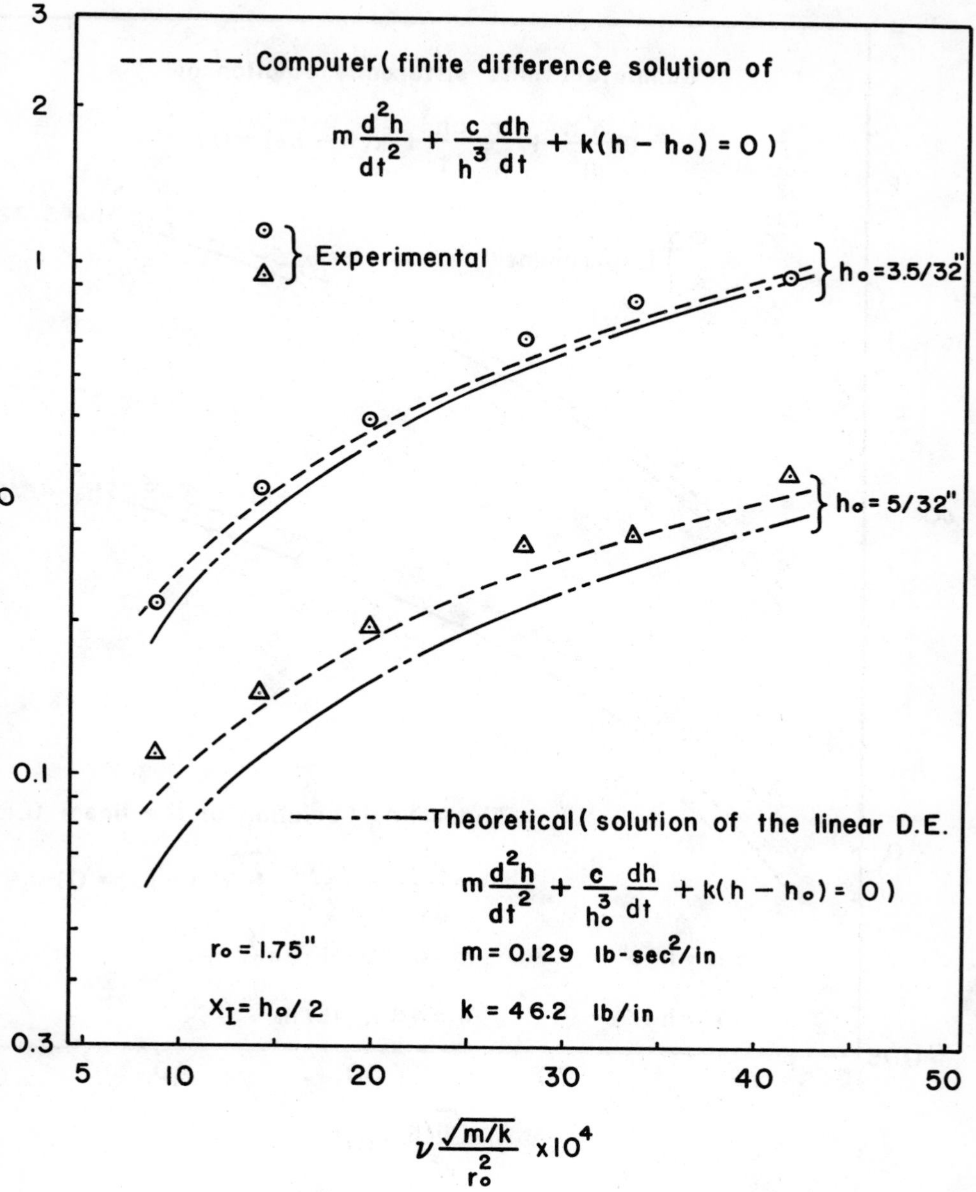

Fig. 14. Damping Factor Versus Viscosity for h_o = 3.5/32" and 5/32".

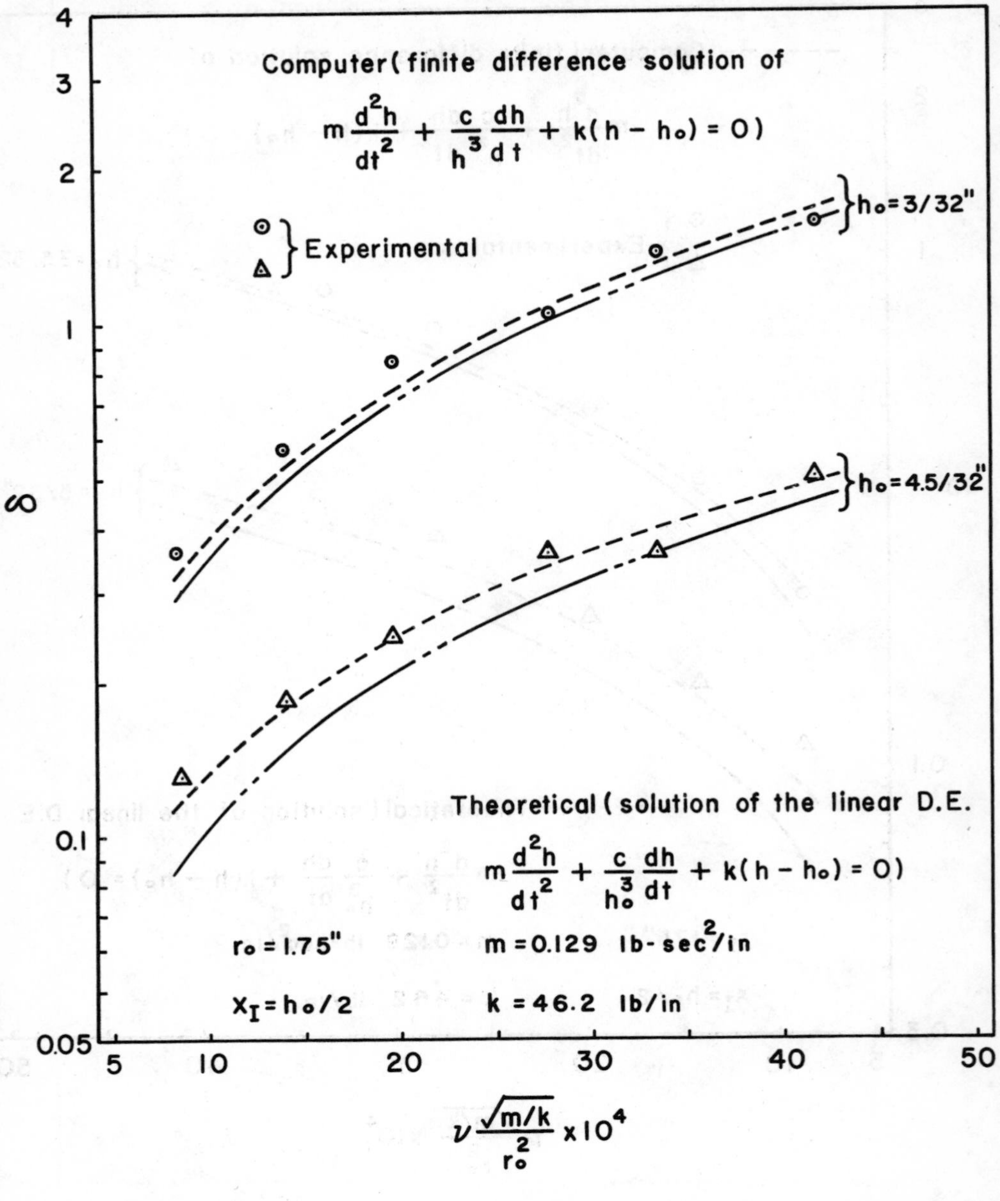

Fig. 15. Damping Factor Versus Viscosity for h_o = 3/32" and 4.5/32".

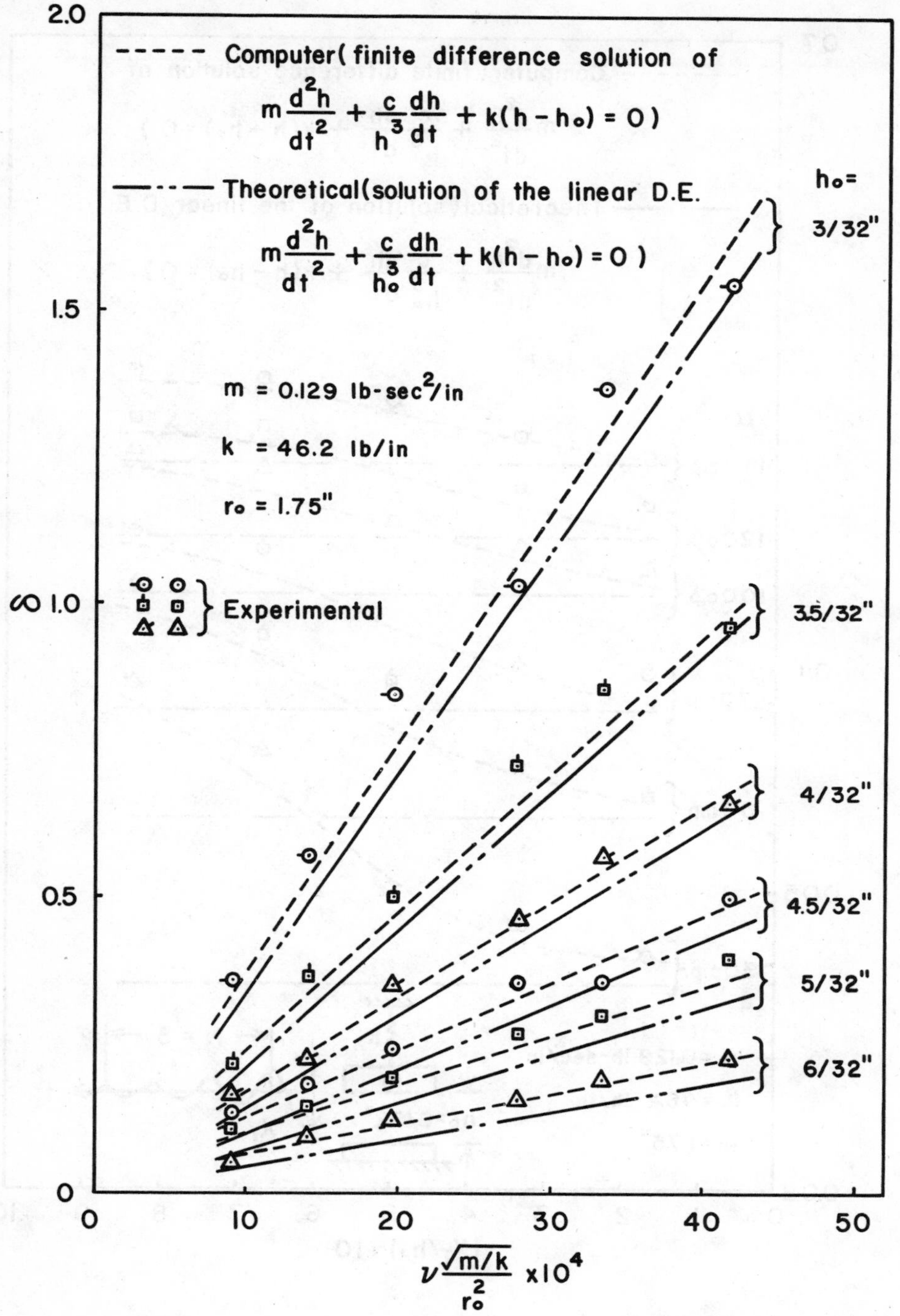

Fig. 16. Damping Factor Versus Viscosity for h_o = 3/32" to 6/32".

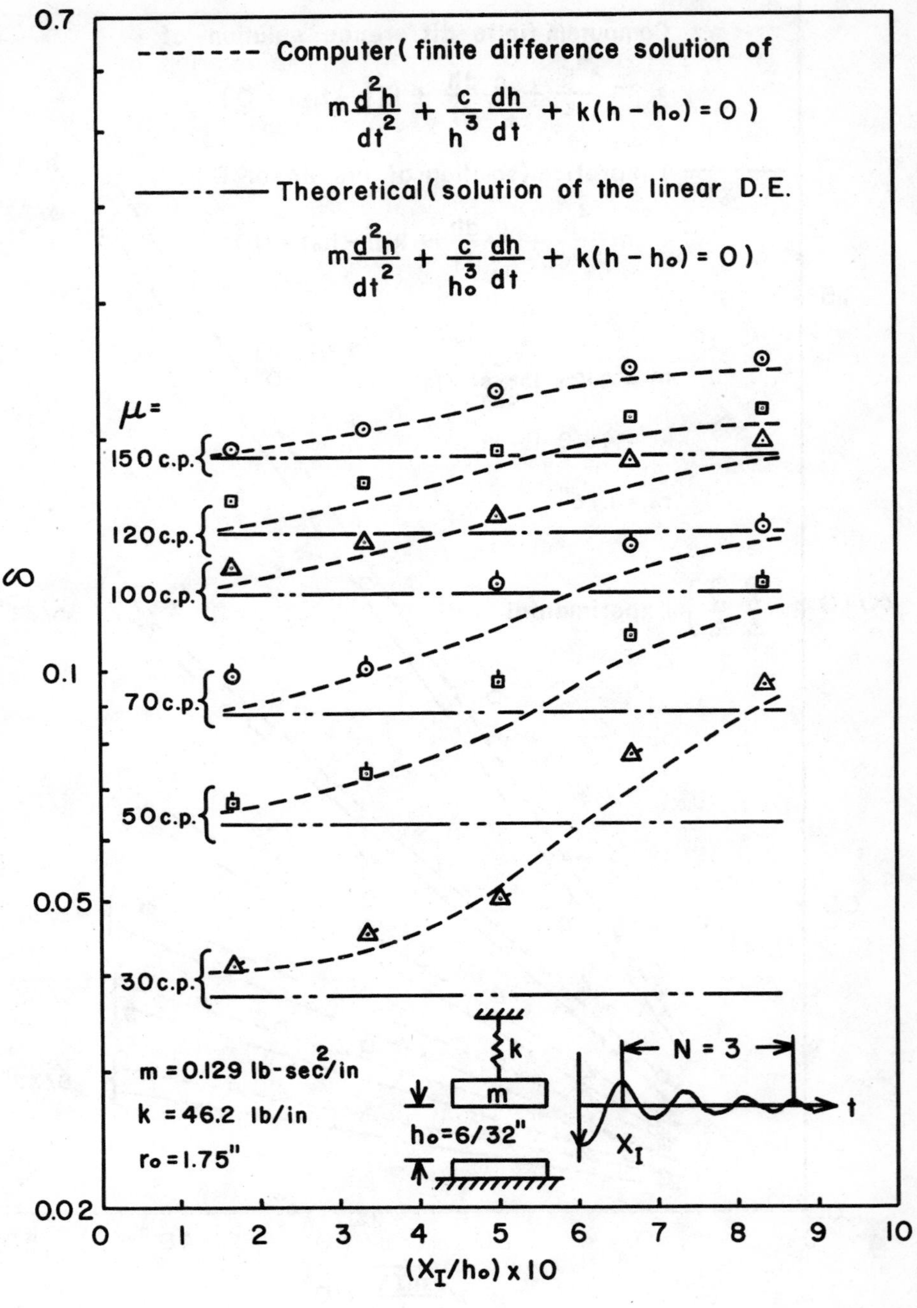

Fig. 17. Damping Factor Versus Initial Displacement.

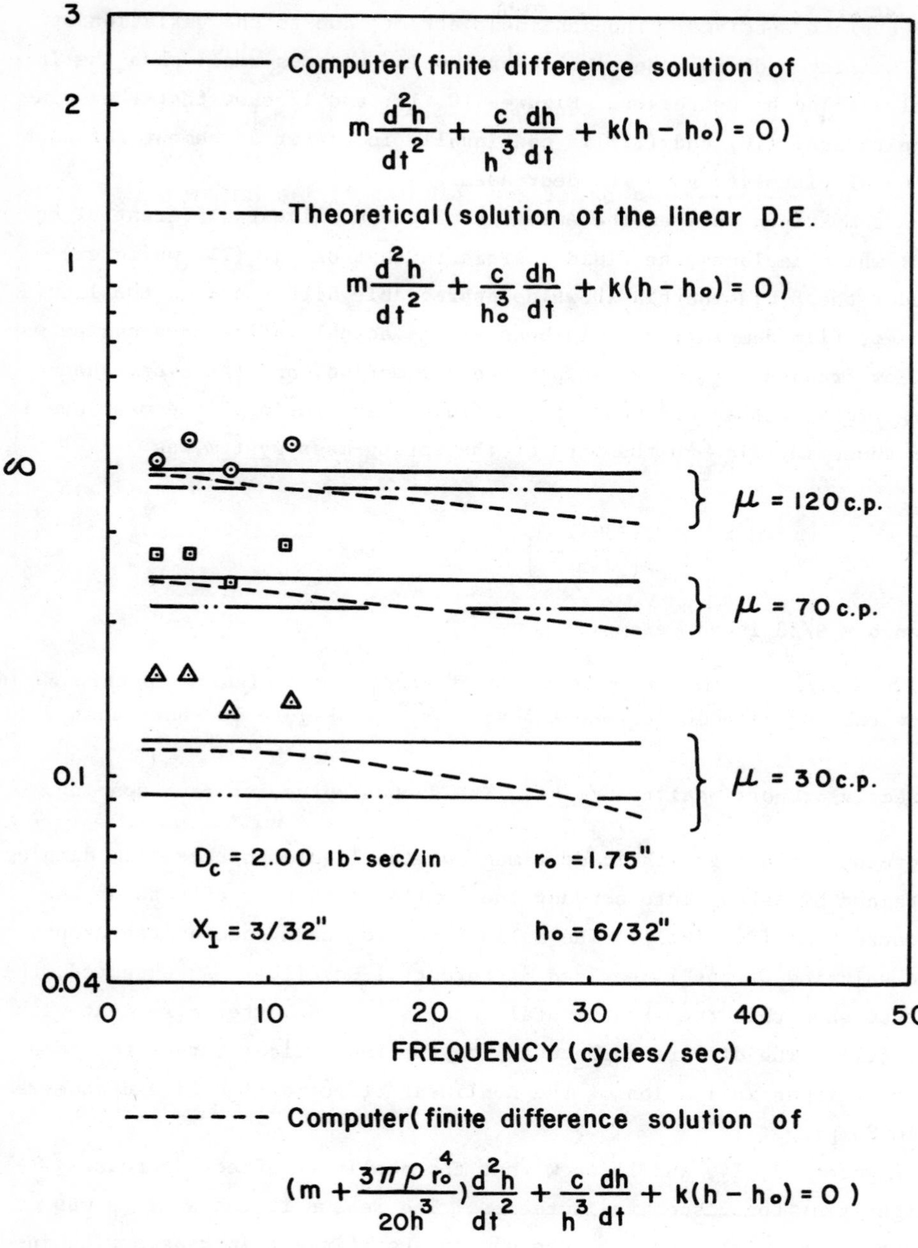

Fig. 18. Damping Factor Versus Frequency.

large plate spacings. The nonlinear effect due to the variation of the spacing h during the oscillatory motion becomes small when the initial spacing h_o decreases. Figures 10, 11, and 12 show that the solution to Eqs. (10) and (21) is continually in better agreement for each value of viscosity as h_o/r_o decreases.

A comparison between the solution of the nonlinear differential Eq. (20) which includes the fluid inertia to that of Eq. (21) which excludes the fluid inertia shows no appreciable difference on the liquid squeeze film damping; this is because the actual spring-mass system was in low frequency (3.0 cycles per second) motion, and the system had a larger mass m than the mass of the fluid. The ratio of the mass due to the squeezing flow to the mass of the spring-mass system was

$$\left(\frac{3\pi\rho r_o^4/m}{20h^3}\right) \times 100 = 1.64\%$$

when h = 6/32 in. for example.

b) Damping Factor as a Function of Viscosity / Figures 13 through 16 show the logarithmic decrement δ vs. $\frac{\nu\sqrt{m/k}}{r_o^2}$. Figure 16 shows that δ is directly proportional to $\frac{\nu\sqrt{m/k}}{r_o^2}$. The dashed curve for each spacing represents the logarithmic decrement of the liquid squeeze film damping obtained by taking into account the nonlinear damping effects of the squeeze film [Eq. (21)]. The solid curve for each spacing represents the solution of the linearized differential Eq. (10). As expected, the curves show that the experimental results are in better agreement with Eq. (21). The difference between the two theoretical curves for each spacing is an indication of the nonlinear effect of the liquid squeeze film damping.

Figures 13, 14, and 15 show that the nonlinear effect decreases slightly as the viscosity increases. The reason is the same as was given in part (a); that is, the damping coefficient increases with increasing viscosity so that the oscillating motion of the plates with a high viscosity liquid squeeze film decays faster than that with smaller viscosity liquids. The amplitude of h during the oscillatory motion becomes smaller as the viscosity increases. Hence the nonlinear effects due to the variation of h decrease slightly as the viscosity increases when δ is calculated using Eq. (17).

c) Damping Factor as a Function of the Initial Displacement / Figure 17 shows that the nonlinear effect of liquid squeeze film damping becomes quite significant when the initial displacement X_I approaches the value of h_o. Two theoretical curves are presented for each viscosity; the solid curve represents the solution to Eq. (10) and the dashed curve is the solution to Eq. (21). The initial spacing h_o was chosen as 6/32 in. for all the experiments. The initial displacement X_I was varied from 1/32 to 5/32 in. in order to generate the oscillating motion of different amplitudes.

The nonlinear differential equation representing the spring-mass system with squeeze film damping may be linearized only when the amplitude of the oscillating motion is small such that $h \simeq h_o$ during the vibratory motion. The data show good agreement between the logarithmic decrements of the solution of the nonlinear and linearized differential equations when the amplitude is small. Therefore the nonlinear effects may be negligible when the amplitude of the oscillating motion is small compared to the spacing h_o but the data clearly show that nonlinear effects must be taken into account for the liquid squeeze film damping when $X_I/h_o \geq 0.1$.

The experimental results agree with the solution to Eq. (21) for each viscosity much better than with Eq. (10) because of the nonlinear characteristics of the actual liquid squeeze film damping. No appreciable fluid inertia effects due to the squeezing flow were found in this part because of low frequency motion.

d) Damping Factor as a Function of Frequency / From the solution of Eq. (10), the logarithmic decrement δ is given as

$$\delta = \frac{2\zeta}{\sqrt{1 - \zeta^2}} \tag{22}$$

where $\zeta = \frac{D}{D_c}$. D_c represents the critical damping coefficient of the spring-mass system and is defined as

$$D_c = 2\sqrt{mk} \tag{23}$$

If D is assumed to be constant, δ is a function of D_c only. The damping coefficient D and frequency of the oscillating motion do not change for two different spring-mass systems while δ is different for each system unless the value of D_c is the same. Hence it was necessary to keep the critical damping coefficient D_c constant throughout the frequency range in order to investigate the frequency effect of liquid squeeze film damping.

Three theoretical curves were obtained by solving Eqs. (10), (20), and (21); the solutions are shown graphically in Figure 18. These differential equations are the linearized differential Eq. (10), the nonlinear differential Eq. (21) in which the fluid inertia is not taken into account, and the nonlinear differential Eq. (20) which includes the nonlinear fluid inertia terms.

The logarithmic decrement δ evaluated from the solutions of the linearized and nonlinear differential equations without the fluid inertia terms do not vary with the frequency under certain conditions (see Table II and Fig. 18). However, the logarithmic decrement obtained from the finite difference solution of the nonlinear differential equation including the nonlinear fluid inertia terms varies slightly and inversely with frequency. If the inertia terms due to the squeezing flow are taken into account in the governing differential equation, the apparent mass of the system increases and consequently the critical damping coefficient $D_c(2\sqrt{mk})$ in the system increases. For example, when one of these terms is included the governing equation becomes

$$\left(m + \frac{3\pi\rho r_o^4}{20h}\right)\frac{d^2h}{dt^2} + \frac{3\pi\mu r_o^4}{2h^3}\frac{dh}{dt} + k(h - h_o) = 0 \tag{24}$$

The effect of the fluid inertia increases with frequency because the mass of the high frequency oscillation is small compared to that of the lower frequency oscillation in the spring-mass system, and yet the fluid inertia term remains the same. The logarithmic decrement δ is expressed as

$$\delta = \frac{\pi}{\sqrt{\frac{D_c^2}{4D^2} - \frac{1}{4}}} \tag{25}$$

which shows that δ varies inversely with D_c when D is held constant. Thus δ decreases with frequency for the conditions listed in Fig. 18.

The amount that the fluid inertia affects the damping factor depends on the ratio of the mass in the spring-mass system and the mass of the fluid. In part (a), (b), and (c) no appreciable inertia effect was found since the system was in low frequency oscillation (3.0 cycles per second) and had a large critical damping coefficient D_c (4.88 lb-sec/in) compared to the D_c(2.00 lb-sec/in) in part (d).

The data were taken in the frequency range of from 3 to 12 cycles per second holding D_c of the spring-mass system constant throughout the experiments. The different frequencies were obtained by changing the ratio k/m. The experimental results show that δ changes little within the frequency range of from 3 to 12 cycles per second since the variation of δ due to the inertia effect is small in that frequency range.

CONCLUSIONS

The following conclusions can be drawn from the research reported herein:

(1) The Reynolds theory is valid for the squeeze film motion under low frequency (3 cycles per second) oscillatory motion for the plate spacings, viscosities, and initial displacements used in these experiments.

(2) The logarithmic decrement δ increases as the initial spacing h_o decreases (other independent variables held constant).

(3) The logarithmic decrement δ was found to vary directly with the viscosity (other independent variables held constant).

(4) The logarithmic decrement δ is inversely proportional to the critical damping coefficient D_c of the spring-mass system.

(5) The damping coefficient must be treated as a nonlinear term due to the variation of h during the oscillatory motion when the amplitude of oscillating motion approaches the same magnitude as spacing h_o.

(6) The rate of variation of δ due to the nonlinear effect becomes small when the viscosity is increased and when the initial spacing decreases for low frequency motion in which the Reynolds theory is used to describe the fluid motion.

(7) The fluid inertia effects may be negligible for low frequency of oscillating motion when the mass in the spring-mass system is large compared to the mass of the fluid.

(8) The computer solution of Eq. (20) shows that the fluid inertia effects should be taken into account for oscillatory motion when the added mass due to the fluid is significant compared to the mass in the spring-mass system.

ACKNOWLEDGMENTS

This research was carried out in the Fluid Mechanics Laboratory at Southern Illinois University. The partial support of this work by the National Aeronautical and Space Administration by means of a Grant (NASA-NGR-14-008-019) is gratefully acknowledged.

REFERENCES

1. Reynolds, O., "On the Theory of Lubrication and Its Application to Mr. Beauchamp Tower's Experiments, Including an Experimental Determination of the Viscosity of Olive Oil," Royal Society of London, Part I, Vol. 177, 157-234.
2. Sommer, Eugene A., "Squeeze-Film Damping," Machine Design, Vol. 38, (1966), 163-167.
3. Jackson, J. D., "A Study of Squeezing Flow," Applied Science Research, A, Vol. 11, (1962), 148-152.
4. Kuzma, Dennis C., "Fluid Inertia Effects in Squeeze Films," Applied Science Research, 18, (1967), 15-20.
5. Ishizawa, Shingo, "The Unsteady Laminar Flow between Two Parallel Discs with Arbitrary Varying Gap Width," Transactions of the Japan Society of Mechanical Engineers, Vol. 9, No. 35, (1966), 533-550.

LAMINAR FLOW IN AN ANNULUS WITH POROUS OUTER WALL

M. S. Tsai
University of Tennessee

Harold L. Weissberg
University of Tennessee

ABSTRACT

The equations of motion for steady, incompressible, viscous flow without swirl in an annular duct with constant radial velocity at porous walls can be reduced, by suitable choice of the form of the stream function, to an ordinary fourth order nonlinear differential equation. A practically important case not specifically treated in previous work, although obtainable as a special case of Terrill's perturbation solution, is that of an impermeable inner wall and a porous outer wall at which the uniform fluid injection or suction occurs. Numerical solutions of the governing differential equation with the appropriate two-point boundary conditions are carried out in the present work for radius ratios between 0.5 and unity. A perturbation solution for small suction Reynolds number (presumably equivalent to that obtainable from Terrill's) and an integral approximation are also described. Discussion of velocity and pressure distribution includes the determination, as a function of radius ratio, of the value of suction Reynolds number associated with vanishing wall slope of velocity profiles and with the onset of adverse pressure gradients.

LIST OF NOTATIONS

a	Inner radius of annulus
b	Outer radius of annulus
C	Constant of integration, Eq. (3)

C_n	Constants in perturbation series; n = 1, 2, ...
E	Coefficient for transformation of dependent variable, Eq. (12)
F	Dimensionless stream function; dependent variable in Eqs. (3) and (5)
G	Transformed dependent variable; Eq. (12)
h	Radial distance between walls of annular channel, (b - a)
N_0, N_x	Reynolds numbers based on average axial component of velocity: $h\,\bar{u}(0)/\nu$ and $h\,\bar{u}(x)/\nu$
p	Pressure
r	Radial coordinate
$\mathcal{R}$,R	Reynolds numbers based on the radial velocity through the porous wall: $b\,v_b/(2\nu)$ and $h\,v_b/\nu$
u	Axial component of velocity
$\bar{u}$	Average value of u over a radial cross section of the annular channel: $\frac{2}{(b^2 - a^2)} \int_a^b r\,u\,dr$
v	Radial component of velocity
v_b	Constant value of v at the porous outer wall where r = b
x	Axial coordinate
η	Dimensionless radial coordinate: $(r/b)^2$
η_0	Value of η at the inner wall where r = a
λ	Dimensionless radial coordinate: $\frac{r - a}{b - a}$
μ	Dynamic viscosity
ν	Kinematic viscosity
ξ	Transformed independent variable; Eq. (12)
ρ	Density
σ	Coefficient for transformation of independent variable; Eq. (12)

INTRODUCTION

A class of problems of current theoretical and practical interest involves the flow of fluids in ducts of various shapes with porous walls. The practical interest is related to such diverse applications as the transpiration cooling of rocket engines, the separation of gas mixtures or the desalination of water by diffusion through porous membrances, and the design of bearings or seals incorporating porous surfaces through which either a lubricant or buffering fluid is injected or removed.

Theoretical interest stems from the fact that the equations of motion can be reduced to an ordinary differential equation (for self-similar solutions) for a variety of porous wall configurations; the resulting solutions exhibit the possibility of adverse pressure gradients and of velocity profiles with inflection points or regions of reverse flow -- flow properties which were previously encountered only for boundary layer flows or flows in ducts with varying cross sectional area.

This paper deals with the self-similar solutions obtainable for the steady flow of an incompressible fluid in the annular duct formed by a stationary, impermeable circular shaft and a concentric porous outer wall through which fluid is injected or removed uniformly over the wall surface. The pertinent ordinary differential equation was obtained by Terrill [1] with boundary conditions appropriate for unequal radial velocities at the inner and outer walls. We have obtained numerical solutions of this equation for the special case in which the fluid velocity at the inner wall vanishes, for radius ratios between 0.5 and unity and for a range of wall flows sufficient to exhibit adverse pressure gradients and velocity profiles with vanishing wall slope ("separation" profiles). Related experimental work is in progress and will be reported elsewhere.

In the following section, the differential equation, its two-point boundary conditions, and approximate and numerical solutions are discussed. In subsequent sections these results are used to exhibit the velocity profiles and pressure distributions; the paper is concluded with a discussion and summary of the results.

The Differential Equation for Self-Similar Solutions

For an annular duct with an inner wall of radius $\underline{a}$ and a concentric outer wall of radius $\underline{b}$, let x and r denote axial and radial coordinates and u and v the corresponding velocity components. The outer wall is taken to be porous and, everywhere on it, the radial velocity component is assumed to have the constant value v_b.

If the dimensionless radial coordinate $\eta \equiv (r/b)^2$ is introduced, the average velocity $\bar{u}(x)$ at any cross section can be written as

$$\bar{u}(x) = \frac{2\pi}{\pi(b^2 - a^2)} \int_a^b r\, u(x,r)\, dr$$

$$= \frac{1}{1 - \eta_0} \int_{\eta_0}^{1} u\, d\eta$$

where

$$\eta_0 \equiv (a/b)^2$$

If a function $F(\eta)$ is now introduced such that

$$u(x,r) = (1 - \eta_0)\, \bar{u}(x)\, F'(\eta) \qquad (1)$$

$$v(x,r) = v_b \eta^{-1/2} F(\eta) \qquad (2)$$

then the Navier-Stokes and continuity equations for an incompressible fluid are satisfied provided that $F(\eta)$ satisfies the ordinary differential equation

$$\eta F''' + F'' + R(F'^2 - FF'') = C \qquad (3)$$

Here C is a constant and R denotes a Reynolds number based on the velocity v_b at the outer wall and the radius b of that wall:

$$R = \frac{b\, v_b}{2\nu} \qquad (4)$$

Suction at the wall corresponds to positive values of R and injection to negative values. The function $F(\eta)$ is actually a dimensionless stream function, for if $\psi(x,r)$ denotes the usual Stokes stream function such that $ru = \partial\psi/\partial r$ and $rv = -\partial\psi/\partial x$, then Eqs. (1) and (2) are equivalent to $F(\eta) = \psi(x,r)/\psi(x,b)$.

Eq. (3), or its equivalent after differentiation,

$$\eta F'''' + 2F''' + R(F'F'' - FF''') = 0 \qquad (5)$$

can be obtained by substitution of Eqs. (1) and (2) into the equations of motion; it is the same as the ordinary differential equation obtained by Terrill [1] but the boundary conditions for which we have obtained solutions are less general than those he discusses.

We assume that no-slip boundary conditions are applicable at both the inner impermeable wall and the outer porous wall so that Eq. (1) gives

$$F'(\eta_0) = 0 \text{ and } F'(1) = 0 \tag{6}$$

The other two boundary conditions for the fourth order equation (5) follow from Eq. (2) and the requirement that the radial velocity component v assume the constant value v_b on the porous wall and vanish on the impermeable wall:

$$F(\eta_0) = 0 \text{ and } F(1) = 1 \tag{7}$$

The numerical solution of Eq. (5) with the two-point boundary conditions (6) and (7) was facilitated by first obtaining approximate solutions by two different methods -- an integral approximation and Terrill's first order perturbation solution. It turns out that the former is simpler while the latter is more accurate over a wider range of wall Reynolds numbers.

The Integral Approximation / An approximation method resembling the Karman-Polhausen approach for boundary layers and first applied to porous channel problems by Morduchow [2] is used here. This approach consists essentially of assuming a functional form for the solution of Eq. (5) containing parameters to be determined by satisfying the boundary conditions (6) and (7) but satisfying the differential equation only on the average instead of at each point. Thus a trial expression for $F(\eta)$ is written as

$$F(\eta) = F_0(\eta) + [A + B\eta + C\eta^2 + D\eta^3 + \eta^4]d \tag{8a}$$

Here

$$F_0(\eta) = 1 + C_0\left[\frac{(1-\eta)^2}{2} + \frac{1-\eta_0}{\log \eta_0}(\eta \log \eta - \eta + 1)\right] \tag{8b}$$

with

$$C_0 = -\left[\frac{(1-\eta_0)^2}{\log \eta_0} - \frac{1-\eta_0^2}{2}\right]^{-1} \tag{8c}$$

is the solution for the annulus with impermeable walls, i.e., F_0 is the solution for $R = 0$.

It is found that the trial solution, Eq. (8), satisfies the boundary conditions (6) and (7) if the constants A, B, C, D depend on the radius ratio parameter η_0 as follows:

$$A = \eta_0^{\ 2} \tag{8d}$$

$$B = -2\eta_0\ (1 + \eta_0) \tag{8e}$$

$$C = 1 + 4\eta_0 + \eta_0^{\ 2} \tag{8f}$$

$$D = -2\ (1 + \eta_0) \tag{8g}$$

The R-dependence of the approximate solution must therefore appear in the remaining parameter d. To evaluate d, we require that the average value of the left-hand side of Eq. (5) vanish:

$$\int_{\eta_0}^{1} [\eta F'''' + 2F''' + R\ (F'F'' - FF''')]d\eta = 0$$

or, from Eq. (3),

$$[\eta F''' + F'' + R\ (F'^2 - FF'')]_{\eta_0}^{1} = 0 \tag{9}$$

Substitution of the trial solution (8) and its derivatives into Eq. (9) yields the following expression for the parameter d:

$$d = \frac{RC_0\left(1 + \dfrac{1 - \eta_0}{\log \eta_0}\right)}{12(1 - \eta_0^2) - 2R(1 - \eta_0^2)} \tag{10}$$

with C_0 as given by Eq. (8c).

Equations (8) and (10) constitute one of the approximate solutions used to facilitate the numerical work.

The Perturbation Solution / The second approximate solution which we have employed is obtained by using the series expansions

$$F(\eta) = \sum_{n=0}^{\infty} F_n(\eta)R^n \quad \text{and} \quad C = \sum_{n=0}^{\infty} C_n\ R^n \tag{11}$$

to generate a system of linear differential equations in the F_n functions by substitution in Eq. (3) and collecting coefficients of like powers of the perturbation parameter R. Terrill [1] has worked out the expressions for F_0, C_0, F_1 and C_1; they have also been evaluated by Tsai [3] for the specific boundary conditions of interest here.

Use of more than two terms in Eqs. (11) would of course be desirable, but the procedure becomes prohibitively lengthy. Even the expressions for F_1 and C_1 are rather cumbersome and will not be repeated here. The expressions for F_0 and C_0 (i.e., the "zeroth order" solutions) are the same as in Eqs. (8b) and (8c).

The Numerical Solutions / The main difficulty in the numerical solution of Eq. (5) is of course that values of $F(\eta)$ and its first three derivatives at one point are required to start the solution, whereas the boundary conditions (6) and (7) specify only the function and its first derivative at two points. The available device for alleviating this difficulty, when the differential equation contains a parameter such as R, has been explained for example by Terrill and Shrestha [4] in connection with numerical solutions for a channel with plane porous walls. A transformation of variables is used as follows.

Let

$$\xi = \sigma\eta \quad \text{and } F(\eta) = EG(\xi) \tag{12}$$

Then Eq. (5) becomes

$$\xi G'''' + 2G''' + RE(G'G'' - GG''') = 0 \tag{13a}$$

and the transformed boundary conditions from (6) and (7) are

$$G(\sigma\eta_0) = G'(\sigma\eta_0) = 0 \tag{13b}$$

and

$$G(\sigma) = 1/E, \quad G'(\sigma) = 0 \tag{13c}$$

The numerical solution is started at some chosen value of ξ_0 by use of (13b) along with assumed values of $G''(\xi_0)$ and $G'''(\xi_0)$ and of the product $RE = R_1$. It is in making the latter assumptions that the results of approximate solutions such as described above are useful.

The solution is continued until a value of ξ is found for which G' vanishes. According to (13c) this value of ξ is set equal to σ and the corresponding value of G determines the value of E. This yields a solution of the original problem although the precise values of η_0 and R are not known until the vanishing of G' terminates the numerical integration. After that, the required results are obtained from the relations $\eta_0 = \xi_0/\sigma$, $R = R_1/E$, $\eta = \xi/\sigma$, and $F(\eta) = EG(\xi)$.

Of course this procedure is not satisfactory if results are required for a prescribed value of η_0, corresponding say to a radius ratio selected for laboratory work. Accordingly, the foregoing procedure was used in an iteration program which was terminated when ξ_0/σ attained a prescribed value of η_0. Details are available in [3].

Approximate and numerical solutions were obtained by the three methods discussed above for various values of R, and for values of $\eta_0 \equiv (a/b)^2$ between 0.25 and 1.0.[1]

The range of R values for which the approximate solutions are useful in obtaining starting values of F'' and F''' for numerical solutions varies with η_0; a detailed discussion is given in [3].

Velocity Profiles

It is seen from Eq. (1) that $F'(\eta)$ is proportional to the ratio of the axial velocity component $u(x,r)$ at any point to the average value $\bar{u}(x)$ over the cross section containing the point.

For the purpose of comparing velocity profile shapes corresponding to different annulus radius ratios, it is useful to introduce a wall Reynolds number R based on the radial clearance (b - a); the relation between this wall Reynolds number and the one used previously is

$$R = \frac{b}{2(b-a)}\,\mathrm{R} = \frac{\mathrm{R}}{2(1-\eta_0^{1/2})} \tag{14}$$

For the same purpose, we also define the dimensionless radial coordinate

$$\lambda = \frac{r-a}{b-a} = \frac{\eta^{1/2} - \eta_0^{1/2}}{1 - \eta_0^{1/2}} \tag{15}$$

Velocity profiles for various values of R and η_0 are shown as plots of $u/\bar{u}$ against λ in Fig. 1. It is seen that R is more important than η_0 in determining the profile shapes.

The slopes of the velocity profiles at the inner wall where $\eta = \eta_0$, i.e., at $\lambda = 0$, can be obtained from Eqs. (1) and (15) as

$$\left.\frac{d(u/\bar{u})}{d\lambda}\right|_{\lambda=0} = 2(1-\eta_0)(1-\eta_0^{1/2})\eta_0^{1/2}\,F''(\eta_0) \tag{16}$$

---

1. The solutions corresponding to $\eta_0 = 1$ were actually obtained for the plane wall problem discussed in [3]. The parameter here designated as R is denoted by R_a in that reference.

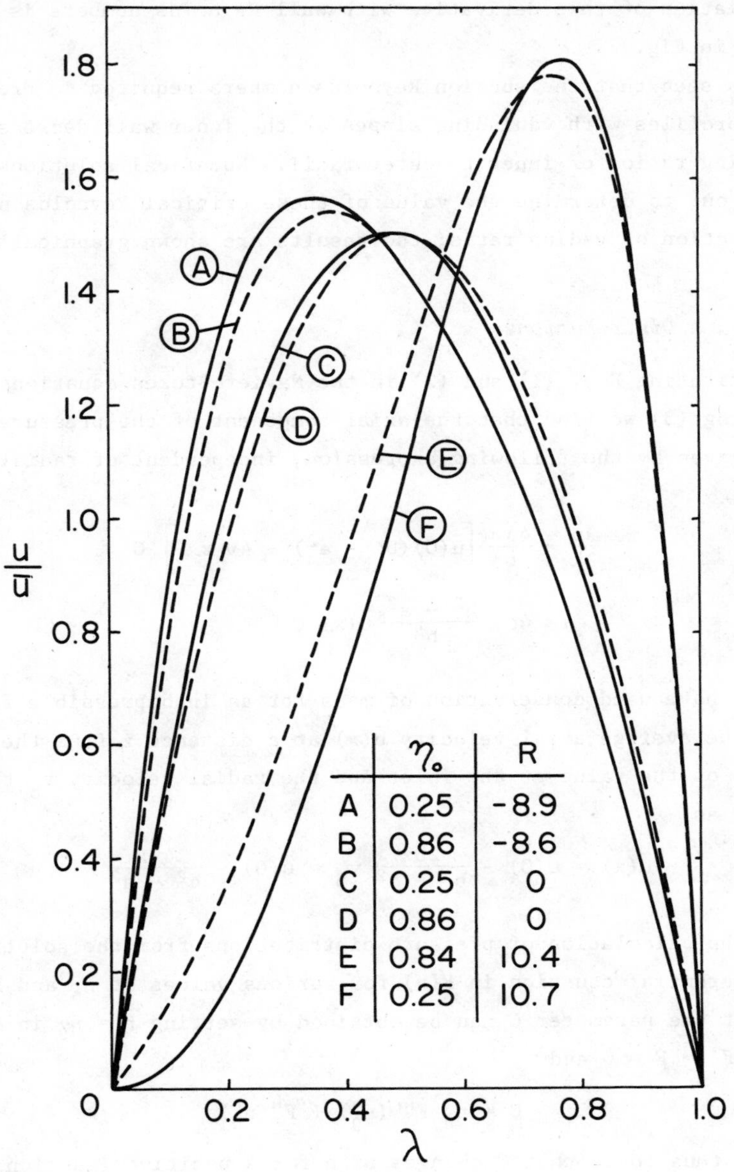

Fig. 1. Axial Velocity Profiles for Various Values of Wall Reynolds Number R and Radius Ratio Parameter η_0 .

The variation of this derivative with wall Reynolds numbers is illustrated in Fig. 2.

It is seen that the suction Reynolds numbers required to produce velocity profiles with vanishing slopes at the inner wall decrease with decreasing ratios of inner to outer radii. Numerical solutions were carried out to determine the value of these critical Reynolds numbers as a function of radius ratio; the results are shown graphically in Fig. 3.

Pressure Distributions

By substituting Eqs. (1) and (2) in the Navier-Stokes equations and then using (3) we find that the axial component of the pressure gradient is given by the following expression, independent of radial position:

$$\frac{\partial p}{\partial x} = \frac{4\rho\nu}{b^4}\left[\bar{u}(0)(b^2 - a^2) - 4\nu\, x\, R\right] C$$

$$= 4\rho\nu \frac{b^2 - a^2}{b^4} \bar{u}(x)\ C \qquad (17)$$

where we have used conservation of mass for an incompressible fluid to obtain the average axial velocity $\bar{u}(x)$ at a distance x from the inlet in terms of the value at the inlet and the radial velocity v_b through the wall as

$$\bar{u}(x) = \bar{u}(0) - \frac{2bx}{b^2 - a^2} v_b = \bar{u}(0) - \frac{4\nu x}{b^2 - a^2} R \qquad (18)$$

For the calculation of pressure distributions from the solutions of the differential equation in $F(\eta)$ for various values of η_0 and R, we note that the parameter C can be obtained by setting $\eta = \eta_0$ in Eq. (3) so that $F' = F = 0$ and

$$C = \eta_0 F'''(\eta_0) + F''(\eta_0) \qquad (19)$$

It is thus found that C changes sign for a positive (suction) value of the wall Reynolds number so that adverse pressure gradients are obtained for sufficiently large suction rates. The dependence of the value of the Reynolds number for which $\partial p/\partial x$ changes sign on the radius ratio parameter η_0 is shown in Fig. 4; the Reynolds number R introduced in Eq. (14) is used in this figure.

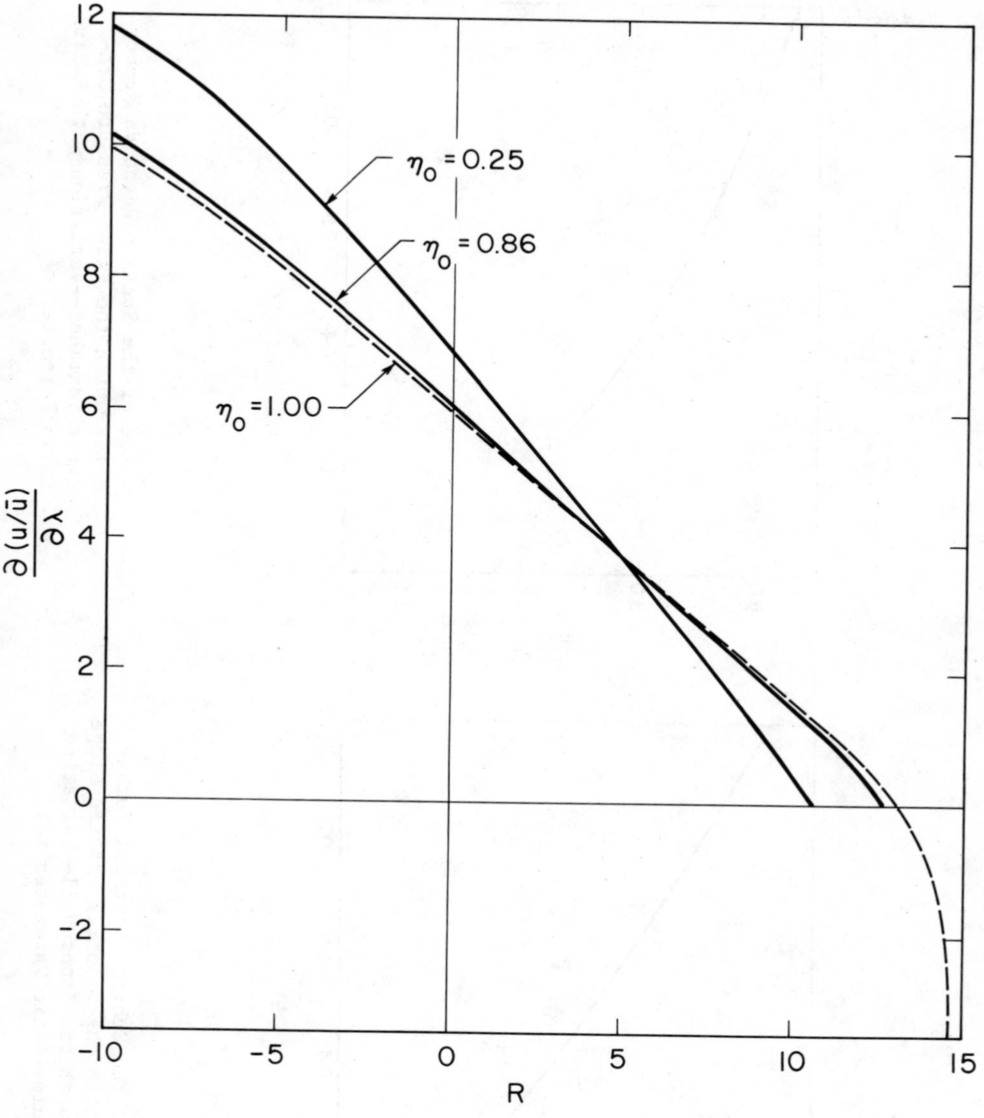

Fig. 2. Variation of Velocity Profile Slope at Inner Wall with Wall Reynolds Number.

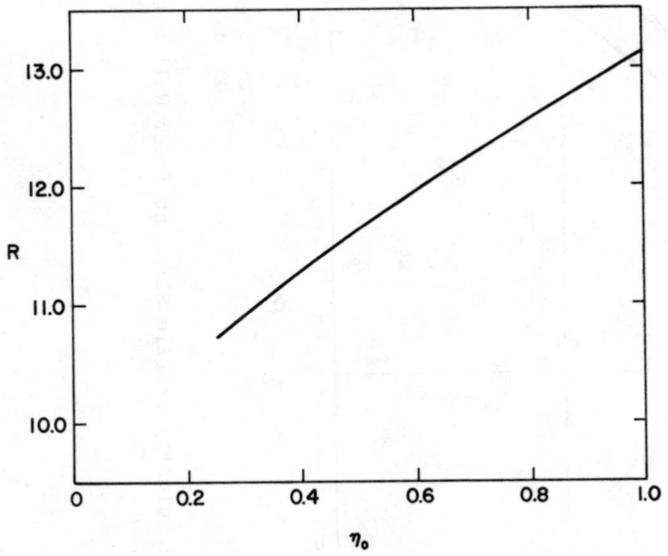

Fig. 3. Value of the Suction Reynolds Number R for which the Velocity Profile Slope Vanishes at the Inner Wall—Variation with Radius Ratio Parameter η_0.

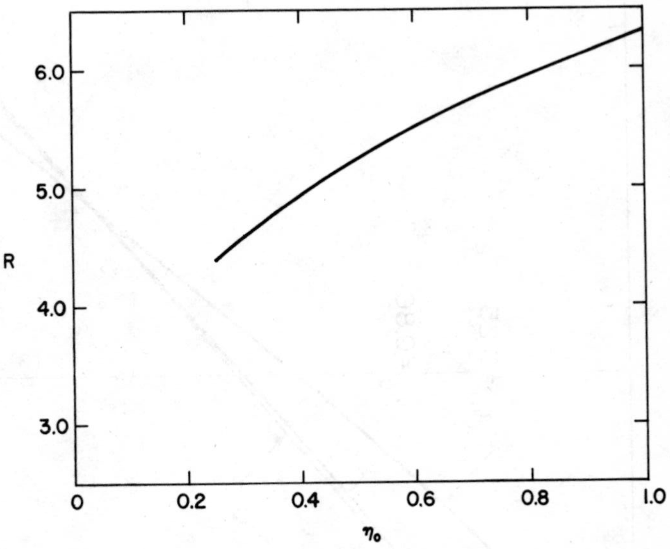

Fig. 4. Value of the Suction Reynolds Number R for which the Axial Pressure Gradient Vanishes—Variation with Radius Ratio Parameter η_0.

Equation (17) is readily integrated to obtain pressure distributions:

$$p(x,\eta) - p(0,\eta) = \frac{4\rho\nu}{b^4}\,[u(0)(b^2 - a^2)\,x - 2\nu\,\mathcal{R}\,x^2]\;C$$

Use of Eqs. (14) and (18) then furnishes the convenient dimensionless expressions

$$\frac{p(x,\eta) - p(0,\eta)}{\frac{1}{2}\,\rho\bar{u}^2(x)} = 8(1-\eta_0^{1/2})^2\;C\,\frac{x}{h\,N_x}\left[1-\eta_0 + R(1-\eta_0^{1/2})\,\frac{x}{h\,N_x}\right] \quad (20)$$

and

$$\frac{p(x,\eta) - p(0,\eta)}{\frac{1}{2}\,\rho\bar{u}^2(0)} = 8(1-\eta_0^{1/2})^2\;C\,\frac{x}{h\,N_0}\left[1-\eta_0 - R(1-\eta_0^{1/2})\,\frac{x}{h\,N_0}\right] \quad (21)$$

where N_x and N_0 are Reynolds numbers based on average axial velocity and the radial distance between the walls $h \equiv b - a$:

$$N_x = h\,\bar{u}(x)/\nu, \qquad N_0 = h\,\bar{u}(0)/\nu$$

Typical graphs showing the variation of pressure with distance along the annulus, obtained from Eqs. (20) and (21), are shown in Figs. 5 and 6. Only one value of η_0 is used here since, as in the case of the velocity profiles, the effect of radius ratio variation down to a/b = 0.5 or η_0 = 0.25 is not very pronounced when the wall Reynolds number R (rather than $\mathcal{R}$) is held fixed in making the comparison.

Summary and Discussion

In this theoretical study of flow in an annulus with the outer wall porous, the two dimensionless parameters which characterize the results are the wall Reynolds number $R \equiv h\,v_b/\nu$ and the radius ratio parameter $\eta_0 \equiv (a/b)^2$. Although another wall Reynolds number $\mathcal{R} \equiv b\,v_b/(2\nu)$ was first introduced in the pertinent differential equation, this was less useful in comparing results for various values of η_0.

For the range $0.25 < \eta_0 < 1.0$ investigated in this work, the effect of the variation of η_0 is found not to be very pronounced for either velocity or pressure distributions. For smaller values of η_0 it can be anticipated that this would no longer be true. For example, with $\mathcal{R}$ = 0 the maximum value of $u/\bar{u}$ stays close to 1.5 for our range of η_0 values -- cf. Fig. 1, whereas it is well known that the maximum $u/\bar{u}$ approaches

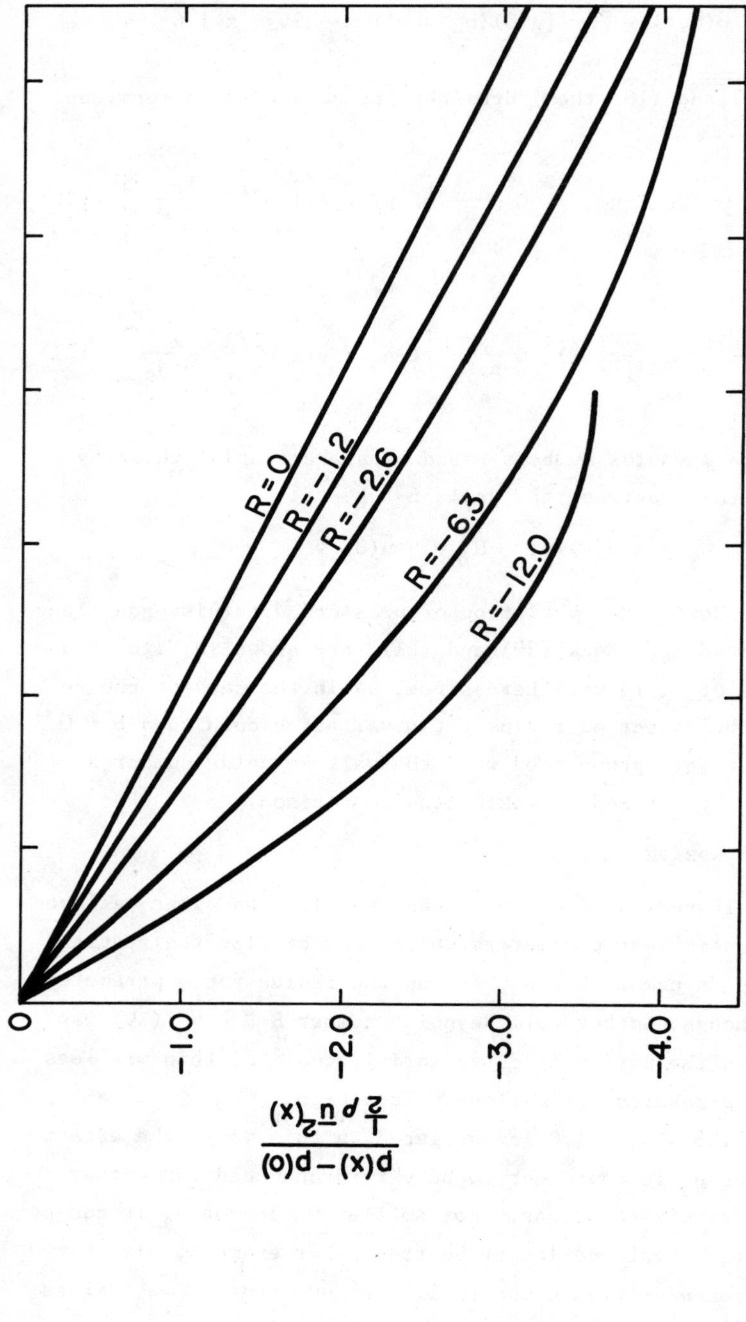

Fig. 5. Pressure Distributions for Various Amounts of Injection at the Porous Wall—Calculated with Negative Values of R in Eq. (20); $\eta_0 = 0.84$.

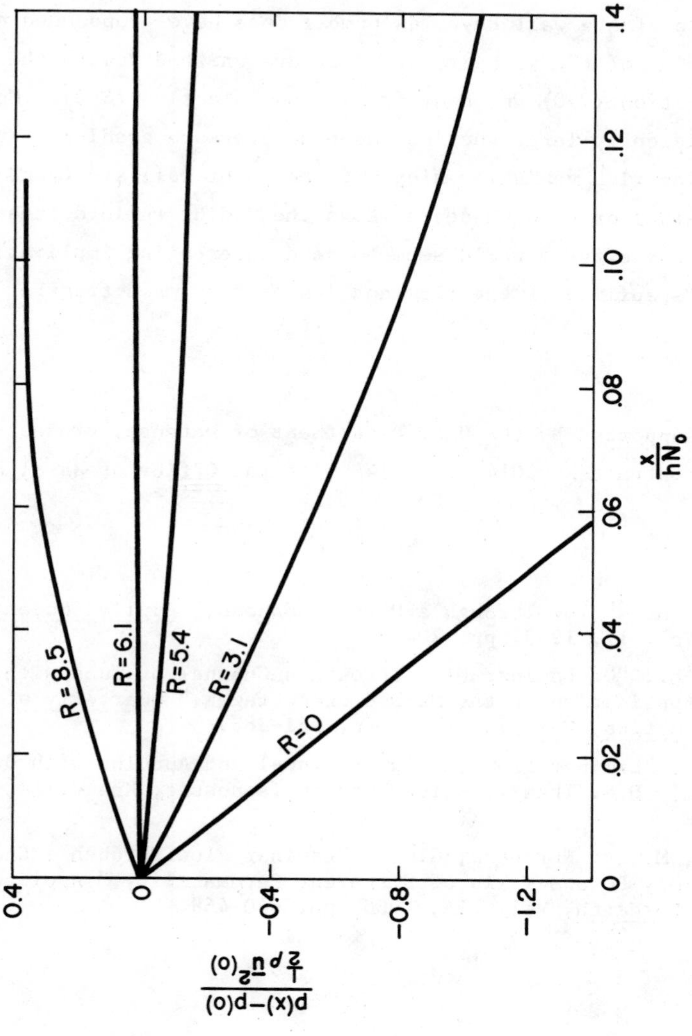

Fig. 6. Pressure Distributions for Various Amounts of Suction at the Porous Wall—Calculated with Positive Values of R in Eq. (21); η_0 = 0.84.

2.0 as η_0 approaches zero. In view of the behavior of the solutions it seems desirable to consider the study of the annulus as a departure either from a channel with plane walls or from a circular tube. It is only the former that has been considered in the present work.

The variation of the wall Reynolds number does have pronounced effects. The maxima of the velocity profiles are shifted toward the porous wall by suction ($R>0$) and away from it by injection ($R<0$). Moreover, for sufficiently large suction, adverse pressure gradients and velocity profiles with vanishing slope at the inner wall are found -- for positive values of R which decrease as the radius ratio decreases from unity. These effects would seem to have interesting implications concerning the stability of the flow and its heat or mass transfer properties.

ACKNOWLEDGEMENT

This work was supported by the U.S. Department of Defense, Project Themis, under contract N 00014-68-A-0144 with the Office of Naval Research.

REFERENCES

1. Terrill, R. M., "Flow Through a Porous Annulus," Applied Scientific Research, Vol. 17, 1967, pp. 204-22.
2. Morduchow, M., "On Laminar Flow Through a Channel or Tube with Injection: Application of the Method of Averages," Quarterly of Applied Mathematics, Vol. 14, 1957, pp. 361-368.
3. Tsai, M. S., "Laminar Flow in Plane Channel and Annulus with One Porous Wall," M.S. Thesis, University of Tennessee, Knoxville, 1968.
4. Terrill, R. M. and Shrestha, G. M., "Laminar Flow Through a Channel with Uniformly Porous Walls of Different Permeability," Applied Scientific Research, Vol. 15A, 1965, pp. 440-468.

UNSTEADY SPHERICAL COUETTE FLOW

Phillip R. Smith
New Mexico State University

Michel Charles
New Mexico State University

ABSTRACT

The equation of motion and the energy equation for unsteady laminar spherical Couette flow of an incompressible, constant viscosity fluid are solved for a general set of boundary conditions. The solutions are in the form of double infinite series of Legendre functions and Bessel's functions. A representative table of eigenvalues is presented for radius ratio of 2.0.

LIST OF NOTATIONS

B_r, B_θ, B_ϕ	Components of the body force, F/L^3
C_v	Specific heat at constant volume, $L^2/T^2\Theta$
$f_1(r)$	Function of r defined by Equation (7)
$f_2(r)$	Function of r defined by Equation (8)
$G(r,\theta,t)$	Function of r, θ, t defined by Equation (21), Θ/T
$H(r,\theta,t)$	Function of r, θ, t defined by Equation (24), Θ/T
$H(\delta_m,\lambda_n,t)$	Integral transform of $H(r,\theta,t)$
$J_p(\delta_m r)$	Bessel function of the first kind
K	Thermal conductivity of the fluid, $F/T\Theta$
$M(r,\theta,t)$	Function of r, θ, t defined by Equation (10), L/T^2
$M(\delta_m,\lambda_n,t)$	Integral transform of $M(r,\theta,t)$, Equation (13)
m	Integer, m = 1, 2, 3, ...
n	Integer, n = 0, 1, 2, 3, ...
$P_n(\cos\theta)$	n^{th} Legendre Polynomial
$P_n^1(\cos\theta)$	Associated Legendre function of order one

p	Pressure, F/L^2
$Q(r,\theta,t)$	Heat generation, Θ/T
r	Radial coordinate, L
r_1	Radius of inner sphere, L
r_2	Radius of outer sphere, L
$T(r,\theta,t)$	Temperature of the fluid, Θ
$T_2(t)$	Temperature of the outer sphere, Θ
$T_i(r,\theta)$	Initial temperature of the fluid, Θ
t	Time, T
$v(r,\theta,t)$	Function defined by Equation (4), L/T
$v_i(r,\theta)$	Initial value of $v(r,\theta,t)$, L/T
$v_i(\delta_m,\lambda_n)$	Integral transform of $v_i(r,\theta)$, Equation (12)
$v_\phi(r,\theta,t)$	Longitudinal velocity of the fluid, L/T
$v_{\phi i}(r,\theta)$	Initial longitudinal velocity, L/T
$w_m(r)$	Characteristic function defined by Equation (14)
α	Thermal diffusivity of fluid, $K/\rho C_v$, L^2/T
δ_m	Eigenvalue defined by Equation (18), 1/L
$\Theta(r,\theta,t)$	Function of r, θ, t defined by Equation (22), Θ
$\Theta_i(r,\theta)$	Initial value of $\Theta(r,\theta,t)$, Θ
$\Theta(\delta_m,\lambda_n)$	Integral transform of $\Theta_i(r,\theta)$, Equation (26)
θ	Colatitude coordinate
λ_n	Eigenvalue, $\lambda_n = n(n+1)$
μ	Dynamic viscosity, FT/L^2
ν	Kinematic viscosity, L^2/T
ρ	Density of the fluid, FT^2/L^4
ϕ	Longitudinal coordinate
$\omega_1(t),\omega_2(t)$	Angular velocities of the inner and outer sphere, respectively, 1/T

INTRODUCTION

Although a few solutions to spherical Couette flow appear in the literature [1,2], the general solution to the laminar, time dependent flow appears to have been neglected. In this paper a general solution is obtained for the motion of an incompressible viscous fluid of constant viscosity contained between two concentric rotating spheres for which the angular velocities are arbitrary functions of time. Further, a general solution to the energy equation for this flow is found where the temperature of the outer sphere is an arbitrary function of time and heat is being generated within the fluid as an arbitrary function of the radius, colatitude, and time.

The Equations of Motion

Consider a Couette flow between two concentric spheres as shown in Fig. 1. The inner sphere is rotating about the z-axis with an angular velocity of $\omega_1(t)$ while the outer sphere rotates about the z-axis with an angular velocity $\omega_2(t)$. The velocity and pressure are assumed to be symmetrical about the z-axis so that $\partial/\partial\phi = 0$. Further, it is assumed that the radial and latitudinal velocities are zero. Thus, the motion of the fluid is only a rotation about the z-axis.

The equations of motion in spherical coordinates are, in this case

$$-\rho \frac{v_\phi^2}{r} = B_r - \frac{\partial p}{\partial r} \tag{1}$$

$$-\rho v_\phi^2 \frac{\cot\theta}{r} = B_\theta - \frac{1}{r}\frac{\partial p}{\partial \theta} \tag{2}$$

and

$$\rho \frac{\partial v_\phi}{\partial t} = B_\phi + \mu\left\{\frac{1}{r^2}\frac{\partial}{\partial r}\left(r^2 \frac{\partial v_\phi}{\partial r}\right) + \frac{1}{r^2 \sin\theta}\frac{\partial}{\partial\theta}\left(\sin\theta \frac{\partial v_\phi}{\partial\theta}\right) - \frac{v_\phi}{r^2 \sin^2\theta}\right\} \tag{3}$$

in which v_ϕ is the longitudinal velocity and B_r, B_θ, and B_ϕ are the components of the body force. The body force is taken to be a known function of the colatitude θ and the radius r. Equations (1), (2), and (3) are not coupled, thus Equation (3) can be solved first for v_ϕ and then the pressure can be determined from Equations (1) and (2).

The boundary conditions for Equation (3) are

1. $v_\phi(r_1, \theta, t) = r_1 \sin\theta\, \omega_1(t)$
2. $v_\phi(r_2, \theta, t) = r_2 \sin\theta\, \omega_2(t)$
3. $v_\phi(r, 0, t) = 0$
4. $v_\phi(r, \pi, t) = 0$

and the initial condition is

5. $v_\phi(r, \theta, 0) = v_{\phi i}(r,\theta)$

where $\omega_1(t)$, $\omega_2(t)$ and $v_{\phi i}(r,\theta)$ are arbitrary functions.

The boundary can be rendered homogeneous by the following technique. Let

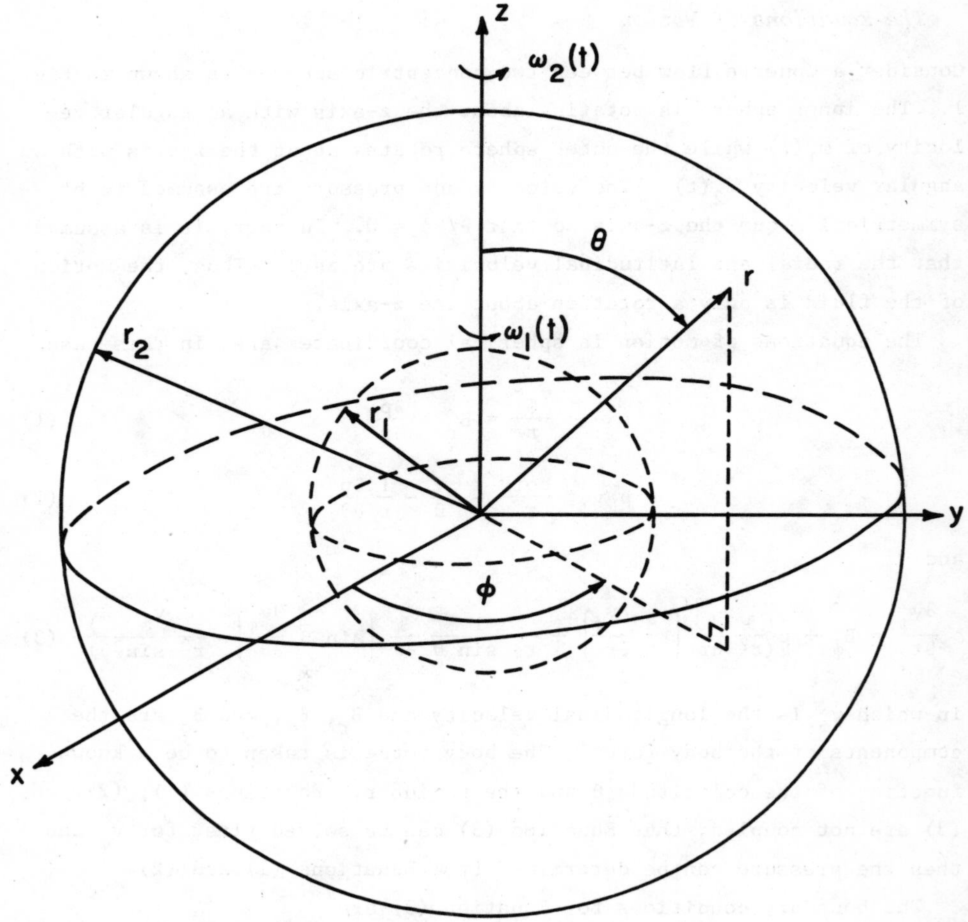

Fig. 1. The Geometry of Concentric Rotating Spheres.

$$v(r,\theta,t) = v_\phi(r,\theta,t) - f_1(r)r_1 \sin\theta\ \omega_1(t) - f_2(r)r_2 \sin\theta\ \omega_2(t) \tag{4}$$

and require that

$$\frac{d}{dr}\left(r^2 \frac{df_1}{dr}\right) = 0 \tag{5}$$

and

$$\frac{d}{dr}\left(r^2 \frac{df_2}{dr}\right) = 0 \tag{6}$$

Further, require that

1. $v(r_1, \theta, t) = 0$
2. $v(r_2, \theta, t) = 0$

These latter conditions in conjunction with Equation (4) yield boundary conditions for $f_1(r)$ and $f_2(r)$:

1. $f_1(r_1) = 1, \quad f_2(r_1) = 0$
2. $f_1(r_2) = 0, \quad f_2(r_2) = 1$

The solution of Equations (5) and (6) now yields

$$f_1(r) = \frac{r_1}{r_2 - r_1}\left(\frac{r_2}{r} - 1\right) \tag{7}$$

and

$$f_2(r) = \frac{r_2}{r_2 - r_1}\left(1 - \frac{r_1}{r}\right) \tag{8}$$

Finally, after substitution of Equations (4), (5), (6), (7), and (8) into Equation (3), one obtains

$$\frac{\partial v}{\partial t}(r,\theta,t) = \nu\left\{\frac{1}{r^2}\frac{\partial}{\partial r}\left[r^2 \frac{\partial v}{\partial r}(r,\theta,t)\right] + \frac{1}{r^2 \sin\theta}\frac{\partial}{\partial\theta}\left[\sin\theta \frac{\partial v}{\partial\theta}(r,\theta,t)\right] - \frac{v(r,\theta,t)}{r^2 \sin^2\theta}\right\} + M(r,\theta,t) \tag{9}$$

with boundary and initial conditions

1. $v(r_1,\theta,t) = 0$
2. $v(r_2,\theta,t) = 0$
3. $v(r,0,t) = 0$
4. $v(r,\pi,t) = 0$
5. $v(r,\theta,0) = v_{\phi i}(r,\theta) - \sin\theta\left[f_1(r)r_1\omega_1(0) + f_2(r)\ r_2\omega_2(0)\right] = v_i(r,\theta)$

and in which

$$M(r,\theta,t) = \frac{B_\phi}{\rho} - f_1(r)\sin\theta\,\omega_1'(t) - f_2(r)\,r_2\sin\theta\,\omega_2'(t)$$

$$+ \frac{\nu}{r^2}\left\{\frac{1}{\sin\theta}\frac{d}{d\theta}\left(\sin\theta\,\frac{d(\sin\theta)}{d\theta}\right) - \frac{\sin\theta}{\sin^2\theta}\right\}\left\{f_1(r)r_1\omega_1(t) + f_2(r)r_2\omega_2(t)\right\} \tag{10}$$

a known function if B_ϕ, $\omega_1(t)$ and $\omega_2(t)$ are specified.

The solution to Equation (9), found by the finite transform method [3], is

$$v(r,\theta,t) = \frac{1}{2}\sum_{n=0}^{\infty}\sum_{m=1}^{\infty}\frac{(2n+1)(n-1)!}{(n+1)!}\left\{v_i(\delta_m,\lambda_n)\,e^{-\nu\delta_m{}^2 t}\right.$$

$$\left.+ M(\delta_m,\lambda_n,t) * e^{-\nu\delta_m{}^2 t}\right\}\frac{w_m(r)\,P_n^1(\cos\theta)}{\left(w_m(r),\,w_m(r)\right)} \tag{11}$$

in which

$$v_i(\delta_m,\lambda_n) = \int_{r_1}^{r_2}\left\{\int_{\pi}^{0} v(r,\theta,0)\,P_n^1(\cos\theta)\,d(\cos\theta)\right\} r^2\,w_m(r)\,dr \tag{12}$$

$$M(\delta_m,\lambda_n,t) = \int_{r_1}^{r_2}\left\{\int_{\pi}^{0} M(r,\theta,t)\,P_n^1(\cos\theta)\,d(\cos\theta)\right\} r^2 w_m(r)\,dr \tag{13}$$

$P_n^1(\cos\theta)$ is the associated Legendre function of degree n and order one, $w_m(r)$ is a characteristic function

$$w_m(r) = r^{-1/2}\,\{J_p(\delta_m r_1)\,J_{-p}(\delta_m r) - J_{-p}(\delta_m r_1)\,J_p(\delta_m r)\} \tag{14}$$

where $J_p(\delta_m r)$ is the Bessel function of the first kind of order p, and $p = n + 1/2$. Further,

$$\left(w_m(r),\,w_m(r)\right) = \int_{r_1}^{r_2} r^2\,w_m^2(r)\,dr \tag{15}$$

is the inner product of $w_m(r)$, and

$$M(\delta_m,\lambda_n,t) * e^{-\nu\delta_m^2 t} = \int_0^t M(\delta_m,\lambda_n,\tau)\,e^{-\nu\delta_m^2(t-\tau)}\,d\tau \tag{16}$$

is the convolution of $M(\delta_m, \lambda_n, t)$ and $e^{-\nu\delta_m^2 t}$. The eigenvalues λ_n are

$$\lambda_n = n(n + 1), \quad n = 0,1,2,3, \ldots \tag{17}$$

while the eigenvalues δ_m, m = 1,2,3, ..., are given by the zeros of the equation

$$J_{-n-1/2}(\delta r_2)\, J_{n+1/2}(\delta r_1) - J_{n+1/2}(\delta r_2)\, J_{-n-1/2}(\delta r_1) = 0 \tag{18}$$

In the Appendix, a representative table of the eigenvalues δ_m is presented for radius ratio r_2/r_1 of 2.0 and n ranging from 0 to 10 and m ranging from 1 to 20.

Finally, the velocity profile is obtained, by substitution of Equation (11), into (4) and solving for v_ϕ, as

$$\begin{aligned} v_\phi(r,\theta,t) &= f_1(r)\, r_1 \sin\theta\, \omega_1(t) + f_2(r)\, r^2 \sin\theta\, \omega_2(t) \\ &+ \frac{1}{2} \sum_{n=0}^{\infty} \sum_{m=1}^{\infty} \frac{(2n+1)(n-1)!}{(n+1)!} \left\{ v_i(\delta_m, \lambda_n)\, e^{-\nu\delta_m^2 t} \right. \\ &\left. + M(\delta_m, \lambda_n, t) * e^{-\nu\delta_m^2 t} \right\} \frac{w_m(r)\, P_n^1(\cos\theta)}{\left(w_m(r), w_m(r)\right)} \end{aligned} \tag{19}$$

where $f_1(r)$ and $f_2(r)$ are given by Equation (7) and (8), respectively.

The Energy Equation

The energy equation in spherical coordinates for an incompressible viscous Couette flow with a constant viscosity is

$$\begin{aligned} \frac{\partial T}{\partial t}(r,\theta,t) &= \alpha \left\{ \frac{1}{r^2} \frac{\partial}{\partial r} \left[r^2 \frac{\partial T(r,\theta,t)}{\partial r} \right] \right. \\ &\left. + \frac{1}{r^2 \sin\theta} \frac{\partial}{\partial\theta} \left(\sin\theta \frac{\partial T}{\partial\theta}(r,\theta,t) \right) \right\} + G(r,\theta,t) \end{aligned} \tag{20}$$

in which

$$G(r,\theta,t) = \frac{\nu}{C_v} \left\{ \left[r \frac{\partial}{\partial r} \left(\frac{v_\phi}{r} \right) \right]^2 + \left[\frac{\sin\theta}{r} \frac{\partial}{\partial\theta} \left(\frac{v_\phi}{\sin\theta} \right) \right]^2 \right\} + Q(r,\theta,t) \tag{21}$$

and where $Q(r,\theta,t)$ is the internal heat generation. Since the velocity is known from Equation (18), then, if $Q(r,\theta,t)$ is given, $G(r,\theta,t)$ is a known function.

The boundary conditions for Equation (20) are assumed to be

1. $T(r_1,\theta,t) = 0$
2. $T(r_2,\theta,t) = T_2(t)$
3. $\frac{\partial T}{\partial \theta}(r,0,t) = 0$
4. $\frac{\partial T}{\partial \theta}(r,\pi,t) = 0$

and the initial condition is taken as

5. $T(r,\theta,0) = T_i(r,\theta)$

The boundary conditions can be made homogeneous by the transformation

$$\Theta(r,\theta,t) = T(r,\theta,t) - \left(\frac{r - r_1}{r_2 - r_1}\right) T_2(t) \tag{22}$$

Equation (20) now becomes

$$\frac{\partial \Theta}{\partial t} = \alpha \left\{\frac{\partial^2 \Theta}{\partial r^2} + \frac{2}{r}\left[\frac{\partial \Theta(r,\theta,t)}{\partial r}\right] + \frac{1}{r^2 \sin\theta}\frac{\partial}{\partial \theta}\left[\sin\theta \frac{\partial \Theta}{\partial \theta}\right]\right\} + H(r,\theta,t) \tag{23}$$

in which

$$H(r,\theta,t) = G(r,\theta,t) + \frac{2\alpha}{r}\frac{T_2(t)}{(r_2 - r_1)} - \left(\frac{r - r_1}{r_2 - r_1}\right) T_2'(t) \tag{24}$$

The boundary and initial conditions are now

1. $\Theta(r_1,\theta,t) = 0$
2. $\Theta(r_2,\theta,t) = 0$
3. $\frac{\partial \Theta}{\partial \theta}(r,0,t) = 0$
4. $\frac{\partial \Theta}{\partial \theta}(r,\pi,t) = 0$
5. $\Theta(r,\theta,0) = T_i(r,\theta) - \left(\frac{r - r_1}{r_2 - r_1}\right) T_2(0) = \Theta_i(r,\theta)$

The solution to Equation (23) is found, by the method of finite transforms, to be

$$\Theta(r,\theta,t) = \sum_{n=0}^{\infty}\sum_{m=1}^{\infty}\left(\frac{2n + 1}{2}\right)\left\{\Theta_i(\delta_m,\lambda_n)\, e^{-\alpha\delta_m^2 t} + H(\delta_m,\lambda_n,t) * e^{-\alpha\delta_m^2 t}\right\}\frac{w_m(r)\, P_n(\cos\theta)}{\left(w_m(r),\, w_m(r)\right)} \tag{25}$$

in which

$$\Theta_i(\delta_m,\lambda_n) = \int_{r_1}^{r_2} \left\{ \int_{\pi}^{0} \Theta(r,\theta,0)\, P_n(\cos\theta)\, d(\cos\theta) \right\} r^2\, w_m(r)\,dr \qquad (26)$$

$$H(\delta_m,\lambda_n,t) = \int_{r_1}^{r_2} \left\{ \int_{\pi}^{0} H(r,\theta,t)\, P_n(\cos\theta)\, d(\cos\theta) \right\} r^2\, w_m(r)\,dr \qquad (27)$$

$P_n(\cos\theta)$ is the nth Legendre polynomial, $w_m(r)$ is the characteristic function defined by Equation (14), $(w_m(r), w_m(r))$ is the inner product of $w_m(r)$ defined by Equation (15), and λ_n and δ_m are eigenvalues defined by Equations (17) and (18), respectively.

The final temperature distribution is obtained by substitution of Equation (25) into Equation (22) and solving for $T(r,\theta,t)$:

$$T(r,\theta,t) = \left(\frac{r - r_1}{r_2 - r_1}\right) T_2(t) + \sum_{n=0}^{\infty} \sum_{m=1}^{\infty} \left(\frac{2n+1}{2}\right) \left\{\Theta_i(\delta_m,\lambda_n)\, e^{-\alpha\delta_m^2 t} + H(\delta_m,\lambda_n,t) * e^{-\alpha\delta_m^2 t}\right\} \frac{w_m(r)\, P_n(\cos\theta)}{(w_m(r), w_m(r))} \qquad (28)$$

Discussion and Conclusion

A general solution for the unsteady motion of an incompressible viscous fluid contained between two concentric rotating spheres has been obtained. If the velocity given by this solution, Equation (19), is substituted into the original differential equation, Equation (3), and into the boundary and initial conditions, they are all satisfied identically.

Further, a general solution to the time dependent energy equation has been found for this flow. When the temperature given by this equation, Equation (28), is substituted into the original differential equation, Equation (20), and into the boundary and initial conditions, they are all satisfied identically.

REFERENCES

1. Langlois, W. E., Slow Viscous Flow, 1st Edition, The Macmillan Company, New York, 1964.

2. Kanwal, K. P., "Slow Steady Rotation of Axially Symmetric Bodies in a Viscous Fluid," Journal of Fluid Mechanics, Vol. 10, 1961.

3. Tsai, C. H. and Smith, P. R., "Finite Transform Solutions of Starting Couette Flow," Proceedings of the 10th Midwestern Mechanics Conference, Fort Collins, Colorado, August, 1967.

BIBLIOGRAPHY

1. Cobble, M. H., "Spherical Shell Heat Exchanger-Dirichlet Problem," Journal of the Franklin Institute, Vol. 276, No. 3, September, 1963.

APPENDIX. Tables of the Eigenvalues δ_m of Eq. (18)

$r_2/r_1 = 2.0$

δ_m (m ↓, n →)	0	1	2	3	4	5
1	0.3141610E 1	0.3286014E 1	0.2021997E-1	0.5087994E-1	0.2101997E-1	0.2101997E-1
2	0.6283186E 1	0.6360679E 1	0.3555788E 1	0.3922531E 1	0.2414597E 0	0.3452994E 0
3	0.9424785E 1	0.9477216E 1	0.6513069E 1	0.6735578E 1	0.4358418E 1	0.4841017E 1
4	0.1256637E 2	0.1260590E 2	0.9581279E 1	0.9735542E 1	0.7021843E 1	0.7364698E 1
5	0.1570796E 2	0.1573967E 2	0.1268462E 2	0.1280191E 2	0.9937942E 1	0.1018592E 2
6	0.1884956E 2	0.1887602E 2	0.1580287E 2	0.1589732E 2	0.1295689E 2	0.1314838E 2
7	0.2199116E 2	0.2201385E 2	0.1892880E 2	0.1900777E 2	0.1602249E 2	0.1617780E 2
8	0.2513276E 2	0.2515261E 2	0.2205915E 2	0.2212699E 2	0.1911262E 2	0.1924301E 2
9	0.2827434E 2	0.2829200E 2	0.2519229E 2	0.2525172E 2	0.2221713E 2	0.2232941E 2
10	0.3141593E 2	0.3143183E 2	0.2832730E 2	0.2838016E 2	0.2533077E 2	0.2542928E 2
15	0.4712390E 2	0.4713450E 2	0.4401638E 2	0.4405045E 2	0.4096293E 2	0.4102391E 2
20	0.6283186E 2	0.6283982E 2	0.5971539E 2	0.5974050E 2	0.5663702E 2	0.5668114E 2

	6	7	8	9	10
1	0.2101997E 1	0.5472781E 0	0.5472781E 0	0.5472781E 0	0.5472781E 0
2	0.3452994E 0	0.5472975E 0	0.5472975E 0	0.5472975E 0	0.5472975E 0
3	0.5353861E 1	0.5935367E 0	0.5935367E 0	0.5935367E 0	0.5935367E 0
4	0.7756644E 1	0.5885415E 1	0.6427878E 1	0.6976055E 1	0.1413954E 1
5	0.1047665E 2	0.8190322E 1	0.8658672E 1	0.9155145E 1	0.1426771E 1
6	0.1337508E 2	0.1080707E 2	0.1117406E 2	0.1157441E 2	0.1626790E 1
7	0.1636252E 2	0.1363550E 2	0.1392806E 2	0.1425107E 2	0.2026807E 1
8	0.1939851E 2	0.1657583E 2	0.1681683E 2	0.1708456E 2	0.7526646E 1
9	0.2246350E 2	0.1957860E 2	0.1978275E 2	0.2001034E 2	0.9673742E 1
10	0.2554709E 2	0.2261910E 2	0.2279586E 2	0.2299336E 2	0.1200499E 2
15	0.4109700E 2	0.3806874E 2	0.3817379E 2	0.3829171E 2	0.2620631E 2
20	0.5673406E 2	0.5366861E 2	0.5374313E 2	0.5382688E 2	0.4150915E 2

S A N D W I C H   M A T E R I A L

SYMMETRICAL AND ANTISYMMETRICAL WRINKLING OF SANDWICH PANELS

I. K. Ebcioglu
University of Florida

S. J. Kim
University of Florida

ABSTRACT

In the present paper, the wrinkling of a sandwich plate is studied by use of the theorem of minimum total potentials. Continuity of displacements at the interface is not neglected and the strain energy due to the initial axial stress is given in its proper form. Furthermore, all the pertinent edge loads, as well as all the three-dimensional stresses in the core, are taken into account.

Four partial differential equations, together with 24 boundary conditions, are obtained and solved for the case of the simply supported boundaries. Critical stresses for symmetrical and antisymmetrical wrinkling are obtained and plotted against various dimensionless parameters. The results are compared with previous papers. A considerable amount of difference is observed in the case of symmetrical wrinkling. The source of such discrepancy is traced and suggestions are made for possible future work.

LIST OF NOTATIONS

a, b	Length and width of the panel
D_f	Bending rigidity of the face
G_c, G_f	Shear moduli of core and face, respectively
$M_{\alpha\beta}$	Bending moments per unit length
$N_{\alpha\beta}$	Axial forces per unit length
P	Lateral load per unit area

Q_α	Transverse shear forces per unit length
u_α, U_α, w, W	Displacement components
V_α, V_3	Displacements
U_f, U_c, U_N	Strain energies
π	Total potential
π_p, π_N, π_M, π_Q	Work done by external loads
α, β, γ	Indices taking on values x or y
t_f, t_c	Thicknesses of face and core, respectively
$f_{cr} = \frac{N_{cr}}{G_f t_f}$	Buckling coefficient of the panel
f_{crf}	Buckling coefficient of the face plate
ν_f, ν_c	Poisson's ratios of face and core, respectively
m	Number of half-wave lengths in the x-direction
', "	Superscripts indicating the lower and the upper quantities, respectively
~, ^	Symbols denoting antisymmetrical and symmetrical instability of the panel, respectively. Thus $\tilde{f}_{crmin}$ is the minimum value of the buckling coefficient f_{cr} for antisymmetrical instability

INTRODUCTION

Stability of rectangular sandwich panels has been exposed to extensive investigations by many authors [1,2,3,4,5,6,7,8]. In most cases, however, the main attention was directed to the antisymmetrical buckling, or buckling as a whole plate. Thus the transverse normal strain in the core was usually neglected. However, when the core of the panel is relatively thick and soft, the core may undergo a substantial deformation due to the transverse normal stretching. Consequently, there exists a possibility that the faces of the sandwich panel may deflect symmetrically with respect to the median plane of the core. When symmetrical buckling does occur, the number of nodes is usually very high; hence the term "wrinkling."

Wrinkling phenomena were first studied by Gough et al. [9], who treated the core to be infinitely thick, thus reducing the problem to a single plate supported by a continuous elastic foundation. March [10] analyzed wrinkling of a sandwich column by using a two-dimensional stress function.

In 1951, Eringen [11] obtained four differential equations and 24 boundary conditions for bending and buckling of a rectangular sandwich panel. The theory is quite general in the sense that all the three-dimensional stress distributions are included. As a result, both types of buckling stresses, symmetrical and antisymmetrical, were obtained.

In the present paper, Eringen's theory is extended by introducing the continuity of displacements across the interface of adjacent layers. Thus a correct geometrical representation of the displacements in the faces is obtained. It is found that Eringen's simplification is justified for the antisymmetrical wrinkling. However, in the case of symmetrical wrinkling, the correct form of the displacements has to be used. The theorem of minimum total potential has been used to derive a variational equation. In so doing, it was found that the form of the potential energy due to axial stresses, as used by Eringen, was not suitable for the present purpose, while permissible for use with the approximate displacements assumed by Eringen. Consequently, a modified form of the total potential has been introduced.

Furthermore, the edge forces and moments acting at the sides of the core have been included in the present paper. This gives a better correspondence between the internal stresses and the external loads at the boundary.

The simplifying assumptions are:

(A-1) Assumptions of the classical thin plate theory hold for the faces;

(A-2) Displacements are linear functions of the distance from the median plane of each layer, and the median place of the core is neutral during small deformations;

(A-3) Each layer is homogeneous and isotropic; linear theory of elasticity holds.

Preliminaries

The configuration of a sandwich panel, together with various applied loads and accompanying Cartesian coordinate system, are shown in Fig. 1. The superscript (') denotes the lower-face quantities and (") the upper-face quantities.

Deformations of the sandwich panel considered here are the small deformations during the deflection. Consequently, the initial

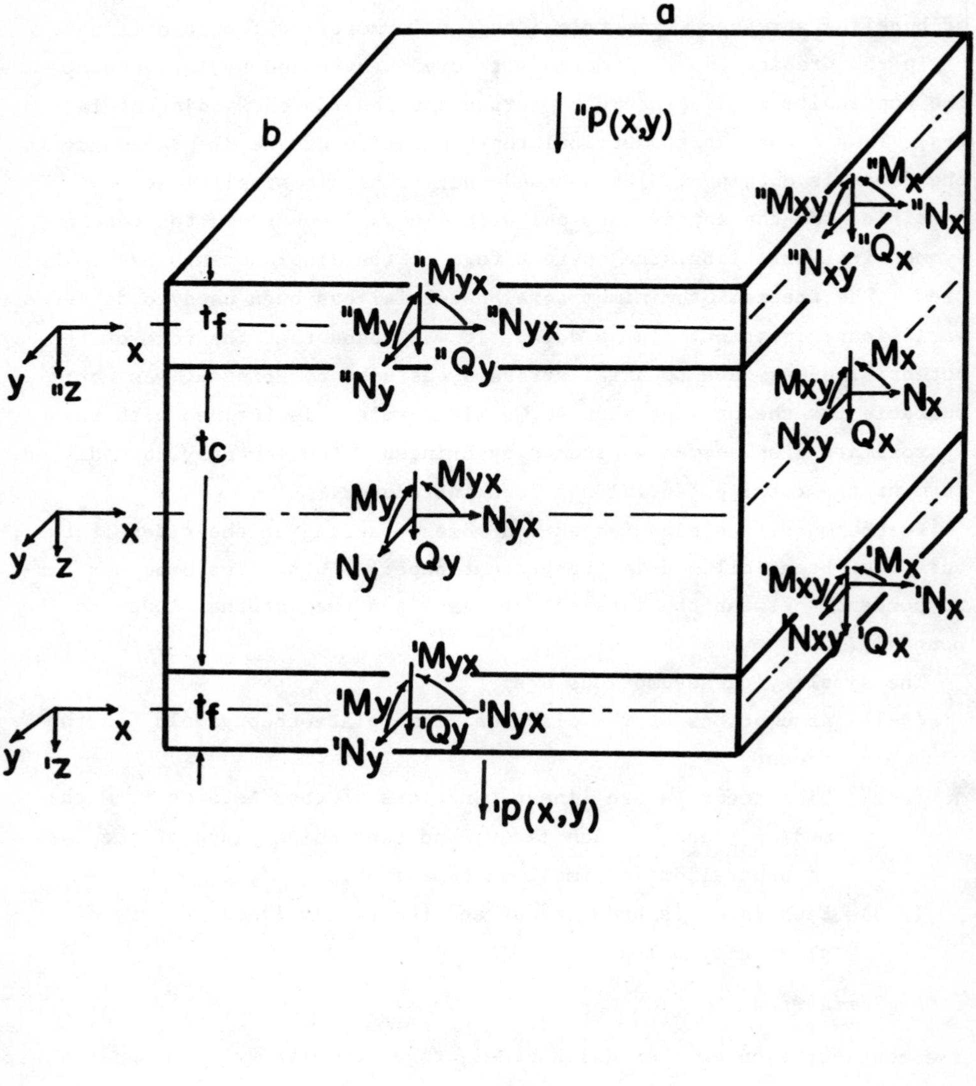

Fig. 1. Rectangular Sandwich Panel with Various Applied Loads.

deformation due to the axial forces acting at the edges is not considered. The initial axial loads may be represented by the axial forces $N_{\alpha\beta}$ acting at the sides of the core and $N^o_{\alpha\beta}$ acting at the sides of the faces, where

$$N^o_{\alpha\beta} = \frac{1}{2}\,({}'N_{\alpha\beta} + {}''N_{\alpha\beta}) \qquad \alpha,\beta = x,\ y \tag{1}$$

Let

$$\begin{aligned} {}'n_{\alpha\beta} &= {}'N_{\alpha\beta} - N^o_{\alpha\beta} \\ {}''n_{\alpha\beta} &= {}''N_{\alpha\beta} - N^o_{\alpha\beta} \end{aligned} \tag{2}$$

Then

$${}'n_{\alpha\beta} = -\,{}''n_{\alpha\beta} = \frac{1}{2}\,({}'N_{\alpha\beta} - {}''N_{\alpha\beta}) \tag{3}$$

Thus the forces ${}'N_{\alpha\beta}$ and ${}''N_{\alpha\beta}$ acting on the edges of the faces are assumed to consist of initial uniform loads of $N^o_{\alpha\beta}$ each and a couple ${}'n_{\alpha\beta}$ which contributes to the bending moment during the small deformations.

As a consequence of the assumptions (A-1) and (A-2), the displacements in each layer can be written as

$$\begin{aligned} {}'V_\alpha(x,y,{}'z) &= {}'u_\alpha(x,y) - {}'z\,{}'w_{,\alpha}(x,y), \quad {}'V_3(x,y,{}'z) = {}'w(x,y) \\ {}''V_\alpha(x,y,{}''z) &= {}''u_\alpha(x,y) - {}''z\,{}''w_{,\alpha}(x,y), \quad {}''V_3(x,y,{}''z) = {}''w(x,y) \\ V_\alpha(x,y,z) &= \frac{2z}{t_c}\,U_\alpha(x,y), \quad V_3(x,y,z) = w(x,y) + \frac{2z}{t_c}\,W(x,y) \end{aligned} \tag{4}$$

where the comma preceding a subscript indicates differentiation with respect to the coordinate variable represented by that subscript, and

$$\begin{aligned} {}'z &= z - \frac{1}{2}\,(t_c + t_f) \\ {}''z &= z + \frac{1}{2}\,(t_c + t_f) \end{aligned} \tag{5}$$

The quantities t_c and t_f are thicknesses of the core and the face, respectively.

Since the displacements must be continuous across the interfaces of any two adjacent layers, we have:

$$\begin{aligned}
{}'V_\alpha(x,y,{}'z = t_f/2) &= V_\alpha(x,y,z = t_c/2) \\
{}'V_3(x,y,{}'z = -\,t_f/2) &= V_3(x,y,z = t_c/2) \\
{}''V_\alpha(x,y,{}''z = t_f/2) &= V_\alpha(x,y,z = -\,t_c/2) \\
{}''V_3(x,y,{}''z = t_f/2) &= V_3(x,y,z = -\,t_c/2)
\end{aligned} \tag{6}$$

Thus from Eq. (4) and Eq. (6), we obtain the following conditions of continuity:

$$\begin{aligned}
{}'u_\alpha &= U_\alpha - \frac{t_f}{2}(w+W)_{,\alpha} \\
{}'w &= w + W \\
{}''u_\alpha &= -\,U_\alpha + \frac{t_f}{2}(w-W)_{,\alpha} \\
{}''w &= w - W
\end{aligned} \tag{7}$$

Theorem of Minimum Total Potential

The total potential π of the sandwich panel shown in Fig. 1 consists of: (a) strain energy U_c stored in the core; (b) strain energy U_f stored in the faces; (c) strain energy U_N stored in the panel due to the presence of initial stresses; (d) work done by external forces, i.e., π_p, π_n, π_M, and π_Q, the work done by the transverse load, the axial loads ${}'n_{\alpha\beta}$ and ${}''n_{\alpha\beta}$ defined by Eq. (3), the edge moments, and the edge shear resultants, respectively. Thus,

$$\pi = U_c + U_f + U_N - \pi_p - \pi_n - \pi_M - \pi_Q \tag{8}$$

Let $({}'V_\alpha, {}'V_3)$, $({}''V_\alpha, {}''V_3)$, and (V_α, V_3) be the displacements in the lower face, the upper face, and the core, respectively. Then the strain energy stored in the panel during small deflections is expressed by:

$$U_c = \frac{1}{2} G_c \int_V \Big\{ \frac{2}{(1-2\nu_c)} [\nu_c V_{\alpha,\alpha}(V_{\beta,\beta}+2V_{3,3}) + (1-\nu_c)(V_{3,3})^3] + V_{\alpha,\beta}(V_{\alpha,\beta}+V_{\beta,\alpha}) + (V_{\alpha,3}+V_{3,\alpha})(V_{\alpha,3}+V_{3,\alpha}) \Big\}\, dv \tag{9}$$

$$U_f = \frac{1}{2} G_f \int_{'V} \left[\frac{2\nu_f}{1-\nu_f}\, 'V_{\alpha,\alpha}\, 'V_{\beta,\beta} + 'V_{\alpha,\beta}('V_{\alpha,\beta} + 'V_{\beta,\alpha})\right] dv$$

$$+ \frac{1}{2} G_f \int_{''V} \left[\frac{2\nu_f}{1-\nu_f}\, ''V_{\alpha,\alpha}\, ''V_{\beta,\beta} + ''V_{\alpha,\beta}(''V_{\alpha,\beta} + ''V_{\beta,\alpha})\right] dv \qquad (10)$$

$$U_N = \frac{1}{2} \int_a (N^o_{\alpha\beta}\, 'w_{,\alpha}\, 'w_{,\beta} + N^o_{\alpha\beta}\, ''w_{,\alpha}\, ''w_{,\beta} + N_{\alpha\beta}\, w_{,\alpha}\, w_{,\beta})\, da \qquad (11)$$

The integrals $\int_{'V}$, $\int_{''V}$, and $\int_V$ denote volume integrals over the volumes of the lower face, the upper face, and the core, respectively, while $\int_a$ denotes area integral over the plane of the panel. G_c and G_f are the shear moduli; ν_c and ν_f are Poisson's ratio; the subscripts c and f denote core and face quantities, respectively. Summation convention is used over the range α, β = x,y.

Work done by the external loads $'p$, $''p$, $'n_{\alpha\beta}$, $''n_{\alpha\beta}$, $'M_{\alpha\beta}$, $''M_{\alpha\beta}$, $M_{\alpha\beta}$, $'Q_\beta$, $''Q_\beta$, and Q_β is:

$$\pi_p = \int_a ('p'w + ''p''w)\, da \qquad (12)$$

$$\pi_n = \oint_c ('n_{\alpha\beta}\, 'u_\alpha + ''n_{\alpha\beta}''u_\alpha)\, n_\beta\, ds \qquad (13)$$

$$\pi_M = \oint_c (-'M_{\alpha\beta}'w_{,\alpha} - ''M_{\alpha\beta}\, 'w_{,\alpha} + M_{\alpha\beta} \frac{2}{t_c} U_\alpha)\, n_\beta\, ds \qquad (14)$$

$$\pi_Q = \oint_c ('Q_\beta'w + ''Q_\beta''w + Q_\beta w)\, n_\beta\, ds \qquad (15)$$

where $\oint_c$ denotes integration along the circumference of the panel plane, and n_β is a unit normal vector along the boundary.

Equations (4), (7), and (9-15) are now substituted in Eq. (8) and the usual method of the variational calculus is used to obtain the variational equation

$$\delta\pi = 0 \qquad (16)$$

$$\delta\pi = \oint_c < \left\{2G_f t_f \left[\frac{2\nu_f}{1-\nu_f} (U_{\gamma,\gamma} - \frac{t_f}{2} w_{,\gamma\gamma})\delta_{\alpha\beta} + U_{\alpha,\beta} + U_{\beta,\alpha} - t_f w_{,\alpha\beta}\right]\right.$$

$$\left. + G_c t_c \left[\frac{2\nu_c}{3(1-2\nu_c)} U_{\gamma,\gamma}\delta_{\alpha\beta} + U_{\alpha,\beta} + U_{\beta,\alpha}\right] - \frac{2}{t_c} M_{\alpha\beta} - ('n_{\alpha\beta} - ''n_{\alpha\beta})\right\} \delta U_\alpha$$

$$+ \Big\{- 8D_f w_{,\alpha\alpha\beta} + G_f t_f^2 \left(\frac{1+\nu_f}{1-\nu_f} U_{\alpha,\alpha\beta} + U_{\beta,\alpha\alpha}\right) + G_c t_c w_{,\beta} + 2G_c U_\beta$$

$$+ (2N^o_{\alpha\beta} + N_{\alpha\beta})\, w_{,\alpha} - ('Q_\beta + ''Q_\beta + Q_\beta)\Big\}\, \delta w$$

$$+ \Big\{- 8D_f W_{,\alpha\alpha\beta} + \frac{G_c t_c}{3} W_{,\beta} + 2N^o_{\alpha\beta} W_{,\alpha} - ('Q_\beta - ''Q_\beta)\Big\}\, \delta W$$

$$+ \Big\{8D_f [\nu_f w_{,\gamma\gamma} \delta_{\alpha\beta} + (1-\nu_f) w_{,\alpha\beta}] - G_f t_f^2 \left(\frac{2\nu_f}{1-\nu_f} U_{\gamma,\gamma} \delta_{\alpha\beta} + U_{\alpha,\beta} + U_{\beta,\alpha}\right)$$

$$+ ('M_{\alpha\beta} + ''M_{\alpha\beta}) + \frac{t_f}{2} ('n_{\alpha\beta} - ''n_{\alpha\beta})\Big\}\, \delta w_{,\alpha}$$

$$+ \Big\{8D_f [\nu_f W_{,\gamma\gamma} \delta_{\alpha\beta} + (1-\nu_f) W_{,\alpha\beta}] + ('M_{\alpha\beta} - ''M_{\alpha\beta})\Big\}\, \delta W_{,\alpha} > n_\beta ds$$

$$- \int_a < \Big\{\left[\frac{2G_f t_f (1+\nu_f)}{1-\nu_f} + \frac{G_c t_c}{3(1-2\nu_c)}\right] U_{\beta,\alpha\beta} + \Big(2G_f t_f + \Big(2G_f t_f$$

$$+ \frac{G_c t_c}{3}\Big) U_{\alpha,\beta\beta}\Big) - \frac{4G_c}{t_c} U_\alpha - 2G_c w_{,\alpha} - \frac{2G_f t_f^2}{1-\nu_f} w_{,\alpha\beta\beta}\Big\}\, \delta U_\alpha$$

$$+ \Big\{-8D_f w_{,\alpha\alpha\beta\beta} + \frac{2G_f t_f^2}{1-\nu_f} U_{\alpha,\alpha\beta\beta} + G_c t_c \left(\frac{2}{t_c} U_{\alpha,\alpha} + w_{,\alpha\alpha}\right)$$

$$+ (2N^o_{\alpha\beta} + N_{\alpha\beta}) w_{,\alpha\beta} + ('P + ''P)\Big\}\, \delta w$$

$$+ \Big\{-8D_f W_{,\alpha\alpha\beta\beta} + \frac{G_c t_c}{3} W_{,\alpha\alpha} - \frac{8G_c (1-\nu_c)}{t_c (1-2\nu_c)} W$$

$$+ 2N^o_{\alpha\beta} W_{,\alpha\beta} + ('P - ''P)\Big\}\, \delta W > da$$

and

$$D_f = \frac{G_f t_f^3}{6(1-\nu_f)}, \qquad \delta_{\alpha\beta} = \begin{cases} 1, & \alpha = \beta \\ 0, & \alpha \neq \beta \end{cases} \tag{17}$$

Equation (16) with Eq. (17) gives a complete description of a sandwich panel in an equilibrium state. The curvilinear integral in Eq. (17) gives 24 boundary conditions along the edges, while the equations of equilibrium are obtained from the area integral of Eq. (17).

From the fundamental lemma of variational calculus, we obtain the following differential equations in the conventional notation:

$$A_1U_{,xx} + A_2U_{,yy} + A_3V_{,xy} + A_4\nabla^2w_{,x} + A_5w_{,x} + A_6U = 0 \tag{18}$$

$$A_1V_{,yy} + A_2V_{,xx} + A_3U_{,xy} + A_4\nabla^2w_{,y} + A_5w_{,y} + A_6V = 0 \tag{19}$$

$$A_7\nabla^4w + A_8\nabla^2(U_{,x}+V_{,y}) + A_9\nabla^2w + A_{10}(U_{,x}+V_{,y}) = \frac{1}{2}\left[('P+''P) + \zeta^{(1)}\right] \tag{20}$$

$$A_7\nabla^4W + A_{11}\nabla^2W + A_{12}W = \frac{1}{2}\left[('P-''P) + \zeta^{(2)}\right] \tag{21}$$

where

$$A_1 = \frac{2}{1-\nu_f} + \frac{G_ct_c(1-\nu_c)}{3G_ft_f(1-2\nu_c)}, \quad A_2 = 1 + \frac{G_ct_c}{6G_ft_f},$$

$$A_3 = \frac{1+\nu_f}{1-\nu_f} + \frac{G_ct_c}{6G_ft_f(1-2\nu_c)}, \quad A_4 = -\frac{t_f}{1-\nu_f}, \quad A_5 = -\frac{G_c}{G_ft_f},$$

$$A_6 = -\frac{2G_c}{G_ft_ft_c}, \quad A_7 = 4D_f, \quad A_8 = -\frac{G_ft_f}{1-\nu_f}, \quad A_9 = -\frac{1}{2}G_ct_c,$$

$$A_{10} = -G_c, \quad A_{11} = -\frac{1}{6}G_ct_c, \quad A_{12} = \frac{4G_c(1-\nu_c)}{t_c(1-2\nu_c)}$$

$$\nabla^2 = \frac{\partial^2}{\partial x^2} + \frac{\partial^2}{\partial y^2}, \quad U_x = U, \quad U_y = V$$

$$\zeta^{(1)} = (2N_x^o+N_x)w_{,xx} + 2(2N_{xy}^o+N_{xy})w_{,xy} + (2N_y^o+N_y)w_{,yy}$$

$$\zeta^{(2)} = 2N_x^oW_{,xx} + 4N_{xy}^oW_{,xy} + 2N_y^oW_{,yy}$$

Eliminating U and V from Eqs. (18-21), we obtain the following equations:

$$-\frac{2D_ft_c}{G_c}\left[\frac{G_ft_f}{1-\nu_f} + \frac{2G_ct_c(1-\nu_c)}{3(1-2\nu_c)}\right]\nabla^6w + \left[\frac{G_ft_f}{1-\nu_f}\left(t_c^2 + 2t_ct_f + \frac{4}{3}t_f^2\right) + \frac{G_ct_c^3(1-\nu_c)}{6(1-2\nu_c)}\right]\nabla^4w$$

$$= \left\{1 - \frac{t_c}{G_c}\left[\frac{G_ft_f}{1-\nu_f} + \frac{G_ct_c(1-\nu_c)}{6(1-2\nu_c)}\right]\nabla^2\right\}('P + ''P + \zeta^{(1)}) \tag{22}$$

$$4D_f\nabla^4 W - \frac{G_c t_c}{6}\nabla^2 W + \frac{4G_c(1-\nu_c)}{t_c(1-2\nu_c)} W = \frac{1}{2}('P - ''P + \zeta^{(2)}) \tag{23}$$

Comparison with Other Theories

Under the similar loading conditions the equations obtained by Eringen in [11] can be written in terms of present notations as:

$$-\frac{2D_f t_c}{G_c}\left[\frac{G_f t_f}{1-\nu_f}(1 + t_f/t_c)^2 + \frac{G_c t_c(1-\nu_c)}{6(1-2\nu_c)}\right]\nabla^6 w$$

$$+\left[\frac{G_f t_f}{1-\nu_f}\left(t_c^2 + 2t_c t_f + \frac{4}{3}t_f^2\right)\right.$$

$$\left.+\frac{G_c t_c^3(1-\nu_c)}{6(1-2\nu_c)}\right]\nabla^4 w = \left\{1 - \frac{t_c}{G_c}\left[\frac{G_f t_f}{1-\nu_f}(1 + t_f/t_c)^2\right.\right.$$

$$\left.\left.+\frac{G_c t_c(1-\nu_c)}{6(1-2\nu_c)}\right]\nabla^2\right\}('P + ''P + \zeta^{(1)}) \tag{22E}$$

$$D_f\nabla^4 W - \frac{G_c t_c}{6(1 + t_f/t_c)^2}\nabla^2 W + \frac{4G_c(1-\nu_c)}{t_c(1 + t_f/t_c)^2(1-2\nu_c)} W$$

$$= \frac{1}{2}('P - ''P + \zeta^{(2)}) \tag{23E}$$

Comparison of Eq. (22) and Eq. (22E) shows that the two equations will coalesce if $(t_f/t_c) \ll 1$ and either $\frac{G_c t_c}{G_f t_f} \ll 1$ or $D_f \simeq 0$. Thus, when the faces are very thin in comparison with the core, the two equations will give similar results for overall deflections of the panel. The difference between Eq. (22) and Eq. (22E) is due to the approximate relations used in [11] for the displacements of the face layers. If all of the preceding conditions are satisified, both Eq. (22) and Eq. (22E) reduce to

$$\frac{G_f t_f t_c^2}{1-\nu_f}\nabla^4 w = \left[1 - \frac{G_f t_f t_c}{G_c(1-\nu_f)}\nabla^2\right]('P + ''P + \zeta^{(1)}) \tag{22R}$$

which is the equation derived by Reissner in [7].

Comparison of Eq. (23) and Eq. (23E) suggests that the two equations will give similar results for the symmetric deflection of the panel if

$t_f/t_c << 1$. However, the bending rigidity of the faces can be neglected in the wrinkling problem only when the faces are extremely thin in comparison with the core.

When the core is assumed to undergo shear deformation only, we have $W = 0$. Then Eq. (7) gives $'u_\alpha = U_\alpha - (t_f/2)w_{,\alpha}$. If the core is further assumed to be weak, i.e., if $G_c t_c << G_f t_f$, then Eqs. (18-20) become:

$$\frac{G_f t_f}{1-\nu_f}\,[2'u_{,xx}+(1-\nu_f)'u_{,yy}+(1+\nu_f)'v_{,xy}] - G_c\left[(2/t_c)'u + \left(1 + \frac{t_f}{t_c}\right)w_{,x}\right] = 0 \tag{18a}$$

$$\frac{G_f t_f}{1-\nu_f}\,[2'v_{,yy}+(1-\nu_f)'v_{,xx}+(1+\nu_f)'u_{,xy}] - G_c\left[(2/t_c)'v + \left(1 + \frac{t_f}{t_c}\right)w_{,y}\right] = 0 \tag{19a}$$

$$2D_f\nabla^4 w - (t_c+t_f)G_c\left[(2/t_c)('u_{,x}+'v_{,y}) + \left(1 + \frac{t_f}{t_c}\right)\nabla^2 w\right] = 'P + ''P + \bar{\zeta}^{(1)} \tag{20a}$$

where

$$\bar{\zeta}^{(1)} = 2N_x^o W_{,xx} + 4N_{xy}^o W_{,xy} + 2N_y^o W_{,yy}$$

Equations (18a-20a) are also obtained from the equations derived by Chang and Ebcioglu [12], which include the effect of different face thicknesses and elastic properties. These equations differ from Hoff's equations [8] by the factor $(1 + t_f/t_c)$ appearing in several places. The difference is due to the approximate displacements used in [8].

Application. Simply Supported Rectangular Sandwich Panel

As an example, let us consider a rectangular sandwich panel, simply supported along the edges and subjected to a uniformly distributed axial compressive load N along the face edges x = 0, a. Using Hoff's approximation [8], i.e., $V = 0$ at $x = 0, a$, and $u = 0$ at $y = 0, b$, we obtain the boundary conditions from Eq. (17) as:

$$\left.\begin{aligned} &U_{,x} = V = w = w_{,xx} = W = W_{,xx} = 0 \quad \text{at} \quad x = 0,\, a \\ &U = V_{,y} = w = w_{,yy} = W = W_{,yy} = 0 \quad \text{at} \quad y = 0,\, b \end{aligned}\right\} \tag{24}$$

These conditions are satisfied by the set

$$\left.\begin{aligned} U &= U_m \cos\frac{m\pi x}{a}\sin\frac{\pi y}{b} \\ V &= V_m \sin\frac{m\pi x}{a}\cos\frac{\pi y}{b} \\ w &= w_m \sin\frac{m\pi x}{a}\sin\frac{\pi y}{b} \\ W &= W_m \sin\frac{m\pi x}{a}\sin\frac{\pi y}{b} \end{aligned}\right\} \tag{25}$$

When the series are substituted in the differential equations (18-21), four homogeneous algebraic equations are obtained. In order to have nontrivial solutions, the determinant of their matrix must vanish. This gives the following conditions:

$$\tilde{f}_{cr} = f_{crf}\left\{1 + \frac{3g\left[(1+r)^2 + \frac{g\alpha_c}{12\alpha_f}\right]}{gr^2 + \alpha_f^2\rho_f^2\left(1 + \frac{g\alpha_c}{12\alpha_f}\right)\left(1 + \frac{1}{\beta^2}\right)}\right\} \tag{26}$$

$$\hat{f}_{cr} = f_{crf}\left[4 + \frac{g}{\alpha_f\rho_f^2\left(1+\frac{1}{\beta^2}\right)} + \frac{12g\alpha_c}{\alpha_f\rho_f^2\rho_c^2\left(1+\frac{1}{\beta^2}\right)^2}\right] \tag{27}$$

where $\tilde{f}_{cr}$ and $\hat{f}_{cr}$ are the critical values of $f = \frac{N}{G_f t_f}$ at which antisymmetrical and symmetrical wrinkling, respectively, of the sandwich panel occur, and

$$\alpha_f = \frac{1}{1-\nu_f}\ , \quad \alpha_c = \frac{2(1-\nu_c)}{1-2\nu_c}\ , \quad \rho_f = \pi t_f/b\ , \quad \rho_c = \pi t_c/b$$

$$\beta = \frac{a}{mb}\ , \qquad r = t_f/t_c\ , \qquad g = G_c t_c/G_f t_f$$

$$f_{crf} = \frac{1}{6}\,\alpha_f\rho_f^2\left(\beta + \frac{1}{\beta}\right)^2$$

When the core is weak, i.e., when $g \ll 1$, we can rewrite Eq. (26) and Eq. (27) as

$$\tilde{f}_{cr} = f_{crf} + \frac{1}{2}\,\alpha_f\rho_f^2\,(1+r)^2\,\frac{\left(\beta + \frac{1}{\beta}\right)^2}{r^2 + \frac{\alpha_f\rho_f^2}{g}\left(1 + \frac{1}{\beta^2}\right)} \tag{26a}$$

$$\hat{f}_{cr} = 4f_{crf} + g\left(\frac{1+\beta^2}{6} + \frac{2\alpha_c\beta^2}{\rho_c^2}\right) \tag{27a}$$

Equation (26a) was also obtained by Chang and Ebcioglu in [12]. When g << 1 [11] gives in terms of present notations,

$$\tilde{f}^E_{cr} = f_{crf} + \frac{1}{2}\alpha_f\rho_f^2\,(1+r)^2\,\frac{\left(\beta+\frac{1}{\beta}\right)^2}{r^2 + \frac{\alpha_f\rho_f^2}{g}(1+r)^2\left(1+\frac{1}{\beta^2}\right)} \tag{26E}$$

$$\hat{f}^E_{cr} = f_{crf} + g(1+r)^2\left(\frac{1+\beta^2}{6} + \frac{2\alpha_c\beta^2}{\rho_c^2}\right) \tag{27E}$$

The superscript E denotes the quantity derived in [11]. Comparison of Eqs. (26a-27a) with Eqs. (26E-27E) again reveals the difference by the factor $(1+r)^2$. Furthermore, there is an additional factor 4 appearing in Eq. (27a). This difference is rather significant.

Discussions of the Numerical Results

As an illustration of foregoing discussions, both types of critical stresses are plotted against various dimensionless parameters and compared with the critical stresses obtained in [11] and [7]. In Figs. 2-9, solid lines represent values obtained from the present theory, dashed lines denote results from [11], and dash and dot lines are those obtained from [7]. The following conclusions may be drawn:

(a) In all cases present theory gives higher values of minimum critical stresses than [7] and [11]. Also, the values of $\beta = a/mb$ at which the minima occur are higher in the present theory.

(b) The minimum critical stresses for antisymmetrical wrinkling are almost linearly increasing functions of the core thickness, while those for symmetrical wrinkling are almost linearly increasing functions of the face thickness.

(c) The number of half-waves $m = a/b\beta$ is much larger for symmetrical wrinkling as can be seen from Figs. 8 and 9. For a square sandwich panel with $t_f/b << 1/200$ several half-waves are present. On the other hand, the number of half-waves become substantially large in the case of antisymmetrical wrinkling only when the core is weak and faces are

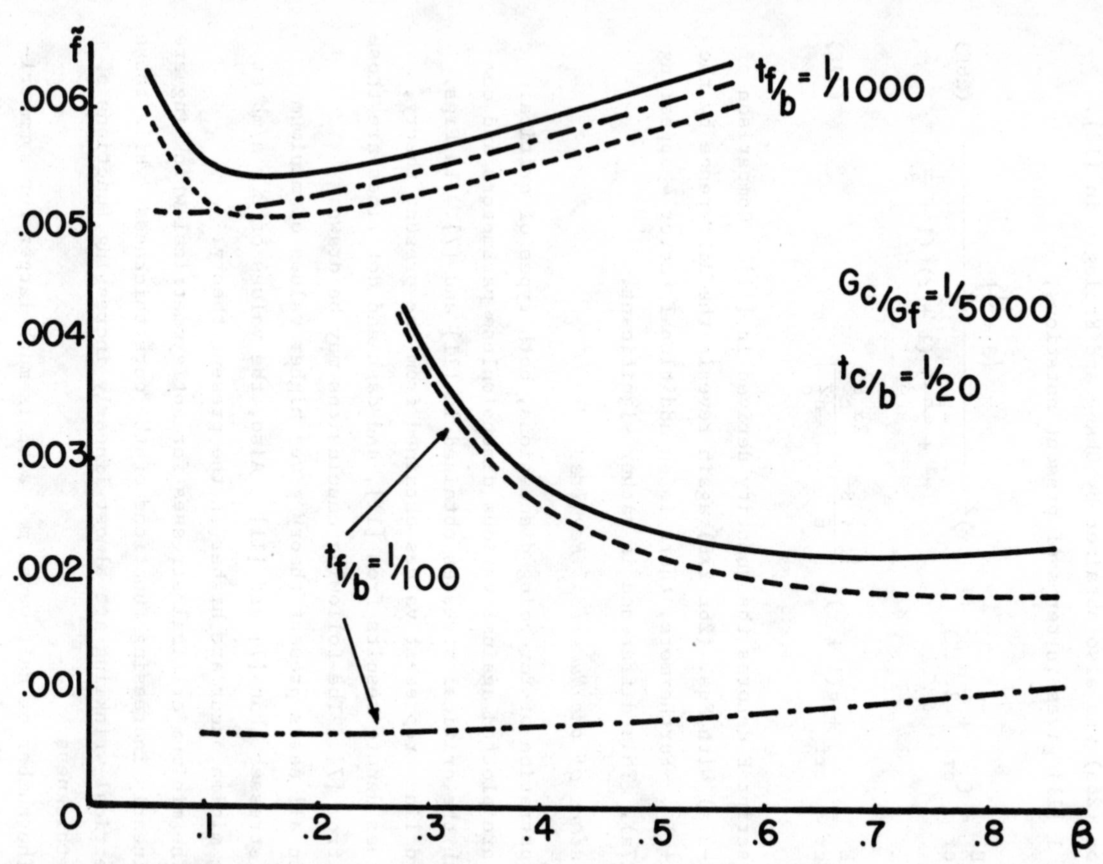

Fig. 2. Critical Values of Buckling Coefficient for Antisymmetrical Instability vs. β. G_c/G_f = 1/5000; t_c/b = 1/20; t_f/b = 1/100, and 1/1000. (-.- [7]; ---- [11])

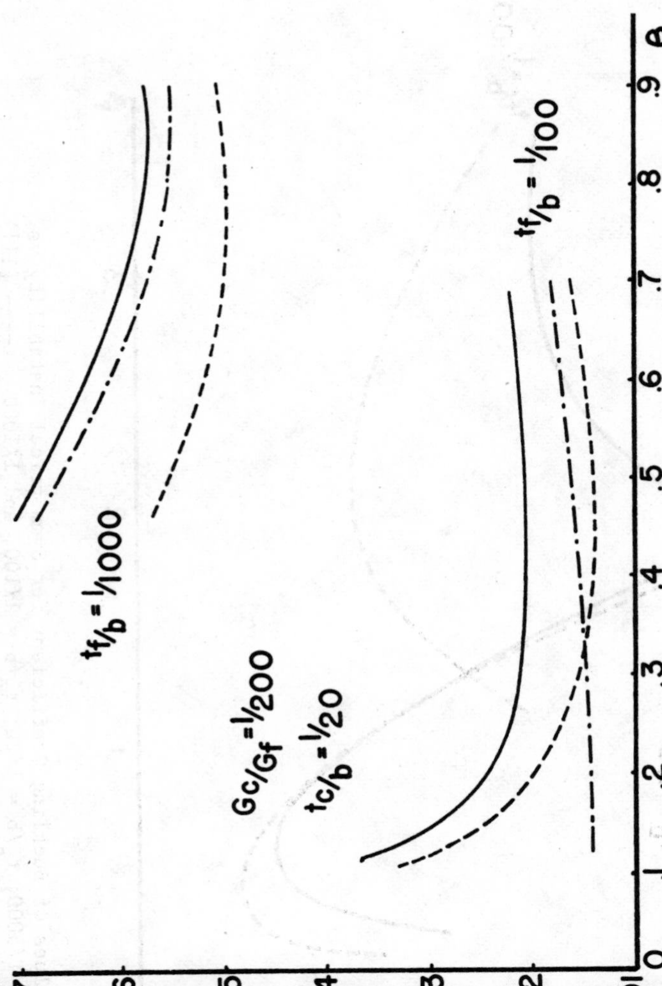

Fig. 3. Critical Values of Buckling Coefficient for Antisymmetrical Instability vs. β. G_c/G_f = 1/200; t_c/b = 1/20; t_f/b = 1/100, and 1/1000. (-.- [7]; ---- [11])

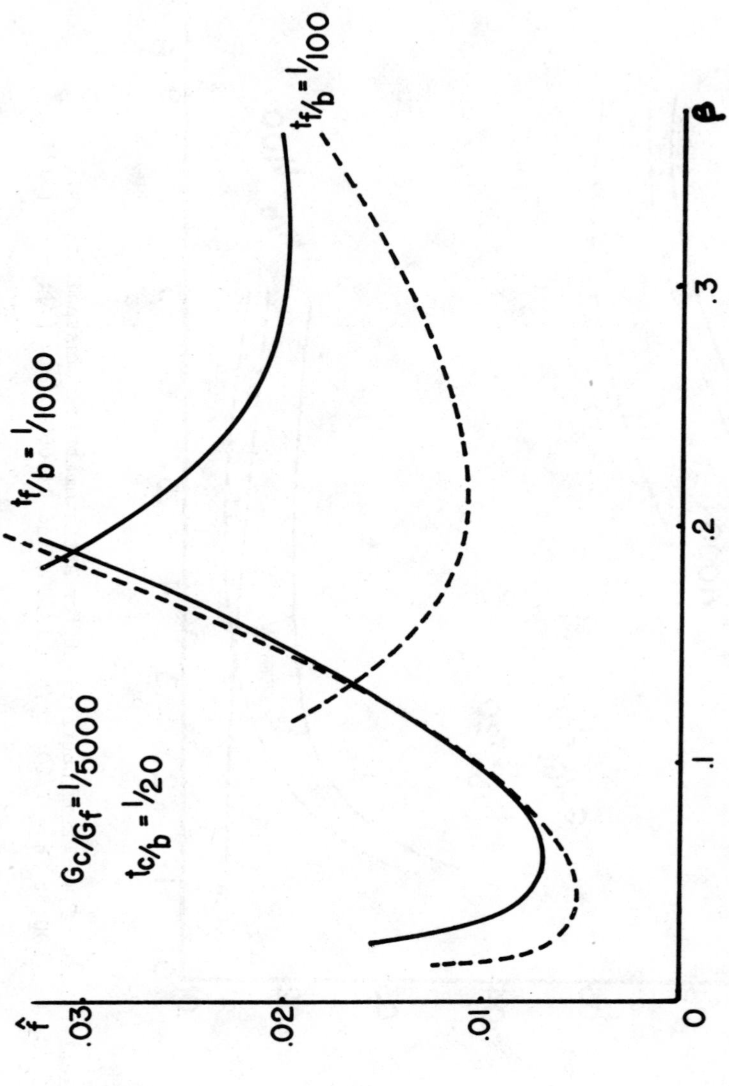

Fig. 4. Critical Values of Buckling Coefficient for Symmetrical Instability vs. β. $G_c/G_f = 1/5000$; $t_c/b = 1/20$; $t_f/b = 1/100$, and 1/1000. (---- [11])

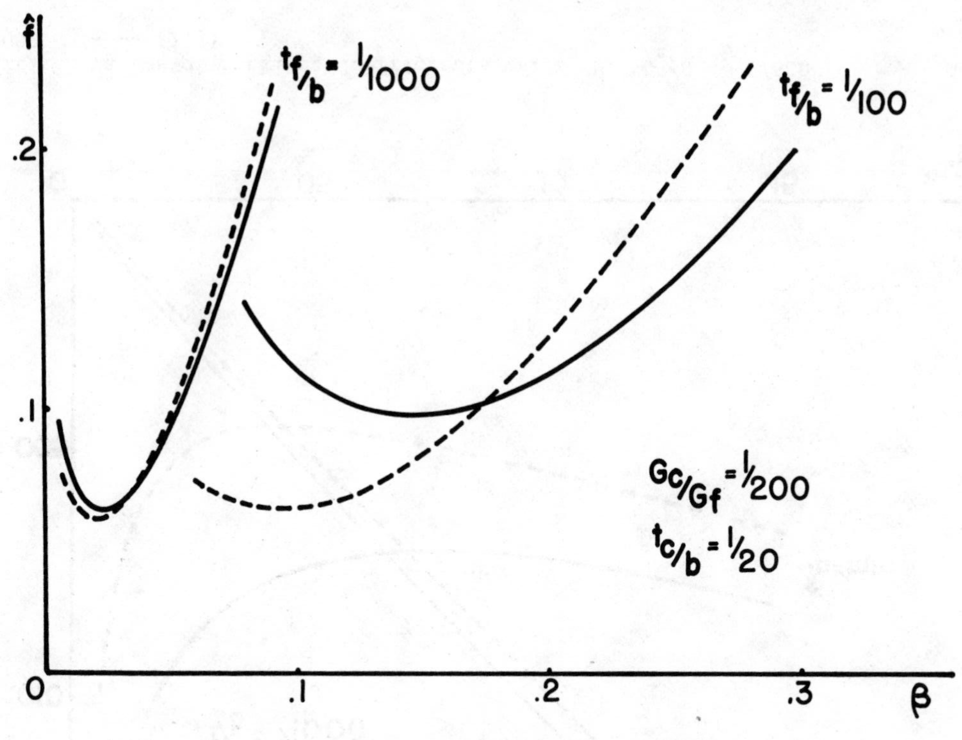

Fig. 5. Critical Values of Buckling Coefficient for Symmetrical Instability vs. β. G_c/G_f = 1/200; t_c/b = 1/20; t_f/b = 1/100, and 1/1000. (---- [11])

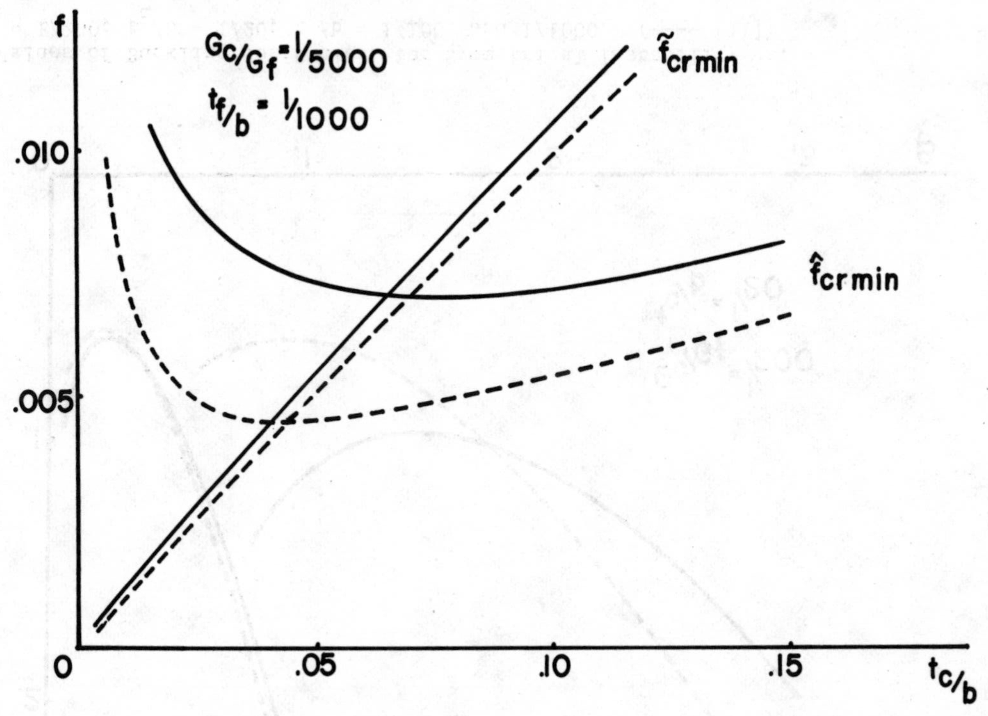

Fig. 6. Minimum Critical Values of Buckling Coefficients vs. t_c/b. $G_c/G_f = 1/5000$; $t_f/b = 1/1000$. (---- [11])

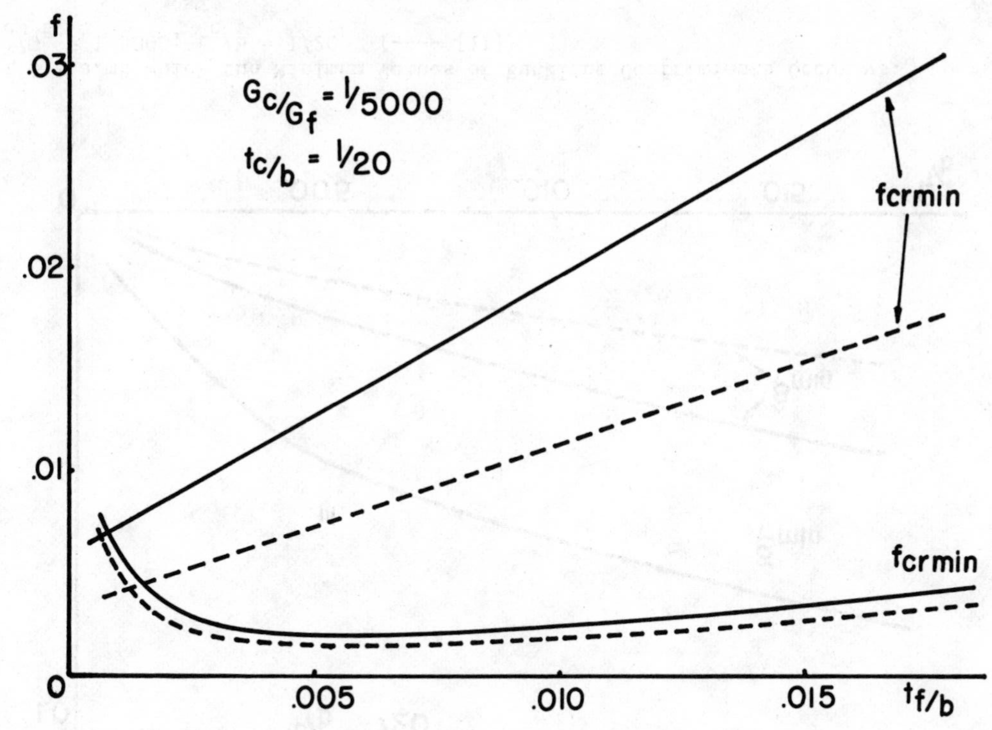

Fig. 7. Minimum Critical Values of Buckling Coefficients vs. t_f/b G_c/G_f = 1/5000; t_c/b = 1/20. (---- [11])

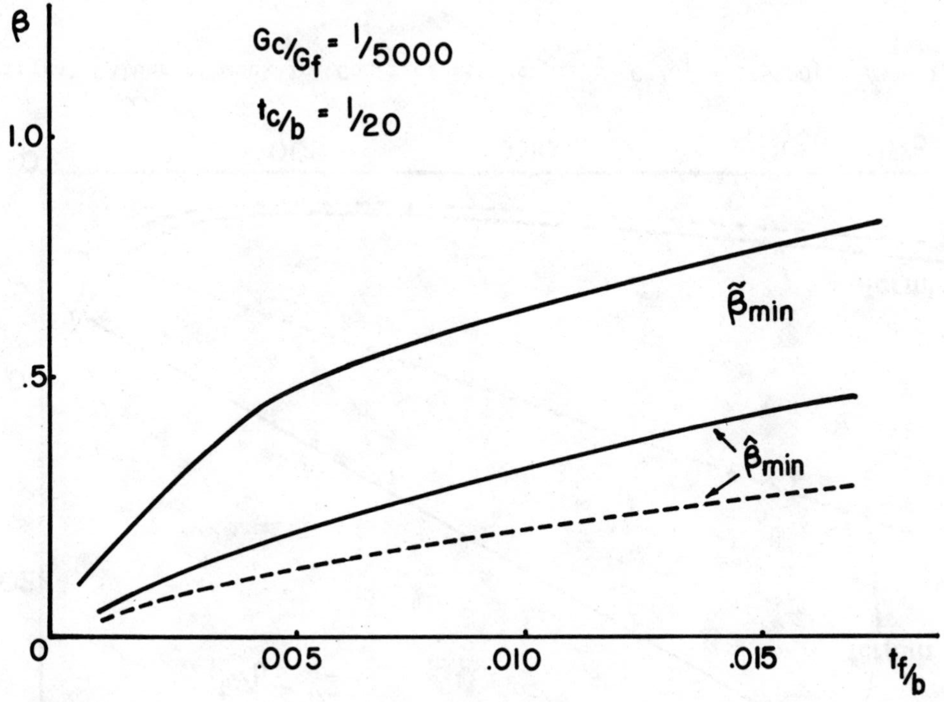

Fig. 8. Values of $\beta = a/mb$ Which the Minimum Values of Buckling Coefficients Occur vs. t_f/b. $G_c/G_f = 1/5000$; $t_c/b = 1/20$. (---- [11])

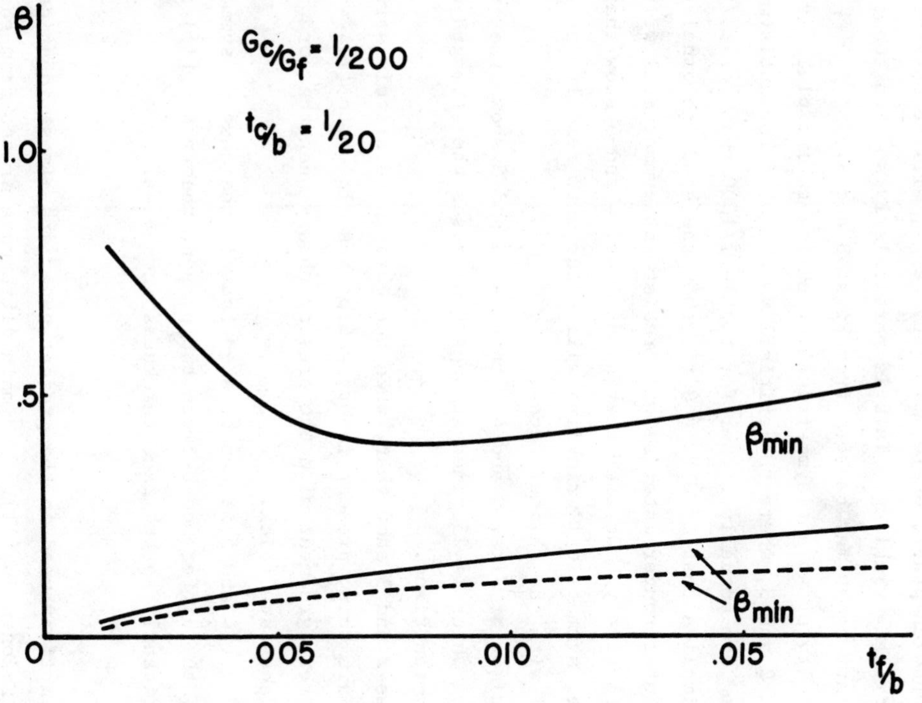

Fig. 9. Values of $\beta = a/mb$ at Which the Minimum Values of Buckling Coefficients Occur vs. t_f/b. $G_c/G_f = 1/200$; $t_c/b = 1/20$. (---- [11])

thin (except in the case of values obtained from [7], which does not consider the bending rigidity of the faces).

(d) However, it can be seen from Figs. 6 and 7 that symmetrical wrinkling will occur first as the thickness of the face becomes very small in comparison with the core thickness. Therefore, wrinkling phenomena of a sandwich panel, where m is very large, will be observed only in symmetrical wrinkling. This is particularly so when the core is relatively strong as may be seen from Figs. 8 and 9.

(e) Difficulty of an antisymmetrical wrinkling taking place is also shown in Figs. 2 and 3, where the critical values of $\tilde{f}$ for antisymmetrical wrinkling are actually higher for $t_f/b = 1/1000$ than for $t_f/b = 1/100$. This implies that if $G_f t_f = G_f' t_f'$, then the sandwich panel with thinner faces of stronger material will resist antisymmetrical wrinkling more effectively. On the other hand, Figs. 4 and 5 show that, in a similar case, symmetrical wrinkling will occur more readily for the sandwich panel with the thinner faces.

(f) Comparison of Figs. 2 and 4 with Figs. 3 and 5 shows that using a core material which is 25 times stronger increases the strength of the panel only ten times.

(g) Figures 2 and 3 show that, when the core is relatively strong and the faces are thin, present theory approaches closer to [7], while [11] gives better agreement with the present theory when the core is weak and the faces are thick.

(h) From Figs. 4 and 5 it can be seen that in the case of symmetrical wrinkling, the difference between the present theory and [11] increases significantly as the face thickness increases.

CONCLUSIONS

The basic assumptions used in the present paper are almost identical to those used by Eringen in [11]. The main difference arises from the introduction of continuity conditions for displacements. Thus, present theory is a modification and a generalization of Eringen's theory through the use of geometrically more correct relations and inclusion of a more general set of external loads. The resulting differential equations and boundary conditions are simple enough to be used for numerical evaluations.

Differences between [11] and the present theory as well as their similarities were discussed in the preceding sections. The difference in the case of antisymmetrical wrinkling of the sandwich panel is negligible for the practical purposes. However, in the case of symmetrical wrinkling, discrepancies between the two theories may be attributed to the approximate displacements used in [11].

Further investigation of the problem of wrinkling, as well as general instability and small deformations of sandwich panel, may be carried out by including the effect of the zeroth order terms in the Taylor expression of the displacements. An alternate approach would be to consider symmetric deflections of the sandwich panel under the lateral loads 'p and "p such that 'p = - "p, and to investigate the behavior of the zeroth and linear displacements at various points of the panel. Furthermore, continued efforts should be directed to the task of obtaining proper justifications of such approximate theories from more exact theories based on either the three-dimensional theory of elasticity or the nonlinear theory.

ACKNOWLEDGMENT

The results presented in this paper were obtained under NSF Grant No. GK-640 of the National Science Foundation to the University of Florida. The paper is based on a part of the second author's dissertation submitted in partial fulfillment of the requirements for the degree of Doctor of Philosophy in the Department of Engineering Science and Mechanics at the University of Florida, Gainesville, Florida.

REFERENCES

1. William, D., Leggett, D. M. A. and Hopkins, H. G., "Flat Sandwich Panels Under Compressive End Load," Aeronautical Research Council, Reports and Memoranda No. 2016, 1941.

2. Hoff, N. J. and Mautner, S. E., "The Buckling of Sandwich-Type Panels," Journal of the Aeronautical Sciences, Vol. 12, No. 3, July 1945, pp. 285-297.

3. Hoff, N. J. and Mautner, S. E., "Bending and Buckling of Sandwich Beams," Journal of the Aeronautical Sciences, Vol. 15, No. 12, December 1948, pp. 707-720.

4. Bijlaard, P. P., "Stability of Sandwich Plates," Journal of Aeronautical Sciences, Vol. 16, No. 9, 1949, pp. 573-574.

5. March, H. W. and Smith, C. B., "Various Types of Edge Conditions--Buckling Loads of Flat Sandwich Panels in Compression," U.S. Forest Products Laboratory, Report No. 1525, 1945.

6. Libove, C. and Batdorf, S. A., "A General Small-Deflection Theory for Flat Sandwich Plates," National Advisory Committee for Aeronautics, Report No. 899, 1948.

7. Reissner, E., "Finite Deflections of Sandwich Plates," Journal of Aeronautical Sciences, Vol. 15, No. 7, 1948, pp. 435-440.

8. Hoff, N. J., "Bending and Buckling of Rectangular Sandwich Plates," National Advisory Committee for Aeronautics, Technical Note 2225, November 1950, p. 28.

9. Gough, C. S., Elam, C. F. and De Bruyne, N. A., "Stabilization of a Thin Sheet by a Continuous Supporting Medium," Journal of the Royal Aeronautical Society, Vol. 44, 1940, pp. 1-32.

10. March, H. W., "Elastic Stability of the Facings of Sandwich Columns," Proceedings of the Symposium of Applied Mathematics, Vol. 3, pp. 85-106, 1950.

11. Eringen, A. C., "Bending and Buckling of Rectangular Sandwich Plates," Proceedings of the First U.S. National Congress of Applied Mechanics, 1952, pp. 381-390.

12. Chang, C. C. and Ebcioglu, I. K., "Elastic Instability of Rectangular Sandwich Panel of Orthotropic Core with Different Face Thicknesses and Materials," Transactions of the American Society of Mechanical Engineers, Journal of Applied Mechanics, Vol. 27, No. 3, September 1960, pp. 474-480.

THEORY OF MICROPOLAR SANDWICH PLATES

M. Cengiz Dökmeci
Cornell University

ABSTRACT

A consistent derivation of the sandwich plate theory is presented within the framework of three dimensional micropolar elasticity theory. A variational procedure deduced from the Hamiltonian principle is employed for the formulation. The transverse shear, transverse normal strains as well as the rotatory inertia are considered in the analysis. The macroscopic equations of motion together with the relevant boundary conditions and the strain energy of the plate are thus obtained. The theory presented herein is in good agreement with those established previously for both the nonpolar and micropolar plates of constant thickness as well as the nonpolar sandwich plates.

LIST OF NOTATIONS

Throughout the paper the Cartesian coordinates x_k (k = 1,2,3) and the Einstein's summation convention are used. Accordingly the repeated Latin indices represent summation over the range of the integers (1,2, 3), while the repeated Greek indices are summed over the range (1,2). A superposed dot and the indices following a comma respectively stand for the partial differentiation with respect to time t and indicated x_k. A star designates the prescribed quantities. The overbars, the primes and the double primes represent the core layer, and the lower and upper facing layers, respectively.

Essentially new quantities are defined when they are first introduced.

The list of notation follows:

$2h$	Uniform thickness of a layer
x_k	Right-handed cartesian coordinates
t	Time
e_{klm}	Usual permutation symbol
ρ	Mass density
u_k, Φ_k	Displacement and microrotation vectors
J_{kl}, I	Microinertia tensor, moment of inertia
f_k, l_k	Body force and body couple per unit mass
v_k, w_k, ϕ_k, ψ_k	Displacement and microrotation components
$\alpha_k \equiv \ddot{u}_k, b_k \equiv J_{kl}\ddot{\Phi}_k$	Acceleration and microrotational acceleration vectors
$e_{kl}, \varepsilon_{kl}, \gamma_{klm}$	Strain and microstrain tensors
$\underset{\sim}{t}, \underset{\sim}{m}$	Stress and couple stress vectors
t_{kl}, m_{kl}	Stress and couple stress tensors
$N_{kl}, M_{kl}, \mathcal{N}_{kl}, \mathcal{M}_{kl}$	Stress and couple stress resultants defined by Eq. (12)
S, A, S_σ, S_u	Total boundary surface, area of the middle plane, surface parts on which stresses and displacements are respectively prescribed
Ω^*, Ω	Strain energies measured per unit volume and per unit area of the middle plane
A_{klmn}, B_{klmn}	Constitutive coefficients for anisotropic micropolar elastic solids

INTRODUCTION

Originating in Cauchy's second law of motion which was established by Fresnel [1] in 1868, Duhem [2] first introduced the concept of directed or oriented media. E. and F. Cosserat [3] systematically constructed the general theories of this media in one, two and three dimensions in 1909. After half a century with very little activity in this area, the concept of Cosserat continuum was revived by a number of scientists in several related theories. Among these theories we specifically consider the micropolar theory [4] for the present investigation. For references and various contributions on this matter, we refer the reader to Truesdell and Noll [5].

The theory of micropolar elasticity independently takes into account the microrotation of the elements of the media, in addition to the conventional macro deformations. The mechanical behavior of certain classes of materials which inherently possess the granular and fibrous structure was characterized by this theory.

In recent papers [6-8], the micropolar elasticity theories in one and two dimensions were derived by means of the direct integration of the three dimensional equations. However, using the generalized Hamiltonian principle, a variational theorem has been established for the alternate derivations [9]. Also the advantage and the application of the theorem have been pointed out in it. As a supplement of [9], our main objective in the present paper is a variational derivation of the theory of micropolar anisotropic sandwich plates. A comparison of the equations obtained with those previously derived for both nonpolar and micropolar plates is studied additionally.

After the kinematic variables and the geometry of sandwich plate are given in section 2, we recall the variational procedure in section 3. New strain measures, strain-displacement and microrotation relations are given in section 4. The load, stress and couple stress resultants are introduced in section 5. Section 6 is devoted to the constitutive relations and the strain energy of the plate. The macroscopic equations of motion and the related natural boundary conditions for micropolar sandwich plates are extensively studied in sections 7 and 8. The results and some special cases, and the approach used in the derivation are briefly discussed in the last section.

The theory presented herein is valid for both the nonpolar and micropolar sandwich plates of constant thickness as well as single plates.

2. *Geometry of the Plate. Kinematic Variables*

Consider a thin sandwich plate of uniform thickness 2H, consisting of three layers. Each layer is referred to a x_k right-hand system of Cartesian coordinates. x_3 is directed positively upward and $x_3 = 0$ is taken as a reference plane which coincides with the middle plane of a layer. Let 2h denote the thickness of a layer.

A simply connected sandwich plate with no singularities of any type is supposed to be present. Every layer is intimately fixed to its adjacent layers. Thus the displacements and microrotations are continuous, including bonding interfaces, throughout the plate.

To develop the sandwich plate theory, we assume the displacement and microrotation vectors of each layer in the form

$$\left.\begin{aligned} \underset{\sim}{u}(x_k,t) &= \underset{\sim}{v}(x_\alpha,t) + x_3\, \underset{\sim}{w}(x_\alpha,t) \\ \underset{\sim}{\Phi}(x_k,t) &= \underset{\sim}{\phi}(x_\alpha,t) + x_3\, \underset{\sim}{\psi}(x_\alpha,t) \end{aligned}\right\} \tag{1}$$

By virtue of these equations, the Kirchoff hypothesis of classical plate theory is abrogated, in contrast to supposed for most plate theories, in a natural fashion.

Using the continuity of displacement and microrotation fields at the bonding interfaces, one obtains

$$\left.\begin{aligned} \bar{\underset{\sim}{v}} &= {}'\underset{\sim}{v} + {}'h'\underset{\sim}{w} + \bar{h}\bar{\underset{\sim}{w}} \quad , \quad & \bar{\underset{\sim}{\phi}} &= {}'\underset{\sim}{\phi} + {}'h'\underset{\sim}{\psi} + \bar{h}\bar{\underset{\sim}{\psi}} \\ {}''\underset{\sim}{v} &= {}'\underset{\sim}{v} + 2\bar{h}\bar{\underset{\sim}{w}} + {}'h'\underset{\sim}{w} + {}''h''\underset{\sim}{w} \quad , \quad & {}''\underset{\sim}{\phi} &= {}'\underset{\sim}{\phi} + {}'h'\underset{\sim}{\psi} + 2\bar{h}\bar{\underset{\sim}{\psi}} + {}''h''\underset{\sim}{\psi} \end{aligned}\right\} \tag{2}$$

Therefore we have the following independent displacement and microrotation functions

$$\begin{aligned} &{}'\underset{\sim}{v}(x_\alpha,t), \quad {}'\underset{\sim}{w}(x_\alpha,t), \quad \bar{\underset{\sim}{w}}(x_\alpha,t), \quad {}''\underset{\sim}{w}(x_\alpha,t), \\ &{}'\underset{\sim}{\phi}(x_\alpha,t), \quad {}'\underset{\sim}{\psi}(x_\alpha,t), \quad \bar{\underset{\sim}{\psi}}(x_\alpha,t), \quad {}''\underset{\sim}{\psi}(x_\alpha,t) \end{aligned} \tag{3}$$

for a three-layered plate.

3. *Variational Procedure*

When the motion of the micropolar continuum is referred to a fixed system of Cartesian axes, the equations of local balance of momentum and moment of momentum are respectively given [4] by

$$\left.\begin{aligned} \underset{\sim}{t}_{k,k} + \rho(\underset{\sim}{f} - \underset{\sim}{\alpha}) &= 0 \\ \underset{\sim}{m}_{k,k} + \underset{\sim}{e}_k \times \underset{\sim}{t}_k + \rho(\underset{\sim}{l} - \underset{\sim}{b}) &= 0 \end{aligned}\right\} \tag{4}$$

where $\underset{\sim}{t}_k$, ρ, $\underset{\sim}{f}$, $\underset{\sim}{m}_k$, $\underset{\sim}{e}_k$, $\underset{\sim}{l}$, $\underset{\sim}{\alpha}$ and $\underset{\sim}{b}$ are respectively the stress vectors, the mass density, the body force, the couple stress vectors, the Cartesian unit base vectors, the body couple, the acceleration and microrotational acceleration vectors.

The stress and couple stress vectors are defined through

$$\underset{\sim}{t} = t_{kl}\, n_k\, \underset{\sim}{e}_l = t_l\, \underset{\sim}{e}_l, \quad \underset{\sim}{m} = m_{kl}\, n_k\, \underset{\sim}{e}_l = m_l\, \underset{\sim}{e}_l \tag{5}$$

where n_k stands for the components of the exterior unit normal vector.

Let S_σ and S_u be the two parts of the boundary surface S where the stress and displacement vectors are prescribed, respectively. Thus, the boundary conditions are

$$\left.\begin{array}{llll} t^*_l - t_{kl}\, n_k = 0, & m^*_l - m_{kl}\, n_k = 0 & \text{on} & S_\sigma \\ u^*_k - u_k = 0 & , \quad \Phi^*_k - \Phi_k = 0 & \text{on} & S_u \end{array}\right\} \tag{6}$$

Let t_o and t_1 indicate two arbitrary instants of time t and δ denote the variation. Then, the variational theorem deduced from the Hamiltonian principle can be written [9] in the form

$$\delta I \equiv \delta I_1 + \delta I_2 + \delta I_3 \tag{7}$$

with

$$\delta I_1 = \int_{t_o}^{t_1} dt \int_V [(t_{lk,l} + \rho f_k - \rho \ddot{u}_k)\, \delta u_k + (m_{lk,l} + e_{kmn} t_{mn} + \rho l_k - \rho J_{lk} \ddot{\Phi}_l)\, \delta\Phi_k]\, dv$$

$$\delta I_2 = \int_{t_o}^{t_1} dt \int_{S_u} [(u_k - u^*_k)\, \delta t_k + (\Phi_k - \Phi^*_k)\, \delta m_k]\, ds \tag{8}$$

$$\delta I_3 = \int_{t_o}^{t_1} dt \int_{S_\sigma} [(t^*_l - t_{kl}\, n_k)\, \delta u_l + (m^*_l - m_{kl}\, n_k)\, \delta\Phi_l]\, ds$$

where e_{klm} and J_{kl} respectively represent the usual permutation symbol and the micro-inertia tensor with $J_{kl}\, \ddot{\Phi}_k \equiv b_l$. For arbitrary and independent variations of the indicated quantities, Eq. (7) leads to Eqs. (4) and (6) as appropriate Euler equations. The counterpart of the variational formulation (7,8) in the classical elastodynamics is clearly discussed in [10].

In the following section we employ this variational theorem to develop a micropolar theory of anisotropic sandwich plates.

4. *Strain-Displacement and Microrotation Relations*

The strain tensor e_{kl} and the microstrain tensors ε_{kl}, γ_{klm} are related to the displacement and microrotation vectors by

$$e_{kl} = \frac{1}{2}(u_{k,l} + u_{l,k}), \quad \varepsilon_k = u_{l,k} + e_{lkm}\Phi_m, \quad \gamma_{klm} = e_{kln}\Phi_{n,m} \qquad (9)$$

Substituting Eq. (1) into (9) we record the following strain distribution for later use.

$$\varepsilon_{kl} = {}_0\varepsilon_{kl} + x_3\, {}_1\varepsilon_{kl} \qquad (10)$$

with

$$\begin{aligned} {}_o\varepsilon_{\alpha\beta} &= v_{\beta,\alpha} + e_{3\beta\alpha}\,\phi_3 , & {}_1\varepsilon_{\alpha\beta} &= w_{\beta,\alpha} + e_{3\beta\alpha}\,\psi_3 , \\ {}_0\varepsilon_{\alpha 3} &= v_{3,\alpha} + e_{3\alpha\beta}\,\phi_\beta , & {}_1\varepsilon_{\alpha 3} &= w_{3,\alpha} + e_{3\alpha\beta}\,\psi_\beta , \\ {}_0\varepsilon_{3\alpha} &= w_\alpha + e_{3\beta\alpha}\,\phi_\beta , & {}_1\varepsilon_{3\alpha} &= e_{3\beta\alpha}\,\psi_\beta , \\ {}_0\varepsilon_{33} &= w_3 , \quad {}_1\varepsilon_{33} = 0 \end{aligned} \qquad (11)$$

Here ${}_0\varepsilon_{kl}$ and ${}_1\varepsilon_{kl}$ are clearly functions of x_α and t.

5. *Load Stress and Couple Stress Resultants*

We recall the two fundamental assumptions of plate theory: (1) the thickness 2H is small as compared to any characteristic length L of the middle plane and (2) the stress and displacement fields do not vary violently across the thickness. Therefore the average and the first moments of the various plate quantities over the thickness can be used in the analysis. Then, for future convenience, we introduce the following definitions for the stress and couple stress resultants per unit length of coordinate curves on A, and the effective external loads per unit area of the middle plane A.

$$\begin{Bmatrix} N_{kl} \\ M_{kl} \end{Bmatrix} = \int_{-h}^{+h} t_{kl} \begin{Bmatrix} 1 \\ x_3 \end{Bmatrix} dx_3 , \quad \begin{Bmatrix} \mathcal{N}_{kl} \\ \mathcal{M}_{kl} \end{Bmatrix} = \int_{-h}^{+h} m_{kl} \begin{Bmatrix} 1 \\ x_3 \end{Bmatrix} dx_3 ,$$

$$t_{3k}\Big]_{x_3=+h} = A_k , \quad t_{3k}\Big]_{x_3=-h} = B_k , \quad m_{3k}\Big]_{x_3=-h}^{x_3=+h} = \begin{bmatrix} \mathcal{A}_k \\ \mathcal{B}_k \end{bmatrix},$$

$$\begin{Bmatrix} F_k \\ H_k \end{Bmatrix} = \int_{-h}^{+h} \rho(f_k - d_k) \begin{Bmatrix} 1 \\ x_3 \end{Bmatrix} dx_3 , \quad \begin{Bmatrix} \mathcal{F}_k \\ \mathcal{H}_k \end{Bmatrix} = \int_{-h}^{+h} \rho(l_k - b_k) \begin{Bmatrix} 1 \\ x_3 \end{Bmatrix} dx_3 ,$$

and

$$\begin{Bmatrix} N^*_k \\ M^*_k \end{Bmatrix} = \int_{-h}^{+h} t^*_k \begin{Bmatrix} 1 \\ x_3 \end{Bmatrix} dx_3 \ , \quad \begin{Bmatrix} \mathcal{N}^*_k \\ \mathcal{M}^*_k \end{Bmatrix} = \int_{-h}^{+h} m^*_k \begin{Bmatrix} 1 \\ x_3 \end{Bmatrix} dx_3$$

$$''t^*_k = ''A^*_k \ , \quad ''m^*_k = ''\mathcal{A}^*_k \ , \quad 't^*_k = -\ 'B^*_k \ , \quad 'm^*_k = -\ '\mathcal{B}^*_k \tag{12}$$

6. Constitutive Relations

For a micropolar elastic body [4], a strain energy or an elastic potential density Ω^* exists, and yields

$$t_{kl} = \frac{\partial \Omega^*}{\partial \varepsilon_{kl}} \ , \quad m_{kl} = \frac{\partial \Omega^*}{\partial \Phi_{l,k}} \tag{13}$$

The elastic potential function of the sandwich plate can be expressed by

$$\Omega = \sum_3 \int_{-h}^{+h} \Omega^* \, dx_3 \tag{14}$$

Here, $\sum_3$ indicates the summation over the three layers, and Ω is measured per unit area of the middle plane A.

Starting with Eq. (13) and using Eqs. (10-12), the general constitutive equations can be developed for the sandwich plate through

$$N_{kl} = \frac{\partial \Omega}{\partial\, _o\varepsilon_{kl}} \ , \quad M_{kl} = \frac{\partial \Omega}{\partial\, _1\varepsilon_{kl}} \ , \quad \mathcal{N}_{kl} = \frac{\partial \Omega}{\partial \phi_{l,k}} \ , \quad \mathcal{M}_{kl} = \frac{\partial \Omega}{\partial \psi_{l,k}} \tag{15}$$

These equations characterize the stress and couple stress resultant - strain relations of the micropolar plate for an arbitrary strain energy function Ω^* and the strain distributions in Eqs. (10, 11).

The following linear version of Eq. (13) is recorded for future use

$$t_{kl} = A_{klmn}\, \varepsilon_{mn} \ , \quad m_{kl} = B_{lkmn}\, \Phi_{m,n} \tag{16}$$

which is produced by the following energy density

$$\Omega^* = \frac{1}{2} (t_{kl}\varepsilon_{kl} + m_{lk}\Phi_{k,l}) = \frac{1}{2} (A_{klmn}\varepsilon_{kl}\varepsilon_{mn} + B_{klmn}\Phi_{k,l}\Phi_{m,n}) \tag{17}$$

Here, A_{klmn} and B_{klmn} are the constitutive coefficients for an anisotropic micropolar elastic solid. They clearly satisfy the following symmetry conditions

$$A_{klmn} = A_{mnkl}\ , \quad B_{klmn} = B_{mnkl} \tag{18}$$

The corresponding linear constitutive equations are written in the form

$$\left.\begin{array}{ll} N_{kl} = 2h\, A_{klmn}\ {}_o\varepsilon_{mn}\ , & M_{kl} = I\, A_{klmn}\ {}_1\varepsilon_{mn} \\ \mathcal{N}_{kl} = 2h\, B_{lkmn}\ \phi_{m,n}\ , & \mathcal{M}_{kl} = I\, B_{lkmn}\ \psi_{m,n} \end{array}\right\} \tag{19}$$

Here I is the inertia moment of a normal cross section of a layer, having thickness 2h and unit length, with respect to the median line, and is given by

$$I = \frac{2}{3}\, h^3 \tag{20}$$

Substituting Eq. (17) into (14), the strain energy of the plate is then obtained as follows

$$\Omega = \frac{1}{2} \sum_3 \Big[(2h\ {}_o\varepsilon_{kl}\ {}_o\varepsilon_{mn} + I\ {}_1\varepsilon_{kl}\ {}_1\varepsilon_{mn})\, A_{klmn} + (2h\ \phi_{k,l}\ \phi_{m,n} + I\ \psi_{k,l}\ \psi_{m,n})\, B_{klmn} \Big]$$

or

$$\Omega = \frac{1}{2} \sum_3 (N_{kl}\ {}_o\varepsilon_{kl} + M_{kl}\ {}_1\varepsilon_{kl} + \mathcal{N}_{kl}\ \phi_{l,k} + \mathcal{M}_{kl}\ \psi_{l,k}) \tag{21}$$

7. Macroscopic Equations of Motion

We now proceed to formulate the macroscopic equations of motion for micropolar sandwich plate. For this purpose, considering Eqs. (1, 12), the volume integral $(8)_1$ is then integrated with respect to x_3 for each layer to obtain

$$\delta I_1 = \int_{t_o}^{t_1} dt \int_A \sum_3 (V_k\ \delta v_k + W_k\ \delta w_k + X_k\ \delta\phi_k + Y_k\ \delta\psi_k)\ dA \tag{22}$$

where

$$\left.\begin{array}{ll} V_k = \Lambda_k + A_k - B_k\ , & W_k = h(\Pi_k + A_k + B_k) \\ X_k = T_k + \mathcal{A}_k - \mathcal{B}_k\ , & Y_k = h(\Xi_k + \mathcal{A}_k + \mathcal{B}_k) \end{array}\right\} \tag{23}$$

with

$$\Lambda_\alpha = N_{\beta\alpha,\beta} + F_\alpha\ , \qquad T_\alpha = \mathcal{N}_{\beta\alpha,\beta} + e_{3\alpha\beta}(N_{\beta 3} - N_{3\beta}) + \mathcal{F}_\alpha$$

$$h\,\Pi_\alpha = M_{\beta\alpha,\beta} - N_{3\alpha} + H_\alpha \,, \quad h\,\Xi_\alpha = \mathcal{M}_{\beta\alpha,\beta} - \mathcal{N}_{3\alpha} + e_{3\alpha\beta}(M_{\beta 3} - M_{3\beta}) + \mathcal{H}_\alpha$$

$$\Lambda_3 = N_{\alpha 3,\alpha} + F_3 \,, \quad T_3 = \mathcal{N}_{\alpha 3,\alpha} + e_{3\alpha\beta}\,N_{\alpha\beta} + \mathcal{F}_3 \qquad (24)$$

$$h\,\Pi_3 = M_{\alpha 3,\alpha} - N_{33} + H_3 \,, \quad h\,\Xi_3 = \mathcal{M}_{\alpha 3,\alpha} - \mathcal{N}_{33} + e_{3\alpha\beta}\,M_{\alpha\beta} + \mathcal{H}_3$$

To set the variational integral (22) to zero for an arbitrary and independent variations of displacement and microrotation components introduced in Eq. (3), one obtains that

$$\left.\begin{aligned}
{}'\Lambda_k + \bar{\Lambda}_k + {}''\Lambda_k + {}'P_k &= 0 \,, & {}'T_k + \bar{T}_k + {}''T_k + {}'R_k &= 0 \,,\\
{}'\Pi_k + {}''\Lambda_k + \bar{\Lambda}_k + {}'Q_k &= 0 \,, & {}'\Xi_k + {}''T_k + \bar{T}_k + {}'S_k &= 0 \,,\\
{}''\Pi_k + {}''\Lambda_k + {}''Q_k &= 0 \,, & {}''\Xi_k + {}''T_k + {}''S_k &= 0 \,,\\
\bar{\Pi}_k + 2{}''\Lambda_k + \bar{\Lambda}_k + \bar{Q}_k &= 0 \,, & \bar{\Xi}_k + 2{}''T_k + \bar{T}_k + \bar{S}_k &= 0
\end{aligned}\right\} \qquad (25)$$

where

$$\left.\begin{aligned}
{}'P_k &= {}''A_k - {}'B_k \,, & {}'Q_k &= {}''A_k + {}'B_k \,, & {}''Q_k &= 2{}''A_k \,, & \bar{Q}_k &= 2{}''A_k\\
{}'R_k &= {}''\mathcal{A}_k - {}'\mathcal{B}_k \,, & {}'S_k &= {}''\mathcal{A}_k + {}'\mathcal{B}_k \,, & {}''S_k &= 2{}''\mathcal{A}_k \,, & \bar{S}_k &= 2{}''\mathcal{A}_k
\end{aligned}\right\} \qquad (26)$$

In Eq. (25) the continuity of tractions at the interfaces is also considered.

Eqs. (25) are the consistent first and second approximate equations of motion for the micropolar sandwich plate. These equations are closely related to several predecessors as pointed out in the last section.

Upon the linearization in the kinematic fields and the continuity conditions at the interfaces, Eqs. (25) consist of the linear combination of the flexural and extensional equations of motion for each layer. The parallel between plate and multilayer plate theories are clearly examined in [11, 12].

8. *Natural Boundary Conditions*

The set of boundary conditions corresponding to (25) are presented in this section. We assume that the tractions are prescribed over the edge boundary surface S_e and over some parts of faces S_f, while the displacement and the microrotations are only prescribed over the remaining parts of the two faces S_u.

First consider the surface integral δI_2 in Eq. (8). Substituting (1) and the prescribed components into δI_2, we obtain, for arbitrary and independent variations of the indicated tractions over S_u, the following boundary conditions

$$\left.\begin{array}{llll} 'v_k = 'v_k^* , & 'w_k = 'w_k^* , & '\phi_k = '\phi_k^* , & '\psi_k = '\psi_k^* \quad \text{on } 'S_u \\ ''v_k = ''v_k^* , & ''w_k = ''w_k^* , & ''\phi_k = ''\phi_k^* , & ''\psi_k = ''\psi_k^* \quad \text{on } ''S_u \end{array}\right\} \tag{27}$$

In addition, as pointed out in [13] and [14], in order to get a unique solution of the boundary value problem considered herein, we must also prescribe the initial values of the components (27) and their velocities over S_u.

The second surface integral δI_3 is split into two parts; δJ_1 for the edge boundary surface S_e, and δJ_2 for the some parts of lower and upper faces S_f. Thus we have

$$\delta I_3 = \delta J_1 + \delta J_2$$

The integral δJ_1 is similarly evaluated to the volume integral δI_1 in section 7. It is then obtained that

$$\delta J_1 = \int_{t_o}^{t_1} dt \oint_C \sum_3 (\Lambda_k^* \, \delta v_k + h \, \Pi_k^* \, \delta W_k + T_k^* \, \delta\phi_k + h \, \Xi_k^* \, \delta\psi_k) ds \tag{28}$$

with

$$\left.\begin{array}{ll} \Lambda_k^* = N_k^* - N_{\alpha k} \, n_\alpha , & h \, \Pi_k^* = M_k^* - M_{\alpha k} \, n_\alpha , \\ T_k^* = \mathcal{N}_k^* - \mathcal{N}_{\alpha k} \, n_\alpha , & h \, \Xi_k^* = \mathcal{M}_k^* - \mathcal{M}_{\alpha k} \, n_\alpha \end{array}\right\} \tag{29}$$

Here C denotes a simply-connected Jordan curve which is the intersection of the middle plane A and the edge boundary surface of layers, and ds represents the element of arc length. Eq. (28) yields the following boundary conditions for arbitrary and independent displacement variations.

$$\left.\begin{array}{ll} {}'\Lambda_k^* + \bar{\Lambda}_k^* + {}''\Lambda_k^* = 0 \; , & {}'T_k^* + \bar{T}_k^* + {}''T_k^* = 0 \; , \\ {}'\Pi_k^* + {}''\Lambda_k^* + \bar{\Lambda}_k^* = 0 \; , & {}'\Xi_k^* + {}''T_k^* + \bar{T}_k^* = 0 \; , \\ {}''\Pi_k^* + {}''\Lambda_k^* = 0 \; , & {}''\Xi_k^* + {}''T_k^* = 0 \; , \\ \bar{\Pi}_k^* + 2{}''\Lambda_k^* + {}'\Lambda_k^* = 0 \; , & \bar{\Xi}_k^* + 2{}''T_k^* + {}'T_k^* = 0 \end{array}\right\} \text{along } C \qquad (30)$$

On the other hand, after evaluating the integral δJ_2 in an analogous fashion we write

$$\delta J_2 = \int_{t_o}^{t_1} dt \left\{ \int_{{}''S_f} \Big[({}''A_k^* - {}''A_k)(\delta{}''v_k + {}''h\ \delta{}''w_k) + ({}''\mathcal{A}_k^* - {}''\mathcal{A}_k)(\delta{}''\phi_k + {}''h\ \delta{}''\psi_k) \Big] dS \right.$$
$$\left. + \int_{{}'S_f} \Big[(-{}'B_k^* + {}'B_k)(\delta{}'v_k - {}'h\ \delta{}'w_k) + (-{}'\mathcal{B}_k^* + {}'\mathcal{B}_k)(\delta{}'\phi_k - {}'h\ \delta{}'\phi_k) \Big] dS \right\} \qquad (31)$$

which yields the boundary conditions at the faces as follows

$${}''A_k^* = {}''A_k \; , \quad {}''\mathcal{A}_k^* = {}''\mathcal{A}_k^* \quad \text{on } {}''S_f \; , \quad {}'B_k^* = {}'B_k \; , \quad {}'\mathcal{B}_k^* = {}'\mathcal{B}_k \quad \text{on } {}'S_f \qquad (32)$$

Here Eq. (12) is considered.

The union of Eqs. (25) together the boundary conditions (27), (30) and (32) constitute the boundary value problem for the consistent first and second approximation steps, corresponding to the independent displacement and microrotation functions (3). The complete set of these equations can be solved by standard methods.

9. *Concluding Remarks*

The field equations of a theory of sandwich plates have been consistently constructed within the framework of three dimensional micropolar elasticity theory. These include the continuity conditions, the strain-displacement and microrotation relations, the macroscopic equations of motion, the mixed natural boundary conditions, the constitutive relations, and the strain energy expression for micropolar anisotropic elastic sandwich plates. A variational theorem [9] which has been already established by the author is employed in the derivation. The theory is formulated for the case when the components of displacement and microrotation varied linearly through the thickness of the plate. Thus the present theory gives rise to shear and rotatory inertia corrections in a rational manner. The contradictions introduced by the usual Kirchhoff's hypothesis are completely abrogated.

Under the assumptions cited in section 5, the method of series representation and the asymptotic expansion method can be used in order to develop a consistent plate theory. The first method together with a variational theorem are employed in this investigation. These methods have been recently re-examined by Green and Naghdi [15] and by Goldenveizer [17].

The analytical advantages of the variational procedure in micropolar elasticity that we have employed have been remarked in [9,10]. A similar variational technique with the stress boundary condition has been employed by Ebcioglu [16] in the derivation of the theory of nonpolar sandwich panels. Omitting the effects of microrotation in the governing equations obtained, our results are in agreement with those of [16] in the case of linear theory.

Although this study is a first attempt in order to develop a micropolar sandwich plate theory, Green and Naghdi [6] have already derived a theory of micropolar plates as has Eringen [7]. Dropping summation in all field equations, we also obtain a theory of micropolar plates for the first approximation as well as the second. Further simplification in our constitutive relations and the kinematic components leads to the theories in [6] and [7], which we formulated here by an alternate procedure.

Finally we note that the theory is approached within a general framework. Therefore, introducing plausible assumptions and convenient approximations for practice, one can obtain a series of results such as the theory of micropolar sandwich plate with weak core, membrane facings and so on. Using the familiar standard methods, the set of these equations can be solved as remarked in [12]. Some special problems of importance are being studied and will be reported elsewhere.

The theory presented herein is valid for both the nonpolar and micropolar plates of constant thickness as well as sandwich plates.

Extension of the present theory to the analysis of micropolar composite beams and layered shells is straight-forward.

ACKNOWLEDGEMENT

The author would like to thank Professor B. A. Boley for his constant encouragement. Acknowledgement is due also to the Office of Naval Research for its financial support and to Professor I. Karacan and Dr. Mgalpd for their enthusiasm.

REFERENCES

1. Fresnel, A., "Second Supplément au Mémoire sur la Double Réfraction," Oeuvres, Vol. 2, 1868, pp. 369-442.
2. Duhem, P., Ann. Ecole Norm., Vol. 10, 1893.
3. Cosserat, E. and F., Théorie des Corps Déformables, Hermann, Paris, 1909.
4. Eringen, A. C., "Theory of Micropolar Elasticity," Fracture, Edited by H. Liebowitz, Vol. 2, Academic Press Ltd., 1968, pp. 621-728.
5. Truesdell, C. and Noll, W., "The Nonlinear Field Theories of Mechanics, Handbuch der Physik, Edited by S. Flügge, Vol. III/3, Springer, Berlin, 1964.
6. Green, A. E. and Naghdi, P. M., "Micropolar and Director Theories of Plates," Quart. Journ. Mech. and Applied Math., Vol. XX, 1967, pp. 183-199.
7. Eringen, A. C., "Theory of Micropolar Plates," ZAMP, Vol. 18, 1967, pp. 12-30.
8. Dökmeci, M. C., "Theory of Micropolar Shells and Plates," Recent Advances in Engineering Science, Edited by A. C. Eringen, Vol. 5, 189-207, Gordon and Breach, 1970.
9. Dökmeci, M. C., "A Variational Theorem in Micropolar Elasticity," to appear.
10. Washizu, K., Variational Methods in Elasticity and Plasticity, Pergamon Press Ltd., 1968.
11. Dökmeci, M. C., "On a Nonlinear Theory of Multilayer Shells and Plates," Abstract of XIIth IUTAM, 32, Stanford, California, 1968.
12. Dökmeci, M. C., "Nonlinear Theory of Multilayer Sandwich Plates," To the Memory of Professor Mustafa Inan, to appear.
13. Mindlin, R. D., "High Frequency Vibrations of Crystal Plates," Quart. Applied Math., Vol. 19, 1961, pp. 51-61.
14. Eringen, A. C., "Linear Theory of Micropolar Elasticity," Journ. Math. and Mechs., Vol. 26, 1965, pp. 909-923.
15. Green, A. E. and Naghdi, P. M., "Some Remarks on the Linear Theory of Shells," Quart. Journ. Mech. and Applied Math., Vol. XVIII, 1965, pp. 257-276.

16. Ebcioḡlu, I. K., "On the Theory of Sandwich Panels in the Reference State," Int. J. Engng. Science, Vol. 2, 1965, pp. 549-564.

17. Goldenveizer, A. L., "The Principles of Reducing Three-Dimensional Problems of Elasticity to Two-Dimensional Problems of the Theory of Plates and Shells," Proc. XIth IUTAM Congress, Springer, 1966, pp. 306-311.

A SANDWICHED LAYER OF DISSIMILAR MATERIAL WEAKENED BY CRACK-LIKE IMPERFECTIONS

P. D. Hilton
Lehigh University

G. C. Sih
Lehigh University

ABSTRACT

An integral representation of the symmetrically and anti-symmetrically loaded problem of a line crack in an elastic layer sandwiched between two elastic half-planes is developed. The elastic properties of the layer are different from those of the half-planes. This problem is of interest in connection with the effect of material and geometric parameters on the mechanics of fracture initiation in laminate composites.

Effective solutions of the stresses and displacements in the layered medium are obtained. In particular, the stress-intensity factor which is associated with the driving force of a crack is calculated numerically from a Fredholm integral equation of the second kind. The results lead to several important conclusions on the interaction of the elastic properties of the composite with its geometry. For given values of the layer thickness to crack length ratio and Poisson's ratio, the stress-intensity factor is found to be higher than the Griffith value of one material when the shear mudulus of the half-planes is lower than that of the layer and the opposite effect is observed when the layer modulus is decreased to a value below the modulus of the surrounding material. The ratio of the layer thickness to crack length also has a strong influence on the force required to propagate a crack. Information of this kind is valuable in selecting the appropriate material properties and layer geometry for which the laminate composite can be best designed against fracture.

INTRODUCTION

It is known that the load-carrying capacity of a laminar composite is much greater than that for a single material of the same geometry. This is because the number of flaws, which tend to lower the strength of structural members, are substantially reduced in a laminate. The strength of individual sheets of a laminate, however, varies over a wide range and in many instances the composite structure will contain a number of weak sheets. These weak sheets will fail first due to cracking and, as a result the load-carrying capacity of the layered composite can be greatly reduced. To examine the failure of the laminate caused by cracking in one of the individual sheets, it suffices to investigate the idealized system of a layer containing an initial flaw sandwiched between two other layers of infinite height. Such a model is adopted in the present work.

While one of the most useful properties of composites is their ability to arrest cracks, relatively little theoretical attention has been given to the fracture analysis of composites. Some of the earlier works [1-4] in this field were concerned with the strength reduction of a crack-like imperfection along the interface of two elastic half-planes made of different materials. Later, Perlman and Sih [5,6] carried out an analysis to study the de-bonding of a fibrous composite. They solved the problem of a circular inclusion (fiber) partially bonded to the interior of medium (matrix) of another material. The unbonded portions of the interface may be regarded as circular arc of discontinuities or curved cracks. The forces required to debond the fiber from the matrix were calculated. Another interesting problem discussed recently by Tamate [7] was concerned with the interaction of a circular fiber with a line crack embedded in the matrix. Since the problem is unmanageable by analytical means, a numerical procedure was used to determine the influence of material properties of the composite on the intensity of the local stress field for various crack-to-fiber distances. The case of a crack oriented perpendicularly to the interface of two dissimilar media was studied by Zak and Williams [8] using the technique of eigenfunction expansions. In their work, only the qualitative character of the stress singularity at the crack tip under plane extension was considered.

The present paper is directed toward the analysis of a laminar composite consisting of a cracked layer bonded between two half-planes with different elastic properties. The crack of finite length is situated in the middle of the layer and parallel to the bond lines. Plane strain conditions are assumed. An integral transform technique is used to reduce the problem to the solution of a Fredholm integral equation which is solved numerically for the crack driving force. The effects of the layer height and the material properties of the composite on the stability or instability behavior of the crack are discussed.

Statement of Problem

Referring to Fig. 1, let the shear modulus and Poisson's ratio of the sandwiched layer of thickness 2h be denoted by μ_1 and ν_1, and those for the half-planes be given by μ_2 and ν_2. In the sequel, the subscripts 1 and 2 will be used to distinguish quantities referred to the layer and its surrounding materials, respectively. The crack of length 2a is centered at the origin along the x-axis. The elastic materials are isotropic and homogeneous.

In the absence of body forces, the governing equations of a two-dimensional elastic body will be solved by application of the Fourier sine or cosine transform depending upon whether the problem is symmetric or anti-symmetric in the variable x. If F_j stands for the transform of the Airy stress function $\phi_j(x,y)$ given by

$$F_j(\xi,y) = \int_0^\infty \phi_j(x,y) \begin{bmatrix}\cos(\xi x)\\ \sin(\xi x)\end{bmatrix} dx, \qquad j = 1,2 \tag{1}$$

whose inverse is

$$\phi_j(x,y) = \frac{2}{\pi}\int_0^\infty F_j(\xi,y) \begin{bmatrix}\cos(x\xi)\\ \sin(x\xi)\end{bmatrix} d\xi, \quad j = 1,2 \tag{2}$$

then the stress components $(\sigma_x)_j$, $(\sigma_y)_j$, and $(\tau_{xy})_j$ may be expressed in terms of $F_j(\xi,y)$ as follows:

$$(\sigma_x)_j = \frac{2}{\pi}\int_0^\infty \frac{d^2F_j}{dy^2} \begin{bmatrix}\cos(x\xi)\\ \sin(x\xi)\end{bmatrix} d\xi$$

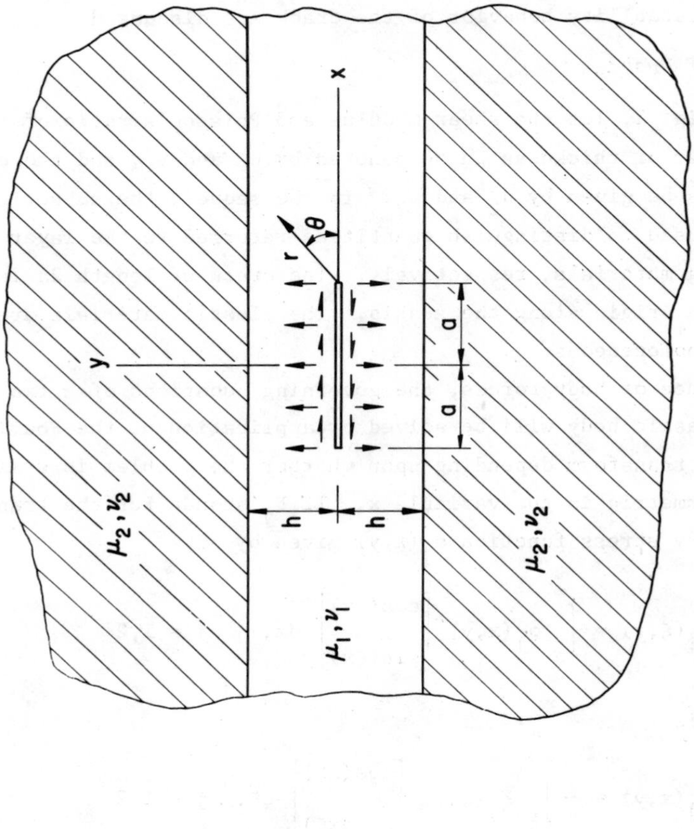

Fig. 1. Layered Composite with a Crack Subjected to Normal and Shear Tractions.

$$(\sigma_y)_j = -\frac{2}{\pi}\int_0^\infty \xi^2 F_j \begin{bmatrix}\cos(x\xi)\\ \sin(x\xi)\end{bmatrix} d\xi \tag{3}$$

$$(\tau_{xy})_j = \frac{2}{\pi}\int_0^\infty \xi \frac{dF_j}{dy} \begin{bmatrix}\sin(x\xi)\\ -\cos(x\xi)\end{bmatrix} d\xi$$

Similarly, the displacement components u_j and v_j become

$$\pi\mu_j u_j = \int_0^\infty \left[(1-\nu_j)\xi^{-1}\frac{d^2F_j}{dy^2} + \nu_j \xi F_j\right] \begin{bmatrix}\sin(x\xi)\\ -\cos(x\xi)\end{bmatrix} d\xi$$

$$\pi\mu_j v_j = \int_0^\infty \left[(1-\nu_j)\xi^{-2}\frac{d^3F_j}{dy^3} + (\nu_j-2)\frac{dF_j}{dy}\right] \begin{bmatrix}\cos(x\xi)\\ \sin(x\xi)\end{bmatrix} d\xi \tag{4}$$

Taking appropriate transform of the biharmonic equation, $F_j (j = 1,2)$ can be found in the usual way (see for example [9]):

$$F_1(\xi,y) = [A_1(\xi) + \xi B_1(\xi)y] \cosh(\xi y) + [C_1(\xi) + \xi D_1(\xi)y] \sinh(\xi y) \tag{5}$$

for the layer bounded by the two parallel planes $y = \pm h$ and

$$F_2(\xi,y) = [A_2(\xi) + \xi B_2(\xi)y] \exp(-\xi y) \;, \quad y>h \tag{6}$$

for the upper half plane $y>h$ while the solution for the lower half plane $y<-h$ can be obtained from symmetry consideration. The unknown functions $A_j(\xi)$, $B_j(\xi)$ $(j=1,2)$ and $C_1(\xi)$, $D_1(\xi)$ are to be determined from the continuity and boundary conditions of the problem.

Assuming that the layer is bonded perfectly to the half-planes, the stresses and displacements must then be continuous across the bond lines $y = \pm h$, i.e.,

$$[\sigma_y(x,\pm h)]_1 = [\sigma_y(x,\pm h)]_2 \;, \quad [\tau_{xy}(x,\pm h)]_1 = [\tau_{xy}(x,\pm h)]_2 \tag{7}$$

and

$$[u(x,\pm h)]_1 = [u(x,\pm h)]_2 \;, \quad [v(x,\pm h)]_1 = [v(x,\pm h)]_2 \tag{8}$$

Without loss in generality[1], the crack is assumed to be opened out by normal tractions p(x) and shear tractions q(x) as shown in Fig. 1. These two cases will be treated separately in the section to follow.

Dual Integral Equations

The problem can be best formulated by setting up a system of dual integral equations which can be solved in a manner established previously.

1. Normal Tractions p(x) / Consider a variable surface pressure p(x) applied to the crack surface. Then the boundary conditions are

$$\begin{aligned} [\sigma_y(x,o)]_1 &= -p(x) \; ; \quad [\tau_{xy}(x,o)]_1 = o \qquad \text{for} \quad |x|<a \\ [v(x,o)]_1 &= o \; ; \quad [\tau_{xy}(x,o)]_1 = o \qquad \text{for} \quad |x|>a \end{aligned} \tag{9}$$

Substituting the appropriate quantities from Eqs. (3) and (4) into Eq. (9) by taking the trigonometric functions appearing at the upper level in the brackets and making use of the continuity conditions (7) and (8), there results the system of dual integral equations

$$\begin{aligned} \int_o^\infty \xi A(\xi) \cos(x\xi)\, d\xi &= o \, , \qquad x>a \\ \int_o^\infty \xi^2 f(\xi) A(\xi) \cos(x\xi)\, d\xi &= \frac{\pi}{2} p(x) \, , \qquad x<a \end{aligned} \tag{10}$$

Since the problem is also symmetric with respect to the y-axis, the absolute value sign on x may be dropped. The function f(ξ) is known in the problem as

$$f(\xi) = \frac{\alpha + [\beta(\xi h)^2 + \gamma] \exp(-2\xi h) + \delta \exp(-4\xi h)}{\alpha - \beta(\xi h) \exp(-2\xi h) - \delta \exp(-4\xi h)} \tag{11}$$

in which α, β, etc. are constants describing the elastic properties of the composite and they are given by

$$\alpha = \frac{1}{2\mu_1^2} \left[3-4\nu_1 + (3-4\nu_2) \left(\frac{\mu_1}{\mu_2}\right)^2 + 2(5 - 6\nu_1 - 6\nu_2 + 8\nu_1\nu_2) \left(\frac{\mu_1}{\mu_2}\right) \right]$$

---

1. The solution for the case when the loads are applied remotely away from the crack can always be found by the principle of superposition.

$$\beta = \frac{2}{\mu_1^2}\left[1-(3-4\nu_2)\left(\frac{\mu_1}{\mu_2}\right)^2 + 2(1-2\nu_2)\left(\frac{\mu_1}{\mu_2}\right)\right]$$

$$\gamma = \frac{1}{\mu_1^2}\left[(5 - 12\nu_1 + 8\nu_1^2) - (3-4\nu_2)\left(\frac{\mu_1}{\mu_2}\right)^2 - 2(1 - 2\nu_1 - 2\nu_2 + 4\nu_1\nu_2)\left(\frac{\mu_1}{\mu_2}\right)\right] \tag{12}$$

$$\delta = \frac{1}{2\mu_1^2}\left[3-4\nu_1 + (3-4\nu_2)\left(\frac{\mu_1}{\mu_2}\right)^2 - 2(3 - 2\nu_1 - 2\nu_2)\left(\frac{\mu_1}{\mu_2}\right)\right]$$

The original unknowns $A_1(\xi)$, $B_1(\xi)$, etc. can be readily expressed in terms of $A(\xi)$ as

$$A_1(\xi) = f(\xi)\,A(\xi)\ ,\quad B_1(\xi) = -C_1(\xi) = A(\xi) \tag{13}$$

and

$$-\mu_1 D_1(\xi) = \left\{(1-2\nu_1)\exp(\xi h) + \cosh(\xi h) - \xi h\exp(-\xi h) + [\sinh(\xi h) + \xi h\exp(-\xi h)]\left(\frac{\mu_1}{\mu_2}\right)\right\}^{-1}$$

$$\cdot\left\{\left(1-\frac{\mu_1}{\mu_2}\right) f(\xi)\exp(-\xi h) + \cosh(\xi h) + (1-2\nu_1)\exp(\xi h) + \xi h\exp(-\xi h) + [\sinh(\xi h) - \xi h\exp(-\xi h)]\left(\frac{\mu_1}{\mu_2}\right)\right\}\cdot A(\xi)$$

from which the stresses and displacements in the layer can be calculated once $A(\xi)$ is known.

2. *Shear Tractions* $q(x)$ / If the upper and lower crack surface is subjected to equal and opposite shear $q(x)$, the conditions to be satisfied on the segment $|x|<a$ and $y=o$ are

$$[\sigma_y(x,o)]_1 = o\ ;\quad [\tau_{xy}(x,o)]_1 = -q(x),\qquad \text{for } x<a$$

and

$$[u(x,o)]_1 = o\ ;\quad [\sigma_y(x,o)]_1 = o\ ,\qquad \text{for } x>a \tag{14}$$

Following the same procedure as in the case of normal tractions, the dual integral equations

$$\int_0^\infty \xi\, B(\xi) \cos(x\xi)\, d\xi = 0 , \qquad x>a$$
$$\int_0^\infty \xi^2\, g(\xi)\, B(\xi) \cos(x\xi)\, d\xi = \frac{\pi}{2}\, q(x) , \qquad x<a \tag{15}$$

are obtained for the determination of the function $B(\xi)$. Here, $g(\xi)$ stands for

$$g(\xi) = \frac{\alpha + [\beta(\xi h)^2 + \gamma] \exp(-2\xi h) + \delta \exp(-4\xi h)}{\alpha + \beta(\xi h) \exp(-2\xi h) - \delta \exp(-4\xi h)} \tag{16}$$

In this case, $A_1(\xi) = 0$ and the remaining unknowns in Eq. (5) are associated with $B(\xi)$ as

$$-\mu_1 B_1(\xi) = \Big\{(1-2\nu_1) \exp(\xi h) + \cosh(\xi h) + \xi h \exp(-\xi h)$$
$$+ [\sinh(\xi h) - \xi h \exp(-\xi h)] \Big(\frac{\mu_1}{\mu_2}\Big)\Big\}^{-1}$$
$$\cdot\Big\{\Big(\frac{\mu_1}{\mu_2} - 1\Big) g(\xi) \exp(-\xi h) + (1-2\nu_1) \exp(\xi h) + \cosh(\xi h) - \xi h \exp(-\xi h)$$
$$+ [\sinh(\xi h) + \xi h \exp(-\xi h)] \Big(\frac{\mu_1}{\mu_2}\Big)\Big\}\cdot B(\xi) \tag{17}$$

and

$$C_1(\xi) = g(\xi)B(\xi) - B(\xi) , \quad D_1(\xi) = B(\xi)$$

The functions $A_2(\xi)$ and $B_2(\xi)$ governing the stress state in the half-planes $y>h$ and $y<-h$ for the two preceeding cases can be obtained from Eqs. (13) and (17) through the continuity conditions as stated by Eqs. (7) and (8). They are

$$A_2(\xi) = \exp(\xi h) \{(A_1 + B_1\xi h) [\cosh(\xi h) - \xi h \exp(\xi h)]$$
$$+ (C_1 + D_1\xi h) [\sinh(\xi h) - \xi h \exp(\xi h)] - \xi h(D_1 \sinh(\xi h) + B_1 \cosh(\xi h)]\}$$
$$B_2(\xi) = \exp(\xi h) \{(A_1 + B_1\xi h) \exp(\xi h) + (C_1 + D_1\xi h) \exp(\xi h)$$
$$+ D_1 \sinh(\xi h) + B_1 \cosh(\xi h)\}\cdot \tag{18}$$

This completes the general formulation of the layered composite crack problem. There remains the task of reducing Eqs. (10) and (15) to a standard form which will be amenable to numerical computation.

Reduction to Fredholm Integral Equation

Note that both Eqs. (10) for the case of normal tractions and Eqs. (15) for the case of shear tractions are of the same form

$$\int_0^\infty C(\xi)\ \cos(x\xi)\ d\xi = 0\ , \qquad x>a$$
$$\int_0^\infty \xi\ h(\xi)\ C(\xi)\ \cos(x\xi)\ d\xi = \frac{\pi}{2}\ F(x)\ , \qquad x<a \tag{19}$$

where $C(\xi)$ is the unknown while $h(\xi)$ and $F(x)$ are given in the problem. With the objective of reducing the system of dual integral equations to a standard form, introduce a new function $w(x)$ related to $C(\xi)$ by

$$w(x) = \frac{2}{\pi}\int_0^\infty C(\xi)\ \cos(x\xi)\ d\xi\ , \qquad x<a \tag{20}$$

and such that $w(x)=0$ for $x>a$ as required by the first of Eqs. (19). Now, applying the Fourier inversion theorem Eq. (20) gives

$$C(\xi) = \int_0^\infty w(x)\ \cos(\xi x)\ dx = \int_0^a w(x)\ \cos(\xi x)\ dx \tag{21}$$

The second of Eqs. (19) may thus be written as

$$\int_0^\infty \xi h(\xi)\left[\int_0^a w(\eta)\ \cos(\xi\eta)\ d\eta\right]\cos(x\xi)\ d\xi = \frac{\pi}{2}\ F(x), \qquad x<a \tag{22}$$

For crack problems in which the stresses become infinite at the end points of the crack it is often advantageous to pre-assign the character of the branch cut into the problem. In this case, since $w(x)$ is associated with the displacement field it must be bounded at $x=\pm a$ and of the order $(x\mp a)^{1/2}$ [10] as $|x|\to a$, i.e.,

$$w(x) = \phi(a)(a^2-x^2)^{1/2} + \text{---} \qquad \text{as} \quad |x|\to a$$

For this reason, let the representation

$$w(x) = \begin{cases} \displaystyle\int_x^a \frac{\tau\phi(\tau)}{\sqrt{\tau^2-x^2}}\ d\tau\ , & 0\le x\le a \\ o\ , & x>a \end{cases} \tag{23}$$

be admitted such that $\phi(\tau)$ is continuous on the interval [o,a]. Inserting Eq. (23) into (22) and then integrating the resulting expression with respect to x from x=o yields, after a formal change of order of integration,

$$\int_0^a \tau\phi(\tau) \int_0^\infty h(\xi)\, J_0(\xi\tau) \sin(\xi x)\, d\xi\, d\tau = \int_0^x F(x)\, dx \ , \quad x<a \qquad (24)$$

where J_0 denotes the Bessel function of the first kind of order zero. Letting $h^*(\xi) = h(\xi)-1$ and applying the elementary integral identity [11]

$$\int_0^\infty J_0(\xi\tau) \sin(\xi x)\, d\xi = \begin{cases} o \ , & x<\tau \\ (x^2-\tau^2)^{-1/2}, & 0<\tau<x \end{cases}$$

leads to

$$\int_0^x \frac{\tau\phi(\tau)}{\sqrt{x^2-\tau^2}}\, d\tau = H(x) \ , \quad x<a \qquad (25)$$

provided that

$$H(x) = -\int_0^a \tau\phi(\tau) \int_0^\infty h^*(\xi)\, J_0(\xi\tau) \sin(\xi x)\, d\xi d\tau + \int_0^x F(x) dx \qquad (26)$$

Equation (25) may be readily converted into an Abel equation and the function $\phi(\tau)$ can be inverted in accordance with

$$\phi(\tau) = \frac{2}{\pi} \int_0^x \frac{d}{dx} [H(x)] \cdot \frac{dx}{\sqrt{\tau^2-x^2}} \ , \quad \tau<a \qquad (27)$$

Putting Eq. (26) into (27) renders

$$\phi(\tau) = \frac{2}{\pi} \int_0^x \frac{F(x)dx}{\sqrt{\tau^2-x^2}} - \int_0^a \eta\phi(\eta) \int_0^\infty \xi h^*(\xi)\, J_0(\xi\eta)\, J_0(\xi x) d\xi d\eta \ , \quad \tau<a \qquad (28)$$

In the subsequent examples, F(x) is taken to be either p=const. or q= const. Thus, by setting $t=\tau/a$ and $s=\xi/a$ the function $\phi(\tau)$ may be non-dimensionalized as

$$\phi(\tau) = \phi(at) = \begin{bmatrix} p\Phi(t) \\ q\Psi(t) \end{bmatrix} t^{-1/2}$$

Under these considerations, Eq. (28) may be recognized as a Fredholm integral equation of the second kind

$$\begin{bmatrix}\Phi(t)\\ \Psi(t)\end{bmatrix} = \sqrt{t} - \int_0^1 K(t,s) \begin{bmatrix}\Phi(s)\\ \Psi(s)\end{bmatrix} ds , \quad t<1 \tag{29}$$

with the symmetric kernel

$$K(t,s) = \sqrt{ts} \int_0^\infty \xi \begin{bmatrix}f^*(\xi/a)\\ g^*(\xi/a)\end{bmatrix} J_0(\xi t)\, J_0(\xi s)\, d\xi, \quad o<t\leq 1; \quad o<s\leq 1 \tag{30}$$

where $f^*(\xi) = f(\xi) - 1$ and $g^*(\xi) = g(\xi) - 1$.

Stress Distribution in the Composite Layer

The theory of linear-elastic fracture mechanics is to provide an ideal way of assisting the understanding of fracture failure and a knowledge for the planning of remedies against fracture in structural elements. Within the uncertainties of applicability, a knowledge of the force required to drive a crack in a composite can be obtained by computing for the stress distribution in the neighborhood of the crack tip. The critical value of this driving force is normally determined experimentally by carrying out a series of destructive tests on composite specimens with initial flaws.

Of interest is the stress field in the layer medium $y=\pm h$. For both cases of normal and shear tractions applied to the crack surface, the two-dimensional stress state can be found by putting Eq. (5) into (3). This gives

$$(\sigma_x)_1 = \frac{2}{\pi} \int_0^\infty [(A_1 + B_1\xi y + 2D_1) \cosh(\xi y) + (C_1 + D_1\xi y + 2B_1) \sinh(\xi y)] \cdot \begin{bmatrix}\cos(x\xi)\\ \sin(x\xi)\end{bmatrix} \xi^2\, d\xi$$

$$(\sigma_y)_1 = -\frac{2}{\pi} \int_0^\infty [(A_1 + B_1\xi y) \cosh(\xi y) + (C_1 + D_1\xi y) \sinh(\xi y)] \cdot \begin{bmatrix}\cos(x\xi)\\ \sin(x\xi)\end{bmatrix} \xi^2\, d\xi \tag{31}$$

$$(\tau_{xy})_1 = \frac{2}{\pi}\int_0^\infty [(A_1 + B_1\xi y + D_1)\sinh(\xi y) + (C_1 + D_1\xi y + B_1)\cosh(\xi y)]$$

$$\cdot \begin{bmatrix} \sin(x\xi) \\ -\cos(x\xi) \end{bmatrix} \xi^2\, d\xi$$

where the $A_1(\xi)$, $B_1(\xi)$, etc. are related to $A(\xi)$ by Eqs. (13) for the problem of normal loading and to $B(\xi)$ by Eqs. (18) for the shear-loading problem. Insertion of the function $w(x)$ into the integrals for $A(\xi)$ and $B(\xi)$ leads to

$$\begin{bmatrix} A(\xi) \\ B(\xi) \end{bmatrix} = \frac{\pi}{2}\frac{a}{\xi}\begin{bmatrix} p \\ q \end{bmatrix}\left\{\begin{bmatrix} \Phi(1) \\ \Psi(1) \end{bmatrix} J_1(a\xi) - \int_0^1 t\, J_1(a\xi t)\frac{d}{dt}\begin{bmatrix} \Phi(t)/\sqrt{t} \\ \Psi(t)/\sqrt{t} \end{bmatrix} dt\right\} \tag{32}$$

where J_1 is the first order Bessel function of the first kind. It is not difficult to show that the integral expression in Eq. (32) remains bounded at the crack tips $x=\pm a$ and that the contribution to the singular behavior of the stresses is fully described by the leading term in Eq. (32). Hence, the singular portion of the stresses takes the form

$$\sigma_{ij} = \begin{bmatrix} p\Phi(1) \\ q\Psi(1) \end{bmatrix}\int_0^\infty S_{ij}(\xi,y)\, J_1(a\xi)\, [\sin(x\xi) \text{ or } \pm\cos(x\xi)]\, d\xi \tag{33}$$

Without going into details, Eqs. (33) may be integrated by keeping only the highest order terms in the expansions of $S_{ij}(\xi,y)$ for large values of ξ. The final results may be expressed in terms of a set of polar coordinates r and θ where r is the distance measured from the crack tip and θ the angle referenced from the line of expected crack extension or the x-axis in Fig. 1. For the case of symmetric loading, the near-field solution is

$$\begin{aligned} \sigma_x &= k_1(2r)^{-1/2}\cos(\theta/2)\,[1 - \sin(\theta/2)\sin(3\theta/2)] + \text{---} \\ \sigma_y &= k_1(2r)^{-1/2}\cos(\theta/2)\,[1 + \sin(\theta/2)\sin(3\theta/2)] + \text{---} \\ \tau_{xy} &= k_1(2r)^{-1/2}\cos(\theta/2)\sin(\theta/2)\cos(3\theta/2) + \text{---} \end{aligned} \tag{34}$$

and for the case of skew-symmetric loading the singular stresses are

$$\sigma_x = k_2(2r)^{-1/2} \sin(\theta/2) \, [2 + \cos(\theta/2) \cos(3\theta/2)] + \text{---}$$

$$\sigma_y = k_2(2r)^{-1/2} \sin(\theta/2) \cos(\theta/2) \cos(3\theta/2) + \text{---} \tag{35}$$

$$\tau_{xy} = k_2(2r)^{-1/2} \cos(\theta/2) \, [1 - \sin(\theta/2) \sin(3\theta/2)] + \text{---}$$

The coefficients k_1 and k_2 in Eqs. (34) and (35) are commonly known as the stress-intensity factors defined as

$$k_1 = \Phi(1)p\sqrt{a} \, , \quad k_2 = \Psi(1)q\sqrt{a} \tag{36}$$

in which $\Phi(1)$ and $\Psi(1)$ stand for the limiting values of $\Phi(t)$ and $\Psi(t)$ as $t \to 1$, the right-hand side crack vertex. Here, the quantities $p\sqrt{a}$ and $q\sqrt{a}$ represent the stress-intensity factors for a geometrically similar body under the same loading conditions but of a single material. In this sense, $\Phi(1)$ and $\Psi(1)$ are the non-dimensionalized stress-intensity factors and they are functions of the parameters ν_1, ν_2, μ_2/μ_1 and h/a which describe the material properties and geometry of the laminar composite.

Before proceeding with the discussion of the numerical results of $\Phi(1)$ and $\Psi(1)$, a few remarks on the physical significance of the parameters k_1 and k_2 are in order. For this purpose, the discussion will be carried out for the symmetric problem and the subscript on the stress-intensity factor may be dropped. The meaning of the k-factor becomes clear in fracture mechanics only when it is associated with the crack extension force G:

$$G = \frac{\pi k^2}{E} \qquad \text{(generalized plane stress)}$$

and (37)

$$G = \frac{\pi(1-\nu^2)k^2}{E} \qquad \text{(plane strain)}$$

where E is the Young's modulus of the material. The quantity G named after Griffith [12] is the rate of energy release per unit extension of the crack under the fixed grips, fixed load or changing load condition. The simple relationships between G and k in Eqs. (37) imply that there is a critical value of G associated with a critical value of k at the point of incipient fracture. In this simple example of a two-dimensional stress state, the fracture theory based on G_{cr} is equivalent to one using k_{cr}. This, however, is not always the case.

The energy concept of G as originally proposed by Griffith is a general one while caution must be exercised in applying the k-factor concept to stress states of a more general character. This arises in higher order plate theories or micro-structure theory of elasticity in which two different stress-intensity factors may appear in the local stress field both of which are coefficients of a $1/\sqrt{r}$ - type of singularity. In such a situation, it is no longer evident as to what is the critical value of the combination of the two stress-intensity factors that will cause unstable crack extension. This combination must then be determined by energy considerations as the basis of formulating fracture theories. For more details, refer to [10].

Discussion of Numerical Results

As mentioned earlier, the values of $\Phi(1)$ and $\Psi(1)$ are found numerically by solving the Fredholm integral equations (29) on the computer. The variations of $\Phi(1)$ and $\Psi(1)$ with the various geometric and material parameters are shown graphically in Figs. 2 through 11.

Figures 2 to 4 exhibit the dependence of $\Phi(1)$ upon μ_2/μ_1 for $\nu_1 = \nu_2 = 0.2$, 0.3, 0.4 and different values of the layer thickness to crack length ratio, h/a. Note that when $\nu_1 = \nu_2$ all the curves intersect at the point $\Phi(1) = 1.0$ and $\mu_2/\mu_1 = 1$ which corresponds to the solution for a single material. Generally speaking, the stress-intensity factor in the cracked layer is higher than the one material solution $p\sqrt{a}$ for $\mu_2/\mu_1 < 1$ and lower for $\mu_2/\mu_1 > 1$. The magnitude of this effect is amplified as the ratio h/a is decreased.

Figures 5 and 6 illustrate plots of $\Phi(1)$ against h/a for curves with various values of μ_2/μ_1. The limiting cases of h/a being equal to infinity or zero may be obtained analytically. When $h/a=\infty$, the composite problem reduces to the one material case where $k_1/p\sqrt{a}=1$. This limit can be observed by noting that the function $f(\xi)$ in Eq. (11) approaches unity as $h/a \to \infty$ and hence $\Phi(1) = 1.0$ in the first of Eqs. (36). Similarly, for the skew-symmetric case, the stress-intensity factor k_2 becomes $q\sqrt{a}$. By letting h/a to approach zero, then both Eq. (11) for the symmetric problem and Eq. (16) for the skew-symmetric problem reduce to the same limit

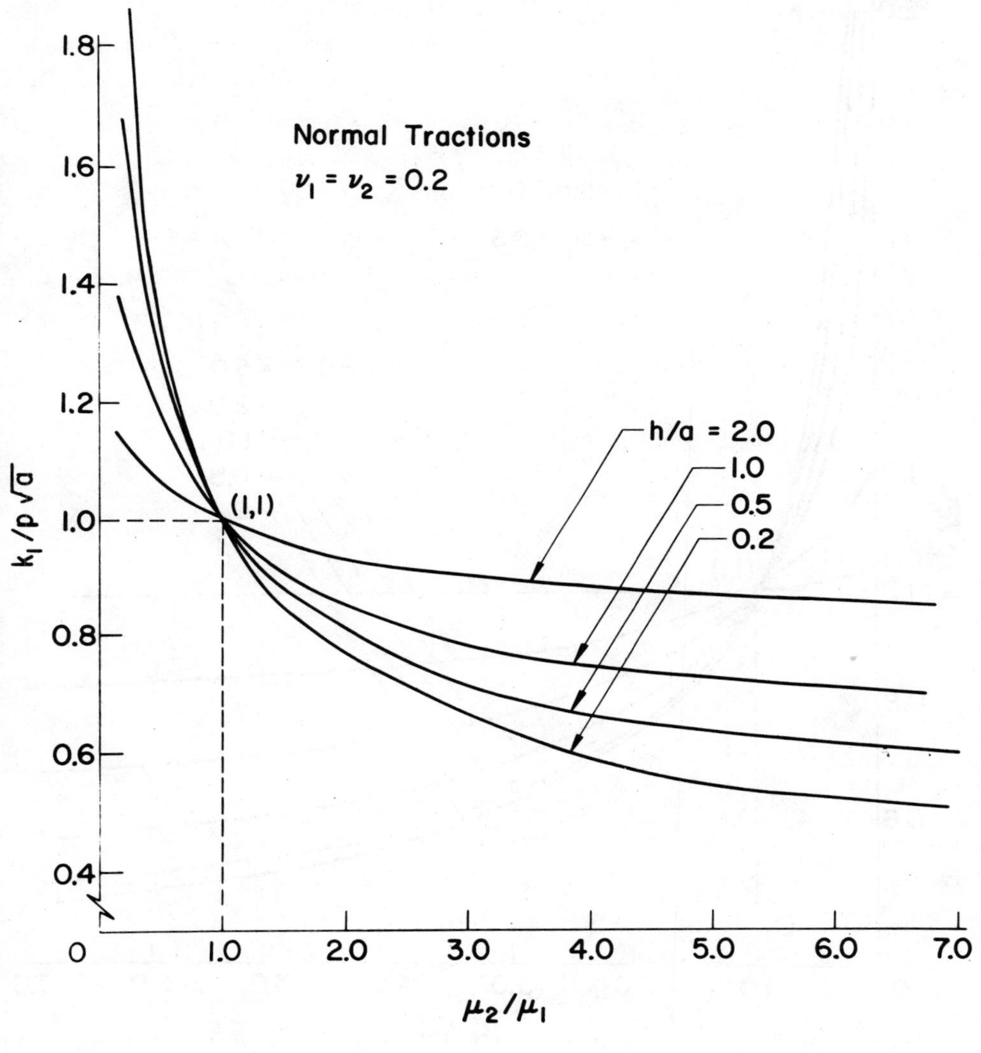

Fig. 2. Normalized Stress-Intensity Factor k_1 versus μ_2/μ_1 for $\nu_1 = \nu_2 = 0.2$.

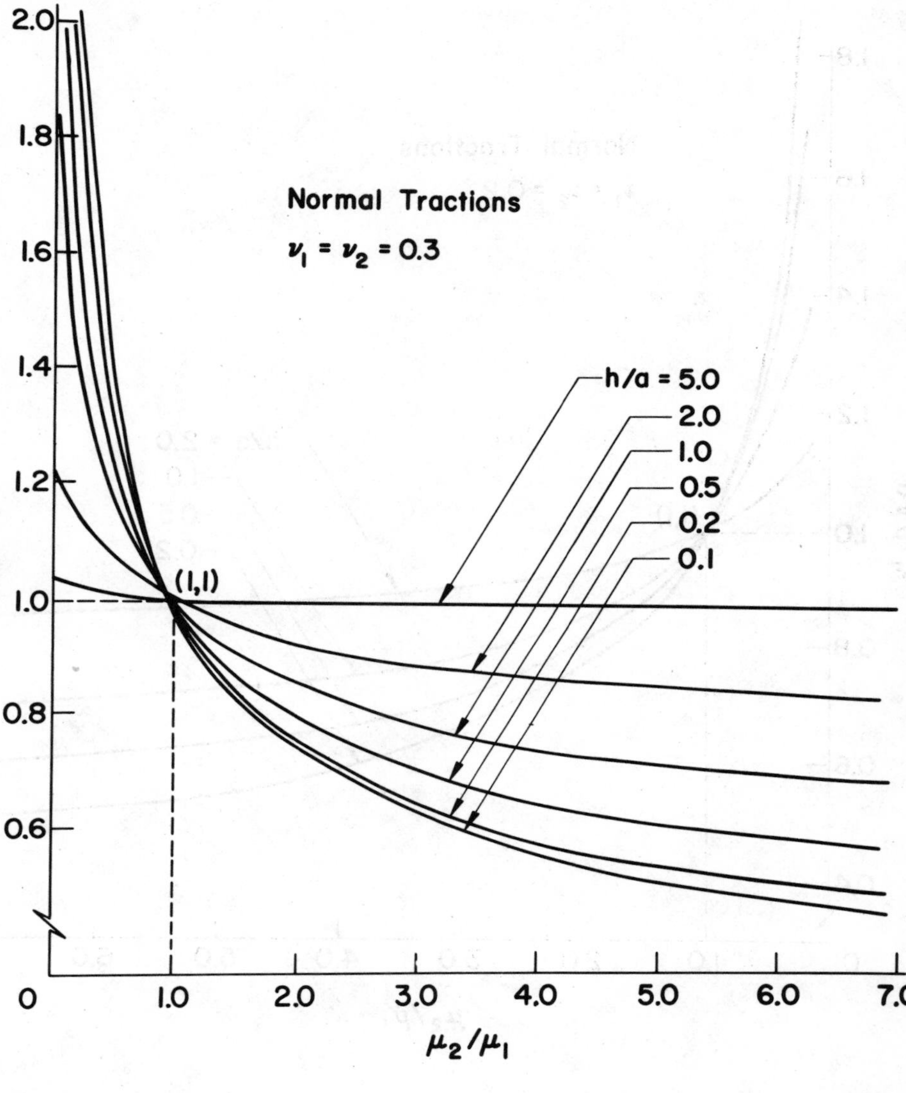

Fig. 3. Normalized Stress-Intensity Factor k_1 versus μ_2/μ_1 for $\nu_1=\nu_2=0.3$.

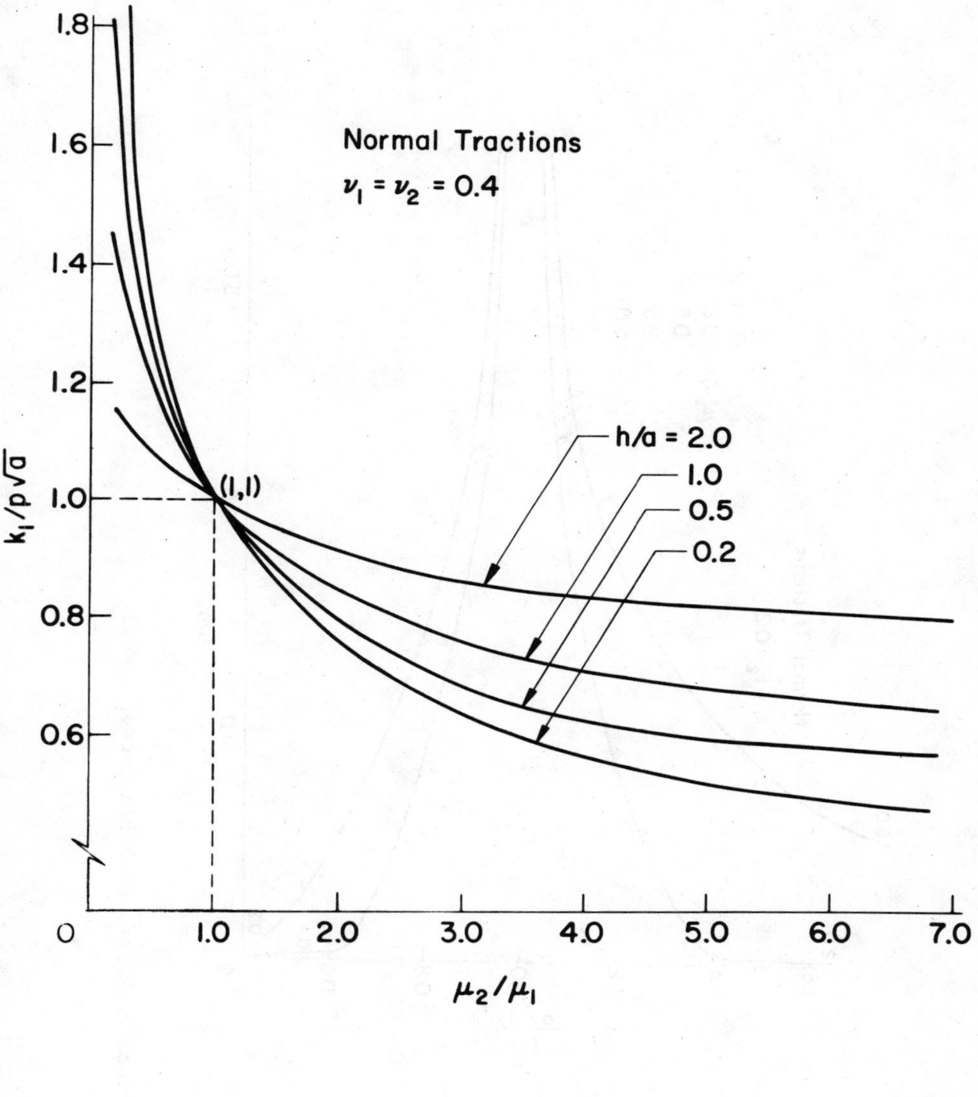

Fig. 4. Normalized Stress-Intensity Factor k_1 versus μ_2/μ_1 for $\nu_1=\nu_2=0.4$.

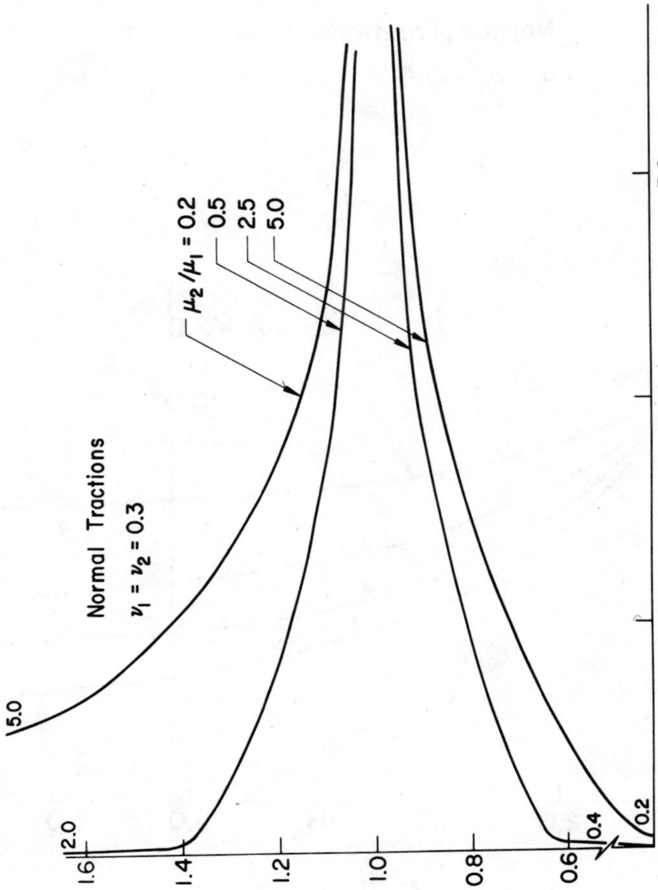

Fig. 5. Variations of $k_1/p\sqrt{a}$ with h/a for $\nu_1=\nu_2=0.3$.

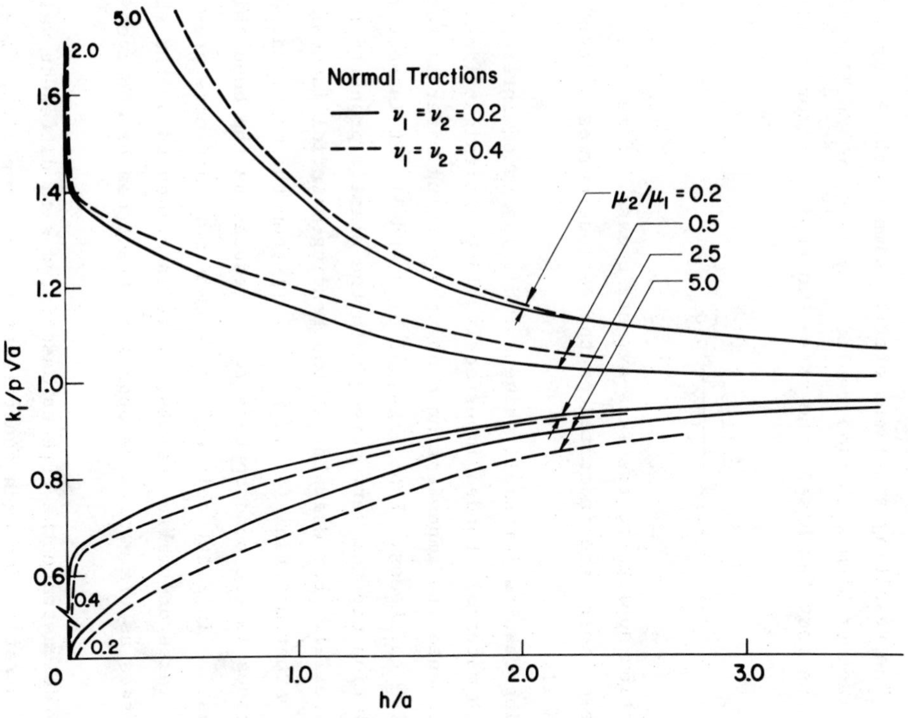

Fig. 6. Variations of $k_1/p\sqrt{a}$ with h/a for $\nu_1=\nu_2=0.2$ and $\nu_1=\nu_2=0.4$.

$$f(\xi) = q(\xi) = \frac{\mu_2(1-\nu_1)}{\mu_1(1-\nu_2)}$$

For the purpose of illustration, consider the system of integral equations (10) for the symmetric problem. Note that since $f(\xi)$ is a constant for h/a=0, it can be moved to the right hand side of the second of Eqs. (10). The resulting equations are the same as those for a single material crack problem with p(x) replaced by $[\mu_1(1-\nu_2)/\mu_2(1-\nu_1)]$ p(x). It follows that for h/a=0, the stress-intensity factor simply becomes

$$k_1 = \frac{\mu_1(1-\nu_2)}{\mu_2(1-\nu_1)} p\sqrt{a}$$

The same deduction applies to the skew-symmetric case. Numerical values for these limits are indicated on the various curves plotted in Figs. 5, 6 and 11.

The foregoing results for small values of h/a may be of interest in connection with materials bonded imperfectly along a straight line. The crack represents the imperfection along the bonding material having small but finite thickness. From Figs. 5, 6, 9 and 11, it is seen that the stress solution depends very strongly on the elastic properties of the bonding material. For example, if the bonding material is weak relative to the parent material (i.e., $\mu_1/\mu_2 < 1$) then the magnitude of the local stresses in the bond appears to be reduced as the bond thickness is decreased. In fact, this effect becomes more and more pronounced as h/a takes on smaller values. This is evidenced by the sharp drop of the curves as $h/a \to o$. The opposite effect can be observed for $\mu_1/\mu_2 > 1$.

In order to demonstrate the effects associated with different values of the Poisson's ratios for each constituent of the composite, Figs. 7 and 8 are plotted for $\nu_1 = 0.2$, $\nu_2 = 0.4$ and $\nu_1 = 0.4$, $\nu_2 = 0.2$, respectively. When ν_2 is greater than ν_1, the curves of $\Phi(1)$ versus μ_2/μ_1 are shifted to the left of the point $\Phi(1) = \mu_2/\mu_1 = 1$. Thus increasing the Poisson's ratio of the material surrounding the cracked layer has the effect of decreasing the stress-intensity factor. The opposite effect is observed in Fig. 8 for $\nu_2 < \nu_1$ where the curves shift to the right of the solution for a single material. Similarly,

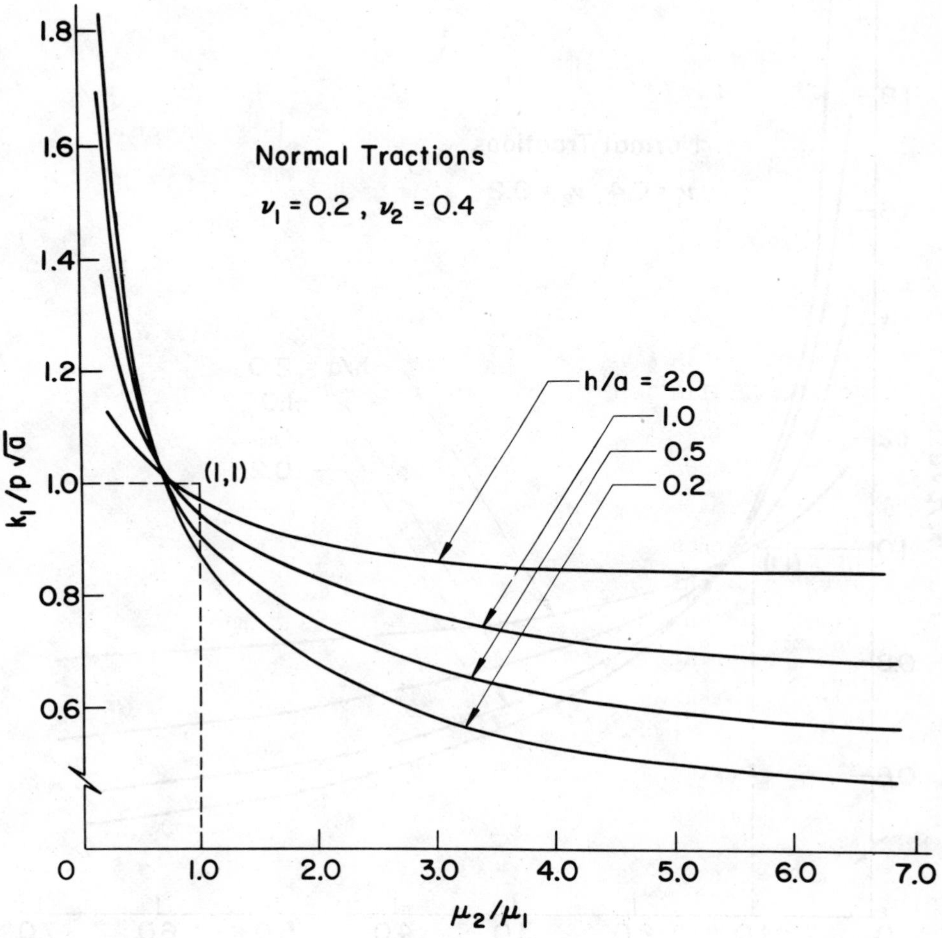

Fig. 7. Plot of $k_1/p\sqrt{a}$ versus μ_2/μ_1 for ν_1=0.2 and ν_2=0.4.

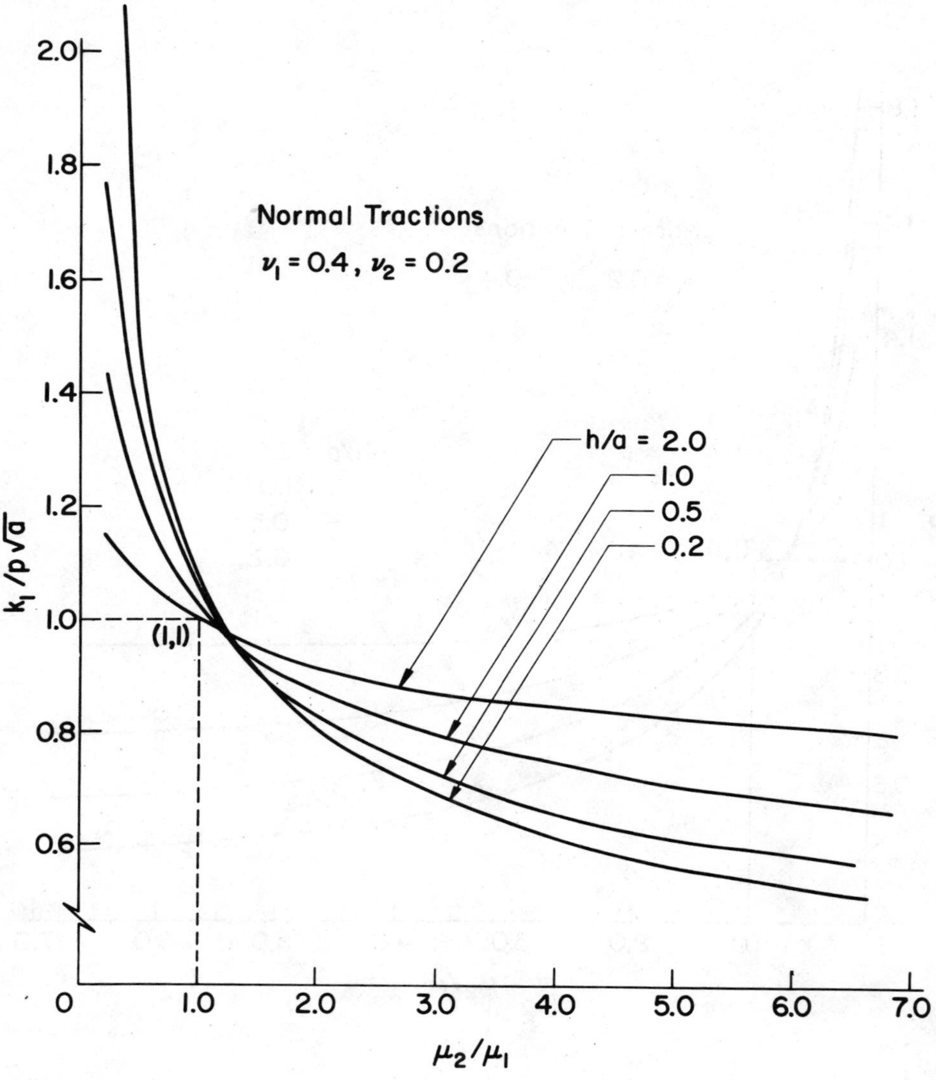

Fig. 8. Plot of $k_1/p\sqrt{a}$ versus μ_2/μ_1 for $\nu_1=0.4$ and $\nu_2=0.2$.

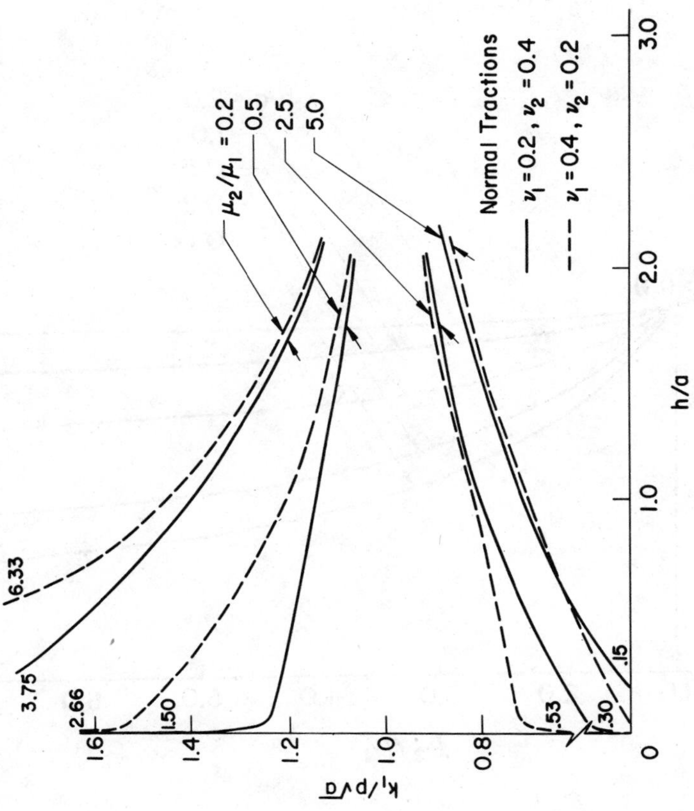

Fig. 9. Variations of $k_1/p\sqrt{a}$ with h/a for ν_1=0.2, ν_2=0.4, and ν_1=0.4, ν_2=0.2.

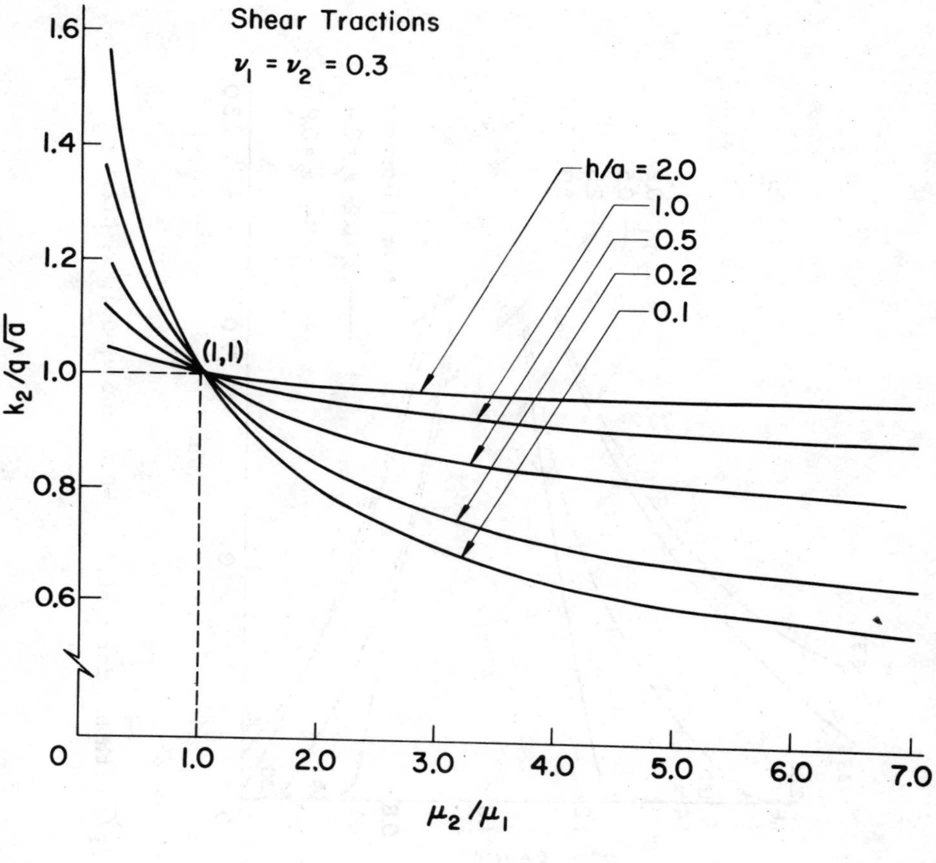

Fig. 10. Non-Dimensionalized Stress-Intensity Factor k_2 versus μ_2/μ_1 for $\nu_1=\nu_2=0.3$.

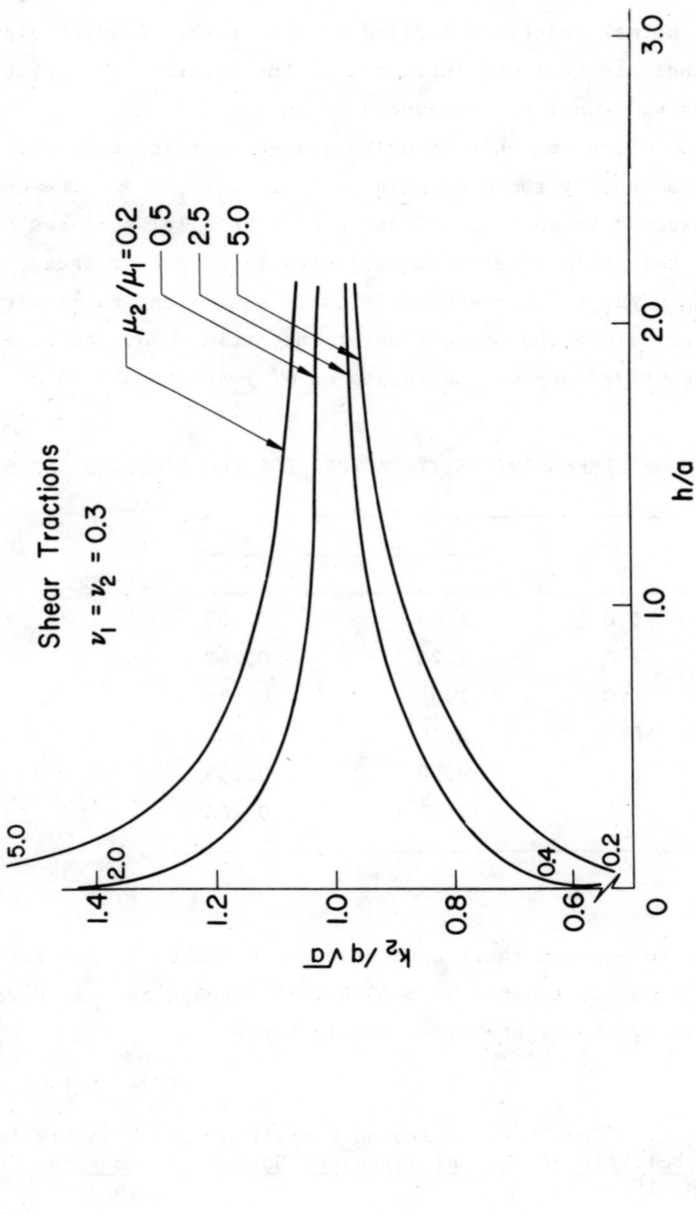

Fig. 11. Variations of $k_2/q\sqrt{a}$ with h/a for $\nu_1=\nu_2=0.3$.

Fig. 9 shows the variation of $\Phi(1)$ with h/a for the case when ν_1 and ν_2 are unequal.

Figures 10 and 11 refer to the crack problem involving shear tractions. Numerical results are given only for $\nu_1 = \nu_2 = 0.3$ since the variations of $\Psi(1)$ with μ_2/μ_1 or h/a are very similar to those found for the case of normal tractions applied to the crack. A quick glance, however, does indicate that the influence of the material properties of the composite on k_2 is not as pronounced as on k_1.

The present solution for the composite system contains two additional limiting cases, namely those of $\mu_2/\mu_1 = 0$ and $\mu_2/\mu_1 = \infty$. The case $\mu_2/\mu_1 = 0$ corresponds to an infinite strip with parallel surfaces free of tractions containing a line crack subjected to normal or shear loads. Allowing μ_2/μ_1 to approach infinity is equivalent to requiring zero displacements along the boundaries of the strip. For the case of a uniformly pressurized crack, the values of $\Phi(1)$ are tabulated as follows:

TABLE 1. VALUES OF STRESS-INTENSITY FACTORS FOR TWO LIMITING CASES

$\frac{h}{a}$	μ_2/μ_1	
	0	∞
5.0	1.05	0.990
2.0	1.25	0.744
1.0	1.84	0.523
0.5	3.30	0.360
0.2	9.50	0.235
0.1	24.50	0.166

ACKNOWLEDGEMENT

The authors wish to express their appreciation to the U. S. Air Force for its support under Contract F33615-69-C-1417 through the Air Force Materials Laboratory at Wright-Patterson Air Force Base.

REFERENCES

1. Williams, M. L., "The Stresses Around a Fault or Crack in Dissimilar Media," Bulletin of the Seismological Society of America, Vol. 49, 1959, pp. 199-204.

2. Sih, G. C. and Rice, J. R., "The Bending of Plates of Dissimilar Materials with Cracks," Journal of Applied Mechanics, Vol. 31, 1964, pp. 477-482.

3. Sih, G. C., "Flexural Problems of Cracks in Mixed Media," Proceedings of the First International Conference on Fracture, Vol. 1, Sendai, Japan, 1965, pp. 391-409.

4. Rice, J. R. and Sih, G. C., "Plane Problems of Cracks in Dissimilar Materials," Journal of Applied Mechanics, Vol. 32, 1965, pp. 418-423.

5. Perlman, A. B. and Sih, G. C., "Circular-Arc Cracks in Bi-Material Plates under Bending," International Journal of Fracture Mechanics, Vol. 3, 1967, pp. 193-206.

6. Perlman, A. B. and Sih, G. C., "Elastostatic Problems of Curvilinear Cracks in Bonded Dissimilar Materials," International Journal of Engineering Science, Vol. 5, 1967, pp. 845-867.

7. Tamate, O., "The Effect of a Circular Inclusion on the Stresses Around a Line Crack in a Sheet Under Tension," International Journal of Fracture Mechanics, Vol. 4, 1968, pp. 257-266.

8. Zak, A. R. and Williams, M. L., "Crack Point Stress Singularities at a Bi-Material Interface," Journal of Applied Mechanics, Vol. 30, 1963, pp. 142-143.

9. Sneddon, I. N., Fourier Transforms, McGraw-Hill Book Company, New York, 1951.

10. Sih, G. C. and Liebowitz, H., "Mathematical Theories of Brittle Fracture," Mathematical Fundamentals of Fracture, Edited by H. Liebowitz, Vol. 2, Academic Press, New York, 1968, pp. 67-190.

11. Watson, G. N., Theory of Bessel Functions, Second Edition, Cambridge University Press, London, 1958.

12. Griffith, A. A., "The Phenomena of Rupture and Flow in Solids," Philosophical Transactions of Royal Society, Vol. A221, 1921, pp. 163-198.

INTERNAL BUCKLING OF A LAMINATED MEDIUM

J. Kiusalaas
The Pennsylvania State University

W. Jaunzemis
The Pennsylvania State University

ABSTRACT

A continuum theory is developed for static problems in composite materials consisting of thin, elastic reinforcing sheets sandwiched between layers of an elastic matrix. Other investigators, using the classical beam and elasticity theories for reinforcement and matrix, respectively, have shown the existence of two basic modes of internal buckling for such composites. The present paper develops the simplest possible continuum model capable of predicting these modes in homogeneously prestrained bodies. The resulting theory is similar to the theories proposed for wave propagation in laminates. The incremental strain energy of the material is obtained by treating the reinforcing layers as plates, and restricting the displacements of each matrix layer to linear functions of local coordinates. Continuity conditions between adjacent layers, and an averaging process are then used to arrive at an incremental strain energy function. Incremental equations of equilibrium and boundary conditions are derived by the usual methods of calculus of variations. It is also shown that the same incremental equations of equilibrium can be derived outright from a general continuum theory of microstructure. However, this approach will not yield explicit expressions for the elastic constants of the continuum in terms of the properties of its constituent components.

The basic modes of internal buckling appear as two special, simple cases of the theory. Further, the characteristic equation for these modes exhibits clearly the influences of microstructure and initial strain, as well as indicating the limits of applicability of a continuum model. A certain uncoupling occurs if Poisson's ratio is negligible. This, in turn, enables one to judge the usefulness of the conventional strain-gradient theories for laminated materials.

LIST OF NOTATIONS

a	Wavelength of buckling
c,d	Parameters in characteristic equation
E	Young's modulus; label identifying extensional buckling modes
e	Compressive prestrain; components of incremental strain tensor
f,g	Auxiliary kinematical variables
h	Thickness of reinforcement
k	Label identifying material layers
K	$= E_R\alpha/(1 - \nu_R^2)$
ℓ	Half-thickness of matrix layers
p,q	Wave numbers of buckling modes
R	Label identifying reinforcement
S	Label identifying shear buckling modes
U	Micro-displacement field of matrix
u	Macro-displacement field of composite
V	Incremental strain energy
v	Displacement field of reinforcement
x	Macro-coordinates
α	$= h/(2\ell)$
Γ	$= K/\mu$
η	Micro-coordinate
κ	$= (\lambda + 2\mu)/2\mu$
λ,μ	Lame's constants
ν	Poisson's ratio
ϕ	Kinematical variables related to ψ
ψ	Micro-displacement gradients

INTRODUCTION

The classical continuum theories employ a single, gross shape deformation in terms of which the mechanical behavior of a body is described. To be practicable, this deformation must possess a high degree of "smoothness" (continuity and differentiability); but then it can reproduce, locally, no more than homogeneous conditions. If the effects of local nonhomogeneity are important, then it is necessary to introduce one or more "micro-deformations," which, when superposed on the gross deformation, will reproduce the local conditions more accurately. For instance, a layer of a laminated material will function not unlike a beam on elastic foundation, so that application of a uniform normal loading may produce an internal buckling of the kind conjectured by Biot [1]. This particular problem lends itself to a continuum-theoretic analysis, whereas others (e.g., local delamination) may not.

Continuum theories of microstructure can be formulated outright, as will be done in Section 6, or else they can be obtained by explicit averaging methods. For the latter approach, the basic ideas were formulated several years ago by Bolotin [2] and Mindlin [3]. As in any continuum theory, the local deformations of constituents of a composite must be considerably restricted - in a manner analogous to the development of theories of rods, plates and shells. Specifically, the micro-deformations are expressed as explicit functions of micro-coordinates and additional kinematical variables, the latter being independent of the micro-coordinates. Using the known mechanical properties of the constituents, it is then possible to describe the energy stored in a typical "elementary cell" of the composite.

The finite-difference form of strain energy can now be transformed into a differential expression, whereby it is necessary to use continuity conditions between constituents, and a "smoothing" procedure based on the assumption that the kinematical variables change sufficiently slowly from one cell to the next. In this way the energy stored in a cell yields the strain energy density of the composite, from which equations of equilibrium and the natural boundary conditions can be derived by the usual methods of calculus of variations.

It should be noted that application of the Bolotin-Mindlin method to a given composite is not straightforward, because neither the constraints to be placed on the micro-displacements, nor the smoothing procedure are unique. The details of these operations, which exert a great influence on the form of the final equations, must be chosen with care to suit the particular problem. For instance, a smoothing procedure employed to describe the propagation of time-harmonic waves may be inappropriate for investigating internal buckling of the same material.

The present paper develops a continuum theory suitable for describing buckling of a laminated medium consisting of alternating reinforcement and matrix layers, as shown in Fig. 1. Deformations are limited to plane strain, and only a homogeneous uniaxial pre-buckling strain is considered. This problem was suggested by the work of Chung and Testa [4], who used classical beam and elasticity theories for the reinforcement and matrix, respectively.

Chung and Testa showed the existence of two distinct modes of internal buckling in laminated bodies, and derived expressions for the critical strain and wavelength associated with each mode in the limiting case of long-wave buckling. The aim of our work is to arrive at the simplest possible continuum theory, using the Bolotin-Mindlin approach, which exhibits the same basic buckling modes. In particular, we wish to demonstrate that continuum theories can indeed provide a realistic description of internal buckling in composite materials. Further, it is possible to judge the limits of applicability of continuum theories and the usefulness of certain special theories (e.g., strain-gradient theories).

To avoid algebraic complications that might otherwise obscure the contents of the theory, a set of restrictions, suggested by the results of [4], is placed on the properties and dimensions of the reinforcement. These restrictions are discussed in Section 1. The incremental strain energy of a cell of the composite is derived in Section 2 by treating the reinforcement as plates, and restricting the micro-displacements to linear functions of the micro-coordinates[1]. Section 3 contains the continuity conditions and a smoothing operation, the latter differing substantially from the procedure used in [5,6]. Incremental equations of equilibrium and boundary conditions are listed in Section 4, the former being utilized in Section 5 to investigate internal buckling. It is shown that two fundamental buckling modes exist, and that they coincide with the modes described in [4].

---

1. This procedure is similar to the work of Sun et al. [5,6] on wave propagation in laminates.

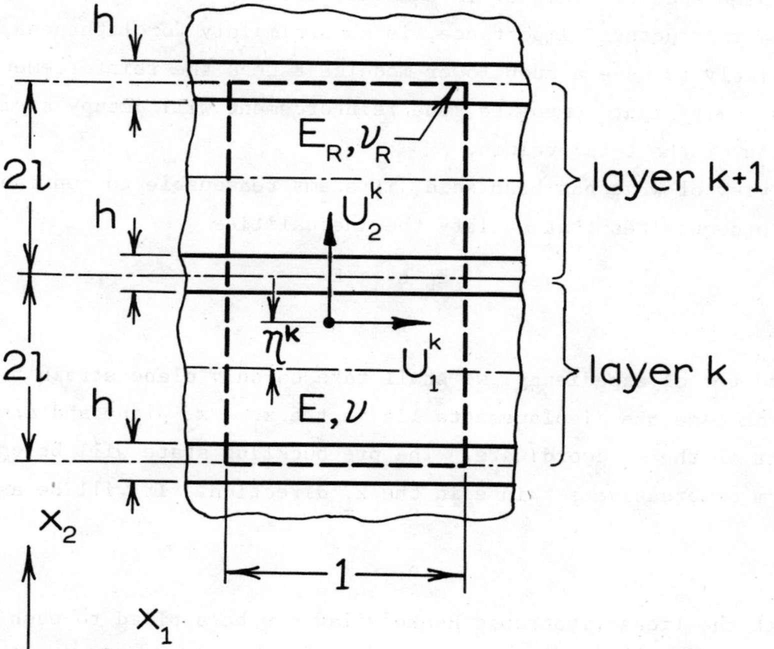

Fig. 1. Laminated Medium; "Macro-Cell" Shown by Dashed Lines.

1. Limitations of the Theory

The model of composites considered here is shown in Fig. 1, and consists of elastic reinforcing sheets of thickness h that are sandwiched between layers of an elastic matrix at intervals 2ℓ. Because the reinforcement should provide the composite with adequate strength and rigidity, a material with a very high Young's modulus E_R (and consequently of high specific weight) is commonly used. The matrix, being of secondary structural importance, is chosen mainly for lightness, and is thus likely to have a much lower modulus E than the reinforcement. In a relatively light composite, the reinforcement will occupy a small fraction of the total volume.

In view of what has been said, it seems reasonable to confine our work to composites that satisfy the inequalities

$$E_R h \gg E\ell \tag{1}$$

$$\ell \gg h \tag{2}$$

As a matter of expediency, we shall take up only plane strain problems, in which case the displacements lie in the $x_1 - x_2$ plane and are independent of the x_3 coordinate. The pre-buckling state will be one of uniform compressive strain e in the x_1 direction. It will be assumed that

$$e \ll 1 \tag{3}$$

so that the linear, isotropic Hooke's law can be applied to each constituent. The Eq. (1) will turn out to be a necessary condition for the pre-buckling strain e to be small.

It has been shown in [4] that if the inequality (2) is sufficiently strong, buckling of the reinforcement will occur in one of the two modes shown in Fig. 2. In case (a) buckling is resisted mainly by an extensional strain of the matrix, producing a close analogy with a plate on an elastic foundation. In case (b) shear deformation of the matrix is chiefly responsible for support of the reinforcement. Following [7], we shall refer to these cases as extensional and shear modes, respectively.

It is important to note that the preceeding description of the buckling modes is valid only so long as the wavelength a is not too small. For $a \ll \ell$ the deformation of the matrix will be confined to a small

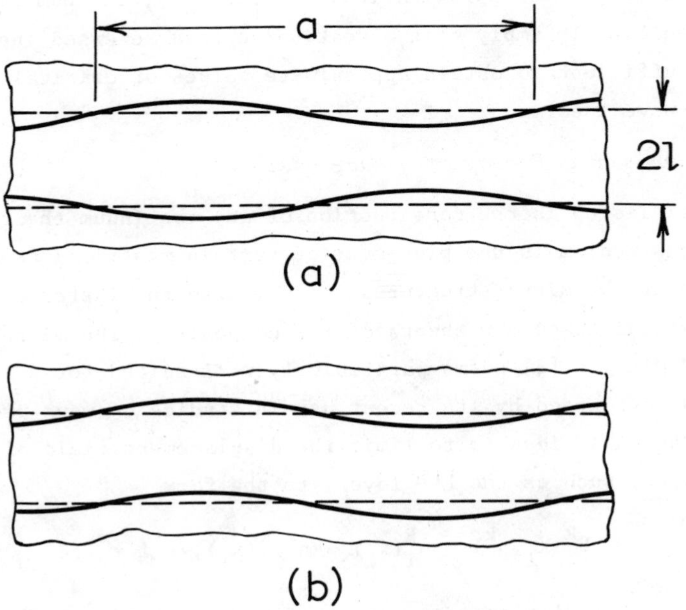

Fig. 2. Basic Buckling Modes: (a) Extensional Mode, (b) Shear Mode.

neighborhood of the reinforcement. Consequently, buckling of one reinforcing sheet will not be influenced by the deformation of its neighbors, and the distinction between the extensional and shear modes will be lost. Because any continuum theory of a composite is based on some averaging process, it is not capable of describing the highly localized deformations of short-wave buckling.

From the analysis in [4] it appears that the condition $E_R h^3 >> E\ell^3$ should also be imposed on the material, as this inequality formally yields the long-wave approximation. Fortunately, the numerical results prescribed clearly imply that a weak, or even a reversed inequality will be sufficient to obtain approximate values of critical loads by the long-wave theory.

2. Incremental Energy of a Macro-Cell

An essential step in the construction of any continuum theory of a nonhomogeneous medium is the placement of certain restrictions on the deformation of the micro-structure. In our case the latter consists of the individual component sheets of the composite. The micro-structure theory of Mindlin [3] seems particularly well-suited for a laminated medium, as evidenced by its recent use in studies of wave propagation [5,6]. The basic idea is to limit the displacement field of a typical matrix layer, such as the kth layer, to the form

$$U_i^k(x_1,\eta^k) = u_i^k(x_1) + \eta^k \psi_i^k(x_1), \quad i = 1,2 \tag{4}$$

where u_i^k are the displacement components of the middle surface of that matrix layer, and η^k represents a local micro-coordinate measuring distance from the middle plane. The functions u_i^k and ψ_i^k are commonly referred to as the macro-displacement and micro-displacement gradient, respectively.[2] It is to be understood that U_i^k represent small, or incremental displacements superimposed on the pre-buckling strain e, and are not to be confused with the components of the total displacement field.

---

2. Because the micro-displacement gradients form a second rank tensor, the proper notation would be ψ_{2i}. For economy of notation, the first index has been dropped in the text.

The components of the incremental strain tensor are, in view of Eq. (4),

$$e_{11}^k = u_{1,1}^k + \eta^k \psi_{1,1}^k \qquad e_{22}^k = \psi_2^k$$
$$e_{12}^k = \frac{1}{2}(\psi_1^k + u_{2,1}^k + \eta^k \psi_{2,1}^k) \tag{5}$$

where comma has been used to denote differentiation with respect to the macro-coordinate x_i.

The strain energy density function for plane strain

$$V_M = (\frac{1}{2}\lambda + \mu)(e_{11} + e_{22})^2 + 2\mu(e_{12}^2 - e_{11}e_{22}) \tag{6}$$

is used to calculate the change in the energy of a matrix layer. Here λ and μ are Lame's constants of the matrix:

$$\lambda = \frac{\nu E}{(1 - 2\nu)(1 + \nu)} \qquad \mu = \frac{E}{2(1 + \nu)} \tag{7}$$

ν being the Poisson's ratio. By using the incremental strains only in Eq. (6), we are in effect neglecting the work done by the pre-buckling strain e. This approximation produces a considerable saving in algebra, and, according to the results of [4], does not have a significant influence on the buckling load.

Substituting Eq. (5) in Eq. (6), and integrating over the approximate thickness 2ℓ yields the incremental strain energy of the kth matrix layer, per unit area of the middle surface:

$$V_M^k = \ell\left[(\lambda + 2\mu)(u_{1,1}^k + \psi_2^k)^2 + \mu(\psi_1^k + u_{2,1}^k)^2 - 4\mu\, u_{1,1}^k\, \psi_2^k\right]$$
$$+ \frac{\ell^3}{3}\left[(\lambda + 2\mu)(\psi_{1,1}^k)^2 + \mu(\psi_{2,1}^k)^2\right] \tag{8}$$

The middle planes of the two reinforcing sheets bounding the kth matrix layer undergo the following displacements, approximately

$$v_i^k(x_1) = U_i^k(x_1, \pm\ell) = u_i^k(x_1) \pm \ell\psi_i^k(x_1) \tag{9}$$

We postulate that equations of the thin plate theory are applicable to the reinforcement, and use the appropriate form of the incremental strain energy per unit area of the middle surface:

$$V_R = \frac{1}{2} \frac{E_R h}{1 - \nu_R^2} \left[(-e \, v_{2,1}^2 + v_{1,1}^2) + \frac{h^2}{12} v_{2,11}^2 \right] \tag{10}$$

where ν_R is the Poisson's ratio of the reinforcing material. The contribution of the reinforcement to the kth material layer (see Fig. 1) consists of half the energy of each reinforcing sheet at its boundary. Using Eq. (9) and Eq. (10), this energy is

$$V_R^k = \frac{1}{2} \frac{E_R h}{1 - \nu_R^2} \left\{ -e \left[(u_{2,1}^k)^2 + \ell^2 (\psi_{2,1}^k)^2 \right] + (u_{1,1}^k)^2 + \ell^2 (\psi_{1,1}^k)^2 \right\}$$

$$+ \frac{1}{24} \frac{E_R h^3}{1 - \nu_R^2} \left[(u_{2,11}^k)^2 + \ell^2 (\psi_{2,11}^k)^2 \right] \tag{11}$$

The total incremental strain energy of the kth layer in the micro-cell is given by $V^k = V_M^k + V_R^k$.

3. *Smoothing Procedure*

In order to arrive at a continuum theory, the discrete sets of functions u_i^k, u_i^{k+1}, ...; ψ_i^k, ψ_i^{k+1}, ... must be replaced by functions which vary smoothly with the x_2 coordinate. Of course, these field variables would have physical meaning only at discrete values of x_2. Such "smoothing" operations must be handled with care, since they exert a great influence on the form of the resultant equilibrium equations and boundary conditions. For example, we observe that the extensional buckling mode, shown in Fig. 2(a), involves an alternating sign of the strain e_{22} in successive matrix layers. Therefore, according to Eq. (5), ψ_2 must be able to attain opposite signs in any two adjacent material cells, if our continuum model is to be capable of reproducing that buckling mode. This can be achieved only by replacing the sets ψ_2^k, ψ_2^{k+2}, ... and ψ_2^{k+1}, ψ_2^{k+3}, ... by two different field variables. For the sake of consistency, a similar smoothing procedure should be employed for ψ_1. No such elaboration is needed for u_i^k, u_i^{k+1}, ..., which will be simply replaced by the functions $u_i(x_1, x_2)$.

Before carrying out the smoothing procedure in detail, we exploit the conditions of continuity between cells k and k+1:

$$U_i^k(x_1, \ell) = U_i^{k+1}(x_1, -\ell) \tag{12}$$

Substituting from Eq. (4), we get

$$\frac{1}{2}(\psi_i^{k+1} + \psi_i^k) = \frac{1}{2\ell}(u_i^{k+1} - u_i^k) \tag{13}$$

Replacing the finite difference on the right side of Eq. (13) by the derivative of u_i, i.e., using the smoothing procedure

$$\frac{1}{2\ell}(u_i^{k+1} - u_i^k) \rightarrow u_{i,2}(x_1,x_2) \tag{14a}$$

results in

$$\frac{1}{2}(\psi_i^{k+1} + \psi_i^k) \rightarrow u_{i,2}(x_1,x_2) \tag{14b}$$

Now the following additional operations become mandatory

$$\frac{1}{2}(u_i^{k+1} + u_i^k) \rightarrow u_i(x_1,x_2) \tag{14c}$$

$$\frac{1}{2\ell}(\psi_i^{k+1} - \psi_i^k) \rightarrow \phi_i(x_1,x_2) \tag{14d}$$

The functions u_i are identified with the mean displacement of the macro-cell at (x_1,x_2), and give rise to macro-strains of the composite. On the other hand, ϕ_i represent micro-deformations within that cell, as demonstrated in Fig. 3.[3]

The mean incremental strain energy density $V^{k,k+1}$ of the cell is obtained by adding the energies of layers k and k+1, and dividing the result by the volume of the element, i.e., by the operation

$$V^{k,k+1} = \frac{1}{4\ell}(V_R^k + V_R^{k+1} + V_M^k + V_M^{k+1}) \tag{15}$$

Upon using the smoothing operations defined in Eq. (14), $V^{k,k+1}$ is identified with the incremental strain energy density function $V(x_1,x_2)$ of the continuum model of the composite. After some tedious algebra, we obtain

$$V = \frac{1}{2}\Big[(\lambda + 2\mu + K)u_{1,1}^2 + 2\lambda u_{1,1}u_{2,2} + (\lambda + 2\mu)u_{2,2}^2$$
$$+ (\mu - eK)u_{2,1}^2 + 2\mu u_{2,1}u_{1,2} + \mu u_{1,2}^2\Big]$$

3. The proper indexing ϕ_{2i2} has again been abbreviated.

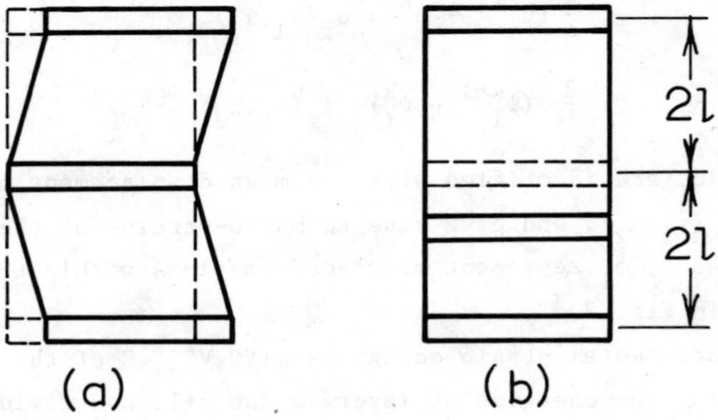

Fig. 3. Deformations of macro-cell described by (a) variable ϕ_1, (b) variable ϕ_2.

$$+ \frac{1}{2} \ell^2 \left[\frac{2}{3} (2\lambda + 4\mu + 3K) u_{1,12}^2 + \lambda u_{1,12} \phi_2 + (\lambda + 2\mu) \phi_2^2 \right.$$

$$\left. + (\frac{4\mu}{3} - 2eK) u_{2,12}^2 + 2\mu u_{2,12} \phi_1 + \mu \phi_1^2 + \frac{K}{3} \alpha^2 u_{2,11}^2 \right]$$

$$+ \frac{1}{2} \ell^4 \left[\frac{2K}{3} \alpha^2 u_{2,112}^2 + \frac{1}{3} (\lambda + 2\mu + 3K) \phi_{1,1}^2 + (\frac{\mu}{3} - eK) \phi_{2,1}^2 \right] \tag{16}$$

$$+ \frac{K}{6} \ell^6 \alpha^2 \phi_{2,11}^2$$

where we used the abbreviations

$$K = \frac{E_R}{1 - \nu_R^2} \frac{h}{2\ell} \tag{17a}$$

$$\alpha = \frac{h}{2\ell} \tag{17b}$$

4. *Incremental Equations of Equilibrium and Boundary Conditions*

Buckling will occur when the material can assume equilibrium configurations other than the initial state without a change in the external loads (method of adjacent equilibria). According to the principle of stationary potential energy, the buckling criterion is thus equivalent to the requirement that the variational equation

$$\delta \iint V \, dx_1 \, dx_2 = 0 \tag{18}$$

must possess at least one non-trivial solution, where the variation is taken with respect to all the kinematically admissible functions u_i and ϕ_i. Employing the conventional techniques of calculus of variations, Eq. (18) yields the following Euler equations, representing the incremental equations of equilibrium:

$$(\lambda + 2\mu + K) u_{1,11} + \mu u_{1,22} + (\lambda + \mu) u_{2,12}$$

$$- \ell^2 \left[\frac{2}{3} (2\lambda + 4\mu + 3K) u_{1,1122} + \lambda \phi_{2,12} \right] = 0 \tag{19a}$$

$$(\lambda + 2\mu) u_{2,22} + (\mu - eK) u_{2,11} + (\lambda + \mu) u_{1,12}$$

$$- \ell^2 \left[(\frac{4\mu}{3} - 2eK) u_{2,1122} + \frac{K}{3} \alpha^2 u_{2,1111} + \mu \phi_{1,12} \right]$$

$$+ \frac{2}{3} K \ell^4 \alpha^2 u_{2,111122} = 0 \tag{19b}$$

$$\ell^2\mu(u_{2,12} + \phi_1) - \ell^4\left(\frac{\lambda + 2\mu + 3K}{3}\right)\phi_{1,11} = 0 \qquad \text{(19c)}$$

$$\ell^2[\lambda\, u_{1,12} + (\lambda + 2\mu)\phi_2] - \ell^4(\frac{\mu}{3} - eK)\phi_{2,11} + \ell^6\,\frac{K\alpha^2}{3}\,\phi_{2,1111} = 0 \qquad \text{(19d)}$$

The boundary conditions derivable from Eq. (18) for boundaries which follow x_1 = const. coordinate lines are

$$(\lambda + 2\mu + K)u_{1,1} + \mu\, u_{2,2} - \ell^2\left[\frac{2(2\lambda + 4\mu + 3K)}{3}\,u_{1,122} + \lambda\,\phi_{2,2}\right] = 0 \quad \text{or} \quad u_1 = 0 \qquad \text{(20a)}$$

$$(\mu - eK)u_{2,1} + \mu\, u_{1,2} - \ell^2\left[(\frac{4\mu}{3} - 2eK)u_{2,122} + \mu\,\phi_{1,2} + \frac{K\alpha^2}{3}\,u_{2,111}\right] + \ell^4\,\frac{2K\alpha^2}{3}\,u_{2,11122} = 0 \quad \text{or} \quad u_2 = 0 \qquad \text{(20b)}$$

$$\frac{K\alpha^2}{3}\,(\ell^2 u_{2,11} - 2\ell^4\, u_{2,1122}) = 0 \quad \text{or} \quad u_{2,1} = 0 \qquad \text{(20c)}$$

$$\ell^4\,\frac{(\lambda + 2\mu + 3K)}{3}\,\phi_{1,1} = 0 \quad \text{or} \quad \phi_1 = 0 \qquad \text{(20d)}$$

$$\ell^4\,(\frac{\mu}{3} - eK)\phi_{2,1} - \ell^6\,\frac{K\alpha^2}{3}\,\phi_{2,111} = 0 \quad \text{or} \quad \phi_2 = 0 \qquad \text{(20e)}$$

$$\ell^6\,\frac{K\alpha^2}{3}\,\phi_{2,11} = 0 \quad \text{or} \quad \phi_{2,1} = 0 \qquad \text{(20f)}$$

Similarily, for x_2 = const. boundaries we get

$$\mu(u_{2,1} + u_{1,2}) - \ell^2\left[\frac{2(2\lambda + 4\mu + 3K)}{3}\,u_{1,112} + \lambda\,\phi_{2,1}\right] = 0 \text{ or } u_1 = 0 \qquad \text{(21a)}$$

$$\lambda\, u_{1,1} + (\lambda + 2\mu)u_{2,2} - \ell^2\left[(\frac{4\mu}{3} - 2eK)u_{2,112} + \mu\,\phi_{1,1}\right] + \ell^4\,\frac{2K\alpha^2}{3}\,u_{2,11112} = 0 \text{ or } u_2 = 0 \qquad \text{(21b)}$$

At corners formed by the intersection of boundaries the following conditions must be satisfied

$$\ell^2\left[\frac{2(2\lambda + 4\mu + 3K)}{3}\,u_{1,12} + \lambda\,\phi_2\right] = 0 \quad \text{or} \quad u_1 = 0 \qquad \text{(22a)}$$

$$\ell^2\left[\left(\frac{4\mu}{3} - 2eK\right)u_{2,12} + \mu\,\phi_1\right] - \ell^4\,\frac{2K\alpha^2}{3}\,u_{2,1112} = 0 \quad \text{or } u_2 = 0 \qquad (22b)$$

$$\ell^4\,\frac{2K\alpha^2}{3}\,u_{2,112} = 0 \quad \text{or } u_{2,1} = 0 \qquad (22c)$$

It is of interest to note that the equations of classical orthotropic elasticity theory are recovered by setting $\ell = 0$ in Eq. (19a) to Eq. (22c). These equations possess a nontrivial solution $u_1 = 0$, $u_2 = f_2(x_1)$ if $\mu - eK = 0$. The last relationship signifies the vanishing of what Biot [7] calls the "slide modulus" of the material. It can be seen that the buckling strain $e = \mu/K$ is small only for materials which are highly anisotropic, such as laminates for which the inequality, Eq. (1) is strong.

Another noteworthy feature of the equations is the uncoupling of ϕ_2 from the remaining variables when $\lambda = 0$, i.e., $\nu = 0$. It means that all the buckling modes are either purely extensional or expressible in terms of u_1, u_2, ϕ_1 only. Since the sole argument for introducing the variables ϕ_1, ϕ_2 was based on the need to express the extensional component of buckling modes, the smoothing procedure Eq. (14d) could now be replaced by $(\psi_1^{k+1} - \psi_1^k)/(2\ell) = u_{1,22}(x_1,x_2)$. Eqs. (19a-c) would then be replaced by two equations in u_i and their gradients, resulting in a simplification of the continuum theory (strain-gradient theory). The uncoupling effect has a particular significance in cases where porous materials, which frequently possess a very small Poisson's ratio, are used in the matrix.

5. *Internal Buckling*

By internal buckling we mean a global instability of the pre-buckling state, as opposed to surface wrinkling (instability near a boundary). Internal buckling is thus manifested only by those nontrivial solutions of the incremental equilibrium equations which remain bounded as $x_i \to \pm\infty$. The system of equations (19a-d), being linear with constant coefficients, admits solutions of the type $\exp[i(px_1 + qx_2)]$. It follows that the critical prestrain is the smallest value of e which admits solutions where p and q are both real.

The two fundamental buckling modes described in [4] can be extracted from the special case $q = 0$, i.e., by assuming u_i and ϕ_i to be functions of x_1 only. Eqs. (19a-d) then become uncoupled:

$$u_{1,11} = 0 \tag{23a}$$

$$(1 - e\Gamma)u_{2,11} - \frac{1}{3}\Gamma\alpha^2\ell^2 u_{2,1111} = 0 \tag{23b}$$

$$\phi_1 - (\frac{2}{3}\kappa + \Gamma)\ell^2\phi_{1,11} = 0 \tag{23c}$$

$$2\kappa\phi_2 - (\frac{1}{3} - e\Gamma)\ell^2\phi_{2,11} + \frac{1}{3}\Gamma\alpha^2\ell^4\phi_{2,1111} = 0 \tag{23d}$$

where we introduced the dimensionless parameters

$$\kappa = \frac{\lambda + 2\mu}{2\mu} = \frac{1 - \nu}{1 - 2\nu} \tag{24a}$$

$$\Gamma = \frac{K}{\mu} = \frac{1 + \nu}{1 - \nu_R^2}\frac{E_R h}{E\ell} \tag{24b}$$

The constants appearing in Eqs. (23a-d) have greatly differing magnitudes, which can be established by reference to Eqs. (1-3). For the sake of future convenience, we restate these inequalities in terms of the notation introduced in previous pages:

$$\Gamma >> 1 \qquad \alpha << 1 \qquad e << 1 \tag{25}$$

Since Eqs. (23a,c) do not admit solutions of the internal buckling type, they are of no further interest. Eq. (23b), on the other hand, provides us with the <u>shear buckling modes</u>. Substituting

$$u_2 = A\exp(ipx_1)$$

p being real, we obtain the characteristic equation

$$(1 - e\Gamma) + \frac{1}{3}\Gamma\alpha^2(p\ell)^2 = 0 \tag{26}$$

Solution of Eq. (26) for e is

$$e = \frac{1}{\Gamma} + \frac{1}{3}\alpha^2(p\ell)^2$$

from which we obtain the critical prestrain

$$e_S = \min_{p\ell} e = \frac{1}{\Gamma} \tag{27a}$$

the critical wave-number being given by

$$(p\ell)_S = 0 \tag{27b}$$

We can directly compare Eqs. (27a,b) with the results of [4] only for $\nu = \nu_R = 0$, the latter being based on the plane stress assumption. In that case we find that Eqs. (27a,b) of [4], representing the long wavelength approximation for shear modes, is indeed in agreement with our results. It is of interest to note that the same critical prestrain is also predicted by classical elasticity theory discussed in Section 2.

The extensional modes can be investigated by setting

$$\phi_2 = B \exp(ipx_1)$$

in Eq. (23d), resulting in the characteristic equation

$$2\kappa + (\frac{1}{3} - e\Gamma)(p\ell)^2 + \frac{1}{3}\Gamma\alpha^2(p\ell)^4 = 0 \tag{28}$$

or

$$e = \frac{2\kappa}{\Gamma(p\ell)^2} + \frac{1}{3\Gamma} + \frac{1}{3}\alpha^2 (p\ell)^2$$

The critical values are found to be

$$e_E = \min_{p\ell} e = \frac{1}{3\Gamma}\left[1 + 2(6\kappa\Gamma\alpha^2)^{\frac{1}{2}}\right] \tag{29a}$$

$$(p\ell)_E = \left(\frac{6\kappa}{\Gamma\alpha^2}\right)^{\frac{1}{4}} \tag{29b}$$

These results should be compared with Eqs. (28a,b) of [4], the long wavelength approximation of extensional modes. With $\nu = \nu_R = 0$, the latter can be reduced to the form

$$e_E = \frac{1}{3\Gamma}\left[6 + 2(6\Gamma\alpha^2)^{\frac{1}{2}}\right] (p\ell)_E = \left(\frac{6}{\Gamma\alpha^2}\right)^{\frac{1}{4}}$$

There exists a discrepancy in the first term of the expression for e_E. The origin of this term can be traced to the shear deformation of the matrix, implying that the continuum theory underestimates the shear rigidity of the matrix. The conclusion is difficult to accept, however, as the placement of constraints on deformation, such as specified in Section 2, invariably increases the apparent rigidity of the material. Consequently, we do not rule out the possibility of a numerical error in [4].

Whether buckling will take place in shear of extensional modes is determined by the magnitude of the parameter $\Gamma\alpha^2$. The former will occur when $\Gamma\alpha^2 < \frac{1}{6\kappa}$, since this inequality yields $e_S < e_E$. If $\Gamma\alpha^2 < \frac{1}{6\kappa}$, the extensional mode dominates, but then we find from Eq. (29b) that $(p\ell)_E > (6\kappa)^{1/2} \geq 6$, which places us uncomfortably close to the short wavelength region of buckling. It follows that if $\Gamma\alpha^2$ greatly exceeds unity, buckling cannot be realistically treated by the continuum theory.

The possible existence of other buckling modes is studied by setting

$$u_i = A_i \exp[i(px_1 + qx_2)] \qquad \phi_i = B_i \exp[i(px_1 + qx_2)]$$

(p and q are real) in Eqs. (19a-d). The resulting characteristic equation is

$$c_1c_2q^4 + (c_1d_2 + c_2d_1 - 1)p^2q^2 + d_1d_2p^4 = 0 \tag{30}$$

where we used the abbreviations

$$c_1 = 1 + \left[\frac{8\kappa + 6\Gamma}{3} - \frac{4(\kappa - 1)^2}{2\kappa + (\frac{1}{3} - e\Gamma)(p\ell)^2 + \frac{1}{3}\Gamma\alpha^2(p\ell)^4}\right](p\ell)^2 \tag{31a}$$

$$c_2 = 2\kappa + \left[(\frac{4}{3} - 2e\Gamma) - \frac{1}{1 + \frac{2\kappa + 3\Gamma}{3}(p\ell)^2}\right](p\ell)^2 + \frac{2}{3}\Gamma\alpha^2(p\ell)^4 \tag{31b}$$

$$d_1 = 2\kappa + \Gamma \tag{31c}$$

$$d_2 = (1 - e\Gamma) + \frac{1}{3}\Gamma\alpha^2(p\ell)^2 \tag{31d}$$

Eq. (30) is, upon solving it for q^2

$$(\frac{q}{p})^2 = \frac{-(c_1d_2 + c_2d_1 - 1) \pm [(c_1d_2 + c_2d_1 - 1)^2 - 4c_1c_2d_1d_2]^{\frac{1}{2}}}{2c_1c_2} \tag{32}$$

Critical prestrain will be the smallest value of e for which Eq. (32) yields at least one pair of real values of q for real p. A necessary condition for q to be real is that the discriminant of Eq. (32) must not be negative. Fortunately, evaluation of the discriminant turns out to be unnecessary. We simply make the provisional assumption that it is positive or zero, and proceed to investigate the remaining stability conditions.

We note that d_1 is always positive, and that for sufficiently small prestrain c_1, c_2, d_2 and $c_1d_2 + c_2d_1 - 1$ are also positive. The last conclusion follows from the observation that Γ is a term in the product c_1d_2; hence the first inequality of Eq. (25) enables us to simplify

$$c_1d_2 + c_2d_1 - 1 \approx c_1d_2 + c_2d_1 \tag{33}$$

We can now deduce from Eq. (32), assuming a non-negative discriminant, that all values of q will be imaginary for sufficiently small e, i.e., the prebuckling state is stable. If e is increased such that any one of the parameters c_1, c_2, or d_2 becomes negative, then Eq. (32) will yield at least two values of real q for real p, and the initial state is unstable. The critical load, therefore, is the smallest value of e which satisfies one of the following equations: $d_2 = 0$, $c_1 = 0$, $c_2 = 0$.

The first equation is identical to Eq. (26); it represented the criterion for buckling by shear modes which was already investigated. From Eq. (31a) we see that c_1 vanishes only when the second term in brackets becomes very large in comparison to unity (note that the first term, containing Γ, is large). This condition is equivalent to Eq. (28), the buckling criterion for extensional modes derived previously.

With $c_2 = 0$ the characteristic equation (30) yields

$$\left(\frac{q}{p}\right)^2 = -\frac{d_1d_2}{c_1d_2 - 1} \approx -\frac{d_1}{c_1}$$

where we used the approximation Eq. (33) in the last step. It follows that for real p, q can be real only when $c_1 < 0$, which means $e > e_E$. Consequently, the critical load associated with $c_2 = 0$ is not a fundamental one in the sense that the buckling mode cannot be realized without first suppressing the extensional mode by some means.

We hasten to add that the critical loads associated with $c_1 = 0$ and $c_2 = 0$ can be calculated from Eqs. (31a,b) to any desired accuracy.

The application of the inequalities in Eq. (25) then formally yields the conclusions drawn above.

6. Formal Methods

In a formal approach to continuum theories of microstructure, a (static) constitutive potential of the form given by Eq. (16) is postulated outright. For dynamic problems it would be necessary to adjoin a second constitutive potential - the kinetic energy function. The viewpoints and techniques of the formal approach have been repeatedly discussed in the literature (cf. [8], pp. 394-409); therefore, we shall consider only the special features of our work.

For two-dimensional problems in laminated materials, the x_1 and x_2 axes are preferred directions, i.e., there are no material symmetries present other than reflections of the x_1 and x_2 axes. Therefore, the "material" tensors are subject to two requirements only. First, these tensors must be of even rank - meaning that in Eq. (16) there can be no cross terms involving deformation tensors of unlike parity. Second, the material tensors must have the symmetries $C_{ijkm} = C_{kmij}$, $D_{ijkmnp} = D_{mnpijk}$, etc. implied by the existence of a strain energy function. Recalling that ϕ_i has been used as an abbreviation for ϕ_{2i2}, we see that Eq. (16) is consistent with these requirements. In particular, the term $G\ell^2 u_{2,12}\phi_1 = D_{212212}u_{2,12}\phi_{212}$ is certainly admissible; on the other hand, a term $u_{2,12}\phi_2$ would also require the presence of $u_{2,22}\phi_1$. Except for such conditions, the complete anisotropy of the problem permits us to keep any term we want, and discard any term we do not want.

At a first glance, the formal approach may seem to have, in the words of Lord Russell, all the advantages of thievery over honest toil. But that is not really so, because we would be left in a sea of moduli C_{ijkm}, D_{ijkmnp}, $E_{ijkmnpqr}$, ... without any idea about their relative importance. In fact, it seems fair to say that for elaborate microstructures, requiring strain gradients and micro-strains of various orders, a general approach is out of the question. Rather, each continuum theory must be developed from the model that it is supposed to describe.

The most interesting aspect of Eq. (16) is the way in which the initial compressive strain e enters into the "effective moduli". The "classical" part of V, i.e., the part that does not depend on ℓ, reduces to the isotropic strain energy function if K is set equal to zero. Further, some anisotropy, namely the modulus K, is needed if the initial strain is to influence the subsequent behavior. To obtain the term $(\mu - eK)u^2_{2,1}$ by the formal method, we assume that V depends on deformation gradients $F_{ij} = \partial x_i/\partial X_j$, where x_i are the final coordinates of a particle with the material coordinates X_i. A routine calculation then yields[4]

$$\delta^2 V = (\delta_{ik} V^0_{jm} + F^0_{in} F^0_{kp} V^0_{jnmp}) F^0_{qj} F^0_{rm} u_{i,q} u_{k,r} \tag{34}$$

where δ_{ik} is the Kronecker delta, V_{jm}, V_{jnmp} are first and second derivatives of V with respect to strains, and the superscript 0 indicates values in the state of initial deformation (thus $F^0_{ij} = \delta_{ij} - e\,\delta_{1i}\delta_{1j}$). Assuming that strain energy is given in terms of strains E_{ij} by the following expression,

$$V = \frac{1}{2}(\lambda E_{ii}E_{kk} + 2\mu E_{ij}E_{ij} + K E^2_{11})$$

we find that the first term in Eq. (34) gives rise to

$$- K e(u^2_{1,1} + u^2_{2,1})$$

From the second term we get

$$K u^2_{1,1} + \mu u^2_{2,1}$$

Therefore, in view of $K(1 - e) \approx K$, the influence of prestraining is felt only in $\mu - iK$, and there only if $K >> \mu$.

In quite the same way the initial strain may appear also in terms proportional to ℓ^4. The term

$$\ell^2(\frac{2\mu}{3} - Ke)u^2_{2,12}$$

is less plausible, at least in a centro-symmetric material. There are various ways in which one may seek to reproduce this term, but they have not been pursued here.

Any theory containing a material property ℓ with the dimension of length will describe a dispersion of waves and "boundary layer effects". To illustrate the latter, one may consider Lame's problem for

4. In what follows the Cartesian tensor notation will be used.

thick-walled spherical shells in the context of a strain-gradient theory (cf. [9]). The radial displacements are then given by

$$u = Ax + \frac{B}{x^2} + \frac{C}{x}\left(\sinh x - \frac{\cosh x}{x}\right) + \frac{D}{x}\left(\cosh x - \frac{\sinh x}{x}\right)$$

where $x = r/\ell$. The first two terms are the classical solution, whereas the remaining two terms represent deviations from the classical solution that are noticeable only at the boundaries.

Internal buckling is rather the opposite of boundary layer effects. It is a global instability, that is, its existence is determined from the field equations alone. The question is then whether initial prestraining can modify the field equations to the extent that they would admit solutions radically different from the solutions obtained for initially unstrained bodies. It has been conjectured by Biot [1] that this is possible even in homogeneous, isotropic bodies when the initial strains are large (and so the response to incremental deformations is, in effect, anisotropic). There is as yet no conclusive evidence for this conjecture. For materials that have both anisotropy and nonhomogeneity (described by strain gradients and micro-strains), this paper and other investigations have clearly shown that internal buckling is a possible mode of instability.

As is readily apparent, the equations of microstructure theories are rather complicated, despite our use of all admissible simplifications. Therefore, it would be highly desirable to discover further simplifications, while retaining the essential content of the theory. This would make it possible to attack problems like boundary wrinkling that may be intractable by direct methods.

The possibility of a different smoothing operation, resulting in a strain gradient theory, was noted before. Whether or not the order of the field equations can be reduced remains to be investigated.

Finally, the discrepancy in the critical prestrain for the extensional buckling modes that was pointed out in Section 5, remains to be resolved. We are convinced that the source of the discrepancy is a numerical, rather than a conceptual error.

ACKNOWLEDGEMENT

This work was supported by the Air Force Office of Scientific Research (AFOSR Grant 69-1626).

REFERENCES

1. Biot, M. A., Mechanics of Incremental Deformations, John Wiley and Sons, Inc., New York, 1965.

2. Bolotin, V. V., "Basic Equations for the Theory of Reinforced Media," Mekhanika Polimerov, Vol. 1, 1965, pp. 27-37.

3. Mindlin, R. D., "Micro-Structure in Linear Elasticity," Archives of Rational Mechanics and Analysis, Vol. 16, 1964, pp. 57-78.

4. Chung, W. Y. and Testa, R. B., "The Elastic Stability of Fibers in a Composite Plate," Journal of Composite Materials, Vol. 3, 1969, pp. 58-80.

5. Sun, C. T., Achenbach, J. D. and Herrmann, G., "Continuum Theory for a Laminated Medium," Journal of Applied Mechanics, Vol. 35, Transactions of the American Society of Mechanical Engineers, Vol. 90, Series E, 1968, pp. 467-475.

6. Sun, C. T., Achenbach, J. D. and Herrmann, G., "Dispersion of Time-Harmonic Waves in a Laminated Plate," AIAA Paper No. 68-353, AIAA/ASME 9th Structures, Structural Dynamics and Materials Conference, Palm Springs, California, April 1968.

7. Rosen, B. W., "Mechanics of Composite Strengthening," Fiber Composite Materials, American Society for Metals, Metals Park, Ohio, 1965.

8. Jaunzemis, W., Continuum Mechanics, The MacMillan Co., New York, 1967.

9. Jaunzemis, W., "An Application of Strain-Gradient Theory to Nonhomogeneous Materials," Fibre Science and Technology 1, 11-17 (1967).

D Y N A M I C S

A THEORETICAL AND EXPERIMENTAL INVESTIGATION OF IMPACT LOADS IN STRANDED STEEL CABLES DURING LONGITUDINAL EXCITATION

Jacques E. Goeller
U. S. Naval Ordnance Laboratory

Patricio A. Laura
Catholic University of America

ABSTRACT

One of the problems encountered in supporting large payloads by a cable system exposed to longitudinal excitation simulating ocean wave motion is referred to as cable snap. This is due to a combination of wave amplitude and frequency that causes slack in the cable which subsequently becomes taut and experiences a severe impact load. This phenomenon has been modeled on an analog computer assuming elastic behavior of the cables and nonlinear damping of the payload and cable. A mathematical model which considers segmented viscoelastic cables is also considered in the present paper. Experiments were performed on 0.0625 inch and 0.09375 inch stranded steel cables of length up to 70 feet with a 27 pound spherical payload attached to the lower end. The cable system was suspended in a tank to a water depth of 65 feet and excited sinusoidally at the top at amplitudes of one to three inches and frequencies from zero up to 3Hz. The cable forces at the top and bottom of the cable were monitored by load cells.

Typical response of the cable forces showed it to gradually increase with frequency until a critical frequency was reached at which impending slack occurs. The critical frequency was well below the resonant frequency of the system. A slight increase in frequency resulted in a drastic increase in cable force which was caused by cable snap.

Cable forces as high as nine times the static force from the payload were encountered. The mathematical solution is in good agreement with the experimental results. It is also shown that these snap loads can be significantly mitigated by the addition of a small length of nylon rope to the bottom of the steel cable. This shock absorber then makes it possible to get through the snap condition by increasing the frequency in much the same way it is possible to get through a resonant condition. This physical condition is also predictable by the mathematical model.

LIST OF NOTATIONS

A_p	Projected cross sectional area of spherical payload $A_p = .785\ D^2$
A_c	Wetted area of cable $A_c = \pi\ d\ L$
C	Damping coefficient
C_{CR}	Critical damping ratio $C_{CR} = 2\sqrt{k_e M_e}$
C_{DP}	Drag coefficient of payload
C_{DC}	Drag coefficient of cable
D	Diameter of payload mass
d	Diameter of cable
E	Modulus of elasticity
F_s	Preload in foundation spring
g	Gravitation constant
k	Spring constant
k_e	Effective spring constant of segmented cable $\frac{1}{k_e} = \frac{1}{k_3} + \frac{1}{k_2}$
L	Length of cable
ℓ	Length of drive rod
M_C	Effective mass of cable
M_e	Effective mass $= M_p + M_{vm}$
M_p	Mass of payload
M_{vm}	Virtual mass of displaced water
P	Axial force in cable
p	Perimeter of cable

W_B Buoyancy force due to displaced payload

W_p Weight of payload

x Spatial variable

x_o Maximum amplitude of displacement function

δ_{sp} Static deflection of payload

δ_{sc} Static deflection of lumped cable mass

τ Time constant of viscoelastic model

ω_{ne} Natural frequency of simple spring mass system;

$$\omega_{ne} = \sqrt{\frac{K_e}{M_e}}$$

ω Circular frequency of forcing function

Subscripts

p Payload

c Cable

e Effective

s External spring

1,2,3 Applies to segments of cable (see Fig. 1 and Fig. 4)

INTRODUCTION

Cable systems using stranded wire rope are frequently used in a number of commercial and military applications. In salvage and towing operations, for example, large objects are suspended from a ship which is exposed to ocean wave motion. The approximate sinusoidal motion of the waves can cause dynamic stresses in the cable which are significantly higher than the static force due to the payload weight.

One of the problems in supporting large payloads by a cable which is excited sinusoidally at the upper end is often referred to as cable snap [1]. The net cable force is composed of the static tensile force due to the payload weight (minus buoyancy force) and the dynamic force which is either compressive or tensile. When the compressive component exceeds the static tensile force the cable goes slack. The cable is subsequently subjected to severe impact stresses when it again becomes taut. Impending slack occurs when the net cable force reaches zero.

The present paper develops mathematical models which predict the phenomenon observed and compares the analytical results with experimental evidence. In order to have generality, a segmented cable system of nylon and steel was considered. Nylon is frequently used because of its light weight and ease of handling. It will be shown in this report that it has the added feature of being a good material for mitigating snap loads. Conventional steel stranded cable is considered since it is frequently used in salvage operations and moreover it is generally used in the upper portion of most deep ocean cable systems to prevent fishbite [2].

Mathematical Models

Two models were used to compute the cable force before and during snap conditions. The first model which is similar to that of [1] is the simplest in that it is a single degree of freedom system with nonlinear payload damping. The model applies only to elastic cables. The second model is more general in that it applies to a segmented cable of two viscoelastic materials and considers nonlinear damping of both the cable and the payload. A distributed mass model [3] was investigated by the authors and it was found that the lumped parameter models yield a good approximation to the distributed mass model over the fundamental frequency range provided slack does not occur in the cable and the mass of the cable is small compared to the mass of the payload.

a. Model No. 1: Analog Simulation

The first model consists of a simple single degree of freedom system as shown in Figure (1). The dynamic equation of motion with respect to the equilibrium position is

$$M_e \ddot{x}_2 + \frac{1}{2} \rho C_{DP} A_P |\dot{x}_2| \dot{x}_2 + K_c(x_2 - x_1) = 0 \qquad (1)$$

The inertia force $M_e \ddot{x}_2$ included the mass of the payload which is considered to be a sphere and the virtual mass of water.[1] An effective cable mass of 1/3 the actual mass was lumped with the payload mass. The virtual mass of the cable is negligible.

[1] Other shapes can be handled provided the virtual mass of water is known.

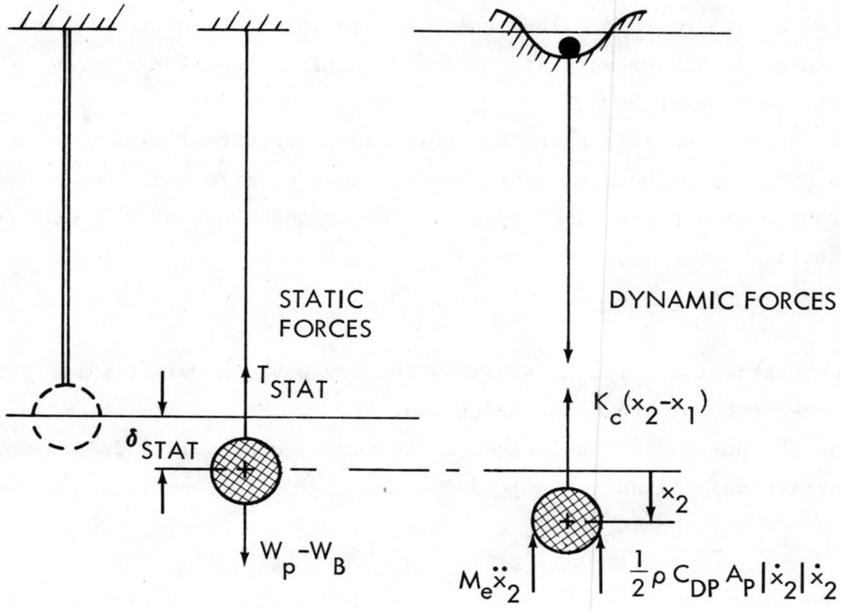

Fig. 1. Static and Dynamic Forces and Displacements for Analog Model.

The drag force is considered to be proportional to the square of the payload velocity. The drag coefficient is taken as constant at 0.50. The basis for this selection can be seen from Fig. 22 of [4] showing the drag coefficient for a sphere versus Reynolds' number. The drag coefficient is fairly constant over a range of Reynolds' number of 500 to 3×10^5. For the experiments conducted, the Reynolds' number was well within this range. Absolute value on velocity is used so that the drag force is always opposite to the direction of motion for both positive and negative $\dot{x}_2$.

The spring force is based on the spring constant of the cable and the supporting structure. For the experiments performed, the spring constant of the cable was very much greater than that of the support structure. Hence

$$K_c = \frac{AE}{L}$$

The static force T_{STAT} is simply the dry payload weight minus the buoyancy force of the displaced fluid.

For the purposes of solution on the analog computer it is convenient to rewrite Eq. (1) as

$$\ddot{x}_2 = - \frac{1}{2} \frac{\rho C_{DP} A_P}{M_e} \left| \dot{x}_2 \right| \dot{x}_2 - \frac{K_c}{M_e} (x_2 - x_1) \qquad (2)$$

The forcing function for simulation of an ocean wave is generally taken as sinusoidal. In the experiments performed, a bell crank device was used as shown in Fig. 2 which generates a forcing function which for a constant rotational speed ω can be shown to be

$$x_p = x_o \sin \omega t + \frac{x_o^2}{4\iota} (\cos \omega t - 1) \qquad (3)$$

the function is very nearly sinusoidal when $x_o/4\iota$ is made very small compared to 1.0 where x_o is the amplitude of the wave (radius of fly-wheel) and ι is the length of the driving rod. For the experiments performed $x_o/4\iota$ has a maximum value of 0.019, this results in a very small deviation from purely sinusoidal input. Computations using a purely sinusoidal function were compared to those using Eq. (3) and little difference was observed.

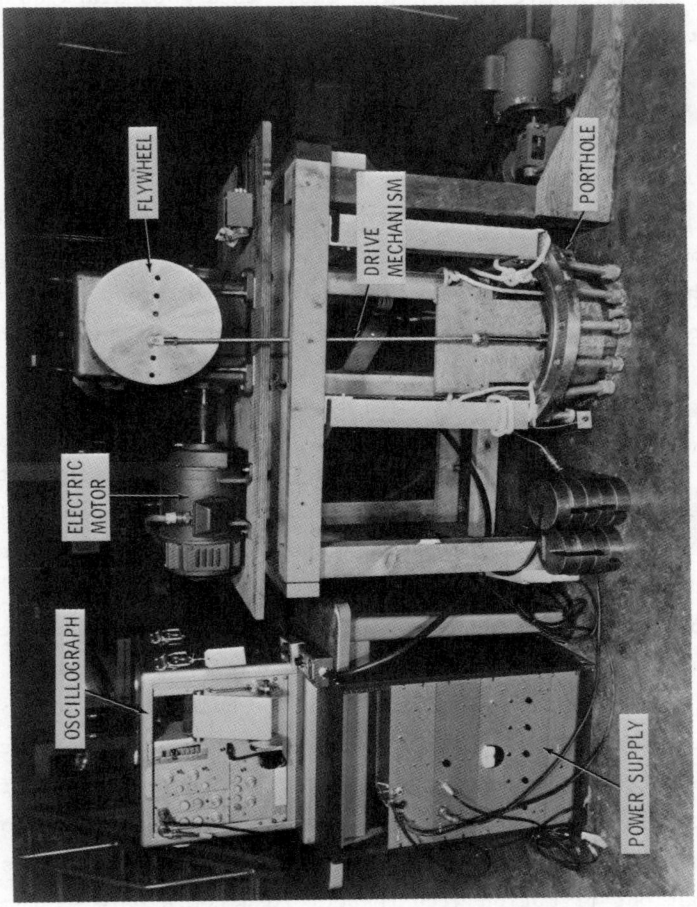

Fig. 2. Test Apparatus.

Equation (2) is valid provided the total cable force given by

$$P_c = W_P - W_B + K_c\,(x_2 - x_1) \tag{4}$$

is greater than or equal to zero. When this force attempts to go compressive (negative) it must be set equal to zero since the cable cannot support a compressive force. The cable then goes slack so that during the slack regime the equation of motion is

$$\ddot{x}_2 = -\frac{\rho\, C_{DP}A_P}{2M_e}\left|\dot{x}_2\right|\dot{x}_2 - \frac{W_P - W_B}{M_e} \tag{5}$$

This is the equation of a body in free flight given an initial acceleration. It eventually reaches a peak, then it descends, until the cable becomes taut at which time it again feels the spring force. Equation (2) then applies again with the initial conditions the same as the final conditions of the slack regime. The previous equations were solved on an analog computer.

b. Model No. 2: Digital Program Solution

The details of the model are illustrated in Fig. 3. The viscoelastic behavior of each cable segment is approximated by a Voigt model. The cable mass is considered as a lumped parameter along with the cable damping. The drag force on the cable and payload is considered to be proportional to the velocity squared with a constant drag coefficient. The payload mass is considered to be held to a rigid foundation by an elastic spring and dashpot to simulate an object held by the ocean sediments. These were included to solve other problems such as breakaway of an object held by the ocean sediments. A constant static force "F_s" is added to simulate a lifting force during a salvage operation. For free oscillation, $K_s = F_s = C_s = 0$. It is convenient to express the dynamic equations of motion with respect to a coordinate system relative to the end of the cable in an unstressed configuration. The equation of motion of the payload then becomes

$$M_e\ddot{x}_2 + \frac{1}{2}\,\rho C_{DP}A_P\left|\dot{x}_2\right|\dot{x}_2 + K_2(x_2 - x_3) + C_2(\dot{x}_2 - \dot{x}_3)$$
$$+ K_s x_2 + C_s\dot{x}_2 - (W_p - W_B) - F_s = 0 \tag{6}$$

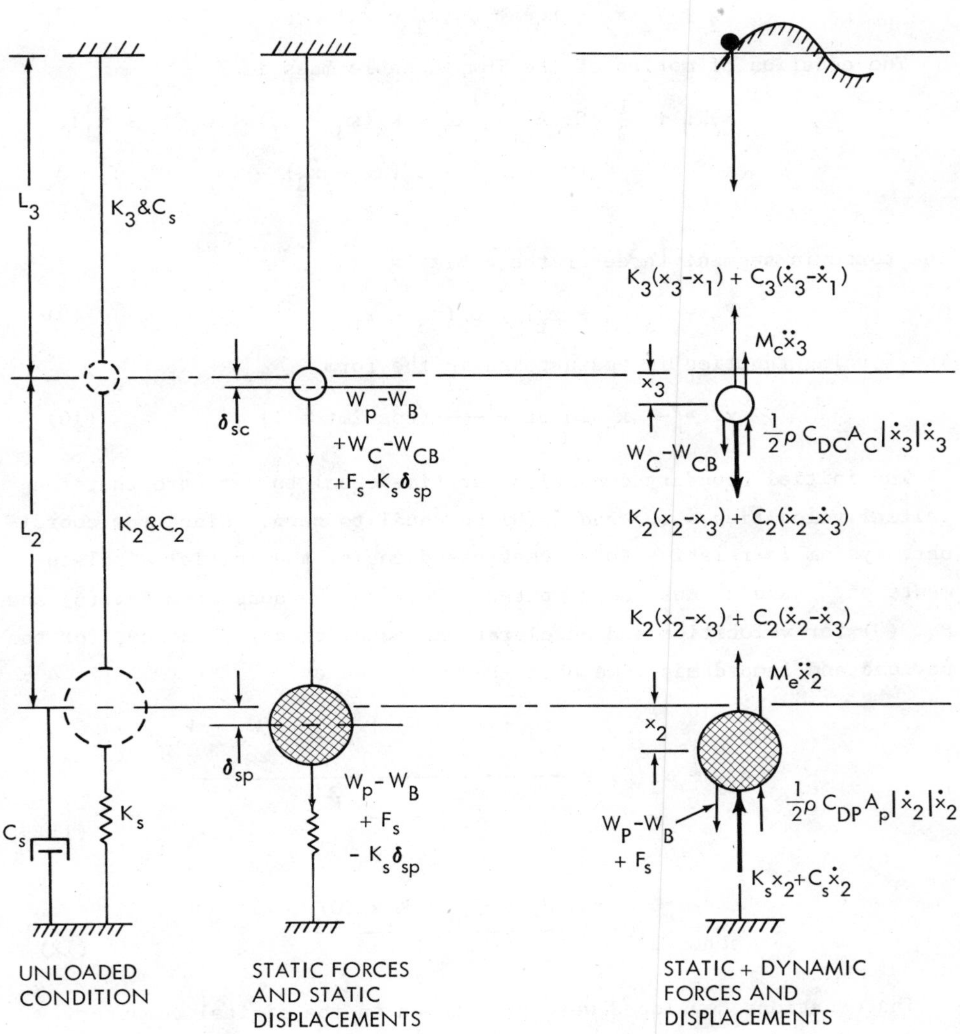

Fig. 3. Illustration of Forces and Displacements in Segmented Cable System - Model (No. 2).

The force in segment two of the cable is

$$P_2 = K_2(x_2 - x_3) + C_2(\dot{x}_2 - \dot{x}_3) \tag{7}$$

The equation of motion of the lumped cable mass is

$$M_c\ddot{x}_3 + \frac{1}{2}\rho C_{DC}A_C|\dot{x}_3|\dot{x}_3 + K_3(x_3 - x_1) + C_3(\dot{x}_3 - \dot{x}_1) - K_2(x_2 - x_3) - C_2(\dot{x}_2 - \dot{x}_3) - (W_c - W_{cB}) = 0 \tag{8}$$

The force in segment three of the cable is

$$P_3 = K_3(x_3 - x_1) + C_3(\dot{x}_3 - \dot{x}_1) \tag{9}$$

The forcing function is again taken in the form

$$x_1 = -[\, x_o \sin \omega t + \frac{x_o^2}{4l} (\cos 2\omega t - 1)\,] \tag{10}$$

The initial boundary conditions at time equal to zero are that the initial velocities $\dot{x}_2(0)$ and $\dot{x}_3(0)$ be equal to zero. Since the coordinate system is relative to an unstressed cable, the initial displacements of x_2 and x_3 must be computed. This can be done from Eq. (6) and Eq. (8) for velocities and accelerations equal to zero. Hence, for the payload and lumped mass, we obtain:

$$\delta_{sp} = x_2(0) = \frac{F_s + W_p - W_B + \dfrac{K_2}{K_2+K_3}(W_c - W_{cB})}{K_s + K_2 - \dfrac{K_2^2}{K_2+K_3}} \tag{11}$$

$$\delta_{sc} = x_3(0) = \frac{W_c - W_{cB} + K_2 x_2(0)}{K_2 + K_3} \tag{12}$$

The equations developed were programmed on the digital computer. However, the equations must be modified in the regime of slack which subsequently causes the snap loads.

There are three possible conditions for snap in the cable as modeled. They are as follows:

(1) The bottom cable segment goes slack ($P_2 = 0$)

(2) The top cable segment goes slack ($P_3 = 0$)

(3) Both the top and bottom segment go slack ($P_2 = P_3 = 0$)
The equations of motion for each of these conditions during the time period of slack can be obtained by setting the appropriate cable force equal to zero. In effect the cable force in each segment must always be positive or zero, but never negative, since the cable cannot support a compressive load (note that in the convention used tension is positive).

Now consider condition one where only the bottom segment goes slack. The appropriate equations in the non-slack time regime are:

$$\ddot{x}_2 = -\frac{\rho C_{DP} A_P}{2M_e}\left|\dot{x}_2\right|\dot{x}_2 - \frac{K_2}{M_e}(x_2 - x_3) - \frac{C_2}{M_e}(\dot{x}_2 - \dot{x}_3) + \frac{W_P - W_B}{M_e} + \frac{F_s}{M_e} - \frac{K_s x_2}{M_e} - \frac{C_s \dot{x}_2}{M_e} \quad (13)$$

$$\ddot{x}_3 = -\frac{\rho C_{DC} A_C}{2M_c}\left|\dot{x}_3\right|\dot{x}_3 - \frac{K_3}{M_c}(x_3 - x_1) - \frac{C_3}{M_c}(\dot{x}_3 - \dot{x}_1) + \frac{K_2}{M_c}(x_2 - x_3) + \frac{C_2}{M_c}(\dot{x}_2 - \dot{x}_3) + \frac{W_c - W_{cB}}{M_c} \quad (14)$$

Impending slack occurs when P_2 tries to go negative while P_3 is still positive viz.

$$P_2 = K_2(x_2 - x_3) + C_2(\dot{x}_2 - \dot{x}_3) \leq 0$$

$$P_3 = K_3(x_3 - x_1) + C_3(\dot{x}_3 - \dot{x}_1) \geq 0$$

Then during the slack regime $P_2 = 0$. Hence

$$\ddot{x}_2 = -\frac{\rho C_{DP} A_P}{2M_e}\left|\dot{x}_2\right|\dot{x}_2 + \frac{W_P - W_B}{M_e} + \frac{F_s}{M_e} - \frac{K_s x_2}{M_e} - \frac{C_s \dot{x}_2}{M_e}$$

$$\ddot{x}_3 = -\frac{\rho C_{DC} A_c}{2M_c}\left|\dot{x}_3\right|\dot{x}_3 - \frac{K_3}{M_c}(x_3 - x_1) - \frac{C_3}{M_c}(\dot{x}_3 - \dot{x}_1) + \frac{W_c - W_{cB}}{M_c} \quad (15)$$

Now consider condition two where only the top segment goes slack. Equations (13) and (14) still apply in the nonslack regime. For slack to initiate in the top segment only it is necessary that:

$$P_2 = K_2(x_2 - x_3) + C_2(\dot{x}_2 - \dot{x}_3) \geq 0$$

$$P_3 = K_3(x_3 - x_1) + C_3(\dot{x}_3 - \dot{x}_1) \leq 0$$

Then in the slack time regime x_2 is still given by Eq. (13) while P_3 is set equal to zero in Eq. (14) yielding the following

$$\ddot{x}_3 = - \frac{\rho C_{DC} A_C}{2M_c} \left|\dot{x}_3\right| \dot{x}_3 + \frac{K_2}{M_c}(x_2 - x_3) + \frac{C_2}{M_c}(\dot{x}_2 - \dot{x}_3) + \frac{W_c - W_{cB}}{M_c} \tag{16}$$

For impending slack in both top and bottom segments, the equations of motion for the slack region are obtained by setting both P_2 and P_3 equal to zero. Hence in the slack regime we obtain:

$$\ddot{x}_2 = - \frac{\rho C_{DP} A_P}{2M_e} \left|\dot{x}_2\right| \dot{x}_2 + \frac{W_P - W_B}{M_e} + \frac{F_s}{M_e} - \frac{K_s x_2}{M_e} - \frac{C_s \dot{x}_2}{M_e} \tag{17}$$

$$\ddot{x}_3 = - \frac{\rho C_{DP} A_c}{2M_c} \left|\dot{x}_3\right| \dot{x}_3 + \frac{W_c - W_{CB}}{M_c} \tag{18}$$

The previous equations were programmed on the 7090 computer. Basically, the program computes the cable forces and displacements from the differential equations of motion (Eq. (13) and Eq. (14)) which are initialized according to the boundary conditions of displacement and velocity. Then forces in the cable are computed and checked to determine if the force in either cable segment is negative. If either or both forces are negative, the program switches to applicable equations which have no cable force; viz the slack regime. It then computes the displacement according to these equations for the following time steps until the cable force becomes positive at which time it switches back to the original equations. The program is written to permit the frequency to be put in as a step function, ramp function, or a combination of ramps and steps. Printout is given for both transient and steady state phases.

Test Apparatus

The tests were performed at the Naval Ordnance Laboratory using the

Hydroballistics Tank shown in Fig. 4. The tank is approximately 35 feet wide by 100 feet long with a water level of up to 65 feet. The water is of high purity. The driving mechanism for oscillating the cable was located on the top deck with the cable inserted through a porthole in the deck. A portion of the cable length was in air while the major portion was immersed in the water. The payload could be photographed through ports in the sides of the tank.

The driving mechanism for oscillating the cable is shown in Fig. 2. It is essentially a crank type device with a drive rod attached to the flywheel. The prime mover consisted of a d-c shunt electric motor with a reduction gear for reducing the speed and increasing the torque capability. The motor had adjustable speed, but at a given setting the speed was insensitive to changes in the applied torque.

The force in the cable specimens was measured by load cells located at top and bottom of the cable. The load cell used was model A 8293 as manufactured by Schaevity with a maximum load capability of 1000 pounds. The voltage output was fed to a Beckman type R oscillograph where a trace of force versus time was obtained. Prior to each test, the instrument was calibrated by applying known weights to the load cells. In tests involving short rise times during impact a Honeywell Visicorder oscillograph was used with a frequency response of 50 KC.

Test Specimens

Two basic types of cables were studied; namely, steel and segmented cables of steel and nylon braided rope. The steel cables can best be described as "aircraft type." This type was used because of its availability in small sizes. The diameters of cable studied were 0.0625 inch and 0.09375 inch. All cables were carbon steel of MIL-W-1511 with a galvanized coating and consisted of seven wires per strand with seven strands per cable (7 x 7). Male type fittings were swaged on each end of the cable. A listing of pertinent characteristics of the specimens is shown in Table I. Force versus extension characteristics on full length cables were obtained in order to determine the corresponding spring constants. The unloading phase exhibited some hysteresis. After the cable was loaded to about ten pounds the force-extension curve

WATER TANK - 100 FEET LONG, 75 FEET DEEP, 35 FEET WIDE
WATER DEPTH - MAXIMUM OF 65 FEET
CONSTRUCTION - STAINLESS STEEL LINED TANK, SUPPORTED BY REINFORCED CONCRETE

Fig. 4. Interior of Hydroballistics Facility.

Table I

Characteristics of Cable Test Specimens

Spec. No.	Mat'l	Dia.	Length	No. of Strands	Wt./100 ft.	Dry Wt.	Spring Const. Air	Spring Const. Water	Natural Freq.* Air	Natural Freq.* Water	Break Str.
		Inch	Ft.		lbs.	lbs.	lb/in	lb/in	Hz	Hz	lbs.
1	St'l	3/32	62	7 x 7	1.6	.992	86.4	86.4	5.57	5.12	920
2	St'l	1/16	62	7 x 7	.75	.465	40.5	40.5	3.85	3.5	480
3	St'l	3/32	70	7 x 7	1.6	1.12	76.5	76.5	5.22	4.82	920
4	St'l	1/16	70	7 x 7	.75	.525	35.8	35.8	3.54	3.32	480
5	St'l	3/32	62	7 x 7	1.60	.99	28	16.8	3.16	2.28	920
	Nylon	1/4	6	Braided	1.66	.099					

*Natural Freq. Based on Wt. of Payload + Virtual Mass + 1/3 Cable Wt.

was fairly linear. The results compared reasonable well with those published by the cable manufacturer.

The payload was a sphere of eight inches diameter which was made of solid aluminum with a weight of 26.9 pounds including attachment fittings. Aluminum was used to get a relatively high payload density (173 lbs/ft^3). A high payload density was desired to delay the snap loading condition to as high a frequency ratio ω/ω_{ne} as possible. A high density payload yields a high initial static stress and low natural frequency. Both effects delay the snap condition. The weight of the sphere in water is 17.3 pounds, excluding the weight of the attached cable. The virtual mass or added mass of displaced water is 0.15 slugs (4.85 pounds).

Test Results

Forced oscillation tests were conducted on both 0.0625 inch and 0.09375 inch stranded cables of 62 feet and 70 feet in length. The forcing frequency was increased in small steps and held until steady state conditions were achieved. Typical force versus time responses are shown in Fig. 5 for a 0.0625 inch cable 62 feet long excited at various frequencies. At low frequency the force response is approximately sinusoidal. However, as the frequency was increased, nonlinearities were encountered as evidenced by the double peak. This behavior was very reproducible and is believed to be caused primarily by the nonlinear water damping. This same type response was observed in the analog using mathematical model No. 1 previously discussed. The forcing frequency was increased until snap occurred at about 1.27 Hz as shown in Fig. 5d. There was a drastic increase of force in the cable peaking to about 130 pounds. After two minutes or 100 cycles, the cable fitting attached to the mass fractured. The recorded force at the time of failure was about 150 pounds. It is important to point out that the rated strength of the cable is 475 pounds while the rated strength of the swaged on cable fitting is 90% of the cable strength or 410 pounds. A failure analysis indicated that the most probable cause of the premature failure was a combined bending stress and axial stress caused by angular orientation of the payload w when snap occurred. Photographic coverage indicated a tendency for the payload to tilt off the vertical during free flight (slack condition).

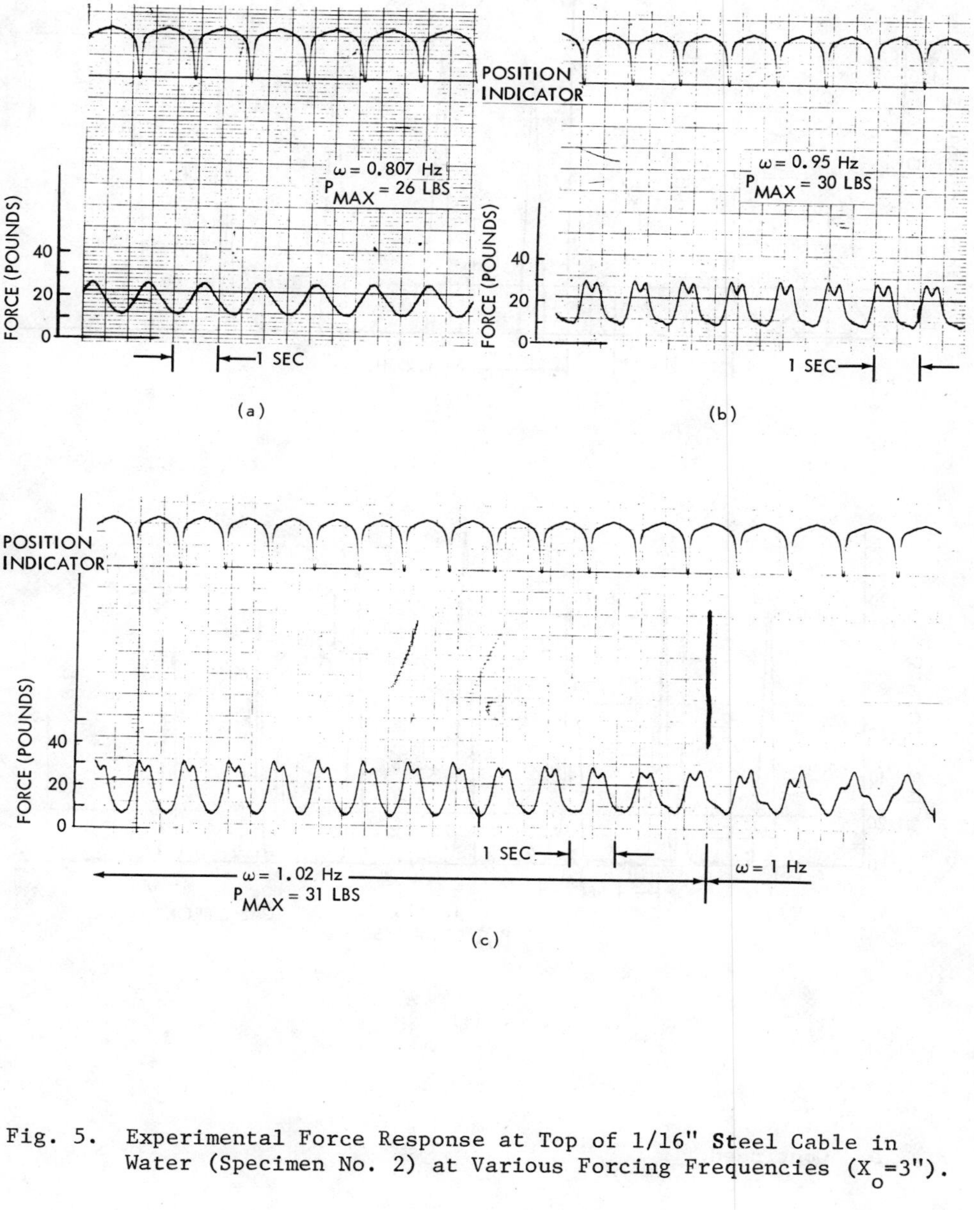

Fig. 5. Experimental Force Response at Top of 1/16" Steel Cable in Water (Specimen No. 2) at Various Forcing Frequencies (X_o=3").

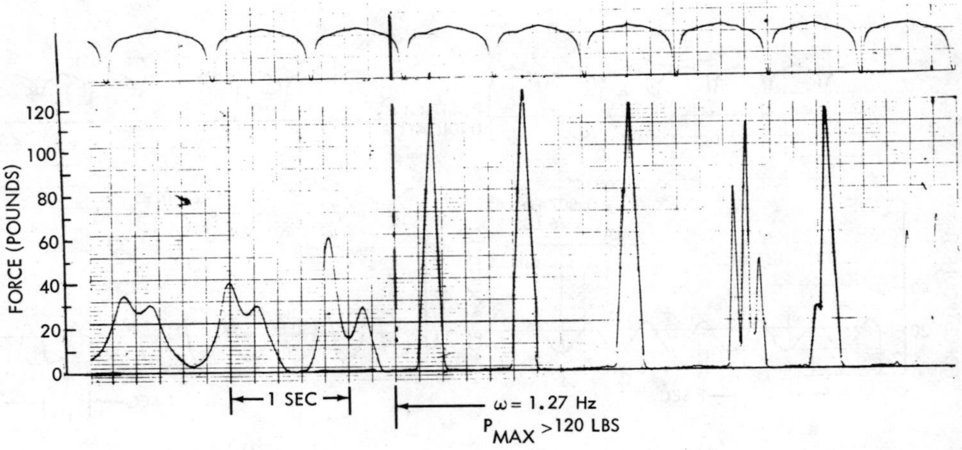

(d)

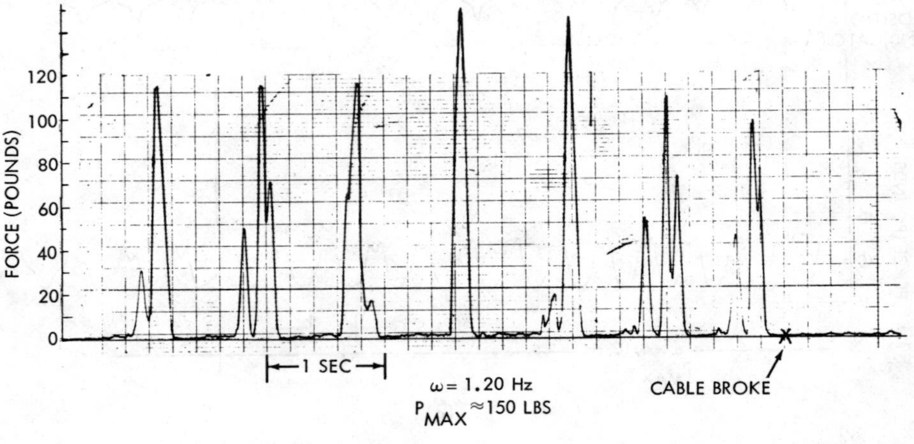

(e)

Fig. 5. Continued.

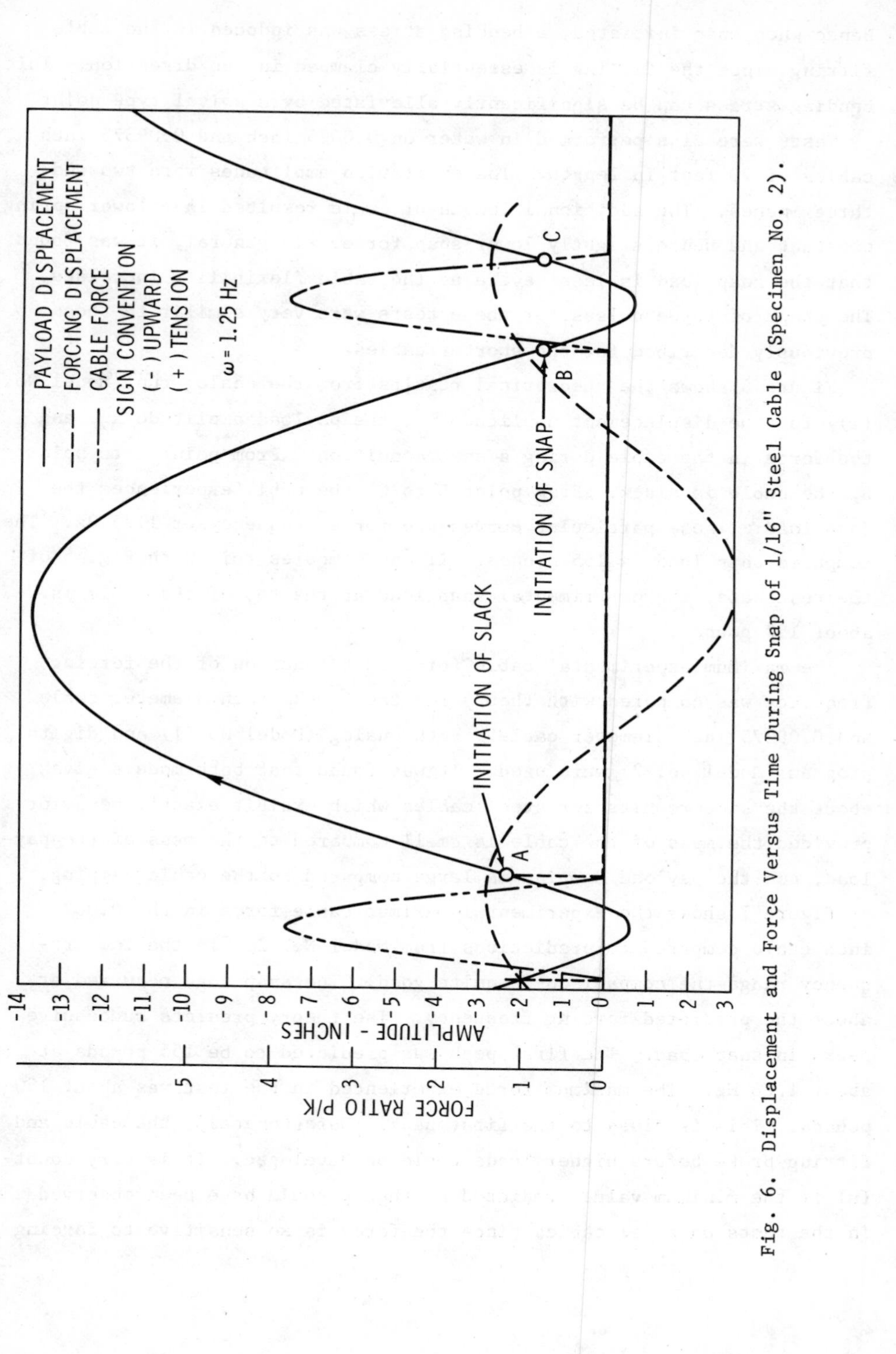

Fig. 6. Displacement and Force Versus Time During Snap of 1/16" Steel Cable (Specimen No. 2).

Hence when snap initiated, a bending stress was induced in the cable fitting since the fitting is essentially clamped in one direction. This bending stress can be significantly alleviated by a swivel type joint.

Tests were also performed in water on 0.0625 inch and 0.09375 inch cables of 70 feet in length. The excitation amplitudes were two and three inches. The additional length of cable resulted in a lower spring constant and hence slightly lower snap force. In general, it was found that the snap load is less severe as the cable flexibility increases. The shape of force pulses for these tests were very similar to those previously described for the shorter cables.

Figure 6 shows the theoretical results from the analog run (Model No. (1)) for the displacement amplitude x_1, the payload amplitude x_2, and the force in the cable during a snap condition. From point A to point B, the cable is slack. From point B to C, the cable experiences the snap load. These particular curves are for a frequency of 1.25 Hz. The computed snap load is 155 pounds. If one compares this with Fig. 5 of the test data, the experimental snap load at the top of the cable is about 150 pounds.

The maximum experimental cable force as a function of the forcing frequency was compared with theory for the 0.0625 inch diameter cable and 0.09375 inch diameter cable. Both analog (Model No. 1) and digital program (Model No. 2) were used. It was found that both models give about the same results for steel cables which exhibit elastic behavior provided the mass of the cable is small compared to the mass of the payload, and the payload damping is large compared to the cable damping.

Figure 7 shows the experimental maximum cable force in the 0.0625 inch cable compared to predictions from Model No. 2. In the low frequency range the comparison is quite good. The snap load occurred at about the predicted forcing frequency. The theory predicts successive peaks in snap load. The first peak was predicted to be 155 pounds at about 1.28 Hz. The maximum force experienced in the test was about 150 pounds. This is close to the first peak. Unfortunately, the cable and fitting broke before higher loads could be developed. It is very doubtful if the minimum value predicted by theory could have been observed in the tests on steel cables since the force is so sensitive to forcing

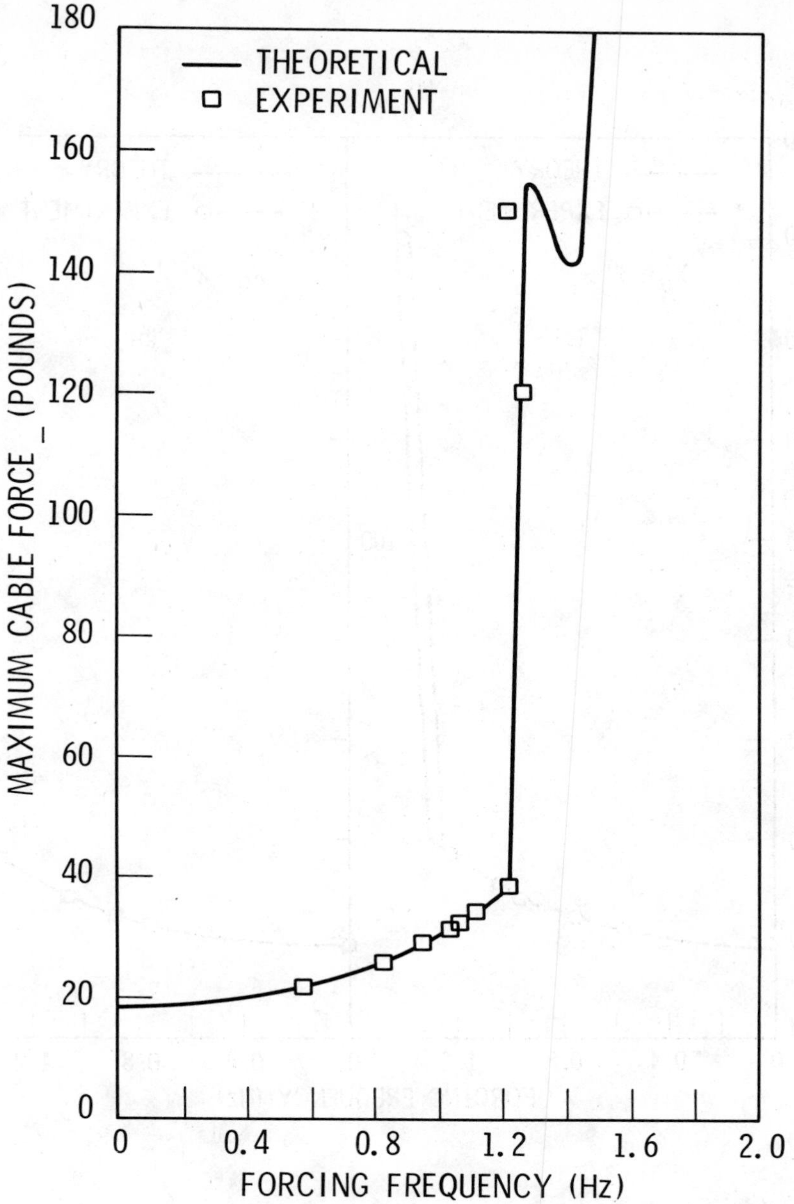

Fig. 7. Force at Top of 1/16" Steel Cable (Specimen No. 2) Versus Forcing Frequency - Comparison of Experiment with Digital Program (Model No. 2).

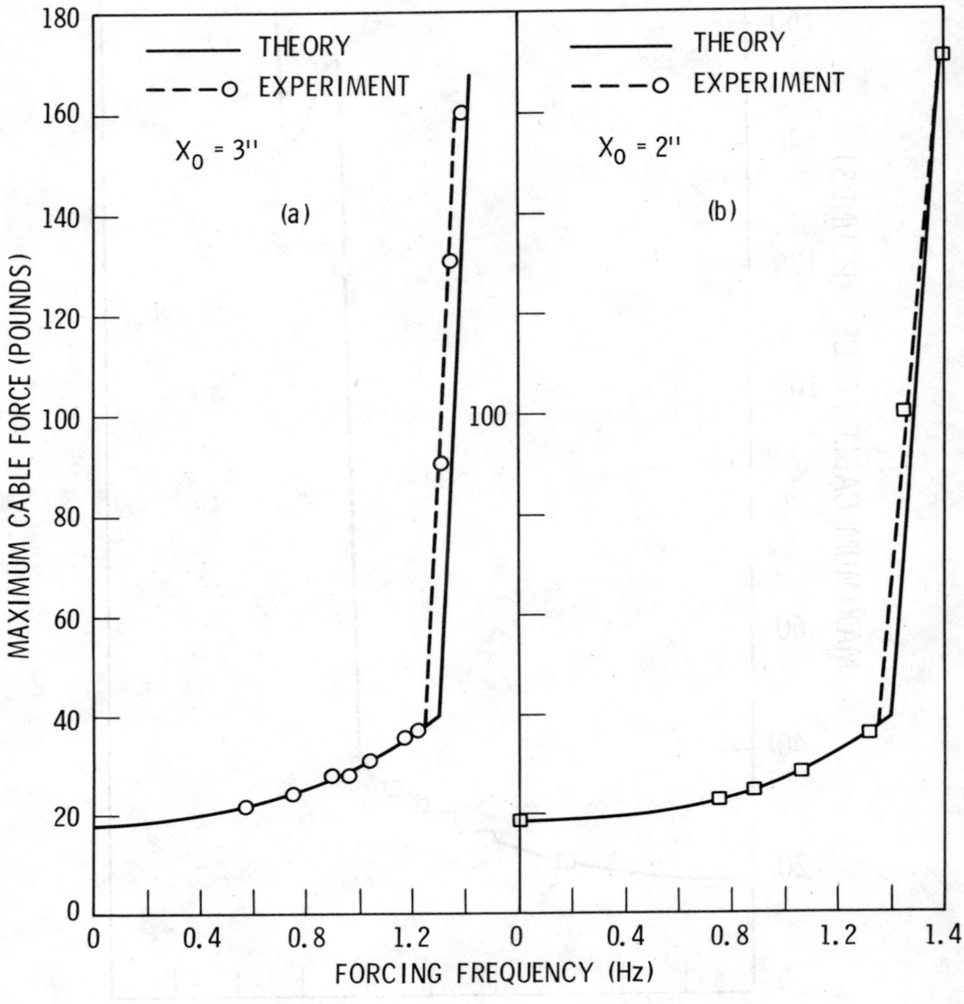

Fig. **8**. Force at Top of 3/32" Steel Cable (Specimen No. 1) Versus Forcing Frequency - Comparison of Experiment with Digital Program (Model No. 2).

frequency once the snap is initiated. A slight increase in frequency results in a significant increase in cable force. However, it was demonstrated later that by adding a small section of nylon rope to the 0.09375 inch steel cable, the snap load could be mitigated by the added flexibility of the nylon. A peak snap load was observed which was followed by a minimum and then a rapid increase in load.

Figure 8 shows analytical and experimental results for 0.09375 inch diameter cable for displacement amplitude of two and three inches. The agreement is good in the low frequency range. The initiation of snap occurs at a slightly lower frequency than expected. For the two inch displacement, the maximum force encountered was 170 pounds. Theoretically, the force should reach a peak of 300 pounds at a frequency of 1.65 Hz, then drop off slightly. Another sharp rise is then predicted. It was not possible to achieve these force levels in the experiment because of fear of damaging the apparatus. During the testing of nylon rope, it was observed that it was possible to get through the snap condition by increasing the frequency in much the same way it is possible to get through a resonance condition. The question then arose as to whether it is possible to get through the snap condition for steel cables by increasing the frequency. Certainly the chances would be improved if a short section of nylon was added to serve as a mitigator or shock absorber. It was hoped that such a test would provide some insight as how to design a shock absorber system for steel cables which might be expected to operate at a frequency near the critical frequency which initiates snap. The 0.09375 inch diameter steel cable previously tested was fitted with a 6-foot addition of 0.25 inch nylon at the bottom. The results could then be compared with those previously obtained for the same cable without the nylon. Typical traces of force at the top of the cable versus time for various forcing frequencies are shown in Fig. 9. The displacement amplitude is two inches. The first snap condition occurred at a forcing frequency of 1.31 Hz and the cable force peaked to 87 pounds. The force then decreased as the frequency was increased, viz, it was possible to get through the snap condition. After getting through the snap condition, photographic coverage showed the payload to exhibit small amplitude vertical oscillation, but also exhibited a rocking motion of the sphere with very little lateral movement at the

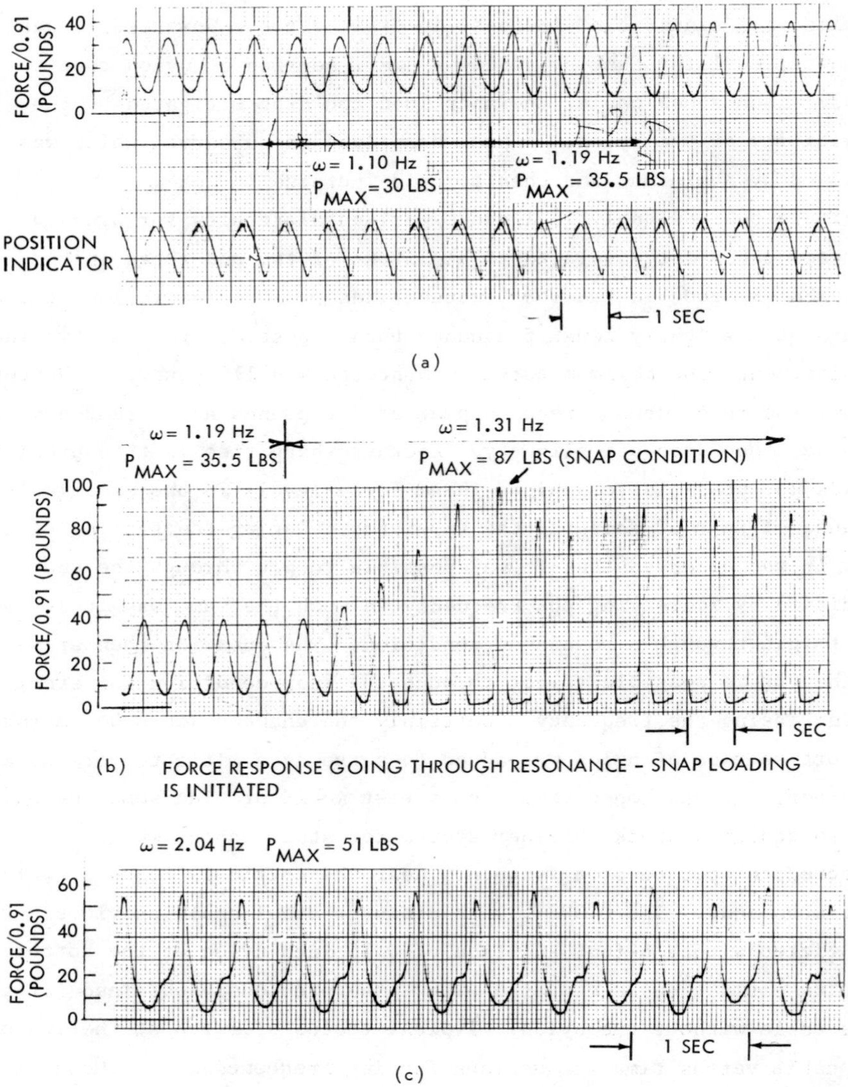

Fig. 9. Experimental Force Response at Top of Specimen No. 5 in Water at Various Frequencies (X_o = 2").

center of gravity. As the frequency was increased to 2.17 Hz, violent snap loads were again encountered. The frequency was then decreased, and the force decreased until the first snap condition was again encountered.

Figure 10 shows the theoretical force at the top of the cable predicted by the digital program (Model No. 2) compared to the experimental results for two inch excitation amplitude at the top. The comparison appears to be quite good considering the complexity of the snap phenomena. It is interesting to note that the cable force does reach a maximum during the first snap condition, followed by a minimum and then a rapid increase at the second snap condition. The second snap condition occurs very near the resonant frequency of the cable system. The theory predicts the same basic type behavior with the largest error occurring in the vicinity of the minimum.

The results prove that it is possible to get through the snap condition by increasing the forcing frequency. However, a second snap condition can follow close behind. It also shows that the two-parameter lumped viscoelastic model used in the digital program (Model No. 2) yields fairly accurate results over a wide frequency range.

The test also shows that the nylon does mitigate the snap load appreciably. The same 0.09375 inch steel cable was tested at two inch amplitude without the nylon (see Fig. 8). The snap load reached 170 pounds at 1.6 Hz and the maximum value had not been reached yet. The predicted maximum for the first snap condition is 300 pounds. The same cable with the nylon addition experienced a maximum force of 90 pounds for a frequency range from 0 to 2.0 Hz.

Pertinent cable characteristics used in the calculations performed in the digital computer are:

K_2 (Nylon) = 20.4 lb/in

K_3 (Steel) = 86.4 lb/in

C_{DC} = .01 (Based on wetted area)

C_{DP} = .5

C_2 (Nylon) = τK_e = .47 lb sec/in

τ (Nylon) = .023 sec

C_2 (Steel) = 0

W_P = 26.9 lbs

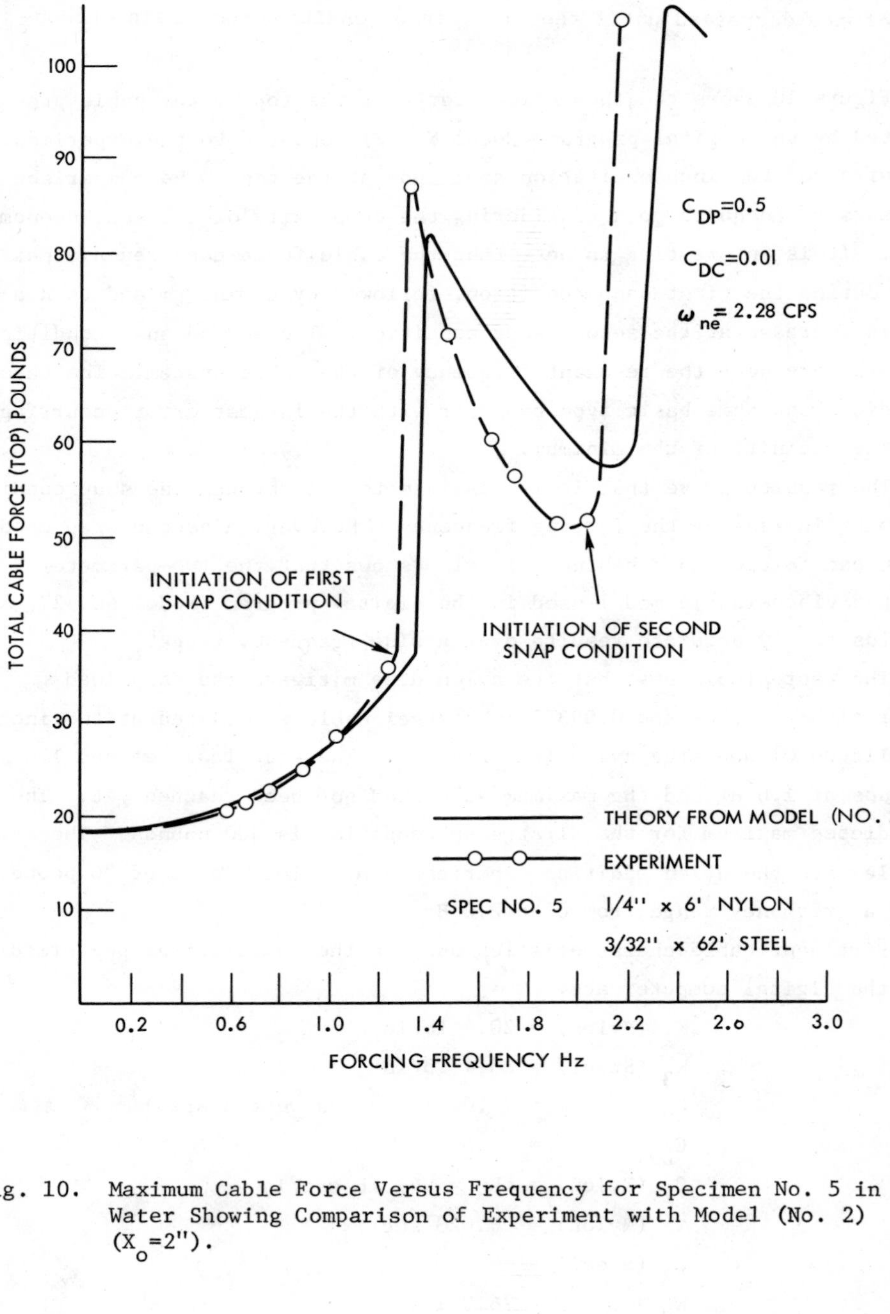

Fig. 10. Maximum Cable Force Versus Frequency for Specimen No. 5 in Water Showing Comparison of Experiment with Model (No. 2) (X_o=2").

W_B = 9.7 lbs

$W_{V.M.}$ = 4.85 lbs

Design Considerations for Minimizing Snap Loads

Normally in designing a cable system, a high safety factor of six to eight is applied on the static wet weight of the payload. This is usually considered adequate for dynamic effects and fatigue. With this in mind, a plot was made of the ratio of maximum cable force to static force as a function of frequency ratio. This is shown in Fig. 11. It is interesting to note a force ratio of six can be easily obtained if a snap condition occurs. This condition can occur at a frequency ratio well below resonance. Hence, it is concluded that the safety factor can be purely fictitious if adequate provisions are not taken for the snap condition. The best solution is to avoid it in the cable system design. This usually means high density payloads so that the static force always exceeds the compressive part of the dynamic force. In cases where this is not possible, there are other possibilities. One is to design a compliant system [5] which takes up the slack by a spring actuated or pneumatic system. The goal is to obtain a constant tension by a feedback automatic control system which makes proper adjustments. A second approach is to design a shock mitigator into the cable system. This can probably be achieved by a spring-dashpot type device. The most simple mitigator which proved to work well is a short section of nylon rope. However, a more compact spring-dashpot mechanical device could be designed. A third approach can be used for payloads which operate near the ocean bottom. This involves hanging a heavy chain off the bottom of the payload. The chain should be long enough to lie on the ocean floor. This provides an appreciable damping effect.

CONCLUSION

As a result of this study, the following conclusions are made in regard to the dynamic behavior of steel-stranded cables:

1. A snap condition is easily initiated in steel cables with resulting drastic increases in force. The onset of snap can be predicted by computing the frequency required to make the dynamic force plus the static force equal to zero, i. e., $T_{STAT} + P_{DYNAMIC} = 0$. The force during the snap condition can be predicted with good accuracy using

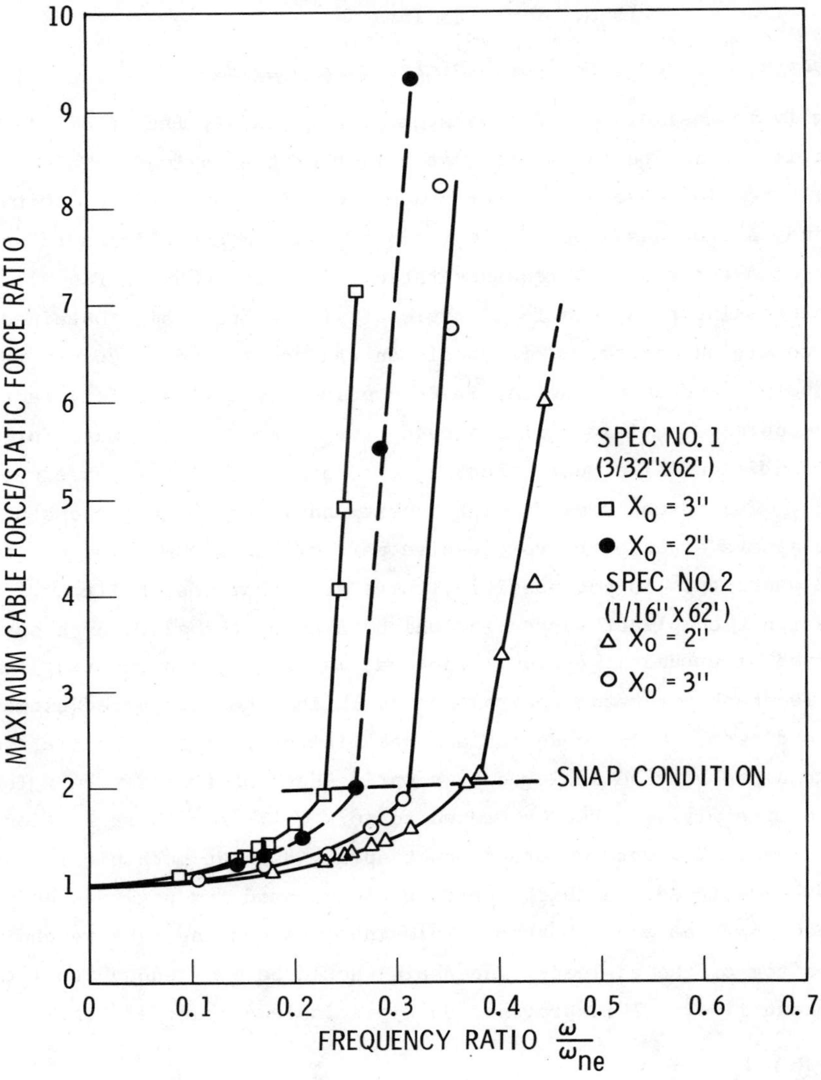

Fig. 11. Experimental Force Ratio P_{MAX}/T_{STAT} Versus Frequency Ratio For 1/16" and 3/32" Steel Cables.

the analytical models presented.

2. Once snap is initiated, the cable force rises sharply with slight increases in frequency. Theoretically, the force reaches a maximum and then decreases with increasing frequency. This was not achieved with purely steel cables, but was demonstrated by adding a small section of nylon to the cable. The maximum load during snap occurs at the top of the cable.

3. A factor of safety of six on the static cable load does not assure safe operation in a snap condition. Peak loads of nine times the static force were achieved in the tests. The magnitude of snap force is strongly dependent on cable stiffness and excitation amplitude. The snap load appears to become more severe as the stiffness of the cable increases.

4. Snap loads can be significantly mitigated by increasing the flexibility with a soft spring-dashpot arrangement.

5. The connection of the cable to the payload is critical in surviving snap loads. Fixity caused by clamping the cable into payload fittings should be avoided because of possible bending stresses during the snap condition.

ACKNOWLEDGEMENT

The present study has been partially supported under the Themis Program titled "Dynamics of Cable Systems" (N00014-68-A-0506-0001). The authors acknowledge the cooperation and encouragement of Dr. Frank Andrews, Director of Acoustics Program and Dr. S. R. Heller, Director of the Institute of Ocean Science and Engineering at the Catholic University of America. They also wish to express their gratitude to Drs. A. Seigel and V. C. Dawson of the Naval Ordnance Laboratory for their cooperation in making various test facilities available.

The authors are also indebted to Mr. C. S. Smith for his help in the programming of the mathematical solutions to the problem.

REFERENCES

(1) Schneider, L., Mahand, T., and Burton, L., "Tow Cable Snap Loads," ASME Paper 64-WA/UNT-8, Dec 1964.

(2) Richardson, William S., "Buoy Mooring Cables, Past, Present and Future," Transactions, Second International Buoy Technology Symposium, 18 Sept 1967.

(3) Goeller, J. E., "A Theoretical and Experimental Investigation of a Flexible Cable System Subjected to Longitudinal Excitation," PhD Dissertation, Catholic University, 1969.

(4) Kuethe, Schetzer, Foundations of Aerodynamics, Second edition, Wiley, 1964.

(5) Snyder, A. E., Jerabek, J. C., and Whitney, C., "Constant-Tension Oceanographic Winch," ASME Paper 63-WA-335, Oct 1963.

SOME PROPERTIES PERTAINING TO THE STABILITY OF CIRCULATORY SYSTEMS

I. C. Jong
University of Arkansas

ABSTRACT

Some theorems on the stability of linear circulatory (nonconservative) systems are proved. One theorem states that the domain of stability of discrete circulatory systems with slight viscous damping is always contained as a subdomain within the domain of stability of the corresponding system with complete absence of damping. Based on this theorem, a more general definition of the term "destabilizing effect" of small viscous damping is proposed. Another theorem states the interrelationship which may exist between the family of flutter boundary curves of the slightly damped circulatory system with two degrees of freedom and the flutter boundary curves of the corresponding undamped system. Corollaries of theorems are established. The various features of the theorems and corollaries are illustrated in an example. An unusual stability phenomenon based on the nonsymmetric definition of the kinetic stability is shown to exist in certain circulatory systems.

LIST OF NOTATIONS

a_{rs}	Elements of a matrix defined in Eq. (7)
A_r	Coefficients of the exponential solution
b_1, b_2	Coefficients of viscous damping
B_1, B_2	Dimensionless coefficients of viscous damping
c	A spring constant
C_{rs}	Elements of a matrix used to specify the direction of the circulatory load

F	A dimensionless loading parameter
G_{rs}	Elements of a matrix used to specify the viscous damping
$\mathrm{Im}(\ )$	Imaginary part of ( )
K_{rs}	Elements of a matrix used to specify the elastic restoring forces or moments
ℓ	Length of the bar of the double pendulum
L	$L = L(F, C_{rs})$
M_{rs}	Elements of the generalized mass matrix
N	An arbitrary integer indicating the degrees of freedom
$O(\varepsilon)$	Order of ε
$p_1, \ldots, p_4$	Coefficients of the characteristic equation
$\bar{p}_1, \bar{p}_3$	Modified coefficients of the characteristic equation
P	Magnitude of the compressive circulatory force
q_r	Generalized coordinates
Q_r	Generalized forces
$\mathrm{Re}(\ )$	Real part of ( )
R_D	Domain of stability of the slightly damped system
R_E	Domain of stability of the undamped system
t	Time variable
T	Kinetic energy function
X	$X = X(F, C_{rs}, \beta)$
α_1, α_2	Parameters used to specify the direction of the compressive circulatory force (P)
β	$\beta = b_1/b_2 = B_1/B_2$
γ_r	Parameters used in $\bar{\lambda}_r = \eta_r + \varepsilon\gamma_r$
$(\Gamma_D)_{div.}$	Divergent boundary curves of R_D
$(\Gamma_D)_{flu.}$	Flutter boundary curves of R_D
Γ_D	$\Gamma_D = (\Gamma_D)_{div.} + (\Gamma_D)_{flu.}$
$(\Gamma_E)_{div.}$	Divergent boundary curves of R_E
$(\Gamma_E)_{flu.}$	Flutter boundary curves of R_E
Γ_E	$\Gamma_E = (\Gamma_E)_{div.} + (\Gamma_E)_{flu.}$
Δ	A determinantal function defined in Eq. (6)
$\bar{\Delta}$	A determinantal function defined in Eq. (5)
ε	A small positive number, $0 < \varepsilon << 1$
η_r	Parameters used in $\bar{\lambda}_r = \eta_r + \varepsilon\gamma_r$
λ	A root parameter of the characteristic equation

λ_r	$\lambda_r = \eta_r$, roots of the characteristic equation of the undamped system
$\bar{\lambda}_r$	$\bar{\lambda}_r = \eta_r + \varepsilon\gamma_r$, roots of the characteristic equation of the slightly damped system
τ	A dimensionless time variable
ϕ_1, ϕ_2	Generalized coordinates of the double pendulum

INTRODUCTION

The trend of using steel and high-strength alloys as materials in modern engineering structures has made the problem of elastic instability increasingly important. Urged by practical requirements, the extensive theoretical and experimental investigations of the conditions governing the stability of elastic structural elements (such as bars, plates, shells,...etc.) in the past century have resulted in a large body of literature in the theory of elastic stability. Moreover, in recent decades, a new branch of the theory of elastic stability has emerged with the characteristic feature that the applied loads are dependent on the deformation of the system and are not derivable from a stationary, single-valued potential. Such loads are nonconservative and are termed circulatory loads [1]. Systems acted on by circulatory loads are termed circulatory systems.

The analysis of the stability of the equilibrium state of an elastic system necessitates the use of a certain stability criterion. Under the classical static stability criterion (Euler method), the critical load is defined as the smallest load under which the system can admit not only its original neutral equilibrium configuration but also an adjacent equilibrium configuration (bifurcation of equilibrium). Such a stability criterion has, however, been found to be inadequate in defining the instability of some circulatory systems whose loss of stability is by flutter (oscillations with increasing amplitudes) and not by divergence (admittance of a neighboring equilibrium configuration, or, static buckling).

Generally, the stability analysis of circulatory systems requires the application of the kinetic stability criterion (method of small oscillations), of which two versions of the definition of stability have been proposed: (a) the nonsymmetric definition, (b) the symmetric definition. Under the nonsymmetric definition, the equilibrium state of an elastic system is said to be stable if, during the motion following a sufficiently small initial disturbance, the magnitudes of displacements of the system remain arbitrarily small for all positive times. In the symmetric definition, the quilibrium state of an elastic system is said to be stable if, during the motion following a sufficiently small initial disturbance, both the magnitudes of displacements and the magnitudes of velocities of the system remain arbitrarily small for all positive times. Loosely speaking, the nonsymmetric definition defines stability in the configuration space (i.e., with respect to the displacement only), while the symmetric definition defines stability in the phase space (i.e., with respect to both the displacement and the velocity). Thus, stability in the sense of the symmetric definition also implies stability in the sense of the nonsymmetric definition, but the reverse is not true. The symmetric definition of the kinetic stability is commonly attributed to Liapunov.

A review of literature in elastic stability indicates that the concept of stability based on the nonsymmetric definition of the kinetic stability has been widely employed and adopted by investigators. Therefore, unless stated otherwise, the word "stability" will, in the sequel, be used to mean stability in the sense of the nonsymmetric definition of the kinetic stability only.

Stability problems of damped as well as undamped circulatory systems have recently received considerable attention of investigators [2-15]. However, it appears that certain properties pertaining to the stability of circulatory systems can still be brought into a broader framework and sharper focus, thus extending the results of [10] and [15].

In the present study, some theorems and corollaries are established for the stability domains and boundaries of linear circulatory systems with N degrees of freedom and two degrees of freedom. As a consequence of the stability theorems, a more appropriate definition for the term "destabilizingeffect" of slight viscous damping is proposed. The various features of the theorems and corollaries are illustrated in an example. The illustrative example reveals that there exists a class of circulatory systems which are stable under the nonsymmetric definition of the kinetic stability, but are unstable under the symmetric definition of the kinetic stability.

Formulation

Let the motion of an N-degree-of-freedom, linear, holonomic, autonomous, dynamic system be described by the generalized coordinates q_r (r = 1,2, ...N) and their time derivatives. The generalized coordinates and their time derivatives are initially zero in the neutral equilibrium state of the system.

The external load acting on the system is a circulatory load of magnitude F. The direction of the circulatory load is assumed to be a linear function of the generalized coordinates. The system itself is viscoelastic, but its viscosity is assumed to be weak. Thus, the generalized forces Q_r associated with the generalized coordinates q_r of this linear system may be written as

$$Q_r = FC_{rs}q_s - (K_{rs}q_s + \varepsilon G_{rs}\dot{q}_s) \qquad (r,s = 1,2,\ldots,N) \qquad (1)$$

where an overdot indicates a differentiation with respect to the time variable t, ε is a small positive number, matrices $[C_{rs}]$ and $[G_{rs}]$ are generally nonsymmetric and the matrix $[K_{rs}]$ is assumed to be symmetric and positive definite. Moreover, in Eq. (1), the range and summation conventions are implied. These two notational conventions will be employed in the sequel. The velocity-dependent forces are dissipative forces if $[G_{rs}]$ is positive definite but are gyroscopic forces if $G_{rs} = - G_{sr}$.

Since the kinetic energy T of the system is

$$T = \frac{1}{2} M_{rs}\dot{q}_r\dot{q}_s \qquad (r,s = 1,2,\ldots,N) \qquad (2)$$

where the matrix $[M_{rs}]$ is symmetric and positive definite, the equations of motion of the system may now be obtained, by using Lagrange's equations, as

$$M_{rs}\ddot{q}_s + \varepsilon G_{rs}\dot{q}_s + (K_{rs} - FC_{rs})q_s = 0 \qquad (r,s = 1,2,\ldots,N) \qquad (3)$$

In the complete absence of velocity-dependent forces, the equations of motion become

$$M_{rs}\ddot{q}_s + (K_{rs} - FC_{rs})q_s = 0 \qquad (r,s = 1,2,\ldots,N) \qquad (4)$$

For the sake of convenience, systems (3) and (4) will hereinafter be referred to as the slightly damped and the undamped systems, respectively.

Systems with N Degrees of Freedom

The quality of being stable or unstable of the neutral equilibrium state of the system may be determined by investigating the possible types of motion which the system may be induced to execute by certain infinitesimal disturbances. Such an investigation is connected with the study of the nature of the roots of the characteristic equation.

To obtain the characteristic equations, we put $q_r = A_r e^{\lambda t}$ in systems (3) and (4) and then set the determinant of the coefficient matrix equal to zero in each system. They are obtained as

$$\bar{\Delta} = \bar{\Delta}(\lambda) = \left| a_{rs} + \varepsilon\lambda G_{rs} \right| = 0 \tag{5}$$

$$\Delta = \Delta(\lambda^2) = \left| a_{rs} \right| = 0 \tag{6}$$

where

$$a_{rs} = \lambda^2 M_{rs} + K_{rs} - FC_{rs} \qquad (r,s = 1,2,\ldots,N) \tag{7}$$

For $F = 0$, it is assumed that small disturbances will cause the slightly damped system to execute asymptotic (diminishing) vibrations and the undamped system undamped free vibrations; i.e., Eq. (5) will yield complex roots with negative real parts for λ, and Eq. (6) will yield pure imaginary roots for λ if $F = 0$. For $F \neq 0$, the nature of the roots λ of the characteristic equations (5) and (6) will depend on the parameters C_{rs} as well as F of the external circulatory load.

In general, when the roots of the characteristic equation are all distinct, the necessary and sufficient conditions of stability are that the real parts of the roots should be all negative or zero. If equal roots occur, the system will be stable if their real parts are negative, but will be unstable if their real parts are zero or positive.

It has been shown [7,9] that the loss of stability of circulatory systems may be either by divergence or by flutter. The divergent critical loads are obtained when the characteristic equation admits a zero root; i.e.,

$$\left| K_{rs} - F_{div.cr.} C_{rs} \right| = 0 \tag{8}$$

Since $[K_{rs}]$ is positive definite, it can be shown [15] that the undamped system cannot lose stability by divergence if $C_{rs} = -C_{sr}$. If the system loses stability by flutter, the characteristic equation must have complex roots with positive real parts or equal pure imaginary roots. Thus, the flutter critical loads are obtained when the positive real parts of the complex roots approach zero (using the Routh-Hurwitz criterion [16,17]) or distinct pure imaginary roots coalesce [17].

Multiple ranges of stability and instability may exist in certain damped or undamped circulatory systems [7,9]. In the present study, some general properties governing the general relationship between the domains (or regions) of stability of the slightly damped (i.e., $0 < \varepsilon << 1$) system and the domains of stability of the corresponding undamped system will be established.

Theorem I. If R_D and R_E are the domains of stability of the slightly damped system (3) and the undamped system (4), respectively, then R_D is contained as a subdomain in R_E.

Proof. For slight damping, the roots of Eq. (5) may differ from the corresponding roots of Eq. (6) by a small amount of $O(\varepsilon)$. Let $\lambda_r = \eta_r$ be the roots of Eq. (6) and $\bar{\lambda}_r = \eta_r + \varepsilon\gamma_r$ be the roots of Eq. (5); $r = 1,2,\ldots,N$. Further, assume that the domain of stability R_E of the undamped system is shown schematically in Fig. 1. Then, at points outside of R_E, at least one of η_r will have a positive real part because the undamped system is unstable when the loading parameters F and C_{rs} take values from these points. Moreover, such a positive real part of η_r is greater than the real part of $\varepsilon\gamma_r$; i.e.,

$$\mathrm{Re}(\eta_r) > \left|\mathrm{Re}(\varepsilon\gamma_r)\right| \qquad \text{outside of } R_E \tag{9}$$

Thus, at points outside of R_E, $\mathrm{Re}(\bar{\lambda}_r) > 0$; i.e., the corresponding slightly damped system is also unstable in regions which are outside of R_E.

To investigate the stability of the slightly damped system inside the domain R_E, let us first express $\bar{\Delta}$ in terms of Δ, from Eqs. (5) and (6), as

$$\bar{\Delta} = \Delta + \varepsilon\lambda \frac{\partial\Delta}{\partial a_{rs}} G_{rs} + \frac{1}{2}\varepsilon^2\lambda^2 \frac{\partial^2\Delta}{\partial a_{rs}\partial a_{jk}} G_{rs}G_{jk} + \ldots = 0 \tag{10}$$

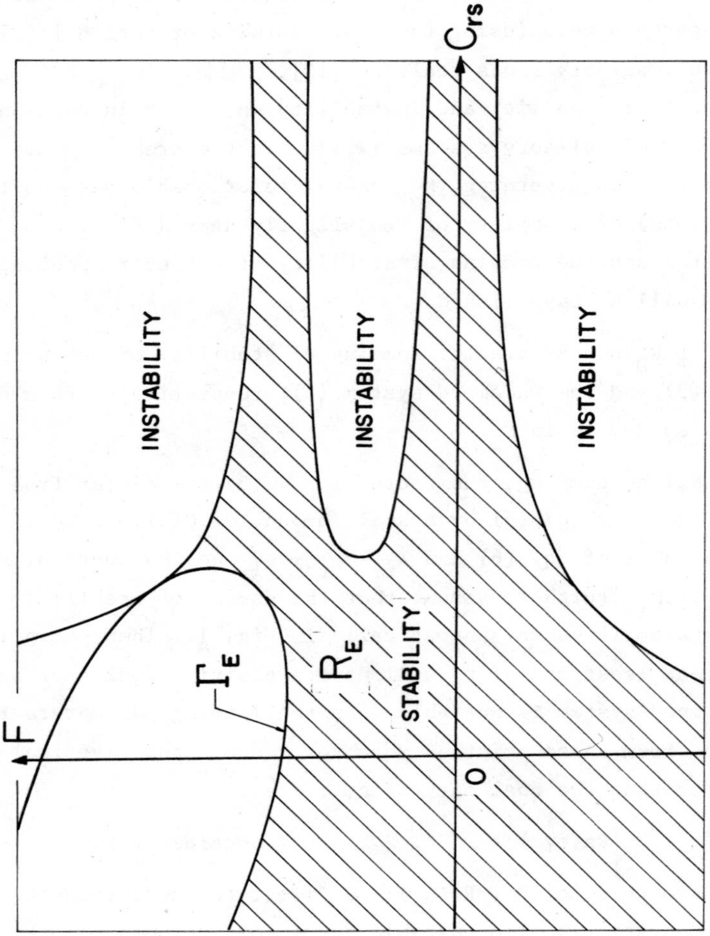

Fig. 1. Stability and Instability Domains and Their Boundaries.

Neglecting terms containing $0(\varepsilon^2)$ and higher in the above expansion, we obtain

$$\bar{\Delta} = \Delta + \varepsilon\lambda \frac{\partial\Delta}{\partial a_{rs}} G_{rs} = 0 \tag{11}$$

as an approximation to Eq. (5). Since $\Delta = \Delta(\lambda^2)$ is a polynomial of degree N in λ^2 and $\frac{\partial\Delta}{\partial a_{rs}} G_{rs}$ a polynomial of degree (N-1) in λ^2, we may write $\bar{\Delta}$ as

$$\bar{\Delta} = \bar{\Delta}(\lambda) = \Delta(\lambda^2) + \varepsilon\lambda\, R(\lambda^2) = 0 \tag{12}$$

where

$$R(\lambda^2) = \frac{\partial\Delta}{\partial a_{rs}} G_{rs} \tag{13}$$

Letting $\lambda_r = \eta_r$ and $\bar{\lambda}_r = \eta_r + \varepsilon\gamma_r$ be the roots of Eqs. (6) and (12), respectively, we have

$$\Delta = \Delta(\eta_r^2) = 0 \tag{14}$$

$$\begin{aligned}\bar{\Delta} &= \Delta[(\eta_r+\varepsilon\gamma_r)^2] + \varepsilon(\eta_r+\varepsilon\gamma_r)R[(\eta_r+\varepsilon\gamma_r)^2] \\ &= \Delta(\eta_r^2) + \varepsilon\eta_r[2\gamma_r \frac{d\Delta(\eta_r^2)}{d(\eta_r^2)} + R(\eta_r^2)] + 0(\varepsilon^2) + \cdots \\ &= 0\end{aligned} \tag{15}$$

Using Eq. (14) and neglecting terms of $0(\varepsilon^2)$ and higher, Eq. (15) becomes

$$\varepsilon\eta_r[2\gamma_r \frac{d\Delta(\eta_r^2)}{d(\eta_r^2)} + R(\eta_r^2)] = 0 \tag{16}$$

which yields

$$\gamma_r = - \frac{R(\eta_r^2)}{2\Delta'(\eta_r^2)} \tag{17}$$

where

$$\Delta'(\eta_r^2) = \frac{d\Delta(\eta_r^2)}{d(\eta_r^2)} \neq 0 \tag{18}$$

The validity of the perturbation method used above lies now in the validity of the inequality $\Delta'(\eta_r^2) \neq 0$ in R_E. For general physical systems, the coefficients of Eqs. (5) and (6) are assumed to be real quantities. Hence, by the theory of equations, the root curves (plotted with $Re(\lambda)$, $Im(\lambda)$, and F as three orthogonal reference axes) of Eq. (5) must be symmetrical about the real plane, and the root curves of Eq. (6) must be symmetrical about: (i) the real plane, (ii) the imaginary plane, and (iii) the F-axis which is the line of intersection of the real and the imaginary planes. By: (i) the properties of the root curves stated above, (ii) the fact that stable undamped systems subjected to general infinitesimal disturbances do not perform asymptotic (diminishing) vibrations, and (iii) the condition under which the critical loads for the undamped system are evaluated, we see that whenever $\Delta(\lambda^2) = 0$ admits equal roots (i.e., $\Delta'(\lambda^2) = 0$) the loading parameters F and C_{rs} must have taken values from some portions of the boundary of R_E or some points as well as some lines outside of R_E. In R_E, all root curves of Eq. (6) are plane curves lying in the imaginary plane. Thus, we have

$$\Delta'(\eta_r^2) \neq 0 \qquad \text{in } R_E \tag{19}$$

and all η_r are distinct pure imaginary roots in R_E. From Eqs. (17) and (19), we see that γ_r are finite real numbers in R_E.

Since η_r are pure imaginary in R_E, the real parts of the roots of Eq. (5) in R_E are given by

$$Re(\bar{\lambda}_r) = Re(\eta_r + \varepsilon\gamma_r) = \varepsilon\gamma_r = -\frac{\varepsilon R(\eta_r^2)}{2\Delta'(\eta_r^2)} \tag{20}$$

Depending on the parameters of the system, $Re(\bar{\lambda}_r)$ may be either negative or positive in R_E. If $Re(\bar{\lambda}_r)$ is negative or zero, the slightly damped system is stable, otherwise, unstable. Thus, the domain of stability R_D of the slightly damped system is generally smaller than R_E and is contained in R_E. This concludes the proof.

Multiple ranges of stability or instability, as delineated in Fig. 1, may frequently occur in circulatory systems. Thus, in allowing the existence of multiple critical loads for the circulatory systems, we have, by Theorem I, the following two corollaries:

Corollary I. If there exist multiple ranges of stability and instability in a certain range of C_{rs}, then some of the critical loads F_d for the slightly damped system (3) may be greater in magnitude than some of the critical loads F_e for the undamped system (4).

Corollary II. If there exist no multiple ranges of stability and instability in a certain range of C_{rs}, then $F_d \leq F_e$ in this range of C_{rs}.

The various features of the above theorem and corollaries are illustrated later.

Systems with Two Degrees of Freedom

Additional general properties relating the stability of slightly damped systems to that of undamped systems can be established when the degrees of freedom are reduced to two. In the following developments, we shall turn our attention to the relationship between the boundary curves of R_E and those of R_D of the two-degree-of-freedom circulatory systems.

The equations of motion of the slightly damped and the undamped systems in the present case may be obtained directly from Eqs. (3) and (4) as:

$$M_{rs}\ddot{q}_s + \varepsilon G_{rs}\dot{q}_s + (K_{rs}-FC_{rs})q_s = 0 \qquad (r,s = 1,2) \tag{21}$$

$$M_{rs}\ddot{q}_s + (K_{rs}-FC_{rs})q_s = 0 \qquad (r,s = 1,2) \tag{22}$$

The boundary curves Γ_D of the domain of stability R_D of the slightly damped system (21) may be divided into the following two types: (i) $(\Gamma_D)_{flu.}$, boundary curves separating R_D from the domain of flutter (dynamic instability); (ii) $(\Gamma_D)_{div.}$, boundary curves separating R_D from the domain of divergence (static instability). Analogously, we may divide the boundary curves Γ_E of the domain of stability R_E of the undamped system (22) into: (i) $(\Gamma_E)_{flu.}$, the flutter boundary curves; (ii) $(\Gamma_E)_{div.}$, the divergent boundary curves. Therefore,

$$\Gamma_D = (\Gamma_D)_{flu.} + (\Gamma_D)_{div.} \tag{23}$$

$$\Gamma_E = (\Gamma_E)_{flu.} + (\Gamma_E)_{div.} \tag{24}$$

The characteristic equations of systems (21) and (22) may be written as:

$$\bar{\Delta} = \bar{\Delta}(\lambda) = p_4\lambda^4 + p_3\lambda^3 + p_2\lambda^2 + p_1\lambda + p_0 = 0 \tag{25}$$

$$\Delta = \Delta(\lambda^2) = p_4\lambda^4 + p_2\lambda^2 + p_0 = 0 \tag{26}$$

The damping parameters εG_{rs} will appear in linear combinations to form as a factor in each of the coefficients p_1 and p_3, but may appear in quadratic form in the coefficient p_2. Since $0 < \varepsilon << 1$, the damping parameters appearing in quadratic form in p_2 may be neglected. Thus, p_2 may here be regarded as free of damping parameters, while p_1 and p_3 are small quantities of $O(\varepsilon)$. The loading parameters F and C_{rs} are contained in p_0, p_1 and p_2 only. Other parameters M_{rs} and K_{rs} of the system are distributed among the five coefficients p_0, p_1, p_2, p_3, and p_4 and are regarded as given constants. From Eqs. (25) and (26) it is obvious that the divergent boundary curves $(\Gamma_D)_{div.}$ and $(\Gamma_E)_{div.}$ are both given by:

$$p_0 = 0 \tag{27}$$

The roots of Eq. (26) are given by

$$\lambda^2 = \frac{1}{p_4}\left[-\frac{p_2}{2} \pm \left(\frac{1}{4}p_2^2 - p_0p_4\right)^{1/2}\right] \tag{28}$$

Thus, flutter boundary curves $(\Gamma_E)_{flu.}$ of the undamped system (22) are obtained by setting the expression inside $(\ )^{1/2}$ in Eq. (28) equal to zero; i.e.,

$$L = L(F, C_{rs}) = \frac{1}{4}p_2^2 - p_0p_4 = 0 \qquad \text{along } (\Gamma_E)_{flu.} \tag{29}$$

The flutter boundary curves $(\Gamma_D)_{flu.}$ of system (21) can be examined by studying the following inequalities in the Routh-Hurwitz criterion for stability:

$$D_0 = p_0 > 0 \tag{30}$$

$$D_1 = p_1 > 0 \tag{31}$$

$$D_2 = \begin{vmatrix} p_1 & p_0 \\ p_3 & p_2 \end{vmatrix} = p_1p_2 - p_0p_3 > 0 \tag{32}$$

$$D_3 = \begin{vmatrix} p_1 & p_0 & 0 \\ p_3 & p_2 & p_1 \\ 0 & p_4 & p_3 \end{vmatrix} = D_2p_3 - p_1^2p_4 > 0 \tag{33}$$

$$D_4 = \begin{vmatrix} p_1 & p_0 & 0 & 0 \\ p_3 & p_2 & p_1 & p_0 \\ 0 & p_4 & p_3 & p_2 \\ 0 & 0 & 0 & p_4 \end{vmatrix} = p_4 D_3 > 0 \tag{34}$$

By Theorem I, we know that R_D is contained in R_E; hence, p_0, p_2, and p_4 must be all positive [17] in R_D as well as in R_E. Moreover, we assume that p_3, which does not contain any loading parameters, is always positive in R_E for positive slight damping. These conditions assure that $D_0 > 0$ is identically satisfied in R_E, and other inequalities $D_4 > 0$, $D_2 > 0$, and $D_1 > 0$ are also satisfied in R_E if the inequality $D_3 > 0$ holds true. Thus, in R_E, inequality (33) is the governing condition for the stability of system (21). The flutter boundary curves $(\Gamma_D)_{flu.}$ of this system are, therefore, given by

$$D_3 = p_1 p_2 p_3 - p_0 p_3^2 - p_1^2 p_4 = 0 \tag{35}$$

Recalling that p_0, p_2, and p_4 are free from any damping parameters and p_1 and p_3 only are linear functions of two independent damping parameters of the two-degree-of freedom system, we may regard Eq. (35) as a homogenous quadratic equation in the damping parameters. Therefore, dividing both sides of Eq. (35) by the square of one of the two independent damping parameters, the two independent damping parameters can be combined (in the form of a ratio) to form a single parameter in the equation.

Assume that the two independent damping parameters are εb_1 and εb_2. Then defining and noting that

$$\frac{D_3}{\varepsilon^2 b_2^2} = X \tag{36}$$

$$\frac{b_1}{b_2} = \beta \tag{37}$$

$$p_0 = p_0(F, C_{rs}) \tag{38}$$

$$\frac{p_1}{\varepsilon b_2} = \bar{p}_1 = \bar{p}_1(F, C_{rs}, \beta) \tag{39}$$

$$p_2 = p_2\ (F, C_{rs}) \tag{40}$$

$$\frac{p_3}{\varepsilon b_2} = \bar{p}_3(\beta) \tag{41}$$

$$p_4 = \text{constant} \tag{42}$$

we may say that the flutter boundary curves $(\Gamma_D)_{flu.}$ of system (21) are given by

$$X = X(F,C_{rs},\beta) = \bar{p}_1 p_2 \bar{p}_3 - p_0 \bar{p}_3^2 - \bar{p}_1^2 p_4 = 0 \tag{43}$$

which is a modified version of Eq. (35). Equation (43) represents a family of curves in the F-C_{rs} space, where each curve of the family corresponds to a specific value of the damping ratio β. In other words, the flutter boundary curves $(\Gamma_D)_{flu.}$ are highly dependent on the damping ratio β.

It is known [18] that, if there exists an envelope of the family of curves defined by Eq. (43), it must satisfy both Eq. (43) and

$$\frac{\partial}{\partial\beta}X(F,C_{rs},\beta) = 0 \tag{44}$$

Elimination of β in Eqs. (43) and (44) yields

$$p_0^2\left(\frac{1}{4}p_2^2 - p_0p_4\right)\left[p_0\left(\frac{\partial\bar{p}_3}{\partial\beta}\right)^2 - p_2\left(\frac{\partial\bar{p}_1}{\partial\beta}\right)\left(\frac{\partial\bar{p}_3}{\partial\beta}\right) + p_4\left(\frac{\partial\bar{p}_1}{\partial\beta}\right)^2\right] = 0 \tag{45}$$

where the partial derivatives do not contain β because $\bar{p}_1$ and $\bar{p}_3$ are linear functions of β. All curves given by Eq. (45) are not guaranteed to constitute the envelope. However, if there is an envelope, it will be part (perhaps all) of the complete locus defined by Eq. (45).

Comparing Eq. (29) with Eq. (45), we see that the locus of the flutter boundary curves $(\Gamma_E)_{flu.}$ of system (22) is part of the locus defined by Eq. (45). The conditions that $L(F,C_{rs}) = 0$ is the envelope of the family of curves $X(F,C_{rs},\beta) = 0$ are [18]: (a) $\frac{\partial X}{\partial F}$ and $\frac{\partial X}{\partial C_{rs}}$ are not simultaneously zero, (b) $\frac{\partial L}{\partial F}$ and $\frac{\partial L}{\partial C_{rs}}$ are not simultaneously zero. These two conditions are dependent on the behavior of the circulatory loading and are not capable of yielding additional general information without the knowledge of the loading. Therefore, we state the following theorem.

Theorem II. The flutter boundary curves $(\Gamma_E)_{flu.}$ of the undamped system (22) are the envelope of the family of flutter boundary curves

$(\Gamma_D)_{flu.}$ of the slightly damped system (21), unless $\frac{\partial X}{\partial F}$ and $\frac{\partial X}{\partial C_{rs}}$ vanish simultaneously or $\frac{\partial L}{\partial F}$ and $\frac{\partial L}{\partial C_{rs}}$ vanish simultaneously at each point of the curve $L(F, C_{rs}) = 0$.

This theorem implies that it is frequently possible to make the two boundary curves $(\Gamma_D)_{flu.}$ and $(\Gamma_E)_{flu.}$ coincide at a point for a given set of C_{rs} by choosing an appropriate value of the damping ratio β. This feature is illustrated in the example.

Illustrative Example

The various features of the foregoing theorems and corollaries may be demonstrated with the following example.

Let a double pendulum in a smooth horizontal plane be employed as a two-degree-of-freedom model. It has two rigid bars of negligible weights and equal lengths ℓ, which carry concentrated masses $m_1 = 2m$, $m_2 = m$, as shown schematically in Fig. 2. A circulatory force P is applied at the free end at an angle $\alpha_1\phi_1 + \alpha_2\phi_2$ with respect to the line of neutral equilibrium position. At the hinges, the viscoelastic restoring moments $c\phi_1 + \varepsilon b_1\dot{\phi}_1$ and $c\phi_2 + \varepsilon b_2\dot{\phi}_2$ are induced, where c, b_1, and b_2 are constants ε is a small parameter, and an overdot again indicates a differentiation with respect to the time variable t. Thus, it can be shown that the equations of small-amplitude motions are

$$6\phi_1'' + 2\phi_2'' = -\phi_1 - \varepsilon B_1\phi_1' + F[2(1-\alpha_1)\phi_1 + (1-2\alpha_2)\phi_2] \tag{46a}$$

$$2\phi_1'' + \phi_2'' = -\phi_2 - \varepsilon B_2\phi_2' + F[(1-\alpha_1)\phi_1 + (1-\alpha_2)\phi_2] \tag{46b}$$

where

$$F = \frac{P\ell}{c} \tag{47a}$$

$$B_r = \frac{b_r}{\ell(cm)^{1/2}} \qquad (r = 1,2) \tag{47b}$$

$$\tau = \frac{1}{\ell}\left(\frac{c}{m}\right)^{\frac{1}{2}} t \tag{47c}$$

and a prime indicates a differentiation with respect to the dimensionless time variable τ. The characteristic equation of system (46) may be written as

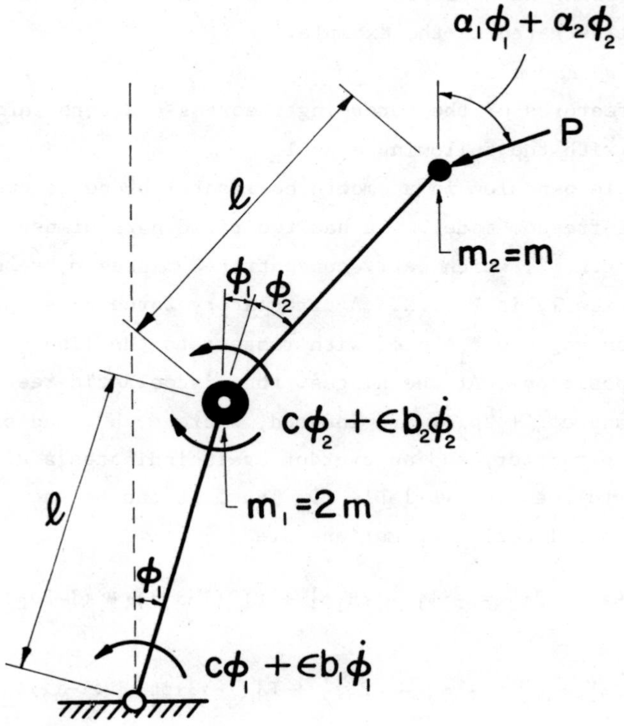

Fig. 2. Two-Degree-of-Freedom Model.

$$p_4\lambda^4 + p_3\lambda^3 + p_2\lambda^2 + p_1\lambda + p_0 = 0 \tag{48}$$

with coefficients

$$p_4 = 2 \tag{49a}$$

$$p_3 = \varepsilon(B_1 + 6B_2) \tag{49b}$$

$$p_2 = 7 + 2(\alpha_2-2)F + \varepsilon^2 B_1B_2 \simeq 7 + 2(\alpha_2-2)F \tag{49c}$$

$$p_1 = \varepsilon\{[1+(\alpha_2-1)F]B_1 + [1 + 2(\alpha_1-1)F]B_2\} \tag{49d}$$

$$p_0 = 1 + (2\alpha_1+\alpha_2-3)F - (\alpha_1-1)F^2 \tag{49e}$$

The divergent critical loads (and hence the divergent boundary curves $(\Gamma_E)_{div.}$ and $(\Gamma_D)_{div.}$) are given by Eq. (27) as

$$p_0 = 1 + (2\alpha_1+\alpha_2-3)F - (\alpha_1-1)F^2 = 0 \tag{50}$$

The flutter critical loads (and hence the fluter boundary curves $(\Gamma_D)_{flu.}$) for this slightly damped system are given by Eq. (43) as

$$\begin{aligned} X = {} & [(\alpha_1-2\alpha_2+1)\beta^2 + 4(3\alpha_2^2-\alpha_1\alpha_2+3\alpha_1-8\alpha_2+3)\beta \\ & - 4(2\alpha_1^2-6\alpha_1\alpha_2-\alpha_1+6\alpha_2-1)]F^2 - 2[(\alpha_1-2\alpha_2+2)\beta^2 \\ & + (9\alpha_1-20\alpha_2+18)\beta - 2(\alpha_1-6\alpha_2+2)]F + (4\beta^2+33\beta+4) \\ = {} & 0 \end{aligned} \tag{51}$$

where $\beta = B_1/B_2 = b_1/b_2$. In the case of complete absence of velocity-dependent forces (i.e., $\varepsilon = 0$), the flutter critical loads (and hence the flutter boundary curves $(\Gamma_E)_{flu.}$) for the undamped system are given by Eq. (29) as

$$L = \tfrac{1}{4}\{4(2+2\alpha_1-4\alpha_2+\alpha_2^2)F^2 - 4(8+4\alpha_1-5\alpha_2)F + 41\} = 0 \tag{52}$$

The stability domains (R_E and R_D) and their boundaries ($(\Gamma_E)_{div.}$, $(\Gamma_D)_{div.}$, $(\Gamma_E)_{flu.}$, and $(\Gamma_D)_{flu.}$) may now be obtained by examining Eqs. (50), (51), and (52).

For convenience in discussing the results presented in Figs. 3 through 9, the following legends are adopted: (i) the loci of divergent

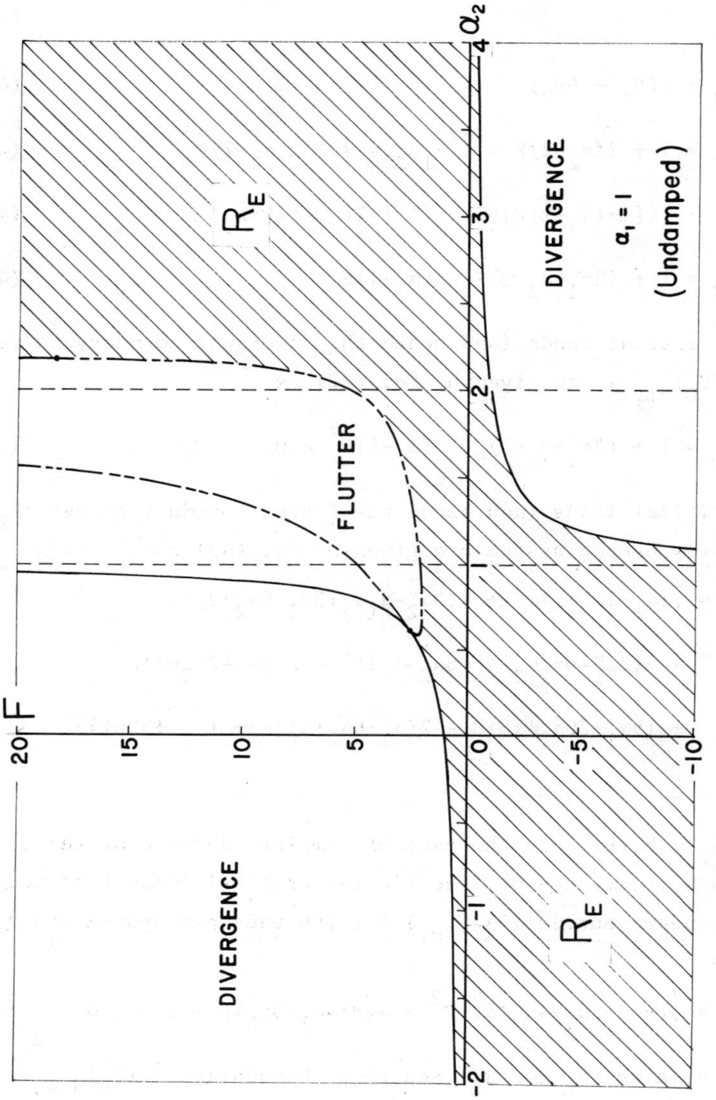

Fig. 3. Stability Diagram for the Undamped System with $\alpha_1 = 1$.

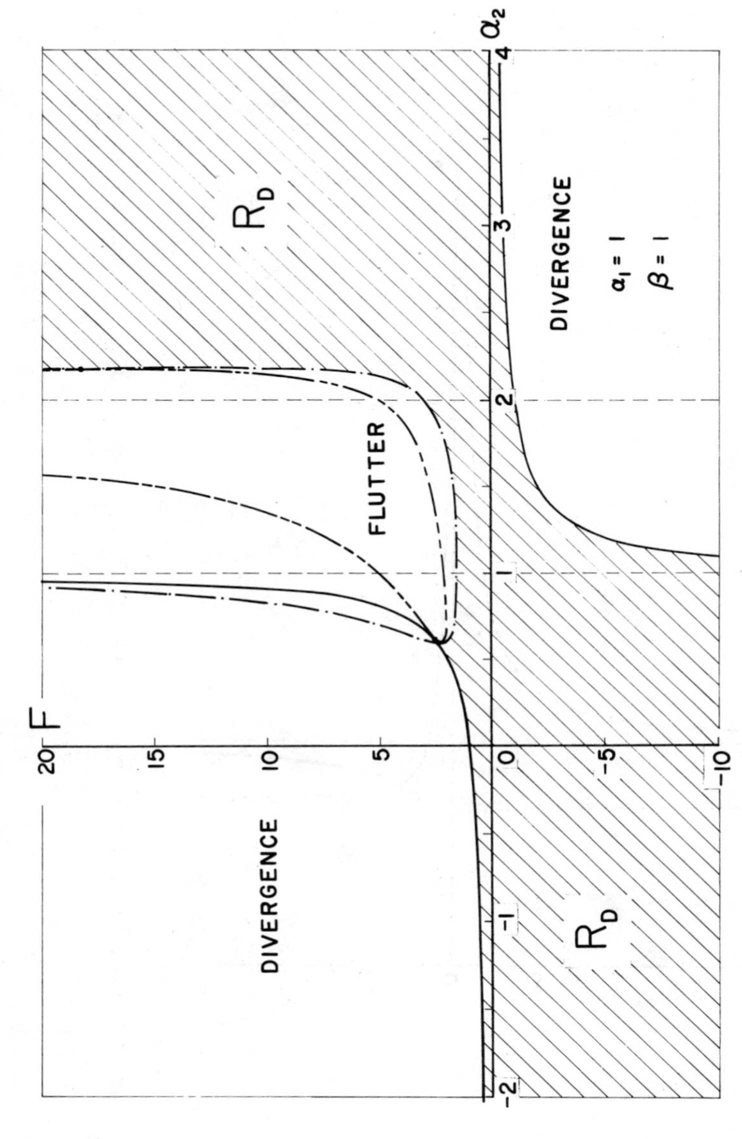

Fig. 4. Stability Diagram for the Slightly Damped System with $\alpha_1 = 1$ and $\beta = 1$.

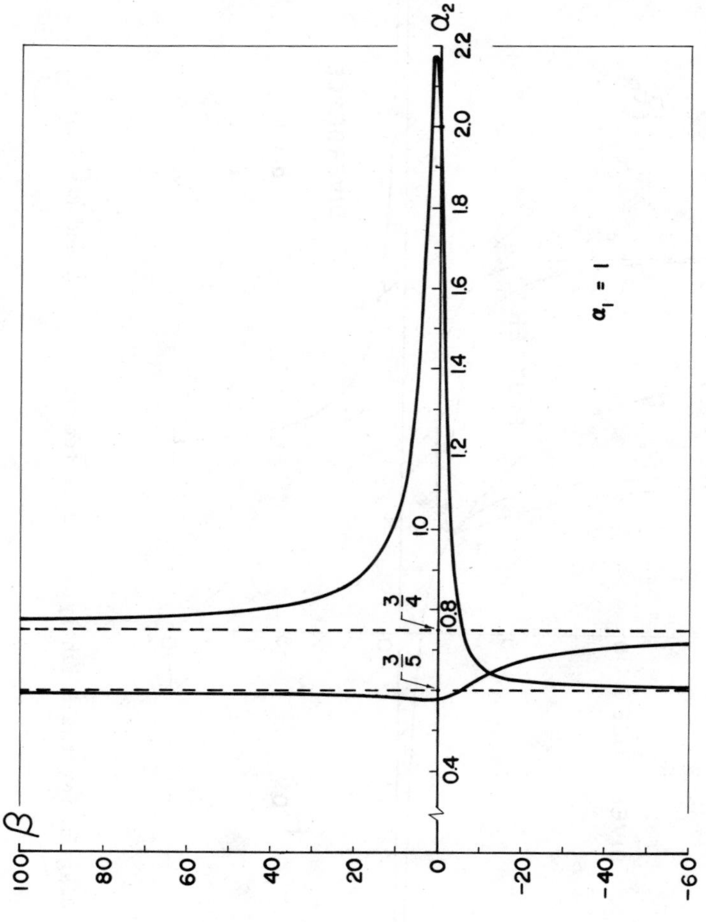

Fig. 5. Appropriate Values of β Versus α_2 for Making $(\Gamma_D)_{flu.}$ and $(\Gamma_E)_{flu.}$ Coincide when $\alpha_1 = 1$.

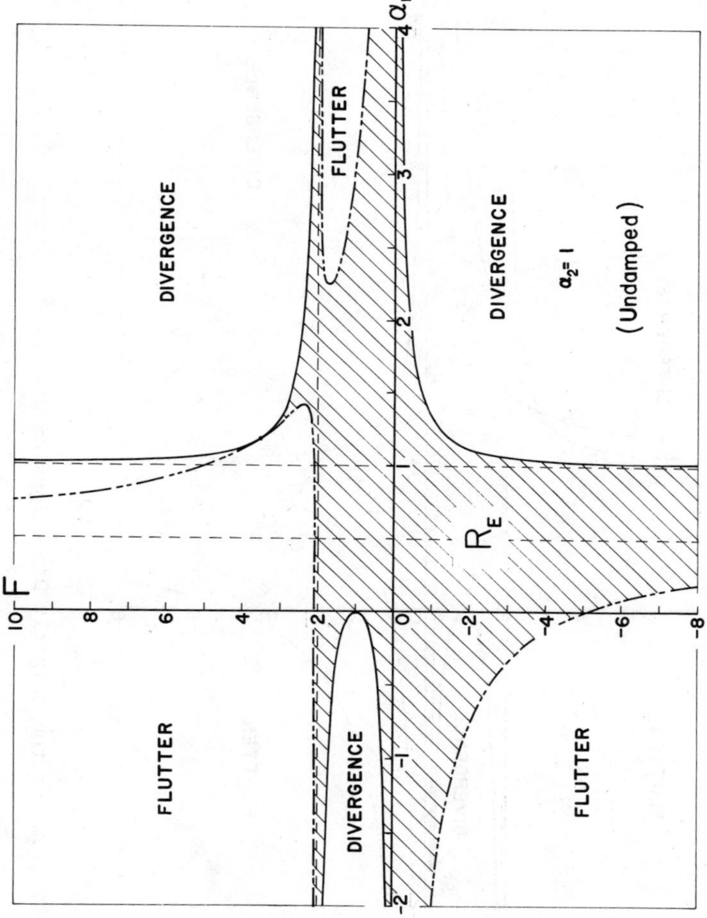

Fig. 6. Stability Diagram for the Undamped System with $\alpha_2 = 1$.

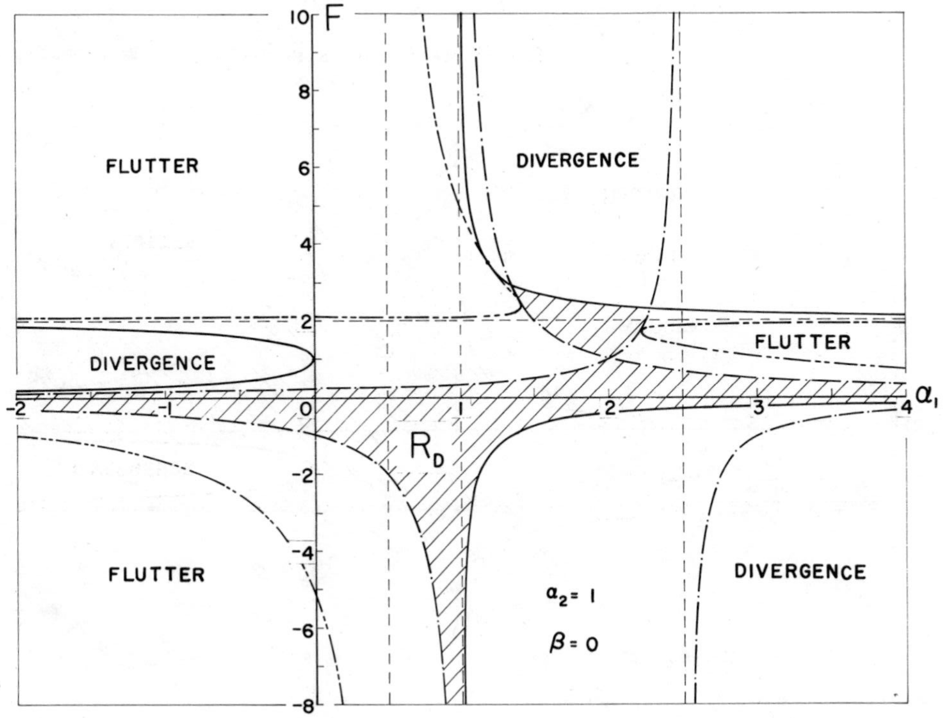

Fig. 7. Stability Diagram for the Slightly Damped System with $\alpha_2 = 1$ and $\beta = 0$.

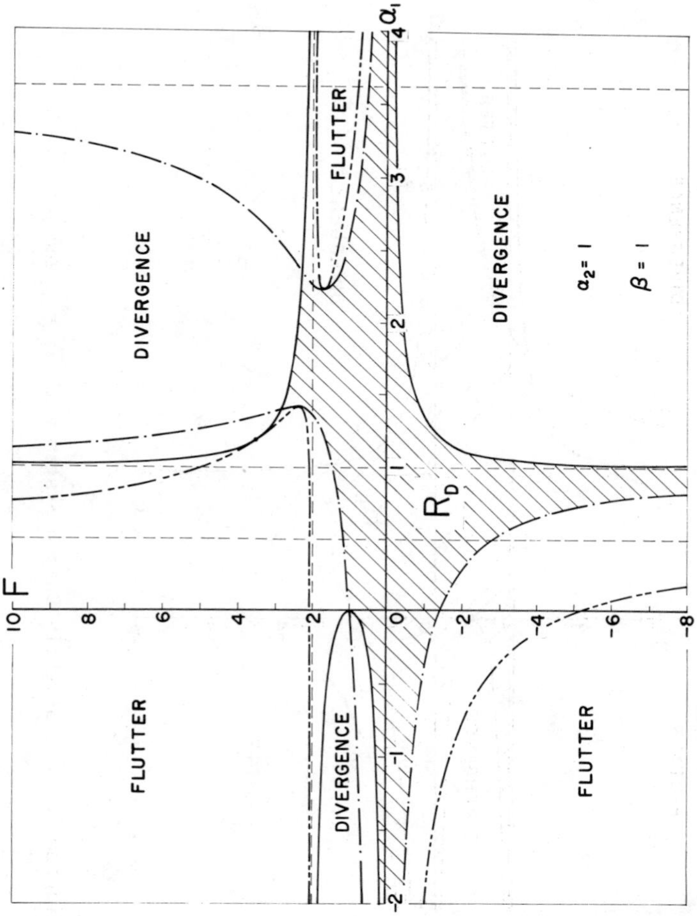

Fig. 8. Stability Diagram for the Slightly Damped System with $\alpha_2 = 1$ and $\beta = 1$.

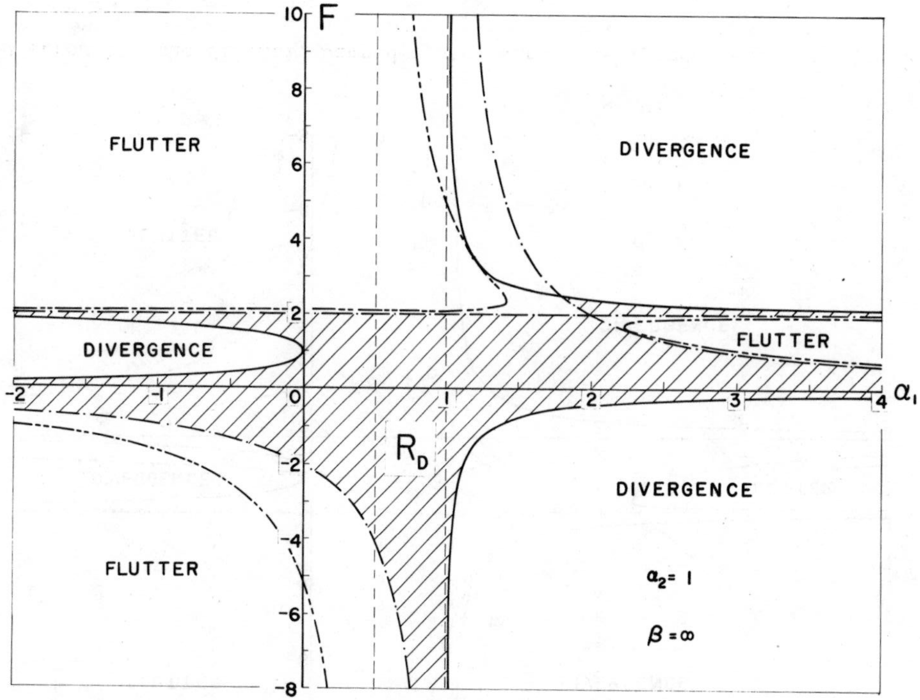

Fig. 9. Stability Diagram for the Slightly Damped System with $\alpha_2 = 1$ and $\beta = \infty$.

boundary curves $(\Gamma_D)_{div.}$ and $(\Gamma_E)_{div.}$ as defined by Eq. (50) are marked by solid curves; (ii) the loci of flutter boundary curves $(\Gamma_D)_{flu.}$ as defined by Eq. (51) are marked by curves with a repeated pattern of one long dash followed by a dot; (iii) the loci of flutter boundary curves $(\Gamma_E)_{flu.}$ as defined by Eq. (52) are marked by curves with a repeated pattern of one long dash followed by two short dashes; (iv) asymptotes of curves are marked by straight lines composed of short dashes; (v) the stability domains R_E and R_D are shaded by diagonal lines.

(A) Case of $\alpha_1 = 1$ / The stability diagrams for the system with α_1 set equal to one are shown in Figs. 3 and 4. With the legends defined above, these two figures are self-explanatory. However, based on the nonsymmetric definition of the kinetic stability, these figures have demonstrated a certain unusual stability phenomenon that may exist in circulatory systems. Figures 3 and 4 distinctly show that when $\alpha_1 = 1$, $\alpha_2 > 2.175$, the external compressive circulatory force can have any magnitudes (including infinity) without making the undamped or the slightly damped system flutter or buckle. In other words, there exists a large class of supertangential $(\alpha_1\phi + \alpha_2\phi > \phi_1 + \phi_2)$ circulatory compressive forces which, no matter how large in magnitudes, cannot induce dynamic instability (vibrations with increasing amplitudes) or static instability (divergent motion or buckling) of the undamped or slightly damped system upon which they act. This is an example of the interesting and unusual nature of the nonconservative problems in the theory of elastic stability.

The consequences of Theorems I and II and Corollary II have been verified in Fig. 4 as shown. The possibility of making the two boundary curves $(\Gamma_D)_{flu.}$ and $(\Gamma_E)_{flu.}$ coincide for $\alpha_1 = 1$ and a given value of α_2 $(0.575<\alpha_2<2.175)$ by choosing an appropriate value of the damping ratio β is exhibited in Fig. 5. This figure indicates that there exists a class of subtangential $(\alpha_1\phi_2+\alpha_1\phi_2 < \phi_1+\phi_2)$ circulatory systems (such as those having $\alpha_1 = 1$ and $\frac{3}{5} < \alpha_2 < \frac{3}{4}$) whose $(\Gamma_D)_{flu.}$ can never be made coincident with $(\Gamma_E)_{flu.}$ if the system is to experience positive viscous damping (i.e., $b_1>0$, $b_2>0$) only.

(B) Case of $\alpha_2 = 1$ / The stability diagrams for the system with α_2 set equal to one are displayed in Figs. 6 through 9. With the legends defined earlier, these figures are also self-explanatory. A clear exposition of multiple ranges of stability and instability existing in the undamped

system is shown in Fig. 6. The presence of slight viscous damping has, by Theorem I, a "destabilizing effect" in the sense that it always reduces the stability domain from R_E to a smaller one R_D as manifested in Figs. 7, 8, and 9. (Note that this is also true with the case shown in Fig. 4.)

The "destabilizing effect" of slight viscous damping in circulatory systems has heretofore been used to mean the decrease of the magnitude of the flutter critical load due to the presence of slight viscous damping [10,15]. However, in the light of the results exhibited in Figs. 7, 8, and 9, it appears that, in allowing the existence of multiple critical loads for circulatory systems, a more appropriate definition for the term "destabilizing effect" of slight viscous damping should be "an effect which decreases the domain of stability" (rather than the magnitude of the critical load).

In Figs. 7, 8, and 9, it is clearly seen that, when $\alpha_2 = 1$ and in the neighborhood of $\alpha_1 > 2.213$, the upper flutter critical load F_d for the slightly damped system is greater in magnitude than any of the two corresponding flutter critical loads F_e for the undamped system. This attests to the validity of Corollary I. The occurrence of points of tangency of $(\Gamma_D)_{flu.}$ and $(\Gamma_E)_{flu.}$ as shown in Figs. 7, 8, and 9 is due to Theorem II.

CONCLUDING REMARKS

The general properties established in the foregoing study for the stability of discrete circulatory systems include: one theorem on the domain of stability, one theorem on the boundary of the domain of stability, two corollaries on critical loads for the slightly damped and the undamped systems. An example is used to illustrate and discuss the various features of the theorems and the corollaries.

Although the unusual stability phenomenon shown in the example is interesting in itself, it should be emphasized that it is based on a nonsymmetric definition of the kinetic stability. Such a definition of stability requires that all functions $|q_r(t)|$ remain arbitrarily small for any time $t > 0$ provided that the initial values $|q_r(0)|$ and $|\dot{q}_r(0)|$ have been chosen sufficiently small. In other words, although the $|\dot{q}_r(0)|$, in addition to the $|q_r(0)|$, are required to be sufficiently small, no restriction resembling the one for $q_r(t)$ is formulated for the $\dot{q}_r(t)$. In the symmetric definition for the kinetic stability, the stable equilibrium state of a system is defined by the conditions that the $|q_r(t)|$ and the $|\dot{q}_r(t)|$ remain arbitrarily small for any time $t > 0$ provided that the $|q_r(0)|$ and the $|\dot{q}_r(0)|$ are chosen sufficiently small.

In the case of $\alpha_1 = 1$, $\alpha_2 > 2.175$ as shown in Figs. 3 and 4, it is to be noted that the frequency (and hence the velocity) of oscillations of the system tends to infinity as $F \to \infty$. Thus, as $F \to \infty$, the system is stable by the nonsymmetric definition of the kinetic stability, but is unstable by the symmetric definition of the kinetic stability because the $|\dot{q}_r(t)|$ become unbounded (although the $|q_r(t)|$ remain bounded) with F. In this case, the phase-plane diagram becomes a long strip along the velocity axis. Stability problems of such a class of circulatory systems require a separate study and will be treated in the future.

ACKNOWLEDGMENT

This work was supported by the National Science Foundation under Grants GK - 1480 and GK - 13533.

REFERENCES

1. Ziegler, H., Principles of Structural Stability, Blaisdell Publishing Company, Mass., 1968.

2. Ziegler, H., "On the Concept of Elastic Stability," Advances in Applied Mechanics, Vol. 4, edited by H. L. Dryden and T. von Karman, Academic Press, Inc., N. Y., 1956, pp. 351-403.

3. Ziegler, H., "Linear Elastic Stability," Zeitschrift für angewandte Mathematik und Physik, Vol. 4, 1953, pp. 89-121, 168-185.

4. Ziegler, H., "Die Stabilitätskriterien der Elastomechanik," Ingenieur-Archiv, Vol. 20, 1952, pp. 49-56.

5. Bolotin, V. V., Nonconservative Problems of the Theory of Elastic Stability, Moscow, 1961, English translation published by Pergamon Press, Inc., N. Y., 1963.

6. Leipholz, H., "Über den Einfluss der Dämpfung bei nichtkonservativen Stabilitätsproblemen elastischer Stäbe," Ingenieur-Archiv, Vol. 33, 1964, pp. 308-321.

7. Herrmann, G., and Bungay, R. W., "On the Stability of Elastic Systems Subjected to Nonconservative Forces," Journal of Applied Mechanics, Vol. 31, Transactions American Society of Mechanical Engineers, Vol. 87, Series E, 1964, pp. 435-440.

8. Herrmann, G., and Jong, I. C., "On the Destabilizing Effect of Damping in Nonconservative Elastic Systems," Journal of Applied Mechanics, Vol. 32, Transactions American Society of Mechanical Engineers, Vol. 87, Series E, 1965, pp. 592-597.

9. Herrmann, G., and Jong, I. C., "On Nonconservative Stability Problems of Elastic Systems with Slight Damping," Journal of Applied Mechanics, Vol. 33, Transactions American Society of Mechanical Engineers, Vol. 88, Series E, 1966, pp. 125-133.

10. Nemat-Nasser, S., and Herrmann, G., "Some General Considerations Concerning the Destabilizing Effect in Nonconservative Systems," Zeitschrift für angewandte Mathematik und Physik, Vol. 17, 1966, pp. 305-313.

11. Nemat-Nasser, S., "On the Stability of the Equilibrium of Nonconservative Continuous Systems with Slight Damping," Journal of Applied Mechanics, Vol. 34, Transactions American Society of Mechanical Engineers, Vol. 89, Series E, 1967, pp. 344-348.

12. Herrmann, G., and Nemat-Nasser, S., "Energy Considerations in the Analysis of Stability of Nonconservative Structural Systems," Dynamic Stability of Structures, edited by G. Herrmann, Pergamon Press, Inc, N. Y., 1967.

13. Jong, I. C., "On Stability of a Circulatory System with Bilinear Hysteresis Damping," Journal of Applied Mechanics, Vol. 36, Transactions American Society of Mechanical Engineers, Vol. 91, Series E, 1969, pp. 76-82.

14. Jong, I. C., "On Stability of a Circulatory System with Weak Distributed Yielding Effects," Journal of Applied Mechanics, ASME, forthcoming.

15. Prasad, S. N., and Herrmann, G., "Some Theorems on Stability of Discrete Circulatory Systems," Acta Mechanica, Vol. 6, 1968, pp. 208-216.

16. Uspensky, J. V., Theory of Equations, McGraw-Hill Book Company, Inc., N. Y., 1948.

17. Routy, E. J., Advanced Dynamics of a System of Rigid Bodies, Dover Publications, N. Y., 1955.

18. Taylor, A. G., Advanced Calculus, Ginn and Company, N. Y., 1955.

NUMERICAL SOLUTION FOR THE MEAN FIRST-PASSAGE-TIME FOR SNAP-THROUGH OF SHELLS

H. N. Pi
University of Waterloo

S. T. Ariaratnam
University of Waterloo

W. C. Lennox
University of Waterloo

ABSTRACT

The mean first-passage-time for the snap-through of a shallow cylindrical shell subjected to wide-band stochastic loading is studied in this paper.

Snap-through of the shell is associated with the departure of the system trajectory from a "safe" region in the state space of the resulting system and the problem is to find the probability of remaining within this specified region. This reduces to the classical first-passage problem and the solution of the related Kolmogorov equation. No solution to this equation is known yet and the only approach to this problem has been by using simulation techniques. However, the mean first-passage-time for the corresponding problem is governed by the Pontriagin-Vitt partial differential equation and this has been solved in this paper by using finite difference techniques. Zero start conditions are assumed so that the problem is non-stationary. Results of this analysis are compared with known approximate solutions and simulation results. While satisfactory agreement is obtained between the present results and those from a simulation study, it is found that the approximate method suggested by Bolotin for solving the Pontriagin-Vitt equation can lead to appreciable errors.

INTRODUCTION

The dynamic stability of structures has often been studied by assuming that the external loads are deterministic functions of time. While this is valid for many actual loadings, it does not adequately describe the type of loads that act on modern aircraft and missile structures that are propelled by jet and rocket engines. These loads fluctuate in a random manner over a wide range of frequencies and have to be considered as stochastic functions of time. An investigation of the stability of structures under such loading is therefore necessary as well as realistic. The behaviour of the structure should then be analysed using the concepts of probability theory and mathematical statistics.

The concepts of stability and probability are closely related. The stable states of equilibrium of a structure are the most probable ones; the unstable states are improbable. The more stable a state is, the greater is the probability of its realization. These ideas are also closely related to the concept of reliability of the structure. In the statistical approach, the aim is to determine the probability distribution for certain parameters of interest which describe the state of the system. Failure of the structure is associated with the departure of these parameters from some "safe" region in parameter space. The probability of staying within this region is then a measure of the reliability.

In this paper we investigate the influence of random loadings on thin shell-type structures capable of exhibiting snap-through. If the state of the shell is described by its representative point in state-space, then snap-through is associated with the departure of the state trajectory from a "safe" region in the state space. The problem is to find the probability that the trajectory remains within this specified region, starting from a given initial state in the neighborhood of the stable unsnapped-equilibrium state.

If the random excitation is a broad-band process, the system response can be approximated by a vector Markov-process. The probability distribution of the time of first snap-through is then given by the Kolmogorov backward equation with appropriate initial and boundary conditions. The non-stationary solution of this equation is difficult to obtain for the present non-linear system. However, the mean time to snap-through can be obtained by solving the Pontriagin-Vitt equation which can be derived from the aforementioned equation. An approximate solution of this equation by using a Galerkin technique has been suggested by Bolotin [1]. In this paper the mean time is obtained by numerically solving the Pontriagin-Vitt equation using a finite-difference technique. These results are compared with those obtained by Bolotin and with those obtained by simulating the system on a digital computer [2].

Formulation of the Problem

We consider a shallow cylindrical shell of thickness h, radius R, width b and curvature parameter $K = b^2/Rh$. The shell edges are hinged to immovable supports. At time $t = 0$ the shell is subjected to a uniformly distributed pressure field of intensity $F(t)$, where $F(t)$ is a stationary random process with mean value F_o. Under the assumption that the shell is sufficiently flat, the deflection is represented by the fundamental mode whose amplitude is given by $q(t)$. Lagrange's equation of motion for the shell can then be written as

$$\frac{d}{dt}\left(\frac{\partial T}{\partial \dot{q}}\right) + \frac{\partial D}{\partial \dot{q}} - \frac{\partial T}{\partial q} + \frac{\partial V}{\partial q} = Q(t) \tag{1}$$

where T is the kinetic energy, D the dissipation function, V the potential energy and Q the generalized force corresponding to the time dependent random loading. The expressions for T, D, V and Q(t) are calculated to be [2]

$$\begin{aligned} T &= \frac{b\, m\, h^2}{4}\, \dot{q}^2 \\ D &= \frac{b\, h^2\, \varepsilon}{2}\, \dot{q}^2 \\ V &= \frac{E\, h^5}{b^3\, (1-\nu^2)}\left[C_1\left(\frac{1}{2} q^2 + \frac{\alpha}{3} q^3 + \frac{\beta}{4} q^4\right) - \frac{2}{\pi} \lambda\, q\right] \\ Q(t) &= \frac{2bh}{\pi}\left[F(t) - F_o\right] \end{aligned} \tag{2}$$

where
$$C_1 = \frac{4\, K^2}{\pi^2} + \frac{\pi^4}{24}$$

$$\alpha = -\frac{3}{2}\,\frac{\pi\, K}{C_1}$$

$$\beta = \frac{1}{8}\,\frac{\pi^4}{C_1}$$

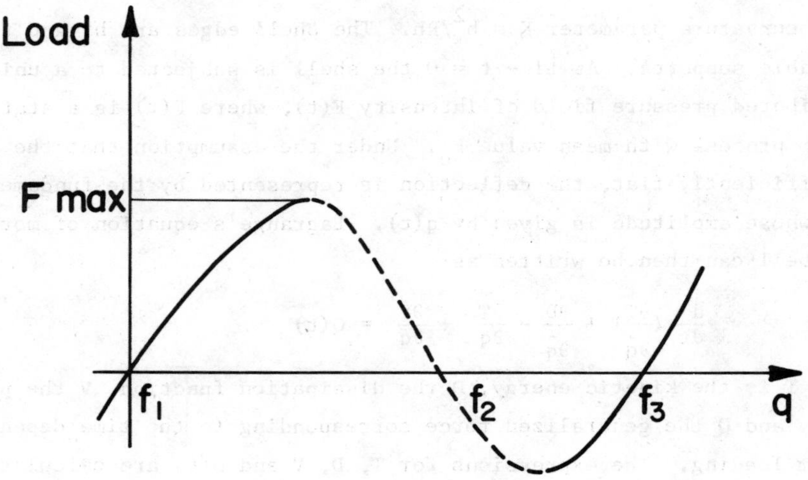

Fig. 1. Static Load-Deflection Diagram.

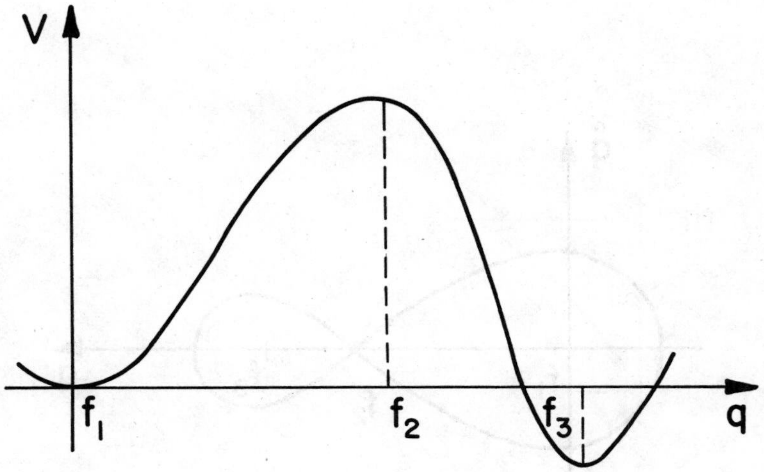

Fig. 2. Section of the Potential Energy Surface.

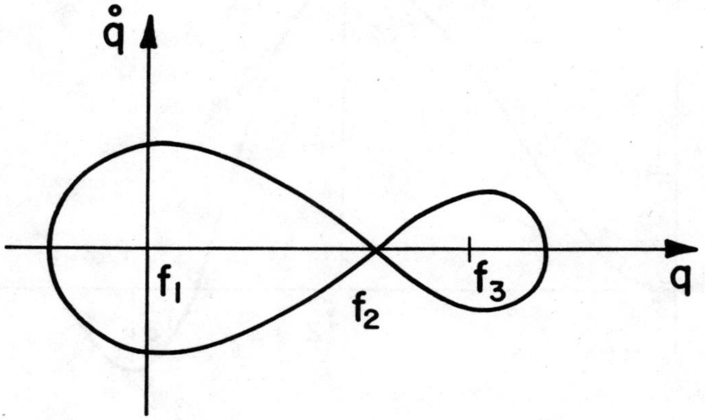

Fig. 3. Separatrix.

and $$\lambda = \frac{F_o}{E} \left(\frac{b}{h}\right)^4 (1 - \nu^2)$$

Here, m is the mass per unit area of middle surface of the shell, ε is the coefficient of viscous damping, ν and E are Poisson's ratio and Young's modulus respectively. Substituting Eq. (2) into Eq. (1) gives

$$\ddot{q} + 2 \zeta \omega \dot{q} + \omega^2 [q + \alpha q^2 + \beta q^3 - \frac{4F_o}{\pi m h}] = \frac{4}{\pi m h} \xi(t) \tag{3}$$

where $$\zeta \omega = \frac{\varepsilon}{m}$$

$$\omega^2 = \frac{2 E h^3}{b^4 m (1 - \nu^2)} C_1$$

and $$\xi(t) = F(t) - F_o$$

In the static case, for any fixed external load $F_o < F_{max}$, where F_{max} is the static snap-through load, the system described by Eq. (3) can possess three equilibrium configurations f_1, f_2 and f_3 which are the roots of the load - deflection equation for the shell obtained by setting

$$\frac{dV}{dq} = 0$$

The static load-deflection curve is sketched in Fig. 1 and the form of the associated potential energy curve for $F = F_o$ is shown in Fig. 2. It can be seen that both f_1 and f_3 are stable equilibrium configurations whereas f_2 is unstable. The equilibrium configuration f_3 corresponds to the snapped-through state of the shell with a reversed curvature.

For the case of dynamic snap-through, we assume that the safe domain for the shell is described by the region inside the left loop of the separatrix in the state plane as shown in Fig. 3. That is, snap-through is assumed not to occur until the trajectory leaves this region. The problem then is to calculate the mean time that a trajectory will take to leave this region for the first time.

Suppose that the shell is initially in the neighborhood of the stable equilibrium configuration f_1 corresponding to the load F_o, when the stochastic fluctuation $\xi(t)$ is applied. The dynamic state of the shell will change with time and accordingly the representative point [described by the state variables $(q, \dot{q})$] in the state-plane will describe a path in this plane. Since $\xi(t)$ is a random process, the state vector $(q, \dot{q})$ will also be a random process and can be described only in terms of its various probability distributions.

Unfortunately, for an arbitrary random process $\xi(t)$, the equation governing the transition probability $p(q, \dot{q} ; t|q_o, \dot{q}_o; t_o)$ is not known. However, if the fluctuation has a reasonably flat spectrum over a wide range of frequencies, the response process $(q, \dot{q})$ can be approximated by a Markov-process and the transition probability $p(q, \dot{q}; t|q_o, \dot{q}_o; t_o)$ is then given by the Fokker-Planck (forward) equation:

$$\frac{\partial p}{\partial t} = - \sum_{i=1}^{2} \frac{\partial}{\partial q_i} (A_i p) + \frac{1}{2} \sum_{i=1}^{2} \sum_{j=1}^{2} \frac{\partial^2}{\partial q_i \, \partial q_j} (B_{ij} p) \tag{4}$$

where A_i and B_{ij} are incremental moments defined by:

$$A_i = \lim_{\delta t \to 0} \frac{< \partial q_i >}{\partial t}$$

$$B_{ij} = \lim_{\delta t \to 0} \frac{< \partial q_i \partial q_j >}{\partial t}$$

The angular brackets <> denotes the ensemble average and the notation $q_1 = q$, $q_2 = \dot{q}$ has been used.

Moreover, if we regard the transition probability as a function of the initial values q_o, $\dot{q}_o$ and t_o, the transition probability satisfies another partial differential equation known as the Kolmogorov (backward) equation:

$$\frac{\partial p}{\partial t_o} = - \sum_{i=1}^{2} \frac{\partial p}{\partial q_{oi}} A_i - \frac{1}{2} \sum_{i=1}^{2} \sum_{j=1}^{2} \frac{\partial^2 p}{\partial q_{oi} \, \partial q_{oj}} B_{ij} \tag{5}$$

i.e.

$$\frac{\partial p}{\partial t_o} = - L[p]$$

where L is the differential operator defined by:

$$L = \sum_{i=1}^{2} \frac{\partial}{\partial q_{oi}} A_i + \frac{1}{2} \sum_{i=1}^{2} \sum_{j=1}^{2} \frac{\partial^2}{\partial q_{oi} \, \partial q_{oj}} B_{ij}$$

Equation (5) is the adjoint of Eq. (4).
In the present case, the coefficients A_i and B_{ij} do not depend on time, and the transition probability depends only on the time difference $\tau = t - t_o$. Hence, Eq. (5) can be rewritten as:

$$\frac{\partial p_\tau}{\partial \tau} = L[p_\tau] \tag{6}$$

Equation (6) is valid for state vectors $\underset{\sim}{q}$, $\underset{\sim}{q}_o$ lying inside a "safe" simply-connected domain D and on the boundary Γ of D. The initial and boundary conditions to be satisfied by p_τ are as follows:

$$p(\underset{\sim}{q}, t_o | \underset{\sim}{q}_o, t_o) = \delta(\underset{\sim}{q} - \underset{\sim}{q}_o) \tag{7}$$

$$p(\underset{\sim}{q}, \tau + t_o | \underset{\sim}{q}_o, t_o) = 0 \quad \text{for } \underset{\sim}{q}_o \; \varepsilon\Gamma \tag{8}$$

The initial condition (7) is obvious while the boundary condition (8) follows from the fact that only those trajectories that have not crossed the boundary up to the time interval τ are taken into consideration.

Let $P(\tau, \underset{\sim}{q}_o)$ denote the probability that a trajectory has not reached the boundary during a time interval τ. Then

$$\begin{aligned} P(\tau, \underset{\sim}{q}_o) &= P_r\{\underset{\sim}{q}(s) \; \varepsilon D, \; t_o \leq s < t_o + \tau | \underset{\sim}{q}(o) = \underset{\sim}{q}_o\} \\ &= \int_D p(\underset{\sim}{q}, t_o + \tau | \underset{\sim}{q}_o, t_o) \, dq_1 dq_2 \end{aligned} \tag{9}$$

If $T(\underset{\sim}{q}_o)$ denotes the time taken for a trajectory starting at $\underset{\sim}{q} = \underset{\sim}{q}_o$ to reach the boundary Γ for the first time, then clearly

$$P(\tau, \underset{\sim}{q}_o) = P_r\{T(\underset{\sim}{q}_o) \geq \tau\}$$

By integrating the Kolmogorov equation (6) as well as the initial and boundary conditions (7) and (8) with respect to q over the domain D, it is seen that $P(\tau, \underset{\sim}{q}_o)$ satisfies the equation

$$L[P(\tau, \underset{\sim}{q}_o)] = \frac{\partial P(\tau, \underset{\sim}{q}_o)}{\partial \tau} \qquad \tau > 0; \; \underset{\sim}{q}_o \; \varepsilon D \tag{10}$$

with initial and boundary conditions

$$P(o, \underset{\sim}{q}_o) = 1, \qquad \underset{\sim}{q}_o \; \varepsilon D \tag{11}$$

$$P(\tau, \underset{\sim}{q}_o) = 0, \qquad \tau > 0, \; \underset{\sim}{q}_o \; \varepsilon\Gamma \tag{12}$$

The closed form solution to this initial-boundary value problem is not known. A partial answer consists in calculating the mean time of reaching the unsafe boundary Γ.

The distribution function of the first passage time T is $1 - P(\tau, \underset{\sim}{q}_o)$. Hence, the mean first-passage time $M(\underset{\sim}{q}_o) = < T(\underset{\sim}{q}_o) >$ is given by

$$M(\underset{\sim}{q}_o) = -\int_o^\infty \tau \frac{\partial P}{\partial \tau} d\tau = \int_o^\infty P(\tau, \underset{\sim}{q}_o)\, d\tau$$

on integration by parts. Integrating Eq. (10) with respect to τ and making use of the initial condition (11) results in the following differential equation for M:

$$L[M(\underset{\sim}{q}_o)] = -1, \qquad \underset{\sim}{q}_o \varepsilon D \tag{13}$$

with boundary condition

$$M(\underset{\sim}{q}_o) = 0 \qquad \underset{\sim}{q}_o \varepsilon \Gamma$$

Equation (13) is the well-known Pontriagin-Vitt equation [3]. Its derivation here is given for the sake of completeness. For the present shell problem, the Pontriagin-Vitt equation for the mean first-passage time of snap-through takes the form:

$$\frac{8S_o}{\pi^2 m^2 h^2} \frac{\partial^2 M}{\partial \dot{q}_o^2} + \dot{q}\frac{\partial M}{\partial q_o} - [2\zeta\omega\dot{q}_o + \omega^2(q_o + \alpha q_o^2 + \beta q_o^3) - \frac{4F_o}{\pi m h}] \frac{\partial M}{\partial \dot{q}_o} = -1 \tag{14}$$

with boundary condition:

$$M(q_o, \dot{q}_o) = 0 \qquad \text{on } \Gamma \tag{15}$$

where Γ denotes the left loop of the separatrix shown in Fig. (4) and S_o is the intensity coefficient of the random excitation F(t) defined by

$$< [F(t + \tau) - F_o][F(t) - F_o] > = S_o \delta(\tau)$$

The analytical solution of Eq. (14) satisfying the boundary condition (15) is not available in the literature. However, due to the simplicity of the boundary condition (15), Bolotin [1] suggested an approximate method of solving Eq. (14). The method consists of replacing the left loop of the separatrix by an ellipse with its center placed on the q-axis. The interior of the ellipse is then mapped onto a unit circle and the solution of the Eq. (14) is found by using Galerkin's method. In this

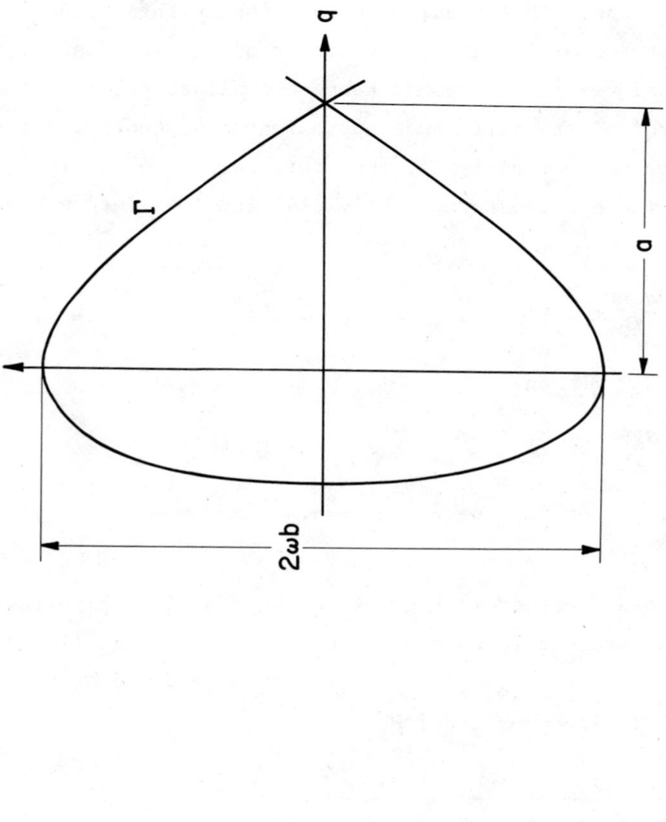

Fig. 4. Safe Region for Snap-Through Problem.

paper Eq. (14) is solved numerically by using a finite-difference technique and the results are compared with those obtained by Bolotin. Also the results are compared with those obtained by a simulation technique [2].

Numerical Solution of the Pontriagin-Vitt Equation

The finite-difference method consists of the replacement of a continuous domain D by a system of rectangular meshes with the result that the governing partial differential equation is converted into a set of algebraic equations. The solution of the problem then reduces to that of solving a system of linear or non-linear algebraic equations by numerical techniques. In order to keep as small as possible the local truncation error of the difference approximations, central differences are used in the present analysis, (see for example [4]). The computation can be simplified by transforming Eqs. (14) and (15) into nondimensional form, i.e.,:

$$\frac{1}{\mu}\frac{\partial^2 M_1}{\partial y^2} + \gamma^2 y\frac{\partial M_1}{\partial x} - [2\zeta\gamma y + (x + \alpha^* x^2 + \beta^* x^3) - \delta]\frac{\partial M_1}{\partial y} = -\gamma \tag{16}$$

$$M_1(x, y) = 0 \qquad \text{on } \Gamma \tag{17}$$

where $x = \frac{q_o}{a}$, $y = \frac{\dot{q}_o}{\omega b}$, $M_1 = \omega M$, $\gamma = \frac{b}{a}$

$$\alpha^* = a\alpha, \quad \beta^* = a^2\beta, \quad \mu = \frac{\pi^2 m^2 h^2 \omega^3 ab}{8S_o}, \quad \delta = \frac{4F_o}{\pi m h a \omega^2}$$

and a and b are as defined in Fig. 4 . The transformation to finite-differences is straight forward with the result that Eq. (16) becomes:

$$[-\gamma^2 (j-1)\frac{v\theta_1}{u(1+\theta_1)}]\, M_{1_{i-1,j}}$$

$$+ [\frac{2}{\mu v^2\theta_2(1+\theta_2)} - \frac{A^*}{v\theta_2(1+\theta_2)}]\, M_{1_{i,j+1}}$$

$$+ [\frac{A^*(1-\theta_2)}{v\theta_2} - \frac{2}{\mu v^2\theta_2} - \frac{\gamma^2 v(j-1)(1-\theta_1)}{u\theta_1}]M_{1_{i,j}}$$

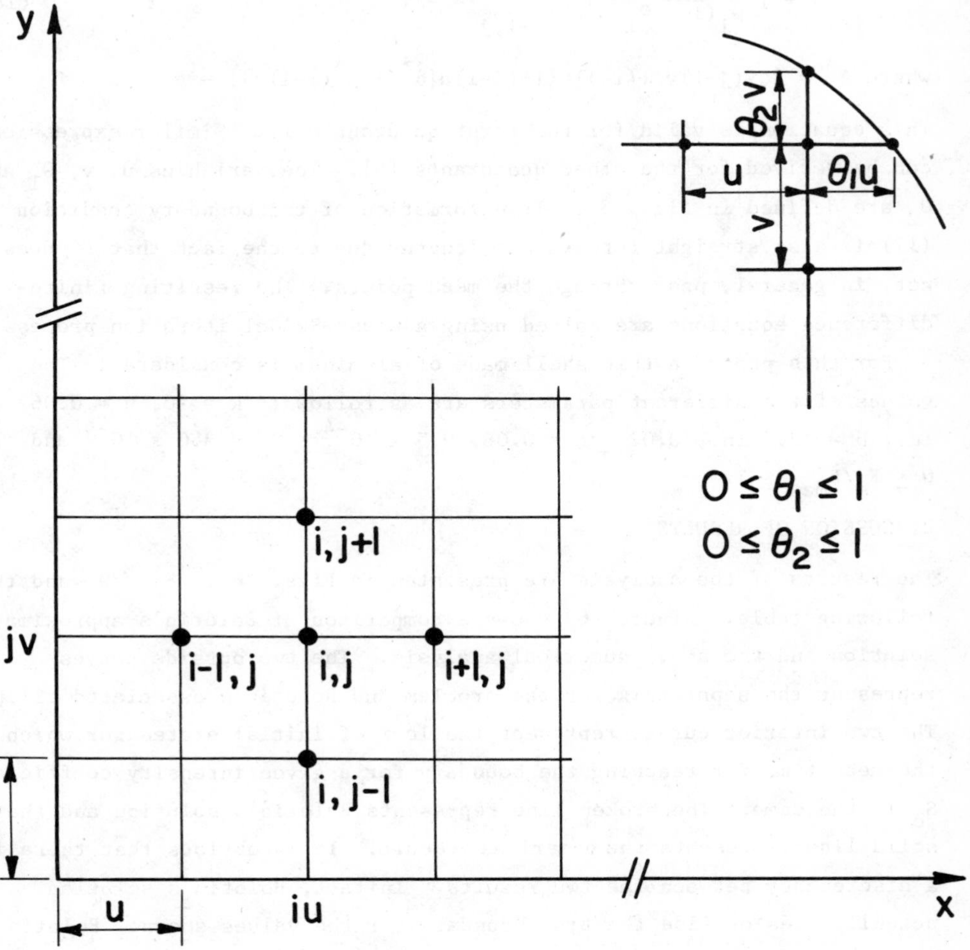

Fig. 5. Grid for Finite-Difference Method Showing Typical Point Near Boundry.

$$+ \left[\frac{2}{\mu v^2(1+\theta_2)} + \frac{A^*\theta_2}{v(1+\theta_2)} \right] M_{1_{i,j-1}}$$

$$+ \left[\frac{\gamma^2(j-1)v}{u\theta_1(1+\theta_1)}\right] M_{1_{i+1,j}} = -\gamma \qquad (18)$$

where $A^* = 2\zeta\gamma(j-1)v + (i-1)u\{1+(i-1)u[\alpha^* + \beta^*(i-1)u]\} - \delta$

This equation is valid for the first quadrant only. Similar expressions can be derived for the other quandrants [5]. The variables u, v, θ_1 and θ_2 are defined in Fig. 5 . Transformation of the boundary condition (17) is also straight forward but lengthy due to the fact that Γ does not, in general, pass through the mesh points. The resulting finite-difference equations are solved using a Gauss-Seidel iteration process.

For this paper, a thin shell made of aluminum is considered. The values of the different parameters are as follows: k = 10, h = 0.063 in., b = 12.6 in., $0.02 \leq \zeta \leq 0.08$, $0.5 \times 10^{-4} \leq S_o \leq 3.0 \times 10^{-4}$ and $0 \leq F_o/F_{max} \leq 1$.

DISCUSSION OF RESULTS

The results of the analysis are presented in Figs. 6 , 8 , 9 and the following table. Figure 6 shows a comparison of Bolotin's approximate solution and the above numerical analysis. The two outside curves represent the separatrix for the problem and Bolotin's associated ellipse. The two interior curves represent the loci of initial states for which the mean time for reaching the boundary for a given intensity coefficient S_o is the same. The broken line represents Bolotin's solution and the solid line represents the numerical result. It is obvious that there is a discrepancy between the two results. In fact, Bolotin's solution actually lies outside the true boundary for the values shown. Bolotin also concluded that the mean time for reaching the boundary for the case when an initial state point is in the second quadrant is less than that when the corresponding initial point is in any of the other quadrants of the state-plane. The numerical analysis indicates that this may not be so, since for the particular case considered, the least mean time occurs for initial states lying in the third quadrant. However, the actual differences in mean times obtained for corresponding points in the second and third quadrants are not significant. The error associated with the numerical integration is of the order 0.001.

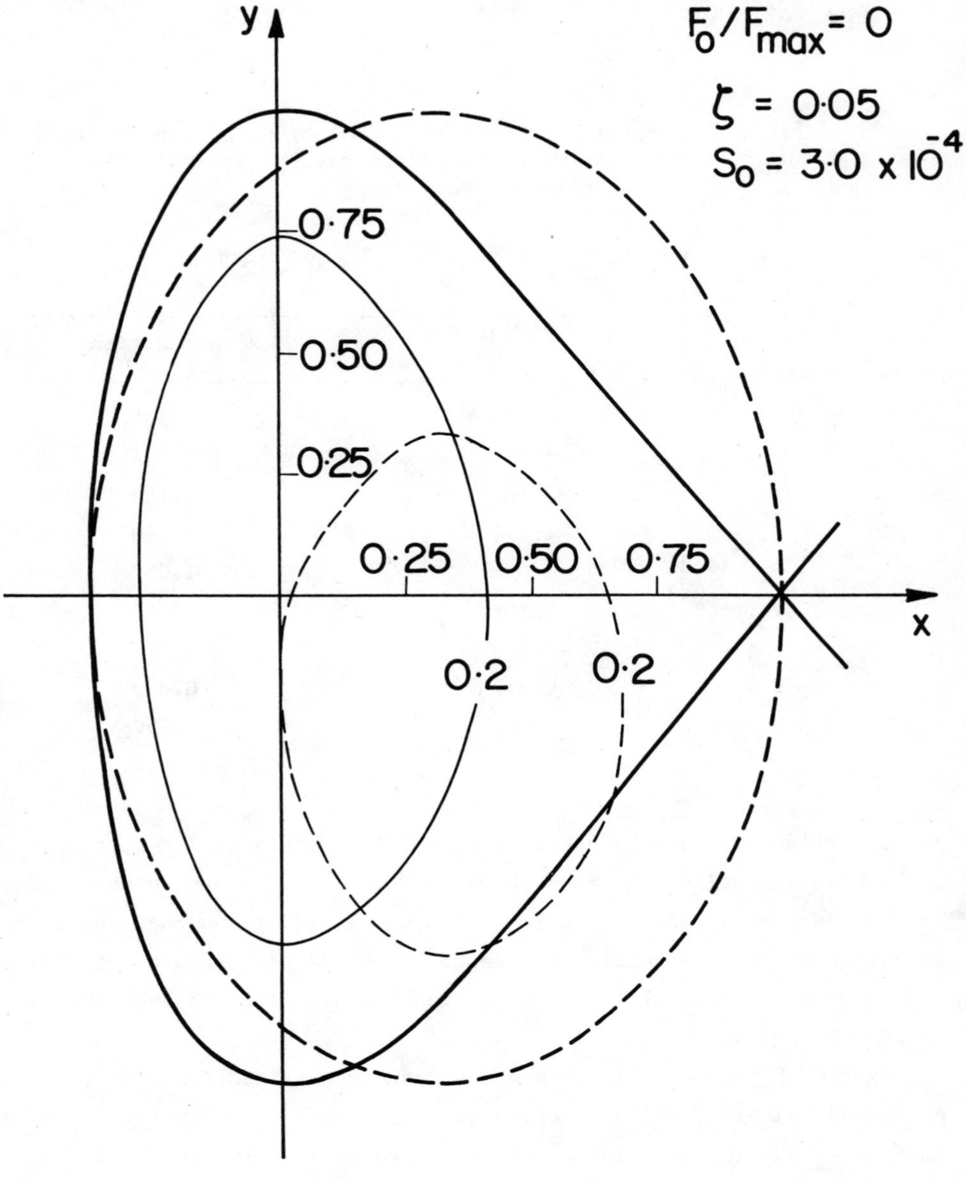

Fig. 6. Contours of Equal Mean Time (Cycles).

These numerical results are also compared with values obtained by a digital simulation of the system [2]. This is presented in the following table.

Table - Comparison of numerical solutions of Pontriagin's equation with simulation results for the mean first-passage time (cycles)

$\zeta = 0.05$, $F_o/F_{max} = 0$ $S_o = 1.0 \times 10^{-4}$

Point	M_1 Pontriagin-Vitt equation	M_1 Simulation
P_0	1.364	1.336
P_1	1.194	1.134
P_2	1.167	1.149
P_3	1.177	1.180
P_4	1.096	1.087
P_5	1.156	1.172
P_6	1.146	1.178
P_7	0.817	0.879
P_8	1.005	0.990
P_9	1.133	1.062

The comparison is made by choosing as initial points $q(o) = 0$, $q(\dot{o}) = 0$ and nine neighboring points as shown in Fig. 7 . As can be seen there is good agreement between the two methods. It was found that the discrepancy between the two results decreased as the sample size for simulation was increased. The variance for the mean values given in the table is of the order 0.5.

Figures 8 and 9 illustrate the results obtained for M_1 for different values of the parameters ζ, S_o and F_o/F_{max}. For large values of F_o/F_{max} damping has little effect as can be seen in Fig. 8 . As may be seen from Fig. 9 , the system is obviously sensitive to the value of S_o.

ACKNOWLEDGMENT

The research reported in this paper was supported by Grant No. A-1815 from the National Research Council of Canada.

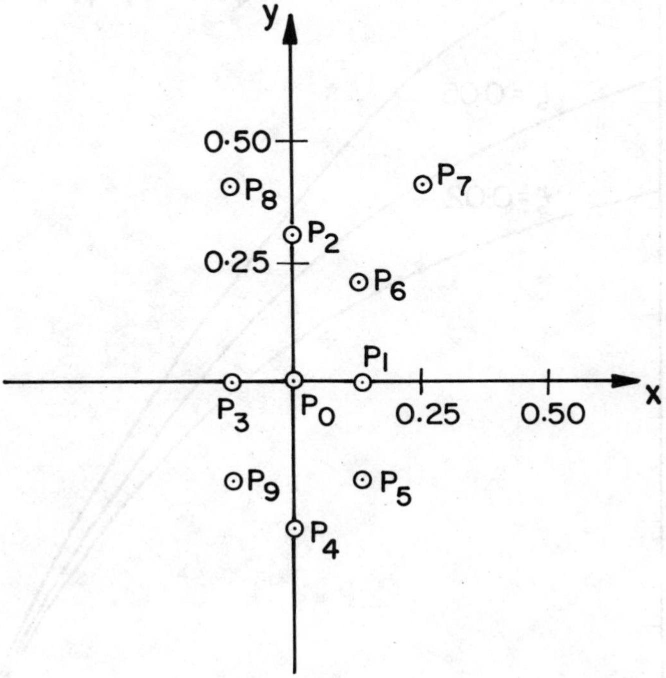

Fig. 7. Array of Initial States.

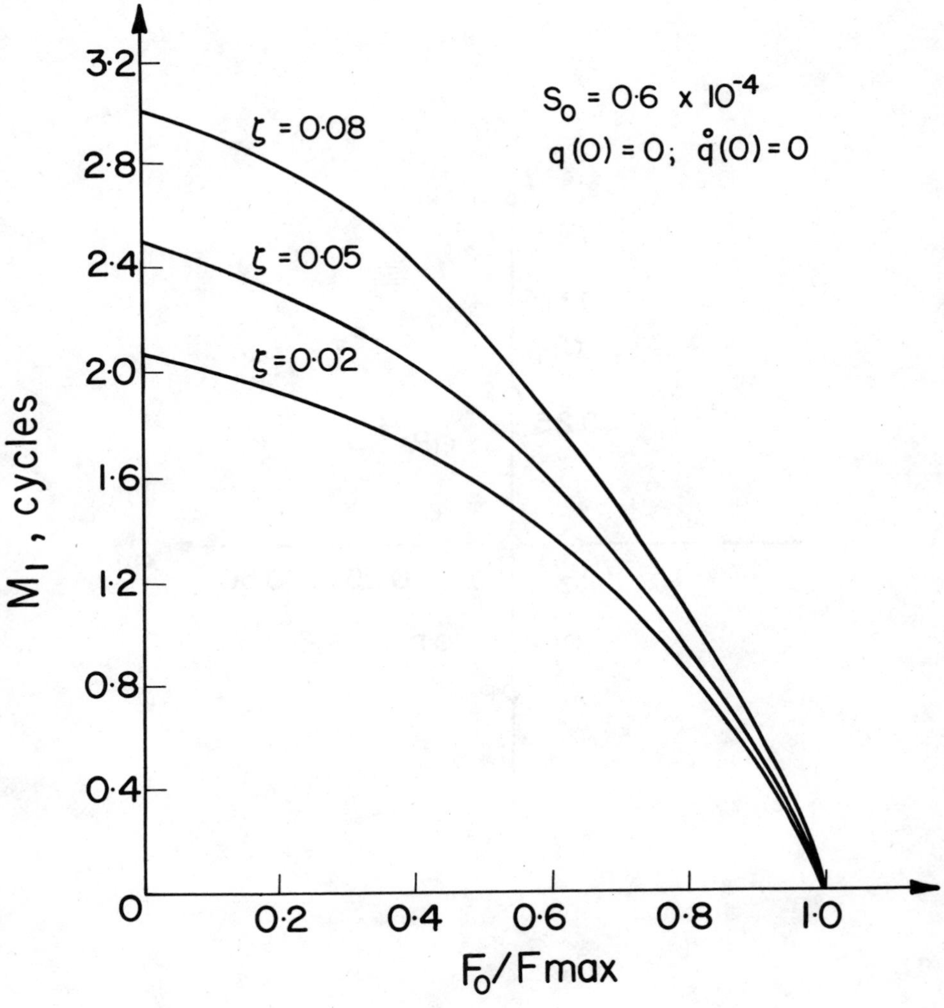

Fig. 8. Mean Time M_1 vs F_o/F_{max} for Various Values of Damping.

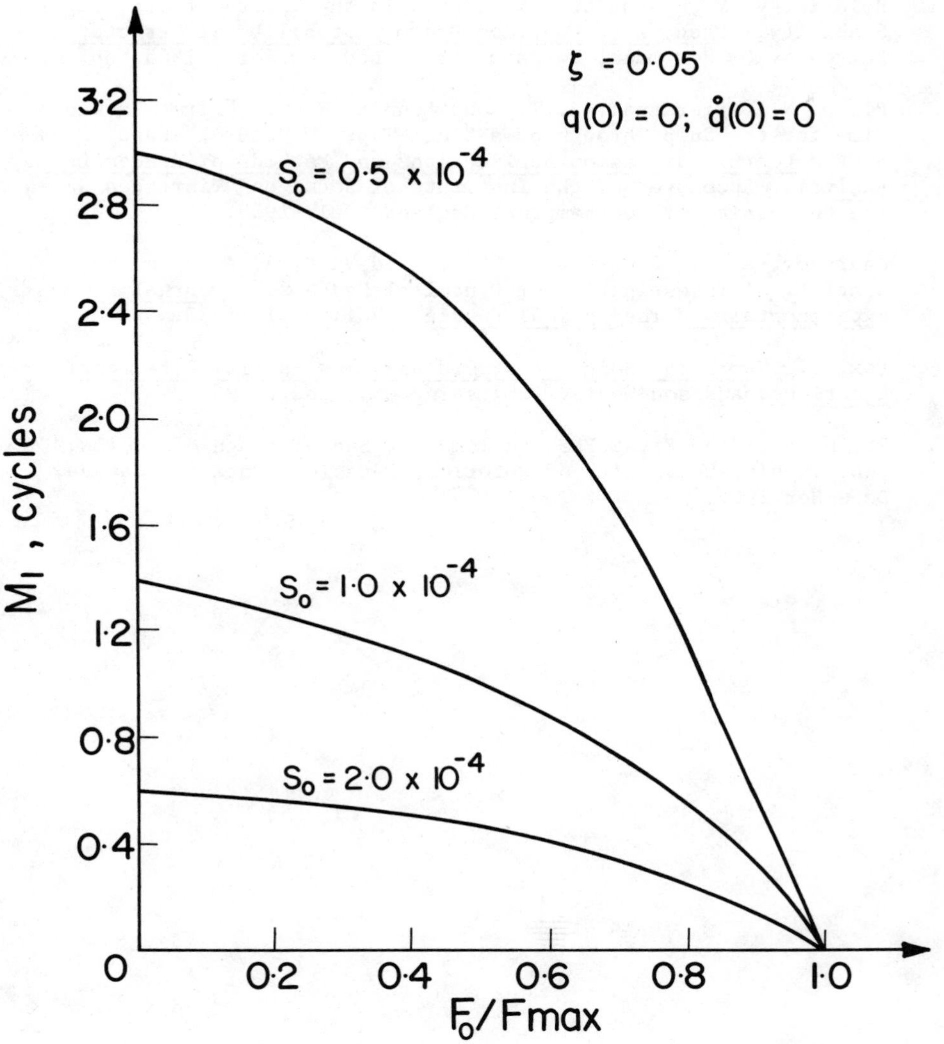

Fig. 9. Mean Time M_1 vs F_o/F_{max} for Various Values of Intensity Coefficent S_o.

REFERENCES

1. Bolotin, V. V., "Statistical Aspects in the Theory of Structural Stability," Proc, Int. Conf. on Dynamic Stability of Structures, Edited by G. Herrmann, Pergamon Press Ltd., Oxford, 1965, pp. 67-81.

2. Pi, H. N., Ariaratnam, S. T., and Lennox, W. C., "First-Passage Time for the Snap Through of a Shell-Type Structure," Paper Presented at the Lecture Series on Applications and Methods of Random Data Analysis, Sponsored by the Institute of Sound and Vibration Research, The University of Southampton, England, July 1969.

3. Andranov, A. A., Pontriagin, L. S., and Vitt, A. A., "On the Statistical Investigation of Dynamical Systems," Journal of Experimental and Theoretical Physics, Vol. 3(3), 1933.

4. Fox, L., Numerical Solution of Ordinary and Partial Differential Equations, Addison-Wesley Publishing Co., Inc., 1962.

5. Pi, H. N., "The First-Passage Time for Snap-Through of Shells." PhD. Thesis, University of Waterloo, Waterloo, Ontario, Canada, December 1969.

FLUID OSCILLATIONS IN A PARTIALLY FILLED CYLINDRICAL TANK WITH A SPRING SUPPORTED ELASTIC FLOOR

Julius Siekmann[1]
Georgia Institute of Technology

Shih-chih Chang
Georgia Institute of Technology

ABSTRACT

The sloshing of a homogeneous, incompressible, nonviscous fluid in a vertical circular cylindrical container with rigid side walls and a spring supported flexible floor is investigated. It is demonstrated that the elastic bottom, being a spring supported thin plate, lowers the frequencies of the system as compared with their respective values in a completely rigid tank. Moreover, an exact solution of the problem is obtained.

LIST OF NOTATIONS

A_n, B_n	Constants
a_n, b_n	Amplitude of n-th sloshing mode
a	Radius of tank
D	Plate stiffness
E	Young's modulus
F	Force in vertical direction
f	Amplitude of imposed axial acceleration
g	Gravitational acceleration
h	Height of liquid
$\bar{h}$	Tank bottom plate thickness

1. Now Technische Hochschule, Darmstadt, Germany.

J_o, J_1	Bessel functions of first kind
k	Spring stiffness
k_n	nth root of the equation $J_1(k_n a) = 0$
p	Pressure
(r, θ, z)	Cylindrical coordinates
t	Time
w	Transverse deflection of plate
ζ	Free surface elevation as referred to static equilibrium configuration of the liquid
ψ	Velocity potential
ρ	Density of liquid
$\bar{\rho}$	Density of tank bottom material
ν	Poisson's ratio
ω	Frequency of liquid-tank system
Ω	Forcing frequency
Δ	Laplace operator in (r,θ)
$\Delta\Delta$	Biharmonic operator in (r,θ)

INTRODUCTION

The advance of rocketry has revived interest in the classical problem of liquid oscillations in rigid or elastic containers as demonstrated recently by a number of comprehensive survey articles and monographs [1,2,3,4]. This is due to the fact that the sloshing characteristics of propellants contained in missile and rocket tanks are of considerable practical importance because of the possibilities of interaction with the control system responses, development of excessive forces and moments due to liquid motion, etc.

It is the purpose of the present paper to study the change of frequencies of the oscillations of an ideal fluid which is contained in a cylindrical vessel of constant circular cross section closed by a spring supported flexible floor at depth h below the free surface as compared with the values for a sloshing liquid in a rigid tank. It will be shown that this spring-mat device lowers the frequencies. Besides, an exact solution of the problem formulated below can be obtained. For the sake of simplicity, the discussion of the solution is restricted to vertical sloshing only. The case of the free oscillations of an ideal incompressible fluid in a partially filled cylindrical tank with rigid side walls and an elastic bottom, the latter being a thin elastic plate clamped at the edge, has been treated elsewhere [5].

Formulation of the Problem

Consider a frictionless, homogeneous and incompressible liquid which partially fills an upright circular cylindrical tank with rigid side walls and an elastic thin plate bottom on an elastic foundation (spring supported plate-mat) (Fig. 1). We assume that viscous and capillary contact effects between the liquid and the tank wall are negligible and that the fluid motion is irrotational. The (r,θ,z) frame of reference is fixed to the container as illustrated in the sketch.

The basic equations describing the motion of the liquid are the usual ones for irrotational sloshing:

Within the liquid the velocity potential must satisfy the Laplace equation

$$\nabla^2\psi \equiv \frac{\partial^2\psi}{\partial r^2} + \frac{1}{r}\frac{\partial\psi}{\partial r} + \frac{1}{r^2}\frac{\partial^2\psi}{\partial\theta^2} + \frac{\partial^2\psi}{\partial z^2} = 0. \tag{1}$$

At the wetted impenetrable tank wall the velocity perpendicular to the wall must be zero

$$\left.\frac{\partial\psi}{\partial r}\right|_{r=a} = 0. \tag{2}$$

At the free surface a dynamic boundary condition, which is obtained from the unsteady state Bernoulli equation, and a kinematic boundary condition, which connects the motion of the free surface with the velocity potential, have to be fulfilled. Both conditions combined yield

$$\left[\frac{\partial^2\psi}{\partial t^2} + g\,\frac{\partial\psi}{\partial z}\right]_{z=h} = 0. \tag{3}$$

Next, we turn to the conditions at the flexible floor. Assuming non-cavitating flow the coupling condition between the liquid and the elastic structure is given by

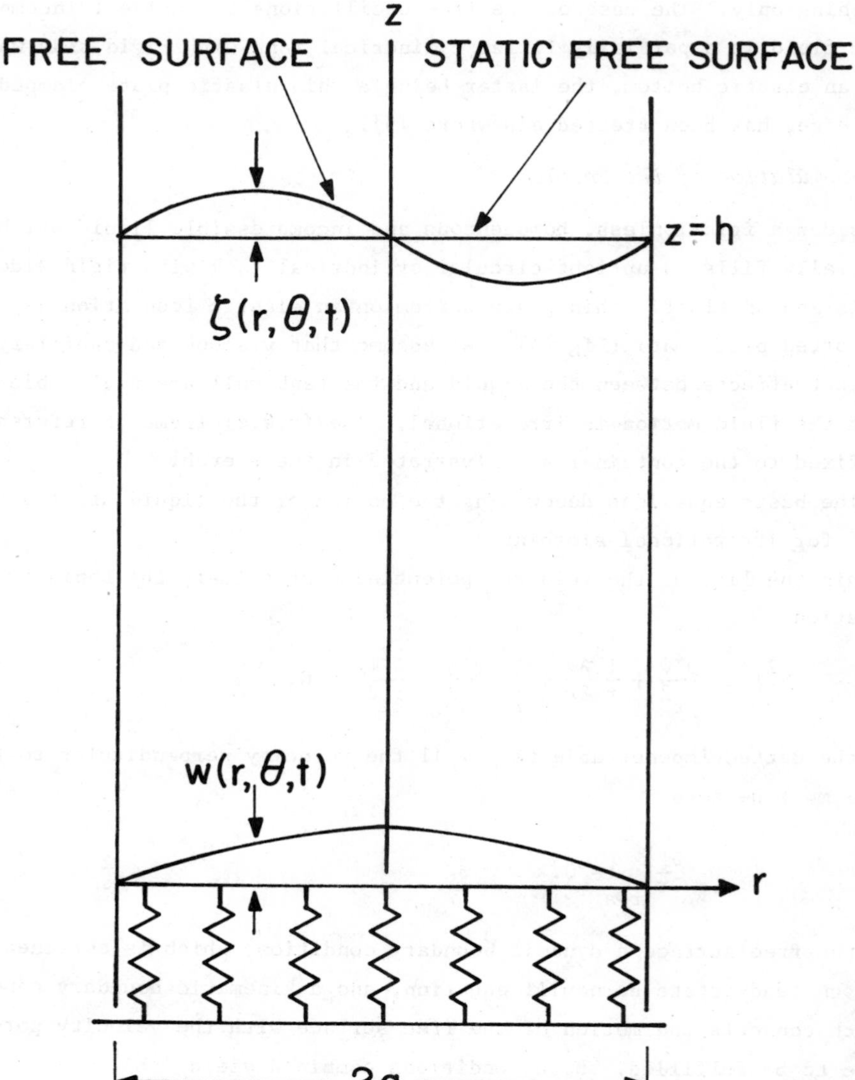

Fig. 1. Tank Geometry and Notations.

$$\frac{\partial w}{\partial t} = \left.\frac{\partial \psi}{\partial z}\right|_{z=0} , \tag{4}$$

where the vertical displacement of a point of the bottom, assumed to be infinitesimally small, is considered to be positive upward.

Finally, the governing differential equation for the bottom is that of a vibrating thin elastic plate resting on springs. Hence

$$\left(\frac{\partial^2}{\partial r^2} + \frac{1}{r}\frac{\partial}{\partial r} + \frac{1}{r^2}\frac{\partial^2}{\partial \theta^2}\right)\left(\frac{\partial^2 w}{\partial r^2} + \frac{1}{r}\frac{\partial w}{\partial r} + \frac{1}{r^2}\frac{\partial^2 w}{\partial \theta^2}\right) + \frac{\bar{\rho}\bar{h}}{D}\frac{\partial^2 w}{\partial t^2} = -\frac{1}{D}(p-q) \tag{5}$$

with

$$D = \frac{E\bar{h}^3}{12(1-\nu^2)} .$$

The fluid pressure acting on the plate follows from the linearized unsteady Bernoulli equation and is given by

$$p = -\rho \left.\frac{\partial \psi}{\partial t}\right|_{z=0} , \tag{6a}$$ [1]

while for the spring force per unit area we have

$$q = -kw . \tag{6b}$$

Thus

$$\Delta\Delta w + \frac{\bar{\rho}\bar{h}}{D}\frac{\partial^2 w}{\partial t^2} = \frac{\rho}{D}\left.\frac{\partial \psi}{\partial t}\right|_{z=0} - \frac{k}{D} w , \tag{7}$$

where $\Delta\Delta$ is the biharmonic operator in (r,θ).

Solution

Restricting the analysis to axisymmetric modes of oscillations only, with

$$\psi(r,z,t) = \Phi(r,z)e^{i\omega t} , \tag{8}$$

we arrive at the following solution for the field equation (1), subject to the zero normal velocity boundary condition (2) at the rigid tank wall

1. A static pressure term has been disregarded since only vibrations about the equilibrium position are considered.

$$\Phi(r,z) = \sum_{n=1}^{\infty} [A_n e^{-k_n z} + B_n e^{k_n z}] J_0(k_n r) \;, \tag{9}$$

where k_n is the n-th root of $J_1(k_n a) = 0$. From equations (3) and (8) there follows

$$\left[g \frac{\partial \Phi}{\partial z} - \omega^2 \Phi \right]_{z=h} = 0 \;, \tag{10}$$

or, after insertion of the solution for the velocity potential,

$$\sum_{n=1}^{\infty} \{ (k_n g + \omega^2) e^{-k_n h} A_n - (k_n g - \omega^2) e^{k_n h} B_n \} J_0(k_n r) = 0 \;. \tag{11}$$

Therefore, for each n the relation

$$(k_n g + \omega^2) A_n - (k_n g - \omega^2) e^{2k_n h} B_n = 0 \quad , \tag{12}$$

or

$$\frac{A_n}{B_n} = \frac{k_n g - \omega^2}{k_n g + \omega^2} e^{2k_n h} \tag{13}$$

holds.

Differentiation of the plate equation (7) with respect to time together with the coupling condition (4) and equation (8) leads to

$$\left[\left(\frac{\partial^2}{\partial r^2} + \frac{1}{r} \frac{\partial}{\partial r} \right)^2 \frac{\partial \Phi}{\partial z} - \frac{\bar{\rho} \bar{h}}{D} \omega^2 \frac{\partial \Phi}{\partial z} + \frac{\rho}{D} \omega^2 \Phi + \frac{k}{D} \frac{\partial \Phi}{\partial z} \right]_{z=0} = 0 \;. \tag{14}$$

By virtue of $\nabla = \Delta^2 - \frac{\partial^2}{\partial z^2}$ and $\nabla^2 \Phi = 0$ we find

$$\left[\frac{\partial^5 \Phi}{\partial z^5} - \left(\frac{\bar{\rho} \bar{h}}{D} \omega^2 - \frac{k}{D} \right) \frac{\partial \Phi}{\partial z} + \frac{\rho}{D} \omega^2 \Phi \right]_{z=0} = 0 \;. \tag{15}$$

Upon substitution of equation (9) and after a few standard manipulations, there results for each n

$$\left[- k_n^5 + \left(\frac{\bar{\rho}\bar{h}}{D}\,\omega^2 + \frac{k}{D}\right) k_n + \frac{\rho}{D}\,\omega^2\right] A_n$$

$$+ \left[k_n^5 - \left(\frac{\bar{\rho}\bar{h}}{D}\,\omega^2 - \frac{k}{D}\right) k_n + \frac{\rho}{D}\,\omega^2\right] B_n = 0 . \tag{16}$$

Together with equation (13) this yields the frequency equation

$$\frac{k_n g - \omega^2}{k_n g + \omega^2}\, e^{2k_n h} = \frac{k_n^5 - \left(\frac{\bar{\rho}\bar{h}}{D}\,\omega^2 - \frac{k}{D}\right) k_n + \frac{\rho}{D}\,\omega^2}{k_n^5 - \left(\frac{\bar{\rho}\bar{h}}{D}\,\omega^2 - \frac{k}{D}\right) k_n - \frac{\rho}{D}\,\omega^2} . \tag{17}$$

Of special interest are, of course, the limiting cases.

a) $D \to 0,\ \bar{\rho} \to 0$, i.e. the completely flexible mat.
From the frequency equation (17) we obtain

$$\frac{k_n g - \omega^2}{k_n g + \omega^2}\, e^{2k_n h} = \frac{k k_n + \rho\omega^2}{k k_n - \rho\omega^2} . \tag{18}$$

b) $D \to \infty$, i.e. the completely rigid mat.
Again, from the frequency equation (17) we find

$$\frac{k_n g - \omega^2}{k_n g + \omega^2}\, e^{2k_n h} = 1 . \tag{19}$$

This result is nothing else than the well known frequency equation for a sloshing liquid in a rigid tank. Because of

$$F = - \int_o^a \int_o^{2\pi} \rho \left.\frac{\partial\psi}{\partial t}\right|_{z=o} r\, d\theta\, dr$$

$$= - 2\pi\rho i\omega e^{i\omega t} \sum_{n=1}^{\infty} (A_n + B_n) \int_o^a J_o(k_n r)\, r\, dr = 0 ,$$

there is no liquid force acting on the plate bottom. Therefore the spring support does not affect the slosh motion whatsoever.

In order to complete the study of free oscillations, certain boundary conditions have to be fulfilled. Assuming that the edge of the plate is entirely free, we can write the boundary conditions as follows [6]

$$\int\{(1-\nu)\left[\frac{\partial^2 w}{\partial x^2}\cos^2\alpha + 2\frac{\partial^2 w}{\partial x\partial y}\sin\alpha\cos\alpha + \frac{\partial^2 w}{\partial y^2}\sin^2\alpha\right] + \nu\Delta w\}\frac{\partial\delta w}{\partial\bar{n}}\,ds = 0\,, \tag{20}$$

$$\int\{(1-\nu)\frac{\partial}{\partial s}\left[\left(\frac{\partial^2 w}{\partial x^2} - \frac{\partial^2 w}{\partial y^2}\right)\sin\alpha\cos\alpha - \frac{\partial^2 w}{\partial x\partial y}(\cos^2\alpha - \sin^2\alpha)\right] - \left(\frac{\partial^3 w}{\partial x^3} + \frac{\partial^3 w}{\partial x\partial y^2}\right)\cos\alpha - \left(\frac{\partial^3 w}{\partial y^3} + \frac{\partial^3 w}{\partial x^2\partial y}\right)\sin\alpha\}\delta w\,ds = 0\,, \tag{21}$$

where the integral is extended along the curvilinear boundary of the plate. For a point P of the edge the coordinate axes in the direction of the tangent $\bar{t}$ and the normal $\bar{n}$ are shown in Fig. 2. The operator Δ denotes the Laplacian in (x,y), δw indicates a virtual displacement, and α is the angle between the outer normal and the x-axis. However, $\frac{\partial\delta w}{\partial\bar{n}}$ corresponds to $\delta\left.\frac{\partial\Phi}{\partial r}\right|_{r=a}$, but this quantity certainly has to vanish because of the liquid boundary condition (2) for an impermeable rigid tank wall. Thus the condition (20) is fulfilled.

The second integral (21) yields the boundary condition[2]

$$\frac{d}{dr}\left(\frac{d^2 w}{dr^2} + \frac{1}{r}\frac{dw}{dr}\right)\bigg|_{r=a} = 0\,. \tag{22}$$

It is readily shown that with the coupling condition (4) there results for each n

$$\left[\frac{d}{dr}\left(\frac{d^2}{dr^2} + \frac{1}{r}\frac{d}{dr}\right)J_0(k_n r)\right]_{r=a} = 0\,. \tag{23}$$

Recalling now that k_n is the nth zero of $J_0'(k_n a)$, where the prime denotes differentiation with respect to the argument, and that $J_0(k_n r)$ is a solution of the Bessel differential equation, one verifies that the condition (23) for the free edge of the plate is satisfied.

2. cf. [6], p. 263.

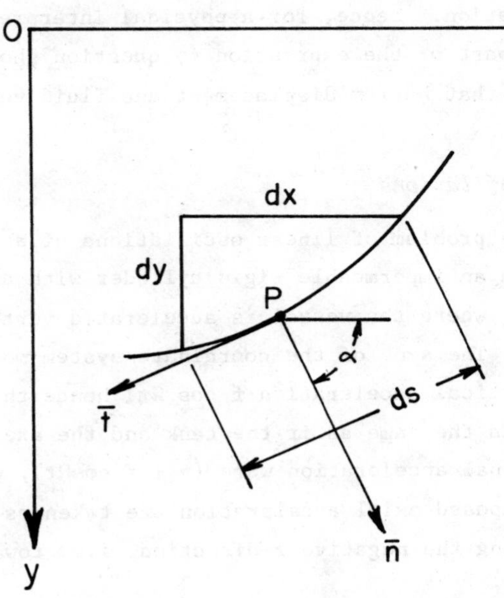

Fig. 2. Sketch of Geometry.

Hence with

$$w(r,t) = W(r)e^{i\omega t} \tag{24}$$

and the coupling condition (4) there follows for the deflection of the bottom

$$W(r) = \frac{1}{i\omega}\frac{\partial\Phi}{\partial z}\bigg|_{z=o} = \frac{i}{\omega}\sum_{n=1}^{\infty}(A_n-B_n)k_n\, J_o(k_n r)\ . \tag{25}$$

For the analysis of the vibration problem it was found convenient to make use of complex notation. Hence, for a physical interpretation of the phenomena the real part of the expression in question should be taken. We thus observe that bottom displacement and fluid velocity are out of phase.

Remarks on Forced Oscillations

We shall discuss now the problem of linear oscillations of a mass of heavy liquid enclosed in an impermeable rigid cylinder with an elastic spring supported bottom, where the vessel is accelerated vertically in simple harmonic motion. The axes of the coordinate system move with the container and with a vertical acceleration f cos Ωt, hence the motion relative to these axes is the same as if the tank and the axes were at rest, and the gravitational acceleration were (g + f cosΩt), where the gravitational and the imposed axial acceleration are taken as positive, if they are directed along the negative z-direction, i.e. toward the tank bottom.

If the deflection and slope of the free surface are small everywhere, the kinematical free surface condition can be linearized to yield

$$\frac{\partial\psi}{\partial z}\bigg|_{z=h} = \frac{\partial\zeta}{\partial t}\ , \tag{26}$$

while the dynamical surface condition leads to

$$\frac{\partial\psi}{\partial t}\bigg|_{z=h} + (g + f\cos\Omega t)\ (h+\zeta) = 0\ . \tag{27}$$

Inasmuch as surface tension and capillary contact effects between liquid and cylinder are ignored, the pressure at the free surface is constant and can be put equal to zero without loss of generality.

A solution of the Laplace equation $\nabla^2\psi = 0$ is posed in the form

$$\psi(r,z,t) = \sum_{n=1}^{\infty} [\dot{a}_n(t)e^{-k_n z} + \dot{b}_n(t)e^{k_n z}]J_0(k_n r) , \tag{28}$$

where the coefficients $a_n(t)$ and $b_n(t)$ are functions of time and a dot denotes differentiation with respect to time. Thus from equation (26) there follows

$$\frac{\partial\zeta}{\partial t} = \sum_{n=1}^{\infty} k_n[\dot{b}_n(t)e^{k_n h} - \dot{a}(t)e^{-k_n h}]J_0(k_n r) \quad , \tag{29}$$

or, after integration,

$$\zeta(r,t) = \sum_{n=1}^{\infty} k_n[b_n(t)e^{k_n h} - a_n(t)e^{-k_n h}]J_0(k_n r) . \tag{30}$$

Since the total volume of the liquid remains constant, an arbitrary function of r as a result of the integration must vanish.

Substitution of equations (28) and (30) into (27) results in

$$e^{-2k_n h}[\ddot{a}_n - (g + f\cos\Omega t)k_n a_n] + \ddot{b}_n + (g + f\cos\Omega t)k_n b_n = 0 \tag{31}$$

for each $n = 1,2,\ldots$ An additive term $(g + f\cos\Omega t)h$ has been omitted since it plays no essential role in the analysis. It could be absorbed either in an arbitrary function of time occurring in the unsteady state Bernoulli equation or by redefinition of the potential function.

For the bottom we obtain from equation (5), with (6a,b), (28) and

$$w(r,t) = \sum_{n=1}^{\infty} [b_n(t) - a_n(t)]k_n J_0(k_n r) , \tag{32}$$

where the coupling condition (4) has been applied, after a few steps of standard calculations

$$\left(\frac{\rho}{D} + \frac{\overline{\rho h}}{D}k_n\right)\ddot{a}_n + \left(k_n^5 + \frac{kk_n}{D}\right)a_n + \left(\frac{\rho}{D} - \frac{\overline{\rho h}}{D}k_n\right)\ddot{b}_n$$

$$- \left(k_n^5 + \frac{kk_n}{D}\right)b_n = 0 , \qquad n = 1,2,\ldots \quad . \tag{33}$$

Equations (31) and (33) represent a coupled system of differential equations of second order. The solution together with the Ince-Strutt stability chart for the Mathieu equation determines whether the motion of the free surface is stable.

It is, of course, of interest to study the case $D \to \infty$, i.e. the circular cylindrical tank with a rigid plane floor. Then from equation (33) there follows $a_n = b_n$, and hence from equation (31)

$$\ddot{a}_n + k_n \tanh k_n h \, (g + f \cos \Omega t) a_n = 0, \quad n = 1,2,\ldots \,. \tag{34}$$

With $T = \frac{1}{2}\Omega t$ and parameters

$$\gamma_n = \frac{4k_n g \tanh k_n h}{\Omega^2}, \qquad \delta_n = -\frac{2k_n f \tanh k_n h}{\Omega^2}$$

equation (34) can be transformed into

$$\frac{d^2 a_n}{dT^2} + (\gamma_n - 2\delta_n \cos 2T) a_n = 0, \tag{36}$$

which is the standard form of Mathieu's equation and discussed in detail by Benjamin and Ursell [7]. If we put f equal to zero (36) takes the form of the equation of simple harmonic motion corresponding to free oscillations of the liquid with a frequency of $(\frac{1}{2}\pi)(k_n g \tan k_n h)^{1/2}$.

Numerical Examples

In order to draw conclusions from the analytical findings of this study, a few numerical examples have been worked out. We took the liquid as water (ρ = 1000 kg/m^3). The radius of the tank was assumed to be 5m, the height of the undisturbed liquid column 1m. In the first example (Table 1) we considered the limiting case $D \to o$, $\bar{\rho} \to o$ and varied the values of the spring constant. With $g = 9.81$ m/sec^2, $k_1 = 3.832/a = 0.7664$ [1/m], $k_2 = 7.0156/a = 1.4031$[1/m], the results obtained from equation (18) show that with increasing spring stiffness the frequencies increase also and approach the respective values for the rigid tank ($\omega_1 = 2.202$, $\omega_2 = 3.492$). In the second example (Table 2) the spring constant was held constant and the plate stiffness was varied. For the sake of simplicity small terms $\bar{\rho}\bar{h}/D$ occurrring in equation (17) were neglected. As the reported numerical data as computed from (17) indicate, there is, for increasing plate stiffness, an increase in the frequencies also and their values again tend toward the respective values for a rigid tank.

It thus follows that a flexible bottom (elastic thin plate) supported by an elastic foundation (springs) lowers the frequencies of the sloshing liquid as compared with their respective values in a rigid container.

TABLE 1

Natural Frequencies in Cycles Per Second for Tank With Completely Flexible Floor Supported by Springs

k[N/m]	ω_1	ω_2
10^5	2.139	3.453
2×10^5	2.170	3.473
4×10^5	2.186	3.483

TABLE 2

Natural Frequencies in Cycles Per Second for Tank With Plate Bottom Supported by Springs ($k = 10^5$ N/m)

D[Nm]	ω_1	ω_2
10^5	2.155	3.484
2×10^5	2.165	3.487
4×10^5	2.175	3.490
∞	2.202	3.492

ACKNOWLEDGMENT

This work was supported in part under National Aeronautics and Space Administration Grant No. NsG-657 to the Georgia Institute of Technology.

REFERENCES

1. Moiseev, N. N., "Introduction to the Theory of Oscillations of Liquid-Containing Bodies," Advances in Applied Mechanics, Edited by H. L. Dryden and Th. v. Kármán, Vol. 8, Academic Press, New York, 1964, pp. 233-289.

2. Moiseev, N. N., and Petrov, A. A., "The Calculation of Free Oxcillations of a Liquid in a Motionless Container," Advances in Applied Mechanics, Edited by G. Chernyi et al., Vol. 9, Academic Press, New York, 1966, pp. 91-154.

3. Abramson, N. H. (ed.), "The Dynamic Behavior of Liquids in Moving Containers," NASA SP-106, Washington, D. C., 1966.

4. Rapoport, I. M., Dynamics of Elastic Containers Partially Filled with Liquid, Applied Physics and Engineering, Vol. 5, New York, 1968.

5. Siekmann, J., and Chang Shih-Chih, "On Liquid Sloshing in a Cylindrical Tank with a Flexible Bottom Under Strong Capillary and Weak Gravity Conditions," The Journal of the Astronautical Sciences, Vol. 14, No. 4, pp. 167-172, July-Aug. 1967.

6. Timoshenko, S., Woinowsky-Krieger, S., Theory of Plates and Shells, Second Edition, MeGraw Hill, New York, 1959, p. 91.

7. Benjamin, T. B., and Ursell, F., "The Stability of the Plane Free Surface of a Liquid in Vertical Periodic Motion," Proc. Roy. Soc. Series A, Vol. 225, 1954, pp. 505-515.

INVITED LECTURE

CANCER: AN UNSTABLE BIODYNAMIC FIELD

Okan Gurel
IBM New York Scientific Center

ABSTRACT

Dynamics of a cancerous cell is discussed in two parts; cellular level and molecular level. In the first part, some experimental observations which form the motivation are discussed. Stability theory of dynamical systems is mentioned, and the unexpected biodynamic field around an individual cancerous cell is introduced. Certain additional experimental results are also mentioned. In the second part, a search for the cause of this biodynamic field is explored. In connection with this, some structural properties of the biological macromolecules are discussed. In the final section, the concept of weak topology leads to the main proposition for malignant state.

INTRODUCTION

In this article we will report some of the recent developments in the course of exploring the dynamic behavior of cells of abnormal nature. The discussion will be divided into two main parts: (a) Cellular level, (b) Molecular Level.

A. Cellular Level

(1) Some Experimental Observations as Motivation [*1*] / In his experiments, Sherwin has made some interesting observations which he labeled as "phenomena" implying that they were strange happenings with no obvious explanations. These experiments were carried out with human pulmonary carcinoma resected and explanted in vitro, and all the observations were at a cellular level. The relationship between these observations and some of the concepts from the stability theory of dynamical

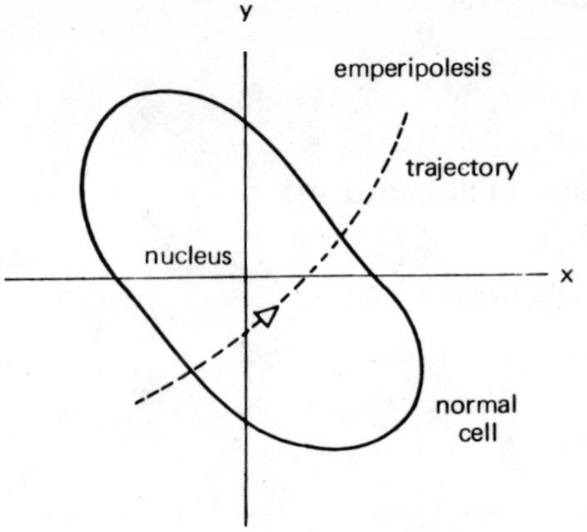

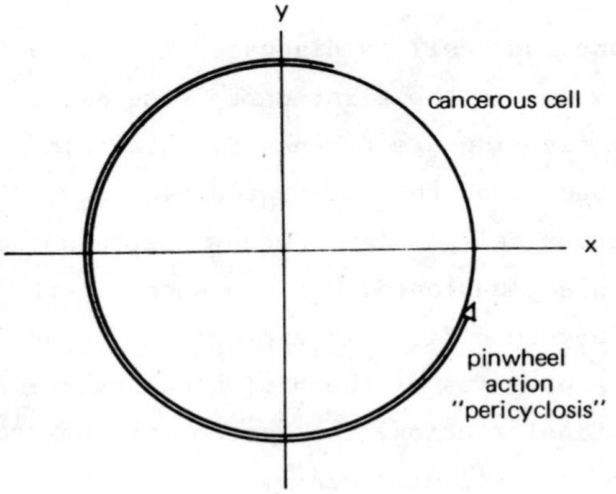

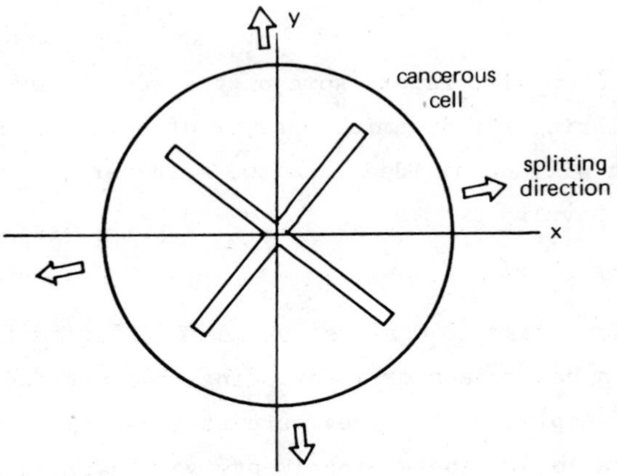

Fig. 1. Emperipolesis.

Fig. 2. Pericyclosis.

Fig. 3. Mitosis.

systems may, at first, seem to be remote. However, a detailed description of Sherwin's observations may prove convincing. Here are the highlights of Sherwin's observations.

(1) Emperipolesis. This is the motion of the ameboid lymphocyte moving in the intercellular fluid reaching, entering, and later leaving a normal cell, Figure 1.

(2) Migration toward and Congregation. Lymphocytes migrate toward certain cells resulting in clustering around these "target" cells.

(3) Migration away and Pericyclosis. Lymphocytes migrate away from cancerous cells; in certain cases a motion involving pinwheeling action (rotation) of the peripheral portion (outside rim) of the cytoplasm is observed; this is called pericyclosis, Figure 2.

(4) Mitosis. Cancerous cells eventually shatter eratically and thus multiply, Figure 3.

These observations made by phase photomicromography clearly indicate that they must be related to certain dynamical concepts.

(2) Stability of Dynamical Systems [1] / Stability theory of differential equations describing a dynamical system is well established. Its application to the problems from various fields have also been flourished. The basis of the theory is the study of singular solutions of the differential equations. A singular point, satisfying the equations of a dynamical system is a solution of the system. Moreover, while a regular point is an element of a single trajectory, a set of regular points, a singular point belongs to more than one trajectory, it is in fact an accumulation point of all those trajectories.

In a two dimensional system, the governing differential equations are expressed as $\dot{x} = dx/dt = P(x,y)$ and $\dot{y} = dy/dt = Q(x,y)$ where P and Q are nonlinear functions of the two independent variables x and y, and t is the time element.

The singular point corresponds to the solution of $P(x,y) = Q(x,y) = 0$. The two basic classes of singular points are stable singular points and unstable singular points. Trajectories in the neighborhood of a stable point approach it while those around an unstable point run away from it.

If it exists, a closed trajectory, a limit cycle, surrounds a singular point and is stable (or unstable) from the inside as well as from the outside, Figure 4.

(3) An Unexpected Biodynamic Field [*1*] / Observing the dynamics involved in the experiments conducted and reported by Sherwin and keeping in mind the already developed theory of stability, one can reach certain conclusions and try to understand their further implications and the causes behind them.

We should picture two different activities quite distinct from each other.

(1) The normal activities of a cell in performing its physiological functions.

(2) The abnormal activities of a cancerous cell which not only differ from those activities of a normal cell but also are in addition to them.

In fact, emperipolesis is explained as a part of activity of a normal cell. The influence of the cell, on the lymphocytes and other substances is of a normal nature. A trajectory followed by a lymphocyte for example is a regular one. On the other hand, migration toward a cell indicates the existence of a bundle of trajectories merging together at certain points thus implies a "sink" in the system, which is a stable point.

The significant observation is the repelled lymphocytes implying the existence of a "source" in the region of that particular cancerous cell.

Then, we can conclude that:

(1) A dynamic field must exist in the volume in which a cancerous cell lies.

(2) The effect of this field is detected by observing the motion of particles and lymphocytes which enter the influence region of this field.

(3) The cause of this "individual" field in and around an individual cell must lie in the field itself.

This dynamic field appearing in a biological environment can be named as a biodynamic field. Characteristics of the field are:

(i) It is localized around each individual cancerous cell.

(ii) It has an unstable singular point, possibly located in an area corresponding to the nucleus of the particular cell.

(iii) The biodynamic field may be expected to exhibit various forms of instabilities.

An important remark must be made here. The very nature of this dynamic field being an additional field, it should not be confused with the general dynamics of a cell, and it exists as a by-product of the abnormalities of the cell, thus wherever the cell goes this additional field moves with it. A simple analogy can be made as the gravitational field of each planet moving together with that particular planet.

(4) Implications of the Biodynamic Field: Additional Results [2,3] / The existence of the biodynamic field as described above has certain further implications. Knowing that this dynamical field is of an unstable nature, we expect to observe different possibilities of instabilities. In addition to a singular point with spiraling trajectories around it, Figure 4a, we can expect it with also limit cylces, Figure 4b. This, in fact, is the mathematical model of the phenomenon observed and named by Sherwin as pericyclosis. It is well known that a limit cycle can be stable or unstable from the inside and outside. The pericyclosis corresponds to a limit cycle stable from the inside and unstable from the outside, Figure 4b.

An additional important class of unstable points are that of saddle points, Figure 5. In this case there are a finite number of separatrices; accepting the singular point as a limiting point and depending on the trajectories between them they may be of the following three types: elliptic, hyperbolic, parabolic [2]. An example of this prediction is given by Cone [2]. Independently from Sherwin, Cone observed the following phenomena:

(1) In experiments with the sarcoma cells, it is observed that the cells were as being attached to each other by linking bridges, which Cone named cytopons, Figure 6a.

(2) During the period of mitosis one cell trigers the mitosis of the other chain-linked cells. This mitotic stimulus is illustrated in Figure 6b.

An explanation of these phenomena can be given in terms of the existence of biodynamic field which exhibits behavior of a saddle point.

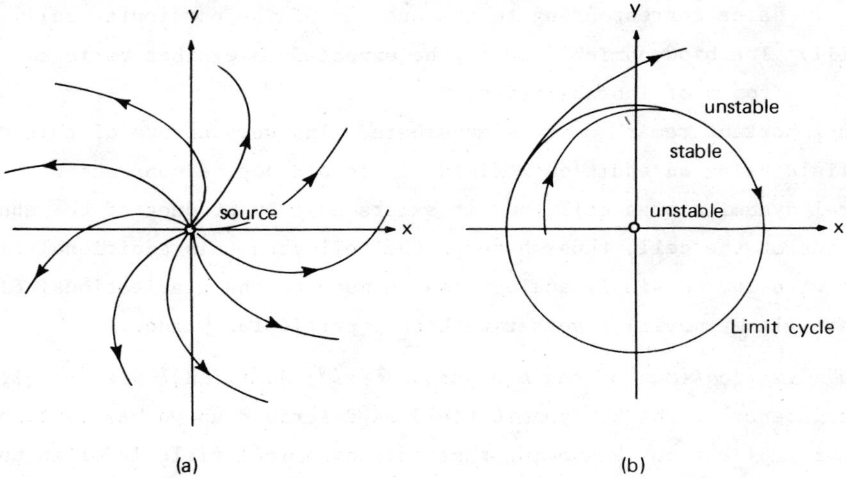

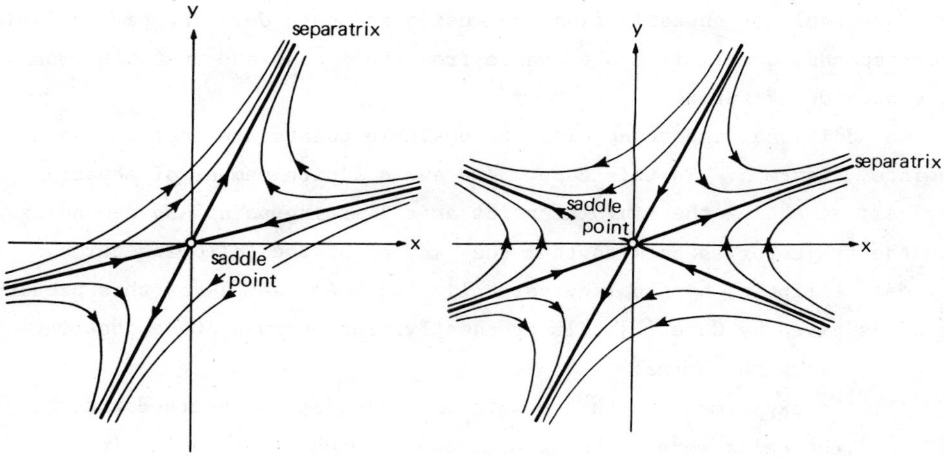

Fig. 4. (a) Stable Singular Point (b) Unstable Singular Point.
Fig. 5. Saddle Points.

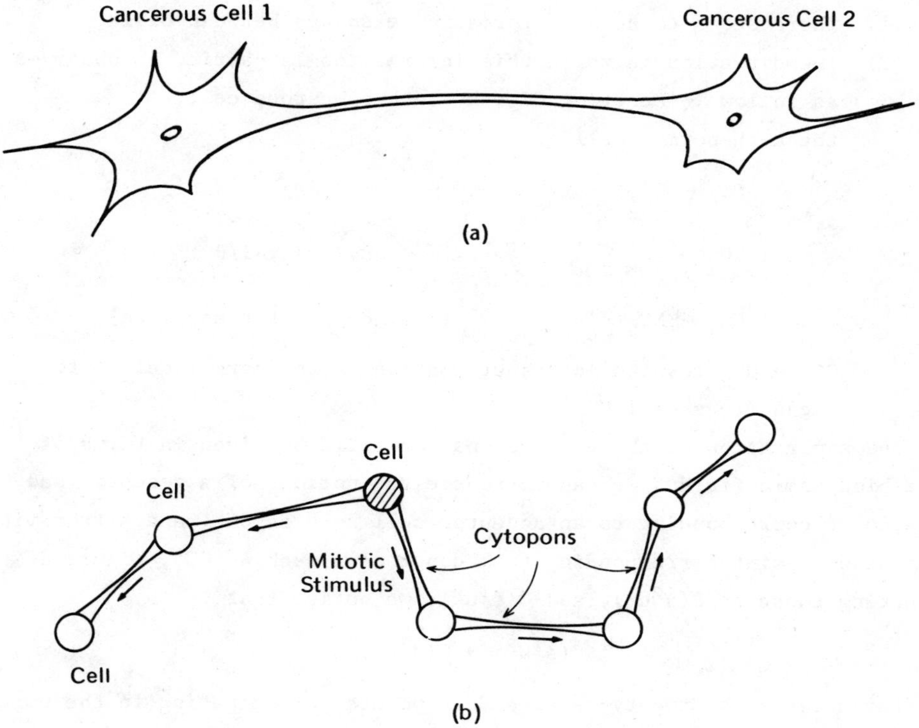

Fig. 6. (a) Cytopons (b) Mitosis.

The experimentally observed cells in sketch form and the corresponding mathematical model showing individual dynamic fields around each cell are illustrated in Figure 7.

Yet another set of independent studies has been conducted by Bendich and his associates [3]. The highlights of these observations are:

(1) There seems to be an information exchange between cells.

(2) The direction in which this information is carried is observed as follows. Denoting CC_i the i-th cancerous cell, NC_k the k-th normal cell

$$CC_i \rightarrow CC_j \qquad i \neq j$$

$$CC_i \rightarrow NC_k \qquad \text{obviously } i \neq k$$

$$CC_i \not\leftarrow NC_k \qquad \text{(i.e. does not take place)}$$

$CC_i \rightarrow NC_k$ results in transformation of the normal cell into a cancerous cell CC_k.

The explanation of these phenomena can still be given in terms of the biodynamic field. We can introduce the notions of a receptor saddle point corresponding to an acceptor cell such as CC_j, and a transmitter saddle point corresponding to a donor cell such as CC_i, Figure 8. Denoting these as $C(s^2u^1)$, and $C(s^1u^2)$, we notice that

$$C(s^1u^2) \rightarrow C(s^2u^1)$$

differentiates the two types of saddle points participating in the emitting and receiving ends of a separatrix. It may be asserted that the triggering-like spontaneous information exchange is achieved by the motion of an atomic element "funneled" through a separatrix in the above defined direction. Otherwise the information exchange between nuclei, as reported by Bendich may be provided by the motion of a molecular element through the separatrix joining them (e.g. a DNA molecule). Transformation is then the absorption of this information not by another cancerous cell, but by a normal cell.

B. Molecular Level

(5) Cause of the Biodynamic Field [3] / The experimental results which were interpreted to point out the existence of an unstable biodynamic field in and around an individual cancerous cell are not

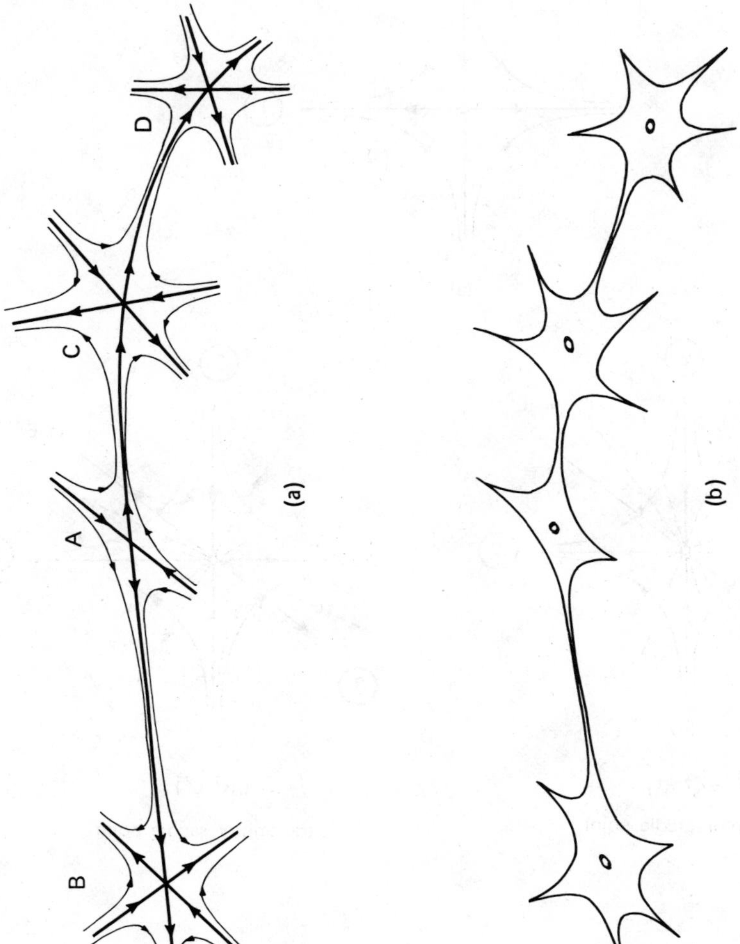

Fig. 7. Biodynamic Field.

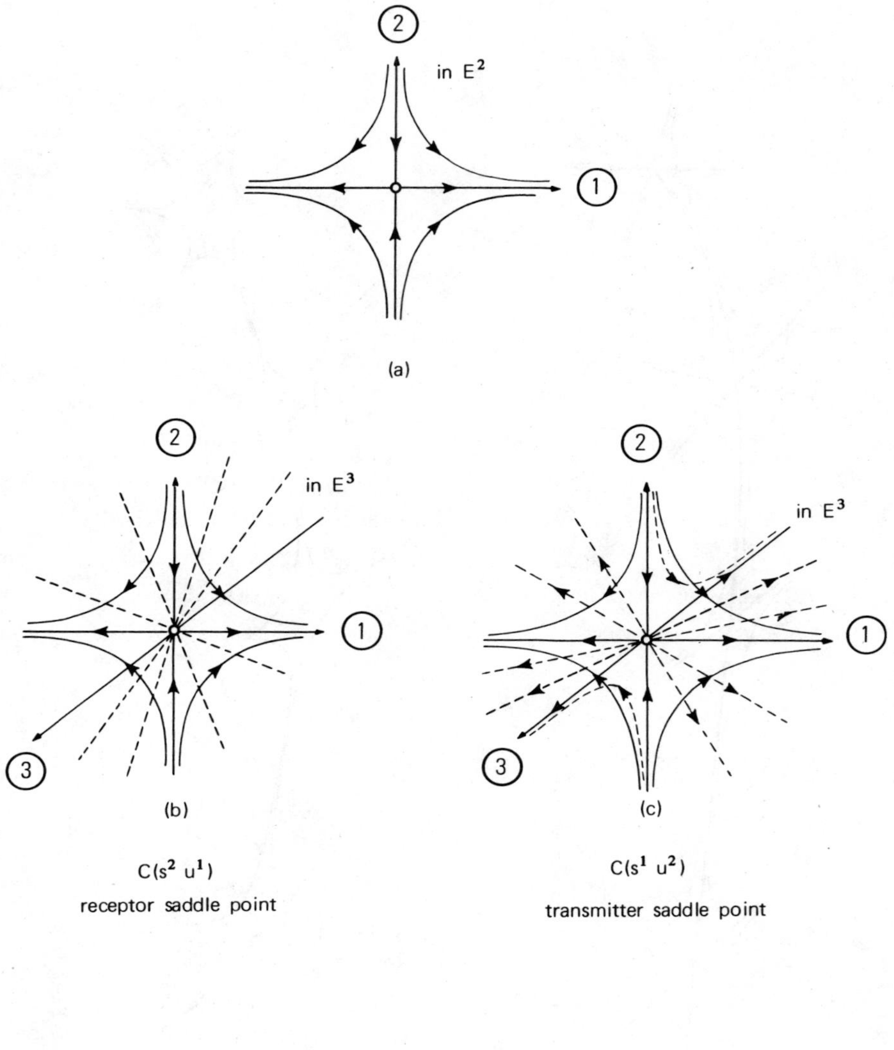

Fig. 8. Biodynamic Field Saddle Points.

sufficient for explaining the cause of the field. The basic reason behind this is that

(i) the observations related to the biodynamic field are at a cellular (cytologic) level,

(ii) the cause of this field may probably lie at a molecular (chemical) level.

In order to pursue in this direction the following steps will be taken. In order to justify the existence of a dynamic field, we must consider the concepts of mass, force and accleleration. To derive the differential equations governing the motion pattern of a particle lying in the created biodynamic field, we can refer to the consideration of energy levels corresponding to the malignant state.

Let us assume that the kinetic energy T and the potential energy V involved in the problem are known. If the energy $E = T + V$ is increased by an additional incoming energy supplied from outside ΔE, this corresponds similarly to the change in kinetic energy ΔT and the change in the potential energy ΔV. For the purpose of illustration, we give Figure 9 where an energy absorber illustrates a storage for ΔV. The basic energy of the system is used up for the physiological functions of the cell. Over and above this, there is now ΔE composed of ΔT and ΔV. The Lagrangian is formed for these additional terms as

$$L = \Delta T - \Delta V \quad .$$

Minimizing the integral $\int L\,dt$ between the time limits t_i (initial) and t_f(final), we arrive at the well known result from the calculus of variations as

$$\frac{\partial L}{\partial x} - \frac{d}{dt}\,\frac{\partial L}{\partial \dot{x}} = 0$$

where $L = \Delta T - \Delta V = m\dot{x}^2/2 - V$, thus

$$\ddot{x} = -m^{-1}\,\frac{\Delta V}{x}$$

Here m is of course the mass of a particle in the influence area of the biodynamic field created by the potential ΔV, and the acceleration of that particle is a linear function of the gradient of the potential energy. If an unstable point at the nucleus of the cell is expected, then this implies $\partial \Delta V/\partial x < 0$ should be involved.

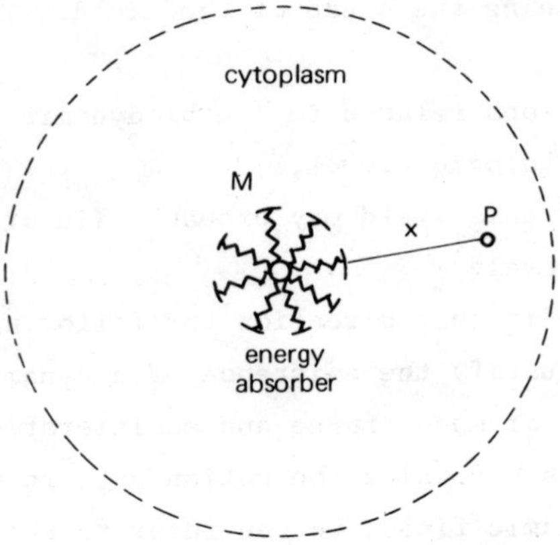

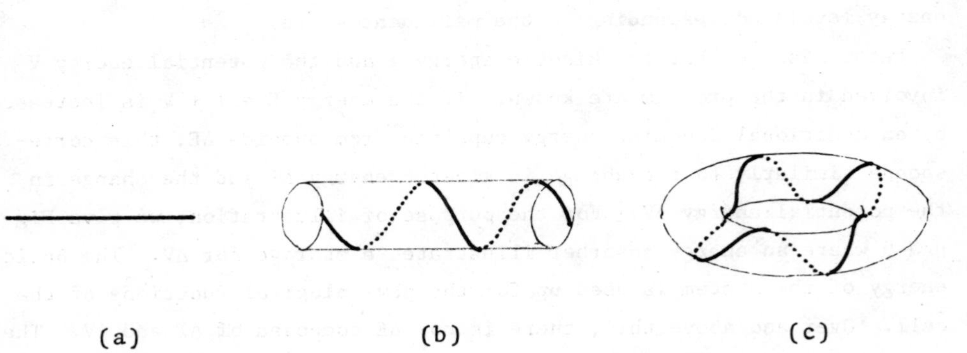

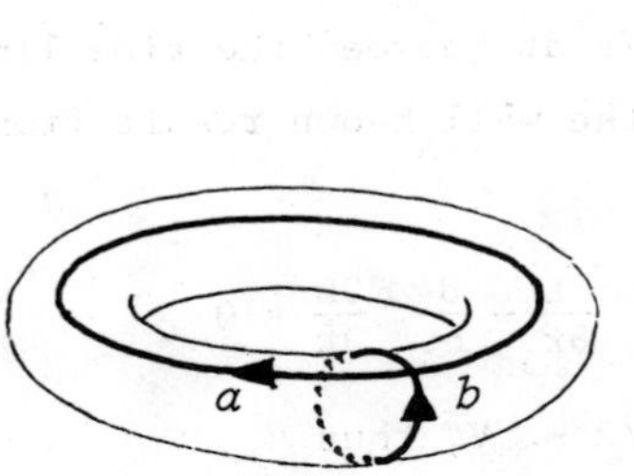

Fig. 9. Cell as Energy Absorber.

Fig. 10. (a) Primary Structure of Molecule.
(b) Secondary Structure of Molecule.
(c) Tertiary Structure of Molecule.

Fig. 11. Quaternary Structure of Molecule.

(6) Some Structural Orders in Biological Macromolecules [4] / After introducing the concept of a biodynamic field, discussion of the necessity of an additional potential energy was in order. Next comes the question of how this may be achieved in the biological system such as the malignant cell. For this, it seems that one must study the components of the cell, namely various biochemical macromolecules constituting the cell, and performing certain physiological functions. To achieve the goal of physiological functioning, the macromolecules must take part in certain chemical reactions. Mechanisms for most of these reactions are unraveled by biochemists, however, the story is certainly not yet completed. Here we will recapitulate these experimental findings in a formal setting for the purpose of using them as a stepping stone for further discussion.

The biological macromolecules such as DNA, RNA, and various proteins exhibit the following basic structure:

(a) They are composed as a linear sequence of a finite number of building blocks. In the case of DNA, there are four bases; in that of proteins, twenty amino acids are the building blocks.

(b) The chain of linearly sequenced building blocks then form a specific geometric configuration such as a helix.

(c) The folding of the helical or remaining sections about themselves also takes place.

(d) In some cases various portions of the same macromolecule are homologous (equivalent).

These four items, in fact, are named as the (1) primary structure, (2) secondary structure, (3) tertiary structure, (4) quaternary structure of the molecules. All molecules obviously are placed in a three dimensional euclidean space E^3. The following notation will be introduced for these structures, Figure 10a,b,c.

(1) $L(\ell)$ indicates the primary structure where l is the coordinate describing the sequence.

(2) $H^i(d,p)$ indicates the secondary structure where d and p are the diameter and the pitch of the helix respectively. The superscript i indicates a single stranded (i=1) and double stranded (i=2) helix.

(3) T(m,n) indicates the tertiary structure as being topologically equivalent to a torus, and m is the parameter corresponding to the number of turns around the torus in the sense of a, and represents the parameter corresponding to the number of turns around the torus in the sense of b, Figure 11.

For the quaternary structure, especially significant in functioning of enzymes, one must either take a single torus or a combination of tori. However, this structure is related more to the physiological function of the enzyme than to its structural characteristics.

On these three structures, we can define transformations altering the structure, which however may not necessarily affect the physiological functions of the molecules. These transformations will be denoted as ϕ_L, ϕ_H^i, and ϕ_T, such that

$$\phi_L: L(\ell) \rightarrow L(\ell')$$

$$\phi_H^i: H^i(d,p) \rightarrow H^i(d',p')$$

$$\phi_T: T(m,n) \rightarrow T(m',n')$$

where the primed parameters are those corresponding to the transformed states. In biological terms, there are examples of each of these transformations. ϕ_L is called in general mutation; while intercalation is an example of ϕ_H^i. Vinograd and his associates at the California Institute of Technology have discovered a number of transformations which can be classified as ϕ_T and are known as chemical topology (topological chemical bonds), Figure 12.

In a number of cases, these transformations are related to cancerous states, implying that if ℓ, d, p, m, n are the parameters at a normal state of a molecule, one or combinations of the parameters ℓ', d', p', m', and n' may indicate a malignant state.

(7) The Concept of Weak Topology [5] / Further relationship between the macromolecules in a living cell and the dynamic field representing the malignancy of this cell can be formed by introducing the concept of weak topology. For this we consider a space of energies, V_a corresponding to the space of molecules, B.

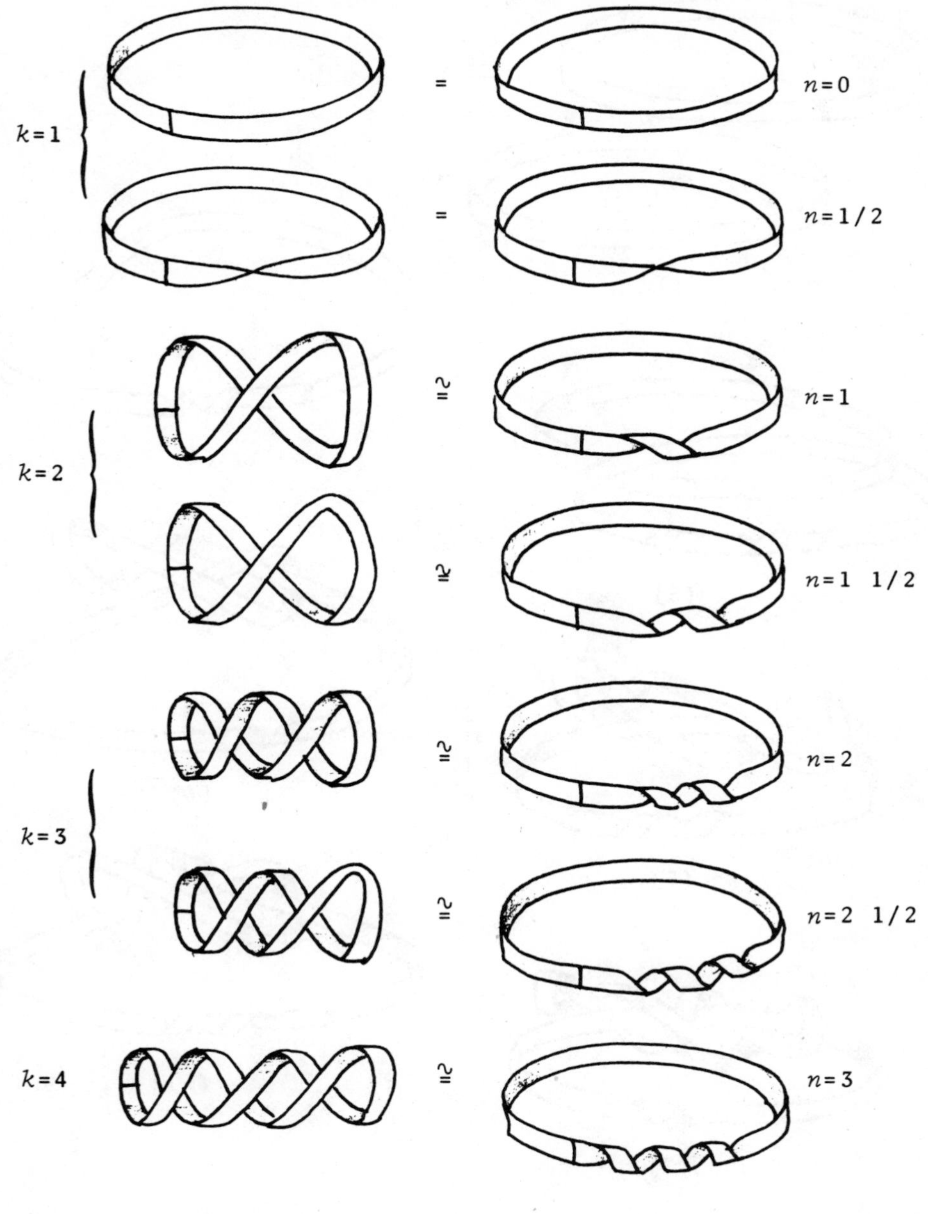

Fig. 12a. Topological Chemical Bonds.

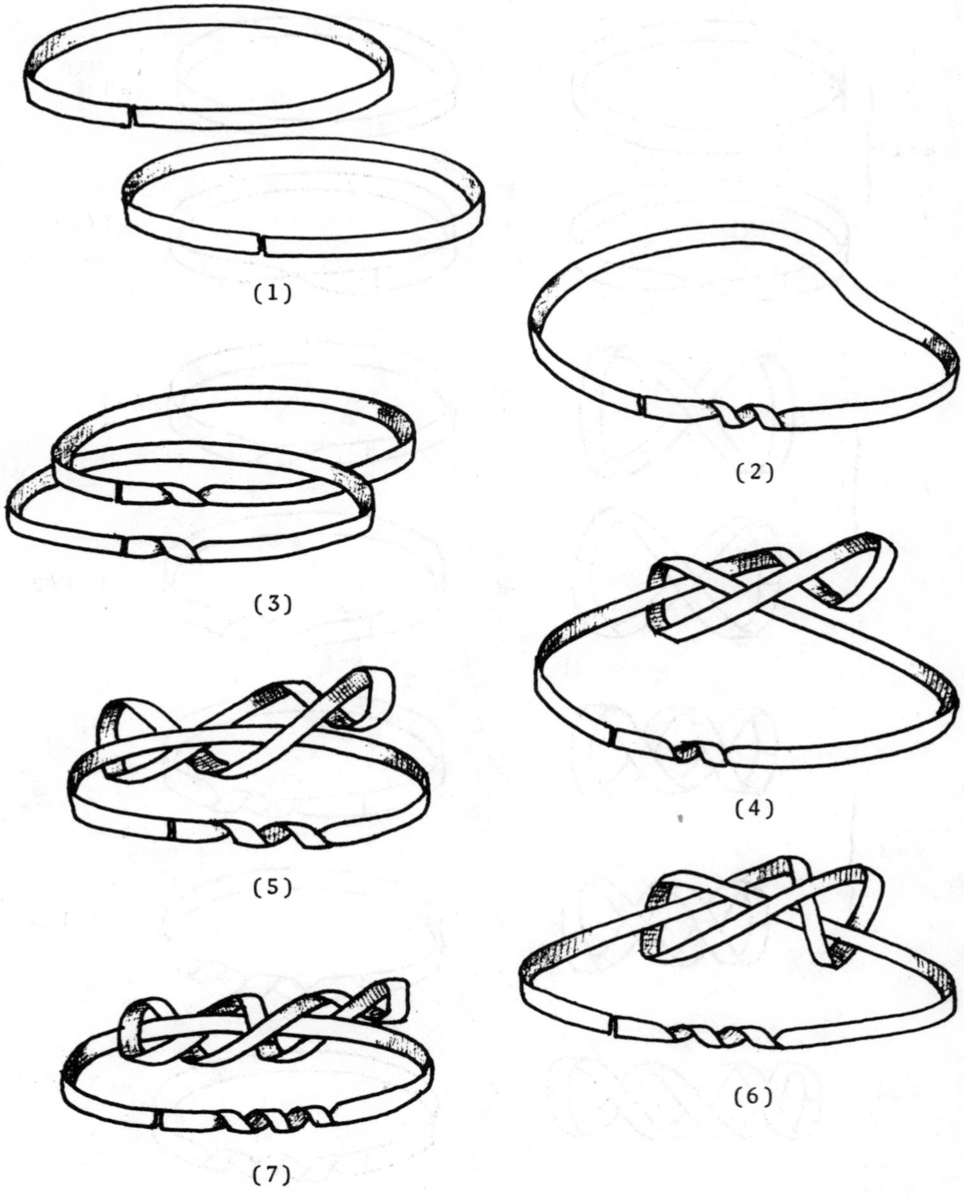

Fig. 12b. Topological Chemical Bonds.

One way of defining a topology in B is done by considering a family of functions $\{f_a\}$ on B with values each in its topological space V_a. A basis in B is all possible intersections of a finite number of sets $f^{-1}\{U_a\}$ where U_a are open sets in V_a. The topology on B defined by this basis will be called the weak topology on B defined by the family of functions $\{f_a\}$ and denoted by $\sigma(B, V_a)$. Then the following complementarity principle is stated:

> Complementarity Principle. The complementarity between the spaces B and V_a is defined by the weak topology $\sigma(B, V_a)$.

By studying various properties of the energy space V_a, we can arrive at certain conclusions on the space B. The space V_a is considered as a product topological space as $V_a = \pi_i V_i$, where V_i, i=1,2,... are topological spaces. The topology of V_a is defined by the projections $\pi_i: V_a \rightarrow V_i$. Considering V_i as the bond energies, say between two atoms, V_i can be expressed in terms of the distance between the two atoms as shown in Figure 13. The derivative of V_i with respect to the interatomic distance will be denoted by DV_i, thus the three important subspaces of the space V_i are

(1) H^+ corresponding to $DV_i > 0$,
(2) H^- corresponding to $DV_i < 0$,
(3) H° corresponding to $DV_i = 0$.

These properties are carried over to the product space.

Defining the set corresponding to the DNA molecules by B_1 and denoting $B_1{}^1$, $B_1{}^2$, and $B_1{}^3$ as the primary, secondary, and tertiary structures of B_1, we can note that

$$\sigma(B_1{}^1, V_a)$$
$$\sigma(B_1{}^2, V_a)$$
$$\sigma(B_1{}^3, V_a)$$

can be defined as corresponding weak topologies. In addition, for all proteins B_k, k=2,3,..., we can define similar weak topologies.

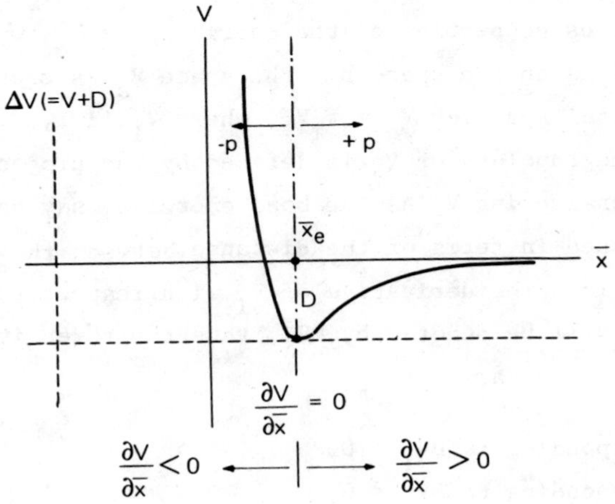

Fig. 13. Bond Energies.

An equilibrium state in B_1 (or in B_k, for k=2,3,...) can be achieved by minimizing

$$\sum_{B_1} \{f_a\} \quad (\text{or } \sum_{B_k} \{f_a\} \text{ for } k-2,3,\ldots)$$

This corresponds to H^o of the representative energy space.

Variations in the structure of B_k may correspond to either H^+ or H^-. Referring to the result derived in Section 5 above, the following proposition can be stated:

> Proposition. A cancerous state corresponds to a variation belonging to the set H^-.

REFERENCES

1. Gurel, Okan, "Dynamics of Cancerous Cells," Cancer, Vol. 23, No. 2, February, 1969, pp. 497-505.

2. Gurel, Okan, "Qualitative Study of Unstable Behavior of Cancerous Cells," Cancer, Vol. 24, No. 5, November, 1969, pp. 945-947.

3. Gurel, Okan, "Unstable Dynamic Field of an Individual Cancerous Cell," Physiol. Chem. Physics 2, 1970, pp. 570-580. Presented at the 10th International Cancer Congress, May 22-29, 1970, Houston, Texas.

4. Gurel, Okan, "Topological Classification of Certain Biological Macromolecules," To appear in Physiol. Chem. Physics, and presented at the 3rd International Biophysical Congress (IUPAB), August 29 - September 3, 1969, Cambridge, Massachusetts.

5. Gurel, Okan, "Fundamental Weak Topologies in Living Systems," IBM New York Scientific Center Technical Report No. 320-2983, March, 1970. To appear in Physiol. Chem. Physics.

B I O M E C H A N I C S

FORCED AXISYMMETRIC RESPONSE OF FLUID FILLED SPHERICAL SHELLS

Yu Chung Lee
West Virginia University

Sunder H. Advani
West Virginia University

ABSTRACT

A general solution for the forced, linear axisymmetric response of a fluid filled spherical shell is derived with the effects of shell transverse shear and rotational inertia included. The fluid is assumed to be inviscid and compressible. Expressions for the shell radial displacement are computed for the problem of a uniform radial Heaviside load on a cap of the shell surface. In addition, the time history of the shell inner fiber stresses at the impact pole is obtained. Some comparisons with the <u>in vacuo</u> shell theory are also given.

LIST OF NOTATIONS

a	Inner shell radius of curvature
a_{jk}	Constants in orthogonality relation
A_{nm}	Modal constants
$c_s=[E/\rho(1-\nu^2)]^{\frac{1}{2}}$	Shell wave speed
c_f	Fluid compressional velocity
E	Young's modulus
h	Shell thickness
$i=(-1)^{\frac{1}{2}}$	Imaginary unit
$j_n(\ )$	Spherical Bessel function
$\varepsilon=h^2/12R^2$	Shell thickness parameter

$k_1 = 1 + \varepsilon$	Shell translational inertia constant
$k_r = 1 + 1.8\varepsilon$	Shell rotational inertia constant
k_s	Averaging shear coefficient
$K_s = 2k_s/(1-\nu)$	Modified averaging shear coefficient
m_θ	External moment intensity
M_θ, M_ϕ	Stress couple resultants
n	Mode number
N_θ, N_ϕ	Stress resultants
$p_\theta = \bar{p}_{,\theta}$	External Tangential Load Intensity
$P_n()$, $P_n^1()$	Legendre function and associated Legendre function of order one respectively
q	External radial load intensity
Q_θ	Transverse shear stress resultant
r, θ, ϕ	Spherical co-ordinates
R	Radius of curvature of shell mid-surface
t	Time
u,w	Meridional and radial displacements of shell mid-surface respectively
α_{nm}	Radial load modifying coefficient
ρ, ρ_f	Shell and fluid mass densities respectively
ψ_θ	Mean rotation angle originally normal to shell mid-surface
Φ	Fluid potential function
$\zeta(r)$	Radial function describing fluid potential
Ω_{nm}	Shell frequencies
γ_{nm}	Fluid added mass constants
ν	Poisson's ratio
$\kappa^2 = \frac{1}{k_s}$	Shear coefficient
$\tau_{\theta\theta}$, $\tau_{\phi\phi}$	Shell fiber stresses
$\nabla^2(\,)$	$= \frac{1}{r^2}\frac{\partial}{\partial r}(r^2 \frac{\partial}{\partial r}) + \frac{1}{r^2 \sin\theta}\frac{\partial}{\partial\theta}(\sin\theta \frac{\partial}{\partial\theta})$
∇_1^2	$= \frac{\partial^2}{\partial\theta^2} + \cot\theta \frac{\partial}{\partial\theta}$
$\partial_t^2 = \frac{R^2}{c_s^2}\frac{\partial^2}{\partial t^2}$	Non-dimensional differential operator
$(\,)_{,\alpha}$	$= \frac{\partial}{\partial\alpha}(\,)$

$(\dot{\ })$ Differentiation with respect to time

INTRODUCTION

The earliest dynamic theory of elastic in vacuo spherical shells including the effects of both bending and stretching is due to Love [1]. Subsequent research on free or forced response of complete spherical shells includes investigations by Nagdhi and Kalnins [2], Kalnins [3], Prasad [4], Baker, et al [5], and Vekslar and Nigul [6]. The effects of fluid coupling on shell vibration frequencies have received considerable attention. Studies on external and/or internal fluid shell interaction have been conducted by Junger [7], Gontkevich [8], Rand and DiMaggio [9], and Sonstegard [10]. Recently, Engin [11] using Laplace transformations has obtained response solutions for fluid filled spherical shells subjected to an axisymmetric radial Dirac load. His solutions ignore transverse shear and rotational inertia effects (elementary theory).

This paper examines the forced axisymmetric response of moderately thick elastic spherical shells completely filled with an inviscid compressible fluid. The retention of transverse shear and rotational inertia effects in the governing equations is based on the premise that the elementary theory results are in error when the forced shell wave length magnitudes are comparable to the shell thickness. The response solutions, obtained by the mode superposition method, are numerically illustrated for a uniform radial Heaviside load on a cap of the shell surface. The rationale for this investigation stems from its applicability as a preliminary impact model of the human head.

Equations Governing Shell Motion

The governing equations of motion and natural boundary conditions for an elastic spherical shell completely filled with an inviscid compressible fluid can be derived by use of Hamilton's principle. In employing this variational formulation, we consider the energy associated with the shell-fluid interaction, the strain and kinetic energies of the deformed shell, and the work due to the external force and moment intensities on the shell. The analysis presented here includes the effects of shell transverse shear and rotational inertia. However, we introduce the following simplifying assumptions: (a) the shell is taken to be axisymmetrically loaded and deformed, (b) the meridional displacement term is neglected in the transverse shear resultant expression, (c) the transverse shear resultant term is ignored in the membrane equation, and (d) meridional inertia is neglected in the moment equations. With these considerations, the equations of motion become

$$N_{\theta,\theta} + (N_\theta - N_\phi)\cot\theta = \rho hRk_1\ddot{u} - Rp_\theta \tag{1}$$

$$Q_{\theta.\theta} + Q_\theta \cot\theta - (N_\theta + N_\phi) = \rho hRk_1\ddot{w} - Rq + \rho_f\, R\left(1-\frac{h}{2R}\right)\dot{\Phi}\,(a,\theta,t) \tag{2}$$

$$M_{\theta,\theta} + (M_\theta - M_\phi)\cot\theta - RQ_\theta = \rho\varepsilon hR^3 k_r\ddot{\psi}_\theta - Rm_\theta \tag{3}$$

where the stress and stress couple resultants are defined by

$$\begin{aligned}
N_\theta &= \frac{Eh}{(1-\nu^2)R}\,[u,_\theta + w + \nu(u\cot\theta + w)] \\
N_\phi &= \frac{Eh}{(1-\nu^2)R}\,[\nu(u,_\theta + w) + u\cot\theta + w] \\
Q_\theta &= \frac{Eh}{2(1+\nu)k_s}\,\left(\psi,_\theta + \frac{w,_\theta}{R}\right) \\
M_\theta &= \frac{Eh^3}{12(1-\nu^2)R}\,(\psi_{\theta,\theta} + \nu\psi_\theta\cot\theta) \\
M_\phi &= \frac{Eh^3}{12(1-\nu^2)R}\,(\nu\psi_{\theta,\theta} + \psi_\theta\cot\theta)
\end{aligned} \tag{4}$$

The axisymmetric fluid velocity potential function $\Phi(r,\theta,t)$ in Eq. 2 is governed by the wave equation

$$\nabla^2\Phi = \ddot{\Phi}/c_f^2 \tag{5}$$

In addition, we impose the velocity boundary condition at the fluid-shell interface

$$\Phi,_r\big|_{r=a} = \dot{w} \tag{6}$$

Referring to Eqs. (2), (5), and (6), we assume Φ to be separable in the form

$$\phi(r,\theta,t) = \zeta(r)\,\overline{\phi}\,(\theta,t) \tag{7}$$

As a result, the interface condition (6) can be re-written as

$$\dot{\phi}\ (a,\theta,t) = \frac{\zeta(a)}{\zeta'(a)}\ \ddot{w}\ (\theta,t) \tag{8}$$

where primes denote differentiation with respect to r. From Eqs. (2) and (8), we can note that the inviscid liquid-shell interaction can be treated as an added mass term which contributes to the radial transverse shell inertia.

We introduce the definitions

$$u = \overline{u}_{,\theta}\ , \quad \psi_\theta = \overline{\psi}_{,\theta} \tag{9}$$

in Eqs. (1), (2), (3), (4), and (8) and proceed in a manner similar to that of Prasad [4], to obtain a secondary set of differential equations governing $\overline{u}$, $\overline{\psi}$ and w in the form

$$\varepsilon\nabla_1^6 w + \varepsilon r_1\nabla_1^4\ w + r_2\nabla_1^2 w + r_3 w + \overline{p}_r = 0 \tag{10}$$

where

$$r_1 = 3 - \nu - 2k_s(1+\nu) - [k_1 + k_r + K_s(k_1 + \gamma)\partial_t^2]$$

$$r_2 = 1 - \nu^2 + \gamma(k_1 + \gamma)\partial_t^2 - \varepsilon[(1 - \nu)^2 - 2(3 + 2\nu - \nu^2)k_s]$$

$$- \varepsilon\,[(1 - \nu)k_1 + 2k_r - 2(1 + \nu)k_r k_s - 4\nu k_1 K_s + 4k_s\gamma]\partial_t^2$$

$$+ \varepsilon[k_1 k_r + (k_1 + k_r)\ (k_1 + \gamma)]\partial_t^4$$

$$r_3 = 2(1 - \nu^2) - [(1 + 3\nu)k_1 - (1 - \nu)\gamma]\partial_t^2 - (k_1 + \gamma)\partial_t^4$$

$$- 4\varepsilon(1 - \nu^2)k_s + 2\varepsilon k_s[(1 + 3\nu)k_1 + 2(1 + \nu)k_r - (1 - \nu)\gamma]\partial_t^2$$

$$+ \varepsilon[2k_1^2 k_s - (1 + 3\nu)\ k_1 k_r K_s + K_s(1 - \nu)(k_1 + k_r)\gamma]\partial_t^4$$

$$- \varepsilon k_1 k_r K_s(k_1 + \gamma)\partial_t^6$$

$$\overline{p}_r = - \frac{(1-\nu^2)R^2}{Eh}\ [1 - \varepsilon K_s(\nabla_1^2 + 1 - \nu - k_r\partial_t^2)] \times$$

$$[(\nabla_1^2 + 1 - \nu - k_1\partial_t^2)\ q + \frac{1+\nu}{\sin\theta}\ (p_\theta \sin\theta)_{,\theta}]$$

$$- \frac{12\varepsilon R^2(1-\nu^2)}{Eh^3} (\nabla_1^2 + 2 - 2\nu - k_1\partial_t^2) \frac{(m_\theta \sin\theta),_\theta}{\sin\theta}$$

with

$$\gamma = \frac{\rho_f}{\rho h} \frac{\zeta(a)}{\zeta'(a)} (1 - \frac{h}{2R}) \tag{11}$$

$$s_1 R\bar{\psi} + s_2 w + s_3 \nabla_1^2 w + \varepsilon^2 K_s \nabla_1^4 w + \varepsilon^2 K_s^2 H_1 = 0 \tag{12}$$

where

$$s_1 = 1 + \varepsilon K_s[\nu - 1 + (2k_r - k_1)\partial_t^2]$$
$$+ \varepsilon K_s^2[-(1-\nu)(k_r - k_1)\partial_t^2 + (k_r - k_1)k_r\partial_t^4]$$

$$s_2 = 1 + \varepsilon K_s(k_r - k_1)\partial_t^2 + \varepsilon^2 K_s^2 \{-4(1+\nu)k_s$$
$$+ [(1+3\nu)k_1 - (1-\nu)\gamma]K_s + k_1 K_s(k_1 + \gamma)\partial_t^4\}$$

$$s_3 = \varepsilon K_s + \varepsilon^2 K_s^2 \{1 - \nu - 2(1+\nu)k_s - [k_1 + K_s(k_1 + \gamma)]\partial_t^2\}$$

$$H_1 = \frac{(1-\nu^2)R^2}{Eh} \{K_s(\nabla_1^2 + 1 - \nu - k_1\partial_t^2)q + \frac{(1+\nu)K_s}{\sin\theta}(p_\theta \sin\theta),_\theta$$
$$- \frac{12R}{h^2}[\frac{(m_\theta \sin\theta),_\theta}{\sin\theta} + (k_r - k_1 + \frac{1}{\varepsilon K_s})m,_\theta]\}$$

and

$$e_1\bar{u} + e_2 R\bar{\psi} + e_3 w + \varepsilon K_s \nabla_1^2 w + \varepsilon K_s H_2 = 0 \tag{13}$$

where

$$e_1 = \varepsilon K_s(1+\nu)(2k_s - k_1 K_s \partial_t^2)$$

$$e_2 = 1 + \varepsilon K_s(\nu - 1 + k_r\partial_t^2)$$

$$e_3 = 1 - \varepsilon K_s[2(1+\nu)k_s + K_s(k_1 + \gamma)\partial_t^2]$$

$$H_2 = \frac{(1-\nu^2)R^2}{Eh}[K_s q + (1+\nu)K_s\bar{p} - \frac{12R}{h^2} m_{\theta,\theta}]$$

Free Vibration Analysis

The subsequent solution to the problem of the forced axisymmetric response of the shell, using a normal mode expansion technique, requires basic relations obtained from the free vibration analysis. We assume the free vibration response to be

$$(w,\ R\psi_\theta,\ u,\ \Phi) = \left(W^{(nm)},\ R\Psi_\theta^{(nm)},\ U^{(nm)},\ \Phi^{(nm)}\right) e^{i\Omega_{nm} t} \tag{14}$$

where n refers to the mode number and m designates the associated frequency ordering number.

The free vibration mode shapes which satisfy Eqs. (10), (12), (13), and (14) are taken as

$$\left(W^{(nm)},\ R\Psi_\theta^{(nm)},\ U^{(nm)}\right)$$

$$= A_{nm}[P_n(\cos\theta),\ g_{nm}P_n^1(\cos\theta),\ d_{nm}P_n^1(\cos\theta)] \tag{15}$$

where

$$g_{nm} = \frac{1}{s_1}(-s_2 + s_3\lambda - \varepsilon^2 K_s\lambda^2)$$

$$d_{nm} = \frac{1}{e_1}(-e_2 g_{nm} - e_3 + \varepsilon K_s\lambda)$$

and

$$\lambda = n(n+1)$$

Substituting Eq. (15) into (10), we obtain the equation

$$c_1\overline{\Omega}_{nm}^6 + c_2\overline{\Omega}_{nm}^4 + c_3\overline{\Omega}_{nm}^2 + c_4 = 0 \tag{16}$$

where $\overline{\Omega}_{nm} = \Omega_{nm} R/C_s$

$$c_1 = \varepsilon K_s k_1 k_r(k_1 + \gamma_{nm})$$

$$c_2 = -(k_1 + \gamma_{nm}) - \varepsilon[k_1k_r + (k_1 + k_r)(k_1 + \gamma_{nm})K_s]\lambda$$
$$+ \varepsilon[2k_1^2k_s - (1 + 3\nu)k_1k_rK_s + (1 - \nu)(k_1 + k_r)K_s\gamma_{nm}]$$

$$c_3 = k_1 + (1 + 3\nu)k_1 - 2\varepsilon k_s[(1 + 3\nu)k_1 + 2(1 + \nu)k_r]$$
$$+ \varepsilon\lambda[2(1 + \nu)k_rk_s + 4\nu k_1k_s - 2k_r - (1 - \nu)k_1]$$

$$+ \varepsilon(k_1 + k_r + k_1 K_s)\lambda^2$$

$$- (1 - \nu - \lambda)[1 - \varepsilon K_s(1 - \nu - \lambda)]\gamma_{nm}$$

and

$$c_4 = 2(1 - \nu^2) - 4\varepsilon(1 - \nu^2)k_s - (1 - \nu^2)\lambda$$

$$- \varepsilon\lambda[(1 - \nu)^2 - 2(3 + 2\nu - \nu^2)k_s]$$

$$+ \varepsilon\lambda^2[3 - \nu - 2(1 + \nu)k_s] - \varepsilon\lambda^3$$

It can be noted that the transcendental character of the frequency equation (16) arises from the retention of the γ_{nm} term which is given by

$$\gamma_{nm} = \frac{\rho_f}{\rho h}\left(1 - \frac{h}{2R}\right)\left[\frac{j_n(\Omega_{nm} r/c_f)}{\frac{d}{dr} j_n(\Omega_{nm} r/c_f)}\right]_{r = a} \tag{17}$$

The pertinent orthogonality relation for the principal modes of vibration can be proven to be (see Appendix)

$$\rho h R \int_0^{\pi}\left[k_1 U^{(j)} U^{(k)} + (k_1 + a_{jk}) W^{(j)} W^{(k)} + \varepsilon k_r R^2 \Psi_\theta^{(j)} \Psi_\theta^{(k)}\right] \sin\theta d\theta = 0 \tag{18}$$

$$\text{provided } \Omega_j \neq \Omega_k$$

where j and k refer to specific modes of vibration and a_{jk} is the fluid orthogonality constant.

To obtain unique expressions for the mode shape functions $U^{(j)}$, $W^{(j)}$, and $\Psi_\theta^{(j)}$, an arbitrary mode normalization condition is adjoined. It is

$$\rho h R \int_0^{\pi}\left[k_1 U^{(j)} U^{(j)} + (k_1 + a_{jj}) W^{(j)} W^{(j)} + \varepsilon k_r R^2 \Psi_\theta^{(j)} \Psi_\theta^{(j)}\right] \sin\theta d\theta = 1 \tag{19}$$

Forced Motion Response

The solution to the forced motion shell response is taken in the form

$$(u, w, \psi_\theta) = \sum_{j=1}^{\infty}\left\{U^{(j)}, W^{(j)}, \Psi_\theta^{(j)}\right\} f_j(t) \tag{20}$$

where

$$\ddot{f}_j + \Omega_j^2 f_j = \int_0^\pi R \left[p_\theta U^{(j)} + \alpha_j q W^{(j)}, m_\theta \Psi_\theta^{(j)} \right] \sin\theta \, d\theta \qquad (21)$$

with $\alpha_j = (k_1 + a_{jj}) \,/\, (k_1 + \gamma_j)$.

Equation (19) can be proven by appropriate manipulation of Eqs. (1) through (4) and use of the orthogonality and normalization conditions (18) and (19) respectively. For a shell initially at rest, the solution to Eq. (20) is

$$f_j(t) = \frac{1}{\Omega_j} \int_0^t \int_0^\pi R \left(p_\theta U^{(j)} + \alpha_j q W^{(j)} + m_\theta \Psi_\theta^{(j)} \right) \sin\theta \, d\theta \, \sin \Omega_j (t - t_1) dt_1 \qquad (22)$$

The preceeding analysis concludes the formal solution of the forced axisymmetric motion of a spherical shell completely filled with an inviscid fluid. The solution incorporates the effects of shell transverse shear and rotational inertia. The elementary theory results can be deduced by ignoring the rotational inertia term $\ddot{\psi}_\theta$ in Eq. (3), eliminating the transverse shear Q_θ between Eqs. (3) and (4), and lastly neglecting shear deformations by letting $R\psi_\theta = -W,_\theta$. An equation governing $\bar{u}$ can be obtained by introducing these simplifications and $k_s = k_r = 0$ to yield

$$\left[1 - \nu^2 - (1 + \nu) k_1 \partial_t^2\right] \bar{u} = \{ 1 - \nu^2 + (k_1 + \gamma) \partial_t^2 + \varepsilon \left[(1 - \nu) \nabla_1^2 + \nabla_1^4\right] \} W$$
$$- \frac{(1-\nu^2)}{Eh} R^2 \, [(1 + \nu) \bar{p} + q] \qquad (23)$$

An equation governing W can be deduced from Eq. (10) with the above assumptions. The forced motion response of the shell using the elementary theory can then be determined in a manner similar to that for the improved theory. The corresponding results for an <u>in vacuo</u> shell are obtainable by letting $\gamma_{nm} = 0$.

A Numerical Example

We apply the preceeding analysis to the problem of a spherical shell filled with a compressible fluid and subjected to an axisymmetric Heaviside load on a cap of the shell surface (Fig. 1). Geometric and material properties of the shell are chosen from typical values reported on the human skull. The contained liquid properties are characterized by those of water. The following data is selected for this

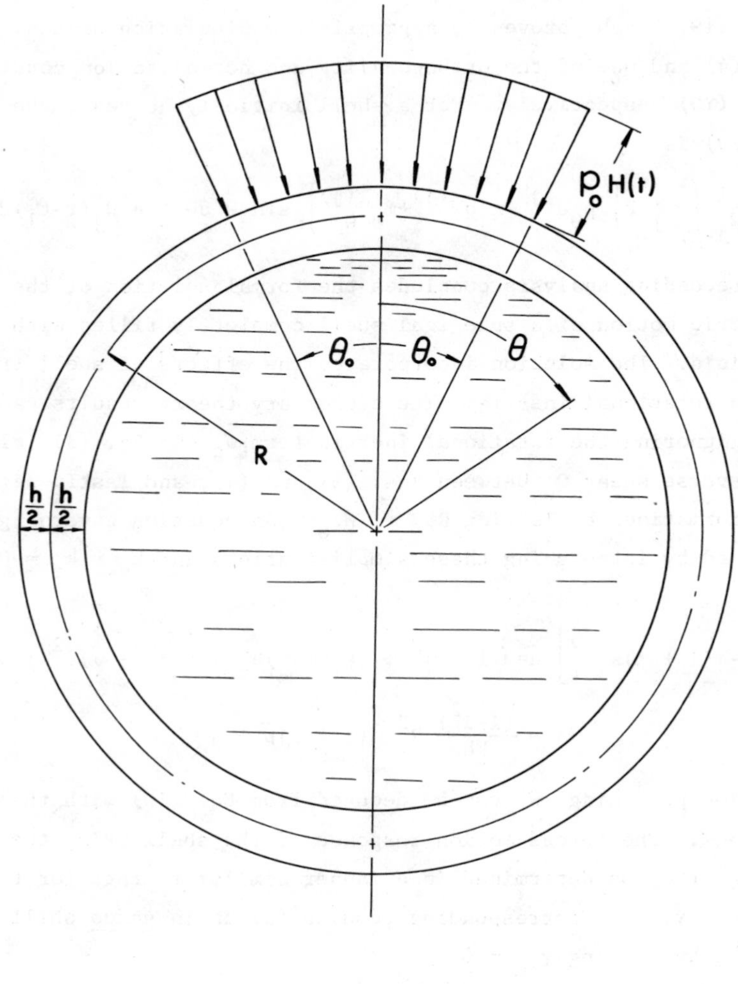

Fig. 1. Fluid Filled Spherical Shell Subjected to Axisymmetric Impact.

preliminary head model:

Shell: $\nu = 0.2$, $\kappa^2 = 0.81$, $h/R = 0.1$, $\rho = 0.077\ \text{lbm/in}^3$, and $c_s = 10^5$ in/sec.

Fluid: $\rho_f = 0.036\ \text{lbm/in}^3$, and $c_f = 47{,}500$ in/sec.

Figure 2 illustrates a plot of the frequency spectrum computed from Eq. 16.

The solution to the forced motion shell problem is taken as

$$W(\theta,t) = \sum_{n=0}^{\infty}\sum_{m=1}^{\infty} A_{nm}P_n(\cos\theta)\, f_{nm}(t)$$
$$\psi_\theta(\theta,t) = \sum_{n=0}^{\infty}\sum_{m=1}^{\infty} g_{nm}A_{nm}P_n^1(\cos\theta)\, f_{nm}(t) \qquad (24)$$
$$u(\theta,t) = \sum_{n=0}^{\infty}\sum_{m=1}^{\infty} d_{nm}A_{nm}P_n^1(\cos\theta)\, f_{nm}(t)$$

where $f_{nm}(t)$ is governed by equation (22) with $p_\theta = m_\theta = 0$ and q given by

$$q(\theta,t) = -p_oH(t) \qquad 0 \le \theta \le \theta_o$$
$$= 0 \qquad \theta_o < \theta \le \pi \qquad (25)$$

Equation (25), expanded in terms of an infinite Legendre series, can be represented as

$$q(\theta,t) = \frac{-p_oH(t)}{2}\sum_{n=0}^{\infty} P_n(\cos\theta)\left[P_{n-1}(\cos\theta_o) - P_{n+1}(\cos\theta_o)\right] \qquad (26)$$

Inserting Eq. (26) in (22), we obtain after integration

$$f_{nm}(t) = \frac{-Rp_oA_{nm}\alpha_{nm}}{(2n+1)\Omega_{nm}^2}\left[P_{n-1}(\cos\theta_o) - P_{n+1}(\cos\theta_o)\right](1-\cos\Omega_{nm}t) \qquad (27)$$

Equations (24), re-written by introducing (27) and the normalized modal constants A_{nm} obtained from Eq. (19) becomes

$$(w, R\psi_\theta, u) = \frac{2(1-\nu^2)p_oR}{E}\sum_{n=0}^{\infty}\sum_{m=1}^{\infty}(P_n(\cos\theta), g_{nm}P_n^1(\cos\theta), d_{nm}P_n^1(\cos\theta)S_{nm}(t) \qquad (28)$$

where

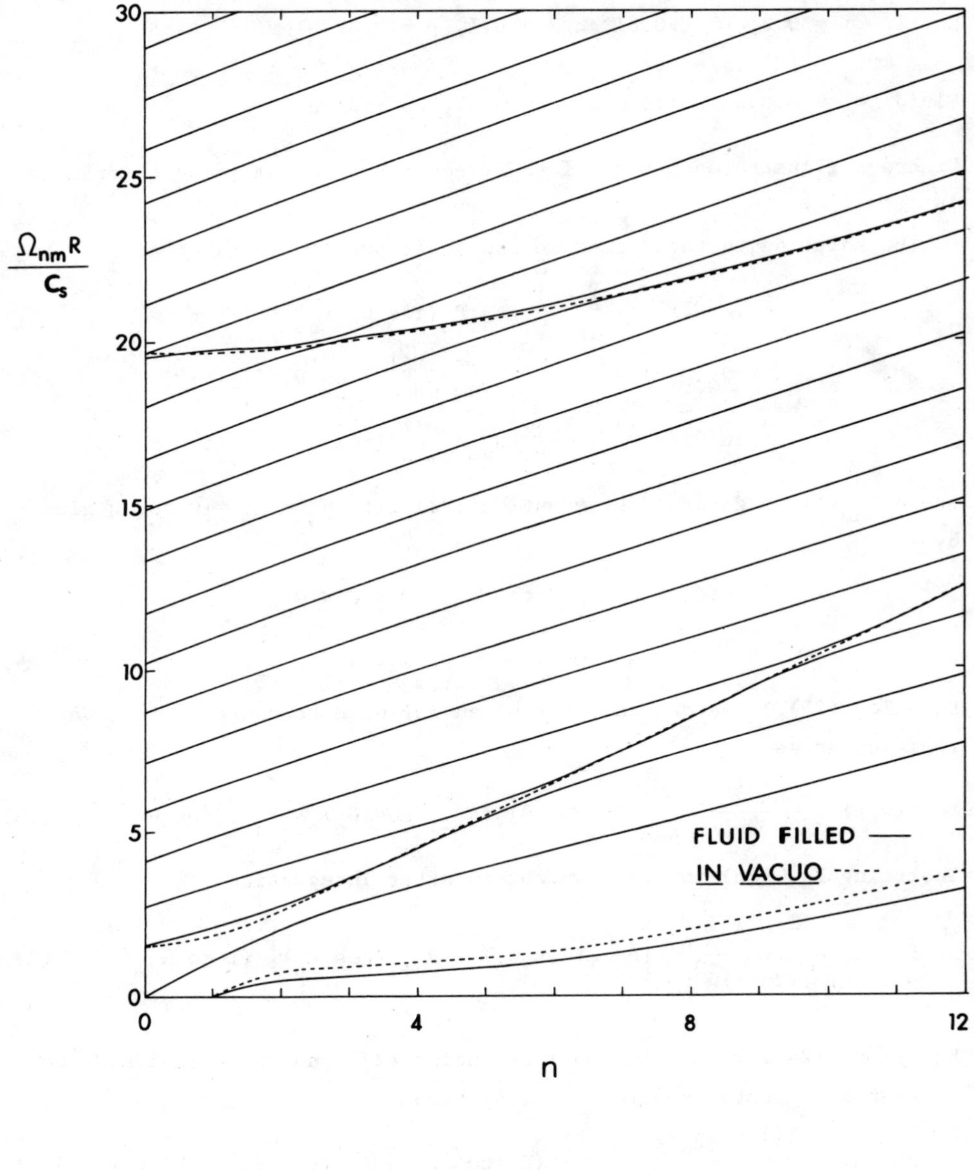

Fig. 2. Frequency Spectrum.

$$S_{nm}(t) = \frac{\alpha_{nm}\left[P_{n+1}(\cos\theta_o) - P_{n-1}(\cos\theta_o)\right](1-\cos\Omega_{nm}t)}{2\left(\frac{\Omega_{nm}R}{c_s}\right)^2\left(\frac{h}{R}\right)\left[(k_1 + a_{nm}) + \lambda(k_1 d_{nm}^2 + k_1 g_{nm}^2)\right]}$$

The stress and stress couple resultants can be obtained by substituting Eqs. (28) into Eqs. (4). They are[1]

$$N_\theta = p_o h \sum_{n=0}^{\infty}\sum_{m=1}^{\infty}\left[d_{nm}(\nu - 1)\cot\theta\, P_n^1(\cos\theta) + (1 + \nu - \lambda d_{nm})\, P_n(\cos\theta)\right] S_{nm}$$

$$N_\phi = p_o h \sum_{n=0}^{\infty}\sum_{m=1}^{\infty}\left[d_{nm}(1 - \nu)\cot\theta P_n^1(\cos\theta) + (1 + \nu - \nu\lambda d_{nm})\, P_n(\cos\theta)\right] S_{nm} \quad (29)$$

$$M_\theta = p_o hR\varepsilon \sum_{n=0}^{\infty}\sum_{m=1}^{\infty}\left[(\nu - 1)\cot\theta\, P_n^1(\cos\theta) - \lambda P_n(\cos\theta)\right] g_{nm} S_{nm}$$

$$M_\phi = p_o hR\varepsilon \sum_{n=0}^{\infty}\sum_{m=1}^{\infty}\left[(1 - \nu)\cot\theta\, P_n^1(\cos\theta) - \lambda\nu P_n(\cos\theta)\right] g_{nm} S_{nm}$$

and

$$K_s Q_\theta = p_o h \sum_{n=0}^{\infty}\sum_{m=1}^{\infty}(1+ g_{nm})\sin\theta\, P_n^1(\cos\theta)\, S_{nm}$$

Figures 3 and 4 illustrate the shell radial displacement computed from Eq. (38). Figure 5 is a time history plot of the shell inner fiber stress $\tau_{\theta\theta}/p_0$ vs. θ obtained from Eqs. (29) and the relation

$$\tau_{jj} = \frac{N_{jj}}{h} - \frac{6M_{jj}}{h^2} \quad (30)$$

In these computations, the radial load expansion (26) was summed up to $n = 12$. The corresponding shell frequencies were summed up to $\Omega_{nm}R/C_s = 30$.

---

1. It may be noted that the $\cot\theta P_n(\cos\theta)$ term in Eqs. (29) has the values $\frac{-n(n+1)}{2}$, 0, and $(-1)^{n+1}\frac{n(n+1)}{2}$ at $\theta = 0°$, 90°, and 180° respectively.

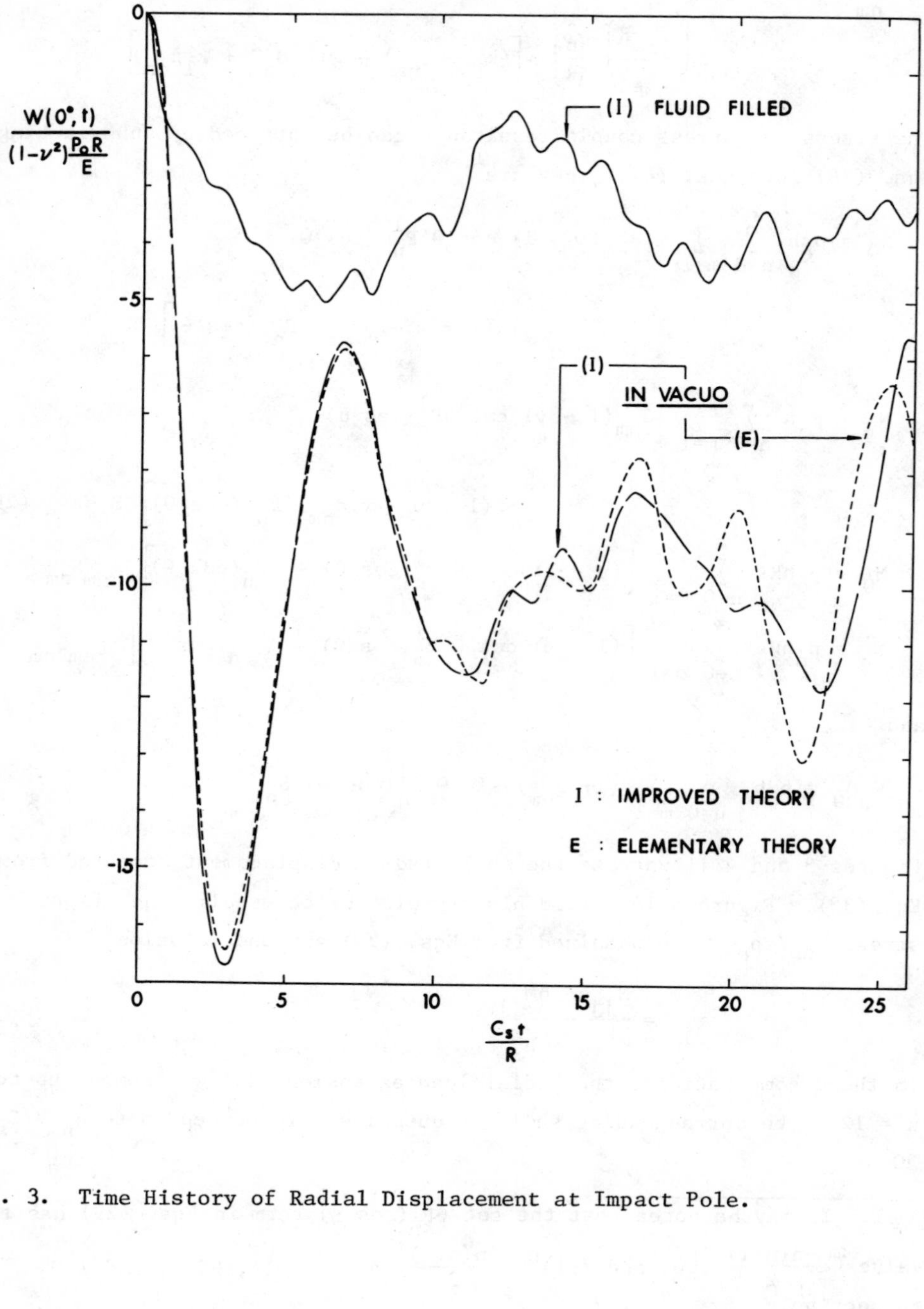

Fig. 3. Time History of Radial Displacement at Impact Pole.

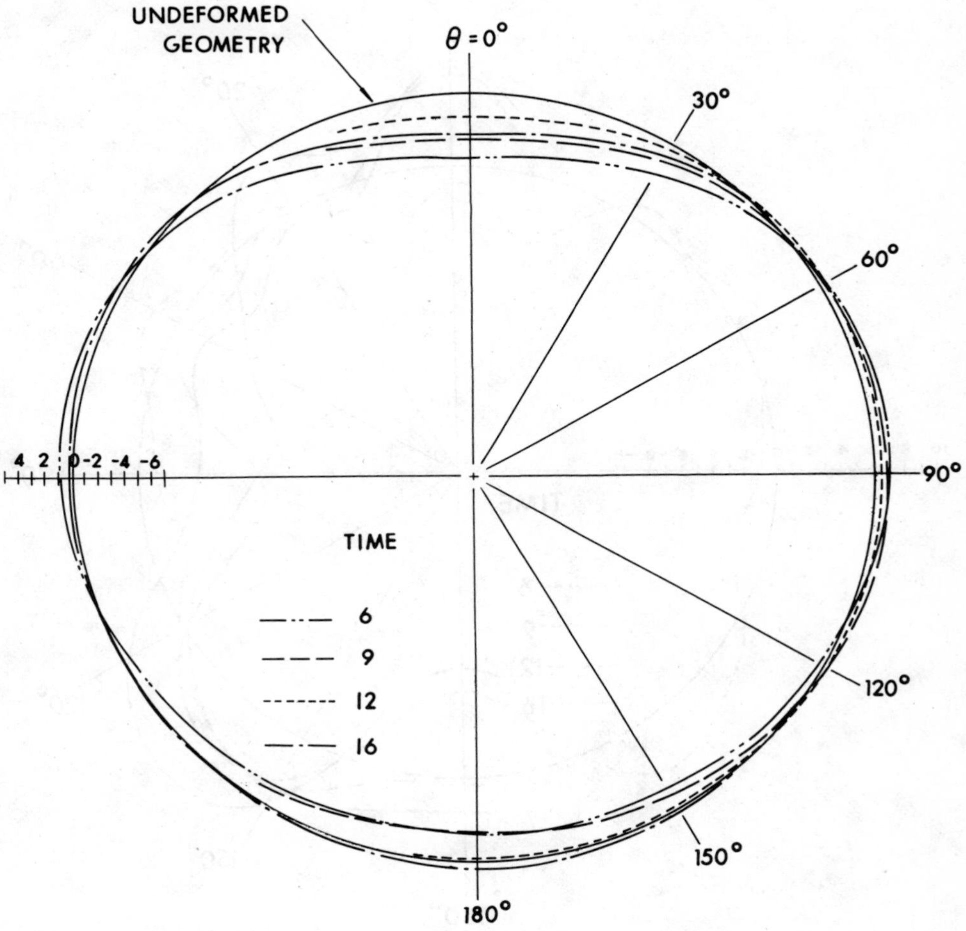

Fig. 4. Radial Displacement vs. θ.

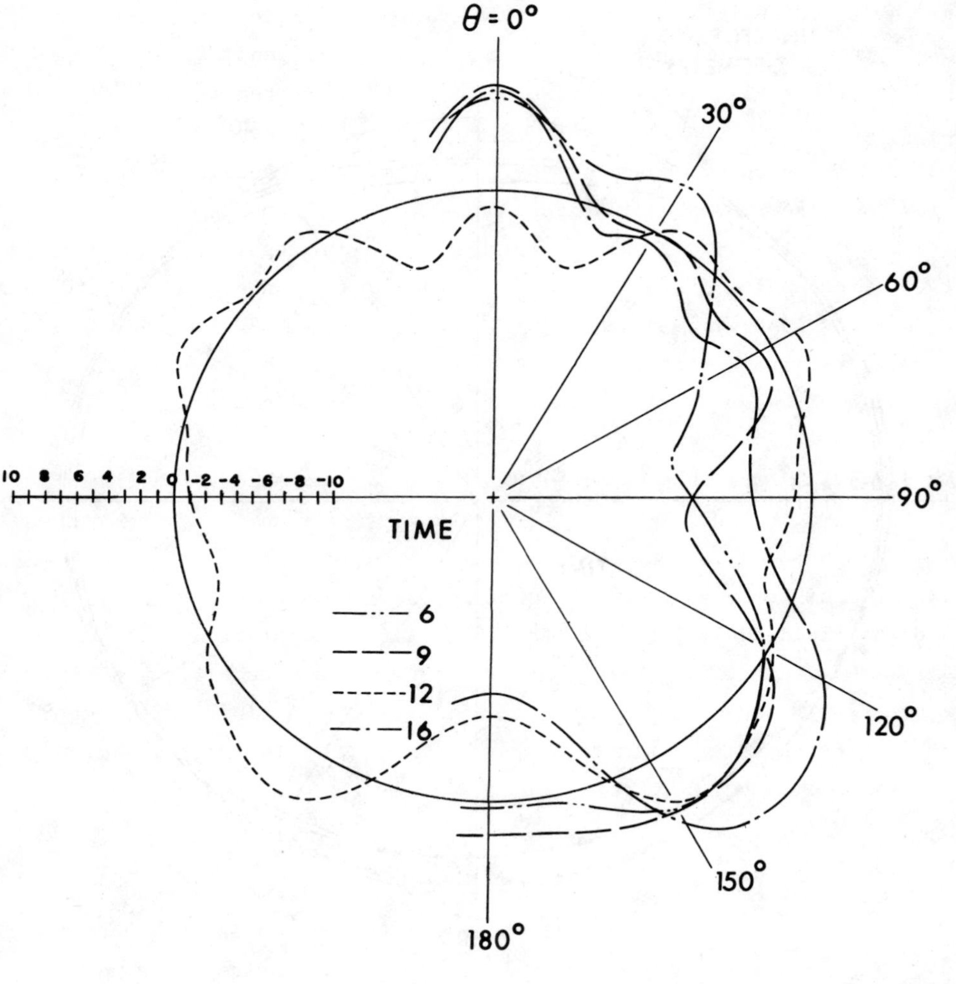

Fig. 5. Inner Fiber Stress vs. θ.

DISCUSSION

The results of the free vibration analysis (Figure 2) indicate the nature of the fluid shell interaction. The fundamental mode frequencies are lower than the corresponding in vacuo bending frequencies. The coupled nature of the shell-fluid composite modes is exhibited by the asymptotic alignment of the curves in the vicinity of the corresponding in vacuo membrane stretch and shear distortion modes. The radial displacement time histories revealed in Figure 3 indicate the "cushioned" response of the fluid filled shell when compared to in vacuo results. The ratio of the corresponding maximum radial displacement responses is approximately 0.30. The magnitudes of the fiber stresses in Fig. 5 result primarily from the membrane stretch mode. For the in vacuo shell, however, the computed stresses arising from bending and extension are comparable in magnitude.

It is believed that the fluid filled shell responses illustrated by Figs. 3, 4, and 5 furnish preliminary information for a highly idealized impact model of the head. Results pertaining to the fluid pressures are obtainable by solving the boundary value problem posed in Eq. (5) and the fluid-shell interface Eq. (6). These computations are in progress. In addition, the response solutions for an arbitrary impact time profile can be deduced by Duhamel's representation. A spherical shell with a viscoelastic core appears to be a logical refinement of the inviscid fluid model.

ACKNOWLEDGMENTS

The work communicated in this manuscript was performed pursuant to Contract No. PH-43-67-1137 with the National Institutes of Health and NASA Sustaining Grant NGL 49-001-001. Computer services were made available by the Computer Center of West Virginia University.

REFERENCES

1. Love, A. E. H., "The Small Free Vibrations and Deformation of a Thin Elastic Shell," Philosophical Transactions of the Royal Society, London, England, Series A, Vol. 179, 1888, pp. 491-546.

2. Naghdi, P. M., and Kalnins, A., "On Vibrations of Elastic Spherical Shells," Journal of Applied Mechanics, Vol. 29, Transactions American Society of Mechanical Engineers, Vol. 84, Series E, 1962, pp. 65-72.

3. Kalnins, A., "Effect of Bending on Vibrations of Spherical Shells," Journal of the Acoustical Society of America, Vol. 36, 1964, pp. 74-81.

4. Prasad, C., "On Vibrations of Spherical Shells," Journal of the Acoustical Society of America, Vol. 36, 1964, pp. 489-494.

5. Baker, W., Hu, W. C., Jackson, T., "Elastic Response of Thin Shperical Shells to Axisymmetric Blast Loading," Journal of Applied Mechanics. Vol. 33, Transactions American Society of Mechanical Engineers, Vol. 88, Series E, 1966, pp. 800-806.

6. Vekslar, N., and Nigul, U., "Theory of Wave Processes in the Axisymmetric Deformation of a Spherical Shell," Mekhanik Tverdogo Tela, Vol. 1, 1966, pp. 74-80.

7. Junger, M. C., "Vibrations of Elastic Shells in a Fluid Medium and the Associated Radiation of Sound," Journal of Applied Mechanics, Vol. 19, Transactions American Society of Mechanical Engineers, Vol. 74, Series E, pp. 439-445.

8. Gontekevich, V. S., "Natural Vibrations of Shells in a Fluid," Akademiya Nauk Ukrainskoy SSR Khar'Kovskiy Filial Institute Mekhaniki, Report, Kiyev, 1964, 103 pages.

9. Rand, R., and DiMaggio, F., "Vibrations of Fluid Filled Spherical and Spheroidal Shells," Journal of the Acoustical Society of America, Vol. 42, 1967, pp. 1278-1286.

10. Sonstegard, D., "Effects of a Surrounding Fluid on the Free, Axisymmetric Vibrations on Thin Elastic Spherical Shells," Journal of the Acoustical Society of America, Vol. 45, 1969, pp. 506-.

11. Engin, A. E., "The Axisymmetric Response of a Fluid-Filled Spherical Shell," Ph.D. Dissertation, University of Michigan, Ann Arbor, 1968.

APPENDIX

Introducing Eq. (8) into Eqs. (1), (2), and (3), we can write the modal equations governing free axisymmetric vibrations of a fluid filled spherical shell as

$$N^{(j)}_{\theta,\theta} + (N^{(j)}_{\theta} - N^{(j)}_{\phi}) \cot \theta = - \rho h R k_1 \Omega^2_j U^{(j)}$$

$$Q_{\theta,\theta}^{(j)} + Q_{\theta}^{(j)} \cot\theta - (N_{\theta}^{(j)} + N_{\phi}^{(j)}) = -\rho h R k_1 \Omega_j^2 W^{(j)}$$

$$- \rho_f R\left(1 - \frac{h}{2R}\right) \frac{\zeta_j(a)}{\zeta_j'(a)} \Omega_j^2 W^{(j)} \tag{A.1}$$

$$M_{\theta,\theta}^{(j)} + (M_{\theta}^{(j)} - M_{\phi}^{(j)}) \cot\theta - RQ_{\theta}^{(j)} = -\rho\varepsilon h R^3 k_r \Omega_j^2 \Psi_{\theta}^{(j)}$$

where $\zeta_j(r)$, defined by Eq. (7), is governed by

$$\frac{d}{dr}\left[\frac{r^2 d\zeta_j}{dr}\right] + \left[\frac{\Omega_j^2 r^2}{c_f^2}\right] - n(n+1) \quad \zeta_j = 0 \tag{A.2}$$

Using the modal form of relations (4) in Eqs. (A.1), we obtain after suitable manipulation and integration of Eqs. (A.1) and (A.2)

$$\rho h R \int_0^{\pi} \left[k_1 U^{(j)} U^{(k)} + (k_1 + a_{jk}) W^{(j)} W^{(k)} + \varepsilon k_r R^2 \Psi_{\theta}^{(j)} \Psi_{\theta}^{(k)}\right] \cdot \sin\theta \, d\theta = 0 \tag{A.3}$$

provided $\Omega_j \neq \Omega_k$

where

$$a_{jk} = \frac{\rho_f\left(1 - \frac{h}{2R}\right)}{\rho h a^2} \quad \frac{\int_0^a \left[r^2 \zeta_j' \zeta_k' + n(n+1)\zeta_j \zeta_k\right] dr}{\zeta_j'(a) \zeta_k'(a)}$$

OSCILLATORY FLOW OF A VISCOUS FLUID IN A FLEXIBLE WALLED TWO DIMENSIONAL CHANNEL

M. Varner
University of South Florida

B. Ross
University of South Florida

ABSTRACT

This paper presents the results of the analysis of three separate but related flows. An analysis is made of the oscillatory motion of a viscous fluid within a rigid walled channel, an elastic walled channel, and the oscillatory motion of a inviscid liquid within an elastic walled channel.

It is shown that the general character of the flow may be described by reference to three dimensionless parameters; m, which describes the inertia effects of the fluid with respect to the membrane, α which describes the relative importance of viscous effects, and k_o, which relates the elastic properties of the membrane to the flow situation.

LIST OF NOTATIONS

u	Velocity of the fluid in the longitudinal direction
v	Velocity of the fluid in the transverse direction
t	Time coordinate
x	Longitudinal coordinate
y	Transverse coordinate
h	$\frac{1}{2}$ depth of channel
w	Width of channel
ν	Kinematic viscosity of the fluid
ρ_o	Density of the fluid

p	Thermodynamic pressure of the fluid
α	A dimensionless parameter
r	A dimensionless coordinate
μ	Absolute viscosity of fluid
b	Membrane thickness
τ_w	Shear stress at the membrane fluid interface
σ_{xx}	Longitudinal stress within the membrane
p'	Normal stress component at the membrane fluid interface
η	Local displacement of membrane in the x direction
ζ	Local displacement of the membrane in the y direction
ρ	Density of the membrane
R	$\frac{1}{2}$ instantaneous channel height
E_c	Elastic modulus of the membrane
σ	Poisson's ratio
ε_{xx}	Longitudinal strain within the membrane
ε_{yy}	Transverse strain within the membrane
c	Complex wave speed
k	Dimensionless wave number
κ	A dimensionless parameter
m	A dimensionless parameter
k_o	Dimensionless wave number for $\nu = 0$
ϕ	Velocity potential function
$\overline{V}$	Velocity vector
γ	Local wall slope

INTRODUCTION

As a first approximation to the pulsatile flow problem, laminar, Newtonian flows down elastic walled tubes have been studied. A number of existing theories by J. R. Womersley [1,2], D. A. McDonald [3], Herman Branson [4], Victor L. Streeter, W. Ford Keitzer, and David F. Bohr [5], and G. W. Morgan and J. P. Kiely [6] have been offered as to the velocity and pressure fields found in the elastic walled tubes.

The problem of this investigation is the study of a two-dimensional, Cartesian flow of a viscous fluid within an elastic walled channel. The method of solution follows along the same lines as the previously solved elastic tube problem. An auxiliary problem of the oscillation flow of a viscous fluid in a two dimensional rigid walled channel is solved first to establish the principle of solution and to introduce the dimensionless parameter α. The parameter α relates to the channel dimension and the viscosity of the fluid. The elastic walled problem is then solved in terms of a complex wave speed and complex pressure gradient. Two additional dimensionless parameters are developed; m, which relates the inertia of the fluid and the walls, and k_o which relates to the elastic properties of the membrane in the flow channel.

Finally, the oscillatory inviscid flow in a flexible walled channel is solved. Under the condition μ=o, the viscous flow solution converges to the inviscid flow solution.

Oscillatory Viscous Flow Within a Rigid Walled Channel

Consider an infinitely long channel of depth 2h and width w. Within this channel, a Newtonian, laminar flow is caused by a pressure gradient of known magnitude. Of particular interest, in this case, is a periodically varying pressure gradient. Thus, solutions of the form $u(y,t) = f(y)\exp(int), \frac{\partial p}{\partial x}(x,t)=A\exp(int)$ where u(y,t) and p(x,t) is the velocity in the x direction and pressure respectively and n is the circular frequency in radians/second will be assumed.

The governing equations of the flow are characterized by the linearized Navier Stokes equations (equation 1).

$$\nu \frac{\partial^2 u}{\partial y^2} - \frac{1}{\rho_o}\frac{\partial p}{\partial x} = \frac{\partial u}{\partial t} \qquad (1)$$

where ν is the kinematic viscosity and ρ_o is the density. It will be noticed that the solutions given above also satisfy continuity and the second equation of motion for the y direction.

To help simplify the final form of the assumed solutions, the non-dimensional parameter r, where y = hr, will be introduced into the equation of motion.

$$\frac{\nu}{h^2}\frac{\partial^2 u}{\partial r^2} - \frac{\partial u}{\partial t} = \frac{1}{\rho_o}\frac{\partial p}{\partial x} \qquad (2)$$

By assuming that the form of A is known, a second order linear equation in u(r) will be formed from the substitution of the assumed solutions into the Navier Stokes equation (equation 3).

$$\frac{\partial^2 u(r)}{\partial r^2} - i\alpha^2 u(r) = \frac{h^2 A}{\nu\rho_0} \qquad (3)$$

where $\alpha = h(n/\nu)^{1/2}$ and $i = \sqrt{-1}$

A general solution to equation 3 is

$$u(r,t) = \{A_0 \exp(\sqrt{i}\alpha r) + A_1 \exp(-\sqrt{i}\alpha r) + \frac{iAh^2}{\rho_0 \alpha^2 \nu}\} \exp(int) \qquad (4)$$

where A_0 and A_1 are arbitrary constants.

The number of undertermined coefficients may be reduced by employing the boundary conditions on the flow.

For

$$u(r,t) = u(-r,t) \text{ and } u(1) = o$$

the velocity distribution reduces to the form given below.

$$u(r,t) = \frac{iA}{\rho_0 n} \{1 - \frac{\cosh(\sqrt{i}\alpha r)}{\cosh(\sqrt{i}\,\alpha)}\} \exp(int) \qquad (5)$$

At this point some observations may be made concerning the character of the flow. Referring to the theoretical velocity distribution, a heavy dependence on the non-dimensional parameter α is seen to exist. Thus, the character of the flow, for the rigid wall case, is mainly controlled by the magnitude of the viscosity, circular frequency, and depth of the channel. The observed pressure gradient, which must be determined experimentally, is also seen to affect, in a linear fashion, the magnitude of the velocity field.

A graph of the velocity field versus r for particular instances in time and typical values of α is given in Figure 1. As can be seen, a slight change in the magnitude of α drastically changes the velocity profile at the instants in time given.

Oscillatory Viscous Flow Within An Elastic Walled Channel

In developing the equations of motion, it will be assumed that the membrane material is elastic, homogeneous and isotropic and that the variation of stress over a cross section may be assumed to be zero.

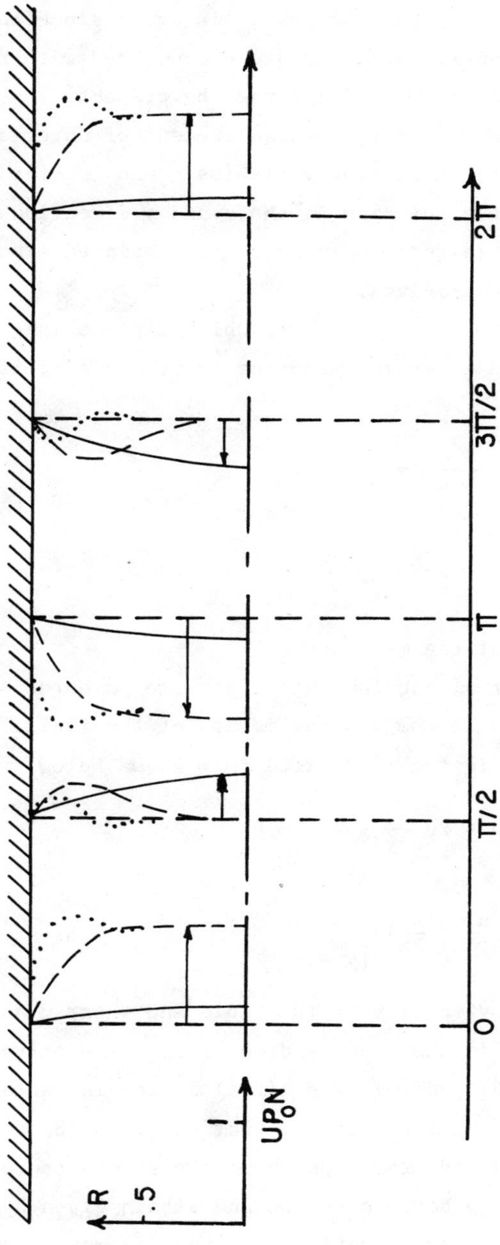

Fig. 1. Variation in Velocity Profile for the Rigid Wall Case as a Function of α and Time.

The assumption of constant stress over a cross section naturally implies thin membrane theory ($b/h<<1$) where b is the membrane thickness. It is also assumed that the moment produced by τ_w is small since the membrane is thin and that only tensile stresses are encountered with respect to σ_{xx} which implies that no buckling forces be present.

Consider all of the forces acting on an element of material in the x-y plane as shown in Figure 2. The variables η and ζ refer to the local displacements of the membrane in the x and y directions, respectively. Employing a simple force balance on the isolated element, the equation of motion may be derived.

If it is assumed that γ is very small, which implies long walls or small perturbations, the governing membrane equations simplify to the form given below.

$$\rho \frac{\partial^2 \zeta}{\partial t^2} = \frac{p'}{b} \tag{6}$$

$$\rho \frac{\partial^2 \eta}{\partial t^2} = \frac{\partial \sigma_{xx}}{\partial x} - \frac{\tau_w}{b} \tag{7}$$

where ρ is the density of the membrane.

p' and τ_w are the normal and tangential stresses exerted on the interface of the membrane due to the viscous motion of the fluid. These stresses may be written in the linearized form given below.

$$p' = \left(p - 2\mu \frac{\partial v}{\partial y}\right)\Big|_{y = R} \tag{8}$$

$$\tau_w = \mu \left(\frac{\partial u}{\partial y} + \frac{\partial v}{\partial x}\right)\Big|_{y = R} \tag{9}$$

where μ is the absolute viscosity of the fluid and where u and v are the velocity components in the x and y directions, respectively. As indicated in equation (8) and (9), $R = R(x,t)$ is the instantaneous channel half height. It will be noticed that equation (8) contains both the hydrostatic and deviatoric parts of the stress tensor.

Noting the relationship between stress and strain given by Hooke's law for the plane stress case, equations (6) and (7) may be written in terms of the displacements ζ and η for the plane stress case.

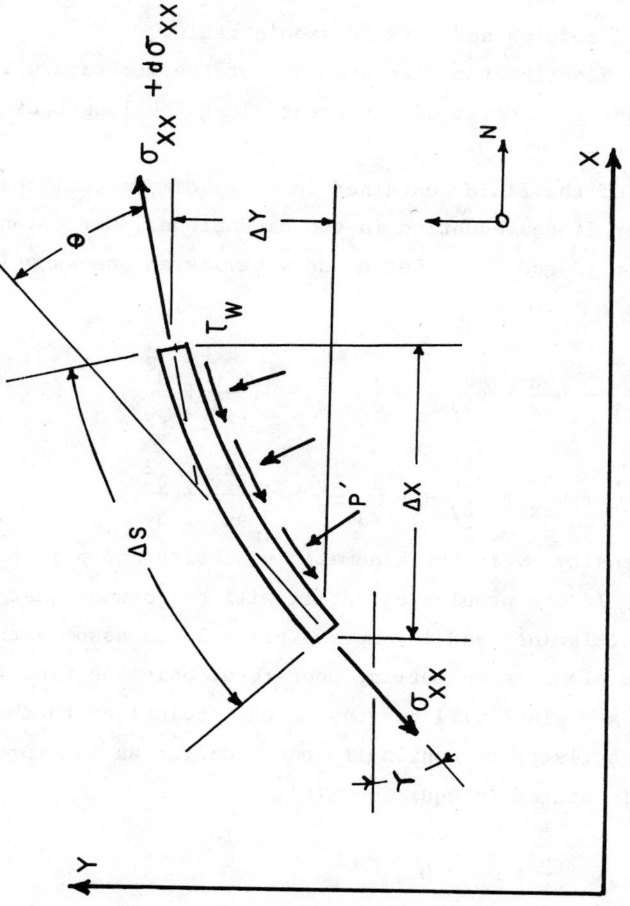

Fig. 2. Typical Membrane Element under Load.

$$\rho \frac{\partial^2 \eta}{\partial t^2} = \frac{E_c}{1-\sigma^2} \{\frac{\partial^2 \eta}{\partial x^2} + \sigma \frac{\partial^2 \zeta}{\partial x \partial y}\} - \frac{\mu}{b} (\frac{\partial u}{\partial y} + \frac{\partial v}{\partial x}) \Big|_{y = R} \quad (10)$$

$$\rho \frac{\partial^2 \zeta}{\partial t^2} = \frac{1}{B} (p - 2\mu \frac{\partial v}{\partial y}) \Big|_{y = R} \quad (11)$$

where E_c is Young's modulus and σ is Poisson's ratio.

These equations describe the displacements of the membrane wall as a function of time and transverse displacement along the length of the channel.

For the motion of the fluid contained in a two dimensional channel, consider the Navier Stokes equation in two dimensional, Cartesian coordinates (equation 12 and 13). Let u and v be instantaneous velocities, See Figure 3, then

$$\frac{\partial u}{\partial t} + u\frac{\partial u}{\partial x} + v\frac{\partial u}{\partial y} = - \frac{1}{\rho_o} \frac{\partial p}{\partial x} + \nu(\frac{\partial^2 u}{\partial x^2} + \frac{\partial^2 u}{\partial y^2}) \quad (12)$$

$$\frac{\partial v}{\partial t} + u\frac{\partial v}{\partial x} + v\frac{\partial v}{\partial y} = - \frac{1}{\rho_o} \frac{\partial p}{\partial y} + \nu(\frac{\partial^2 v}{\partial x^2} + \frac{\partial^2 v}{\partial y^2}) \quad (13)$$

where ρ_o is the density, ν is the kinematic viscosity and p is the thermodynamic pressure. In the problem cited, it will be assumed that the fluid is Newtonian, laminar and incompressible. It is assumed that the flow about the x-z plane is symmetric, therefore, only the flow in the upper half of the x-y plane will be considered. Solutions to the flow problem must also satisfy the continuity equation for an incompressible fluid. This law is stated in equation (14).

$$\frac{\partial u}{\partial x} + \frac{\partial v}{\partial y} = 0 \quad (14)$$

For oscillatory flow, a general solution for the velocity and pressure distributions u, v and p may be assumed by analogy with the rigid wall case.

The assumed solutions are

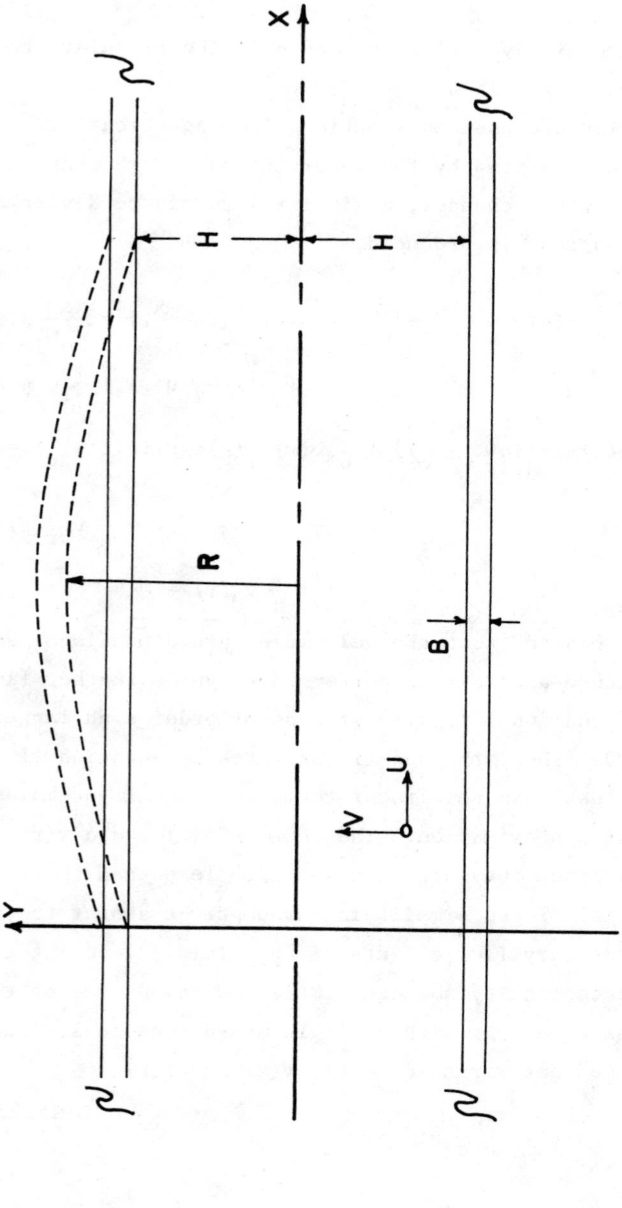

Fig. 3. Coordinate Orientation along Channel.

$$u = u(y)\exp\{in(t - \frac{x}{c})\}; \quad v = v(y)\exp\{in(t - \frac{x}{c})\}$$
$$p = p(y)\exp\{in(t - x)\} \tag{15}$$

where c is the complex wave velocity, and n is the circular frequency in radians per second.

Upon substituting the assumed solutions into equations (12), (13) and (14) and non-dimensionalizing by the substitution y = rh where h is 1/2 the average depth of the channel, a simpler form of the Navier Stokes and continuity equations is produced.

$$inu(r) - \frac{in}{c} u^2(r)\exp\{in(t - \frac{x}{c}\} + \frac{1}{h} v(r)\exp\{in(t - \frac{x}{c})\} = \frac{in}{\rho_0 c} p(r) + \nu(- \frac{n}{c^2} u(r) + \frac{1}{h^2}u_{rr}(r)) \tag{16}$$

$$inv(r) - \frac{in}{c} u(r)v(r)\exp\{in(t - \frac{x}{c})\} + \frac{1}{h} v(r)v_r(r)\exp\{in(t - \frac{x}{c})\} = - \frac{1}{\rho_0 h}p_r(r) + \nu(- \frac{n}{c^2} v(r) + \frac{1}{h^2}u_{rr}(r)) \tag{17}$$

$$- \frac{in}{c} u(r) + \frac{1}{h} v_r(r) = 0 \tag{18}$$

While it is recognized that the velocities are dimensional and complex, an order of magnitude analysis is performed to guide further linearization from continuity (equation 18), u(r) will be of order c/nh larger in general than $v_r(r)$. Then, the non-linear terms in equation (16) and (17) are of order 1/c less than the linear terms in general and may be neglected for a first approximation. The terms $n^2u(r)$ and $n^2v(r)$ will also be neglected since they are of order $1/c^2$ less than their neighboring linear terms. These simplifying assumptions amount to essentially neglecting the secondary flow effects of the fluid. Imposing these restrictions, the continuity and equilibrium equations reduce to linear mixed differential equations with a single non-dimensional, independent variable r and dependent variables u(r), v(r) and p(r).

$$inu(r) = \frac{in}{\rho_0 c} p(r) + \frac{\nu}{h^2} u_{rr}(r) \tag{19}$$

$$inv(r) = - \frac{1}{\rho_0 h} p_r(r) + \frac{\nu}{h^2} v_{rr}(r) \tag{20}$$

$$-\frac{in}{c}u(r) + \frac{1}{h}v_r(r) = 0 \tag{21}$$

If it is now assumed that the pressure varies exponentially with r, or p(r) = Acosh(kr) where k must be determined and A is a constant of known magnitude, keeping in mind the symmetry of p with respect to x, then the equations of equilibrium (equations (19) and (20)) can be solved for u(r) and v(r). Thus,

$$u_{rr}(r) - \frac{inh^2}{\nu}u(r) = -\frac{inh^2}{\nu\rho_o c}A\cosh(kr) \tag{22}$$

$$v_{rr}(r) - \frac{inh^2}{\nu}v(r) = \frac{hk}{\rho_o\nu}A\sinh(kr) \tag{23}$$

The general solutions of these two equations are as follows,

$$u(r) = A_o\exp(\sqrt{i}\alpha r) + A_1\exp(-\sqrt{i}\alpha r) - \frac{i\alpha^2 A}{\rho_o\nu}\frac{\cosh(kr)}{k^2 - i\alpha^2} \tag{24}$$

$$v(r) = B_o\exp(\sqrt{i}\alpha r) + B_1\exp(-\sqrt{i}\alpha r) + \frac{hkA}{\rho_o\nu}\frac{\sinh(kr)}{k^2 - i\alpha^2} \tag{25}$$

where $\alpha = h(n/v)^{1/2}$ is a dimensionless parameter that characterizes the flow field and the ratios $\frac{A_o}{B_o}$ and $\frac{A_1}{B_1}$.

The constant k^λ are evaluated by considering the continuity equation (equation (21)). Thus

$$\frac{A_o}{B_o} = \frac{c}{\sqrt{in\nu}}\ ;\ \frac{A_1}{B_1} = \frac{c}{\sqrt{in\nu}}\ ;\ k = \frac{hn}{c}$$

By considering the boundary condition v(x,o,t) = o and noting that for $k \ll \alpha, k^2 - i\alpha^2$ may be approximated by $i\alpha^2$, the velocity and pressure distributions become,

$$u(x,r,t) = \{A_o\cosh(\sqrt{i}\alpha r) + \frac{1}{\rho_o c}\}A\exp\{in(t - \frac{x}{c})\} \tag{26}$$

$$v(x,r,t) = \{A_o\kappa\sinh(\sqrt{i}\alpha r) + \frac{ikr}{\rho_o c}\}A\exp\{in(t - \frac{x}{c})\} \tag{27}$$

$$p(x,r,t) = A\exp\{in(t - \frac{x}{c})\} \tag{28}$$

where the approximation $\cosh(kr) \simeq 1$ and $\sinh(kr) \simeq kr$ for $k \ll 1$ has been made.

To evaluate the constant A_o in terms of A and the complex wave speed c, the boundary conditions on the velocity at the wall must be used. At the wall, the velocity of the fluid, due to the admission of viscous effects, must be continuous. This condition on the flow field stated mathematically is

$$\left.\frac{\partial\zeta}{\partial t} = v\right|_{r=1} \qquad \left.\frac{\partial\eta}{\partial t} = u\right|_{r=1} \tag{29}$$

where η and ζ are the displacements in the x and y directions respectively.

The boundary conditions stated above assume that the displacements η and ζ are small. Thus, long waves have been included in the basic assumptions. This necessarily implies 1/c<<1 which also indicates a limitation on the modulus of the elastic membrane.

Before these boundary conditions can be used to evaluate the constants A_o and c, the form of η and ζ must be determined. Noting the assumption of long waves - or small displacements - a solution of the form

$$\zeta = D\exp\{in(t - \frac{x}{c})\} \qquad \eta = E\exp\{in(t - \frac{x}{c})\} \tag{30}$$

is assumed.

By substituting the assumed general solutions into the equations of motion for the elastic membrane (equations 10 and 11), the form of D and E may be determined. Hence,

$$(-n^2 p + \frac{E_c n^2}{c^2(1-\sigma^2)})E + \frac{\mu}{b}(\frac{\sqrt{i}\alpha}{h} - \frac{in\kappa}{c})\sinh(\sqrt{i}\alpha)A_o + \frac{\mu nkA}{bc^2\rho_o} = 0 \tag{31}$$

$$-n^2 D + \frac{2\mu\sqrt{i}\alpha\kappa}{hb}\cosh(\sqrt{i}\alpha)A_o - \frac{1}{b}(1 - \frac{2\mu ni}{c^2\rho_o})A = 0 \tag{32}$$

Thus, two additional equations will be needed to solve for all of the complex constants. These two equations will be produced as a result of the boundary conditions at the wall.

Then:

$$inD - A_o \kappa \sinh(\sqrt{i}\alpha) - \frac{ikA}{\rho_o c} = 0 \tag{33}$$

$$inE - A_o \cosh(\sqrt{i}\alpha) - \frac{1}{\rho_o c} A = 0 \tag{34}$$

Equations (31), (32), (33) and (34) are four homogeneous equations in four independent, undertermined constants A_o, A,D, and E. For a non-trivial solution to exist, the determinant of the coefficients must be zero. Using this fact, the functional form of c, the complex wave speed, may be determined.

$$\begin{bmatrix} 0 & -n^2 p + B'\frac{n^2}{c^2} & \frac{\mu}{b}\left(\frac{\sqrt{i}\alpha}{h} - \frac{in\kappa}{c}\right)\sinh(\sqrt{i}\alpha) & \frac{\nu n^2 h}{bc^3} \\ -n^2 & 0 & \frac{2\mu\sqrt{i}\alpha\ \kappa}{hb}\cosh(\sqrt{i}\alpha) & -\frac{1}{b}\left(1 - \frac{2\mu n i}{\rho_o c^2}\right) \\ in & 0 & -\kappa\sinh(\sqrt{i}\alpha) & \frac{-inh}{\rho_o c^2} \\ 0 & in & -\cosh(\sqrt{i}\alpha) & \frac{-1}{\rho_o c} \end{bmatrix} = 0$$

where $B' = \frac{E_c}{1-\sigma^2}$

The complex wave number, $k = \frac{hn}{c}$, may be evaluated from the above determinant by employing the approximation 1/c>>1 to reduce the complexity.

$$k^2 = k_o^2 \left\{1 - \frac{\sqrt[3]{i}\, m}{\alpha} \tanh(\sqrt{i}\alpha)\right\} \tag{35}$$

where

$$m = \frac{h\rho_o}{b\rho};\quad k_o = \frac{hn}{c_o} \text{ for } c_o = \sqrt{B'/\rho} \text{ are defined.}$$

As can be seen, the complex wave number is a function of k_o which describes the importance of the elastic properties of the membrane in determining the character of the flow, α, which describes the importance of viscous effects and m which relates the inertia of the fluid as compared to the inertia of the membrane.

The form of the complex constants A_o, D, and E may now be established by solving equations (31), (32), (33), and (34) for these constants in terms of A. The results of these manipulations are given below.

$$\frac{A_o}{A} = \frac{1}{bn\rho k} \frac{1 + ik^2/m}{\frac{2m}{\alpha}G_\alpha + iH_\alpha}$$

$$\frac{D}{A} = \frac{1}{bn^2\rho} \{\frac{2mkG_\alpha}{\alpha} (bn\rho \frac{A_o}{A}) - 1\}$$

$$\frac{E}{A} = \frac{-1}{bn^2\rho} \{\alpha G_\alpha (bn\rho \frac{A_o}{A}) + \frac{ik}{m}\}$$

where: $G_\alpha = \frac{i}{\alpha}\cosh(\sqrt{i}\alpha)$, $H_\alpha = \frac{\sqrt{i}}{\alpha} \sinh(\sqrt{i}\alpha)$

With the substitution of these relations into the velocity, pressure and displacement distributions, as given by equations (26), (27), (28) and (30) respectively, the problem is completely solved.

Oscillatory Inviscid Motion in an Elastic Walled Channel

Consideration of the inviscid flow problem will add insight into the correctness of the viscous flow problem. By examining the results derived from the inviscid flow analysis, a comparison will be made to check for convergence of the two solutions; the potential flow solution as compared to the viscous flow solution under the assumption of vanishing viscosity.

To accomplish this task, use will be made of Euler's equations written along a streamline in an irrotational field. A simplified form of Euler's equation, written in terms of the velocity potential, will be employed. Use of the velocity potential function for incompressible flow necessarily implies that $\phi(x,y,t)$ be harmonic. The Euler equation and Laplace equation governing the inviscid, incompressible flow case are given in equations (36) and (37) respectively.

$$\frac{p}{\rho_o} + \frac{\partial\phi}{\partial t} + \frac{1}{2} \{\frac{(\partial\phi)^2}{\partial x} + \frac{(\partial\phi)^2}{\partial y}\} = B(t) \quad (36)$$

$$\nabla^2\phi = \frac{\partial^2\phi}{\partial x^2} + \frac{\partial^2\phi}{\partial y^2} = 0 \quad (37)$$

By analogy with the viscous flow problem, a form of ϕ will be assumed such that the assumed form satisfies both the governing equations within the assumptions made and satisfies the boundary conditions on the flow itself. The assumed form of ϕ is given in relation (38).

$$\phi = A(y)\exp\{in(t - \frac{x}{c_o})\} \tag{38}$$

where c_o is the wave speed for the inviscid flow problem.

By substituting the assumed form of ϕ into Laplace's equation and noting that $\frac{\partial\phi}{\partial r} = 0$ at r=o, the functional A(y) may be evaluated. Thus

$$\phi = D \cosh (k_o r)\exp\{in(t-x/c_o)\} \tag{39}$$

The action of the membrane upon the fluid contained within will also generate a boundary condition that must be satisfied by the form of ϕ chosen. Recalling the membrane equations from the viscous flow solution, with the added assumption that no viscous forces are present, the membrane equations become

$$\rho \frac{\partial^2\eta}{\partial t^2} = B' \frac{\partial^2\eta}{\partial x^2} \tag{40}$$

$$\rho \frac{\partial^2\zeta}{\partial t^2} = \frac{p}{b}\Big|_{r = 1} \tag{41}$$

where for small perturbations or long waves, it is assumed that both η and ζ are independent of r.

The motion of the membrane wall and the fluid at r=1 may be linked by an equation of the form given below

$$\frac{1}{h} \frac{\partial\phi}{\partial r}\Big|_{r=1} = v = \frac{\partial\zeta}{\partial t} \tag{42}$$

The constant c_o may be evaluated by employing equation (40) where η is assumed to be of the form η=Mexp{in(t-x)}. Thus,

$$c_o = B'/f$$

By elimination of the pressure between equations (36) and (41), Euler's equation becomes,

$$\frac{1}{m}\frac{\partial^3\phi}{\partial r\partial x\partial t} + \frac{\partial^2\phi}{\partial x\partial t} + \frac{1}{2}\frac{\partial}{\partial x}\{(\frac{\partial\phi}{\partial x})^2 + \frac{1}{h^2}(\frac{\partial\phi}{\partial r})^2\}\Big|_{r=1} = 0 \tag{43}$$

Under the assumption $1/c<<1$, equation (43), for the assumed form of ϕ given, is satisfied. Hence, the boundary condition on ϕ at the wall is satisfied by the assumed solution.

To evaluate the pressure distribution, Euler's equation (equation (36)) will be employed. Substituting the known form of ϕ into equation (36) and simplifying under the restriction $1/c<<1$ the thermodynamic pressure becomes

$$p(x,r,t) = J\cosh(k_o r)\exp\{in(t - \frac{x}{c_o})\} \tag{44}$$

where the complex constant $-\eta\rho_o D$ has been replaced by a new complex constant J. Since the fluid velocity is related to the velocity potential ϕ (equation 45), the analytic nature of the velocity components, u and v, may be developed (equation 46).

$$\nabla\phi = \overline{V} \tag{45}$$

$$v(x,r,t) = \frac{i}{\rho_o c_o} J\sinh(k_o r)\exp\{in(t - \frac{x}{c_o})\}$$

$$u(x,r,t) = \frac{1}{\rho_o c_o} J\cosh(k_o r)\exp\{in(t - \frac{x}{c_o})\} \tag{46}$$

From the form of the pressure distribution given in equation (44), the membrane wall displacements may be evaluated. Referring to equation (41) and the assumptions made, one finds:

$$\zeta(x,t) = -\frac{J}{\rho n^2 b}\exp\{in(t - \frac{x}{c_o})\} \tag{47}$$

For small perturbations or long waves, the loading function p(x,1,t) acting tangential to the membrane is essentially zero. Therefore, one would expect only small perturbations of the membrane in the x direction, if any.

Thus, under this argument, M=0. This gives.

$$\eta(x,t) = M\exp\{in(t - \frac{x}{c_o})\} = 0 \tag{48}$$

As can be seen, the velocity, pressure and displacement fields are all functions of a single, undetermined constant J. This constant, as in the viscous flow problem, is assumed known from experimental pressure field investigations conducted on the flow in question.

By the comparison of equations (44), (46), (47), and (48) with their viscous flow counterparts under the assumption of zero viscosity, confirmation as to the correctness of the viscous flow solution under the assumptions made is guaranteed.

RESULTS AND CONCLUSIONS

In the theoretical development presented, the variation in the velocity, displacement and pressure fields was studied for oscillatory viscous motion within an elastic and rigid walled channel. It was found that the variation in these quantities could be described by referring to three dimensionless parameters characteristic of the flow.

The solution of the elastic walled problem, it was shown, emphasized the importance of the parameter α which describes viscous effects. The dimensionless parameters m and k_o where m describes the importance of the inertia effects of the fluid compared to the membrane and where k_o, the wave number, describes the elastic properties of the membrane, also were shown to be of importance in the description of the elastic walled problem.

The fact that only the wave speed exists for $\nu \to 0$ points out the basic difference between the solution for an elastic walled channel and for an elastic walled tube. The elastic walled tube solution predicts for $\nu \to 0$, as pointed out by Womersley, a wave number of the fluid in the form $k_o - qn/c'_o = jE_c/2q\rho_o$ where j is the thickness of the tube, q is the radius of the tube and ρ_o is the density of the fluid. The only wave number predicted for $\nu \to 0$ for the elastic walled channel is $k_o = hn/c_o$ the wave number of the membrane.

A typical plot of k_r, k_i, and the damping ratio for m = 30 is shown in Figures 4, 5 and 6, respectively. Tables of the complex constants involved in the solutions may be obtained from the author upon request.

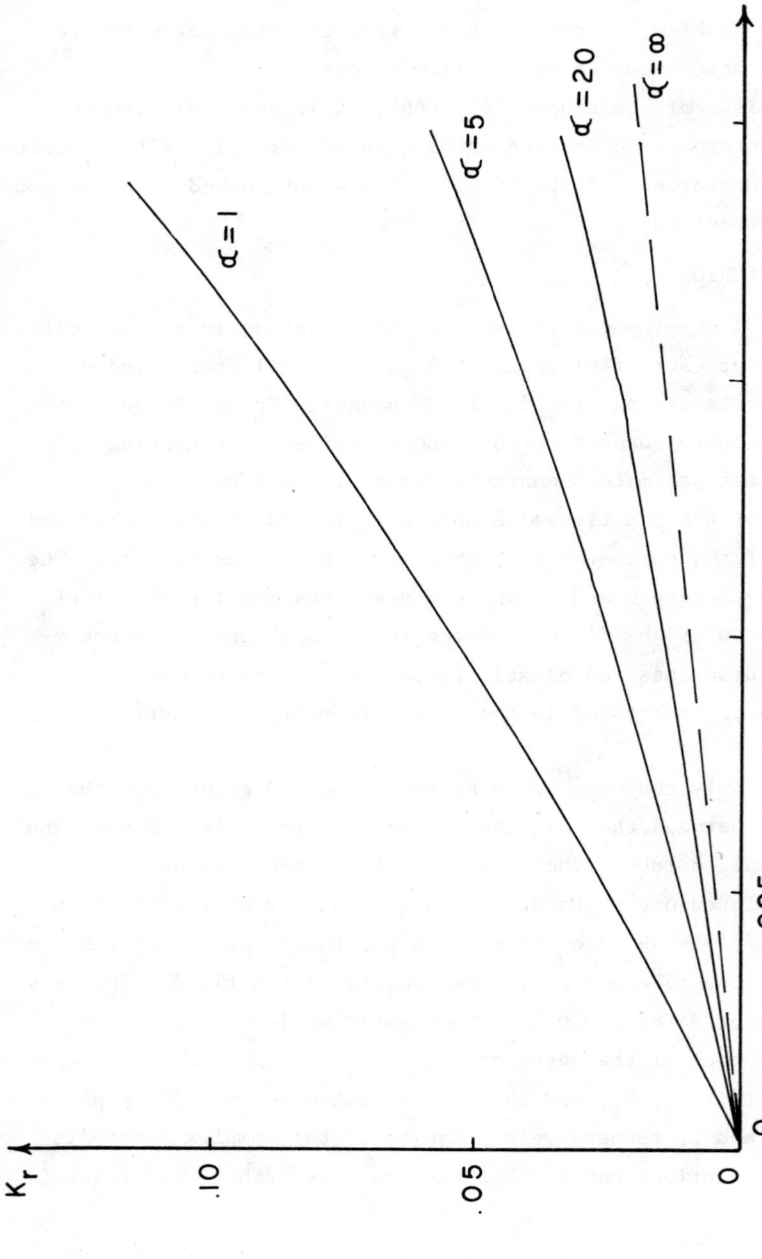

Fig. 4. Theoretical Variation of k_r with α for m = 30.

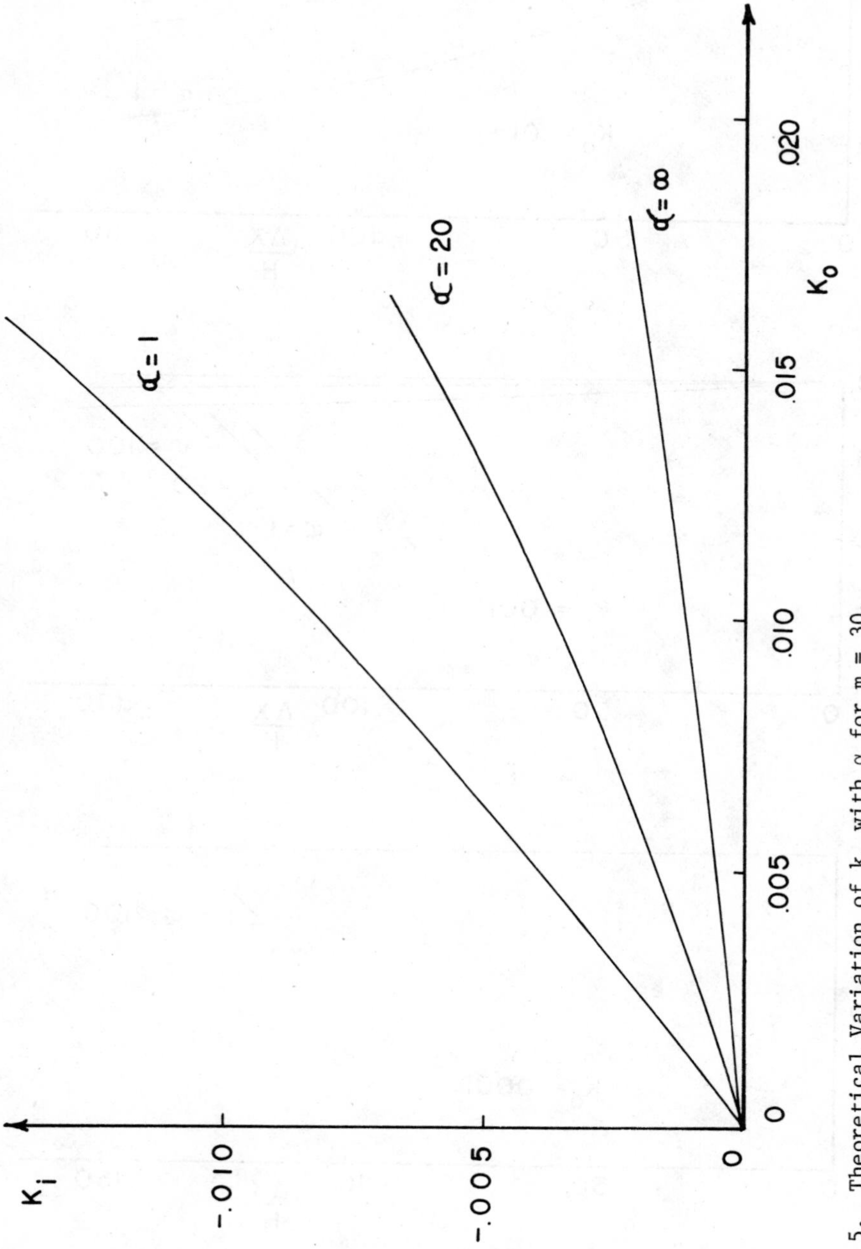

Fig. 5. Theoretical Variation of k_i with α for m = 30.

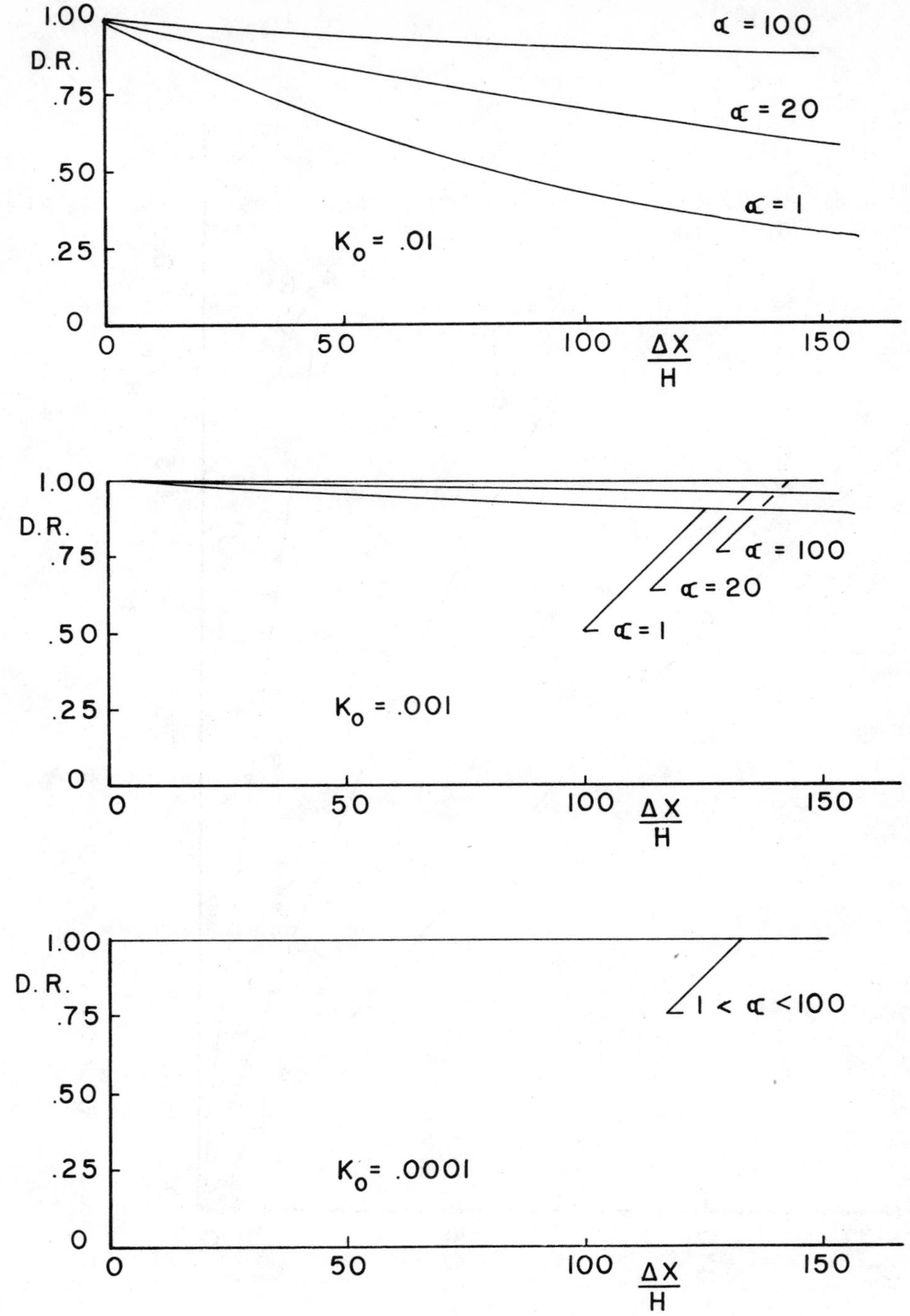

Fig. 6. Damping Ratio Versus $\frac{\Delta x}{h}$ for m = 30.

REFERENCES

1. Womersley, J. R., "Oscillatory Motion of a Viscous Liquid in a Thin Walled Plastic Tube - I. The Linear Approximation for Long Waves," Phil. Mag., 46, 199(1955).

2. Womersley, J. R., "Oscillatory Flow in Arteries: The Constrained Plastic Tube as a Model of Arterial Flow and Pulse Transmission," Phy. Med. Biol., 2, 178(1957).

3. McDonald, D. A., "Relation of Pulsating Pressure to Flow in Arteries," J. Physiol., (London), 127, 533(1955).

4. Branson, H., "The Flow of a Viscous Fluid in an Elastic Tube: A Model of the Femoral Artery," Bull. Math. Biophys., 7, 181(1945).

5. Bohr, D. R., W. F. Keitzer, and V. L. Streeter, "Pulsatile Pressure and Flow through Distensible Vessels," Circulation Res., 13, 3-20 (1963).

6. Kiely, J. P., and G. W. Morgan, "Wave Propagation in a Viscous Liquid Contained in a Flexible Tube," J. Acoust. Soc. Am., 26, 323(1954).

BIBLIOGRAPHY

1. Brest, A. N., Heart Substitutes, Springfield, Ill.: Charles C. Thomas (1966).

2. Bergel, D. H., "The Static and Elastic Properties of the Arterial Wall," J. Physiol., (London), 156, 445(1961).

3. Bergel, D. H., "The Dynamic Elastic Properties of the Arterial Wall," J. Physiol., (London), 156, 458(1961).

4. Fry, D. L., A. J. Mallos, and D. J. Patel, "Aortic Mechanics in the Living Dog," J. Appl. Physiol., 16, 293(1961).

5. Merrill, E. W., and R. E. Wells, Jr., "Influence of Flow Properties of Blood Upon Viscosity - Hermatocrit Relationships," J. Clin. Invest., 41, 1591(1962).

6. Peterson, L. H., "Dynamics of Pulsatile Blood Flow," Circulation Res., 2, 127(1954).

7. Jenson, R. E., J. Parnell, and L. H. Peterson, "Mechanical Properties of Arteries in Vivo," Circulation Res., 8, 622(1960).

8. Feigl, E. O., A. W. Jones, and L. H. Peterson, "Mechanical and Chemical Properties of Arteries in Experimental Hypertension," J. Clin. Invest., 42, 1640(1963).

9. Jacobs, R. B., "On the Propagation of a Disturbance Through a Viscous Liquid Flowing in a Distensible Tube of Appreciable Mass," Bull. Math. Biophys., 15, 395(1953).

10. Herrmann, G., and J. E. Russell, "Resonant Velocities in Steady-State Coupled Shell-Fluid Response," Proceedings of the Army Symposium on Solid Mechanics, 1968, 221-233.

CYLINDRICAL BONES AS ANISOTROPIC POROELASTIC MEMBERS SUBJECTED TO HYDROSTATIC PRESSURE

J. L. Nowinski
University of Delaware

ABSTRACT

Two-phase poroelastic material is taken as a model of a living bone in the sense that the osseous tissue is treated as a linear transversely isotropic perfectly elastic solid, and the fluid substances filling the pores as a Newtonian viscous fluid. Using Biot equations, derived in his consolidation theory and assuming a plane state of strain three governing equations involving fluid excess pressure and the stress function are derived for a circular cylindrical bone subjected to a uniform external pressure. Laplace transform technique enables one to find explicit solutions for stresses and displacements. Four illustrative examples are analyzed involving a purely elastic case, an infinite poroelastic medium with a cylindrical cavity and a solid and hollow cylinders. Viscoelastic properties of the adopted bone model seem to be in agreement with the experimental findings of Sedlin.

LIST OF NOTATIONS

r, θ, z	Cylindrical coordinates
a, b	Inner and outer radius of the tube
t	Time
σ	Liquid excess pressure
$\sigma_{rr}, \sigma_{\theta\theta}, \sigma_{zz}$	Radial, azimuthal and longitudinal stress
σ_i, σ_o	Liquid excess pressures at r=a and r=b

p_o	Outer uniform normal load
e, ε	Dilatation of solid and liquid phase
u, U	Radial displacement of solid and liquid phase
F(r,t)	Stress function
A,D,M,N,Q,R	Elastic coefficients
$S = A-Q^2/R$	

$K = (PR-Q^2)/(A+2N+R+2Q)$ and $P = A+2N$, $L = (PR-Q^2)/2N(Q+R)$

C	Coefficient of permeability
$\alpha = (C\xi/K)^{1/2}$	
ξ	Laplace transform coefficient
$\overline{f}(r,\xi)$	Laplace transform of f(r,t)
D_i (i=1,2,3,4)	Integration constants
A*,B*,D	Defined by Eqs. (33a) and (33b)

INTRODUCTION

It is well known that the osseous tissue resembles the lattice-work in the sense that it forms a solid skeleton containing innumerable cavities. The cavities (pores) are filled with bone marrow and various fluids such as blood, synovial fluid and others. The microscopic examination reveals that also the skeleton itself is perforated by tiny passages. Consequently, a living bone may be considered as a two-phase solid-fluid material pervaded by interconnected pores. Actually, like all biological materials a real bone represents a highly complex material: it is nonhomogeneous, anisotropic, with the solid phase governed by nonlinear constitutive equations and the liquid phase behaving like a non-Newtonian fluid. To facilitate the calculations, in the present study, we make the following rather natural simplifications:

(1) First, that the volume concentration of pores is uniform, so that the bulk material may be regarded as statistically homogeneous. It follows that the porosity of the material, defined as the percentage of the pore volume in the unit bulk volume, remains constant.

(2) Secondly, it is assumed that in the two-phase bone material the solid skeleton is linearly and perfectly elastic and undergoing small deformations.

(3) Third, the liquid phase is treated as Newtonian viscous, the pores as interconnected, and the flow of the fluid, produced by the deformation of the bone, as governed by Darcy's law.

(4) With regard to the internal forces it is postulated that the stresses in the bulk material are smoothly divided between the solid phase, as the stresses σ_{ij}, and the liquid phase, as the excess pressure σ (both per unit area of the bulk material).

It is nowadays a prevailing opinion (see e.g. [1]) that the crystallographic structure of bones is of the hexagonal class. In other words, bone elements have one axis of elastic symmetry of infinite order, so that they behave like transversely isotropic. Such a model is assumed also in the present analysis.

From the above assumptions, the homogeneity of the material and the smoothness of the stress distribution are the most vulnerable assumptions. While the first may be abandoned at a cost of some (in fact, considerable) computational labor, the second is difficult both to avoid and to defend.

In very truth, the presence of cavities in the bone certainly contributes to the local concentrations of stress, so that the mechanical picture of the phenomenon is extremely complicated. As a consolation, one may accept Currey's opinion [18], see also [10], p. 181, that the discontinuities in the bone are generally arranged in such a fashion, that they create minimum stress concentrations. Furthermore, the propagation of the cracks is eventually prevented much in the same way as in the Bowie's crack model (holes drilled at the tips of the crack).

Following the idea of two earlier papers [2], [3], this paper represents likewise an attempt at a more scrupulous quantitative analysis of mechanical behavior of bones than it could be done in the past by such authors as Wertheim [4], Rauber [5], Koch [6] and Marique [7] [1]. Except Marique's, all this work is from fifty to hundred years old, and concerns mostly the femur (thigh-bone) treated as an elastic beam. It involves some inacuracies brought about by a rather elementary, and occasionally naive, stress analysis based on simplified rules of the Strength of Materials.

---

1. Compare in this connection the comprehensive studies by Evans [8], Fung [9] and Kraus [10].

As the model of the poroelastic body we adopt the model developed by Terzaghi and Biot in their theory of consolidation, cf. e.g. [11]-[13]. A somewhat similar aspect was analyzed qualitatively by Zarek and Edwards [19] with regard to the articular cartilage.

We first give a brief derivation of the three governing equations involving the stress function and the excess liquid pressure referred to cylindrical coordinates. We assume that the load is axisymmetric and that the deformation is equivalent to a plane state of strain.

The bone element analyzed is represented by an infinitely long circular tube with a uniform annular cross-section. The load consists of a hydrostatic pressure on the outer surface of the tube. Both curved faces of the tube are taken as permeable, with the liquid phase subjected to a different pressure on each face. Such situations can arise during dives, which are recently reported to reach pressures equivalent to 1,000 ft. of sea water.

Using the Laplace transform technique, explicit solutions for stresses and displacements in the L-subspace are found. Four illustrative limit cases are analyzed in more detail involving a purely elastic case, an infinite poroelastic medium with a cylindrical cavity, and a solid and hollow poroelastic cylinder.

Viscoelastic properties of the adopted bone model show the pattern followed by the standard linear three-parameter rheological model (elastic spring in series with a Kelvin-Voigt element). Thus under a sudden application of constant load, an instantaneous deformation originates which, with elapsing time, increases asymptotically to a final bounded value. This phenomenon of creep taking place under the action of constant load, as well as our earlier findings of stress relaxation under a constant strain [2], seem to be in full agreement with the model proposed by Sedlin on the basis of his experimental observations [14], [15]. In fact, according to Sedlin, under loads well below the fracture load, the actual behavior of bones is well qualitatively characterized by the standard linear viscoelastic model. This is just the model suggested by the application of the consolidation theory. Of course, it belongs to future investigations to determine whether such an approach fully describes the actual behavior of bones in vivo.

General Equations

As already mentioned, the present analysis is based on the consolidation theory of Terzaghi and Biot. For details of the theory the reader is referred to the original papers of Biot, e.g. [11] - [13]. For future reference, however, and to make the study self-contained, we start with a brief recapitulation of the main equations of the theory adapted to the case under discussion.

Let us consider an infinite circular cylindrical tube of poroelastic material referred to a system of cylindrical coordinates, r,θ,z. Let the inner and the outer radius of the tube be a and b, respectively, Fig. 1. Assume that, at time $t = +0$, the outer surface of the tube is suddenly subjected to a uniform hydrostatic pressure p_o acting upon the skeleton of the bulk material, and that the surfaces $r=a$ and $r=b$ are unsealed (which seems to be a realistic assumption for a living bone) and subjected to sudden local uniform excess pressures $\sigma = \sigma_i$ and $\sigma = \sigma_o$, respectively, (also at the instant $t = +0$). It is assumed that the pressures p_o, σ_i and σ_o are maintained constant at all times $t > 0$. The solid phase on the inner surface of the tube should be free from load.

In view of the axial symmetry and the existing state of plane strain, the only components of the total stress that do not vanish identically are $\sigma_{rr} + \sigma$, $\sigma_{\theta\theta} + \sigma$ and $\sigma_{zz} + \sigma$. The non-vanishing components of strain are

$$e_{rr} = \frac{\partial u}{\partial r}, \quad e_{\theta\theta} = \frac{u}{r} \tag{1}$$

with u as the radial component of the displacement vector of the solid phase $\vec{u}$. If the displacement vector of the fluid phase be denoted by $\vec{U}$, then the dilatation of the solid and the fluid phases, respectively, is

$$e = e_{rr} + e_{\theta\theta}, \quad \varepsilon = \frac{\partial U}{\partial r} + \frac{U}{r} \tag{2}$$

(U = radial component of $\vec{U}$).

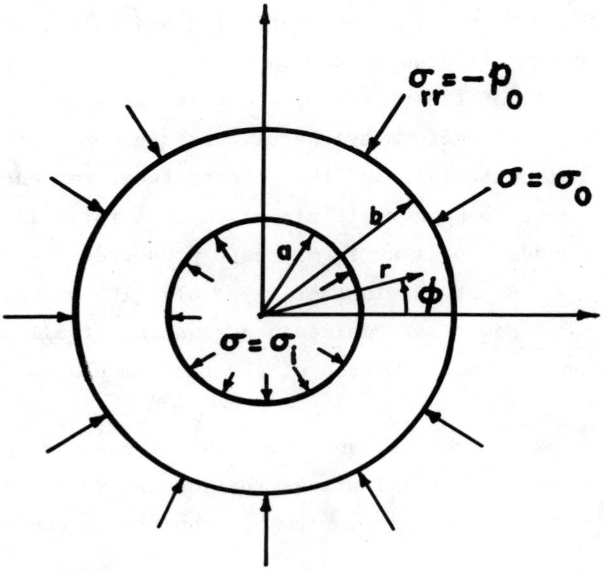

Fig. 1. Geometry and Load.

For a transversely isotropic poroelastic body the constitutive relations, in the coordinate system considered, become[2]

$$\begin{aligned} \sigma_{rr} &= 2Ne_{rr} + Ae + Q\varepsilon \\ \sigma_{\theta\theta} &= 2Ne_{\theta\theta} + Ae + Q\varepsilon \\ \sigma_{zz} &= De + M\varepsilon \\ \sigma &= Qe + R\varepsilon \end{aligned} \tag{3}$$

so that the four stress and three strain components are related to each other by means of six elastic constants denoted by majuscules [12]. The equation of flow is assumed to be expressed properly by Darcy's law

$$\frac{\partial\sigma}{\partial r} = C\frac{\partial}{\partial t}(U-u) \tag{4}$$

with C as coefficient of permeability in the radial direction. Here, in harmony with the assumption of the plane state of strain, the flow of the fluid phase is supposed to remain plane.

The only remaining equation of equilibrium

$$\frac{\partial(\sigma_{rr}+\sigma)}{\partial r} + \frac{\sigma_{rr}-\sigma_{\theta\theta}}{r} = 0 \tag{5}$$

is satisfied if we introduce the stress function F=F(r,t) defined by the relations

$$\sigma_{rr} + \sigma = \frac{F}{r}, \quad \sigma_{\theta\theta} + \sigma = \frac{\partial F}{\partial r} \tag{6}$$

Upon combining (3) and (6), we get the strain components in the form

$$\begin{aligned} e_{rr} &= \frac{1}{2N}\left(\frac{F}{r} - Se + \frac{Q+R}{R}\sigma\right) \\ e_{\theta\theta} &= \frac{1}{2N}\left(\frac{\partial F}{\partial r} - Se + \frac{Q+R}{R}\sigma\right) \end{aligned} \tag{7}$$

with $S = A-Q^2/R$, so that the dilatation of the solid phase becomes

$$e = \frac{1}{N+S}\left[\frac{1}{2}\nabla_1 F - \frac{Q+R}{R}\sigma\right] \tag{8}$$

2. In equations (3.2) in [12] the present symbol Q is denoted by M and vice versa. In the plane strain considered the transverse isotropy is reflected solely in the stress component σ_{zz}, which in the isotropic case becomes equal to Ae + Qε, leaving four constants unknown.

where $(\nabla_1 \equiv \frac{\partial}{\partial r} + \frac{1}{r})$.

The problem being solved in terms of stresses, the associated strains (7) should satisfy the compatibility equation

$$\frac{\partial}{\partial r}(r\, e_{\theta\theta}) - e_{rr} = 0 \tag{9}$$

After some manipulations we obtain the following first governing equation involving a single function σ,

$$K \frac{\partial}{\partial r}(\nabla_1 \frac{\partial \sigma}{\partial r}) - C \frac{\partial}{\partial t}\frac{\partial \sigma}{\partial r} = 0 \tag{10}$$

where $K = (PR-Q^2)/\ (A+2N+R+2Q)$ and $P = A+2N$.

Similarly the elimination of the excess pressure function leads to the equation for the stress function

$$K \frac{\partial}{\partial r} \nabla_1 (\frac{\partial}{\partial r} \nabla_1 F) - C \frac{\partial}{\partial t}\frac{\partial}{\partial r} \nabla_1 F = 0 \tag{11}$$

We apply Laplace transformation

$$\bar{f}\ (r,\xi) = \int_0^\infty f(r,t) e^{-\xi t} dt \tag{12}$$

to Eq. (10) with the notation $\tau = \partial\bar{\sigma}/\partial r$, and arrive at the equation of the modified Bessel functions,

$$r^2 \frac{\partial^2 \tau}{\partial r^2} + r \frac{\partial \tau}{\partial r} - (1 + \frac{C\xi}{K} r^2)\tau = 0 \tag{13}$$

Its solution is

$$\tau\ (r,\xi) = \tilde{C}_1 I_1(\alpha r) + \tilde{C}_2 K_1(\alpha r) \tag{14}$$

so that $\bar{\sigma}(r,\xi)$ is found in the form

$$\bar{\sigma}(r,\xi) = C_1 I_0(\alpha r) + C_2 K_0(\alpha r) \tag{15}$$

where $\alpha = (C\xi/K)^{\frac{1}{2}}$ and the free integration constant is rejected.

The solution of (11) transformed to L-space is readily obtained by first using the auxilary function

$$v(r,\xi) \equiv \frac{\partial}{\partial r} \nabla_1 \bar{F} \tag{16}$$

which satisfies an equation similar to (10). This gives directly

$$v(r,\xi) = \tilde{D}_1 I_1(\alpha r) + \tilde{D}_2 K_1(\alpha r) \tag{17}$$

and reduces the problem to the solution of the non-homogeneous differential equation

$$\frac{\partial^2 \bar{F}}{\partial r^2} + \frac{1}{r}\frac{\partial \bar{F}}{\partial r} - \frac{\bar{F}}{r^2} = v(r,\xi) \qquad (18)$$

A relatively trivial calculation using standard properties of the cylindrical functions yields the transform of the stress function of the following final form,

$$\bar{F}(r,\xi) = D_1 I_1(\alpha r) + D_2 K_1(\alpha r) + D_3 r + D_4 r^{-1} \qquad (19)$$

It is now required for the solutions (15) and (19) to satisfy identically the equation (9). This furnishes the relations between the parametric constants (clearly depending on the L-parameter ξ) C_i and D_i, $i = 1,3$. In this way we gain

$$C_1 = L\alpha D_1, \; C_2 = - L\alpha D_2 \qquad (20)$$

where $L = (PR - Q^2)/2N(Q+R)$. Thus

$$\bar{\sigma}(r,\xi) = D_1 \alpha L I_0(\alpha r) - D_2 \alpha L K_0(\alpha r) \qquad (21)$$

This, in fact, completes the construction of the general solution, which must now fulfill the prescribed boundary conditions. In the present case, these conditions in their transformed form are,

$$\left.\begin{aligned} \bar{\sigma}(a,\xi) &= \frac{\sigma_i}{\xi} \\ \bar{\sigma}(b,\xi) &= \frac{\sigma_o}{\xi} \\ \bar{\sigma}_{rr}(a,\xi) &= 0 \\ \bar{\sigma}_{rr}(b,\xi) &= \frac{-p_o}{\xi} \end{aligned}\right\} \quad \begin{aligned} &\text{at any time} \\ &t \geq +0\,, \end{aligned} \qquad (22)$$

where the opposite signs of σ_1, σ_o and p_o follow from our earlier convention by which the fluid stress is defined as the negative pressure on the fluid.

With (19) and (21) in mind, Eq. (6) provides the final form of the transformed radial stress.

$$\bar{\sigma}_{rr} = D_1[\frac{I_1(\alpha r)}{r} - \alpha L I_0(\alpha r)] + D_2[\frac{K_1(\alpha r)}{r} + \alpha L K_0(\alpha r)] + \\ + D_4\frac{1}{r^2} + D_3 \tag{23}$$

Upon substitution of (21) and (23) into the boundary conditions (22), we get a system of four nonhomogeneous linear algebraic equations from which by some straight-forward manipulations the values at the unknown integration constants D_i, $i = 1,2,3,4$, may be found. This brings to light the final expression for the stress function (19) and consequently for the radial and azimuthal stresses (6), the excess fluid pressure (21) and - if desired - for the radial displacement u from $(1)_2$ and $(7)_2$. Clearly, all these equations are obtained in their transformed form, so that a retransformation to the ordinary space is demanded.

Since the integration constants D_i represent involved functions of the Laplace parameter ξ, application of the contour integration for derivation of the inverse Laplace transforms is, in the general case just described, rather clumsy. This would rather obscure than clarify the discussion, so that instead, we content ourselves with the analysis of some particular cases.

Illustrative Examples

1. Let us first consider the limit case of a purely elastic tube. Then $\bar{\sigma} \equiv 0$ throughout and $D_1 = D_2 = 0$. It follows from (19), (16) upon rejecting the redundant transformation signs that

$$\sigma_{rr} = D_4 r^{-2} + D_3, \quad \sigma_{\theta\theta} = - D_4 r^{-2} + D_3 \tag{24}$$

which is the well known solution to the Lamé problem for a cylindrical tube under normal pressures. Since in this case the material constants N and A become Lamé elastic constants μ and λ, the associated radial displacement takes the classical form

$$u = p_0 \frac{[\mu r^2 + (\mu+\lambda)a^2]b^2}{2\mu(\mu+\lambda)\ (a^2-b^2)r} \tag{25}$$

2. Let us now increase indefinitely the outer radius b of the clyinder, thus passing to the limit case of an infinite poroelastic space with an infinitely long circular cylindrical hole. Since the deformation should vanish at the infinite distance from the hole, one should pose $D_1=D_3=0$ in order to suppress the r-term and the modified Bessel function of the first kind that become unbounded as $r \to \infty$. Apart from the notation, the general solution (23) degenerates in this particular case into the solution obtained directly by Jana [16] upon using the displacement function. For instance, disregarding the immaterial (in the axially symmetric case) Jana's displacement function ψ, Eq. $(3.5)_1$ in [16] reads in our notation

$$\bar{\sigma}_{rr} = - c\alpha^2 L K_o(\alpha r) - c\alpha \frac{K_1(\alpha r)}{r} + \frac{B}{r^2}$$

which is precisely the equation (23) with $D_1=D_3=0$ and $c\alpha = - D_2$, $B = D_4$.

3. In analyzing the case of a solid cylinder we have to guarantee the boundedness of the pertinent function at r=0, so that D_2 and D_4 are posed equal to zero. The fluid excess pressure and the radial stress then become

$$\bar{\sigma} = D_1 \ \alpha L I_o(\alpha r)$$
$$\bar{\alpha}_{rr} = D_1 \left[\frac{I_1(\alpha r)}{r} - \alpha L I_o(\alpha r)\right] + D_3. \tag{26}$$

Fulfillment of the boundary conditions $(22)_2$ and $(22)_4$ furnishes the values of the parametric constants,

$$D_1 = \sigma_o/\xi \ \alpha L I_o(\alpha b)$$
$$D_3 = -\frac{p_o}{\xi} - \frac{\sigma_o}{\alpha \xi L I_o(\alpha b)} \left[\frac{I_1(\alpha b)}{b} - \alpha L I_o(\alpha b)\right] \tag{27}$$

It is instructive to analyze the evolution in time of the deformation of the cylinder. As a pertinent characteristic let us choose the radial displacement u. After a rather longer but trivial calculation we arrive at the equation,

$$\bar{u}(r,\xi) = -\frac{\sigma_o I_1(\alpha r)}{\alpha\xi 2NL\, I_o(\alpha b)} - \frac{r}{2(N+S)\xi}\{p_o + \frac{\sigma_o}{\alpha L\, I_o(\alpha b)}[\frac{I_1(\alpha b)}{b} - \alpha L\, I_o(\alpha b)]\} \tag{28}$$

where as earlier $\alpha = (C/K\xi)^{1/2}$.

The inverse transformation of the above formula does not provide a formula suitable for small values of time (cf. [16], p. 141). A more convenient result is obtained upon application of two limit theorems of the operational calculus expressed symbolically by

$$f(t=+0) = \lim_{\xi \to \infty} \xi\bar{f}(\xi)$$
$$f(t=\infty) = \lim_{\xi \to 0} \xi\bar{f}(\xi) \tag{29}$$

It is clear that the above formulae furnish the values of the deformation characteristics in two time instants: directly after the application of the load, and after elapse of an infinitely long time. In the first case, the modified Bessel functions $I_\nu(x)$ may be represented by their asymptotic form $e^x/\sqrt{2\pi x}$, valid for any value of ν. In the second case, the approximations $I_o(x) \approx 1$ and $I_1(x) \approx \frac{x}{2}$ are adequate. As a final result, we arrive at the following equations,

$$u_{t=+0} = -\frac{p_o - \sigma_o}{2(N+S)} r$$
$$u_{t=\infty} = -\frac{p_o + \sigma_o Q/R}{2(N+S)} r \tag{30}$$

First of these equations, for vanishing fluid pressure, represents the static purely elastic displacement (25)[3]. The second equation is

3. In which $a \equiv 0$ and S is equivalent to λ, see [13], p. 93.

the asymptotic value of the radial displacement. Biot in [17] has analyzed the relative values of the poroelastic coefficients and found, among others, that $Q/R = (\alpha-f)/f$, where f is the porosity, and α in a number of cases may be approximately set equal to 1. If one considers the materials with a limited degree of porosity so that $f < 1/2$, then $Q/R > 1$ and the absolute value of $u_{t=\infty}$ is greater than the absolute value of $u_{t=+0}$. In this case for a fixed load the bony materials reveal the phenomenon of creep. On the other hand, in the moment of sudden application of load an instantaneous deformation originates equal to $u_{t=+0}$. Such viscoelastic properties are associated with the rheological model known as the standard linear three-parameter viscoelastic system and represented by an elastic spring in series with the Kelvin-Voigt element, Fig. 2. This phenomenon of creep occuring under the action of constant load, as well as our earlier findings of stress relaxation under a constant strain [2] show a full agreement with the model proposed by Sedlin on the basis of his experimental observations [14], [15], (see also [10]). In fact, according to Sedlin, under loads well below the ultimate load, the actual behavior of bones is well qualitatively characterized by the standard linear viscoelastic model. This is just the model suggested by the consolidation theory applied in the present analysis. It is instructive to evaluate also the evolution in time of a stress characteristic such as, say, the normal stress at the axis of the cylinder $\sigma_{rr}(r=0,t)$.

From (26) and (27) using the limit formulae (29), we easily obtain,

$$\bar{\sigma}(0,\xi) = D_1\ \alpha L$$

$$\bar{\sigma}_{rr}(0,\xi) = D_1\ \alpha(\frac{1}{2} - L) + D_3 \tag{31}$$

and for inverted fluid excess pressure and normal stress,

$$\sigma(0,\ +0) = 0$$

$$\sigma(0,\ \infty) = \sigma_o \tag{32a}$$

and

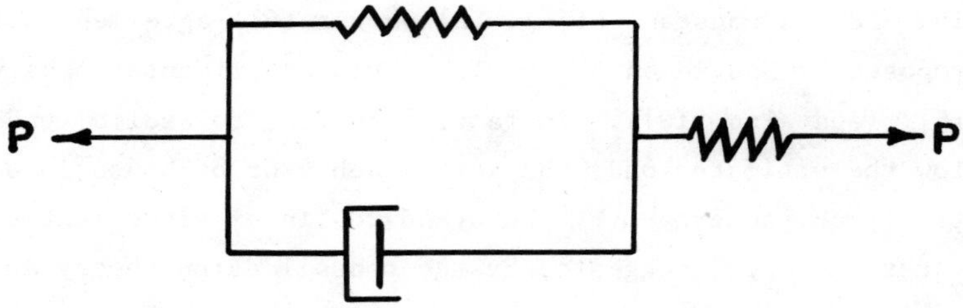

Fig. 2. Viscoelastic Model of Osseous Materials.

$$\sigma_{rr}(0, +0) = -(p_o - \sigma_o)$$
$$\sigma_{rr}(0, \infty) = -p_o \tag{32b}$$

respectively. It is seen that at the moment of application of load no fluid excess pressure reaches the axis of the body. As time goes by, however, the pressure at $r = 0$ increases to its final value equal to the outer fluid pressure. In contrast, the normal stress in the solid phase is brought forth simultaneously with the external load; its original intensity $p_o - \sigma_o$ increases with elapsing time to the final value p_o equal to the intensity of the external load.

4. Let us now return to the general case of a hollow cylinder. Assume for definiteness that $\sigma_i = \sigma_o$ which is a reasonable guess for a living bone. Upon using Eqs. (22), the first two of which are not coupled with the last two, we arrive after some manipulations at the following equations for the constants of integration,

$$\begin{aligned} D_1 &= \sigma_o[K_o(\alpha a) - K_o(\alpha b)]/D \\ D_2 &= \sigma_o[I_o(\alpha a) - I_o(\alpha b)]/D \\ D_3 &= [A^* a^2 \xi - b^2(B^* + p_o)]/\xi\,(b^2 - a^2) \\ D_4 &= [-A^* b^2 \xi + b^2(B^* + p_o]a^2/\xi(b^2 - a^2) \end{aligned} \tag{33}$$

where

$$D = \xi\alpha L[I_o(\alpha b)K_o(\alpha a) - I_o(\alpha a)K_o(\alpha b)] \tag{33a}$$

and

$$\begin{aligned} A^* &= D_1[\frac{I_1(\alpha a)}{a} - \alpha L I_o(\alpha a)] + D_2[\frac{K_1(\alpha a)}{a} + \alpha L K_o(\alpha a)] \\ B^* &= D_1\xi\ [\frac{I_1(\alpha b)}{b} - \alpha L I_o(\alpha b)] + D_2\xi\ [\frac{K_1(\alpha b)}{b} + \alpha L K_o(\alpha b)] \end{aligned} \tag{33b}$$

With these equations in mind, the fluid excess pressure and the radial stress, both in their transformed form, can be found immediately from Eqs. (21) and (23). We then use the procedure indicated by (29) and, after some calculations, we find the following limit values of the excess fluid pressure,

$$\sigma(r,0) = \begin{cases} 0 & \text{for } r \neq a \neq b \\ \sigma_o & \text{for } r = a,\ b \end{cases} \tag{34}$$

$$\sigma(r,\infty) = \sigma_o \quad \text{for } a \leq r \leq b$$

It is seen that at the moment of application of load no fluid pressure reaches the inside of the cylinder. As time goes by, however, the inside pressure increases asymptotically to its final value equal to the values of the outside fluid pressure. The radial stress variation can be found in a similar fashion upon inserting Eqs. (33) into (23) and passing to the appropriate limits. This procedure yields the following final results,

$$\sigma_{rr}(r, +0) = -p_o \frac{(r^2-a^2)b^2}{(b^2-a^2)r^2} + \begin{cases} \sigma_o & \text{for } r \neq a \neq b \\ 0 & \text{for } r=a,\ r=b \end{cases} \tag{36}$$

$$\sigma_{rr}(r,\infty) = -p_o \frac{(r^2-a^2)b^2}{(b^2-a^2)r^2} \quad \text{for } a \leq r \leq b \tag{37}$$

First of these equations shows that, in contrast to the fluid pressure, the stress in the solid originates simultaneously with the application of the external load. It tends with time toward a final bounded value absolutely larger than the original one. In fact, the essentially negative part of σ_{rr} is at time $t = +0$ reduced by the presence of the positive term σ_o. The time variation of a deformation characteristic such as the radial displacement may be found by inverting the following equation obtained from $(7)_2$

$$\frac{\bar{u}}{r} = \frac{2N+S}{4N(N+S)} \frac{\partial \bar{F}}{\partial r} - \frac{S}{4N(N+S)} \frac{\bar{F}}{r} - \frac{Q+R}{2R(N+S)} \bar{\sigma} \tag{38}$$

The final results of the related transformations are

$$u(r, +0) = -\frac{p_o[Nr^2+(N+S)a^2]b^2 - \sigma_o Nr^2(b^2-a^2)}{2N(N+S)\ (b^2-a^2)r} \tag{39}$$

$$u(r,\infty) = -\frac{p_o[Nr^2+(N+S)a^2]R\ b^2 + \sigma_o NQr^2(b^2-a^2)}{2NR(N+S)\ (b^2-a^2)r} \tag{40}$$

Since the absolute value of $u(r,\infty)$ is greater than that of $u(r,+0)$, one notices here the same linear three-parameter viscoelastic behavior as the one pointed at in the case of the solid cylinder. Clearly, in view of the assumed particular boundary conditions Eqs. (39) and (40) transform into Eqs. (30) if the hollow cylinder degenerates into a solid cylinder.

CONCLUSIONS

The results of the three illustrative examples discussed in the subsections 2 to 4 and involving poroelastic models of bone elements (medium with an infinite cylindrical hole, a solid cylinder and a thick-walled tube) seem to lead to the following conclusions for all three examples.

1. In the case of a load suddenly applied and then kept constant the poroelastic model adopted for the osseous material reveals the phenomenon of an instantaneous deformation followed by a creep tending toward a final asymptotic value. Such a behavior combined with our earlier findings, for the same model, of stress relaxation that under the action of constant strain [2], indicates that the adopted rheological model is equivalent to the standard linear three-parameter viscoelastic model.
2. It seems, therefore, reasonable to assume that the adopted rheological model may probably serve as a model of the bony material, since such a model for the bony tissue was proposed independently earlier on the basis of laboratory tests on bones [14], [15], (cf. also [10] and [20]). While it is nowadays universally accepted that the bone is a viscoelastic material, further studies are, clearly, necessary to determine whether the adopted approach fully describes the actual behavior of bones in vivo.
3. Since in the adopted model, which reflects the actual behavior of bones, both the deformation and the internal stress in solid and

liquid phase increase with elapsing time, the bones are "less vulnerable" to loadings of shorter duration than to those of prolonged action. This should be interpreted in the sense that relatively brief loadings "have not enough time" to develop peak (that is, asymptotic) values of the internal stresses and deformations, so that the effort of the loaded elements is below its possible maximum (at time $t = \infty$).

ACKNOWLEDGEMENT

This work was supported by a grant of the National Science Foundation.

REFERENCES

1. Lang, S. B., "Elastic Coefficients of Animal Bone," Science, Vol. 165, 1969, p. 287.

2. Nowinski, J. L., "The Flexure and Torsion of Cancellous Bones as Poroelastic Materials," Tech. Rep. No. 101, Department of Mechanical and Aerospace Engineering, University of Delaware, Newark, Delaware, 1969.

3. Nowinski, J. L., "Bone Articulations as Systems of Poroelastic Bodies in Contact," Tech. Rep. No. 102, Department of Mechanical and Aerospace Engineering, University of Delaware, Newark, Delaware, 1969, AIAA Journal, Vol. 9, No. 1, 1971, pp. 62-67.

4. Wertheim, M. G., "Memoire sur l'elasticite et la cohesion des principaux tissus du corps humain," Annals de Chimie Physique, Vol. 21, 1847, p. 385.

5. Rauber, A. A., "Elastizitaet und Festigkeit der Knochen," Engelmann, Leipzig, 1876.

6. Koch, J. C., "The Laws of Bone Architecture," American Journal of Anatomy, Vol. 21, 1917, pp. 177-298.

7. Marique, P., "Etudes sur le femur," Librairie des Sciences, Bruxelles, 1945.

8. Evans, F. G., "Stress and Strain in Bones," C. C. Thomas, 1957.

9. Fung, Y-C. B., "Biomechanics," Applied Mechanics Reviews, Vol. 21, 1968, pp. 1-20.

10. Kraus, H., "On the Mechanical Properties and Behavior of Human Compact Bone," Advances in Biomedical Engineering and Medical Physics, Vol. 2, 1968, pp. 169-204.

11. Biot, M. S., "General Theory of Three-Dimensional Consolidation," Journal of Applied Physics, Vol. 12, 1941, pp. 155-164.

12. Biot, M. A., "Theory of Elasticity and Consolidation for a Porous Anisotropic Solid," Journal of Applied Physics, Vol. 26, 1955, pp. 182-185.

13. Biot, M. S., "General Solutions of the Equations of Elasticity and Consolidation for a Porous Material," Journal of Applied Mechanics, Vol. 23, 1956, pp. 91-96.

14. Sedlin, E. D., "A Rheological Model for Cortical Bone," Acta Orthopaedica Scandinavica, Suppl. 83, Munksgaard, Copenhagen, 1965, pp. 1-77.

15. Sedlin, E. D. and Sonnerup, L., "Rheological Considerations in the Physical Properties of Bone," Proceedings European Symposium on Calcified Tissues, 3rd, 1965, pp. 98-101.

16. Jana, R. N., "Deformation in an Infinite Poroelastic Medium with a Long Circular Cylindrical Hole," Quarterly Journal of Mechanics and Applied Mathematics, Vol. 16, 1963, pp. 137-148.

17. Biot, M. A., "The Elastic Coefficients of the Theory of Consolidation," Journal of Applied Mechanics, Vol. 24, 1957, pp. 594-601.

18. Currey, J. D., "Stress Concentrations in Bone," Quarterly Journal of Microscopic Sciences, Vol. 103, 1962, pp. 111-133.

19. Zarek, J. M. and Edwards, J., "Dynamic Considerations of the Human Skeletal System," Biomechanics and Related Bio-Engineering Topics, ed. R. M. Kendi, Proceedings of the Symposium, Glasgow, September 1964, Pergamon Press, 1965, pp. 187-203.

20. Burnstein, A. H. and Frankel, V. H., "The Viscoelastic Properties of Some Biological Materials," Annals of the New York Academy of Sciences, Vol. 146, Art. 1, 1968, pp. 158-165.

DYNAMICS OF PLATES

REFLECTION AND REFRACTION OF ELASTIC WAVES IN EDGE-IMPACTED RECTANGULAR PLATES

William F. Hartman
The Johns Hopkins University

ABSTRACT

Axial edge impact of rectangular metal plates provides conditions for studying reflection and refraction of plane stress waves at an elastic interface. Strain-time data are compared with shock wave predictions using a plane stress hypothesis. Release waves from the free sides of the plates are observed to differ from analytical predictions. For oblique supercritical incidence upon an interface between dissimilar plates it is found that the waves refracted in the faster medium do not become separated from the incident and reflected waves along the interface.

LIST OF NOTATIONS

$\alpha_1, \alpha_2, \ldots$	Angles between wave normals and interface
$\underset{\sim}{a}_1, \underset{\sim}{a}_2, \ldots$	Amplitude vector of shock wave
E	Young's modulus
ν	Poisson's ratio
$E^* = E/(1-\nu^2)$	
G	Shear modulus
$\underset{\sim}{n}_1, \underset{\sim}{n}_2, \ldots$	Unit vectors normal to wave fronts
$\underset{\sim}{N}$	Unit vector normal to interface
s	Wave speed
$\underset{\sim}{T}$	Unit vector tangent to interface
t_{ij}	Stress tensor
ρ	Density

u_i	Components of displacement vector
$u_{i,j} \equiv \partial u_i/\partial x_j$	
$\dot{u}_i \equiv \partial u_i/\partial t$	
β^+	Value of β ahead of wave
β^-	Value of β behind the wave
$[\beta] = \beta^+ - \beta^-$	
$2V_0$	Speed of impacting plate
$2w$	Width of plates

INTRODUCTION

The reflection and refraction of elastic waves at an interface have been traditionally studied from several points of view including those of the seismologist, the acoustician and the vibrationist. The types of waves considered are usually oscillatory and a steady state analysis is rather conventional. The medium of propagation is most often assumed to be infinite or semi-infinite, while applications frequently require one be more than aware of the complexities in bounded media. The experimentalist, interested in studying the behavior of materials subjected to impact, can be faced with the dilemma of extracting from several theoretical approaches a tractable indicator of the transient response of a bounded medium to a shock-like input. Furthermore, for situations involving waves obliquely incident on a boundary or interface, the existence of critical angles necessitates certain "patched" solutions, the physical meaning of which is often ambiguous. Interfacial problems are relevant not only when studying the response of composite bodies but whenever a transducer is employed. Inability to recognize the geometric wave effects could lead to a serious misinterpretation of material dissipation in attenuation studies. Some knowledge of the reflection and refraction at grain boundaries in multicrystals should correlate with the smoothing of step-inputs in such materials. Anticipated research on a similar topic motivated the experimental study described here.

Axial edge impacts of metal plates provide conditions for experimentally studying the reflection and refraction at a solid-solid interface of impact-generated waves. The experimentalist, aided by some basic theory, can then compare his observations with the behavior suggested by analytical treatments of similar problems. In particular, some hypotheses of wave behavior for supercritical incidence may be resolved. Critical angles were first studied in the reflection and refraction of light. In 1611 Kepler published the results of some simple experiments in which he discovered the phenomenon of "total reflection", a term which should be used cautiously when discussing elastic waves. Without proper measurement or tractable theory, the refraction behavior for supercritical incidence is of course unknown; but even if we accept the classical treatment for oscillatory waves, the behavior for shock-like waves remains obscure.

For elastic waves there are two general critical angle problems, the oblique incidence of a transverse wave on a free boundary or interface and the oblique incidence of a longitudinal wave on an interface. This first type consists of several special cases such as the five possible situations discussed by McNiven and Mengi [1]. They consider a train of plane harmonic shear waves striking a plane interface and show that there result "Rayleigh-like" waves at the interface. Their treatment does not suggest what happens for non-periodic motions. The case of a plane transverse wave of arbitrary shape incident upon an interface has been treated by Friedlander [2]. For a step shear wave with amplitude perpendicular to the plane of propagation and incident at an interface beyond the critical angle he obtained a transmitted wave which decays inversely as the distance from the interface in contrast to the exponential decay of oscillatory waves.

Critical incidence of longitudinal pulses which involve no transverse waves exist for pressure pulses obliquely incident at the interface of two fluids. Arons and Yennie [3] studied the phase distortion of acoustic pulses reflected from a sea floor which was assumed to be a dense fluid. They found good agreement with measured pressure time curves, although their analysis, which is patterned after Rayleigh's, yields both reflected and transmitted pressures having parts which exist for all time, that is, do not propagate.

There is a more subtle critical angle problem which must be specially considered when dealing with bounded media, such as plates. This concerns waves propagating parallel to a free surface. For example, as the obliquity to a free boundary of a longitudinal wave diminishes to zero, that is, grazing incidence, there no longer exists an elementary wave solution which satisfies the boundary conditions. This problem was discussed by Goodier and Bishop [4], who were unable to resolve it for the impact problem. Recently, Wright [5] has obtained a solution for impact on an elastic quarter space. A comparison of his results with some data for plate impacts will be provided in this paper.

When an impact wave or shock wave is supercritically incident upon an interface it is a reasonable hypothesis that a transmitted wave breaks away from the incident wave, preceding it along the interface and therefore generating nonuniform, time dependent boundary conditions. Such a situation entails severe analytical difficulties. On the other hand this hypothesis can easily be tested experimentally. Simply look for the "break away" effect.

In this paper a shock wave formulation of impact waves is used to guide the description of three distinct interfacial problems. These consist of an impact wave propagating in a rectangular brass plate and incident to an aluminum plate:

i) normally

ii) obliquely at a subcritical angle,

iii) obliquely at a supercritical angle.

The objectives will be to determine the applicability of the shock wave description for cases (i) and (ii) and to suggest what is desirable in a theory for the description of (iii).

Experimental Procedure

In order to achieve axial edge impacts, a Stull-Ealing linear air track has been adapted as a frictionless guiding device for an impacting plate. This brass plate is ten inches long, six inches wide and one quarter inch thick. It is mounted on a specially made glider and propelled by a spring device so that it uniformly speeds down the tract and strikes a similar brass plate which is supported in mechanical isolation from the tract. The apparatus is sketched in Fig. 1. The glider speed ranges from 50 in/sec to 80 in/sec, and is measured by an electronic time interval meter. The 6" × 1/4" meeting surfaces of the plates are carefully machined and honed. Alignment can be achieved by holding the impacting plate A fixed near the end of the track and carefully adjusting the orientation of plate B until the interface is optically closed. The rails which support plates B and C are lubricated

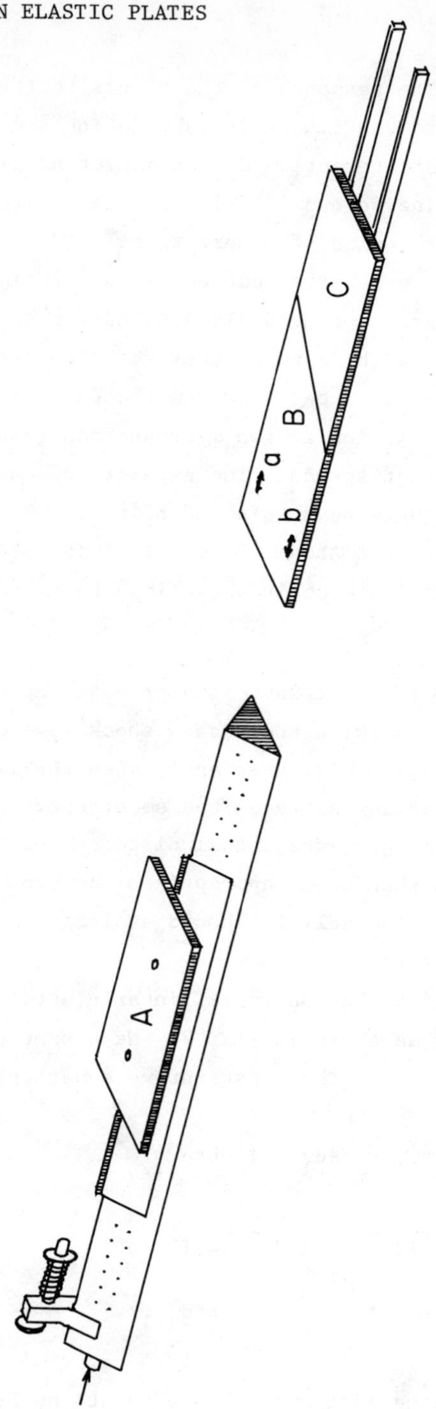

Fig. 1. Plate A is Propelled on the Airbearing and Strikes Plate B on Edge. The Response of Strain Gages at a and b Indicates the Degree of Axiality of the Impact.

precision steel flats. The response of the plates to the first pass of the wave is insensitive to variations in lubrication and position of these supports. Also the interaction of the impacting plate with the glider through the mounting screws is delayed long enough so as not to affect B during the short period of observation.

Foil-resistance strain gages are mounted on the specimens at desired locations. These gages are type Budd 314-350, having a gage length of 1/16 inch, and are bonded with Eastman adhesive. The response of the gages are photographically recorded from the traces of a Tektronik 556 oscilloscope. Rise times as low as two microseconds (μsec) are observed for the higher impact speeds. The axiality of each impact is checked by observing if gages such as a and b in Fig. 1 respond simultaneously to the shock front. About 20% of all impacts are axial to within two μsec. The results of only these impacts are discussed here.

Shock Wave Formulation

We will treat the incident impact wave as a propagating discontinuity surface of first order, otherwise known as a shock wave or stress wave. Of course this representation will best apply when the impacting speed is greatest and the contacting surfaces the smoothest. As the reflections and refractions multiply, the actual disturbances become smoother and a weak wave analysis then seems appropriate; however for the short time response the shock wave analysis should at least loosely agree with the reality of the situation.

The plates are assumed to be isotropic linear elastic solids. We choose the x_1, x_2, x_3 axes as shown in Fig. 2. We assume plane stress, that is, $t_{33} = t_{32} = t_{31} = 0$. The constitutive equations then reduce to

$$
\begin{aligned}
t_{11} &= E^* u_{1,1} + \nu E^* u_{2,2} \\
t_{12} &= G(u_{1,2} + u_{2,1}) \qquad (1) \\
t_{22} &= E^* u_{2,2} + \nu E^* u_{1,1} \, .
\end{aligned}
$$

A development of the kinematical and balance equations for propagating singular surfaces of the first order is given by Truesdell and Toupin [6]. We write them as the following:

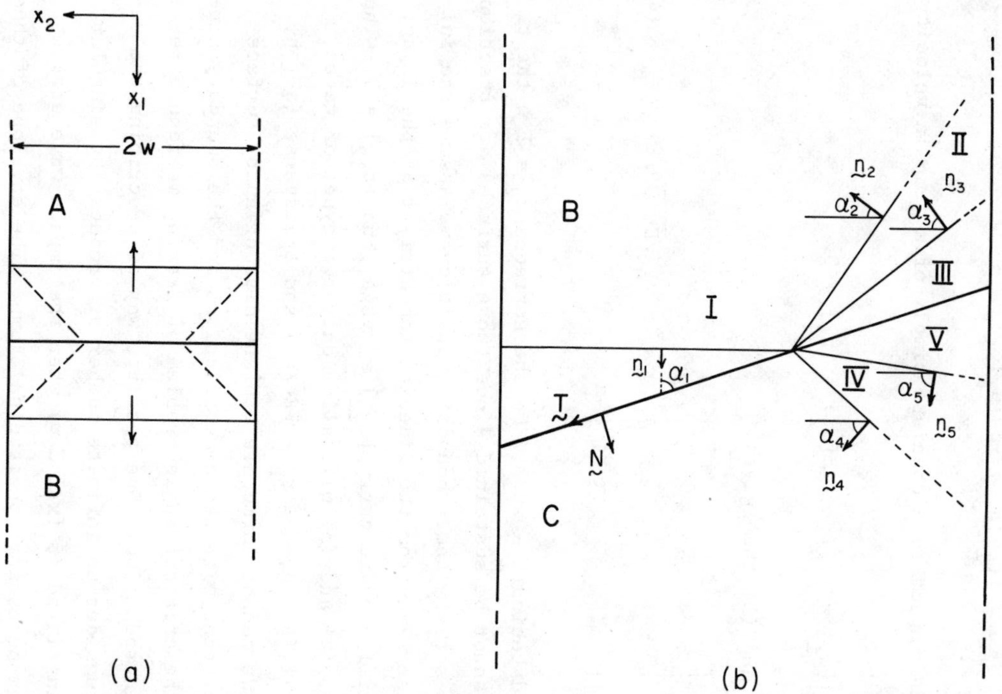

Fig. 2. a) For a Symmetrical Axial Impact of Plate A onto B the Shock Waves Propagate from the Impact Face as Shown. The Dashed Lines Represent the Location of the Release Waves which are Propagating from the Free Edges.

b) A General Representation of the Reflected ($\underset{\sim}{n}_2, \underset{\sim}{n}_3$) and Refracted ($\underset{\sim}{n}_4, \underset{\sim}{n}_5$) Waves Resulting from the Incident Wave ($\underset{\sim}{n}_1$) at the Interface (Normal $\underset{\sim}{N}$) of Two Contiguous Dissimilar Plates. The Dashed Lines Delineate Regions wherein Additional Waves are Necessary.

$$[u_{i,j}] = a_i\, n_j$$
$$[\dot{u}_i] = -a_i s \tag{2}$$

$$[t_{ij}]n_j = -\rho s[\dot{u}_i] \, . \tag{3}$$

The condition at the impact face consists simply of a jump in velocity in the x_1 direction,

$$[\dot{u}_1] = -v_0, \qquad [\dot{u}_2] = [\dot{u}_3] = 0.$$

Equations (1), (2) and (3) then give:

$$t^I_{ij} = \begin{pmatrix} -E^*a_1 & 0 \\ 0 & -\nu E^* a_1 \end{pmatrix} , \quad a_1 = v_0/\sqrt{E^*/\rho} \, , \tag{4}$$

as the stress field behind the wave. On the surfaces $x_2 = \pm\, w$ the t_{22} stress component cannot be sustained since those surfaces are traction free. In order to satisfy their boundary condition we assume the initiation of a release wave from the sides at the arrival of the impact wave. This wave will need to carry $[t_{22}] = -\nu E^*a_1$ and $[t_{12}] = 0$. The nature of Eqs. (1), (2) and (3) will allow only two types of waves, namely, longitudinal ($\underset{\sim}{a} \propto \underset{\sim}{n}$, $s \equiv s_L = \sqrt{E^*/\rho}$) and transverse ($\underset{\sim}{a} \perp \underset{\sim}{n}$, $s \equiv s_T = \sqrt{G/\rho}$). We cannot formulate a plane discontinuity surface which will be consistent with these restrictions and the boundary condition. This is the critical angle problem of grazing incidence referred to in the introduction. One possible way of describing the release wave is to consider an infinite number of propagating singular <u>points</u> which are initiated at (x_1, $\pm$ w) when the impact wave arrives there and carry the necessary longitudinal jump. The envelope of these points appears as the dotted lines in Fig. 2a. Across one of these lines the strain $u_{2,2}$ changes by a magnitude of νa_1. These lines themselves act as plane singular surfaces, but the amplitude vectors are neither parallel nor perpendicular to the normal vectors. Therefore it is emphasized that this is just a convenient way of picturing the release waves; it is not theory.

Although the above perspective of the release wave will be seen to provide a fair description near the impact face it does not predict the $u_{2,2}$ response at distances beyond $x_1 = w$. Wright [5] has obtained a solution to this problem, for a quarter space, by using a decomposition into a trivial quarter space problem and a half space problem. The negative of the moving reactive stresses on the free boundary are used as boundary conditions to obtain an interior solution which can be superposed with the stress field caused by the impact on the quarter space. Some results, directly applicable to normal velocity edge impact of plates, are given in [5] and are discussed in the next section.

A general interfacial configuration is pictured in Fig. 2b. We will consider the plates to be smoothly contiguous at this interface. The reflected (refracted) waves with normals $\underset{\sim}{n}_2$, $\underset{\sim}{n}_3(\underset{\sim}{n}_4,\underset{\sim}{n}_5)$ are longitudinal and transverse waves respectively. Their speeds are denoted by s_L, $s_T(\bar{s}_L, \bar{s}_T)$. The segmented part of these waves is used to denote the fact that additional hypotheses of wave initiation are needed in these areas in order to preserve stress continuity there. These complications will not be discussed here. If we assume that the illustrated waves move such that they all intersect the interface at a common point, that is, that the reflected and refracted waves initiate at every point on the surface with the arrival of the incident wave at that point, then

$$\frac{\cos \alpha_1}{s_L} = \frac{\cos \alpha_2}{s_L} = \frac{\cos \alpha_3}{s_T} = \frac{\cos \alpha_4}{\bar{s}_L} = \frac{\cos \alpha_5}{\bar{s}_T} . \tag{5}$$

These relations cannot always be satisfied; for example, when $\bar{s}_L > s_L$ there exists an α^* such that $\bar{s}_L/s_L \cos \alpha_1 \geq 1$ for $0 \leq \alpha_1 \leq \alpha^*$. The angle of α^* is then called the critical angle and incidence at any angle less than α^* is called supercritical. The appropriate method of resolving this dilemma remains obscure. One open conjecture is that a refracted longitudinal wave will form and break away, leading the incident wave along the interface and thereby producing time dependent boundary conditions along the interface. Such a situation could no longer be described with elementary stress waves.

The interfacial configurations here studied experimentally consist of three:

1) $\alpha_1 = \pi/2$

2) $\alpha_1 = \alpha', \ \alpha^* < \alpha' < \pi/2$

3) $\alpha_1 = \alpha'', \ 0 < \alpha'' < \alpha^*.$

For each of these, the conditions to be satisfied at the interface are

$$(t_{ij}^{III} + t_{ij}^{V})N_iN_j = 0$$

$$t_{ij}^{III}\,N_jT_i = t_{ij}^{V}\,N_jT_i = 0 \tag{6}$$

$$(\dot{u}_i^{III} + \dot{u}_i^{V})N_i = 0.$$

Equations (6) correspond respectively to equality of normal component of the stress vector across the interface, the vanishing of the shear stress on the interface, and the equality of the normal particle speed across the interface.

For a brass plate A and an aluminum plate B:

$$s_L = 150{,}000 \text{ in/sec}, \quad s_T = 86{,}000 \text{ in/sec}, \quad \bar{s}_L = 208{,}000 \text{ in/sec},$$

$$\bar{s}_T = 125{,}000 \text{ in/sec}, \ \rho = 8.0\times10^{-4}\,\frac{\text{lbs sec}^2}{\text{in}^4}, \ \bar{\rho} = 2.52\times10^{-4}\,\frac{\text{lbs sec}^2}{\text{in}^4}.$$

As one indicator of the applicability of the shock wave formulation, we can now easily calculate the reflected (refracted) strain amplitudes for two special cases, normal incidence at the interface and oblique incidence at $\alpha_1 = 60°$ with plate B removed. For the former case, Eqs. (1) through (6) give $a_3 = a_5 = 0$, $u_{1,1}^{III} = -0.6a_1$, $u_{1,1}^{V} = -a_1$. For the latter case we replace Eqs. (6) with the condition $t_{ij}^{III}N_j = 0$ and get $u_{1,1}^{II} = -0.904a_1$, $u_{1,1}^{III} = 0.10a_1$. If these calculated strains agree with those measured for such impacts, then the shock wave formulation may be assumed applicable for the other interfacial conditions. It is important to realize that the regions III and V do not extend to the side boundaries, for in that neighborhood additional waves are being formed both to maintain continuity of particle velocity within each plate and to satisfy zero traction on the boundary. However, the short-time response away from the free edges should be calculable by the above technique.

Experimental Results

i) Normal Incidence / In order to check the applicability of the plane stress assumption and the shock formulation, we can consider simple normal impacts of free-ended rectangular plates. An instrumented configuration is shown in Fig. 3. The axiality of the impact is implied by the symmetry of the responses of gages 1 and 2. The shock predictions are good in spite of this being a very weak impact. The plane stress assumption is consistent with the strain-time record at location 4. Figure 4 displays good axiality and depicts fair agreement of the transverse gages with the release-wave concept. The strain $u_{2,2}$ at location 4 does not show the doubling of the amplitude because of its proximity to the edge, approximately three μsec away.

As shown in Fig. 5, observations made along the plate axis, x_1, indicate that the transverse response becomes segmented as x_1 increases. Results obtained by Wright [5] imply that the transverse strain will exhibit a changing shape similar to the data curves of Fig. 5. Figure 6 shows a direct comparison of the strains calculated from [5] with aluminum data. The general shape of the transverse response curve loosely agrees; however the theoretical amplitude of the first plateau is too high. The longitudinal response is similar to the shock wave response except for an appreciable perturbation occurring at the arrival time of the "head" wave. No effect such as this is observed in axial impacts. This can be better seen in Fig. 7, which shows no appreciable variation in the longitudinal strain while the transverse straining occurs.

Some data for normal incidence of the impact wave on a brass-aluminum interface is shown in Fig. 8. The predicted strain values are those obtained above. The time interval in which the transmitted wave increases to its predicted maximum could be associated with the presence of the oil lubricant at the interface.

ii) Subcritical Incidence / Observation of the reflection and refraction of impact waves for subcritical incidence is important as a guide in describing the phenomenon occurring at supercritical incidence. Figure 9 shows that the shock wave predictions give some

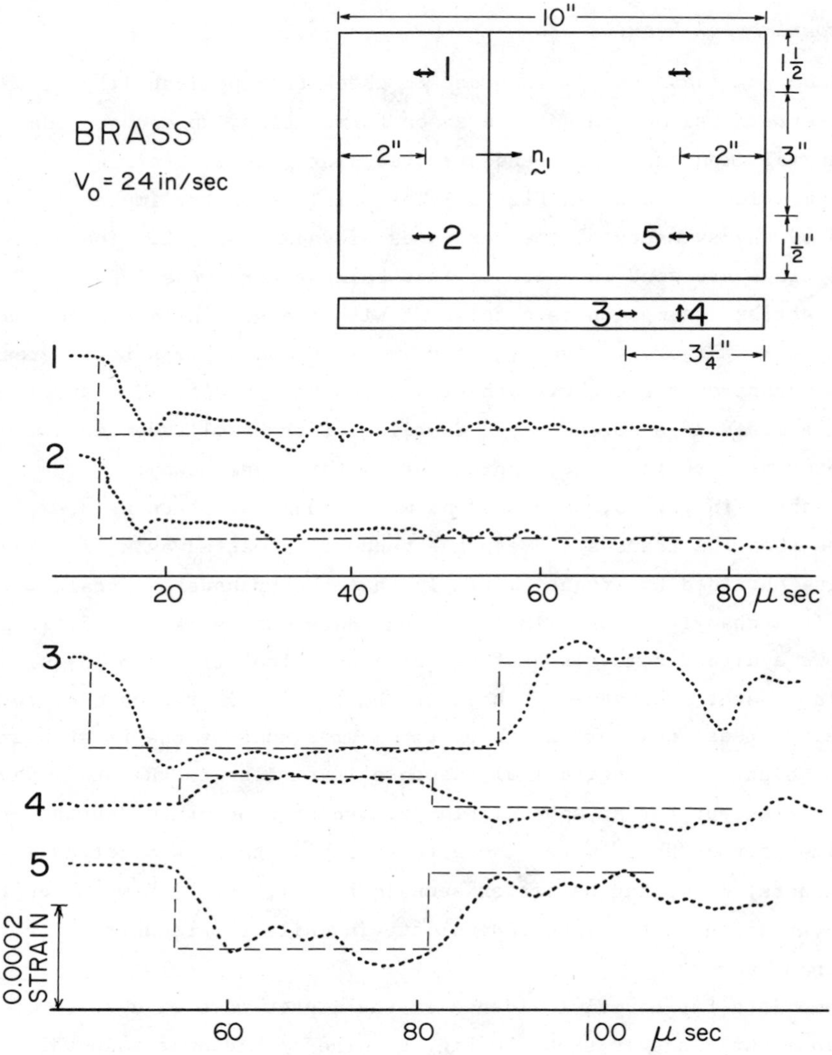

Fig. 3. The Observed Strain Response (Dotted Lines) Resulting from Axial Impact by an Identical Plate is Compared with the Shock Wave Strains (Dashed Lines) Predicted from the Measured Impact Speed.

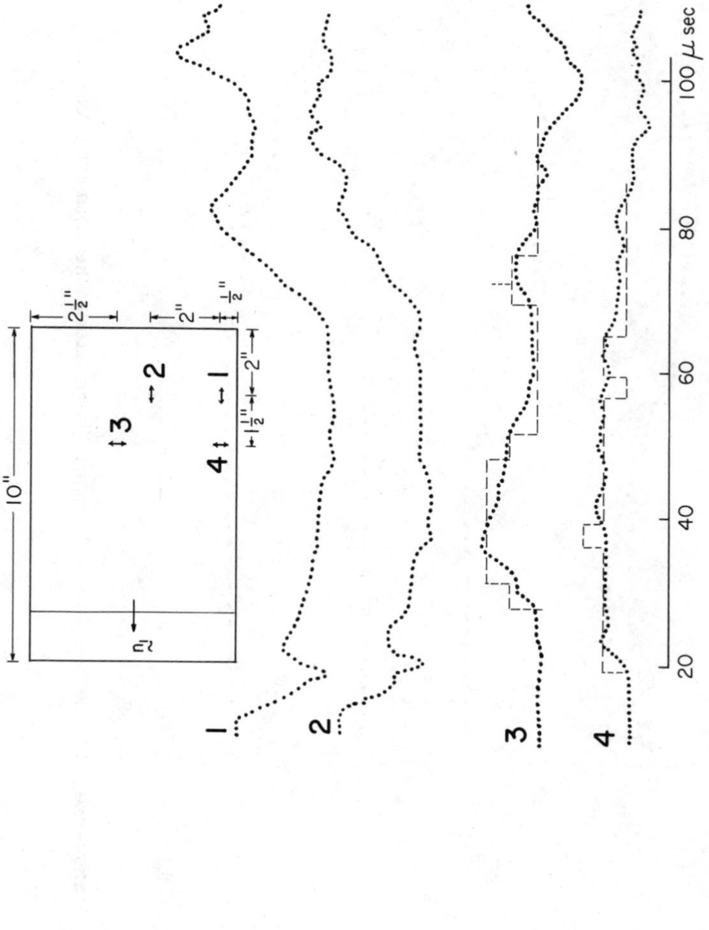

Fig. 4. Brass Plate-Normal Incidence. The Dotted Lines are Experimental Data. The Dashed Lines are Shock Wave Predictions of the Transverse Strain Caused by the Release Waves.

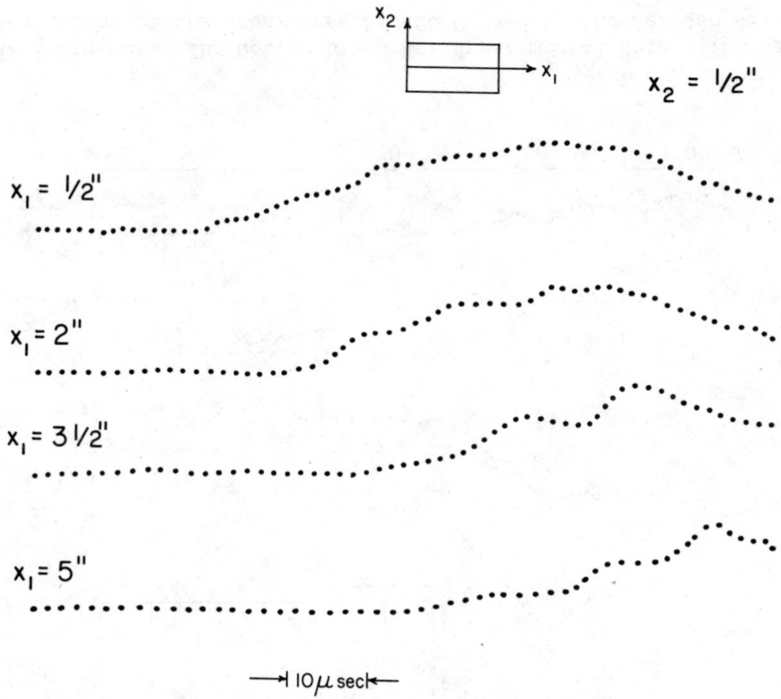

Fig. 5. The Transverse Strain-Time Curve Changes Shape Along the Symmetry Axis.

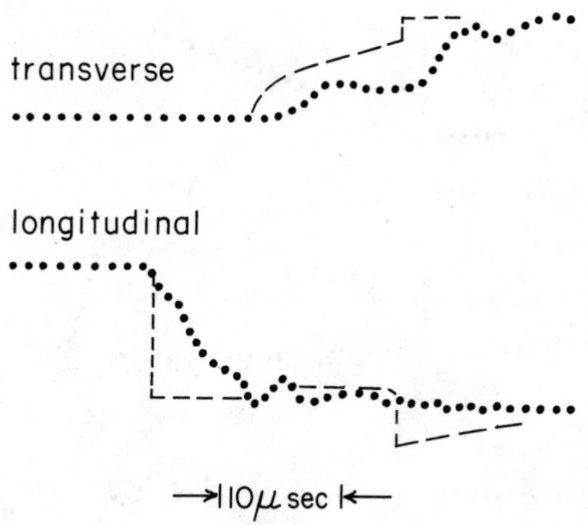

Fig . 6. Measured Strains, Dotted Lines, at $x_1 = 2$ Inches, $x_2 = 0$, in Aluminum Plate are Compared with Predictions Obtained from Reference [5].

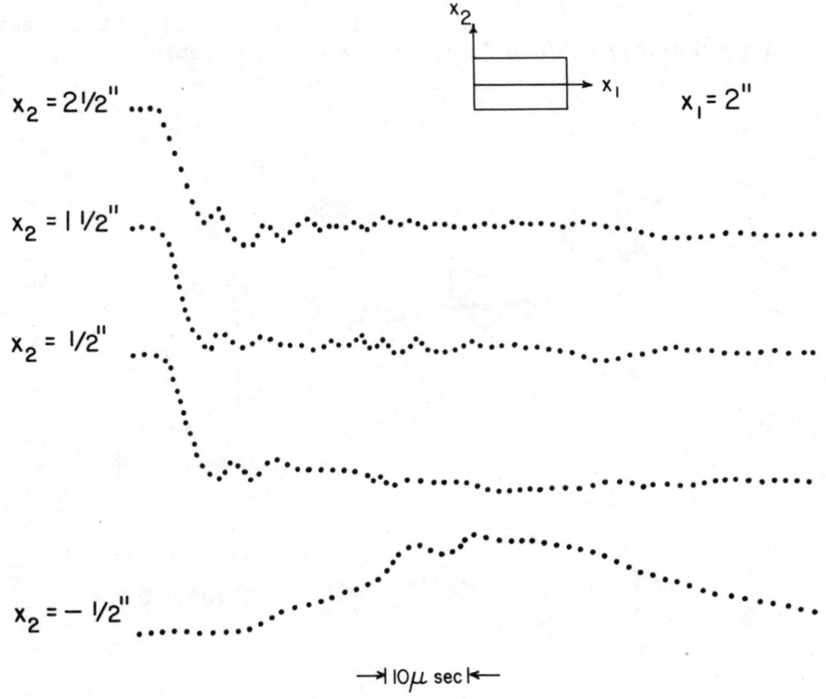

Fig. 7. Longitudinal Strains at Three Positions Across Width of Brass Plate Do Not Appreciably Change as Transverse Strain Develops and Disappears.

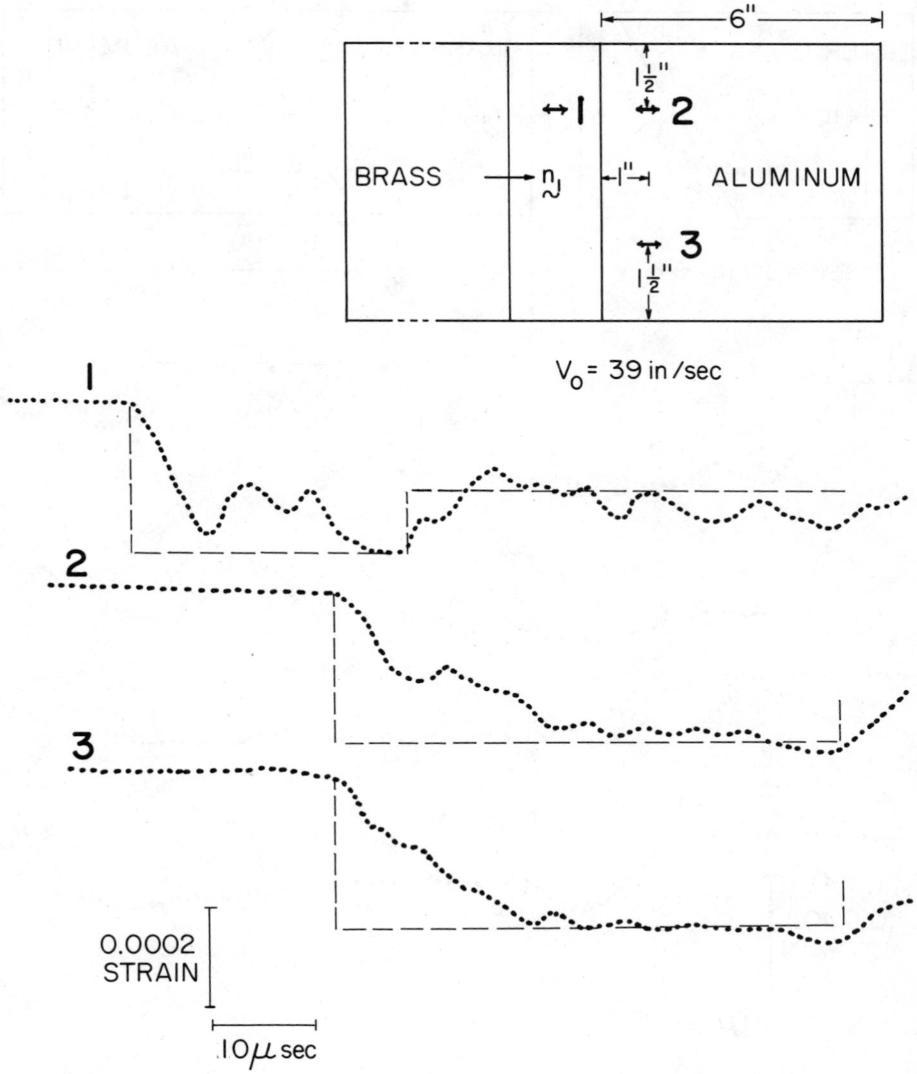

Fig. 8. The Longitudinal Strain Amplitudes Predicted by the Shock Equations for Normal Incidence at the Interface are Compared with Those Observed (Dotted Lines).

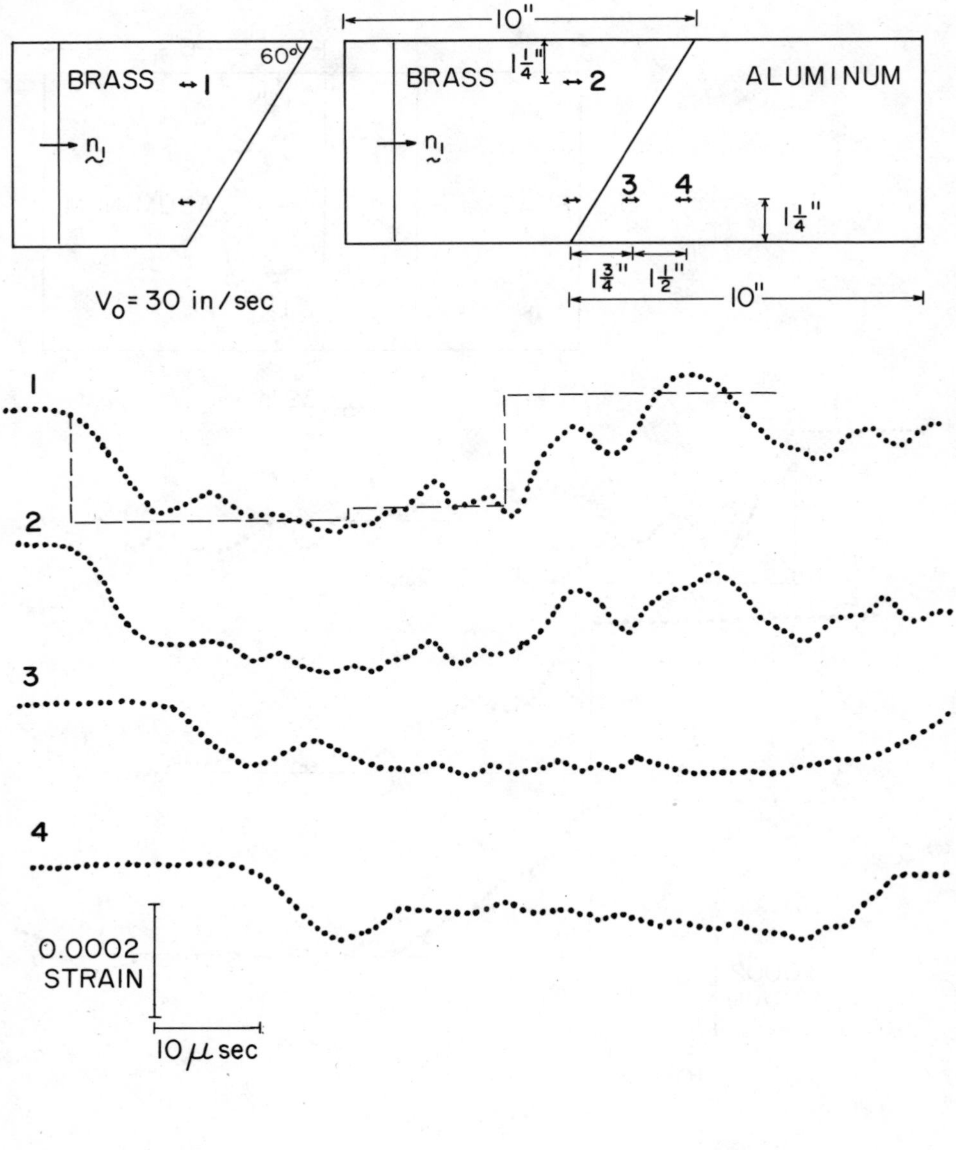

Fig. 9. Response 1 is for 60° Incidence at Free Surface. The Large Reflection is Predicted as Being Caused by the Reflected Transverse Wave. The Same Location Responds Similarly when the Reflection Originates at the Brass-Aluminum Interface.

indication of the actual response of the free-ended plate. The discrepancies can be correlated with the increased effect of the side release waves on the interface. It can be seen that the reflected transverse wave has a large amplitude for both the free-ended plate and the two-plate combination. The strain $u_{1,1}$ caused by the transmitted waves is 60% of the strength of the incident wave.

iii) Supercritical Incidence / The critical angle α^* for the plates used here is 44°. Figure 10 shows some data for an interfacial angle of 40°. The unusual shape of the incident wave, as portrayed by gages 1 and 2, is caused by the arrival of a flexural pulse, which trails behind the longitudinal wave in a dispersive way. This is caused by out-of-plane misalignment. The small departures of 1, 2 and 3 from the responses for the free-ended brass plate indicate that the same reflected waves occur, only their amplitudes are less. Notice that gage 4 begins responding about two μsec after gage 3. The calculated difference based on the arrival of the transverse wave at 4 is 3 μsec. This is an important observation. It suggests that a refracted longitudinal wave does not break away and precede the incident wave along the interface. If this did occur, then gage 4 would respond before gage 3.

The response of gages 1, 2, 3 in Fig. 11 can be correlated with the arrival time of the refracted transverse wave. Gages 4 and 5 should also respond to this wave with an amplitude equal to that of 1 and 3. The difference is indicative of some longitudinal wave in the tangential direction.

CONCLUSIONS

The shock wave formulation of impact waves in bounded plates predicts both arrival times and maximum strains for normal incidence to an elastic interface and oblique incidence to a free edge. The arrival times for some of the reflected and refracted waves for oblique incidence to an interface can also be correlated with shock fronts. The problem of grazing incidence, which is always present in bounded plates, has not been completely resolved. Although the transverse strains agree qualitatively with a recent analysis, the release waves do not affect the longitudinal strains in the manner predicted in that analysis. For the supercritical incidence studied here there is no indication of the

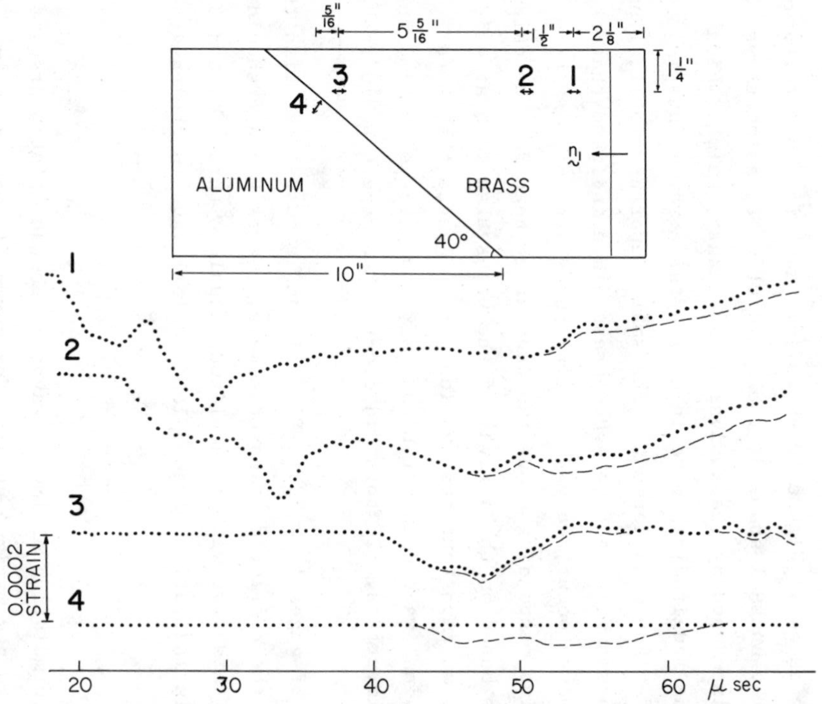

Fig. 10. Supercritical Incidence. The Dotted Lines Correspond to the Observed Responses when the Plates are Not Touching. The Dashed Lines are the Only Differences in the Responses when the Interface is Lubricated. The Arrival of a Wave at Location 4 Occurs Appreciably Later than the Response at 3.

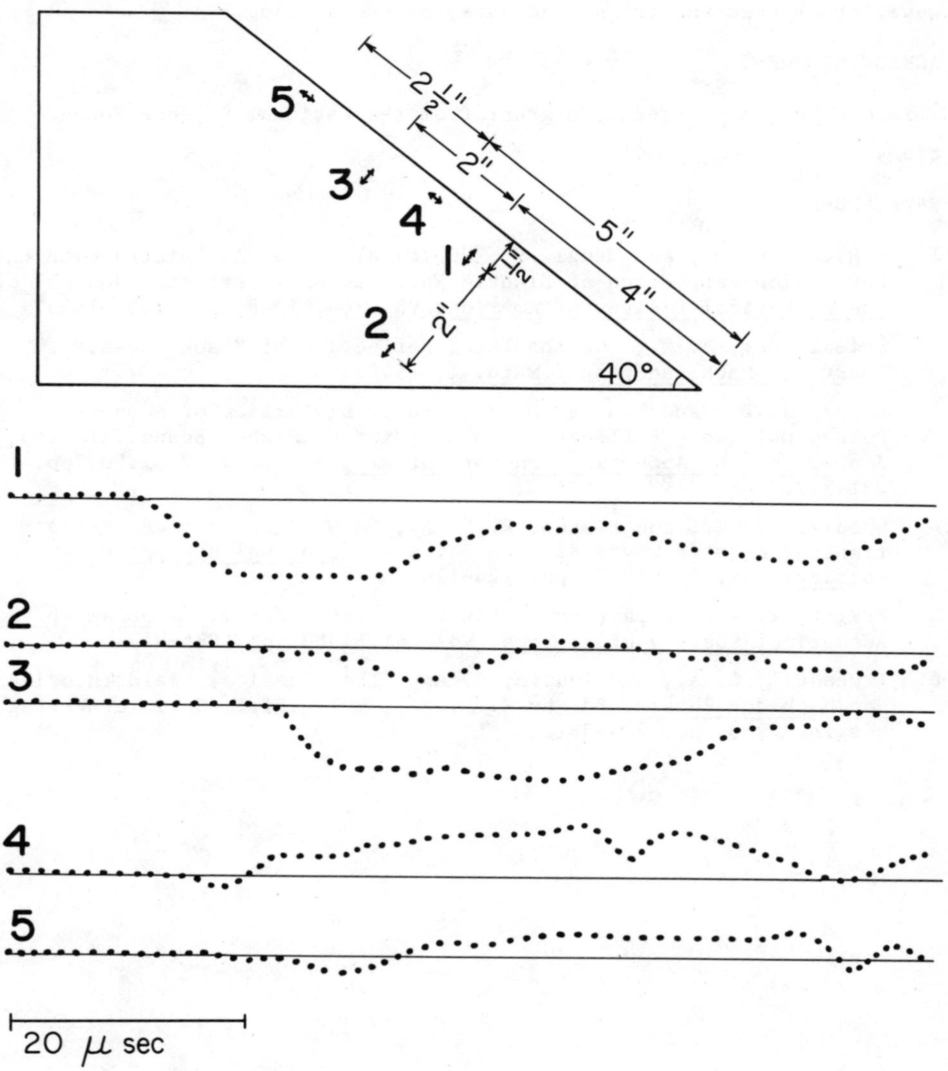

Fig. 11. Strains Resulting from the Refracted Waves in the Aluminum Plate for the Same Configuration as Fig. 10.

longitudinal wave breaking away in the faster medium. However, some wave, other than the transverse wave, is propagating.

ACKNOWLEDGEMENT

This work was supported by a grant from the National Science Foundation.

REFERENCES

1. McNiven, H. D., and Mengi, Y., "Critical Angles Associated with the Reflection-Refraction of Elastic Waves at an Interface," Journal of the Acoustical Society of America, Vol. 44, 1968, pp. 1658-1663.

2. Friedlander, F. G., "On the Total Reflection of Plane Waves," Quart. J. Mech. and Appl. Math. 1, 1948.

3. Arons, A. B., and Yennie, D. R., "Phase Distortion of Acoustic Pulses Obliquely Reflected from a Medium of Higher Sound Velocity," Journal of the Acoustical Society of America, Vol. 22, 1950, pp. 231-237.

4. Goodier, J. N., and Bishop, R. E. D., "A Note on Critical Reflections of Elastic Waves at Free Surfaces," Journal of Applied Physics, Vol. 23, 1952, pp. 124-126.

5. Wright, T. W., "Impact on an Elastic Quarter Space," Journal of the Acoustical Society of America, Vol. 45, 1969, pp. 935-943.

6. Truesdell, C. A., and Toupin, R. A., "The Classical Field Theories," Handbuch der Physik, Ed. by S. Flugge, Vol. III/1, Springer-Verlag, Berlin, 1960, pp. 226-881.

THE EFFECT OF AN ELASTIC EDGE RESTRAINT ON THE FORCED VIBRATION OF A RECTANGULAR PLATE

F. D. Henry
The University of Oklahoma

D. M. Egle
The University of Oklahoma

ABSTRACT

The steady state reponse of a thin rectangular plate subjected to a concentrated load with simple harmonic time variation is evaluated by normal mode superposition. The plate is simply supported on three edges and restrained by an arbitrary elastic structure on the fourth edge. Numerical results are presented showing the effects of varying the elastic restraint on the plate response at resonance for two natural frequencies and several load positions.

LIST OF NOTATIONS

D	Plate flexural rigidity = $Eh^3/12(1-\nu^2)$
E	Young's modulus
G	Magnitude of point load
M_x, V_x	Bending moment, vertical force per unit length (see Fig. 1)
W_{mn}, W_{jk}	Plate eigenfunctions
W_M	Displacement amplitude
Z_{pq}	Stiffness of edge restraint - see Eqs. (6,7)
a,b	Plate dimensions (see Fig. 1)
h	Plate thickness
j,k; m,n	Vibration modal number (1,2,3 etc.) associated with the x,y directions
t	Time

$w(x,y,t)$	Plate deflection normal to the x-y plane
x,y	Rectangular coordinates in plane of the plate
α_m, α_j	Wave number associated with x direction, see Eq. (15)
γ_n, γ_k	Wave number associated with y direction, see Eq. (15)
ζ	Structural damping factor
λ_{mn}, λ_{jk}	Eigenvalue expression, $\lambda_{mn} = \alpha_m^2 + 2\ \gamma_n^2$
ν	Poisson's ratio
ξ_{mn}, ξ_{jk}	Generalized time dependent coordinates
ρ	Mass per unit area of plate
ϕ_{mn}, ϕ_{jk}	Normalized eigenfunctions
ω_{mn}, ω_{jk}	Plate natural frequencies
ω	Frequency of excitation

INTRODUCTION

It is well known that the boundary conditions imposed on a structure have a varying effect on the dynamic response of that structure. If the forces applied to the structure excite predominately the lower modes of free vibration, the boundary conditions will probably have a significant effect on the response. On the other hand, if the higher frequency modes are those excited, the response will be affected to a lesser degree by a change in the boundary conditions. The purpose of this study is to investigate the influence of boundary conditions on the steady state response of a typical structure and to formulate the criteria for determining the conditions under which the boundary conditions do not affect the response.

To illustrate a practical application of this information, consider the following. Assume that a subsystem has undergone specified testing to determine its individual vibration characteristics or to determine environmental specifications within the subsystem. This subsystem will eventually be mated with a parent structure which will, in all probability, change the subsystem's boundary conditions from those encountered in the testing. If the effect of the new boundary conditions could be assessed without retesting the mated system, a saving in time and cost would result.

The particular problem to be considered here is that of a thin rectangular plate subjected to a concentrated load with a simple harmonic time variation. Three of the plate's edges are simply supported, the fourth is assumed to be attached to an elastic supporting structure. The free vibration problem is solved neglecting energy dissipation in the plate. The forced vibration problem, including damping effects through the use of a complex elastic modulus, is solved using a normal mode expansion. Numerical results are presented to show the effect of varying the boundary conditions on the plate displacement at resonance for the lowest and third lowest natural frequencies.

Although there have been several published studies [1-7] dealing with the forced response of plates of several configurations, none of these have incorporated the elastic edge restraint. The reader may be interested in a rather complete survey [8] of the free vibration of plates.

Analysis

Natural Frequencies and Normal Modes / Consider the homogeneous, isotropic rectangular plate shown in Fig. 1. For free vibration, the displacement normal to the plate may be expressed in the form

$$w(x,y,t) = W(x,y)\, e^{i\omega t} \tag{1}$$

and the equation of motion is

$$\nabla^4 W(x,y) - \beta^4 W(x,y) = 0 \tag{2}$$

where $\beta^4 = \rho\omega^2/D$.

The plate is to be simply supported along three edges, the fourth edge $x = b$ having an elastic support. The three simply supported conditions require

$$W = 0 \text{ and } W,_{yy} = 0 \text{ along } y = 0 \tag{3}$$

$$W = 0 \text{ and } W,_{yy} = 0 \text{ along } y = a \tag{4}$$

$$W = 0 \text{ and } W,_{xx} = 0 \text{ along } x = 0 \tag{5}$$

The boundary conditions along the fourth edge are taken in the form

$$M_x(b,y) = [Z_{11}\, W,_x + Z_{12}\, W]_{x\, =\, b} \tag{6}$$

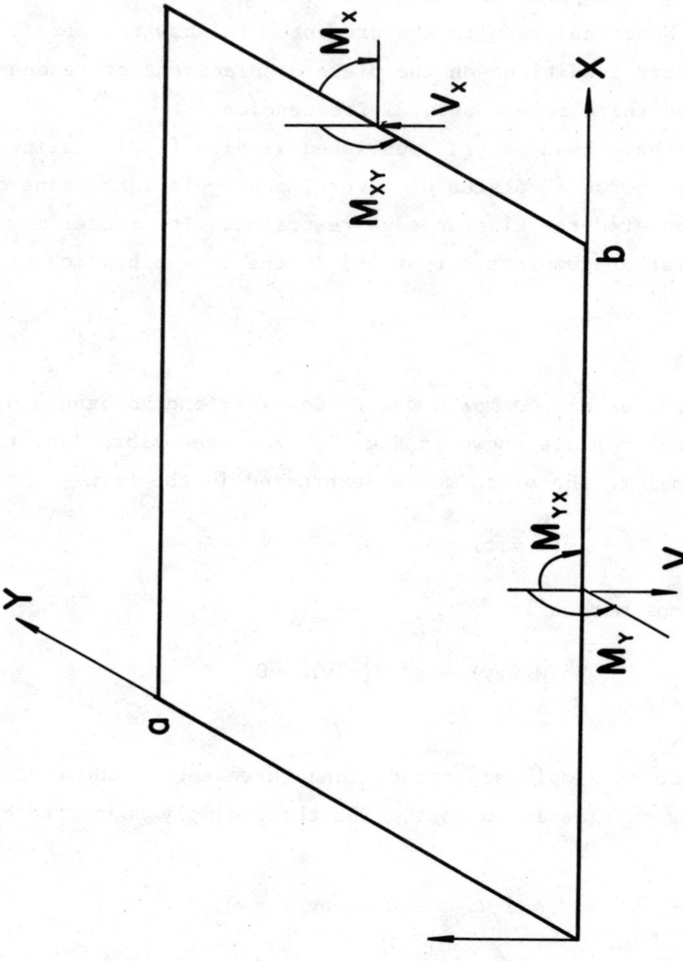

Fig. 1. Plate Geometry and Notation.

$$V_x(b,y) = [-Z_{21} W,_x - Z_{22} W]_{x = b} \qquad (7)$$

The edge restraints represented by Eqs. (6,7) are not all inclusive in that the moment and force at position y depends only on the displacement and slope at the same position, whereas, in general, the moments and forces at y would be a function of the displacements and slopes along the entire edge, $0 \leq y \leq a$. Physically, Eqs. (6,7) represent a set of closely spaced and equal, but independent, elastic supports having a linear and a rotary restraint and cross coupling between linear and rotary motions.

The quantities Z_{11}, Z_{12}, Z_{21}, and Z_{22} are the stiffnesses per unit length of the boundary structure and are assumed to be independent of frequency. If it is further assumed that the boundary structure obeys Betti's law for elastic structures, then Z_{12} and Z_{21} are equal. The magnitude of the stiffnesses may be further restricted if the boundary structure is passive (no energy sources) and stable for then the work done by the moments and forces on the boundary structure must be positive definite. The work done (per unit length) on the restraining structure is

$$U = \frac{1}{2} \begin{Bmatrix} M_x \\ -V_x \end{Bmatrix}_b^T \begin{Bmatrix} W,_x \\ W \end{Bmatrix}_b \qquad (8)$$

where the subscript b indicates the quantities are evaluated at x = b. Combining Eqs. (6,7,8) will give

$$U = \frac{1}{2} \begin{Bmatrix} W,_x \\ W \end{Bmatrix}_b^T \begin{bmatrix} Z_{11} & Z_{12} \\ Z_{21} & Z_{22} \end{bmatrix} \begin{Bmatrix} W,_x \\ W \end{Bmatrix}_b \qquad (9)$$

The necessary and sufficient conditions for U to be positive-definite are

$$\begin{aligned} Z_{22} &> 0 \\ Z_{11} Z_{22} - Z_{12}^2 &> 0 \end{aligned} \qquad (10)$$

The end conditions, Eqs. (6,7) may be written in terms of displacements and slopes by combining the moment-vertical force-displacement-slope relationships at the edge of the plate

$$M_x(b,y) = -D[W(x,y)_{,xx} + \nu W(x,y)_{,yy}]_{x=b} \tag{11}$$

$$V_x(b,y) = -D[W(x,y)_{,xxx} + (2-\nu)W(x,y)_{,xyy}]_{x=b} \tag{12}$$

with Eqs. (6,7). Thus the boundary conditions are

$$\left\{Z_{11}\, W_{,x} + Z_{12}\, W + D(W_{,xx} + \nu W_{,yy})\right\}_{x=b} = 0 \tag{13}$$

$$\left\{-Z_{21}\, W_{,x} - Z_{22}\, W + D[W_{,xxx} + (2-\nu)\, W_{,xyy}]\right\}_{x=b} = 0 \tag{14}$$

The solutions to Eq. (2) which satisfy the end conditions, Eqs. (3, 4,5,13,14) may be shown to be

$$W_{mn} = \sin \gamma_n\, y\{\sin \alpha_m x - C_{mn} \sinh \lambda_{mn} x\} \tag{15}$$

$$m = 1,2 \ldots ;\ n = 1,2 \ldots$$

where

$$C_{mn} = \frac{-Z_{22} \sin \alpha_m b - \{Z_{21} + D[\alpha_m^2 + (2-\nu)\, \gamma_n^2]\}\, \alpha_m \cos \alpha_m b}{-Z_{22} \sinh \lambda_{mn} b + \{-Z_{21} + D(\alpha_m^2 + \nu\, \gamma_n^2)\}\, \lambda_{mn} \cosh \lambda_{mn} b} \tag{16}$$

$$\alpha_{mn}^2 + \gamma_n^2 = \beta^2$$

$$\gamma_n = \frac{n\pi}{a}$$

$$\lambda_{mn}^2 = \alpha_{mn}^2 + 2\gamma_n^2 ,$$

and α_{mn}, λ_{mn} are the roots of

$$D_{11}\, D_{22} - D_{12}\, D_{21} = 0 \tag{17}$$

where

$$D_{11} = Z_{11}\, \alpha \cos \alpha\, b + [Z_{12} - D(\alpha^2 + \nu\, \gamma_n^2)] \sin \alpha\, b$$

$$D_{22} = Z_{22} \sinh \lambda b + [Z_{21} - D(\alpha^2 + \nu \gamma_n^2)] \lambda \cosh \lambda b$$

$$D_{12} = Z_{11} \lambda \cosh \lambda b + [Z_{12} - D(-\lambda^2 + \nu \gamma_n^2)] \sinh \lambda b$$

$$D_{21} = -Z_{22} \sin \alpha b - [Z_{21} + D(\alpha^2 + (2-\nu)\gamma_n^2)] \alpha \cos \alpha b$$

The natural frequencies of the plate are given by

$$\omega_{mn} = \sqrt{D/\rho}\, (\alpha_m^2 + \gamma_n^2) \tag{18}$$

Orthonormality of the Eigenfunctions / In order to use the modal expansion technique, the eigenfunctions, Eq. (15), must be orthogonal. To show orthogonality, Eq. (2) is used to form the identity

$$(\beta_{mn}^4 - \beta_{jk}^4) \int_o^b \int_o^a W_{mn} W_{jk}\, dy\, dx$$

$$= \int_o^b \int_o^a \left\{ W_{jk} \nabla^4 W_{mn} - W_{mn} \nabla^4 W_{jk} \right\} dy\, dx \tag{19}$$

Integrating the right hand side of Eq. (19) by parts twice and utilizing the boundary conditions, Eqs. (3,4,5,13,14), Eq. (19) may be shown to be

$$(\beta_{mn}^4 - \beta_{jk}^4) \int_o^b \int_o^a W_{mn} W_{jk}\, dy\, dx$$

$$= \frac{Z_{12} - Z_{21}}{D} \left[W_{mn} \frac{\partial W_{jk}}{\partial x} - W_{jk} \frac{\partial W_{mn}}{\partial x} \right]_{x=b}$$

$$+ \nu \int_o^a \left[W_{jk} \frac{\partial^3 W_{mn}}{\partial x \partial y^2} - W_{mn} \frac{\partial^3 W_{jk}}{\partial x \partial y^2} + \frac{\partial W_{jk}}{\partial x} \frac{\partial^2 W_{mn}}{\partial y^2} - \frac{\partial W_{mn}}{\partial x} \frac{\partial^2 W_{jk}}{\partial y^2} \right]_{x=b} dy \tag{20}$$

The first term on the right hand side of Eq. (20) vanishes only if $Z_{12} = Z_{21}$. The integral on the right hand side of Eq. (20) may also be shown to vanish by integrating the last two terms by parts twice and employing Eqs. (3,4). Thus the eigenfunctions, Eq. (15) satisfy the orthogonality integral

$$\int_0^b \int_0^a W_{mn} W_{jk} \, dy \, dx = 0; \quad m \neq j, \; n \neq k \tag{21}$$

if $\beta_{mn} \neq \beta_{jk}$ and $Z_{12} = Z_{21}$. Note that Eq. (21) is not valid if the stiffness Z_{ij} are frequency dependent.

The eigenfunctions may be normalized in the usual manner by requiring

$$\int_0^b \int_0^a \phi_{mn}^2 \, dy \, dx = 1 \tag{22}$$

where $\phi_{mn} = W_{mn}/K_{mn}$ and K_{mn} is a constant. The normalized eigenfunctions ϕ_{mn} are

$$\phi_{mn}(x,y) = \frac{\sin \gamma_n y[\sin \alpha_m x - C_{mn} \sinh \lambda_{mn} x]}{K_{mn}} \tag{23}$$

where

$$K_{mn} = \sqrt{a/2} \left\{ \frac{b}{2} (1-C_{mn}^2) + \frac{1}{4} \left[\frac{C_{mn}}{\lambda_{mn}} \sinh (2\lambda_{mn} b) \right. \right.$$

$$\left. - \frac{1}{\alpha_m} \sin (2\alpha_m b) \right] - \frac{2\, C_{mn}}{\lambda_{mn}^2 + \alpha_m^2} [\lambda_{mn} \sin \alpha_m b \cosh \lambda_{mn} b$$

$$\left. - \alpha_m \cos \alpha_m b \sinh \lambda_{mn} b] \right\}^{1/2}$$

Solution of the Forced Vibration Problem / Consider a plate which possesses some degree of structural damping being excited by a force per unit area p(x,y,t). The damping may be incorporated in the analysis by use of the complex elastic modulus. Doing so changes the equation of motion to

$$D^* \nabla^4 w(x,y,t) + \rho \frac{\partial^2 w(x,y,t)}{\partial t^2} = p(x,y,t) \tag{24}$$

where $D^* = D(1 + i\zeta)$ and $i = \sqrt{-1}$, ζ is defined as a structural damping factor assumed independent of frequency.

Using the normal mode expansion technique, assume the solution to Eq. (24) in the form

$$w(x,y,t) = \sum_{m=1}^{\infty} \sum_{n=1}^{\infty} \phi_{mn}(x,y)\ \xi_{mn}(t) \tag{25}$$

The ϕ_{mn} functions are orthonormal mode functions obtained by solving the free vibration problem; $\xi_{mn}(t)$ are generalized coordinates which remain to be determined.

The exciting force is taken to be simple harmonic of frequency ω, thus

$$P(x,y,t) = p(x,y)\ e^{i\omega t} \tag{26}$$

Substituting Eq. (25) into (24), multiplying by ϕ_{jk}, integrating over the surface of the plate and noting Eq. (2,21,22) eventually yields

$$\ddot{\xi}_{jk}(t) + (1 + i\zeta)\ \omega_{jk}^2\ \xi_{jk}(t) = P_{jk}\ e^{i\omega t} \tag{27}$$

where

$$P_{jk} = \frac{1}{\rho} \int_{x=0}^{b} \int_{x=0}^{a} p(x,y)\ \phi_{jk}(x,y)\ dy\ dx \tag{28}$$

The steady-state solution of the forced vibration problem is of the form

$$w(x,y,t) = \sum_{j=1}^{\infty} \sum_{k=1}^{\infty} \phi_{jk}(x,y)\ R_{jk}(t) + i \sum_{j=1}^{\infty} \sum_{k=1}^{\infty} \phi_{jk}(x,y)\ I_{jk}(t) \tag{29}$$

where

$$R_{jk}(t) = \frac{P_{jk}}{(\omega_{jk}^2 - \omega^2)^2 + (\zeta\ \omega_{jk}^2)^2} \left\{(\omega_{jk}^2 - \omega^2)\cos \omega t + (\zeta\ \omega_{jk}^2)\sin \omega t\right\}$$

and

$$I_{jk}(t) = \frac{P_{jk}}{(\omega_{jk}^2 - \omega^2)^2 + (\zeta\ \omega_{jk}^2)^2} \left\{(\omega_{jk}^2 - \omega^2)\sin \omega t - (\zeta\ \omega_{jk}^2)\cos \omega t\right\}$$

Forced Reponse to a Point Load / Consider the loading to be a concentrated force of magnitude G, with a simple harmonic time variation, applied at position (x_o, y_o). The load per unit area then takes the form

$$p(x,y,t) = G\,\delta(x-x_o)\,\delta(y-y_o)\sin\omega t \tag{30}$$

where $\delta(x-x_o)$ is the Dirac delta function. Applying Eq. (30) to (28), and using the imaginary part of Eq. (29), the steady-state solution may be written

$$w(x,y,t) = \frac{G}{\rho}\left\{H(x,y)\sin\omega t + L(x,y)\cos\omega t\right\} \tag{31}$$

where

$$H(x,y) = \sum_{j=1}^{\infty}\sum_{k=1}^{\infty}\left\{\frac{\phi_{jk}(x,y)\,\phi_{jk}(x_o,y_o)(\omega_{jk}^2 - \omega^2)}{(\omega_{jk}^2 - \omega^2)^2 + (\zeta\,\omega_{jk}^2)^2}\right\}$$

and

$$L(x,y) = -\sum_{j=1}^{\infty}\sum_{k=1}^{\infty}\left\{\frac{\phi_{jk}(x,y)\,\phi_{jk}(x_o,y_o)(\zeta\,\omega_{jk}^2)}{(\omega_{jk}^2 - \omega^2)^2 + (\zeta\,\omega_{jk}^2)^2}\right\}$$

Numerical Results

The numerical calculations of the preceding analysis were directed toward answering two questions:

(1) How are the natural frequencies affected by changing the boundary conditions?

(2) What influence do the general boundary properties have on the location and magnitude of the maximum deflection?

In order to do this both the natural frequency equation and the displacement magnitude (i.e., $W_m = \sqrt{H^2 + L^2}$) expression were programmed for a computer study. A one eighth inch, steel plate (a = 15 inches, b = 30 inches, $\nu = 0.286$, $E = 29 \times 10^6$ psi, $\rho/h = 7.34 \times 10^{-4}$ lb sec^2/in^4 was chosen as the model. To simulate various boundary conditions, variations were made in the restraint stiffnesses. Since the concern is with maximum displacement, only resonant frequency excitations were used. A unit load (i.e., G = 1) was positioned near the anti-node locations for the free-vibration frequency. In all studies both the load and monitoring positions in the y direction were taken to be at y = a/2, the wave number (n) in the same direction being set equal to 1. Figures 2-8 summarize the results of the study. The range on both m,n was 1-5. Comparison of these results with those calculated with m,n ranging from 1-10 showed no appreciable differences.

Natural Frequencies / To determine the relative influence of various boundary conditions on the natural frequencies, Z_{22} was varied from zero to 10^7 lbs/in^2, all other Z's being set equal to zero. This range represents a variation from a free edge to one that is nearly simply supported. Similar variations were implemented for Z_{11}. A rotationally restrained but linearly free support is simulated by letting $Z_{11} = 10^7$ lbs. Figure 2 shows the results of these calculations. From these curves it is seen that the stiffness Z_{22} has a much greater influence on the natural frequencies than does the Z_{11} value. As Z_{22} increases from 0 to 10^7 lb/in^2 the fundamental frequency increases by approximately 20 percent whereas the same variation in Z_{11} causes an increase of less than 2 percent. At the higher natural frequencies the predominant effect of Z_{22} over Z_{11} is even greater. It also appears that the change of natural frequency as a function of Z occurs over a smaller numerical range of Z_{22} than it does for Z_{11}.

The fundamental natural frequencies for the three cases in which the fourth edge was free, simply supported, and clamped were computed using the frequency equation (17). These results compared favorably with the values given by Fletcher [9] and Hearmon [10].

Influence of Z_{11} / In order to evaluate the influence of Z_{11} on the plate displacement at resonance, this stiffness parameter was varied through a range from 0 to 10^7 lbs. Figure 3 shows the relative influence of Z_{11} on the deflection magnitude for various loads (x_o = 10, 15, and 20 in.). In all of these cases the frequency of the exciting force was that of the fundamental natural frequency. It is interesting to note that large variations in Z_{11} do not cause large changes in either the displacement magnitudes nor the elastically restrained boundary. Actually the position of the load has a much greater influence on the maximum displacement than does the magnitude of the Z_{11} stiffness function.

Figure 4 shows the plate resonant response for a somewhat higher forcing frequency, $\omega = \omega_{31}$. It is again noted that large variations in the value of Z_{11} have only a localized effect near the boundary on the

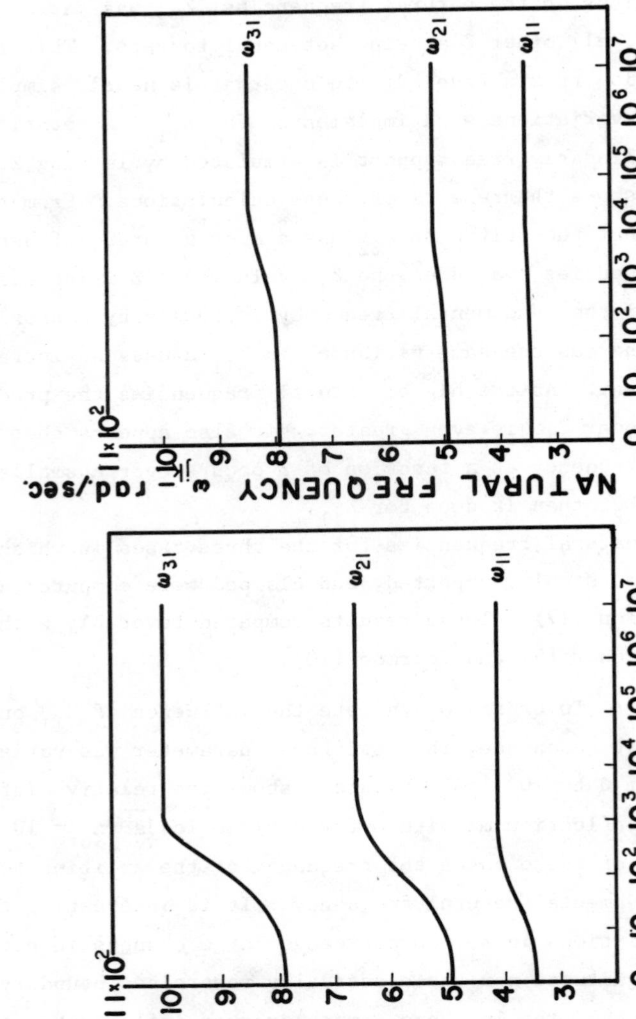

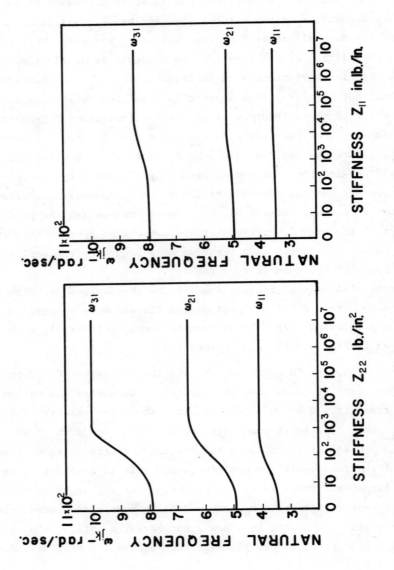

Fig. 2. Influence of Z_{11} and Z_{22} on the Resonant Frequencies of a Rectangular Plate (3 sides simply supported).

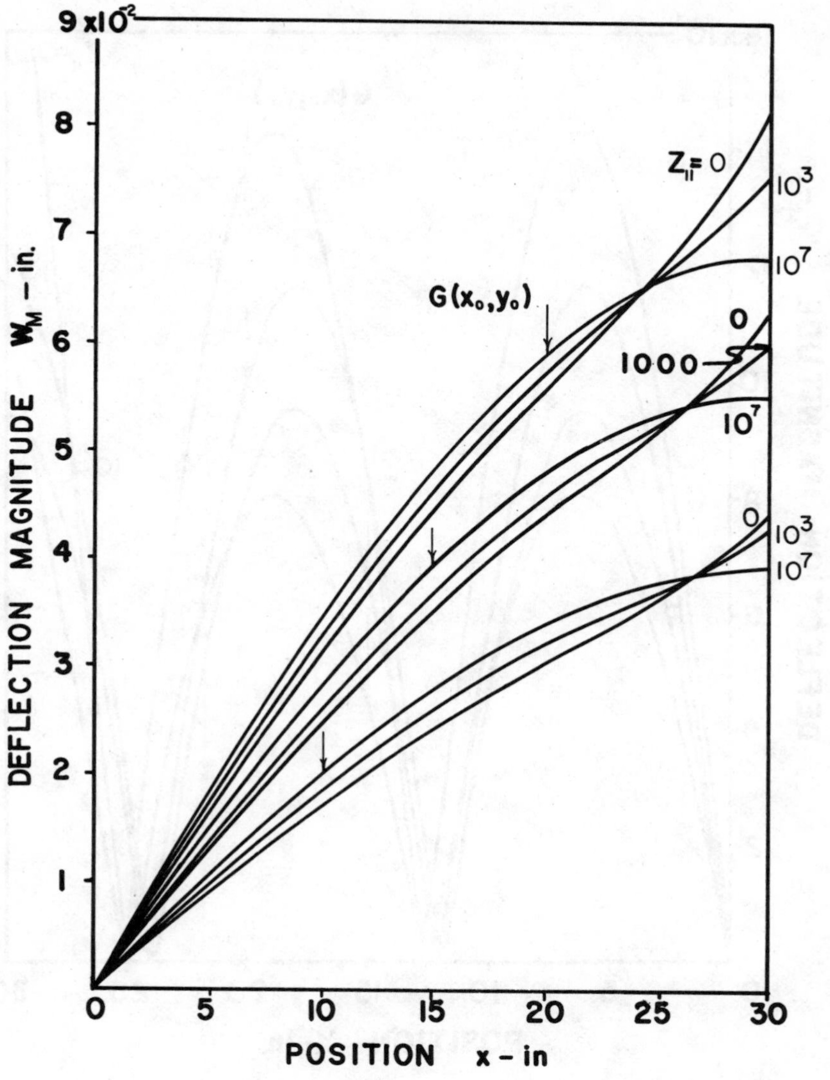

Fig. 3. Influence of Z_{11} on the Deflection at Resonance of a Vibrating Plate ($Z_{12} = Z_{21} = Z_{22} = 0$, $\omega = \omega_{11}$).

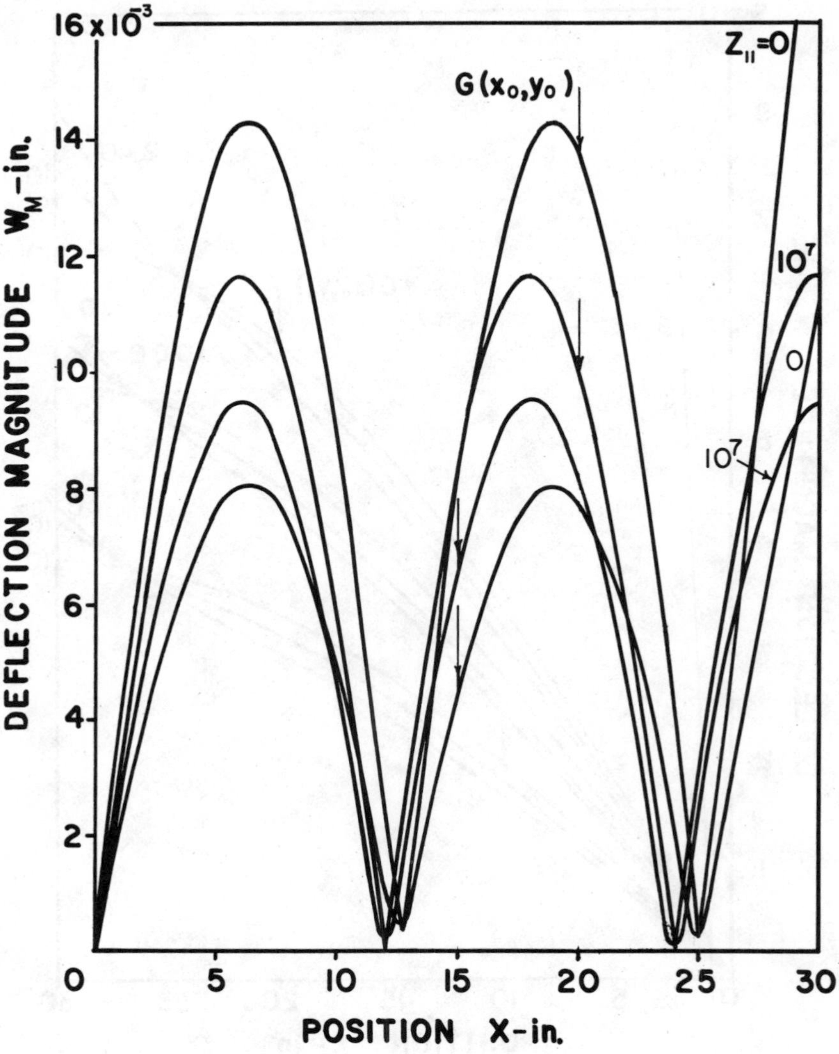

Fig. 4. Influence of Z_{11} on the Deflection at Resonance of a Vibrating Plate ($Z_{12} = Z_{21} = Z_{22} = 0$, $\omega = \omega_{31}$).

shape of the displacement curves. Also, it is important to observe that again the predominant effect is that of varying the load position.

Influence of Z_{22} / The influence of Z_{22} is much more pronounced than that of Z_{11}, as shown in Fig. 5. Previously it was observed that Z_{11} had little influence on the shape of the displacement curve; however, in this figure it is seen that large variations in Z_{22} cause very significant changes in the shape and magnitude of the displacement curves. The major changes occur in the half of the plate near the changing boundary conditions; nevertheless, the changes are not nearly as localized as they were for the cases obtained for the Z_{11} variations. Load position variations result in a change of the magnitude of the maximum deflections, but they no longer dominate the stiffness change effects.

As the resonant frequency increases to ω_{31} (see Fig. 6), the ability of Z_{22} to influence the magnitude of the deflection is greatly localized to an area near the support. It is noted, however, that for small values of Z_{22}, the major influence is that of changing the location of maximum deflection.

Figure 7 illustrates the influence of changing the load position in the case where the arbitrary boundary acts as a clamped edge ($Z_{11} = 10^7$ lbs, $Z_{21} = Z_{12} = 10^{-6}$ lb/in, $Z_{22} = 10^7$ lbs/in^2). Although the magnitudes and shapes of the deflection curves are not exactly the same as those for the cases when $Z_{22} = 10^7$ lbs/in^2 (see Fig. 5), the similarities suggest the dominance of the Z_{22} stiffness.

Influence of Z_{12}, Z_{21} / The stiffness terms Z_{12} and Z_{21} represent cross-coupling which relate angular displacements to vertical forces and linear displacements to moments, see Eqs. (6,7). To investigate the effect of these terms, the stiffness values were taken to be

$$Z_{11} = 2\,F\,\mu^2$$

$$Z_{12} = Z_{21} = 3\,F\mu$$

$$Z_{22} = 6\,F$$

These stiffnesses represent an edge restraint consisting of a large number of closely spaced, equal but independent cantilever beams supporting the edge of the plate. The parameters F and μ are,

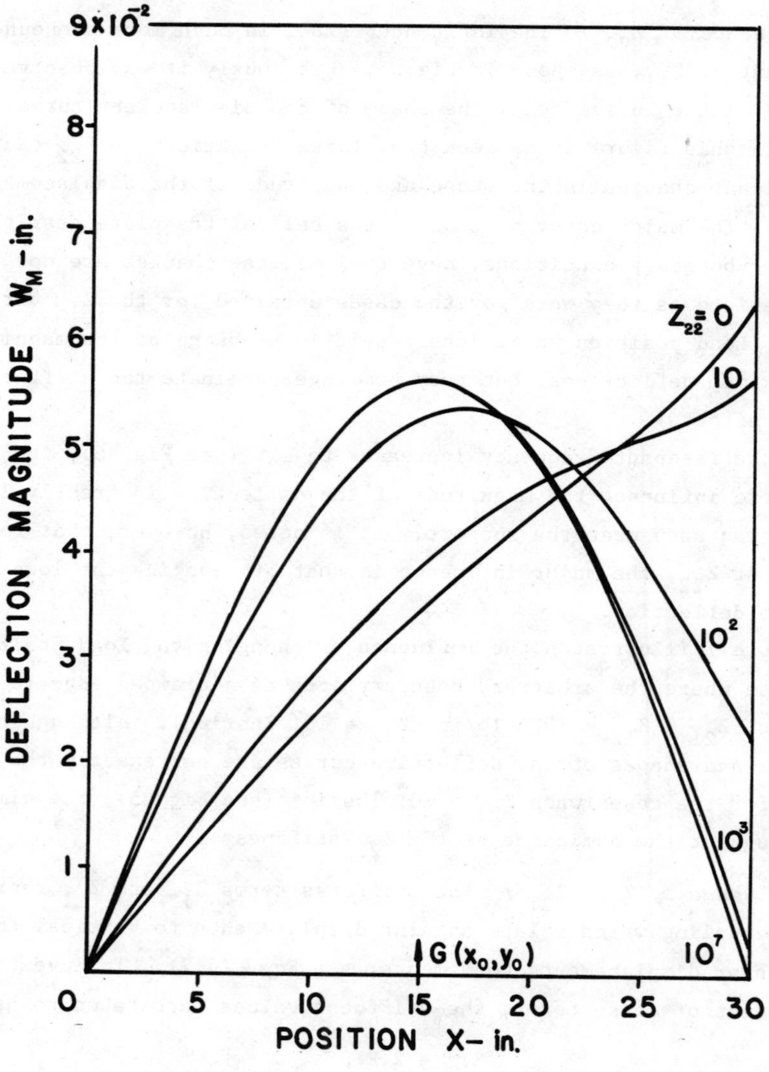

Fig. 5. Influence of Z_{22} on the Deflection at Resonance of a Vibrating Plate ($Z_{11} = Z_{12} = Z_{21} = 0$, $\omega = \omega_{11}$, $x_o = 15"$).

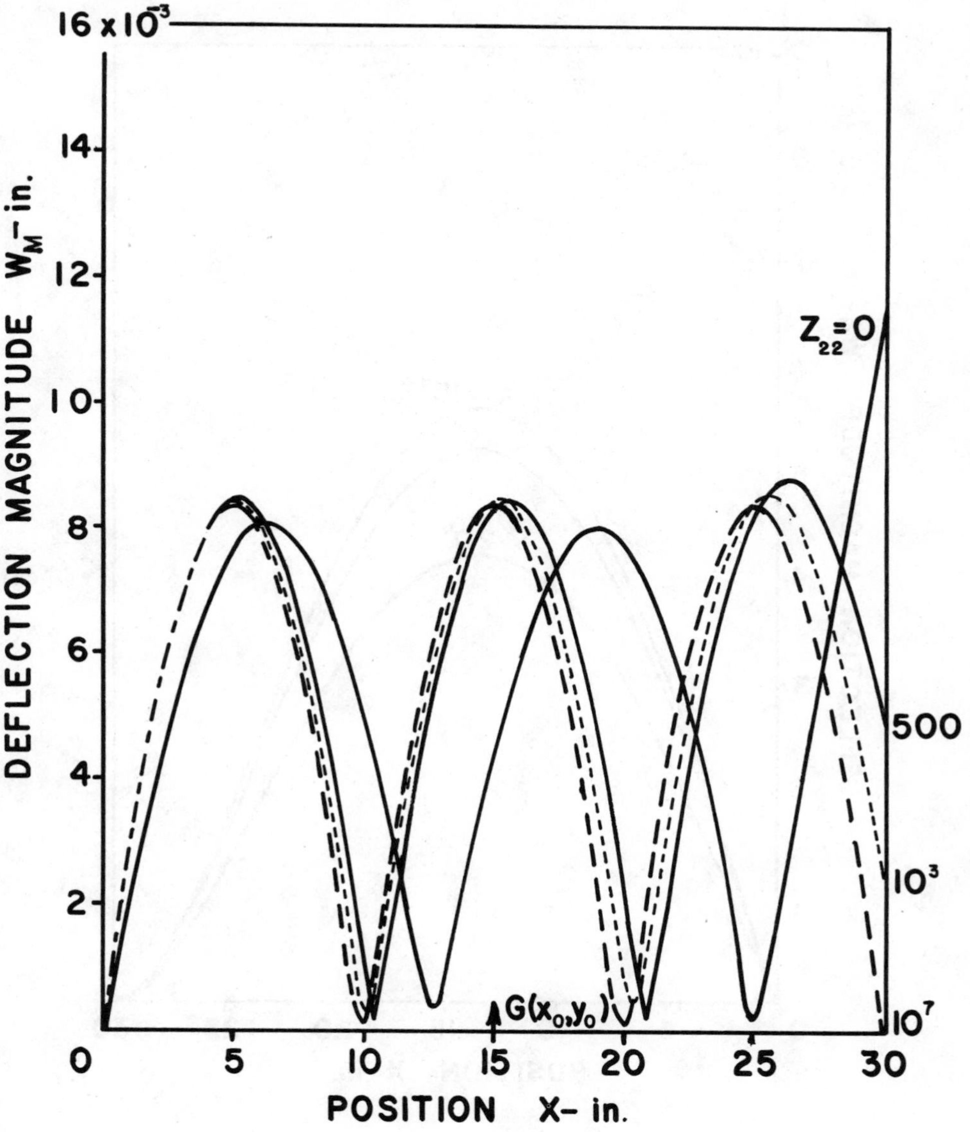

Fig. 6. Influence of Z_{22} on the Deflection at Resonance of a Vibrating Plate ($Z_{11} = Z_{12} = Z_{21} = 0$, $\omega = \omega_{31}$, $x_o = 15''$).

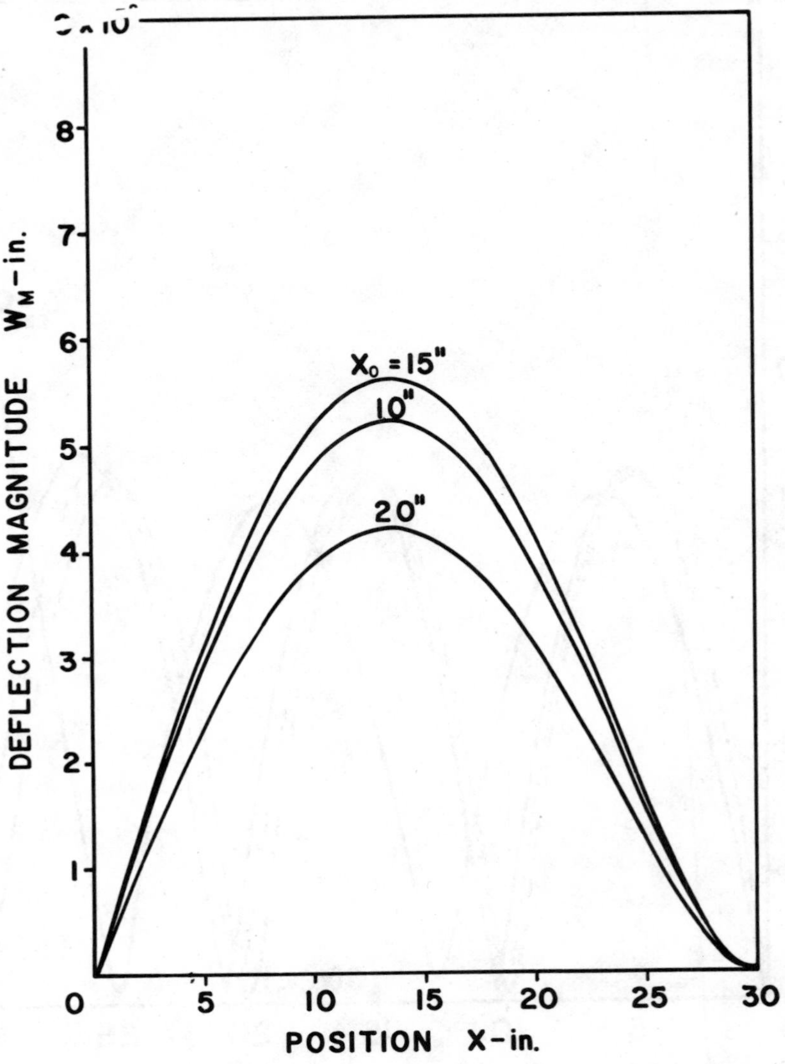

Fig. 7. Influence of Z_{22} on the Deflection at Resonance of a Vibrating Plate (clamped edge, $Z_{11} = 10^7$ lb/in^2, $Z_{12}=Z_{21} = 10^7$ lb/in; $\omega = \omega_{11}$).

respectively, the combined geometric and material property, and the length of the beams. By holding Z_{22} = 1200 lb/in^2 and varying the remaining stiffness values as a function of μ, several studies were performed using an exciting frequency equal to the fundamental natural frequency. The results of these studies are shown in Fig. 8. Case 1 illustrates the effect of removing the cross-coupling by setting μ equal to zero. In case 2 (μ = 10 in) both the Z_{11} and Z_{12} terms appear very large compared to Z_{22}; however, Eq. (10) remains satisfied. Studies were performed also for values of μ = 0.1 and 1.0 inches. In both of these cases the curves fell between those shown in Fig. 8.

Several calculations were done for stiffness values which did not satisfy Eq. (10). It is interesting to note that the results obtained seem anomalous in that the natural frequencies increase to unrealistic values and abrupt changes in slope appear in the deflection curves. However, in view of the fact that a restraint which violates Eq. (10) would have to have a negative potential energy function and thus would be statically unstable, such behavior is not anomalous only unexpected.

CONCLUSIONS

Of particular interest in this analysis is the fact that as both Z_{11} and Z_{12} grow exceedingly large compared to Z_{22}, the influence of Z_{22} continues to be the dominating factor in determining the shape of the deflection curve. This suggests that if the Z_{22} stiffness characteristic of a boundary is accurately matched for the purpose of vibration testing, a close approximation of the actual boundary is obtained.

Based on the preceding results, the following conclusions are drawn:

(1) The most important stiffness property of a boundary is that associated with Z_{22}. Accuracy in obtaining both natural frequencies and displacement profiles will be directly related to the ability to simulate the actual Z_{22} stiffness value.

(2) Proper positioning of the load in a forced vibration problem is more important than matching the Z_{11} stiffness property.

(3) The influence which Z_{11} exerts in determining the magnitude of the displacement is localized to an area near the boundary. This is true independent of the resonant forcing frequency.

(4) Load positioning and matching of the Z_{22} impedance value are both essential when the forcing frequency is near the fundamental

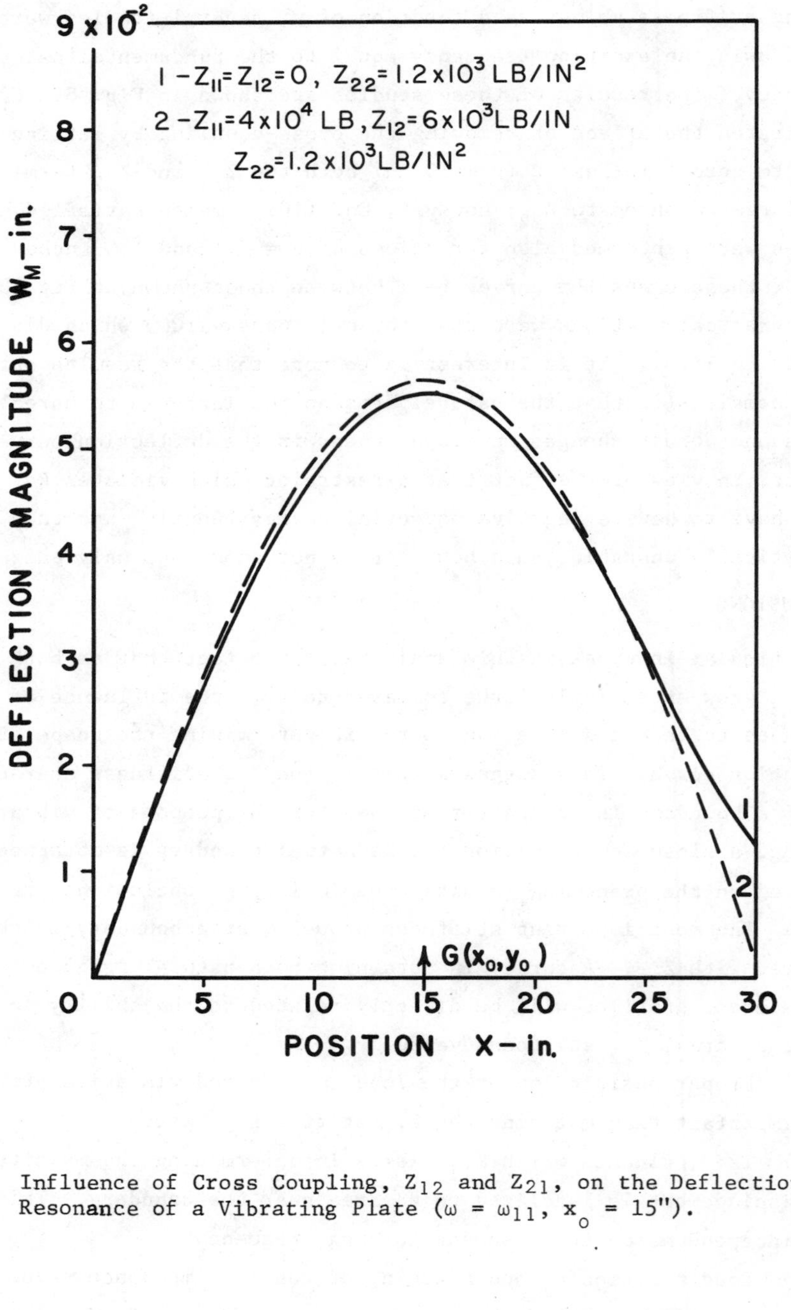

Fig. 8. Influence of Cross Coupling, Z_{12} and Z_{21}, on the Deflection at Resonance of a Vibrating Plate ($\omega = \omega_{11}$, $x_o = 15"$).

natural frequency. As the forcing frequency increases, the ability of Z_{22} to influence the maximum displacement is localized nearer the boundary and becomes of lesser importance.

ACKNOWLEDGEMENT

This study was supported in part by NASA under grant NGR 37-003-041.

REFERENCES

1. Reismann, H., "Forced Motion of Elastic Plates," Journal of Applied Mechanics, Vol. 35, 1968, pp. 510-515.
2. Jones, J. P., "Forced Motion of a Thin Bonded Plate," Journal of the Acoustical Society of America, Vol. 37, 1965, pp. 1008-1015.
3. Thomas, D. A., "Mechanical Impedance for Thin Plate," Journal of the Acoustical Society of America, Vol. 32, 1960, pp. 1302-1304.
4. Kalnins, A., "On Fundamental Solutions and Green's Functions in the Theory of Elastic Plates," Journal of Applied Mechanics, Vol. 33, 1966, pp. 31-38.
5. Weiner, R. S., "Forced Axisymmetric Motions of Circular Elastic Plates," Journal of Applied Mechanics, Vol. 32, 1965, pp. 893-898.
6. Williams, C. J. H., and Tobias, S. A., "Forced Undamped Nonlinear Vibrations of Imperfect Circular Disks," Journal of Mechanical Engineering Sciences, Vol. 5, 1963, pp. 325-335.
7. McLeod, A. J., and Bishop, R. E. D., "The Forced Vibration of Circular Flat Plate," Mechanical Engineering Sciences Monograph No. 1, 1965.
8. Leissa, A. W., "Free Vibrations of Elastic Plates," American Institute of Aeronautics and Astronautics Paper No. 69-24, 1969.
9. Fletcher, H. J., Addendum to "The Frequency of Vibration of Rectangular Isotropic Plates," Journal of Applied Mechanics, Vol. 26, 1959, p. 290.
10. Hearmon, R. F. S., "The Frequency of Vibration of Rectangular Isotropic Plates," Transactions of the American Society of Mechanical Engineers, Vol. 74, Journal of Applied Mechanics, 1952, pp. 402-403.

THE DYNAMIC CHARACTERISTICS OF CLAMPED RECTANGULAR PLATES OF ORTHOTROPIC MATERIAL

James E. Ashton
General Dynamics

ABSTRACT

The advent of the widespread use of fiber-reinforced composite materials has introduced a renewed interest in the analysis of plates composed of laminated orthotropic materials. This paper presents an analysis of the natural frequencies and characteristic shapes of rectangular plates clamped on all four edges. The plates considered are orthotropic, but the principal axis of orthotropy is not maintained parallel to the edges of the plate. The influence of anisotropy on the dynamic frequencies and characteristic shapes is investigated, as is the effect of varying the orientation of the principal axis of orthotropy.

INTRODUCTION

Recent interest and increased usage of advanced fibrous composite materials has made mandatory an assessment of the effects of orthotropy on the behavior of these fibrous composites. However, most plate solutions obtained in the past have been limited to isotropic or specially oriented orthotropic materials. Since an efficient use of orthotropic materials requires a variable orientation to be considered, there is a great need for solutions which can assess the effects of such orientations. This paper considers such a solution for the case of clamped rectangular plates.

Analysis Technique

The method of solution used in this analysis is Hamilton's principle, with the energy solution obtained by means of the Ritz method. A 49 term series of beam characteristic shapes is used to approximate the deflected shape.

The potential energy due to bending, for the plate shown in Figure 1, can be written as follows:

$$V = \frac{1}{2} \int_0^a \int_0^b [M]^T [\chi] \, dxdy \tag{1}$$

where

$$[M] = \begin{bmatrix} M_x \\ M_y \\ M_{xy} \end{bmatrix} = \text{plate moment resultants}$$

$$[\chi] = \begin{bmatrix} \chi_x \\ \chi_y \\ 2\chi_{xy} \end{bmatrix} = \text{plate curvatures} = \begin{bmatrix} -w,_{xx} \\ -w,_{yy} \\ -2w,_{xy} \end{bmatrix}$$

w = transverse deflection

and a comma denotes partial differentiation.

For anisotropic materials

$$[M] = [D] [\chi] \tag{2}$$

where [D] is in general a fully populated matrix of stiffness coefficients which are defined in terms of the elastic constants of the orthotropic ply (E_1, E_2, $\nu_{12} = \nu_{21} E_1/E_2$, G_{12}) and the angle of orientation of the principal axis of orthotropy ϕ:

$$D_{ij} = \frac{1}{12} \overline{Q}_{ij} h^3 \tag{3}$$

where, in the usual notation (reference [1]):

$$\overline{Q}_{11} = Q_{11} \cos^4\phi + 2(Q_{12} + 2Q_{66}) \sin^2\phi \cos^2\phi + Q_{22} \sin^4\phi$$

$$\overline{Q}_{12} = (Q_{11} + Q_{22} - 4Q_{66}) \sin^2\phi \cos^2\phi + Q_{12} (\sin^4\phi + \cos^4\phi)$$

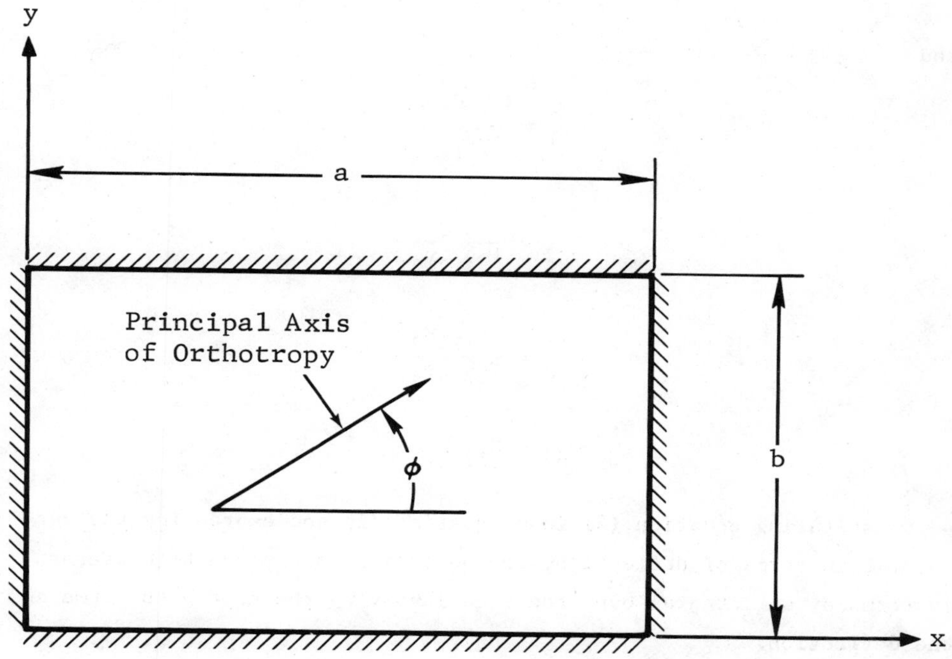

Fig. 1. Plate Geometry.

$$\overline{Q}_{22} = Q_{11} \sin^4\phi + 2(Q_{12} + 2Q_{66}) \sin^2\phi \cos^2\phi + Q_{22} \cos^4\phi$$

$$\overline{Q}_{16} = (Q_{11} - Q_{12} - 2Q_{66}) \sin\phi \cos^3\phi + (Q_{12} - Q_{22} + 2Q_{66}) \sin^3\phi \cos\phi$$

$$\overline{Q}_{26} = (Q_{11} - Q_{12} - 2Q_{66}) \sin^3\phi \cos\phi + (Q_{12} - Q_{22} + 2Q_{66}) \sin\phi \cos^3\phi$$

$$\overline{Q}_{66} = (Q_{11} + Q_{22} - 2Q_{12} - 2Q_{66}) \sin^2\phi \cos^2\phi + Q_{66} (\sin^4\phi + \cos^4\phi)$$

and

$$Q_{11} = \frac{E_1}{1-\nu_{12}\nu_{21}}$$

$$Q_{22} = \frac{E_2}{1-\nu_{12}\nu_{21}}$$

$$Q_{12} = \frac{\nu_{12} E_2}{1-\nu_{12}\nu_{21}}$$

$$Q_{66} = G_{12}$$

Substituting equation (2) into equation (1) and expressing the curvatures in terms of deflection, the potential energy can be expressed in terms of an integral over the area involving the stiffness terms and the deflection.

The kinetic energy is given in terms of the deflection by the following expression:

$$T = \frac{1}{2} \omega^2 \rho h \int_0^a \int_0^b w^2 \, dxdy \qquad (4)$$

where

ρ = mass density

h = plate thickness

ω = angular frequency of vibration.

An approximate solution can be obtained by equating the potential energy to the kinetic energy and requiring this energy balance to be (approximately) stationary. In the present analysis, the deflection is assumed in a series:

$$w = \sum_{i=1}^{7} \sum_{j=1}^{7} a_{ij} \; Z_i(x) \; Z_j(y) \tag{5}$$

where

a_{ij} = parameters to be determined

$Z_i(y)$ = characteristic shape for the ith natural mode of a clamped-clamped beam.

Adequate convergence should be obtained with this 49 term series, based on the results obtained in references [2] and [3]. A further investigation of this convergence is presented in the next section.

The series Eq. (5) satisfies the boundary conditions of zero deflection and zero slope at the plate edges. The use of the series (5) reduces the problem of finding a stationary energy balance to an ordinary maximum-minimum problem in the 49 variables a_{ij}. Differentiating the energy balance with respect to each a_{ij} then leads to a system of 49 simultaneous equations which define a discrete eigenvalue problem from which the natural frequencies and characteristic shapes may be determined:

$$\sum_{m=1}^{7} \sum_{n=1}^{7} d_{ikmn} \; a_{mn} = \omega^2 \rho h \sum_{m=1}^{7} \sum_{n=1}^{7} ab \; \Psi_{1im} \; \Psi_{1kn} \; a_{mn} \tag{6}$$

$$i = 1 \ldots 7$$
$$k = 1 \ldots 7$$

where

$$\begin{aligned} d_{ikmn} = {} & D_{11} \Psi_{3im} \Psi_{1kn} \frac{b}{a^3} + D_{12}(\Psi_{5im} \Psi_{5nk} + \Psi_{5mi} \Psi_{5kn}) \frac{1}{ab} \\ & + D_{22} \Psi_{1im} \Psi_{3kn} \frac{a}{b^3} + 2D_{16}(\Psi_{6mi} \Psi_{4kn} + \Psi_{6im} \Psi_{4nk}) \frac{1}{a^2} \\ & + 2D_{26}(\Psi_{4im} \Psi_{6nk} + \Psi_{4mi} \Psi_{6kn}) \frac{1}{b^2} + 4D_{66} \Psi_{2im} \Psi_{2kn} \frac{1}{ab} \end{aligned}$$

$$\Psi_{1mn} = \int_0^1 Z_m(\zeta)\, Z_n(\zeta)\, d\zeta$$

$$\Psi_{2mn} = \int_0^1 Z_m(\zeta),_\zeta\, Z_n(\zeta),_\zeta\, d\zeta$$

$$\Psi_{3mn} = \int_0^1 Z_m(\zeta),_{\zeta\zeta}\, Z_n(\zeta),_{\zeta\zeta}\, d\zeta$$

$$\Psi_{4mn} = \int_0^1 Z_m(\zeta),_\zeta\, Z_n(\zeta)\, d\zeta$$

$$\Psi_{5mn} = \int_0^1 Z_m(\zeta),_{\zeta\zeta}\, Z_n(\zeta)\, d\zeta$$

$$\Psi_{6mn} = \int_0^1 Z_m(\zeta),_{\zeta\zeta}\, Z_n(\zeta),_\zeta\, d\zeta$$

The integrals above have been tabulated in reference [4]. The equations have been programmed for an IBM digital computer. Some interesting results are presented below.

Results and Conclusions

The first four natural frequencies of square or rectangular plates obtained using the above described technique have been found to vary significantly as the principal axis of orthotropy is oriented at different angles with respect to the plate edges for the following ratios of the elastic constants:

$$\frac{E_1}{E_2} = 10 \qquad \frac{G_{12}}{E_2} = .25 \qquad \nu_{12} = .3 \tag{7}$$

Two planforms (a = b and a = 2b) have been investigated. The results are tabulated in Table I and Figures 2 and 3 for a variety of orientations ϕ of the principal axis of orthotropy with respect to the x axis. The node lines of the characteristic shapes are presented in Figures 4, 5, and 6. Also presented in the Table and figures are results neglecting the anisotropic stiffness terms D_{16} and D_{26} (that is, the plate is at all times considered specially orthotropic). The calculated

TABLE I. NATURAL FREQUENCIES OF ANISOTROPIC PLATE

$$a = b \qquad D_{\phi\phi} = \frac{E_1 h^3}{12(1-\nu_{12}\nu_{21})}$$

Orientation ϕ	$\omega/\sqrt{D_{\phi\phi}/\rho h b^4}$							
	Mode 1		Mode 2		Mode 3		Mode 4	
	Aniso-tropic	Ortho-tropic	Aniso-tropic	Ortho-tropic	Aniso-tropic	Ortho-tropic	Aniso-tropic	Ortho-tropic
0°	23.97	23.97	31.15	31.15	46.41	46.41	62.77	62.77
15°	23.10	23.80	31.52	33.31	47.65	50.30	59.46	60.17
30°	21.35	23.42	33.18	38.96	50.72	54.63	51.87	62.15
45°	20.51	23.23	35.01	46.69	47.07	46.69	52.21	74.44

$$a = 2b$$

Orientation ϕ	$\omega/\sqrt{D_{\phi\phi}/\rho h b^4}$			
	Mode 1	Mode 2	Mode 3	Mode 4
0°	9.34	17.61	20.83	26.49
15°	9.68	17.19	22.02	26.44
26.6°	10.57	16.93	25.11	25.46
45°	13.88	17.73	23.85	31.73
60°	17.87	19.86	23.75	29.75
75°	21.27	22.32	24.69	28.94
90°	22.57	23.38	25.30	28.87

frequency from the specially orthotropic analysis is markedly different from that calculated including the anisotropic coupling terms D_{16} and D_{26}.

The effect of anisotropy on the characteristic shapes is especially significant. The node lines, which for an orthotropic plate are parallel to the edges, are found to become skewed to the edges and often curved.

All of the results presented above were obtained using 49 terms in the assumed series for w. Quite adequate convergence was obtained using this number of terms. To illustrate this, the results for the

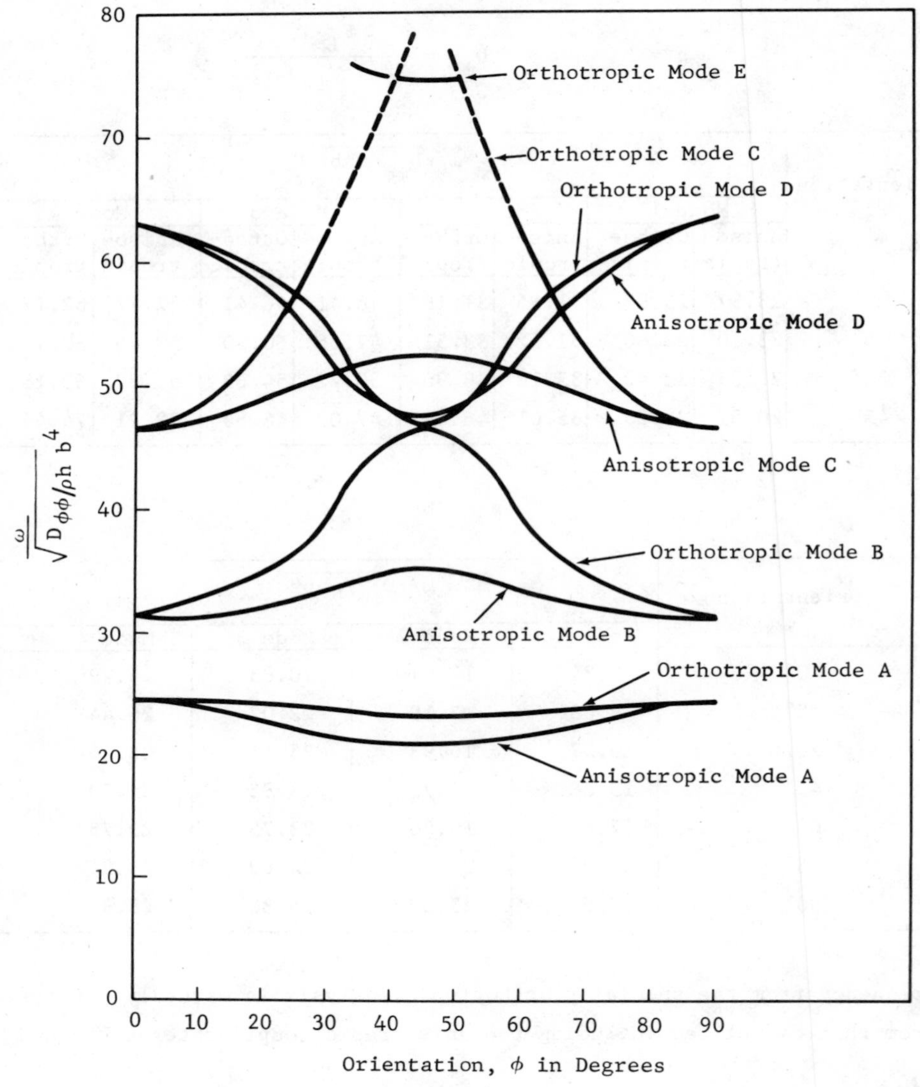

Fig. 2. Natural Frequency Variation with Orientation, Square Anisotropic Plate.

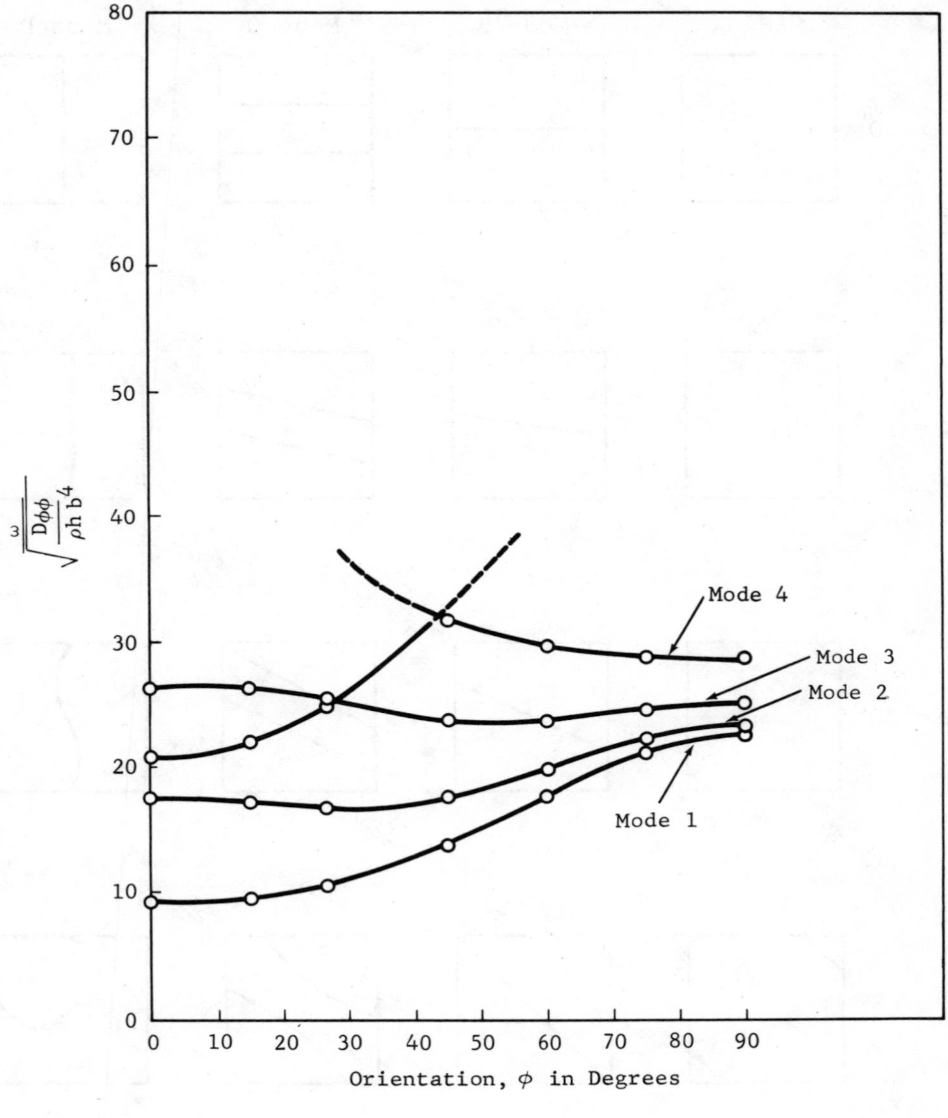

Fig. 3. Natural Frequency Variation with Orientation, Rectangular Anisotropic Plate.

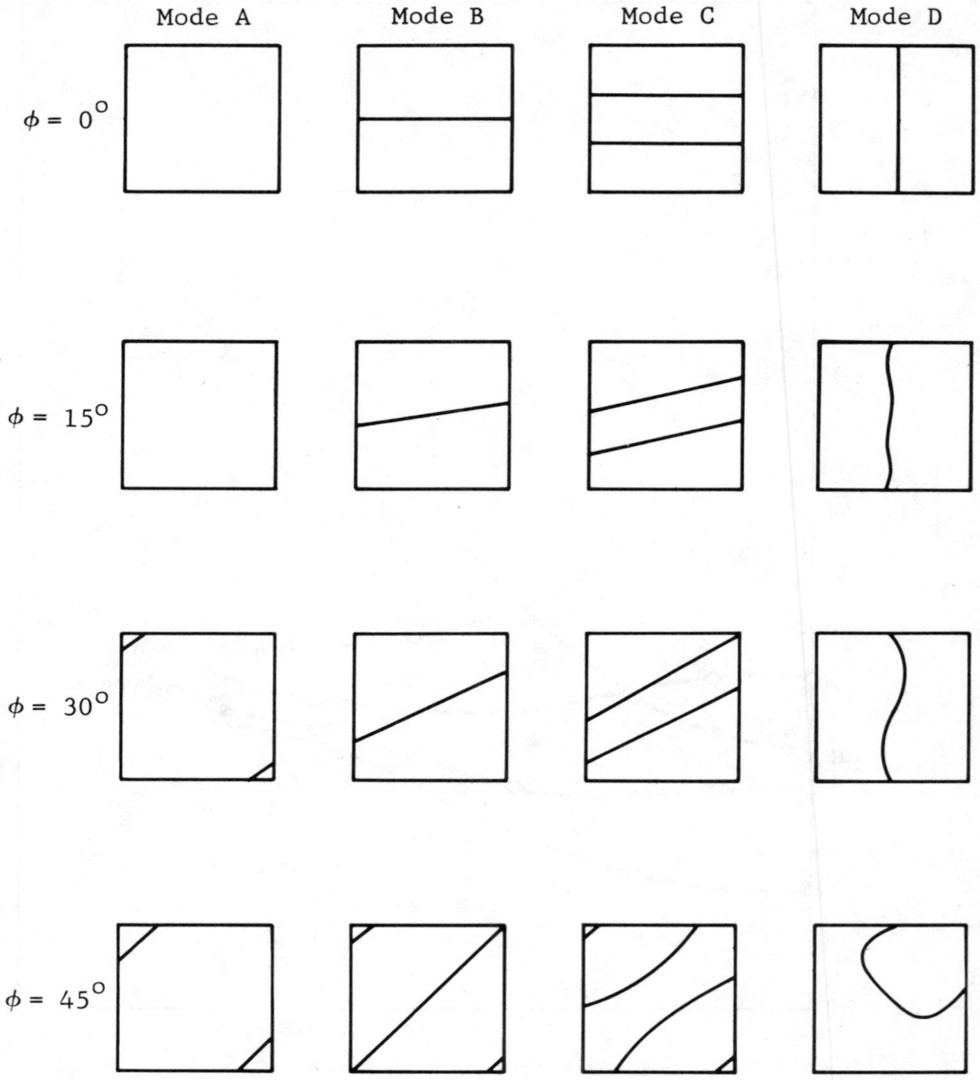

Fig. 4. Square Anisotropic Plate Node Lines.

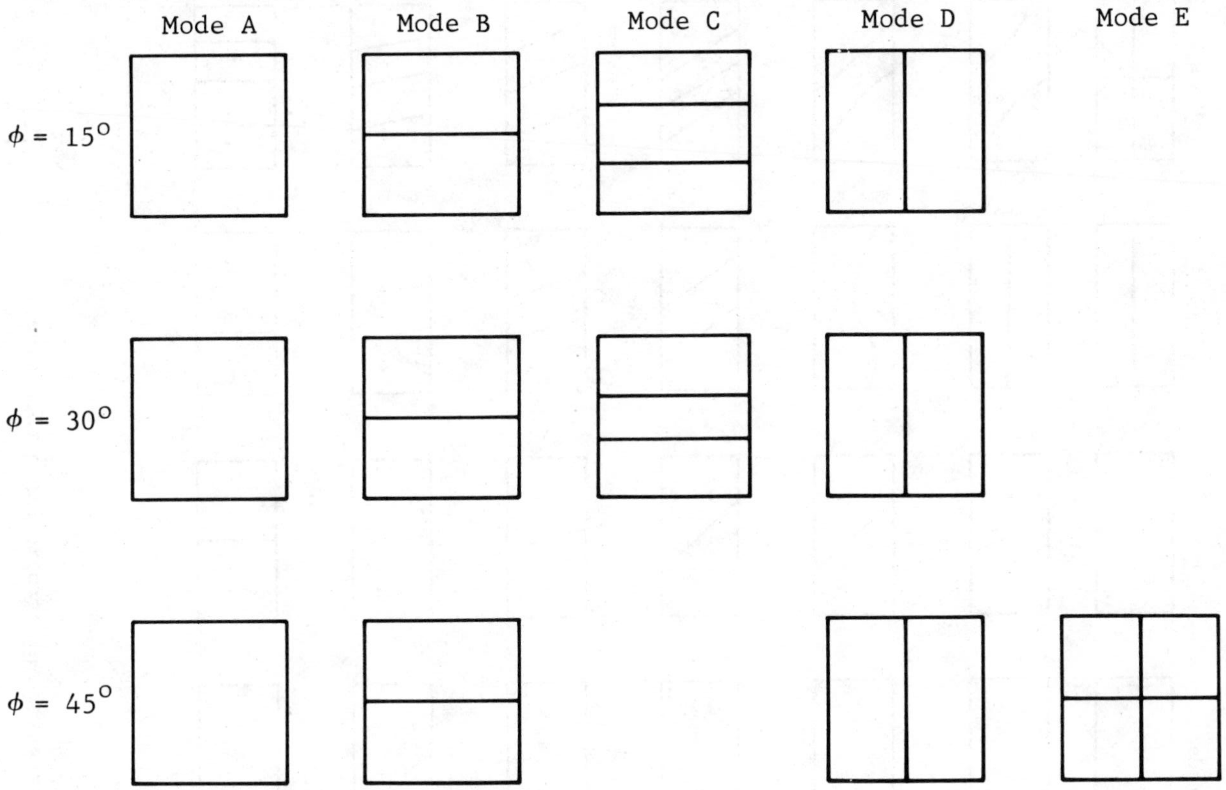

Fig. 5. Square Plate, Orthotropic Analysis Node Lines.

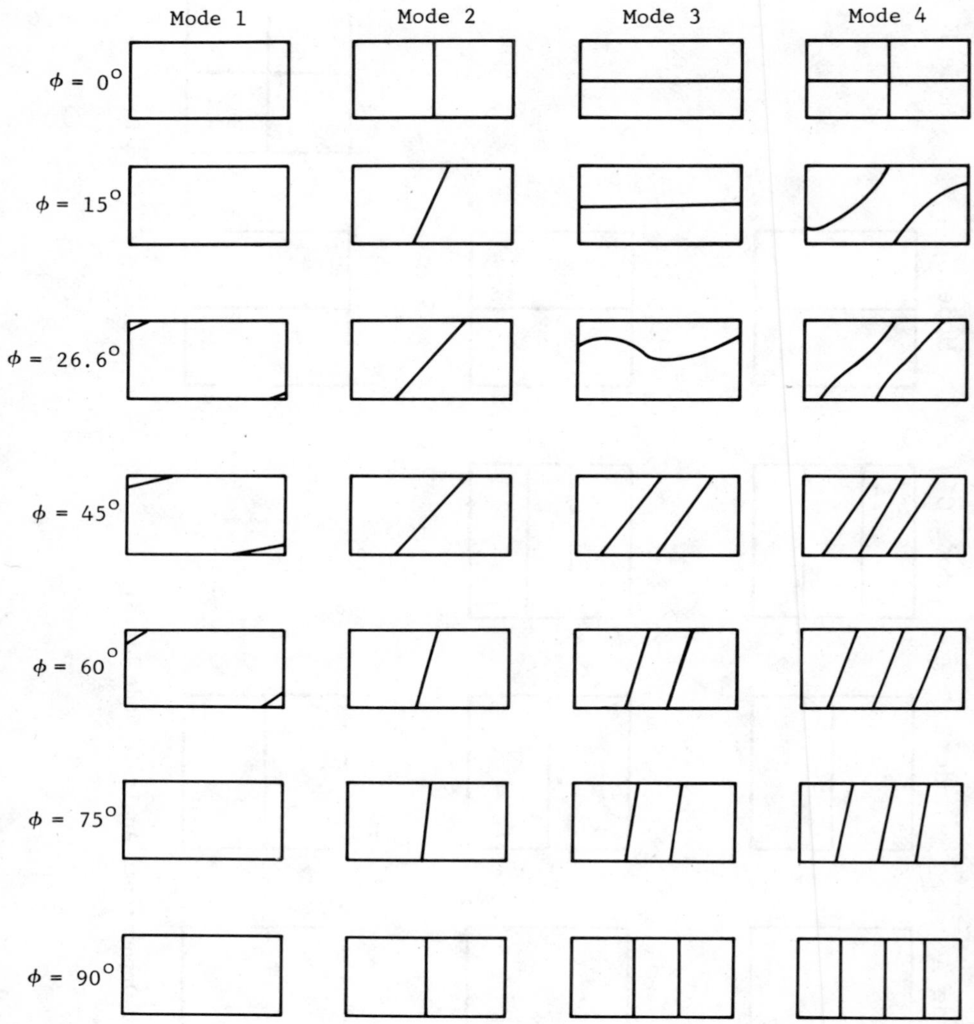

Fig. 6. Rectangular Anisotropic Plate Node Lines.

square plate with ϕ = 45 degrees are tabulated in Table II for series of 9, 16, 25, 36, and 49 terms.

TABLE II. CONVERGENCE OF THE SOLUTION

$a = b \qquad \phi = 45°$

Number of Terms in Series	$\omega/\sqrt{D_{\phi\phi}/\rho h b^4}$			
	Mode 1	Mode 2	Mode 3	Mode 4
9	20.79	35.35	49.75	55.75
16	20.64	35.25	47.80	52.53
25	20.53	35.04	47.37	52.49
36	20.51	35.01	47.11	52.25
49	20.51	35.01	47.07	52.21

The results presented in Tables I and II and Figures 2-6 illustrate that the Ritz procedure as outlined herein can adequately predict the lower modes of both specially orthotropic and generally orthotropic clamped rectangular plates. Furthermore, the numerical results, which were obtained for elastic constants representative of high modulus fiber reinforced composite materials (such as boron and graphite epoxy) indicate that the effects of the D_{16} and D_{26} terms in the plate bending stiffness matrix can be quite important. Such results show that the dynamic response of such generally orthotropic plates can be easily predicted as long as proper attention is paid to the full characterization of the plate bending behavior.

ACKNOWLEDGEMENT

This work was sponsored by the Air Force Materiels Laboratory, Research and Technology Division, Air Force Systems Command, United States Air Force under Contract No. AF33(615)-5257.

REFERENCES

1. Ashton, J. E., Halpin, J. C., and Petit, P. H., Primer on Composite Materials: Analysis, Technomic, 1969.

2. Iyengar, S. R., and Srinivasan, R. S., "Clamped Skew Plates under Uniform Loading," Journal of Royal Aeronautical Society, Vol. 71, February, 1967.

3. Ashton, J. E., and Waddoups, M. E., "Analysis of Anisotropic Plates," Journal of Composite Materials, Vol. III, No. 1, January, 1969.

4. Young, D., "Vibration of Rectangular Plates by the Ritz Method," Journal of Applied Mechanics, December, 1950.

WAVE PROPAGATION

A STUDY OF THERMOELASTIC WAVES BY THE METHOD OF CHARACTERISTICS

A. A. Lopez
Michigan Technological University

H. W. Lord
Michigan Technological University

ABSTRACT

The propagation of temperature, strain, and stress waves in solids is studied using the method of characteristics. A numerical procedure, previously developed for weakly coupled systems of hyperbolic partial differential equations, is extended to treat strongly coupled systems of equations. This procedure is then applied to the governing equations of the generalized dynamical theory of thermoelasticity which predicts finite propagation velocities for thermal and mechanical disturbances. Several one dimensional problems are treated and the results compared with existing work of the generalized and classical theories of thermoelasticity.

LIST OF NOTATIONS

$\underline{a}$	Frequency
$c_{1,2}$	Characteristic roots or wave velocities
$C^{\pm}_{1,2}$	Characteristic lines
C_v	Specific heat
$\tilde{e}$	Thermomechanical coupling constant
k	Thermal conductivity

t	Time
T	Absolute temperature
T_o	Reference temperature
u	Displacement
U	Dimensionless displacement
x	Space variable
z	Dimensionless space variable
α	Linear thermal expansion coefficient
β	Relaxation constant
ε	Strain
θ	Dimensionless temperature
λ, μ	Lamé elastic constants
ξ	Dimensionless strain
ρ	Mass density
σ	Stress
$\sum$	Dimensionless stress
τ	Dimensionless time
τ_o	Relaxation time

INTRODUCTION

The classical theory of thermoelasticity results in temperature and strain fields governed by two coupled partial differential equations, one equation being parabolic and the other hyperbolic. Because of the nature of the parabolic field equation, the classical theory predicts that a sudden mechanical or thermal disturbance will propagate as a wave with a small percursory effect leading the wave front infinitely far into the medium [1]. Kaliski [2] and Lord and Shulman [3] presented a generalized dynamical theory of thermoelasticity which introduces the effect of thermal inertia and results in temperature and strain fields governed by two coupled hyperbolic second order linear partial differential equations, thus predicting pure wave-type propagation of thermal and mechanical disturbances.

Studies of boundary value problems using the governing equations of the generalized dynamical theory of thermoelasticity have been restricted to investigations of the response of one-dimensional problems of a half-space subjected to thermal and mechanical disturbances at its free surface. Popov [4] investigated the problem of a step-temperature input at the free boundary by using the method of Laplace transforms. Norwood and Warren [5] made an analysis similar to that of Popov, extending the analysis to include step-inputs in strain, temperature, and stress at the free surface. Achenbach [6] used the theory of propagating surfaces of discontinuity to study the effect of heat conduction on jumps in the responses due to a step-stress at the free surface.

In the above references, the solutions given are valid only at the wave fronts, and yield expressions for the discontinuities and propagation velocities of the wave fronts. More recently, Lord and Lopez [7] obtained an approximate solution using Laplace transforms which yielded an integral equation for the response, valid for all times and for arbitrary inputs at the boundary. In the work presented here, a numerical procedure is developed, using the method of characteristics, which yields solutions to one-dimensional problems governed by the equations of the generalized theory of thermoelasticity valid for all times.

The application of the method of characteristics to systems of second order partial differential equations has recently received considerable attention. The solutions to several one-dimensional elastic wave problems were treated in a unified manner by Chou and Mortimer [8] who developed numerical procedures to handle the propagation of discontinuities along the characteristic curves. The procedure developed by Chou and Mortimer is extended in this paper to treat the strongly coupled system of equations, as defined by Chou and Perry [9], that arise in the generalized theory of thermoelasticity. The one-dimensional thermoelastic half-space, subjected to several types of mechanical and thermal inputs at the free boundary, is considered and the results compared with existing work of the generalized and classical theories.

Statement of the Problem

The work presented here considers an initially quiescent isotropic elastic half-space subjected to thermal and mechanical disturbances at its free surface. Furthermore, it is assumed that the resulting temperature and strain fields in the medium are governed by the one-dimensional equations of the generalized dynamical theory of thermoelasticity, as given by Lord and Shulman [3].

$$k \frac{\partial^2 T}{\partial x^2} = \rho C_v \left(\frac{\partial T}{\partial t} + \tau_o \frac{\partial^2 T}{\partial t^2} \right) + (3\lambda + 2\mu)\alpha T_o \left(\frac{\partial \varepsilon}{\partial t} + \tau_o \frac{\partial^2 \varepsilon}{\partial t^2} \right) \quad (1)$$

$$\rho \frac{\partial^2 u}{\partial t^2} = (\lambda + 2\mu) \frac{\partial^2 u}{\partial x^2} - (3\lambda + 2\mu)\alpha \frac{\partial T}{\partial x} \quad (2)$$

$$\sigma = (\lambda + 2\mu)\varepsilon - (3\lambda + 2\mu)\, \alpha(T - T_o) \quad (3)$$

These equations are restricted to small changes in strain and temperature and when τ_o is set equal to zero, reduce to the coupled equations of the classical theory of thermoelasticity.

Equations (1), (2), and (3) can be put in a more convenient form by defining the following nondimensional variables:

$$z = \left(\frac{\lambda + 2\mu}{\rho} \right)^{1/2} \frac{\rho C_v}{k} x \qquad \tau = \left(\frac{\lambda + 2\mu}{\rho} \right) \frac{\rho C_v}{k} t$$

$$\theta = \frac{T - T_o}{T_o} \qquad \Sigma = \frac{\sigma}{\alpha(3\lambda + 2\mu)T_o} \quad (4)$$

$$U = \rho \left(\frac{\lambda + 2\mu}{\rho} \right)^{3/2} \frac{1}{\alpha(3\lambda + 2\mu)T_o} \frac{\rho C_v}{k} u$$

Substitution of these variables into the one-dimensional governing equations yields:

Energy equation $\theta'' - \dot{\theta} - \beta\ddot{\theta} = \tilde{e}(\dot{U}' + \ddot{U}')$ (5)

Equation of motion $U'' - \ddot{U} = \theta'$ (6)

Stress-strain-temperature equation $\Sigma = U' - \theta$ (7)

where the primes and dots denote partial differentiation with respect to the dimensionless space and time variables z and τ, respectively. Expressions for the constants $\tilde{e}$ and β, in Eq. (5), are given below.

$$\tilde{e} = \frac{(3\lambda + 2\mu)^2 \alpha^2 T_o}{(\lambda + 2\mu)\rho C_v} \tag{8}$$

$$\beta = \left(\frac{\lambda + 2\mu}{\rho} \right) \left(\frac{\rho C_v}{k} \right) \tau_o \tag{9}$$

Equations (5) through (7) can be written in a form that is amenable to treatment by the method of characteristics by introducing the dimensionless strain variable $\xi = U'$ in the energy equation (5)

$$\theta'' - \dot{\theta} - \beta \ddot{\theta} = \tilde{e} (\dot{\xi} + \beta \ddot{\xi}) \tag{10}$$

and in the equation of motion (6), after taking its derivative with respect to z,

$$\xi'' - \ddot{\xi} = \theta'' \tag{11}$$

Equations (10) and (11), which govern the temperature and strain fields, constitute a system of strongly coupled second order partial differential equations of the hyperbolic type, to which the method of characteristics is readily applied. In addition, the stress equation (7) becomes

$$\sum = \xi - \theta \tag{12}$$

The boundary and initial conditions of the problem can now be stated. The elastic half-space is subjected to strain and temperature inputs at its free surface, z = 0. Moreover, it is assumed that the response of the medium remains bounded at $z = \infty$. Hence, the boundary conditions may be written as

$$\begin{aligned} \theta(0,\tau) &= \theta_o(\tau) \quad ; \quad & \xi(0,\tau) &= \xi_o(\tau) \\ \theta(\infty,\tau) &< M & \xi(\infty,\tau) &< M \end{aligned} \tag{13}$$

where $\theta_o(\tau)$ and $\xi_o(\tau)$ are arbitrary continuous input functions, whose first order derivatives may be discontinuous, and M is any positive constant. The medium is assumed to be initially quiescent and at a uniform reference temperature T_o. Thus, the initial conditions may be written as

$$\begin{aligned} \theta(z,0) &= \dot{\theta}(z,0) = \theta'(z,0) = 0 \\ \xi(z,0) &= \dot{\xi}(z,0) = \xi'(z,0) = 0 \end{aligned} \tag{14}$$

Equations (10) through (14) represent the boundary value problem which is treated here by the method of characteristics.

The Method of Characteristics

The method of characteristics, as presented here, is restricted to continuous temperature and strain fields, although discontinuities in the first order derivatives are allowed. In applying this method to a system of second order partial differential equations, curves along which the second order derivatives are of indeterminate form are sought in the z-τ plane. These curves are obtained in the following manner. The governing equations (10) and (11) give two equations relating the six second order derivatives of θ and ξ,

$$\theta'' - \beta\ddot{\theta} - \tilde{e}\beta\ddot{\xi} = \dot{\theta} + \tilde{e}\,\dot{\xi} \tag{10}$$

$$\theta'' - \xi'' + \ddot{\xi} = 0 \tag{11}$$

Additional equations are obtained by considering the regions of the z-τ plane in which $\dot{\theta}$, θ', $\dot{\xi}$, and ξ' are continuous. Then, the following equations are valid:

$$d(\theta') = \theta''\,dz + \dot{\theta}'\,d\tau \tag{15}$$

$$d(\dot{\theta}) = \dot{\theta}'\,dz + \ddot{\theta}\,d\tau \tag{16}$$

$$d(\xi') = \xi''\,dz + \dot{\xi}'\,d\tau \tag{17}$$

$$d(\dot{\xi}) = \dot{\xi}'\,dz + \ddot{\xi}\,d\tau \tag{18}$$

Equations (10), (11), and (15) through (18) form a set of six equations relating the six second order derivatives θ'', $\dot{\theta}'$, $\ddot{\theta}$, ξ'', $\dot{\xi}'$, $\ddot{\xi}$ and which can be written in matrix form as

$$\begin{bmatrix} 1 & 0 & -\beta & 0 & 0 & -\tilde{e}\beta \\ 1 & 0 & 0 & -1 & 0 & 1 \\ dz & d\tau & 0 & 0 & 0 & 0 \\ 0 & dz & d\tau & 0 & 0 & 0 \\ 0 & 0 & 0 & dz & d\tau & 0 \\ 0 & 0 & 0 & 0 & dz & d\tau \end{bmatrix} \begin{Bmatrix} \theta'' \\ \dot{\theta}' \\ \ddot{\theta} \\ \xi'' \\ \dot{\xi}' \\ \ddot{\xi} \end{Bmatrix} = \begin{Bmatrix} \dot{\theta}+\tilde{e}\dot{\xi} \\ 0 \\ d\theta' \\ d\dot{\theta} \\ d\xi' \\ d\dot{\xi} \end{Bmatrix} \tag{19}$$

The second order derivatives in Eq. (19) are of indeterminate form if the determinant of the coefficient matrix on the left-hand side of Eq. (19) and the determinant of the matrix formed by replacing in the coefficient matrix one of its columns by the column matrix on the right-hand side of Eq. (19) vanish simultaneously. The first condition yields the characteristic equation from which the characteristic curves are determined. The second condition gives the compatibility equations that must be satisfied along the characteristics curves.

Setting the determinant of the coefficient matrix equal to zero yields the characteristic equation

$$[(dz)^2 - (d\tau)^2]\,[(d\tau)^2 - \beta(dz)^2] + \tilde{e}\beta(dz)^2\,(d\tau)^2 = 0 \tag{20}$$

Dividing through by $\beta(d\tau)^4$ gives

$$\left(\frac{dz}{d\tau}\right)^4 - \left(\frac{1}{\beta} + 1 + \tilde{e}\right)\left(\frac{dz}{d\tau}\right)^2 + \frac{1}{\beta} = 0$$

from which the characteristic roots are obtained

$$\left(\frac{dz}{d\tau}\right)_{1,2,3,4} = \pm\sqrt{\frac{\left(\frac{1}{\beta} + 1 + \tilde{e}\right) \pm \sqrt{\left(\frac{1}{\beta} + 1 + \tilde{e}\right)^2 - \frac{4}{\beta}}}{2}} \tag{21}$$

These characteristic roots define a set of characteristic curves in the z-τ plane. For the homogeneous medium treated here, subjected to small perturbations in temperature, β and $\tilde{e}$ are constants. Thus, the characteristic curves are straight lines. The characteristic roots are the wave velocities and are in agreement with those published by Achenbach [6] and Norwood and Warren [5].

The compatibility equation obtained by replacing the first column in the coefficient matrix of Eq. (19) by the column matrix appearing on the right-hand side of that same equation is

$$[(dz)^2 - (d\tau)^2][(d\tau)^2 (\tilde{e}\,\dot{\xi} + \dot{\theta}) - \beta\, dz d\theta' + \beta\, d\tau d\dot{\theta}]$$

$$+ \tilde{e}\,\beta\, dz (d\tau)^2\, d\,\xi' - \tilde{e}\,\beta\,(d\tau)^3\, d\,\dot{\xi} = 0 \tag{22}$$

This equation is in agreement with the general form of the compatibility equations given by Chou and Perry [9]. Five other compatibility equations could be obtained by replacing each of the remaining five columns of the coefficient matrix by the column matrix and setting the determinant equal to zero. However, in our case, each compatibility equation contains the same differentials and consequently, as pointed out by Chou and Perry, can be reduced to the same compatibility conditions. The compatibility conditions are obtained by substituting the characteristic roots of Eq. (21) into the compatibility equation (22).

Numerical Procedures

The procedure used to obtain numerical solutions when the input functions $\theta_o(\tau)$ and $\xi_o(\tau)$ of Eq. (13) have continuous first order derivatives is identical to that presented by Chou and Mortimer [8] for the weakly coupled set of partial differential equations. For each mesh ABCD (Fig. 1) the values of θ, $\dot{\theta}$, θ', ξ, $\dot{\xi}$, and ξ' are assumed to be known at A,

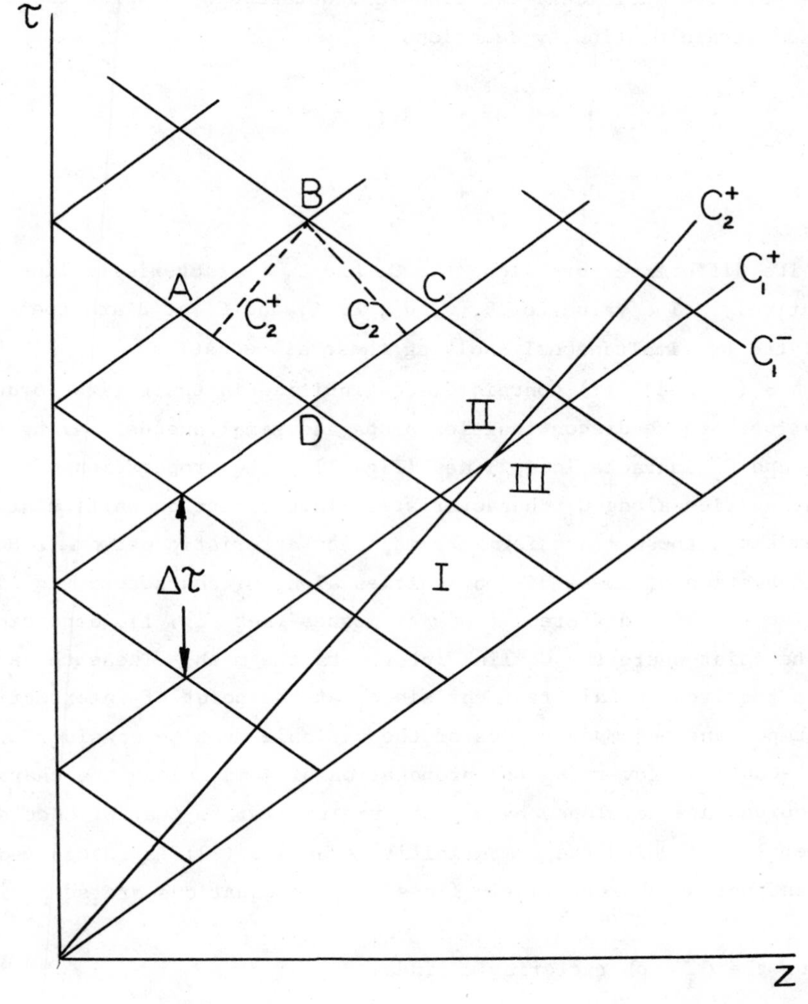

Fig. 1. Characteristic Network.

C, and D. To calculate the values at B, the compatibility equation (22) is written in finite difference form along the four characteristic lines through B. Two additional equations are obtained by writing the temperature and strain continuity equations

$$d\theta = \theta' dz + \dot{\theta}\, d\tau \tag{23}$$

$$d\xi = \xi' dz + \dot{\xi}\, d\tau \tag{24}$$

in finite difference form along the C_2^- and C_1^- characteristic lines[1], respectively. The values of θ, $\dot{\theta}$, θ', ξ, $\dot{\xi}$, and ξ' at B are then calculated by simultaneously solving these six equations.

When $\theta_0(\tau)$ and $\xi_0(\tau)$ contain discontinuities in their first order derivatives, these discontinuities propagate simultaneously along both the C_1 and C_2 characteristic lines (Fig. 1). The propagation of discontinuities along C_1 characteristic lines create no particular problem since these lines form the main characteristic network. However, the propagation of these discontinuities along C_2 characteristic lines give rise to three different types of meshes (see Fig. 1), depending upon the point where the C_2 line intersects the mesh. These three types of mesh require special treatment since, at the point of intersection, both jumped and unjumped values of the variable must be considered.

The equations governing the propagation of jumps along the characteristic curves are developed by a procedure similar to that of Chou and Mortimer [8] in which the compatibility equation (22) is integrated along and across characteristic lines. These equations are summarized below.

Along the $C_1^{\pm}$ characteristic lines,

$$[\dot{\theta}] \pm c_1 [\theta'] = 0$$

1. Here c_1 and c_2 are used to represent the positive radical on the right-hand side of Eq. (21). $C_1^{\pm}$ or simply C_1 is used to represent the characteristic lines whose slope is $\pm c_1$.

$$[\dot{\xi}] = \frac{(c_2^2 - 1)}{\tilde{e}} [\dot{\theta}]$$

$$[\xi'] = \frac{(c_2^2 - 1)}{\tilde{e}} [\theta'] \tag{25}$$

$$[\dot{\theta}] = K_1 \exp\left(- \int \frac{c_2^2 (c_1^2 - 1)}{2\beta(c_1^2 - c_2^2)} d\tau \right)$$

and along the $C_2^{\pm}$ characteristic lines

$$[\dot{\theta}] \pm c_2 [\theta'] = 0$$

$$[\dot{\xi}] = \frac{(c_1^2 - 1)}{\tilde{e}} [\dot{\theta}]$$

$$[\xi'] = \frac{(c_1^2 - 1)}{\tilde{e}} [\theta'] \tag{26}$$

$$[\dot{\theta}] = K_2 \exp\left(\int \frac{c_1^2 (c_2^2 - 1)}{2\beta(c_1^2 - c_2^2)} d\tau \right)$$

where K_1 and K_2 are constants of integration calculated from the boundary conditions, and the brackets [] are used to represent jumps defined by

$$[\dot{\theta}] = \lim_{B \to A} \dot{\theta}(B) - \dot{\theta}(A)$$

Equations (25) and (26) predict that if a discontinuity in one of the derivatives, say, $\dot{\theta}$, is introduced, this automatically gives rise to discontinuities in the other derivatives. Furthermore, these discontinuities propagate along both C_1 and C_2 characteristic lines simultaneously. This is unlike the weakly coupled problems treated by Chou and Mortimer in which there was no coupling between the discontinuities of the first order derivatives of the dependent variables. Due to the coupling and simultaneous propagation of discontinuities in the thermoelastic problem, all boundary conditions must be considered simultaneously when calculating the constants of integration K_1 and K_2 in Eqs. (25) and (26).

The numerical procedure used to evaluate the dependent variables and their first order derivatives, for the problem with discontinuous boundary conditions, is similar to that used for the problem with continuous boundary conditions. Compatibility and continuity equations (22) through (24), are written in finite difference form along characteristic lines. However, for the meshes intersected by the C_2 characteristic, along which discontinuities propagate, the variables at point B (see Fig. 2) must be calculated in two steps. The first step consists of solving for the values of the variables at point F. In the second step, the values of the variables at point B are calculated using the values at point F and taking into account the jumps in the variables across C_2. The equations used to obtain the values of θ, $\dot{\theta}$, θ', ξ, $\dot{\xi}$, and ξ' at points F and B for types I and II meshes are given in Appendix A. An analogous procedure is used for type III meshes.

Applications

The numerical procedure developed in the previous sections is applied here to four problems. The first two problems treated involve step-inputs in stress and temperature, respectively. Since the numerical procedure associated with the method of characteristics is restricted to continuous strain and temperature inputs, it was necessary to approximate the Heaviside unit step function $H(\tau)$ by

$$H_{\underline{a}}(\tau) = \begin{cases} 0, & \tau < 0 \\ \sin^2(\underline{a}\tau), & 0 < \underline{a}\tau < \pi/2 \\ 1, & \underline{a}\tau > \pi/2 \end{cases} \tag{27}$$

where $\underline{a}$ is the frequency. The use of large values of $\underline{a}$ in Eq. (27) results in a fast rise time, similar to that of the Heaviside function, while preserving the continuity of the input function and its first order derivatives. A value of $\underline{a}$ equal to 10.0 was used in our computations. The boundary conditions for step-stress and step-temperature inputs can then be written as

$$\text{Step-stress} \qquad \theta(0,\tau) = 0 \quad ; \quad \textstyle\sum(0,\tau) = H_{\underline{a}}(\tau) \tag{28}$$

$$\text{Step-temperature} \qquad \theta(0,\tau) = H_{\underline{a}}(\tau) \quad ; \quad \textstyle\sum(0,\tau) = 0 \tag{29}$$

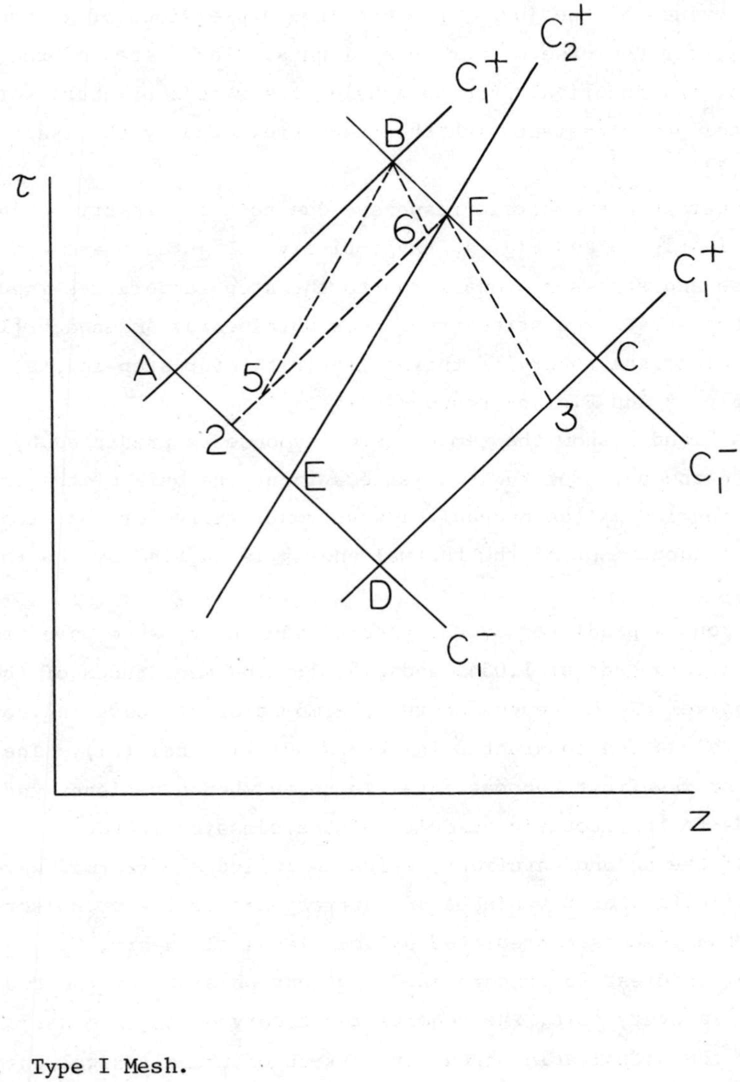

Fig. 2. Type I Mesh.

The temperature, strain and stress responses of the above two problems were computed at $z = 0.5137$ for $\tilde{e} = 0.0733$ (corresponding to lead at room temperature) and $\beta = 2.6$, using a grid size for which $\Delta\tau \simeq 0.005$ (see Fig. 1). The jumps in the temperature and strain responses occurring at the wave-fronts are shown in Tables I and II. These tables also list the exact values of the jumps, given by the expressions of Norwood and Warren [5], for the case of pure step-inputs. The values of the jumps obtained by the numerical procedure using the method of characteristics are in excellent agreement with the jumps predicted by the exact expressions of [5].

The temperature and strain responses due to the step-stress input are shown in Fig. 3 and Fig. 4, respectively. Figures 5 and 6 show the temperature and stress responses due to the step-temperature input. In addition the strain and stress responses obtained by Achenbach [10] using the classical theory of thermoelasticity, for step-inputs, are shown in Fig. 4 and Fig. 6, respectively.

Figures 3 and 5 show the temperature response as predicted by the generalized theory. For the step-stress input the bulk of the thermal energy is carried by the mechanical wavefront, while for the step-temperature input most of the thermal energy is carried by the thermal wavefront.

The responses predicted by the generalized theory show wave fronts traveling with speeds of 1.0545 and 0.5881. The magnitudes of these propagation velocities depend on the thermomechanical coupling constant $\tilde{e}$ and the relaxation constant β in accordance with Eq. (21). The velocity of the first wavefront becomes equal to unity when β vanishes and corresponds to the acoustic velocity of the classical theory. The velocity of the second wavefront, which is called the thermal wavefront, becomes infinite when β vanishes and corresponds to the precursory effect in the responses predicted by the classical theory.

It is of interest to compare the solutions obtained by the two theories. In every case, the generalized theory of thermoelasticity eliminates the undesirable precursory effect of the classical theory and predicts two wavefronts. For the step-temperature input the two theories predict responses in stress which are very different in form, as shown

Table I. Value of the Jumps at z = 0.5137 due to a Unit Step-Stress Input

Wave Front	Exact Solution (Norwood and Warren)	Numerical Procedure (Method of Characteristics)
TEMPERATURE		
First	-0.0952	-0.095
Second	0.0815	0.081
STRAIN		
First	0.8497	0.851
Second	0.1247	0.127

Table II. Value of the Jumps at z = 0.5137 due to a Unit Step-Temperature Input

Wave Front	Exact Solution (Norwood and Warren)	Numerical Procedure (Method of Characteristics)
TEMPERATURE		
First	0.0503	0.049
Second	0.809	0.806
STRAIN		
First	-0.4493	-0.442
Second	1.237	1.25

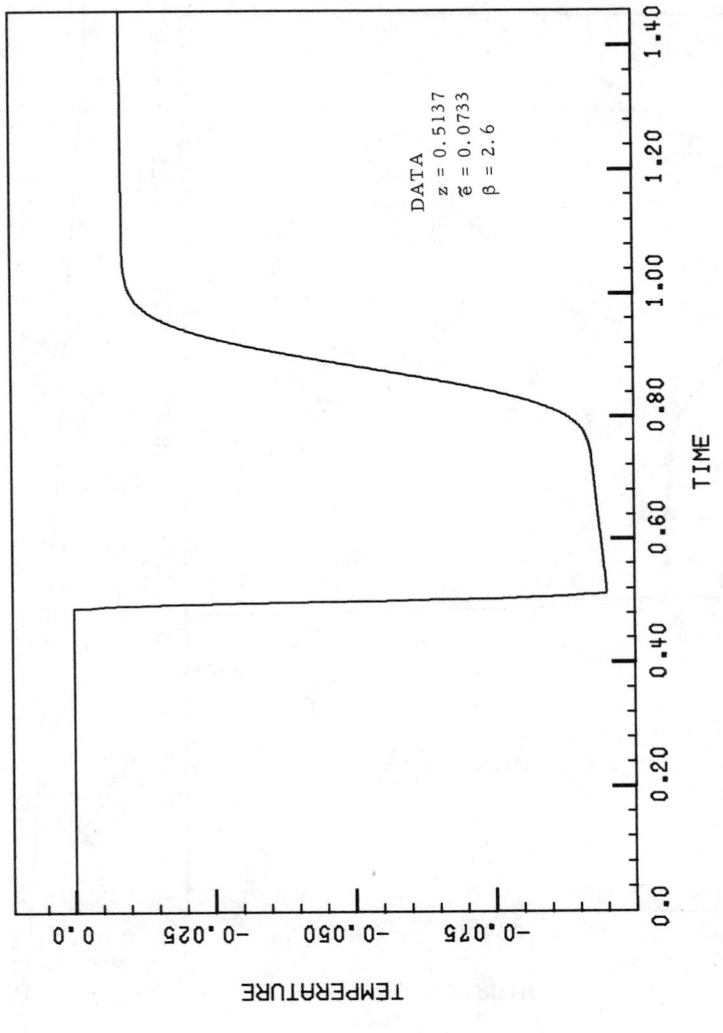

Fig. 3. Temperature Response to a Unit Step-Stress.

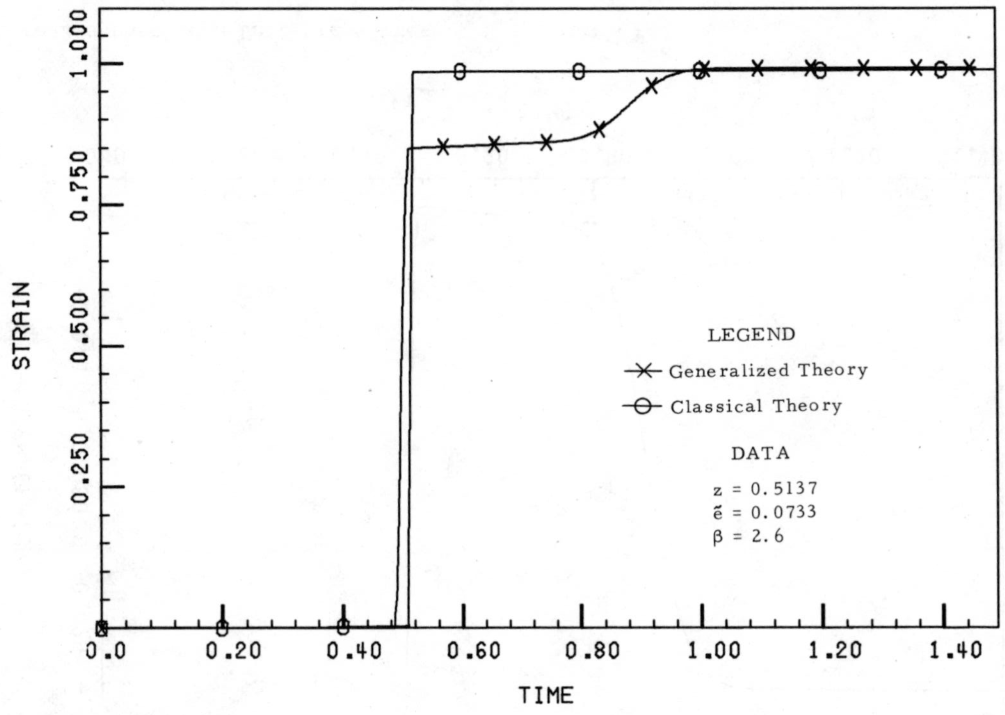

Fig. 4. Strain Response to a Unit Step-Stress.

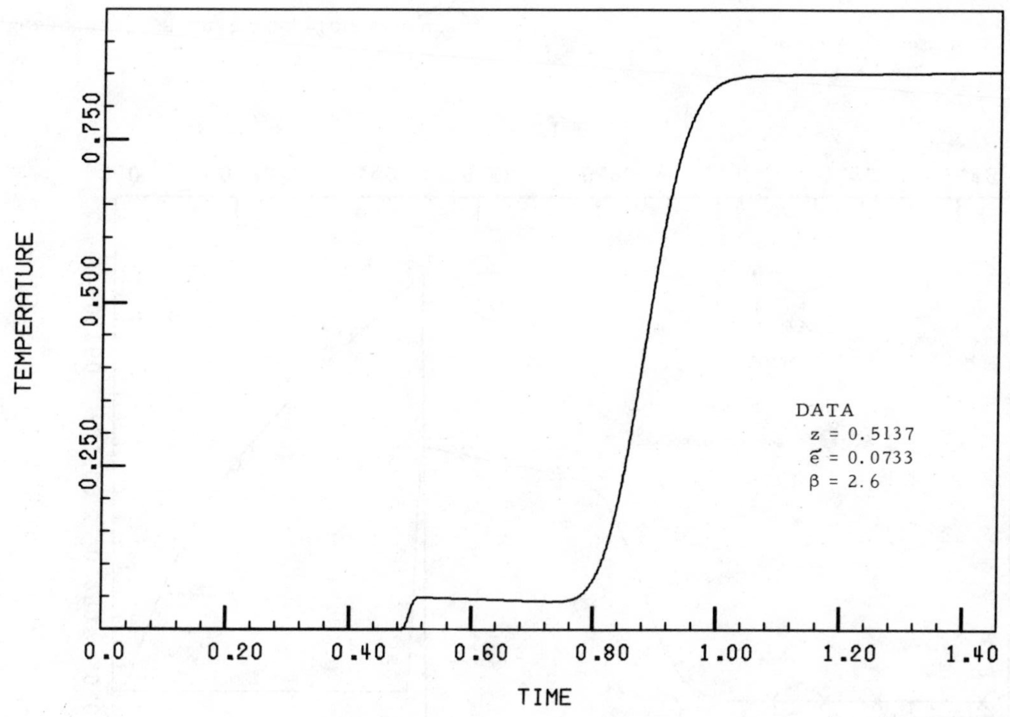

Fig. 5. Temperature Response to a Unit Step-Temperature.

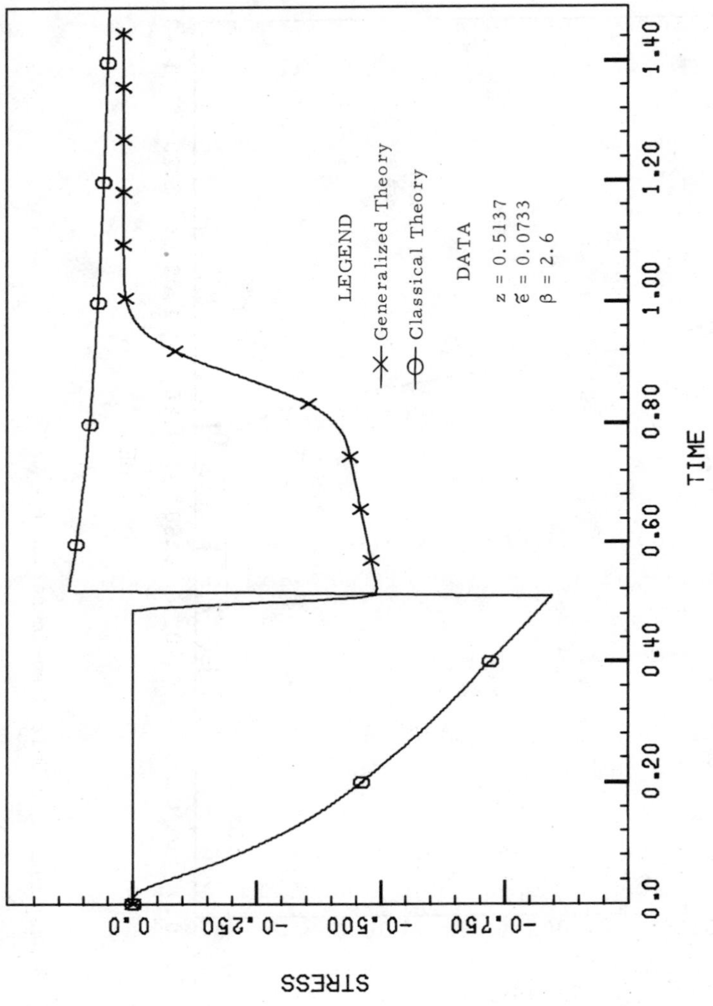

Fig. 6. Stress Response to a Unit Step-Temperature.

in Fig. 6. The classical theory shows a large compressive pulse preceding the acoustic wavefront, which is physically inadmissible. The response obtained by the generalized theory shows a relatively large compressive stress pulse contained between the acoustic and thermal wavefronts. This is contrary to the response predicted by the classical theory which shows only tensile stresses occurring behind the acoustic wavefronts.

The third problem treated is that of an elastic half-space subjected to a half-sine-squared temperature pulse and zero stress at the free boundary. Thus, the boundary conditions become

$$\theta(0,\tau) = \xi(0,\tau) = \begin{cases} 0 & \underline{a}\tau < 0;\ \underline{a}\tau > \pi \\ \sin^2 \underline{a}\tau & 0 < \underline{a}\tau < \pi \end{cases} \qquad (30)$$

where $\underline{a}$ is the frequency of the pulse.

The temperature and strain responses, due to a temperature pulse input of frequency $\underline{a} = 2.$, are shown in Figs. 7 and 8. These responses were computed at $z = 0.5137$ for $\tilde{e} = 0.0733$ and $\beta = 2.6$, using a grid size for which $\Delta\tau \simeq 0.0025$. The value of β used was determined from the experimental propagation velocities of the heat pulse studies of Rogers and Rollefson [11] on NaF at 7.2°K. However, β can be related to the unknown relaxation constant τ_o by Eq. (9). Using the known physical properties of NaF at this temperature yields a value of $\tau_o = 6 \times 10^{-8}$ sec.

The generalized theory predicts that a temperature pulse input will generate a small thermal pulse traveling with the acoustic velocity followed by an initially large pulse propagating with the thermal velocity. The magnitude of the first pulse is small, being proportional to the coupling constant $\tilde{e}$, with most of the thermal energy being carried by the second pulse. However, the magnitude of the second pulse decays very rapidly as the pulse propagates into the medium, as shown in [7].

It is interesting to note that in a large number of the heat pulse experiments performed at low temperatures in solids two temperature pulses have been measured. Temperature pulse responses have been

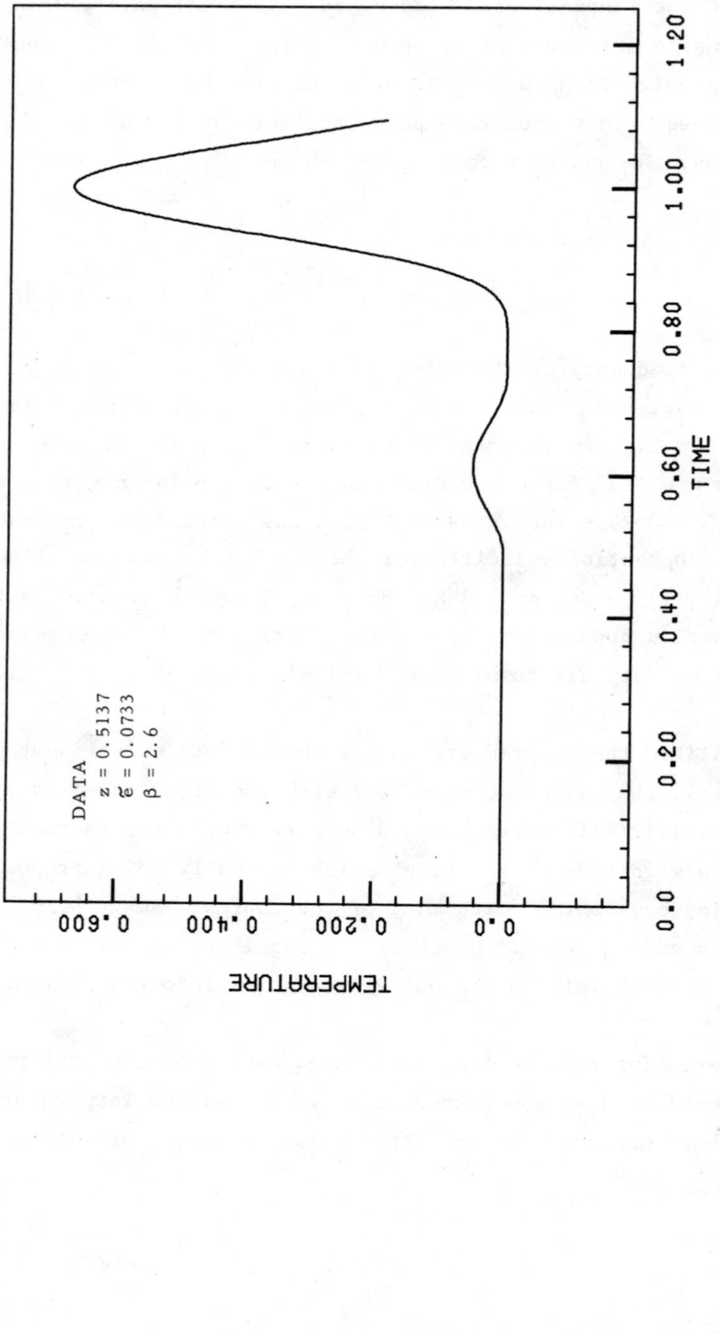

Fig. 7. Temperature Response to a Sine-Squared Temperature Pulse.

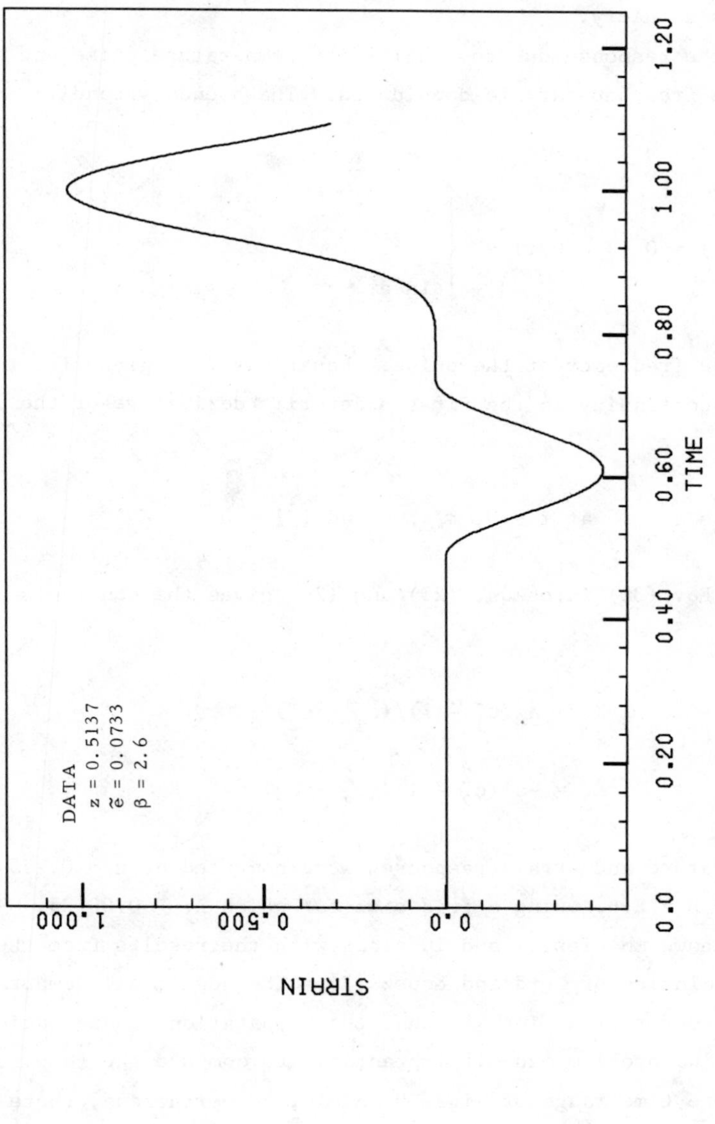

Fig. 8. Strain Response to a Sine-Squared Temperature Pulse.

obtained, using the generalized theory, which are strikingly similar to those reported by Rogers and Rollefson. However, it is realized that the validity of the macroscopic theory can only be established by a series of experiments carefully designed to isolate certain characteristics of the proposed theory.

Finally, the response due to a half-sine temperature pulse and zero strain at the free boundary is considered. The boundary conditions become

$$\xi(0,\tau) = 0 \; ; \quad \theta(0,\tau) = \begin{cases} 0, & \underline{a}\tau < 0 \; ; \; \underline{a}\tau > \pi \\ \sin \underline{a}\tau, & 0 < \underline{a}\tau < \pi \end{cases} \tag{31}$$

where a is the frequency of the pulse. Equations (31) give rise to the following discontinuity in the first order time derivative of the temperature

$$[\dot{\theta}] = \underline{a}, \qquad \text{at } \tau = 0, \; \pi/\underline{a}; \quad \text{and } [\dot{\xi}] = 0 \tag{32}$$

Substituting Eq. (32) into Eqs. (25) and (26) gives the constants of integration

$$\begin{aligned} K_1 &= \underline{a}\ (c_1^2 - 1)/(c_1^2 - c_2^2) \\ K_2 &= -\underline{a}\ (c_2^2 - 1)/(c_1^2 - c_2^2) \end{aligned} \tag{33}$$

The temperature and strain responses were computed at z = 0.125 for $\tilde{e} = 0.001$ and $\beta = 2.6$, using a grid size for which $\Delta\tau \approx 0.00125$. These results are shown in Figs. 9 and 10 along with the results from the approximate solution of Lord and Lopez [7]. The additional computations required in order to take into account the propagation of discontinuities in the half-sine problem made it impractical to compute the responses over the entire time range of Figs. 9 and 10. Nevertheless, there is good agreement between the computed solution and the approximate solution over the time region for which the numerical procedure was applied.

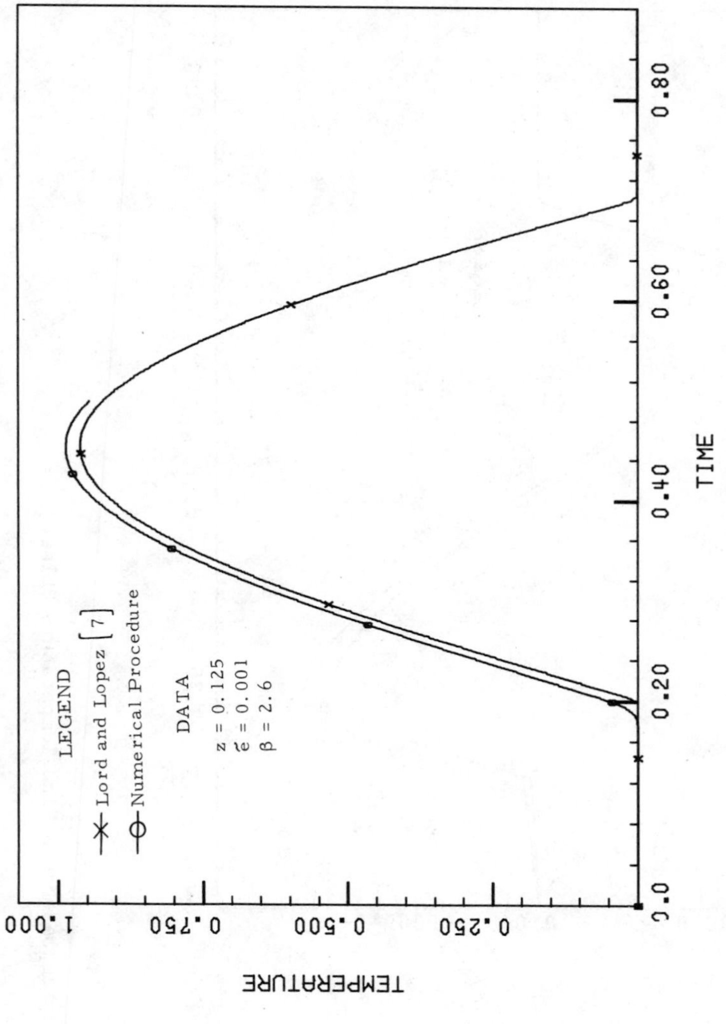

Fig. 9. Temperature Response to a Sine Temperature Pulse.

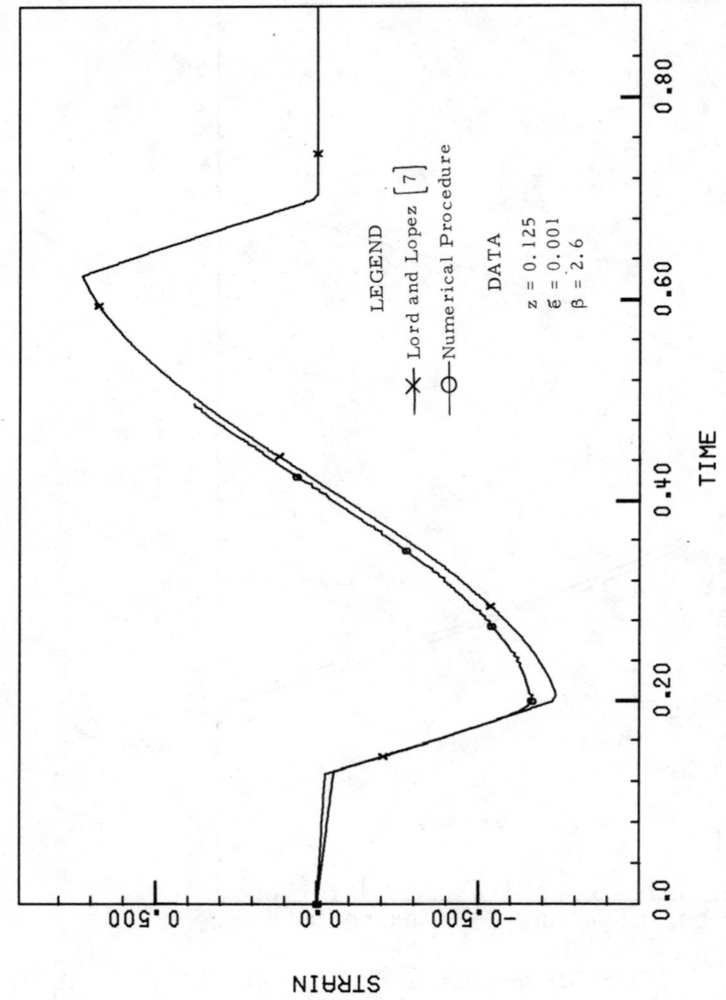

Fig. 10. Strain Response to a Sine Temperature Pulse.

DISCUSSION

The numerical procedure developed in this paper applies the method of characteristics to a strongly coupled set of linear second order hyperbolic partial differential equations, giving solutions valid for all times. The mesh size required in order to obtain accurate solutions, using this numerical procedure, depends upon the type of problem considered. There is very little difference between the solutions obtained for the step-input problems using a mesh size for which $\Delta\tau \approx 0.01$ and those obtained using a mesh size for which $\Delta\tau \approx 0.005$. On the other hand, the calculation of accurate solutions for the pulse problems requires the use of very fine meshes relative to that required for the step-input problems. This is particularly true for problems with input functions having discontinuous first order derivatives. Moreover, it was found that finer and finer grids are necessary in order to obtain satisfactory solutions as the response progresses further into the medium. Consequently, the procedure developed using the method of characteristics is best suited for problems for which the input functions applied at the boundary vary at a fixed rate, such as step and ramp inputs, or for problems for which the response is required at a very short distance into the medium. However, good qualitative results can be obtained for problems requiring the response at larger distances into the medium by using the approximate solution introduced by Lord and Lopez [7].

The computer programs used to calculate the solutions presented in this paper require about one minute of computer run time (on an IBM 360 Model 44 computer) for every 5000 grid points used in the characteristic mesh. As an example, computation of the responses of Figs. 3 and 4, using a grid size for which $\Delta\tau \approx 0.005$, required the calculation of the variables at 40,000 grid points and took about 8 minutes of run time.

ACKNOWLEDGEMENT

The authors are grateful for the support of this work given by the National Science Foundation under Grant GK-3312. We also wish to thank Dr. R. J. Pomazal for carefully reading the manuscript of this paper.

REFERENCES

1. Boley, B. A. and Tolins, I. S., "Transient Coupled Thermoelastic Boundary Value Problems in the Half-Space," Journal of Applied Mechanics, Vol. 29, 1962, pp. 637-646.

2. Kaliski, S., "Wave Equations in Thermoelasticity," Bulletin De L'Academie Polonaise Des Sciences, Serie des sciences techniques Vol. 13, No. 4, 1965, pp. 253-260.

3. Lord, H. W. and Shulman, Y., "A Generalized Dynamical Theory of Thermoelasticity," Journal of the Mechanics and Physics of Solids, Vol. 15, 1967, pp. 299-309.

4. Popov, E. B., "Dynamic Coupled Problem of Thermoelasticity for a Half-Space Taking Account of the Finiteness of the Heat Propagation Velocity," Journal of Applied Mathematics and Mechanics (PMM), Vol. 31, 1967, pp. 349-355.

5. Norwood, F. R. and Warren, W. E., "Wave Propagation in the Generalized Dynamical Theory of Thermoelasticity," Quarterly Journal of Mechanics and Applied Mathematics, Vol. 22, 1969, pp. 283-290.

6. Achenbach, J. D., "The Influence of Heat Conduction on Propagating Stress Jumps," Journal of the Mechanics and Physics of Solids, Vol. 16, 1968, pp. 273-282.

7. Lord, H. W. and Lopez, A. A., "Wave Propagation in Thermoelastic Solids at Very Low Temperature," Acta Mechanica, Vol. 10, June 1970, pp. 85-95.

8. Chou, P. C. and Mortimer, R. W., "Solution of One-Dimensional Elastic Wave Problem by the Method of Characteristics," Journal of Applied Mechanics, Vol. 34, 1967, pp. 745-750.

9. Chou, P. C. and Perry, R. F., "The Classification of Partial Differential Equations in Structural Dynamics," Proceedings of ASME/AIAA Tenth Structures, Structural Dynamics, and Materials Conference, 1969, pp. 185-194.

10. Achenbach, J. D., "Approximate Transient Solutions for the Coupled Equations of Thermoelasticity," The Journal of the Acoustical Society of America, Vol. 36, 1964, pp. 10-18.

11. Rogers, S. J. and Rollefson, R. J., "Heat Pulses and Phonon Scattering in N_aF," Bulletin of American Physical Society, Vol. 12, 1967, p. 339.

APPENDIX A

The equations required to solve for the values of the variables at points F and B, for types I and II meshes, are presented in this Appendix. As a point of departure the values of the variables at points A, C, and D in the mesh (see Fig. 2) are assumed to be known. Then a C_1^+ line is drawn through F, the intersection of this line with AD being labeled point 2. Similarly a C_2^- line, drawn through F, intersects CD at point 3. The values of the variables at points 2 and 3 are calculated by linear interpolation of their values at points A, C, and D.

Jumped and unjumped values of the variables appear at F, depending upon which side of the characteristic line C_2^+ the point is being viewed. Let the jumped values of the variables be denoted by the subscript j, then the jumped and unjumped values of the variables at point F are related by equations of the form,

$$\dot{\theta}_{Fj} = \dot{\theta}_F + [\dot{\theta}]_F$$

The compatibility equation (22) is written below in finite difference form along the four characteristic lines passing through F

$$(c_1^2 - 1)\ \{\beta(\dot{\theta}_{Fj} - \dot{\theta}_2 - c_1\ (\theta'_{Fj} - \theta'_2)) + (\frac{\dot{\theta}_{Fj}+\dot{\theta}_2}{2} + \tilde{e}\frac{\dot{\xi}_{Fj}+\dot{\xi}_2}{2})(\tau_F - \tau_2)\}$$

$$+ \tilde{e}\beta\ \{\ c_1(\xi'_{Fj} - \xi'_2) - (\dot{\xi}_{Fj} - \dot{\xi}_2)\ \} = 0 \qquad \text{(A1)}$$

$$(c_1^2 - 1)\{\beta(\dot{\theta}_F - \dot{\theta}_C + c_1(\theta'_F - \theta'_C)) + (\frac{\dot{\theta}_F+\dot{\theta}_C}{2} + \tilde{e}\frac{\dot{\xi}_F+\dot{\xi}_C}{2})\ (\tau_F - \tau_C)\}$$

$$+ \tilde{e}\beta\ \{\ -\ c_1\ (\xi'_F - \xi'_C) - (\dot{\xi}_F - \dot{\xi}_C)\ \} = 0 \qquad \text{(A2)}$$

$$(c_2^2 - 1)\ \{\beta(\dot{\theta}_{Fj} - \dot{\theta}_{Ej} - c_2(\theta'_{Fj} - \theta'_{Ej})) + (\frac{\dot{\theta}_{Fj}+\dot{\theta}_{Ej}}{2} + \tilde{e}\ \frac{\dot{\xi}_{Fj}+\dot{\xi}_{Ej}}{2})(\tau_F - \tau_E)\}$$

$$+ \tilde{e}\beta\ \{c_2(\xi'_{Fj} - \xi'_{Ej}) - (\dot{\xi}_{Fj} - \dot{\xi}_{Ej})\ \} = 0 \qquad \text{(A3)}$$

$$(c_2^2 - 1)\{\beta\ (\dot{\theta}_F - \dot{\theta}_3 + c_2(\theta'_F - \theta'_3)) + (\frac{\dot{\theta}_F+\dot{\theta}_3}{2} + \tilde{e}\ \frac{\dot{\xi}_F+\dot{\xi}_3}{2})(\tau_F - \tau_3)\}$$

$$+ \tilde{e}\beta\{\ - c_2(\xi'_F - \xi'_3) - (\dot{\xi}_F - \dot{\xi}_3)\ \} = 0 \qquad \text{(A4)}$$

In addition, the continuity equations (Eqs. (23) and (24)) are written along the C_2^- and C_1^- lines,

$$\theta_F - \theta_3 = \frac{\dot{\theta}_F + \dot{\theta}_3}{2}(\tau_F - \tau_3) + \frac{\theta'_F + \theta'_3}{2}(z_F - z_3) \qquad \text{(A5)}$$

$$\xi_F - \xi_C = \frac{\dot{\xi}_F + \dot{\xi}_C}{2}(\tau_F - \tau_C) + \frac{\xi'_F + \xi'_C}{2}(z_F - z_C) \qquad \text{(A6)}$$

In Eqs. (A1) and (A3) the jumped values of the variables at F have been used since the line of discontinuity C_2^+ has already been crossed. Equations (A1) to (A6) can now be solved for the values of the variables at point F.

To proceed to point B, a C_2^- line is drawn through B, its intersection with the line F2 being labeled point 6. Similarly, a C_2^+ line is drawn through point B intersecting F2 or AD at point 5. The values of the variables at points 5 and 6 are obtained by linear interpolation of known values of the variables. The compatibility and continuity equations, written in finite difference form along these lines passing through point B, then provide a set of equations from which the values of the variables at B can be determined. These equations are listed below.

$$(c_1^2 - 1)\{\beta\,(\dot\theta_B - \dot\theta_A) - c_1(\theta_B' - \theta_A')) + (\frac{\dot\theta_B+\dot\theta_A}{2} + \tilde e\,\frac{\dot\xi_B+\dot\xi_A}{2})(\tau_B - \tau_A)\}$$

$$+ \tilde e\beta\{\, c_1(\xi_B' - \xi_A') - (\dot\xi_B - \dot\xi_A)\} = 0 \qquad \text{(A7)}$$

$$(c_1^2 - 1)\{\,\beta\,(\dot\theta_B - \dot\theta_{Fj} + c_1(\theta_B' - \theta_{Fj}')) + (\frac{\dot\theta_B+\dot\theta_{Fj}}{2} + \tilde e\,\frac{\dot\xi_B+\dot\xi_{Fj}}{2})(\tau_B-\tau_F)\}$$

$$+ \tilde e\beta\{\, - c_1(\xi_B' - \xi_{Fj}') - (\dot\xi_B - \dot\xi_{Fj})\,\} = 0 \qquad \text{(A8)}$$

$$(c_2^2 - 1)\{\beta\,(\dot\theta_B - \dot\theta_5 - c_2(\theta_B' - \theta_5')) + (\frac{\dot\theta_B+\dot\theta_5}{2} + \tilde e\,\frac{\dot\xi_B+\dot\xi_5}{2})(\tau_B - \tau_5)\}$$

$$+ \tilde e\beta\{\, + c_2(\xi_B' - \xi_5') - (\dot\xi_B - \dot\xi_5)\,\} = 0 \qquad \text{(A9)}$$

$$(c_2^2 - 1)\{\beta\,(\dot\theta_B - \dot\theta_6 + c_2(\theta_B' - \theta_6')) + (\frac{\dot\theta_B+\dot\theta_6}{2} + \tilde e\,\frac{\dot\xi_B+\dot\xi_6}{2})(\tau_B - \tau_6)\}$$

$$+ \tilde e\beta\,\{- c_2(\xi_B' - \xi_6') - (\dot\xi_B - \dot\xi_6)\,\} = 0 \qquad \text{(A10)}$$

$$\theta_B - \theta_6 = \frac{\dot\theta_B+\dot\theta_6}{2}\,(\tau_B - \tau_6) + \frac{\theta_B'+\theta_6'}{2}(z_B - z_6) \qquad \text{(A11)}$$

$$\xi_B - \xi_F = \frac{\dot\xi_B+\dot\xi_{Fj}}{2}(\tau_B - \tau_F) + \frac{\xi_B'+\xi_{Fj}'}{2}(z_B - z_F) \qquad \text{(A12)}$$

The procedure required for a Type III mesh is similar to that outlined above.

WAVE PROPAGATION IN TWO JOINED ELASTIC QUARTER-SPACES

L. M. Brock
Northwestern University

J. D. Achenbach
Northwestern University

ABSTRACT

A half-plane consisting of two joined elastic quarter-planes is subjected to in-plane disturbances that are applied normal to the free surface. The wave motion in the composite half-plane is analyzed by means of Laplace and Fourier transform techniques. Inversion of the transforms is achieved by Cagniard's method. The stresses at the interface of the two quarter-planes are worked out in detail, and numerical results are presented. The appearance of singularities in the stresses due to typical interface effects is discussed.

LIST OF NOTATIONS

a	Inverse of dilatational wave velocity
b	Inverse of shear wave velocity
$f(t)$	Time-dependence of external particle velocity
i	$(-1)^{\frac{1}{2}}$
m	Inverse of Lamé elastic constant μ
r, θ, z	Polar coordinates of system
s	Laplace transform variable
t	Time
U_o	Magnitude of external particle velocity

u, v	Displacements in x and y directions, respectively
x, y, z	Rectangular cartesian coordinates in system
$\delta(t)$	Dirac delta function in time
κ	Inverse of Stoneley wave velocity
λ, μ	Lamé elastic constants
ξ	Fourier-sine and Fourier-cosine transform variable
ρ	Mass density
σ_{ij}	Stresses; subscripts refer to rectangular cartesian coordinates
Σ_{ij}	Interface stresses; subscripts refer to rectangular cartesian coordinates
PV()	Cauchy principal value
Im()	Imaginary part of complex quantity
Re()	Real part of complex quantity
$(\dot{\ })$	$\partial/\partial t$
$()_p$	Quantity associated with primary waves
$()_d$	Quantity associated with diffracted waves
$()_1$	Denotes field variable or material constant in the region y < 0
$()^c$	Fourier-cosine transform
$()^s$	Fourier-sine transform
$L()$, $(\bar{\ })$	Laplace transform
$\lvert\ \rvert$	Absolute value

INTRODUCTION

Among the problems encountered in actual use of laminated materials is the problem of delamination, i.e., separation at the interfaces of the constituents. This problem is important because delamination may drastically reduce the load-bearing capacity of the laminated body. Delamination is caused by excessive tensile and/or shear stresses at the interfaces.

If a laminated medium is suddenly subjected to high-rate surface disturbances on a boundary normal to the layering, see Fig. 1, the discontinuities in the material properties give rise to a complicated pattern of transient waves immediately after application of the loads. For small enough times, the dynamic interaction is limited to neighboring layers, and one can obtain the interface stresses by

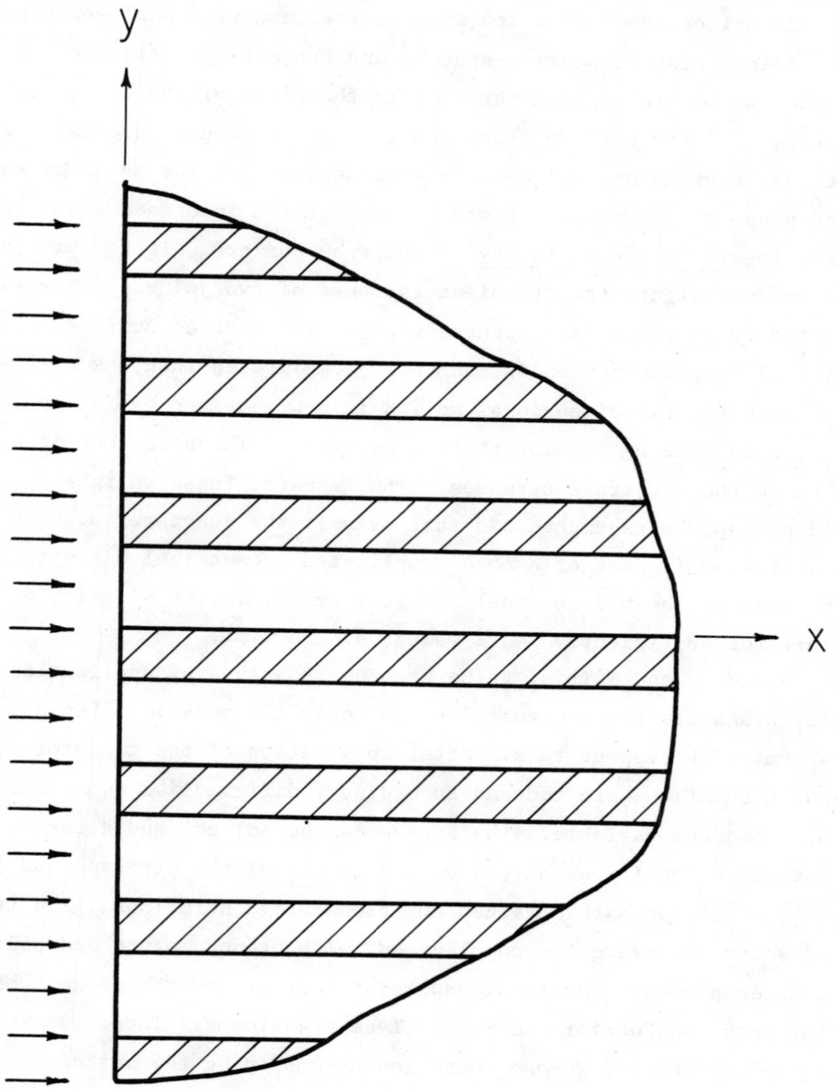

Fig. 1. Laminated Medium Subjected to Normal Disturbances.

considering two joined quarter-spaces.

In an earlier paper [1], the dynamic response of a half-space composed of two joined elastic quarter-spaces, and subjected to time-varying shear tractions which are applied parallel to the plane of juncture, was investigated. For surface tractions varying in time as Heaviside step functions, closed-form expressions were derived for the shear stress in the plane of juncture. It was found that the interface shear stress shows a logarithmic singularity at the free surface. In the present paper we investigate the transient response of two joined quarter-spaces subjected to in-plane disturbances applied at the free surface. This problem of in-plane motion is much more complicated than the problem of [1] because the two-dimensional motion is now governed by four potentials which are coupled by the interface conditions. The attention is again focused on the interface stresses. The geometry is shown in Fig. 2. It should perhaps be re-emphasized that even if the juncture shown in Fig. 2 is just a small part of a more complicated geometrical situation, the results of the present analysis still apply in the vicinity of the juncture for sufficiently small values of the time.

The boundary and initial value problem is solved by application of Fourier transform techniques. Thus we apply the one-sided Laplace transforms with respect to x. After application of the transforms, the governing equations are reduced to ordinary differential equations with y as independent variable. The system can be solved, and after using the interface conditions at y = 0 (continuity of the stresses and the displacements), we have obtained the transformed solutions. The transformed solutions are quite complicated, with branch points and poles in the complex planes. The final and major task is now the process of inverting both the Fourier and the Laplace transforms. These two inversions can be achieved in one operation by employing the method of Cagniard [2], whereby the inverse Laplace transform can be obtained by inspection along an appropriate contour in the complex plane of the Fourier transform parameter.

The problem formulated in this paper was also considered by Peck and Gurtmann [3], who presented a head-of-the-pulse approximation which is valid at some distance from the loaded surface. Wave propagation in

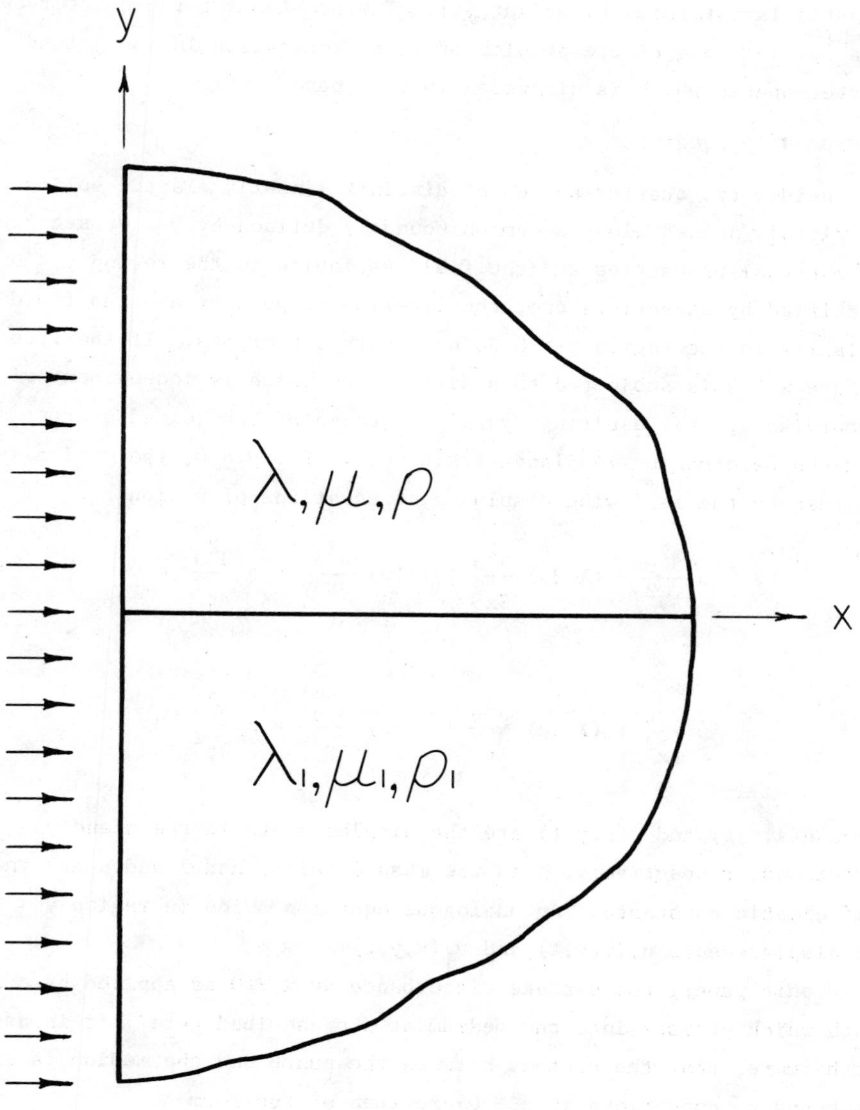

Fig. 2. Two Joined Elastic Quarter-Spaces.

a quarter-space subjected to mixed boundary conditions on one face was recently investigated by Wright [4]. The problem for the quarter-space is a special case of the problem of wave propagation in tow joined quarter-spaces which is discussed in this paper.

Governing Equations

We consider two quarter-spaces of distinct linearly elastic solids which are rigidly joined along a common boundary defined by $y \equiv 0$, see Fig. 2. The material properties and the field variables in the region $y \leq 0$ are identified by subscripts one; the material properties and the field variables in the region $y \geq 0$ do not carry subscripts. If the free surface $x \equiv 0$ is subjected to a disturbance which is independent of the z coordinate, the resulting dynamic response of the joined quarter-spaces involves deformation in plane strain only. For $y \geq 0$, the motion is then governed by the following displacement equations of motion

$$\mu \frac{\partial^2 u}{\partial y^2} + (\lambda+2\mu) \frac{\partial^2 u}{\partial x^2} + (\lambda+\mu) \frac{\partial^2 v}{\partial x \partial y} = \rho \frac{\partial^2 u}{\partial t^2} \qquad (1)$$

$$\mu \frac{\partial^2 v}{\partial x^2} + (\lambda+2\mu) \frac{\partial^2 v}{\partial y^2} + (\lambda+\mu) \frac{\partial^2 u}{\partial x \partial y} = \rho \frac{\partial^2 v}{\partial t^2} \qquad (2)$$

where $u(x,y,t)$ and $v(x,y,t)$ are the displacements in the x and y directions, respectively, ρ is the mass density, and λ and μ are the Lamé elastic constants. An analogous equation holds in region $y \leq 0$ for the displacements $u_1(x,y,t)$ and $v_1(x,y,t)$.

In this paper, the surface disturbance at $x \equiv 0$ is applied by a rigid punch which presses into the medium at a prescribed rate. It is assumed, furthermore, that the contact between the punch and the medium is smooth. The boundary conditions at $x \equiv 0$ are then of the form

$$\dot{u}(0,y,t) = \dot{u}_1(0,y,t) = f(t) \qquad (3)$$

$$\sigma_{xy}(0,y,t) = \sigma_{xy1}(0,y,t) = 0 \qquad (4)$$

Since the displacements and the stresses are continuous at $y \equiv 0$, the interface conditions are

$$u(x,0,t) = u_1(x,0,t) \tag{5}$$

$$v(x,0,t) = v_1(x,0,t) \tag{6}$$

$$\sigma_{yx}(x,0,t) = \sigma_{yx1}(x,0,t) \tag{7}$$

$$\sigma_{yy}(x,0,t) = \sigma_{yy1}(x,0,t) \tag{8}$$

Assuming that the quarter-spaces are at rest prior to time $t = 0$, the initial conditions may be written as

$$u(x,y,0) = u_1(x,y,0) = v(x,y,0) = v_1(x,y,0) \equiv 0 \tag{9}$$

$$\dot{u}(x,y,0) = \dot{u}_1(x,y,0) = \dot{v}(x,y,0) = \dot{v}_1(x,y,0) \equiv 0 \tag{10}$$

The system of governing equations is completed by the stress-strain relations. For a homogeneous isotropic linearly elastic medium, the relevant stress-strain relations in the region $y \geq 0$ are

$$\sigma_{xx} = (\lambda+2\mu) \frac{\partial u}{\partial x} + \lambda \frac{\partial v}{\partial y} \tag{11}$$

$$\sigma_{xy} = \mu \left(\frac{\partial u}{\partial y} + \frac{\partial v}{\partial x}\right) \tag{12}$$

$$\sigma_{yy} = (\lambda+2\mu) \frac{\partial v}{\partial y} + \lambda \frac{\partial u}{\partial x} \tag{13}$$

Analogous stress-strain relations hold in the region $y \leq 0$.

Method of Solution

The problem is solved by application of Fourier transform techniques. Thus, we employ a Laplace transform with respect to time, and Fourier-sine and cosine transforms with respect to the x coordinate.

The Laplace transform with respect to time is defined in the following manner

$$L[f(t)] = \overline{f}(s) = \int_0^\infty f(t)e^{-st}dt \tag{14}$$

It is expedient to employ the Fourier-sine transform with respect to x for the displacement components in the x direction. Thus

$$u^s(\xi,y,t) = \left(\frac{2}{\pi}\right)^{\frac{1}{2}} \int_0^\infty u(x,y,t) \sin \xi x \, dx \tag{15}$$

with inverse transform

$$u(x,y,t) = \left(\frac{2}{\pi}\right)^{\frac{1}{2}} \int_0^\infty u^s(\xi,y,t) \sin \xi x \, d\xi \tag{16}$$

For the displacement components in the y direction the Fourier-cosine transform should be used

$$v^c(\xi,y,t) = \left(\frac{2}{\pi}\right)^{\frac{1}{2}} \int_0^\infty v(x,y,t) \cos \xi x \, dx \tag{17}$$

with inverse transform

$$v(x,y,t) = \left(\frac{2}{\pi}\right)^{\frac{1}{2}} \int_0^\infty v^c(\xi,y,t) \cos \xi x \, d\xi \tag{18}$$

To determine the Laplace-Fourier transforms of the displacement components we first apply the Laplace transform to the governing equations, Eqs. (1)-(13), and to the corresponding equations for $y \leq 0$, whereby the initial conditions (9) and (10) are used to evaluate the Laplace transforms of the first- and second-order derivatives with respect to time. The Fourier-sine transform is subsequently applied to Eqs. (1), (5), (7) and (12), and to the corresponding equations in region two. The Fourier-cosine transform is applied to Eqs. (2), (6), (8), (11) and (13). To express the results in a convenient form it proves useful to introduce the following new symbols

$$m = 1/\mu \qquad m_1 = 1/\mu_1 \tag{19a,b}$$

$$a^2 = \rho/(\lambda+2\mu) \qquad a_1^2 = \mu_1/(\lambda_1+2\mu_1) \tag{20a,b}$$

$$b^2 = \rho/\mu \qquad b_1^2 = \rho_1/\mu_1 \tag{21a,b}$$

$$\alpha^2 = \xi^2 + a^2 s^2 \qquad \alpha_1^2 = \xi^2 + a_1^2 s^2 \tag{22a,b}$$

$$\beta^2 = \xi^2 + b^2 s^2 \qquad \beta_1^2 = \xi^2 + b_1^2 s^2 \tag{23a,b}$$

It should be noted that $1/a$, $1/a_1$ and $1/b$, $1/b_1$ are dilatational and shear wave velocities, respectively.

After application of the transforms, and after some subsequent manipulations, Eqs. (1) and (2) can be written as

$$a^2 \frac{d^2\bar{u}^s}{dy^2} - b^2\alpha^2\bar{u}^s - (b^2 - a^2)\xi \frac{d\bar{v}^c}{dy} = -\left(\frac{2}{\pi}\right)^{\frac{1}{2}} \frac{b^2\xi\bar{f}(s)}{s} \tag{24}$$

$$(b^2 - a^2)\xi \frac{d\bar{u}^s}{dy} + b^2 \frac{d^2\bar{v}^c}{dy^2} - a^2\beta^2\bar{v}^c = 0 \tag{25}$$

where the Laplace transforms of boundary conditions (3) and (4) have been used. An analogous pair of equations is found for $y \leq 0$, and we thus have to find the solutions to two pairs of coupled, second-order ordinary differential equations in y, which satisfy four interface conditions at $y = 0$. The general solutions of Eqs. (24) and (25) which show the appropriate behavior as $|y|$ increases beyond bounds are easily obtained as

$$\bar{u}^s = Be^{-\alpha y} + De^{-\beta y} + \left(\frac{2}{\pi}\right)^{\frac{1}{2}} \frac{\xi\bar{f}(s)}{s\alpha^2} \tag{26}$$

$$\bar{v}^{c} = \frac{\alpha}{\xi} Be^{-\alpha y} + \frac{\xi}{\beta} De^{-\beta y} \tag{27}$$

Similarly, we find for $y \leq 0$

$$\bar{u}_1^{s} = A_1 e^{\alpha_1 y} + C_1 e^{\beta_1 y} + \left(\frac{2}{\pi}\right)^{\frac{1}{2}} \frac{\xi \bar{f}(s)}{s\alpha_1^2} \tag{28}$$

$$\bar{v}_1^{c} = -\frac{\alpha_1}{\xi} A_1 e^{\alpha_1 y} - \frac{\xi}{\beta_1} C_1 e^{\beta_1 y} \tag{29}$$

In Eqs. (26)-(29), the branches of the radical have been chosen such that

$$\mathrm{Re}(\alpha) > 0, \quad \mathrm{Re}(\beta) > 0, \quad \mathrm{Re}(\alpha_1) > 0, \quad \mathrm{Re}(\beta_1) > 0 \tag{30}$$

where

$$\mathrm{Re}(\xi) > 0$$

The four constants A_1, C_1, B and D are obtained by employing the interface conditions at $y = 0$. The set of four equations, which is easily obtained, may be written as

$$\begin{bmatrix} 1 & \beta_1 & -1 & \beta \\ \alpha_1 & \xi^2 & \alpha & -\xi^2 \\ \frac{\mu_1}{2}(\xi^2+\beta_1^2) & \mu_1\xi^2\beta_1 & -\frac{\mu}{2}(\xi^2+\beta^2) & \mu\xi^2\beta \\ \mu_1\alpha_1 & \frac{\mu_1}{2}(\xi^2+\beta_1^2) & \mu\alpha & -\frac{\mu}{2}(\xi^2+\beta^2) \end{bmatrix} \begin{bmatrix} -\frac{A_1}{\xi} \\ -\frac{C_1}{\xi\beta_1} \\ -\frac{B}{\xi} \\ \frac{D}{\xi\beta} \end{bmatrix} = \begin{bmatrix} F_1 \\ 0 \\ F_2 \\ 0 \end{bmatrix} \tag{32}$$

where

$$F_1 = \left(\frac{2}{\pi}\right)^{\frac{1}{2}} \frac{\bar{f}(s)}{s} \left(\frac{1}{\alpha_1^2} - \frac{1}{\alpha^2}\right) \tag{33}$$

$$F_2 = \left(\frac{2}{\pi}\right)^{\frac{1}{2}} \frac{s\overline{f}(s)}{2} [(b_1^2-2a_1^2) \frac{\mu_1}{\alpha_1^2} - (b^2-2a^2) \frac{\mu}{\alpha^2}] \tag{34}$$

The coefficients are solved for by using Cramer's rule. They can be written as follows:

$$A_1 = -\frac{\xi\Delta_A}{\Delta}, \quad B = -\frac{\xi\Delta_B}{\Delta}, \quad C_1 = \frac{\xi\beta_1\Delta_C}{\Delta}, \quad D = \frac{\xi\beta\Delta_D}{\Delta}, \tag{35a,b,c,d}$$

where

$$\Delta(\xi,s) = [\xi^2(\xi^2 + c_1b_1^2s^2 + c_2b^2s^2)^2 + \xi^2\alpha_1\beta_1\alpha\beta - \alpha\beta(\xi^2 + c_1b_1^2s^2)^2$$
$$- \alpha_1\beta_1(\xi^2 + c_2b^2s^2)^2 + c_1b_1^2s^2c_2b^2s^2(\alpha_1\beta + \alpha\beta_1)] \tag{36}$$

$$\Delta_B(\xi,s) = \left(\frac{2}{\pi}\right)^{\frac{1}{2}} \frac{\overline{f}(s)}{s} \{[\alpha_1\beta_1(\xi^2 + c_2b^2s^2) - \xi^2(\xi^2 + c_1b_1^2s^2 + c_2b^2s^2)$$
$$- \alpha_1\beta c_1b_1^2s^2] + \frac{1}{\alpha^2} [\xi^2(\xi^2 + c_1b_1^2s^2 + c_2b^2s^2)^2$$
$$+ c_2b^2s^2c_1b_1^2s^2\alpha_1\beta - \alpha_1\beta_1(\xi^2 + c_2b^2s^2)^2]$$

$$+ \frac{c_1b_1^2s^2}{\alpha_1} [\beta(\xi^2 + c_1b_1^2s^2) - \beta_1(\xi^2 + c_2b^2s^2)]\} \tag{37}$$

$$\Delta_D(\xi,s) = \left(\frac{2}{\pi}\right)^{\frac{1}{2}} \frac{\overline{f}(s)}{s} \{[\alpha\alpha_1\beta_1 - \alpha_1c_1b_1^2s^2 - \alpha(\xi^2 + c_1b_1^2s^2)]$$
$$+ \frac{1}{\alpha} [(\xi^2 + c_1b_1^2s^2)(\xi^2 + c_1b_1^2s^2 + c_2b^2s^2) - \alpha_1\beta_1(\xi^2 + c_2b^2s^2$$
$$+ \frac{c_1b_1^2s^2}{\alpha_1} [(\xi^2 + c_1b_1^2s^2 + c_2b^2s^2) - \alpha\beta_1]\} \tag{38}$$

and

$$c_1 = \frac{\mu_1}{2(\mu_1 - \mu)}, \qquad c_2 = \frac{1}{2} - c_1 = \frac{\mu}{2(\mu - \mu_1)} \tag{39a,b}$$

The expressions for Δ_A and Δ_C are obtained from Eqs. (37) and (38), respectively, by replacing c_1 by c_2, and vice versa, and removing the subscripts one from the quantities with subscripts, and appending subscripts one to the quantities in Eqs. (37) and (38) that do not have subscripts.

The remaining, and most difficult task consists of inverting the Laplace-Fourier transforms.

The Transforms of the Stresses

For practical purposes one is particularly interested in the dynamic stress-distributions in the two joined elastic quarter-spaces. Since no restrictions have yet been placed on material properties, no generality is lost by dealing only with the stresses in the quarter-space defined by $y \geq 0$. Substituting Eqs. (28) and (29) into the expressions for the stress transforms, we obtain

$$\bar{\sigma}^c_{xx} = \left(\bar{\sigma}^c_{xx}\right)_p + \left(\bar{\sigma}^c_{xx}\right)_d \tag{40}$$

$$\bar{\sigma}^c_{yy} = \left(\bar{\sigma}^c_{yy}\right)_p + \left(\bar{\sigma}^c_{xx}\right)_d \tag{41}$$

$$\bar{\sigma}^s_{xy} = \left(\bar{\sigma}^s_{xy}\right)_p + \left(\bar{\sigma}^s_{xy}\right)_d \tag{42}$$

where

$$m\left(\bar{\sigma}^c_{xx}\right)_d = \frac{1}{\xi}(2\alpha^2 - b^2 s^2)Be^{-\alpha y} + 2\xi De^{-\beta y} \tag{43}$$

$$m\left(\bar{\sigma}^c_{yy}\right)_d = -\frac{1}{\xi}(\xi^2 + \beta^2)Be^{-\alpha y} - 2\xi De^{-\beta y} \tag{44}$$

$$m\left(\bar{\sigma}^s_{xy}\right)_d = -2\alpha Be^{-\alpha y} - \frac{1}{\beta}(\xi^2 + \beta^2)De^{-\beta y} \tag{45}$$

$$m\left(\bar{\sigma}^c_{xx}\right)_p = -\frac{b^2 s}{\alpha^2}\left(\frac{2}{\pi}\right)^{\frac{1}{2}}\bar{f}(s) \tag{46}$$

$$m\left(\bar{\sigma}^c_{yy}\right)_p = -(b^2 - 2a^2)\frac{s}{\alpha^2}\left(\frac{2}{\pi}\right)^{\frac{1}{2}}\bar{f}(s) \tag{47}$$

$$m\left(\bar{\sigma}^s_{xy}\right)_p = 0 \tag{48}$$

In Eqs. (43)-(48), m is defined by Eq. (19a), and B and D are given by Eqs. (35b) and (35d), respectively.

The inversions of $\left(\bar{\sigma}^c_{xx}\right)_p$ and $\left(\bar{\sigma}^c_{yy}\right)_p$ are straightforward and can be obtained by using tables of integral transforms [5]. The results are

$$m(\sigma_{xx})_p = -\frac{b^2}{a^2} f(t-ax) \tag{49}$$

$$m(\sigma_{yy})_p = -\left(\frac{b^2}{a^2} - 2\right) f(t-ax) \tag{50}$$

It should be noted that Eqs. (49) and (50) are, in fact, the stresses that would occur in elastic half-spaces if the surfaces were subjected to surface disturbances defined by Eqs. (3) and (4). We call these solutions the primary waves. The second terms in Eqs. (40) and (41) represent the modifications of the pattern of primary waves due to the discontinuity of the material properties at y = 0. The expressions for $(\bar{\sigma}^c_{xx})_d$, etc., represent the Laplace-Fourier transforms of the diffracted waves, and their inverse transforms are much more difficult to obtain.

By employing Eqs. (18) and (43), the Laplace transform of the stress component $(\sigma_{xx})_d$ may formally be written as

$$m\left(\bar{\sigma}_{xx}\right)_d = \left(\frac{2}{\pi}\right)^{\frac{1}{2}} \int_0^\infty [(2\alpha^2 - b^2s^2)Be^{-\alpha y} + 2\xi^2 De^{-\beta y}] \frac{\cos \xi x}{\xi} d\xi \tag{51}$$

Similar expressions can be written for $\left(\bar{\sigma}_{yy}\right)_d$ and $\left(\bar{\sigma}_{xy}\right)_d$.

It is now convenient to define a new variable η such that

$$\xi = s\eta \tag{52}$$

Because s is real and positive, it can be considered as acting simply as a scaling factor relating η and ξ. It now becomes possible to rewrite the Laplace transforms of the stresses in the following manner

$$m\left(\bar{\sigma}_{xx}\right)_d = \frac{2}{\pi}\,\bar{f}(s)\,(I_1 - I_4) \tag{53}$$

$$m\left(\bar{\sigma}_{yy}\right)_d = \frac{2}{\pi}\,\bar{f}(s)\,(I_2 + I_4) \tag{54}$$

$$m\left(\bar{\sigma}_{xy}\right)_d = \frac{2}{\pi}\,\bar{f}(s)\,(I_3 + I_5) \tag{55}$$

where

$$\bar{I}_1(x,y,s) = \mathrm{Re}\Big[\int_0^\infty (b^2 - 2p^2)M_B e^{-s(py-i\eta x)}\,d\eta\Big] \tag{56}$$

$$\bar{I}_2(x,y,s) = \mathrm{Re}\Big[\int_0^\infty (\eta^2 + q^2)M_B e^{-s(py-i\eta x)}\,d\eta\Big] \tag{57}$$

$$\bar{I}_3(x,y,s) = \mathrm{Im}\Big[\int_0^\infty 2\eta p M_B e^{-s(py-i\eta x)}\,d\eta\Big] \tag{58}$$

$$\bar{I}_4(x,y,s) = \mathrm{Re}\Big[\int_0^\infty 2\eta^2 q M_D e^{-s(qy-i\eta x)}\,d\eta\Big] \tag{59}$$

$$\bar{I}_5(x,y,s) = \mathrm{Im}\Big[\int_0^\infty \eta(\eta^2 + q^2)M_D e^{-s(qy-i\eta x)}\,d\eta\Big] \tag{60}$$

In Eqs. (56)-(60),

$$M_B = m_B/M\,, \qquad M_D = m_D/M \tag{61a,b}$$

$$m_B(\eta) = (p_1q_1T_2 - \eta^2T_{12} - c_1b_1^2p_1q) + c_1b_1^2(qT_1 - q_1T_2)/p_1$$
$$+ (\eta^2T_{12}^2 + c_1b_1^2c_2b^2p_1q - p_1q_1T_2^2)\,/\,p^2 \tag{62}$$

$$m_D(\eta) = (pT_1 + c_1b_1^2p_1 - pp_1q_1) + c_1b_1^2(pq_1 - T_{12})/p_1$$
$$+ (p_1q_1T_2 - T_1T_{12})/p \tag{63}$$

$$M(\eta) = \eta^2T_{12}^2 + \eta^2p_1q_1pq - pqT_1^2 - p_1q_1T_2^2 + c_1b_1^2c_2b^2(pq_1 + p_1q) \tag{64}$$

Also

$$p_1 = (\eta^2 + a_1^2)^{\frac{1}{2}} , \qquad q_1 = (\eta^2 + b_1^2)^{\frac{1}{2}} \qquad (65a,b)$$

$$p = (\eta^2 + a^2)^{\frac{1}{2}} , \qquad q = (\eta^2 + b^2)^{\frac{1}{2}} \qquad (66a,b)$$

$$T_1 = \eta^2 + c_1 b_1^2 , \qquad T_2 = \eta^2 + c_2 b^2 \qquad (67a,b)$$

$$T_{12} = \eta^2 + c_1 b_1^2 + c_2 b^2 \qquad (68)$$

With the transforms of the stress components in the forms (53)-(55), Cagniard's method is used to find their inverses [2], [6]. This method invokes the Cauchy integral theorem to deform the paths of integration of the above integrals from along the real axis onto paths in the complex η-plane. These paths, known as Cagniard contours, are parameterized such that the exponential terms in the integrals assume the form $e^{-s\tau}$, where τ is real and positive. In this manner, the integrals become explicit Laplace transforms over the real variable τ, and the inverses can be written by inspection.

Before performing these operations, the analyticity of the integrands in the complex η-plane should be discussed. Due to the presence of the radicals p, q, p_1 and q_1, the integrands of I_1, I_2, I_3, I_4 and I_5 are multiple-valued. Thus, the integrands are analytic only in the cut η-plane. It is convenient to choose a Riemann sheet with branch cuts of the type shown in Fig. 3. The sheet illustrated is for the case when the four inverse wave speeds obey the inequalities

$$b_1 > b > a > a_1 \qquad (69)$$

but with appropriate relabeling it is equally valid for any of the six actually possible cases.

With the single-valuedness of the integrands in the cut η-plane established, the possibility of singularities must be investigated. It is observed that poles in the cut η-plane can occur only at the zeros of $M(\eta)$, where $M(\eta)$ is defined by Eq. (64). Although closed-form expressions for these zeros cannot be found, explicit information

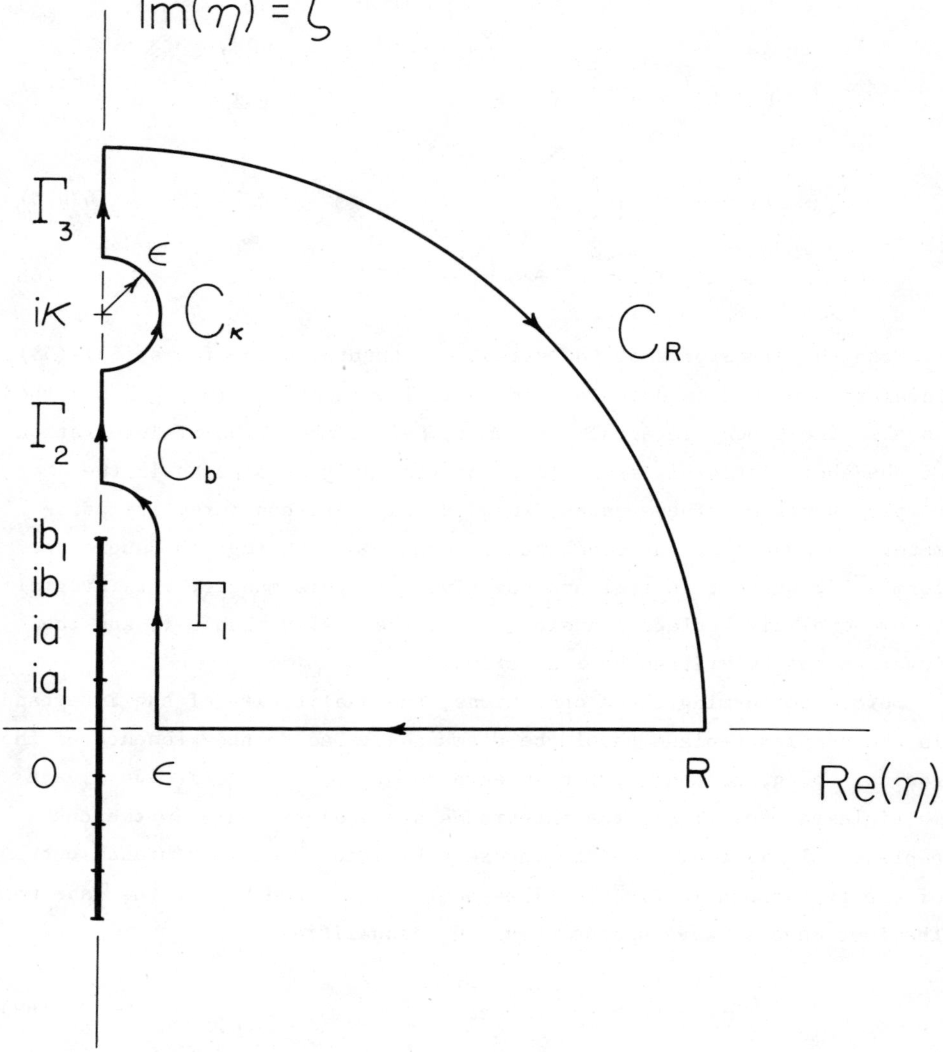

Fig. 3. Branch Cuts and Contours in η-Plane for $b_1 > b > a > a_1$.

on the number of roots and on their location can be obtained by employing the principle of the argument. The roots of $M(\eta) = 0$ were investigated by Cagniard [7], who showed that on the Riemann sheet that is considered here, roots exist if:

For $b > b_1$:

$$- b^2(c_1b_1^2 + c_2b^2 - b^2)^2 + (b^2 - a_1^2)^{\frac{1}{2}} (b^2 - b_1^2)^{\frac{1}{2}} (c_2b^2 - b^2)^2$$
$$- c_1c_2b_1^2b^2(b^2 - a^2)^{\frac{1}{2}} (b^2 - b_1^2)^{\frac{1}{2}} < 0 \qquad (70)$$

For $b_1 > b$:

$$- b_1^2(c_2b^2 + c_1b_1^2 - b_1^2)^2 + (b_1^2 - a^2)^{\frac{1}{2}}(b_1^2 - b^2)^{\frac{1}{2}}(c_1b_1^2 - b_1^2)^2$$
$$- c_2c_1b^2b_1^2(b_1^2 - a_1^2)^{\frac{1}{2}}(b_1^2 - b^2)^{\frac{1}{2}} < 0 \qquad (71)$$

If roots exist, then there are always two roots, which are located on the imaginary axis, i.e.,

$$\eta_o = \pm i\kappa \qquad (72)$$

where, moreover,

$$\max(b,b_1) < \kappa < \infty \qquad (73)$$

A complete treatment of the problem, with detailed evaluation of the stresses in the (x,y)-plane, is beyond the scope of this paper. Here, we focus on the interface stresses at $y = 0$, which will be worked out in detail in the next section. It is, however, of interest to show the pattern of the wavefronts in the (x,y)-plane at a time t. Referring to Fig. 4, where the pattern of wavefronts is shown for the case defined by Eq. (69), we note a system of plane, cylindrical and wedge-like waves. The cylindrical waves radiate outward from the origin $(x,y = 0)$ and are of two types. There are the dilatational waves which propagate with

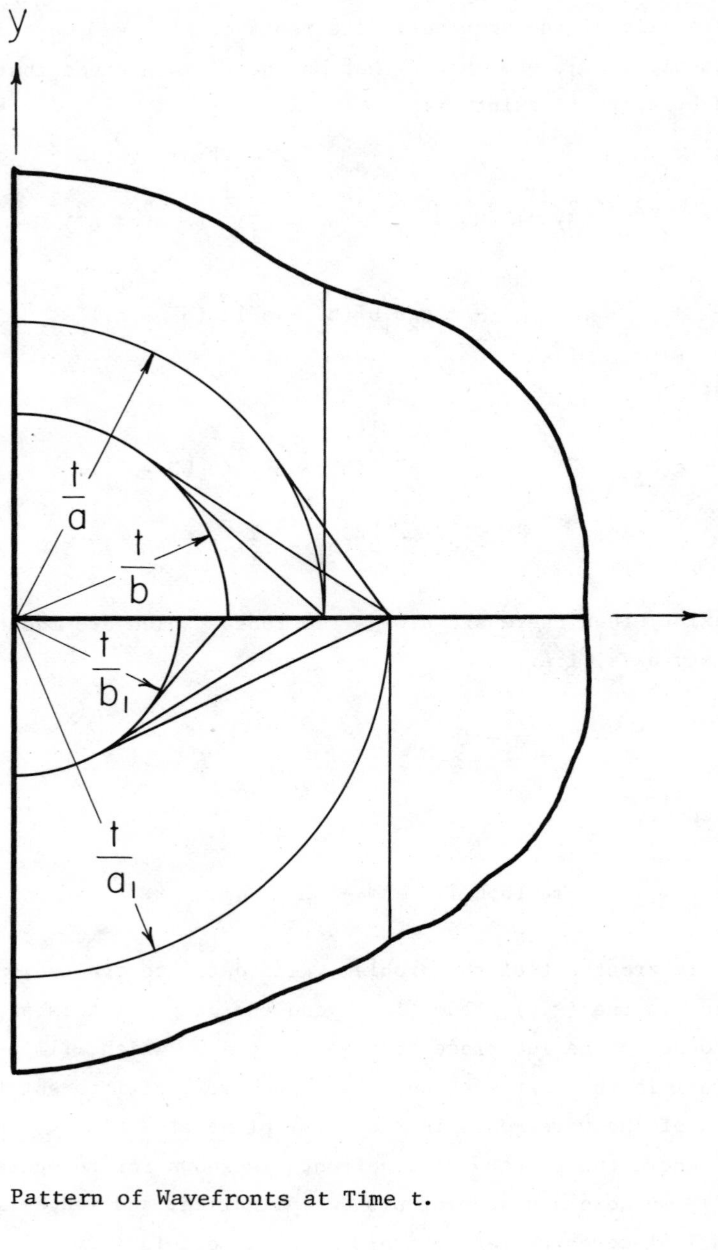

Fig. 4. Pattern of Wavefronts at Time t.

velocity 1/a, and the shear waves which travel with velocity 1/b. For values of θ large enough, these systems of cylindrical waves, together with the plane waves, form the total contribution of the stress components. However, for values of θ whose cosines are greater than certain ratios involving the various inverse wave velocities, a pattern of wedge-like waves must be superimposed upon the cylindrical waves. These waves, known as head waves, arise because of the differences in the wave velocities in the two quarter-spaces. As the faster-traveling stress waves propagate along the interface (y = 0), they create a continuous line of point disturbances which, obeying Huygen's principle, emit cylindrical waves into the slower medium. The envelopes of these waves form the wavefronts of the head waves which, as can be seen from Fig. 4, are tangent to the wavefronts of the slower-traveling cylindrical waves.

Interface Stresses

The Laplace transforms of the interface stresses are obtained by substituting $y \equiv 0$ into the expressions (40)-(42). It is noted that the primary waves are independent of y, and we thus focus on the stresses associated with the diffracted waves. Since the stress response for more complicated variation of the particle velocity at the surface x = 0 can be obtained by Duhamel superposition, the attention is restricted to the special case when at x = 0, Eq. (3) is of the form

$$\dot{u}(0,y,t) = \dot{u}_1(0,y,t) = U_o\delta(t) \tag{74}$$

The Laplace transforms of the relevant interface stresses may then be written as

$$\frac{\pi m}{2U_o}\overline{\Sigma}_{yy}(x,s) = \mathrm{Re}\ \{ \int_0^\infty [(\eta^2 + q^2)M_B + 2\eta^2 q M_D]e^{is\eta x}d\eta\} \tag{75}$$

$$\frac{\pi m}{2U_o}\overline{\Sigma}_{xy}(x,s) = \mathrm{Im}\ \{ \int_0^\infty [2p\eta M_B + \eta(\eta^2 + q^2)M_D]e^{is\eta x}d\eta \tag{76}$$

where, for simplicity of notation, we have introduced $\overline{\sum}_{yy}(x,s) = [\bar{\sigma}_{yy}(x,s)]_d$, and $\overline{\sum}_{xy}(x,s) = [\bar{\sigma}_{xy}(x,s)]_d$, where M_B and M_D are defined by Eqs. (61a) and 61b), respectively.

The process of obtaining the inverse Laplace transforms of Eqs. (75) and (76) is now discussed in some detail for $\overline{\sum}_{yy}(x,s)$. We start out by defining

$$S = \int_{\varepsilon}^{R} [(\eta^2 + q^2)M_B + 2\eta^2 qM_D]e^{is\eta x}d\eta \tag{77}$$

where

$$0 < \varepsilon < R < \infty \tag{78}$$

and we note that

$$\operatorname{Re}(\lim_{\substack{\varepsilon \to 0 \\ R \to \infty}} S) = \frac{\pi m}{2U_o} \overline{\sum}_{yy}(x,s) \tag{79}$$

By employing the Cauchy theorem, the path of integration of S is now deformed into a Cagniard contour. Although all the arguments hold equally well for other cases, we consider here the particular case defined by Eq. (69), and we also assume that the condition (71) is met. The integration along the real axis may then be replaced by an integration along the contours Γ_1, C_b, Γ_2, C_κ, Γ_3 and C_R, as shown in Fig. 3. It can now easily be shown that the integrations along C_R and C_b vanish as $R \to \infty$ and $\varepsilon \to 0$, respectively. The remaining integrals yield contributions in the limit $\varepsilon \to 0$, and the result may be written as

$$\begin{aligned} \frac{\pi m}{2U_o} \overline{\sum}_{yy} = &- \int_0^{b_1} \operatorname{Im} \{[(\eta^2 + q^2)M_B + 2\eta^2 qM_D]_{\eta=i\zeta}\}e^{-s\zeta x}d\zeta \\ &- PV \int_{b_1}^{\infty} \operatorname{Im}\{[(\eta^2 + q^2)M_B + 2\eta^2 qM_D]_{\eta=i\zeta}\}e^{-s\zeta x}d\zeta \\ &+ \pi R(\kappa)e^{-s\kappa x} \end{aligned} \tag{80}$$

where PV denotes the principal value of the integral over the real variable ζ, and where $R(\kappa)$ is computed by means of residue theory as

$$R(\kappa) = R_1(\kappa)/R_2(\kappa) \tag{81}$$

where

$$\begin{aligned} R_1(\kappa) = {} & (\kappa^2 + \psi^2)[\phi_1\phi^2(\phi_1\psi_1V_2 - c_1b_1^2\phi_1\psi - \kappa^2V_{12}) + \phi^2c_1b_1^2(\psi_1V_2 - \psi V_1) \\ & + \phi_1(\phi_1\psi_1V_2^2 - \kappa^2V_{12}^2 - c_1c_2b_1^2b_2^2\phi_1\psi)] + 2\kappa^2\psi[\phi_1\phi^2(\phi V_1 + c_1b_1^2\phi_1 \\ & + \phi\phi_1\psi_1) + c_1b_1^2\phi_1(\phi\psi_1 + V_{12}) + \phi_1\phi(\phi_1\psi_1V_2 + V_1V_{12})] \end{aligned} \tag{82}$$

$$\begin{aligned} R_2(\kappa) = {} & \phi_1\phi^2\kappa[2(\phi_1\psi_1V_2 + \phi\psi V_1 + \phi\psi\phi_1\psi_1 + V_{12}^2 - 2\kappa^2V_{12}) \\ & + (\kappa^2\phi\psi\phi_1 + \phi c_1c_2b_1^2b^2 - \phi_1V_2^2)/\psi_1 \\ & + (\kappa^2\phi\psi\psi_1 + \psi c_1c_2b_1^2b^2 - \psi_1V_2^2)/\phi_1 \\ & + (\kappa^2\phi_1\psi_1\phi + \phi_1c_1c_2b_1^2b^2 - \phi V_1^2)/\psi \\ & + (\kappa^2\phi_1\psi_1\psi + \psi_1c_1c_2b_1^2b^2 - \psi V_1^2)/\phi] \end{aligned} \tag{83}$$

In Eqs. (82) and (83),

$$\phi = (\kappa^2 - a^2)^{\frac{1}{2}}, \qquad \psi = (\kappa^2 - b^2)^{\frac{1}{2}} \tag{84a,b}$$

$$\phi_1 = (\kappa^2 - a_1^2)^{\frac{1}{2}}, \qquad \psi_1 = (\kappa^2 - b_1^2)^{\frac{1}{2}} \tag{85a,b}$$

$$V_1 = c_1b_1^2 - \kappa^2, \quad V_2 = c_2b^2 - \kappa^2, \quad V_{12} = c_1b_1^2 + c_2b^2 - \kappa^2 \tag{86a,b}$$

Equation (80) can be simplified further by the observation that the integrands are real in the intervals $0 \leq \zeta \leq a_1$ and $b_1 \leq \zeta < \infty$. The principal value term thus vanishes altogether, and the range of integration of the remaining integral is $a_1 \leq \zeta \leq b_1$. Upon introduction of the substitution

$$t = \zeta x \tag{87}$$

where $0 \leq t,\ x < \infty$, the integral is then finally cast in the form of an integral whose inverse Laplace transform can be obtained by inspection as

$$\frac{\pi m}{2U_o} \sum_{yy}(x,t) = -\frac{1}{x}\,\mathrm{Im}[P_1(\frac{it}{x}) + P_2(\frac{it}{x})]\ H(t-a_1x)H(b_1x-t)$$

$$+ \pi R(\kappa)\delta(t-\kappa x) \tag{88}$$

where

$$P_1(\eta) = (\eta^2 + q^2)M_B(\eta) \tag{89}$$

$$P_2(\eta) = 2\eta^2 q M_D(\eta) \tag{90}$$

In the same manner we can find

$$\frac{\pi m}{2U_o} \sum_{xy}(x,t) = \frac{1}{x}\,\mathrm{Re}[P_3(\frac{it}{x}) + P_4(\frac{it}{x})]H(t-a_1x) \tag{91}$$

where

$$P_3(\eta) = 2p\eta M_B(\eta) \tag{92}$$

$$P_4(\eta) = \eta(\eta^2 + q^2)M_D(\eta) \tag{93}$$

Several observations can be made regarding $\sum_{yy}$ and $\sum_{xy}$. The most noticeable feature is the appearance of a discontinuity which propagates along the interface with velocity $1/\kappa$. In $\sum_{yy}$, this discontinuity manifests itself as a propagating delta function of constant amplitude, $2\mu U_o R(\kappa)$. In $\sum_{xy}$, the effect is that of an infinite discontinuity at $x = t/\kappa$. These propagating discontinuities, which are known as Stoneley waves, are strictly interface phenomena. Mathematically, the Stoneley waves arise because of the presence of a pole in the cut η-plane at $\eta = i\kappa$. Thus, the conditions for the existence of Stoneley waves are given by Eq. (70) or Eq. (71). Since $\max(b,b_1) < \kappa < \infty$, it is evident that the velocity of Stoneley waves is always less than the lowest shear wave velocity.

Another feature of the expressions for Σ_{yy} and Σ_{xy} is that, with the exception of the Stoneley wave contributions, the normal stress vanishes identically in the range $0 \le x \le t/b_1$. On the other hand the shear stress Σ_{xy} vanishes only at $x = t/\kappa$ and $x = 0$. The point $x = 0$ is on the surface of the half-space where the shear stress is prescribed to vanish. It can be shown that Σ_{xy} approaches this zero value linearly as $x/t \to 0$.

Regarding the behavior of Σ_{yy} and Σ_{xy} at the various wavefronts, it can be shown that the stresses are continuous at the shear wavefronts, which are defined by $x = t/b$ and $x = t/b_1$. At the dilatational wavefronts $x = t/a$ and $x = t/a_1$, however, not only are the interface stresses discontinuous but their absolute values tend to infinity in the manner shown below:

$$\left|\Sigma_{yy},\Sigma_{xy}\right| \sim 1 \Big/ \left|\frac{t^2}{x^2} - a^2\right|^{\frac{1}{2}} \qquad \text{as } x \to t/a \tag{94}$$

and

$$\left|\Sigma_{yy},\Sigma_{xy}\right| \sim 1 \Big/ \left|\frac{t^2}{x^2} - a_1^2\right|^{\frac{1}{2}} \qquad \text{as } x \to t/a_1 \tag{95}$$

Numerical Results

The interface stresses Σ_{yy} and Σ_{xy} have been calculated for two materials which do indeed obey the prescribed inequalities given by Eq. (69). The material chosen for the quarter-space defined by $y > 0$ is stainless steel, which has the following properties: $\mu = 11 \times 10^6$ lb/in^2, $\rho = 7.26 \times 10^{-4}$ slug/in^3, and $\nu = 0.34$. The material closen for the quarter-space defined by $y < 0$ is aluminum, whose properties are as follows: $\mu_1 = 3.8 \times 10^6$ lb/in^2, $\rho_1 = 7.49 \times 10^{-4}$ slug/in^3, and $\nu_1 = 0.29$. It can be checked that Stoneley waves do exist for this combination of material properties.

Figures 5, 6, and 7 show graphs plotting $t\sum_{yy}/U_o$ and $t\sum_{xy}/U_o$ versus the dimensionless variable a_1x/t. It should be noted that due to the choice of materials, the values of the two shear wave velocities and that of the Stoneley wave velocity lie extremely close together. Thus, with the scale chosen for the various graphs, it is difficult to distinguish the individual wavefronts associated with these waves. To six-place accuracy, the values of the ordinate at these wavefronts are: $a_1/\kappa = 0.492356$, $a_1/b_1 = 0.492366$, and $a_1/b = 0.506260$.

CONCLUDING REMARKS

The main conclusions of this work pertain to the appearance of singularities in the interface stresses. Thus, for an impact-type load, i.e., for an applied particle velocity normal to the surface which varies in time as a Dirac delta function, while the surface is free of shear tractions, the normal interface stress is unbounded at the wavefronts of the two dilatational waves, and it behaves as a delta function at a point which propagates with the velocity of Stoneley waves, provided that the latter waves exist. The shear stress is also singular at the wavefronts of the dilatational waves, but the singularity propagating with the velocity of Stoneley waves is of a "pole"-type.

The interface stresses for more general time-dependence of the externally applied surface velocity can be obtained by integration. Since the singularities at the wavefronts of the dilatational waves are integrable, the normal stress at the interface is bounded for more gradually applied surface disturbances. The interface shear-stress, however, still shows a singularity propagating with the velocity of Stoneley waves. For finite times, both interface stresses remain bounded near the free surface.

The character of the singularities may be significantly affected by the fact that the boundary conditions are mixed, i.e., a particle velocity and a stress component are prescribed. It is very well possible that singularities will appear at the interface near the free surface if the boundary conditions are in terms of surface tractions.

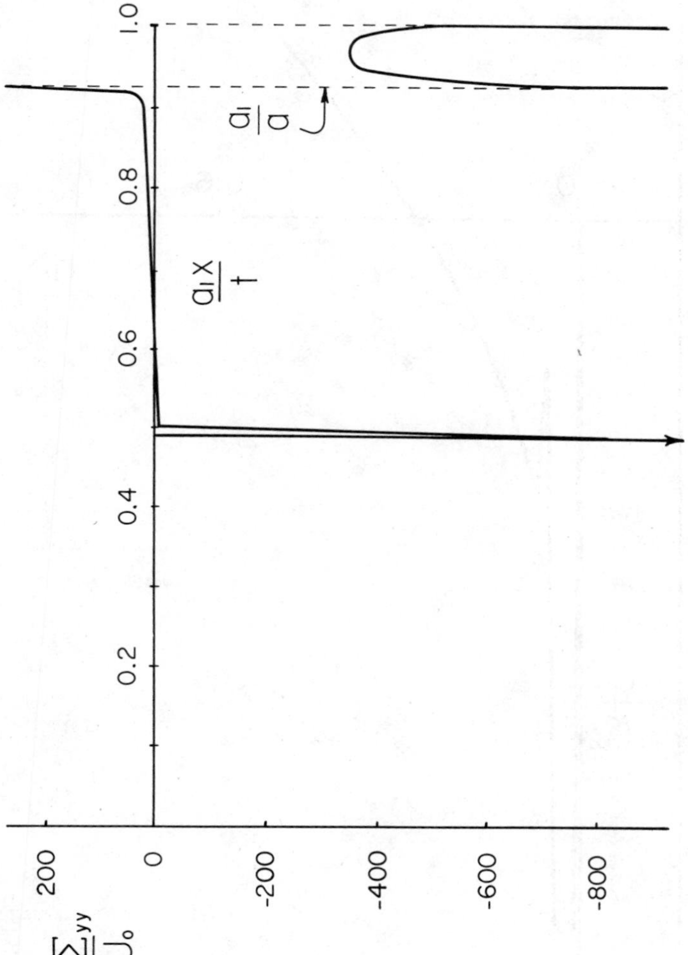

Fig. 5. Normal Stresses at the Interface.

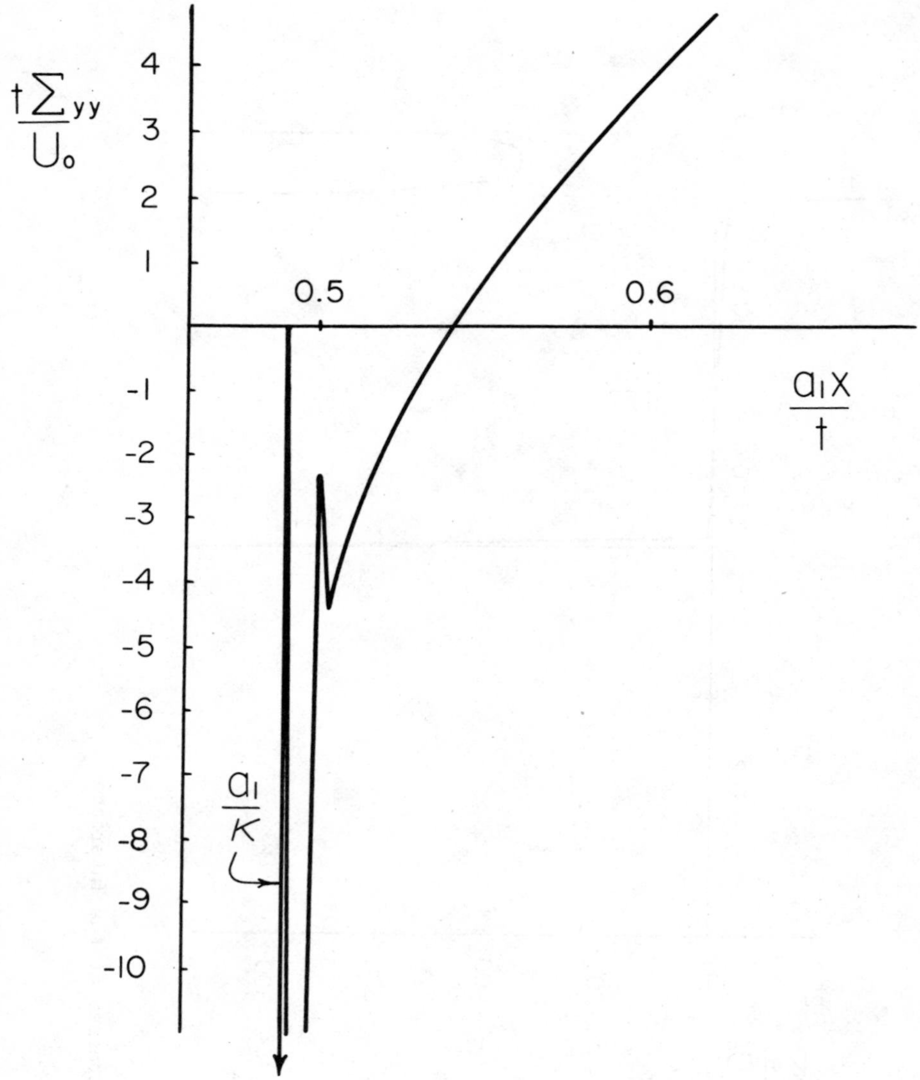

Fig. 6. Normal Stresses at the Interface Near the Stoneley Waves.

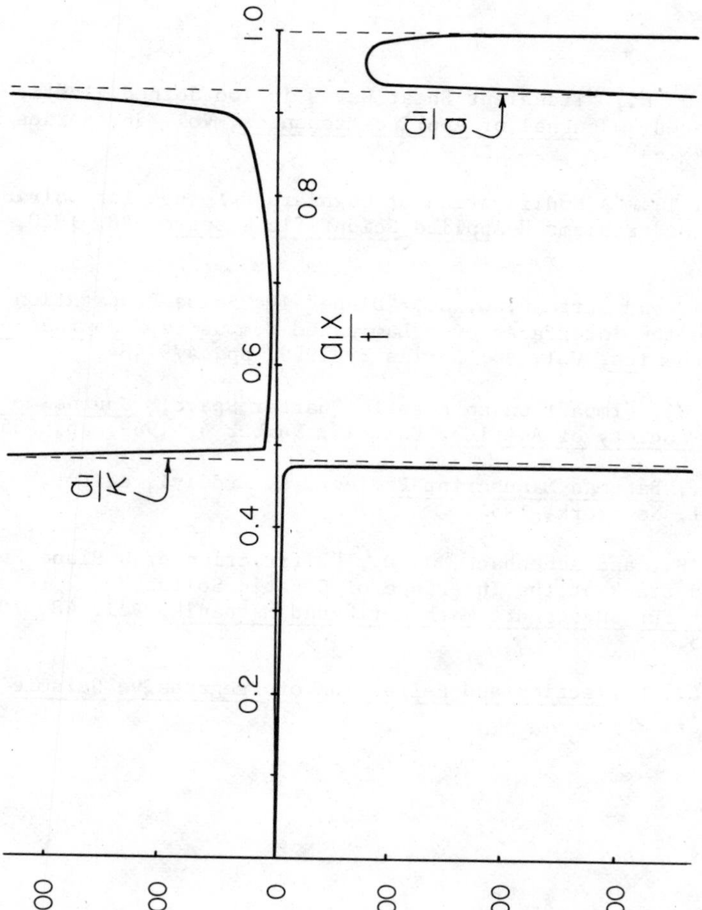

Fig. 7. Shear Stresses at the Interface.

ACKNOWLEDGMENT

This work was sponsored by the Air Force Materials Laboratory, Air Force Systems Command, Wright-Patterson Air Force Base, under Contract F33615-68-C-1290.

REFERENCES

1. Achenbach, J. D., "Transient Shear Waves in Two Joined Elastic Quarter-Spaces," Journal of Applied Mechanics, Vol. 36, Series E, 1969, pp. 491-496.

2. de Hoop, A. T., "A Modification of Cagniard's Method for Solving Seismic Pulse Problems," Applied Scientific Research B8, 1960, pp. 349-356.

3. Peck, J. C., and Gurtman, G. A., "Dispersive Pulse Propagation Parallel to the Interfaces of a Laminated Composite," Journal of Applied Mechanics, Vol. 36, Series E, 1969, pp. 479-484.

4. Wright, T. M., "Impact on an Elastic Quarter Space," Journal of the Acoustical Society of America, Vol. 45, Number 4, 1969, pp. 935-943.

5. Bateman, H., Bateman Manuscript Project, A. Erdélyi, editor, McGraw-Hill, New York, 1954.

6. Freund, L. B., and Achenbach, J. D., "Diffraction of a Plane Pulse by a Closed Crack at the Interface of Elastic Solids," Zeitschrift für angewandte Mathematik und Mechanik, Vol. 48, 1968, pp. 173-185.

7. Cagniard, L., Reflection and Refraction of Progressive Seismic Waves, McGraw-Hill, 1962.

PROPAGATION AND ATTENUATION OF HARMONIC WAVES IN A VISCOELASTIC CIRCULAR CYLINDER

J. L. Lai
The B. F. Goodrich Company

T. R. Tauchert and E. H. Dowell
Princeton University

ABSTRACT

Using the correspondence principle of dynamic viscoelasticity, the characteristic equation for the propagation of harmonic waves with arbitrary circumferential nodes in an infinite viscoelastic circular rod is derived. The wave number is complex with real part yielding the phase velocity and imaginary part being the attenuation constant. The equations for longitudinal, torsional and flexural motions are found from the general equation. Simplified solutions for waves with very long wave length are presented and a discussion on the applications of these results is given. Numerical results in the form of dispersion and attenuation curves for polystyrene are presented. The results are compared with those based upon the one-dimensional theory, and with the corresponding elastic solutions.

LIST OF NOTATIONS

a	Radius of the cylinder
c	$= \omega/k_r$ phase velocity of propagation
c_1	Dilatational wave velocity
c_2	Shear wave velocity
i	$= (-1)^{1/2}$

k	$= k_r - ik_i$ complex wave number
k_1	$= (\omega^2/c_1^2 - k^2)^{1/2}$
k_2	$= (\omega^2/c_2^2 - k^2)^{1/2}$
n	Number of circumferential nodes
r, θ, z	Polar coordinates
t	Time
C_0	= 6400 fps, bar velocity of polystyrene at room temperature and at ω = 10,000 cps
C_p	Dimensionless phase velocity in polystyrene cylinder
$\overline{E}(\omega)$	$= \overline{E}_R + i\overline{E}_I$ frequency-dependent complex Young's Modulus
J_n	Nth order Bessel function of first kind
$G(t)$, $L(t)$	Stress relaxation functions
$\overline{G}(\omega)$, $\overline{L}(\omega)$	Frequency-dependent complex moduli for viscoelastic medium
α	$= ak_i$ nondimensional attenuation
ρ	Mass density
ν	Poisson's ratio
ω	Circular frequency
Ω	$= a\omega/C_0$ dimensionless frequency

INTRODUCTION

Recently, viscoelastic materials such as plastics and high polymers have become extremely important as engineering materials. The viscoelastic theory is required in order to study the dynamic behavior of structures which are made of these materials. Hence, the attenuation and the propagation of viscoelastic waves has received considerable attention.

The analysis of wave propagation in viscoelastic media is an extension of the corresponding elastic problem. Using complex, frequency-dependent moduli instead of elastic constants in the frequency equations of elastic problems, we may obtain the characteristic equations for viscoelastic bodies. Wave numbers obtained from the viscoelastic solutions are complex with the real part determining the phase velocity and the imaginary part being the attenuation constant. Because the equations based upon the three-dimensional theory are very complicated, most problems studied to date have been simplified to the one-dimensional case [1, 2, 3].

In the earlier works on harmonic viscoelastic waves in rods, the one-dimensional theory and the spring-dashpot model representation were used to obtain dispersions and attenuations. Recently, Coquin [4] used the corresponding Pochhammer solutions and an approximate method to obtain the attenuations of longitudinal waves in a Voigt-solid rod. Kawatate [5] derived a steady-state solution for stress waves traveling in a linear viscoelastic cylinder of infinite length by a method similar to Pochhammer's. The study of torsional harmonic wave propagation in a circular viscoelastic rod can be found in [6]. However, a general formulation for the harmonic waves in linear viscoelastic rods has not been presented before. The numerical calculations for dispersions and attenuations based on the three-dimensional linear viscoelastic theory have not appeared in the literature.

In this paper, we will first use the principle of correspondence to obtain the general characteristic equation for viscoelastic harmonic waves in an infinitely long circular cylinder. The dimension and the coordinates of the cylinder are shown in Fig. 1. Three special cases, longitudinal, torsional and flexural motions, are reduced from the general equation. Simplified equations corresponding to very long wave length solutions are obtained. The application of these simplified equations is also discussed. Using experimental data for polystyrene with the assumption that Poisson's ratio is real and constant, the dispersion curves and the attenuations are obtained with the aid of a digital computer. The results are compared with those for corresponding elastic problems and those based on the one-dimensional theory. The effects of geometry and material properties on the dispersion and the attenuation are also investigated.

Basic Equations for Viscoelastic Solids

The dynamics of viscoelastic solids are governed by the laws of conservation of mass, momentum, and moment of momentum; stress-strain relations, boundary conditions and initial conditions [7]. Let u_k, e_{kl}, τ_{kl}, f_k and ρ denote displacement, strain, stress, body force per

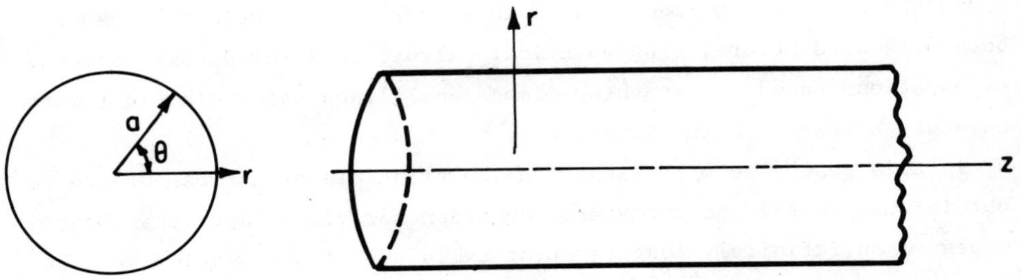

Fig. 1. The Coordinate System.

unit volume and mass density, respectively. The constitutive equation of a homogeneous, non heat-conducting, linear isotropic viscoelastic body is

$$\tau_{kl}(t) = 2 \int_{-\infty}^{t} G(t-\tau) \frac{\partial e_{kl}}{\partial \tau} d\tau + \delta_{kl} \int_{-\infty}^{t} L(t-\tau) \frac{\partial e_{ii}}{\partial \tau} d\tau \quad (1)$$

where G(t) and L(t) are the stress relaxation functions which decrease monotonically with t; δ_{kl} is the ordinary Kronecker delta function. If $G(t) = \mu$, $L(t) = \lambda$, where μ and λ are the Lame constants, one has the usual constitutive equation for elasticity. The strain-displacement relations are

$$e_{kl} = \frac{1}{2} (u_{k;l} + u_{l;k}) \quad (2)$$

where ; is the notation for covariant differentiation. The equations of balance are

$$\tau_{kl;l} - \rho \left(f_k - \frac{\partial^2 u_k}{\partial \tau^2}\right) = 0 \quad (3)$$

$$\tau_{kl} = \tau_{lk} \quad (4)$$

After the substitution of Eq. (2) into Eq. (1), then into Eq. (3) and the neglect of the body forces, we can write the equation of motion in terms of vectorial displacement $\vec{u}$ as follows

$$\int_{-\infty}^{t} \{G(t-\tau)\nabla^2 + [L(t-\tau) + 2G(t-\tau)] \vec{\nabla}\vec{\nabla}\cdot\} \frac{\partial \vec{u}}{\partial \tau} d\tau = \rho \frac{\partial^2 u}{\partial t^2} \quad (5)$$

Equation (5) has the same form as the Navier equation of motion for elasticity [7]. For harmonic waves in a viscoelastic material, we may write the displacement in the form

$$\vec{u}(\vec{x},t) = \vec{U}(\vec{x})\, e^{i\omega t} \quad (6)$$

where $\vec{x}$ is the vector coordinate of a point in an undeformed body and $\vec{U}$ is the amplitude of the displacement of the viscoelastic solid and is a function of the coordinate $\vec{x}$ only. Substituting Eq. (6) into Eq. (5), the harmonic motion of a viscoelastic solid is governed by

$$\overline{G}(\omega)\ \nabla^2\ \vec{U} + \{\overline{L}(\omega) + 2\overline{G}(\omega)\}\ \vec{\nabla}(\vec{\nabla}\cdot\vec{U}) = -\ \rho\omega^2\vec{U} \tag{7}$$

where

$$\begin{aligned} \overline{G}(\omega) &\equiv i\omega \int_0^\infty G(t)\ e^{-i\omega t} dt \\ \overline{L}(\omega) &\equiv i\omega \int_0^\infty L(t)\ e^{-i\omega t} dt \end{aligned} \tag{8}$$

From Eq. (7), we can see that the difference between the dynamics of viscoelastic and elastic bodies is that the former has frequency-dependent moduli. Hence, viscoelastic solutions may be readily obtained once the analogous elastic solutions are known, simply by replacing the elastic constants by complex and frequency-dependent moduli which characterize the viscoelastic material. The propagating wave number obtained from the viscoelastic frequency equation is also complex.

Simple Plane Guided Waves in a Linear Isotropic Viscoelastic Cylinder

Since the material moduli for viscoelastic materials are complex and frequency-dependent, we have separate directions for attenuations and propagations of general plane waves in a viscoelastic medium [8, 9]. However, we will only consider the case of a "simple plane wave" in a viscoelastic cylinder. That is, the direction of propagation is coincident with that of attenuation.

We may apply the principle of correspondence to the solution of the elastic case which has been presented by Meeker and Meitzler [10] in order to obtain the characteristic equation for the general case of a simple plane wave propagating in a viscoelastic cylinder. That is, the frequency-dependent complex wave velocities replace the constant real wave velocities for the viscoelastic cylinder. The real propagating wave number k in the elastic case must also be replaced by a complex wave number $k = k_r - ik_i$. However, we may also use the method used in [10] to derive the general characteristic equation for the propagation and the attenuation of harmonic waves in a viscoelastic cylinder. According to [11], the characteristic equation is

$$|C_{km}| = 0 \qquad (k, m = 1, 2 \text{ and } 3) \tag{9}$$

where C_{km} are the elements of the determinant defined as

$$
\begin{aligned}
C_{11} &= \frac{2k_1}{a} J_{n-1}(k_1 a) - \left[\frac{2n(n+1)}{a^2} + k^2 - k_2^2\right] J_n(k_1 a) \\
C_{12} &= \frac{-2nk_2}{a} J_{n-1}(k_2 a) + \frac{2n(n+1)}{a^2} J_n(k_2 a) \\
C_{13} &= \frac{2(n+1)k}{a} J_{n+1}(k_2 a) - 2kk_2 J_n(k_2 a) \\
C_{21} &= 2kk_1 J_{n-1}(k_2 a) - \frac{2kn}{a} J_n(k_1 a) \\
C_{22} &= \frac{nk}{a} J_n(k_2 a) \\
C_{23} &= (k^2 - k_2^2) J_{n+1}(k_2 a) + \frac{k_2 n}{a} J_n(k_2 a) \\
C_{31} &= \frac{2n}{a} k_1 J_{n-1}(k_1 a) - \frac{2n(n+1)}{a^2} J_n(k_1 a) \\
C_{32} &= \frac{-2k_2}{a} J_{n-1}(k_2 a) - \left(k_2^2 - \frac{2n}{a^2}\right) J_n(k_2 a) \\
C_{33} &= -kk_2 J_n(k_2 a) + 2k \frac{(n+1)}{a} J_{n+1}(k_2 a)
\end{aligned}
\tag{10}
$$

where n is the number of circumferential nodes, J_n is the first kind of Bessel function of nth order and

$$k_1^2 \equiv \omega^2/c_1^2 - k^2$$

$$k_2^2 \equiv \omega^2/c_2^2 - k^2$$

$$c_1^2 \equiv \frac{\overline{L}(\omega) + 2\overline{G}(\omega)}{\rho}$$

$$c_2^2 \equiv \frac{\overline{G}(\omega)}{\rho}$$

Therefore c_1 and c_2, the dilatational and the shear wave velocities in an infinite viscoelastic medium, are complex and frequency-dependent. The propagation wave number $k = k_r - ik_i$ is complex; the real part corresponds to the propagation constant and gives the phase velocity; the imaginary part gives the attenuation of waves in the direction of propagation. The arguments of the Bessel functions given in Eqs. (10) are complex. Therefore, a simple plane-wave in a viscoelastic material is attenuated in the direction of propagation and is dispersive due to geometrical and material effects. The characteristic Eq. (9) may be written symbolically as

$$F(k, \omega, c_1, c_2, a, n) = 0 \tag{11}$$

Some Special Cases

Several special cases may be obtained by reduction of Eq. (9). The simplified solution for each case which is good for the long wave length region will also be obtained by retaining the first few terms of the expansion of Bessel functions.

A. Longitudinal Waves

By substituting n = 0 into Eq. (9), the frequency Eq. (9) is reduced to the product of

$$E_1 \cdot E_2 = 0 \tag{12}$$

where
$$E_1 \equiv \frac{2k_1}{a}(k_2^2+k^2)\, J_1(k_1a)\, J_1(k_2a) - (k^2-k_2^2)\, J_0(k_1a)\, J_1(k_2a)$$
$$-4k^2k_1\, k_2\, J_1(k_1a)\, J_0\,(k_2a) \tag{13}$$
$$E_2 \equiv \frac{2k_2}{a} J_1\,(k_2a) - k_2^2\, J_0\,(k_2a)$$

When $E_1 = 0$, we have the characteristic equation for longitudinal waves which involves only longitudinal and radial displacements u_z and u_r. This equation is analogous to the Pockhammer-Chree equation [12] for the elastic case.

The characteristic equation for longitudinal waves $E_1 = 0$ is still very complicated and is a transcendental equation in terms of the Bessel functions with complex arguments. Without the aid of a digital computer, the dispersive relations and the attenuations cannot be obtained except when simplifications are made. Should the radius of the cylinder be small relative to the wave length, the characteristic equation $E_1 = 0$ may be reduced to the simplified solutions for longitudinal waves. These solutions depend upon the number of series terms retained from the expansion of the Bessel functions in the characteristic equation. The ratio of Bessel functions of zero and first order when the arguments are small can be expanded in series form as

$$\frac{J_0(x)}{J_1(x)} = \frac{2}{x}\left(1 - \frac{x^2}{8} - \frac{x^4}{192} + 0(x^6)\right) \tag{14}$$

If we retain only the first term of the series, we have the approximate solution,

$$\frac{\omega^2}{\overline{E}(\omega)/\rho} \cong k^2 \tag{15}$$

where $\overline{E}(\omega)$ is the complex Young's modulus of viscoelastic solids and equals $2\overline{G}(\omega)\,(1+\nu)$ with ν being a complex and frequency-dependent Poisson's ratio [13]. This solution is the same as that based on the elementary, one-dimensional theory [14]. It shows no geometrical dispersion effects. If we put the real and the imaginary parts of Eq. (15) equal to zero, we obtain two equations

$$\overline{E}_R = \frac{\rho\omega^2\ (1-k_1^2\ c^2/\omega^2)}{[1+k_i^{\ 2}\ c^2/\omega^2]^2}$$

$$\overline{E}_I = \frac{2\rho c\ \omega k_i}{[1+k_i^{\ 2}\ c^2/\omega^2]^2} \tag{16}$$

where $c = \omega/k_r$ is the velocity of the propagation, k_i is the attenuation and $\overline{E}_R$ and $\overline{E}_I$ are the real and the imaginary parts of Young's modulus of the viscoelastic solid. These equations can be used to find Young's modulus of viscoelastic solids if measurements of the attenuation and the velocity of the propagation of longitudinal waves are made, provided the ratio (radius of specimen/wave length) is much smaller than one. If the first two terms of the series expansion for Bessel functions are retained, a more accurate approximate solution is obtained in the form

$$\frac{\omega^2}{\overline{E}/\rho} = k^2(1 - \frac{\nu^2}{2}\, k^2 a^2) \tag{17}$$

This solution corresponds to the longitudinal elastic waves based upon Rayleigh's theory [15], in which lateral inertia effects are considered. The dispersion is affected by geometry.

B. Torsional Waves

Torsional waves as well as longitudinal waves give an axisymmetric motion which involves only the torsional displacement u_θ and is independent of the angular coordinate θ. The characteristic equation is $E_2 = 0$ given in Eq. (13). The values of k_2 which satisfy $E_2 = 0$ are

$$k_2 a = 0, \qquad 5.135, \qquad 8.4172, \; .....$$

The torsional waves are generated by the equivoluminal mode only. The first mode is free of any geometrical effects. The attenuations and the propagation constants may be expressed by the following equations:

$$k_i = \beta \sin \gamma$$

$$k_r = \beta \cos \gamma \qquad (18)$$

where $\beta \equiv \{(\omega^2/c_s^2 - k_2^2)^2 + (\omega^2/c_s^2 \tan \delta)^2\}^{1/2}$

$$\gamma \equiv \frac{1}{2} \tan^{-1} \frac{\omega^2/c_s^2 \tan 2\delta}{\omega^2/c_s^2 - k_2^2}$$

$$c_s^2 \equiv \frac{\overline{G}(\omega)}{\rho} \sec 2\delta \qquad \text{and}$$

$$\delta \equiv \frac{1}{2} \tan^{-1} \frac{\text{Im } \overline{G}(\omega)}{\text{Re } \overline{G}(\omega)}$$

Once the material shear modulus is known, we may obtain the attenuations and the propagation constants for each mode through the substitution of the corresponding k_2 values into Eqs. (18).

C. Flexural Waves

When we put n = 1, Eq. (9) becomes the solution for flexural waves. This motion involves all three displacement components. If the ratio of the radius of the cylinder to wave length is small, the first two terms of the expansion are retained. An approximate solution is found to be

$$\frac{\omega^2}{\overline{E}(\omega)/\rho} \cong \frac{k^4 a^2}{4} \qquad (19)$$

This is the solution analogous to the one based on the Bernoulli-Euler Classical lateral vibration theory [16] of a rod.

When the real and the imaginary parts of Eq. (19) are set equal to zero, we obtain

$$\overline{E}_R(\omega) = \frac{4\rho\omega^2}{a^2q^4}\cos 4\theta$$
$$\overline{E}_I(\omega) = \frac{4\rho\omega^2}{a^2q^4}\sin 4\theta \quad (20)$$

where $q^2 = k_r^2+k_i^2$, $\theta = \tan^{-1} k_i/k_r$.

If we measure the attenuation and the propagating velocity of flexural waves along a thin rod with low frequency (radius of rod/wave length << 1), we can use Eqs. (20) to calculate $\overline{E}_R$ and $\overline{E}_I$.

If the first three terms of the series expansion are retained, the result of this second approximation is

$$\frac{\omega^2}{\overline{E}(\omega)/\rho} \cong \frac{k^4a^2}{4}\left(1 - \frac{5+2\nu}{6}k^2a^2\right) \quad (21)$$

This result corresponds to the one which is found on the basis of Rayleigh theory [15] involving a consideration of rotatory inertia for flexural vibration.

Nemerical Solutions

As discussed earlier the characteristic Equation (11) is complex. The solutions of k and ω must be such that both the real and the imaginary parts of the equation will be zero. Hence, from the two equations Re F = 0 and Im F = 0, the frequency spectrum and the attenuation curve are obtained. Since the characteristic equations for either general or special cases are very complicated, utilization of a digital computer is unavoidable.

In order to calculate typical dispersion curves and attenuations, we use the experimental data for polystyrene shown in Figure 2 which

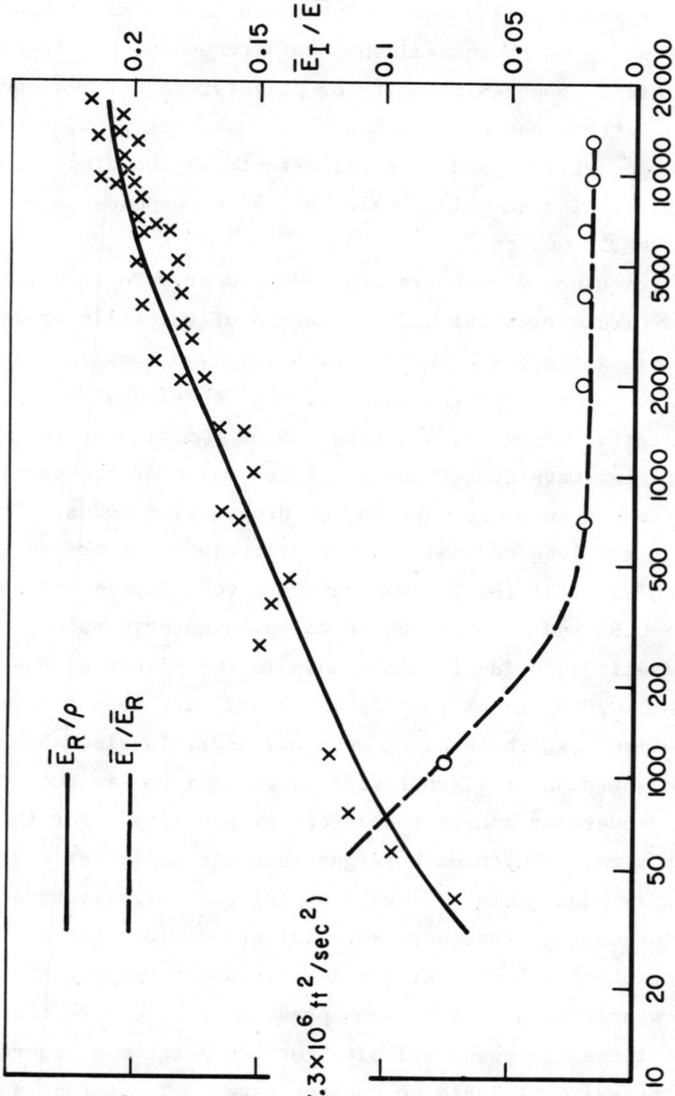

Fig. 2. Complex Moduli of Polystyrene.

was measured by Lai [11].[1] We assume that the Poisson's ratio of polystyrene is real and constant. With these data the dispersion curves for longitudinal viscoelastic waves are obtained in the range $0.0156 < \Omega < 6$, where $\Omega = a\omega/C_o$ is the non-dimensional frequency. C_0 is equal to 6400 fps, a reference phase velocity of polystyrene at frequency ω = 10,000 cps. In this paper, we use a = 4.9" so that we can investigate both geometrical and material effects on the dispersion and the attenuation. The numerical value $\Omega = 6$ corresponds to a frequency equal to 15,000 cps.

Substituting frequency ω, the frequency-dependent velocities C_1 and C_2, radius a and circumferential nodes number n of the cylinder into Eq. (11), we obtain a complex equation which involves complex k as its variables. Then we search for the roots of the equation with the aid of an IBM 7094 digital computer. It takes about ten minutes to calculate the values of complex wave number for the fixed value of frequency. In this paper, we present only the results for propagating modes. The dispersion curves for longitudinal viscoelastic waves are presented in Figure 3. We can see that the first mode phase velocity increases to a maximum at $\Omega = 0.93$ and then decreases to an asymptotic value. The corresponding elastic solution is also shown in the Figure by dashed lines (with $\overline{E}_R$ at 10,000 cps as Young's modulus). The result termed "Elementary Solution", which is based upon Eq. (15), is also shown in Figure 3. The dispersion of viscoelastic waves in a rod is due both to the material properties and to the effect of geometry. For the lowest mode with a wave length much larger than the radius of rod, the geometric effect is negligible. Since the real part of polystyrene increases with increasing frequency, material properties contribute to the increasing phase velocity at the low frequency range. At higher frequencies the geometric effect becomes predominant. Due to the effect of boundary conditions the phase velocity for the first mode decreases and approaches the value of Rayleigh surface waves. The second and the

1. The experimental data are obtained through a series of vibration tests on various polystyrene beams at room temperature. Resonant frequencies on the response curves and their log decrements are measured. Then, using Timoshenko beam theory and these results, we calculate the mechanical properties of polystyrene.

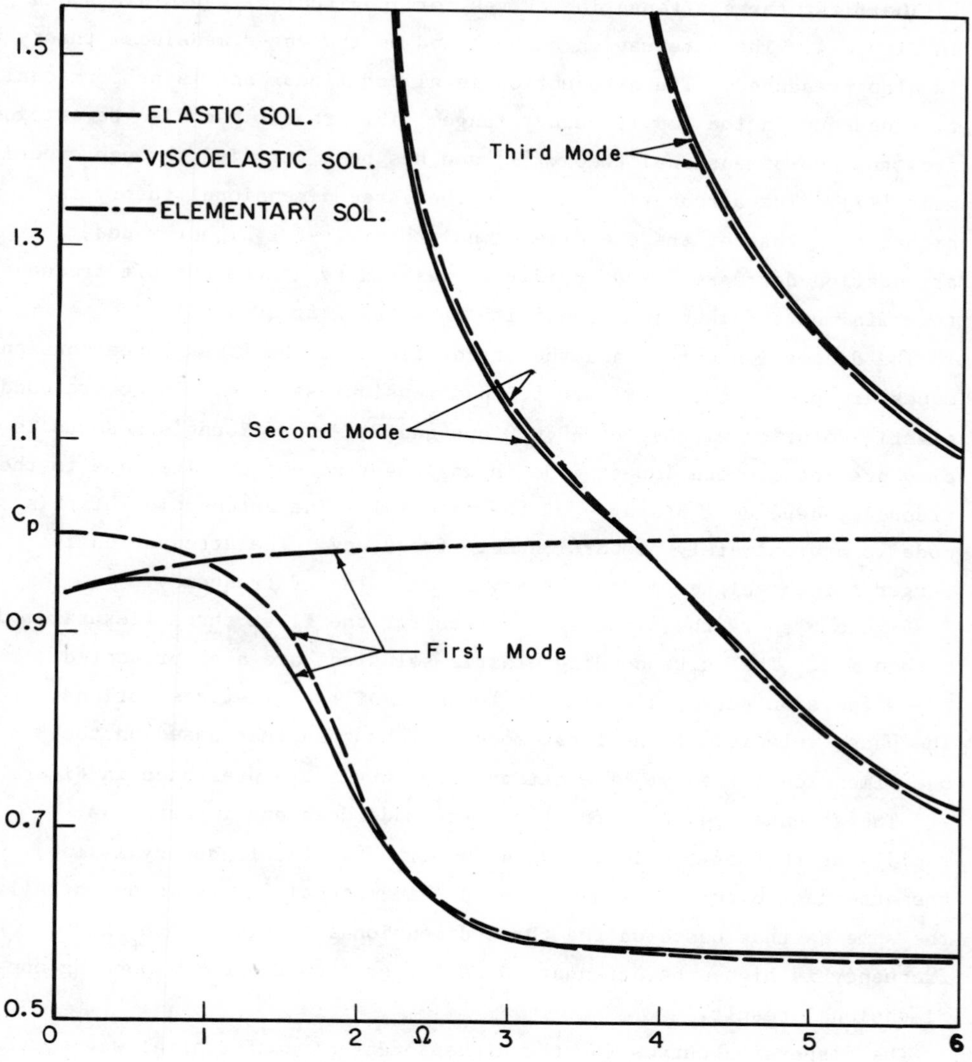

Fig. 3. Dispersion Curves of Longitudinal Modes.

third modes are similar to those of longitudinal waves in elastic rods.

The first three attenuation curves for longitudinal waves are shown in Figure 4. The attenuation curve based on the one-dimensional theory is also presented. The attenuation is almost linear and is proportional to frequency in the low frequency range. This result can also be obtained from the one-dimensional theory [1] and has been verified through experiment [17]. The attenuation based on the three-dimensional theory is higher than that of the one-dimensional theory. For higher modes, the attenuation decreases very rapidly from infinity at the cut-off frequency to a minimum and then increases with increasing frequency.

The dispersion curves and the attenuations of the first three torsional modes are presented, in Figure 5, in dimensionless form. The corresponding elastic solution with $\overline{E}_R$ at 10,000 cps and $\overline{E}_I = 0$ as Young's modulus is also presented. The lowest mode is no longer non-dispersive, due to the frequency-dependent property of the material. The attenuation of this mode is approximately proportional to frequency. The attenuation is larger for the higher modes for any fixed value of frequency.

Figure 6 shows the dispersion curves for the first three flexural modes with $n = 1$. The corresponding elastic solutions are also presented. The dispersion curves are similar to those of the elastic solutions. The phase velocity of the first mode is less than that based on the one-dimensional theory. The attenuation curves are presented in Figure 7. The attenuation curve for the first mode does not increase as rapidly as that of the longitudinal mode. When the frequency is low, the attenuation curve based on the one-dimensional theory is essentially the same as that based on the three-dimensional theory. When the frequency is high, the attenuation is larger than the corresponding one-dimensional result.

The dispersion curves for the higher order circumferential waves, $n=2$ and 3, are given in Figure 8. None of the higher order circumferential waves can propagate when the non-dimensional frequency is less than 1.17. The asymptotic values of both waves at short wave length are that of Rayleigh surface waves. The attenuation curves for $n = 2$ and 3 waves are presented in Figure 9. The shapes of the curves are similar to those of the higher modes of longitudinal or flexural waves.

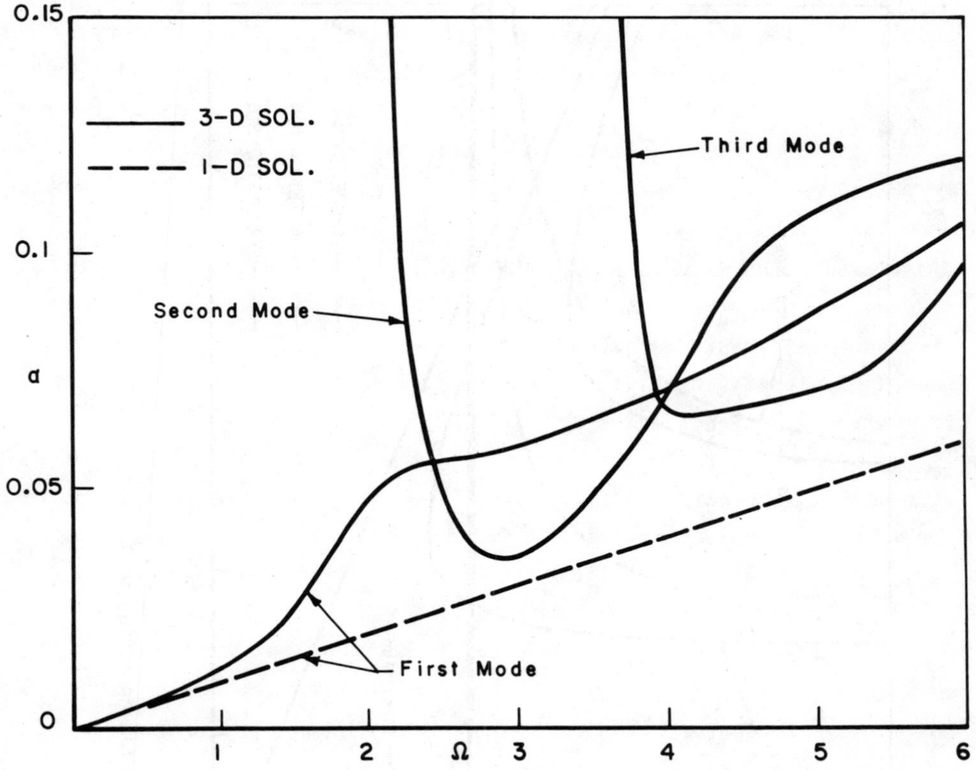

Fig. 4. Attenuations of Longitudinal Waves.

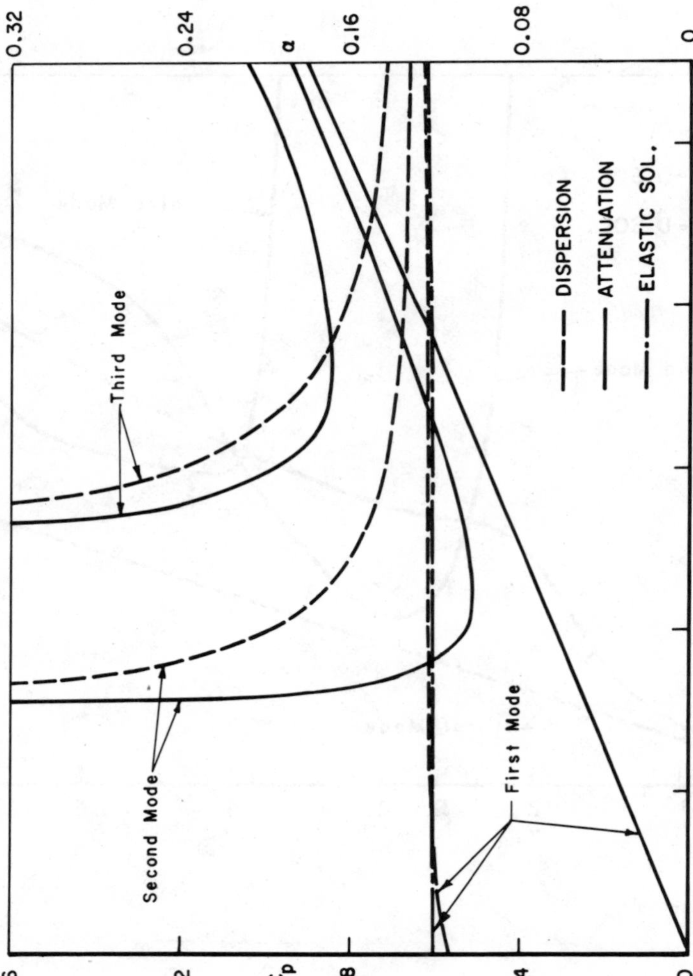

Fig. 5. Dispersion Curves and Attenuations of Torsional Modes.

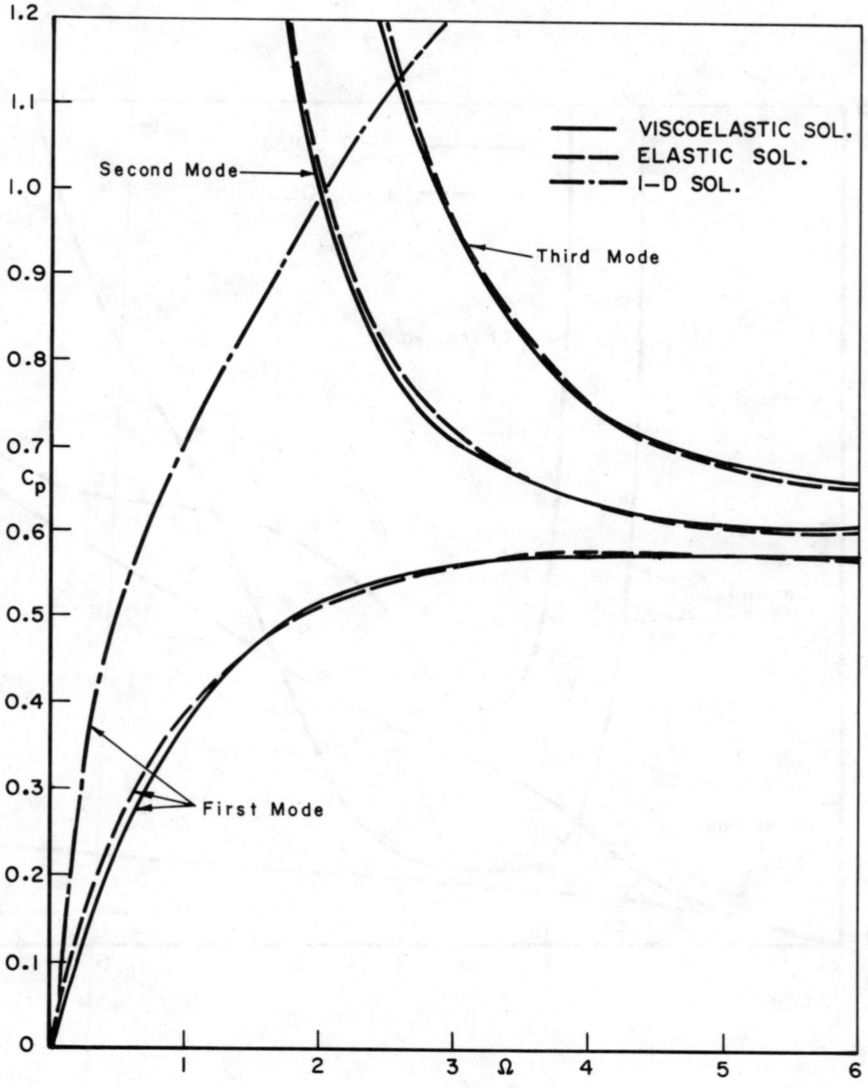

Fig. 6. Dispersion Curves of Flexural Modes with n = 1.

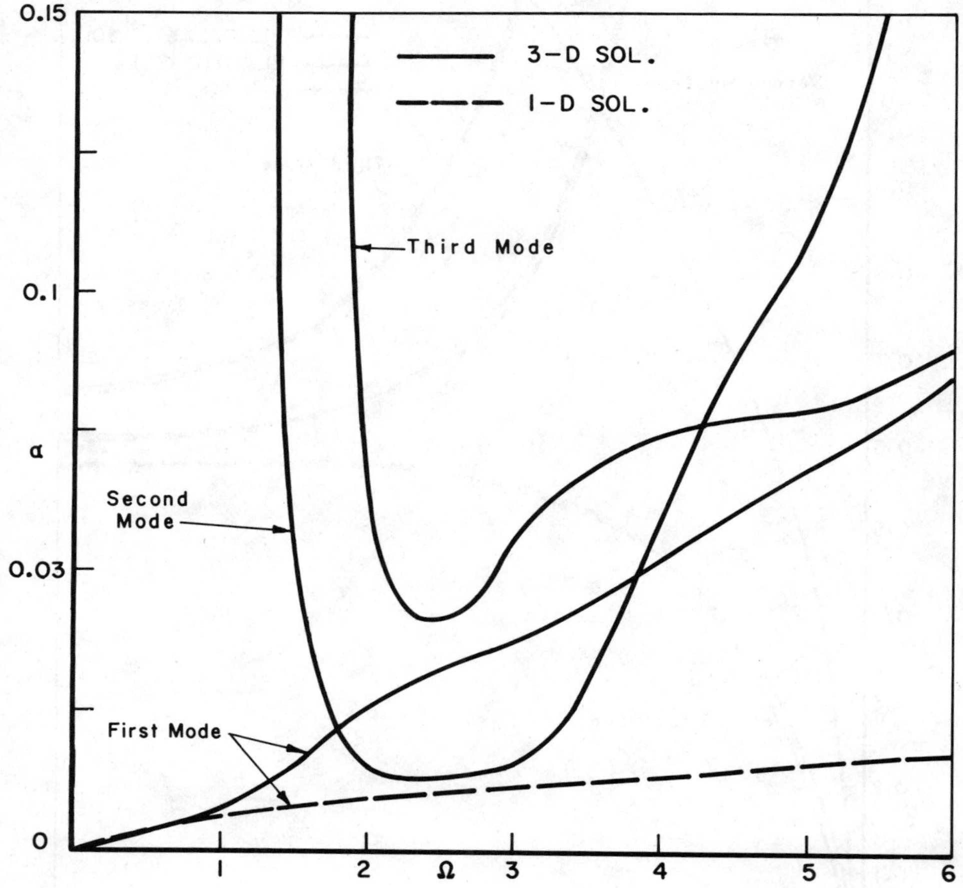

Fig. 7. Attenuations of Flexural Modes with n = 1.

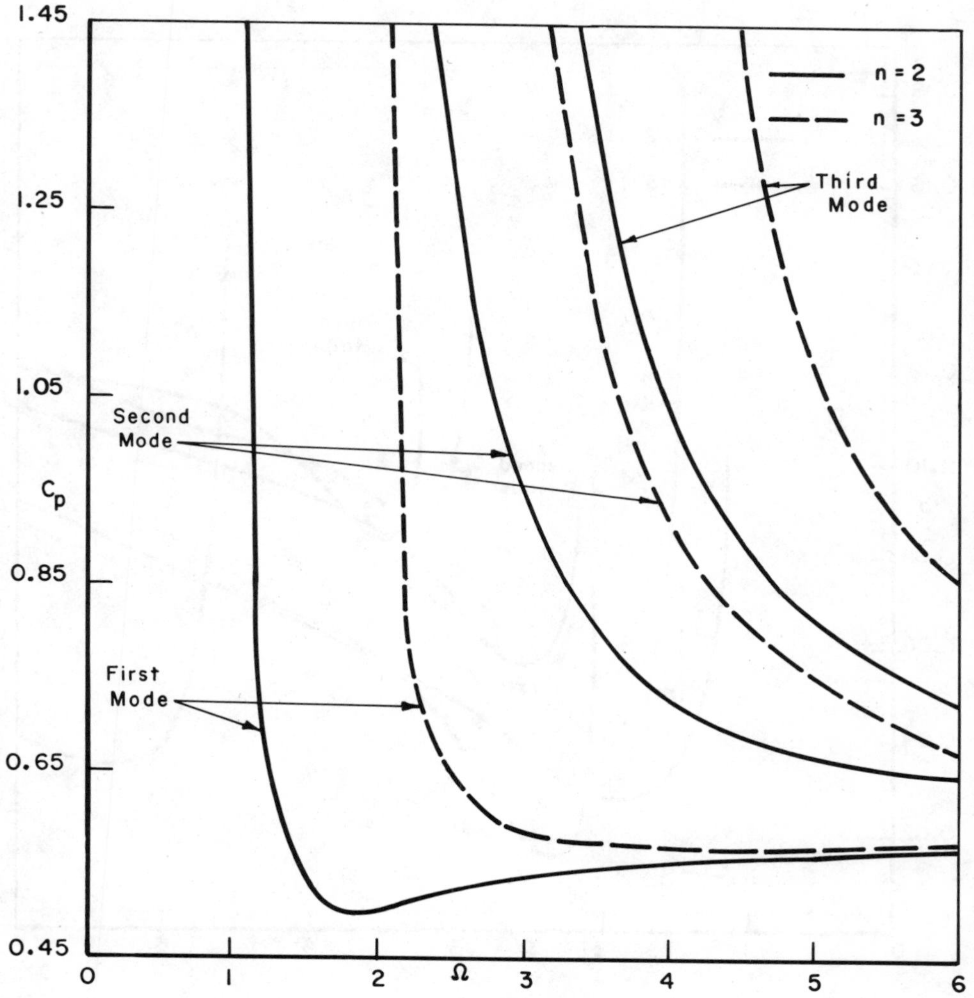

Fig. 8. Dispersion Curves for the Higher Order Circumferential Waves.

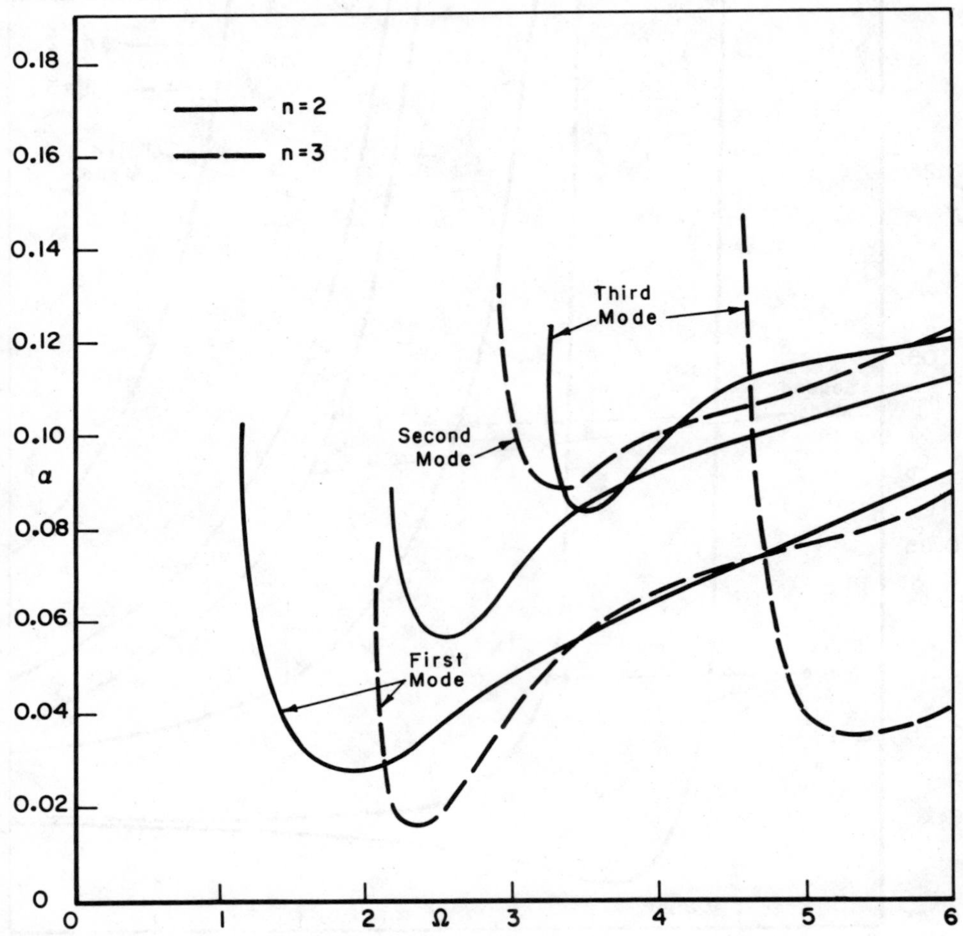

Fig. 9. Attenuations for the Higher Order Circumferential Waves.

DISCUSSION AND CONCLUSIONS

The dispersion and the attenuation of viscoelastic waves in a wave guide arise from the effects of the material properties and the boundary conditions or geometry. If the imaginary part of the moduli is much less than that of the real part (say 0.1), the loss moduli affect the dispersion very slightly (less than one percent). The dispersion in the low frequency range is mainly attributed to the frequency-dependent property of material. However, the dispersion effect in the high frequency range is mainly contributed by geometry.

Polystyrene was used as a physical example for our numerical calculation. Since the variation of the real part of the moduli with frequency is small, the dispersion due to material properties is not very significant. When the frequency is high, the asymptotic phase velocities for the first modes of longitudinal and flexural waves are that of Rayleigh surface waves. As for torsional waves, the non-dispersive lowest mode which appears in the elastic problem is now dispersive solely due to the effect of the frequency-dependent material properties.

Because the first mode of each motion is generally dominant, it is of interest to compare the attenuations of the first mode for different types of waves. When the harmonic frequencies are identical, the attenuation for the first longitudinal mode is the largest among longitudinal, torsional and flexural waves. On the other hand, the attenuation is the least for the first mode of flexural waves with $n = 1$. The attenuation of the lowest torsional mode is independent of the geometrical conditions and is governed by the material properties only. The attenuations of both the lowest mode of longitudinal and flexural waves are attributed to both geometry and material properties. Moreover, the attenuations of longitudinal and flexural waves based on the one-dimensional theory are less than those of the three-dimensional theory.

ACKNOWLEDGMENT

Part of this work was sponsored by NASA Grant NGR 31-001-124.

REFERENCES

1. Hunter, S. G., "Viscoelastic Waves," Progress in Solid Mechanics I, Edited by I. N. Sneddon and R. Hill, North Holland Publishing Co., Amsterdam, 1959, pp. 1-57.

2. Kolsky, H., Stress Waves in Solids, Dover Publications, New York, 1963.

3. Davis, R. M., "Stress Waves in Solids," Surveys in Mechanics, G. I. Taylor 70th Anniversary Volume, University Press, Cambridge, 1956, pp. 64-138.

4. Coquin, G. A., "Attenuation of Guided Waves in Isotropic Viscoelastic Materials," Journal of Acoustic Society of America, Vol. 36, 1964, pp. 1074-1080.

5. Kawatate, K., "Stress Waves in a Linear Viscoelastic Cylinder," International Journal of Engineering Science, Vol. 4, 1966, pp. 605-610.

6. Wolosewick, R. M. and Raynor, S., "Axisymmetric Torsional Wave Propagation in Circular Viscoelastic Rods," Journal of Acoustic Society of America, Vol. 42, 1967, pp. 417-421.

7. Eringen, A. C., Mechanics of Continua, John Wiley & Sons, Inc., New York, 1967.

8. Lockett, F. J., "The Reflection and Refraction of Waves at an Interface Between Viscoelastic Materials," Journal of Mechanics and Physics for Solids, Vol. 10, 1962, pp. 53-64.

9. Cooper, H. F. and Reiss, E. L., "Reflection of Plane Viscoelastic Waves from Plane Boundaries," Journal of Acoustic Society of America, Vol. 39, 1966, pp. 1133-1138.

10. Meeker, T. R. and Meitzler, A. H., "Guided Wave Propagation in Elongated Cylinders and Plates," Physical Acoustics, Edited by W. P. Mason, Vol. 1, Part A, Academic Press, New York, 1964, pp. 111-167.

11. Lai, J. L., "The Propagation of Waves in Composite Elastic Rods and Viscoelastic Rods," Ph.D. Dissertation, Princeton University, Princeton, N. J., Sept. 1968.

12. Redwood, M., Mechanical Waveguides, Pergamon Press, New York, 1960.

13. Ferry, J. D., Viscoelastic Properties of Polymers, John Wiley & Sons, Inc., New York, 1961.

14. Fung, Y. C., Foundations of Solid Mechanics, Prentice-Hall, Inc., Englewood, N. Y., 1965.

15. Rayleigh, J. W. S., The Theory of Sound, Vol. 1, Dover Publications, New York, 1945, pp. 252.

16. Timoshenko, S., Vibration Problems in Engineering, D. Van Nostrand Co., Inc., Princeton, N. J., 1956.

17. Kolsky, H., "The Propagation of Stress Pulses in Viscoelastic Solids," The Philosophical Magazine, Vol. 1, 1956, pp. 693-710.

PLATES

INFINITE PLATE WITH A SUPPORTED REINFORCED CIRCULAR HOLE

R. Amon
University of Illinois

O. E. Widera
University of Illinois

ABSTRACT

The deflection of an infinite plate with a hole which is reinforced with a simply supported beam and loaded by a concentrated force is determined. The problem is formulated within the framework of classical plate theory and the Euler-Bernoulli hypothesis for beams. The solution is obtained by superimposing on a particular solution (which includes the proper singularity for a concentrated force) a series of biharmonic functions. The fact that the plate and beam may possess different elastic properties is included in the solution.

LIST OF NOTATIONS

a	Radius of the hole
D	Flexural rigidity of plate
K	Flexural rigidity of reinforcing beam
L	Torsional rigidity of reinforcing beam
M	Bending moment in reinforcing beam
M_r	Radial bending moment in plate
m	Distributed moment on reinforcing beam
P	Magnitude of concentrated force
p	Distributed load on reinforcing beam
Q	Shear force in reinforcing beam

q	Transverse load on plate
R	Support reaction
r, θ	Polar coordinates
T	Twisting moment in reinforcing beam
V_r	Kirchoff shear force
v	Deflection of reinforcing beam
w	Deflection of plate
βa	Distance from load to center of plate
χ	K/aD
$\bar{\chi}$	Change in curvature of reinforcing beam
λ	L/aD
ν	Poisson's ratio
ϕ	Rotation of the principal axis of reinforcing beam
$\bar{\tau}$	Change in twist of reinforcing beam

INTRODUCTION

The circular plate because of its importance in applications has received considerable attention from researchers in thin plate theory. According to the Poisson-Kirchoff theory, the deflection w of the middle surface of such a plate is given by

$$\nabla^4 w = \frac{q}{D} \tag{1}$$

where ∇^4 denotes the Laplacian operator $\nabla^2 = \frac{\partial^2}{\partial r^2} + \frac{1}{r}\frac{\partial}{\partial r} + \frac{1}{r^2}\frac{\partial^2}{\partial \theta^2}$

applied twice, q is the transverse load and D is the flexural rigidity of the plate. In the above and in what is to follow, the sign conventions and symbols used agree with those employed by Timoshenko and Woinowsky-Krieger [1].

The solution of the plate problem in general presents no particular difficulty unless a singularity at a point other than the origin is present. In this case the solution can be expressed in the form

$$w = w_S + w_R \tag{2}$$

where w_s denotes the singular solution state, while w_R represents the regular solution state. The determination of w_s for various circular plate problems has been the object of many papers, such as, for example, those of Clebsch [2], Föppl [3], Michell [4], Reissner [5] and Washizu [6]. Once a singular solution is found, then the regular solution is determined such that the boundary conditions on w are satisfied.

In this paper we will study the problem of an infinite plate with a reinforced circular hole under the action of a concentrated force P. The support is in the shape of an edge-beam which can be either simply supported or vertically guided so as to maintain zero radial slope. The problem of the non-reinforced plate has been studied by Symonds [7] for the case of a clamped edge, while Bassali [8] has treated the simply supported edge problem. Dundurs and Lee [9] recovered both of these solutions by a proper specialization of the elastic constants. Savin [10] has treated the problem of a reinforced hole by assimilating the reinforcement around the hole to a thicker annular plate; Savin and Fleyshman [11] considered the reinforcement as a circular beam as in the sense of strength of materials. However, neither work discussed the case of the load singularity.

For the problems under consideration, the singular solution is taken as

$$w_s = \frac{P}{8\pi D} r_1^2 \operatorname{Log} \frac{r_1}{\beta r_2} \qquad (3)$$

where the coordinates and symbols shown in Fig. 1 are used. This expression contains the proper singularity for a concentrated force $(P/8\pi D)r_1^2 \log r_1$ and it vanishes at the edge of the hole. The derivatives of w_s also have simple series expansions in θ at $r = a$ and are recorded here for later reference:

$$\left(\frac{\partial w_s}{\partial r}\right)_{r=a} = \frac{Pa}{8\pi D}(1 - \beta^2)$$

$$\left(\frac{\partial^n w_s}{\partial \theta^n}\right)_{r=a} = \left(\frac{\partial^{n+1} w_s}{\partial r \partial \theta^n}\right)_{r=a} = 0 \quad (n=1,2,\ldots) \qquad (4)$$

$$(M_{rs})_{r=a} = \frac{P}{8\pi D}(1 - \beta^2)(1-\nu - 4\sum_{n=0}^{\infty} \beta^n \cos n\theta)$$

$$(V_{rs})_{r=a} = \frac{P}{2\pi a}\{1 - \sum_{n=0}^{\infty}[(1-\beta^2)n+2]\beta^n \cos n\theta\} \qquad (4) \text{ cont'd}$$

Here, M_r is the radial bending moment and V_r the supplemented shearing force. Details of their derivation can be found in [12].

Relations for Circular Beams

Before continuing on with the solution of our problems, we set down some of the basic relations pertaining to the edge-beam. A more detailed discussion can be found in the papers by Federhofer [13] and Amon and Dundurs [14].

We assume that one of the principal axes of the cross-sectional area of the edge beam is perpendicular to the middle surface of the plate and that the transfer of forces between the beam and the plate takes place at the location of the axis of the beam. The beam is loaded by a transverse load per unit length p, distributed moment-load per unit length m, bending moment M, twisting moment T and shearing force Q as shown in Fig. 2. The equations of equilibrium are

$$\frac{dQ}{d\theta} + ap = 0 \qquad (5)$$

$$\frac{dT}{d\theta} - M - am = 0 \qquad (6)$$

$$\frac{dM}{d\theta} + T - aQ = 0 \qquad (7)$$

The relations between the deflection v of the center line, the rotation ϕ of the principal axis and the changes in curvature $\bar{\chi}$ and in twist $\bar{\tau}$ of the beam axis are given by

$$\bar{\chi} = \frac{1}{a}\left(-\frac{1}{a}\frac{d^2v}{d\theta^2} + \phi\right)$$

$$\bar{\tau} = \frac{1}{a}\left(\frac{1}{a}\frac{dv}{d\theta} + \frac{d\phi}{d\theta}\right) \qquad (8)$$

The stress resultants expressed in terms of changes in curvature and twist are given by

$$r_1^2 = r^2 - 2\beta a r \cos\theta + \beta^2 a^2$$

$$r_2^2 = r^2 - 2\frac{a}{\beta} r \cos\theta + \frac{a^2}{\beta^2}$$

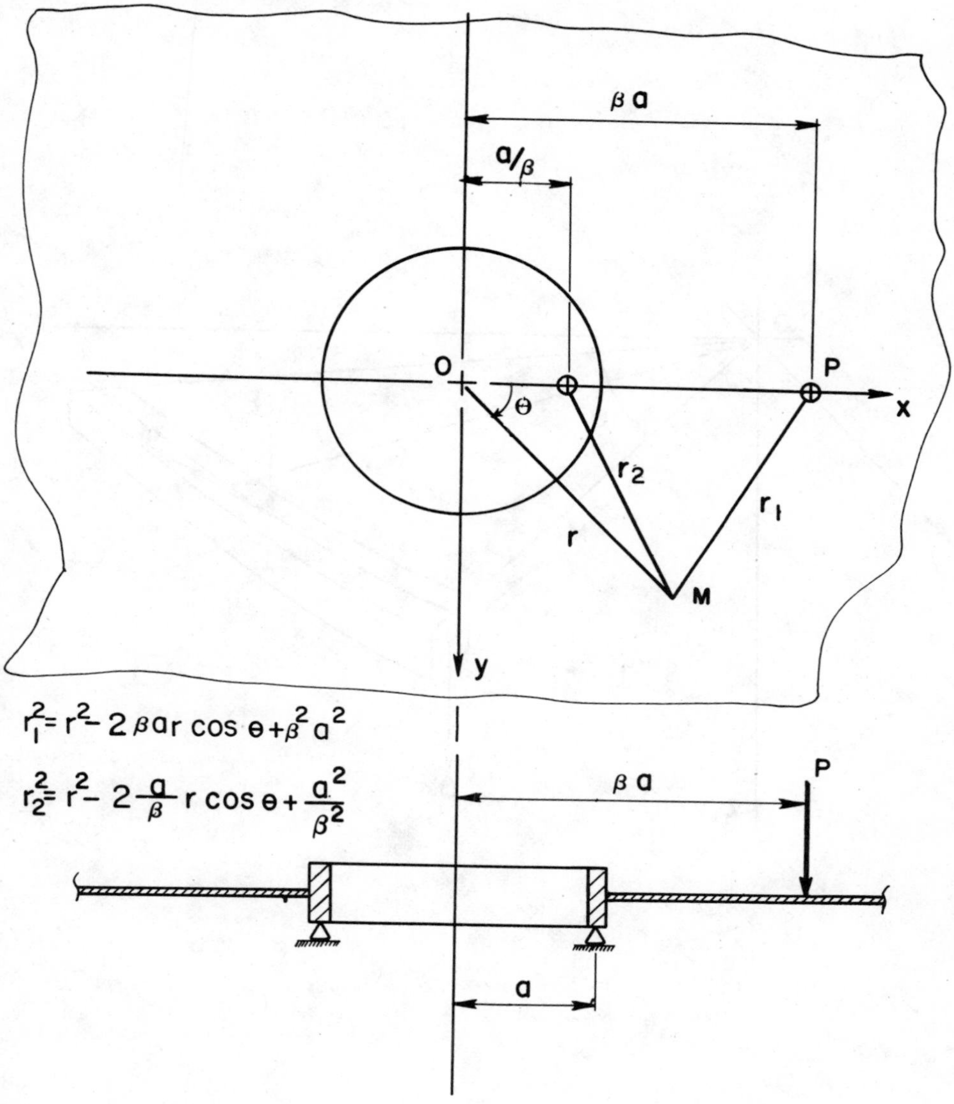

Fig. 1.   Infinite Plate with Reinforced Circular Hole.

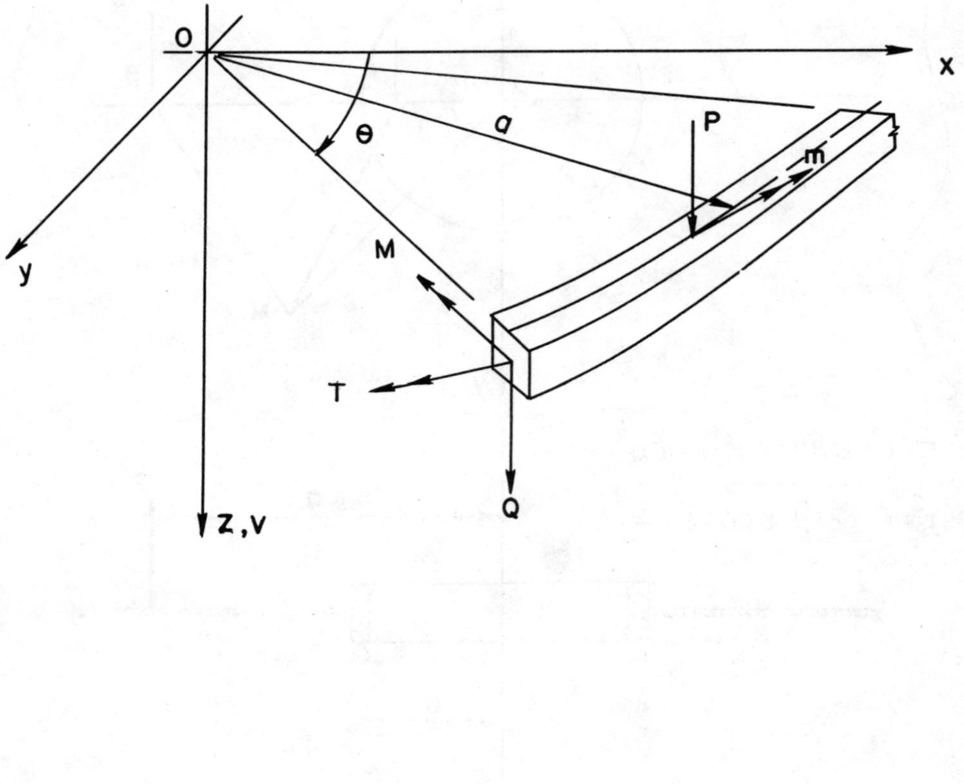

Fig. 2. Stress Resultants for Reinforcing Beam.

$$M = K\bar{\chi}, \qquad T = L\bar{\tau} \tag{9}$$

where K and L are the bending and torsional stiffness, respectively. Substitution of Eq. (8) into Eq. (9) yields

$$\begin{aligned} M &= D\chi \left(-\frac{1}{a}\frac{d^2v}{d\theta^2} + \phi\right) \\ T &= D\lambda \left(\frac{1}{a}\frac{dv}{d\theta} + \frac{d\phi}{d\theta}\right) \end{aligned} \tag{10}$$

where

$$\chi = \frac{K}{aD}, \qquad \lambda = \frac{L}{aD} \tag{11}$$

From Eq. (7) we now obtain

$$Q = \frac{D}{a}\left[\frac{1}{a}\left(\frac{dv}{d\theta}\lambda - \frac{d^3v}{d\theta^3}\chi\right) + \frac{d\phi}{d\theta}(\chi+\lambda)\right] \tag{12}$$

Simply Supported Edge-Beam

For a simply supported edge beam, the conditions at $r = a$ can be written as

$$\begin{aligned} w &= v = 0 \\ \frac{\partial w}{\partial r} &= -\phi \\ M_r &= -m \end{aligned} \tag{13}$$

On substituting Eq. (13) into Eq. (10) and using relation (6), we obtain the following two boundary conditions for the plate at $r = a$:

$$\begin{aligned} &w = 0 \\ &\chi\frac{\partial w}{\partial r} - \lambda\frac{\partial^3 w}{\partial r\partial\theta^2} + \frac{a}{D}M_r = 0 \end{aligned} \tag{14}$$

We assume the deflection of the plate to be given by

$$w = w_s + \frac{Pa^2}{8\pi D}\left[A \log\frac{r}{a} + \left(\frac{r}{a}\right)^2 \sum_{n=0}^{\infty} a_n\left(\frac{\beta r}{a}\right)^{-n}\cos n\theta + \sum_{n=0}^{\infty} b_n\left(\frac{Br}{a}\right)^{-n}\cos n\theta\right] \tag{15}$$

Satisfaction of boundary conditions (14) by (15) yields

$$a_n = -b_n = \frac{-2(1-\beta^2)}{\chi^2+n^2\lambda+2n-1-\nu} \tag{16}$$

The constant A is determined from the condition

$$M_r = 0 \qquad (r \to \infty) \tag{17}$$

This yields

$$A = \beta^2-1-2(\frac{\chi-\nu-1}{\chi+\nu-1}) \log \beta \tag{18}$$

The final form of the solution state is thus given by

$$w = \frac{Pa^2}{8\pi D} \{ \frac{r_1^2}{a^2} \log \frac{r_1}{\beta r_2} + [\beta^2-1-2(\frac{x-\nu-1}{x+\nu-1}) \log \beta]\log \frac{r}{a}$$

$$+ (\frac{r^2}{a^2} - 1)[\log \beta + 2(\beta^2-1) \sum_{n=1}^{\infty} \frac{1}{x+a^2\lambda+2n-1-\nu} (\frac{a}{\beta r})^n \cos n\theta]\} \tag{19}$$

Guided Edge-Beam

For a plate with a guided edge-beam the conditions at the internal boundary $r = a$ are

$$w = v, \frac{\partial w}{\partial r} = 0 \tag{20}$$

$$\phi = 0 \tag{21}$$

$$V_r = \frac{P}{\pi a} (\frac{1}{2} + \beta\cos\theta) + p \tag{22}$$

where the term $\frac{P}{\pi a} (\frac{1}{2} + \beta\cos\theta)$ represents the reaction on the beam. Use of Eq. (20), (21) and (7) yields the following expressions for the stress resultants at the edge,

$$M = -\frac{D}{a} \chi \frac{\partial^2 w}{\partial \theta^2} \tag{23}$$

$$T = \frac{D}{a} \lambda \frac{\partial w}{\partial \theta} \tag{24}$$

$$Q = \frac{D}{a^2} \left(\lambda \frac{\partial w}{\partial \theta} - \chi \frac{\partial^3 w}{\partial \theta^3}\right) \tag{25}$$

On substituting Eq. (25) into (5) and then substituting the resulting expression for p into Eq. (22), we obtain

$$V_r = \frac{P}{a\pi D} \left(\frac{1}{2} + \beta\cos\theta\right) + \frac{D}{a^3} \left(\chi \frac{\partial^4 w}{\partial \theta^4} - \lambda \frac{\partial^2 w}{\partial \theta^2}\right) \tag{26}$$

Equations (20) and (26) represent the boundary conditions for the plate.

The deflection is assumed to have the form

$$w = w_s + \frac{Pa^2}{8\pi D} \Big[A \log \frac{r}{a} + \left(\frac{r}{a}\right)^2 \sum_{n=0}^{\infty} a_n \left(\frac{\beta r}{a}\right)^n \cos n\theta$$

$$+ \sum_{n=1}^{\infty} b_n \left(\frac{a}{\beta r}\right)^n \cos n\theta + a_0 \left(\frac{r}{a}\right)^2 + b_0\Big] \tag{27}$$

Satisfaction of boundary conditions (22) and (28) yields

$$a_0 = -\frac{1}{2} (1-\beta^2+A)$$

$$b_0 = \text{arbitrary}$$

$$b_n = -2\left(\frac{n-2}{n^2}\right) \left[\frac{2-(1-\beta^2)n}{\chi n^2+\lambda+2n-1-\nu}\right] \tag{28}$$

$$a_n = -\left(\frac{n}{n-2}\right) b_n$$

The condition of vanishing radial moment at $r = \infty$ yields

$$A = \beta^2 - 1 - 2 \log\beta \tag{29}$$

The final form of the deflection function is thus

$$w = \frac{Pa^2}{8\pi D}\left\{\frac{r_1^2}{a^2}\log\frac{r_1}{\beta r_2} + (\beta^2-1-2\log\beta)\log\frac{r}{a}\right.$$

$$-2\sum_{n=1}^{\infty}\frac{2-(1-\beta^2)n}{(\chi n^2+2n+\lambda-1-\nu)}\left[n-2-n\left(\frac{r^2}{a^2}\right)\right]\left(\frac{a}{\beta r}\right)^n \cos n\theta$$

$$\left. + \left(\frac{r^2}{a^2}-1\right)\log\beta\right\} \qquad (30)$$

The special case of χ or $\lambda = \infty$ yields

$$w = \frac{Pa^2}{8\pi D}\left\{\frac{r_1^2}{a^2}\log\frac{r_1}{\beta r_2} + (\beta^2-1-2\log\beta)\log\frac{r}{a}\right.$$

$$\left. + \left(\frac{r^2}{a^2}-1\right)\log\beta + b_o\right\} \qquad (31)$$

which represents the deflection of an infinite plate clamped at the inner boundary and undergoing an arbitrary rigid body displacement b_o.

DISCUSSION AND CONCLUSION

To illustrate the results obtained in the above analysis, we show in Figs. 3 and 4 the deflection along the load-carrying diameter for the plate loaded at $\beta = 1.5$ and 2.0, respectively. The flexural and torsional stiffnesses of the beam have been assumed to be equal.

For some special values of χ and λ, previously known results can be recovered. For example, if we set $\chi = \lambda = 0$ in the result for the simply supported case we obtain

$$w = \frac{Pa^2}{8\pi D}\left\{\frac{r_1^2}{a^2}\log\frac{r_1}{\beta r_2} + \left[\beta^2 - 1 + 2\left(\frac{1+\nu}{1-\nu}\right)\log\beta\right]\log\frac{r}{a}\right.$$

$$+ \left(\frac{r^2}{a^2}-1\right)\left[2(\beta^2-1)\sum_{n=1}^{\infty}\frac{1}{2n-1-\nu}\left(\frac{a}{\beta r}\right)^n\cos n\theta\right.$$

$$\left. + \left(\frac{r^2}{a^2}-1\right)\log\beta\right\} \qquad (32)$$

This expression agrees with that obtained by Bassali [8] and Dundurs and Lee [9] for an infinite plate with a circular hole and simply supported at the edge of the hole.

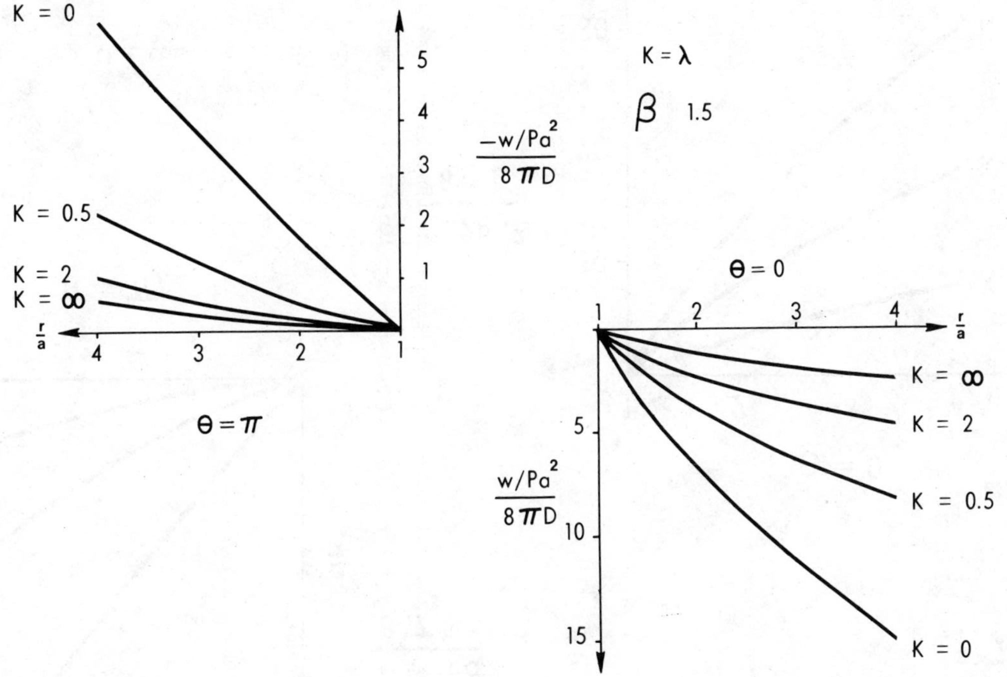

Fig. 3. Deflection Along the Load Carrying Diameter.

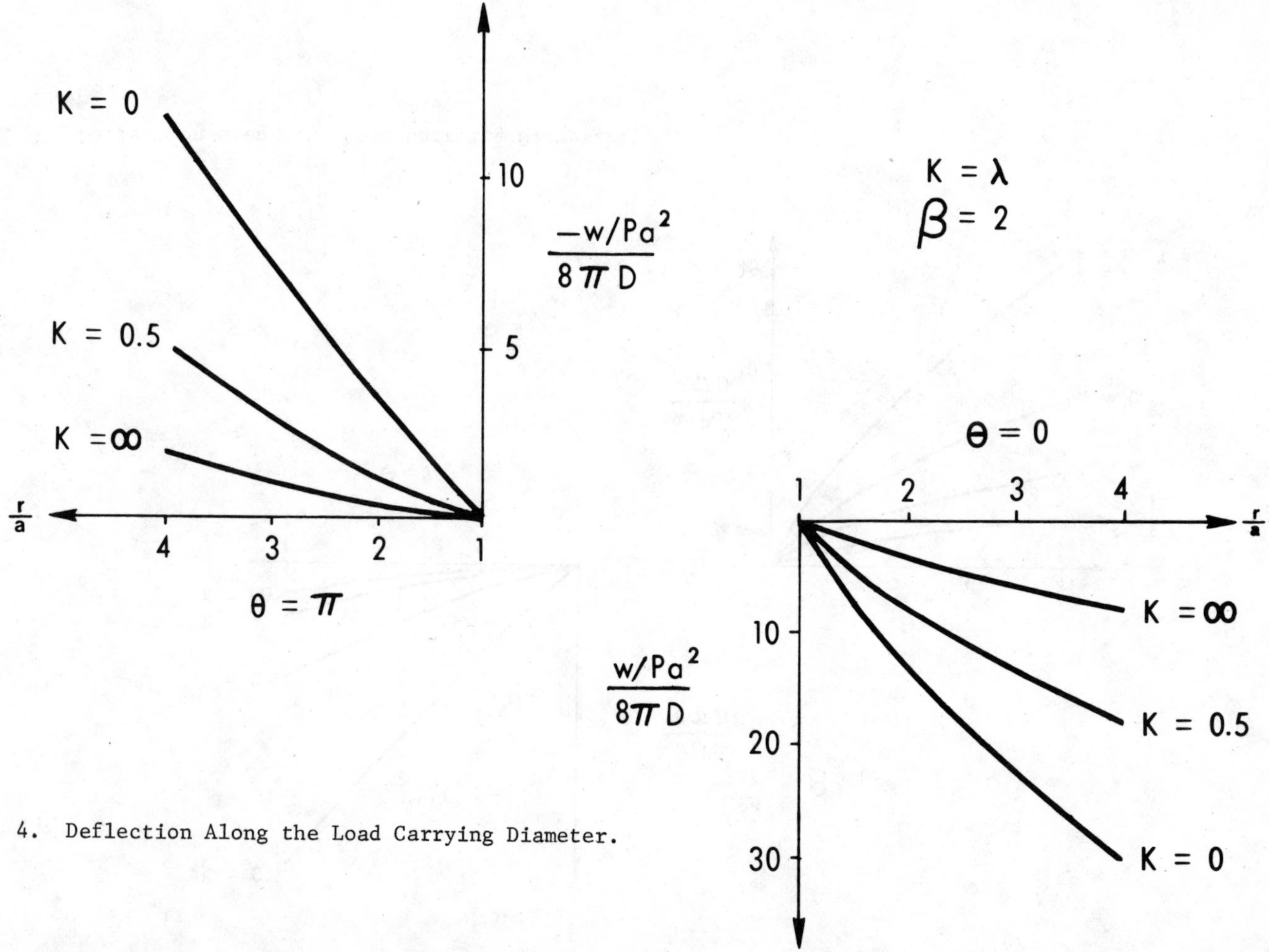

Fig. 4. Deflection Along the Load Carrying Diameter.

Setting $\chi = \infty$ in Eq. (19) we obtain

$$w = \frac{Pa^2}{8\pi D} \{ \frac{r_1^2}{a^2} \log \frac{r_1}{\beta r_2} + (\beta^2 - 1 - 2\log\beta) \log \frac{r}{a} + (\frac{r^2}{a^2} - 1) \log \beta \}. \quad (33)$$

which is identical to the result obtained by Symonds [7] for the infinite plate clamped at the internal boundary.

The results obtained in this paper can be applied to large plates with reinforced circular holes in the neighborhood of the hole. Although the loading was in terms of a concentrated force, the results for other types of loading can readily be obtained by a proper integration of the concentrated force solution.

REFERENCES

1. Timoshenko, S. and Woinowsky-Krieger, S., Theory of Plates and Shells, Second Edition, McGraw-Hill Book Co., Inc., New York, 1959.

2. Clebsch, A., Theorie der Elastizitaet fester Koerper, Leipzig, Germany, 1862.

3. Foeppl, A., "Die Biegung einer kreis-foermigen Platte," Sitzungsberichte der mathematisch-physikalischen Klasse der K. B. Akademie zu Muenchen, 1912, pp. 155-190.

4. Mitchell, J. H., "The Flexure of a Circular Plate," Proceedings of the London Mathematical Society, Vol. 34, 1902, pp. 223-228.

5. Reissner, E., "Ueber die Biegung der Kreisplatte mit exzentrischer Einzellast," Mathematische Annalen, Vol. 111, 1935, pp. 777-780.

6. Washizu, K., "On the Bending of Isotropic Plates," Transactions of the Japan Society of Mechanical Engineers, Vol. 18, 1952, pp. 41-47.

7. Symonds, P. S., "Concentrated-Force Problems in Plane Strain, Plane Stress and Transverse Bending of Plates," Journal of Applied Mechanics, Vol. 13, Transactions American Society of Mechanical Engineers, Vol. 68, 1946, pp. 183-197.

8. Bassali, W. A., "Transverse Bending of Infinite and Semi-Infinite Thin Elastic Plates, I, "Proceedings of the Cambridge Philosophical Society, Vol. 53, 1957, pp. 248-255.

9. Dundurs, J., and Lee, T. M., "Flexure of an Infinite Plate on a Circular Support," Journal of Applied Mechanics, Vol. 30, 1963, pp. 225-231.

10. Savin, G. N., Stress Concentration around Holes, Pergamon Press, London, 1961.

11. Savin, G. N. and Fleyshman, N. P., Plates and Shells with Stiffened Edges, Kiev, 1964.

12. Amon, R., "Bending by a Concentrated Force of a Circular Plate with a Reinforced Edge," Ph.D. Thesis, Northwestern University, Evanston, 1966.

13. Federhofer, K., "Berechnung des senkrecht zu seiner Ebene belasteten Bogentraegers," Zeitschrift fuer Mathematik und Physik, Vol. 62, 1913, pp. 40-63.

14. Amon, R. and Dundurs, J., "Circular Plate with Supported Edge-Beam," Journal of the Engineering Mechanics Division, Proceedings of the American Society of Civil Engineers, Vol. 94, No. EM3, 1968, pp. 731-742.

ON THE CONTACT OF AXISYMMETRIC PLATES OF VARIABLE THICKNESS

M. B. McGrath
University of Colorado

F. Essenburg
University of Colorado

ABSTRACT

Both the problem of an axisymmetric circular plate of variable thickness partially contacting a rigid smooth surface and the problem of two axisymmetric circular plates partially in contact are considered. The analysis is carried out within the framework of a plate theory which includes both the effects of transverse shear deformation and thickness variation. A general method of solution of both classes of problems considered is given and both the practical and conceptual advantages of the treatment of the present paper over the treatment of such problems within the framework of classical plate theory are discussed.

Specific examples illustrate the application of the method of the paper. Numerical results of these examples point out the significance of the relaxation of the Kirchoff hypothesis in (1) giving a physically consistent expression for the surface load in the region of contact, (2) improving the estimate for the size of the region of contact, and (3) removing the physically inconsistent requirement of the classical treatment of the transmission of a line load at periphery of the region of contact.

INTRODUCTION

The present paper is concerned with problems of isotropic elastic axisymmetric circular plates of variable thickness -- portions of which are in contact with smooth, rigid surfaces of revolution, as well as problems involving two such plates in contact with each other. Apparently problems of these types have not been previously discussed in the literature. The treatment of corresponding problems involving plates of uniform thickness within the framework of classical plate theory [1] invokes certain conceptual difficulties in that the classical theory treatment is incapable of providing a physically consistent expression for the surface traction transmitted by the constraining surface to the plate (or transmitted between the plates in the case of the contact of two plates). In addition, the classical theory treatment also requires the assumption of the transmission of a line load at the periphery of the region of contact, and does not provide an adequate estimate for the size of the region of contact. It has been demonstrated [2,3] that these difficulties can be overcome by the use of a plate theory which relaxes the Kirchhoff hypothesis in the manner of the Reissner plate theory [4]. It is the purpose of the present paper to point out the occurrence of these same difficulties in the types of problems considered here and to provide a method of treating such problems which eliminates these conceptual difficulties.

The extension of the application of Reissner plate theory to problems of plates of non-uniform thickness was considered in [5] where it was concluded that, from a practical point of view at least, an adequate theory is obtained through the use of the basic equations of the Reissner theory for uniform plates with the effect of thickness variation accounted for by regarding the thickness as a function of the middle surface coordinates in the subsequent differentiation of these basic equations and by neglecting the effect of transverse normal stress. For purposes of the present investigation, it is significant that such a treatment adequately relaxes the Kirchhoff hypothesis and accounts for the effect of transverse shear deformation, as well as thickness variation.

In problems involving an axisymmetric plate of non-uniform thickness, a portion of which is in contact with a smooth, rigid surface of revolution, throughout a contact region the middle surface deflection is a prescribed function which depends upon both the plate thickness as a function of the radial coordinate and the geometry of the constraining surface. Under the assumptions of the classical non-uniform plate theory, all other parameters of the problem, including the surface traction transmitted by the constraining surface to the plate, are expressed in terms of the derivatives of the middle surface deflection and the thickness function together with its derivatives. The integration constants for the non-contact regions (or region) as well as the boundaries (or boundary) separating the contact and non-contact regions are determined from the boundary conditions at the edges (or edge) of the plate, as well as the continuity conditions on the deflection, its derivative, and the radial bending moment. The shear stress resultant is regarded as discontinuous at such boundaries and this discontinuity is accounted for by the assumption that the constraining surface transmits a line load to the plate at the boundaries of the contact region. The use of a shear deformation theory, however, provides a differential equation for the parameters of the problem in the contact region and thus provides for the expression at these parameters in terms of two integration constants. These constants, together with the integration constants for the non-contact regions, are determined from the edge boundary conditions, together with the continuity of all parameters of the problem (including the transverse shear stress resultant) at the boundaries of the contact regions. In this manner a physically consistent expression for the transmitted surface traction throughout the contact region is obtained and there is no prediction of the transmission of a line load at the peripheries of the contact regions.

In problems involving the contact of two non-uniform axisymmetric plates, in a contact region the difference in the deflections of the two plates depends upon the sum of the thickness functions for the two plates and the surface tractions transmitted between the two plates are equal in magnitude and opposite in direction. Under the assumptions of classical non-uniform plate theory, it is then found that all of the parameters governing the two plates are determined from the solution of a fourth order differential equation and, hence, involve four constants of integration. In a non-contact region the solution for each plate involves four constants of integration. The integration constants, together with the unknown radii of the boundaries of the regions of contact, are determined from the edge boundary conditions on the two plates together with continuity conditions on the plate deflections, their derivatives, and the radial bending moments at the boundaries of the regions of contact. The shear stress resultant is regarded as discontinuous at such boundaries and this discontinuity is accounted for by assuming that a line load is transmitted between the plates at such boundaries. We find that the use of shear deformation theory provides a sixth order differential equation governing the parameters of the problem in a contact region and thus expresses these parameters in terms of six integration constants. In this manner continuity in all parameters, including the shear stress resultant, is permitted at the boundaries of the contact regions and the transmission of a line load between the plates at these boundaries is not predicted. The shear deformation also provides a physically consistent expression for the transmitted surface tractions in many cases where the classical theory prediction fails to do so. In some specific problems the shear deformation theory will predict an annular or circular region of contact where the classical theory predicts a circular line of contact.

It should be noted that in problems of both of the types considered here the method of solution consists of finding appropriate solutions to the basic equations in the contact and non-contact regions. The integration constants and the radii of the boundaries of the contact regions are then determined from the simultaneous solutions of the equations resulting from the boundary and continuity conditions. The unknown radii are governed by a system of equations which are usually (depending upon the prescribed form of the thickness variation) highly transcendental in character. Even in simple problems where the number of contact and non-contact regions is minimal such a process is extremely tedious; and in problems where the number of such regions is in any way substantial, the process is almost hopeless except for the computational facility provided by a modern, high-speed computer. It is highly probable that this is the reason for the previous lack of attention to problems of these types in the classical plate theory literature.

The Basic Equations

Under the assumptions of axial symmetry and in terms of a dimensionless radius $\rho = r/a$, where r is the radial coordinate and a is a characteristic radius, the basic equations of the Reissner Plate Theory [4] are[1]:

$$M_r' + \frac{M_r - M_\theta}{\rho} = aV$$

$$(\rho V)' = a\rho(q^+ - q^-)$$

$$M_r = \frac{D_o h^3}{a}(\beta' + \nu\beta/\rho) \qquad (1)$$

$$M_\theta = \frac{D_o h^3}{a}(\beta/\rho + \nu\beta')$$

$$\beta + w'/a = \frac{1}{\mu^2 D_o h} V ,$$

where

$$D_o = E/12(1 - \nu^2), \qquad \mu^2 = 5(1 - \nu).$$

In these equations prime denotes differentiation with respect to ρ; M_r and M_θ are respectively the radial and circumferential bending moments; V is the shear stress resultant; β is the average radial rotation; w is the middle surface deflection; $h = h(\rho)$ is the thickness of the plate; and q^+ and q^- are respectively the normal surface tractions at the surfaces $z = + h/2$ and $z = - h/2$. Young's modulus, denoted by E, and Poisson's ratio, denoted by ν, will be regarded as constants and the coordinate system is chosen so that the deflection is positive when measured downward. The natural edge boundary conditions consistent with the foregoing set of equations are (i) either M_r specified or β specified and (ii) either V specified or w specified.

It follows from the first, third, and fourth of Eqs. (1) that

$$L(\beta) = \frac{a^2 V}{D_o h^3} , \qquad (2)$$

where

1. In the equations recorded here, the effect of transverse normal stress has not been included.

$$L(\ ) = (\ )'' + (3\rho\frac{h'}{h} + 1)\frac{(\ )'}{\rho} + (3\rho\nu\frac{h'}{h} - 1)\frac{(\ )}{\rho^2} ,$$

and from the last that

$$M(\beta) = \mu^2 \frac{a}{h^2} w' , \quad (3)$$

where

$$M(\ ) = L(\ ) - \mu^2 \frac{a^2}{h^2} (\ )$$

The equations appropriate to the classical plate theory may be deduced from the above by letting $\mu^2 \to \infty$. The first four of Eqs. (1) and Eq. (2) are unaltered while the last of Eqs. (1) and Eq. (3) both become

$$\beta = - w'/a \quad (4)$$

The boundary conditions are modified by the specification of w' rather than β.

For a region of a plate which is not contacting either a smooth rigid surface or another plate the method of solution is perfectly straightforward. Since, in such a region the surface tractions are prescribed, an expression for V is obtained from an integration of the second of Eqs. (1). An expression for β is then obtained from the solution of Eqs. (2), and the deflection, w, is given by the solution of the last of Eqs. (1). The solution under the assumptions of the classical theory is identical except that the expression for w is given by the solution of Eq. (4). It will be noted that both the shear deformation theory solution and the classical theory solutions involve four integration constants.

Although the character of both Eqs. (2) and (3) is heavily dependent upon the form of the thickness h as a function of the radial coordinate some observations with regard to their solutions can be made. If the quantities $(3\rho\frac{h'}{h} + 1)$, $(3\rho\nu\frac{h'}{h} - 1)$ and $(3\rho\nu\frac{h'}{h} - 1 - \rho^2\mu^2 \frac{a^2}{h^2})$ have convergent power series for some radius of convergence, then Eqs. (2) and (3) have a regular singular point at $\rho = 0$. In this case, by a well known theorem [6], two series solutions for each equation will exist and will be uniformly convergent within the region of convergence. It also follows that if $1/h^2$ and h'/h remain finite as $\rho \to 0$ one of the solutions of both Eqs. (2) and (3) will contain a logarithmic term. The requirement that $1/h^2$ and h'/h remain finite as $\rho \to 0$ is a sufficient condition (but not a necessary condition) for the existence and convergence of solutions of these equations.

Contact with Smooth Rigid Surface

Throughout a circular or annular region in which a non-uniform axisymmetric plate contacts a smooth rigid surface, the surface traction transmitted by the constraining surface to the plate is an unknown of the problem, whereas the middle surface deflection is a prescribed function which depends upon both the plate thickness and constraining surface geometry as prescribed functions of the radial coordinate. With the middle surface deflection w prescribed, an expression for β is given by the solution of Eq. (3). Expressions for M_r and M_θ are then given by the third and fourth of Eqs. (1), and V and the unknown transmitted surface traction are given by the first two of Eqs. (1). It will be noted that the solution thus obtained involves two integration constants.

If there are N such regions of contact and M annular (or circular) regions of non-contact, the problem obviously involves 2N + 4M integration constants. In addition, there will be N + M - 1 circular boundaries separating the N regions of contact from the M regions of non-contact. The radii of these boundaries, together with the integration constants, constitute 3N + 5M - 1 unknown constants.

We now have three possible cases. If N = M, the unknown constants are 8N - 1 in number and one plate boundary will be in a region of non-contact with two boundary conditions and the other plate boundary will be in a region of contact with the condition either M_r specified or β specified (since w is prescribed at that boundary). Obviously, if the origin is included, the appropriate set of boundary conditions or boundary condition will be replaced with a condition that the parameters of the problem remain bounded at the origin. In addition, at each of the N + M - 1 boundaries separating the regions of contact and non-contact continuity requirements are imposed on M_r, V, β, and w. Thus, we have a total of three boundary (or boundedness) conditions and 4(N + M - 1) continuity requirements, a total of 4(N + M) - 1 = 8N - 1 conditions.

Now consider the case where M = N + 1. The number of unknown constants is then 8N + 4. Since both plate boundaries are in regions of non-contact, there will be a total of four boundary conditions (or two boundary conditions and two boundedness conditions), which, together with the 4(N + M - 1) continuity requirements, gives a total of 4(N + M) = 8N + 4 conditions.

The remaining possible case is M = N - 1. In this case, there will be 8N -6 unknown constants. Since both plate boundaries must be in contact regions, there will be a total of two boundary conditions (or one boundary condition and one boundedness condition) which, together with the 4(N + M - 1) continuity conditions, gives a total of 4(N + M) - 2 = 8N - 6 conditions. Thus, in all possible cases, the number of conditions equals the number of unknown constants and the solution of the problem will satisfy the boundary conditions and admit the continuity of M_r, V, β, and w at the boundaries between the regions of contact and non-contact.

Now let us consider the treatment of problems of this type under the assumptions appropriate to the classical plate theory. Since, in a contact region, w is a prescribed function, the other parameters, including the surface traction transmitted to the plate by the constraining surface, are given by Eq. (4) and the first four of Eqs. (1). The expressions for these parameters do not involve any integration constants. The solution for each non-contact region will involve four integration constants. The radii of the circular lines bounding the contact regions are also unknowns of the problem. An analysis of the type given above for the shear deformation theory treatment shows that these integration constants and unknown radii are determined from the appropriate edge boundary conditions (or boundedness conditions at the origin) and three continuity conditions at each boundary separating the contact and non-contact regions. It would appear that, following the method of the classical treatment of similar problems involving uniform plates, M_r, w', and w should be regarded as continous and that the discontinuity in

V is accounted for by assuming the transmission of a line load by the constraining surface at such circular boundaries. This discontinuity in V may also be established by deducing the classical theory solution from the shear deformation theory solution by letting $\mu^2 \to \infty$.

It should be noted that in a specific problem the number of contact and non-contact regions is determined by the surface and edge loading, as well as the plate and constraining surface geometries. If the intensity of the loading is regarded as increasing monotonically, a contact region will be initiated as either a point contact at the origin or a line contact on a circular line. Usually, with further increase in loading intensity, the point contact will propagate to a circular contact region and the circular line of contact will propagate to annular contact region. The validity of any assumption with regard to the existence of a contact region is established by verification that the value of the transmitted surface traction is positive (in the sign convention used here). It is possible, as in the classical treatment of the example of the next section, that a line (or point) of contact does not propagate to a region with an increase of loading intensity. In such cases, the radius of the circular line of contact changes with a change in loading intensity.

An Example

We now consider the specific example of a circular non-uniform plate with the thickness given by

$$h = h_o y(\rho)$$

$$y(\rho) = \sqrt{1 - k\rho^2} \tag{5}$$

where h_o and k are positive constants, clamped at its edge, and loaded at its top surface through a plane smooth rigid surface as shown in Fig. 1. We then have $q^+ = 0$ everywhere and the appropriate boundary conditions are

$$w(1) = \beta(1) = 0 \tag{6}$$

The contact region will be circular of outer radius $\rho = m$.

For the region $0 < \rho \leq m$ we have

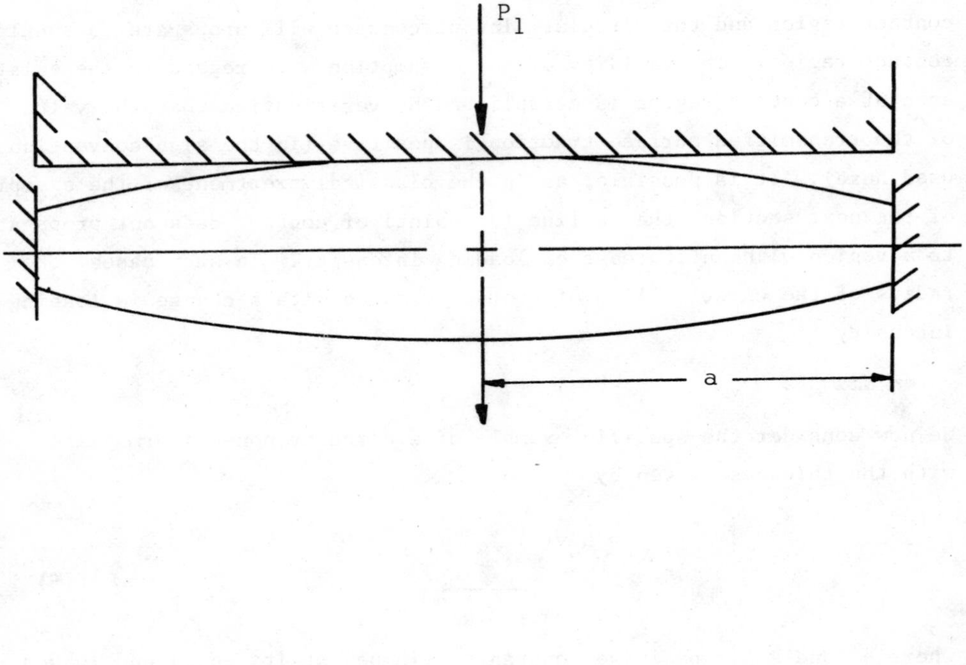

Fig. 1. Non-uniform Plate Contacting Rigid Surface.

$$w = \frac{h - h_o}{2} + \delta \tag{7}$$

where δ is the displacement of the constraining surface from the configuration at which it just touches the plate. It then follows from Eq. (3) that

$$\beta = A\rho\beta_{11} + \beta_{1\rho} \tag{8}$$

where

$$\beta_{11} = F(a_1, b_1, 2, k\rho^2)$$

$$a_1 = \frac{1}{4}(5 + i\sqrt{4\lambda^2 - 9})$$

$$b_1 = \frac{1}{4}(5 - i\sqrt{4\lambda^2 - 9})$$

$$\lambda^2 = (3\nu - 1) + \frac{1}{k}\left(\frac{\mu a}{h}\right)^2$$

$$\beta_{1\rho} = -\frac{\mu^2 ak}{2h_o} \sum_{n=o}^{\infty} c_n \rho^{n+3}$$

$$c_n = \frac{e_n + k(n^2 + 5n + 4 + \lambda^2)c_{n-2}}{(n^2 + 6n + 8)}$$

$$e_n = k\,\frac{n - 1}{n}\; e_{n-2}$$

$$c_o = \frac{1}{8} \qquad e_o = 1$$

$$c = c_3 = \ldots = 0$$

The function $F(a,b,c,x)$ is the hypergeometric function and a second solution of the homogeneous part of Eq. (3) is inadmissible since it is unbounded at the origin. It then follows from Eqs. (1) that

$$V = \mu^2 D_o\{\, h_o y(A\rho\beta_{11} + \beta_{1\rho}) - \frac{h_o^2 k\rho}{2a}\,\}$$

$$M_r = \frac{D_o h^3}{a} y^3 \{ A[(1+\nu)\beta_{11} + \rho\beta_{11}'] + \beta_{1\rho}' + \frac{\beta_{1\rho}}{\rho} \tag{9}$$

$$q^- = \frac{\mu^2 D_o h_o}{a} \{ \frac{h_o^2 k}{a} - A[y\rho\beta_{11}' + \beta_{11}(2y - \frac{k\rho}{y})]$$

$$- y\beta_{1\rho}' - \beta_{1\rho}(y + \frac{k\rho}{y})\}$$

In the region $m < \rho \leq 1$, $q^- = 0$ and

$$V = -\frac{P_1}{2\pi a\rho} \tag{10}$$

where the integration constant P_1 is the total load transmitted by the constraining surface. It then follows from Eq. (2) that

$$\beta = \frac{a P_1}{2\pi D_o h_o^3} [B_1\beta_{21} + B_2\beta_{22} + \beta_{2\rho}] \tag{11}$$

where

$$\beta_{21} = \rho F(a_2, b_2, 2, k\rho^2)$$

$$a_2 = \frac{1}{4}(5 + \sqrt{9 - 4(3\nu - 1)})$$

$$b_2 = \frac{1}{4}(5 - \sqrt{9 - 4(3\nu - 1)})$$

$$\beta_{22} = \beta_{21} \log k\rho^2 + \frac{1}{(1 - a_2)(1 - b_2)k\rho}$$

$$+ \rho \sum_{n=1}^{\infty} \frac{(a_2)_n (b_2)_n}{(2)_n n!} (k\rho^2)^n \{ N(a_2,n) + N(b_2,n)$$

$$- N(2,n) - N(1,n)\}$$

$$N(a_2,n) = \frac{1}{a_2} + \frac{1}{a_2 + 1} + \ldots + \frac{1}{a_2 + n - 1}$$

$$\beta_{2\rho} = \sum_{n=0} d_n \rho^{n+1}$$

$$d_n = \frac{e_n + k(n^2 + 5n + 3 + 3\nu)d_{n-2}}{n^2 + 6n + 8}$$

$$d_o = \frac{1}{8}$$

$$d_1 = d_3 = \ldots = 0$$

It then follows from Eqs. (1) that

$$\frac{w}{a} = -\frac{a P_1}{2\pi D_o h_o^3}\{\int[\beta(n) + (\frac{h_a}{\mu a})^2 \frac{1}{ny(n)}]d\eta + B_3\}$$

$$M_r = -\frac{P_1}{2\pi}\{B_1(\beta_{21}' + \nu\frac{\beta_{21}}{\rho}) + B_2(\beta_{22}' + \nu\frac{\beta_{22}}{\rho}) + \beta_{2\rho}' + \frac{\nu\beta_{2\rho}}{\rho}\} \quad (12)$$

The integration constants A, P_1, B_1, B_2, B_3 and the radius m are determined from the boundary conditions given in Eq. (6) and the continuity of w, β, M_r and V at $\rho = m$. The transcendental equation relating P_1 and m is

$$\frac{aP_1}{2\pi D_o h_o^3} = \{[-\beta_{1\rho}(m) + \frac{h_o k}{2a}\frac{m}{y(m)}][\Delta_1 + \beta_{21}'(m)\beta_{22}(1)$$

$$-\beta_{22}'(m)\beta_{21}(1)] + \beta_{13}'(m)\Delta_1 + (\beta_{21}'(m)\beta_{22}(1)$$

$$-\beta_{21}(1)\beta_{22}'(m))\beta_{1\rho}(m)\} = \{\frac{1}{\mu^2 my(m)}[\Delta_1$$

$$+\beta_{21}'(m)\beta_{22}(1) - \beta_{22}'(m)\beta_{21}(1)]$$

$$+\beta_{21}'(m)\ (\beta_{22}(1)\beta_{23}(m) - \beta_{22}(m)\beta_{23}(1))$$

$$+\beta_{22}'(m)\ (\beta_{21}(m)\beta_{2\rho}(1) - \beta_{21}(1)\beta_{2\rho}(m))$$

$$+\Delta_1 \beta_{2\rho}{}'(m)\}^{-1} \tag{13}$$

where $\Delta_1 = \beta_{21}(1)\beta_{22}(m) - \beta_{21}(m)\beta_{22}(1)$

The other constants are significant only with respect to a numerical example and the involved analytical expressions for them will not be given.

The classical theory solution for this example is also of interest. For the region $m < \rho \leq 1$ it is given by letting $\mu^2 \to \infty$ in Eqs. (10), (11) and (12). For the region $0 < \rho \leq m$ and $\nu \geq \frac{1}{3}$ we have

$$\begin{aligned} w'/a &= -\frac{h_o k}{2a} \frac{\rho}{y} \\ M_r &= \frac{D_o h_o^4 k}{2a^2} (1 + \nu - \nu k \rho^2) \\ V &= \frac{D_o h_o^4}{2a^3} k^2 (1 - 3\nu)\rho \\ q^- &= \frac{D_o h_o^4}{a^4} k^2 (3\nu - 1) \end{aligned} \tag{14}$$

It will be observed that if $\nu < \frac{1}{3}$ the last of Eqs. (13) gives a negative value for q^-. Acordingly, if $\nu < \frac{1}{3}$ we have

$$\begin{aligned} q^- &= 0 \\ V &= 0 \end{aligned} \tag{15}$$

Equation (2) is then homogeneous and

$$\begin{aligned} \frac{w'}{a} &= -\frac{h_o k}{2a} \beta_{21}(\rho) \\ M_r &= -\frac{D_o h_o^4}{2a^4} y^3 \left(\beta_{21}{}' + \frac{\nu}{\rho} \beta_{21}\right) \end{aligned} \tag{16}$$

The transcendental equation relating P_o and m is independent of ν and is

$$\frac{aP_1}{2\pi D_o h_o^3} = \{ \frac{h_o k}{2a} \frac{m}{y(m)} [\Delta_1 \frac{1}{my^2(m)} + \beta_{21}'(m)\beta_{22}(1)$$

$$- \beta_{22}'(m)\beta_{21}(1)]\} \times \{\beta_{21}'(m)(\beta_{22}(1)\beta_{2\rho}(m)$$

$$- \beta_{22}(m)\beta_{2\rho}(1)) + \beta_{22}'(m)(\beta_{21}(m)\beta_{2\rho}(1)$$

$$- \beta_{21}(1)\beta_{23}(m)) + \Delta_1\beta_{2\rho}'(m)\}^{-1} \quad (17)$$

It should be emphasized that if $\nu < \frac{1}{3}$ the solution of Eqs. (17) gives the radius of the circle of contact while if $\nu \geq \frac{1}{3}$ it gives the radius of the region. If $m \to 0$ Eq. (17) gives a finite positive value for P_1, say, P_1*. Thus the classical theory predicts the propagation of a contact region if $\nu \geq \frac{1}{3}$ or a circle of contact if $\nu < \frac{1}{3}$ only if P_1 is greater than P_1*. For $P_1 \leq P_1*$ a point of contact is predicted.

For $\nu = \frac{1}{3}$, $\frac{2a}{h_o} = 10$, $k = 0.8$ the solutions of Eqs. (13) and (17) are shown in Fig. 2. The substantial discrepancy between the classical theory and shear deformation theory predictions for the value of m for any given value of P_1 will be observed. For m = 0.3 the bending moments and shear resultants are shown in Fig. 3 and Fig. 4, respectively. Again a substantial discrepancy in the predictions of the two theories is observed. For this case the classical theory predicts a zero value for the shear resultant in the contact region and a line load of intensity $P_1/2\pi am$ at the edge of that region. The shear deformation theory prediction for the transmitted surface traction for m = 0.3 is shown in Fig. 5. Obviously, apart from the line load, the classical theory predicts no surface traction for this case.

Two Plates in Contact

Now let us consider two axisymmetric circular plates, circular or annular portions of which are in contact under the assumption that in the contact regions only normal tractions are transmitted between the

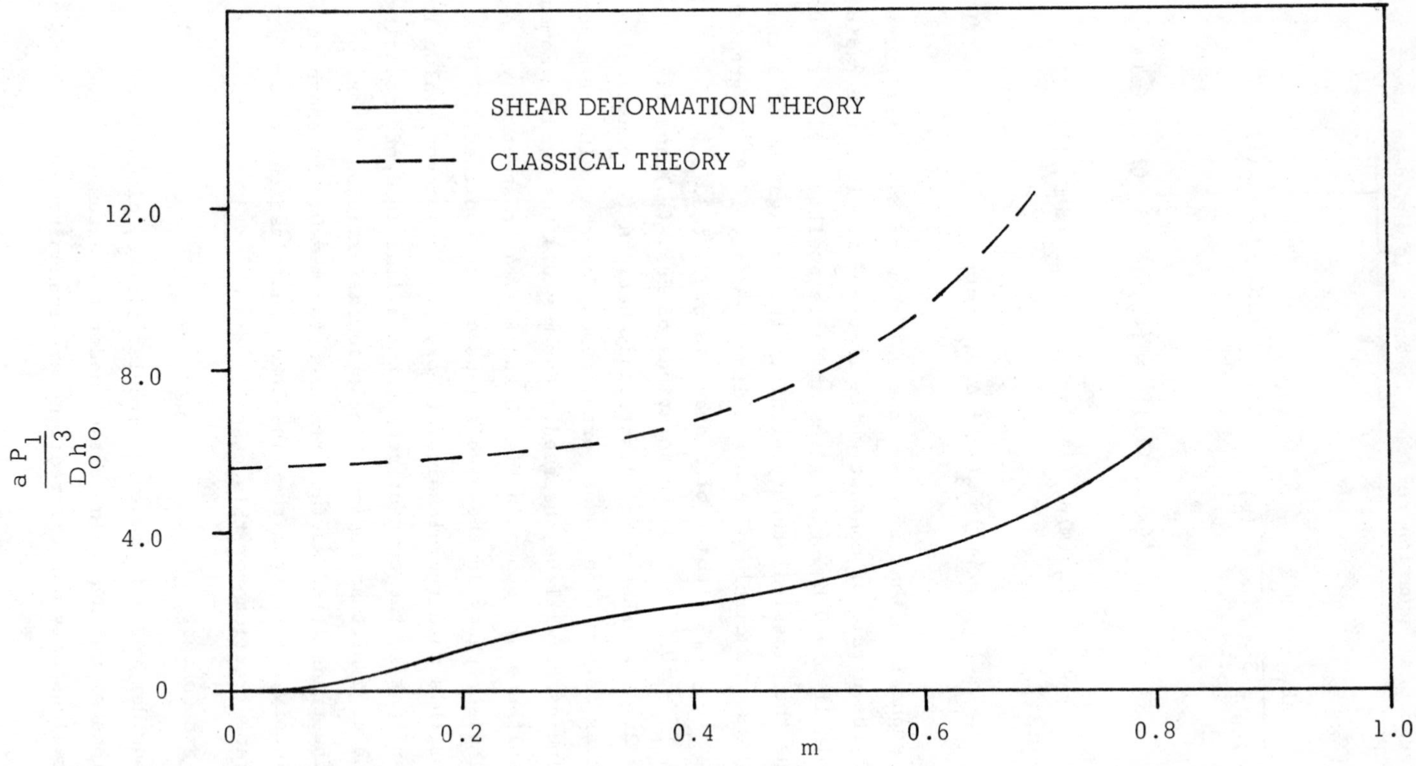

Fig. 2. Variation of Dimensionless Radius of Contact Region, m, with Applied Load, P_1, for Example of Non-uniform Plate Contacting Rigid Surface.

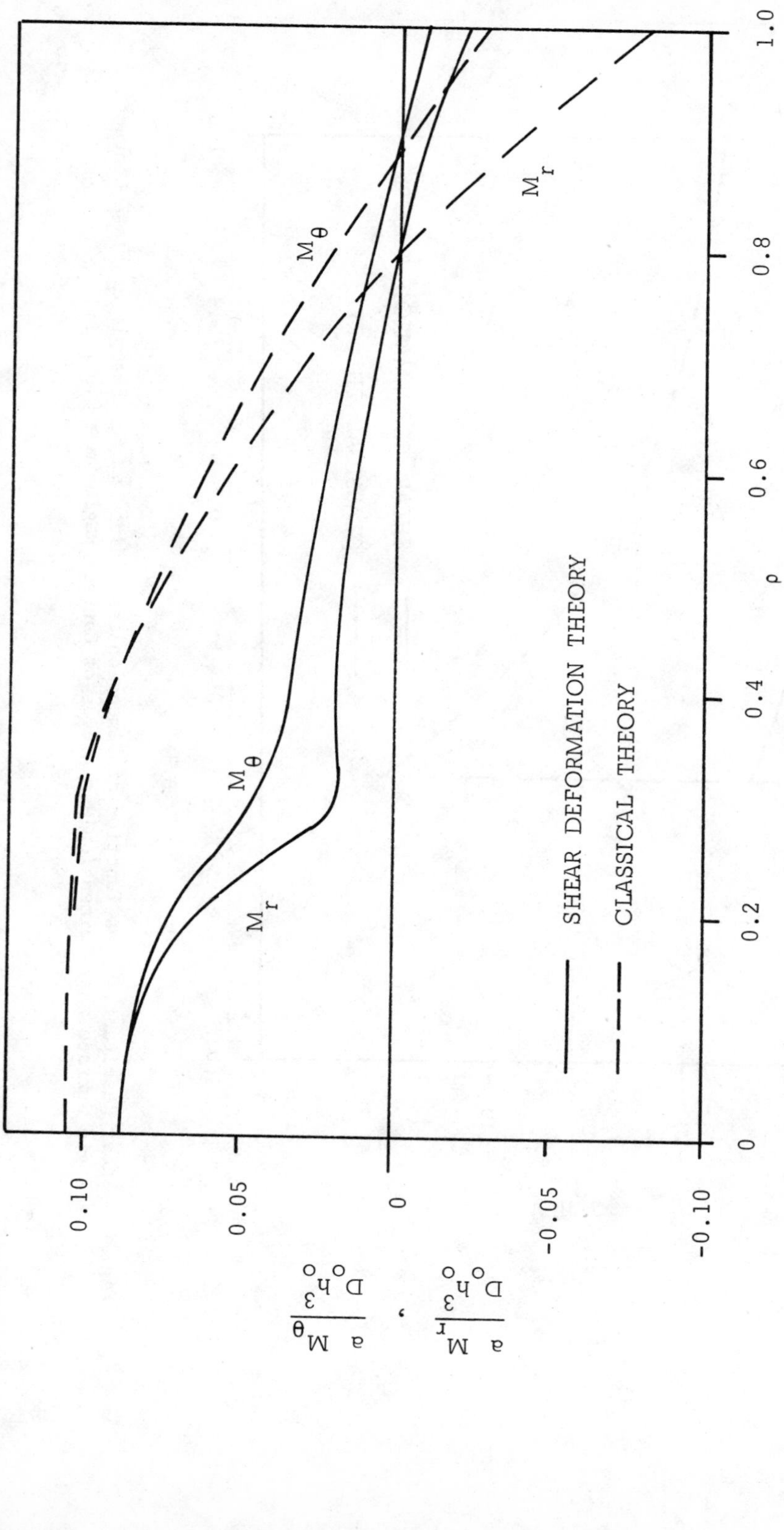

Fig. 3. Bending Moments, M_r and M_θ, as Functions of Dimensionless Radius of Contact Region m = 0.3.

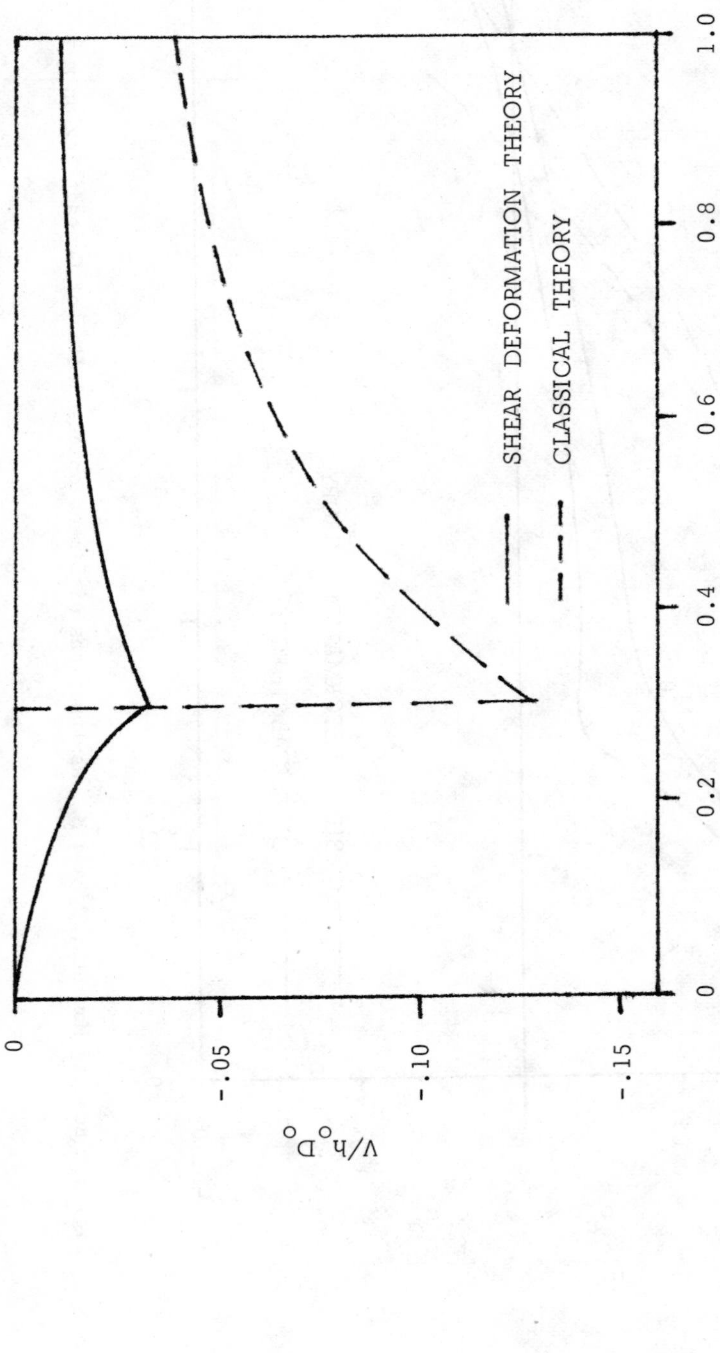

Fig. 4. Shear Resultant, V, as Function of Dimensionless Radius, ρ, for Example of Plate Contacting Rigid Surface where Dimensionless Radius of Contact Region m = 0.3.

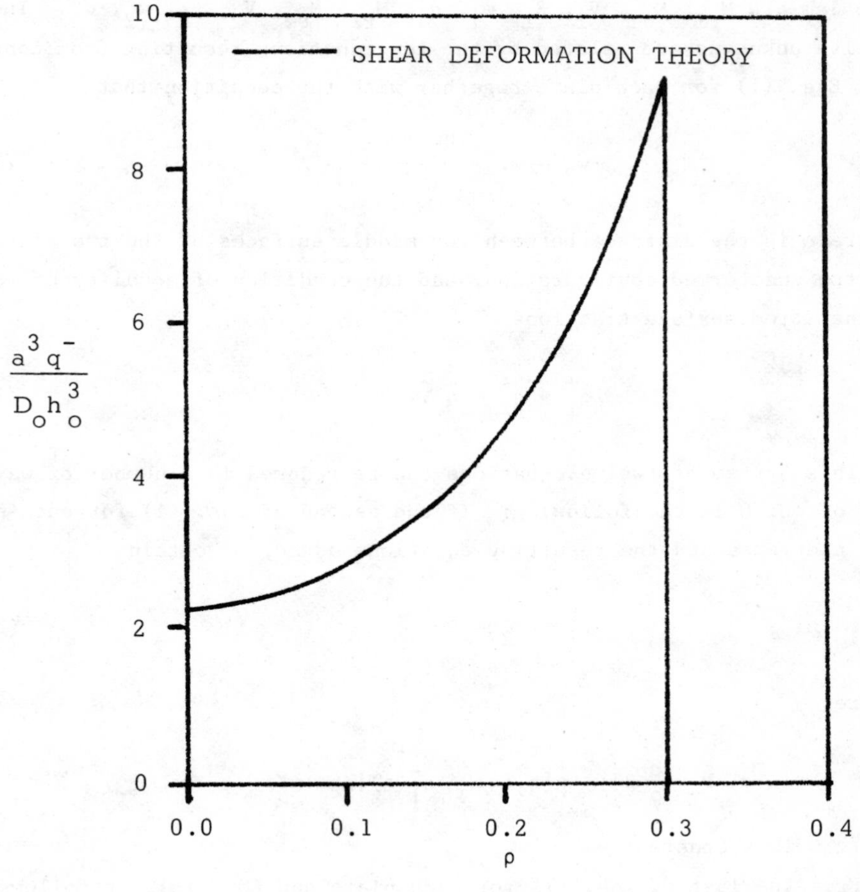

Fig. 5. Normal Surface Traction, $\bar{q}$, as Function of Dimensionless Radius, ρ, for Example of Plate Contacting Rigid Surface Whose Dimensionless Radius of Contact Region $m = 0.3$.

plates. We denote the parameters of one of the plates, say the upper plate, with the subscript 1 and those of the other plate with a subscript 2. In a contact region the transmitted surface tractions are unknowns of the problem and, thus, in the region the unknown parameters of the problem are M_{r1}, $M_{\theta 1}$, V_1, β_1, w_1, q_1^+, M_{r2}, $M_{\theta 2}$, V_2, β_2, w_2, q_2^-. These twelve unknowns are related by the ten equations resulting from considering Eqs. (1) for each plate together with the condition that

$$w_2 - w_1 = \frac{h_1 + h_2}{2} - \Delta \tag{18}$$

where Δ is the distance between the middle surfaces of the two plates in the undeformed configuration, and the condition of equality of the transmitted surface tractions

$$q_1^+ = q_2^- = q \; . \tag{19}$$

This system of twelve equations can be reduced in a number of ways, one of which is the following: If the second of Eqs. (1) for each plate is integrated and the resulting equations added, we obtain

$$V_1 + V_2 = P \tag{20}$$

where

$$P = \frac{a}{\rho} \int^{\rho} \eta[q_2^+(\eta) - q_1^-(\eta)]d\eta + \frac{C}{\rho}$$

where C is a constant.

From the last of Eqs. (1) for each plate and Eq. (18), it follows that

$$\beta_2 - \beta_1 + (h_1 + h_2)'/2a = \frac{V_2}{\mu_2^2 D_{o2} h_2} - \frac{V_1}{\mu_1^2 D_{o1} h_1} \tag{21}$$

The addition of Eq. (2) written for each plate gives

$$(V_1 + V_2) = \frac{D_{o1}h_1^3}{a^2} L_1(\beta_1) + \frac{D_{o2}h_2^3}{a^2} L_2(\beta_2) \tag{22}$$

Straightforward elimination between Eqs. (20), (21), and (22), and the relation between β_1 and V_1 given by Eq. (2) then gives

$$L_2\left[\frac{1}{a^2}\left(\frac{1}{\mu_1^2 D_{o1}h_1} + \frac{1}{\mu_2^2 D_{o2}h_2}\right) h_1^3 L_1(\beta_1)\right] - \frac{1}{D_{o2}}\left(\frac{h_1}{h_2}\right)^3 L_1(\beta_1)$$

$$- \frac{1}{D_{o1}} L_2(\beta_1) = \frac{1}{D_{o1}} L_2\left[\frac{P}{\mu_2^2 D_{o2}h_2} - \frac{(h_1 + h_2)'}{2a}\right] - \frac{a^2 P}{D_{o1}D_{o2}h_2^3} \tag{23}$$

The solution of Eq. (23) will give an expression for β_1 in terms of five arbitrary integration constants since Eq. (23) is fourth order and P involves an arbitrary constant. Expressions for M_{r1}, $M_{\theta 1}$, V_1 and q are obtained from the first four of Eqs. (1). With β_1 and V_1 determined, w_1 is obtained from an integration of the last of Eqs.(1) and a sixth integration constant is introduced. With the aid of Eqs. (20) and (21), expressions for β_2 and V_2 are obtained and w_2 is given by Eq. (18). Expressions for M_{r2} and $M_{\theta 2}$ are then given by the third and fourth of Eqs. (1). It should be noted that the expressions for the twelve unknown parameters in the contact region involve six arbitrary integration constants.

In a non-contact region, the solution for each of the plates involves four integration constants. An analysis of the type given above for the plate contacting a rigid surface shows that, in all cases, the number of integration constants, together with the unknown radii of the circular boundaries of the contact regions equals the number of boundary conditions (or boundedness conditions if the origin in included), together with the number of continuity conditions on the parameters M_{r1}, V_1, β_1, w_1, M_{r2}, V_2, β_2, w_2 at the boundaries of the regions of contact.

In the case of the classical treatment of problems of this kind, the reduction of the basic equations is far less complicated. It is readily shown that w_1 is governed by

$$\frac{D_{o1}}{D_{o2}}\left(\frac{h_1}{h_2}\right)^3 L_1\left(\frac{w_1'}{a}\right) + L_2\left(\frac{w_1'}{a}\right) = -L_2\left(\frac{(h_1+h_2)'}{2a}\right) - \frac{a^2 P}{D_{o2}h_2^3} \qquad (24)$$

With w_1 determined from Eq. (24), w_2 is given by Eq. (18). The remaining parameters, including the transmitted surface traction, are then obtained from Eqs. (1). The classical theory solution for a contact region thus involves four integration constants. In a non-contact region, eight integration constants (four for each plate) are introduced. It is easily shown that these constants, together with the unknown radii, are determined from the appropriate boundary conditions (or boundedness conditions at the origin), together with continuity requirements, on w_1, w_1', M_{r1}, w_2, w_2', M_{r2} at the circular boundaries of the contact regions. At these boundaries the shear resultants V_1 and V_2 are discontinuous and the discontinuity is accounted for by the transmission of a line load between the plates.

If $h_1 = h_2 = h$ and $\nu_1 = \nu_2 = \nu$ it follows that $\mu_1 = \mu_2 = \mu$ and $L_1()$ $= L_2() = L()$. In this case Eq. (23) is substantially simplified. If we write

$$\Psi = -\frac{(D_{o1}\beta_1 + D_{o2}\beta_2)}{(D_{o1} + D_{o2})} \qquad (25)$$

it readily follows that Eq. (23) is equivalent to the two second order equations

$$L(\psi) = -\frac{a^2}{h^3}\frac{P}{(D_{o1} + D_{o2})}$$

and

$$\frac{h^2}{\mu^2 a} M(\beta_1) = \Psi - \frac{D_{o2}}{(D_{o1} + D_{o2})}\frac{h'}{a} + \frac{P}{\mu^2 (D_{o1} + D_{o2})h} . \qquad (26)$$

For the classical treatment for this case the second of Eqs. (26) is replaced by

$$\frac{w_1'}{a} = \Psi - \frac{D_{o2}h'}{(D_{o1} + D_{o2})a} \quad . \tag{27}$$

An Example

We now consider a specific example in which

$$\begin{aligned} &h_1 = h_2 = h = h_o \sqrt{1-k\rho^2} = h_o y(\rho) \\ &\nu_1 = \nu_2 = \nu \\ &E_1 = E_2 = E \\ &\mu_1 = \mu_2 = \mu \\ &D_{o1} = D_{o2} = D_o \end{aligned} \tag{28}$$

Let the lower plate be clamped so that

$$w_2(1) = \beta_2(1) = 0 \tag{29}$$

and let the boundary conditions of the upper plate be

$$w_1(1) = \bar{w}_1 \qquad M_{r1}(1) = 0 \tag{30}$$

where $\bar{w}_1 = 0$ in the configuration in which the plates just touch as shown in Fig. 6. Both plates are free from surface traction, other than the traction transmitted in the contact region.

Then, for the contact region $0 \leq \rho \leq m$, it follows from Eqs. (26) that

$$\begin{aligned} &\psi = G_1\rho F(a_2, b_2, 2, k\rho^2) \\ &\beta_1 = G_2\beta_{11} + G_1\beta_{13} + \beta_{14} \end{aligned} \tag{31}$$

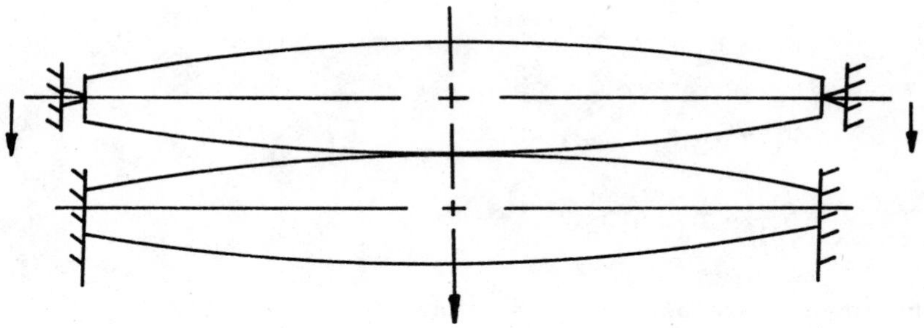

Fig. 6. Two Non-uniform Plates in Contact.

where β_{11}, a_1, a_2, b_1, b_2 are given by Eqs. (8) and (11) and

$$\beta_{13} = \left(\frac{\mu a}{h_o}\right)^2 \sum g_n \rho^{n+3}$$

$$\beta_{14} = \left(\frac{\mu a}{h_o}\right)^2 \frac{k}{2} \sum C_n \rho^{n+3}$$

$$g_n = \frac{f_n + [k(n^2 + 5n + 4) + \lambda^2]\, g_{n-2}}{(n^2 + 6n + 8)}$$

$$f_n = 4\,\frac{(a_2 + n/2 - 1)(b_2 + n/2 - 1)kf_{n-2}}{n(n + 2)}$$

$$f_o = 8g_o = 1$$

$$g_1 = g_3 = \ldots = 0$$

and C_n is given in Eq. (8). It then follows that

$$\frac{w_1'}{a} = \Psi - \frac{h_o y'}{2a} \qquad (32)$$

$$\frac{w_1}{a} = \int \Psi(n)\,dn - \frac{h_o' y}{2a} + G_3$$

It also follows that

$$\beta_2 = \beta_1 + 2\psi$$

$$\frac{w_2}{a} = \int \psi(n)\,dn + \frac{h_o y}{2a} + G_4 \qquad (33)$$

The expressions for $V_1 = - V_2$, M_{r1}, M_{r2}, $M_{\theta 1}$, $M_{\theta 2}$, and q are readily deduced by substitution in Eqs. (1) and little purpose is served by recording them here.

For the region $\rho < m \leq 1$ the equations governing each plate are identical in form to the equations governing the non-contact region of the previous specific example. Accordingly, their solutions will be of that form and the solution will involve eight integration constants, four for each plate.

Expressions for these eight constants, the constants G_1, G_2, G_3, G_4, and the transcendental equation relating m and $\bar{w}_1$ are determined from the eight continuity conditions at $\rho = m$, the four boundary conditions given by Eqs. (29) and (30), and Eq. (18) with $\Delta = h_o$. Obviously, the obtaining of such expressions involves the solution of thirteen simultaneous, extremely cumbersome, algebraic equations. For a numerical example, the solution is advantageously obtained from a computer program. Accordingly, such expressions serve little purpose and will not be recorded here.

The classical theory solution for $o \leq \rho \leq m$ and $\nu \geq \frac{1}{3}$ is given by

$$\frac{w_1'}{a} = G_1\beta_{21}(\rho) + \frac{h_o k\rho}{2a\ y}$$

$$\frac{w_2'}{a} = \psi + \frac{h_o y'}{2a} \tag{34}$$

$$V_1 = -V_2 = \frac{h_o^4 k^2 D_o}{2}(3\nu - 1)\rho$$

$$q_1^+ = q_2^- = \frac{D_o h_o^4 k^2}{a^4}(3\nu - 1)$$

The other parameters are obtained by straightforward substitution. As in the case of the previous specific example, the value of the transmitted surface traction of Eqs. (34) will be negative if $\nu < 1/3$ and, accordingly, Eq. (34) is not valid if $\nu < 1/3$. For such a case, the classical theory predicts that the plates will not be in contact in the region $\rho < m$ but will be in contact at the line $\rho = m$. It can be shown that the transcendental equation relating $\bar{V}_1$ and m is independent of the form of the solution for $\rho < m$ and, hence, is independent of the value of ν. As in the previous example, the classical theory predicts the propagation of the region or circle of contact only after a finite value of $\bar{w}_1$ is attained.

For the case $\frac{2a}{h_o} = 10$, $k = 0.8$, $\nu = 1/3$, the predicted variation of m with $\bar{w}_1$ of the shear deformation and classical theories is shown in

Fig. 7 . For m = 0.4, the radial bending moment distribution is shown in Fig. 8, and the shear resultant and surface traction distributions are shown in Figs. 9 and 10. The substantial discrepancies between the predictions of the two theories are clearly evident. Obviously, for this case the classical theory predicts a zero value for the shear resultant and surface traction in the contact region, and the transmission of a line load between the plates at the edge of that region.

CONCLUSIONS

In the treatment of problems of the types considered here, the solutions are dependent upon the specification of the plate thickness as a function of the radial coordinate and thus, unlike the analysis of corresponding problems involving plates of uniform thickness, general conclusions are difficult to draw. However, a few observations can be made.

It would appear that the conceptual difficulties inherent in the classical theory treatment of problems of these types prescribe a practical limitation upon the use of the classical theory in such analyses as well. On the basis of the illustrative examples considered, it is clear that, at least in the case of some problems, there is a substantial discrepancy between the predictions of the classical theory and those of the shear deformation theory. Particularly significant in these examples are the discrepancies in the predictions for the radius of the contact region as a function of the applied load. In both examples, if $\nu < 1/3$ the classical theory predicts a line of contact whereas the shear deformation theory predicts a contact region. If $\nu \geq 1/3$ both theories predict a contact region, but there is a substantial discrepancy in the size of the region, as well as the distribution of the surface tractions transmitted in the contact region.

In investigations where the transmitted surface tractions are of interest, it is significant that the classical treatment requirement of the transmission of a line load at the periphery of the contact region is eliminated through the use of the shear deformation theory. It is also significant that, for both examples, there is a range of values of the externally applied loads for which the classical theory predicts a point of contact, whereas the shear deformation theory predicts a region of contact.

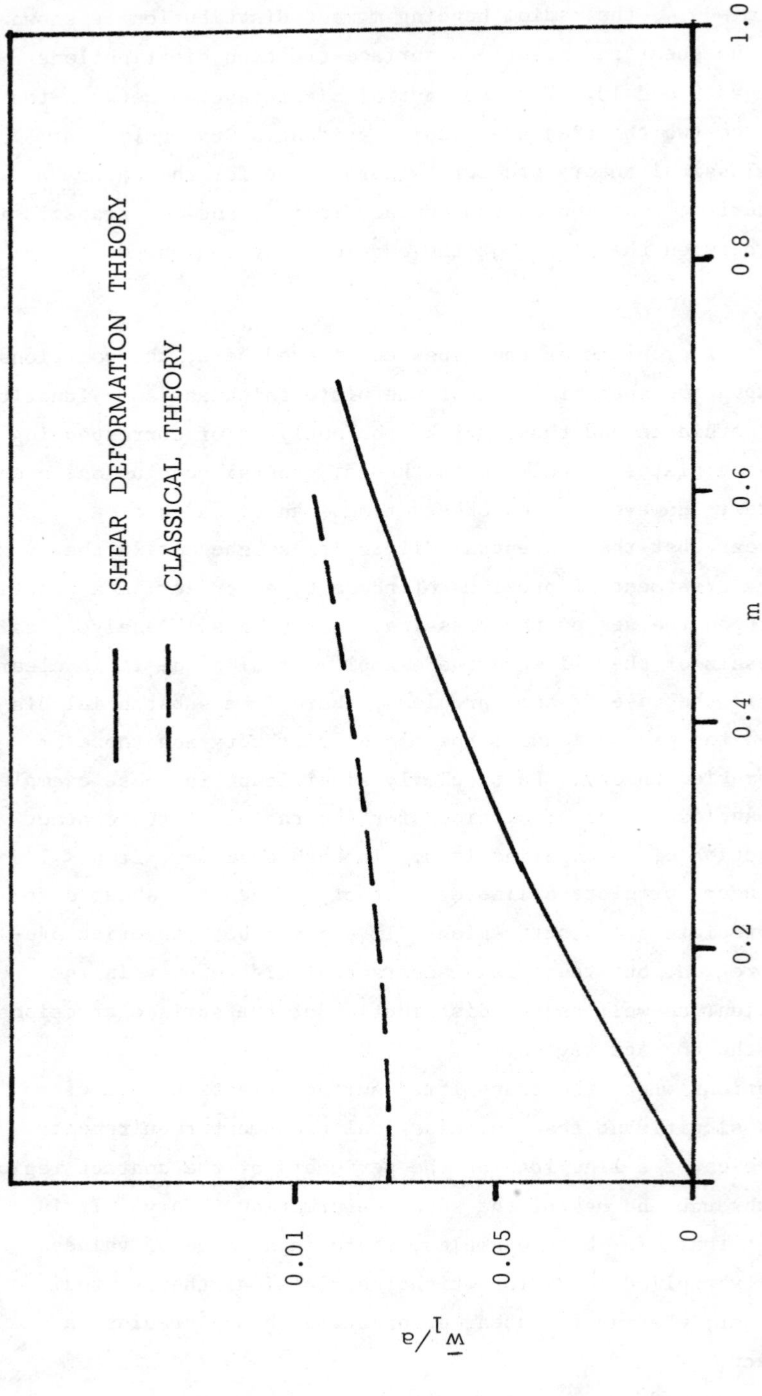

Fig. 7. Variation of Dimensionless Radius of Contact Region, m, with Prescribed Edge Deflection of Upper Plate, $\bar{w}_1$, for Example of Two Plates in Contact.

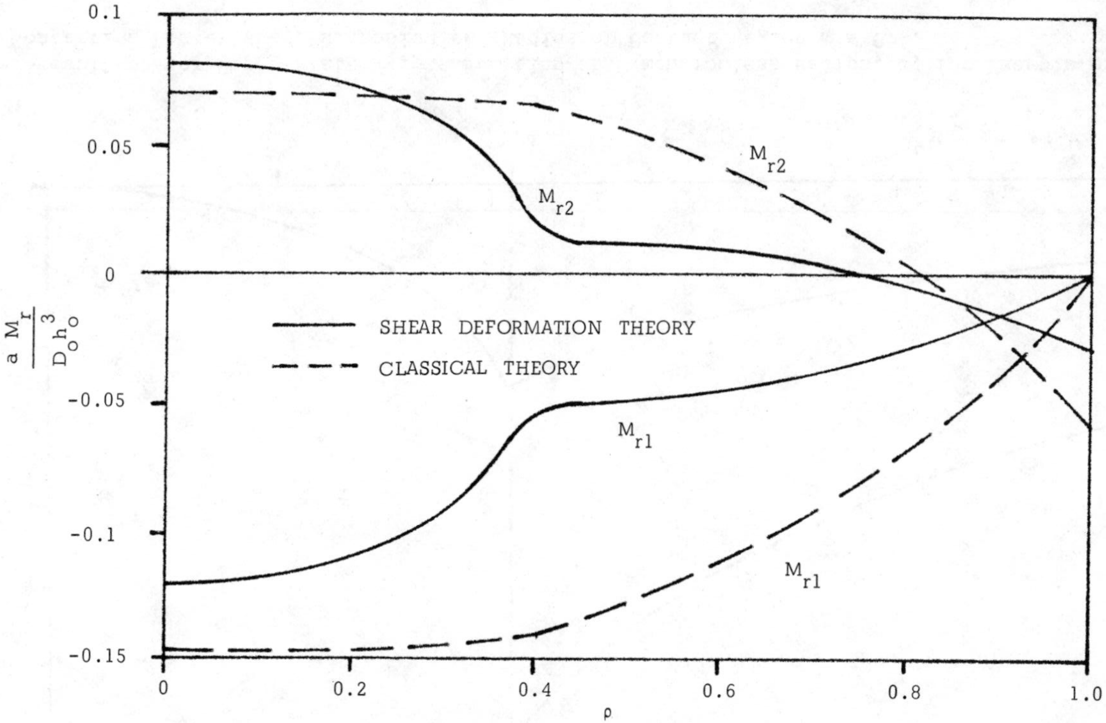

Fig. 8. Radial Bending Moments, M_{r1} and M_{r2}, as Functions of Dimensionless Radius, ρ, for Example of Two Contacting Plates where Dimensionless Radius of Contact Region $m = 0.4$.

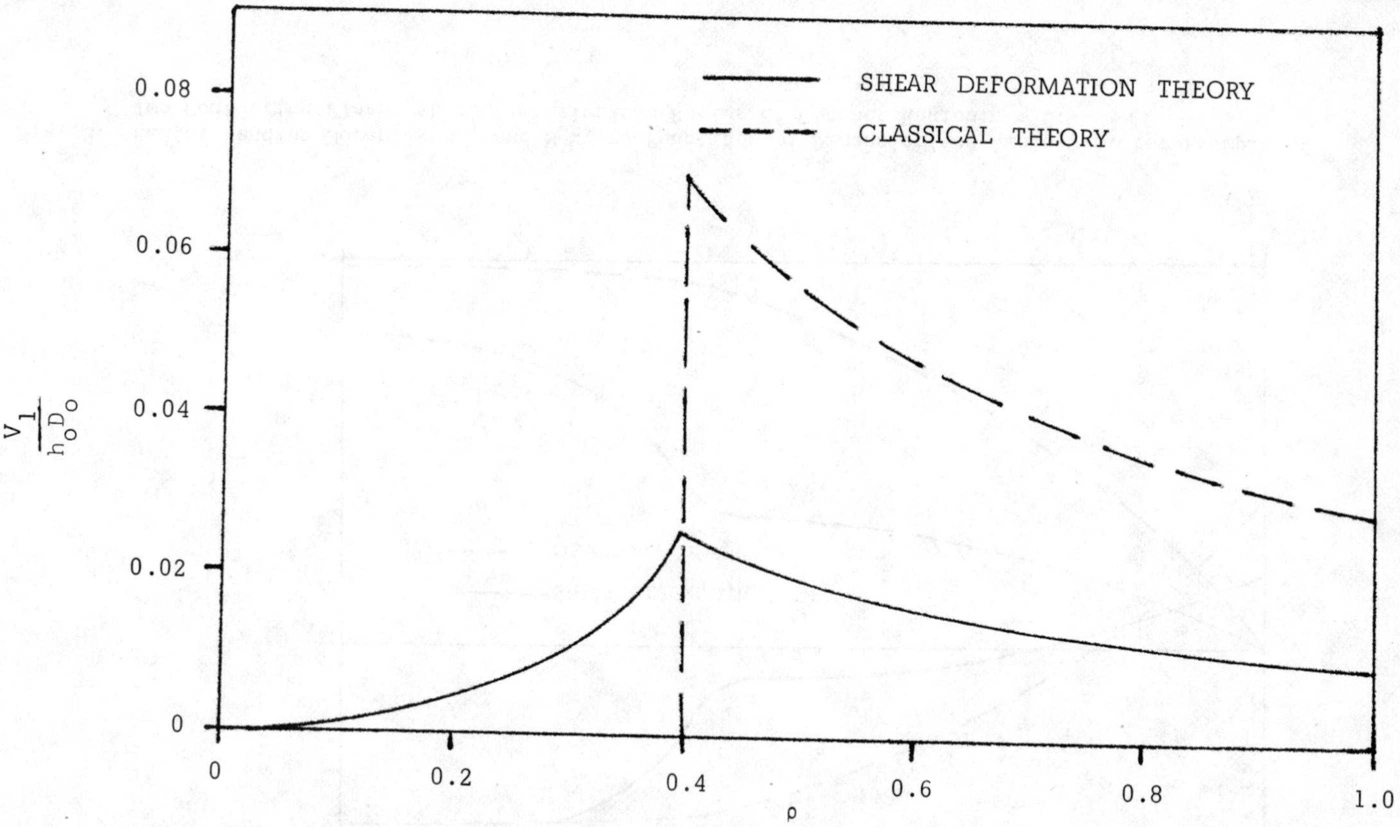

Fig. 9. Shear Resultant for Upper Plate V_1, as Function of Dimensionless Radius, ρ, for Example of Two Contacting Plates where Dimensionless Radius of Contact Region m = 0.4.

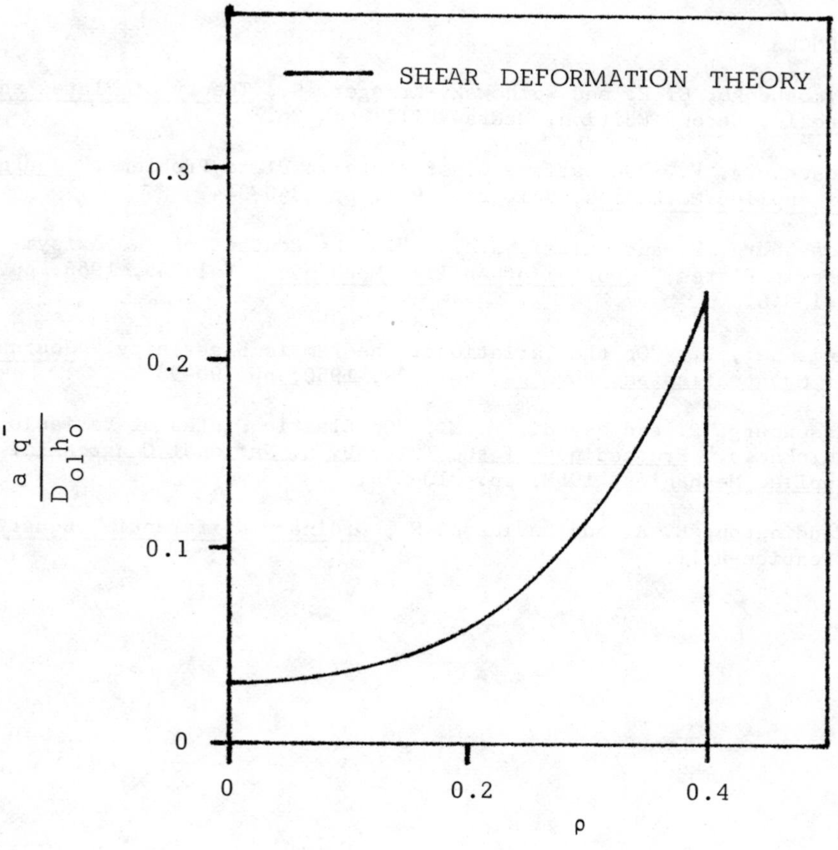

Fig. 10. Normal Surface Traction Transmitted between the Two Plates, q, as Function of Dimensionless Radius, ρ, for Example of Two Contacting Plates where Dimensionless Radius of Contact Region m = 0.4.

ACKNOWLEDGMENT

The results reported here were obtained in the course of an investigation supported by the National Science Foundation Grant No. GK-21 to the University of Colorado.

REFERENCES

1. Timoshenko, S. P. and Woinowsky-Krieger, S., Theory of Plates and Shells, Second Edition, McGraw-Hill Book Co.

2. Essenburg, F., "On Surface Constraints in Plate Problems," Journal of Applied Mechanics, Vol. 29, 1962, pp. 340-344.

3. Essenburg, F. and Gulati, S. T., "On the Contact of Two Axisymmetric Plates," Journal of Applied Mechanics, Vol. 35, 1966, pp. 341-346.

4. Reissner, E., "On the Variational Theorem in Elasticity," Journal of Mathematics and Physics, Vol. 29, 1950, pp. 90-95.

5. Essenburg, F. and Naghdi, P. M., "On Elastic Plates of Variable Thickness," Proceedings of the Third U. S. National Congress of Applied Mechanics, 1958, pp. 313-319.

6. Caddington, E. A. and Levinson, N., Ordinary Differential Equations, Prentice-Hall.

ELASTIC STABILITY OF FOLDED PLATE STRUCTURES OF TRIANGULAR CROSS-SECTION

S. E. Swartz[1]
Kansas State University

S. A. Guralnick
Illinois Institute of Technology

ABSTRACT

Single and multiple cell folded plate structures of triangular cross-section are widely used as a structural system for roofing large floor areas. These structures are generally constructed of reinforced concrete, plywood or steel. Herein is presented an approximate analysis of the elastic stability of this type of structure with regard to local buckling in a plate element. This method of solution is based upon "beam" theory for the folded plate stress analysis and is of a closed form which can be readily applied by hand or desk calculator computations. A comparison of this method is made with a more general approach based upon the theory of elasticity. In addition, numerical results for stresses and buckling loads are correlated with those obtained from seven aluminum model specimens of single-cell, triangular cross-section subjected to uniformly distributed surface loads and uniform intensity line loads.

LIST OF NOTATIONS

E	Young's Modulus.
I	Beam moment of inertia of cross-section.
I_o	Moment of inertia of inclined plate element about a horizontal axis through the plate centroid.
M	Transverse moment.

1. Formerly Post Doctoral Research Associate, Illinois Institute of Technology.

M_x	Beam bending moment.
M_{xa}	Average beam moment.
$Q(y)$	Beam cross-section area moment.
V_x	Beam shear.
V_{xa}	Average beam shear.
a	Length of the structure.
b	Width of plate element.
d_1	Depth of structure.
d_2	Width of a cell.
h	Thickness of plate element.
k_{ca}, k_{c1}, k_{c2}	Compression buckling coefficients.
k_{sa}, k_{s1}, k_{s2}	Shear buckling coefficients.
n	Number of cells.
q	A uniform load.
q_d	A uniform dead load.
x, y, z	Coordinate directions.
α	Plate inclination from horizontal
ε	$\frac{6\,b\,(1-\nu^2)}{E\,h^3}\,\frac{M}{\theta}$
θ	Transverse rotation in plate element.
ν	Poisson's Ratio.
σ_x	Longitudinal stress in the outer fiber.
σ_{xa}	Average longitudinal stress in the plate strip.
$\sigma_{x_{cr}}$	Critical longitudinal stress in the plate strip.
τ_{xy}	Shearing stress.
τ_{xya}	Average shearing stress in the plate strip.
$\tau_{xy_{cr}}$	Critical shearing stress in the plate strip.

INTRODUCTION

Several acceptable methods for the analysis of folded plate structures for stresses and deflections have been developed [1], [2], [3], [4], [5], [6] in the recent past. In addition, several experimental studies [2], [7], [8], [9] have been reported which indicate satisfactory agreement between measured and predicted values of strains (and, by inference, stresses) induced in such structures by the presence of transverse applied loads. Generally speaking, these theoretical and experimental studies were directed toward providing information which would enable a practicing engineer to predict the "safe" load carrying capacity of an arbitrary folded plate structure based upon its geometry and its support conditions and upon the stress-strain characteristics of the material used in its fabrication. Because information concerning the possibility of local or general instability of transversely-loaded, folded plate structures has hitherto been lacking, it has not ordinarily been possible in the past to attempt a rational analysis of buckling strength in making a prediction of "safe" carrying capacity. Of course, a practicing engineer can make use of certain empirical rules obtained from a consideration of ordinary plate buckling in designing a folded plate structure; however, there is, to the writers' knowledge, little or no information available at the present time which deals with the buckling behavior of folded plate structures per se as distinct from shells and/or thin-walled beams. It is the purpose of this paper to present an approximate analysis of the elastic stability of transversely-loaded, prismatic folded plate structures of single or multiple-cell triangular cross-section. It must, of course, be recognized that such an analysis can, at best, yield merely an upper bound estimate of the actual critical load and can, furthermore, yield no information on possible post-buckling reserve strength.

Analysis

Consider the structure shown in Fig. 1. According to conventional [1], [2], [4], [6] folded plate analysis no "joint displacement correction" is needed in order to determine the membrane stress distribution throughout the plate members of the structure. In fact, for the purpose of determining membrane stresses, one may treat such a structure as a "beam" spanning the distance between its end diaphragms to obtain transverse normal stresses. Once the transverse normal stresses have been obtained, one may use the equation of Guralnick and Swartz [10] to obtain the complete distribution of membrane stresses throughout each plate of the structure.

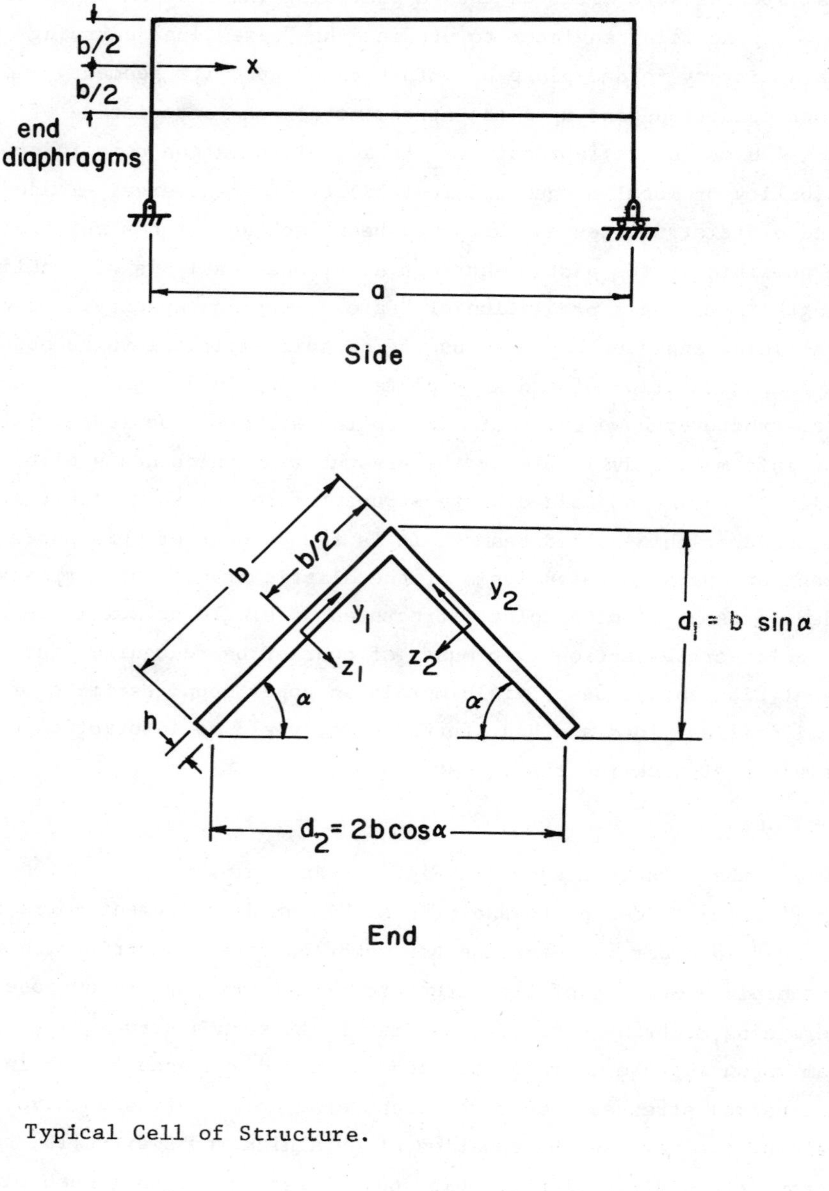

Fig. 1. Typical Cell of Structure.

Conrado and Schnobrich [11] have reported results of an analysis of multi-celled triangular folded plate structures utilizing a generalized numerical technique which employs the same basic assumptions with regard to a structural action as those employed by Goldberg and Leve [3]. A comparison of the membrane stresses in a series of single cell and in five cell folded plate structural models obtained by the method of Conrado and Schnobrich [11] and those obtained by "beam" theory is given in Table I. The maximum discrepancy between any pair of corresponding values of normal stress is smaller than 4.3 percent of the value obtained by the numerical technique and the maximum discrepancy between any pair of corresponding values of shearing stress is smaller than 13.5 percent of the value obtained by the numerical technique. Because of this fact, it appears reasonable to assume, for the purpose of estimating buckling strength, that membrane stresses in each plate of a simply-supported, single or multi-celled (not in excess of five cells) folded plate structure may be computed with sufficient accuracy by applying "beam" theory.

Because of its simplicity, the "beam" theory for membrane stresses is employed in this paper in order to permit clarity in the exposition of the buckling analysis. It should be noted, however, that the buckling analysis presented herein is independent of the technique used to obtain the membrane stresses prior to the onset of buckling and hence, this buckling analysis may be used with any appropriate technique of flexural analysis.

A typical cell of a folded plate structure together with a coordinate system is shown in Fig. 1. The structure is assumed to be supported at its ends by "diaphragms" which are perfectly rigid with respect to in-plane deformations and perfectly flexible with respect to out-of-plane deformations.

Referring to Fig. 2, the "beam" cross-section properties of the section are determined as follows:

The moment of inertia of an inclined element is

$$I_o = I_X \sin^2 \alpha + I_Y \cos^2 \alpha$$

The first statical moment of the cross-sectional area to be used in shear stress calculation for an inclined element is

TABLE I

Comparison of Maximum Longitudinal Normal and Shearing Stresses Obtained by Beam Theory and "Elasticity" Theory [3, 11]

Plate Inclination, α, degrees	Span Length, a, in.	Maximum Percent Difference in σ_x		Maximum Percent Difference in τ_{xy}	
		Single Cell	Average of 5 Cells	Single Cell	Average of 5 Cells
25	27	4.3	3.8	13.5	11.0
	54	2.1	1.3	7.8	7.9
	81	0.8	1.2	7.6	7.2
	108	1.0	1.0	7.2	7.3
35	27	3.9	3.3	12.8	10.4
	54	1.6	1.2	8.2	8.0
	81	0.4	0.6	7.9	7.5
	108	0.3	0.4	7.7	7.3
45	27	4.1	2.9	11.9	7.5
	54	1.3	1.3	7.7	7.7
	81	0.4	0.5	7.6	7.5
	108	0.3	0.3	7.5	7.7
55	27	3.9	2.9	10.2	9.4
	54	1.3	1.0	7.8	7.8
	81	0.5	0.7	7.6	7.6
	108	0.6	0.4	7.4	8.0
65	27	4.4	4.4	8.7	8.7
	54	1.1	0.9	7.0	7.0
	81	0.6	0.5	6.9	6.9
	108	0.8	0.4	7.6	6.7

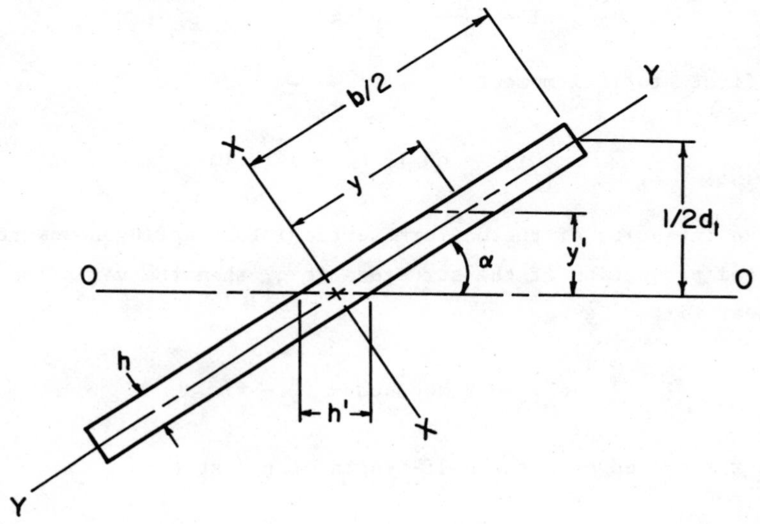

Fig. 2. Inclined Plate Element.

$$Q_o\ (y) = \frac{1}{2}\, h\ (\frac{1}{4}\, b^2\ - y^2)\ \sin\ \alpha$$

In the above

$$I_X = \frac{1}{12}\ hb^3; \qquad I_Y = \frac{1}{12}\ bh^3$$

Assuming $\frac{h}{b} \leq \frac{1}{10}$, then I_Y may be neglected in comparison to I_X and if there are n cells, the moment of inertia of the cross-section is

$$I = \frac{nhb^3}{6}\ \sin^2\ \alpha \tag{1}$$

The first statical moment is

$$Q(y) = nh\ (\frac{1}{4}\ b^2\ -\ y^2)\ \sin\ \alpha \tag{2}$$

If the intensity of the uniform vertical load acting downward on the horizontal projection of the structure is q, then the variation of the beam shear with x is

$$V_x = 2\ nbq\ \cos\ \alpha\ (\frac{a}{2}\ -\ x) \tag{3}$$

The shear averaged over the half-length of the structure is

$$V_{xa} = \frac{1}{2}\ nbaq\ \cos\ \alpha \tag{4}$$

The variation of external moment with x is

$$M_x = nbq\ \cos\ \alpha\ (a\ -\ x)\ x \tag{5}$$

The external moment averaged over the length of the structure is

$$M_{xa} = \frac{1}{6}\ nba^2q\ \cos\ \alpha \tag{6}$$

The in-plane shearing stress at any cross-section x-distant from the origin of coordinates is

$$\tau_{xy} = \frac{V_x Q(y)}{I(2nh)}$$

or,

$$\tau_{xy} = \frac{6\left(\frac{a}{2} - x\right)\left(\frac{1}{4} b^2 - y^2\right) q \cot \alpha}{b^2 h} \tag{7}$$

The shear stress averaged over the half-length of the structure and the half-width of the plate is

$$\tau_{xya} = \frac{aq \cot \alpha}{4\ h} \tag{8}$$

The longitudinal normal stress is

$$\sigma_x = -\frac{M_x Y'}{I}$$

or,

$$\sigma_x = -\frac{6q\ (a - x)\ xy}{hb^2} \cot \alpha \tag{9}$$

The absolute value of the longitudinal compressive normal stress averaged over the length and half-width of the plate is

$$\sigma_{xa} = \frac{a^2 q \cot \alpha}{4\ bh} \tag{10}$$

For the case of an n-celled structure subjected to a uniform intensity line load W applied to each of its ridges other than its free edges, the equations for the relevant stresses become

$$\tau_{xy} = \frac{3W\ (2n - 1)\left(\frac{a}{2} - x\right)\left(\frac{1}{4}b^2 - y^2\right)}{nhb^3 \sin \alpha} \tag{7a}$$

$$\tau_{xya} = \frac{(2n - 1)\ aW}{8\ nbh \sin \alpha} \tag{8a}$$

$$\sigma_x = -\frac{3W\ (2n - 1)\ (a - x)\ xy}{nhb^3 \sin \alpha} \tag{9a}$$

$$\sigma_{xa} = \frac{(2n - 1)\, a^2 W}{8\, nhb^2 \sin \alpha} \tag{10a}$$

The interaction between the average shearing stress and the longitudinal normal stress on the local buckling strength of a plate is, as suggested by Bleich [19], assumed to be given with sufficient accuracy by

$$\left(\frac{\tau_{xya}}{\tau_{xy_{cr}}}\right)^2 + \frac{\sigma_{xa}}{\sigma_{x_{cr}}} = 1 \tag{11}$$

in which,

$$\tau_{xy_{cr}} = k_{sa} \frac{\pi^2 E}{12\,(1-\nu^2)} \left(\frac{2h}{b}\right)^2 \tag{12}$$

and,

$$\sigma_{x_{cr}} = k_{ca} \frac{\pi^2 E}{12\,(1-\nu^2)} \left(\frac{2h}{b}\right)^2 \tag{13}$$

The coefficients k_{sa}, k_{ca} are the average shear buckling and longitudinal buckling coefficients for the plate strip, E is Young's Modulus and ν is Poisson's Ratio. The coefficients k_{sa} and k_{ca} may be determined by using the method given by Lundquist, Stowell and Schwartz [13], [14]. Following Bleich [19], the buckling zone is assumed to be approximated with sufficient accuracy by a strip of length a and width b/2 in the compression portion of the plate. This strip is assumed to be simply supported along its transverse edges and elastically supported with regard to rotation only along its longitudinal edges. Using the method of Lundquist, et. al. involves the determination of the bending stiffness along each longitudinal edge of the strip. This bending stiffness is given in non-dimensional form by [13], [14]:

$$\varepsilon = \frac{6\, b\, (1-\nu^2)\, M}{E\, h^3\, \theta} \tag{14}$$

in which M is the transverse moment and θ is the corresponding rotation. M and θ are assumed to vary longitudinally in the same manner.

For the structures being analyzed in this paper it is necessary to consider two cases:

a. The plate is exterior.

b. The plate is interior.

Denoting the strip edge by 1 at the center of the plate and the strip edge at ridge by 2 and assuming one-way slab action it may be observed that for case a,

$$M_1 = \frac{q\, b^2 \cos^2 \alpha}{8}$$

and

$$\theta_1 = \frac{7\, q\, b^3 \cos^2 \alpha}{4\, E\, h^3}$$

or

$$\varepsilon_1 = \frac{3\,(1-\nu^2)}{7} \qquad (15)$$

At edge 2 for case a, and at edges 1 and 2 for case b, $\theta = 0$ due to symmetry but $M \neq 0$. Therefore at these edges $\varepsilon = \infty$.

The coefficients k_{sa}, k_{ca} may be approximated according to Stowell [12] as

$$k_{sa} = \frac{1}{2}\,(k_{s1} + k_{s2}) \qquad (16)$$

and,

$$k_{ca} = \frac{1}{2}\,(k_{c1} + k_{c2}) \qquad (17)$$

Case a - Exterior Plate

$$k_{s1} \approx \frac{2}{\sqrt{3}} \left[2 \sqrt{\frac{\left(\frac{1}{2} - \frac{2}{\pi^2}\right) \varepsilon_1 + \frac{1}{2}}{\left(\frac{1}{2} - \frac{4}{\pi^2}\right) \varepsilon_1 + \frac{1}{2}}} + 3 \right] \qquad (18)$$

and,

$$k_{c1} \approx 2 \left[\sqrt{\frac{\varepsilon_1 \left(1 - \frac{4}{\pi^2}\right) + 1}{\varepsilon_1 \left(1 - \frac{8}{\pi^2}\right) + 1}} + 1 \right] \qquad (19)$$

These expressions may be obtained from the equations given by Lundquist [13] and by Stowell and Schwartz [15] by neglecting second order terms in ε_1, by assuming that the length to width ratio of the buckling zone is greater than five to one and that the width to half-wave length ratio of the buckling zone is approximately unity.

For values of ν between 0.05 and 0.35, k_{s1} and k_{c1} do not differ by more than $\pm$ 0.25% from the values 5.95 and 4.15 respectively.

For edge 2, fixity is assumed and,

$$k_{s2} = 8.98 \qquad (20)$$

and,

$$k_{c2} = 6.97 \qquad (21)$$

Case b - Interior Plate

$$k_{sa} = 8.98 \text{ and } k_{ca} = 6.97$$

For the case of a uniformly-distributed load, substituting Eqs. (8) and (10) into Eq. (11) and solving for q_{cr} yields:

$$\frac{q_{cr}}{E} = \frac{k_{sa}^2 \pi^2 h^3}{1.5\, k_{ca} (1-\nu^2)\, b^3 \cot \alpha} \left[-1 + \sqrt{1 + 4 \left(\frac{k_{ca}}{k_{sa}} \frac{b}{a}\right)^2} \right] \qquad (22)$$

For the case of uniform line load, the critical value of W is

$$\frac{W_{cr}}{E} = \frac{4\, k_{sa}^2\, n\, \pi^2 h^3 \sin \alpha}{3\, k_{ca} (1-\nu^2) (2n - 1)\, b^2} \left[-1 + \sqrt{1 + 4 \left(\frac{k_{ca} b}{k_{sa} a}\right)^2} \right] \qquad (23)$$

Eqs. (22) and (23) may be used directly to predict buckling loads; however, these expressions require the use of a desk calculator or a digital computer rather than a slide rule to obtain accurate numerical results.

Swartz [16], [20] has given a general analysis for the buckling of single-cell, folded plate structures of arbitrary cross-section. Because of the complexity of the expressions utilized in Swartz's analysis, cumbersome numerical techniques requiring the use of a high-speed digital computer must be employed to obtain a solution for the critical load of any particular structure. Graphs of buckling load versus span to depth ratio obtained from Eq. (22) and by Swartz's technique are shown in Fig. 3. By comparing these two curves, it may be observed that for any particular value of the a/d ratio, Eq. (22) yields a slightly smaller (i.e. conservative) prediction of the buckling load than the more refined technique of Swartz. Since the discrepancy between corresponding predictions of buckling load is not large over the whole a/d range shown in Fig. 3, the advantages of the closed form solution given by Eq. (22) or Eq. (23) are obvious.

Test Results

In order to check the reliability of predictions of buckling load made by means of Eqs. (22) or (23) seven aluminum model specimens of single-cell triangular cross-section were fabricated and load tested. Four models were subjected to a series of point loads distributed over their entire surface to simulate the effects of a uniformly-distributed surface load and the remaining three models were subjected to a series of point loads applied along the top ridge to simulate the effects of a uniform-intensity line load. Specimen dimensions together with measured and predicted values of buckling loads are given in Table II. Each model was extensively instrumented with electric resistance strain gages of the "rosette" type and with a large number of linear travel dial gages having a one-inch range and a least reading of .001 inch. Details of the experimental setup and some buckling results for the uniformly loaded models are presented elsewhere [18].

Representative examples of graphs of the growth of measured longitudinal normal stress σ_x at midspan of the model specimen with applied loads

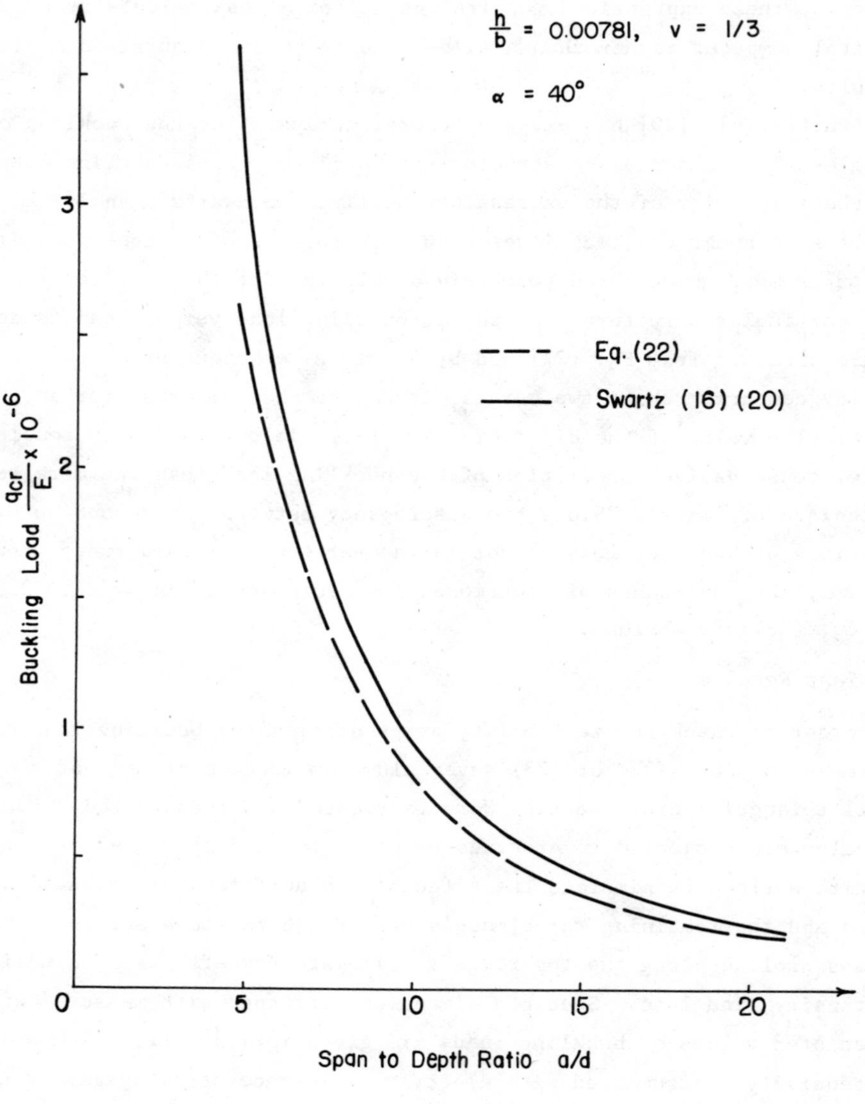

Fig. 3. Buckling Load vs. Span to Depth Ratio.

TABLE II

TEST RESULTS***

Model No.	Plate Thickness, h, in.	Plate Width, b, in.	Span Length, a, in.	$\frac{q_{cr}}{E} \times 10^{-6}$		$\frac{W_{cr}}{E\,h} \times 10^{-6}$		Ratio of observed to predicted buckling loads
				Eq. 25	Observed	Eq. 27	Observed	
III A3*	0.0625	8	81	0.319	0.1596			0.500
III A4*	0.0625	8	108	0.180	0.0827			0.459
III B4*	0.125	8	108	1.438	0.4210			0.293
III C4*	0.090	8	108	0.537	0.1796			0.334
L III A1S**	0.0625	8	54			141.44	48.64	0.344
L III A2S**	0.0625	8	81			62.88	20.74	0.330
L III A3S**	0.0625	8	108			35.20	13.33	0.378

* Structure Subjected to **Uniformly**-Distributed Load over Entire Surface

** Structure Subjected to Uniform-Intensity Line Loads at Each Ridge other than Free Edges

*** All models were simply-supported, single-cell structures with $\alpha = 40^{\circ}$, $E = 10.13 \times 10^{6}$ and $\nu = 0.333$

are shown in Figs. 4 and 5. In addition, graphs of predicted normal stress versus applied load are shown in each of these figures for comparison purposes. It may be observed that agreement between measured and predicted stresses is satisfactory. Similar results were obtained with each specimen at all load levels below that at which buckling commenced. At the buckling load and beyond, strain measurements became meaningless due to partial or complete destruction of those gages attached to the structure in the vicinity of developing "buckles".

Normal deflection surface "profiles" measured by a single line of dial gages located on a line in the upper third of the plate parallel to the long axis of the specimen are shown in Figs. 6 through 8. Previously reported results [18] for the uniformly loaded models showed that the initial buckling took the form of an approximately square "dimple" located adjacent to the midspan of the structure in the upper half of the plate. As the load was increased another dimple formed at about the quarter span of the structure in the upper half of the plate. The measured value of the buckling load reported in Table II was obtained in each instance from a "reading" of the corresponding measured deflection profiles. Or, in other words, the measured buckling load was taken to be the load which caused the deflection profile to change from a "regular" pattern to an "irregular" pattern. In all cases the model specimens were able to sustain a load at least fifty percent greater than that which caused initial buckling behavior to appear.

CONCLUSIONS

The procedure presented herein for predicting the buckling load of an arbitrary plate of a triangular cross-section folded plate structure yields an upper bound solution for the critical load. This procedure is based on the assumption that the structural material is perfectly homogeneous, isotropic, and elastic, that each plate is perfectly plane and centrally-loaded in its own plane and that all deflections are "small" compared to the lateral dimensions of the plate. It may be observed from the data presented in Table II that measured buckling loads were, in all instances, considerably smaller than those predicted. This discrepancy between the observed buckling loads and those predicted by a purely elastic, small deflection theory analysis is not unusual in experiments

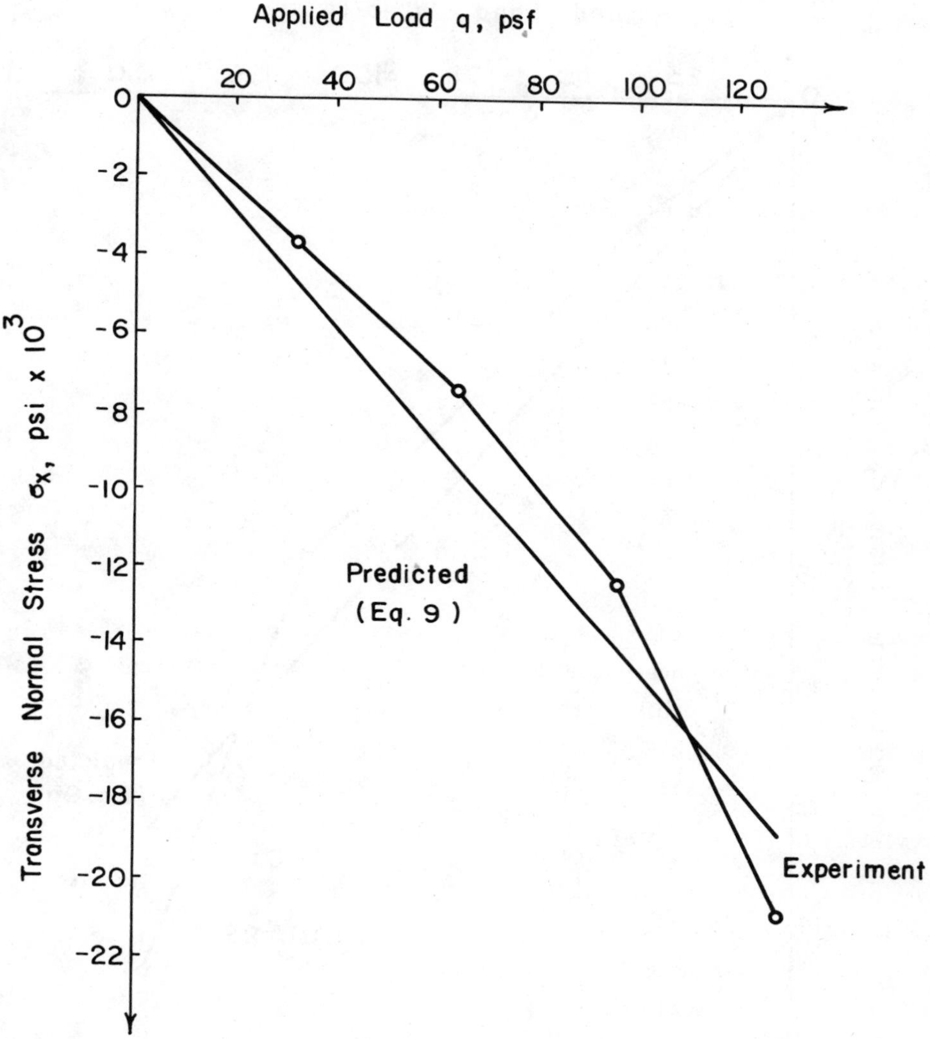

Fig. 4. Transverse Normal Stress Versus Applied Load (Top Edge, Midspan, Specimen No. III A-4).

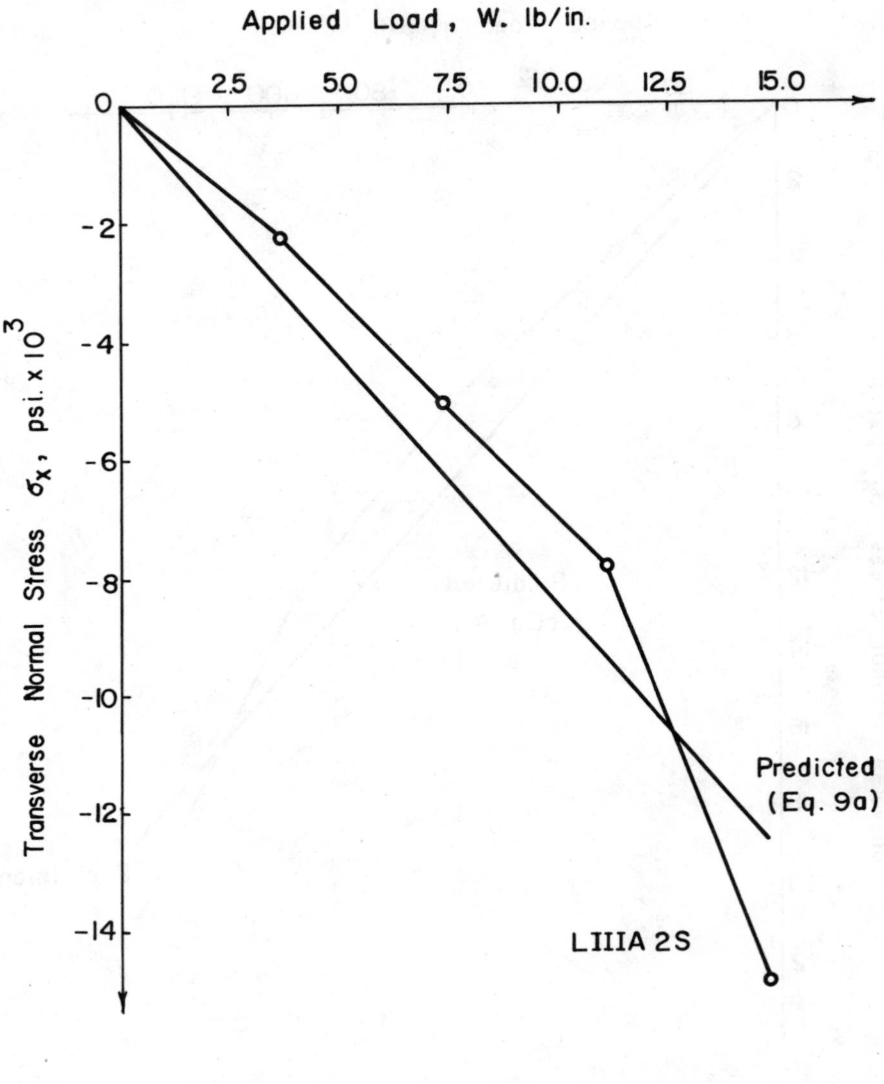

Fig. 5. Transverse Normal Stress Versus Applied Load (Third-span, Top Edge, Specimen No. LIIIA-2S).

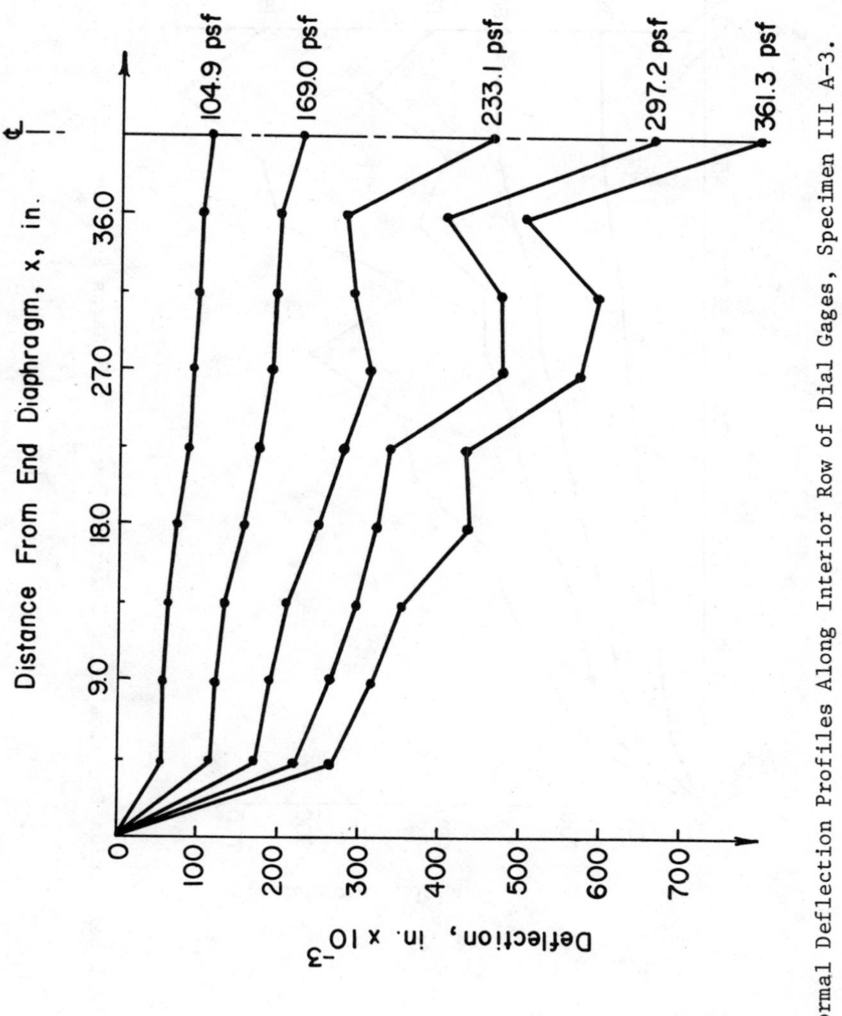

Fig. 6. Normal Deflection Profiles Along Interior Row of Dial Gages, Specimen III A-3.

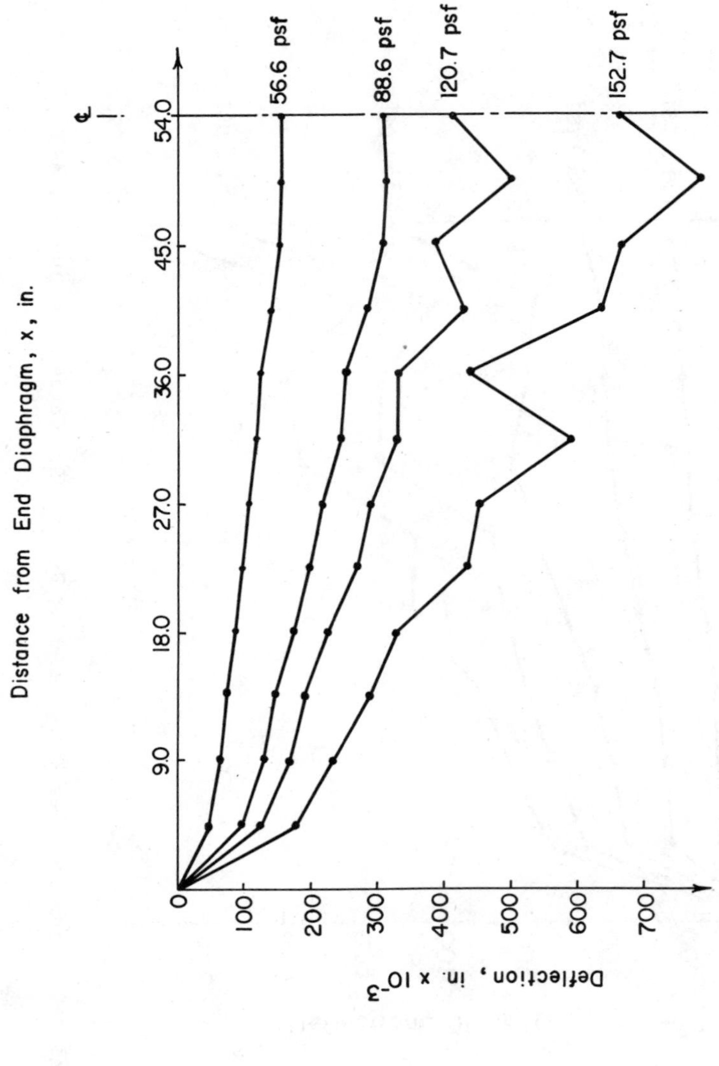

Fig. 7. Normal Deflection Profiles Along Interior Row of Dial Gages Speciman IIIA-4.

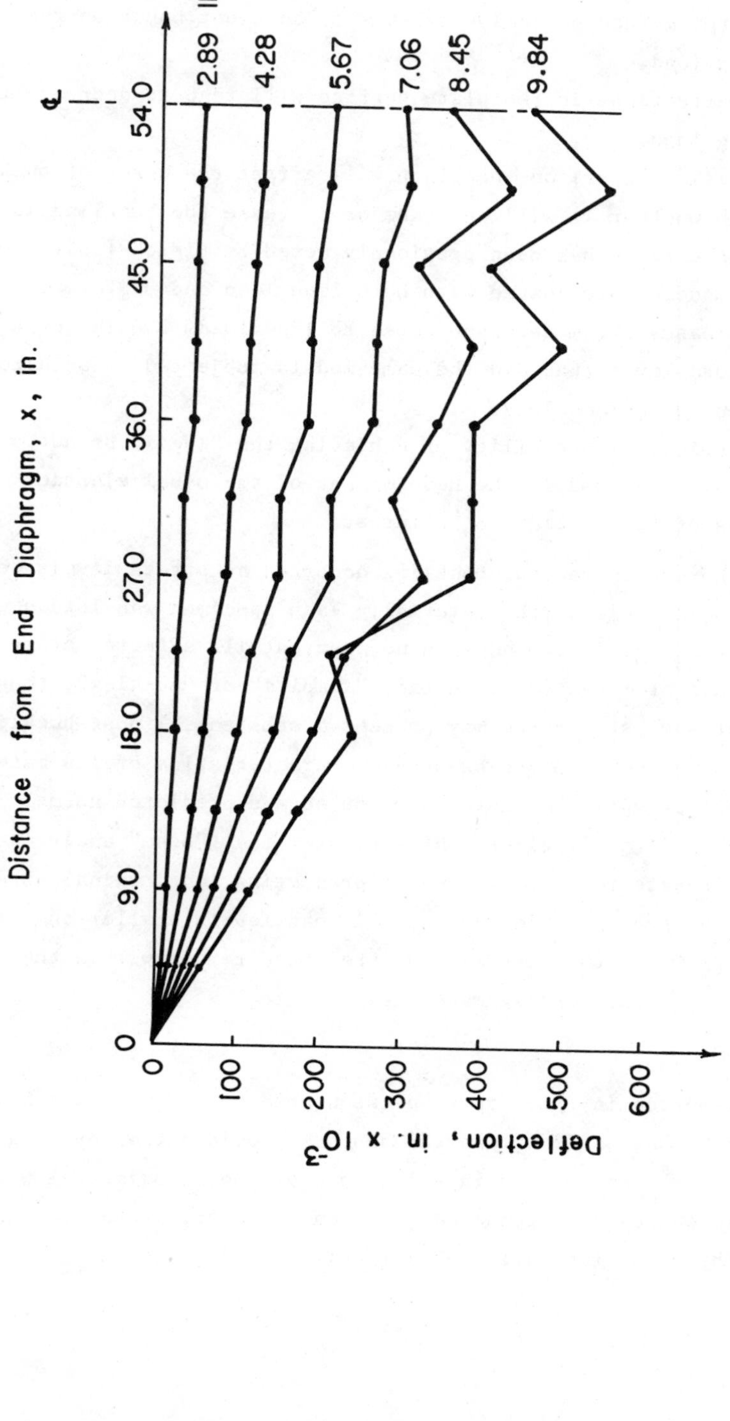

Fig. 8. Normal Deflection Profiles Along Interior Row of Dial Gages Specimen LIII A 3S.

with plate structures and such discrepancies have also been noted by Timoshenko and Gere [17]. These discrepancies may be attributed in part to the following factors:

1. The energy method of analysis leads to an upper bound on the buckling load.
2. The imperfections in the plate surface will tend to decrease the buckling load.
3. The normal pressure on the plate will affect the onset of buckling, although whether it will decrease or increase the buckling load is not clear, as has been previously noted by Bleich [19]. Two of the models were tested with both line load and uniform load. In both cases the models subjected to line loads buckled at a lower load level than did the same models subjected to a uniformly distributed surface load.
4. The practical impossibility of achieving the "ideal" boundary conditions presumed in the development of the usual elastic analysis of folded plate structures.

In all of the models tested, buckling occurred at stress levels well within the elastic range of the material. Each specimen was loaded well beyond its initial critical load with no apparent ill effects, other than the presence of large scale surface "dimples" or "buckles", thus indicating that such structures may possess a substantial post-buckling strength depending upon the stress-strain characteristics of its material.

The satisfactory agreement between measured and predicted normal stresses observed in every experiment indicates that "beam" analysis is sufficiently accurate for the purpose of predicting longitudinal normal stresses in structures of this type at all load levels smaller than the buckling load provided that stresses so predicted remain within the elastic range of the structural material.

ACKNOWLEDGMENTS

The research reported in this paper was sponsored by the National Science Foundation, Grant No. GK 1280, and the support provided thereby is gratefully acknowledged. Assistance in all phases of the experimental work reported herein was capably rendered by Anton Ketterer, technician and Bahman Shahrokhizadeh, laboratory assistant.

REFERENCES

1. Winter, G. and Pei, M., "Hipped Plate Construction", ACI Journal, Proceedings, Vol. 18, January, 1947, pp. 505-531.

2. Gaafar, I., "Hipped Plate Analysis Considering Joint Displacements," Transactions, A.S.C.E., Vol. 119, 1954, pp. 743-770.

3. Goldberg, J. E. and Leve, H. L., "Theory of Prismatic Folded Plate Structures", Publications, I.A.B.S.E., No. 17, 1957, Zurich, Switzerland.

4. Simpson, H., "Design of Folded Plate Roofs", Proceedings, A.S.C.E., Vol. 84, No. ST1, January, 1958, pp. 1-21.

5. Yitzhaki, D., Prismatic and Cylindrical Shell Roofs, Haifa Science Publishers, Haifa, Israel, 1958.

6. Anon., "Phase I Report on Folded Plate Construction," Report of the Task Committee on Folded Plate Construction of the Committee on Masonry and Reinforced Concrete of the Structural Division, Proceedings, A.S.C.E., Vol. 89, No. ST6, December, 1963, pp. 365-406.

7. Scordelis, A. C., Croy, E. L. and Stubbs, I. R., "Experimental and Analytical Study of a Folded Plate," Proceedings, A. S. C. E., Vol. 87, December, 1961.

8. Beaufait, F. W. and Gray, G. A., "Experimental Analysis of Continuous Folded Plates," Proceedings, A.S.C.E., Vol. 92, No. ST1, February, 1966, pp. 11-20.

9. Scordelis, A. C. and Gerasimenko, P. V., "Strength of Reinforced Concrete Folded Plate Models," Proceedings A.S.C.E., Vol. 92, No. ST1. February, 1966, pp. 351-364.

10. Guralnick, S. A. and Swartz, S. E., "Reinforcement of Folded Plates," Journal of the American Concrete Institute Proceedings, Vol. 62, May, 1965, pp. 587-604.

11. Conrado, A. K. and Schnobrich, W. C., "Discrete Analysis of Continuous Folded Plates," Civil Engineering Studies, Structural Research Series No. 321, University of Illinois, Urbana, March, 1967.

12. Stowell, E. Z., "Buckling Stresses for Flat Plates and Sections," Transactions, A.S.C.E., Vol. 117, 1952.

13. Lundquist, E. E. and Stowell, E. Z., "Critical Compressive Stresses for Flat Rectangular Plates Supported Along All Edges and Elastically Restrained Against Rotation Along the Unloaded Edges," N.A.C.A. Report, No. 733.

14. Stowell, E. Z., "Critical Shear Stress of an Infinitely Long Flat Plate with Equal Restraint Against Rotation Along the Parallel Edges," N.A.C.A. Wartime Report, No. 1-476, 1943.

15. Stowell, E. Z. and Schwartz, E. B., "Critical Stress for an Infinitely Long Flat Plate with Elastically Restrained Edges Under Combined Shear and Direct Stress," N.A.C.A. Wartime Report, No. L-340, 1943.

16. Swartz, S. E., "Buckling of Folded Plates," A thesis presented to Illinois Institute of Technology, at Chicago, Illinois, in partial fulfillment of the requirements for the degree of Doctor of Philosophy, June, 1967.

17. Timoshenko, S. P. and Gere, J. M., Theory of Elastic Stability, McGraw-Hill Book Company, Inc., New York, N. Y., 1961, pp. 424.

18. Swartz, S. E., Mikhail, M. L. and Guralnick, S. A., "Buckling of Folded Plate Structures," Experimental Mechanics, Vol. 9, No. 6, June, 1969.

19. Bleich, J., Buckling Strength of Metal Structures, MeGraw-Hill Book Company, Inc., New York, N. Y., 1952.

20. Swartz, S. E. and Guralnick, S. A., "Approximate Analysis of the Stability of Folded Plate Structures," Publications, I.A.B.S.E., Vol. 29, part 2, Zurich, Switzerland, December, 1969.

APPLICATION OF CONFORMAL TRANSFORMATION TO THE VARIATIONAL METHOD: BUCKLING LOADS OF POLYGONAL PLATES

James C. M. Yu
Auburn University

ABSTRACT

The minimal problem of the potential energy of an elastic polygonal plate under a distributive load and in-plane hydrostatic pressure is transformed by a holomorphic function into an equivalent problem of a plate with a circular boundary. The equivalent problem is then explicitly solved by the Rayleigh-Ritz method. The formulation is independent of the actual shape of the plate and thus holds for a large class of plates with boundaries which are conformal images of a unit circle. The numerical results calculated for buckling loads on plates of various shapes are in good agreement with the available data.

LIST OF NOTATIONS

a_c	Characteristic dimension of a polygonal plate
a_i, b_i, c_i	Coefficients in series expansions
A^{mnpq}	Set of constants
D	Flexural rigidity of a plate
P	In-plane hydrostatic pressure per unit boundary length
q_n	Normal distributive loading
$\|\|Q\|\| = Q\bar{Q}$	Square of the modulus of any quantity Q
$Q^{(jn)}$	Symmetric part of Q^{jn}
$\text{Det}\|Q^{jn}\| = \text{Det}\|Q\|$	Determinant with the elements Q^{jn}
R + C	Region R with the boundary C in the z-plane

$R_\zeta + C_\zeta$	Region R_ζ with the boundary C_ζ in the ζ-plane
$V(a_j)$	Function of the undetermined coefficients a_j
$V[W]$	Functional of any function W
W, W_{xy}	Displacement and its derivative with respect to the subscripts
$z = f(\zeta)$	Conformal mapping function
ν	Poisson's ratio
$\phi^m(\zeta,\bar{\zeta})$	Coordinate functions

INTRODUCTION

Timoshenko introduced the Rayleigh-Ritz method of minimizing potential energy to the study of deflection and buckling of an elastic plate and gave extensive applications in his well known texts [1,2]. M. Yoshiko and T. Kawai [3] used the same approach to formulate a general eigenvalue problem for a plate which is bounded by a finite number of smooth arcs. In their formulation, the coordinate functions become unwieldy in manipulations for a many-sided plate. Furthermore, these complicated manipulations must be repeated for each plate. This makes the formulation even less desirable. It is, therefore, the purpose of this paper to develop a procedure for which these complicated manipulations need be done only once for a large class of plates.

The application of conformal mapping to engineering problems has a very long history. But its application to the direct method was probably first made by K. Munakata [4] in the study of vibration and stability of a rectangular clamped plate. G. N. Savin [5] applied a similar idea to a complicated problem in the study of a stress concentration caused by an irregular hole in a shallow shell. S. B. Roberts [6] studied a general eigenvalue problem for the Helmholtz differential equation with a mixed homogeneous condition in a plane region with an irregular boundary. With certain technical modifications P. A. Laura *et al.* [7,8] used Munakata's approach to solve many important engineering problems.

The authors mentioned above transform the differential equation into another region for the greater ease in the choice of coordinate functions provided in the transformed plane. And then, the transformed equation is either solved exactly in an asymptotic sense as Savin did or approximated by the Galerkin method as Munakata and Laura did. In this paper, an application of conformal transformation to the variational method will be introduced. The basic idea is to transform the potential energy of an elastic plate with an irregular boundary by a holomorphic function into a unit circular region in another plane. Thus, the minimal problem for the potential energy of the actual plate is replaced by an equivalent problem for a plate with a circular boundary. The coordinate functions for the equivalent problem can be easily chosen, and the problem can then be solved by the Rayleigh-Ritz method. The coordinate functions chosen in the transformed plane also satisfy the required homogeneous conditions along the actual boundary of the plate as a result of the holomorphic property of the mapping function. The choice of the coordinate functions is independent of the actual shape of the plate. Therefore, the formulation is valid for all plates with boundaries which form the conformal images of a unit circle. The parameters characterizing the actual shape of the plate are needed only at the very end of the problem when a numerical result is required.

With the introduction of the local potential [9], the method presented in this paper can not only be applied directly to solid and fluid mechanics but also to heat and mass transfer and to other transport phenomena in a plane region with an irregular boundary. The author has also applied this method to the determination of the natural frequencies of polygonal plates [10]. A nonlinear cooling problem of polygonal plates in which conductivity is a function of temperature is currently under investigation.

General Formulation

Let an elastic plate with a boundary C occupy a region R in the z-plane, as shown in Fig. 1a. The potential energy of an elastic plate under a distributive load $q_n(x,y)$ and in-plane hydrostatic pressure P is given as follows:

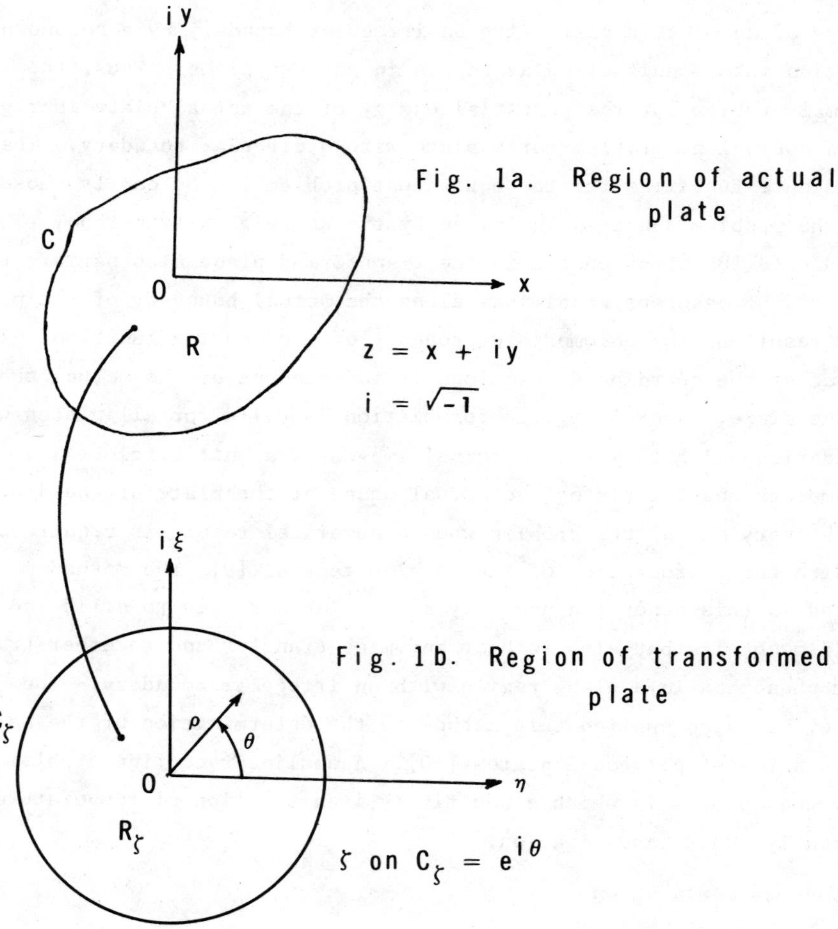

Fig. 1. Conformal Transformation of Region R onto a Unit Circular Region R_ζ.

$$V[w] = \int\int_R \{\frac{D}{2}[(\nabla^2 w)^2 - 2(1-\nu)(w_{xx}w_{yy} - w_{xy}{}^2)] - q_n w - \frac{P}{2}(w_x{}^2 + w_y{}^2)\}\, dxdy \quad (1)$$

If the region R can be obtained by transforming a unit circular region in the ζ-plane by a holomorphic function, as shown in Fig. 1b,

$$z = f(\zeta) \qquad \text{with } f'(\zeta) \neq 0 \text{ in } R_\zeta \quad (2)$$

then Eq. (1) can be rewritten as

$$V[w] = 4D(1+\nu)\int_0^{2\pi}\int_0^1\left[\left|\left|\frac{w_{\zeta\bar{\zeta}}}{f'(\zeta)}\right|\right|^2 + \alpha\left|\left|\frac{\partial}{\partial\zeta}\frac{w_\zeta}{f'(\zeta)}\right|\right|^2 - \frac{q_n w}{4D(1+\nu)}||f'(\zeta)||^2 - \frac{P}{2D(1+\nu)}||w_\zeta||^2\right]\rho d\rho d\theta \quad (3)$$

where $\zeta = \rho e^{i\theta}$, and $\alpha = (1-\nu)/(1+\nu)$. The minimum value of the potential energy is an invariant with respect to the conformal transformation. Therefore, the minimal problem of the potential energy in the z-plane is replaced by an equivalent problem in the ζ-plane. The equivalent problem will be solved by the Rayleigh-Ritz method.

The N-term approximation of $w(\zeta,\bar{\zeta})$ denoted by $w_N(\zeta,\bar{\zeta})$ can be represented as follows:

$$w_N(\zeta,\bar{\zeta}) = \sum_{m=1}^{N} a_m\phi^m(\zeta,\bar{\zeta}) \quad (4)$$

where a_m are the N undetermined coefficients and $\phi^m(\zeta,\bar{\zeta})$ are the coordinate functions which satisfy the required homogeneous conditions on C_ζ. As a result of the holomorphic property of the transformation function $z = f(\zeta)$ with its reversion $\zeta = g(z)$, $\phi^m(\zeta,\bar{\zeta})$ and $\Phi^m(z,\bar{z})$ also satisfy the corresponding conditions on C in the z-plane.

The transformation function and its derivative are assumed to be holomorphic in R_ζ. Therefore, the derivative of the transformation function can be expanded in a power series of ζ [11, p. 363],

$$f'(\zeta) = \sum_{n=0}^{\infty} b_n\zeta^n \quad (5)$$

That only the derivative is needed is seen from Eq. (3). For application, the series in Eq. (5) can be truncated with finite terms to obtain the preassigned degree of accuracy between the transformed image of a unit circle and the actual boundary. By the assumption that $f'(\zeta) \neq 0$ in R_ζ, the reciprocal of $f'(\zeta)$ exists. And thus, it can also be expanded in a power series of ζ. Use of the binomial formula yields

$$\frac{b_0}{f'(\zeta)} = \sum_{m=0}^{\infty} c_m \zeta^m \tag{6}$$

where

$$c_0 = 1$$

$$c_m = \sum_{n=1}^{m} \Gamma_m^n$$

for $m \geq 1$, and

$$\Gamma_m^n = \sum_{i,j\ldots q=1} (-1)^i C_j^i C_k^j \cdots C_q^p \left(\frac{b_1}{b}\right)^i \left(\frac{b_2}{b_1}\right)^j \cdots \left(\frac{b_n}{b_{n-1}}\right)^q$$

with the condition that the sum of the exponents is equal to m; that is, $(i + j + \ldots + q) = m$. C_j^i are the binomial coefficients.

Substitution of Eqs. (4), (5), and (6) into Eq. (3) gives the following expression for potential energy

$$V(a_j) = \frac{4D(1+\nu)}{(b_0)^2} \sum_{m,n=1}^{N} a_m a_n (B^{mn} + \alpha D^{mn} - \lambda G^{mn}) - \sum_{m=1}^{N} a_m F^m \tag{7}$$

where

$$\left.\begin{aligned} B^{mn} &= \sum_{p,q=0}^{\infty} c_p c_q A^{mnpq} \\ D^{mn} &= \sum_{p,q=0}^{\infty} c_p c_q C^{mnpq} \\ F^{m} &= \sum_{p,q=0}^{\infty} b_p b_q E^{mnpq} \end{aligned}\right\} \qquad (8a)$$

$$\left.\begin{aligned} A^{mnpq} &= \int_0^{2\pi}\int_0^1 \phi^m_{\zeta\bar{\zeta}}\ \overline{\phi^n_{\zeta\bar{\zeta}}}\ \zeta^p\ \overline{\zeta^q}\ \rho d\rho d\theta \\ C^{mnpq} &= \int_0^{2\pi}\int_0^1 \left(\zeta^p \phi^m_{\zeta\zeta} + p\zeta^{p-1}\phi^m_{\zeta}\right) \times \left(\overline{\zeta^q}\ \overline{\phi^n_{\zeta\zeta}} \right. \\ &\qquad \left. + q\overline{\zeta^{q-1}}\ \overline{\phi^n_{\zeta}}\right) \rho d\rho d\theta \\ E^{mpq} &= \int_0^{2} \int_0^{1} q_n \phi^m \zeta^p \overline{\zeta^q}\ \rho d\rho d\theta \\ G^{mn} &= \int_0^{2} \int_0^{1} \phi^m_{\zeta} \overline{\phi^n_{\zeta}}\ \rho d\rho d\theta \end{aligned}\right\} \qquad (8b)$$

and

$$\lambda = \frac{(b_0)^2}{2\ (1 + \nu)}$$

From Eq. (7) with the condition that

$$\frac{\partial V}{\partial a_j} = 0 \qquad j=1,2,\ldots,N \qquad (9)$$

for a stationary value of the potential energy, one obtains

$$\sum_{n=1}^{N} a_n [B^{(jn)} + \alpha D^{(jn)} - \lambda G^{(jn)}] = \frac{(b_0)^2}{8D(1+\nu)} F^j \tag{10}$$

When the distributive load $q_n(\zeta,\bar{\zeta})$ and P are given, Eq. (10) yields a system of N linear algebraic equations for the N undetermined constants a_n. The property of linear independence of the coordinate functions ensures that the solution be unique. Thus, an N-term approximation for the deflection $w(\zeta,\bar{\zeta})$ is obtained. The deflection $w(\zeta,\bar{\zeta})$ can be transformed into $w(z,\bar{z})$ by $\zeta = g(z)$ whose existence is assumed. Then, the forces and moments can be easily calculated at any position of the actual plate. It would be desirable to express the force system in terms of $w(\zeta,\bar{\zeta})$ directly instead of reversing $w(\zeta,\bar{\zeta})$ to $w(z,\bar{z})$. However, that problem will not be examined in this paper.

When $q_n = 0$ and, consequently, $F^j = 0$, there is no non-trivial solution of a_n except when P reaches its critical value, which is determined by the condition

$$\mathrm{Det}\left|B^{(jn)} + \alpha D^{(jn)} - \lambda G^{(jn)}\right| = 0 \qquad j,n=1,2,\ldots,N \tag{11}$$

The value of P corresponding to the smallest root of λ in Eq. (11) is the buckling load denoted by P_{cr}.

Explicit Formulas

Further progress can be made only when the coordinate functions are explicitly chosen. The following coordinate functions were selected to satisfy the geometrical boundary conditions along the edge:

$$\phi^m(\zeta,\bar{\zeta}) = [1 - (\zeta\bar{\zeta})^m]^s \tag{12}$$

where

s = 1 for the simply supported plate, and

s = 2 for the clamped plate.

The coordinate functions $\phi^m(\zeta,\bar{\zeta})$ in Eq. (12) are independent of θ; thus, they can be used only for problems in which the images of the concentric circles in the ζ-plane are the contour lines of the deflection. Otherwise, the requirement of completeness of the coordinate functions is not satisfied. Consequently, the approximation cannot be improved by simply increasing the number of terms in the series expansion. For example, these coordinate functions are not satisfactory for a study of the deflection of a polygonal plate under an arbitrary load, since the contour lines of the actual plane are not the images of the concentric circles in the ζ-plane.

It is worthwhile to mention at this point that the choice of coordinate functions in the ζ-plane is independent of the actual shape of the plate. This makes the formulation applicable to a large class of plates.

As a result of the particular choice of the coordinate functions in Eq. (12), it can be shown that $A^{(mn)pq} = C^{(mn)pq} = 0$ if $p \neq q$. Therefore, Eq. (8a) is simplified from a double summation to a single one as follows:

$$B^{(mn)} = \sum_{p=0}^{\infty} (c_p)^2 A^{(mn)p}$$

$$D^{(mn)} = \sum_{p=0}^{\infty} (c_p)^2 C^{(mn)p} \tag{13}$$

$$F^m = \sum_{p=0}^{\infty} (b_p)^2 E^{mp}$$

The quantities $A^{(mn)p}$, $C^{(mn)p}$, E^{mp}, and $G^{(mn)}$ for $\phi^m(\zeta,\bar{\zeta})$ given in Eq. (12) can be explicitly evaluated from Eq. (8b). They are

$$A^{(mn)p} = \pi(mns)^2 \{\frac{1}{m+n+p-1} + 2(s-1)[\frac{2}{2m+2n+p-1} - \frac{1}{2m+n+p-1} - \frac{1}{m+2n+p-1}]\} \tag{14}$$

$$C^{(mn)p} = \pi mns^2\{\frac{(m-1)(n-1)}{m+n+p-1} + (s-1)[\frac{1-2m-2n+4mn}{2m+2n+p-1} - \frac{(2m-1)(n-1)}{2m+n+p-1} - \frac{(m-1)(2n-1)}{m+2n+p-1}]\}$$

$$+ \pi mnps^2\{\frac{m+n-2}{m+n+p-1} + (s-1)[\frac{2(m+n-1)}{2m+2n+p-1} - \frac{2m+n-2}{2m+n+p-1} - \frac{m+2n-2}{m+2n+p-1}]\}$$

$$+ \pi mn(ps)^2\{\frac{1}{m+n+p-1} + (s-1)[\frac{1}{2m+2n+p-1} - \frac{1}{2m+n+p-1} - \frac{1}{m+2n+p-1}]\} \quad (15)$$

$$G^{(mn)} = \pi mns^2\{\frac{1}{m+n} + (s-1)[\frac{1}{2m+2n} - \frac{1}{2m+n} - \frac{1}{m+2n}]\} \quad (16)$$

$$E^{mp} = \pi q_n\{\frac{1}{p+1} - \frac{1}{m+p+1} + (s-1)[\frac{1}{2m+p+1} - \frac{1}{m+p+1}]\} \quad (17)$$

When $\phi^m(\zeta,\bar{\zeta})$ in Eq. (12) are selected, Eqs. (14), (15), and (16) are valid for any shape of plate having a boundary which is a conformal image of a unit circle. Even the edge conditions, simply supported or clamped, have been explicitly included. Equation (17) holds only for constant q_n.

Numerical Results of Buckling Loads

For convenience in computation, Eq. (11) is expanded in a polynomial of λ as follows:

$$\lambda^N \text{Det}|G| - \lambda^{N-1}\sum_{j=1}^{N} \text{Det}|G(h,j)| + \ldots.$$

$$+ (-1)^k \lambda^{N-k} \sum_{j_1 \cdots j_k=1}^{N} \mathrm{Det}|G(H, j_1 \cdots j_k)|$$

$$+ \ldots + (-1)^N \mathrm{Det}|H| = 0 \tag{18}$$

where

$$H^{(jn)} = B^{(jn)} + \alpha D^{(jn)}$$

The indices $j_1 \cdots j_k$ in $\mathrm{Det}|G(H, j_1 \cdots j_k)|$ only take the natural order of 1, 2, 3, . . ., N, and $\mathrm{Det}|G(H, j_1 \cdots j_k)|$ represents a determinant obtained by erasing the $j_1 \cdots j_k$*th* rows of Det|G| and filling the blanks with the corresponding $j_1 \cdots j_k$*th* rows of Det|H|.

The derivatives of the transformation functions used for computation are:

$$f'(\zeta) = a_c \Gamma (1 - \zeta^\beta)^{-2/\beta} \tag{19}$$

for a regular polygon with number of sides β and apothem a_c [7], Γ are the coefficients given in Table I.

TABLE I. COEFFICIENTS Γ FOR REGULAR POLYGONS

Shape	Γ
Triangle	1.135
Square	1.079
Pentagon	1.052
Hexagon	1.038
Heptagon	1.028
Octagon	1.022

$$f'(\zeta) = 0.9202a_c(1 + 0.2812\zeta^3 + 0.0981\zeta^6 + 0.0315\zeta^9) \tag{20}$$

for a three-lobe profile with rounded joints [12]; and

$$f'(\zeta) = 0.99a_c(1 + 0.36\zeta^2 + 0.15\zeta^4 + 0.07\zeta^6) \qquad (21)$$

for an ellipse [11, p. 421].

Equation (18) was solved for both a two-term (N = 2) and a three-term (N = 3) approximation. The results are summarized in Table II. In all calculations, $\nu = 0.3$. The results in Table 2 for simply supported plates (s = 1) show satisfactory agreement with those of Laura and Shahady in [7]. For clamped plates (s = 2), the results obtained in this paper by a two-term approximation are in excellent agreement with those obtained by a three-term approximation in [7].

TABLE II. BUCKLING LOAD COEFFICIENTS $(a_c^2/D)P_{cr}$

Shape	s = 1			s = 2		
	N = 2	N = 3	[7]	N = 2	N = 3	[7]
Triangle	4.580	4.553	4.487	12.439	12.299	--
Square	4.985	4.965	4.935	13.226	13.128	13.226
Pentagon	5.187	5.171	5.213	13.675	13.590	13.692
Hexagon	5.272	5.251	5.361	13.924	13.841	13.926
Heptagon	5.316	5.295	5.465	14.127	14.045	14.127
Octagon	5.320	5.297	5.529	14.251	14.169	14.250
3-Lobes	5.339	5.331	--	17.739	17.617	--
Ellipse	4.638	4.629	--	15.567	15.443	15.250

Equations (13), (14), and (15) show that $H^{(mn)}$ are monotonic functions of the coefficients c_i. If $B(c_i)$ denotes the number of the first non-vanishing terms in the sequence c_i, then an increase of $B(c_i)$ will simultaneously increase the value of the buckling load. To indicate this behavior, the buckling loads of a simply supported square plate corresponding to different $B(c_i)$ are plotted in Fig. 2 with the exact value of $(a_c2/D)P_{cr} = 4.9346$ as a referential zero. Since $B(c_i)$ is a

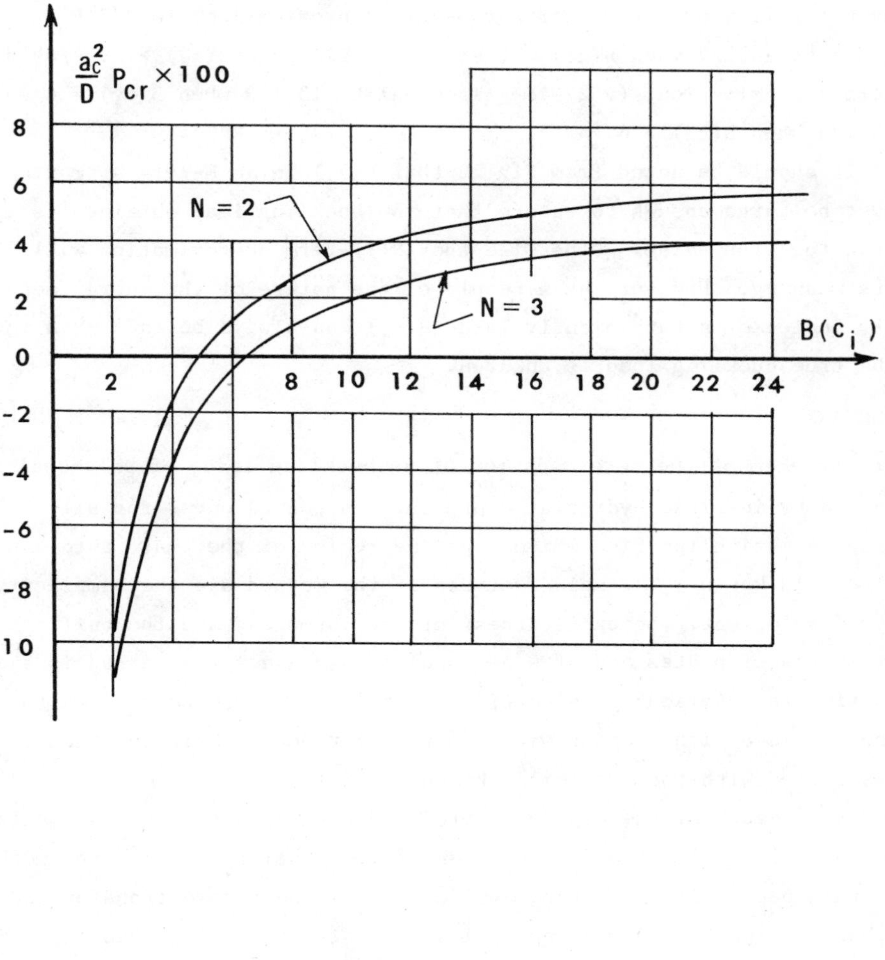

Fig. 2. Variation of Buckling Load Coefficients vs. $B(c_i)$ for a Simply Supported Square Plate.

discrete point set, the continuous curve in Fig. 2 is only provided for a better indication of its tendency. The convergence is fast with respect to both $B(c_i)$ and N.

Buckling loads of a square, clamped plate have been calculated for various $B(c_i)$ and, in contrast to the case of a simply supported edge condition, show insensitivity to $B(c_i)$. This insensitivity is indicated by the following data: For a two-term approximation, $(a_c 2/D)P_{cr}$ is equal to 13.223 when $B(c_i) = 2$ and to 13,226 when $B(c_i) \geq 4$. For a three-term approximation, $(a_c 2/D)P_{cr}$ is equal to 13,123 when $B(c_i) = 4$ and to 13.128 when $B(c_i) \geq 6$.

It should be noted from Fig. 2 that $B(c_i)$ in an N-term approximation must be large enough to ensure that the buckling load obtained is larger than the true value. Otherwise the (N+1)-term approximation will lose its meaning. However, as a result of the nature of the energy method, the choice of a sufficiently large $B(c_i)$ can always be made even though the true buckling load is unknown.

SUMMARY

The problem of the determination of the buckling loads of polygonal plates caused by in-plane hydrostatic pressure is solved once, for all, if the transformation function which maps the region of the plate onto a unit circle is known. The main features of the method are the simplicity of its development, the explicitness of its formulas, and the unification of shapes of plates and of edge conditions. Since the method is simply to find the stationary value of a functional, it can be applied to any problem in a plane region with an irregular boundary if the functional associated with the problem is known.

As a result of the rapid and profound development of the variational method, especially the introduction of the local potential, the method in this paper will have many applications in heat-mass transfer and in other transport phenomena as well as its direct applications in solid and fluid mechanics.

ACKNOWLEDGMENT

The author wishes to express his gratitude to Mr. C. H. Chen for his constant help in computer programming. The computations were performed on the IBM 360 at the Auburn University Computer Center.

REFERENCES

1. Timoshenko, S. P., and Woinowsky-Krieger, S., *Theory of Plates and Shells*, McGraw-Hill, New York, 1959.

2. Timoshenko, S. P., and Gere, J. M., *Theory of Elastic Stability*, McGraw-Hill, New York, 1961.

3. Yoshiko, M., and Kawai, T., "On the Method of Application of Energy Principles to Problems of Elastic Plates," *Proceedings of the Eleventh International Congress of Applied Mechanics*, Münich, 1964, pp. 461-468.

4. Munakata, K., "On the Vibration and Elastic Stability of a Rectangular Plate Clamped at Its Four Edges," *Journal of Mathematics and Physics*, Vol. 31, 1953, pp. 69-74.

5. Savin, G. N., "The Stress Distribution in a Thin Shell with an Arbitrary Hole," *Problems of Continuum Mechanics*, American Society for Industrial and Applied Mathematics, New York, 1961, pp. 382-405.

6. Roberts, S. B., "The Eigenvalue Problem for Two-Dimensional Regions with Irregular Boundaries," *Journal of Applied Mechanics, Transactions of American Society of Mechanical Engineers*, Vol. 34, Series E, 1967, pp. 618-622.

7. Laura, P. A., and Shahady, P. A., "Compex Variable Theory and Elastic Stability Problems," *Journal of the Engineering Mechanics Division, American Society of Civil Engineers*, Vol. 95, 1969, pp. 59-67.

8. Laura, P. A., and Shahady, P. A., "Longitudinal Vibration of a Solid Propellant Rocket Motor," *Developments in Theoretical and Applied Mechanics*, Edited by W. A. Shaw, Vol. 3, Pergamon Press Ltd., Oxford, 1966, pp. 623-633.

9. Donnelly, R. J., Herman, R., and Prigonine, I., *Non-Equilibrium Thermodynamics, Variational Techniques and Stability*, University of Chicago Press, Chicago and London, 1966.

10. Yu, James C. M., "Application of Conformal Transformation to the Variational Method: Natural Frequencies of Polygonal Plates," Submitted for Publication.

11. Kantrovich, L. V., and Krylov, V. I., *Approximate Methods of Higher Analysis*, P. Noordhoff, Ltd., The Netherlands, 1964, pp. 363-421.

12. Axelrad, D. R., "An Approximate Solution for the Torsional Properties of Cylindrical Shafts with Multi-Symmetrical Curved Boundaries," *Zeitschrift für Angewandte Mathematik und Physik*, Vol. 13, 1962, pp. 105-117.

CONTINUUM MECHANICS

A NON-LINEAR INTEGRAL-TYPE THEORY OF INELASTICITY FOR TRANSVERSELY ISOTROPIC MATERIALS

Robert D. Snyder
West Virginia University

Alvin Strauss
University of Kentucky

T. L. Ho
West Virginia University

ABSTRACT

A non-linear integral-type theory of inelasticity is developed based on the following assumptions: i) that permanent plastic deformation is produced even at the lowest stress levels; ii) that upon cyclic loading and unloading the uniaxial stress-strain curve exhibits a stable hysteresis loop; iii) the material is transversely isotropic; iv) the response (stress) is essentially independent of the rate of strain. Some basic boundary value problems are discussed and the theory is compared with some experimental data for compression and flexure of ATJ graphite.

LIST OF NOTATIONS

T	Nine dimensional inner product space
S	Six dimensional space of symmetric tensors
$\underline{T}$, $\underline{F}$, $\underline{E}$, etc.	Tensors and elements of T or S
T_{ij}, F_{ij}, S_{ij}, etc.	Components of $\underline{T}$, $\underline{F}$, and $\underline{S}$
R	Real number field
H	Hilbert space of mappings from R into T or S
$\underline{T}(\cdot)$, $\underline{F}(\cdot)$, $\underline{E}(\cdot)$	Mappings from R into T or S and elements of H
$\underline{F}(\ )$	Functionals, mapping H into T or S
$s(\tau)$, S	Strain arc length at time τ and the present time t, respectively

$(\ )'$, $(\dot{\ })$	Derivative with respect to time τ and arc length s, respectively
G	Symmetry group
$\underline{Q}$	An element of G
I_α	Tensor invariants
k, c_i, a, b, r	Material parameters
$K_i(\cdot)$	Material response functions
E_i	Initial tangent moduli
ε	Longitudinal bending strain
ρ	Radius of curvature
u	Distance from neutral bending surface
M_c	Bending moment

INTRODUCTION

This work arose out of a study of the room-temperature mechanical response of nuclear reactor grade graphite. The essential characteristics of this response are i) permanent plastic deformation is produced even at the lowest stress levels, ii) that upon cyclic loading and unloading the material exhibits a stable hysteresis loop, and iii) the symmetry of the material is transversely isotropic. Features (i) and (ii) are illustrated in the cyclic loading stress-strain curve of Fig. 1, in which the starred quantities represent residual strain after unloading. We adjoin to these characteristics that short of impact rates the stress-strain relationship is rate independent and that other time dependent phenomena are absent at room temperature. Thus we describe room temperature graphite as a nonlinear, transversely isotropic, rate independent inelastic material whose degree of inelasticity is governed by some previously attained state of strain. In a previous paper [1] the authors have developed a one-dimensional theory for such response under cyclic loading. In this paper we develop a nonlinear integral-type three-dimensional constitutive theory capable of exhibiting the aforementioned characteristics and obtain a constitutive equation for cyclic loading conditions. Finally, some experiments are discussed and the theory compared with some experimental data for ATJ graphite.

The terminology and notation employed are that of modern continuum mechanics and functional analysis. Bold face (underscored) letters

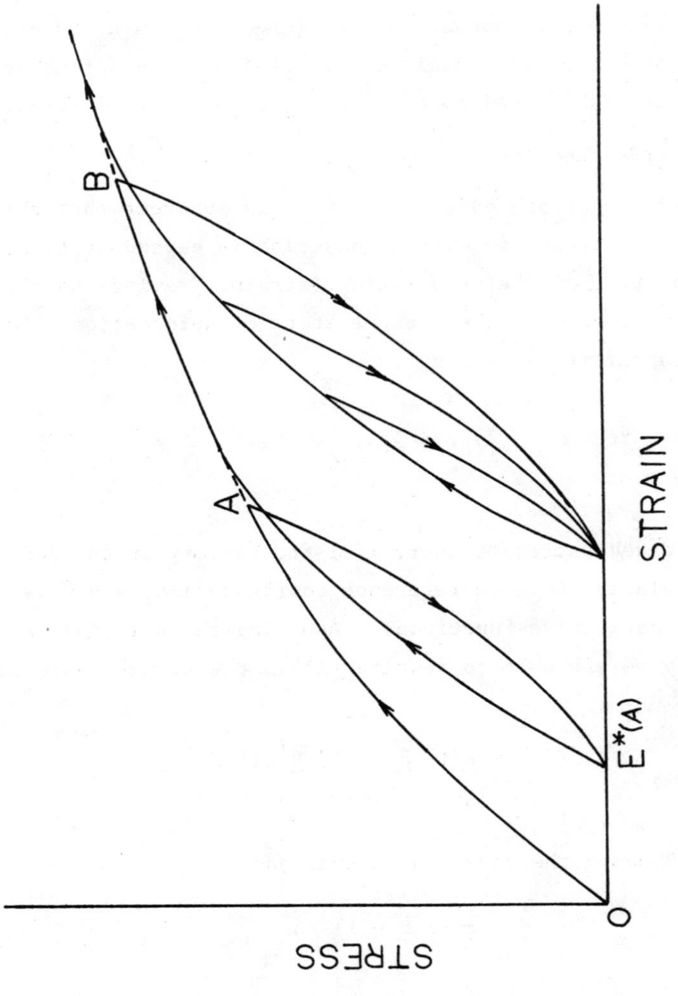

Fig. 1. Cyclic Stress-Strain.

denote linear transformations (tensors) in the nine-dimensional inner product space T or the six-dimensional space S of symmetric tensors. The trace of a tensor is denoted by tr and the transpose with a superscript T. We consider the tensor valued functions (histories) $\underline{F}(\ )$ to be mappings from R (reals) into T (or S) and to be elements of a Hilbert space H and whose components are elements of an L_2 space. Finally, the constitutive functionals are denoted with bold face script majuscules and are considered to be mappings from H into T (or S).

The Constitutive Functional

From the remarks of the preceding section it is apparent that the mechanical response (stress) we wish to describe is dependent to some extent upon the history of the deformation (strain) previous to the present time t as well as upon the present state of deformation. We make this statement explicit by writing

$$\hat{\underline{T}}(t) = \underset{\tau=-\infty}{\overset{\tau=t}{\hat{\underline{F}}}}[\underline{F}(\tau)] \tag{1}$$

where $\hat{\underline{T}}$ is the Cauchy stress tensor, $F(\tau)$ the history of the deformation gradient relative to some reference configuration, and $\hat{\underline{F}}$ is the tensor-valued constitutive functional. Applying the principle of material objectivity we are able to rewrite (1) in the frame-invariant form

$$\hat{\underline{T}}(t) = \underline{R}(t)\ \underset{\tau=-\infty}{\overset{\tau=t}{\hat{\underline{F}}}}[E(\tau)]\ \underline{R}^T(t) \tag{2}$$

where $\underline{F} = \underline{R}\ \underline{U}$, R being the rotation tensor, and

$$\underline{E} = \frac{1}{2}\ (\underline{F}^T\underline{F} - \underline{I})\ \varepsilon S$$

is the Cauchy-Green strain tensor. We now assume that our material has been physically standardized at $\tau = 0$ so that we may write

$$\underline{T}(t) = \underset{\tau=0}{\overset{\tau=t}{\hat{\underline{F}}}}[E(\tau)] \tag{3}$$

where $\underline{T} = \underline{R}^T\ \hat{\underline{T}}\ \underline{R}$ is the rotated stress tensor.

Since we wish the response to be time-rate-independent, in the manner of Pipkin and Rivlin [2] we introduce the non-negative monontonic increasing time invariant parameter

$$s(\tau) = \int_0^{\tau} \sqrt{\text{tr}\ \underline{E}'(\tau')\ \underline{E}'(\tau')}\ d\tau' \tag{4}$$

where

$$\underline{E}'(\tau) = \frac{d\underline{E}(\tau')}{d\tau'} .$$

Thus s represents the arc length of the strain path in the six-dimensional inner product space S. We now write our constitutive functional in the time-invariant form

$$\underline{T}(S) = \underset{s=0}{\overset{s=S}{\underline{F}}}[\underline{E}(s)] \tag{5}$$

where S is the arc length corresponding to $\tau=t$ the present time. In effect we have replaced the wall clock by a material clock which moves only when the material is strained. Thus all time dependent phenomena such as rate-dependence, creep, relaxation, etc., are absent in such a representation.

We note that $\underline{E}(s)$ is intrinsically continuous in s [3]. We further restrict our attention to strain paths for which the right and left-hand derivatives $d\underline{E}(s)/ds$ exist at each point in the interval $(0,\infty)$. Then, by assuming $\underline{E}(0) = \underline{0}$ we may write (4) in the equivalent form

$$\underline{T}(S) = \underset{s=0}{\overset{s=S}{\underline{F}}}[\dot{\underline{E}}(s)] \tag{6}$$

where F( ) is a new functional and

$$\dot{\underline{E}}(s) = \frac{d\underline{E}(s)}{ds}$$

We now consider the requirements imposed by whatever symmetry the material exhibits in its reference state. We say an orthogonal tensor $\underline{Q}$ belongs to the symmetry group G if

$$\underline{Q}\ \underline{F}[\dot{\underline{E}}(s)]_{s=0}^{s=S}\ \underline{Q}^T = \underline{F}[\underline{Q}\ \dot{\underline{E}}(s)\ \underline{Q}^T]_{s=0}^{s=S} \tag{7}$$

We note that s is invariant under a change of reference configuration specified by $\underline{Q}$. Transversely isotropic materials are characterized by an axis of rotational symmetry. If the X_1 axes of a set of rectangular cartesian coordinates (X_1, X_2, X_3) is taken as the symmetry axis, then the transverse isotropy group is made up of all tensors with matrix coefficients of the form

$$Q_{ij} = \begin{bmatrix} 1 & 0 & 0 \\ 0 & \cos\theta & \sin\theta \\ 0 & -\sin\theta & \cos\theta \end{bmatrix} \quad \text{and} \quad \begin{bmatrix} 1 & 0 & 0 \\ 0 & -1 & 0 \\ 0 & 0 & 1 \end{bmatrix}$$

Wineman and Pipkin [4] have shown that every form-invariant functional $\underline{F}$ of a tensor history $\underline{\psi}$ can be expressed in the form

$$\underline{F}[\underline{\psi}(\tau)] = \sum_{\beta=1}^{B} L^{(\beta)} \left\{ \underline{f}^{(\beta)};\ I_1, I_2, \ldots I_A \right\} \tag{8}$$

where $L^{(\beta)}$ is a functional of the basic form-invariant tensor $\underline{f}^{(\beta)}$ and the basic invariants I_α ($\alpha = 1, 2, \ldots A$) of the history, and $L^{(\beta)}$ is linear with respect to $\underline{f}^{(\beta)}$. Lianis and DeHoff [5] have shown that the basic invariants for a set of tensors $\{\underline{T}\}$ under the transverse isotropy group coincide with those of the set $\{\underline{1}, \underline{T}\}$ for the full isotropy group where

$$\underline{1} = \begin{bmatrix} 1 & 0 & 0 \\ 0 & 0 & 0 \\ 0 & 0 & 0 \end{bmatrix}.$$

Using this and the results of Spencer and Rivlin [6] we can write a table of basic invariants for the history $\dot{\underline{E}}(s)$ under the transverse isotropy group. Such a table is given by

$$\{I_\alpha\} = \left\{ \text{tr}\ \underline{M}^{(1)},\ \text{tr}\ \underline{M}^{(1)}\underline{M}^{(2)},\ \ldots,\ \text{tr}\ \underline{M}^{(1)}\underline{M}^{(2)}\underline{M}^{(3)}\underline{M}^{(4)}\underline{M}^{(5)}\underline{M}^{(6)} \right\} \tag{9}$$

where the $\underline{M}^{(i)}$ are all elements in the set

$$\{\underline{1},\ \underline{\dot{E}}(s_1),\ \underline{\dot{E}}(s_2),\ \underline{\dot{E}}(s_3),\ \ldots\ \underline{\dot{E}}(s_6)\}$$

In a similar manner, the tensor invariants $\underline{f}^{(\beta)}$ are obtained from the basic invariants formed from the set

$$\{\underline{\psi},\ \underline{1},\ \underline{\dot{E}}(s_1),\ \underline{\dot{E}}(s_2),\ \ldots\ \underline{\dot{E}}(s_6)\}$$

which are linear in the symmetric tensor $\underline{\psi}$. Thus, with these results we could now write the most general functional exhibiting transverse isotropy. Instead, however, we restrict our attention to those invariants and form-invariant tensors which are of degree one or less in $\underline{\dot{E}}$. These are

$$\{I_\alpha\} = \{\mathrm{tr}\ \underline{\dot{E}}(s),\ \mathrm{tr}\ \underline{1}\ \underline{\dot{E}}(s)\}$$
$$\{\underline{f}^{(\beta)}\} = \{\underline{I},\ \underline{1},\ \underline{\dot{E}}(s),\ \underline{\dot{E}}(s)\ \underline{1} + \underline{1}\ \underline{\dot{E}}(s)\} \qquad (10)$$

Now, using the theorem of Wineman and Pipkin [4] and assuming that $\underline{F}[\underline{\dot{E}}(s)]$ is first order in $\underline{\dot{E}}(s)$ we see that

$$\underline{F}[\underline{\dot{E}}(s)] = L^{(1)}[\underline{I}\ \mathrm{tr}\ \underline{\dot{E}}(s)] + L^{(2)}[\underline{1}\ \mathrm{tr}\ \underline{\dot{E}}(s)]$$
$$+ L^{(3)}[\underline{I}\ \mathrm{tr}\ \underline{1}\ \underline{\dot{E}}(s)] + L^{(4)}[\underline{1}\ \mathrm{tr}\ \underline{1}\ \underline{\dot{E}}(s)]$$
$$+ L^{(5)}[\underline{\dot{E}}(s)] + L^{(6)}[\underline{\dot{E}}(s)\ \underline{1} + \underline{1}\ \underline{\dot{E}}(s)] \qquad (11)$$

where $L^{(\beta)}$ ($\beta = 1, 2, \ldots 6$) are linear[1] in their respective argument functions. Finally, using the Riesz Representation Theorem for bounded linear functionals we arrive at the form of the constitutive functional which we will consider in the remainder of this paper.

$$\underset{s=0}{\overset{s=S}{\underline{F}}}[\underline{\dot{E}}(s)] = \int_0^S K_1(s)\ \underline{\dot{E}}(s)\ ds + \int_0^S K_2(s)\ [\underline{\dot{E}}(s)\ \underline{1} + \underline{1}\ \underline{\dot{E}}(s)]\ ds$$
$$+ \underline{I}\int_0^S K_3(s)\ \mathrm{tr}\ \underline{\dot{E}}(s)\ ds + \underline{1}\int_0^S K_4(s)\ \mathrm{tr}\ \underline{\dot{E}}(s)\ ds$$

(equation continued on the next page)

1. Linear in the sense that we consider $\underline{\dot{E}}(s)$: R → S and for fixed s we define $\underline{\dot{E}}_1(s) + \underline{\dot{E}}_2(s) = (\dot{E}_1 + \dot{E}_2)\ (s)$. Of course, since s depends intrinsically on $\underline{E}$, the response functional is actually nonlinear.

$$+ \underline{I} \int_0^S K_5(s) \text{ tr } \underline{1}\, \dot{\underline{E}}(s)\, ds + \underline{1} \int_0^S K_6(s) \text{ tr } \underline{1}\, \dot{\underline{E}}(s)\, ds \qquad (12)$$

when $K_\alpha(s)$ ($\alpha = 1, 2, \ldots 6$) are scalar valued piecewise continuous functions of s called the material response functions.

Before proceeding to the discussion of the material response functions, we make the following observation. The time invariant parameter $s(\tau)$ can be constructed in an infinite number of ways, the usual one being that employed in Eq. (4). However, in dealing with transversely isotropic materials we feel it is more reasonable to introduce the parameter $s(\tau)$ defined by

$$s(\tau) = \int_0^\tau \left[\sqrt{\text{tr } \underline{E}'(\tau')\, \underline{E}'(\tau')} - k\sqrt{\text{tr } \underline{1}\, \underline{E}'(\tau')\, \underline{E}'(\tau')}\,\right] d\tau' \qquad (13)$$

where $k \leq 1$ is a scalar constant which physically reflects the degree of transverse isotropy of the particular material. In the subsequent work, we will use (13) for our definition of arc length s.

Response Functions for Cyclic Loading

Although our constitutive functional is valid for all histories $\underline{E}(\tau) \varepsilon H$, in order to determine an explicit form for the material response functions $K_i(s)$, we will consider histories of the form

$$\underline{E}(\tau) = \underline{E}\, h(\tau) + \underline{E}_o \qquad (14)$$

where $h(\tau)$ is piecewise differentiable and $\underline{E}$ and $\underline{E}_o$ are constant tensors in S. Then

$$\underline{E}'(\tau) = \underline{E}\, h'(\tau)$$

and

$$s(\tau) - s(0) = \{\sqrt{\text{tr } \underline{E}\, \underline{E}} - k\sqrt{\text{tr } \underline{1}\, \underline{E}\, \underline{E}}\,\} \int_0^\tau |h'(\tau')|\, d\tau' \qquad (15)$$

Thus, we can choose any convenient straining program specified by $h(\tau)$ and determine the arc length s from Eq. (15).

We now define a straining program (14) as a <u>loading</u> process if $h(\tau)$ is a monotone increasing function. Then $h'(\tau) > 0$ and if $h(0) = 0$ and $\underline{E}_o = \underline{0}$ (15) becomes

$$s(\tau) = M\, h(\tau)$$

and

$$\underline{E}(s) = \underline{E}\,\frac{s}{M}$$

$$\dot{\underline{E}}(s) = \underline{E}\,\frac{1}{M} \qquad (16)$$

where $M = \sqrt{\mathrm{tr}\,\underline{E}\,\underline{E}} - k\sqrt{\mathrm{tr}\,\underline{1}\,\underline{E}\,\underline{E}}$

Consider now a typical term in the constitutive functional (12), the first term, say. For a loading program

$$\int_0^S K_1(s)\,\frac{\underline{E}}{M}\,ds = \frac{\underline{E}}{M}\int_0^S K_1(s)\,ds \qquad (17)$$

Now, Woolley [7] and others have shown that an exponential form describes the one-dimensional uniaxial loading response of graphite rather well. Thus, to illustrate our theory we are motivated to choose some exponential form for each $K_i(s)$. However, since we wish to describe unloading and reloading processes as well as loading, the response function must reflect some sort of explicit dependence on straining history to distinguish loading from unloading. In general, this would call for some type of criterion analogous to the yield functions of plasticity theory. However, for cyclic processes with strain histories of the form (14), we choose response functions of the form

$$K_i(s) = C_i\,\exp\{[a + bn(r - 1)]\,\hat{S} - bs\} \qquad (18)$$

where C_i, a, b, and r are material parameters, n is the number of complete reversals of the cyclic straining process, and $\hat{S}$ is the value of the arc length parameter corresponding to the previous maximum strain state experienced by the graphite. We remark that for strain histories of the form (14), the quantities n and $\hat{S}$ are easily identified since all six components of strain are reversed at the same instant of time and value of arc length.

The material parameters C_i (i = 1, 2, 3, 4, 5, 6) can be physically interpreted in terms of axial and shear moduli, a and b are indexes of the nonlinearity of the material, and r is an index of the inelasticity or strain damage.

To illustrate, let

$$\underline{E} = \begin{bmatrix} m_1 & 0 & 0 \\ 0 & m_2 & 0 \\ 0 & 0 & m_3 \end{bmatrix} \tag{19}$$

which corresponds to an arbitrary triaxial state of axial strains parallel to the principal material axes. Then by (16)

$$M = \sqrt{m_1^2 + m_2^2 + m_3^2} - k\sqrt{m_1^2} \tag{20}$$

and

$$\dot{\underline{E}}(s) = \frac{1}{M}\begin{bmatrix} m_1 & 0 & 0 \\ 0 & m_2 & 0 \\ 0 & 0 & m_3 \end{bmatrix} \tag{21}$$

Then for such a loading program n and $\hat{S}$ in (18) are zero and the constitutive functional (12) yields

$$\underline{T}(S) = \frac{1}{M}\int_0^S \left\{ C_1 \begin{bmatrix} m_1 & 0 & 0 \\ 0 & m_2 & 0 \\ 0 & 0 & m_3 \end{bmatrix} + (2C_2 + C_6) \begin{bmatrix} m_1 & 0 & 0 \\ 0 & 0 & 0 \\ 0 & 0 & 0 \end{bmatrix} \right.$$

$$+ C_3 \begin{bmatrix} m_1 + m_2 + m_3 & 0 & 0 \\ 0 & m_1 + m_2 + m_3 & 0 \\ 0 & 0 & m_1 + m_2 + m_3 \end{bmatrix}$$

$$\left. + C_4 \begin{bmatrix} m_1 + m_2 + m_3 & 0 & 0 \\ 0 & 0 & 0 \\ 0 & 0 & 0 \end{bmatrix} + C_5 \begin{bmatrix} m_1 & 0 & 0 \\ 0 & m_1 & 0 \\ 0 & 0 & m_1 \end{bmatrix} \right\} e^{-bs}\, ds$$

or

$$T_{11} = \frac{1}{Mb}\{(C_1 + 2C_2 + C_5 + C_6)m_1 + (C_3 + C_4)(m_1 + m_2 + m_3)\}(1 - e^{-bS}) \tag{22a}$$

$$T_{22} = \frac{1}{Mb}\{C_3(m_1 + m_2 + m_3) + C_1 m_2 + C_5 m_1\}(1 - e^{-bS}) \tag{22b}$$

$$T_{33} = \frac{1}{Mb}\{C_3(m_1 + m_2 + m_3) + C_1 m_3 + C_5 m_1\}(1 - e^{-bS}) \tag{22c}$$

$$T_{12} = T_{13} = T_{23} \equiv 0 \tag{22d}$$

Then, utilizing (16)

$$\left.\frac{dT_{11}}{dE_{11}}\right]_{S=0} = \frac{1}{m_1}\{(C_1 + 2C_2 + C_5 + C_6)m_1 + (C_3 + C_4)(m_1 + m_2 + m_3)\} \tag{23a}$$

$$\left.\frac{dT_{22}}{dE_{22}}\right]_{S=0} = \frac{1}{m_2}\{C_3(m_1 + m_2 + m_3) + C_1m_2 + C_5m_1\} \tag{23b}$$

$$\left.\frac{dT_{33}}{dE_{33}}\right]_{S=0} = \frac{1}{m_3}\{C_3(m_1 + m_2 + m_3) + C_1m_3 + C_5m_1\} \tag{23c}$$

which, in uniaxial loading experiments, can be interpreted as the initial tangent moduli of the stress-strain curves. For example, in a uniaxial test loading parallel to the 1 axis

$$\left.\frac{dT_{11}}{dE_{11}}\right]_{S=0} = E_1 \text{ modulus}$$

while

$$T_{22} = T_{33} = 0 \qquad \text{all } s.$$

Letting

$$A = (C_1 + 2C_2 + C_5 + C_6), \qquad B = (C_3 + C_4) \tag{24}$$

uniaxial experiments parallel to the 1 and 2 or 3 axes are sufficient to determine A, B, C_1, C_3, C_4, and C_5 leaving C_2 and C_6 to be determined from a shear or some other experiment. The parameter b appearing in (22) is then selected to provide the best fit for the uniaxial loading data.

The parameters n, a, and r come into play only when the material undergoes an unloading process after reaching some $\hat{\underline{E}}$ and $\hat{S}$. In Eq. (14) an unloading process would be one for which $h'(\tau) < 0$. Hence we write

$$\underline{E}(\tau) = \hat{\underline{E}} + (\hat{\underline{E}} - \underline{E}^*)\, h(\tau) = \hat{\underline{E}} + \underline{B}\, h(\tau) \tag{25}$$

where $\underline{B} = \hat{\underline{E}} - \underline{E}^*$ and $\underline{E}^*$ is the residual strain in the material when the load has been removed. Then by (15) and assuming $h(0) = 0$

$$s(\tau) - \hat{S} = \{\sqrt{\mathrm{tr}\ \underline{B}\ \underline{B}} - k\sqrt{\mathrm{tr}\ \underline{1}\ \underline{B}\ \underline{B}}\} \int_0^{\tau} - h'(\tau)d\tau = -N\ h(\tau) \tag{26}$$

thus

$$\begin{aligned} \underline{E}(s) &= \hat{\underline{E}} - \frac{s - \hat{S}}{N}\underline{B} \\ \dot{\underline{E}}(s) &= -\frac{\underline{B}}{N} \end{aligned} \qquad S \geq \hat{S} \tag{27}$$

where

$$N = \sqrt{\mathrm{tr}\ \underline{B}\ \underline{B}} - k\sqrt{\mathrm{tr}\ \underline{1}\ \underline{B}\ \underline{B}}$$

We consider a typical term of (12), say the first. Then

$$\begin{aligned} \int_0^S K_1(s)\ \dot{\underline{E}}(s)\ ds &= \int_0^{\hat{S}} + \int_{\hat{S}}^S K_1(s)\ (-\frac{\underline{B}}{N})ds \\ &= \int_0^{\hat{S}} + (-\frac{\underline{B}}{N})\int_{\hat{S}}^S K_1(s)\ ds \end{aligned} \tag{28}$$

The first term on the right is just (17) for $S = \hat{S}$, and thus corresponds to the stress $\underline{T}(\hat{S})$. Using (18), the second term becomes

$$C_1 \frac{\underline{B}}{Nb} \exp\{[a + b(1)(r - 1)]\hat{S}\}\ \{\exp(-bS) - \exp(-b\hat{S})\}$$

and similar expressions for the other terms in (12). Hence if

$$\underline{B} = \begin{bmatrix} b_1 & 0 & 0 \\ 0 & b_2 & 0 \\ 0 & 0 & b_3 \end{bmatrix}$$

then

$$\begin{aligned} \underline{T}(S) = \underline{T}(\hat{S}) + \frac{1}{Nb}\{C_1\underline{B} + (2C_2 + C_6)\ \underline{1}\ \underline{B} + C_3\ \underline{I}\ \mathrm{tr}\ \underline{B} + C_4\ \underline{1}\ \mathrm{tr}\ \underline{B} \\ + C_5\ \underline{I}\ \mathrm{tr}\ \underline{1}\ \underline{B}\}\ \exp\ \{[a + b(r - 1)]\hat{S}\} \\ \{\exp\ (-bS) - \exp\ (-b\hat{S})\} \end{aligned} \tag{29}$$

Assuming that C_1, C_3, C_4, and C_5 have been determined from the loading data, the parameter a can now be determined from the condition that $\underline{T} = \underline{0}$ when $S = S^*$. Also, to guarantee that the stress will cycle in a loop as the strain is cycled, we let $r = S^*/\hat{S}$. In the next section we illustrate the procedure outlined in this section with some actual experimental data.

Comparison with Experimental Data

Uniaxial Compression / We consider some load versus axial and Poisson strain obtained for cyclic loading of an ATJ type of molded graphite. Uniaxial compressive loading, unloading, and reloading was performed in a series of tests on 3/4 inch diameter cylindrical specimens oriented parallel to each of the principal material axes. Figure 2 presents some typical data for the tests parallel to the 1 direction. Similar data were available for loading parallel to the 2 and 3 axes. For convenience of demonstration we will use the units of the raw data curves; that is, the load (stress) is in pounds, the strain is in microinches per inch, and the moduli in pounds per microinches per inch.

For the initial loading portion of the curves, our theory requires the values of the tangent moduli E_1 and E_2 and the maximum strains m_1, m_2, and m_3. These are:

Loading in 1 direction

$$E_1 = 0.4, \qquad m_1 = 25{,}000, \qquad m_2 = m_3 = -2500$$

Loading in 2 direction

$$E_2 = 0.7, \qquad m_1 = -2000, \qquad m_2 = 12{,}800, \qquad m_3 = -1800.$$

Then, using the procedure outlined in the previous section we get

$$A = 0.340, \qquad B = 0.075, \qquad C_1 = 0.614$$

$$C_3 = 0.116, \qquad C_4 = -0.041, \qquad C_5 = -0.0314$$

Now, since k is to reflect the anisotropy and yet equal zero for the isotropic case, we let

$$k = \frac{E_2 - E_1}{E_2} = \frac{3}{7}$$

Then for loading in 1 direction

$$\hat{S}_1 = M_1 = 14{,}500$$

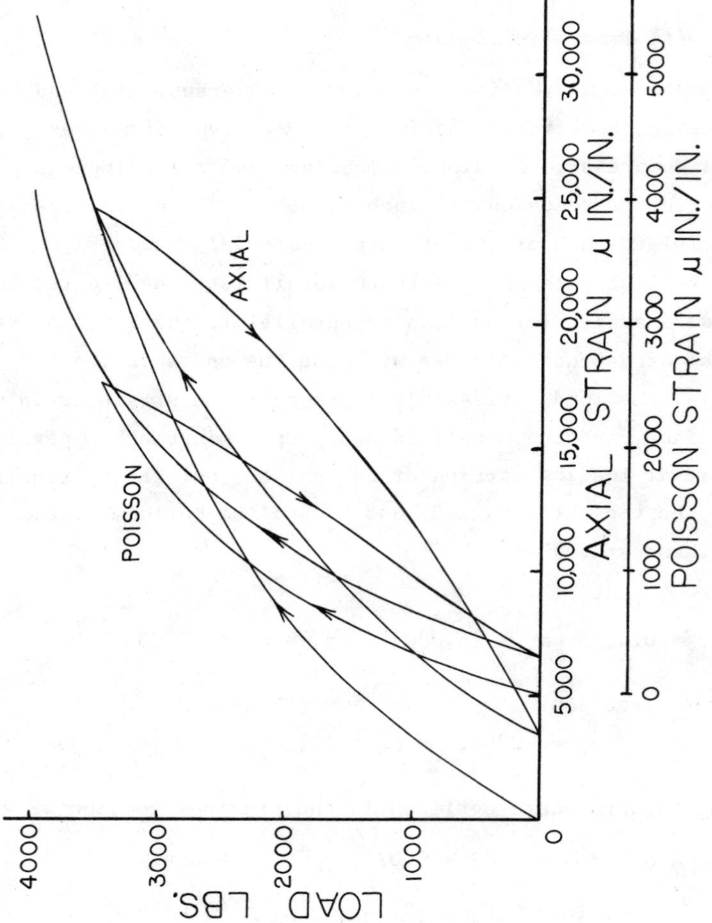

Fig. 2. Load-Axial and Poisson Strain.

and for 2 direction

$$\hat{S}_2 = M_2 = 12,200$$

Then since from experiment

$$T_{11}(\hat{S}_1) = 3550 \quad \text{and} \quad T_{22}(\hat{S}_2) = 3570$$

the "best fit" is obtained for b = 0.00018 for which

$$T_{11}(\hat{S}_1) = 3540 \,, \qquad T_{22}(\hat{S}_2) = 3610$$

For the unloading portion of the data we require the residual strains $\underline{E}^*$ which are:

Unloading in 1 direction

$$E^*_{11} = 3300, \qquad E^*_{22} = E^*_{33} = -300$$

Thus, recalling the definition of $\underline{B}$, for the 1 direction

$$\underline{B}_1 = \begin{bmatrix} 21,700 & 0 & 0 \\ 0 & -2200 & 0 \\ 0 & 0 & -2200 \end{bmatrix} \therefore N_1 = 12,600$$

and for the 2 direction

$$\underline{B}_2 = \begin{bmatrix} -1700 & 0 & 0 \\ 0 & 11,000 & 0 \\ 0 & 0 & -1550 \end{bmatrix} \therefore N_2 = 10,500$$

Then

$$S^*_1 = M_1 + N_1 = 27,100$$

$$S^*_2 = M_2 + N_2 = 22,700$$

Now $\underline{T}(S^*)$ should be zero. Hence if we choose a = 0.000027 we find that

$$T_{11}(S^*) = -20 \qquad T_{22}(S^*) = 80 \,.$$

Thus all the material parameters in (18) have now been determined with the exception of C_2 and C_6 which require some additional experiments. Figures 3 and 4 show the comparison between the experimental

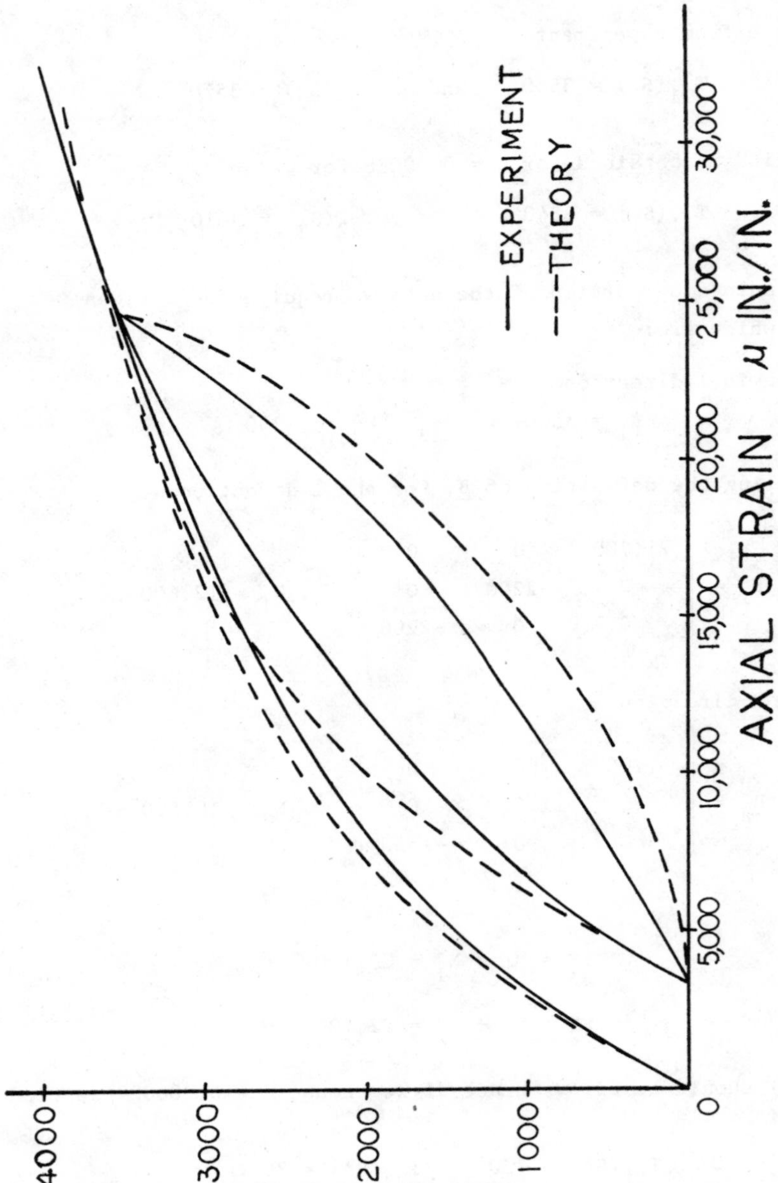

Fig. 3. Load-Strain in 1 Direction.

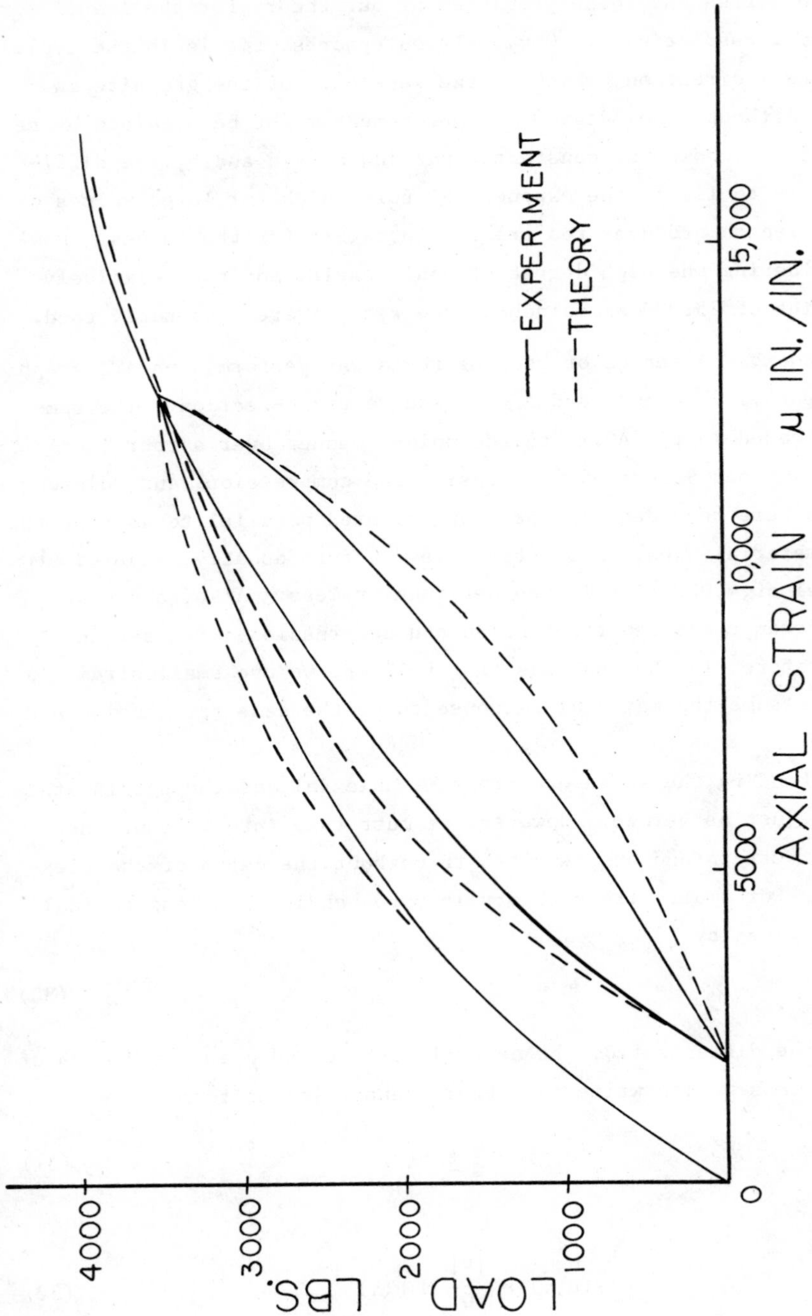

Fig. 4. Load-Strain in 2 or 3 Direction.

load-strain curves and those predicted by our theory for the 1 and 2 or 3 directions, respectively. Obviously our poorest fit is in the cycle loop for the 1 direction, which is the weak axis of the graphite in question. Although some degree of improvement might be obtained by refinement of the choice of constants, particularly a and b, the difficulty appears to lie in the exponential form which for large values of strain arc length produces too great a curvature for the curves. However, considering the high degree of nonlinearity and the relatively large strains of 25,000 microinches, the results are reasonably good.

Pure Bending / A series of bending tests was performed on ATJ graphite specimen 4-1/2 in long and 3/4 in square cross-section. The samples were loaded in the ASTM "thirds-point" manner over a four inch span length. Load versus axial (tension and compression) and Poisson strain data were recorded for specimen oriented parallel to each of the principal material axes. A brittle type fracture usually occurred at a strain level of 4,000 microinches per inch or less. Also, there was little difference between the tension and compression axial strain data. Therefore, in the analysis that follows, we use small strain theory and assume the material response to be the same for tension and compression.

In pure bending the state of stress is uniaxial and the strain state is triaxial just as before. However, we must take into account the variation of strain and arc length s throughout the depth of the flexure sample. For small strain theory in pure bending the longitudinal strain ε is given by

$$\varepsilon = \frac{u}{\rho} \tag{30}$$

where u is the distance from the neutral surface and ρ is the radius of curvature. Thus we can write the strain tensor in the form

$$\underline{E}(u,\tau) = \frac{u}{C}\,\underline{E}\,h(\tau) \tag{31}$$

so that

$$s(u,\tau) = \frac{|u|}{C}\,M\,h(\tau) \tag{32}$$

$$\underline{E}(s) = \pm\,\frac{\underline{E}}{M}\,s \tag{33}$$

where C is one half the depth of the beam and E and M are given by (19) and (20), respectively. Hence, to within the proper sign the stresses are given by (22) with

$$S = \frac{|u|}{C} M\, h(t) = \frac{|u|}{C} M_t \tag{34}$$

The boundary conditions for pure bending are obviously satisfied with the moment M_c given by

$$M_c = 2 \int_0^C T_{\alpha\alpha}(u)\, u da$$

where α = 1, 2, or 3 depending upon the orientation of the specimen. If the longitudinal axis is the 1 axis,

$$M_c = \frac{2C^2 d}{Mb} [A\, m_1 + B(m_1 + m_2 + m_3)] \left[\frac{1}{2} - \frac{1}{M_t^2 b^2} + e^{-bM_t} \frac{1}{M_t b} + \frac{1}{M_t^2 b^2} \right] \tag{35}$$

while for the 2 axis

$$M_c = \frac{2C^2 d}{Mb} [C_3\, (m_1 + m_2 + m_3) + C_1\, m_2 + C_5\, m_1] \left[\frac{1}{2} - \frac{1}{M_t^2 b^2} + e^{-bM_t} \left(\frac{1}{M_t b} + \frac{1}{M_t^2 b^2} \right) \right] \tag{36}$$

where A and B are given by (24) and d is the width of the specimen.

Using the values of A, B, C_1, C_3, C_5, and b determined from the compression tests we can predict the load versus strain curve for the flexure tests. Figure 5 compares the theory with experiment for the 1 direction while Fig. 6 is for the 2 direction. Although the 2 direction gives good agreement between experiment and theory, it is obvious that the 1 direction gives rather poor agreement. We believe that the fault lies primarily in the fact that graphite actually behaves quite differently in tension than in compression particularly in regard to the Poisson effects. Thus, one should not expect uniaxial compression data to accurately predict the response in bending. Actually, the main reason for including the flexure problem was to demonstrate the

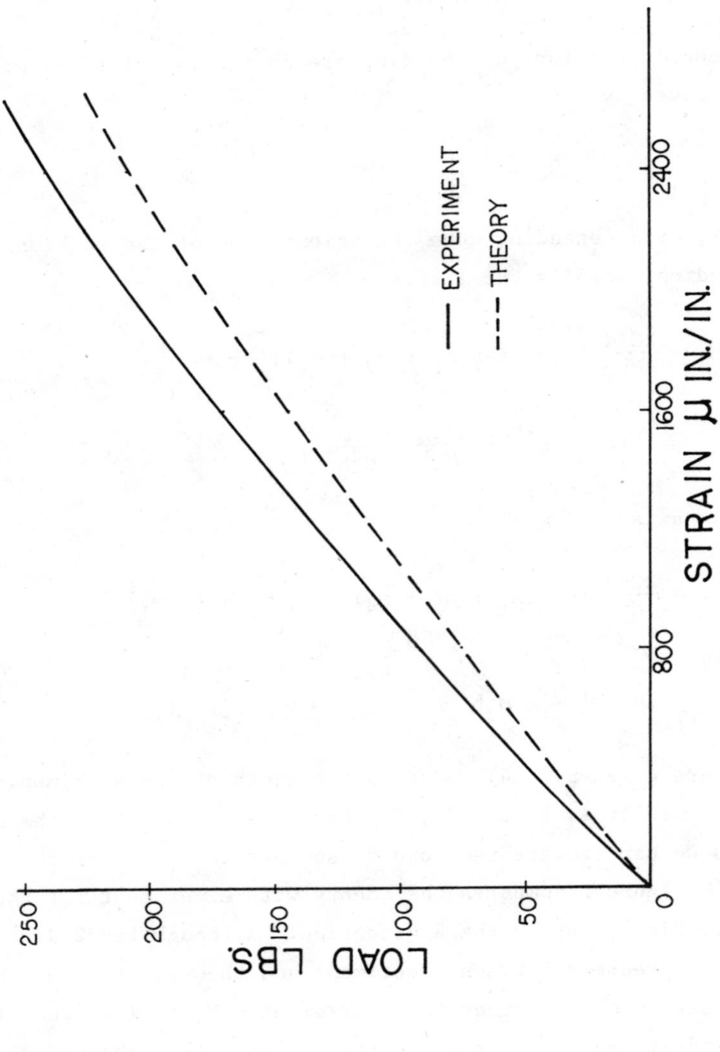

Fig. 5. Flexure Load-Strain in 1 Direction.

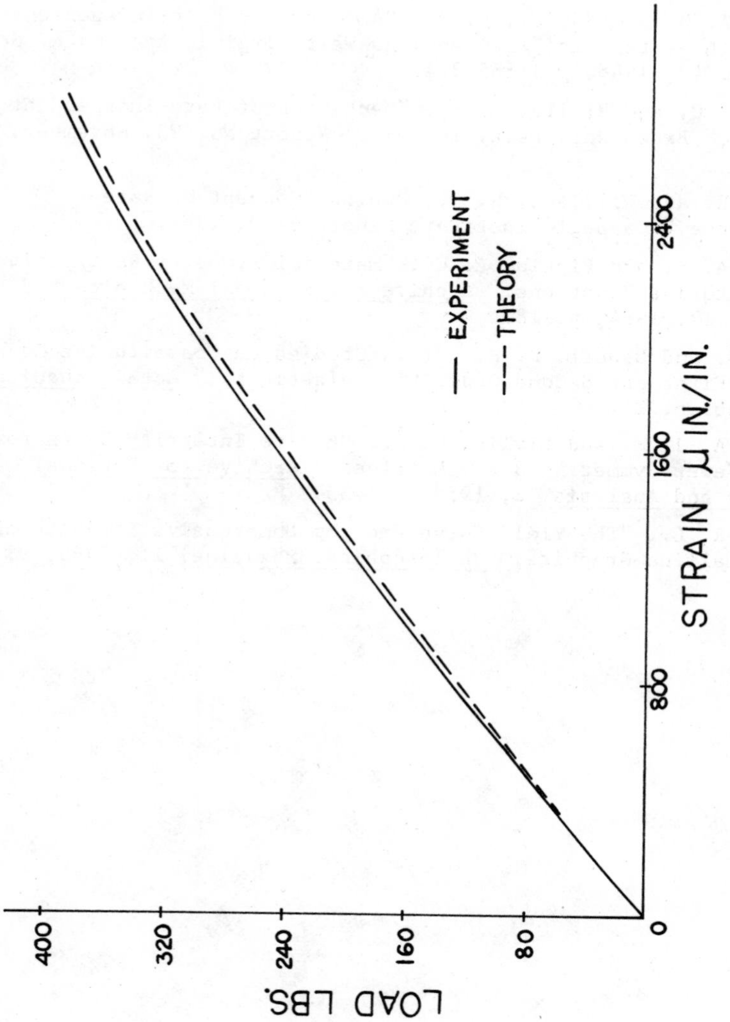

Fig. 6. Flexure Load-Strain in 2 or 3 Direction.

solution of a problem involving a non-homogeneous strain field as we have done.

REFERENCES

1. Strauss, A. M. and Snyder, R. D., "A Theory of Rate-Independent Response with Hysteresis," Proceedings West Virginia Academy of Science, Vol. 40, 1968, pp. 365-374.

2. Pipkin, A. C. and Rivlin, R. S., "Mechanics of Rate-Independent Materials," Brown University Technical Report No. 95, November, 1964.

3. Owen, D. R. and Williams, W. O., "On the Concept of Rate-Independence," Carnegie Institute Report 67-9, 1967.

4. Wineman, A. S. and Pipkin, A. C., "Material Symmetry Restrictions on Constitutive Equations," Archive for Rational Mechanics and Analysis, 17, 1964, p. 183.

5. Lianis, G. and DeHoff, P. H., Jr., "Studies on Constitutive Equations of First and Second Order Viscoelasticity," Acta Mechanica, 2(1), 1966, p. 21.

6. Spencer, A. J. M. and Rivlin, R. S., "Finite Integrity Basis for Five or Fewer Symmetric 3 x 3 Matrices," Archive for Rational Mechanics and Analysis, 2, 1959, p. 435.

7. Woolley, R. L., "The Yield Curve and the Compressive Strength of Polycrystalline Graphite," Philosophical Magazine, 11, 1965, p. 799.

ON THE ROLE OF DENSITY GRADIENTS IN THE CONTINUUM THEORY OF MIXTURES

G. Aguirre Ramirez
Research Institute
University of Alabama in Huntsville

S. T. Wu
Research Institute
University of Alabama in Huntsville

ABSTRACT

Recent developments in the continuum theory of mixtures indicate that the diffusive force depends on density gradients. In this paper it is demonstrated by using Boltzmann's kinetic equation that the transport properties of a mixture of gases are dependent on the gradients of mean molecular properties. In particular, it is shown that diffusion is controlled by the density gradients of the constituent gas in the mixture.

LIST OF NOTATIONS

$\underset{\sim}{x}$ Position vector
ρ Total mass density of mixture
ρ_α Mass density of the α-species
$\dot{\underset{\sim}{x}}$ Mean velocity of mixture
$\dot{x}_\alpha$ Velocity of the α-species
$\underset{\sim}{u}_\alpha$ Diffusion velocity of the α-species
c_α Mass supply for the α-species
$\underset{\sim}{P}_\alpha$ Diffusive force for α-species
$\underset{\sim}{T}_\alpha$ Partial stress tensor
$\underset{\sim}{f}_\alpha$ Partial body force
f Total body force
e_α Energy supply for α-species
ε_α Partial specific internal energy

r_α Partial energy source
$\underset{\sim}{L}_\alpha$ Gradient of the velocity
$\underset{\sim}{h}_\alpha$ Partial heat flux
r Total energy source
$\underset{\sim}{h}$ Total heat flux
$\underset{\sim}{L}$ Gradient of mean velocity
θ Temperature of the mixture
η Total entropy
η_α Partial entropy
Φ Entropy flux
s Entropy supply
$\underset{\sim}{q}_\alpha$ Partial entropy flux
$\underset{\sim}{F}_\alpha$ Deformation gradient of α-species
F_α Singlet local velocity distribution function of α-species
p Total static pressure
p_α Partial static pressure of α-species
m_α Mass of the α-species
θ_α Temperature of the α-species

In this paper, direct tensor notation is used in preference to component notation. For the most part vectors in the three-dimensional inner product vector space U and points in the Euclidean 3-space are indicated by boldface Latin minuscules: $\underset{\sim}{x}$, $\grave{\underset{\sim}{x}}$, .., $\underset{\sim}{u}$. Linear transformations from U into U are indicated by boldface Latin majuscules: $\underset{\sim}{T}$, .., M. We regard second order tensors and linear transformations as the same. If $\underset{\sim}{T}$ is a linear transformation, $\underset{\sim}{T}^T$ denotes its transpose, $\underset{\sim}{T}^{-1}$ its inverse, tr $\underset{\sim}{T}$ its trace and det $\underset{\sim}{T}$ its determinant. The gradient with respect to spatial coordinates is denoted by grad.

INTRODUCTION

In recent years several thermo-mechanical theories of mixtures subject to diffusion have appeared. Most of these theories were introduced in the literature as improvements on a theory introduced by Truesdell [1]. Truesdell's theory in itself was an improvement of the mechanical theory of diffusion put forth by Maxwell and Stefan.

Based on a new general approach to non-equilibrium thermodynamics originally proposed by Coleman and Noll [5], Green and Naghdi [4, 8],

Ingram and Eringen [6], and Bowen [7], made efforts to unite the mechanical and thermodynamical theories of diffusion. Motivated by what he considered, "the failure of these authors to produce a theory which is both well motivated physically and also consistent with classical thermostatics," Müller [2] proposed a theory for a binary mixture of viscous fluids. The theory presented by Müller has two significant features one of which is the consistent allowance of dependence of the constitutive equations on the density gradients of each species. Bowen and Wiese [3] have also recently presented a theory for a mixture of diffusing elastic materials which also has this particular important feature.

Upon reading Truesdell's Socony Mobil lectures, it becomes apparent that he was guided by Maxwell's kinetic theory of monatomic gases when he first proposed his theory. In this paper the Boltzmann equation and the successive approximations introduced by Chapman and Enskog [9] are used to demonstrate that the kinetic theory of mixtures of gases also shows that the diffusive force on each species depends on density gradients, and thereby the arguments of Müller [2] and Bowen and Wiese [3] are strengthened.

Preliminaries

In this section we briefly review the equations of balance for mixtures of continua proposed by Truesdell [1].

We consider a mixture of α species. The fundamental hypothesis underlying the theory of mixtures is that each place $\mathbf{x}$ of the region of Euclidean 3-space occupied by the mixture of time t is simultaneously occupied by particles of all α species. We denote the density and velocity of the α species respectively by[1] $\rho_\alpha, \grave{\mathbf{x}}_\alpha$. The following definitions are made: the density ρ of the mixture is defined by

$$\rho = \sum_\alpha \rho_\alpha \tag{1}$$

and the mean velocity $\dot{\mathbf{x}}$ of the mixture and diffusion velocity $\mathbf{u}_\alpha$ of the α species by

$$\rho \dot{\mathbf{x}} = \sum_\alpha \rho_\alpha \grave{\mathbf{x}}_\alpha \tag{2}$$

---

1. Since we shall be using direct tensor notation, subscripts and superscripts appearing in a quantity will have no tensorial meaning.

$$\mathbf{u}_\alpha = \grave{\mathbf{x}}_\alpha - \dot{\mathbf{x}} \tag{3}$$

For a given function Ψ of $\mathbf{x}$, t two different time derivatives, $\dot{\Psi}$ and $\grave{\Psi}_{(\alpha)}$ are introduced. $\dot{\Psi}$ is computed following the mean motion of the mixture while $\grave{\Psi}_{(\alpha)}$ is computed following the individual motion of the α species:

$$\dot{\Psi} = \frac{\partial \Psi}{\partial t}(\mathbf{x}, t) + \left(\operatorname{grad} \Psi(\mathbf{x}, t)\right)\dot{\mathbf{x}} \tag{4}$$

$$\grave{\Psi}_{(\alpha)} = \frac{\partial \Psi}{\partial t}(\mathbf{x}, t) + \left(\operatorname{grad} \Psi(\mathbf{x}, t)\right)\grave{\mathbf{x}}_\alpha \tag{5}$$

Given a quantity Ψ_α associated with the α species, the mass-weighted mean of Ψ_α is defined by

$$\rho\Psi = \sum_\alpha \rho_\alpha \Psi_\alpha \tag{6}$$

In the kinetic theory of a mixture of gases, Maxwell's equation of transfer is an expression for the time-rate of change of a mean quantity following the mean motion of the mixture in terms of means of certain time rates for the individual molecules. In the continuum theory of mixtures the equation of transfer is obtained from previously introduced definitions as

$$\rho\dot{\Psi} = \sum_\alpha \left\{\rho_\alpha \grave{\Psi}_\alpha + \left(\frac{\partial \rho_\alpha}{\partial t} + \operatorname{div}(\rho_\alpha \grave{\mathbf{x}}_\alpha)\right)\Psi_\alpha - \operatorname{div}(\rho_\alpha \Psi_\alpha \mathbf{u}_\alpha)\right\}$$
$$- \left(\frac{\partial \rho}{\partial t} + \operatorname{div}(\rho\dot{\mathbf{x}})\right)\Psi \tag{7}$$

The mass supply c_α of the α species is defined by the equation

$$\rho c_\alpha = \frac{\partial \rho_\alpha}{\partial t} + \operatorname{div}(\rho_\alpha \grave{\mathbf{x}}_\alpha) \tag{8}$$

Equation (8) is the balance of mass of the α species.

The equation

$$\sum_\alpha c_\alpha = 0 \tag{9}$$

is the mathematical statement that over the whole mixture no mass is created. Equation (9) is equivalent to the balance equation

$$\frac{\partial\rho}{\partial t} + \text{div}(\rho\dot{\underset{\sim}{x}}) = 0 \qquad (10)$$

for the mass density of the mixture.

Truesdell [1] defines the supply of momentum $\underset{\sim}{P}_\alpha$ of species α as follows:

$$\rho\underset{\sim}{P}_\alpha = \rho_\alpha(\grave{\grave{\underset{\sim}{x}}}_\alpha - \underset{\sim}{f}_\alpha) - \text{div}\ \underset{\sim}{T}_\alpha \qquad (11)$$

where $\underset{\sim}{T}_\alpha$ is the partial stress tensor and $\underset{\sim}{f}_\alpha$ the body force acting on the α species. The momentum supply $\underset{\sim}{P}_\alpha$ is due to interaction of the α species with the other species. The fact that the total linear momentum is not affected by internal interaction is expressed by

$$\sum_\alpha \underset{\sim}{P}_\alpha = \underset{\sim}{0} \qquad (12)$$

The total stress tensor $\underset{\sim}{T}$ for the mixture is introduced according to the definition

$$\underset{\sim}{T} = \sum_\alpha(\underset{\sim}{T}_\alpha - \rho_\alpha\ \grave{\underset{\sim}{u}}_\alpha \otimes \grave{\underset{\sim}{u}}_\alpha) \qquad (13)$$

The total stress tensor $\underset{\sim}{T}$ is symmetric but the partial stress $\underset{\sim}{T}_\alpha$ need not be so. Introducing the total body force $\underset{\sim}{f}$ through

$$\rho\underset{\sim}{f} = \sum_\alpha \rho_\alpha\ \underset{\sim}{f}_\alpha \qquad (14)$$

it can be shown [1] that the total stress satisfies Cauchy's first equation of motion with respect to the mean velocity,

$$\text{div}\ \underset{\sim}{T} + \rho\underset{\sim}{f} = \rho\ddot{\underset{\sim}{x}} \qquad (15)$$

if and only, if

$$\sum_\alpha(\underset{\sim}{P}_\alpha + c_\alpha\ \underset{\sim}{u}_\alpha) = \underset{\sim}{0} \qquad (16)$$

The energy supply e_α of the α species is defined by Truesdell [1] to be given by

$$\rho\ e_\alpha = \rho_\alpha(\grave{\varepsilon}_\alpha - r_\alpha) - \text{tr}\ \underset{\sim}{T}^T_\alpha\ \underset{\sim}{L}_\alpha - \text{div}\ \underset{\sim}{h}_\alpha \qquad (17)$$

where e_α is the partial specific internal energy, r_α the partial energy source, $\underset{\sim}{L}_\alpha$ the gradient of the velocity, $\grave{\underset{\sim}{x}}_\alpha$ and $\underset{\sim}{h}_\alpha$ the partial heat flux. The total internal energy ε for the mixture is then defined by

$$\rho\ \varepsilon = \sum_\alpha \rho_\alpha(\varepsilon_\alpha + \frac{1}{2}\ \underset{\sim}{u}^2_\alpha) \qquad (18)$$

and the total energy source r by

$$\rho\ r = \sum_\alpha \rho_\alpha (r_\alpha + \underset{\sim}{f}_\alpha \cdot \underset{\sim}{u}_\alpha) \tag{19}$$

It can then be shown [1] if the total heat flux $\underset{\sim}{h}$ to the mixture is defined by

$$\underset{\sim}{h} = \sum_\alpha \left[\underset{\sim}{h} + \underset{\sim}{T}_\alpha^T\ \underset{\sim}{u}_\alpha - \rho_\alpha (\varepsilon_\alpha + \frac{1}{2}\underset{\sim}{u}_\alpha^2)\underset{\sim}{u}_\alpha \right] \tag{20}$$

the total energy ε will satisfy the balance equation

$$\rho\ \dot{\varepsilon} = \text{tr}\ \underset{\sim}{T}\ \underset{\sim}{L} + \text{div}\ \underset{\sim}{h} + p\ r \tag{21}$$

if and only if

$$\sum_\alpha \left(e_\alpha + \underset{\sim}{P}_\alpha \cdot \underset{\sim}{u}_\alpha + c_\alpha (r_\alpha + \frac{1}{2}\underset{\sim}{u}_\alpha^2) \right) = 0 \tag{21.a}$$

In Eq. (21), $\underset{\sim}{L}$ is the gradient of the mean velocity.

Equations (8), (11), and (17) are respectively the local balance equations of mass, linear momentum, and energy for the α species while Eqs. (10), (15), and (21) are respectively the local balance equations of total mass, linear momentum, and energy for the mixture.

The Second Law of Thermodynamics

In this section we discuss the second law of thermodynamics for the mixture. In continuum mechanics the second law of thermodynamics is given in the form of an inequality, the Clausius-Duhem inequality. However, the final form of this inequality in terms of previously introduced quantity plays a key role in the continuum thermodynamics of mixtures.

A temperature $\theta = \theta(\underset{\sim}{x}, t)$ which is assumed positive is assigned to every point $\underset{\sim}{x}$ of the region occupied by the mixture at time t. Also, letting η_α denote the partial entropy, the entropy η for the mixture is defined by

$$\rho\ \eta = \sum_\alpha \rho_\alpha\ \eta_\alpha \tag{22}$$

The entropy inequality is postulated for the whole mixture in the form [2]

$$\rho\ \dot{\eta} + \text{div}\ \underset{\sim}{\Phi} - \rho\ s \geq 0 \tag{23}$$

where Φ is the entropy flux and s is the entropy supply to the mixture from the external world. Letting r_R be defined by

$$\rho\, r_R = \sum_\alpha \rho_\alpha\, r_\alpha \tag{24}$$

both Müller [2] and Bowen and Wiese [3] define s by[2]

$$s = \frac{r_R}{\theta} \tag{25}$$

Green and Naghdi [4] do not introduce partial energy sources so that they do not need the definition given by Eq. (24). However, r_R plays the same role in their theory as it does in [2] and [3]. In [4] the entropy source for the mixture is also defined by Eq. (25).

Bowen and Wiese [3] introduce partial entropy fluxes $\underset{\sim}{q}_\alpha$ and define the total entropy flux by

$$\underset{\sim}{\Phi} = \sum_\alpha \underset{\sim}{q}_\alpha \tag{26}$$

Müller [2], on the other hand, considers $\underset{\sim}{\Phi}$ to be a quantity for which a constitutive relation is needed. Green and Naghdi [4] define Φ by

$$\underset{\sim}{\Phi} = \frac{\underset{\sim}{h}}{\theta} \tag{27}$$

However in the theory of Green and Naghdi [4], $\underset{\sim}{h}$ is not related to partial entities since they do not introduce these. Bowen and Wiese [3] define the partial entropy flux by

$$\underset{\sim}{q}_\alpha = \frac{\underset{\sim}{h}_\alpha}{\theta} + \rho_\alpha\, \eta_\alpha\, \underset{\sim}{u}_\alpha \tag{28}$$

and arrive at the form of the inequality

$$\rho\,\dot{\eta} + \operatorname{div} \sum_\alpha \frac{1}{\theta}\left(\underset{\sim}{h}_\alpha + \rho_\alpha\, \theta\eta_\alpha\, \underset{\sim}{u}_\alpha\right) - \frac{\rho r_R}{\theta} \ge 0 \tag{29}$$

while Green and Naghdi [4] arrive at

$$\rho\,\dot{\eta} + \operatorname{div}\left(\frac{\underset{\sim}{h}}{\theta}\right) - \frac{\rho r_R}{\theta} \ge 0 \tag{30}$$

Müller [2] on the other hand arrives at

---

2. Actually in [3], different temperatures θ_α are assigned to each species. Eq. (25) results as a special case when all species have the same temperature.

$$\rho\,\dot{\eta} + \text{div}\,\underset{\sim}{\Phi} - \frac{\rho r_R}{\theta} \geq 0 \tag{31}$$

Bowen and Wiese [3] introduce the partial free energy Ψ_α by

$$\Psi_\alpha = \varepsilon_\alpha - \theta\,\eta_\alpha \tag{32}$$

and define the inner part of the free energy Ψ_I by

$$\rho\,\Psi_I = \sum_\alpha \rho_\alpha\,\Psi_\alpha \tag{33}$$

Through previously introduced definitions, it can be shown that

$$\Psi_I = \varepsilon_I - \theta\eta \tag{34}$$

where ε_I is the inner part of the free energy given by

$$\rho\,\varepsilon_I = \sum_\alpha \rho_\alpha\,\varepsilon_\alpha \tag{35}$$

Müller[3] [2] and Green and Naghdi [4] choose to introduce the total free energy Ψ by the definition

$$\Psi = \varepsilon - \theta\eta \tag{36}$$

Ψ and Ψ_I are related by

$$\Psi = \Psi_I + \frac{1}{\rho}\sum_\alpha \rho_\alpha \frac{\underset{\sim}{u}_\alpha^2}{2} \tag{37}$$

Through some previously introduced definitions and Eq. (21), Müller [2] arrives at the final form of the entropy inequality

$$\begin{aligned} &- \rho\,\dot{\Psi} + \theta\,\text{div}\,\hat{\underset{\sim}{k}} - \eta\,\dot{\theta} + \sum_\alpha \rho_\alpha\,\overline{\grave{\underset{\sim}{x}}_\alpha}^{\,\bullet} \cdot \underset{\sim}{u}_\alpha \\ &+ \text{tr}(\underset{\sim}{T} - \sum_\alpha \underset{\sim}{T}_\alpha)(\sum_\lambda \rho_\lambda\,\underset{\sim}{D}_\lambda + \text{grad}\,\rho_\lambda \otimes \underset{\sim}{u}_\lambda) + \sum_\alpha \text{t r}\,\underset{\sim}{T}_\alpha\,\underset{\sim}{L}_\alpha \\ &+ \sum_\alpha \rho_\alpha\ \text{tr}\,\underset{\sim}{D}_\alpha\,\underset{\sim}{u}_\alpha \otimes \underset{\sim}{u}_\alpha - \frac{\underset{\sim}{g}}{\theta} \cdot (\underset{\sim}{h} - \sum_\alpha \underset{\sim}{T}_\alpha^T\,\underset{\sim}{u}_\alpha) \\ &- \rho \sum_\alpha (\underset{\sim}{P}_\alpha - c_\alpha \grave{\underset{\sim}{x}}_\alpha) \cdot \underset{\sim}{u}_\alpha \geq 0 \end{aligned} \tag{38}$$

3. In [2], Ψ is not called the total free energy. We have reasoned that Ψ in [2] is the total free energy by the definition Eq. (36) and the fact that ε appearing therein also appears in Eq. (2.16) of [2] which is Eq. (21) here.

where $\underset{\sim}{g} = \text{grad}\ \theta$, $2\ \underset{\sim}{D}_\alpha = \underset{\sim}{L}_\alpha + \underset{\sim}{L}_\alpha^T$, and

$$\hat{\underset{\sim}{k}} = \underset{\sim}{\Phi} - \frac{\underset{\sim}{h}}{\theta} - \frac{1}{\theta} \sum_\alpha \underset{\sim}{T}_\alpha^T \underset{\sim}{u}_\alpha \tag{39}$$

We call the reader's attention to the appearance of grad ρ_α in the fifth term on the left hand side of Eq. (38).

Through identities which can be established from the introduced definitions and Eq. (21), Bowen and Wiese [3] arrive at the final form of the entropy inequality

$$-\overline{(\rho\ \Psi_I)}^{\boldsymbol{\cdot}} - \rho\eta\dot{\theta} - \text{tr} \sum_\alpha \rho_\alpha \underset{\sim}{K}_\alpha \underset{\sim}{L}_\alpha - \sum_\alpha \underset{\sim}{u}_\alpha \cdot \left(P_\alpha + \text{grad}(\rho_\alpha\ \Psi_\alpha)\right)$$

$$- \sum_\alpha c_\alpha \frac{\underset{\sim}{u}_\alpha^2}{2} - \frac{\underset{\sim}{g}}{\theta} \cdot \left[\underset{\sim}{h} - \sum_\alpha \rho_\alpha \left(\underset{\sim}{K}_\alpha + \frac{\underset{\sim}{u}_\alpha^2}{2} \underset{\sim}{1}\right) \underset{\sim}{u}_\alpha\right] \geq 0 \tag{40}$$

where

$$\underset{\sim}{K}_\alpha = \Psi_\alpha \underset{\sim}{1} - \frac{1}{\rho_\alpha} \underset{\sim}{T}_\alpha^T \tag{41}$$

We call the reader's attention to the appearance of grad $(\rho_\alpha\ \Psi_\alpha)$ in Eq. (40). It is through this term that grad ρ_α enters into Bowen and Wiese's formulation of the entropy inequality.

Therefore even though Müller and Bowen and Wiese arrive at different forms of the entropy inequality for the mixture, both inequalities have the feature that the density gradients appear therein. In modern continuum mechanics the entropy inequality is used to find restrictions on proposed constitutive equations [5]. For this reason the form that the inequality takes is very important. In addition the inequality also gives a clue as to what independent variables one should take to describe a particular material behavior. For instance Müller examines a binary mixture of ideal fluids and starts his investigation of the constitutive equations by requiring the constitutive response functions to depend on

$$\rho_\alpha,\ \text{grad}\ \rho_\alpha,\ \grave{\underset{\sim}{x}}_\alpha,\ \underset{\sim}{L}_\alpha,\ \theta,\ \underset{\sim}{g}$$

with $\alpha = 1,2$. Bowen and Wiese examine a mixture of elastic materials and require that the constitutive response functions depend on

$$\theta,\ \underset{\sim}{g},\ \underset{\sim}{F}_\alpha,\ \nabla\underset{\sim}{F}_\alpha,\ \grave{\underset{\sim}{x}}_\alpha$$

where $\underset{\sim}{F}_\alpha$ is the deformation gradient of the α species and $\nabla\underset{\sim}{F}_\alpha$ its gradient with respect to material points. The dependence on density gradients in [3] is implied through $\nabla\underset{\sim}{F}_\alpha$.

The entropy inequality used by Green and Naghdi [4] does not contain density gradients. They examine the linear constitutive equations for a binary mixture of Newtonian fluids and take as independent variables

$$\rho_\alpha,\ \grave{\underset{\sim}{x}}_1 - \grave{\underset{\sim}{x}}_2,\ \underset{\sim}{D}_\alpha,\ \underset{\sim}{W}_1 - \underset{\sim}{W}_2,\ \theta,\ \underset{\sim}{g}$$

where $2\underset{\sim}{W}_\alpha = \underset{\sim}{L}_\alpha - \underset{\sim}{L}_\alpha^T$. Green and Naghdi [4] do not consider the density gradients as independent variables in most of their constitutive relations. However, as pointed out by Bowen [5], in [4] one quantity is allowed to depend on density gradients. This is the momentum supply $\rho\underset{\sim}{P}_\alpha$. Bowen and Wiese [3] point out that if the momentum supply in [4] were not allowed to depend on density gradients, then one would have to accept unusual results.

Kinetic Description for a Mixture

In this section we shall demonstrate, by using the Boltzmann kinetic equation, that the transport properties of a mixture of gases are dependent on the gradients of mean molecular properties. In particular we shall show that diffusion is controlled by the density gradients of the constituent gas in the mixture. To this purpose we consider the Boltzmann kinetic equation with body force $\underset{\sim}{f}_\alpha$ for the α constituent of a gas mixture:

$$D\,F_\alpha = \frac{\partial F_\alpha}{\partial t} + \dot{\underset{\sim}{X}}_\alpha \cdot \operatorname{grad} F_\alpha + \underset{\sim}{f}_\alpha \cdot \frac{\partial F_\alpha}{\partial \dot{\underset{\sim}{X}}_\alpha} = \left(\frac{\delta F_\alpha}{\delta t}\right)_{\text{coll.}} = \sum_\beta J_{\alpha\beta} \qquad (42)$$

with

$$\left(\frac{\delta F_\alpha}{\delta t}\right)_{\text{coll.}} = \sum_\beta J_{\alpha\beta} = \sum_\beta \int (F'_\alpha F'_\beta - F_\alpha F_\beta)\, \underset{\sim}{g}_{\alpha\beta}\, \sigma_{\alpha\beta}\, d\Omega\, d\dot{\underset{\sim}{X}}_\beta$$

where $F_\alpha = F_\alpha(\dot{\underset{\sim}{X}}_\alpha, \underset{\sim}{x}, t)$ is the singlet local distribution function of the velocity $\dot{\underset{\sim}{X}}_\alpha$ of the α component of the mixture, $\underset{\sim}{g}_{\alpha\beta} = \dot{\underset{\sim}{X}}_\alpha - \dot{\underset{\sim}{X}}_\beta$ is the relative velocity between two colliding particles α and β. $\sigma_{\alpha\beta}$ represents the measure of the interaction between α,β particles and is called the differential scattering cross-section and the element of solid angle $d\Omega$ is defined by

$$d\Omega = \sin \chi \, d\chi \, d\gamma \tag{43}$$

where χ represents the scattering angle (i.e., the angle between $\underset{\sim}{g}_{\alpha\beta}$ and $\underset{\sim}{g}'_{\alpha\beta}$) and γ is the azimuthal angle measured in the plane perpendicular to the vector $\underset{\sim}{g}_{\alpha\beta}$. Finally primed and unprimed quantities indicate the quantities post- and pre-collision respectively.

The solution of Eq. (42) can be carried out by adopting the Chapman-Enskog procedure [9]. Since the details are available elsewhere [9], [10], [11] we shall merely indicate the main steps. A perturbation expansion for the distribution function is written

$$F_\alpha = F_\alpha^{(0)} \; (1 + \Phi_\alpha + \ldots) \tag{44}$$

where $F_\alpha^{(0)}$ is the equilibrium Maxwellian distribution normalized such that

$$\int F_\alpha^{(0)} \; (\dot{\underset{\sim}{X}}_\alpha, \underset{\sim}{x}, t) \; d\dot{\underset{\sim}{X}}_\alpha = \eta_\alpha(\underset{\sim}{x}, t) = \text{number density}. \tag{45}$$

The mass density for each constituent is defined by $\rho_\alpha = \eta_\alpha m_\alpha$, with m_α being the mass of the constituent α. The continuum velocity field $\grave{\underset{\sim}{x}}_\alpha$ is then defined as the mean of $\dot{\underset{\sim}{X}}_\alpha$, i.e., $\grave{\underset{\sim}{x}}_\alpha = \overline{\dot{\underset{\sim}{X}}}_\alpha$. Also the velocity field $\dot{\underset{\sim}{x}}$ of the mixture is defined by

$$\rho \, \dot{\underset{\sim}{x}} = \sum_\alpha \rho_\alpha \grave{\underset{\sim}{x}}_\alpha = \sum_\alpha m_\alpha \int \dot{\underset{\sim}{X}}_\alpha \, F_\alpha^{(0)} \; (\dot{\underset{\sim}{X}}_\alpha, \underset{\sim}{x}, t) \; d\dot{\underset{\sim}{X}}_\alpha \tag{46}$$

The equilibrium Maxwellian distribution for which the constituent gas has its own temperature T_α and mean velocity $\grave{\underset{\sim}{x}}_\alpha$ was developed by Wu [11] and is given by

$$F_\alpha^{(0)} = \mathcal{F}_\alpha^{(0)} \left[1 + \left(\frac{m_\alpha \underset{\sim}{U}_\alpha^2}{2k\theta} - \frac{3}{2}\right) \Theta_\alpha + \frac{m_\alpha}{k\theta} \underset{\sim}{U}_\alpha \cdot \underset{\sim}{\beta}_\alpha\right] \tag{47}$$

with

$$\mathcal{F}_\alpha^{(0)} = n_\alpha \left(\frac{m_\alpha}{2\pi k\theta}\right)^{\frac{3}{2}} \exp\left(-\frac{m_\alpha \underset{\sim}{U}_\alpha^2}{2k\theta}\right) \tag{48}$$

Here k denotes the Boltzmann constant, and $\underset{\sim}{U}_\alpha$ the peculiar velocity given by

$$\underset{\sim}{U}_\alpha = \dot{\underset{\sim}{X}}_\alpha - \dot{\underset{\sim}{x}} \; . \tag{49}$$

Also

$$\Theta_\alpha = \frac{\theta_\alpha - \theta}{\theta}, \qquad \underset{\sim}{\beta}_\alpha = \dot{\underset{\sim}{x}}_\alpha - \dot{\underset{\sim}{x}} \tag{50}$$

with θ being the temperature of the mixture given by

$$\theta = \frac{1}{n} \sum_\alpha n_\alpha \theta_\alpha \tag{51}$$

By using Eq. (42) and transforming it to the $\dot{\underset{\sim}{x}}$, θ system, i.e., colliding center of mass system, we can seek higher order solutions. Thus

$$\frac{DF_\alpha}{Dt} + \underset{\sim}{U}_\alpha \cdot \text{grad } F_\alpha - \frac{D\dot{\underset{\sim}{x}}}{Dt} \cdot \frac{\partial F_\alpha}{\partial \underset{\sim}{U}_\alpha} - \text{tr} \frac{\partial F_\alpha}{\partial \underset{\sim}{U}_\alpha} \underset{\sim}{U}_\alpha \text{ grad } \dot{\underset{\sim}{X}}_\alpha = \sum_\beta J_{\alpha\beta} \tag{52}$$

where D/Dt indicates the time derivative following the motion $\dot{\underset{\sim}{X}}_\alpha$, i.e.,

$$\frac{D}{Dt} = \frac{\partial}{\partial t} + \dot{\underset{\sim}{X}}_\alpha \cdot \text{grad} \tag{53}$$

Using Eqs. (44), (47), (48) together with the conservation theorems and expanding the collision integrals as such

$$\sum_\beta J_{\alpha\beta} = \sum_\beta \left(J^{(0)}_{\alpha\beta} + J^{(1)}_{\alpha\beta} + \ldots\right) \tag{54}$$

we find the equations for the successive orders of approximation to the Boltzmann equation. Thus, for the zeroth order approximation

$$J^{(0)}_{\alpha\beta} = 0 \tag{55}$$

which leads to the determination of the Maxwellian distribution. For the first order approximation

$$J^{(1)}_{\alpha\beta} = \mathcal{F}^{(0)}_\alpha \Bigg\{ \left[(1 - \Theta_\alpha) \frac{m_\alpha \underset{\sim}{U}^2_\alpha}{2\, k\theta} - \frac{5}{2}\right] \underset{\sim}{U}_\alpha \cdot \text{grad } 1\text{n } \theta$$

$$+ \frac{n}{n_\alpha} \Theta_\alpha \underset{\sim}{U}_\alpha \cdot \left[\left(\frac{\rho_\alpha}{\rho} - \frac{n_\alpha}{n}\right) \text{grad } 1\text{n } p - \text{grad} \left(\frac{n_\alpha}{n}\right) - \sum_\beta \frac{\rho_\alpha \rho_\beta}{\rho\, p} (\underset{\sim}{f}_\alpha - \underset{\sim}{f}_\beta)\right]$$

$$+ \left(\frac{m_\alpha \underset{\sim}{U}^2_\alpha}{2\, k\, \theta} - \frac{5}{2}\right) \underset{\sim}{U}_\alpha \cdot \text{grad } \Theta_\alpha + (1 - \Theta_\alpha) \frac{m_\alpha}{n\theta} \text{ tr } \underset{\sim}{U}^0_\alpha \otimes \underset{\sim}{U}_\alpha \text{ grad } \dot{\underset{\sim}{x}}$$

$$+ \frac{m_\alpha}{n\theta} \text{ tr } \underset{\sim}{U}^0_\alpha \otimes \underset{\sim}{U}_\alpha \text{ grad } \underset{\sim}{\beta}_\alpha \Bigg\} \tag{56}$$

This leads to the solution of Eq. (52) to the first order approximation as

$$\Phi_\alpha = - \mathbf{A}_\alpha \cdot \text{grad } \theta - \text{tr } \mathbf{B}_\alpha \text{ grad } \dot{\mathbf{x}} - \mathbf{G}_\alpha \cdot \mathbf{d}_\alpha - \mathbf{D}_\alpha \cdot \text{grad } \Theta_\alpha - \text{tr } \mathbf{H}_\alpha \text{ grad } \mathbf{B}_\alpha \tag{57}$$

where

$$\mathbf{d}_\alpha = \left(\frac{\rho_\alpha}{\rho} - \frac{n_\alpha}{n}\right) \text{grad ln } p - \text{grad}\left(\frac{n_\alpha}{n}\right) - \sum_\beta \frac{\rho_\alpha \rho_\beta}{\rho \, p} (\mathbf{f}_\alpha - \mathbf{f}_\beta) \tag{58}$$

The coefficients $\mathbf{A}_\alpha$, $\mathbf{G}_\alpha$, and $\mathbf{D}_\alpha$ are vectors, $\mathbf{B}_\alpha$ and $\mathbf{H}_\alpha$ are second order tensors. These coefficients are functions of the local velocity, composition, and temperature. The coefficients are expanded as a finite series of orthogonal polynomials after Chapman and Cowling [9],

$$\mathbf{A}_\alpha = \left(\frac{2k\theta}{m_\alpha}\right)^{\frac{1}{2}} \left[(1 - \Theta_\alpha) \mathcal{C}_\alpha \sum_m a_m S^m_{\frac{3}{2}} (\mathcal{C}^2_\alpha) - \Theta_\alpha \sum_m a'_m S^m_{\frac{3}{2}} (\mathcal{C}^2_\alpha)\right],$$

$$\mathbf{B}_\alpha = (1 - \Theta_\alpha) \overset{0}{\mathcal{C}_\alpha \mathcal{C}_\alpha} \sum_m b_m S^m_{\frac{5}{2}} (\mathcal{C}^2_\alpha),$$

$$\mathbf{G}_\alpha = \left(\frac{2k\theta}{m_\alpha}\right)^{\frac{1}{2}} \Theta_\alpha \mathcal{C}_\alpha \sum_m g_m S^m_{\frac{3}{2}} (\mathcal{C}^2_\alpha),$$

$$\mathbf{D}_\alpha = \left(\frac{2k\theta}{m_\alpha}\right)^{\frac{1}{2}} \mathcal{C}_\alpha \sum_m d_m S^m_{\frac{3}{2}} (\mathcal{C}^2_\alpha),$$

$$\mathbf{H}_\alpha = \overset{0}{\mathcal{C}_\alpha \mathcal{C}_\alpha} \sum_m h_m S^m_{\frac{5}{2}} (\mathcal{C}^2_\alpha) . \tag{59}$$

where $S^m_n (\mathcal{C}^2_\alpha)$ is a Sonine polynomial used by Chapman and Cowling [9] and Burnett [12]. Only even terms of Sonine polynomials are chosen in order to satisfy the solubility conditions, i.e., the conservation laws.

According to the definition given by Chapman and Cowling, the diffusion velocity to the first order of approximation is

$$
\begin{aligned}
\underset{\sim\alpha}{u} &= \dot{\underset{\sim\alpha}{x}} - \dot{\underset{\sim}{x}} = \overline{\underset{\sim\alpha}{U}} = \overline{\dot{\underset{\sim\alpha}{X}}} - \dot{\underset{\sim}{x}} \\
&= m_\alpha \int \underset{\sim\alpha}{U} F_\alpha \, d\underset{\sim\alpha}{\mathbf{U}} \\
&= m_\alpha \int U_\alpha \left(F_\alpha^{(0)} + F_\alpha^{(0)} \Phi_\alpha \right) dU_\alpha \\
&= \rho_\alpha \underset{\sim\alpha}{\beta} - D_\alpha \underset{\sim\alpha}{d} - D_\alpha^T \frac{\partial \theta}{\partial \underset{\sim}{x}} \,,
\end{aligned}
\tag{60}
$$

where D_α and D_α^T are the ordinary and thermal diffusion coefficients respectively.

The expression of equation (60) is the diffusion equation giving the fluxes of component in terms of gradients. Thus, in the present formalism, we indeed show the diffusion velocity as function of gradients of molecular properties. If we have an isothermal medium, the mean velocity of the constituent gas $\dot{\underset{\sim\alpha}{x}}$ which is approximately the mean velocity of the mixture $\dot{\underset{\sim}{x}}$, and without body force, then

$$
\begin{aligned}
\underset{\sim\alpha}{\beta} &= 0, \\
\frac{\partial \theta}{\partial \underset{\sim}{x}} &= 0, \\
\underset{\sim\alpha}{f} &= \underset{\sim\beta}{f} = 0
\end{aligned}
\tag{61}
$$

thus,

$$
\begin{aligned}
\underset{\sim\alpha}{u} &= - D_\alpha \underset{\sim\alpha}{d} \\
&= - D_\alpha \left[\left(\frac{p_\alpha}{\rho} - \frac{n_\alpha}{n} \right) k\theta \frac{\partial n}{\partial \underset{\sim}{x}} - \frac{\partial}{\partial \underset{\sim}{x}} \left(\frac{n_\alpha}{n} \right) \right] .
\end{aligned}
\tag{62}
$$

Hence, the arguments given by Bowen and Wiese [3] and Müller [2] are proved by using the Boltzmann kinetic equation.

CONCLUSION

We have briefly reviewed the continuum mechanical theory of a mixture of continua with diffusion. It was shown that density gradients appear in the second axiom of thermodynamics used in continuum mechanics to restrict proposed constitutive equations. The equations of the continuum mechanics theory of mixtures are established through definitions introduced. However, we have shown through the kinetic theory of a mixture of gases that indeed the diffusive force on each species depends on the density gradients. Therefore the arguments of Müller [2] and Bowen and Wiese [3] are strengthened.

REFERENCES

1. Truesdell, C., "Sulle basi della termomeccanica," Accad. Lincei Rendiconti 22, Ser. 8, 33, 158 (1957).
2. Müller, I., "A Thermodynamic Theory of Mixtures of Fluids," Arch. ration. Mech. Analysis, 28, 1 (1968).
3. Bowen, R. M., and Wiese, J. C., "Diffusion in Mixtures of Elastic Materials," Int. J. Engr. Sci., 7, 689 (1969).
4. Green, A. E., and Naghdi, P. M., "A Dynamic Theory of Interacting Continua," Int. J. Engr. Sci., 3, 231 (1965).
5. Coleman, B., and Noll, W., "The Thermodynamics of Elastic Materials with Heat Conduction and Viscosity," Arch. ration. Mech. Analysis 13, 167 (1963).
6. Eringen, A. C., and Ingram, J. D., "A Continuum Theory of Chemically Reacting Media-I," Int. J. Engr. Sci. 3, 197 (1965).
7. Bowen, R. M., "Toward a Thermodynamics and Mechanics of Mixtures," Arch. ration. Mech. Analysis, 24, 370 (1967).
8. Green, A. E., and Naghdi, P. M., "A Theory of Mixtures," Arch. ration. Mech. Analysis 24, 243 (1967).
9. Chapman, S., and Cowling, T. G., The Mathematical Theory of Non-Uniform Gases, Cambridge at the University Press (1960).
10. Hirschfelder, J. O., Curtiss, C. F., and Bird, R. B., Molecular Theory of Gases and Liquids, John Wiley and Sons, Inc., New York (1954).
11. Wu, S. T., "Kinetic Theory of Macroscopic Transport Phenomena in Multifluid Systems," J. of Phys. Soc. Japan 27, No. 1, 8 (1969).
12. Burnett, D., "The Distribution of Velocities in a Slightly Non-Uniform Gas," Proc. London Math. Soc. 39, Ser. 2, 385 (1935).

DYNAMIC RESPONSE OF VISCOELASTIC FLUID LINES

Wen-Jei Yang
University of Michigan

ABSTRACT

A theory is developed to predict the dynamic characteristics of viscoelastic fluid lines. The three-parameter Oldroyd model is employed to describe the rheological characteristics of the viscoelastic fluid. The effects of fluid viscosity, stress and strain relaxation times and compressibility are included to derive transfer functions relating the pressure and velocity variable at the two cross sections of a transmission line. The numerical results of the theoretical analysis are obtained for the frequency response of the line. The analysis includes the important effect on the dynamic response induced by the vibration of the line in the longitudinal direction. It is disclosed that in small-diameter lines, the influence of the rheological properties is significant. The systems to which these results may apply include the transmission lines of polymer solutions and plastics melts and the circulatory lines of some biological fluids.

LIST OF NOTATIONS

A(s)	Integration constant
A_1	Flow cross sectional area of pipe
A_2	Cross sectional area of pipe wall
A_3	Area of orifice
B(s)	Integration constant
B	Bulk modulus of fluid
b	Function defined by Eqs. (15) and (26)
c	Speed of sound in fluid

c_s	Speed of sound in the material of pipe
E	Modulus of elasticity of pipe
e_{ij}	Component of the symmetrical rate of deformation tensor
$f(x,s)$	Function defined by Eq. (16)
$G(s)$	Transfer matrix
I_o, I_1	Modified Bessel functions of first kind
j	$\sqrt{-1}$
K	Constant defined by Eq. (24)
ℓ	Distance between sections 1 and 2
m	Mass of orifice block
N	Dimensionless parameter defined by Eq. (27)
$\overline{P}(x,s)$	Laplace transform of $\overline{p}(x,t)$
$p(x,r,t)$	Pressure deviation
$\overline{p}(x,t)$	Average value of $p(x,r,t)$ across flow cross-sectional area
R	Inside radius of tube
r	Coordinate in radial direction
s	Laplace variable
t	Time
$\overline{U}(x,s)$	Laplace transform of $\overline{u}(x,t)$
$u(x,r,t)$	Deviation of x-component velocity
$\overline{u}(x,t)$	Average value of $u(x,r,t)$ across flow cross-sectional area
$v(x,r,t)$	Deviation of r-component velocity
x	Coordinate in axial direction
$y(x,t)$	Displacement of pipe in axial direction
$Y(x,s)$	Laplace transform of $y(x,t)$
$\delta(s)$	$\nu(1 + \lambda_1 s)/(1 + \lambda_2 s)$
ζ	Coefficient of damping
Λ_1, Λ_2	Dimensionless parameters defined by Eq. (27)
λ_1	Stress relaxation time
λ_2	Strain relaxation time
μ	Coefficient of viscosity
ν	μ/ρ
ρ	Fluid density
ρ_s	Density of material of pipe
τ_{ij}	Shear stress
Ω	Dimensionless frequency defined by Eq. (27)
ω	Frequency, radians per second

Subscripts

1 Upstream section 1

2 Downstream section 2

INTRODUCTION

The purpose of early investigations on unsteady fluid flow in pipes was to analyze the surging phenomena or water hammer in power plants, to determine the velocity of sound in the fluid and to analyze the dynamic characteristics of hydraulic transmission lines in automatic control, liquid-propellant rockets and other systems [1, 2]. In previous studies, the fluid is taken as either nonviscous or Newtonian (which obey Newton's law of viscosity). It is obvious that the nonviscous and viscous water-hammer theories cannot predict the dynamic behavior of viscoelastic fluid transmission lines because of the differences in flow properties.

The two chief readily observed characteristics exhibited by viscoelastic fluids are the dependency of apparent viscosity (values of viscosity obtained experimentally) on the rate of shear and a capacity for elastic recovery when stress is suddenly removed. Under unsteady-state conditions, the linear viscoelastic (or Oldroyd) model can describe to some extent the rhelogical properties of the viscoelastic fluid. The relevant tensor equation, according to Eirich [3], is

$$\tau_{ij} + \lambda_1 \frac{D\tau_{ij}}{Dt} = \mu\left(e_{ij} + \lambda_2 \frac{De_{ij}}{Dt}\right) \tag{1}$$

where τ_{ij} is the shear stress, e_{ij} is the component of the symmetrical rate of deformation tensor and μ is a coefficient of viscosity. λ_1 and λ_2 are the stress and strain relaxation times, respectively, and D/Dt is the substantial derivative.

In the present paper, a theory is developed to predict transfer functions relating the pressure and velocity variables at two cross sections in the hydraulic transmission line of viscoelastic fluids.

Analysis

Consider the laminar flow of a viscoelastic fluid in a pipe of radius R. It is convenient to use cylindrical coordinates whose x-axis is identified with the center line of the tube. Let r be the coordinate in the radial direction and t denote time. The deviations of the velocities in the x- and r-directions from their steady-state values are denoted by u(x,r,t) and v(x,r,t), respectively, and the deviation of the pressure by p(x,r,t). Under the assumptions of negligible elastic effect of the tube and constant coefficient of viscosity together with the neglect of relatively unimportant terms, the governing differential equations for the deviations may be written as follows.

Continuity equation:

$$\frac{\partial \rho}{\partial t} + \rho\left[\frac{\partial u}{\partial x} + \frac{1}{r}\frac{\partial}{\partial r}(rv)\right] = 0 \tag{2}$$

Equation of motion in x-direction:

$$\rho \frac{\partial u}{\partial t} = -\frac{\partial p}{\partial x} + \frac{1}{r}\frac{\partial}{\partial r}(r\tau_{rx}) \tag{3}$$

Thermodynamic equation of state for a liquid:

$$\frac{\partial \rho}{\rho} = \frac{\partial p}{B} \tag{4}$$

The equation of motion in the r-direction is neglected since u >> v. This implies that the pressure is constant across the cross section of the tube and becomes a function only of x and t. The nonlinear inertia terms $u\frac{\partial u}{\partial x}$ and $v\frac{\partial u}{\partial y}$ are considerably small compared with the local acceleration term $\frac{\partial u}{\partial t}$ and thus are neglected in Eq. (3). Also neglected in Eq. (3) is the viscous term $\frac{\partial \tau_{xx}}{\partial x}$, which is small compared with the viscous shear term $\frac{1}{r}\frac{\partial}{\partial r}(r\tau_{rx})$. The terms $v\frac{\partial \rho}{\partial r}$ and $u\frac{\partial \rho}{\partial x}$ are neglected in Eq. (2) as they are small compared with those terms appearing in the equation. The last simplification is justified since viscoelastic fluids have a high bulk modulus.

Now, Eqs. (2) and (4) may be combined to eliminate ρ. It yields

$$\frac{1}{B}\frac{\partial p}{\partial t} + \frac{\partial u}{\partial x} + \frac{\partial v}{\partial r} + \frac{v}{r} = 0 \tag{5}$$

Let the average pressure $\overline{p}$ and the average velocity $\overline{u}$ in the x-direction across the tube cross section be defined as

$$\overline{p}(x,t) = \frac{1}{\pi R^2}\int_0^R 2\pi r\, p\, dr \tag{6}$$

and

$$\bar{u}(x,t) = \frac{1}{\pi R^2}\int_0^R 2\pi r\ u\ dt \qquad (7)$$

It is obvious that $p = \bar{p}$. The governing equations are subject to the initial and boundary conditions

$$u(x,r,0) = 0, \qquad \bar{p}(x,0) = 0 \qquad (8)$$

$$u(x,R,t) = 0, \qquad \frac{\partial u(x,0,t)}{\partial r} = 0 \qquad (9a)$$

$$v(x,R,t) = 0 \qquad (9b)$$

Taking the Laplace transform of Eq. (1) and (3) followed by a combination of the resulting equations to eliminate $L[\tau_{rx}(x,r,t)]$, it yields

$$\frac{\partial^2 U}{\partial r^2} + \frac{1}{r}\frac{\partial U}{\partial r} - \frac{s}{\delta}\left(U + \frac{c^2}{Bs}\frac{d\bar{P}}{dx}\right) = 0 \qquad (10)$$

where $U(x,r,s) = L[u(x,r,t)]$, $\bar{P}(x,s) = L[\bar{p}(x,t)]$ and $\delta = \frac{\mu}{\rho}\left(\frac{1+\lambda_2 s}{1+\lambda_1 s}\right)$.
The solution of Eq. (8) which satisfies Eq. (9a) is

$$U = f(x,s)\left\{ I_0\left[r\left(\frac{s}{\delta}\right)^{1/2}\right] - I_0\left[R\left(\frac{s}{\delta}\right)^{1/2}\right]\right\} \qquad (11)$$

where I_0 is the modified Bessel function of first kind and order zero and $f(x,s)$ is a function to be determined. $\bar{U}$ may be obtained by multiplying both sides of Eq. (11) by $2\pi r$ followed by integrating with respect to r from 0 to R:

$$\bar{U} = f\left\{\frac{2}{R\left(\frac{s}{\delta}\right)^{1/2}} I_1\left[R\left(\frac{s}{\delta}\right)^{1/2}\right] - I_0\left[R\left(\frac{s}{\delta}\right)^{1/2}\right]\right\} \qquad (12)$$

Next, both sides of Eq. (5) are multiplied by $2\pi r$ and then integrated with respect to r from 0 to R. It yields

$$\frac{\partial\bar{p}}{\partial t} = -B\frac{\partial\bar{u}}{\partial x} \qquad (13)$$

Taking the Laplace transform of Eq. (13) followed by the substitution of Eq. (12) into the resulting equation, one gets

$$\frac{d^2 f}{dx^2} + \left(\frac{bs}{c}\right)^2 f = 0 \qquad (14)$$

where

$$\frac{1}{b^2} = \frac{2}{R\left(\frac{s}{\delta}\right)^{1/2}} \; \frac{I_1\left[R \frac{s}{\delta}^{1/2}\right]}{I_o\left[R\left(\frac{s}{\delta}\right)^{1/2}\right]} - 1 \tag{15}$$

The solution of Eq. (14) is

$$f(x,s) = A(s) \cos \frac{sb}{c} x + B(s) \sin \frac{sb}{c} x \tag{16}$$

where A(s) and B(s) are the integration constants to be determined by the conditions of $\overline{p}$ and $\overline{u}$ at a cross section of the tube.

Hence

$$\overline{U}(x,s) = [A(s) \cos \frac{sb}{c} x + B(s) \sin \frac{sb}{c} x] \; \frac{I_o\left[R\left(\frac{s}{\delta}\right)^{1/2}\right]}{b^2} \tag{17}$$

and

$$\overline{P}(x,s) = [A(s) \sin \frac{sb}{c} x - B(s) \cos \frac{sb}{c} x] \; \frac{B}{bc} \; I_o\left[R\left(\frac{s}{\delta}\right)^{1/2}\right] \tag{18}$$

Let $\overline{P}_1(s)$ and $\overline{U}_1(s)$ be the Laplace transforms of the pressure and velocity, respectively at the upstream section where x = 0. Then A(s) and B(s) can be obtained from Eqs. (17) and (18) to be

$$A(s) = \frac{\overline{U}b^2}{I_o\left[R\left(\frac{s}{\delta}\right)^{1/2}\right]}$$

and

$$B(s) = \frac{-\overline{P}_1 \, bc}{BI_o\left[R\left(\frac{s}{\delta}\right)^{1/2}\right]}$$

Therefore,

$$\overline{U}(x,s) = \overline{U}_1 \cos \frac{sb}{c} x - \overline{P}_1 \frac{c}{Bb} \sin \frac{sb}{c} x$$

$$\overline{P}(x,s) = \overline{U} \, \frac{bB}{c} \sin \frac{sb}{c} x + \overline{P}_1 \cos \frac{sb}{c} x$$

At the downstream cross section x = ℓ, the Laplace transforms of velocity $\overline{U}_2$ and pressure $\overline{P}_2$ may be related to those at the upstream cross section by

$$\overline{U}_2 = \overline{U}_1 \cos \frac{sb\ell}{c} - \overline{P}_1 \frac{c}{Bb} \sin \frac{sb\ell}{c} \tag{19}$$

$$\overline{P}_2 = \overline{U}_1 \frac{bB}{c} \sin \frac{sb\ell}{c} + \overline{P}_1 \cos \frac{sb\ell}{c} \tag{20}$$

Equations (19) and (20) may be expressed in matrix form as

$$F(s) \begin{Bmatrix} \overline{U}_1 \\ \overline{P}_1 \end{Bmatrix} = \begin{Bmatrix} \overline{U}_2 \\ \overline{P}_2 \end{Bmatrix} \qquad (21)$$

where F(s) is the transfer matrix defined as

$$F(s) = \begin{bmatrix} \cos \frac{sb\ell}{c} & -\frac{c}{Bb} \sin \frac{sb\ell}{c} \\ \frac{Bb}{c} \sin \frac{sb\ell}{c} & \cos \frac{sb\ell}{c} \end{bmatrix}$$

From Eqs. (19), (20) and (21), one gets the transfer functions

$$\frac{B}{C}\frac{\overline{U}_1}{\overline{P}_1} = \frac{\left(\frac{B}{C}\frac{\overline{U}_2}{\overline{P}_2}\right) \cos \frac{sb\ell}{c} + \frac{1}{b} \sin \frac{sb\ell}{c}}{\cos \frac{sb\ell}{c} - \left(\frac{\overline{U}_2}{\overline{P}_2}\frac{B}{C}\right) b \sin \frac{sb\ell}{c}} \qquad (22)$$

and

$$\frac{\overline{P}_2}{\overline{P}_1} = \frac{1}{\cos \frac{sb\ell}{c} - \left(\frac{\overline{U}_2}{\overline{P}_2}\frac{B}{C}\right) b \sin \frac{sb\ell}{c}} \qquad (23)$$

in which the pressure-flow relationship at $x = \ell$, i.e., $\overline{U}_2/\overline{P}_2$, is yet to be specified. Here, consideration is given to the case where a flow restriction or a fixed orifice is placed at one end of the flow line. For such a case, $\overline{U}_2/\overline{P}_2$ may be expressed as [2]

$$\frac{\overline{U}_2}{\overline{P}_2} = \frac{1}{K} + \frac{sY(\ell,s)}{\overline{P}_2} \qquad (24)$$

where K is a constant depending on the orifice characteristics and $sY(\ell,s)$ is the Laplace transform of $\partial y(\ell,t)/\partial t$ which is the velocity (or the rate of displacement) of the end of the pipe in the axial direction induced by the undamped longitudinal vibrations of the pipe with the upstream end (x = 0) bolted. Hence, if the flow line is securely fastened to a stationary frame, the last term in Eq. (24) vanishes, i.e., $\overline{U}_2/\overline{P}_2 = 1/K$. The expression of $sY(\ell,s)/\overline{P}_2$ is shown in [1] to be

$$\frac{sY(\ell,s)}{\overline{P}_2} = \frac{A_1 - A_3}{ms + \zeta + \frac{A_2E}{c_s} \coth \frac{s\ell}{c_s}} \tag{25}$$

where A_1 is the flow cross-sectional area, A_2 the cross-sectional area of the pipe wall, A_3 the area of the orifice, m the mass of the orifice block, ζ the damping coefficient, E the modulus of elasticity of the pipe and c_s the velocity of sound in the material of pipe. Equation (25) is obtained by solving the equation for the undamped longitudinal vibrations of the pipe

$$\frac{\partial^2 y}{\partial t^2} = c_s^2 \frac{\partial^2 y}{\partial x^2}$$

subject to the initial conditions $y(x,0) = 0$ and $\partial y(x,0)/\partial t = 0$, and the boundary conditions $y(0,t) = 0$ and

$$A_2E \frac{\partial y(\ell,t)}{\partial x} + m \frac{\partial^2 y(\ell,t)}{\partial t^2} + \zeta \frac{\partial y(\ell,t)}{\partial t} = \overline{p}_2(A_1-A_2) \ .$$

Results and Discussion

The frequency response of the flow line may be obtained by substituting s for $j\omega$ in Eqs. (22) and (23). The resulting equations may be reduced to a form consisting of the real part R and the imaginary part I. Then the amplitude-ratio and phase-shift responses can be expressed as $\sqrt{R^2 + I^2}$ and $\tan^{-1}(-R/I)$, respectively. However, the complexity resulting from the dependence of the parameter b on the modified Bessel functions I_o and I_1, as shown in Eq. (15), makes the numerical computation for frequency or transient response a formidable task. For this reason, two asymptotic numerical solutions of Eqs. (22) and (23) were obtained, one being valid for small values of ω and the other for large values of ω. The numerical solution for intermediate frequency range was obtained through the matching of these two asymptotic solutions by a simple extrapolation procedure.

For small values of s, the modified Bessel functions may be approximated as

$$I_o\left(\sqrt{\frac{s}{\delta}}\,R\right) \simeq 1 + \left(\sqrt{\frac{s}{\delta}}\,\frac{R}{2}\right)^2$$

$$I_1\left(\sqrt{\frac{s}{\delta}}\,R\right) \simeq \sqrt{\frac{s}{\delta}}\,\frac{R}{2}$$

Therefore, Eq. (15) is reduced to

$$\frac{1}{b^2} \simeq \frac{1}{1 + \left(\sqrt{\frac{s}{\delta}}\frac{R}{2}\right)^2} - 1 \tag{26a}$$

For large values of s, the asymptotic expression of the modified Bessel function

$$I_n\left(\sqrt{\frac{s}{\delta}}\,R\right) \sim \frac{e^{\sqrt{\frac{s}{\delta}}\,R}}{\sqrt{2\pi\sqrt{\frac{s}{\delta}}\,R}} \qquad \text{(for n = any integer)}$$

leads to

$$\frac{1}{b^2} \simeq \frac{1}{\sqrt{\frac{s}{\delta}}\frac{R}{2}} - 1 \tag{26b}$$

It is convenient to express the parameter $\sqrt{\frac{s}{\delta}}\frac{R}{2}$ in Eq. (26) as

$$\sqrt{\frac{s}{\delta}}\frac{R}{2} = \left[\frac{1}{4}\left(\frac{j\Omega}{N}\,\frac{1 + j\Lambda_1\Omega}{1 + j\Lambda_2\Omega}\right)\right]^{1/2} \tag{27}$$

where

$$\Omega = \frac{\omega\ell}{c}, \quad \Lambda_1 = \frac{\lambda_1 c}{\ell}, \quad \Lambda_2 = \frac{\lambda_2 c}{\ell}, \quad N = \frac{\nu\ell}{cR^2}$$

are all dimensionless. $\overline{U}_1/\overline{P}_1$, $\overline{U}_2/\overline{P}_2$, 1/K and c/B have the same physical units. Each one can be made dimensionless if multiplied by a conversion factor, say $c_o\rho_o/g_o$, where c_o is the reference velocity, ρ_o the reference density and g_o a dimensional constant (32.17 lbm-ft/lbf-sec^2). In the following discussion, $\overline{U}_1/\overline{P}_1$, $\overline{U}_2/\overline{P}_2$, 1/K and c/B will be treated as if they were dimensionless.

An examination of Eqs. (22) and (23) reveals that the responses of the pressure and velocity in a rigidly-bolted line are functions of the six dimensionless parameters: Ω for frequency response or ℓ/ct for transient response, Λ_1, Λ_2, N, K and B/c. The amplitude ratios and phase shifts for both $\overline{U}_1/\overline{P}_1$ and $\overline{P}_2/\overline{P}_1$ have been computed by means of an IBM 360 digital computer for values of Λ_1, Λ_2, N = 0.01, 0.1 and 1.0, K, B/c = 1.0 and 10, and Ω in the ranges 0.001 to 0.1 for the small Ω solution and 0.1 to 100 for the large Ω solution. $\Lambda_1 = \Lambda_2$ corresponds to a Newtonian fluid. Some representative results are shown in Figs.

1, 2, 3 and 4. The table gives a list of the five dimensionless parameters for each response curve illustrated in the figures. Of significance in these results is the phenomena of "resonance" in the amplitude ratios and phase shifts of the velocity deviation at section 1 and of the pressure deviation at section 2. These phenomena were also observed in the flow line of Newtonian fluids [2]. The "resonance" phenomena are more pronounced in the viscoelastic fluid line as the ratio of Λ_1/Λ_2 is increased or as the value of N is decreased. A result worth mentioning is that the phase-lead can exist in certain ranges of Ω for the response of pressure deviation at section 2 and over most of the frequency ranges for the response of velocity deviation at section 1.

TABLE . LIST OF DIMENSIONLESS PARAMETERS FOR RESPONSE CURVE ILLUSTRATED IN FIGS. 1, 2, 3 AND 4

Curve	Λ_1	Λ_2	N	B/c	K
1A	1	1	1	1	1
B	1	1	1	1	10
C	1	1	1	10	1
D	1	1	1	10	10
2A	0.01	0.01	1	1	1
B	0.01	0.01	1	1	10
C	0.01	0.01	1	10	1
D	0.01	0.01	1	10	10
3A	0.1	0.01	1	1	1
B	0.1	0.01	1	1	10
C	0.1	0.01	1	10	1
D	0.1	0.01	1	10	10
4A	1	0.01	1	1	1
B	1	0.01	1	1	10
C	1	0.01	1	10	1
D	1	0.01	1	10	10

The effects of the parameters Λ_1, Λ_2, N, K and B/c are briefly summarized in the following:

a. Effects of Λ_1 and Λ_2: At low frequencies the effects of Λ_1 and Λ_2 on both the amplitude ratios and phase shifts are entirely negligible. This means that there is practically no effect due to Λ_1 and Λ_2 on the transient response of the flow line for large times. In high

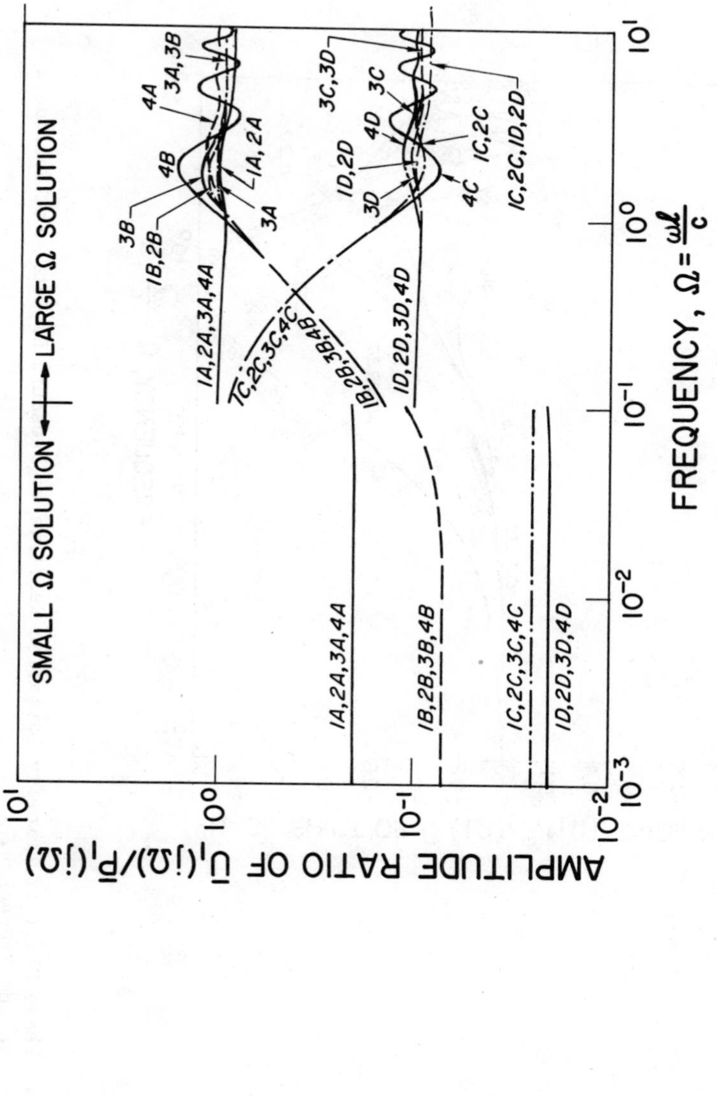

Fig. 1. Amplitude Ratio of Velocity to Pressure Deviations at Section 1 Versus Frequency.

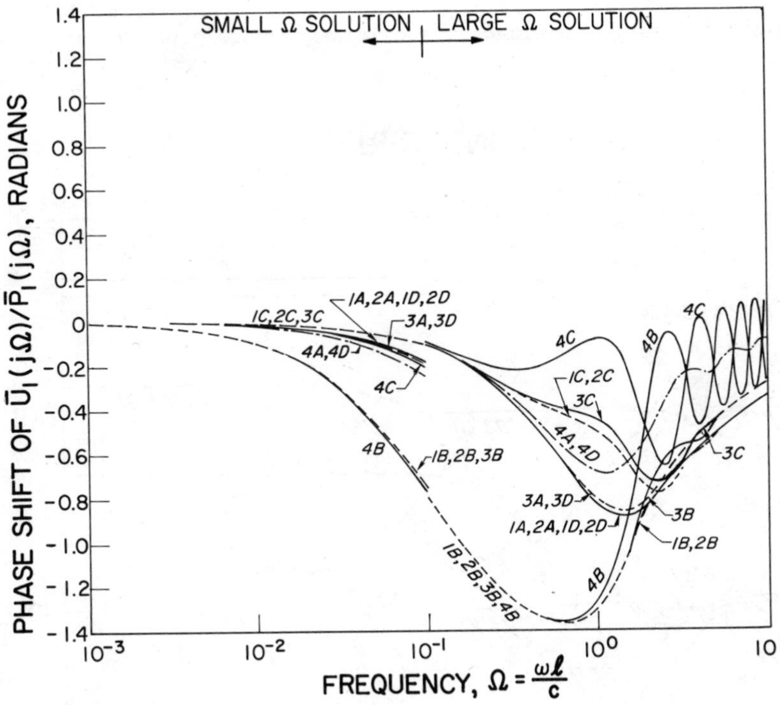

Fig. 2. Phase Shift of Velocity Deviation Relative to Pressure Deviation at Section 1 Versus Frequency.

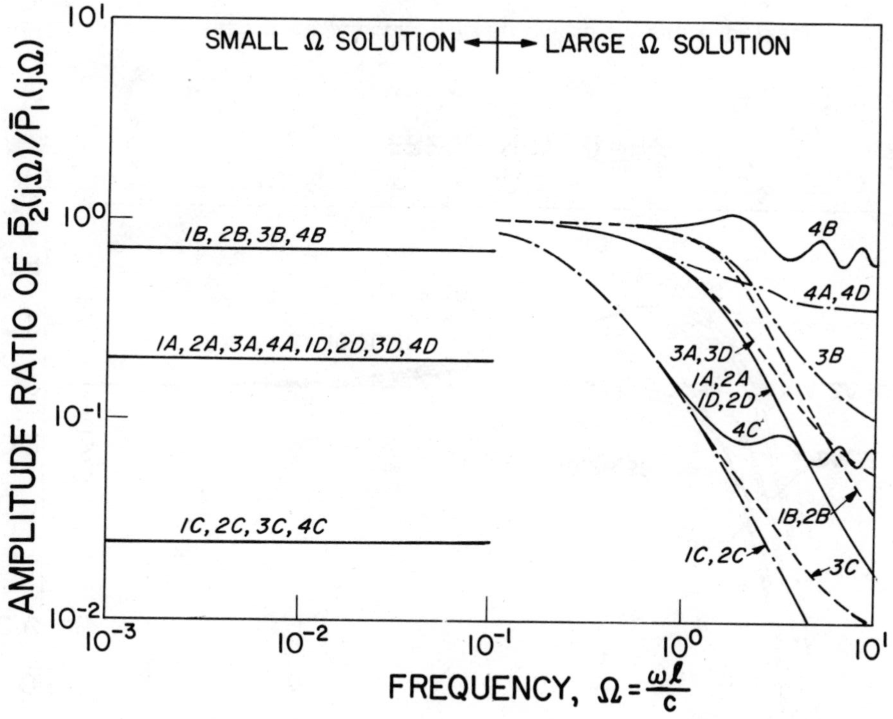

Fig. 3. Amplitude Ratio of Pressure Deviation at Section 2 to Pressure Deviation at Section 1 Versus Frequency.

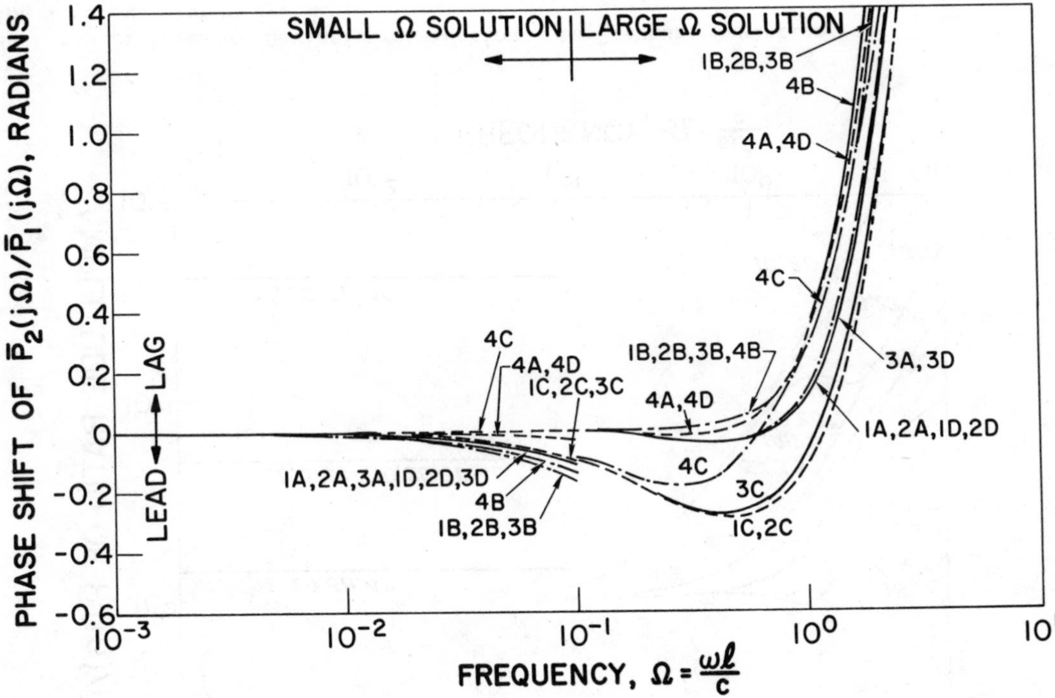

Fig. 4. Phase Shift of Pressure Deviation at Section 2 Relative to Pressure Deviation at Section 1 Versus Frequency.

frequency range, however, the responses of two systems having the same value of Λ_1/Λ_2 are identical. As Λ_1/Λ_2 increases, the amplitude ratios of both $\overline{U}_1/\overline{P}_1$ and $\overline{P}_2/\overline{P}_1$ increase, while their phase leads decrease. A maximum or a minimum appears in the response curves at an interval of approximately π in Ω. The oscillation in the response curves is amplified as the value of Λ_1/Λ_2 increases and/or as N decreases.

b. Effects of K: As the value of K increases in low frequency domain, the amplitude ratio of $\overline{U}_1/\overline{P}_1$ decreases while that of $\overline{P}_2/\overline{P}_1$ increases. The effects of K on phase shifts are very small when Ω is less than 10^{-2}. In high frequency domain, however, the effects of K on the amplitude ratios or their mean values are negligible. On the contrary, the phase shifts of both $\overline{U}_1/\overline{P}_1$ and $\overline{P}_2/\overline{P}_1$ are significantly influenced by the value of K.

c. Effects of N: N is large when a fluid with a large coefficient of viscosity oscillates at a small frequency in a small-diameter line, while N is small when a liquid with low viscosity coefficient oscillates at very high frequency in a large-diameter tube. As $N \rightarrow 0$, $(\sqrt{S/\delta})(R/2)$ and thus b approaches infinity, which results in $\overline{U}_1/\overline{P}_1 = 0$ and $\overline{P}_2/\overline{P}_1 = 0$. In other words, the influence of the rheological properties Λ_1, Λ_2 and N are important in case of small diameter tubes. It is disclosed from the figures not included in the paper that at low frequencies, a decrease in N causes an increase in the amplitude ratios of both $\overline{U}_1/\overline{P}_1$ and $\overline{P}_2/\overline{P}_1$. The effects of N on the phase shifts are negligible for values of less than 10^{-2}. In high frequency domain when $\Omega > 1$ the amplitude ratios of $\overline{U}_1/\overline{P}_1$ or their mean values are unaffected by a variation in N, but the maximum or minimum amplitude at "resonance" increases with a decrease in N. However, a decrease in N will cause an increase in the amplitude ratio of $\overline{P}_2/\overline{P}_1$. The parameter N also plays an important role in the phase shifts of $\overline{U}_1/\overline{P}_1$ and $\overline{P}_2/\overline{P}_1$.

d. Effects of B/c: In both low and high frequency domains, the amplitude ratios and phase shifts of both $\overline{U}_1/\overline{P}_1$ and $\overline{P}_2/\overline{P}_1$ decrease with an increase in B/c. It is worth mentioning that the corresponding response curves of series A and D coincide except the amplitude ratio response of $\overline{U}_1/\overline{P}_1$ for low values of N. These two series of response curves have the same value of B/cK.

Fig. 5 shows the amplitude ratio and phase shift of $\overline{P}_2/\overline{P}_1$ in the presence of line vibrations. The theoretical curves were computed from

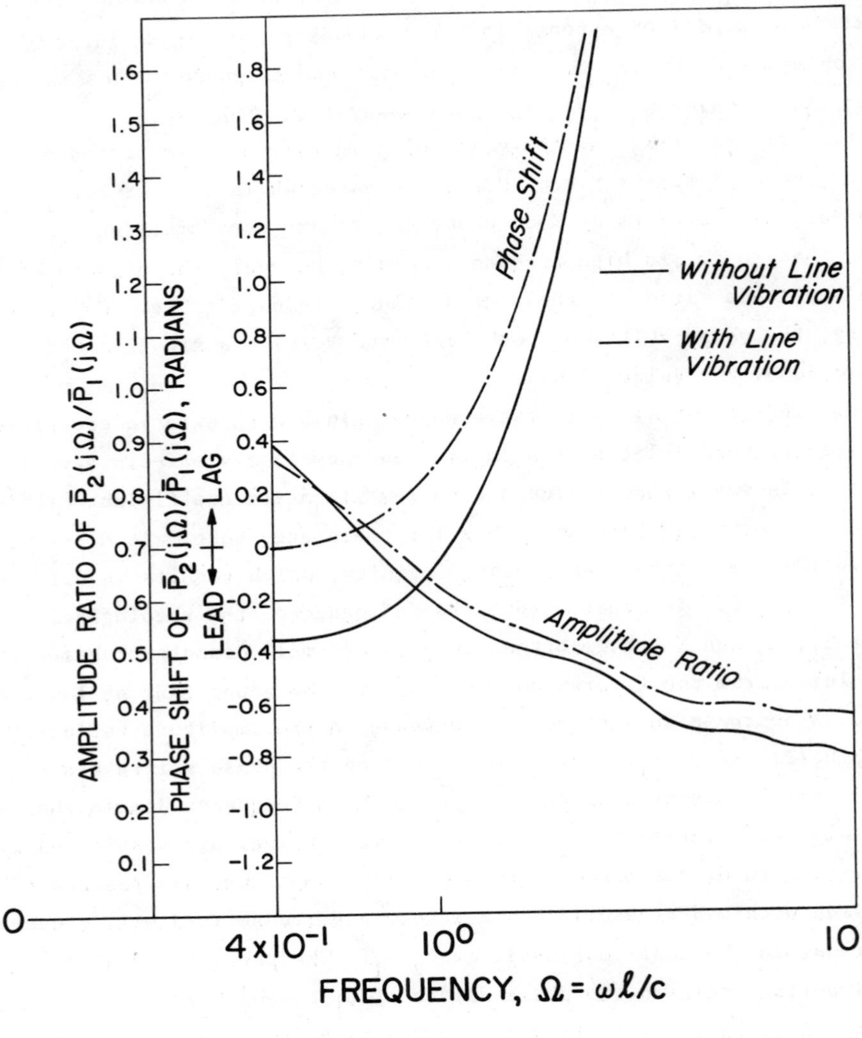

Fig. 5. Amplitude Ratio and Phase Shift of Pressure Deviation at Section 2 to Pressure Deviation at Section 1 Versus Frequency with Vibration.

Eqs. (23) and (24) corresponding to the case where $A_2 = 0$, $\zeta = 0$, and $(A_1-A_3)\ell/mc = 1.0$. The figure also illustrates the results of $\overline{P}_2/\overline{P}_1$ in the absence of line vibrations corresponding to response curves 5A in Figs. 3 and 4. It is shown that the deviations in amplitude ratio and phase shift are affected by line vibrations. In case of a pure viscous fluid [2] the maximum deviations in amplitude and phase angle occur near the natural frequency of longitudinal vibrations of the line. Although it is not shown here, the present study has also disclosed that the line vibration does not appreciably change the dynamic response of velocity deviation at section 1.

Illustrative Example

The following illustrative example is constructed to show the engineering scientist how to apply the results obtained in this investigation.

Consider a flow of a solution of poly (methyl) methacrylate in n-butyl acetate through a stainless-steel tube of 0.672-in. ID and 765-ft. long. At 25°C and a polymer concentration of 29.15 gm/liter, the solution has the following rheological properties [4]: $\lambda_1 = 0.18$ sec, $\lambda_2 = 0.01$ sec, $n = 16.0$ poise, $\rho = 61.7$ lbm/ft^3, and $C = 4250$ ft/sec (approximate value). The downstream end of the line is connected through an orifice to an outlet tank. The experimental results in [2] have indicated that for a line with a fixed orifice the amplitude ratio of velocity to pressure deviations at the discharge end is approximately constant and their relative phase angle is almost negligible. Thus the flow-pressure relationship at the discharge end is assumed to be $\overline{U}_2/P_2 = 1/K$. Let the orifice characteristics be such that $K = 8{,}140$ lbf-sec/ft^3. (This value has been selected for convenience so that K becomes unity in dimensionless form).

The numerical values of the dimensionless parameters are $\Lambda_1 = 1.0$, $\Lambda_2 = 0.0555$, $B/c = 1.0$, $K = 1.0$, and $N = 1.0$. It is found in the table that the response curves corresponding to this physical system should lie between curves 1A and 4A and may be found by interpolation.

It must be noted that the curves presented in Figs. 1 through 4 are prepared mainly for the purpose of examining the effects of the dimensionless parameters on the velocity and pressure responses of viscoelastic transmission lines. Separate numerical calculations may be required for specific applications since the ranges of the parameters represented by the curves in the four figures are rather limited.

CONCLUDING REMARKS

A linearlized theory is developed to predict the dynamic response of viscoelastic fluid transmission lines by employing a three-parameter Oldroyd model for the shear-stress-shear-strain relationship. A transfer function is derived relating the pressure and velocity variables. Theoretical results are obtained for frequency response.

The roles of the five dimensionless parameters Λ_1, Λ_2, N, B/c and K are identified. It is concluded that the phenomena of "resonance" become more pronounced as the ratio of the stress- and strain-relaxation times is increased or as the coefficient of viscosity is decreased. The amplitude ratios and phase shifts of both the pressure and velocity responses decrease with an increase in the ratio of bulk modulus to sonic velocity in the fluid. As expected, the constant K representing orifice characteristics can significantly affect the dynamic behavior of the flow line.

The longitudinal vibrations of the viscoelastic fluid flow line may modify the dynamic characteristics of pressure deviation at downstream sections.

REFERENCES

1. Yang, W. J. and Masubuch, M., Dynamics for Process and System Control, Gordon Breach, London, 1969.
2. D'souza, A. F. and Oldenburger, R., "Dynamic Response of Fluid Lines," Journal of Basic Engineering, Vol. 86, Transactions American Society of Mechanical Engineers, Series D, 1964, pp. 589-598.
3. Eirich, F. R., Rheology, Theory and Applications, Vol. 1, Academic Press, New York, 1955.
4. Toms, B. A., "Elastic and Viscous Properties of Dilute Solution of Poly(methyl) methacrylate in Certain Solvent/non-Solvent Mixtures," Rheologica, Acta, Vol. 2/3, p. 137, 1958.

ON THE NUMERICAL SOLUTION OF A CLASS OF NONLINEAR PROBLEMS IN DYNAMIC COUPLED THERMOELASTICITY

J. T. Oden
Research Institute, University of Alabama

J. Poe
Research Institute, University of Alabama

ABSTRACT

This paper concerns the application of the finite-element method to the solution of certain nonlinear problems in thermoelasticity. Numerical solutions of transient, coupled thermoelasticity problems involving bodies which exhibit material nonlinearities and temperature-dependent thermal conductivity and specific heat are presented. General equations of motion and heat conduction of an arbitrary finite element are reduced so as to apply to the problem of transient response of a nonlinear thermoelastic half space subjected to a time-dependent temperature over its boundary.

LIST OF NOTATIONS

a_o, a_1, ...	Material constants
c_D	Specific heat at constant deformation
C_o	Reference configuration
F_m	Components of body force per unit mass in C_o
G	Green deformation tensor
h	Internal heat supplied per unit undeformed volume
I, II, III	Strain invariants
K_{ij}	Temperature dependent thermal conductivity tensor
K_o	Conventional thermal conductivity
ℓ	Nondimensional length
m^{NM}	Consistent mass matrix for the element

P_{Nk}	Components of nodal generalized forces
q^i	Components of heat flux
q_N	Generalized nodal heat flux at node N
S^m	Components of surface traction
T	Temperature
T_o	Temperature of the reference configuration
u_m	Cartesian components of displacement relative to C_o
$\overline{U}$	Nondimensional displacement
x_i	Coordinates describing the motion of the body
X_i	Rectangular cartesian coordinates in the undeformed body
α	Linear coefficient of thermal expansion
γ_{ij}	Green-Saint Venant strain tensor
δ	Thermomechanical coupling parameter
ε	Term governing variation of thermal conductivity with temperature
ζ	Nondimensional time
η	Entropy per unit undeformed volume
θ	Absolute temperature
$\overline{\theta}$	Nondimensional temperature
λ, μ	Lamé constants
ξ	Internal energy per unit undeformed volume
ρ, ρ_o	Mass densities in the configurations C_o and C respectively
σ	Internal dissipation
σ^{ij}	Stress per unit initial area
τ	Time parameter
ϕ	Free energy per unit undeformed volume
$\psi_N(\underset{\sim}{x})$	Finite element interpolation function

INTRODUCTION

It is widely known that many physical properties of common materials are dependent on temperature. A casual glance at any good handbook on physical properties of materials, for example, will show that quantities such as specific heat, thermal conductivity, thermal expansion coefficients, etc., which are treated as constants in classical theories, may change significantly with a change in temperature. The description of the behavior of such materials becomes further complicated if it is also recognized that their ability to conduct heat may be dependent on deformation. Indeed, the interconvertibility of mechanical work and heat was recognized long ago by Joule; hence, it is reasonable to take into account the effects of temperature in the equations of motion of a body and to include the effects of motion in the equations of heat conduction.

Experimental observations indicate that many thermomechanical phenomena associated with fairly common materials are decidedly nonlinear in nature. As such, their analytical description falls well outside the scope of the classical theory of thermoelasticity. Reiner [1] proposed a nonlinear stress-strain law for a limited class of thermoelastic solids and Jindra [2] used a perturbation procedure to solve a problem in static, uncoupled thermoelasticity wherein certain material nonlinearities were assumed. Recognizing that many materials exhibit deviations from standard linear constitutive laws even for infinitesimal strains, Dillon [3] developed a theory which included mild material nonlinearities by retaining certain higher-order terms in a series expansion of the free energy density. Dillon studied the influence of nonlinear terms in the deviatoric strains by calculating the temperature generated in a circular bar subjected to prescribed time-dependent twisting.

Owing to the extreme mathematical difficulties usually involved in treating nonlinear equations, no analytical solutions to nonlinear boundary and initial value problems in dynamic-coupled thermoelasticity appear to be available. It is natural, therefore, to consider numerical methods for solving such problems. This is the viewpoint adopted in the present investigation.

This paper is concerned with the application of the finite-element concept to the analysis of a class of nonlinear problems in dynamic-coupled thermoelasticity. After a brief review of certain fundamental equations governing the behavior of thermoelastic solids, we present rather general coupled equations of motion and heat conduction for a typical element of a discrete model of the continuum. The form of the free energy function and the constitutive equation for heat flux is not specified in these equations; nor are restrictions imposed on magnitudes of the displacement gradients. We then obtain special forms of these equations by assuming infinitesimal strains, expanding the free energy in a power series, and retaining terms of higher order than the second, in the manner described by Dillon [3]. We also account for temperature dependent specific heat and thermal conductivity, the latter being incorporated in a nonlinear version of Fourier's law wherein the thermal conductivity is assumed to be a linear function of temperature. By linearizing these equations, we show that the finite-element models of Nickell and Sackman [4] and Oden and Kross [5] are obtained.

To demonstrate the influence of various nonlinearities, we then consider applications of the theory to selected problems for which solutions to the linearized problem are known. In particular, we solve several nonlinear versions of the coupled Danilovskaya problem [6], which involves the transient response of a thermoelastic half-space subjected to a time-dependent temperature field applied uniformly over its plane boundary. This problem was solved using linear theory by Sternberg and Chakravorty [7]; numerical solutions of the linearized problem have also been presented [4, 5]. Our results indicate that material nonlinearities, as manifested by nonlinear dilatational terms in the constitutive equation for stress, temperature-dependent thermal conductivity, and temperature-dependent specific heat, may lead to significant differences from the linear theories. Parametric studies are performed in those cases in which insufficient experimental data is available to estimate the relative magnitudes of higher-order material constants. The present finite-element formulation of the problem leads to several hundred simultaneous nonlinear first- and second-order differential equations in the nodal values of displacements and temperatures. These are solved by a Runge-Kutta-Gill integration scheme.

Nonlinear Thermoelasticity

Consider a deformable, thermoelastic continuum under the action of a general system of external forces and prescribed temperatures. The reference configuration C_o is ideally selected to correspond to a natural unstrained state and to be at a uniform temperature T_o. To trace the motion of the continuum and its variations in temperature, we introduce a system of intrinsic coordinates X^i which are rectangular cartesian at $\tau = 0$, τ being a time parameter. At $\tau = t > 0$, cartesian coordinates of a particle X^i are denoted x_i and the temperature at x^i

is $T_o + T(X^i, t)$, where $T(X^i, t)$ is the temperature change. The relations $x_i = x_i(X^1, X^2, X^3, t)$ describe the motion of the body.

The thermomechanical behavior of the contimuum must be such that the following physical laws are satisfied locally at every particle X^i:

$$(\sigma^{ij} x_{m,j})_{,i} + \rho_o F_m = \rho_o \ddot{u}_m, \quad \sigma^{ij} = \sigma^{ji} \tag{1}$$

$$\rho\sqrt{G} = \rho_o \tag{2}$$

$$\dot{\xi} = \sigma^{ij}\gamma_{ij} + q^i_{;i} + h \tag{3}$$

$$\theta\dot{\eta} \geq q^i_{;i} + h - \frac{1}{\theta} q^i T_{,i} \tag{4}$$

Here σ^{ij} is the stress per unit initial area A_o referred to the convected coordinate lines X^i; F_m are the components of body force per unit mass in C_o; u_m are the cartesian components of displacement relative to C_o; ξ, η, and h denote the internal energy, entropy, and internal heat supplied per unit undeformed volume; γ_{ij} is the Green-Saint Venant strain tensor; q^i are components of heat flux; and $\theta = T_o + T$ is the absolute temperature. Superposed dots indicate time rates, commas partial differentiation with respect to X^i, and semi-colons denote covariant differentiation with respect to X^i. We also have

$$G = \det(\delta_{ij} + 2\gamma_{ij}) \tag{5}$$

where

$$2\gamma_{ij} = u_{i,j} + u_{j,i} + u_{m,i}u_{m,j} \tag{6}$$

Equations (1) represent local forms of the laws of balance of linear and angular momentum; (2) insures that mass is conserved during the motion; (3) is a local form of the law of conservation of energy, and (4) is the Clausius-Duhem inequality.

It is convenient to introduce the free energy ϕ per unit undeformed volume:

$$\phi = \xi - \eta\theta \tag{7}$$

Then (3) can be recast in the alternate forms

$$\dot{\phi} = \sigma^{ij}\dot{\gamma}_{ij} - \eta\dot{\theta} - \sigma \tag{8}$$

$$\theta\dot{\eta} = q^i_{;i} + h + \sigma \tag{9}$$

where (8) defines σ, the internal dissipation. The theory of thermoelasticity is based on the assumption that σ is zero and that ϕ is a differentiable function of the current values of γ_{ij} and T. It then follows from (8) that

$$\sigma^{ij} = \frac{\partial\phi(\gamma_{ij}, T)}{\partial\gamma_{ij}} \qquad \eta = -\frac{\partial\phi(\gamma_{ij}, T)}{\partial T} \tag{10}$$

Therefore, the equations of motion and heat conduction at a point in a thermoelastic continuum are

$$\left[\frac{\partial\phi(\gamma_{ij}, T)}{\partial\gamma_{ij}} x_{m,i}\right]_{,j} + \rho_o F_m = \rho_o \ddot{u}_m \tag{11}$$

$$-\theta \frac{d}{dt}\left[\frac{\partial\phi(\gamma_{ij}, T)}{\partial T}\right] = q^i_{;i} + h \tag{12}$$

Specific forms of (11) and (12) can be obtained when the form of the function $\phi(\gamma_{ij}, T)$ and the constitutive equation for q^i for the material are identified.

Finite-Element Models

We shall now outline the development of general discrete models of thermoelastic behavior based on the finite-element concept. Following the usual procedure, we view the continuum as a collection of a finite number of component parts called finite elements, which are connected continuously together. Ordinarily, the elements are of relatively simple geometric shapes (e.g., tetrahedra, prisms, quadrilaterals, triangles, etc.) and the connectivity of the model is accomplished by regarding the elements to be attached to one another at preselected nodal points. Since the process of connecting elements appropriately together is based on purely topological properties of the model, it suffices to isolate a typical finite element and to first describe its behavior independent of the rest.

In the present investigation, a typical element e is viewed as a subdomain of the displacement and temperature fields $u_i(\tilde{X}, t)$ and $T(\tilde{X}, t)$. The local displacements and temperatures over a typical element are assumed to be of the form

$$u_i = \psi_N(\underset{\sim}{X})u_{Ni} \qquad T = \psi_N(\underset{\sim}{X})T_N \tag{13}$$

where u_{Ni} and T_N are the displacement components and the temperature change at node N of the element. Here the dependence of u_{Ni} and T_N on t is understood and the repreated nodal index is summed from 1 to N_e, N_e being the total number of nodes of element e. The interpolation functions $\psi_N(\underset{\sim}{X})$ form a basis for the N_e-dimensional subspace, described by (13), which is a projection of the space to which the continuum displacement and temperature functions belong; they are assumed to have the following properties:

$$\psi_N(\underset{\sim}{X}) \geq 0 \; ; \quad \psi_N(\underset{\sim}{X}^M) = \delta^M_N, \quad \sum_{N=1}^{N_e} \psi_N(\underset{\sim}{X}) = 1 \tag{14}$$

Following a procedure described in previous investigations [8, 9, 10], we introduce the local approximations (13) into appropriately modified forms of the energy balances (8) and (9) and require that the results hold for arbitrary nodal values $\dot{u}_{Ni}$ and $\dot{T}_N$. In this way we obtain general equations of motion and heat conduction for a typical finite element e:

$$m^{NM}\ddot{u}_{Mk} + \int_{\upsilon_{o(e)}} \frac{\partial\phi(\gamma_{ij}, T)}{\partial\gamma_{ij}} (\delta_{ik} + \psi_{M,k}u_{Mi})\psi_{N,j}\, d\upsilon = P_{Nk} \tag{15}$$

$$-\int_{\upsilon_{o(e)}} \left[\psi_N(\underset{\sim}{X})(T_o + \psi_M T_M)\frac{d}{dt}\left(\frac{\partial\phi(\gamma_{ij}, T)}{\partial T}\right) - q^i\psi_{N,i}\right]d\upsilon = q_N \tag{16}$$

Here M, N = 1, 2, ..., N_e; i, j, k = 1, 2, 3; $\psi_{N,i} = \partial\psi_N(\underset{\sim}{X})\, X^i$;

$$m^{NM} = \int_{\upsilon_{o(e)}} \psi_N(\underset{\sim}{X})\psi_M(\underset{\sim}{X})d\upsilon \tag{17}$$

$$P_{Nk} = \int_{\upsilon_{o(e)}} \psi_N(\underset{\sim}{X})F_k\rho_o d\upsilon + \int_{A_{o(e)}} S^m(\delta_{km} + \psi_{M,k}u_{Mm})\psi_N(\underset{\sim}{X})dA \tag{18}$$

$$q_N = \int_{\upsilon_{o(e)}} \psi_N(\underset{\sim}{X})hd\upsilon + \int_{A_{o(e)}} q^i n_i\psi_N(\underset{\sim}{X})dA \tag{19}$$

The array m^{NM} is the consistent mass matrix for the element, P_{Nk} is the kth component of generalized force at node N, and q_N is the normal generalized heat flux at node N. The surface tractions S^m and heat flux components q^i per unit undeformed area are referred to coordinate directions X^i in the deformed body. Equation (15) is the discrete analogue of (11) and (16) is the discrete analogue of (12). Again, specific forms of (15) and (16) can be obtained once forms of $\phi(\gamma_{ij}, T)$ and $q^i(\gamma_{ij}, T, T_{,i})$ appropriate for the material under consideration are specified.

Constitutive Equations for Thermoelastic Solids

For isotropic thermoelastic materials, the free energy can be expressed as a function of the strain invariants and temperature:

$$\phi = (I, II, III, T) \tag{20}$$

where

$$I = \gamma_{ii}$$

$$II = \frac{1}{2}(\gamma_{ii}\gamma_{jj} - \gamma_{ij}\gamma_{ij}) \tag{21}$$

$$III = \det(\gamma_{ij})$$

Following a standard approach, we assume that the free energy can be expanded in a power series in the strain invariants and temperature increments;[1]

$$\phi = a_o + a_1 I + a_2 II + a_3 III + a_5 I^2 + a_6 I^3 + a_7 T^2$$

$$+ a_8 IT + a_9 I\ II + a_{10} IT^2 + a_{11} IIT + a_{12} T^3$$

$$+ a_{13} I^2 T + a_{14} I^4 + a_{15} II^2 + a_{16} I\ II + \ldots \tag{22}$$

where a_o, a_1, a_2 ... are material constants. If we assume the material to be stress free in the reference state and to not be dependent on terms in the free energy of higher than fourth order, $a_o = a_1 = 0$ and a_{17}, a_{18}, a_{19}, ... do not appear. We may regard this form as having no

1. The term $a_4 T$ is omitted because it does not influence either σ_{ij} or $\dot{\xi}$.

restriction on the magnitude of the strains and temperature but as a free energy function of a certain class of thermoelastic materials.

Obviously we can obtain many forms of the free energy function by simply adding or deleting terms in (22). For example, an incompresible thermoelastic material of the Mooney-type is described by a relatively simple form of the free energy function;

$$\phi = a_o + a_1 I + a_2 II + a_7 T^2 + a_8 IT \tag{23}$$

where

$$a_1 = 2(C_1 + C_2) \qquad a_2 = 4C_2 \tag{24}$$

and C_1 and C_2 are the usual Mooney constants for the isothermal case. Another example is provided by the classical thermoelastic solids, for which

$$\phi = \frac{1}{2} E^{ijkm} \gamma_{ij}\gamma_{km} + B^{ij}\gamma_{ij}T + \frac{1}{2}\frac{a}{T_o} T^2 \tag{25}$$

where E^{ijkm} and B^{ij} are arrays of material parameters which are assumed constant for isotropic homogeneous bodies, and have the properties of symmetry

$$E^{ijkm} = E^{jikm} = E^{ijmk} = E^{kmij} \quad \text{and} \quad B^{ij} = B^{ji} \tag{26}$$

These material parameters may be rewritten as

$$\begin{gathered} \lambda = E^{1122},\ -\mu = \frac{1}{2}(E^{1111} - \lambda),\ \alpha(3\lambda + 2\mu) = B^{11} \\ \rho_o c_D = -\ 2aT \end{gathered} \tag{27}$$

where α is the linear coefficient of thermal expansion, c_D is the specific heat at constant deformation, and λ and μ are Lamé constants. However, only relatively simple forms of the free energy can be utilized in the development of manageable nonlinear theories of thermoelasticity. We shall confine our attention to thermoelastic materials for which the constitutive equations of stress are nonlinear but the strains are infinitesimal:

$$\gamma_{ij} = \frac{1}{2}(u_{i,j} + u_{j,i}) \tag{28}$$

So as to obtain quantitative solutions, we follow the example of Dillon [3] and assume that the quadratic version of the free energy function coincides with the quadratic form (25) formulated in classical thermoelasticity. Then

$$a_2 = -2\mu, \; a_5 = \frac{1}{2}(\lambda + 2\mu), \; a_8 = -\alpha(3\lambda + 2\mu) \tag{29}$$

However, we obtain a more general form of specific heat:

$$\rho_o c_D = -2\theta(a_7 + 2a_{12}T + 2a_{10}I) \tag{30}$$

Conclusive data on the variation of c_D with deformation is not readily available and as a further simplification we set $a_{10} = 0$. We shall include, however, the effects of temperature on c_D and assume that it varies linearly with temperature. In order to include mild nonlinearities in the constitutive equations for stress, we retain terms of third degree in γ_{ij} and T. With these simplifications the free energy is reduced to

$$\phi = -2\mu II + a_3 III + (\lambda + 2\mu)I^2 + a_6 I^3 + a_7 T^2 - \alpha(3\lambda + 2\mu)IT$$
$$+ a_9 I\, II + a_{11} IIT + a_{12} T^3 + a_{13} I^2 T \tag{31}$$

The stress and entropy are then

$$\sigma^{ij} = \delta_{ij}[\lambda I + a_3 II + 3a_6 I^2 - \alpha(3\lambda + 2\mu)T + a_9(I^2 + II)$$
$$+ a_{11} IT + 2a_{13} IT] - \gamma_{ij}(-2\mu + a_3 I + a_9 I + a_{11} T)$$
$$+ a_3 \gamma_{ik}\gamma_{jk} \tag{32}$$

$$\eta = -2a_7 T + \alpha(3\lambda + 2\mu)I - 2a_{11} II + 3a_{12} T^2 - a_{13} I^2 \tag{33}$$

Equations (31)-(33) reduce to the classical equations of linear thermoelasticity if we delete nonlinear terms a_3, a_6, a_9, a_{11}, a_{12}, and a_{13}. If either a_3, a_6, or $a_9 \neq 0$, the material is mildly nonlinear in dilatation. It is recognized that for small strains in some metallic-type materials the relation between the dilatational components of stress and strain is linear to a larger extent than the deviatoric components [3]. We have nevertheless retained these terms in order to quantitatively assess the effects of nonlinearities in the dilatational strain components on the behavior of the material. Dillon [3] observed that for a material under oscillating dilatational strains the heating in compression should equal the cooling in tension, which requires $a_{13} = 0$. However, we know that when a body is worked heat is generated which is not completely dissipated. Recognizing that this property may not fall within the province of thermoelastic materials, we nevertheless retain the term in order to study its effect on the materials behavior, if indeed small.

We now turn to the problem of identifying the constitutive equation for heat flux in a thermoelastic solid. Fourier's law seems to work for a wide range of materials and as in the specific heat appears to be independent of deformation, but may vary with temperature. With this in mind we introduce a modified Fourier Law:

$$q_i = K_{ij}(T)\, T_{,j} \tag{34}$$

where K_{ij} is the temperature dependent thermal conductivity tensor. We shall assume as a first approximation for isotropic materials that K_{ij} is given by the linear form.

$$K_{ij} = \delta_{ij}(K_o)(1 + \varepsilon T) \tag{35}$$

Here K_o is the conventional thermal conductivity of the media and ε is a material constant of dimension 1/Temperature.

For materials described by (31) and (34), the equations of motion and heat conduction for a typical finite element are

$$m^{NM}\ddot{u}_{Mk} + \int_{\upsilon_o(e)} \Big\{[(-2\mu + 2(\lambda + 2\mu) + 3a_6\gamma_{rr} + a_9\gamma_{rr} + a_{11}T + 2a_{13}T)\gamma_{ss}$$

$$+ a_9(\gamma_{rr}\gamma_{ss} - \gamma_{rs}\gamma_{rs}) - \alpha(3\lambda + 2\mu)T]\delta_{ij}$$

$$- [2\mu + a_3(\gamma_{rr} - \frac{1}{2}\gamma_{rr}\gamma_{ss} - \frac{1}{2}\gamma_{rs}\gamma_{rs}) + a_9\gamma_{rr} + a_{11}T]\gamma_{ij}$$

$$+ a_3\gamma_{ir}\gamma_{jr}\Big\}\delta_{ik}\psi_{N,j}\,d\upsilon = P_{Nk}$$

$$- T_o \int_{\upsilon_o(e)} \psi_N(x)\Big\{2a_7T - \alpha(3\lambda + 2\mu)\dot{\gamma}_{rr} + a_{11}(\gamma_{rr}\dot{\gamma}_{ss} - \gamma_{rs}\dot{\gamma}_{rs})$$

$$+ 6a_{12}T\dot{T} + a_{13}\gamma_{rr}\dot{\gamma}_{ss}\Big\}d\upsilon$$

$$- \int_{\upsilon_{o(e)}} K_o(1 + \varepsilon T)\delta_{ij}\psi_{N,i}T_{,j}\,d\upsilon = q_N \tag{36}$$

where

$$\gamma_{rs} = \frac{1}{2}\,[\psi_{N,s}(\underset{\sim}{x})u_{Nr} + \psi_{N,s}(\underset{\sim}{x})u_{Ns}]$$
$$T = \psi_N(\underset{\sim}{x})T_N \tag{37}$$

The Elastic Half Space Problem

At present, detailed studies of practical problems in nonlinear thermoelasticity are handicapped by the lack of experimental data for real materials on the magnitudes of the constants $a_3 - a_{16}$. To demonstrate the influence of various nonlinear terms in (31) we have chosen to investigate nonlinear versions of the Danilovskaya [6] problem for which comparable solutions of the linearized problem are known. The particular example considered involves a materially nonlinear elastic half space subjected to a linear time dependent change in temperature over the entire boundary which is assumed to be initially stress free. After a specified change in temperature has occurred the temperature is held constant over the surface.

The linearized version of this type ramp heating problem was first investigated by Sternberg and Chakravorty [7] for the thermoelastically uncoupled case. Solutions for the coupled case were obtained by Nickell and Sackman [4] and Oden and Kross [5] through finite element techniques.

Consider a materially nonlinear elastic half space ($x_1 \geq 0$) constrained to only uniaxial motion characterized by the displacement field

$$u_1 = u(x, t), \quad u_2 = u_3 = 0 \tag{38}$$

The bounding surface at $x_1 = 0$ is assumed to be stress free and is subjected to a uniformly distributed ramp heating of the form

$$T_1 = 0 \qquad -\infty < t \leq 0$$
$$T_1 = \frac{T_f}{t_o}\,t \qquad 0 \leq t \leq t_o \tag{39}$$
$$T_1 = T_f \qquad t_o \leq t < \infty$$

where T_1 is the initial surface temperature, T_f is the final surface temperature, and t_o is the rise time of the boundary temperature. Since the body is assumed to be initially at rest, the displacements and stresses resulting from the temperature field T_1 are governed by the initial conditions

$$u_1(x, 0) = 0, \quad \frac{\partial u_1(x, 0)}{\partial t} = 0 \quad (0 < x < \infty) \tag{40}$$

These boundary conditions are supplemented by the regularity conditions

$$u_1(x, t), \sigma_1(x, t) \to 0$$

and

$$T(x, t) \to 0 \quad \text{as} \quad x \to \infty \tag{41}$$

We assume that the material in the half space is characterized by a free energy function of the form given in (31). Since the body is constrained to only uniaxial motion the second and third strain invariants vanish reducing (31) to

$$\phi = (\lambda + 2\mu)I^2 + a_6 I^3 + a_7 T^2 - \alpha(3\lambda + 2\mu)IT + a_{12}T^3 + a_{13}I^2 T \tag{42}$$

For simplicity we use simplex approximations of element displacement and temperature fields so that

$$u_i = \psi_N(\underset{\sim}{x})u_N, \quad T = \psi_N(\underset{\sim}{x})T_N \tag{43}$$

where

$$\psi_N(\underset{\sim}{x}) = \alpha_N + \beta_{iN}x^i, \quad N = 1, 2 \tag{44}$$

With these selections, the equations of motion (15) and heat conduction (16) for a typical finite element become

$$P_1 = \frac{\rho_o L}{6}(2\ddot{u}_1 + \ddot{u}_2) + \frac{\lambda + 2\mu}{L}(u_1 - u_2) + \frac{\alpha}{2}(3\lambda + 2\mu)(T_1 + T_2)$$
$$- \frac{3}{L^2} a_6 (u_1 - u_2)^2 + \frac{a_{13}}{L}(T_1 + T_2)(\dot{u}_1 - \dot{u}_2) \tag{45}$$

$$P_2 = \frac{\rho_o L}{6}(\ddot{u}_1 + 2\ddot{u}_2) - \frac{1}{L}(\lambda + 2\mu)(u_1 - u_2) - \frac{\alpha}{2}(3\lambda + 2\mu)(T_1 + T_2)$$
$$+ \frac{3}{L^2} a_6 (u_1 - u_2)^2 - \frac{a_{13}}{L}(T_1 + T_2)(\dot{u}_1 - \dot{u}_2) \tag{46}$$

$$q_1 = \frac{\rho_o c_D(T)T_o}{6}(2\dot{T}_1 + \dot{T}_2) + \frac{K_o}{L}[1 + \frac{\varepsilon}{2L}(T_1 + T_2)](T_1 - T_2)$$
$$- \frac{T_o}{2}\alpha(3\lambda + 2\mu)(\dot{u}_1 - \dot{u}_2) - \frac{T_o}{L}a_{13}(u_1 - u_2)(\dot{u}_1 - \dot{u}_2) \quad (47)$$

$$q_2 = \frac{\rho_o c_D(\dot{T})\dot{T}_o}{6}(\dot{T}_1 + 2\dot{T}_2) - \frac{K_o}{L}[1 + \frac{\varepsilon}{2L}(T_1 + T_2)](T_1 - T_2)$$
$$- \frac{T_o}{2}\alpha(3\lambda + 2\mu)(\dot{u}_1 - \dot{u}_2) - \frac{T_o}{L}a_{13}(u_1 - u_2)(\dot{u}_1 - \dot{u}_2) \quad (48)$$

where L is the length of the element. We introduce the usual dimensionless variables as follows:

$$\ell = \frac{a}{\kappa}x_1 \qquad \zeta = \frac{a^2}{\kappa}t$$
$$\overline{\theta} = \frac{T}{T_o} \qquad \overline{U} = \frac{a(\lambda + 2\mu)}{\kappa\beta T_o}U \quad (49)$$

where

$$\kappa = \frac{K_o}{p_o c_D} \qquad a^2 = \frac{\lambda + 2}{\rho}$$
$$\beta = \overline{\alpha}(3\lambda + 2\mu) \qquad \delta = \frac{\beta^2 T_o}{\rho c_D(\lambda + 2\mu)} \quad (50)$$

In the above relations, x_1, is a characteristic length, t the real time, K_o thermal conductivity, $c_D(T)$ temperature dependent specific heat at constant deformation, λ and μ are Lamé constants, α is the linear coefficient of thermal expansion, and the quantity δ is the thermomechanical coupling parameter.

Numerical Results

Numerical results showing the influence of thermomechanical coupling, material nonlinearities, and temperature dependent specific heat and thermal conductivity in the solution of the half space problem are presented in Figures 1 - 8.

Solutions of the finite element differential equations (45) - (48) were obtained by a Runge-Kutta-Gill integration scheme. In the solutions the masses and temperatures of each element were lumped at the nodes in order to uncouple the elemental acceleration and time rate of temperature change terms. This method of approximation proved very satisfactory for a large number of elements and is illustrated in Figs. 1 and 2 which contain numerical results for the linearized material as well as the "exact" solutions [10]. Figures 1 and 2 contain the dimensionless temperature $\overline{\theta}$ and displacement $\overline{U}$ at $\ell = 1.0$ with the thermomechanical coupling parameter $\delta = 0.0$ and $\delta = 1.0$ as a function of dimensionless time ζ, for the cases $\zeta_o = 1.0$ and $\zeta = 0.25$ respectively. These results were obtained using a fifty element model having 10 elements between the bounding surface and $\ell = 1.0$.

A qualitative description of the effect of material nonlinearities in the half space is illustrated in Figs. 3 and 4. These data were generated using the same fifty element model for a material having $\varepsilon = 0.0$, $\delta = 1.0$ for the case $\zeta_o = 1.0$. It should be noted that a coupling parameter of the magnitude used represents a high degree of thermomechanical coupling for metallic materials. The influence of the nonlinearities introduced by the a_6 and a_{13} terms on the heat conduction equation must be transmitted through this coupling term. The magnitudes of these terms in (45) - (48), which when non-dimensionalized according to (49), are denoted A_6 and A_{13}. Figure 3 shows variations in temperature at $\ell = 1.0$ as a function of ζ for the four cases: $A_6 = 0.05$, $A_{13} = 0.0$; $A_6 = 0.25$, $A_{13} = 0.0$; $A_6 = 0.0$, $A_{13} = 0.05$; $A_6 = 0.0$, $A_{13} = 0.05$. Figure 4 depicts the variation in displacement at $\ell = 1.0$ versus time for the same four cases. Very little variation in the temperature is observed for $A_6 = A_{13} = 0.05$. For the case $A_6 = 0.25$ no significant departure from the linear theory occurs until $\zeta \geq 1.2$. This is due to the fact that this nonlinearity manifests itself only in terms of second order in the displacements and apparently requires a rather large value for A_6 in order to influence the temperature equations. The effect of the A_{13} is much more pronounced in the temperature variations due to the fact that it appears in the elemental heat conduction equations as well as in the equations of motion. The temperature variations become apparent at $\zeta \geq 0.8$ for $A_{13} \geq 0.25$. Noticeable deviations in the displacements occur at $\zeta = 1.0$ for both the A_6 and A_{13} terms and increase significantly with time. For values of A_6 and A_{13} greater than 0.25 the material becomes highly nonlinear. We note again that the effects of shear do not appear in this example problem.

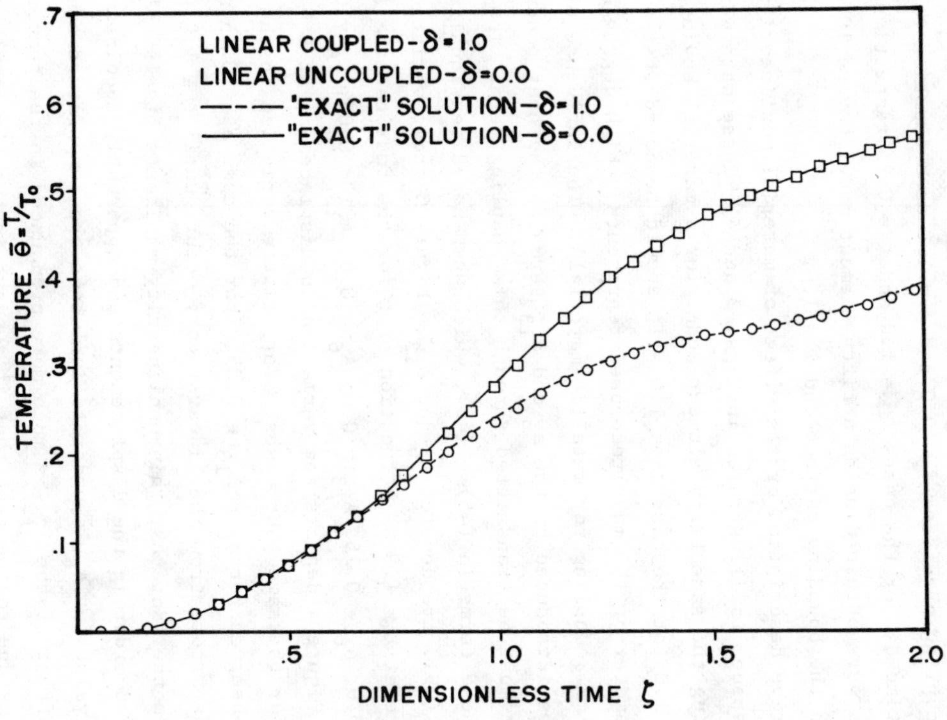

Fig. 1. Temperature at $\ell = 1.0$ Linear Coupled and Uncoupled Half Space with $\xi_0 = 1.0$.

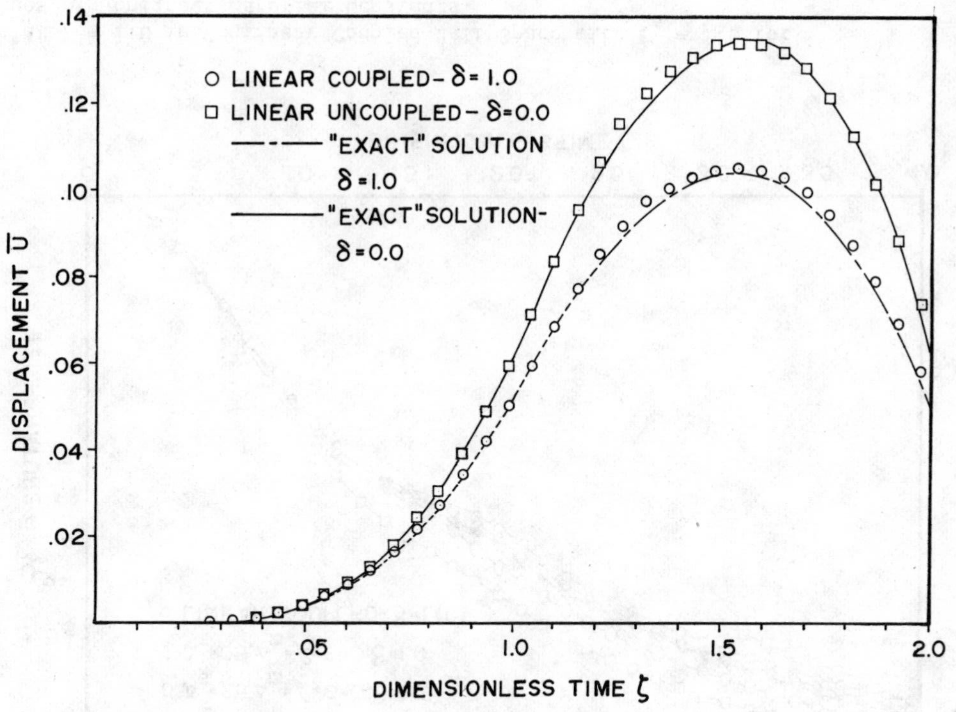

Fig. 2. Displacement at ℓ = 1.0 in Linear Coupled and Uncoupled Half Space with ξ_o = 1.0.

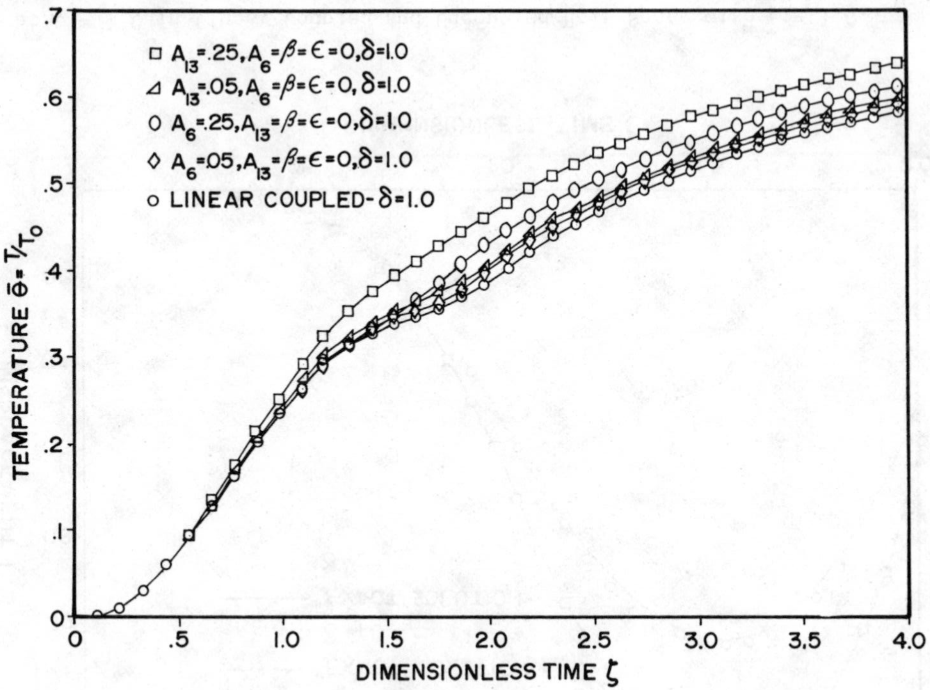

Fig. 3. Temperature at ℓ = 1.0 in Nonlinear Coupled Half Space with ξ_0 = 1.0 for Various Values of Nonlinear Material Constants.

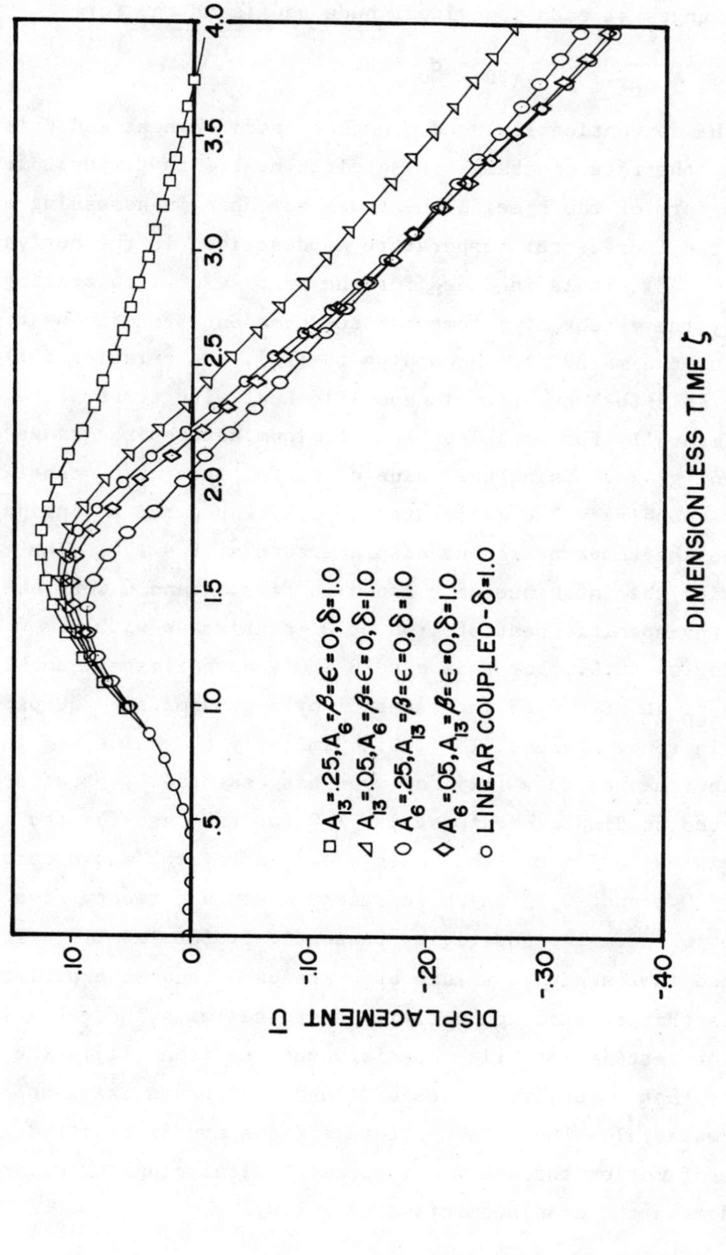

Fig. 4. Displacement at $\ell = 1.0$ in Nonlinear Coupled Half Space with $\xi_o = 1.0$ for Various Values of Nonlinear Material Constants.

Figures 5 and 6 display the effects of temperature dependent coefficients of specific heat and thermal conductivity for a material with $\delta = 1.0$ and $A_6 = A_{13} = 0$ subjected to a ramp heating corresponding to $\zeta_o = 1.0$. For simplicity, we assume the specific heat varies only with temperature changes at each individual node and is of the form

$$c_D = c_o + \beta T \tag{51}$$

where c_o is the conventionally used constant specific heat and β is the term governing the rate of change in specific heat with temperature. Although this form of the specific heat was not used in assessing the magnitude of the incremental temperature as described in the derivation of Eqs. (45) - (48), it is included for the purpose of illustrating quantitatively the effect of a temperature-dependent specific heat on the response of the material. According to [11], the relation (51) accurately describes the variation in specific heat with temperature obtained experimentally for both iron and aluminum between the range of 0° to 400° centigrade. Using the value of c_o for iron at 0° centigrade [11] the corresponding value calculated in (51) for β had an insignificant effect on the temperatures or displacements at $\ell = 1.0$. The results displaying the influence of β shown in Figs. 5 and 6 were obtained using the specific heat of iron at 0° centigrade with $\beta = 0.25$ and $\beta = 0.1$ for $\varepsilon = 0.0$. For this case $\beta = 0.1$ approximately doubles the magnitude c_D and $\beta = 0.25$ increases c_D by approximately 250 percent for a change in temperature of $T = 1.0$. Similarly the value ε calculated from experimental data [12] for iron has essentially no effect on the temperatures or displacements at $\ell = 1.0$ for the case for the linearized material with $\beta = 0$. The cases shown in Figs. 5 and 6 correspond to $\varepsilon = -0.1$ and -0.25 which represent a ten and twenty-five percent decrease in thermal conductivity respectively for $T = 1.0$. It should be noted that negative values of ε are used because experimental data indicates that thermal conductivity decreases with increases in temperature for certain metallic materials such as iron [12]. The results indicate that effective values of ε and β decrease the temperatures in the material. These temperature effects are transmitted into the equations of motion through the thermomechanical coupling parameter and tend to dampen the displacements at $\ell = 1.0$.

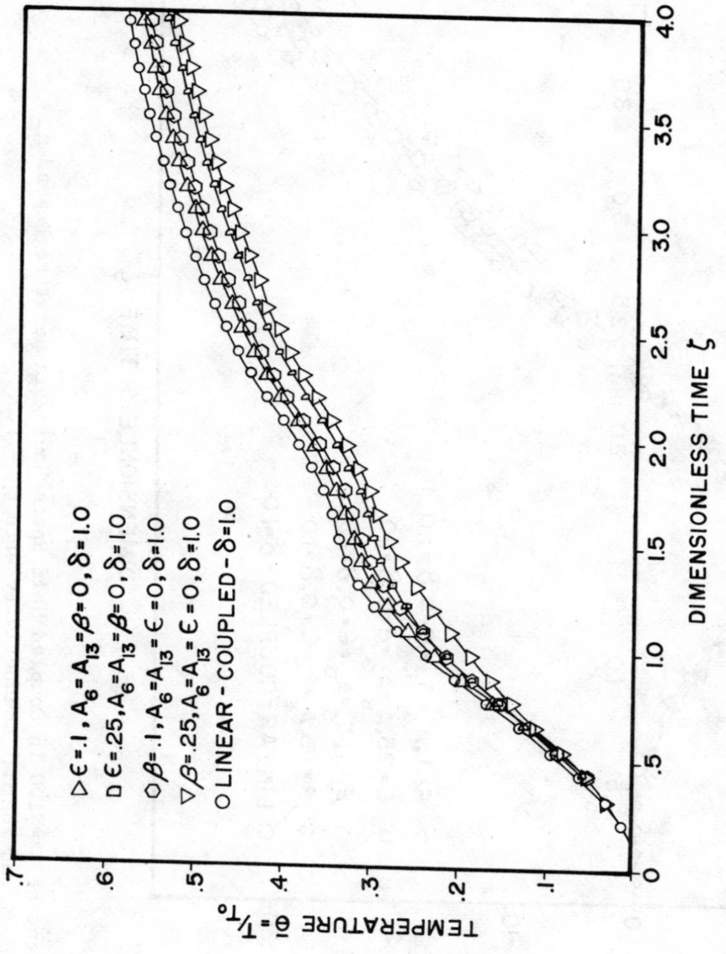

Fig. 5. Temperature at ℓ = 1.0 in Coupled Half Space Having Temperature Dependent Specific Heat and Thermal Conductivity with ξ_0 = 1.0.

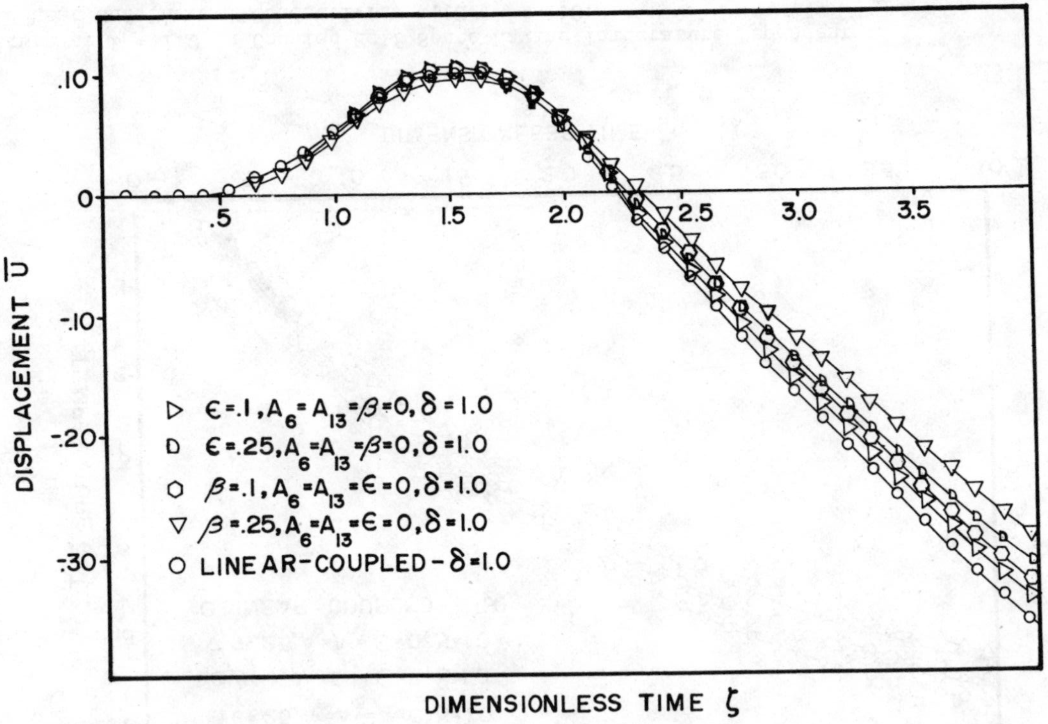

Fig. 6. Displacement at ℓ = 1.0 in Coupled Half Space Having Temperature Dependent Specific Heat and Thermal Conductivity with ξ_0 = 1.0.

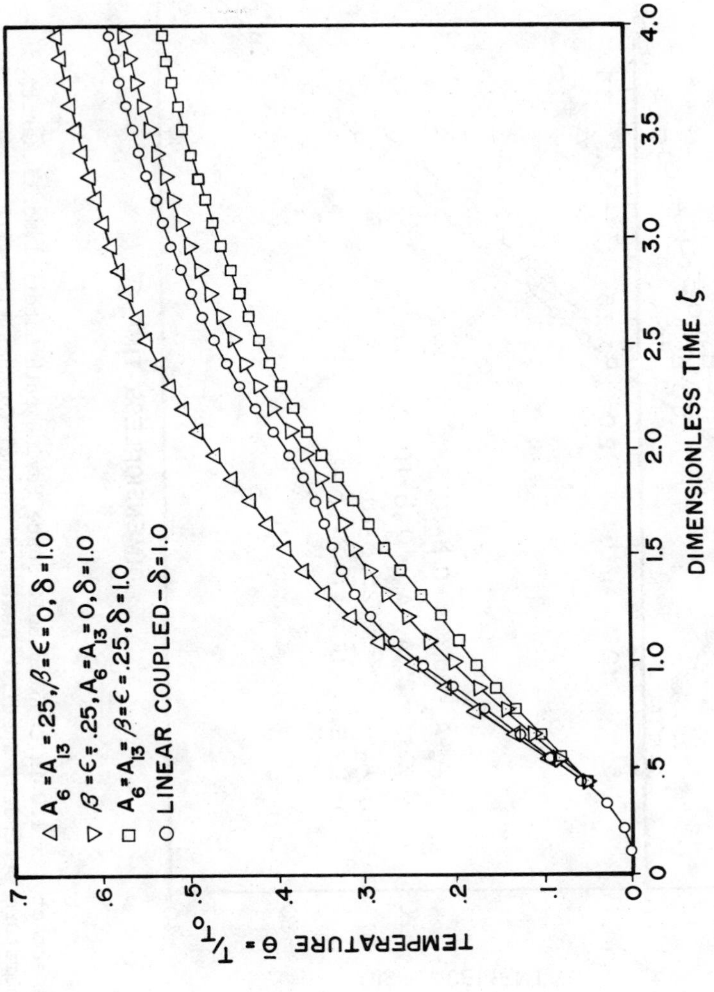

Fig. 7. Temperature at $\ell = 1.0$ in Coupled Half Space Having both Material Nonlinearities and Temperature Dependent Specific Heat and Thermal Conductivity with $\xi_0 = 1.0$.

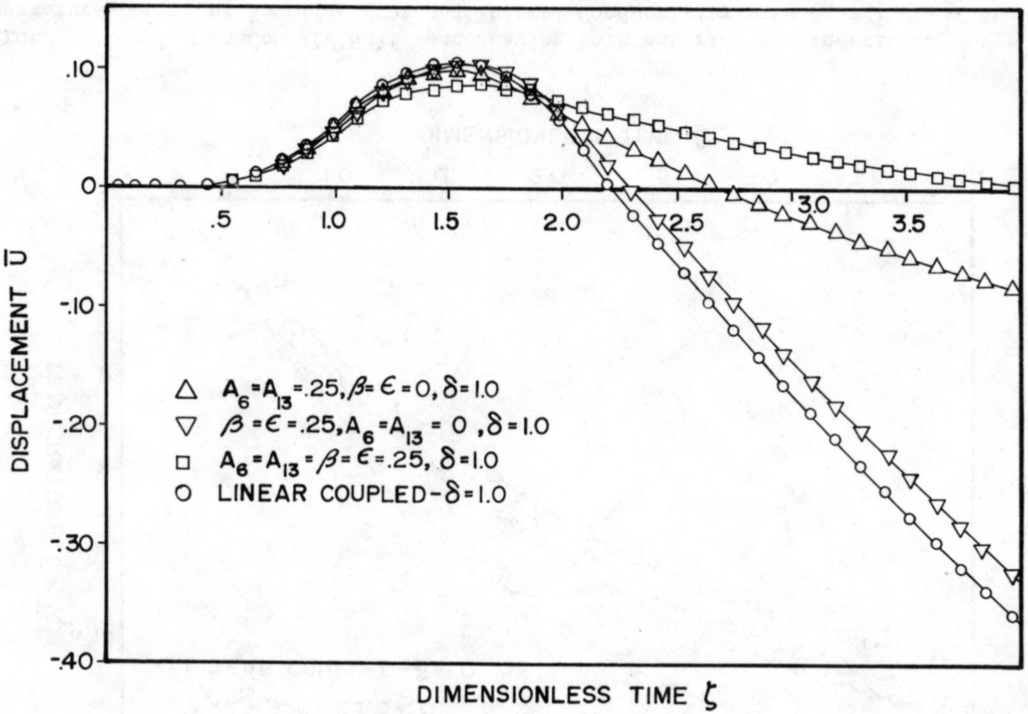

Fig. 8. Displacement at $\ell = 1.0$ in Coupled Half Space Having both Material Nonlinearities and Temperature Dependent Specific Heat and Thermal Conductivity with $\xi_o = 1.0$.

Figures 7-8 display the combined quantitative effects of the nonlinear terms A_6 and A_{13}, and the temperature dependent thermal conductivity and specific heat on the response of the material to ramp heating $\zeta_0 = 1.0$. The cases shown are: $A_6 = A_{13} = 0.25$; $\beta = \varepsilon = 0$; $A_6 = A_{13} = 0$; $\beta = 0.25$, $\varepsilon = -0.25$; $A_6 = A_{13} = \beta = 0.25$, $\varepsilon = -0.25$. We note that experimental data indicate that the values of ε and β used in this study are very unrealistic for metallic materials. Also, the values used for the A_6 and A_{13} terms are thought to indicate a much larger influence on the response of a metallic material than actually exists in nature.

ACKNOWLEDGEMENTS

The research reported in this paper was supported through Contract F44620-69-C-0124 under Project Themis at the University of Alabama Research Institute.

REFERENCES

1. Reiner, M., "Rheology," Encyclopedia of Physics, Vol. VI, Springer-Verlag, Berlin, 1958, p. 507.
2. Jindra, F., "Wärmespannungen bei einem nichtlinearen Elastizitätsgesetz," Ingenieur Archiv, Vol. 38, 1959, p. 109.
3. Dillon, O. W., Jr., "A Nonlinear Thermoelasticity Theory," Journal of the Mechanics and Physics of Solids, Vol. 10, 1962, pp. 123-131.
4. Nickell, R. E. and Sackman, J. J., "Approximate Solutions in Linear, Coupled Thermoelasticity," Journal of Applied Mechanics, Vol. 35, Series E, No. 2, 1968, pp. 255-266.
5. Oden, J. T. and Kross, D. A., "Analysis of the General Coupled Thermoelasticity Problems by the Finite Element Method," Proceedings, Second Conference on Matrix Methods in Structural Mechanics, Air Force Flight Dynamics Laboratory, (15-17 October 1968), Wright-Patterson AFB, Ohio (in press).
6. Danilovskaya, V. I., "On a Dynamical Problem of Thermoelasticity" (in Russian), Prikladnaya Matematika i Mekhanika, Vol. 16, No. 3, 1962, pp. 341-344.
7. Sternberg, E. and Chakravorty, J. G., "On Inertia Effects in a Transient Thermoelastic Problem," Journal of Applied Mechanics, Vol. 26, No. 4, Transactions ASME, Vol. 81, Series E, 1959, pp. 503-509.
8. Oden, J. T., "A General Theory of Finite Elements; II. Applications," International Journal for Numerical Methods in Engineering, Vol. 1, 1969, pp. 247-259.

9. Oden, J. T., "Finite Element Formulation of Problems of Finite Deformation and Irreversible Thermodynamics of Nonlinear Continua — A Survey and Extension of Recent Developments," Proceedings, Japan-U.S. Seminar on Matrix Methods in Structural Analysis and Design, Tokyo, August 1969.

10. Oden, J. T. and Aguirre-Ramirez, G., "Formulation of General Discrete Models of Thermomechanical Behavior of Materials with Memory," International Journal of Solids and Structures, November, 1969 (to appear).

11. Hodgman, C. D., Weast, R. C., and Selby, S. M., Handbook of Chemistry and Physics, Chemical Rubber Publishing Co., Cleveland, Ohio, 1956.

12. Jakob, M., Heat Transfer, Vol. I, John Wiley and Sons, New York, 1962.

BARS

STABILITY OF PARAMETRICALLY EXCITED VIBRATIONS OF AN ELASTIC ROD

Edward C. Haight
The MITRE Corporation

Wilton W. King
Georgia Institute of Technology

ABSTRACT

A theoretical and experimental examination is presented of the loss due to parametric coupling of the stability of the steady-state plane transverse response of a slender elastic rod subjected to a harmonic longitudinal excitation. The analysis shows that, provided an arbitrarily small viscous damping term is present, plane motion is stable for all values of the parameters when the natural frequency ratio for motions in the two principal planes is unity. Only when the natural frequencies are detuned does the original planar response lose its stability. It is shown that when the frequency ratio is near unity there is a critical excitation frequency which causes the original planar response to exhibit an amplitude jump and a simultaneous plane shift to stable motions in the other principal plane.

LIST OF NOTATIONS

A	Area of the rod cross-section
A_b	Amplitude of the base excitation function
$\overline{A}_b$	A_b/ℓ . Nondimensional base amplitude
A_n	Steady-state amplitude of the planar response
$\overline{A}_n$	A_n/ℓ . Nondimensional steady-state amplitude
$(A_n)_{cr}$	Steady-state amplitude of the planar response for which motion changes from a stable to an unstable state
A_{1n}, A_{2n}	$A_{1n}^2 + A_{2n}^2 = A_n^2$

$\overline{A}_{1n}$, $\overline{A}_{2n}$	$\overline{A}_{1n} = A_{1n}/\ell$, $\overline{A}_{2n} = A_{2n}/\ell$
E	Modulus of elasticity
I_η, I_2, I_3	Moments of inertia of the rod cross-section about the η, χ_2, and χ_3 axes, respectively
L	Lagrangian function
M	Mass per unit length of the rod
N	Normal force on the rod cross-section
S	Deformed arc length
T	Kinetic energy
T_{2n}, T_{3m}	n^{th} and m^{th} generalized coordinates
V	Potential energy
X_1, X_2, X_3	Inertial coordinates of the rod centerline in its undeformed configuration
$X_n(S)$, $X_m(S)$	n^{th} and m^{th} spatial modes
b_m	$b_m = \frac{4\gamma_m \ell}{\alpha}$
c_m	$c_m = \frac{\delta_m \ell^2}{\alpha}$
f_n	$f_n = \frac{4\varepsilon_n}{\alpha}$
ℓ	Length of rod
m,n	Mode numbers
s	Undeformed arc length
t	Time
u,v,w	Displacement components in the x_1, x_2, x_3 directions, respectively
x_1, x_2, x_3	Inertial coordinates of the rod centerline in its deformed configuration
x_{3m}	Perturbation function
β_n	$\beta_n = (M\omega_n^2/EI)^{1/4}$
$\alpha, \beta_j^{(i)}, \gamma_j, \delta_j, \Delta_{ij}$	Constants defined in the paper
Δ_n	Logarithmic decrement for the nth mode
ε	Extensional strain of the centerline
ε_1, ε_2	Coefficients in the Mathieu equation
ε_n	Damping constant
η	2τ
κ	Principal curvature of the rod centerline

τ	Nondimensional time, $\tau = \frac{\omega t}{2}$
ϕ_n	Parameter, given in Table I
ω	Frequency of the excitation
$\omega_n^{(i)}$	n^{th} eigenfrequency for the response in the x_1, x_i - plane, i = 2,3
$\Omega_n^{(i)}$	$\Omega_n^{(i)} = \omega/2\omega_n^{(i)}$, i = 2,3
$\dot{(\ )}$	$\frac{\partial()}{\partial t}$
$(\ )'$	$\frac{\partial()}{\partial s}$ or $\frac{d()}{d\tau}$. The distinction is clear from the context.

INTRODUCTION

A widely studied phenomenon is the parametric excitation of planar transverse responses of axially driven strings and rods. The present study shows that for certain values of the parameters, the parametrically excited planar motions may in turn parametrically excite a mode which does not lie in the original plane. The coupling which exists between the original planar response and its parametrically coupled nonplanar motion is solely due to the presence of certain nonlinear terms. That is to say, linear formulation of the problem is incapable of predicting the phenomenon of interest.

Parametric coupling of these nonplanar motions to the original planar response for the axially excited rod occurs only over a narrow range of the parameters which describe the rod. In fact, it is shown that no coupling will exist for rods having a natural frequency ratio of unity for motions in the two principal planes. Furthermore, if the natural frequency ratio is much different from one, no coupling will exist due to the presence of damping.

The object of this study is to determine, for the axially excited rod, a set of equations of motion which is capable of predicting the coupling between motions in the two principal planes. That is, we seek to determine the range of frequencies of the harmonic driving function for which plane motion of the rod is unstable with respect to small disturbances in a direction normal to the initial response plane.

Before proceeding to the equations of motion, we present a brief summary of the relevant literature.

A Review of Earlier Work

Early studies were simplified by assumptions or approximations which caused the governing differential equations to be linear. However, Gol'denblat [1] showed that while a linear formulation is sufficient for the prediction of the instability regions, it is incapable of determining the amplitudes of the vibrations in the resonance regions. Bolotin, in a number of articles, incorporated a nonlinear theory to more satisfactorily explain the phenomenon; these studies are summarized in his book [2]. The (nonlinear) effect of longitudinal inertia upon the parametric response of columns was discussed by Evensen and Evan-Iwanowski [3]. For a comprehensive literature review relating to parametric behavior of elastic bodies, the reader is referred to Beylin and Dzhaneldize [4] and Evan-Iwanowski [5].

Material dealing with parametric coupling between motions in two different modes is less plentiful. Perhaps the most relevant article on this specialization of dynamic stability is a study by Henry and Tobias [6] of a pair of quasi-linear, coupled, ordinary differential equations of a special form, representing free vibration of an undamped, two degree-of-freedom system. This paper was prompted by an earlier one by Tobias [7] concerning the coupling effects in imperfect discs. In [6] Henry and Tobias demonstrated that it is possible for motion to be confined entirely to one mode and they determined a criterion for stability of the mode at rest.

The majority of the literature dealing with mode coupling incorporates direct rather than parametric excitation of the initial response. The principal response, however, is frequently parametrically coupled to another mode of interest. For example, Murthy and Ramakrishna [8] showed that a string excited in a direction perpendicular to the axis may reach a condition for which the particles cease to vibrate solely in the plane of the driving force. That is, planar motion is unstable over some frequency interval of the driving frequency. Quick [9] excited an elastic string longitudinally and showed that elastic asymmetry causes the string to move out of the plane of vibration and into thin elliptical orbits. Ebner [10] studied the parametric oscillation of imperfect simply supported thin-walled columns with open cross-sections and included in his analysis twisting deformations as well as lateral bending deformation. Tso [11] analyzed the related topic of the stability of parametrically induced torsional motion of a bar subjected to axial excitation.

The Equations of Motion

Consider a long, slender, initially straight, perfectly elastic rod oriented so that the base is clamped and the opposite end is free. Note here that these end conditions are chosen to expedite the experiments; other end conditions can be handled analytically in a similar manner. Let the undeformed arc length be s(S,t). Assume the cross-sectional dimensions and the material properties of the rod to be constant with S.

In order to insure that twisting motions of the rod will be small, the restriction is made that the cross-section is closed; furthermore, it is assumed that the lowest eigenfrequency of twisting motion about the longitudinal axis is much larger than any of the bending response eigenfrequencies of concern. In light of these assumptions, we omit the twisting response from the analysis.

Let x_2 and x_3 be the principal centroidal axes of the cross-section and let the base be excited harmonically according to $A_b \cos \omega t$. The coordinate system is shown in Fig. 1. The problem is formulated in Lagrangian or material coordinates and Hamilton's Principle is used to obtain the equations of motion. After neglecting shear deformation, rotatory inertia, and simplifying the curvature expression in the usual manner, the equations of motion are (see [12] for a complete development)

$$EI_3 v''''(S,t) - M\ddot{u}(S,t)v'(S,t) + v''(S,t)\int_S^{\ell} \ddot{u}(\xi,t)d\xi + M\ddot{v}(S,t) = 0 \quad (1)$$

$$EI_2 w''''(S,t) - M\ddot{u}(S,t)w'(S,t) + w''(S,t)\int_S^{\ell} \ddot{u}(\xi,t)d\xi + M\ddot{w}(S,t) = 0 \quad (2)$$

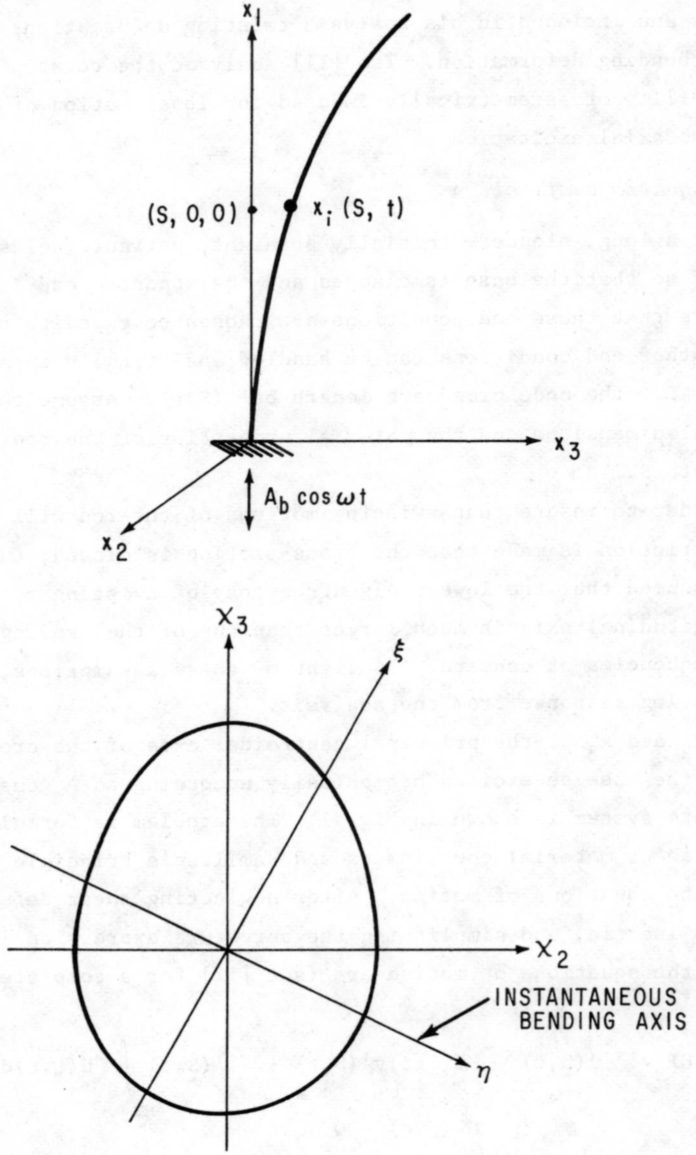

Fig. 1. Orientation of the Coordinate System.

This pair of equations agrees with the one found by Evensen and Evan-Iwanowski [3] when the above equations are reduced to the plane motion case by letting $w(S,t) \equiv 0$.

The function u can be expressed in terms of v and w by noting that

$$ds^2 = dx_1^2 + dx_2^2 = dx_3^2$$

$$x_1(S,t) = S + u(S,t)$$

$$x_2(S,t) = v(S,t)$$

$$x_3(S,t) = w(S,t)$$

hence,

$$dx_1^2 = \left[\left(\frac{\partial s}{\partial S}\right)^2 - \left(\frac{\partial v}{\partial S}\right)^2 - \left(\frac{\partial w}{\partial S}\right)^2\right] dS^2 \tag{3}$$

Assuming small strains

$$\left(\frac{\partial s}{\partial S}\right)^2 \doteq 1 \tag{4}$$

The use of Eq. (4) in Eq. (3) and one integration with respect to S shows that

$$x_1(S,t) = \int_0^S [1-v'^2(\xi,t) - w'^2(\xi,t)]^{1/2}\, d\xi + C_1(t)$$

If $x_1(o,t) = A_b \cos \omega t$, then $C_1(t) = A_b \cos \omega t$ and

$$u(S,t) = \int_0^S [1-v'^2(\xi,t) - w^{2}(\xi,t)]^{1/2}\, d\xi - S + A_b \cos \omega t \tag{5}$$

In keeping with the first order approximation policy used herein, we expand the integrand of Eq. (5) in a binomial series and retain only terms up to, and including, the linear one in $v'^2 + w'^2$. This shows that

$$u(S,t) = -\frac{1}{2}\int_0^S [v'^2(\xi,t) + w'^2(\xi,t)]\, d\xi + A_b \cos \omega t \tag{6}$$

The governing integro-differential equations which determine v(S,t) and w(S,t) are found by using Eq. (6) in Eq. (1) and Eq. (2). They are:

$$EI_3 v'''' + M\ddot{v} + \frac{Mv'}{2}\frac{\partial^2}{\partial t^2}\int_0^S (v'^2 + w'^2)\, d\xi + Mv'\, A_b\omega^2 \cos \omega t$$

$$- \frac{Mv'}{2}\int_0^\ell \left\{\frac{\partial^2}{\partial t^2}\int_0^\xi (v'^2 + w'^2)\, d\eta\right\} d\xi$$

$$- Mv''\, A_b\omega^2\, (\ell - S) \cos \omega t = 0 \tag{7}$$

$$EI_2 w'''' + M\ddot{w} + \frac{Mw'}{2}\frac{\partial^2}{\partial t^2}\int_0^S (v'^2 + w'^2)\, d\xi + Mw' A_b\omega^2 \cos \omega t$$

$$- \frac{Mw''}{2}\int_0^\ell \left\{\frac{\partial^2}{\partial t^2}\int_0^\xi (v'^2 + w'^2)\, d\eta\right\} d\xi$$

$$- Mw''\, A_b\omega^2\, (\ell - S) \cos \omega t = 0 \tag{8}$$

Notice that these equations are symmetric in v and w when $I_2 = I_3$.

The Galerkin Method

The Galerkin method is used to reduce Eq. (7) and Eq. (8) to ordinary differential equations. A one term approximation to the solution of the equations, using the eigenfunctions of the linear fixed-free vibrating rod as coordinate functions, is sought in the form

$$v(S,t) \doteq T_{2n}(t) X_n(S) \tag{9}$$

$$w(S,t) \doteq T_{3m}(t) X_m(S) \tag{10}$$

Notice that this solution form admits (when $m \neq n$) the possibility that the spatial mode shape in the x_1, x_3-plane is different from the mode shape in the x_1, x_2-plane.

This choice of coordinate functions for the Galerkin analysis is convenient due to the fact that many of the resulting integrals have been tabulated by Young and Felgar [13]. The functions $X_n(S)$ are

$$X_n(S) = \cosh \beta_n S - \cos \beta_n S - \phi_n(\sinh \beta_n S - \sin \beta_n S),\ n = 1,2,\ldots,$$

where

$$\beta_n{}^4 = \frac{M\omega_n{}^2}{EI}$$

and ϕ_n is a parameter, the values of which are given in Table I.

TABLE I. VALUES OF ϕ_n AND $\beta_n \ell$ (From Young and Felgar)

n	ϕ_n	$\beta_n \ell$
1	0.7341	1.8751
2	1.0185	4.6941
3	0.9992	7.8548

An application of Galerkin's method and introduction of nondimensional time $\tau = \frac{\omega t}{2}$ gives

$$\alpha\ddot{T}_{2n} + (\beta_n^{(3)} + \gamma_n A_b \omega^2 \cos \omega t)\ T_{2n} + \delta_n T_{2n}(T_{2n}\ddot{T}_{2n} + \dot{T}_{2n}^2)$$
$$+ \Delta_{nm} T_{2n}(T_{3m}\ddot{T}_{3m} + \dot{T}_{3m}^2) = 0 \tag{11}$$

$$\alpha\ddot{T}_{3m} + (\beta_m^{(2)} + \gamma_m A_b \omega^2 \cos \omega t)\ T_{3m} + \delta_m T_{3m}(T_{3m}\ddot{T}_{3m} + \dot{T}_{3m}^2)$$
$$+ \Delta_{mn} T_{3m}(T_{2n}\ddot{T}_{2n} + \dot{T}_{2n}^2) = 0 \tag{12}$$

The constants which appear in Eqs. (11) and (12) are defined by

$$\alpha = M\ell$$

$$\beta_j^{(i)} = EI_i \beta_j^4 \ell \qquad i = 2,\ j = m \text{ or } i = 3,\ j = n$$

$$\gamma_j = 2M - \frac{1}{2} M\ell\phi_j \beta_j (2 - \phi_j \beta_j \ell), \qquad j = m,n$$

$$\delta_j = \int_o^{\ell} \left[M \int_o^S X_j'^2(\xi)d\xi\right] X_j(S)X_j'(S)\ dS$$

$$- \int_o^{\ell} \left\{M \int_S^{\ell} \left[\int_o^{\xi} X_j'^2(\eta)d\eta\right] d\xi\right\} X_j(S)X_j\ (S)dS, \qquad j = m,n$$

$$\Delta_{ij} = \int_o^{\ell} \left[M \int_o^S X_j'^2(\xi)d\xi\right] X_i(S)X_i'(S)dS$$

$$- \int_o^{\ell} \left\{M \int_S^{\ell} \left[\int_o^{\xi} X_j'^2(\eta)d\eta\right] d\xi\right\} X_i(S)X_i''(S)dS, \qquad \begin{matrix} i = m,\ j = n \\ \text{or} \\ i = n,\ j = m \end{matrix}$$

The constants δ_j and Δ_{ij} are evaluated by numerical integration on a digital computer. It is convenient to form the dimensionless numbers

$$c_n = \frac{\delta_n \ell^2}{\alpha} \qquad \text{and} \qquad c_{mn} = \frac{\Delta_{mn}\ell^2}{\alpha}$$

and tabulate these instead. Some values are given in Tables II and III.

TABLE II. VALUES OF b_n AND c_n

n	b_n	c_n
1	6.28	4.60
2	34.6	145
3	99.8	998

TABLE III. VALUES c_{mn}

m	n	c_{mn}
1	2	25.2
1	3	66.7
2	3	369

Integration by parts shows that $c_{mn} = c_{nm}$.

Equations (11) and (12) can be compared with results derived by others by observing that the plane motion case $T_{3m}(\tau) \equiv 0$ is a solution of the equations. This reduces them to

$$T_{2n}'' + \left(\frac{4\beta_n^{(3)}}{\alpha\omega^2} + \frac{4\gamma_n}{\alpha} A_b \cos 2\tau\right) T_{2n} + \frac{\delta_n}{\alpha} T_{2n}(T_{2n}'' + T_{2n}'^2) = 0 \qquad (13)$$

which is again the form obtained by Evensen and Evan-Iwanowski [3].

Simplifying assumptions pertaining to the curvature have reduced the curvature expression to the one used in small deflection beam theory. This has resulted in the disappearance of the nonlinear elasticity terms[1] from Eq. (13). When retained, this effect appears, in the first approximation, as a cubic term in T_{2n} [2]. The only nonlinearity present in our equations is the so-called nonlinear inertia term $(\delta n/\alpha)T_{2n}(T_{2n}T''_{2n} + T'^2_{2n})$ which arises because the longitudinal inertia of an element of the rod is included. Bolotin [2] has shown that, for rods of this type, the predominant nonlinear effect is that of nonlinear inertia. Moody [14] also concludes that nonlinear inertia effects are far more significant than nonlinear elasticity effects on the parametric response of thin rods. Equations (11) and (12) further show that the essential coupling between motions in the two perpendicular planes is due exclusively to nonlinear terms.

The Subharmonic Response and the Stability Analysis

The principal planar motion of the axially excited long slender rod is the plane steady-state, half-order subharmonic response [2]. It is the stability of this planar motion to out-of-plane perturbations that we investigate.

The starting assumption is that the initially straight rod is executing the abovementioned motion of the form

$$T_{2n}(\tau) = A_{1n} \sin \tau + A_{2n} \cos \tau$$
$$T_{3m}(\tau) = 0 \qquad (14)$$

The use of Eq. (14) and Eqs. (11) and (12) and the application of the Ritz averaging method [15] produces the amplitude-frequency or response relation for plane motion. The stability of the plane motion solution to disturbances perpendicular to that plane can be investigated by substituting the perturbed solution

1. Here we use Bolotin's terminology and define nonlinear elasticity terms as nonlinear terms that do not contain derivatives of displacements with respect to time.

$$T_{2n}(\tau) = A_{1n} \sin \tau + A_{2n} \cos \tau + 0$$
$$T_{3m}(\tau) = 0 + x_{3m}(\tau) \tag{15}$$

into Eqs. (11) and (12) and applying the "infinitesimal" stability criterion as described by Stoker [16], Chapter IV.

The solution Eq. (14) combined with the Ritz averaging method shows that the response relation is

$$\bar{A}_{1n}\left[\bar{A}^2_{1n} + \bar{A}^2_{2n} - \frac{2}{c_n}\left(\frac{1}{\Omega_n^{(3)2}} - 1 - \frac{b_n\bar{A}_b}{2}\right)\right] = 0$$
$$\bar{A}_{2n}\left[\bar{A}^2_{1n} + \bar{A}^2_{2n} - \frac{2}{c_n}\left(\frac{1}{\Omega_n^{(3)2}} - 1 + \frac{b_n\bar{A}_b}{2}\right)\right] = 0 \tag{16}$$

where

$$\Omega_n^{(3)} = \frac{\omega}{2\omega_n^{(3)}} \qquad \text{and} \qquad b_n = \frac{4\gamma_n \ell}{\alpha}$$

This pair of equations determines the relationship between the amplitude of the response and the frequency of the exciting function when $T_{3m}(\tau) \equiv 0$. Each quantity in Eq. (16) is dimensionless.

Two useful cases are present in Eq. (16). ($\bar{A}_{1n} = \bar{A}_{2n} = 0$ is a trivial case.) For the first case, choose $\bar{A}_{1n} \neq 0$, $\bar{A}_{2n} = 0$ to obtain

$$\bar{A}^2_{1n} - \frac{2}{c_n}\left(\frac{1}{\Omega_n^{(3)2}} - 1 - \frac{b_n\bar{A}_b}{2}\right) = 0 \tag{17}$$

For the second case, $\bar{A}_{1n} = 0$, $\bar{A}_{2n} \neq 0$ implies

$$\bar{A}^2_{2n} - \frac{2}{c_n}\left(\frac{1}{\Omega_n^{(3)2}} - 1 + \frac{b_n\bar{A}_b}{2}\right) = 0 \tag{18}$$

A third case, the one for which both $\bar{A}_{1n} \neq 0$ and $\bar{A}_{2n} \neq 0$, is not present unless $b_n\bar{A}_b = 0$. If $b_n\bar{A}_b = 0$ (which occurs only if the base excitation amplitude $A_b = 0$), the two equations are identical and yield the "backbone" or free vibration response curve. Let $\bar{A}^2_n = \bar{A}^2_{1n} + \bar{A}^2_{2n}$ and combine Eqs. (17) and (18) to obtain the concise form

$$\overline{A}_n^2 - \frac{2}{c_n}\left(\frac{1}{\Omega_n^{(3)2}} - 1 \mp \frac{b_n\overline{A}_b}{2}\right) = 0 \tag{19}$$

In order to relate $\overline{A}_n$ to an actual amplitude on the rod, we refer to Young and Felgar [13] and note that $X_n(\ell) = 2.000$. This means that $2A_n$ equals the actual steady-state amplitude of the rod at its free end.

Equation (19) represents the two branches of the response relation and is shown in Fig. 2. Bolotin and others have discussed the well-known result that the left-most curve is unstable with respect to small in-plane disturbances and hence is never physically realized.

Before proceeding to the nonplanar aspect of the stability analysis, one should understand the results of an analysis which tests the stability of the straight rod with respect to disturbances in the direction of the planar response with which we are concerned. There are regions for which two or more amplitudes are predicted by the theory for a single given frequency (see Fig. 2). For instance, if the exciting frequency has the value given by point F, the theory predicts three possible response amplitudes. They are the zero amplitude response (that is, the rod remains straight), the amplitude given by point E (which is unstable and is never physically realized), and the amplitude given by C. Whether the amplitude at F or at C is the one which is present depends upon whether the frequency is being increased to F or decreased to F. In the region between A and B the straight configuration is unstable. Hence, if the frequency at G is selected, the rod can only respond with a steady-state amplitude given by H.

For increasing frequency, a point in Fig. 2 follows path OA (straight configuration) until a vertical amplitude jump to I occurs. Then as frequency is further increased, the plane steady-state response amplitude decreases along path IHBJ until the rod remains straight once more. Decreasing the exciting frequency causes the rod to remain straight until the frequency at B is reached; a further frequency decrease causes the amplitude to follow path BHICD. Theoretically, the response amplitude continues to increase without bound, but in practice the damping which is inherent in all physical systems causes a downward jump to zero amplitude. The addition of damping to the theory causes

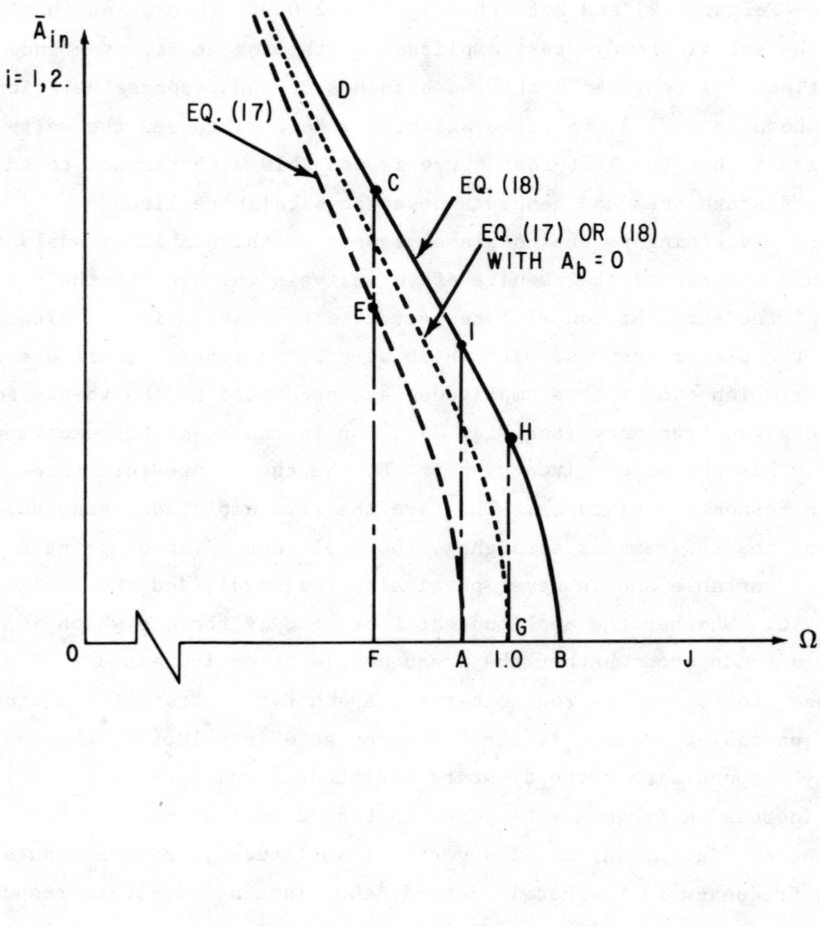

Fig. 2. The Response Relation for Plane Motion of the Axially Excited Rod.

the curves given by Eq. (19) to be smoothly connected at some maximum amplitude.

The investigation of the planar response to out-of-plane disturbances is conducted by using the "infinitesimal" stability criterion. The names "variational method" and "method of small oscillations" are also applied to this technique. According to this method, a solution to the variational or stability equation (which is a linear, homogeneous, non-constant coefficient differential equation) is said to be stable if all solutions to it remain bounded for $t \geq 0$; otherwise, the motion is unstable.

The application to this problem proceeds as follows: A known solution to Eqs. (11) and (12) is given by Eq. (14) and a neighboring solution is given by Eq. (15). The perturbation function $x_{3m}(\tau)$ is assumed to be so small that powers of it higher than the first can be neglected. Upon substituting the perturbed solution into Eqs. (11) and (12), neglecting terms of higher order than the first in x_{3m}, and using the solution Eq. (14), we obtain

$$x''_{3m}(\tau) + \left[\frac{1}{\Omega_m^{(2)2}} + \left(b_m\bar{A}_b + c_{mn}\bar{A}_{1n}^2 - c_{mn}\bar{A}_{2n}^2\right)\cos 2\tau - 2c_{mn}\bar{A}_{1n}\bar{A}_{2n}\sin 2\tau\right] x_{3m}(\tau) = 0 \qquad (20)$$

This is called the stability equation; its solutions determine whether or not the system is stable with respect to disturbances in the x_3 (out-of-plane) direction.

The stability equation can be put into the form of the Mathieu equation by making use of the two cases $\bar{A}_{1n} \neq 0$, $\bar{A}_{2n} = 0$ and $\bar{A}_{1n} = 0$, $\bar{A}_{2n} \neq 0$. However, since the former case is always unstable with respect to in-plane disturbances, there is no need to test its out-of-plane stability. The latter case reduces Eq. (20) to

$$x''_{3m}(\tau) + \left[\frac{1}{\Omega_m^{(2)2}} + (b_m\bar{A}_b - c_{mn}\bar{A}_n^2)\cos 2\tau\right] x_{3m}(\tau) = 0$$

Since $\bar{A}_{1n} = 0$, we have used the fact that $\bar{A}_{2n}^2$ is the same as $\bar{A}_n^2$.

Now the standard form of the Mathieu equation can be obtained by letting

$$\eta = 2\tau \tag{21}$$

$$\varepsilon_1 = \frac{1}{4\Omega_m^{(2)2}} \tag{22}$$

$$\varepsilon_2 = \frac{1}{4}\,(b_m\bar{A}_b - c_{mn}\bar{A}_n^2) \tag{23}$$

This gives

$$\frac{d^2x_{3m}(\eta)}{d\eta^2} + (\varepsilon_1 + \varepsilon_2 \cos \eta)\, x_{3m}(\eta) = 0$$

As has been shown by McLachlan [17] and others, the solutions to the Mathieu equation are either bounded or unbounded depending on the values of the parameters ε_1 and ε_2. In Fig. 3 the values of ε_1 and ε_2 corresponding to unstable solutions are shown as shaded regions in the plane.

Each point in the ε_1, ε_2-plane will be called a stability point. We say that a given motion is stable if the parameters which define the motion cause the stability point to fall in the portion (unshaded in Fig. 3) of the ε_1, ε_2-plane which corresponds to bounded solutions of the Mathieu equation. Stability points lying in the shaded portion of the plane correspond to unbounded solutions (unstable motions). Points which lie on the boundaries of the regions are also identified with unbounded solutions.

If one restricts his attention to the portion of the ε_1, ε_2-plane in the neighborhood of $\varepsilon_1 = \frac{1}{4}$, $\varepsilon_2 = 0$, Cunningham [18] and others have shown that for small values of ε_2 a good first order approximation to the principal instability zone is given by

$$\varepsilon_1 = \frac{1}{4} \pm \frac{1}{2}\,\varepsilon_2$$

These boundaries are shown in Fig. 4. Since we are interested in excitation frequencies near twice the linear natural frequency of the rod, it is clear from Eq. (22) that ε_1 is near $\frac{1}{4}$. To see that ε_2 is small for this problem, we restrict the base excitation amplitude to $0 \le \bar{A}_b \le 0.005$ and the steady-state response amplitude to $0 \le \bar{A}_n \le 0.10$. Tables

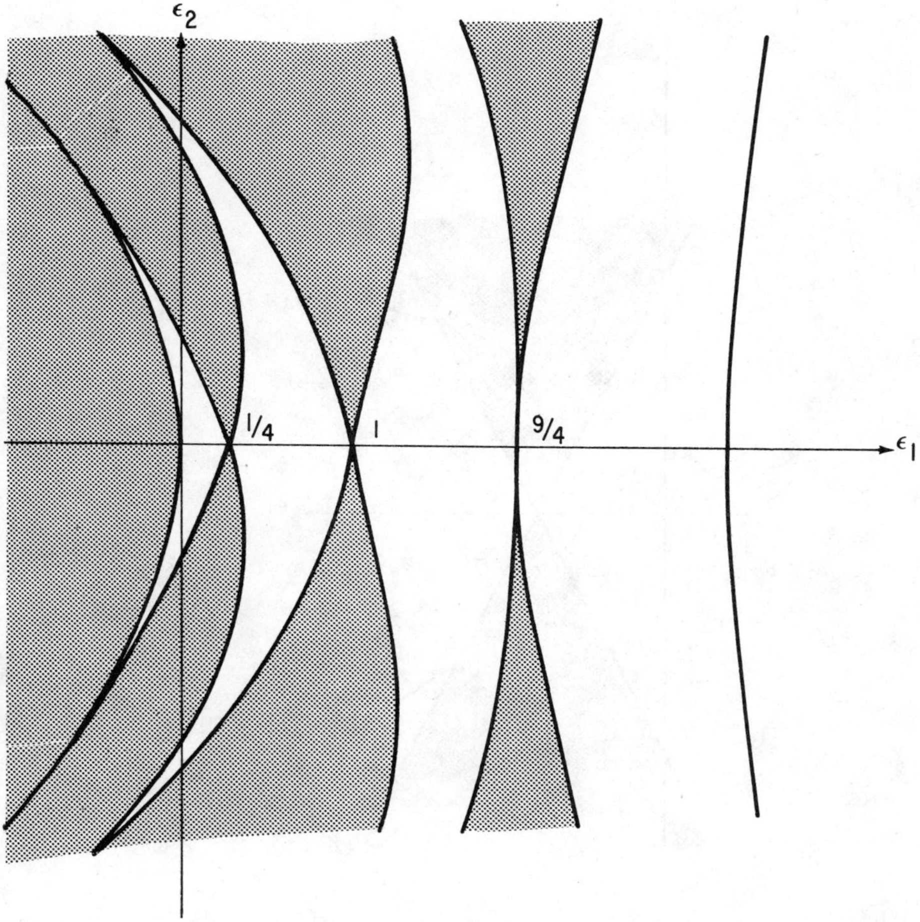

Fig. 3. Stable and Unstable Regions for the Mathieu Equation.

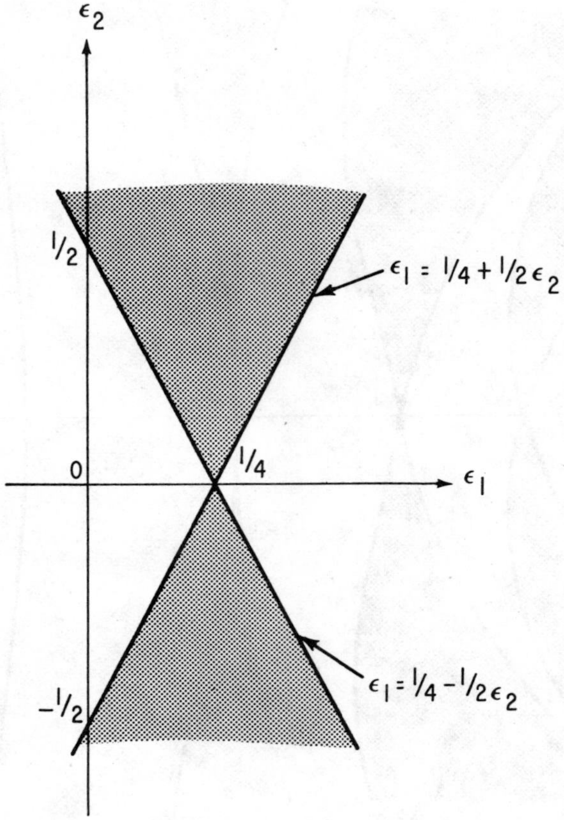

Fig. 4. Approximate Principal Instability Region for the Mathieu Equation for Small Values ε_2.

II and III show the first three values of b_n and c_{mn}. Substituting the above values into Eq. (22) shows that

$$-\frac{1}{2} < \varepsilon_2 < \frac{1}{2}$$

for this problem.

Since the values of the parameters ε_1 and ε_2 determine the stability of a planar motion, one must determine which pairs of numbers $\overline{A}_n$ and $\Omega_n^{(3)}$ satisfying the response relation Eq. (19) lead to stable solutions of the stability equation (20). To accomplish this, we map the ε_1, ε_2-plane onto the $\Omega_n^{(3)}$, $\overline{A}_n$-plane. This transformation is effected by eliminating ε_1 and ε_2 between Eqs. (22) and (23) and the stability boundaries $\varepsilon_1 = \frac{1}{4} \pm \frac{1}{2}\varepsilon_2$. This gives

$$\Omega_m^{(2)^2} = \frac{1}{1 + \frac{1}{2}(b_m\overline{A}_b - c_{mn}\overline{A}_n^2)} \tag{24}$$

for the boundary given by $\varepsilon_1 = \frac{1}{4} + \frac{1}{2}\varepsilon_2$ and

$$\Omega_m^{(2)^2} = \frac{1}{1 - \frac{1}{2}(b_m\overline{A}_b - c_{mn}\overline{A}_n^2)} \tag{25}$$

for the boundary given by $\varepsilon_1 = \frac{1}{4} - \frac{1}{2}\varepsilon_2$. Note the similarity between Eq. (25) and the response relation when written in the form

$$\Omega_m^{(3)^2} = \frac{1}{1 - \frac{1}{2}(\pm\, b_n\overline{A}_b - c_n\overline{A}_n^2)} \tag{26}$$

Thus far we have discussed only planar responses of the rod in the x_1, x_2-plane and disturbances in the x_3-direction. Of course, it may be possible for the rod to respond in the x_1, x_3-plane as well, and when it does, we shall then be concerned with disturbances in the x_2-direction. These latter stability equations and the response relations can be found from Eqs. (24), (25), and (26) by substituting n for m and 3 for 2 in the subscripts and superscripts.

The stability information contained in Eqs. (24), (25), and (26) together with their counterparts obtained by changing the subscripts and superscripts can be interpreted by plotting these eight equations for some selection of the parameters involved. Only the case for which $m = n$ is treated from this point on. The reason is as follows: If the stability point determined by Eqs. (22) and (23) lies in an unstable region which is in the neighborhood of $\varepsilon_1 = \frac{1}{4}$, $\varepsilon_2 = 0$, then the small nonplanar disturbance $x_{3m}(\tau)$ occurs initially at half the exciting frequency [6], [7], [18]. This frequency is the same as the frequency of the planar response; that is, $m = n$. Experimental evidence accumulated during this research indicates the validity of this observation.

The eight equations with $m = n$ are

$$\Omega_n^{(3)\,2} = \frac{1}{1 - \frac{1}{2}(\pm\, b_n\bar{A}_b - c_n\bar{A}_n^2)} \qquad \text{(response curves for } x_1\text{, } x_2\text{-plane motion)} \tag{27}$$

$$\Omega_n^{(2)\,2} = \frac{1}{1 - \frac{1}{2}(\pm\, b_n\bar{A}_b - c_n\bar{A}_n^2)} \qquad \text{(response curves for } x_1\text{, } x_3\text{-plane motion)} \tag{28}$$

$$\Omega_n^{(2)\,2} = \frac{1}{1 \pm \frac{1}{2}(b_n\bar{A}_b - c_n\bar{A}_n^2)} \qquad \text{(stability boundaries associated with Eq. (27))} \tag{29}$$

$$\Omega_n^{(3)\,2} = \frac{1}{1 \pm \frac{1}{2}(b_n\bar{A}_b - c_n\bar{A}_n^2)} \qquad \text{(stability boundaries associated with Eq. (28))} \tag{30}$$

Note that we have used the fact that, when $m = n$, $c_{mn} = c_m = c_n$. The graph of these equations on the $\Omega_2^{(2)}$, $\bar{A}_2$-plane is shown in Fig. 5. The constants used are:

$\ell = 32.9$ inches

$A_b = 0.075$ inches

$m = n = 2$

$E = 30 \times 10^6$ psi

Specific weight of material = 485 lb/ft^3

$\omega_2^{(2)}/\omega_2^{(3)} = 0.973$

$b_2 = 34.6$, $c_2 = 145$ (From Table II)

It is now possible to follow the response of the initially straight rod to an increasing or a decreasing excitation frequency. Suppose the frequency is slowly and continuously increased from zero. The rod

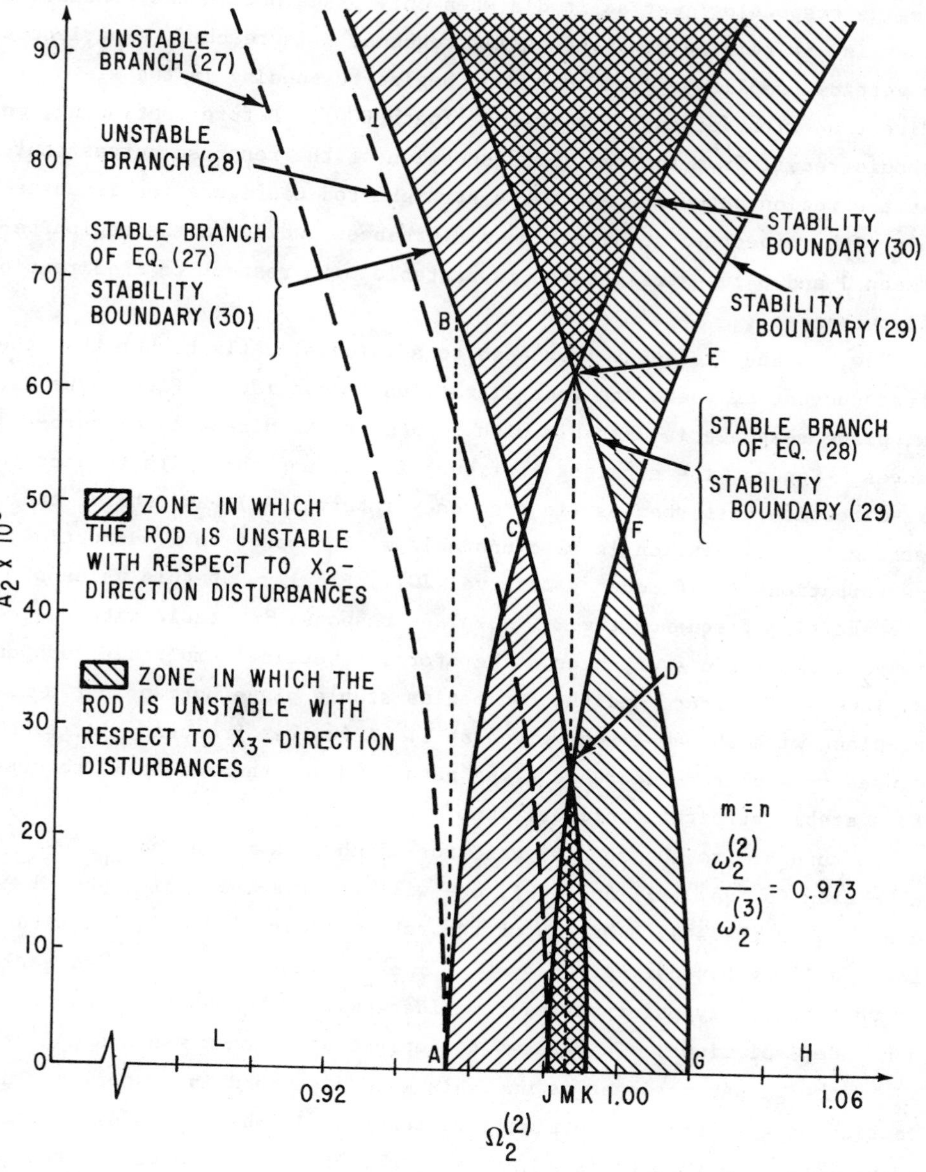

Fig. 5. Response Equations and Stability Boundaries.

begins responding just as it did when only plane motion was considered. That is, it remains straight until frequency A is reached, experiences a vertical amplitude jump to B, and begins responding in the x_2-direction with decreasing amplitude (path BCD). Before continuing, one should recall from the earlier discussion of the response curves that in the region between A and K the straight rod configuration is unstable with respect to x_2-direction disturbances, while in the region between J and G the straight rod is unstable with respect to x_3-direction disturbances.

Now, as the frequency increases to a value slightly higher than the frequency at D, there are four situations to consider. First, the x_1, x_2-plane response is unstable with respect to x_3-direction disturbances. Second, the straight configuration is unstable with respect to x_2-direction disturbances (in frequency interval AK), and third, the straight configuration is also unstable with respect to x_3-direction perturbations (in frequency interval JG). Finally, at this value of the exciting frequency the x_1, x_3-plane response is stable with respect to x_2-direction disturbances. Therefore, a vertical amplitude jump and a plane shift occur, and the rod begins stable plane motion in the x_1, x_3-plane with the amplitude given by E. A further frequency increase causes an amplitude decrease along path EFGH and the rod again returns to a stable straight configuration.

We turn now to the special case for which both m = n and $\omega_n^{(3)} = \omega_m^{(2)}$. Referring to Eqs. (27) and (29), one will observe that this special case causes the stable branch of the response curve to coincide with the stability boundary given by $\varepsilon_1 = \frac{1}{4} - \frac{1}{2}\varepsilon_2$. It was indicated earlier that stability points lying coincident with a boundary correspond to unbounded solutions. This seems to imply that, when m = n and $\omega_n^{(3)} = \omega_m^{(2)}$, the planar response is unstable when disturbed in a nonplanar direction, regardless of the planar response amplitude. In addition to being intuitively unrealistic, this situation fails to occur in the laboratory. However, the apparent paradox can be resolved by the addition to the theory of a damping term. This damping term, no matter how small, causes the m = n and $\omega_n^{(3)} = \omega_m^{(2)}$ case to have a planar response which is always stable with respect to nonplanar disturbances. In the Appendix, Fig. 9, the effect of damping on the curves in the Ω_n, $\overline{A}_n$-plane for this special case is shown.

Another special situation arises when the detuning is large, that is, when $\omega_n^{(3)}$ is much different from $\omega_n^{(2)}$. As the detuning increases, the cross-hatched regions in Fig. 5 tend to separate. At some value of the detuning, the region of overlapping JDK decreases to zero and a qualitatively different response arises. We concentrate briefly on the case in which $K \leq J$. The overlapping zone JDK disappears provided

$$\Omega_n^{(3)} \leq \Omega_m^{(2)}$$

that is, provided the natural frequency ratio is such that

$$\left(\frac{\omega_n^{(3)}}{\omega_m^{(2)}}\right)^2 \leq \frac{1 - \frac{1}{2} b_n \bar{A}_b}{1 + \frac{1}{2} b_m \bar{A}_b} \tag{31}$$

The stability information for the previous example with the moments of inertia adjusted so that Eq. (31) is satisfied is shown in Fig. 6. Now, for increasing frequency, a stability point follows path OABCD; that is, the rod begins responding in the x_1, x_2-plane and remains in that plane until it returns to the stable straight configuration. The rod remains straight until frequency D' is reached after which it jumps into an x_1, x_3-plane response. When the frequency is diminished, the rod follows path HGFJE (x_1, x_3-plane response), experiences a downward amplitude jump to M (the straight configuration), remains straight until frequency D is reached, and then follows path DCBI (x_1, x_2-plane response) until damping causes a downward amplitude jump to the stable straight configuration.

As a final item of interest, we show that a "whirling motion" of the type predicted by Murthy and Ramakrishna [8] in their analysis of the transversely excited elastic string is not possible for the axially excited rod. In order to account for the "whirling motion," a phase difference of $\pi/2$ is assumed between motions in the two planes. Hence we assume, as did Murthy and Ramakrishna, a solution of the form

$$v(S,t) = T_{2n}(t)\, X_n(S) = a_{n2}\, X_n(S) \cos \frac{\omega t}{2}$$

$$w(S,t) = T_{3n}(t)\, X_n(S) = a_{n3}\, X_n(S) \sin \frac{\omega t}{2}$$

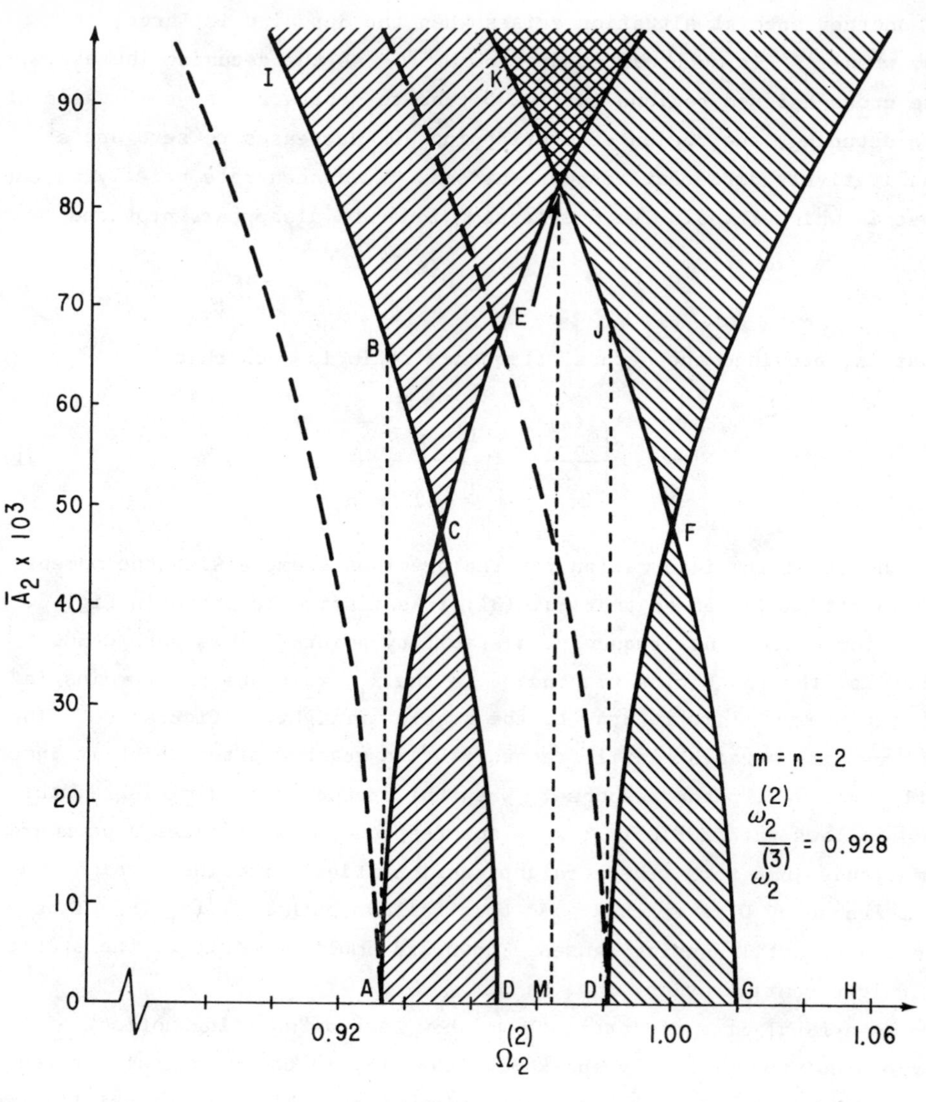

Fig. 6. Response Equations and Stability Boundaries when

$$\frac{\left\{\omega_n^{(3)}\right\}^2}{\left\{\omega_n^{(2)}\right\}^2} \le \frac{1 - \frac{1}{2}\, b_n\, \overline{A}_b}{1 + \frac{1}{2}\, b_n\, \overline{A}_b} \, .$$

The Galerkin method applied to the spatial variable yields Eqs. (11) and (12) as shown earlier. Now let $T_{2n}(\tau) = a_{n2}\cos\tau$ and $T_{3n}(\tau) = a_{n3}\sin\tau$ and apply the method of harmonic balance (Cunningham [18]). This gives

$$a_{n2}\left[\frac{1}{\Omega_n^{(3)2}} - 1 + \frac{b_n\bar{A}_b}{2} + \frac{c_n(a_{n3}^2 - a_{n2}^2)}{2\ell^2}\right] = 0 \tag{32}$$

$$a_{n3}\left[\frac{1}{\Omega_n^{(2)2}} - 1 - \frac{b_n\bar{A}_n}{2} - \frac{c_n(a_{n3}^2 - a_{n2}^2)}{2\ell^2}\right] = 0 \tag{33}$$

Since we are restricting our attention to the case $a_{n2} \neq 0$, $a_{n3} \neq 0$ (this insures the "whirling motion"), we divide Eq. (32) by a_{n2} and Eq. (33) by a_{n3} and add to obtain

$$\omega^2 = 2\left(\omega_n^{(2)2} + \omega_n^{(3)2}\right) \tag{34}$$

In other words, there is predicted a single frequency at which the "whirling motion" could occur. This is tantamount to saying that the "whirling motion" cannot be generated in the laboratory since Eq. (34) can never be satisfied exactly in practice. It is interesting to note that the frequency given by Eq. (34) is the frequency M for which the previously discussed plane shift occurs.

To calculate the values of the amplitude such as D and E in Fig. 5 at which the vertical amplitude jumps occur, one needs only to substitute Eq. (34) into the appropriate stable branch of the response curves. The amplitude at E is

$$\left(\bar{A}_n^2\right)_{\substack{cr\\m=n}} = \frac{1}{c_n}\left[b_n\bar{A}_b + 2\left(\frac{\omega_n^{(2)2} - \omega_n^{(3)2}}{\omega_n^{(2)2} + \omega_n^{(3)2}}\right)\right]$$

and the amplitude at D is

$$\left(\bar{A}_n^2\right)_{\substack{cr\\m=n}} = \frac{1}{c_n}\left[b_n\bar{A}_b - 2\left(\frac{\omega_n^{(2)2} - \omega_n^{(3)2}}{\omega_n^{(2)2} + \omega_n^{(3)2}}\right)\right]$$

Experiments

The purpose of the experiments is to test the validity of the foregoing analysis that predicts the inception of nonplanar responses of axially forced rods. The primary objective is to determine the frequency of the excitation and the amplitude of the planar response which marks transition to a nonplanar motion.

The specimens were made from 0.188 inch diameter steel rod having a useable length after clamping of 32.9 inches. The rods had parallel flats ground on two sides since the theory shows that circular cross-section rods will only respond in one plane. Experiments verified this conclusion. All rods were carefully selected for initial straightness and were rigidly clamped by means of shaped blocks to the table of the shaker.

In testing the rods, the frequency was slowly and continuously increased along path OLA (Fig. 5) until A was reached. At A, a vertical amplitude jump to B occurred. The frequency which corresponded to A and B was measured (Ω_A) and the steady-state x_1, x_2-plane response amplitude ($\bar{A}_{n_B}$) after the jump to B was measured. Frequency was further increased (and a corresponding decrease in amplitude was witnessed) until the frequency at D was reached. At D, a vertical amplitude jump and a 90° plane-shift to E was observed. Both the frequency at D (Ω_D) and the steady-state amplitude of the x_1, x_3-plane response at E ($\bar{A}_{n_{E_{inc}}}$, the amplitude at E when frequency is increased) were measured. Analogous measurements were made as frequency was decreased. The frequency Ω_G (Fig. 5) for increasing frequency was averaged with Ω_G for decreasing frequency since the two values were substantially the same. These data were acquired for four rods, each having a different natural frequency ratio. Because of the limited frequency range of the testing machine, only the second mode could be excited. The comparison of experimental data with theoretical values of the critical amplitudes and frequencies is shown in Table IV. Damping has not been included in the theoretical calculations.

The formulas used to calculate the amplitudes and frequencies listed in Table IV are found from the earlier equations. They are:

$$\left(\bar{A}_{2_B}\right)^2 = \frac{2}{c_2}\, b_2 \bar{A}_b$$

$$\left(\bar{A}_{2_E}\right)^2_{\text{inc.}} = \left(\bar{A}_{2_E}\right)^2_{\text{dec.}} = \frac{1}{c_2}\left[b_2\bar{A}_b + 2\left(\frac{\omega_2^{(2)^2} - \omega_2^{(3)^2}}{\omega_2^{(2)^2} + \omega_2^{(3)^2}}\right)\right]$$

$$\left(\bar{A}_{2_D}\right)^2 = \frac{1}{c_2}\left[b_2\bar{A}_b - 2\left(\frac{\omega_2^{(2)^2} - \omega_2^{(3)^2}}{\omega_2^{(2)^2} + \omega_2^{(3)^2}}\right)\right]$$

$$\omega_A^2 = \frac{2(\omega_2^{(3)})^2}{2 + b_2\bar{A}_b}$$

$$\omega_D^2 = \omega_E^2 = 2(\omega_2^{(2)^2} + \omega_2^{(3)^2})$$

$$\omega_G^2 = \frac{2(\omega_2^{(2)})^2}{2 - b_2\bar{A}_b}$$

The data in Table IV indicate that the theory correctly models the qualitative response of the rod. However, the theoretical amplitudes are greater than the experimentally obtained amplitudes with the error increasing with amplitude. Of course, a damping term tends to decrease the theoretical amplitude, but we have shown in the Appendix that if damping forces are assumed to be proportional to velocity, the effect only becomes noticeable for much larger amplitudes than those present. Possibly a nonlinear damping term would allow the theory to more accurately predict the response amplitudes.

Note, for the first three cases listed, that $\bar{A}_{2_E\,\text{inc.}} < \bar{A}_{2_E\,\text{dec.}}$ for the experiments. These amplitudes theoretically should be the same provided damping is not present. Also note that $\omega_D > \omega_E$ in the experiments; these, too, should be equal in the absence of damping. Even if damping proportional to velocity is included in the analysis, the alteration to the above-mentioned quantities is very small for the amount of damping indicated by the viscous damping hypothesis. Again, a nonlinear damping term might cause better agreement between theory and experiments. The experimental data suggest that the response curves and stability boundaries have the shape indicated in Fig. 7.

TABLE IV. COMPARISON OF THE EXPERIMENTS WITH THE THEORY; $m = n = 2$, $\ell = 32.9$ inches

Parameters	Source of Data	$\Omega^{(2)}_{2_A}$	$\overline{A}_{2_B}$	$\Omega^{(2)}_{2_D}$	$\overline{A}_{2_E}$ inc.	$\Omega^{(2)}_{2_G}$	$\overline{A}_{2_E}$ dec.	$\Omega^{(2)}_{2_E}$	$\overline{A}_{2_D}$
$\overline{A}_b = 2.28 \times 10^{-3}$	Experiments	0.985	0.013	1.005	0.015	1.045	0.019	0.974	0.016
$\omega_2^{(2)}/\omega_2^{(3)} = 0.973$	Theory	0.967	0.033	0.993	0.027	1.020	0.027	0.993	0.019
$\overline{A}_b = 1.52 \times 10^{-3}$	Experiments	0.993	0.010	1.007	0.011	1.036	0.016	0.985	0.011
$\omega_2^{(2)}/\omega_2^{(3)} = 0.973$	Theory	0.974	0.022	0.993	0.023	1.013	0.023	0.993	0.013
$\overline{A}_b = 2.28 \times 10^{-3}$	Experiments	0.929	0.015	0.959	0.015	1.000	0.021	0.937	0.013
$\omega_2^{(2)}/\omega_2^{(3)} = 0.946$	Theory	0.954	0.033	0.987	0.030	1.020	0.030	0.987	0.013
$\overline{A}_b = 1.52 \times 10^{-3}$	Experiments	0.935	0.010	(1)	(3)	0.997	0.017	0.942	0.002
$\omega_2^{(2)}/\omega_2^{(3)} = 0.946$	Theory	0.960	0.022	(1)	(3)	1.013	0.027	0.987	(2)
$\overline{A}_b = 2.28 \times 10^{-3}$	Experiments	0.908	0.016	(1)	(3)	1.007	0.022	0.928	0.003
$\omega_2^{(2)}/\omega_2^{(3)} = 0.897$	Theory	0.929	0.033	(1)	(3)	1.020	0.036	0.974	(2)
$\overline{A}_b = 1.52 \times 10^{-3}$	Experiments	0.917	0.010	(1)	(3)	1.000	0.017	0.940	(2)
$\omega_2^{(2)}/\omega_2^{(3)} = 0.897$	Theory	0.935	0.022	(1)	(3)	1.013	0.033	0.974	(2)
$\overline{A}_b = 2.28 \times 10^{-3}$	Experiments	0.894	0.015	(1)	(3)	1.003	0.022	0.926	(2)
$\omega_2^{(2)}/\omega_2^{(3)} = 0.861$	Theory	0.909	0.033	(1)	(3)	1.020	0.039	1.004	(2)

TABLE IV. (continued)

$\overline{A}_b = 1.52 \times 10^{-3}$	Experiments	0.900	0.010	(1)	(3)	0.997	0.020	0.948	(2)
$\omega_2^{(2)}/\omega_2^{(3)} = 0.861$	Theory	0.916	0.022	(1)	(3)	1.013	0.037	1.004	(2)

(1) In these cases, the rods were sufficiently detuned so that zone JDK, Fig. 5, disappeared. Hence there is no frequency which corresponds to point D. See Fig. 6.

(2) No amplitude exists at point D for the reason mentioned in (1). See Fig. 6.

(3) The amplitude at E cannot be reached by increasing frequency. See Fig. 6.

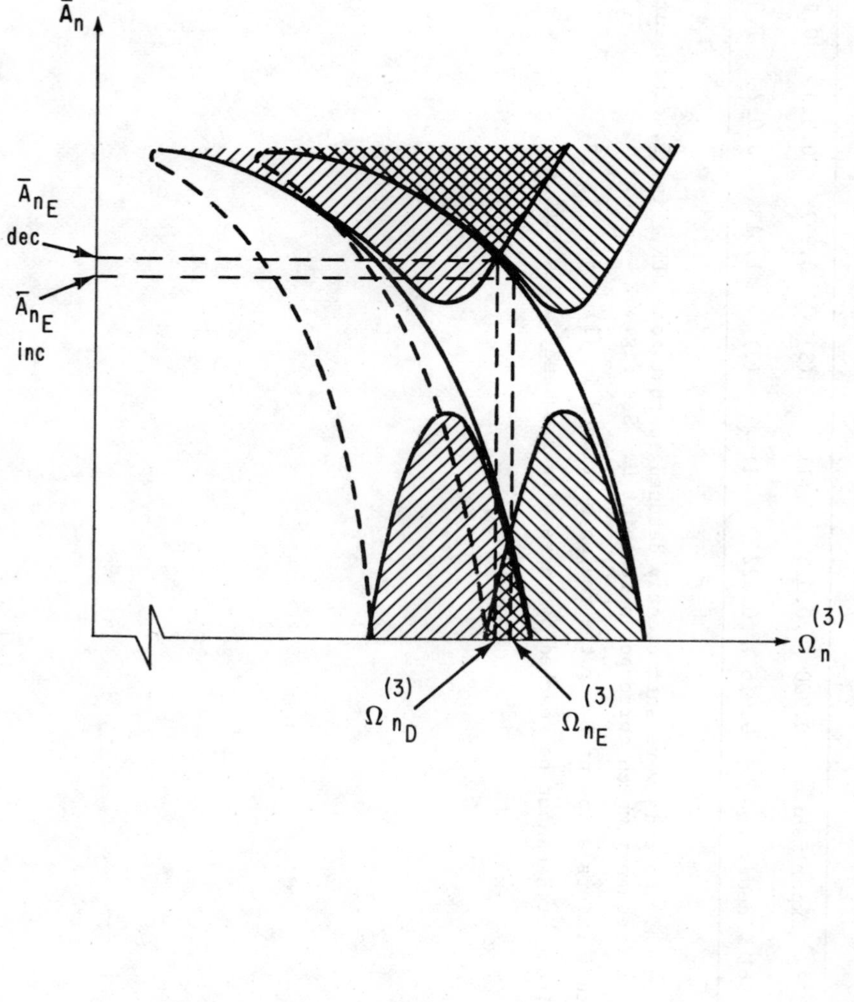

Fig. 7. Shape of the Response Curves and Stability Boundaries as Suggested by the Experimental Data.

Conclusions

A study has been made of the conditions under which parametrically induced planar vibrations of a long slender axially excited elastic rod become unstable when the rod is subjected to out-of-plane disturbances. We have shown that nonplanar motion is parametrically coupled to the planar response.

The analysis shows that there are values of the base excitation amplitude, driving frequency, and natural frequency ratio for which the plane subharmonic solution is unstable with respect to nonplanar perturbations. Only when the natural frequency ratio is near unity does the amplitude jump and accompanying plane change occur both for increasing and decreasing frequency. The effect of increasing the detuning is to cause the response curves for plane motion to become more widely separated in frequency. For large enough detuning, the jump from motion in one plane to motion in a perpendicular plane is eliminated. We have shown that if the detuning is sufficiently large and damping is considered, the two perpendicular plane motions can be separated by a region in which the straight configuration is stable.

When m = n and $\omega_m^{(2)} = \omega_n^{(3)}$, the planar response is stable over the whole frequency range provided that damping, no matter how small, is considered. The writers suggest that this result has application to the problem of the vertical excitation of an upright, rigid, right circular cylindrical tank partially filled with liquid. Dodge, Kana, and Abramson [19] point out that there is "no evidence of any time-dependent rotation, periodic or otherwise, of the plane of the liquid motion as occurs with large-amplitude sloshing resulting from transverse excitation." This result is similar to the one we have obtained for the axially excited rod. It is conceivable that the plane shift and amplitude jump analogous to that obtained for the rod when $\omega_m^{(2)} \neq \omega_n^{(3)}$ could occur in an axially excited tank having a nearly circular cross-section.

The experiments show that the theory qualitatively predicts the correct rod response. However, a significant difference exists between theoretical and experimental amplitudes which cannot be accounted for by the addition to the theory of a damping term proportional to velocity. A nonlinear damping term or a higher order Galerkin analysis might better the agreement between theory and experiments; however a comparable analysis [12] of resonant response of a rod subjected to lateral harmonic excitation has produced excellent predictions of amplitudes as well as frequencies.

ACKNOWLEDGEMENTS

This research was supported by NSF Grant GK-1484 to the Georgia Institute of Technology.

REFERENCES

1. Gol'denblat, I. I., Contemporary Problems of Vibrations and Stability of Engineering Structures, Stroiizdat, Moscow, 1947.

2. Bolotin, V. V., The Dynamic Stability of Elastic Systems, Translated by V. I. Weingarten, et al., Holden-Day, Inc., San Francisco, 1964.

3. Evensen, H. A. and Evan-Iwanowski, R. M., "Effects of Longitudinal Inertia Upon the Parametric Response of Elastic Columns," Journal of Applied Mechanics, Vol. 33, March, 1966, pp. 141-148.

4. Beylin, Ye. A. and Dzhaneldize, G. Yu., "A Survey of Writings on the Dynamic Stability of Elastic Bodies," Prikladnaya Matematika i Mekhanika (Applied Mathematics and Mechanics), Vol. 16, 1952, pp. 635-648.

5. Evan-Iwanowski, R. M., "On the Parametric Response of Structures," Applied Mechanics Reviews, Vol. 18, No. 9, September, 1965, pp. 699-702.

6. Henry, R. F. and Tobias, S. A., "Modes at Rest and Their Stability in Coupled Non-Linear Systems," Journal of Mechanical Engineering Science, Vol. 3, No. 2, 1961, pp. 163-173.

7. Tobias, S. A., "Free Undamped Non-Linear Vibrations of Imperfect Circular Discs," Proceedings of the Institution of Mechanical Engineers, Vol. 171, No. 22, 1957, pp. 691-715.

8. Murthy, G. and Ramakrishna, B., "Nonlinear Character of Resonance in Stretched Strings," Journal of the Acoustical Society of America, Vol. 38, September, 1965, pp. 461-471.

9. Quick, W. H., "Theory of the Vibrating String as an Angular Motion Sensor," Journal of Applied Mechanics, Vol. 31, September, 1964, pp. 523-534.

10. Ebner, S. G., "Elastic Oscillations of Imperfect Columns of Thin-Walled Open Sections Subjected to Axial Periodic Loads," Ph.D. Thesis, University of Colorado, Boulder, 1968.

11. Tso, W. K., "Parametric Torsional Stability of a Bar Under Axial Excitation," Journal of Applied Mechanics, Vol. 35, March, 1968, pp. 13-19.

12. Haight, E. C., "Parametric Excitation of Nonplanar Motions of an Elastic Rod," Ph.D. Thesis, Georgia Institute of Technology, Atlanta, 1969.

13. Young, D. and Felgar, R. P., "Tables of Characteristic Functions Representing Normal Modes of Vibration of a Beam," Engineering Research Bulletin No. 4913, Bureau of Engineering Research, The University of Texas, Austin, July, 1949.

14. Moody, M. L., "The Parametric Response of Imperfect Columns," Developments in Mechanics, Vol. 4, Proceedings of the Tenth Midwestern Mechanics Conference, 1967, pp. 329-346.

15. Klotter, K., "Non-Linear Vibration Problems Treated by the Averaging Method of W. Ritz," Proceedings of the 1st U.S. National Congress of Applied Mechanics, J. W. Edwards, Ann Arbor, Michigan, 1952, pp. 125-131.

16. Stoker, J. J., Nonlinear Vibrations, Interscience Publishers, New York, 1950.

17. McLachlan, Ordinary Non-Linear Differential Equations in Engineering and Physical Sciences, Second Edition, Oxford at the Clarendon Press, 1958.

18. Cunningham, W. J., Nonlinear Analysis, McGraw-Hill Book Company, Inc., New York, 1958.

19. Dodge, F., Kana, D. and Abramson, H. N., "Liquid Surface Oscillations in Longitudinally Excited Rigid Cylindrical Containers, AIAA Journal, Vol. 3, No. 4, April, 1965, pp. 685-695.

APPENDIX

Addition of Damping

There are at least three different sources of damping effects in this rod problem. There is the dissipation of energy due to internal friction, the resistance imparted by the surrounding air to the motion of the rod through it, and the external loss of energy due to relative motion between the rod and its support system. In short, a meaningful mathematical model of damping for this system is difficult to construct. However, some particular trends can be found by adding certain suitable terms to the equations of motion for the undamped problem and then by making adjustments based on experimental data to these terms so that the theoretical result shows acceptable agreement with the experiments. This indirect method follows.

Assume that damping forces are directly proportional to velocity. Then the equations of motion take the form

$$\alpha \ddot{T}_{2n} + 2\varepsilon_n \dot{T}_{2n} + (\beta_n^{(3)} + \gamma_n A_b \omega^2 \cos \omega t)\, T_{2n} + \delta_n T_{2n}(T_{2n}\ddot{T}_{2n} + \dot{T}_{2n}^2)$$

$$+ \Delta_{nm} T_{2n}(T_{3m}\ddot{T}_{3m} + \dot{T}_{3m}^2) = 0$$

$$\alpha\ddot{T}_{3m} + 2\varepsilon_m\dot{T}_{3m} + (\beta_m^{(2)} + \gamma_m A_b\omega^2 \cos \omega t)\, T_{3m} + \delta_m T_{3m}(T_{3m}\ddot{T}_{3m} + \dot{T}_{3m}^2)$$
$$+ \Delta_{mn} T_{3m}(T_{2n}\ddot{T}_{2n} + \dot{T}_{2n}^2) = 0$$

Using the Ritz averaging method on the planar response equation ($T_{3m}(t) \equiv 0$) shows that the amplitude-frequency relation is

$$\left(\Omega_n^{(3)}\right)^4 - \left[\frac{4\left(c_n\bar{A}_n^2 + 2 - \dfrac{f_n^2}{\left(2\omega_n^{(3)}\right)^2}\right)}{c_n^2\bar{A}_n^4 + 4c_n\bar{A}_n^2 + 4 - b_n^2\bar{A}_b^2}\right]\left(\Omega_n^{(3)}\right)^2$$

$$+ \frac{4}{c_n^2\bar{A}_n^4 + 4c_n\bar{A}_n^2 + 4 - b_n^2\bar{A}_b^2} = 0 \qquad (35)$$

where $f_n = \dfrac{4\varepsilon_n}{\alpha}$.

For small values of $\left(\dfrac{f_n}{2\omega_n^{(3)}}\right)^2$ and for small values of $\bar{A}_n$, the effect of damping on the response curves is small if handled in the above manner. For large values of $\bar{A}_n$, damping has an important qualitative effect on the response relation; it causes the two formerly separate branches to become joined at high values of $\bar{A}_n$. The branches become joined when the discriminant of quadratic Eq. (35) is zero. This occurs when

$$\bar{A}_n^2 = \frac{1}{2c_n}\left[\frac{b_n^2\bar{A}_b^2 + \left(\dfrac{f_n}{2\omega_n^{(3)}}\right)^4 - 2\left(\dfrac{f_n}{2\omega_n^{(3)}}\right)^2}{\left(\dfrac{f_n}{2\omega_n^{(3)}}\right)^2}\right]$$

Because the linear damping term has a negligible effect on the response curves for small values of $\bar{A}_n$ and $\left(\dfrac{f_n}{2\omega_n^{(3)}}\right)^2$ and because the plane shift described earlier occurs for relatively low values of $\bar{A}_n$ when $\omega_n^{(2)}/\omega_n^{(3)}$ is near unity, we do not include the damping term in the response equation. That is, only the effect of damping on the zone for which plane motion is unstable is included.

The result of applying an analysis for stability of the planar response is

$$x''_{3m}(\tau) + \frac{f_n}{\omega} x'_{3m}(\tau) + \left[\frac{1}{\Omega_m^{(2)2}} + (b_m \overline{A}_b - c_{mn} \overline{A}_n^2) \cos 2\tau\right] x_{3m}(\tau) = 0$$

where $x_{3m}(\tau)$ is a small x_3-direction disturbance. Following Bolotin [2], Chapter 2, one finds that the stability boundary equations are approximated by

$$\left(\Omega_m^{(2)}\right)^2 = \left[1 \pm \frac{1}{4}\left(\Omega_m^{(2)}\right)^4 \left(b_m \overline{A}_b - c_{mn} \overline{A}_n^2\right) - \left(\frac{\Delta_n}{\pi}\right)^2\right]^{\frac{1}{2}} \tag{36}$$

where Δ_n is the logarithmic decrement defined by

$$\Delta_n = \frac{1}{T} \ln \frac{T_{2m}(\tau)}{T_{2m}(\tau + T)}$$

T is the period of the steady-state response.

In elementary theory of vibrations, one shows that the logarithmic decrement Δ_n is related to the damping constant $2\varepsilon_n$ approximately by

$$\Delta_n \doteq \frac{2\pi\, \varepsilon_n}{\alpha\omega_n^{(3)}}$$

A graph of Eq. (36) with $\Delta_n = 0.02$ and the other physical parameters given earlier is shown in Fig. 8.

As a final observation on the effect of damping, we note that damping is responsible for causing the special case m = n, $\omega_n^{(3)} = \omega_m^{(2)}$ to execute stable plane motion for all values of ω. This can be attributed to the fact that damping shrinks the size of the instability zones so that the response curves now lie entirely within the stable zone. The response curves and stability boundaries for this special case are shown in Fig. 9.

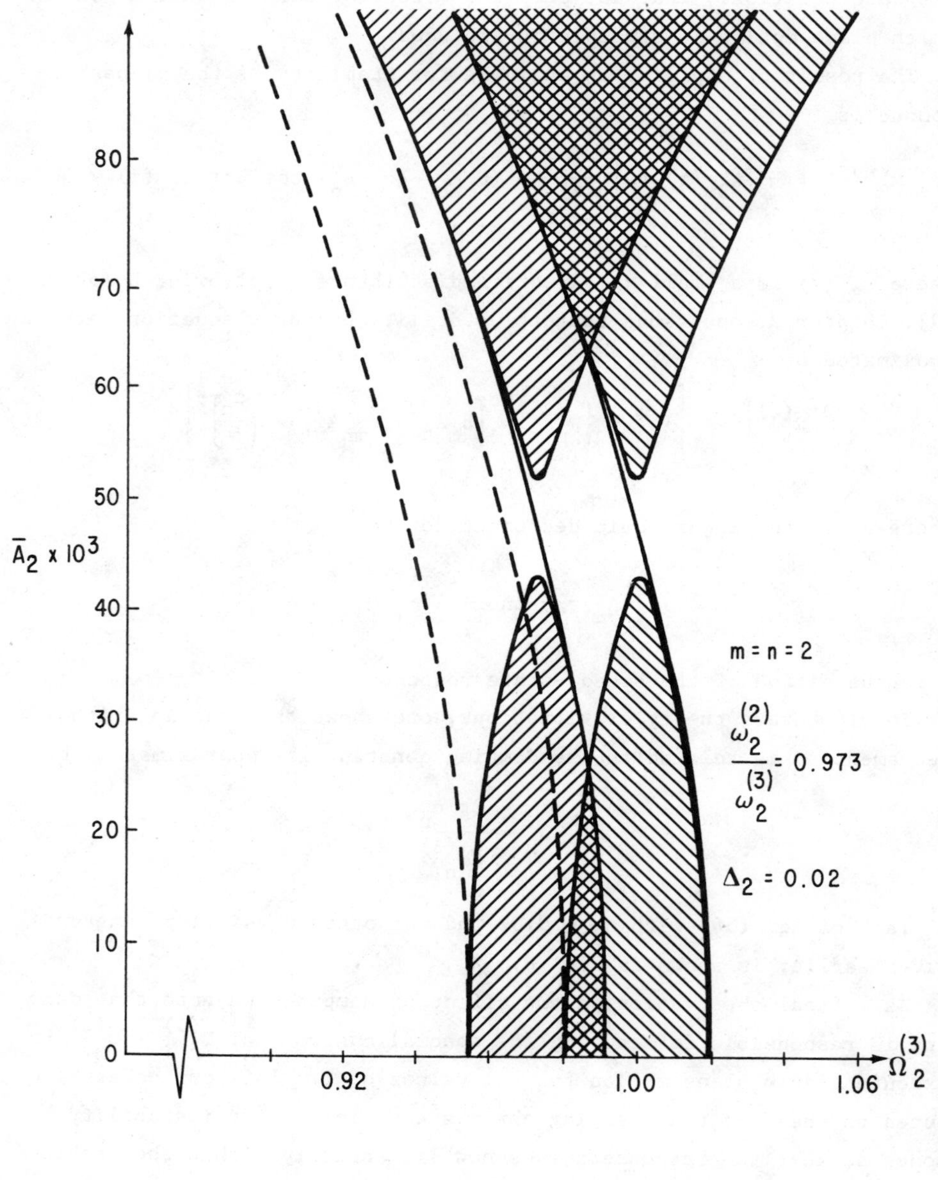

Fig. 8. Effect of Damping on the Instability Region for the Axially Excited Rod.

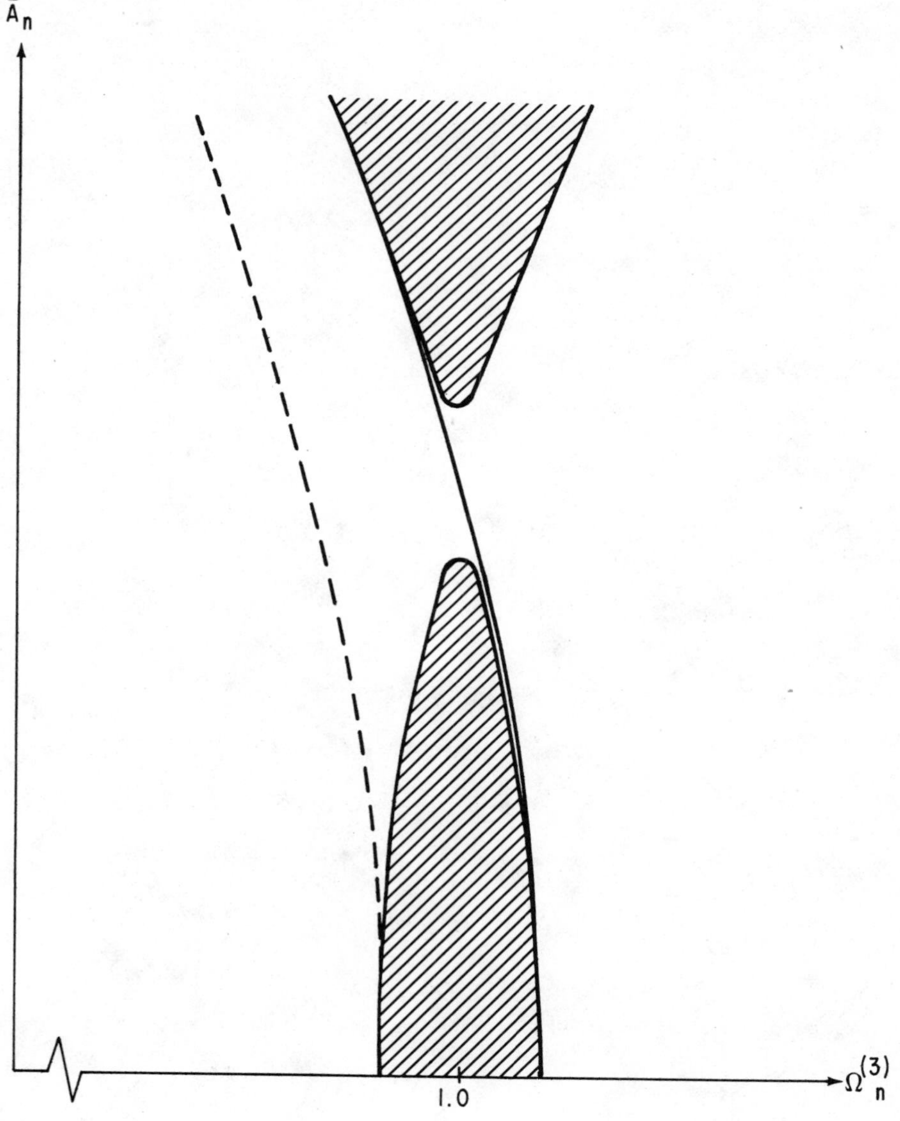

Fig. 9. Effect of Damping on the Instability Region when m = n and $\omega_n^{(3)} = \omega_n^{(2)}$.

NONSTATIONARY PARAMETRIC RESPONSE OF A NONLINEAR COLUMN

R. M. Evan-Iwanowski
Syracuse University

W. F. Sanford
Syracuse University

T. Kehagioglou
IBM, Poughkeepsie, New York

ABSTRACT

An analytical and experimental study has been performed for the nonstationary dynamic responses of columns subject to axial load of the form, $P(t) = P_o + P_1(t) \cos\theta(t)$, where $P_1(t)$ and $\dot{\theta} = \nu(t)$, are functions of time.

The following was investigated: Nonstationary parametric responses of a straight column with nonlinear elasticity (hard "spring" effect), with longitudinal inertia, (soft "spring" effect), and linear and nonlinear damping. The effects on the columns responses of time varying external excitation frequency, $\nu(t)$, were studied independently and in combination with time dependent amplitude of excitation $P_1(t)$.

Characteristic "peaking" of nonstationary responses, accompanied by beat phenomenon have been observed. Marked differences exist for increasing and decreasing sweeps of excitation frequencies depending on the direction of overhang.

Experiments show excellent qualitative agreement with theoretical results. However, some experimentally observed phenomena, such as the phenomenon of nonstationary "penetration," was not predicted theoretically.

LIST OF NOTATIONS

Symbols Related to External Excitation

$P(t)$	Applied axial force $= P_o + P_1(t) \cos \theta(t)$
P_o	Static load
$P_1(t)$	Amplitude of harmonic load
$\theta(t)$	Angular displacement
$\dot{\theta}(t) = \nu(t)$	Excitation frequency
P_E	Euler's load for first spatial mode, $= (\Pi^2 EI)/\ell^2$
μ	Dimensionless load parameter, $= \frac{P_1}{2(P_E - P_o)}$
ν_o	Initial excitation frequency
ν_1	Speed of linear nonstationary frequency sweep
μ_o	Initial excitation amplitude
μ_1	Speed of linear amplitude sweep
t	Time
$\overline{\alpha}, \overline{\beta}$	Amplitude and frequency of cyclic sweep

Symbols Related to Column Response

$f(t)$	Lateral displacement
$a(t)$	Amplitude of lateral displacement
$\phi(t)$	Angular displacement
$\psi(t)$	Phase angle
ω	Natural frequency of unloaded column, $= \frac{\Pi^2}{\ell^2} \left(\frac{EI}{m}\right)^{1/2}$
Ω	Natural frequency of column with static load P_o, $= \omega(1 - P_o/P_E)^{1/2}$

Symbols Related to Column Parameters and Physical Constants

M, M_E	Concentrated end mass
β	Coefficient of linear damping
d	Coefficient of nonlinear damping
K	Coefficient of nonlinear longitudinal inertia, $= K_1 + K_2$
γ	Coefficient of nonlinear elasticity
$\underline{\psi}$	Nonlinear terms
c	Spring constant
F	Perturbing terms
ρ	$= K - 3\gamma/4\Omega^2$
$\varepsilon > 0$	Small parameter ($\varepsilon << 1$)

INTRODUCTION

The term parametric resonance in this paper is used in a classical sense proposed by the Russian School, whereby the excitation frequency ν is related to the natural frequency of the response of a system, Ω, as follows:

$$\frac{\nu}{2\Omega} = \frac{1}{m}$$

m is a positive integer. This kind of resonance is exhibited by a column subjected to an axial loading. In the stationary regime, all parameters are constant, and in the nonstationary regime some parameters, such as amplitude and frequency of external excitation may be functions of time.

It seems that the existence of stationary responses, in its strict sense of the word, is rather unusual in practice. True, the stationary analysis may be adequate for sets of given problems. Manifestations of nonstationary responses, that is, the appearance of nonstationary systems in practice, are quite common, such as: start up and slow down of engines driving shafts in post-critical operation; effects of earthquake on structures; effects of impinging water waves with varying frequency on shore structures and ships; impinging sound waves on ear drums, etc. In all these cases, the frequency or the amplitude or both of external excitation are functions of time.

Apparently, the first paper on the subject of nonstationary responses of mechanical systems is due to Lewis [1], where the analysis of a linear one degree of freedom system excited by a force with time dependent frequency was presented. A similar problem for a system with n degrees of freedom has been solved by Filippov [2]. Analytical solutions for a parametrically excited column in a nonstationary regime are found in Mitropolskii's monograph [3]. These solutions pertain to a limited number of cases, viz., an elastic linear column and for a linear form of excitation frequency $\nu(t) = \nu_0 + \nu_1 t$; $\nu_1 > 0$.

Experiments for the stationary parametric response of a column are presented in [4]. A recent review of the state of the art of nonstationary systems is given in [5].

The present paper treats analytically and experimentally a set of problems of nonstationary responses of parametrically excited columns including effects of longitudinal inertia and geometric nonlinearities for certain forms of time variation of the frequency and amplitude of external excitation. Table I presents the parameters used and their time forms. It is expected that the most pronounced modifications of stationary responses in the presence of nonstationary components will be near resonance. Thus, the main attention in this analysis is directed toward the determination of nonstationary responses near resonance. Asymptotic methods are used in solving the differential equations of motion. Experimental work was performed with an objective to verify, at least qualitatively, the nonstationary effects and to determine whether some phenomena not accounted for in the analytical model may present themselves experimentally.

TABLE I. VARIATIONS OF $\nu(t)$ AND $\mu(t)$

Case	Frequency $\nu(t)$	Amplitude $\mu(t)$	Figures
1	19.5 - 4t	Cont.	4,5,11
2	19.5 - 2t	"	4,5,11
3	19.5 - 1t	"	4,5,11
4	19.5 - 0.5t	"	4,5,11
5	19.5 + 0.5t	"	4,5,11
6	19.5 + 1t	"	4,5,11
7	19.5 + 2t	"	4,5,11
8	19.5 + 4t	"	4,5,11
9	1.00 - 0.1 sin t/2	"	6
10	1.00 - 0.1 sin t	"	7
11	1.00 - 0.1 sin 2t	"	8
12	1.95	0.01 + 0.01t	9
13	1.95	0.5 - 0.01t	9
14	1.90 - 0.1 sin t	0.01 + 0.01t	10
15	1.90 - 0.1 sin t	Cont.	12
16	1.95 - 0.1t	"	13

Statement of Problem / Consider a slender, simply supported column subjected to a periodic axial loading of the form, Figure 1:

$$P(t) = P_o + P_1(t) \cos \theta(t) \tag{1}$$

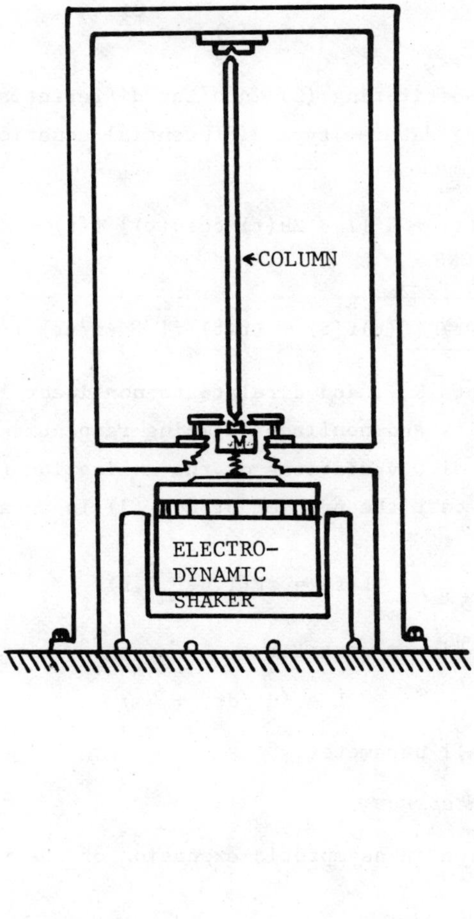

Fig. 1. Experimental Apparatus.

where $\dot{\theta}(t) = \nu(t)$, and $P_1(t)$ are the frequency and amplitude of external excitation. In stationary regimes these quantities are constant, and for the nonstationary regimes they are functions of time. Assuming spatial-temporal mode of lateral (parametric) displacements of the form (first mode)

$$x(t) = f(t) \sin \frac{\pi x}{\ell} \tag{2}$$

we obtain after substituting (2) into the differential equation of motion, the following Mathieu type differential equation for f(t): (see [8],[9])

$$\ddot{f}(t) + 2\beta\dot{f}(t) + \Omega^2[1 - 2\mu(t) \cos\theta(t)]\, f(t) + \underline{\psi}(f,\dot{f},\ddot{f}) = 0 \tag{3}$$

where

$$\underline{\psi}(f,\dot{f},\ddot{f}) = 2Kf(t)\ [f(t)\ddot{f}(t) + (\dot{f}(t))^2] + \gamma f^3(t) + 2df^2(t)\dot{f}(t) \tag{4}$$

and the coefficients K,γ, and d relate to nonlinear inertia, nonlinear geometric elasticity and nonlinear damping respectively. With the usual assumptions of slow variations of the excitation functions and the responses [3], we cast the problem of Eq. (3) in an asymptotic form as follows:

$$L\{f\} = \varepsilon F(T,\theta,f,\dot{f},\ddot{f}) \tag{5}$$

Where L(f) is the linear operator

$$L = (d^2/dt^2 + \Omega^2) \tag{6}$$

and $\varepsilon > 0$ is a small parameter.

Nonstationary Response

We seek the solution in asymptotic expansion of the first approximation in the form

$$f(t) = a(t) \cos \phi(t) \tag{7}$$

where a(t) and $\phi(t)$ are the amplitude and displacement angle of the response and

$$\phi = \Omega t + \psi \tag{8}$$

where $\psi(t)$ is the phase shift.

The method of asymptotic expansions (i) permits the determination of types or resonances possible in a given system, and (ii) provides the means for a relatively simple analysis of a rather complex problem. (As a check, Eq. (3) has been solved directly using numerical analysis).

After performing well-known steps in the application of asymptotic methods, we obtain the following results: (For detailed calculation see [8-9]).

For resonance

$$\Omega \doteq \nu/2 \tag{9}$$

and

$$\dot{a} = -\frac{\Omega^2 \varepsilon\mu(T)a}{\nu(T)} \sin 2\psi - (\varepsilon\beta a + \frac{1}{4}\varepsilon d a^3) \tag{10}$$

$$\dot{\psi} = \Omega - \frac{1}{2}\nu(T) - \frac{\Omega^2\varepsilon\mu(T)}{\nu(T)} \cos 2\psi - \frac{1}{2}\Omega(\varepsilon K - \frac{3}{4}\frac{\varepsilon\gamma}{\Omega^2})a^2 \tag{11}$$

Next, we solve simultaneously differential Eqs. (10) and (11).

Stationary Responses / For stationary responses the left-hand side of (10) and (11) is set equal to zero. Expressing the amplitude as a function of excitation frequency ν we obtain for the stationary amplitude

$$a = \left[\frac{\Omega\rho(\Omega - \frac{\nu}{2}) - \frac{\rho d}{2} \pm \sqrt{\frac{\Omega^2\mu^2}{4\nu^2}(d^2 + 4\Omega^2\rho^2) - [\beta\Omega\rho + \frac{1}{2}d(\Omega - \frac{\nu}{2})]^2}}{\frac{1}{8}(d^2 + 4\Omega^2\rho^2)}\right]^{\frac{1}{2}} \tag{12}$$

where $\rho = K - 3\gamma/4\Omega^2$ and the stationary phase angle

$$\psi = \frac{1}{2}\sin^{-1}\left[-\frac{(\beta + \frac{1}{4}da^2)\nu}{\Omega^2\mu}\right] \tag{13}$$

where

$$0 \geq \psi > -\frac{\Pi}{4} \quad \text{when} \quad \rho < 0 \tag{14a}$$

$$-\frac{\Pi}{4} > \psi \geq -\frac{\Pi}{2} \qquad \rho > 0 \tag{14b}$$

Stability / The $\pm$ sign in the stationary amplitude Eq. (12) denotes two branches of the response curve. Stability analysis indicates that one branch is stable and another unstable. The following are stability criteria:

The solution (branch) is stable if

$$2\Omega - \nu - \rho\Omega a^2 - \frac{4\Omega^4\mu^2}{\nu^3} > 0 \quad \text{when } da/d\nu > 0 \text{ hence } \rho < 0 \tag{15a}$$

$$2\Omega - \nu - \rho\Omega a^2 - \frac{4\Omega^4\mu^2}{\nu^3} < 0 \quad \text{when } da/d\nu < 0 \text{ hence } \rho > 0 \tag{15b}$$

otherwise, the solution (branch) is unstable.

The discussion of stability (instability) carried here can be extended to the determination of stable (unstable) regions in a three dimensional space (ν,a,μ). Schematic representation of the first such instability region is shown in Fig. 2 which yields the Strutt diagram for $a \to 0$, Fig. 3.

Complete information on stability (instability) of a given equilibrium state of a system may be obtained from a phase diagram, i.e., plots of f vs. $\dot{f}$ presented in this paper.

Experimental Investigation

Experimental Set-Up / A steel column 38 inches long with a rectangular 1/2 × 1/4 in. cross section was mounted as shown in Fig. 1. An exchangeable end mass was attached to the lower end of the column in order to increase the longitudinal inertia. The leveled ends of the column were placed in v-grooves of 90° to simulate simply-supported boundary conditions.

To record lateral column displacements, two strain gauges were mounted on either side of the center of the column. The axial force on the column was measured by two strain gauges placed upon the loading bar. Both lateral displacement and axial force were recorded on a strip chart recorder.

Dynamic axial loading was applied to the column by means of an electro-dynamic shaker.

Experimental Procedure / Upon mounting the column, dead weight load, P_o, was applied by compressing the end spring. Stationary response was achieved by changing the frequency of ν to approximately twice Ω. With initial conditions $2a \doteq 1/2$ in., nonstationary response was produced by sweeping the excitation frequency $\nu(t) = \nu_o + \nu_1 t$; where ν_1 is the speed of sweep.

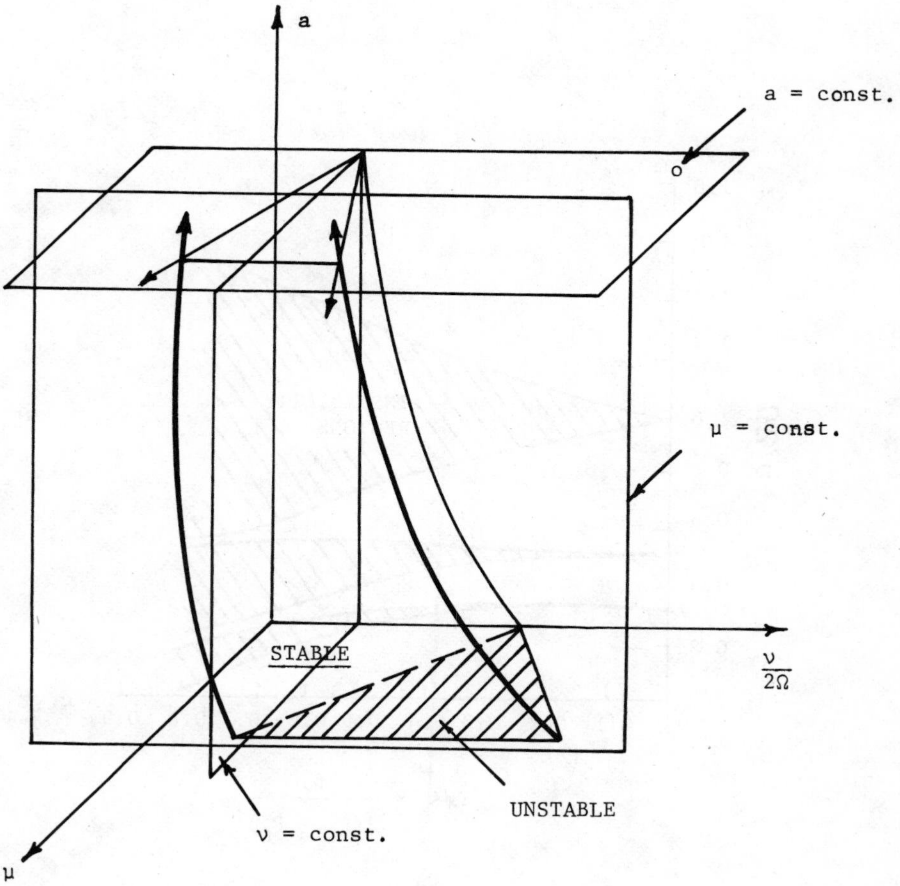

Fig. 2. Principal Region of Parameteric Instability in (ν, a, μ) Space.

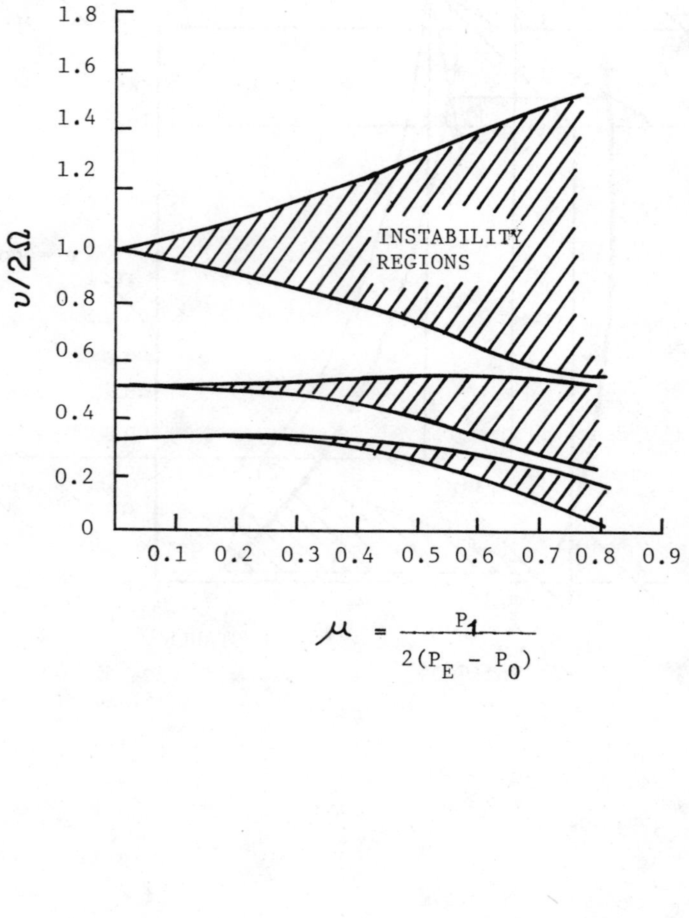

Fig. 3. Regions of Parametric Instability of the Standard Mathieu-Hill Solutions.

The parameter ρ was altered by varying the end mass M = 10.2, 6.4, 0.2 lb. and the end spring constant $\bar{c}$ = 13, 37.5 lb/in. Four different values of ρ, two positive and two negative, were used experimentally, corresponding to hard spring type systems, and negative to soft spring type systems.

Results / The main parameters responsible for modification of the parametric responses in nonstationary regimes are the magnitude and sign of the sweep rate ν_1, in linear variations of ν, i.e., $\nu = \nu_o \pm \nu_1 t$; and the frequency of sweep $\bar{\beta}$ in cyclic variation of ν, i.e., $\nu = \nu_o + \bar{\alpha}(t) \sin \bar{\beta}t$. The effect of the direction of the linear sweep, sign of ν_1, is related to the direction of overhang, sign of ρ. Linear variations of the amplitude of excitations were considered of the form $\mu(t) = \mu_o \pm \mu_1 t$. Functional forms and values of the system parameters and excitation forms used in this paper are given in Table I.

The most obvious manifestation of nonstationary responses, when compared with stationary responses, is a peaky variation of the envelope of the amplitude and subsequent beat. As a rule, the faster the sweep the lower are the peaks of the response, all other conditions being equal. In the case of linear systems with main resonance, peaks appear for higher frequencies for faster sweeps [1]. No such regularity can be observed for nonlinear systems [3]. In the case of parametric resonance, the situation is even more complex, and three cases can be distinguished (Figs. 4,5): (1) For relatively slow sweep speeds in the direction of overhang, the nonstationary response follows the stable branch of the stationary response, thus rendering the system unstable. For low sweep speed in the opposite direction, the nonstationary response follows the stationary response curve downwards. (2) For moderate speeds the nonstationary response stays in the neighborhood of the initial stationary value. It may also be observed from Fig. 4 that for the faster sweep speeds (the larger absolute values of ν_1), zero amplitude was reached quickest with respect to time [neglecting the response described in (1)]. (3) Finally, for relatively high speeds the nonstationary motion approaches the static equilibrium state. The latter phenomenon of leaving a resonance state (parametric in this case) is termed drag out. Experimentally observed drag-in phenomenon, whereby an additional perturbation of a stable column pushes it into

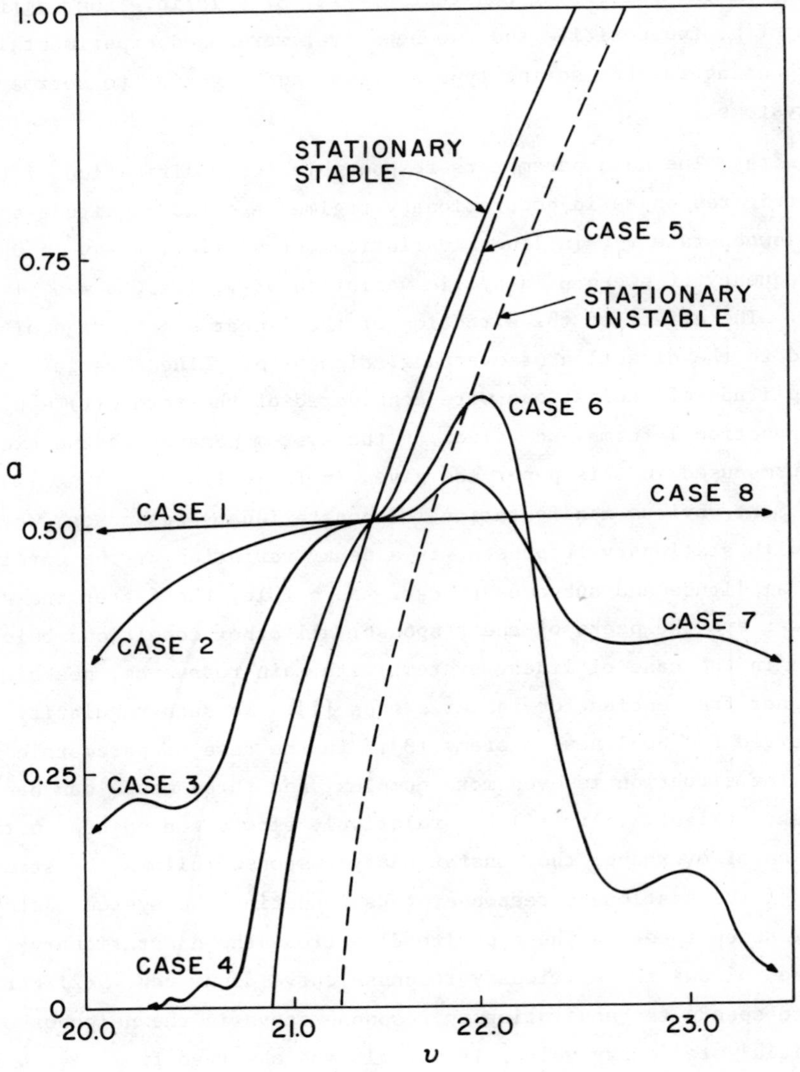

Fig. 4. Nonstationary Amplitude Response for Dominant Nonlinear Elastic System, $\rho = -4$.

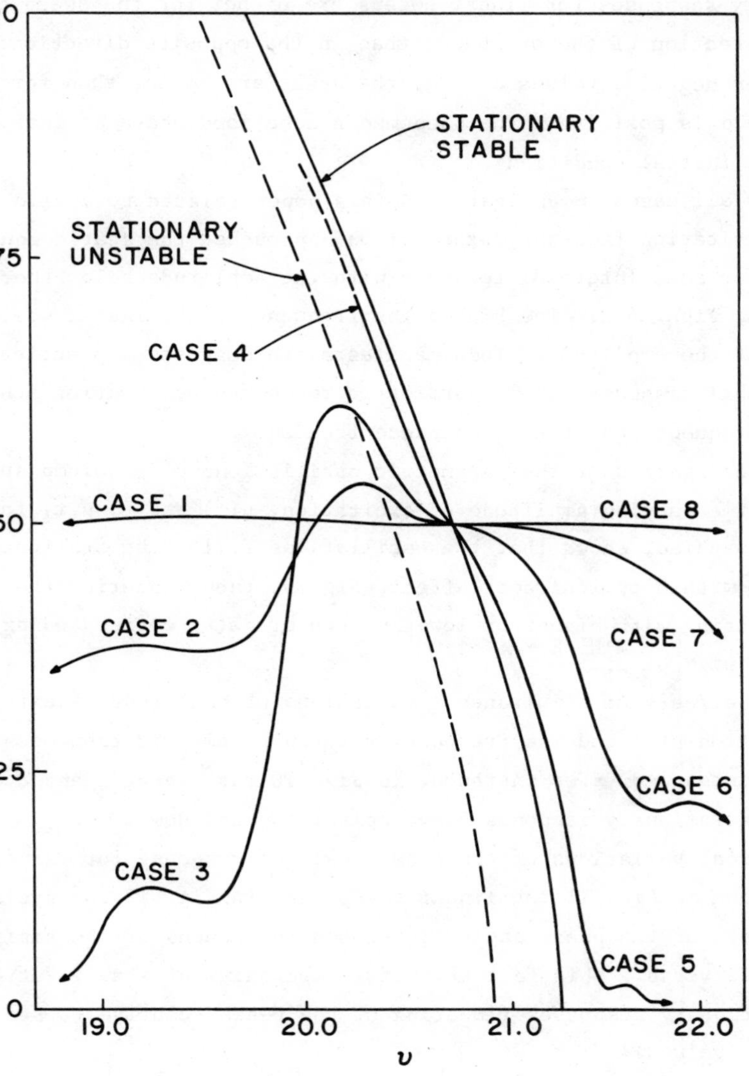

Fig. 5. Nonstationary Amplitude Response for Dominant Nonlinear Inertia System, $\rho = 4$.

an instability zone, has been reported in [4]. The peaks of nonstationary responses for linear sweeps are higher for the sweep being in the direction of the overhang, than in the opposite direction. That is, for negative values of $\nu_1\rho$, the peaks are higher than for the case when $\nu_1\rho$ is positive. The phenomenon described above is independent of the initial conditions.

For all cases investigated in this paper related to cyclic sweep of the excitation frequency, the column approached the static equilibrium state or some intermediate state with the amplitude below the initial values, Figs. 6-8. The higher the frequency $\bar{\beta}$ the faster was the reduction of the amplitude. This manifestation suggests a practical means of stabilizing systems in parametric resonance by "hunting" the excitation frequency about the resonance frequency.

Investigation of the parametric oscillations of a column subjected to a time varying amplitude of excitation, $\mu(t) = \mu_0 \pm \mu_1 t$, for the cases studied, shows that the oscillations follow the stationary stable branch with a typical beat effect, Fig. 9, thus rendering the system oscillating with higher or lower values of $a(t)$ corresponding directly to the sign of μ_1.

The effects of simultaneous variations of amplitude of external excitation $\mu(t)$ and its frequency $\nu(t)$ on parametric responses are quite entangled. For instance, in Fig. 10 for linear μ and cyclic ν the nonstationary response curve spirals up and down.

Typical variations of the phase angle of response for various cases are shown in Fig. 11 for linear sweep, and in Fig. 12 for cyclic sweep. The peaks of the phase angle correspond to troughs of the amplitude, and vice versa. This fact suggests a mechanism of stabilization on nonstationary responses (lowering of the peaks relative to stationary initial values).

Figures 13-14 show plots of energy profiles in the phase plane $(f,\dot{f})$. The cases of stable and unstable vibratory motion are clearly seen from these graphs; if the phase-plane curve spirals inward the system is stable, otherwise unstable.

For the sake of comparison of asymptotic solutions with direct solutions, typical results are presented in Fig. 15.

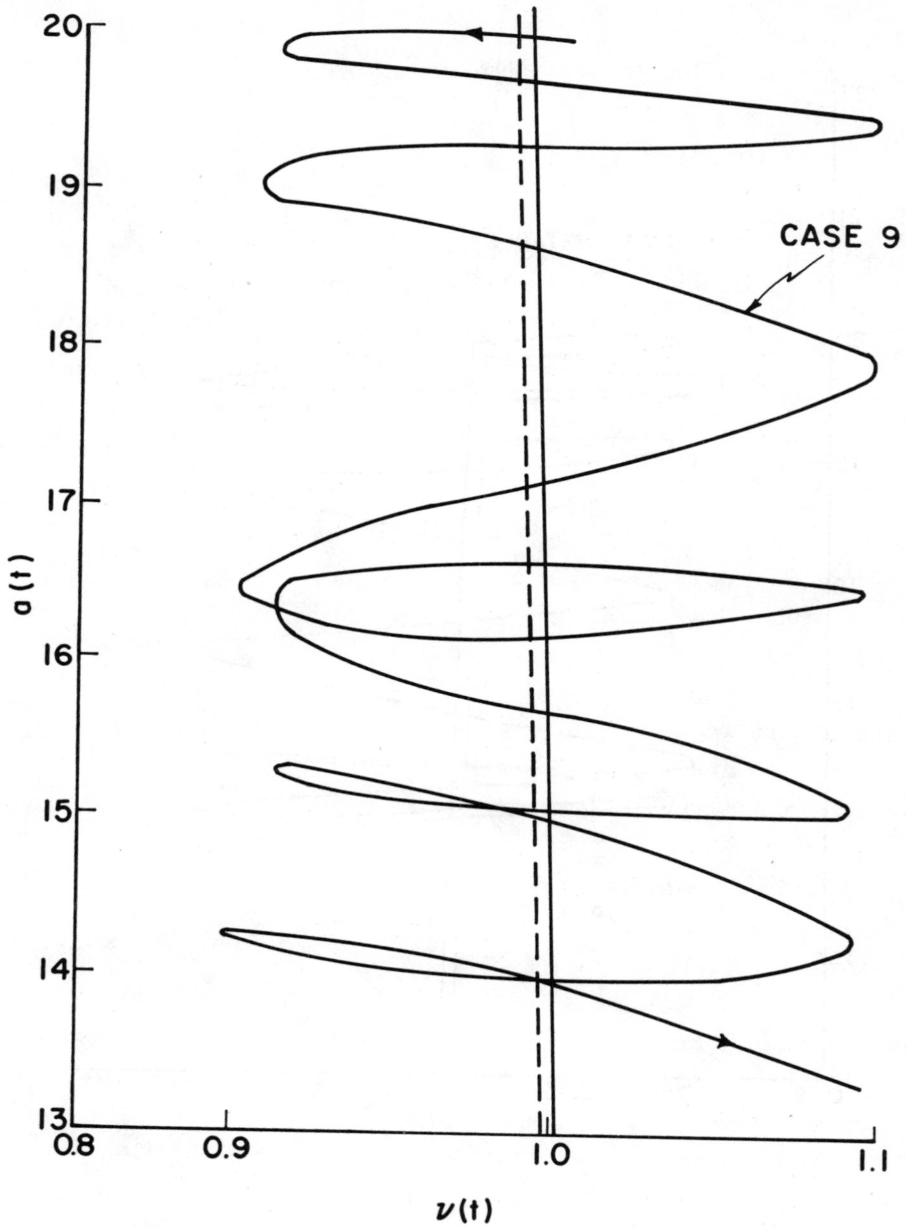

Fig. 6. Nonstationary Response of Column, $\nu = 1.00 - 0.1 \sin t/2$.

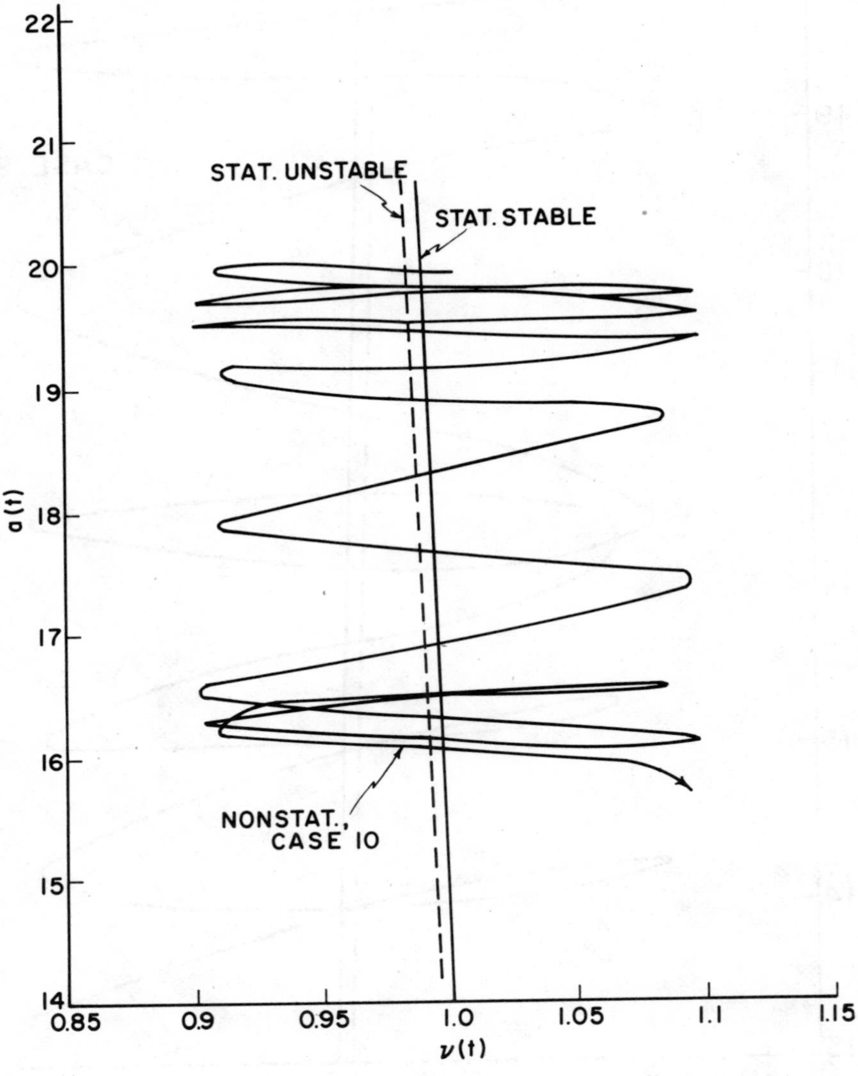

Fig. 7. Nonstationary Response of Column, $\nu = 1.00-0.1 \sin t$.

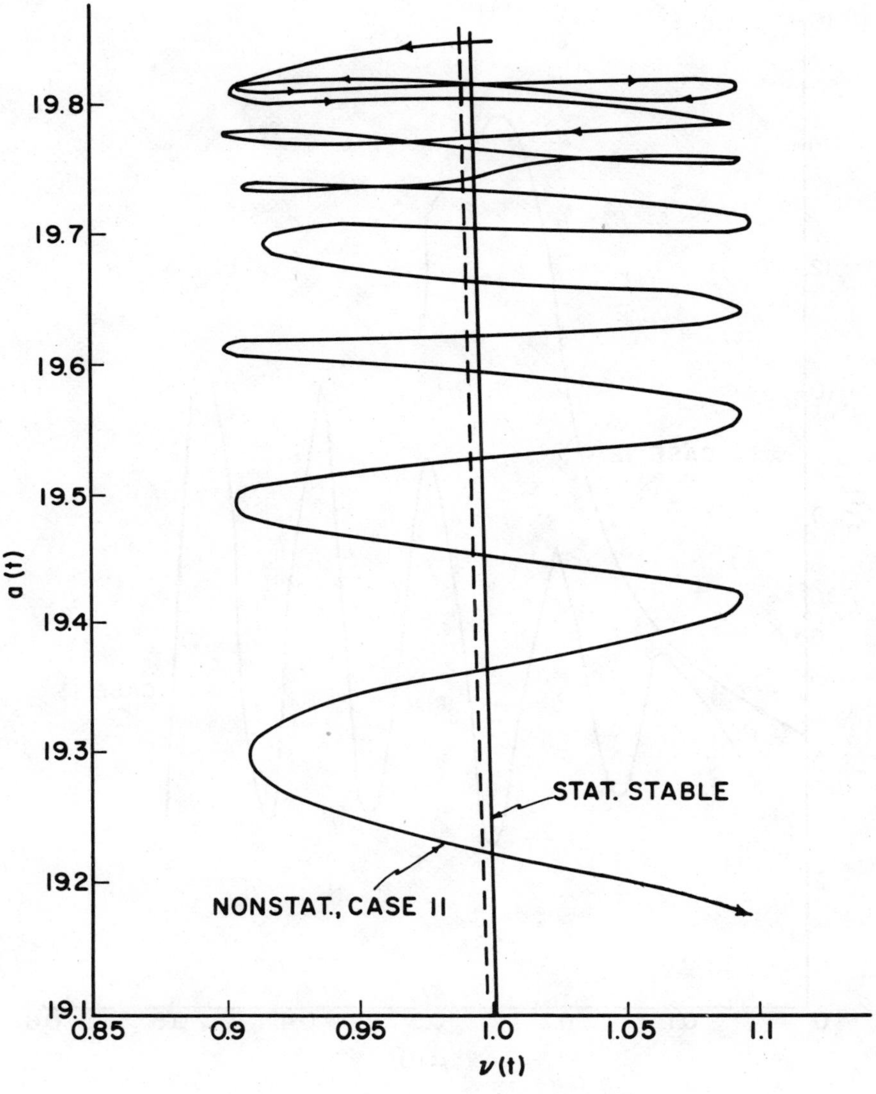

Fig. 8. Nonstationary Response of Column, $\nu = 1.00 - 0.1 \sin 2t$.

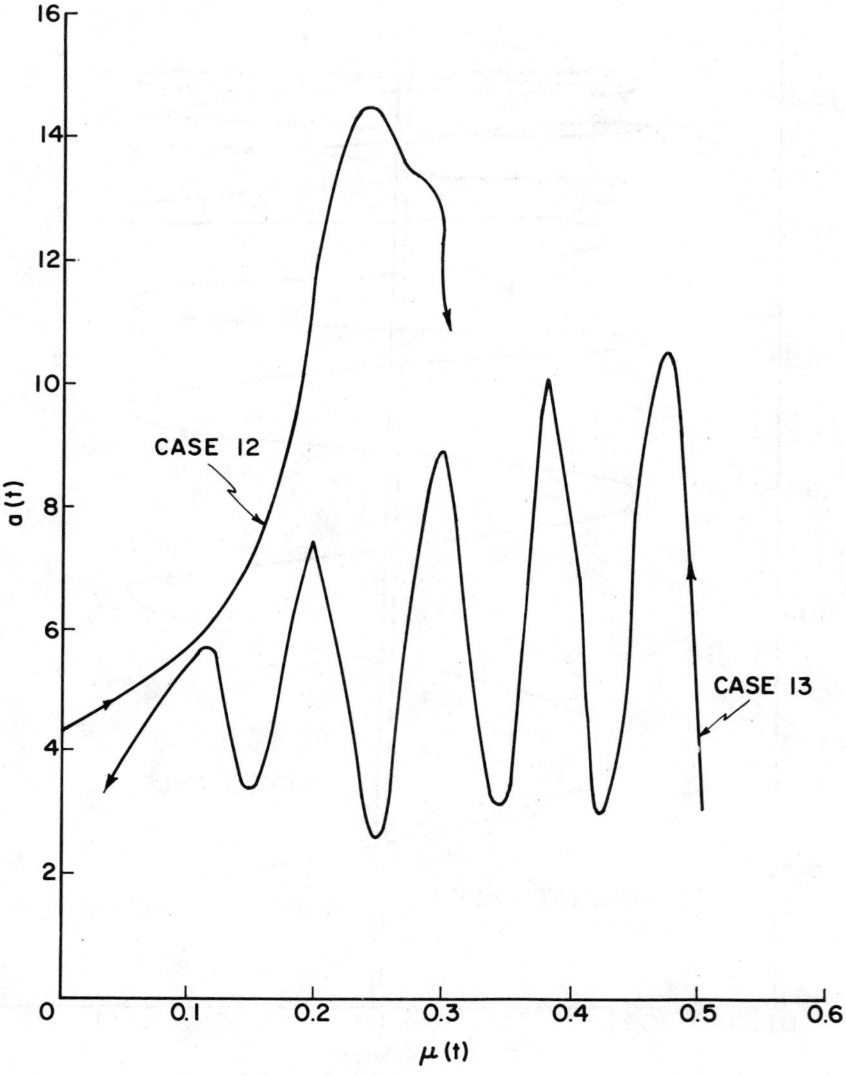

Fig. 9. Nonstationary Response of Column, $\mu = 0.01+0.01t$, case 12; $\mu = 0.5-0.01t$, case 13.

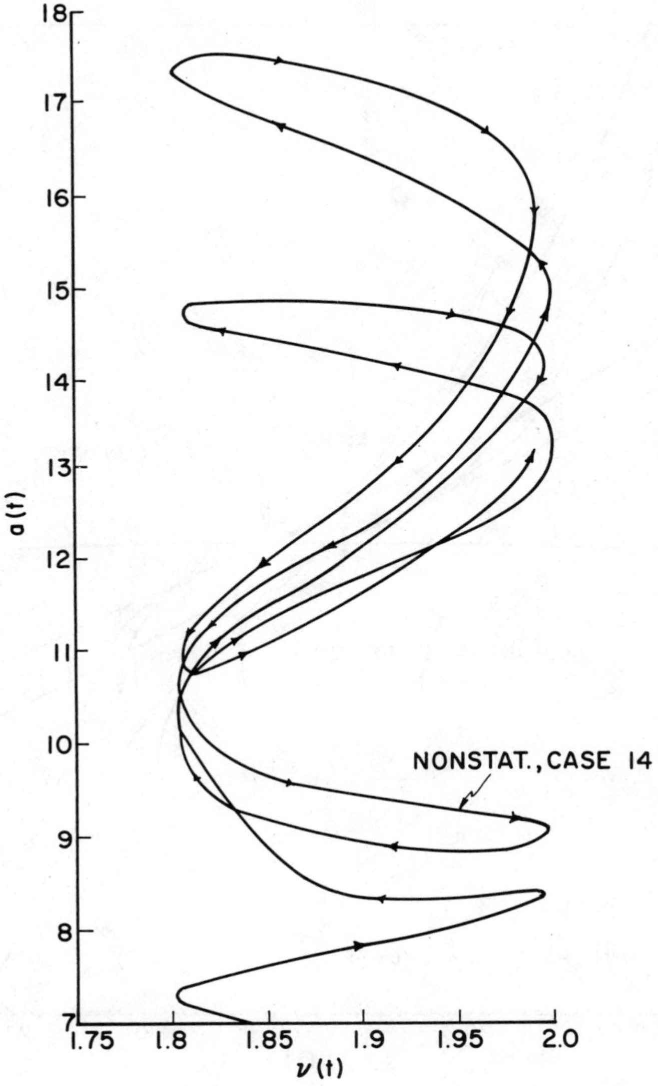

Fig. 10. Nonstationary Response of Column, $\nu = 1.90-0.15 \ln t$; $\mu = 0.01+0.01t$.

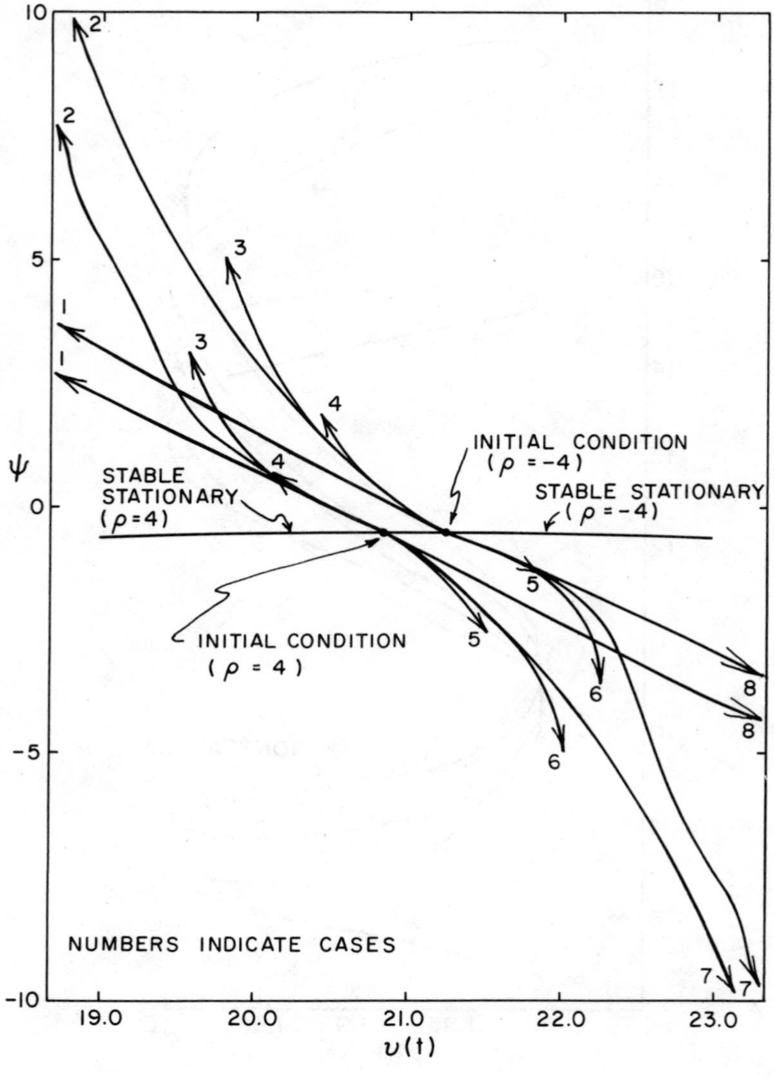

Fig. 11. Nonstationary Phase Angle Response for Nonlinear Inertial ($\rho = 4$) and Elastic ($\rho = -4$) Systems.

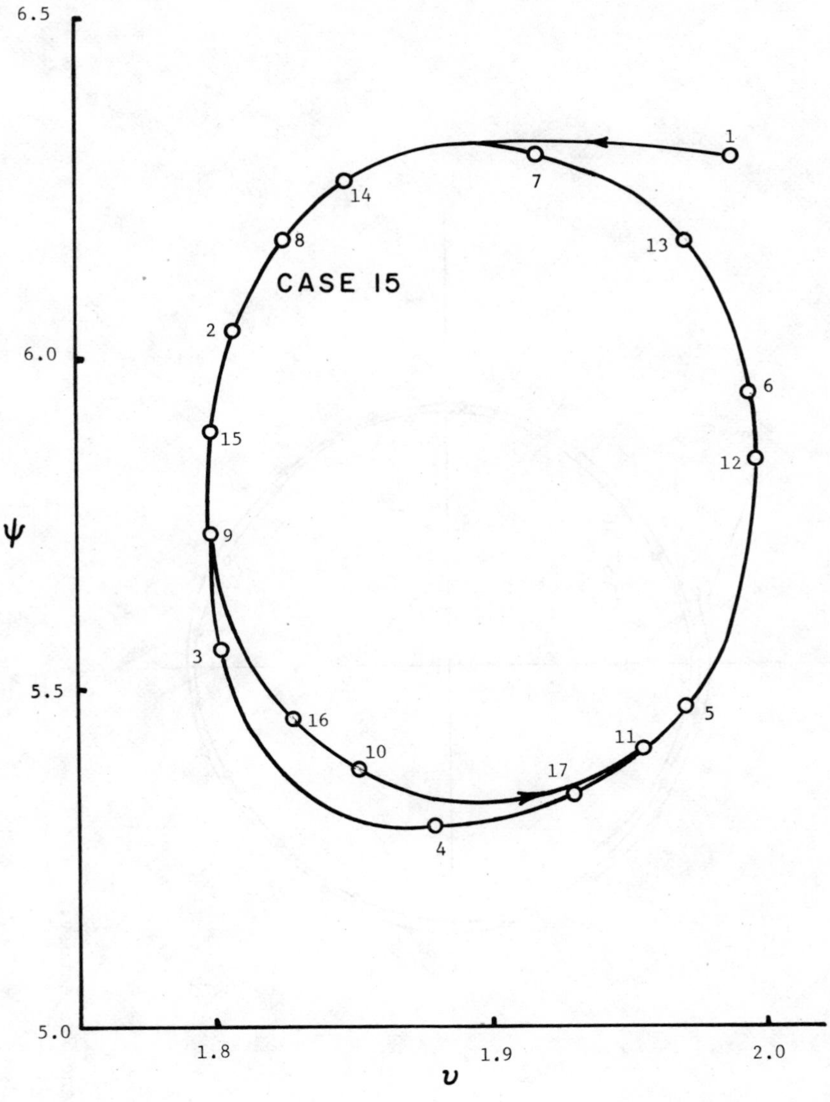

Fig. 12. Phase Angle v/s Sinosoidally Varying Frequency
$\nu(t) = 1.90-0.1 \sin t$.

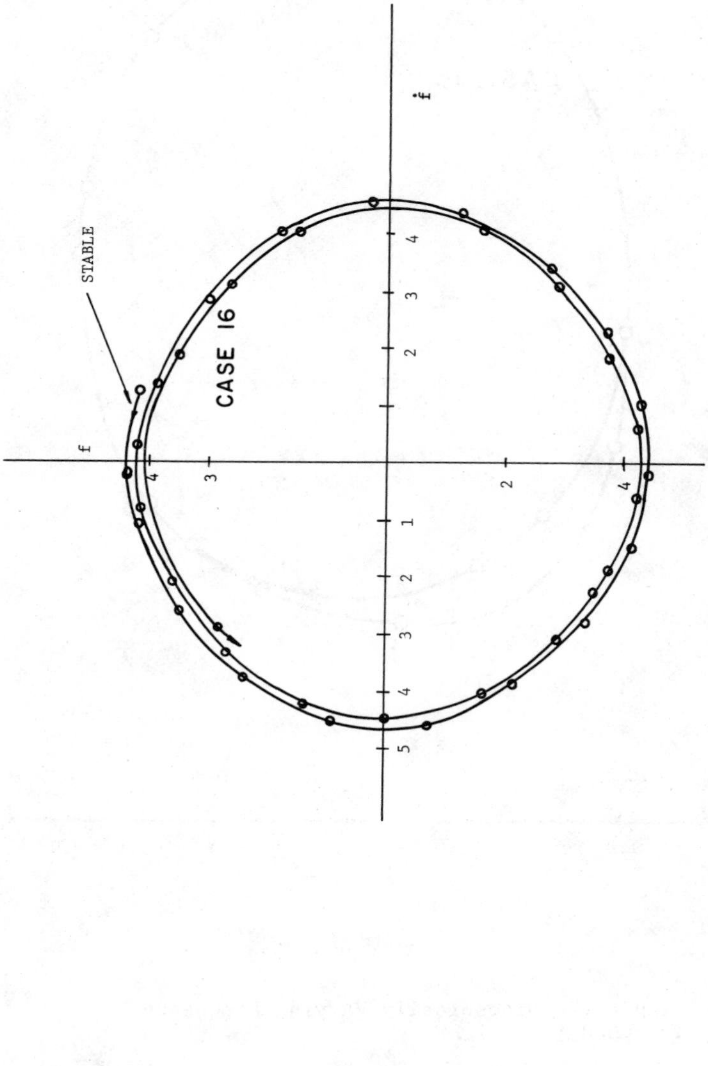

Fig. 13. Phase Plane Trajectory.

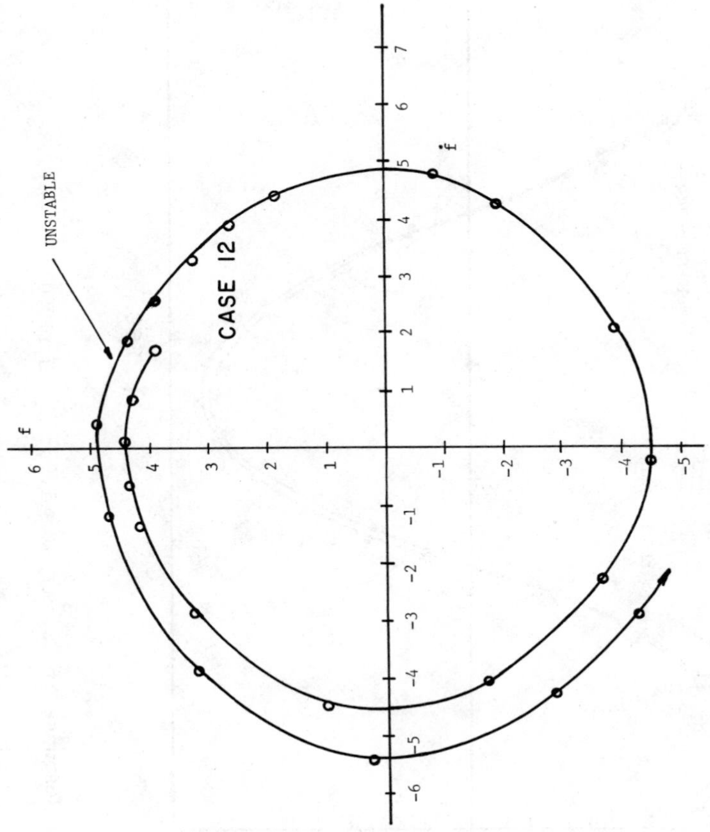

Fig. 14. Phase-Plane Trajectory, Case 12.

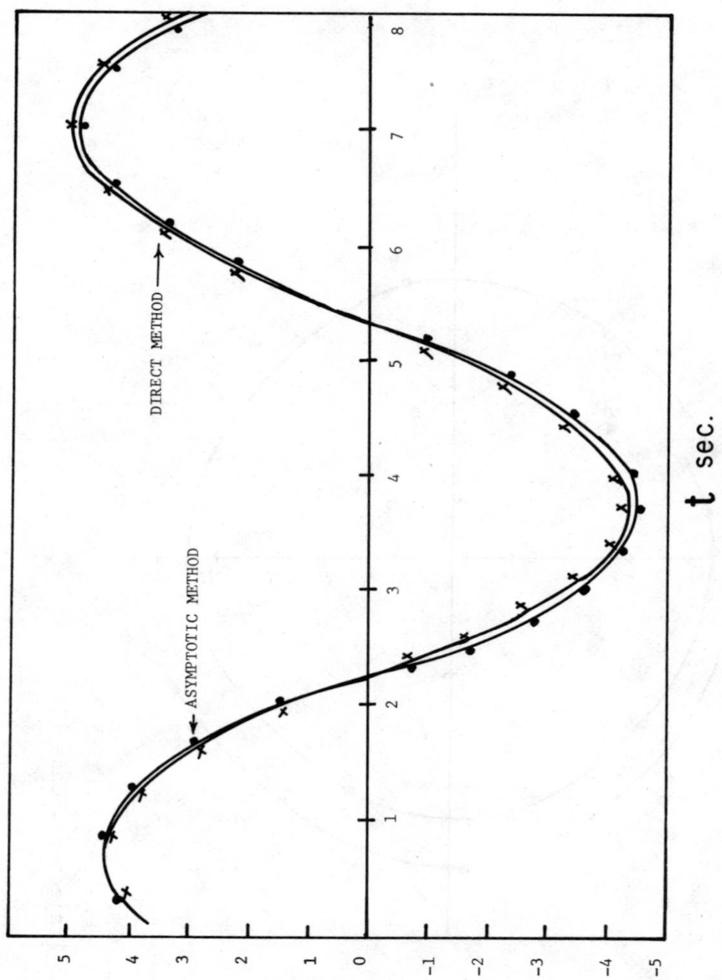

Fig. 15. Nonstationary Response of Column, $\nu = 1.95$, $\mu = 0.1+0.01t$.

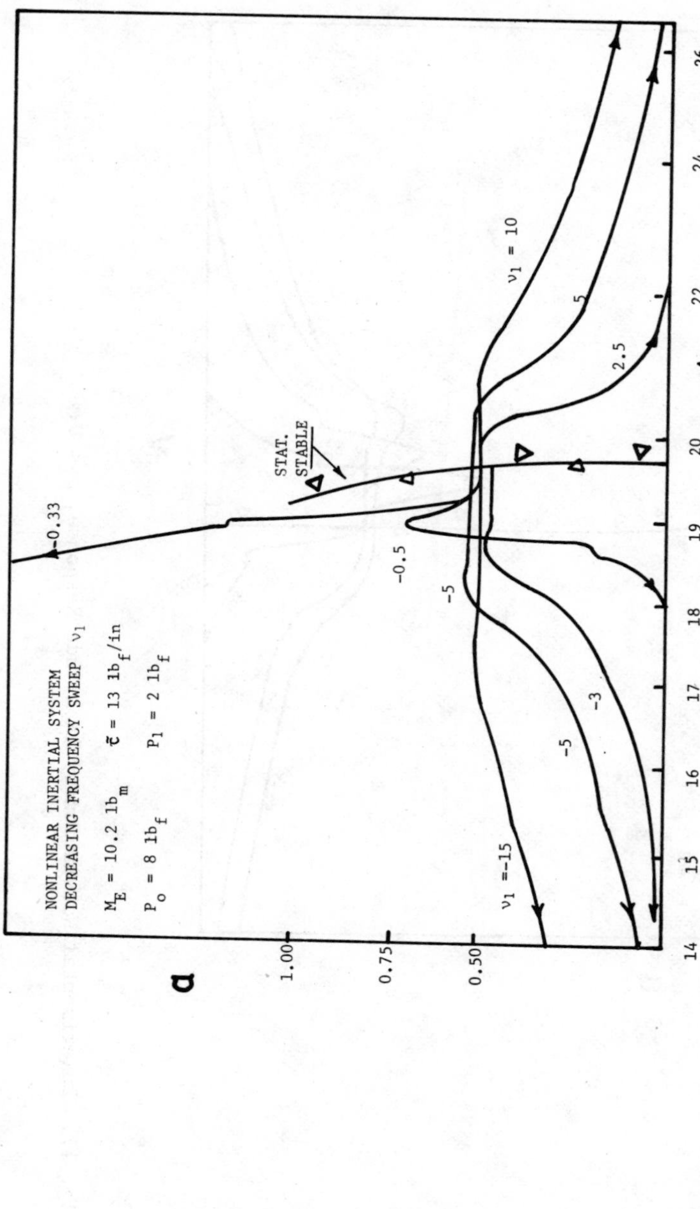

Fig. 16. Experimental Nonstationary Amplitude, $\rho > 0$.

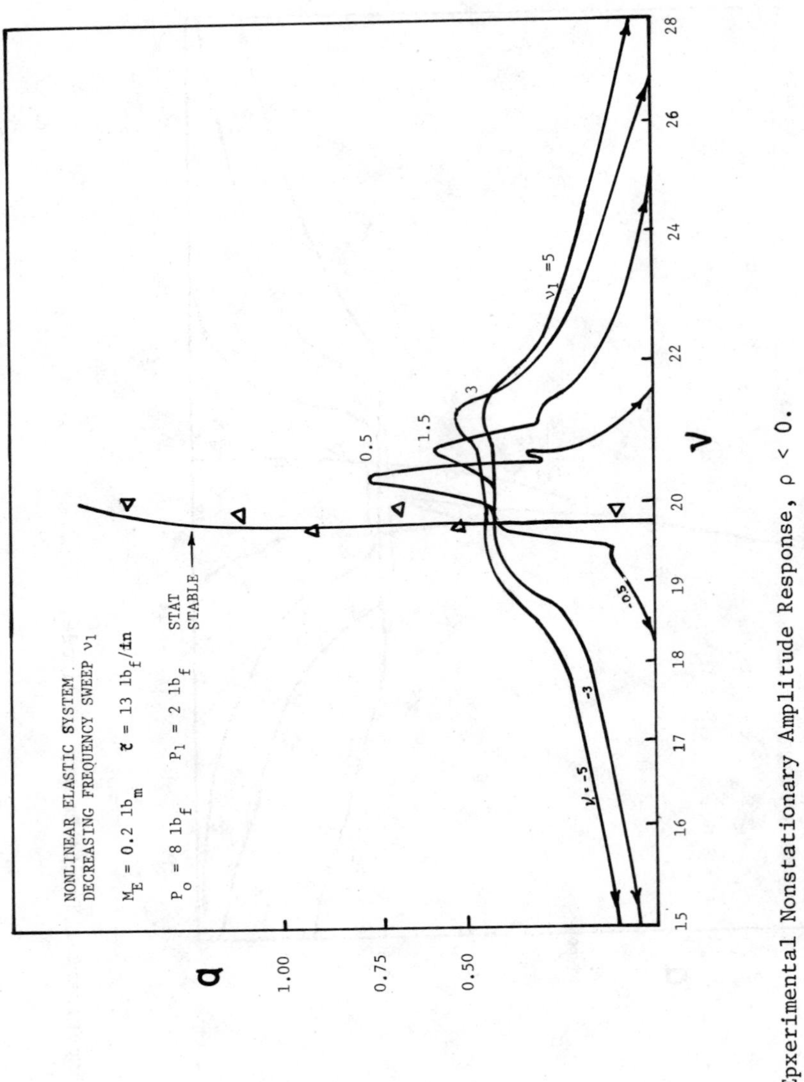

Fig. 17. Epxerimental Nonstationary Amplitude Response, $\rho < 0$.

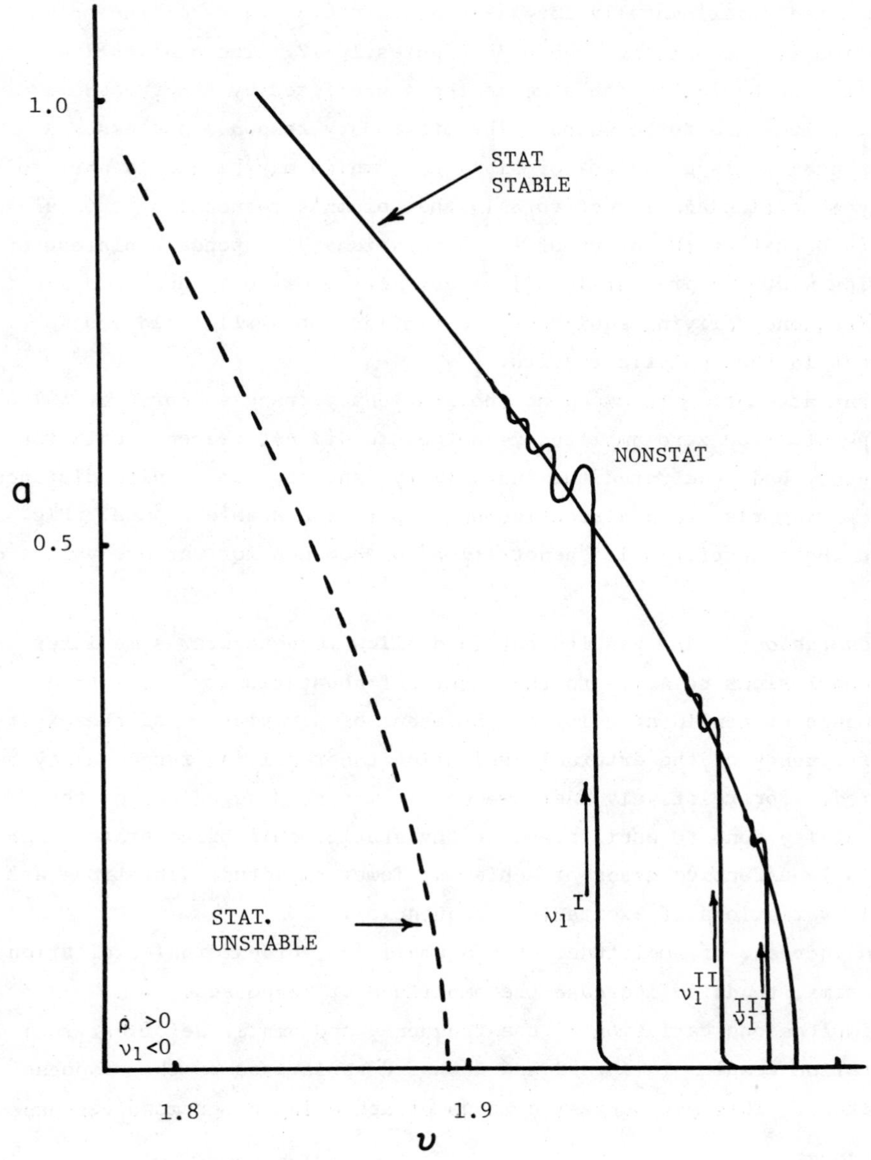

Fig. 18. Nonstationary Penetration Effect for Soft Spring System.

The column's stationary and nonstationary amplitude response was determined experimentally for $\rho > 0$ and $\rho < 0$. Traces of the actual experimental results are shown in Figures 16-17. The qualitative results are basically the same as those predicted by theory. Some observations are to be noted. The stationary response possesses a sharp peak at large values of amplitude, which may be due in part to instrumentation and is not totally the column's response. It is also observed that at the start of the nonstationary response a plateau of varying width is present in all cases. It seems to be due to a lag in the frequency driving equipment. A similar but smaller plateau is present in the analytic results.

When attempting to sweep up the stationary response curve at a low sweep rate from zero amplitude, the column did not respond until the frequency had penetrated the instability zone for some finite distance, thus giving rise to a discontinuous jump to the stable branch. Fig. 18 shows the characteristic "penetration" phenomenon for various values of ν_1.

Conclusions / The results obtained allow one to draw some interesting conclusions relative to the nature of nonstationary parametric responses of nonlinear columns. By means of a variation of the external frequency of the external excitation the resulting response may be lowered. For relatively fast sweeps, it may be dragged out of the instability zone to oscillate near the static equilibrium state. Particularly effective means of achieving lower amplitude vibrations are cyclic variations of excitation frequencies.

An increase of amplitude, even a small one, of external excitation with time, tends to increase the amplitude of responses.

Simultaneous variation of the frequency and amplitude of external excitation results in upward and downward variations of the response amplitude. This may suggest a means of achieving programmed responses.

REFERENCES

1. Lewis, F. M., "Vibration During Accleration Through a Critical Speed," ASME, Vol. 5, No. 23, 1932, p. 03-261.

2. Filippov, A. P., "Vibrations of Elastic Systems," Izd.AN. USSR (1956); AMR 10 (1957), Rev. 3191.

3. Mitropolskii, Y. A., Problems of the Asymptotic Theory of Nonstationary Vibrations, Daniel Davey and Company, New York, 1965.

4. Evenson, H. A., and Evan-Iwanowski, R. M., "Effect of Longitudinal Inertia Upon the Parametric Response of Elastic Columns," Journal of Applied Mechanics, 1966, pp. 969-976.

5. Evan-Iwanowski, R. M., "Nonstationary Vibrations of Mechanical Systems," Applied Mechanics Review, March, 1969, pp. 213-217.

6. Bolotin, V. V., The Dynamic Stability of Elastic Systems, Holden-Day, Inc., San Francisco, London, Amsterdam, 1964.

7. Den Hartog, J. P., Mechanical Vibrations, McGraw-Hill Book Company, Inc., (Fourth Edition), New York, 1956.

8. Sanford, W. F., "Analytical and Experimental Study of the Nonstationary Parametric Response of a Nonlinear Column," M.S. Thesis, Syracuse University, 1969, Syracuse, New York.

9. Kehagioglou, T., "Analytical Investigation of Parametrically Excited Column with Initial Geometric Imperfections and Nonlinearities in Nonstationary Mode," M.S. Thesis, Syracuse University, 1969, Syracuse, New York.

A COMPARISON OF INITIAL VELOCITIES FOR DYNAMIC INSTABILITY OF A SHALLOW ARCH

C. H. Popelar
The Ohio State University

G. M. Abraham
Bell Telephone Laboratories, Inc.

ABSTRACT

The dynamic stability of a simply supported, shallow sinusoidal arch subjected to a nearly symmetric impulsive load is studied. Upper and lower bounds for the critical initial velocity for snap-through and the initial velocity necessary to parametrically excite the unsymmetric mode are compared with the critical initial velocity obtained from direct numerical integration of the equations of motion. For ratios of the rise to thickness of the arch greater than approximately two the difference between the computed upper and lower bounds is appreciable and increased monotonically with this ratio. The critical value is found to be only a few percent greater than the lower bound.

LIST OF NOTATIONS

A	Cross sectional area
a_1, a_2	Generalized coordinates
E	Modulus of elasticity
e	Ratio of rise to radius of gyration
H	Initial rise of the arch at midspan
I	Moment of inertia
L	Distance between supports
P	Axial load
t	Time
v_0	Amplitude of initial velocity

V	Potential energy
V_0	Initial velocity parameter
x	Horizontal coordinate
y	Vertical coordinate
ε	Small parameter
μ	Small quantity
ρ	Radius of gyration
σ	Mass density
τ	Dimensionless time
ϕ	Phase angle

INTRODUCTION

Perhaps one of the simplest mathematical models which exhibits many of the characteristics common to the buckling of shells is the shallow arch. The distinguishing feature of the buckling of these arches, subjected to either static or dynamic loading, is that as the loading is increased a point is reached at which the arch abruptly assumes the inverted configuration, or the arch "snaps through." Even under static loading the actual snap-through is in reality a dynamic phenomenon. Extensive investigations of both the static and dynamic stability have been made. Since it is the latter that is of immediate concern and since it is not the purpose to present here an exhaustive survey of the literature, the reader is referred to papers by Gjelsvik and Bodner [1] Schreyer and Masur [2] and their references for discussions of the static stability of shallow arches.

In 1954 Hoff and Bruce [3] introduced the transverse inertia and investigated the snap-through of a shallow arch from a dynamic point of view. Since then the dynamic stability of shallow arches under various loading conditions has been investigated, for example see Humphreys [4] and Lock [5]. In the latter paper Lock showed that for a uniformly distributed step pressure an unsymmetric mode may be parametrically excited. McIvor and Popelar [6] found that a nearly symmetric impulsive load may parametrically excite only a single unsymmetric mode. Conditions for the initial growth of these modes are based upon linearized equations of motion, but whether or not the parametrically excited motion will lead to snap-through depends upon the discarded nonlinear terms. Computer solutions of the governing nonlinear differential equations were used to obtain the critical values.

A difficulty not restricted only to the aforementioned analyses [4, 5,6] is the lack of a precise definition of dynamic buckling or snap-through. By making use of a phase space Hsu [7] set forth a more rigorous definition of dynamic instability which not only includes the previous definitions but also eliminates the indecisiveness associated with them. According to Hsu [8] snap-through is possible if there exists more than one locally stable equilibrium point; of which one is referred to as the preferred configuration. For an impulsive loading the preferred configuration is the initial unstrained configuration. A further study by Hsu [9] of impulsively loaded arches revealed that for many clamped arches the undeformed state is the only locally stable equilibrium configuration and in particular for clamped parabolic and sinusoidal arches it is the only equilibrium configuration. Therefore within the preceding definition one is led to the astounding conclusion that no elastic snap-through can occur for these arches. For a simply supported sinusoidal arch there exist at most two locally stable equilibrium configurations. These correspond for impulsive loadings to the undeformed state and the mirror image of the configuration.

Hsu [10] also obtained sufficiency conditions for and against snap-through for a simply supported sinusoidal arch under a step pressure. These sufficiency conditions serve to establish upper and lower bounds for the critical load. The former condition is obtained by considering the local stability of the preferred equilibrium configuration. This yielded snap-through in the first mode. The latter condition is obtained by expanding the level surface of total energy until it comes into contact with an equilibrium point other than the preferred one. Since the kinetic energy vanishes at the equilibrium point, then the potential energy there is equal to the total energy, fixed by the initial conditions, and this establishes a lower bound. Since the lower bound is not less than about 85 percent of the upper bound, the critical value appears to be suitably bracketed.

In the preceding problem it was found that modes higher than the second did not influence the sufficiency conditions. A similar conclusion was reached by Hsu [7] for an impulsive loading. However, for most values of a geometric parameter the initial energy sufficient for symmetric snap-through is so much greater than the maximum amount which will insure stability against snap-through, that without further investigation the utility of these bounds is questionable. Identical results, but presented in terms of impulses, were obtained by Simitses [11]. Due to the complexity of this nonlinear phenomenon, the quality of these bounds can be assessed only with a computer or by tedious and laborious graphical techniques [12].

It is the purpose of this study to make a comparison of the critical initial velocity, determined by numerical integration of the equations of motion, with upper and lower bounds for the critical initial velocities, obtained from the previously mentioned sufficiency conditions, for an impulsively loaded, shallow sinusoidal arch. In addition, a comparison of these velocities with that necessary to produce parametric excitation of an unsymmetric mode is included. Through the use of phase trajectories a better qualitative description of dynamic snap-through is presented for, not only the case treated herein, but for other related problems.

Equations of Motion

In the sequel the discussion is restricted to a pinned-pinned, shallow arch that is initially unstressed and whose cross section is uniform (see Fig. 1). The governing nonlinear differential equation of motion [3] for the free, undamped elastic response is

$$EI\left(\frac{\partial^4 y}{\partial x^4} - \frac{\partial^4 y_0}{\partial x^4}\right) + P\,\frac{\partial^2 y}{\partial x^2} + \sigma A\,\frac{\partial^2 y}{\partial t^2} = 0 \qquad (1)$$

where

$$P = \frac{EA}{2L}\int_0^L \left[\left(\frac{\partial y}{\partial x}\right)^2 - \left(\frac{\partial y_0}{\partial x}\right)^2\right] dx \qquad (2)$$

is the axial force. As a consequence of the neglect of the longitudinal inertia this force is spatially constant. The flexural rigidity, extensional rigidity, and the mass density are denoted, respectively, by EI, EA and σ. For an impulsive loading which accelerates every particle of the arch to a finite velocity before any appreciable displacement takes place, the initial conditions are

$$y(x,0) = H \sin \frac{\pi x}{L} \qquad (3)$$

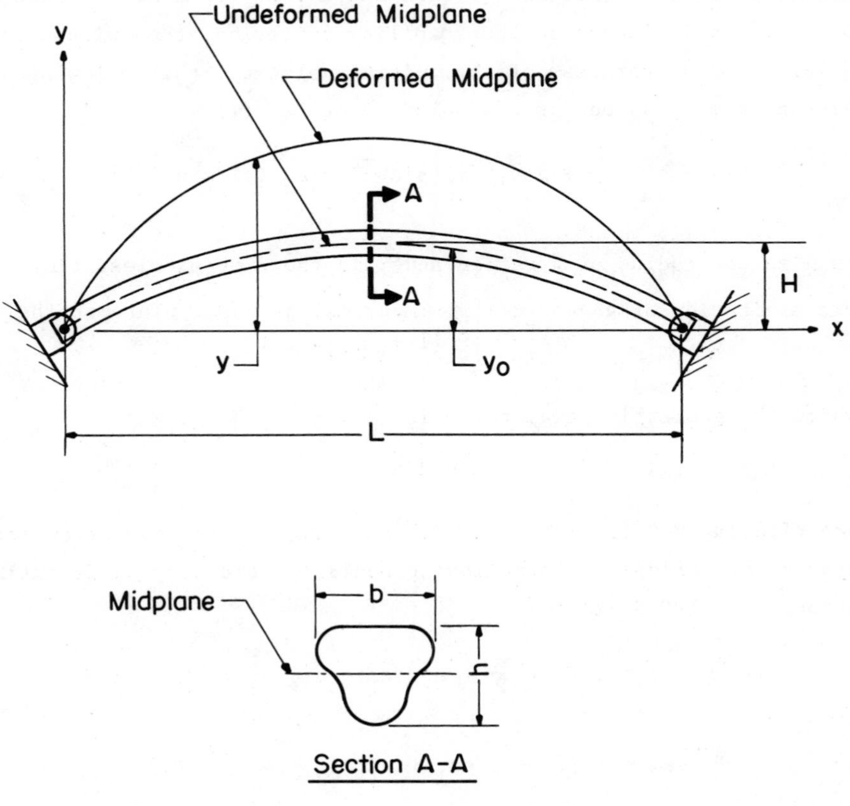

Fig. 1. Arch Geometry.

$$\frac{\partial y}{\partial t}(x,0) = v_0 \, f(x) \tag{4}$$

where f(x) can be expanded in a Fourier series.

It is possible to satisfy the boundary conditions and separate the variables in Eq. (1) with a Fourier sine series whose coefficients are functions of time. Since Hsu [7] has shown that modes higher than the second have no influence on the stability criterion, then with a certain loss of arbitrariness of the initial velocity, the following abbreviated form is taken for the solution of Eq. (1)

$$y = H \sin\frac{\pi x}{L} + \rho\left(a_1(\tau)\sin\frac{\pi x}{L} + a_2(\tau)\sin\frac{2\pi x}{L}\right) \tag{5}$$

where ρ is the radius of gyration and τ is the dimensionless time

$$\tau = \frac{\pi^2\rho}{L^2}\left[\frac{E}{\sigma}\left(1+\frac{e^2}{2}\right)\right]^{1/2} t \tag{6}$$

in which the geometric parameter e is

$$e = H/\rho \; . \tag{7}$$

Substituting Eq. (5) into Eqs. (1) and (2), one achieves from the separation of variables the following nonlinear ordinary differential equations

$$\left(1+\frac{e^2}{2}\right)\ddot{a}_1 = -\left(1+\frac{e^2}{2}+a_2^2\right)a_1 - e\left(\frac{3}{4}a_1^2 + a_2^2\right) - \frac{a_1^3}{4} \tag{8}$$

$$\left(1+\frac{e^2}{2}\right)\ddot{a}_2 = -\left(16 + 2\,ea_1 + a_1^2\right)a_2 - 4\,a_2^3 \tag{9}$$

where the dot denotes differentiation with respect to τ. In view of Eqs. (3), (4) and (5) the initial conditions for a nearly symmetric initial velocity with a slight unsymmetric perturbation are

$$a_1(0) = a_2(0) = 0$$

$$\dot{a}_1(0) = \frac{v_0 L^2}{\pi^2\rho^2}\left[\frac{E}{\sigma}\left(1+\frac{e^2}{2}\right)\right]^{-1/2} \equiv V_0 \tag{10}$$

$$\dot{a}_2(0) = \mu V_0, \quad \mu << 1.$$

Initial Growth of the Unsymmetric Motion

In the initial phase of the motion a_2 is small compared to a_1 since its initial values Eq. (10) are assumed small. As a consequence in this early response only terms of first degree in a_2 in Eqs. (8) and (9) need be retained. Eq. (8) assumes the simplified form

$$\ddot{z} + z = - \varepsilon(3z^2 + z^3) \tag{11}$$

in which

$$z = a_1/e \tag{12}$$

$$\varepsilon = \frac{e^2}{4 + 2e^2}, \quad 0 \leq \varepsilon < 1/2 \tag{13}$$

According to the method of Krylov and Bogoliubov (see, for example Minorsky [13]) a solution to Eq. (11) is taken as a power series in ε

$$z = B \cos \psi + \varepsilon U(B,\psi) + \varepsilon^2 U_2(B,\psi) + \cdots \tag{14}$$

where the U's are periodic functions of period 2π, and B and ψ satisfy

$$\begin{aligned} \dot{B} &= \varepsilon X(B) + \varepsilon^2 X_2(B) + \cdots \\ \dot{\psi} &= 1 + \varepsilon Y(B) + \varepsilon^2 Y_2(B) + \cdots \end{aligned} \tag{15a,b}$$

If Eqs. (14) and (15) are substituted into Eq. (11) and if coefficients of like powers of ε are equated, then the differential equation governing the first order solution is

$$\frac{d^2U}{d\psi^2} + U = - 3B^2 \cos^2 \psi - B^3 \cos^3 \psi + 2X(B) \sin \psi + 2BY(B) \cos \psi \tag{16}$$

Since the function U is assumed to be periodic of period 2π, it may be expanded in a Fourier series with coefficients that are arbitrary functions of B. When this series is substituted into Eq. (16) and coefficients of like harmonics are equated, there results

$$\begin{aligned} Y(B) &= \frac{3}{8} B^2 \\ X(B) &= 0 \end{aligned} \tag{17}$$

Substituting Eq. (17) into Eq. (15) and integrating, one concludes

$$B = \text{const.} \tag{18}$$

$$\psi = \left(1 + \frac{3}{8}\varepsilon B^2\right)\tau + \phi \tag{19}$$

where ϕ is a constant. It can be shown that the first approximate solution of Eq. (11) is

$$z = B\cos\psi - \frac{3}{2}\varepsilon B^2 \tag{20}$$

The initial conditions Eq. (10) are fulfilled provided B and ϕ satisfy

$$V_0 = -eB\left(1 + \frac{3}{8}\varepsilon B^2\right)\left(1 - \frac{9}{4}\varepsilon^2 B^2\right)^{1/2}$$

$$\phi = \tan^{-1}\frac{-V_0}{\frac{3}{2}\varepsilon e B^2\left(1 + \frac{3}{8}\varepsilon B^2\right)} \tag{21a,b}$$

The appropriate root for B must be chosen such that it approaches the linear solution $-V_0/e$ as ε approaches zero.

If Eq. (20) is introduced into Eq. (9), then after some grouping of terms Hill's equation

$$a_2'' + \Omega^2[1 + C\cos\psi + D\cos 2\psi]a_2 = 0 \tag{22}$$

is obtained. The prime in Eq. (22) denotes differentiation with respect to ψ and

$$C = \frac{8B - 12\varepsilon B^3}{64/e^2 + (2-12\varepsilon)B^2 + 9\varepsilon^2 B^4}$$

$$D = \frac{2B^2}{64/e^2 + (2-12\varepsilon)B^2 + 9\varepsilon^2 B^4} \tag{23a-c}$$

$$\Omega^2 = \frac{\varepsilon[64/e^2 + (2-12\varepsilon)B^2 + 9\varepsilon^2 B^4]}{1 + \frac{3}{8}\varepsilon B^2}$$

Whether or not there will be growth of the unsymmetric mode is governed by the instability or stability of the trivial solution $a_2 = 0$ of Eq. (22). According to Bolotin [14] the first approximation of boundaries between regions of stability and instability of the trivial solution of Eq. (22) is

$$1 \pm \frac{1}{2} C - \frac{1}{\Omega^2} = 0 \tag{24}$$

$$1 \pm \frac{1}{2} D - \frac{1}{4\Omega^2} = 0. \tag{25}$$

The approximation amounts to considering the effect of each harmonic in Eq. (22) separately. Equation (24) is a quartic in B with e appearing as a parameter and Eq. (25) is a quadratic in B^2. The latter equation can be solved explicitly for B; whereas Eq. (24) must be solved numerically after the parameter e is specified. In either case the desired value is the root with the smallest absolute value. The critical value of V_0 which will produce growth of the unsymmetric mode is obtained by substituting these values of B and e into Eq. (21).

Bounds for the Critical Velocity

If a locally stable equilibrium point other than the one corresponding to the undeformed configuration exists, then dynamic snap-through is said to be possible. Conversely, if the undeformed equilibrium position is the only one that is locally stable, then no dynamic snap-through will occur. A direct consequence of the assumption of no damping in the present problem is the total energy is a constant and it is equal to the initial kinetic energy. Upper and lower bounds for the critical initial velocity can be found by considering the equilibrium points and an expanding level surface of the total energy enclosing the undeformed equilibrium configuration. The method is essentially that presented by Hsu [7].

Let S be the largest level surface of total energy in the phase space that encloses only the equilibrium point of the undeformed configuration. If the phase trajectory remains in the region enclosed by the surface S, then the system is stable. This will be the case provided the total energy is less than that on S. The first opportunity for the phase trajectory to leave the region bounded by S occurs when the total energy surface makes contact with another equilibrium point. When this occurs the initial kinetic energy is equal to the potential energy of this point and a lower bound for the critical initial velocity is established. This is an extension of the lower bound proposed by Hoff and Bruce [3] for a two-degree-of-freedom system.

On the other hand, it is known in this case that, if the motion is restricted to be symmetric, snap-through will occur when the expanding level surface makes contact with another equilibrium point or, alternately, the separatrix. Therefore, an upper bound is obtained by equating the initial kinetic energy to the potential energy of the saddle point.

In the present problem the equilibrium points in the phase space are those points for which the right-hand sides of Eqs. (8) and (9) vanish simultaneously with $\dot{a}_1$ and $\dot{a}_2$. These points[1] are

$$0 \le e < 4 \qquad a_1 = 0, \quad a_2 = 0 \tag{26}$$

$$4 \le e < \sqrt{18} \qquad \begin{aligned} & a_1 = 0, \quad a_2 = 0 \\ & a_1 = -\frac{3}{2} e + \frac{1}{2} (e^2-16)^{1/2}, \quad a_2 = 0 \\ & a_1 = -\frac{3}{2} e - \frac{1}{2} (e^2-16)^{1/2}, \quad a_2 = 0 \end{aligned} \tag{27a-c}$$

$$e \ge \sqrt{18} \qquad \begin{aligned} & a_1 = 0, \quad a_2 = 0 \\ & a_1 = -\frac{3}{2} e + \frac{1}{2} (e^2-16)^{1/2}, \quad a_2 = 0 \\ & a_1 = -\frac{3}{2} e - \frac{1}{2} (e^2-16)^{1/2}, \quad a_2 = 0 \\ & a_1 = -\frac{4e}{3}, \quad a_2 = \frac{1}{3} (2e^2-36)^{1/2} \\ & a_1 = -\frac{4e}{3}, \quad a_2 = -\frac{1}{3} (2e^2-36)^{1/2}. \end{aligned} \tag{28a-e}$$

The locally stable equilibrium points are Eqs. (26), (27a,c) and (28a,c). Since there is only one locally stable equilibrium point for $e < 4$, then there will be no snap-through as defined here. For an arch with a rectangular cross section with $e = 4$ the arch has a rise only slightly greater than its thickness. It is questionable whether or not such an arch would physically exhibit snap-through.

---

1. See [7] for the location and classification of equilibrium points when the solution is taken in the form of an infinite Fourier series.

If Eqs. (8) and (9) are multiplied, respectively, by da_1 and da_2 and if the resulting sum is integrated with the initial conditions Eq. (10), then there results

$$\frac{1}{2}\left(1 + \frac{e^2}{2}\right)(\dot{a}_1^2 + \dot{a}_2^2) + V(a_1, a_2) = \frac{1}{2}\left(1 + \frac{e^2}{2}\right) V_0^2 \tag{29}$$

where the dimensionless potential energy $V(a_1, a_2)$ is

$$V(a_1, a_2) = \frac{a_1^2}{2}\left[1 + \frac{1}{8}(2e + a_1)^2\right] + a_2^2\left[8 + ea_1 + \frac{1}{2}a_1^2 + a_2^2\right]. \tag{30}$$

In Eq. (29) μ^2 has been neglected compared to unity. Obviously, Eq. (29) is a statement of the conservation of mechanical energy.

To obtain an upper bound for the critical initial velocity only symmetric deformation is considered. The level surface of total energy enclosing the equilibrium point Eq. (27a) is expanded until it comes into contact with another equilibrium point which will be Eq. (27b) or Eq. (28b). At this equilibrium point it follows from Eq. (29) that

$$(V_0)_U^2 = \frac{1}{32(2 + e^2)}\left[-3e + \sqrt{e^2-16}\right]^2\left[8 + e^2 + e\sqrt{e^2-16}\right], \quad e > 4 \tag{31}$$

where $(V_0)_U$ denotes an upper bound for the critical initial velocity.

To obtain a lower bound the procedure is the same except the deformation is no longer restricted to be symmetric. For $4 \le e < \sqrt{18}$ the first equilibrium point with which the expanding level surface comes into contact is Eq. (27b); whereas, for $e \ge \sqrt{18}$ it can be shown that contact is made first with the equilibrium points Eq. (28d,e). A lower bound for the critical initial velocity $(V_0)_L$, identical to [3] and [7], is

$$(V_0)_L^2 = \frac{1}{32(2 + e^2)}\left[-3 + \sqrt{e^2-16}\right]^2\left[8 + e^2 + e\sqrt{e^2-16}\right], \quad 4 \le e \le \sqrt{18} \tag{32}$$

$$(V_0)_L^2 = \frac{32}{2 + e^2}\left(\frac{1}{3}e^2 - 2\right), \quad e \ge \sqrt{18} \tag{33}$$

A comparison of Eqs. (31) and (32) shows that for $4 \le e \le \sqrt{18}$ the upper and lower bounds are identical. Therefore, for this very limited range of geometries the critical initial velocity is given by Eq. (32)

and the snap-through is symmetric. It is observed that $(V_0)_L$ has an asymptote of $(32/3)^{1/2}$ whereas $(V_0)_U$ increases monotonically with e. Therefore potentially large differences between $(V_0)_L$ and $(V_0)_U$ may exist for representative values of e.

To determine the critical initial velocity Eqs. (8) and (9) were numerically integrated by the Hamming's modified predictor-corrector method for the initial conditions Eq. (10) with $\mu = 0.01$ while V_0 was systematically varied. The numerical integration was continued for a dimensionless time of 50. Comparisons of the results of the numerical integration and the preceding analysis follow in the next section.

Results and Discussion

Equations (24) and (25) were solved numerically for the smallest absolute value of B and V_0 was obtained from Eq. (21a). For the range of the geometric parameter e considered, $B < 1$ and V_0 is given with a good approximation by $V_0 = - eB$. This implies that for an investigation of the initial growth of the unsymmetric mode or for an analysis of infinitesimal stability the symmetric motion may be approximated with a sufficient degree of accuracy by the linear response. A plot of V_0 versus e for Eqs. (24) and (25) is presented in Fig. 2. In the e-V_0 plane Eq. (24) governs the larger regions of stability and instability. A characteristic of parametric resonance in the absence of linear viscous damping is that for certain values of a parameter the disturbance required to produce instability can be made as near zero as desired. Such is the case in the present problem for $e \approx \sqrt{30}$ and $e \approx \sqrt{130}$.

Also plotted in Fig. 2 are Eqs. (31), (32) and (33). Over the range of the geometric parameter for which the theory can reasonably thought to be applicable, the lower bound for the critical initial velocity is greater than the velocity necessary to produce growth of the unsymmetric mode. For $4 \lesssim e \lesssim \sqrt{18}$ the upper and lower bounds, as noted earlier, are coincident and they, of course, represent the critical value. However, over a significant range of the geometric parameter e the difference between the bounds is large and the utility of these bounds at this point is open to question. This is in striking contrast to the rather closeness of the bounds, the lower bound never being less than about 85 percent of the upper bound, for a step pressure of infinite

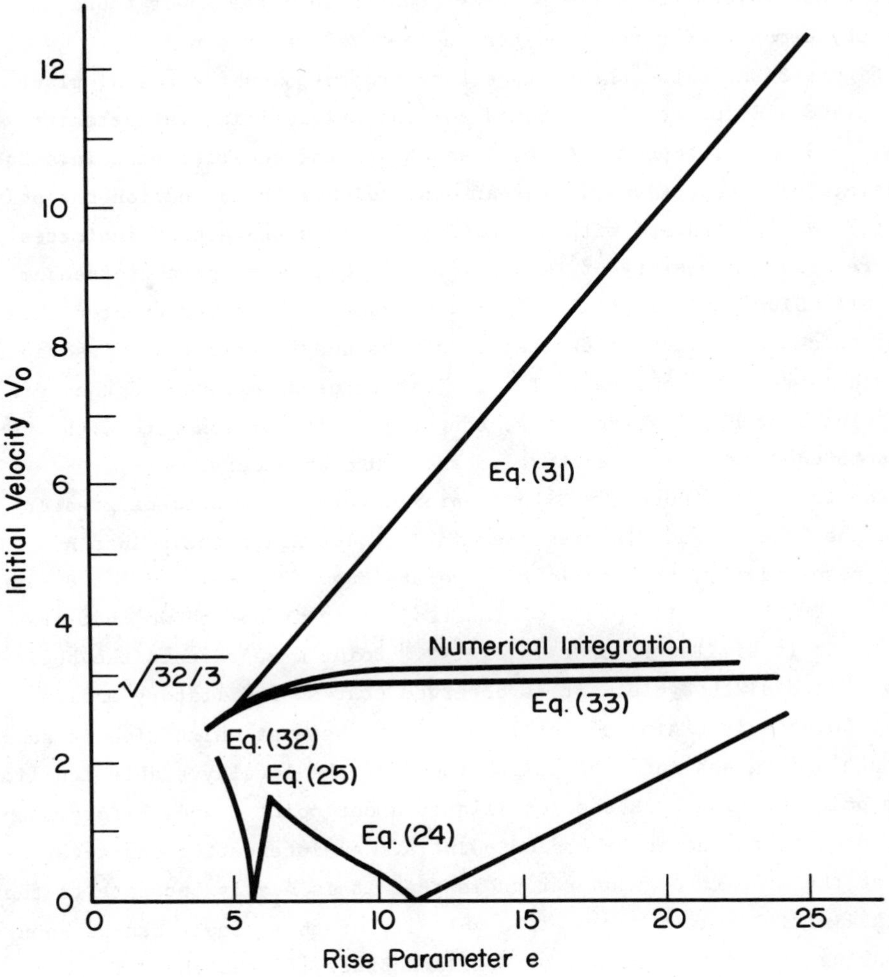

Fig. 2. Comparison of Initial Velocities.

duration [10,11].[2] The critical initial velocity obtained by direct numerical integration of Eqs. (8) and (9) is also shown. It is seen that these values are a few percent greater than the lower bound and thereby demonstrate the need for an improved upper bound.

Figure 3 shows the phase trajectory projected on the a_1, a_2 plane for e = 8 and for the lower bound for the critical initial velocity $(V_0)_L = 3.06$. The points A, B, D and E are the equilibrium points Eqs. (28a,b,d,e), respectively. The arrows indicate the direction the point $\left(a_1(\tau),\ a_2(\tau)\right)$ travels with increasing τ. This trajectory indicates the relative complexity of the motion for this two-degree-of-freedom system. Since this initial velocity is about four times greater than that to cause parametric excitation of the unsymmetric mode, its rapid growth is readily apparent. The trajectory never extends to the left of point D or E; in other words, the trajectory remains within the region bounded by S and therefore no snap-through occurs.

The trajectory for $V_0 = 3.15$, approximately three percent greater than the lower bound, is presented in Fig. 4. Again the points A-E are, respectively, the equilibrium points Eqs. (28 a-e). For the sake of clarity the initial phase of the trajectory is not shown, but its character is similar to that in Fig. 3. Point m represents the beginning of the sixth cycle. It is observed that an oscillatory motion about point A is exhibited until the ninth cycle at which time it snaps through and passes into the neighborhood of the locally stable equilibrium point C. The arch then oscillates about point C once before snapping back to the neighborhood of point A. An interesting characteristic of the snap-through on return is that it is nearly opposite to that of the initial snap-through. The validity of this result can be seen by making use of the analogy of Hoff and Bruce [3] that Eqs. (8) and (9) also govern the motion of a point mass of mass $(1 + e^2/2)$ sliding on a smooth surface whose elevation is described by the potential function Eq. (30). Contour lines of this surface for e = 8 are also included in [3]. After having snapped through and returned the arch simply continues this process. For larger initial velocities the

2. However, it should be noted that the upper bound of [10,11] is the quasistatic buckling load and that Lock [5] found for e > 8.5 that the critical step pressure is greater than this bound by as much as 32 percent.

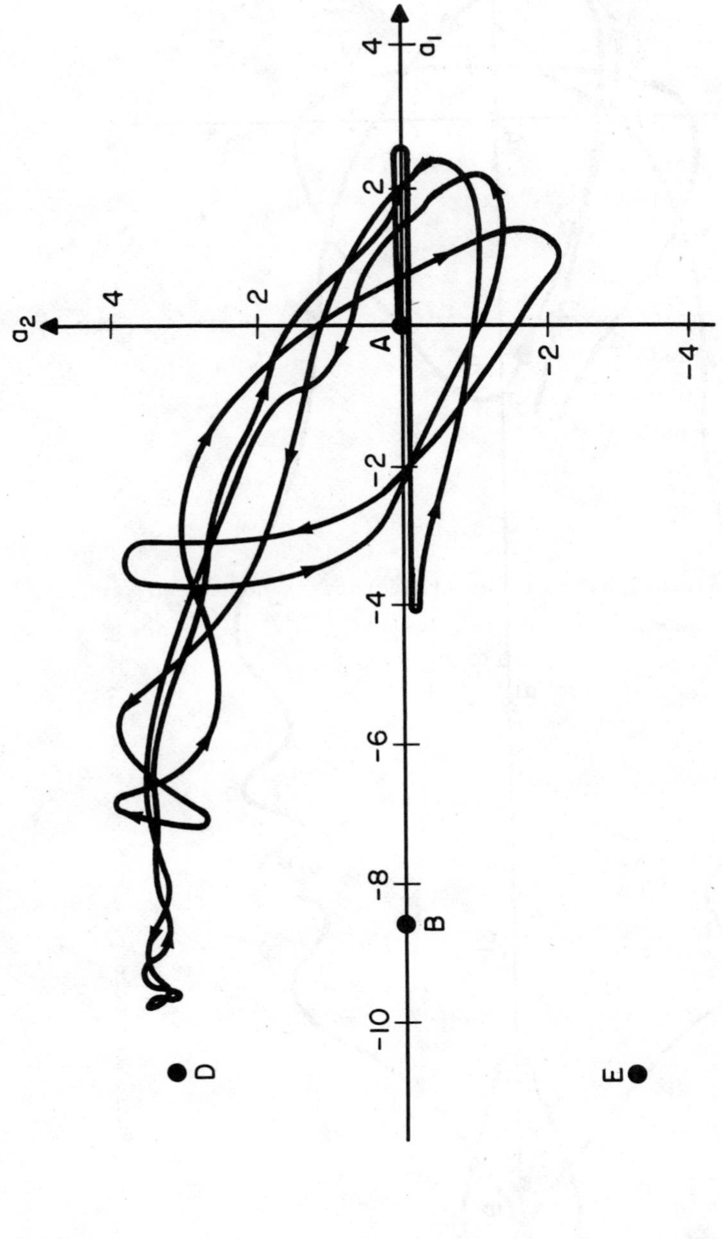

Fig. 3. Phase Trajectory, e = 8, V_o = 3.06.

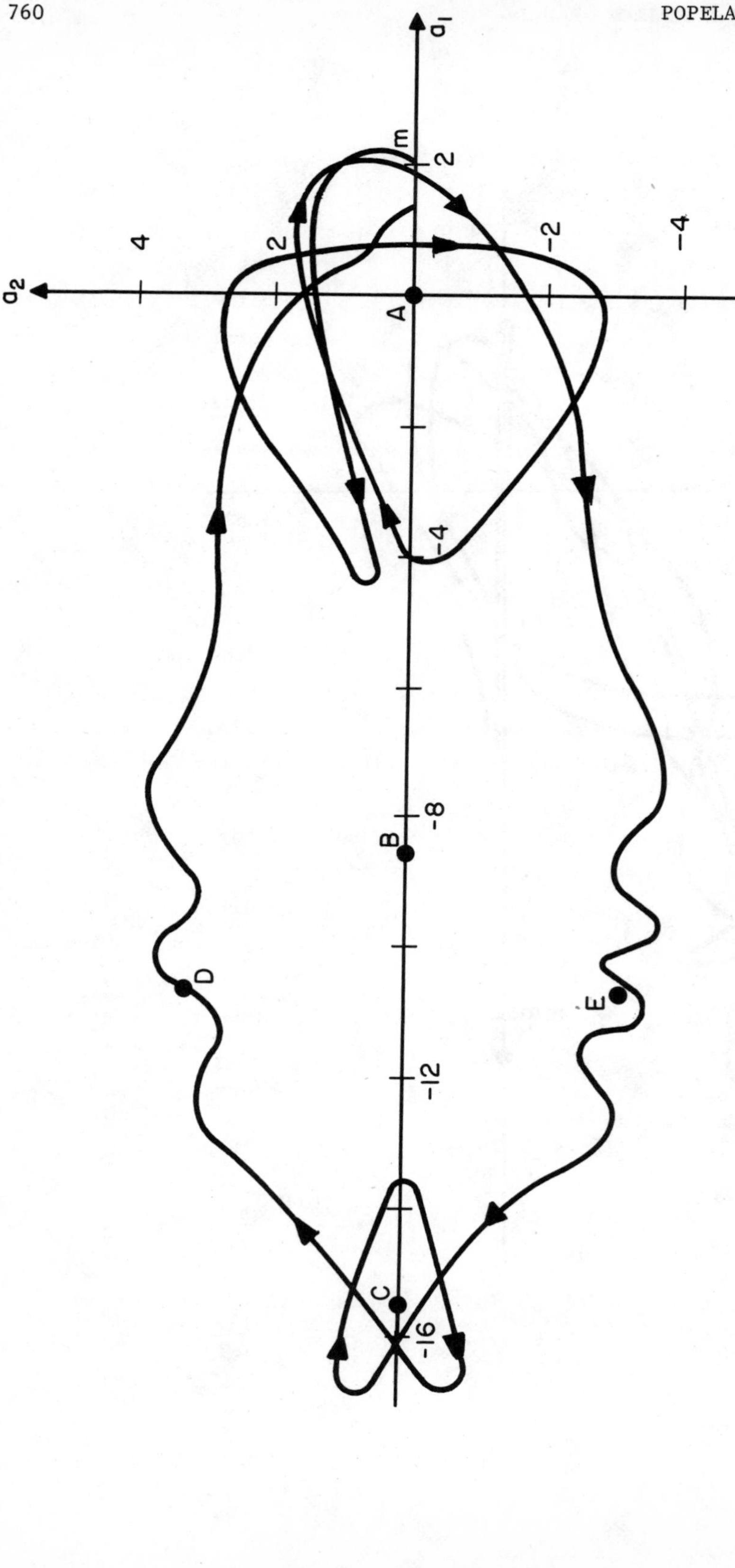

Fig. 4. Phase Trajectory, $e = 8$, $V_o = 3.15$.

snap-through occurs in a shorter time with a more direct path leading towards point C.

The trajectories of a viscoelastic material, e.g., see Huang and Nachbar [15], or in the presence of damping are readily envisioned now in view of Fig. 4. If sufficient energy is dissipated after snap-through and the subsequent oscillation(s) about point C such that the total energy is less than the potential energy of point D or E, then the arch will ultimately come to rest in the symmetric configuration of point C. On the other hand, if enough energy remains to make the return trip, then the arch may after sufficient dissipation of energy resume its original configuration. This phenomenon has been observed experimentally [4,16] in other related structures where plastic deformation was predominately the mode of dissipation of energy.

Conclusions

The initial growth of the unsymmetric mode is produced by parametric resonance. For initial velocities necessary to produce this growth the symmetric motion is described adequately by the linear reponse. The parametric excitation of the unsymmetric mode occurs for an initial velocity less than a lower bound for the critical velocity for snap-through.

For $4 \leq e \leq \sqrt{18}$ the computed upper and lower bounds coincide and the snap-through is symmetric. However, to the right of this limited interval the upper and lower bounds diverge with the difference becoming very large for representative values of e. In the present problem the critical initial velocity determined by numerical integration of the equations of motion is only a few percent greater than the lower bound. Therefore, it is the upper bound that needs improving. For $e < 4$ there is no snap-through and unsymmetric snap-through occurs for $e > \sqrt{18}$.

REFERENCES

1. Gjelsvik, A. and Bodner, S. R., "Energy Criterion and Snap Buckling of Arches," Journal of the Engineering Mechanics Division, Proceedings of the American Society of Civil Engineers, Vol. 88, No. EM2, 1962, pp. 17-36.

2. Schreyer, H. L. and Masur, E. F., "Buckling of Shallow Arches," Journal of the Engineering Mechanics Division, Proceedings of the American Society of Civil Engineers, Vol. 92, No. EM4, 1966, pp. 1-19.

3. Hoff, N. J. and Bruce, V. G., "Dynamic Analysis of the Buckling of Laterally Loaded Flat Arches," Journal of Mathematics and Physics, Vol. 32, 1954, pp. 276-288.

4. Humphreys, J. S., "On Dynamic Snap Buckling of Shallow Arches," AIAA Journal, Vol. 4, 1966, pp. 878-886.

5. Lock, M. H., "The Snapping of a Shallow Sinusoidal Arch under a Step Pressure Load," AIAA Journal, Vol. 4, 1966, pp. 1249-1256.

6. McIvor, I. K. and Popelar, C. H., "Dynamic Stability of a Shallow Cylindrical Shell," Journal of the Engineering Mechanics Division, Proceedings of the American Society of Civil Engineers, Vol. 93, No. EM3, 1967, pp. 109-127.

7. Hsu, C. S., "On Dynamic Stability of Elastic Bodies with Prescribed Initial Conditions," International Journal of Engineering Science, Vol. 4, 1966, pp. 1-21.

8. Hsu, C. S., "The Effects of Various Parameters on the Dynamic Stability of a Shallow Arch," Journal of Applied Mechanics, Vol. 34, No. 2, Transactions of American Society of Mechanical Engineers, Vol. 89, Series E, 1966, pp. 349-358.

9. Hsu, C. S., "Equilibrium Configurations of a Shallow Arch of Arbitrary Shape and their Dynamic Stability Character," International Journal of Non-Linear Mechanics, Vol. 3, 1968, pp. 113-136.

10. Hsu, C. S., "Stability of Shallow Arches Against Snap-Through under Timewise Step Loads," Journal of Applied Mechanics, Vol. 35, No. 1, Transactions of American Society of Mechanical Engineers, Vol. 91, Series E, 1968, pp. 31-39.

11. Simitses, G. J., "Dynamic Snap-Through Buckling of Low Arches and Shallow Spherical Caps," Ph.D. Dissertation, Stanford University, Palo Alto, 1965.

12. Kauderer, Hans, Nichtlineare Mechanik, Springer-Verlag, Berlin, 1958, pp. 593-612.

13. Minorsky, N., Nonlinear Oscillations, D. Van Nostrand Co., Inc., New York, 1962.

14. Bolotin, V. V., The Dynamic Stability of Elastic Systems, Holden-Day, Inc., San Francisco, 1964.

15. Huang, N. C. and Nachbar, W., "Dynamic Snap-Through of Imperfect Viscoelastic Shallow Arches," Journal of Applied Mechanics, Vol. 35, No. 2, Transactions of American Society of Mechanical Engineers, Vol. 91, Series E, 1968, pp. 289-296.

16. Burns, J. J., Popelar, C. H. and Foral, R. F., "Experimental Buckling of Thin Shells under Transient Pressure Pulse Loading," presented to The American Rocket Society Launch Vehicles: Structures and Material Conference, April 3-5, 1962, Phoenix, Arizona, Paper No. 2425-62.

AXIAL-SYMMETRIC DEFORMATIONS OF A RUBBER-LIKE CYLINDER UNDER INITIAL STRESS

C. T. Sun
Iowa State University of Science and Technology

ABSTRACT

The objective of this paper is to formulate and solve the problem of axial-symmetric deformations of a rubber-like solid cylinder under initial stress. The analysis is based on the general theory of mechanics of incremental deformations established by M. A. Biot [1]. The initial stress is uniformly applied at both ends. By introducing a displacement potential function ϕ the field equation is derived. The solution of the field equation is given in terms of modified Bessel functions in r and trigonometric functions of z. The results show that instability does not occur under finite compressive initial stress. The radial displacement at the cylindrical surface is then calculated as a function of the extension ratio in the axial direction and the slenderness ratio of the cylinder. The numerical results indicate that the rigidity of the cylinder increases as the tensile initial stress increases, and decreases as the compressive initial stress increases. Finally it is pointed out that the solution can be extended to a hollow cylinder under initial stress in the axial direction.

LIST OF NOTATIONS

a_o, $2L_o$	Radius and length of the cylinder
a, 2L	Radius and length of the cylinder in the state of initial stress
A,B,C,Q	Incremental elastic coefficients
S_{ij}	Initial stress tensor
s_{ij}	Incremental stress tensor
s	Mean normal stress

P	Initial stress in the axial direction
r,z;	Cylindrical coordinates
u,w	Incremental displacement components
W	Strain energy density in the unstressed state
k	Constant
D_1, D_2	Constants of integration
q	Magnitude of the boundary stress
Δf_r, Δf_z	Incremental boundary stresses in r and z directions respectively
U	Amplitude of the maximum radial displacement when P is different from zero
U_o	Amplitude of the maximum radial displacement when P = 0
α	Constant
β	Constant
ω	Local rotation
ε_{ij}	Incremental strain tensor
λ_r, λ_θ	Extension ratios in the radial and tangential directions, respectively
λ	Extension ratio in the axial direction
μ_o	Shear modulus in the unstressed state
ϕ, $\overline{\phi}$	Displacement potentials
γ	A constant inversely proportional to the slenderness ratio L/a of the cylinder
Δ	A function of γ and λ

INTRODUCTION

To the author's knowledge there are three different approaches in studying the problems of continuous media under initial stress. The classical method, which was established by A. E. Green, R. S. Rivlin and R. T. Shield [2], is to apply the theory of tensor invariants to an elastic medium to derive field equations which govern small deformations superposed on a state of finite strain. As pointed out by M. A. Biot [3], this method is handicapped by an intricate formalism which obscures the physical interpretation. Evident to this is the fact that only a few problems have been solved by means of this approach. Another method used to investigate the initial stress problems was derived by V. V. Novozhilov [4]. The differential equations and the boundary conditions were obtained by using a perturbation technique on the non-linear field equations of the theory of elasticity. By using this method, several instability problems were studied by S. Tang [5], A. D. Kerr and S. Tang [6] and S. Tang [7]. This method is very useful for certain types of problems; however, the author believes that its application is limited to elastic media which are homogeneous and isotropic in the unstressed state.

One of the basic difficulties arising from the initial stress in a continuous medium is that the additional stress, or incremental stress, depends not only on the incremental strain, a purely physical origin, but also on the local rigid body rotation, a purely geometric origin. The method provided by the theory of tensor invariants does not separate the physics from geometry. In order to overcome this difficulty, M. A. Biot [1] introduced the concept of incremental deformations. A small region of the medium is considered to undergo a pure deformation followed by a rigid body rotation. Thus a local rotation is introduced which, in general, varies from point to point and provides a separation of the purely geometric properties of the deformation field (the rigid body rotation) from those which depend on the physics of the material (strain components). Consequently the incremental stress is also defined relative to these locally rotated axes. The general equations governing the dynamics and stability of solids as well as fluids under initial stress are formulated in terms of these quantities. The application of this approach is very broad. It does not require that the medium be elastic or isotropic but is applicable to anisotropic, visco-elastic or plastic media. By using this method, M. A. Biot investigated the problems in the areas such as rubber elasticity [8], internal gravity waves in a fluid [9], and textronic folding in geodynamics [10].

In this paper we first formulate the problem of axial-symmetric deformations of a rubber-like cylinder under uniform initial stress. The initial stress can be applied on the curved surface $r = a$, on both ends $z = \pm L$, or simultaneously. The medium is assumed to be incompressible with Neo-Hookean type strain energy density.

The problem is formulated by the use of the general theory of mechanics of incremental deformations. From the condition of incompressibility, a displacement potential function is introduced. The field equation governing the incremental axial-symmetric deformations superposed on the specified state of initial stress is then derived.

For the purpose of illustration, the problem of axial-symmetric deformations of a solid cylinder under initial stress in the axial direction is solved. The solution shows that instability does not occur under finite compressible initial stress. In order to see the effect of the initial stress, the radial displacement at the surface r = a is calculated as a function of initial stress P in the axial direction and the slenderness ratio of the cylinder. As expected, the numerical results show that the rigidity of the cylinder increases as the tensile initial stress increases and decreases as the compressive initial stress increases. The solution can also be extended to a hollow cylinder under uniform initial stress in the axial direction.

Derivation of the Field Equation

Let us consider a rubber-like solid cylinder of length $2L_o$ and radius a_o as shown in Fig. 1. The cylinder is subjected to the following state of initial stresses

$$S_{rr} = S_{\theta\theta} = S_1$$
$$S_{zz} = S_2 \qquad (1)$$
$$S_{r\theta} = S_{\theta z} = S_{zr} = 0$$

where S_1 and S_2 are constants. It is very easy to see that Eq. (1) satisfies the equations of equilibrium.

We shall investigate the effect of initial stress on the displacement and stress fields of this cylinder under axial-symmetric perturbations from the equilibrium state.

Because of axial-symmetry, the nonvanishing components of incremental displacement vector are the radial displacement u and the axial displacement w which are functions of r and z. The incremental strain components are

$$\varepsilon_{rr} = \frac{\partial u}{\partial r} \qquad \varepsilon_{\theta\theta} = \frac{u}{r}$$
$$\varepsilon_{zz} = \frac{\partial w}{\partial z} \qquad \varepsilon_{rz} = \frac{1}{2}\left(\frac{\partial u}{\partial z} + \frac{\partial w}{\partial r}\right) \qquad (2)$$

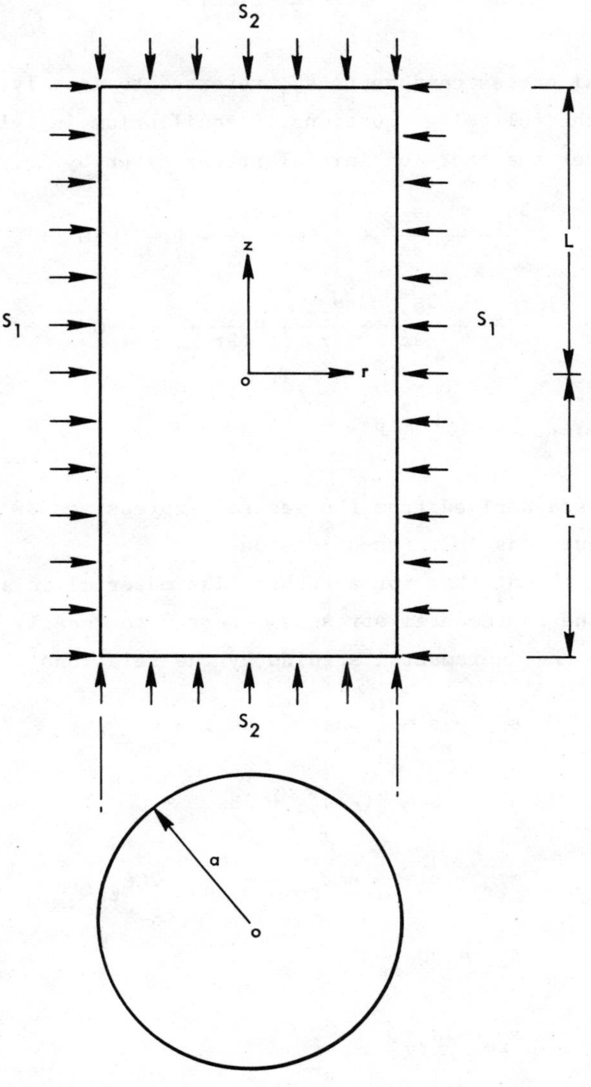

Fig. 1. Solid Cylinder under Initial Stress.

The local rotation is

$$\omega = \frac{1}{2}\left(\frac{\partial u}{\partial z} - \frac{\partial w}{\partial r}\right) \tag{3}$$

The incremental stress components s_{ij} referred to locally rotated axes must satisfy the following equations of equilibrium in cylindrical coordinates (under the state of initial stress given by Eq. (1)):

$$\begin{aligned} &\frac{\partial s_{rr}}{\partial r} + \frac{\partial s_{rz}}{\partial z} + \frac{s_{rr} - s_{\theta\theta}}{r} - P\frac{\partial \omega}{\partial z} = 0 \\ &\frac{\partial s_{rz}}{\partial r} + \frac{\partial s_{zz}}{\partial z} + \frac{s_{rz}}{r} - P\left(\frac{\partial \omega}{\partial r} + \frac{\omega}{r}\right) = 0 \end{aligned} \tag{4}$$

where

$$P = S_{rr} - S_{zz}$$

Equations (4) are derived from the general expressions of incremental equilibrium equations in three-dimensions.[1]

It has been shown[2] that for a rubber-like material in a state of initial stress the incremental stresses referred to locally rotated axes are related to the incremental strains by the relations

$$\begin{aligned} s_{rr} - s &= \frac{1}{3}(2A\varepsilon_{rr} - B\varepsilon_{\theta\theta} - C\varepsilon_{zz}) \\ s_{\theta\theta} - s &= \frac{1}{3}(-A\varepsilon_{rr} + 2B\varepsilon_{\theta\theta} - C\varepsilon_{zz}) \\ s_{zz} - s &= \frac{1}{3}(-A\varepsilon_{rr} - B\varepsilon_{\theta\theta} + 2C\varepsilon_{zz}) \\ s_{rz} &= 2Q\varepsilon_{rz} \\ s_{z\theta} &= s_{r\theta} = 0 \end{aligned} \tag{5}$$

$$s = \frac{1}{3}(s_{rr} + s_{\theta\theta} + s_{zz}) \tag{6}$$

where A, B, and C are the incremental elastic coefficients and Q is the incremental shear modulus. They are, in general, functions of the

1. See Eq. (7.42) p. 50 of [1].
2. See Eq. (8.20) p. 99 of [1].

initial stresses and initial strains. M. A. Biot has shown[3] that for rubber-like materials, A, B, and C are given by

$$A = \lambda_r \frac{\partial W}{\partial \lambda_r} + \lambda_r^2 \frac{\partial^2 W}{\partial \lambda_r^2} - \lambda_r \lambda_\theta \frac{\partial^2 W}{\partial \lambda_\theta^2}$$

$$B = \lambda_\theta \frac{\partial W}{\partial \lambda_\theta} + \lambda_\theta^2 \frac{\partial^2 W}{\partial \lambda_\theta^2} - \lambda_r \lambda_\theta \frac{\partial^2 W}{\partial \lambda_r^2} \qquad (7)$$

$$C = \lambda_r \lambda_\theta \frac{\partial^2 W}{\partial \lambda_r \partial \lambda_\theta}$$

where W represents the strain energy density of the medium in the original unstressed state and λ_r and λ_θ represent the extension ratios in the radial and tangential directions respectively. The extension ratio in the axial direction λ_z is related to λ_r and λ_θ from the condition of incompressibility of rubber-like materials, i.e.,

$$\lambda_r \lambda_\theta \lambda_z = 1 \qquad (8)$$

For an isotropic medium in the unstressed state, the incremental shear modulus Q is given by [11]

$$Q = \frac{1}{2}(S_{zz} - S_{rr}) \frac{\lambda_z^2 + \lambda_r^2}{\lambda_z^2 - \lambda_r^2} \qquad (9)$$

For a rubber-like medium the strain energy density W is a function of three extention ratios. It takes the form

$$W = \frac{\mu_o}{2} (\lambda_r^2 + \lambda_\theta^2 + \lambda_z^2 - 3) \qquad (10)$$

where μ_o is the shear modulus of the medium in the unstressed state. By substituting λ_z from the incompressibility condition as expressed in Eq. (8) into Eq. (10) and then in turn into Eq. (7), we obtain

$$A = 2\mu_o \lambda_r^2$$

$$B = 2\mu_o \lambda_\theta^2 \qquad (11)$$

$$C = 2\mu_o \lambda_z^2$$

---

3. See Eq. (8.13) p. 98 of [1].

The finite stress-strain relations for an incompressible rubber-like material are given by[4]

$$S_{rr} - S_{\theta\theta} = \mu_o(\lambda_r^2 - \lambda_\theta^2)$$
$$S_{\theta\theta} - S_{zz} = \mu_o(\lambda_\theta^2 - \lambda_z^2) \qquad (12)$$
$$S_{zz} - S_{rr} = \mu_o(\lambda_z^2 - \lambda_r^2)$$

Substituting $S_{rr} - S_{\theta\theta} = 0$ and $S_{zz} - S_{rr} = -P$ from Eq. (1) into Eq. (12) we obtain

$$\lambda_r = \lambda_\theta$$
$$P = \mu_o(\lambda_r^2 - \lambda_z^2) \qquad (13)$$

Taking into account of the incompressibility condition in Eq. (8), Eq. (13) can be written as

$$\lambda_r^2 = \lambda_\theta^2 = \frac{1}{\lambda_z} = \frac{1}{\lambda}$$
$$P = \mu_o(\frac{1}{\lambda} - \lambda^2) \qquad (14)$$

where $\lambda = \lambda_z$ represents the extension ratio in the axial direction.

By using Eqs. (12) and (14) the expressions of A, B, C and Q can be simplified as follows:

$$A = B = 2\mu_o \frac{1}{\lambda}$$
$$C = 2\mu_o\lambda^2 \qquad (15)$$
$$Q = \frac{1}{2}\mu_o(\frac{1}{\lambda} + \lambda^2)$$

Eqs. (14) and (15) we can also express Q and P in terms of A and C:

$$P = \mu_o(\frac{1}{\lambda} - \lambda^2) = \frac{1}{2}(A - C)$$
$$Q = \frac{1}{2}\mu_o(\frac{1}{\lambda} + \lambda^2) = \frac{1}{4}(A + C) \qquad (16)$$

4. See Eq. (8.45) p. 104 of [1].

It is worthwhile to mention that, in the case of absence of the initial stresses, i.e., $S_{rr} = S_{\theta\theta} = S_{zz} = 0$ or, in the case under uniform hydrostatic stress, i.e., $S_{rr} = S_{\theta\theta} = S_{zz} = S$, we have

$$\begin{aligned} &\lambda = 1 \\ &A = B = C = 2\mu_o \\ &Q = \mu_o \end{aligned} \tag{17}$$

The condition of incompressibility in the state of incremental deformations requires that

$$\varepsilon_{rr} + \varepsilon_{\theta\theta} + \varepsilon_{zz} = 0 \tag{18}$$

By using the condition in Eq. (18) and Eq. (15), the incremental stress-strain relations in Eq. (5) assume the following form

$$\begin{aligned} s_{rr} &= s + A\varepsilon_{rr} + \frac{1}{3}(A - C)\varepsilon_{zz} \\ s_{\theta\theta} &= s + A\varepsilon_{\theta\theta} + \frac{1}{3}(A - C)\varepsilon_{zz} \\ s_{zz} &= s + \frac{1}{3}(A + 2C)\varepsilon_{zz} \\ s_{rz} &= \frac{1}{2}(A + C)\varepsilon_{rz} \end{aligned} \tag{19}$$

Now let us introduce a displacement potential ϕ such that

$$\begin{aligned} u &= -\frac{1}{r}\frac{\partial\phi}{\partial z} \\ w &= \frac{1}{r}\frac{\partial\phi}{\partial r} \end{aligned} \tag{20}$$

From the incremental strain displacement relation in Eq. (2) we see that the condition of incompressibility in Eq. (18) is identically satisfied by virtue of Eq. (20). For the sake of convenience we write Eq. (20) in a slightly different form:

$$\begin{aligned} u &= -\frac{\partial\overline{\phi}}{\partial z} \\ w &= \frac{\partial\overline{\phi}}{\partial r} + \frac{\overline{\phi}}{r} \end{aligned} \tag{21}$$

where

$$\overline{\phi} = \frac{\phi}{r} \tag{22}$$

Introducing this function $\overline{\phi}$ into Eqs. (2), (3), (19) and (4) respectively, leads, after suitable eliminations, to the equations

$$\frac{\partial s}{\partial r} - \frac{\partial}{\partial z}\left[\frac{1}{12}(5A + C - 6P)\left(\frac{\partial^2\overline{\phi}}{\partial r^2} + \frac{1}{r}\frac{\partial\overline{\phi}}{\partial r} - \frac{\overline{\phi}}{r^2}\right) + \frac{1}{4}(C + A - 2P)\frac{\partial^2\overline{\phi}}{\partial z^2}\right] = 0 \tag{23}$$

and

$$\frac{\partial s}{\partial z} + \frac{1}{12}(5C + A + 6P)\frac{\partial^2}{\partial z^2}\left(\frac{\partial\overline{\phi}}{\partial r} + \frac{\overline{\phi}}{r}\right) + \frac{1}{4}(C + A + 2P)\frac{\partial}{\partial r}\left(\frac{\partial^2\overline{\phi}}{\partial r^2} + \frac{1}{r}\frac{\partial\overline{\phi}}{\partial r} - \frac{\overline{\phi}}{r^2}\right) + \frac{1}{4}(C + A + 2P)\frac{1}{r}\left(\frac{\partial^2\overline{\phi}}{\partial r^2} + \frac{1}{r}\frac{\partial\overline{\phi}}{\partial r} - \frac{\overline{\phi}}{r^2}\right) = 0 \tag{24}$$

Differentiating Eq. (23) with respect to z and Eq. (24) with respect to r we obtain

$$\frac{\partial^2 s}{\partial r\partial z} - \frac{\partial^2}{\partial z^2}\left[\frac{1}{12}(5A + C - 6P)\left(\frac{\partial^2\overline{\phi}}{\partial r^2} + \frac{1}{r}\frac{\partial\overline{\phi}}{\partial r} - \frac{\overline{\phi}}{r^2}\right) + \frac{1}{4}(C + A - 2P)\frac{\partial^2\overline{\phi}}{\partial z^2}\right] = 0 \tag{25}$$

and

$$\frac{\partial^2 s}{\partial r\partial z} + \frac{1}{12}(5C + A + 6P)\frac{\partial^2}{\partial z^2}\left(\frac{\partial^2\overline{\phi}}{\partial r^2} + \frac{1}{r}\frac{\partial\overline{\phi}}{\partial r} - \frac{\overline{\phi}}{r^2}\right) + \frac{1}{4}(C + A + 2P)\frac{\partial^2}{\partial r^2}\left(\frac{\partial^2\overline{\phi}}{\partial r^2} + \frac{1}{r}\frac{\partial\overline{\phi}}{\partial r} - \frac{\overline{\phi}}{r^2}\right) + \frac{1}{4}(C + A + 2P)\frac{1}{r}\frac{\partial}{\partial r}\left(\frac{\partial^2\overline{\phi}}{\partial r^2} + \frac{1}{r}\frac{\partial\overline{\phi}}{\partial r} - \frac{\overline{\phi}}{r^2}\right) - \frac{1}{4}(C + A + 2P)\frac{1}{r^2}\left(\frac{\partial^2\overline{\phi}}{\partial r^2} + \frac{1}{r}\frac{\partial\overline{\phi}}{\partial r} - \frac{\overline{\phi}}{r^2}\right) = 0 \tag{26}$$

Elimination of s from Eqs. (25) and (26) yields

$$\frac{1}{2}(C + A)\ \frac{\partial^2}{\partial z^2}\left(\frac{\partial^2\overline{\phi}}{\partial r^2} + \frac{1}{r}\frac{\partial\overline{\phi}}{\partial r} - \frac{\overline{\phi}}{r^2}\right) + \frac{1}{4}(C + A + 2P)\ \frac{\partial^2}{\partial r^2}\left(\frac{\partial^2\overline{\phi}}{\partial r^2} + \frac{1}{r}\frac{\partial\overline{\phi}}{\partial r} - \frac{\overline{\phi}}{r^2}\right)$$
$$+ \frac{1}{4}(C + A + 2P)\ \frac{1}{r}\frac{\partial}{\partial r}\left(\frac{\partial^2\overline{\phi}}{\partial r^2} + \frac{1}{r}\frac{\partial\overline{\phi}}{\partial r} - \frac{\overline{\phi}}{r^2}\right)$$
$$- \frac{1}{4}(C + A + 2P)\ \frac{1}{r^2}\left(\frac{\partial^2\overline{\phi}}{\partial r^2} + \frac{1}{r}\frac{\partial\overline{\phi}}{\partial r} - \frac{\overline{\phi}}{r^2}\right) + \frac{1}{4}(C + A - 2P)\ \frac{\partial^2\overline{\phi}}{\partial z^2} = 0 \qquad (27)$$

This equation may be written as

$$\frac{\partial^2}{\partial r^2}\,\nabla^2\overline{\phi} + \frac{1}{r}\frac{\partial}{\partial r}\,\nabla^2\overline{\phi} - \frac{1}{r^2}\,\nabla^2\overline{\phi} + \beta^2\,\frac{\partial^2}{\partial z^2}\,\nabla^2\overline{\phi} = 0 \qquad (28)$$

where

$$\nabla^2 = \frac{\partial^2}{\partial r^2} + \frac{1}{r}\frac{\partial}{\partial r} - \frac{1}{r^2} + \frac{\partial^2}{\partial z^2} \qquad (29)$$

and

$$\beta^2 = \frac{C + A - 2P}{C + A + 2P} \qquad (30)$$

Equation (28) can further be simplified by factorization

$$\nabla^2_\beta\ \nabla^2\overline{\phi} = 0 \qquad (31)$$

where

$$\nabla^2_\beta = \frac{\partial^2}{\partial r^2} + \frac{1}{r}\frac{\partial}{\partial r} - \frac{1}{r^2} + \beta^2\,\frac{\partial^2}{\partial z^2} \qquad (32)$$

From Eq. (31) we see that the effect of the initial stress P enters into the problem through β^2. From Eq. (30) we have $\beta^2 = 1$ as $P = 0$. This means that, for an incompressible medium free from initial stress, the field equation of axial-symmetric deformations is reduced to $\nabla^2\nabla^2\overline{\phi} = 0$ where the operator ∇^2 is given by Eq. (29). Equation (31) represents the field equation governing incremental axial-symmetric deformations under the state of initial stress given in Eq. (1).

A Solid Cylinder under Initial Stress S_{zz}

In this section we shall investigate the problem of a solid circular cylinder under initial stress in the axial direction. In this case

$$S_{zz} = -P \qquad\qquad S_{rr} = S_{\theta\theta} = 0 \qquad (33)$$

The incremental boundary conditions are such that on the surface $r = a$ an axial-symmetric normal load of sinusoidal type is applied, and on both ends $z = \pm L$ the surfaces are assumed to be rigid and smooth.[5] Analytically the incremental boundary conditions can be expressed as follows:[6]

$$\left.\begin{aligned} w &= 0 \\ \Delta f_r &= 0 \end{aligned}\right\} \quad \text{for} \quad z = \pm L \tag{34}$$

$$\left.\begin{aligned} \Delta f_r &= q \cos kz \\ \Delta f_z &= 0 \end{aligned}\right\} \quad \text{for} \quad r = a \tag{35}$$

where Δf_r and Δf_z represent the incremental boundary stress in r and z, directions respectively, and q is a constant.

Equation (31) can be solved by using the substitutions

$$\nabla^2 \overline{\phi} = \psi \tag{36}$$

$$\nabla_\beta^2 \psi = 0 \tag{37}$$

The solution of Eq. (37) is given by

$$\psi = DI_1(\alpha r) \sin kz \tag{38}$$

where

$$\alpha^2 = \beta^2 k^2 \tag{39}$$

and $I_1(\alpha r)$ is a modified Bessel function of order one. From Eq. (38) the solution of Eq. (36) is found to be

$$\overline{\phi} = [D_1 I_1(kr) + D_2 I_1(\alpha r)] \sin kz \qquad (\alpha \neq k) \tag{40}$$

where $I_1(kr)$ is a modified Bessel function of order one.

Note that Eq. (40) is not valid for the case when the medium is free from initial stress, i.e., when $P = 0$. As $P = 0$, from Eqs. (30) and (39), we see that $\beta^2 = 1$ and $\alpha = k$. In this case D_1 and D_2 are no longer independent constants. Thus the solution for the same problem

5. Only this kind of boundary conditions at $z = \pm L$ can be satisfied mathematically.

6. 2L and a represent the length and the radius after the initial stress is applied.

without initial stress should be obtained by solving the following equation independently

$$\nabla^2\nabla^2\bar{\phi} = 0$$

To determine s we substitute Eq. (40) into either Eq. (21) or Eq. (22). We find

$$s = \left[\frac{1}{6}(A - C)k^2D_1I_0(kr) + \frac{1}{3}(C - A)\left(\frac{C}{A}\right)^{1/2} k^2D_2I_0(\alpha r)\right]\cos kz \tag{41}$$

where $I_0(kr)$ and $I_0(\alpha r)$ are modified Bessel functions of order zero. In deriving Eq. (39), Eqs. (16) and (30) have been used.

The displacement components can be determined by substituting Eq. (40) into Eq. (21); the following results will be obtained:

$$\begin{aligned} u &= -k[D_1I_1(kr) + D_2I_1(\alpha r)]\cos kz \\ w &= k[D_1I_0(kr) + D_2\beta I_0(\alpha r)]\sin kz \end{aligned} \tag{42}$$

The stress components are determined from Eqs. (42), (2) and (19), respectively. We have

$$\begin{aligned} s_{rr} = {} & \left[-\frac{1}{2}(C + A)k^2I_0(kr) + \frac{AkI_1(kr)}{r}\right] D_1 \cos kz \\ & + \left[\frac{AkI_1(\alpha r)}{r} - Ak^2\beta I_0(\alpha r)\right] D_2 \cos kz \end{aligned} \tag{43}$$

$$\begin{aligned} s_{\theta\theta} = {} & \left[\frac{1}{2}(A - C)k^2I_0(kr) - \frac{AkI_1(kr)}{r}\right] D_1 \cos kz \\ & - \frac{AkD_2I_1(\alpha r)}{r} \cos kz \end{aligned} \tag{44}$$

$$s_{zz} = [\frac{1}{2}(C + A)k^2D_1I_0(kr) + Ck^2\beta D_2I_0(\alpha r)]\cos kz \tag{45}$$

$$s_{rz} = \frac{1}{4} k^2(A + C)[2D_1I_1(kr) + (1 + \beta^2)D_2I_1(\alpha r)]\sin kz \tag{46}$$

In order to determine the constants D_1 and D_2 we use the boundary conditions as expressed in Eqs. (34) and (35). It has been shown by M. A. Biot from the general expressions of the incremental boundary conditions that Eqs. (34) and (35) can be reduced to[7]

$$w = 0, \quad \frac{\partial u}{\partial z} = 0 \qquad \text{for } z = \pm L \tag{47}$$

and

$$s_{rr} = q \cos kz, \quad s_{rz} + P\,\varepsilon_{rz} = 0 \qquad \text{for } r = a \tag{48}$$

From stress-strain relations in Eq. (5) the second equation in Eq. (48) can also be written as

$$(P + 2Q)\varepsilon_{rz} = 0$$

or simply

$$\varepsilon_{rz} = 0 \qquad \text{for } r = a \tag{49}$$

It can be shown from Eqs. (42) and (46) that the boundary conditions as expressed in Eq. (47) are satisfied identically by putting

$$\sin kL = 0 \tag{50}$$

from which we determine

$$k = \frac{\pi}{L} \tag{51}$$

Substituting the solutions of Eqs. (43) and (46) into the boundary conditions of Eqs. (48) and (49) respectively we obtain

$$\left[-\frac{1}{2}(C + A)k^2 I_0(ka) + \frac{AkI_1(ka)}{a}\right]D_1 + \left[\frac{AkI_1(\alpha a)}{a} - Ak^2\beta I_0(\alpha a)\right]D_2 = q \tag{52}$$

$$2I_1(ka)D_1 + (1 + \beta^2)I_1(\alpha a)D_2 = 0 \tag{53}$$

From Eqs. (52) and (53) we determine

$$D_1 = \frac{q}{\mu_o}\frac{a}{k}\frac{(1 + \lambda^3)}{\Delta} I_1(\lambda^{3/2}\gamma), \quad D_2 = \frac{-2q}{\mu_o}\frac{a}{k}\frac{I_1(\gamma)}{\Delta} \tag{54}$$

---

7. See Eq. (7.56) p. 53 of [1].

where

$$\Delta = -(1+\lambda^3)^2\,\gamma I_0(\gamma)I_1(\lambda^{3/2}\gamma) - 2(1-\lambda^3)I_1(\gamma)I_1(\lambda^{3/2}\gamma)$$
$$+ 4\lambda^{3/2}I_1(\gamma)I_0(\lambda^{3/2}\gamma) \qquad (\lambda \neq 1) \tag{55}$$

$$\gamma = \frac{\pi a}{L} = ka \tag{56}$$

In deriving Eqs. (54) and (55), Eqs. (15) and (16) have been used. Notice that γ in Eq. (56) is inversely proportional to the slenderness ratio L/a of the cylinder.

Numerical calculation shows that for a given value of γ, Δ will not vanish for any finite value of λ. Thus, for a solid cylinder, under axial-symmetric deformation, the initial stress does not cause instability.

The radial displacement u as a function of r and z is obtained by substituting Eq. (54) into the first equation of Eq. (42). We have

$$\frac{u}{a} = -\frac{q}{\mu_o}\frac{1}{\Delta}\left[(1+\lambda^3)I_1(\lambda^{3/2}\gamma)I_1(kr) - 2I_1(\gamma)I_1(\alpha\gamma)\right]\cos kz \tag{57}$$

The maximum displacement occurs at r = a. By putting r = a in Eq. (57) we obtain

$$\frac{u_{max}}{a} = U(\gamma,\lambda)\cos kz \tag{58}$$

where

$$U(\gamma,\lambda) = \frac{q}{\mu_o}\frac{1-\lambda^3}{\Delta}I_1(\gamma)I_1(\lambda^{3/2}\gamma) \qquad (\lambda \neq 1) \tag{59}$$

represents the amplitude of the maximum radial displacement.

Discussion of the Numerical Results

In order to see the influence of initial stress P on the rigidity of the cylinder, we evaluate the numerical results of U/U_o as a function of P for various values of γ as shown in Fig. 2. The quantity U_o represents the amplitude of the maximum radial displacement for the case when the medium is free from initial stress (P = 0). It is obtained by solving the following equation

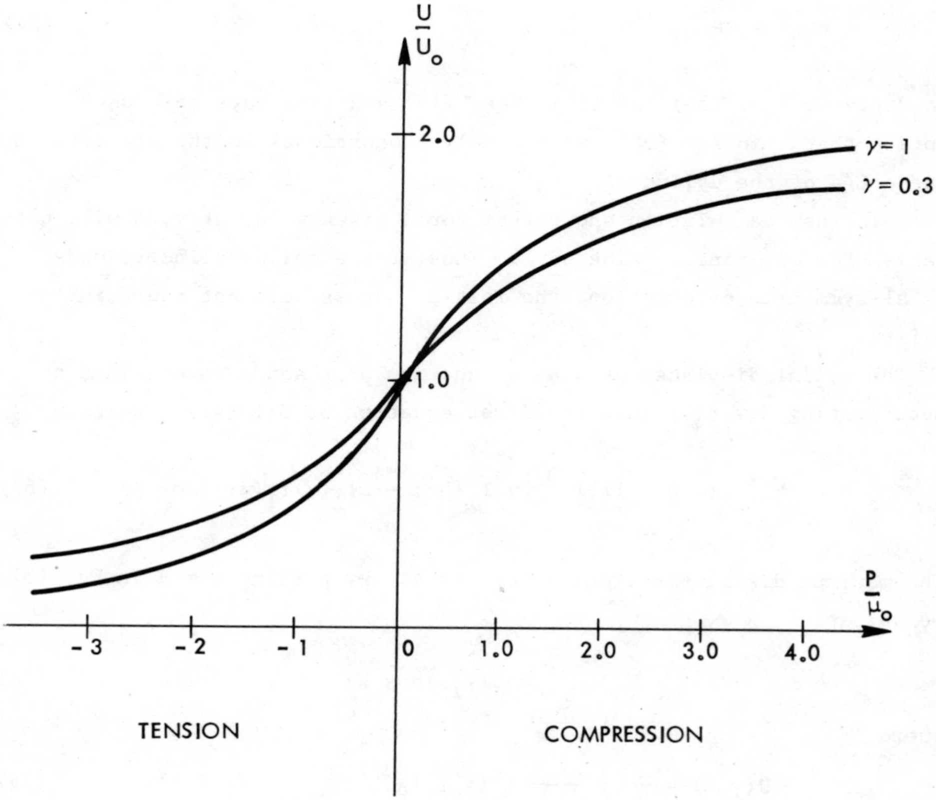

Fig. 2. Plot of U as a Funtion of P for Various Values of ν.

and then using the same boundary conditions to evaluate the constants D_1 and D_2. The result is not shown here.

To plot Fig. 2 we first express U as a function of γ and P by using Eqs. (59) and (14). Positive value of P ($0 < \lambda < 1$) indicates compression and negative P ($\lambda > 1$) indicates tension. Regardless of the value of γ, the numerical results show that the rigidity of the cylinder decreases (i.e., the ratio of U/U_o increases) as the compressive initial stress increases, and the rigidity increases (i.e., the ratio of U/U_o decreases) as the tensile initial stress increases.

Finally it is worthwhile to mention that the above solution can be easily extended to a hollow cylinder under uniform initial stress in the axial direction. We believe that in this case, the initial stress will cause instability of the cylinder. The result will be given in a separate publication.

ACKNOWLEDGEMENTS

This work was partially supported by the Engineering Research Institute, Iowa State University.

REFERENCES

1. Biot, M. A., Mechanics of Incremental Deformations, John Wiley and Sons Inc., New York, 1964.

2. Green, A. E., Rivlin, R. S. and Shield, R. T., "General Theory of Small Elastic Deformations Superposed on Finite Elastic Deformations," Proceedings of the Royal Society A., Vol. 211, 1952, pp. 128-154.

3. Biot, M. A., "Surface Instability in Finite Anisotropic Elasticity Under Initial Stress," Proceedings of the Royal Society A., Vol. 273, 1963, pp. 329-339.

4. Novozhilov, V. V., Foundations of the Nonlinear Theory of Elasticity, Graylock Press, Rochester, N. Y., 1953.

5. Tang, S., "Wave Propagation in Initially-Stressed Elastic Solids," Acta Mechanica, Vol. 4, No. 1, 1968, pp. 92-106.

6. Kerr, A. D. and Tang, S., "The Stability of a Rectangular Elastic Solid," Acta Mechanica, Vol. 4, No. 1, 1968, pp. 43-63.

7. Tang, S., "Elastic Stability of Thick Circular Plates Under Three-Dimensional States of Stress," Acta Mechanica, Vol. 4, No. 4, 1968, pp. 382-297.

8. Biot, M. A., "Surface Instability of Rubber in Compression," Applied Scientific Research A, Vol. 12, 1963, pp. 168-181.

9. Biot, M. A., "General Fluid-Displacement Equations for Acoustic-Gravity Waves," Physics of Fluids, Vol. 6, No. 5, 1965, pp. 621-626.

10. Biot, M. A., "Folding of a Layered Viscoelastic Medium Derived from an Exact Stability Theory of a Continuum Under Initial Stress," Quarterly of Applied Mathematics, Vol. 17, No. 2, 1959, pp. 185-204.

11. Biot, M. A., "Incremental Elastic Coefficients of an Isotropic Medium of Finite Strain," Applied Scientific Research A, Vol. 12, 1963, pp. 151-167.

INVITED LECTURE

SOME PROBLEMS IN ASTROELASTICITY

Yi-Yuan Yu
General Electric Company

INTRODUCTION

In the design and analysis of aircraft, a rigid structure is the exception rather than the rule. Since aerodynamic aspects always come into play, the field of "aeroelasticity" was evolved. With the advent of the space age, some of the concepts and techniques become automatically applicable to space vehicles as well, as the latter still must penetrate the atmosphere before entering into space. For space vehicles and particularly spacecraft, however, problems of dynamics and control do arise which are different from those usually encountered in aeroelasticity. They may properly be said to belong to the field of "astroelasticity." Some such problems that have been studied by the author are reviewed in this paper. Through a discussion of these specific problems an overview of the general problem of dynamics and control of flexible space vehicles and spacecraft is presented. Among other things it depicts the interaction between the disciplines of Structural Mechanics and Control Theory as applied to problems in Astronautics.

The method of linear dynamic analysis of a system based on the characteristics of its subsystems appears to be particularly suited for large flexible space vehicle systems. This is developed by starting with a general three-dimensional elastic solid. Any number of solids or structural components may then be coupled together through the use of the receptance concept. One advantage of doing this lies in the fact that the receptance is essentially the frequency of the structural system and is readily applicable to control and stability studies.

Among the most important dynamic characteristics of a structural component or system are its natural frequencies, because they are intimately related to the frequency response. While frequency or free vibration analysis has been an established discipline in Structural Mechanics, space structures have some unique features such as large size, light weight, and large flexibility. The low natural frequencies that tend to be associated with such features can lead to potential problems of structure-control system interaction. Analysis of a paraboloidal antenna is given as an example.

Based on a knowledge of the natural frequencies and frequency response of a flexible space vehicle or spacecraft, its control and stability in the linear domain can normally be analyzed in a routine manner. However, anomalous behaviors of quite a few spacecraft are known to have developed. One of the most intriguing among these is the phenomenon of thermal flutter of a flexible boom. The basic governing equations are presented. The special case of thermal bending flutter is discussed.

Large finite deflections can develop easily for large flexible space structures. It is important to examine their effect on stability and control, which becomes a nonlinear problem. The method of V. M. Popov in the theory of nonlinear automatic control is adopted, which has the important advantage of being based on the frequency response of the linear part of the nonlinear system. The results given by the receptance technique mentioned earlier are thus still useful. As an example, a thrust-vector control system is considered. In the degenerate linear case, the example also illustrates the usual treatment of the effects of structural flexibility on control stability.

1. *Dynamics of Coupled System of Elastic Solids*

Dynamic analysis of a system based on the subsystem characteristics has several advantages. A direct analysis of the total system may not always be practical, for instance, when different parts of the spacecraft and/or launch vehicle are designed and made by different manufacturers. Since the identity of the subsystems is maintained, the analysis will provide information on the dynamic interaction, leading to proper dynamic loads for the spacecraft. It is hoped that this may also generate useful guidelines on appropriate test inputs for spacecraft.

(1) General Three-Dimensional Elastic Solid / Hamilton's principle for an arbitrary three-dimensional elastic solid has the form

$$\delta \int_{t_o}^{t_1} (T - U + W)\, dt = 0$$

where T is the kinetic energy, U the strain energy, and δW the virtual work. The associated variational equation of motion is [1]

$$\int_V (\rho \ddot{u}_i\, \delta u_i + \delta U_0)\, dV = \int_{S_P} \bar{p}_i\, \delta u_i\, dS + \int_V X_i\, \delta u_i\, dV \qquad (1)$$

where u_i is the displacement, U_o strain-energy density, $\bar{p}_i$ surface traction, X_i body force, V volume of the solid, S_p that part of the surface S of the solid on which traction is given. A repeat subscript i in a term implies summation over the full range of i = 1, 2, 3. Over some regions, s in number, in the surface S, the displacement may be prescribed.

To treat the general forced-vibration problem, two types of associated problems are solved first. The first consists of a group of s separate static problems, in all of which the body under consideration is assumed to be subjected to neither surface nor body forces, and the displacement boundary conditions are prescribed statically. The solution to the static problem is denoted by $u_i^{[k]}(x)$. The second type of associated problem is that of free vibration, whose solution is of the form $u_i(x,t) = u_i^{(n)}(x)e^{i\omega_n t}$, ω_n and $u_i^{(n)}$ being the nth natural frequency and mode, respectively. The modes satisfy the usual relations

$$\int_V \rho u_i^{(m)}\, u_i^{(n)}\, dV = \begin{cases} 0 & (m \neq n) \\ M_n & (m = n) \end{cases} \qquad (2)$$

where M_n is the nth generalized mass.

For the general problem of forced vibration, the displacement is then taken as

$$u_i\,(x,t) = \sum_{n=0}^{\infty} u_i^{(n)}\,(x)\,\phi_n\,(t) + \sum_{k=1}^{s} u_i^{|k|}\,(x)\,f_k^{\,i}\,(t) \tag{3}$$

where n = 0 is associated with rigid-body motion, ϕ_n are the generalized coordinates, and $f_k^{\,i}(t)$ are as prescribed in the original displacement boundary conditions. Through the use of Eqs. (2) and (3), Eq. (1) yields

$$M_n\,\ddot{\phi} + M_n\,\omega_n^2\,\phi = F_n = F_{pn} + F_{Xn} + F_{un} \qquad (n = 0,1,2,\ldots) \tag{4}$$

where F_n is the generalized force, and its components corresponding to surface traction, body force, and motion input are, respectively,

$$F_{pn} = \int_{S_p} \bar{p}_i u_i^{(n)} dS,\quad F_{Xn} = \int_V X_i u_i^{(n)} dV,\quad F_{un} = -\int \rho \sum_{k=1}^{s} u_i^{|k|} \ddot{f}_k^{\,i}\, u_i^{(n)} dV$$

(2) Coupled System of Solids / Consider a coupled system of linear elastic solids, as shown in Fig. 1. Each of the solids by itself can be subjected to surface traction, body force, and motion input. Additional surface traction will be exerted on it by every other solid with which it is in contact, and this will be called the interface traction. To determine the response of the system, only one of the solids is assumed to be subjected to some external excitation at a time, and only one type of excitation need be considered at a time. The total response due to all types of excitation on all solids is then obtained by superposition. Furthermore, since the response to arbitrary periodic, transient, or random excitation can be calculated if the steady-state response to a simple harmonic excitation is known, only the latter will be considered. Last but not least, the treatment enables us to calculate the frequency response of the coupled system based on the frequency responses or receptances of the individual components.

In Fig. 1, let M be the solid that is subjected to a simple harmonic external excitation. For M alone, its response is then, according to Eqs. 3 and 4,

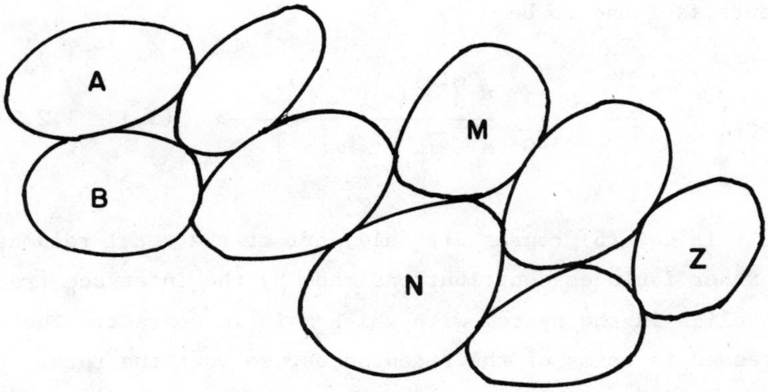

Fig. 1. Coupled System of Solids.

$$u_i^{MM} = \sum_{n=0}^{\infty} \frac{u_i^{M(n)}(x)}{M_n^M[(\omega_n^M)^2 - \omega^2]} F_n^M + \sum_{k=1}^{s} u_i^{M|k|}(x)e^{i\omega t} \tag{5}$$

where ω is the exciting frequency, the superscript M refers to the solid M, and the second superscript M on u_i indicates that the response is due to excitation on M itself. Equation (5) may be used to calculate the receptance of the solid M. Thus, when the excitation consists of a concentrated force having components P_{rj}^M and acting at $x = x_r$, the receptance is found to be

$$\alpha_{ij}^M(x,x_r) = \frac{u_i^{MM}}{P_{rj}^M} = \sum_{n=0}^{\infty} \frac{u_i^{M(n)}(x)u_j^{M(n)}(x_r)}{M_n^M[(\omega_n^M)^2 - \omega^2]} \qquad (i,j = 1,2,3) \tag{6}$$

The result in Eq. (5) represents only part of the total response of M, which further includes contributions made by the interface tractions from other solids in the system with which M is in contact. The latter may be expressed in terms of the receptances, so that the total response of M is

$$u_i^M = u_i^{MM} + \int_{S_{MN}} \alpha_{ij}^M(x_M,x_{MN})\bar{p}_j^{MN}\,dS + \int_{S_{MR}} \alpha_{ij}^M(x_M,x_{MR})\bar{p}_j^{MR}\,dS \tag{7}$$

where, for instance, the superscripts MN indicate the contribution made to M by N, and, similarly, the subscripts MN indicate the part of M in contact with N. The solid N has been singled out; the remaining solids in contact with M are denoted collectively by R. In a similar manner the response of N is written as

$$u_i^N = \int_{S_{NM}} \alpha_{ij}^N(x_N,x_{NM})\bar{p}_j^{NM}\,dS + \int_{S_{NR}} \alpha_{ij}^N(x_N,x_{NR})\bar{p}_j^{NR}\,dS \tag{8}$$

which contains only the interface action, but not any external excitation, and in which α_{ij}^N is similar to α_{ij}^M. If no slipping is assumed and full contact is maintained across the contact surface $S_{MN} = S_{NM}$ between M and N, Eqs. (7) and (8) lead to the result

$$\int_{S_{MN}} \left(\alpha_{ij}^{M} + \alpha_{ij}^{N}\right)\bar{p}_j^{MN}\, dS + \int_{S_{MR}} \alpha_{ij}^{M}\bar{p}_j^{MR} dS - \int_{S_{NR}} \alpha_{ij}^{N}\bar{p}_j^{NR} dS = -u_i^{MM} \text{ on } S_{MN} \quad (9)$$

Equations similar to Eq. 9 may be written for all pairs of solids that are in contact with each other in the system. In general, solving for the interface tractions $\bar{p}_j^{MN}$,... from these equations will be difficult. From a practical standpoint, however, each of the contact surface regions S_{MN},... may be divided into small enough subregions over which the distributed tractions are replaced by concentrated forces acting at discrete points, which will then be tractable at least numerically. After the interface forces become known, the response of the solids may be calculated, although the results are necessarily also approximate.

The natural frequences and modes as well as the receptances of the total system may further be calculated. Since the receptance is essentially the frequency response, the result is then immediately applicable to control and stability analyses, as mentioned earlier.

Based on the above concepts, examples of joined beams and shells have been worked out [1]. These are, of course, continuous systems. Discussion of joining discrete structural subsystems is also available [2]. Useful computer programs have been developed for such purposes by various government agencies and industries.

2. *Vibrations of Paraboloidal Antenna*

As an example of calculating natural frequencies, we consider a rib-stiffened, prestressed shallow spherical membrane. Because of the shallowness, the results are also applicable to a shallow paraboloidal membrane. The problem is of both theoretical interest and practical importance in space applications, since spacecraft antennas often take the shape of a shallow paraboloidal dish, and weight-saving and other constraints necessitate the kind of space-erectable structure which a rib-stiffened membrane can provide. The large size and high flexibility of the structure, however, are likely to be associated with natural frequencies which are so low as to possibly interfere with the proper functioning of the control system of the spacecraft. A thorough and accurate knowledge concerning the natural frequencies, and particularly the lowest frequencies, therefore becomes eminently important.

The paraboloidal antenna consists of a shallow spherical membrane which, when deployed in space, is stretched over a large number of shallow circular ribs. In the deployed position, the ribs extend radially; and the membrane becomes uniformly prestressed, but essentially in the circumferential direction only, because it is made from an interwoven fabric composed of strands in orthogonal directions. Being shallow, the membrane may be represented in the usual manner by the paraboloid $z = H[1-(r/a)^2]$, where H is the rise, a the base radius, and r the radial coordinate, as shown in Fig. 2. The corresponding radius of curvature is given by $R = a^2/2H$.

(1) Equation of Axisymmetrical Motion / Since the lowest axisymmetrical mode of the antenna is predominantly transverse in nature, only the following equation governing the transverse motion of the membrane is considered:

$$N_x + N_y + \bar{N}_y \left(\frac{u}{R} + \frac{\partial w}{\partial r} \right) \frac{R}{r} + qR - \rho h R \ddot{w} = 0 \qquad (10)$$

where $\bar{N}_y$ is the initial membrane stress in the circumferential direction, N_x and N_y are the additional membrane stresses in the radial and circumferential directions, respectively, induced by the motion, q is the distributed transverse load per unit area, ρ the density and h the thickness. Equation (10) can be derived by making use of the equations of spherical shells given in Timoshenko's book [3].

To gain some physical insight we derive directly the $\bar{N}_y$ term in Eq. (10) by considering first an element of a spherical membrane in Fig. 3 which is not necessarily shallow. The axisymmetrical deformation of the membrane element is shown in Fig. 4, where u and w are the displacement components in the meridional and transverse directions, respectively. Corresponding to u and w, each face in a meridional plane undergoes an angle of rotation

$$\chi = \frac{u}{R} + \frac{1}{R} \frac{\partial w}{\partial \theta}$$

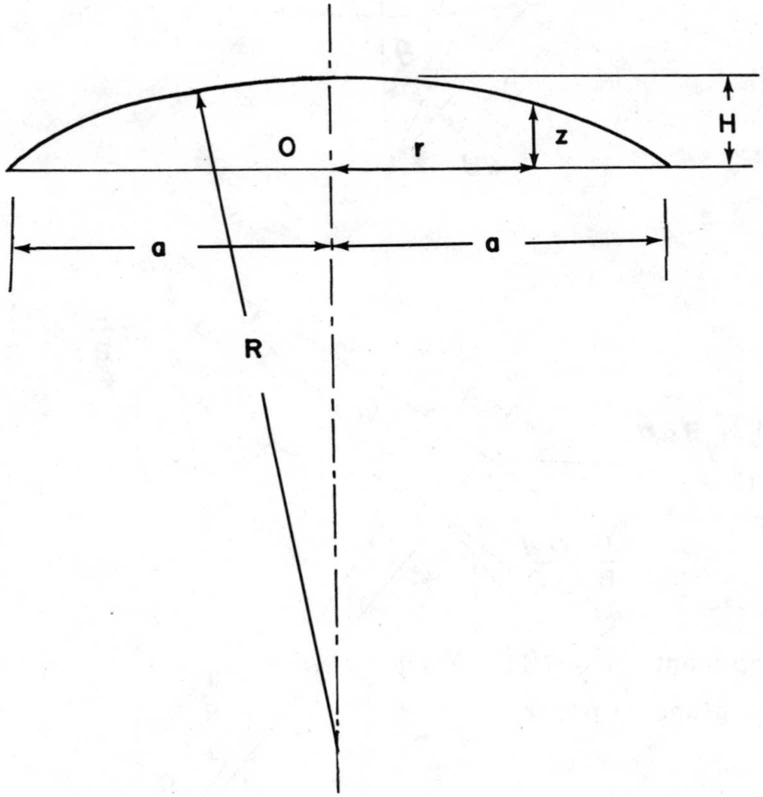

Fig. 2. Shallow Paraboloidal or Spherical Shell.

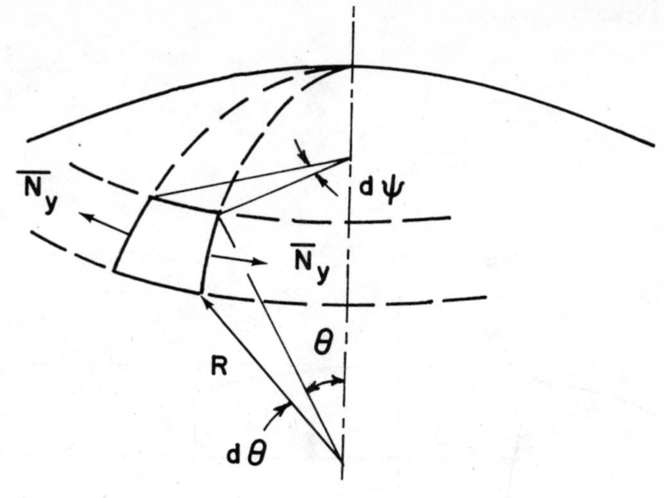

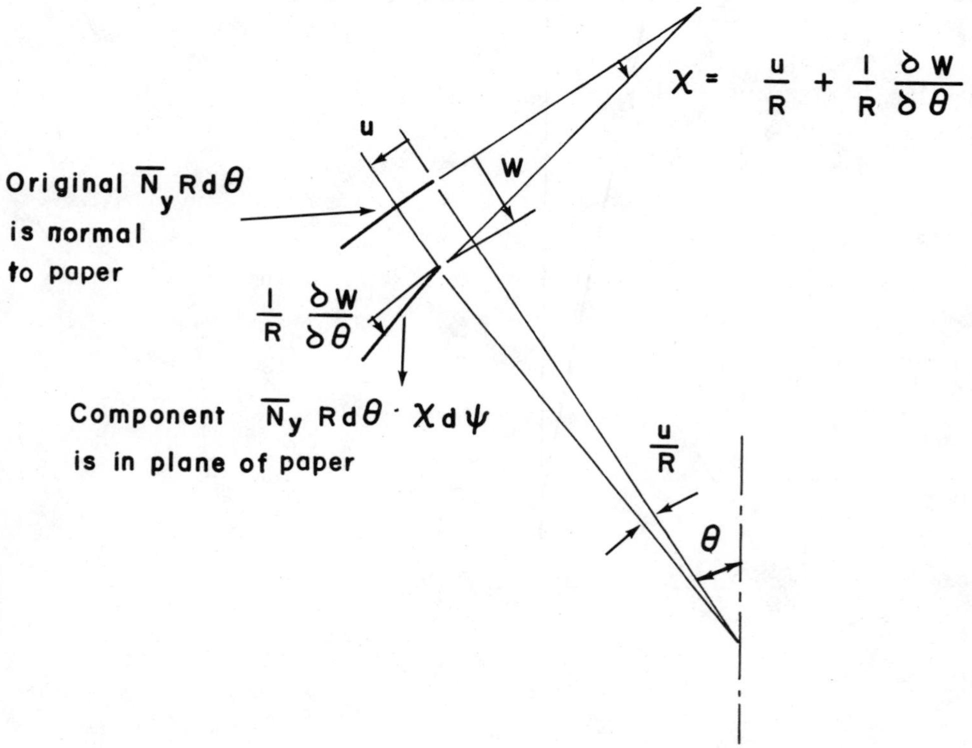

Fig. 3. Spherical Membrane Element. (Above)

Fig. 4. Axisymmetrical Deformation of Spherical Membrane Element. (Below)

Since two adjacent meridional planes make an angle $d\psi$ with each other, there is a relative rotation $\chi d\psi$ between two opposite faces. As a result, the membrane forces $\bar{N}_y R d\theta$ acting on them, each of which is originally normal to a meridional plane, now have a component in the meridional plane. By decomposition the equivalent unit pressure normal to the membrane surface is found to be $(\bar{N}_y/R^2)(u + \partial w/\partial\theta) \cot\theta$, which leads to the $\bar{N}_y$ term in Eq. (10) when the membrane is shallow.

For ordinary membranes there is always some Poisson effect. However, since the membrane material is an interwoven fabric composed of strands in orthogonal directions, the Poisson effect becomes negligible, and we write simply

$$N_x = E_1 \left(\frac{\partial u}{\partial r} - \frac{w}{R}\right), \quad N_y = E_2 \left(\frac{u}{r} - \frac{w}{R}\right)$$

where E_1 and E_2 depend on the elastic properties of the individual strands and number of strands in each direction.

The ribs which are used to stiffen the membrane are thin, shallow circular beams lying in radial planes and equally spaced around the circumference. Since the number of ribs is large, the radially stiffened membrane may be considered to execute axisymmetrical vibration in a gross manner. The ribs will then have identical motion, each vibrating in its plane of curvature. Since the ribs are shallow, the stress equation of motion of each individual rib is essentially the same as that of a straight beam, namely,

$$\frac{\partial^2 M_r}{\partial r^2} + q_r - \rho_r A_r \ddot{w} = 0 \qquad (11)$$

where M_r is the bending moment in the rib, q_r the distributed transverse load per unit length, ρ_r the density of rib material, and A_r the cross-sectional area of the rib. For the ribs and membrane to move together, the displacement w must be the same for both. For a shallow circular rib the relation between M_r and w is further taken to be the same as that for a straight beam, namely, $M_r = -E_r I_r \partial^2 w/\partial r^2$, where E_r is Young's modulus of the rib material and I_r the cross-sectional moment of inertia. For a rib with a variable cross section, A_r and I_r are functions of r.

The rib-stiffened membrane is a composite structure consisting of both the membrane and the ribs. In the separate equations of motion (10) and (11), the transverse displacement w has already been taken to be the same. For the membrane and ribs to execute free vibration together, in the absence of external load on the composite structure, the transverse load on the membrane and the transverse loads on the ribs which appear in these equations become internal forces and must be action and reaction to each other. This condition is made use of by writing from Eq. (10) the equation for a typical membrane sector between two adjacent ribs and adding the result to Eq. (11), which results in

$$\frac{\partial^2 M_r}{\partial r^2} + \frac{2\pi r}{n}\left[\frac{N_x + N_y}{R} + \frac{\bar{N}_y}{r}\left(\frac{u}{R} + \frac{\partial w}{\partial r}\right)\right] - \left(\rho_r A_r + \frac{2\pi r}{n}\rho h\right)\ddot{w} = 0$$

With N_x, N_y and M_r expressed in terms of the displacements, the equation is finally written in the following variational form:

$$\int_a^b \left\{\left(\frac{\partial^2}{\partial r^2} E_r I_r \frac{\partial^2 w}{\partial r^2}\right) - \frac{2\pi}{n}\left[E_1\left(\frac{\partial u}{\partial r} - \frac{w}{R}\right)\frac{r}{R} + E_2\left(\frac{u}{r} - \frac{w}{R}\right)\frac{r}{R}\right.\right.$$

$$\left.\left. + \bar{N}_y\left(\frac{u}{R} + \frac{\partial w}{\partial r}\right)\right] + \left(\rho_r A_r + \frac{2\pi r}{n}\rho h\right)\ddot{w}\right\} \delta w \, dr = 0 \qquad (12)$$

where r = a, b locate the two ends of the rib. Since only a field integral is present in the variational equation of motion, it is implied that the boundary conditions of the structure will have been taken care of. Seeking for an approximate solution on the basis of Eq. (12) will then follow Galerkin's procedure.

(2) Axisymmetrical Vibration / For free vibration we take

$$u = U(r)\, e^{i\omega t}, \qquad w = W(r)\, e^{i\omega t}$$

For an approximate solution, U(r) and W(r) are further assumed. When they are singled-term approximations, Eq. (12) gives immediately

$$\omega^2 = \frac{\int_a^b \left[\frac{n}{2\pi} \frac{d^2}{dr^2} \left(E_r I_r \frac{d^2 W}{dr^2} \right) - E_1 \left(\frac{dU}{dr} - \frac{W}{R} \right) \frac{r}{R} - E_2 \left(\frac{U}{r} - \frac{W}{R} \right) \frac{r}{R} - \bar{N}_y \left(\frac{U}{R} + \frac{dW}{dr} \right) \right] W dr}{\int_a^b \left(\frac{n}{2\pi} \rho_r A_r + \rho h r \right) W^2 dr} \tag{13}$$

For a rib-stiffened membrane spring supported at the hub (r = a) and free at the outside rim (r = b), the boundary conditions are

$$\left.\begin{aligned} u &= w = 0 \\ \frac{\partial w}{\partial r} &= cM_r \text{ or } \frac{\partial w}{\partial r} = \frac{1}{k} \frac{\partial^2 w}{\partial r^2} \end{aligned}\right\} \text{at } r = a$$

$$\left.\begin{aligned} N_x &= E_1 \left(\frac{\partial u}{\partial r} - \frac{w}{R} \right) = 0 \\ M_r &= -E_r I_r \frac{\partial^2 w}{\partial r^2} = 0 \\ Q_r &= -\frac{\partial}{\partial r} \left(E_r I_r \frac{\partial^2 w}{\partial r^2} \right) = 0 \end{aligned}\right\} \text{at } r = b \tag{14}$$

where c and k are constants of proportionality and k is essentially also the spring constant of the support at the hub. When the support is rigidly clamped, k is equal to infinity, and the related boundary condition degenerates into $\partial w/\partial r = 0$ at r = a. The lowest mode may be taken in the form

$$U(r) = \frac{1}{R} \left[6 (r - a)^2 + k (r - a)^3 \right]$$

$$W(r) = 12 (r - a) + 6k (r - a)^2 - 4k \frac{(r - a)^3}{b - a} + k \frac{(r - a)^4}{(b - a)^2}$$

which satisfy all the boundary conditions in Eq. (14). The frequency may now be calculated in a straightforward manner according to Eq. (13).

(3) Torsional Vibration / Since the membrane is made of an interwoven fabric, it is assumed to be incapable of resisting in-plane shear in the directions of the orthogonal strands as well as transverse shear. The equation of torsional motion of a spherical membrane (shallow or deep) under initial stress in the circumferential direction may be deduced accordingly from the general nonlinear equations of spherical shells given by Grossman, Koplik, and Yu [4]. The result is

$$\bar{N}_y \frac{v}{R^2} - p + \rho h \ddot{v} = 0$$

where v is the displacement component in the circumferential direction, p the surface load per unit area in the same direction, and other notations are the same as before. The governing equation of motion of the rib is again taken in a form similar to Eq. (11). By means of the procedure described earlier for the axisymmetrical case, the equation of torsional motion of the rib-stiffened membrane is finally obtained in the following variational form:

$$\int_a^b \left[\frac{\partial^2}{\partial r^2} \left(E_r I_{r'} \frac{\partial^2 v}{\partial r^2} \right) + \frac{2\pi}{n} \bar{N}_y \frac{rv}{R^2} + \left(\rho_r A_r + \frac{2\pi r}{n} \rho h \right) \ddot{v} \right] \delta v dr = 0$$

where $I_{r'}$ is the cross-sectional moment of inertia of the rib for the circumferential direction.

The lowest frequency of torsional vibration may now be calculated in a similar manner as that of axisymmetrical vibration. In the specific numerical example calculated, the former turns out to be much lower than the latter.

(4) Major Conclusions / Equation (13) for axisymmetrical vibration has been applied to a rigidly-clamped, rib-stiffened membrane. The numerical results have led to some important conclusions. On one hand, the membrane acts as an elastic foundation to the ribs, which is to make the natural frequency of the system higher than that of the ribs alone. On the other hand, the circumferential tensile prestress in the

membrane lowers the frequency. With an initial tension large enough, the lowest frequency may theoretically vanish, and the structure buckles. Actually, the effect of prestressing on the frequency of axisymmetrical vibration tends to be very small, and buckling is unlikely.

Since the interwoven fabric from which the membrane is made is assumed to have no resistance to shear, the membrane action during torsional vibration is restricted to that due to the initial tension, which, however, plays a much more important role than in the axisymmetrical case. Furthermore, in contrast to the latter case, the initial tension raises, rather than lowers, the lowest frequency of torsional vibration of the composite structure.

It will be interesting and important to examine the effect of the flexibility or rigidity of the spring support on the frequencies. This has been analyzed for axisymmetrical vibrations. When the spring support degenerates into a hinge support that resists no moment, the lowest frequency reduces to zero, corresponding to a rigid body movement. As the spring support becomes less and less flexible, the frequency increases and approaches the value for the case of a rigidly-clamped edge as an upper limit. From the standpoint of control, therefore, a design goal should be to make the inner support as close to a rigidly-clamped one as possible. This will in turn make the lowest frequency as high as possible.

3. *Thermal Flutter of Spacecraft Boom*

Long, space-erectable booms extending from the main structure of a spacecraft have been used extensively, for instance, as antenna or gravity-gradient stabilization systems. Until recently the widely used type of boom has been an open tubular element formed out of strip metal and heat-treated into a circular section in such a manner that the edges of the strip overlap. Lately such open-section booms on some spacecraft in flight were observed to start oscillating as the spacecraft crossed from the Earth's shadow into sunlight. Although the bending and buckling of an open section has been studied extensively by many authors, the thermoelastic problem of dynamic instability of an open section has received attention only recently, as a result of such anomalies. An explanation is attempted for the bending case. The governing equations for the general case of coupled flexure and torsion are presented first.

(1) Thermoelastic Equations of Motion of Open Section / The thin-walled open cross section of a bar is shown in Fig. 5, where 0 is the shear center and C the centroid. The coordinate x is along the axial direction of the bar; y and z are coordinates in the plane of the cross section with the origin at 0; and y_1 and z_1 are parallel coordinates with the origin at C. The centroid C is located at $y = y_c$, $z = z_c$ relative to the shear center 0 so that $y_1 = y - y_c$, $z_1 = z - z_c$. The lateral surface of the bar is assumed to be free from external loading. In the spirit of Goodier's treatment of coupled flexure and torsion of the open section [5], the displacements in the x, y, z directions are taken in the form [6]

$$U(x, y, z, t) = \phi(y, z)\,\beta'(x, t) - y_1\,v'(x, t) - z_1\,w'(x, t)$$

$$V(x, y, z, t) = v(x, t) - z\beta(x, t)$$

$$W(x, y, z, t) = w(x, t) + y\beta(x, t)$$

where v and w are the displacements of the shear center and β is the angle of rotation about the shear center, as also shown in Fig. 5; ϕ is St. Venant's warping function; and a prime denotes differentiation with respect to x.

The kinetic and strain energies may then be written, and the following variational equation of motion is readily derived from Hamilton's principle [6].

$$\int_{t_o}^{t_1} dt \int_0^{\ell} \left\{ \left[M'_x - \rho I_o \ddot{\beta} + \rho A \left(\dot{z}_c \ddot{v} - y_c \ddot{w} \right) \right] \delta\beta - \left[M''_z + \rho A \left(\ddot{v} - z_c \ddot{\beta} \right) \right] \delta v + \left[M''_y - \rho A \left(\ddot{w} + y_c \ddot{\beta} \right) \right] \delta w \right\} dx$$

$$- \int_{t_o}^{t_1} \left[M_x \delta\beta - M'_z\,\delta v + M'_y\,\delta w + S\delta\beta' + M_z \delta v' - M_y \delta w' \right]_0^{\ell} dt = 0 \qquad (15)$$

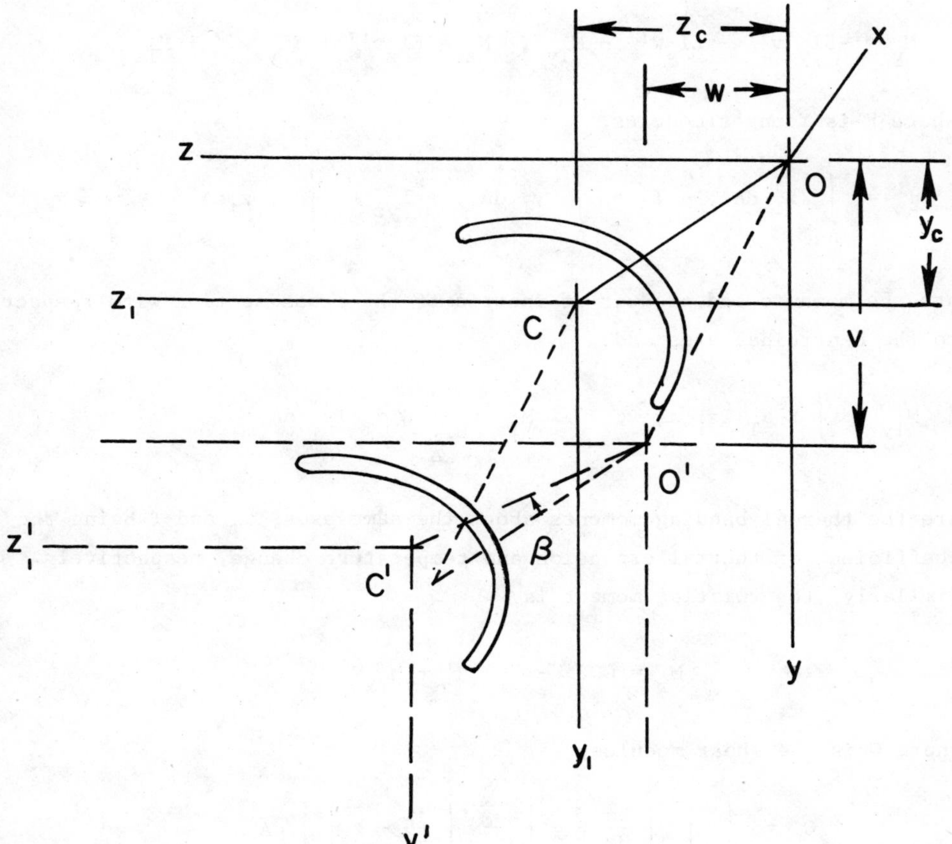

Fig. 5. Bar of Thin-Walled Open Section.

where ρ is the density of the bar material, ℓ the length, A the cross-sectional area, and I_o the polar moment of inertia of A about the shear center.

The bending moments are related to the displacements by

$$M_y = -EI_{yz}v'' - EI_y w'' - M_{Ty} , \quad M_z = EI_z v'' + EI_{yz} w'' + M_{Tz}$$

where E is Young's modulus,

$$I_y = \int_A z_1^2 \, dA , \quad I_z = \int_A y_1^2 \, dA , \quad I_{yz} = \int_A y_1 z_1 dA$$

are the moments and product of inertia of the cross section with respect to the centroidal axes and

$$M_{Ty} = \int_A E \, \alpha_T \, Tz_1 \, dA , \qquad M_{Tz} = \int_A E \, \alpha_T \, Ty_1 \, dA$$

are the thermal bending moments about the same axes, α_T and T being the coefficient of thermal expansion and temperature change, respectively. Similarly, the twisting moment is

$$M_x = GC\beta' - E\Gamma\beta''' + M_{Tx}$$

where G is the shear modulus,

$$C = \int_A \left[\left(\frac{\partial\phi}{\partial z} + y \right)^2 + \left(\frac{\partial\phi}{\partial y} - z \right)^2 \right] dA$$

$$\Gamma = \int_A \phi^2 \, dA$$

are the torsional constant and warping constant, respectively, and

$$M_{Tx} = \int_A E\alpha_T \, T' \, \phi dA$$

is the thermal twisting moment. Finally, we have

$$S = E\Gamma\beta'' - S_T \; , \quad S_T = \int E\alpha_T \, T\phi dA$$

In terms of displacements the equations of motion written from the variational Eq. (15) become

$$\begin{aligned} &GC\beta'' - E\Gamma\beta'''' + S_T'' - \rho I_o\ddot{\beta} + \rho A\left(z_c\ddot{v} - y_c\ddot{w}\right) = 0 \\ &EI_z v'''' + EI_{yz}w'''' + M_{Tz}'' + \rho A\left(\ddot{v} - z_c\ddot{\beta}\right) = 0 \quad \left(0 \le x \le \ell\right) \\ &EI_{yz}v'''' + EI_y w'''' + M_{Ty}'' + \rho A\left(\ddot{w} + y_c\ddot{\beta}\right) = 0 \end{aligned} \tag{16}$$

The boundary conditions may similarly be written from Eq. (15).

If the open section has one axis of symmetry, say, in the z-direction, and if the heat input is further symmetrical with respect to the same axis, pure bending uncoupled from twisting can take place, and Eq. (15) reduces to

$$\begin{aligned} &\int_{t_o}^{t_1} dt \int_0^{\ell} \left(EI_y w'''' + M_{Ty}'' + \rho A\ddot{w} \right) \delta w dx \\ &+ \int_{t_o}^{t_1} \left[\left(EI_y w'' + M_{Ty}\right)\delta w' - \left(EI_y w''' + M_{Ty}'\right)\delta w\right]_{x=0}^{x=\ell} dt = 0 \end{aligned} \tag{17}$$

The corresponding equation of motion is then

$$EI_y w'''' + M_{Ty}'' + \rho A\ddot{w} = 0 \qquad \left(0 \le x \le \ell\right) \tag{18}$$

For a boom fixed to the spacecraft at one end (Fig. 6), the appropriate boundary conditions are

$$\begin{aligned} &w = w' = 0 && \left(x = 0\right) \\ &EI_y w'' + M_{Ty} = EI_y w''' + M_{Ty}' = 0 && \left(x = \ell\right) \end{aligned} \tag{19}$$

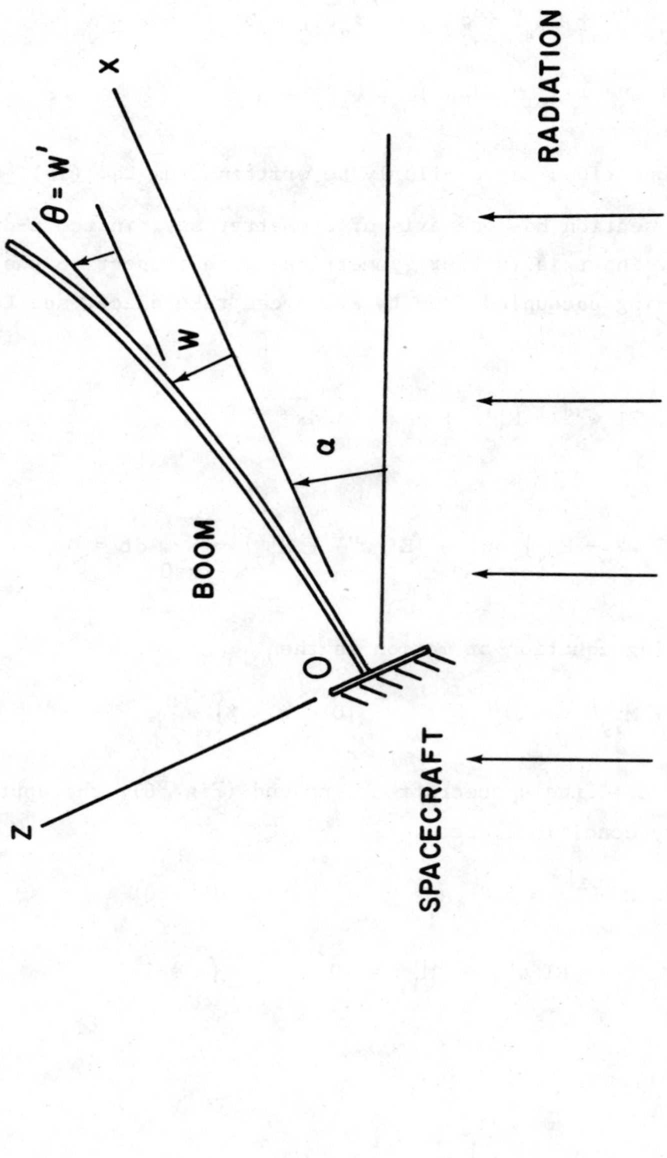

Fig. 6. Spacecraft Boom.

(2) Thermal Bending / For the special case of pure bending just deduced, the thermal curvature $\kappa_T = -M_{Ty}/EI_y$ at a point in the boom is assumed to be governed by the equation

$$\frac{\partial \kappa_T}{\partial t} + \frac{\kappa_T}{\tau} = K\cos(\alpha + \theta) \tag{20}$$

where τ is a characteristic time and K a thermal bending constant, both depending on the construction of the boom; the angle α defines the attitude of the boom, and $\theta = w'$ is the boom slope, as shown in Figure 6. This is the same equation as proposed by Etkin and Hughes [7] for describing the heat-transfer process across the boom. However, in their treatment of the problem of spin decay, the boom slope θ was further neglected in the equation. Such a simplification obviously cannot be tolerated here.

In a previous paper [8], the assumption $\tau^2\theta << \theta$ is made, and Eq. (19) may then be shown to have the solution

$$\kappa_T = k_c - k_s(w' - \tau\dot{w}') \text{ with } k_c \equiv \kappa_o \cos\alpha,\ k_s \equiv \kappa_o \sin\alpha \tag{21}$$

which was used in the equation of motion (18). In the boundary conditions (19) the thermal curvature was further simplified into

$$\kappa_T \doteq k_c = \text{constant} \tag{22}$$

Actually, the use of neither Eqs. (21) nor (22) can be justified, and the previous results [8] have been found to be inadequate. Equation (21) has since been used by other authors, equally without justification. A rigorous solution to the thermal bending flutter problem should be based upon the exact solution to Eq. (20), which has the following series form:

$$\kappa_T = k_c - k_s(w' - \tau\dot{w}' + \tau^2\ddot{w}' - \tau^3\dddot{w}' \ \ldots) \tag{23}$$

For stability analysis the variational equation (17) for the bending case is written in the following modified form:

$$\int_{t_o}^{t_1} dt \int_o^{\ell} \left(EIw'''' + \rho A\ddot{w}\right) \delta w dx + \int_{t_o}^{t_1} dt \int_o^{\ell} M_T \delta w'' dx$$

$$+ \int_{t_o}^{t_1} \Big[EIw''\delta w' - EIw'''\delta w \Big]_{x=0}^{x=\ell} dt = 0 \tag{24}$$

or by introducing Eq. (23) together with $C = \rho A/EI$,

$$\int_{t_o}^{t_1} dt \int_o^{\ell} \left(w'''' + C\ddot{w}\right) \delta w dx$$

$$- \int_{t_o}^{t_1} dt \int_o^{\ell} \Big[k_c - k_s \left(w' - \tau\dot{w}' + \tau^2\ddot{w}' - \tau^3\dddot{w}' + \ldots\right) \Big] \delta w'' dx$$

$$+ \int_{t_o}^{t_1} \Big[w'' \delta w' - w'''\delta w \Big]_{x=0}^{x=\ell} dt = 0 \tag{25}$$

The modified variational equation (24) or (25) differs from the original variational equation (17) in that the field equation and appropriate boundary conditions such as Eqs. (18) and (19) can no longer be deduced. In particular, the boundary integral in Eq. (24) or (25) now has the usual form for the isothermal case, devoid of any thermal effect. However, this enables us to make effective use of the usual solutions for free vibration of a beam which will make the boundary integral vanish exactly. Such solutions will not make the two field integrals in Eq. (24) or (25) vanish simultaneously, but direct integration with respect to x can be carried out. Since the infinite number of solutions of free vibration of a beam form a complete series, a rigorous solution to the thermal problem in the form of an infinite series is obtainable. This method of approach to the problem of thermal bending of a beam based on the modified variational equation is apparently new and can be extended to the general case of coupled thermal bending and twisting.

(3) Stability Analysis / The thermal bending deflection of the boom is thus taken in the form

$$w = \sum_{n=1}^{\infty} X_n(x)\, T_n(t)$$

where $X_n(x)$ are the isothermal cantilever modes. Substitution of w in Eq. (25) and integration then yields

$$c\omega_n^2 T_n + c\ddot{T}_n$$

$$- \sum_{m=1}^{\infty} I_{nm} k_s \left(T_m - \tau\dot{T}_m + \tau^2\ddot{T}_m - \tau^3\dddot{T}_m + \ldots\right)$$

$$= \frac{1}{\ell} k_c X_n(\ell) \qquad (n = 1, 2, \ldots)$$

For stability analysis, the non-homogeneous part on the right-hand side of the equation, which is essentially a forcing function, is not needed. By further taking $T_n(t) = A_n \exp(\lambda t)$, we find

$$C\left(\omega_n^2 + \lambda^2\right)A_n - \sum_{m=1}^{\infty} I_{nm} k_s \left(1 + \tau\lambda\right)^{-1} A_m = 0 \qquad (n = 1, 2, \ldots)$$

from which the characteristic equation can be written immediately.

The characteristic equation is exact if an infinite number of modes are included. When a single mode is used as an approximation, the equation reduces to

$$\left(\tau\lambda^3 + \tau^2 + \omega_n^2\, \tau\lambda + \omega_n^2\right)C - k_s I_{nn} = 0 \qquad (n = 1, 2, \ldots) \qquad (26)$$

Thermal flutter is governed by the Routh discriminant of this result, which is easily shown to be

$$R = \tau k_s I_{nn}/C$$

Since I_{nn} is negative for a cantilever mode, we have

$$R \gtrless 0 \quad \text{if} \quad k_s \gtrless 0$$

Thermal flutter will thus take place only if $k_s > 0$, that is, if the boom is pointed away from the sun. This is the reverse of the previous result [8]. It now agrees with the results given by other authors [9, 10] based on single-degree-of-freedom discrete models.

Stability has further been analyzed [11] by taking a two-mode approximation and truncating the characteristic equation accordingly. The result shows that thermal flutter can take place when the boom is pointed either away or towards the sun. Physically this is not surprising because the second cantilever mode that has been included in the analysis involves curvature reversal. It will be interesting, and important, to investigate the effect on stability due to the simultaneous presence of even more modes and eventually all modes.

4. *Effect of Large Structural Deflection on Control Stability*

Nonlinear components in attitude control systems are the norm rather than exception. The effect of large deflection is to make the vehicle structure a nonlinear one. As an example a thrust vector control system has been treated [12]. The results are summarized below, and the degenerate linear case also serves to illustrate the customary treatment that is carried out for launch vehicles.

(1) Structural System / For simplicity, a single-axis analysis of the pitching motion of a flexible space vehicle will be carried out. As shown in Fig. 7, the vehicle is simulated by a uniform beam whose deflection may be large and finite. After simplification, it is found that the transverse motion of the vehicle is governed by the variational equation

$$\int \left[G\left(\psi' + w''\right) + E \left\{ \frac{1}{2}\left(w' - \psi\right) \left[\frac{1}{8}\left(w' - \psi\right)^2 - \frac{T}{AE}\,\frac{\ell - x}{\ell} \right] \right\}' + \frac{q}{A}\delta(x) - \rho\ddot{w} \right] \delta w dx = 0 \tag{27}$$

where ψ is the rotation of a cross section, T the thrust, q the equivalent lateral load intensity due to T at x = 0, $\delta(x)$ the Dirac delta

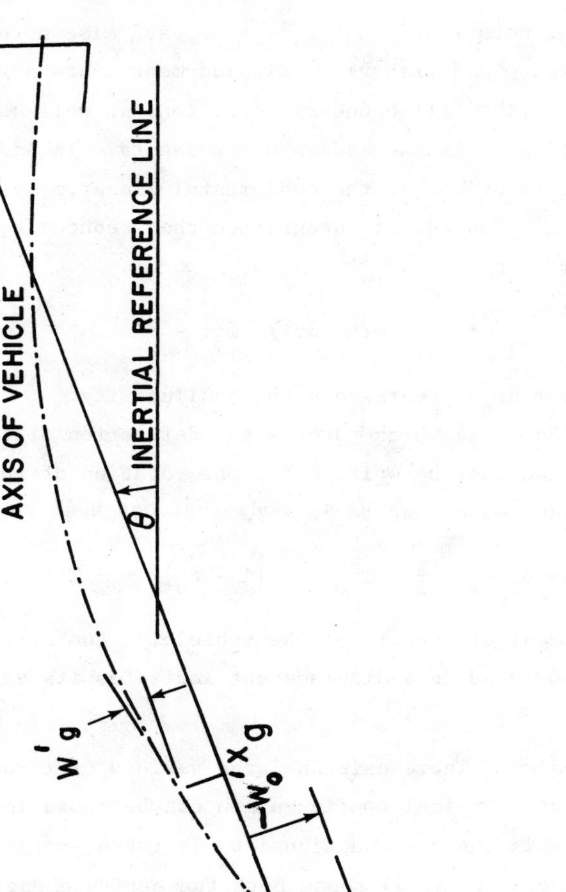

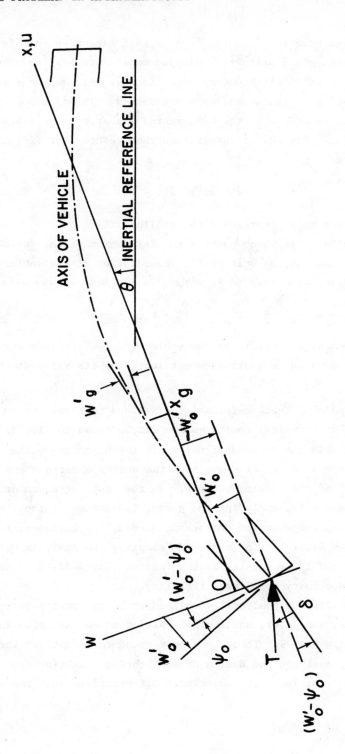

Fig. 7. Flexible Space Vehicle.

function, and other notations are the same as used elsewhere in this paper. The rotation ψ and transverse displacement w are next assumed in such a form as to satisfy all boundary conditions as well as the requirements of conservation of linear and angular momenta. In addition, they may be shown to be reducible to the fundamental linear mode of vibration of a free-free beam. Subsequent integration then reduces Eq. (27) to the following form.

$$\ddot{\tau} + (1 - mr + n\tau^2)\ \omega_o^2\tau = -\Omega\delta \tag{28}$$

where the cubic term $n\omega_o^2\tau^3$ represents the nonlinearity.

In addition to Eq. (28) which governs the deflection of the vehicle, an equation of motion must be written for the rotation of the vehicle as a whole. This is, according to Fig. 7,

$$I_0\ddot{\theta} = -T\left(w_0' - \psi_0 - \delta\right)\frac{\ell}{2} - Tw_0 = T\ell\left(1 - c_o\right)\tau + \frac{1}{2}T\ell\delta \tag{29}$$

where I_0 is the moment of inertia of the vehicle, θ the attitude angle, and the subscript 0 added to a displacement indicates its value at the end $x = 0$.

(2) Control System / There exist a large variety of thrust vector control systems, but a typical configuration can be shown in Fig. 8. For stability analysis the command signal θ_c is taken as zero. The gyros located at $x = x_g$ (Fig. 7) sense both the attitude angle θ and the local slope w_g' of the flexing vehicle. In the usual arrangement in which the instrument unit, including the gyros, is located at the front of a launch vehicle, compensation network is needed, for instance, to phase-stabilize the first bending mode. To simplify the analysis here the gyros are assumed to be located at the rear so that additional compensation is not necessary for linear stability.

To further simplify the analysis, idealized transfer functions are used for the gyros, amplifier, and engine position servo, as shown in the block diagram in Fig. 9. These have been found to be satisfactory in the preliminary analysis and design of most thrust vector-control systems for launch vehicles. The associated differential equations are

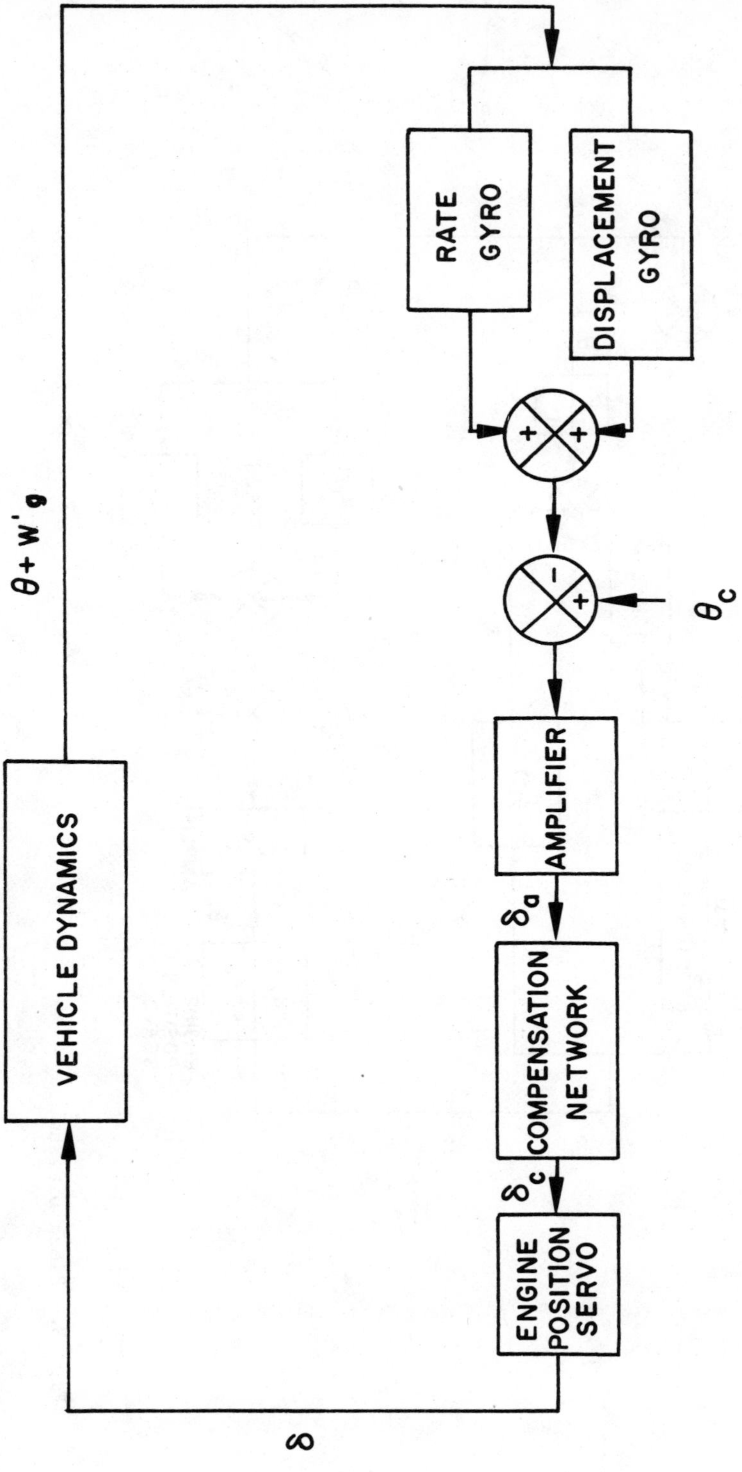

Fig. 8. Typical Control System Configuration.

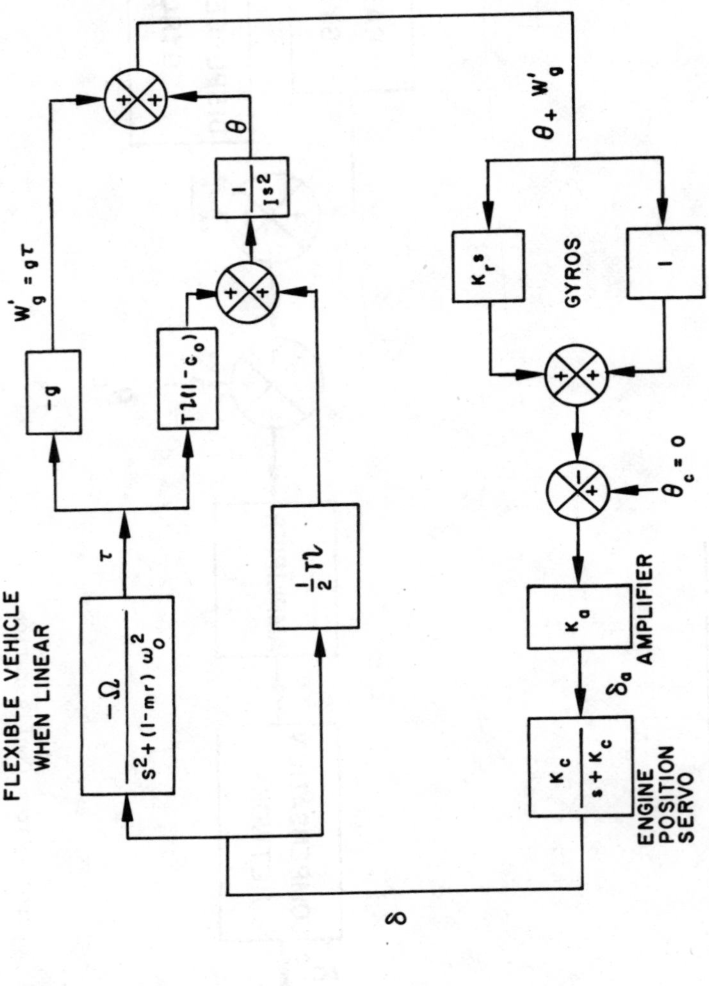

Fig. 9. Block Diagram.

$$\delta_a = -K_a \left[(\theta + w'_g) + K_r (\dot{\theta} + \dot{w}'_g) \right]$$
$$\dot{\delta} + K_c \delta = K_c \delta_a \tag{30}$$

The block diagram in Fig. 9 covers also vehicle dynamics. Transfer function is naturally available for the flexible vehicle only when it is a linear structure. In the linear case the open-loop transfer function for the coupled structure-control system is readily shown to be

$$G(s) = K_a K_c K_r \frac{gI_0\Omega + \frac{1}{2}T\ell}{I_0} \frac{s + 1/K_r}{s^2(s+K_c)} \frac{s^2 + \dfrac{(1-mr)\omega_0^2 - 2(1-c_0)\Omega}{1 + 2gI_0\Omega/T\ell}}{s^2 + (1-mr)\omega_0^2} \tag{31}$$

(3) Nonlinear Stability Analysis / Popov's stability theorem [13] deals with the absolute stability of a nonlinear dynamic system represented by the following equations:

$$\dot{x}_i = \sum_{j=1}^{n} a_{ij}x_j + b_i y \quad (i = 1,2,\ldots,n)$$
$$y = \phi(\sigma) \tag{32}$$
$$\sigma = \sum_{k=1}^{n} c_k x_k$$

The single nonlinearity $\phi(\sigma)$ satisfies the inequality

$$0 \leq \frac{\phi(\sigma)}{\sigma} \leq k \tag{33}$$

k being either a finite positive number or infinity. The block diagram of the nonlinear system is shown in Fig. 10, where N characterizes the nonlinear element and G(s) the linear part of the system. The nonlinearity as prescribed by the inequality (33) is represented graphically in Fig. 11, where $\phi(\sigma)$ is seen to be bounded within the angle or sector [0,k], but its precise form is otherwise unspecified. The dynamic system described by Eq. (32) is said to be absolutely stable

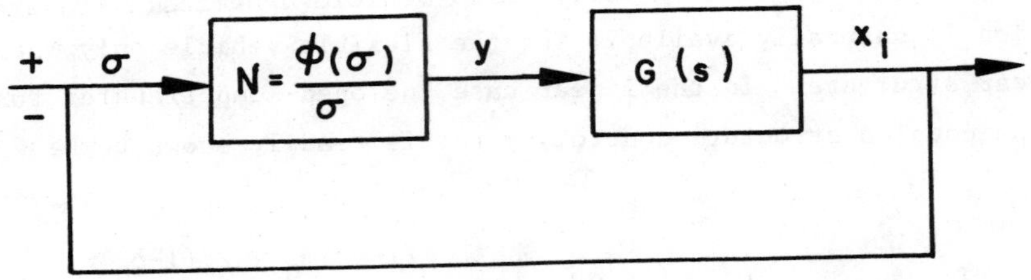

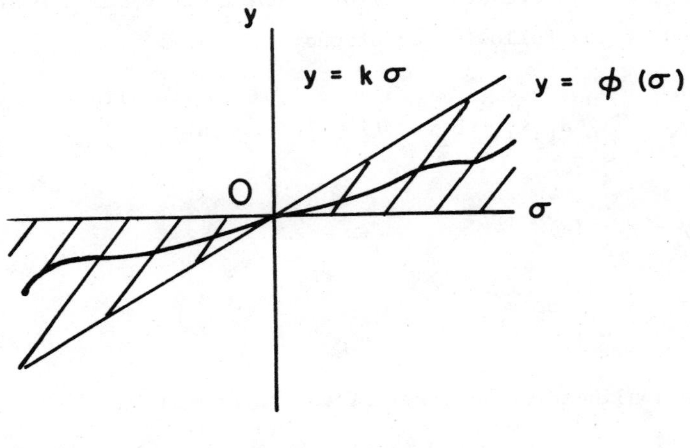

Fig. 10. Block Diagram of Nonlinear Control System. (Above)

Fig. 11. Nonlinearity. (Below)

if asymptotic stability is achieved for perturbation of the initial conditions that can be of arbitrary unbounded amplitude and for any nonlinearity that satisfies the inequality (33).

When all the closed-loop poles of the linear part of a nonlinear system lie to the left of the imaginary axis in the root locus plot; that is, when the associated linear system is asymptotically stable, the nonlinear system is called a principal case. For the principal case Popov's stability theorem states: The system represented by Eqs. (32) and (33) is absolutely stable in the sector [0, k] if there exists a finite real number q such that

$$\mathrm{Re}\ (1 + jq\omega)\ G\ (j\omega) + 1/k > 0 \qquad \text{for all } \omega \geq 0$$

The governing equations (28) through (30) of the thrust vector control system can readily be identified with the form of Eqs. (32) and (33). Since the cubic nonlinearity lies in the sector [0, ∞], we have k = ∞, and Popov's criterion reduces to

$$\mathrm{Re}\ (1 + jq\omega)\ G\ (j\omega) > 0 \qquad \text{for all } \omega \geq 0 \tag{34}$$

The transfer function of the linear part of our nonlinear system as given by Eq. (31) is of the form

$$G\ (s) = \frac{K}{s^2}\ \frac{s^2 + \omega_2^2}{s^2 + \omega_1^2}\ \frac{s + K_2}{s + K_1}$$

from which

$$\mathrm{Re}\ (1+jq\omega)\ G(j\omega) = -\frac{K}{\omega^2}\ \frac{\omega^2-\omega_2^2}{\omega^2-\omega_1^2}\ \frac{1}{\omega^2+K_1^2}\left[\omega^2 + K_1^2K_2 - q\omega^2\left(K_1 - K_2\right)\right]$$

There is no difficulty in making the expression in the square brackets always positive or negative by choosing the proper value of q, but the fraction $(\omega^2 - \omega_2^2)/(\omega^2 - \omega_1^2)$ must change sign as ω changes from a value between ω_1 and ω_2 to a value outside this range. The inequality (34) thus cannot be satisfied, and absolute stability of the nonlinear system cannot be assured even when the associated linear system is stable.

It can be shown [12] that the above situation can be remedied by the insertion of a compensation network, which has further been substantiated by a numerical example. It suffices here to say that, while linear stability does not guarantee nonlinear stability, a non-linearly unstable attitude control system can be made stable through application of Popov's theorem.

Concluding Remarks

While the field of Astroelasticity is relatively new, there are already a sizable number of papers and reports that have been published. No attempt has been made to present a survey of the field. Nevertheless, it is hoped that the specific topics covered in this lecture will, when put together, convey a perspective overview of the general problem. Surveys of related works are available. A recent one in which many references are cited has been prepared under the sponsorship of NASA [14].

REFERENCES

1. Yu, Yi-Yuan, "Dynamic Analysis of Flexible Space Vehicle Systems Subjected to Arbitrary Force and Motion Inputs," Journal of the Astronautical Sciences, Vol. 15, No. 4, August, 1968, pp. 183-193.

2. Przemieniecki, J. S., Theory of Matrix Structural Analysis, McGraw-Hill Book Company, New York, 1968.

3. Timoshenko, S., Theory of Elastic Stability, McGraw-Hill Book Company, New York, 1936.

4. Grossman, P., Koplik, B., Yu, Yi-Yuan, "Nonlinear Vibration of Shallow Spherical Shells," Journal of Applied Mechanics, Vol. 36, 1969, pp. 451-458.

5. Goodier, J. N., "Torsional and Flexural Buckling of Bars of Thin-Walled Open Section Under Compressive and Bending Loads," Journal of Applied Mechanics, Transactions of ASME, Vol. 64, 1964, pp. A-103 to A-107.

6. Yu, Yi-Yuan, "Variational Equation of Motion for Coupled Flexure and Torsion of Bars of Thin-Walled Open Section Including Thermal Effect," General Electric Company, TIS69-SD-238, March, 1969. Also to be published in Journal of Applied Mechanics.

7. Etkin, B., and Hughes, P. C., "Explanation of the Anomalous Spin Behavior of Satellites with Long, Flexible Antennae," Journal of Spacecraft and Rockets, Vol. 4, No. 9, September, 1967, pp. 1139-1145.

8. Yu, Yi-Yuan, "Thermally Induced Vibration and Flutter of a Flexible Boom," Journal of Spacecraft and Rockets, Vol. 6, No. 8, August, 1969, pp. 902-910.

9. Banks, G. F., "Boom Flutter Due to Thermal Lag," NASA-GSFC Memorandum (privately communicated), September, 1967.

10. Augusti, G., "Instability of Struts Subject to Radiant Heat," Meccanica, Vol. 3, September, 1968, pp. 167-176.

11. Yu, Yi-Yuan, "A Rigorous Analysis of Thermal Bending Flutter of a Flexible Boom Based on a Modified Variational Equation of Motion," to be published in Journal of Spacecraft and Rockets.

12. Yu, Yi-Yuan, "Stability of Nonlinear Attitude Control Systems, Including Particularly the Effect of Large Deflection of Space Vehicles," AIAA Paper No. AT35, to be published in the Proceedings of the Nineteenth Congress of the International Astronautical Federation.

13. Popov, V. M., "Absolute Stability of Nonlinear Systems of Automatic Control," Automation and Remote Control, Vol. 22, 1961, pp. 961-979.

14. "Effects of Structural Flexibility on Spacecraft Control Systems," NASA SP-8016, April, 1969.

FLUID DYNAMICS

A NOTE ON FLOW OVER A FLAT PLATE

Arsev H. Eraslan
The University of Tennessee

John A. Benek
The University of Tennessee

ABSTRACT

An alternate singular perturbation theory, with uniformly valid solutions throughout the flow region, is presented for the high Reynolds number flow over a flat plate. The application of the method completely eliminates the superficial and formal mathematical requirements of asymptotic matching of inner and outer expansions and the construction of composite solutions which are associated with the classical singular perturbation theory. Furthermore, it clearly identifies and corrects a fundamental error in the evaluation of the viscous drag according to the classical second order boundary layer theory.

LIST OF NOTATIONS

English Alphabet

a	Constant of Friedrichs equation, Eq. (1)
C_f	Dimensionless drag coefficient, Eq. (73)
F	Principal perturbational solution, Eq. (6)
f	Uniformly valid solution, Eqs. (2) and (13)
$\overline{f}$	Corrective perturbational solution, Eq. (12)
L	Characteristic length
P	Principal perturbational solution for pressure, Eq. (25)
p	Dimensionless pressure, Eq. (20)
$\overline{p}$	Corrective perturbational solution for pressure, Eq. (26)
Re	Reynolds number, Eq. (24)

U Principal perturbational solution for tangential component of velocity, Eq. (25)

u Dimensionless tangential component of velocity, Eq. (20)

$\bar{u}$ Corrective perturbational solution for tangential component of velocity, Eq. (26)

V Principal perturbational solution for normal component of velocity, Eq. (25)

v Dimensionless normal component of velocity, Eq. (20)

$\bar{v}$ Corrective perturbational solution for normal component of velocity, Eq. (26)

X Independent variable associated with the principal perturbational solutions, Eqs. (4) and (25)

x Natural, dimensionless independent variable associated with the uniformly valid solutions, Eq. (20)

$\bar{x}$ Independent variable associated with the corrective perturbational solutions, Eqs. (4) and (26)

Y Independent variable associated with the principal perturbational solutions, Eq. (25)

y Natural, dimensionless independent variable associated with the uniformly valid solutions, Eq. (20)

$\bar{y}$ Independent variable associated with the corrective perturbational solutions, Eq. (26)

Z Complex, independent variable, Eq. (67)

Greek Alphabet

β Constant of Blasius solution, Eq. (55)

ε Small perturbational parameter, Eq. (24)

η Independent similarity variable of Classical solutions, Eq. (54)

μ Viscosity coefficient

ρ Density

τ_w Wall shear stress

Ψ Stream function, Eq. (62)

ω Vorticity component, Eq. (63)

Superscripts

(i) Inner limit behavior

(o) Outer limit behavior

(*) Classical solutions, Eqs. (50) and (64)

Subscripts

n Perturbational order of the solution functions

∞ Free stream conditions

INTRODUCTION

The analysis of the mathematical problem associated with the laminar flow of an incompressible, viscous fluid over a semi-infinite flat plate may be considered as the fundamental example for the application of singular perturbation methods to the solution of Navier-Stokes equation at high Reynolds number conditions.

It is well known that the classical results, obtained according to the direct application of the Prandtl [1] boundary layer concept and the solution of the reduced, parabolic system by Blasius [2], correspond only to the leading first order approximating term in the asymptotic expansion, for large Reynolds number, of the solution to the actual elliptic mathematical problem. Further refinements of the solution to the Navier-Stokes equation by considering higher order perturbational terms in the expansions, e.g., second order boundary layer theory, were discussed in considerable detail by various authors (Lagerstrom and Cole [3], Van Dyke [4,5], Kaplun [6], and Cole [7]).

The systematic applications of the majority of the singular perturbation methods to elliptic problems require three basic concepts. Firstly, the original mathematical system is distinctly separated into two singular mathematical systems associated with the inner and outer asymptotic expansions. Secondly since neither of the solutions for the two regions can satisfy the complete set of the boundary conditions associated with the actual problem, superficial boundary conditions are constructed by matching the inner and outer expansions according to certain formal matching principles, e.g., Lagerstrom's restrictive matching principle. Thirdly, since neither of the two solutions are valid throughout the complete region, intermediate, composite solutions are constructed to render uniformly valid characteristics for the perturbational solutions in the overlapping regions.

The investigations by Erdelyi [8] and Fraenkel [9] present detailed and mathematically rigorous discussions of various new aspects of the classical singular perturbation theories. Further studies which consider various extensions, based on the construction of combined forms of inner and composite expansions, and the development of asymptotic series in terms of perturbational functions of multiple scaled independent variables, were also presented by Van Dyke [4].

The only alternate perturbational theory, which is both conceptually and mathematically different than the methods of the aforementioned investigations, was suggested by Vishik and Lyusternik [10] based on the "corrections" of the "limiting solutions" to satisfy the totality of boundary conditions of the actual elliptic system.

The systematic application of the method to the flow of an incompressible, viscous fluid over a semi-infinite flat plate was presented by Chudov [11] with particular emphasis on the uniformly valid properties of the solutions.

The purpose of the present paper is to illustrate the feasibility of an alternate, formal, asymptotic expansion method which can directly yield uniformly valid perturbational solutions, to any desired degree of accuracy, without necessitating superficial matching principles and the construction of composite expansions in the overlapping intermediate regions.

Fundamental Concept of the Proposed Method

The fundamental idea behind the development of the classical singular perturbation theory is commonly illustrated by the asymptotic solutions of the special form of the well known Friedrichs [12] boundary value problem,

$$\varepsilon \frac{d^2f}{dx^2} + \frac{df}{dx} = a; \quad f(0) = 0, \quad f(1) = 1 \tag{1}$$

with the exact solution of the form,

$$f(x;\varepsilon) = ax + (1 - a)\,\frac{(1 - e^{-x/\varepsilon})}{(1 - e^{-1/\varepsilon})} \tag{2}$$

The alternate, uniform first order approximation for small ε, based on inner and outer asymptotic expansions, is given as:

$$f(x;\varepsilon) \sim \begin{cases} (1-a) + ax & \text{as} \quad \varepsilon\to 0 \text{ with } x > 0 \text{ fixed} \\ (1-a)(1-e^{-\bar{x}}) & \text{as} \quad \varepsilon\to 0 \text{ with } \bar{x} = \dfrac{x}{\varepsilon} \text{ fixed} \end{cases} \tag{3}$$

The pertinent characteristic properties of this solution are well discussed by Van Dyke [4]; hence, we will refrain from further elaboration of this point but rather concentrate on an alternate construction of the solution based on the concept of strained coordinates.

Statement of the Problem / It is required to construct a perturbational solution $f(x;\varepsilon)$, for the original boundary value problem, Eq. (1), such that for a given sufficiently small parameter ε, the solution $f(x;\varepsilon)$ is uniformly valid in the complete range of validity of the mathematical system, $0 \leq x \leq 1$, to any desired accuracy in ε.

It is important to realize that the statement of the problem distinctly requires that the solution be uniformly valid in the complete range $0 \leq x \leq 1$, for all perturbations; hence, it immediately eliminates the possibility of separating the range into inner and outer regions with their associated solutions not necessarily satisfying the boundary conditions of the problem. Consequently, the method of solution must necessarily be different than the classical asymptotic expansions which result in the solutions of Eq. (3).

Postulate 1. The complete range $0 \leq x \leq 1$ of the original boundary value problem, Eq. (1), can be described alternately and simultaneously by the natural coordinate X and the strained coordinate $\bar{x}$, such that,

$$X = x, \quad \bar{x} = x/\varepsilon \tag{4}$$

for any fixed $\varepsilon > 0$.

It is of profound significance that according to postulate 1, the complete range $0 \leq x \leq 1$ is described by two independent variables X and $\bar{x}$ which extend throughout the range by overlapping each other. Consequently, the ranges of the two coordinates are not restricted to different inner and outer regions; but they indeed cover the entire range of validity of the original mathematical system. Furthermore, since the variables cover the entire region, $0 \leq x \leq 1$, the limit points are necessarily included in the simultaneous descriptions, i.e.,

$$x = 0 \underset{\varepsilon \text{ fixed}}{\Longleftrightarrow} X = 0 \underset{\varepsilon \text{ fixed}}{\Longleftrightarrow} \bar{x} = 0$$

$$x = 1 \underset{\varepsilon \text{ fixed}}{\Longleftrightarrow} X = 1 \underset{\varepsilon \text{ fixed}}{\Longleftrightarrow} \bar{x} = 1/\varepsilon \tag{5}$$

Definition 1. The Principal Perturbational Solution $F(X;\varepsilon)$, associated with the outer boundary condition at $x = 1$, is defined as the natural perturbational expansion, in powers of the small parameter $\varepsilon \geq 0$ and the unknown perturbational functions $F_n(X)$ in the natural coordinate $X = x$ of the original system, such that the function $F(X;\varepsilon)$ identically satisfies the outer boundary conditions for all $\varepsilon \geq 0$, i.e.,

$$F(X;\varepsilon) = F_o(X) + \varepsilon F_1(X) + \ldots + \varepsilon^n F_n(X) + \ldots$$

$$F(1;\varepsilon) = 1, \quad \text{for all } \varepsilon \geq 0 \tag{6}$$

As a consequence of the definition 1, it is necessary and sufficient that the perturbational functions $F_n(X)$ satisfy the boundary conditions,

$$F_o(1) = 1, \quad F_n(1) = 0, \quad (n \geq 1) \tag{7}$$

Substituting the expansion, Eq. (6), in the differential equation of the original system, Eq. (1), written in natural coordinates $X = x$, and considering the boundary conditions associated with $F_n(X)$, Eq. (8), the singular perturbational systems associated with the powers of ε, become,

$$\frac{dF_o}{dX} = a \; ; \quad F_o(1) = 1$$

$$\frac{dF_n}{dX} = - \frac{d^2F_{n-1}}{dX^2} = 0 \; ; \quad F_n(1) = 0 \; , \quad (n \geq 1) \tag{8}$$

with the complete set of solutions as:

$$F_o(X) = aX + (1-a) \; , \quad F_n(X) = 0 \; , \quad (n \geq 1) \tag{9}$$

Hence, the principal perturbational solution $F(X;\varepsilon)$ becomes,

$$F(X;\varepsilon) = aX + (1-a) + \sum_{n=1}^{\infty} \varepsilon^n(0) \tag{10}$$

which necessarily violates the inner boundary condition, Eq. (1), according to its zeroth order perturbational functions,

$$F(0;\varepsilon) = (1-a) \neq 0 \; , \quad F_o(0) = 1-a \; ; \quad F_n(0) = 0 \; , \quad (n \geq 1) \tag{11}$$

In view of the consequences of the solution set, Eq. (9), $F(X;\varepsilon)$ cannot be considered as a valid approximation of the actual required solution $f(x;\varepsilon)$ due to the singular properties of the mathematical system, Eq. (8), and the violation of the inner boundary condition, Eq. (11).

Definition 2. The Corrective Perturbational Solution $\overline{f}(\overline{x};\varepsilon)$, associated with the satisfaction of the inner boundary condition at $x = 0$, is defined as the perturbational expansion in terms of the small parameter $\varepsilon > 0$ and the unknown perturbational functions $\overline{f}_n(\overline{x})$ in the strained coordinate $x = \overline{x}/\varepsilon$, i.e.,

$$\overline{f}(\overline{x};\varepsilon) = \overline{f}_o(\overline{x}) + \sum_{n=1}^{\infty} \varepsilon^n \overline{f}_n(\overline{x}) \tag{12}$$

According to definition 2, $f(x;\varepsilon)$ is rather arbitrary; and indeed, it does not necessarily satisfy the inner boundary conditions, Eq. (1). This point is of significant importance since it establishes the fundamental difference of the present approach from the classical asymptotic expansion method.

Postulate 3. (Superposition Postulate). For any $\varepsilon > 0$, the uniformly valid solution $f(x;\varepsilon)$ of the original system, Eq. (10), in the complete range $0 \leq x \leq 1$, is necessarily equal to the sum of the principal perturbational solution $F(X;\varepsilon)$ and the corrective perturbational solution $\overline{f}(\overline{x};\varepsilon)$, i.e.,

$$f(x;\varepsilon) = F(X;\varepsilon) + \overline{f}(\overline{x};\varepsilon) = F_o(x) + \overline{f}_o(\overline{x}) = \sum_{n=1}^{\infty} \varepsilon^n [F_n(x) + \overline{f}_n(\overline{x})] \tag{13}$$

The superposition postulate establishes, once and for all, that the matching of the inner and outer expansions, as in the case of the classical method, is not necessary for the construction of the uniformly valid solution.

Considering the construction of the uniformly valid solution, Eq. (13), from two sets of perturbational functions, $F_n(X)$ and $\overline{f}_n(\overline{x})$, in terms of only one of the two variables X or $\overline{x}$, respectively, the present method is distinctly different than the one proposed by Cochran [13] which employs a single set of functions in terms of both the unstrained and strained variables.

For the solution $f(x;\varepsilon)$ to be uniformly valid in the complete range $0 \le x \le 1$, it must necessarily satisfy both boundary conditions; hence, for any arbitrary $\varepsilon > 0$, and in view of the outer limit boundary conditions for the perturbational functions $F_n(X)$ of the principal perturbational solution, Eq. (7), the perturbational functions $\overline{f}_n(\overline{x})$ of the corrective solution must necessarily satisfy the conditions,

$$\overline{F}_o(0) = - F_o(0), \quad \overline{f}_n(0) = - F_n(0), \quad (n \ge 1) \tag{14}$$

$$\overline{f}_o(1/\varepsilon) = 0, \quad \overline{f}_n(1/\varepsilon) = 0, \quad (n \ge 1) \tag{15}$$

With the two sets of the boundary conditions for the functions $\overline{f}_n(\overline{x})$ determined, Eqs. (14) and (15), the problem reduces to the formulation of the differential equations associated with the function set.

Definition 3. The Inner Limit Behavior, $f^{(i)}(x;\varepsilon)$, is defined as the limit $X \to 0$ with $\varepsilon,\overline{x}$ fixed of the uniformly valid solution, $f(x;\varepsilon)$, i.e.,

$$f^{(i)}(x;\varepsilon) = \lim_{\substack{X\to 0\\ \varepsilon,\overline{x}\ \text{fixed}}} F(X;\varepsilon) + \overline{f}(\overline{x};\varepsilon) = \overline{f}_o(\overline{x}) + F_o(0)$$

$$+ \sum_{n=1}^{\infty} \varepsilon^n \left[\overline{f}_n(\overline{x}) + \sum_{k=0}^{n} \frac{\overline{x}^{-k}}{k!} \frac{d^k F_{n-k}}{dX^k}(0)\right] \tag{16}$$

It is essential to realize that the inner limit behavior $f^{(i)}(x;\varepsilon)$ is defined strictly based on the complete uniformly valid solution $f(x;\varepsilon)$ and not in terms of the principal, $F(X;\varepsilon)$, or the corrective, $\overline{f}(\overline{x};\varepsilon)$ perturbational functions; hence, it clearly represents the behavior of the uniformly valid solution $f(x;\varepsilon)$ of the original system, Eq. (1), in the neighborhood of the inner limit $x = 0$.

Postulate 4. The inner limit behavior $f^{(i)}(x;\varepsilon)$ approximates the uniformly valid solution $f(x;\varepsilon)$ to any desired accuracy in $\varepsilon > 0$ in the neighborhood of the inner limit $x = 0$; hence, it necessarily satisfies the original differential equation, Eq. (1), to any desired accuracy in $\varepsilon > 0$ in the neighborhood of the inner limit $x = 0$.

The postulate implies that in the neighborhood of the inner limit, $x = 0$, the principal perturbational solution $F(X;\varepsilon)$ can be approximated by its neighborhood behavior and that the corrective solution $\bar{f}(\bar{x};\varepsilon)$, in the strained coordinate, $\bar{x} = x/\varepsilon$, is the controlling part of the uniformly valid solution; hence, it clearly conforms with the boundary layer assumption that the corrective perturbational solution, which is associated with the satisfaction of the inner, $f(0;\varepsilon) = 0$ boundary condition, has the significant influence on the solution in the small region near the boundary.

Substituting the inner limit behavior expansion, Eq. (16), in the original system, Eq. (1), written in the strained variable $\bar{x} = x/\varepsilon$, collecting the terms of the powers of ε, and considering the already established boundary conditions for $\bar{f}_n(\bar{x})$, Eqs. (14) and (15), the complete set of boundary value problems for the unknown perturbational functions $\bar{f}_n(\bar{x})$ becomes,

$$\frac{d^2\bar{f}_o}{d\bar{x}^2} + \frac{d\bar{f}_o}{d\bar{x}} = 0; \quad \bar{f}_o(0) = -F_o(0) = -(1-a), \quad \bar{f}_o(1/\varepsilon) = 0$$

$$\frac{d^2\bar{f}_1}{d\bar{x}^2} + \frac{d\bar{f}_1}{d\bar{x}} = a - \frac{dF_o}{dX}(0) = 0; \quad \bar{f}_1(0) = -F_1(0) = 0, \quad f_1(1/\varepsilon) = 0$$

$$\frac{d^2\bar{f}_n}{d\bar{x}^2} + \frac{d\bar{f}_n}{d\bar{x}} = -\sum_{k=1}^{n} \frac{\bar{x}^{k-1}}{(k-1)!} \frac{d^kF_{n-k}}{dX^k}(0) = 0; \quad \bar{f}_n(0) = -F_n(0) = 0, \tag{17}$$

$$\bar{f}_n(1/\varepsilon) = 0, \quad (n \geq 1)$$

with the complete set of solutions as:

$$\bar{f}_o(\bar{x}) = -(1-a)\frac{(e^{-\bar{x}} - e^{-1/\varepsilon})}{(1 - e^{-1/\varepsilon})}, \quad \bar{f}_n(\bar{x}) = 0, \quad (n \geq 1) \tag{18}$$

Hence, the complete uniformly valid solution $f(x;\varepsilon)$ becomes,

$$f(x;\varepsilon) = F_o(x) + \bar{f}_o(\bar{x}) = ax + (1-a) - (1-a)\frac{(e^{-\bar{x}} - e^{-1/\varepsilon})}{(1 - e^{-1/\varepsilon})} \tag{19}$$

which, written in the unstrained coordinate x of the original system, is indeed the exact solution, Eq. (2). It is important to realize that although Eq. (19) contains only zeroth order perturbational terms, it actually is the complete perturbational solution since the series is not truncated but the higher order perturbational terms were evaluated to be trivial solutions according to the systematic application of the method. Indeed, the final result establishes that the perturbational solution immediately converges to the exact solution with only zeroth order perturbational terms.

The present method does not require the separation of the original range $0 \leq x \leq 1$ into two superficial ranges with two sets of inner and outer solutions which are valid only in their corresponding ranges. Since the asymptotic expansion of the proposed method is uniformly valid throughout the range $0 \leq x \leq 1$, it does not necessitate any, implicit or explicit, matching condition. The essential boundary conditions for the perturbational functions $F_n(x)$ and $\overline{f}_n(\overline{x})$ are determined strictly at the limit points of the range, $x = 0$ and $x = 1$, from the natural boundary conditions of the original system, without resorting to any type of matching of the two solutions in intermediate, overlapping ranges. Furthermore, since the solution $f(x;\varepsilon)$ is indeed uniformly valid throughout the range $0 \leq x \leq 1$, the proposed method completely eliminates the necessity of the composite expansion which is significantly important in the construction of the uniformly valid solutions according to the classical methods.

Considering that the zeroth order solution of the present method results in the exact solution, whereas the corresponding order perturbational solution of the classical method only gives an approximation to the solution, it can be concluded that, at least in its application to the Friedrichs boundary value problem, the proposed method is vastly superior to the classical method in all aspects of the perturbational theory.

Application to Flow over a Flat Plate

For the two-dimensional, steady flow of an incompressible, viscous fluid, the well known dimensionless mathematical system consists of the boundary value problem,

$$\frac{\partial u}{\partial x} + \frac{\partial v}{\partial y} = 0 \tag{20}$$

$$u \frac{\partial u}{\partial x} + v \frac{\partial u}{\partial y} = - \frac{\partial p}{\partial x} + \varepsilon^2 \frac{\partial^2 u}{\partial x^2} + \varepsilon^2 \frac{\partial^2 u}{\partial y^2} \tag{21}$$

$$u \frac{\partial v}{\partial x} + v \frac{\partial v}{\partial y} = - \frac{\partial p}{\partial y} + \varepsilon^2 \frac{\partial^2 v}{\partial x^2} + \varepsilon^2 \frac{\partial^2 v}{\partial y^2} \tag{22}$$

$$u(x,0) = 0, \quad v(x,0) = 0, \quad x > 0; \quad \frac{\partial u}{\partial y}(x,0) = 0, \quad v(x,0) = 0, \; x < 0$$

$$\lim_{y\to\infty} u(x,y) = 1, \quad \lim_{y\to\infty} v(x,y) = 0, \quad -\infty \le x \le +\infty \tag{23}$$

where the coordinates x and y are along and normal to the plate, respectively. The unknowns of the problem are the velocity components u, along the plate, and v, normal to the plate and the pressure p. All the quantities are appropriately non-dimensionalized on the characteristic length along the plate L, the free stream velocity U_∞, density ρ_∞, and viscosity μ_∞. The small parameter ε is defined as the inverse of the square root of the Reynolds number Re as:

$$\varepsilon = 1/\sqrt{Re} \;, \quad Re = \rho_\infty U_\infty L/\mu_\infty \tag{24}$$

Following the proposed method of the previous section and considering the Prandtl boundary layer hypothesis, the unstrained and strained coordinates and variables for the solution are,

Unstrained:

$$X = x, \quad Y = y, \quad U(X,Y;\varepsilon) = u(x,y;\varepsilon)$$

$$V(X,Y;\varepsilon) = v(x,y;\varepsilon), \quad P(X,Y;\varepsilon) = p(x,y;\varepsilon) \tag{25}$$

Strained:

$$\bar{x} = x, \quad \bar{y} = y/\varepsilon, \quad \bar{u}(\bar{x},\bar{y};\varepsilon) = u(x,y;\varepsilon)$$

$$\bar{v}(x,y;\varepsilon) = \frac{1}{\varepsilon} v(x,y;\varepsilon), \quad \bar{p}(x,y;\varepsilon) = p(x,y;\varepsilon) \tag{26}$$

Such that,

$$\underset{\varepsilon \text{ fixed}}{y \to \infty} \iff \underset{\varepsilon \text{ fixed}}{Y \to \infty} \iff \bar{y} \to \infty \;; \quad \underset{\varepsilon \text{ fixed}}{y = 0} \iff \underset{\varepsilon \text{ fixed}}{Y = 0} \iff \bar{y} = 0 \tag{27}$$

Considering the unstrained variables $U(X,Y;\varepsilon)$, $V(X,Y;\varepsilon)$, $P(X,Y;\varepsilon)$ as the principal perturbational solutions, and the strained variables $\bar{u}(\bar{x},\bar{y};\varepsilon)$, $\bar{v}(\bar{x},\bar{y};\varepsilon)$, $\bar{p}(\bar{x},\bar{y};\varepsilon)$ as the corrective perturbational solutions, the uniformly valid perturbational expansions to the problem become:

$$u(x,y;\varepsilon) = U_0(X,Y) + \bar{u}_0(\bar{x},\bar{y}) + \varepsilon[U_1(X,Y) + \bar{u}_1(\bar{x},\bar{y})] \tag{28}$$

$$v(x,y;\varepsilon) = V_0(X,Y) + \varepsilon[V_1(x,y) + \bar{v}_0(\bar{x},\bar{y})] + \varepsilon^2[V_2(x,y) + \bar{v}_1(\bar{x},\bar{y})] \tag{29}$$

$$p(x,y;\varepsilon) = P_0(X,Y) + \bar{p}_0(\bar{x},\bar{y}) + \varepsilon[P_1(X,Y) + \bar{p}_1(\bar{x},\bar{y})] \tag{30}$$

In the expansions, Eqs. (28), (29) and (30), the series were truncated after the first order terms in ε; hence, the uniformly valid solutions are of the same order of accuracy as the classical second order boundary layer theory.

Considering the conditions on the plate, $y = 0 \Leftrightarrow Y = 0 \Leftrightarrow \bar{y} = 0$, and noting that the boundary conditions for the original system, Eq. (23), must necessarily be satisfied for any $\varepsilon > 0$ according to the uniformly valid property of the solutions, the appropriate relations for the boundary conditions of the perturbational terms become,

$$\bar{u}_0(\bar{x},0) = - U_0(X,0), \quad \bar{u}_1(\bar{x},0) = - U_1(X,0)$$

$$V_0(X,0) = 0, \quad V_1(X,0) = - \bar{v}_0(\bar{x},0), \quad V_2(X,0) = - \bar{v}_1(\bar{x},0) \tag{31}$$

$$\bar{P}_0(\bar{x},0) = - P_0(X,0), \quad \bar{p}_1(\bar{x},0) = - P_1(X,0)$$

It is important to realize that the limit relations, Eq. (31), do not determine uniquely all the necessary inner boundary conditions; indeed, $U_0(X,0)$, $P_0(X,0)$, $\bar{v}_0(\bar{x},0)$, $U_1(X,0)$, $P_1(X,0)$ are completely arbitrary at this point in the analysis. The concrete specification of the boundary conditions can and must be accomplished after considering the singular characteristics of the perturbational mathematical systems for the unknown functions.

Postulate 5. For sufficiently large distances from the plate, $y \to \infty \Leftrightarrow Y \to \infty \Leftrightarrow \bar{y} \to \infty$, for ε fixed, the viscous effects in the system completely vanish; hence, the boundary conditions at the free stream are necessarily satisfied by the solutions of the inviscid mathematical system, $\varepsilon = 0$, i.e.,

$$\lim_{y\to\infty} u(x,y;\varepsilon) = \lim_{Y\to\infty} U_0(X,Y) = 1, \quad \lim_{y\to\infty} v(x,y;\varepsilon) = \lim_{Y\to\infty} V_0(X,Y) = 0 \tag{32}$$

The postulate, in a sense, is the statement of the boundary layer assumption that the viscous effects are restricted only to regions near the plate.

Considering the conditions at the free stream, $y \to \infty \Leftrightarrow Y \to \infty \Leftrightarrow \bar{y} \to \infty$, and noting that the boundary conditions for the original system, Eq. (23), must necessarily be satisfied for any $\varepsilon > 0$, in view of postulate 5, the appropriate relations for the free stream boundary conditions become,

$$\lim_{Y\to\infty} U_o(X,Y) = 1, \quad \lim_{y\to\infty} \bar{u}_o(\bar{x},\bar{y}) = 0, \quad \lim_{Y\to\infty} \bar{U}_1(x,y) = - \lim_{Y\to\infty} U_1(x,y)$$

$$\lim_{Y\to\infty} V_o(X,Y) = 0, \quad \lim_{Y\to\infty} V_1(X,Y) = - \lim_{\bar{y}\to\infty} \bar{v}_o(\bar{x},\bar{y}) \tag{33}$$

$$\lim_{Y\to\infty} P_o(X,Y) = P_o = \text{const.}, \quad \lim_{\bar{y}\to\infty} \bar{p}_o(\bar{x}_1\bar{y}) = 0, \quad \lim_{\bar{y}\to\infty} \bar{p}_1(\bar{x}_1\bar{y}) = -\lim_{Y\to\infty} P_1(x,Y)$$

Again it should be emphasized that the limit relations, Eq. (33), do not determine uniquely the boundary conditions at the free stream; hence, the arbitrary values for $\lim_{Y\to\infty} U_1(X,Y)$ and the $\lim_{Y\to\infty} P_1(X,Y)$ need to be specified after considering the singular perturbational systems for the particular functions.

Although the arbitrary characteristics of the boundary conditions at the inner and outer limit points can be eliminated by considering the singular properties of the ultimate perturbational systems, substantial simplification in the development can be achieved by formally assuming two additional conditions to be verified later in the analysis.

Postulate 6. The mathematical systems associated with the principal perturbational solutions of higher than zeroth order can be formulated under impermeable wall conditions without any loss of generality, i.e.,

$$V_1(X,0) = 0, \quad V_2(X,0) = 0 \tag{34}$$

Postulate 7. The only nonvanishing influence of the viscous effects associated with the corrective perturbational solutions, at sufficiently large distances from the plate, are the displacement effects, i.e.,

$$\lim_{\bar{y}\to\infty} \bar{u}_1(\bar{x},\bar{y}) = 0, \quad \lim_{\bar{y}\to\infty} \bar{p}_1(\bar{x},\bar{y}) = 0 \tag{35}$$

The postulate 6 in a sense represents the choice of solution to the system and postulate 7 clearly states the well established consequence of the boundary layer effects on the flow field.

The outer limit behaviors of the uniformly valid solutions become,

$$
\begin{aligned}
u^{(o)}(x,y;\varepsilon) &= U_o(X,Y) + \varepsilon U_1(X,Y) \\
v^{(o)}(x,y;\varepsilon) &= V_o(X,Y) + \varepsilon V_1(X,Y) + \varepsilon \bar{v}_{o\infty}(X) \qquad (36) \\
p^{(o)}(x,y;\varepsilon) &= P_o(X,Y) + \varepsilon P_1(X,Y)
\end{aligned}
$$

where the limiting value of the zeroth order transverse velocity component is defined as:

$$
\bar{v}_{o\infty}(X) = \bar{v}_{o\infty}(\bar{x}) = \lim_{\bar{y}\to\infty} \bar{v}_o(\bar{x},\bar{y}) \qquad (37)
$$

Similarly the inner limit behaviors of the uniformly valid solutions become,

$$
\begin{aligned}
u^{(i)}(x,y;\varepsilon) &= U_o(X,0) + \bar{u}_o(\bar{x},\bar{y}) + \varepsilon U_1(X,0) + \varepsilon \bar{u}_1(\bar{x},\bar{y}) \\
v^{(i)}(x,y;\varepsilon) &= V_o(X,0) + \varepsilon V_1(X,0) + \varepsilon \bar{v}_o(\bar{x},\bar{y}) \qquad (38) \\
p^{(i)}(x,y;\varepsilon) &= P_o(X,0) + \bar{p}_o(\bar{x},\bar{y}) + \varepsilon P_1(X,Y) + \varepsilon \bar{p}_1(\bar{x},\bar{y})
\end{aligned}
$$

It is important to note that in the formulation of limit behavior expressions, Eqs. (36) and (38), for the asymptotic expansions, direct limits of $Y \to 0$ and $\bar{y} \to \infty$ were employed without considering Taylor series expansions in the neighborhoods of the limit points. It should be emphasized that further refinement of the solutions can be achieved by the rigorous expansions of the perturbational functions in the neighborhood of the limit points, particularly if higher order approximations are desired for the solutions.

Substituting the limit behavior expressions, Eqs. (40) and (42), in the original system, Eq. (23), written in the appropriate unstrained or strained coordinates, collecting the coefficient terms of the powers of ε, and considering the inner and outer limit boundary conditions, Eqs. (31) and (33), together with postulates 6 and 7, the governing mathematical systems for the unknown perturbational functions of the asympotitic expansions can be systematically determined.

Constraint Equations / The perturbational system corresponding to ε^{-1} power results in two equations,

$$V_o(X,0)\,\frac{\partial \bar{u}_o}{\partial \bar{y}}(\bar{x},\bar{y}) = 0 \tag{39}$$

$$\frac{\partial \bar{p}_o}{\partial \bar{y}} = 0 \tag{40}$$

The first requirement of the ε^{-1} order system is of significant importance. Since $u_o(\bar{x},\bar{y})$ cannot be a function of $\bar{x}$ only due to the boundary conditions, Eqs. (31) and (33), and indeed, it is vastly undesirable due to the excessive singular characteristics of such a solution, $V_o(X,0)$ must necessarily vanish on the wall to satisfy the condition, Eq. (39). This mathematical result establishes, once and for all, that the zeroth order inviscid solutions must be obtained under impermeable plate conditions; consequently, if there exist mass transfer on the plate, it must necessarily be included in the viscous corrective solution. Furthermore, the velocity of mass transfer cannot be of higher order of magnitude than ε in comparison to free stream characteristic velocity. Hence, the perturbational methods, associated with high Reynolds number, Prandtl boundary type mathematical systems, cannot be applied to massive wall mass transfer problems which require the solution of the zeroth order inviscid flow field under non-zero transverse velocity conditions on the wall.

The second requirement, Eq. (40), of the ε^{-1} order system implies the well known condition that there exists no zeroth order pressure gradient across the boundary layer, which is clearly consistent with the results of the classical singular perturbation theory.

Zeroth Order Principal Perturbational Solution / Collecting the terms corresponding to the ε^{o} power, the mathematical system for the zeroth order principal perturbation solution becomes,

$$\frac{\partial U_o}{\partial X} + \frac{\partial V_o}{\partial Y} = 0 \tag{41}$$

$$U_o \frac{\partial U_o}{\partial X} + \frac{\partial U_o}{\partial Y} = - \frac{\partial P_o}{\partial X} \tag{42}$$

$$U_o \frac{\partial V_o}{\partial Y} + \frac{\partial V_o}{\partial Y} = - \frac{\partial P_o}{\partial Y} \tag{43}$$

with the appropriate boundary conditions,

$$\frac{\partial U_o}{\partial Y}(x,0) = 0, \quad X < 0; \quad U_o(X,0) \text{ arbitrary}, \quad X > 0 \tag{44}$$

$$V_o(X,0) = 0, \quad \lim_{Y\to\infty} U_o(X,Y) = 1, \quad \lim_{Y\to\infty} V_o(X,Y) = 0$$

$$\lim_{Y\to\infty} P_o(X,Y) = P_o = \text{const.}$$

which clearly represents the governing equations for the inviscid flow field over the flat plate with the well known solution,

$$U_o(X,Y) = 1, \quad V_o(X,Y) = 0, \quad P(X,Y) = P_o = \text{const.} \tag{45}$$

Zeroth Order Corrective Perturbational Solution / Collecting the terms corresponding to ε^o powers and substituting the results of the zeroth order principal perturbational solution, Eq. (45), the mathematical system for the zeroth order corrective perturbational solution becomes,

$$\frac{\partial \bar{u}_o}{\partial \bar{x}} + \frac{\partial \bar{v}_o}{\partial \bar{y}} = 0 \tag{46}$$

$$(1 + \bar{u}_o) \frac{\partial \bar{u}_o}{\partial \bar{x}} + \bar{v}_o \frac{\partial \bar{u}_o}{\partial \bar{y}} = - \frac{\partial \bar{p}_o}{\partial \bar{x}} + \frac{\partial^2 \bar{u}_o}{\partial \bar{y}^2} \tag{47}$$

$$\frac{\partial \bar{p}_o}{\partial \bar{y}} = 0 \tag{48}$$

$$\bar{u}_o(\bar{x},0) = -1, \quad \bar{v}_o(\bar{x},0) = 0, \quad \lim_{\bar{y}\to\infty} \bar{u}_o(\bar{x},\bar{y}) = 0, \quad \lim_{\bar{y}\to\infty} \bar{p}_o(\bar{x},\bar{y}) = 0 \tag{49}$$

It is evident that the present system has distinctly different form both in momentum equation, Eq. (46), and the boundary condition for the tangential component of velocity, Eq. (49), than the classical first order boundary layer problem for the flat plate.

After considering Eq. (48) and the boundary condition, Eq. (49), the pressure gradient along $\bar{x}$ can be eliminated. To employ the already established solutions to the classical flat plate problem, the velocity components may be reformulated as:

$$u_o^*(\bar{x},\bar{y}) = 1 + \bar{u}_o(\bar{x},\bar{y}), \quad \bar{v}_o^*(\bar{x},\bar{y}) = \bar{v}_o(\bar{x},\bar{y}) \tag{50}$$

which transforms the original mathematical system, Eqs. (46) through (49), into the classical Blasius problem,

$$\frac{\partial \bar{u}_o^*}{\partial \bar{x}} + \frac{\partial \bar{v}_o^*}{\partial \bar{y}} = 0 \tag{51}$$

$$\bar{u}_o^* \frac{\partial \bar{u}_o^*}{\partial \bar{y}} + v_o^* \frac{\partial \bar{u}_o^*}{\partial \bar{y}} = \frac{\partial^2 \bar{u}_o^*}{\partial \bar{y}^2} \tag{52}$$

$$\bar{u}_o(\bar{x},0) = 0, \quad \bar{v}_o^*(\bar{x},0) = 0, \quad \lim_{\bar{y}\to\infty} \bar{u}_o(\bar{x},\bar{y}) = 1 \tag{53}$$

The similar solutions to the system are readily available (Schlichting [2]) as:

$$\eta = \frac{\bar{y}}{\bar{x}^{1/2}}, \quad u_o^*(\bar{x},\bar{y}) = \bar{f}^{*\prime}(\eta), \quad \bar{v}_o^*(\bar{x},\bar{y}) \frac{1}{2\bar{x}^{1/2}} (\eta\bar{f}^{*\prime} - \bar{f}^*) \tag{54}$$

As a consequence of the results, it is immediately evident that the mathematical system for the zeroth corrective perturbational solution of the present method is in a sense equivalent to the classical mathematical problem associated with the flat plate problem.

First Order Principal Perturbational Solution / The mathematical system for the first order principal perturbational solution requires the limit $\bar{y} \to \infty$ of the transverse velocity component, $\bar{v}_o(\bar{x},\bar{y})$, which can be evaluated from the Blasius solution as:

$$\bar{v}_{o\infty}(\bar{x}) = \lim_{\bar{y}\to\infty} \bar{v}_o(\bar{x},\bar{y}) = \lim_{\bar{y}\to\infty} \bar{v}_o^*(\bar{x},\bar{y}) = \frac{1}{2\bar{x}^{1/2}} \lim_{\eta\to\infty}(\eta\bar{f}_o^{*\prime} - \bar{f}_o^*)$$

$$= -\frac{\beta}{2}\bar{x}^{-1/2} = -\frac{\beta}{2}X^{-1/2}, \quad \beta \simeq -0.865 \tag{55}$$

Collecting the terms corresponding to ε^1 power, and substituting the limiting value of the transverse velocity component of the zeroth order corrective perturbational solution, Eq. (55), the mathematical system for the first order principal perturbational solution becomes,

$$\frac{\partial U_1}{\partial X} + \frac{\partial V_1}{\partial Y} = 0; \quad \frac{\partial U_1}{\partial X} = - \frac{\partial P_1}{\partial X}; \quad \frac{\partial V_1}{\partial X} + \frac{1}{4} \beta X^{-3/2} = - \frac{\partial P}{\partial Y} \tag{60}$$

$$\begin{gathered} U_1(X,0) \text{ arbitrary}, \quad V_1(X,0) = 0, \quad X > 0 \\ \lim_{Y\to\infty} U_1(X,Y) = 0, \quad \lim_{Y\to\infty} V_1(X,Y) = \overline{v}_{o\infty}(X) = \frac{\beta}{2} X^{-1/2} \end{gathered} \tag{61}$$

Defining the stream function $\Psi_1(X,Y)$, which identically satisfies the continuity equation, and eliminating the pressure by cross differentiation, the governing differential equation becomes,

$$\nabla^2 \Psi_1(X,Y) = - \omega_1(X,Y) = \frac{1}{4} \beta X^{-3/2} = 0 \tag{62}$$

Equation (61) immediately shows that the first order principal perturbational solution is associated with a mathematical system corresponding to rotational inviscid flow over the plate. This result is of significant importance since it definitely establishes that the complete inviscid flow field for the perturbational system of the present method becomes rotational. The results of the classical perturbational solutions for the corresponding order of accuracy present governing equations associated with the irrotational second order inviscid flow with specified wall mass injection on the flat plate. As clearly discussed by Van Dyke [5], the vorticity interaction due to the displacement effect of the boundary layer is considered indirectly by translating the boundary conditions on the transverse velocity component from the wall to the free stream conditions. However, the application of the proposed perturbational method directly illustrates that the viscous boundary layer affects the flow over the flat plate by inducing vorticity throughout the flow field which includes the regions where the viscous effects are indeed negligible.

The boundary conditions for $\Psi_1(X,Y)$, associated with Eq. (61), can be determined readily from Eq. (60) as:

$$\frac{\partial \Psi_1}{\partial Y}(X,0) = 0, \quad X < 0; \quad \Psi_1(X,0) = 0, \quad X < 0$$

$$\frac{\partial \Psi_1}{\partial Y}(X,0) \text{ arbitrary}, \quad X > 0; \quad \frac{\partial \Psi_1}{\partial X}(X,0) = 0 \text{ or } \Psi_1(X,0) = 0 \quad (63)$$

$$\lim_{Y\to\infty} \frac{\partial \Psi_1}{\partial Y}(X,Y) = 0, \quad \lim_{Y\to\infty} \frac{\partial \Psi_1}{\partial X}(X,Y) = -\frac{\beta}{2} X^{-1/2}$$

To employ the existing solutions of the classical second order theory, the dependent variable $\Psi_1(X,Y)$ may be transformed by defining a pseudo stream function, $\Psi_1^*(X,Y)$, as:

$$\Psi_1^*(X,Y) = \Psi_1(X,Y) + \beta X^{1/2} \quad (64)$$

which transforms the original system, Eqs. (62) and (63) into the classical form,

$$\nabla^2 \Psi_1^* = 0 \quad (65)$$

$$\frac{\partial \Psi_1}{\partial Y}(X,0) = 0, \quad X < 0; \quad \Psi_1^*(X,0) = 0, \quad X < 0$$

$$\frac{\partial \Psi_1}{\partial Y}(X,0) \text{ arbitrary}, \quad X > 0; \quad \frac{\partial \Psi_1}{\partial X}(X,0) = \frac{1}{2}\beta X^{-1/2}, \quad X > 0 \quad (66)$$

$$\lim_{Y\to\infty} \frac{\partial \Psi_1}{\partial Y}(X,Y) = 0, \quad X > 0; \quad \lim_{Y\to\infty} \frac{\partial \Psi_1}{\partial X}(X,Y) = 0, \quad X > 0$$

It is interesting to note that the outer limit condition on the transverse velocity component, $\bar{\mathbf{v}}_{o\infty}$, is replaced by the wall condition at Y = 0; hence, the transformed system, Eqs. (65) and (66), is identical to the mathematical problem associated with the classical second order theory corresponding to flow over a parabolic body.

The complex form of the solution to the system is readily available from potential flow theory as:

$$\Psi_1^*(X,Y) = \beta Z^{1/2} = \beta(X + iY)^{1/2} \quad (67)$$

Hence, substituting Eq. (67) in Eq. (64), the original stream function $\Psi_1(X,Y)$ and the associated velocity component become,

$$\Psi_1(X,Y) = \beta[Z^{1/2} - X^{1/2}] = \beta[(X + iY)^{1/2} - X^{1/2}]$$

$$U_1(X,Y) = \frac{\partial \Psi_1}{\partial Y}(X,Y) = \frac{\beta}{2}\ \text{Imaginary}\left[\frac{1}{(X + iY)^{1/2}}\right] \tag{68}$$

$$V_1(X,Y) = -\frac{\partial \Psi_1}{\partial X}(X,Y) = \frac{\beta}{2}\ \text{Real}\left[\frac{1}{X^{1/2}} - \frac{1}{(X + iY)^{1/2}}\right]$$

which completes the solution to the first order principal perturbational system.

First Order Corrective Perturbational Solution / Collecting the terms corresponding to ε^1 power, substituting the results of the first order principal perturbational solution, Eq. (68), and employing the appropriate boundary conditions, Eq. (31) by considering postulate 6, the mathematical system for the first order corrective perturbational solution becomes,

$$\frac{\partial \bar{u}_1}{\partial \bar{x}_1} + \frac{\partial \bar{v}_1}{\partial \bar{y}} = 0$$

$$(1 + \bar{u}_o)\frac{\partial \bar{u}_1}{\partial \bar{x}} + \bar{u}_1 \frac{\partial \bar{u}_o}{\partial \bar{x}} + \bar{v}_o \frac{\partial \bar{u}_1}{\partial \bar{y}} + \bar{v}_1 \frac{\partial \bar{u}_o}{\partial \bar{y}} = -\frac{\partial \bar{p}_1}{\partial \bar{x}} + \frac{\partial^2 \bar{u}_1}{\partial \bar{y}^2}\ ; \quad \frac{\partial \bar{p}_1}{\partial \bar{y}} = 0 \tag{69}$$

$$\bar{u}_1(\bar{x},0) = -U_1(X,0) = 0, \quad \bar{v}_1(x,0) = 0$$

$$\lim_{y\to\infty} \bar{u}_1(\bar{x},\bar{y}) = 0, \quad \lim_{y\to\infty} \bar{p}_1(\bar{x},\bar{y}) = 0 \tag{70}$$

The mathematical system, Eqs. (69) and (70), represents a homogeneous system with homogeneous boundary conditions; consequently, it only possesses the trivial solution,

$$\bar{u}(x,y) \equiv 0, \quad \bar{v}(\bar{x},\bar{y}) = 0, \quad \bar{p}(\bar{x},\bar{y}) = 0 \tag{71}$$

Hence, the first order corrective perturbational system does not contribute to the first order approximation of the solution. This result is equivalent to the second order inner expansion solution of the classical singular perturbation theory.

Discussion of Results / In view of the principal and corrective perturbational solutions for the zeroth and first order approximations, the velocity components associated with the uniformly valid solutions accurate to first order approximation in ε become:

$$\begin{aligned} u(x,y;\varepsilon) &= U_o(X,Y) + \bar{u}_o(\bar{x},\bar{y}) + \varepsilon U_1(X,Y) + \varepsilon[\bar{u}_1(\bar{x},\bar{y}) \equiv 0] \\ v(x,y;\varepsilon) &= V_o(X,Y) + \varepsilon v_o(x,y) + \varepsilon V_1(X,Y) + \varepsilon^2[v_1(x,y) \equiv 0] \end{aligned} \tag{72}$$

which are valid in the complete range $0 \leq y \leq \infty$.

The results for the tangential and normal velocity components are represented in Figures 1 and 2, respectively, for $x = 1$ and for two values of $\varepsilon = 0.1, 0.2$, according to the present method and the classical singular perturbation theory without the construction of the composite expansions.

It is immediately evident that the uniformly valid property of the present solution is a distinct advantage over the classical results in the sense that the former is continuous with at least continuous first order derivatives; whereas, the latter is only continuous with distinctly discontinuous first order derivatives at the point of intersection of the inner and outer solutions. It is interesting to realize that if one constructs the additive form of the composite expansion according to the rather formal and superficial argument (Van Dyke [4]), the resulting uniformly valid solution of the classical singular perturbation theory becomes identical to the result of the present theory. Hence, it is conclusive that the present method guarantees a uniformly valid solution, in the complete range $0 \leq y \leq \infty$, which is at least as accurate and as valid as the solution to the same order of approximation of the classical theory.

Drag on the Flat Plate / A convenient form of the representation of the drag on the plate is given by the dimensionless drag coefficient, C_f, as:

$$C_f = \frac{2}{\rho U_\infty^2 x} \int_0^x \tau_w(x)dx; \quad \tau_w(x) = \tau_w(x;\varepsilon) = \frac{\mu U_\infty}{L} \frac{\partial u}{\partial y}(x,0;\varepsilon) \tag{73}$$

where the shear stress τ_w must necessarily be evaluated from the complete uniformly valid solution.

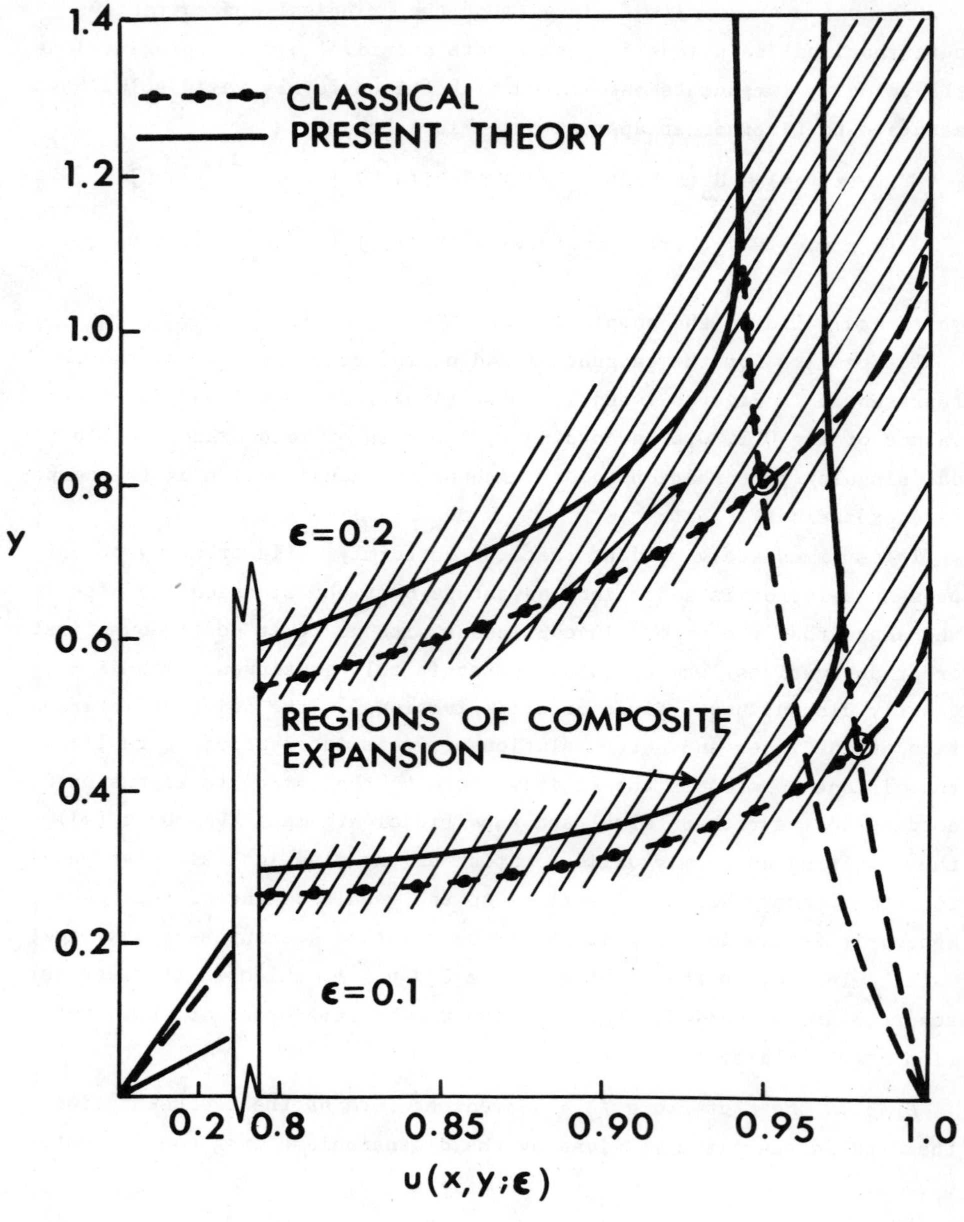

Fig. 1. Variations of Tangential Velocity Component.

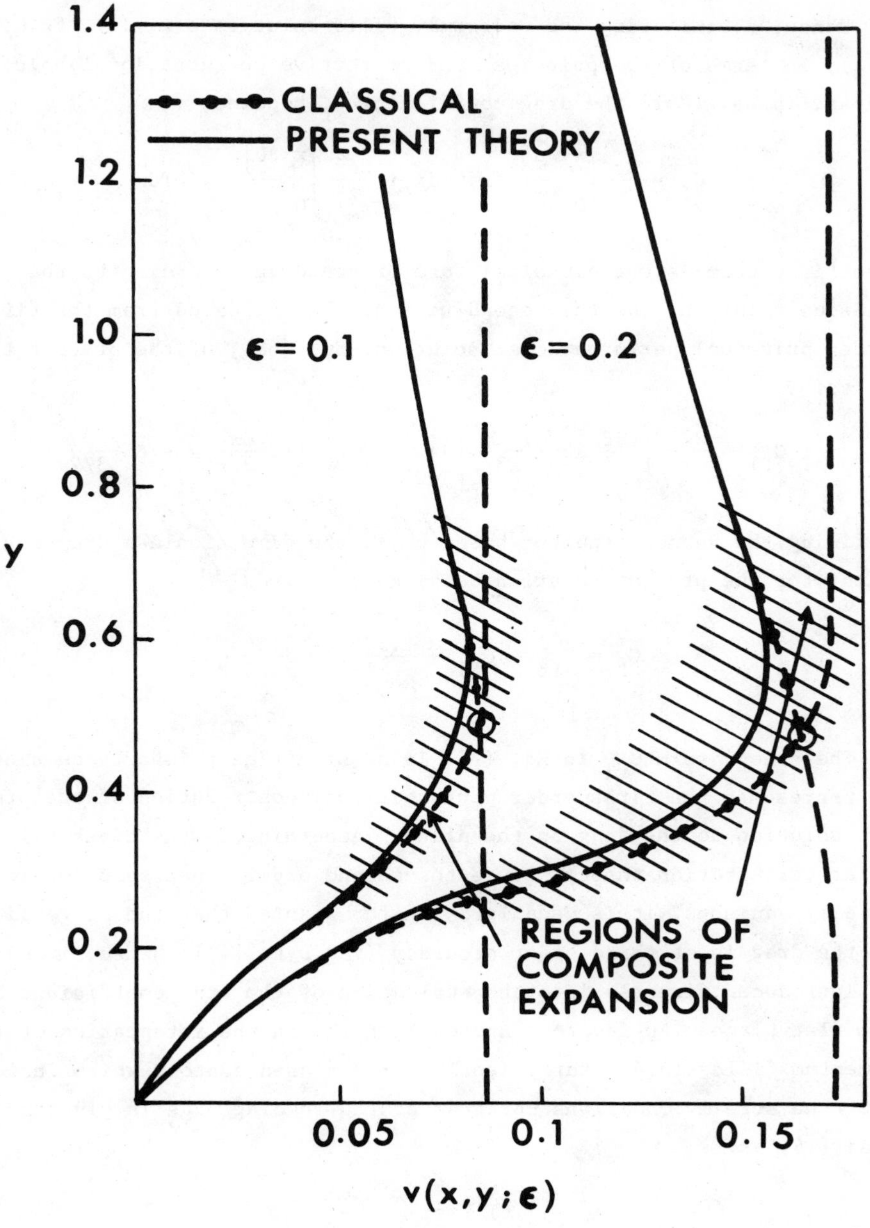

Fig. 2. Variations of Normal Velocity Component.

Hence, substituting the uniformly valid solution u(x,y;ε), from Eq. (72), in terms of the principal and corrective perturbational solutions, in Eq. (73), the drag coefficient C_f becomes,

$$C_f = \frac{2\varepsilon}{x}\int_0^x \frac{\partial \bar{u}_o}{\partial \bar{u}}(x,0)\,dx + \frac{2\varepsilon^3}{x}\int_0^x \frac{\partial U_1}{\partial Y}(x,0)\,dx \tag{74}$$

The first term is the classical form of the drag according to the Blasius solution; and the second term can be evaluated from the first order principal perturbational solution, Eq. (68), of the present theory as:

$$C_{f1} = \frac{2\varepsilon^3}{x}\int \frac{\beta}{4}\,\mathrm{Real}\left[\frac{1}{Z^{3/2}}\right]_{Y=0} dx = \frac{\beta}{2}\frac{\varepsilon^3}{x}\int \frac{dx}{x^{3/2}} = -\,\beta\,\frac{\varepsilon^3}{x^{3/2}} \tag{75}$$

Defining the Reynolds number based on x, the dimensionless drag coefficient for the present solution becomes,

$$C_f = C_{fo} + C_{f1} = \frac{1.328}{Re_x^{1/2}} + \frac{0.865}{Re_x^{3/2}} \tag{76}$$

The second term C_{f1} in Eq. (76) is of significant importance since it represents the first order perturbational contribution of the present solution to the drag on the plate. According to the classical singular perturbation theory, since the second order inner solution identically vanishes, it is usually taken for granted that the correction to the drag is of third order accuracy (Van Dyke [4]); hence, it cannot be introduced directly into the evaluation of the drag coefficient on the flat plate. An indirect approach, based on the integration of the momentum field along a sufficiently large closed contour which includes the free stream conditions upstream of the leading edge is given by Imai [14] as:

$$[C_{f1}]_{Imai} = \frac{2.326}{Re_x} \tag{77}$$

The comparison of Imai's result, Eq. (77) with the present solution, Eq. (76) is given in Fig. 3. The important feature of the comparison is that near the leading edge, $Re_x \to 0$, $\varepsilon \to \infty$, the results of the present theory give considerably higher values of order of $\varepsilon^{1/2}$ than Imai's

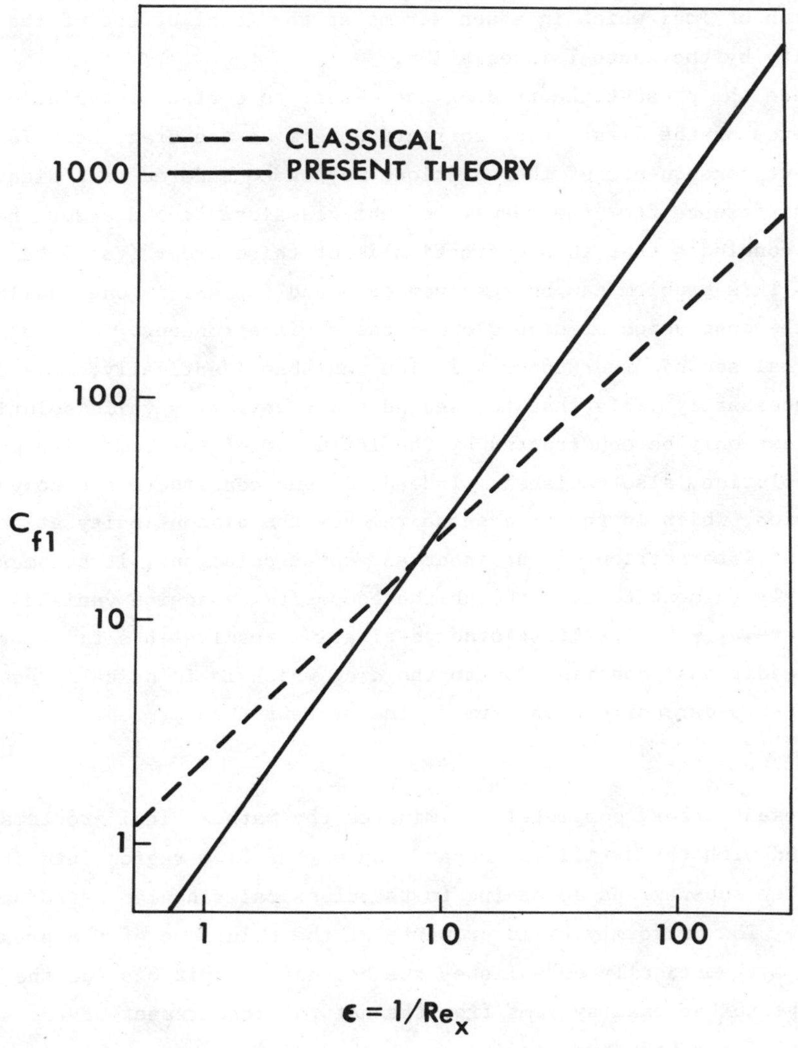

Fig. 3. Comparison of First Order Drag Coefficient.

solution. This implies that the leading edge represents a higher order singular behavior in the present theory in comparison to the integrated solution of Imai which in a sense removes the local effect of the singularity by the contour integration.

Since the present theory does not resort to contour integration, the existence of the first order correction term on the drag, Eq. (76), as a direct consequence of the solution, may be considered as a significant difference from the results of the classical second order theory which concludes that this correction is of third order (Van Dyke [4], [5]). This problem can be resolved once and for all if one realizes that the conclusion of second order theory is erroneous. Although the classical second order inner solution vanishes identically, this does not necessarily imply that the second order uniformly valid solution, which can only be constructed by the inclusion of the composite expansion solution, also vanishes. Indeed, if one constructs the composite expansion, which in the true sense removes the discontinuity at the point of intersection of the inner and outer solutions, it becomes immediately evident that, although the composite expansion vanishes on the plate, $y = 0$, its first order derivative results in a finite value as an additional contribution to the drag which is identically equal to the first order correction term of the present theory.

CONCLUSIONS

The present theory completely eliminates the mathematical problems associated with the artificial separation of the flow region into inner and outer sub-regions according to the classical singular perturbation theory. The uniformly valid property of the solutions of the present theory systematically establishes the boundary conditions for the singular perturbational systems from the natural requirement of the satisfaction of the boundary conditions of the original mathematical problem. Hence, it completely eliminates the necessity of superficial asymptotic matching principles; and, furthermore, it specifies once and for all the set of the boundary conditions which must necessarily remain arbitrary for the solutions of the reduced singular mathematical systems.

Since the solutions are uniformly valid, the present theory does not require any form of composite expansion to overcome the difficulties associated with the construction of uniformly valid solutions in the intermediate, overlapping region of the inner and outer solutions of the classical perturbation theory.

The singular systems associated with the perturbational expansions of the present theory result in mathematical problems of equivalent complexity to the mathematical systems of the classical theory; hence, the proposed method does not introduce any additional mathematical difficulty in the solution of the original problem.

The first order uniformly valid solution, according to the present theory, clearly illustrates the existence of the first order correction on the evaluation of the viscous drag on the flat plate, which is usually overlooked in the solution of the classical second order theory.

In general, it can be concluded that the proposed theory is distinctly superior to the classical singular perturbation methods in all aspects of solution to the flat plate problem; and it is rather evident that its application to the inherently more complicated problems associated with compressible, high Reynolds number flow conditions could ultimately eliminate the mathematical difficulties which are usually encountered in the classical second order boundary layer theory.

ACKNOWLEDGMENT

This work was partially supported by Themis Project No. 57 under ONR Contract N00014-68-A-0144.

REFERENCES

1. Prandtl, L., "Uber Flussigkeitsbewegung bei sehr Kleiner Reibung," Proceedings 3rd International Mathematical Congress, Heidelberg 1914.

2. Schlichting, H., Boundary Layer Theory, McGraw-Hill Book Company, Inc., 1960.

3. Lagerstrom, P. A. and Cole, J. D., "Examples Illustrating Expansion Procedures for the Navier-Stokes Equation," J. Rat. Mech. Anal., Vol. 4, 1955, pp. 817-882.

4. Van Dyke, M., Perturbation Methods in Fluid Mechanics, Academic Press, 1964.

5. Van Dyke, M., "Higher Order Boundary Layer Theory," Annual Review of Fluid Mechanics, Edited by W. A. Sears, Vol. 1, Annual Reviews, Inc., Palo Alto, California, 1969, pp. 265-292.

6. Kaplun, S., Fluid Mechanics and Singular Perturbations, edited by Lagerstrom, P. A., Howard, L. N. and Liu, C., Academic Press, 1967.

7. Cole, J. D., Perturbation Methods in Applied Mathematics, Blaisdell Publishing Co., 1968.

8. Erdelyi, A., "Singular Perturbations of Boundary Value Problems Involving Ordinary Differential Equations," J. Soc. Indust. Appl. Math., Vol. 11, 1963, pp. 105-116.

9. Fraenkel, L. E., "On the Method of Matched Asymptotic Expansions, Parts 1, 11, 111," Proc. Camb. Phil. Soc., Vol. 65, 1969, pp. 209-284.

10. Vishik, M. I. and Lyusternik, L. A., "Regulyarnoe vyrozhdenie i progranichnyi sloi dlya lineinykh differentsial' nykh uravnnii s malym parametram," ("Regular Degeneracy and Boundary-Layers for Linear Differential Equations with a Small Coefficient,") Uspehi Mat. Nauk, Vol. 12, 1957, pp. 30122, (Translated in Amer. Math. Soc. Transl., Vol. 20).

11. Chudov, L. A., "Some Shortcomings of Classical Boundary Layer Theory," (Translation from Russian) NASA TT F-360, TT 65-50138, 1966, pp. 65-73.

12. Friedrichs, K. O., "Asymptotic Phenomena in Mathematical Physics," Bull. Amer. Math. Soc., Vol. 61, 1955, pp. 611-684.

13. Cochran, T., "A New Approach to Singular Perturbation Problems," Ph.D. Dissertation, Stanford Univ., 1962.

14. Imai, I., "Second Order Approximation to the Laminar-Layer Flow over a Flat Plate," J. Aeronaut. Sci., Vol. 24, 1957, pp. 155-156.

A COMPARISON OF THE SOLUTIONS OF PRANDTL'S AND NAVIER-STOKES EQUATIONS IN A SUPERPOSED FLUCTUATING FLOW

Z. U. A. Warsi
Mississippi State University

ABSTRACT

The present paper is concerned with a comparison of the solutions of Prandtl and the corresponding Navier-Stokes equations when a fluctuating flow is superposed over an otherwise steady stream of low viscosity past a body in two-dimensional incompressible flow. The main aim is to analyze the effects of fluctuation parameters like the angular frequency and amplitude on the estimates of the fluctuating flow. It has been shown that in addition to the Reynolds number being large enough to satisfy the steady state estimates, the Reynolds number based on the angular frequency should also satisfy an estimate for the two solutions to be approximately close to one another. The applicability of boundary layer theory at high values of the Reynolds number based on the angular frequency parameter is also discussed.

LIST OF NOTATIONS

a	Amplitude of superposed flow
b	Constant
C, C_o	Constants
C_r, C_i	Functions defined in the text
d	Representative length
i	$(-1)^{1/2}$
j	Integer
k_r, k_i	Functions defined in the text
L_r, L_i, ℓ_r, ℓ_i	Operators
M, N, n	Constants

p	Pressure
Q_r, Q_i	Functions defined in the text
R, R_μ	Reynolds numbers
s	Variable
T	Physical time
t	Non-dimensional time variable
u,v	Velocity components
V	Difference between ω and $\overline{\omega}$
W	Initial velocity profile
X,Y	Physical coordinates
x	Non-dimensional coordinate along X
z	Variable
$\alpha, \beta, \gamma, \gamma_j$	Non-dimensional constants
ε^2	Kinematic viscosity
μ	Angular frequency
η	Non-dimensional coordinate along Y
ξ, ζ, τ	Crocco variables
ω	Non-dimensional derivative of u
θ_r, θ_i, ψ	Functions defined in the text
δ	R/R_μ
λ	Constant, $0 < \lambda < 1$
Φ_{1r}, Φ_{1i}	Functions defined in the text
$\phi(s)$	Function of s

Subscripts and Superscripts

$(\ )_o$	Steady state quantity
$(\ )_1$	Perturbation quantity
$(\ )_\infty$	Free-stream condition
$(\ )^*$	Physical quantity
$\overline{(\ )}$	Boundary layer quantity
$(\ )_{variable}$	Differentiation with respect to the variable
$(\ )_r$	Real part
$(\ )_i$	Imaginary part

INTRODUCTION

Recent efforts in the direction of establishing a mathematical basis for boundary layer theory by Nickel [1], Oleinik [2] and Fife [3] and consequently of establishing a firm mathematical connection between the solutions of the Navier-Stokes and Prandtl's equations by Fife [3] and Serrin [4] has opened a new field of activity where many questions of fundamental and practical importance can be settled. These researches provide certain mathematically valid estimates for comparison of solutions of the two widely used viscous flow models as based on the Navier-Stokes and Prandtl's equations for two-dimensional steady flows. Recently Brzychczy [5] has compared the solutions in a purely unsteady case when the initial conditions are provided and has shown that the difference between the solutions of Prandtl and the corresponding Navier-Stokes equations can be made arbitrarily small by choosing the kinematic viscosity small provided that at some station the two solutions are very close to one another. The last condition is, of course, necessary as is shown by Fife [3].

Most of the available analytical solutions in boundary layer theory, particularly in unsteady flows, have been understood and explained by the expansion of the dependent variables in terms of certain parameters, assumed small. The small parameter represents a flow property like a factor of unsteadiness in unsteady flow or the amplitude of the incident stream in fluctuating flow. It is, therefore, worthwhile to assess the difference between the Prandtl's and Navier-Stokes solutions when expansion procedures are adopted in preference to the direct methods. In the present paper a comparison of the solutions of Prandtl and Navier-Stokes is carried out for the case when a fluctuating flow of small amplitude is superposed in magnitude over an otherwise steady stream of low viscosity in two-dimensional flow. Lighthill [6] has already considered the solutions of the boundary layer equations by the expansion procedures mentioned above. The purpose of this paper is to provide certain mathematically valid estimates for comparison of the boundary layer and Navier-Stokes solutions when the velocity components in both cases are expanded in powers of the amplitude of fluctuating flow. It has been shown that in addition to the requirement that the steady state Reynolds number be large, the Reynolds number based on the angular frequency[1] should also satisfy an estimate as obtained in this paper, for the two solutions to be approximately close to one another. On the basis of this result, it has been possible to establish a criterion for the validity of the boundary layer theory for fluctuating flows at high frequencies.

Equations and Transformations

The Navier-Stokes equations for an incompressible and non-stationary flow are

$$u^*_T + u^* u^*_X + v^* u^*_Y + \frac{1}{\rho} p^* = \varepsilon^2 (u^*_{XX} + u^*_{YY}) \tag{1}$$

$$v^*_T + u^* v^*_X + v^* v^*_Y + \frac{1}{\rho} p^*_Y = \varepsilon^2 (v^*_{XX} + v^*_{YY}) \tag{2}$$

$$u^*_X + v^*_Y = 0 \tag{3}$$

where ε^2 is the kinematic viscosity, (X,Y) are the curvilinear coordinates along and perpendicular to the surface respectively and an asterisk denotes quantities in the physical plane. The corresponding boundary layer equations are

$$\bar{u}^*_T + \bar{u}^* \bar{u}^*_X + \bar{v}^* \bar{u}^*_Y + \frac{1}{\rho} \bar{p}^*_X = \varepsilon^2 \bar{u}^*_{YY} \tag{4}$$

$$\bar{u}^*_X + \bar{v}^*_Y = 0 \tag{5}$$

where an overhead bar denotes a boundary layer quantity. The solutions of equations (1) - (5) are defined in a domain Ω: $\{(T,X,Y): 0 \le X \le X_o, 0 \le Y < \infty, T > 0\}$ with the boundary and initial conditions.

$$\begin{gathered} u^*|_{Y=0} = 0, \quad \bar{u}^*|_{Y=0} = 0, \quad v^*|_{Y=0} = 0, \quad \bar{v}^*|_{Y=0} = 0 \\ u^*|_{X=0} = W^*(T,Y), \quad \bar{u}^*|_{X=0} = \bar{W}^*(T,Y) \end{gathered} \tag{6}$$

We now non-dimensionalize the equations by introducing new variables

1. For the importance of angular frequency in fluctuating fluid flow the reader is referred to the article of J. T. Stuart [7].

$$X = xd, \quad Y = \frac{\varepsilon\eta}{(\mu)^{1/2}}, \quad T = \frac{t}{\mu}, \quad u = \frac{u^*}{u_\infty}, \quad v = \frac{d(\mu)^{1/2}}{\varepsilon}\frac{v^*}{u_\infty}$$

$$p^* = \rho u_\infty^2 p, \quad \bar{u} = \frac{\bar{u}^*}{u_\infty}, \quad \bar{v} = \frac{d(\mu)^{1/2}}{\varepsilon}\frac{\bar{v}^*}{u_\infty}, \quad \bar{p}^* = \rho u_\infty^2 p$$

where d and u_∞ are characteristic length and velocity respectively and μ is the free-stream angular frequency. With these transformations, equations (1) - (3) become

$$u_t + \delta(uu_x + vu_\eta + p_x) - R_\mu^{-1} u_{xx} - u_{\eta\eta} = 0 \qquad (7)$$

$$R^{-1}v_t + \delta R^{-1}(uv_x + vv_\eta) + p_\eta - R^{-1}R_\mu^{-1}v_{xx} - R^{-1}v_{\eta\eta} = 0 \qquad (8)$$

$$u_x + v_\eta = 0 \qquad (9)$$

where $\delta = \dfrac{u_\infty}{\mu d} = \dfrac{R}{R_\mu}$, $R_\mu = \dfrac{\mu d^2}{\varepsilon^2}$ and $R = \dfrac{u_\infty d}{\varepsilon^2}$.

The boundary layer equations (4) and (5) are now

$$\bar{u}_t + \delta(\bar{u}\,\bar{u}_x + \bar{v}\,\bar{u}_\eta + \bar{p}_x) - \bar{u}_{\eta\eta} = 0 \qquad (10)$$

$$\bar{u}_x + \bar{v}_\eta = 0 \qquad (11)$$

The boundary conditions for equations (7) - (11) are

$$u|_{\eta=0} = 0, \quad \bar{u}|_{\eta=0} = 0, \quad v|_{\eta=0} = 0, \quad \bar{v}|_{\eta=0} = 0$$
$$u|_{x=0} = W(t,\eta), \quad \bar{u}|_{x=0} = \bar{W}(t,\eta) \qquad (12)$$

Making Crocco's transformation by taking

$$t = \tau, \quad x = \xi, \quad \zeta = u(t,x,\eta)$$

and

$$\omega = \omega(\tau,\xi,\zeta) = \frac{\partial u}{\partial\eta}, \quad \eta = \int_0^u \frac{dr}{\omega(\tau,\xi,r)}$$

in equation (7), we have

$$\omega^2\omega_{\zeta\zeta} - \omega_\tau - \delta(p_{x\eta} - p_x\omega_\zeta + \zeta\omega_\xi) = R_\mu^{-1}\left(\frac{u_{xx}u_{\eta\eta}}{u_\eta} - u_{xx\eta}\right) \tag{13}$$

defined in a domain Ω_1 : $\{(\tau,\xi,\zeta): 0 \le \xi < \xi_0, 0 \le \zeta < \zeta_1, \zeta_1 = u(\tau,\xi,\infty), \tau > 0\}$ with the boundary conditions

$$\begin{gathered} \omega|_{\xi=0} = \frac{\partial W}{\partial \eta} = \omega(\tau,0,\zeta), \quad \omega|_{\zeta=\zeta_1} = 0 \\ \omega\,\omega_\zeta - \delta p_x = 0 \quad \text{at} \quad \zeta = 0 \end{gathered} \tag{14}$$

Similarly, making the transformation

$$t = \tau, \quad x = \xi, \quad \zeta = \overline{u}(t,x,\eta), \quad \overline{\omega} = \frac{\partial \overline{u}}{\partial \eta}$$

in equation (10), we get

$$\overline{\omega}^2\overline{\omega}_{\zeta\zeta} - \overline{\omega}_\tau - \delta(\zeta\overline{\omega}_\xi - \overline{\omega}_\zeta\overline{p}_x) = 0 \tag{15}$$

defined in the domain Ω_2 : $\{(\tau,\xi,\zeta): 0 \le \xi \le \xi_0, 0 \le \zeta < \overline{U}(\tau,\xi), \tau > 0\}$ with the boundary conditions

$$\begin{gathered} \overline{\omega}|_{\xi=0} = \frac{\partial \overline{W}}{\partial \eta} = \overline{\omega}(\tau,0,\zeta), \quad \overline{\omega}|_{\zeta=\zeta_1} = 0 \\ \overline{\omega}\,\overline{\omega}_\zeta - \delta\overline{p}_x = 0 \quad \text{at} \quad \zeta = 0 \end{gathered} \tag{16}$$

Introducing now the difference

$$V = \omega - \overline{\omega}$$

and using (13) and (15), we have

$$u_\eta\overline{u}_\eta[\omega^2 V_{\zeta\zeta} - V_\tau + (\omega + \overline{\omega})\,V\overline{\omega}_{\zeta\zeta} + \delta(p_x V_\zeta - \zeta V_\xi)] = \psi \tag{17}$$

where

$$\psi = \delta[(\overline{p}_x - p_x)\,u_\eta\overline{u}_{\eta\eta} + p_{x\eta}u_\eta\overline{u}_\eta] + R_\mu^{-1}(u_{xx}u_{\eta\eta}\overline{u}_\eta - u_{xx\eta}u_\eta\overline{u}_\eta) \tag{18}$$

The boundary conditions for the difference V are

$$V|_{\xi=0} = \omega(\tau,0,\zeta) - \overline{\omega}(\tau,0,\zeta)$$

$$\omega V_\zeta + V\overline{\omega}_\zeta = \delta(p_x - \overline{p}_x) \quad \text{at} \quad \zeta = 0 \tag{19}$$

The solutions of equations (17) - (19) are defined in the region $\Omega_\varepsilon/d(\mu)^{1/2} = \Omega_1 \Omega_2$ in which

$$\zeta \leq \zeta_\varepsilon/d(\mu)^{1/2} = \min\left[u\left\{\tau,\xi,\left(\frac{\varepsilon}{d(\mu)^{1/2}}\right)^{-\lambda}\right\}, \overline{u}\left\{\tau,\xi,\left(\frac{\varepsilon}{d(\mu)^{1/2}}\right)^{-\lambda}\right\}\right], \; 0<\lambda<1$$

Comparison of Solutions

As discussed in the introduction, we are interested in the comparison of solutions of the Navier-Stokes and Prandtl's equations in the situation when an oscillating stream of frequency μ and amplitude a is superposed in magnitude over an otherwise steady stream of velocity u_∞. The form of the characteristic stream in this case is

$$u_\infty(1 + a\, e^{i\tau}), \; i = (-1)^{1/2}$$

Consequently we are justified in writing any of the dependent variables χ as

$$\chi = \chi_o + a\chi_1 e^{i\tau} + O(a^2) \tag{20}$$

where a subscript o denotes the steady state and a subscript 1 as the perturbed condition. It should be noted that χ_1 is in general a complex function and we are interested only in the real value. It is also important to remark that if $\overline{\chi}$ is the value of χ in the boundary layer solution then

$$|\chi - \overline{\chi}| = |(\chi_o - \overline{\chi}_o) + ae^{i\tau}(\chi_1 - \overline{\chi}_1)|$$

$$\leq |\chi_o - \overline{\chi}_o| + a|\chi_1 - \overline{\chi}_1|$$

Now, according to Fife [3], the steady state solutions of the boundary layer and Navier-Stokes equations approach one another as $\varepsilon \to 0$, i.e.,

$$|\chi_o - \overline{\chi}_o| \leq C_o\varepsilon^{\gamma_o}$$

where C_o and γ_o are constants, hence, our problem is to consider only the second part, viz., $|\chi_1 - \bar{\chi}_1|$. To facilitate the comparison we adopt the same transformations of the independent variables both for the steady and the fluctuating parts. Thus, for example, the estimate of the difference of the skin friction in the steady state as given by Fife [3] becomes in our present notation

$$\left|\frac{\partial u_o}{\partial \eta} - \frac{\partial \bar{u}_o}{\partial \eta}\right|_{\eta=0} \leq K_2 R_\mu^{-1/2}$$

We now state the following theorem.

Theorem I / If for some $\varepsilon < \varepsilon_o$, the steady state solutions of the Prandtl's and the Navier-Stokes equations approach one another and if in the fluctuating flow field

$$\begin{aligned} |\{p_1(x,0)\}_x - \{\bar{p}_1(x)\}_x| &\leq MR_\mu^{-\gamma_1} \\ |\{p_1(x,Y)\}_{xY}| &\leq M/d \\ |\omega_1(0,\zeta) - \bar{\omega}_1(0,\zeta)| &\leq MR_\mu^{-\gamma_2} \\ |\omega_1(x,\zeta_\varepsilon/d(\mu)^{1/2}) - \bar{\omega}_1(x,\zeta_\varepsilon/d(\mu)^{1/2})| &\leq MR_\mu^{-\gamma_3} \end{aligned} \tag{21}$$

then

$$|\omega_1(x,\zeta) - \bar{\omega}_1(x,\zeta)| \leq CR_\mu^{-\gamma} \tag{22}$$

where M and C are arbitrarily chosen non-dimensional constants and

$\gamma = \min\limits_{j=1,2,3} \left(\frac{1-\lambda}{2}, \gamma_j\right), \quad 0 < \gamma_j < 1,$

Proof: Introducing terms like (20) in equations (17) and (18), we get the steady state equation with a subscript 0 and a perturbed equation with a subscript 1 as,

$$\omega_o^2(V_o)_{\zeta\zeta} + (\omega_o + \bar{\omega}_o)V_o(\bar{\omega}_o)_{\zeta\zeta} + \delta\{(p_o)_x(V_o)_\zeta - \zeta(V_o)_\xi\} = \Phi_o \tag{23}$$

where

$$\Phi_o = \delta\left[\left\{(\bar{p}_o)_x - (p_o)_x\right\} \frac{(\bar{u}_o)_{\eta\eta}}{(\bar{u}_o)_\eta}\right] + R_\mu^{-1}\left\{\frac{(u_o)_{xx}(u_o)_{\eta\eta}}{(u_o)_\eta} - (u_o)_{xx\eta}\right\} \qquad (24)$$

The perturbed equation is

$$\omega_o^2(V_1)_{\zeta\zeta} + (\omega_o + \bar{\omega}_o)V_1(\bar{\omega}_o)_{\zeta\zeta} - iV_1 + \delta\left\{(p_o)_x(V_1)_\zeta - \zeta(V_1)_\xi\right\} = \Phi_1 \qquad (25)$$

where

$$\Phi_1 = \delta\Bigg[\left\{(\bar{p}_1)_x - (p_1)_x\right\}\frac{(\bar{u}_o)_{\eta\eta}}{(\bar{u}_o)_\eta} + \left\{(\bar{p}_o)_x - (p_o)_x\right\}\left\{\frac{(\bar{u}_o)_{\eta\eta}(u_1)_\eta}{(u_o)_\eta(\bar{u}_o)_\eta} + \frac{(\bar{u}_1)_{\eta\eta}}{(\bar{u}_o)_\eta}\right\}$$

$$+ (p_o)_{x\eta}\left\{\frac{(u_1)_\eta}{(u_o)_\eta} + \frac{(\bar{u}_1)_\eta}{(\bar{u}_o)_\eta}\right\} + (p_1)_{x\eta} - (V_o)_\zeta(p_1)_x\Bigg]$$

$$+ R_\mu^{-1}\left\{\frac{(u_1)_{xx}(u_o)_{\eta\eta}}{(u_o)_\eta} - (u_1)_{xx\eta} + \frac{(u_o)_{xx}(u_o)_{\eta\eta}(\bar{u}_1)_\eta}{(u_o)_\eta(\bar{u}_o)_\eta} + \frac{(u_o)_{xx}(u_1)_{\eta\eta}}{(u_o)_\eta}\right.$$

$$\left. - \frac{(u_1)_\eta(u_o)_{xx\eta}}{(u_o)_\eta} - \frac{(\bar{u}_1)_\eta(u_o)_{xx\eta}}{(\bar{u}_o)_\eta}\right\} - 2\omega_o\omega_1(V_o)_{\zeta\zeta} - \left\{(\omega_o + \bar{\omega}_o)(\omega_1)_{\zeta\zeta}\right.$$

$$\left. + (\omega_1 + \bar{\omega}_1)(\bar{\omega}_o)_{\zeta\zeta}\right\}V_o - \Phi_o\left\{\frac{(u_1)_\eta}{(u_o)_\eta} + \frac{(\bar{u}_1)_\eta}{(\bar{u}_o)_\eta}\right\} \qquad (26)$$

Introducing now the complex form of V_1, ω_1, p_1, and u_1 as

$$V_1 = (V_{1r} + iV_{1i})\ \phi\ (\alpha\zeta)\ e^{\beta\xi}$$

$$\omega_1 = (\omega_{1r} + i\omega_{1i}) \qquad (27)$$

$$p_1 = p_{1r} + ip_{1i}$$

$$u_1 = u_{1r} + iu_{1i}$$

where the subscript r is for real part and i for imaginary part and $\phi(s)$ is a second order differentiable function defined by Oleinik [2] for $s \geq 0$ as

$$\phi(s) = 3 - e^{s}, \quad 0 \leq s \leq 1/2$$
$$1 \leq \phi(s) \leq 3, \quad \text{for all} \quad s \geq 0$$

The constants α and β are positive non-dimensional constants. Substituting (27) in (25) and (26) and separating real and imaginary parts, we have

$$L_r(V_{1r},V_{1i}) \equiv \omega_o^2(V_{1r})_{\zeta\zeta} + \left\{2\alpha\omega_o^2\frac{\phi'}{\phi} + \delta(p_o)_x\right\}(V_{1r})_\zeta - \delta\zeta(V_{1r})_\xi + C_rV_{1r} - C_iV_{1i} = \Phi_{1r}\, e^{-\beta\xi}/\phi \tag{28}$$

$$L_i(V_{1r},V_{1i}) \equiv \omega_o^2(V_{1i})_{\zeta\zeta} + \left\{2\alpha\omega_o^2\frac{\phi'}{\phi} + \delta(p_o)_x\right\}(V_{1i})_\zeta - \delta\zeta(V_{1i})_\xi + C_rV_{1i} + C_iV_{1r} = \Phi_{1i}\, e^{-\beta\xi}/\phi \tag{29}$$

where

$$\begin{aligned} C_r &= \alpha^2\omega_o^2\frac{\phi''}{\phi} + \delta\left\{\alpha(p_o)_x\frac{\phi'}{\phi} - \zeta\beta\right\} + (\omega_o + \bar{\omega}_o)(\bar{\omega}_o)_{\zeta\zeta} \\ C_i &= -1 \end{aligned} \tag{30}$$

Here a prime denotes differentiation with respect to ζ, and

$$\Phi_{1r} = \delta\left[\left\{(\bar{p}_{1r})_x - (p_{1r})_x\right\}\frac{(\bar{u}_o)_{\eta\eta}}{(\bar{u}_o)_\eta} + \left\{(\bar{p}_o)_x - (p_o)_x\right\}\left\{\frac{(\bar{u}_o)_{\eta\eta}(u_{1r})_\eta}{(u_o)_\eta(\bar{u}_o)_\eta} + \frac{(\bar{u}_{1r})_{\eta\eta}}{(\bar{u}_o)_\eta}\right\} + (p_o)_{x\eta}\left\{\frac{(u_{1r})_\eta}{(u_o)_\eta} + \frac{(\bar{u}_{1r})_\eta}{(\bar{u}_o)_\eta}\right\} + (p_{1r})_{x\eta} - (V_o)_\zeta(p_{1r})_x\right]$$
$$+ R_\mu^{-1}\left[\frac{(u_{1r})_{xx}(u_o)_{\eta\eta}}{(u_o)_\eta} - (u_{1r})_{xx\eta} + \frac{(u_o)_{xx}(u_o)_{\eta\eta}(\bar{u}_{1r})_\eta}{(u_o)_\eta(\bar{u}_o)_\eta}\right.$$

$$+ \frac{(u_o)_{xx}(u_{1r})_{\eta\eta}}{(u_o)_\eta} - \frac{(u_{1r})_\eta(u_o)_{xx\eta}}{(u_o)_\eta} - \frac{(\bar{u}_{1r})_\eta(u_o)_{xx\eta}}{(\bar{u}_o)_\eta}\Bigg]$$

$$- 2\omega_o\omega_{1r}(V_o)_{\zeta\zeta} - \left\{(\omega_o + \bar{\omega}_o)(\omega_{1r})_{\zeta\zeta} + (\omega_{1r} + \bar{\omega}_{1r})(\bar{\omega}_o)_{\zeta\zeta}\right\} V_o$$

$$- \Phi_o \left\{\frac{(u_{1r})_\eta}{(u_o)_\eta} + \frac{(\bar{u}_{1r})_\eta}{(\bar{u}_o)_\eta}\right\} \tag{31}$$

The terms in Φ_{1i} are the same as in (31) with i in place of r. The subscripts outside braces in equation (28) - (31) indicate differentiation with respect to the particular variables. The boundary conditions (19) become

$$V_{1r}|_{\xi=0} = \{\omega_{1r}(\tau,0,\zeta) - \bar{\omega}_{1r}(\tau,0,\zeta)\}/\phi$$

$$V_{1i}|_{\xi=0} = \{\omega_{1i}(\tau,0,\zeta) - \bar{\omega}_{1i}(\tau,0,\zeta)\}/\phi$$

$$\left.\begin{aligned} \ell_r(V_{1r}) &\equiv \omega_o(V_{1r})_\zeta - k_r V_{1r} = \theta_r\, e^{-\beta\xi}/\phi \\ \ell_i(V_{1i}) &\equiv \omega_o(V_{1i})_\zeta - k_i V_{1i} = \theta_i\, e^{-\beta\xi}/\phi \end{aligned}\right\} \text{ at } \zeta = 0 \tag{32}$$

where

$$k_r = k_i = - \{\alpha\omega_o \frac{\phi'}{\phi} + (\bar{\omega}_o)_\zeta\} \tag{33a}$$

$$\theta_r = \delta\{(p_{1r})_x - (\bar{p}_{1r})_x\} - \omega_{1r}(V_o)_\zeta - V_o(\bar{\omega}_{1r})_\zeta \quad \text{at } \zeta = 0 \tag{33b}$$

The expression for θ_i is obtained by replacing r by i in θ_r.

The proof of Theorem I now depends upon the maximum principle as applied to the differential operations L_r, L_i and the boundary operators ℓ_r, ℓ_i. The maximum principle states that if Q is a certain quantity defined in a particular region and if the differential inequalities $L(Q) < 0$ and $\ell(Q) < 0$ at $\zeta = 0$ hold, then Q cannot have a negative minimum in the region under consideration. Thus, in this region we can choose certain constants such that $Q \geq 0$. Let us now choose $\alpha > 0$ and $\beta > 0$ large enough so that,

$$C_r < -M_{1r}$$

$$C_i < -M_{1i}$$

where $M_{1r} > 0$ and $M_{1i} > 0$. Also in $\Omega_\varepsilon/d(\mu)^{1/2}$ we set

$$Q_{r\pm} = \frac{1}{(2)^{1/2}} C\, R_\mu^{-\gamma} \pm V_{1r}$$

$$Q_{i\pm} = \frac{1}{(2)^{1/2}} C\, R_\mu^{-\gamma} \pm V_{1i}\,, \qquad C > 0$$

then from (28) and (29)

$$\begin{aligned} L_r(Q_{r\pm},Q_{i\pm}) &= \frac{1}{(2)^{1/2}} (C_r - C_i) C R_\mu^{-\gamma} \pm \Phi_{1r} \frac{e^{-\beta\xi}}{\phi} \\ L_i(Q_{r\pm},Q_{i\pm}) &= \frac{1}{(2)^{1/2}} (C_r + C_i) C R_\mu^{-\gamma} \pm \Phi_{1r} \frac{e^{-\beta\xi}}{\phi} \end{aligned} \tag{34}$$

and from (32)

$$\begin{aligned} \ell_r(Q_{r\pm},Q_{i\pm}) &= -\frac{1}{(2)^{1/2}} C k_r R_\mu^{-\gamma} \pm \theta_r \frac{e^{-\beta\xi}}{\phi} \\ \ell_i(Q_{r\pm},Q_{i\pm}) &= -\frac{1}{(2)^{1/2}} C k_i R_\mu^{-\gamma} \pm \theta_i \frac{e^{-\beta\xi}}{\phi} \qquad \text{at} \quad \zeta = 0 \end{aligned} \tag{35}$$

We shall now estimate the order of magnitude of the quantities $|Q_{1r}|$ and $|\theta_r|$ under the assumption that the steady state solutions of the Prandtl and Navier-Stokes equations approach one another for $\varepsilon \to 0$ as $|V_0| \leq C_0 R_\mu^{-\gamma_0}$.

In $\Omega_\varepsilon/d(\mu)^{1/2}$, $\eta \leq \left(\frac{\varepsilon}{d(\mu)^{1/2}}\right)^{-\lambda} = R_\mu^{\lambda/2}$, and the mean value theorem gives

$$\begin{aligned} (p_{1r})_x &= [p_{1r}(x,0)]_x + \eta[p_{1r}(x,z)]_{x\eta} \\ (p_0)_x &= [p_0(x,0)]_x + \eta[p_0(x,z)]_{x\eta}\,, \quad 0 < z < \eta \end{aligned} \tag{36}$$

$$(\bar{p}_{1r})_x = [\bar{p}_{1r}(x)]_x$$
$$(\bar{p}_o)_x = [\bar{p}_o(x)]_x \tag{36}$$

where variable subscripts outside brackets denote differentiation. Substituting (36) in (31) and using (21), we get

$$|\Phi_{1r}| \le \frac{\delta M}{(2)^{1/2}} \left[R_\mu^{-\gamma_1} + R_\mu^{-(1-\lambda)/2}\right]$$

Hence

$$|\phi_{1r}| \le \frac{\delta M}{(2)^{1/2}} R_\mu^{-\gamma} = \frac{MR}{(2)^{1/2}} R_\mu^{-\gamma-1}$$

where γ is the minimum of γ_1, and $(1-\lambda)/2$. Similarly $|\theta_r| \le \frac{\delta M}{(2)^{1/2}} R_\mu^{-\gamma_1}$. Having obtained these estimates and choosing $\alpha > 0$ and $\beta > 0$ large such that $C_r - C_i < 0$, $C_r + C_i < 0$ and $k_r = k_i > 0$, then from (34) and (35) we have

$$L_r(Q_{r\pm}, Q_{i\pm}) < 0, \quad L_i(Q_{r\pm}, Q_{i\pm}) < 0$$

and

$$\ell_r(Q_{r\pm}, Q_{i\pm}) < 0, \quad \ell_i(Q_{r\pm}, Q_{i\pm}) < 0, \quad \text{at} \quad \zeta = 0.$$

Hence on the basis of maximum principle neither $Q_{r\pm}$ nor $Q_{i\pm}$ can have a negative minimum and consequently we choose $C > 0$ large enough so that

$$Q_{r\pm} > 0, \quad Q_{i\pm} > 0 \quad \text{in} \quad \Omega_\varepsilon/d(\mu)^{1/2}$$

for R_μ sufficiently large. Therefore,

$$|\omega_{1r} - \bar{\omega}_{1r}| \le \frac{1}{(2)^{1/2}} CR_\mu^{-\gamma}$$

$$|\omega_{1i} - \bar{\omega}_{1i}| \le \frac{1}{(2)^{1/2}} CR_\mu^{-\gamma}$$

which gives

$$|\omega_1(x,\zeta) - \overline{\omega}_1(x,\zeta)| \leq CR_\mu^{-\gamma}$$

This proves the theorem.

In the proof of Theorem I we choose $\alpha > 0$ and $\beta > 0$ in such a way that

$$C_r - C_i < 0$$

$$C_r + C_i < 0$$

Since $C_r < 0$ and $C_i < 0$, hence it is sufficient to consider the inequality

$$C_r - C_i < -N \tag{37}$$

where $N > 0$ and is arbitrary. Substituting the expressions of C_r and C_i from (30) in (37), we get

$$\alpha^2\omega_o^2 \frac{\phi''}{\phi} + \delta\left\{\frac{\alpha\phi'}{\phi}(p_o)_x - \zeta\beta\right\} + (\omega_o + \overline{\omega}_o)(\overline{\omega}_o)_{\zeta\zeta} + 1 < -N$$

Since most of the non-uniformities in the solutions of the boundary layer and full viscous equations occur near the surface of the body, hence we consider small values of ζ such that $\alpha\zeta < \frac{1}{2}$ and $\alpha > 0$ is chosen large enough. Using the expression of $\phi(s)$ defined earlier we get

$$(\omega_o + \overline{\omega}_o)(\overline{\omega}_o)_{\zeta\zeta} - \delta\zeta\beta + 2\alpha\delta|(p_o)_x| - \frac{1}{3}\alpha^2\omega_o^2 + 1 < -N$$

Since α is large, we get $2\alpha\delta|(p_o)_x| - \frac{1}{3}\alpha^2\omega_o^2 < 0$ and consequently

$$\delta < \frac{1}{6}\frac{\alpha\omega_o^2}{|(p_o)_x|} \tag{38}$$

The choice of α occurring in the estimate (38) can now be made by considering equation (33a). Since k_r and k_i are positive, we can without loss of generality assume them to be greater than $d(\mu)^{1/2}/\varepsilon^{2}$. Therefore,

---

2. The terms in the boundary operators (32) are such that they explicitly involve $\varepsilon/(\mu)^{1/2}$ and therefore,

$$-\left(\alpha\omega_o \frac{\phi'}{\phi} + \frac{\partial\overline{\omega}_o}{\partial\zeta}\right) > \frac{d(\mu)^{1/2}}{\varepsilon}$$

Following the arguments preceding the inequality (38), we get

$$\alpha > \frac{2d(\mu)^{1/2}}{\omega_o \varepsilon} \left\{1 + \frac{\varepsilon}{d(\mu)^{1/2}} \left|\frac{\partial\overline{\omega}_o}{\partial\zeta}\right|\right\} \tag{39}$$

Reverting to physical variables and writing for brevity

$$|(p_o)_x| = b, \quad \max \left|\frac{\partial u_o}{\partial Y}\right| = n$$

the inequality (39) becomes

$$\alpha > \frac{2\mu d}{n\varepsilon^2} \left\{1 + \frac{\varepsilon^2}{d\mu} \left|\frac{\partial^2\overline{u}_o}{\partial\zeta\partial Y}\right|\right\} \tag{40}$$

If we now use the order of magnitude of α as given in (40) in the estimate (38), we get after some simplification

$$R_\mu > \frac{3b}{nd} R \tag{41}$$

Since R is sufficiently large and is such that the solutions of the Navier-Stokes and Prandtl's equations in the steady state approach one another, hence the inequality (41)[3] satisfies all the requirements of Theorem I. In conclusion we can state the following theorem.

Theorem II / Let $\varepsilon < \varepsilon_o$ and let a be the small amplitude of the superposed fluctuating flow. If the Reynolds number R is such that the solutions of the Navier-Stokes and Prandtl's equations in the steady state approach one another, then the difference between the solutions

---

$k_r V_{1r} = \frac{k_r \varepsilon}{d(\mu)^{1/2}} \left(\frac{\partial u_{1r}}{\partial Y_1} - \frac{\partial \overline{u}_{1r}}{\partial Y_1}\right)$, where $Y_1 = \frac{Y}{d}$. Therefore, without loss of generality we take $\frac{k_r \varepsilon}{d(\mu)^{1/2}} > 1$.

3. The inequality (41) has been chosen because it provides stronger conditions than the inequality $R_\mu \leq (3b/nd)\, R$.

for a superposed fluctuating flow of small amplitude can be made as small as desired provided that

$$R_\mu > \frac{3b}{nd} R$$

where $R_\mu = \frac{\mu d^2}{\varepsilon^2}$ and b, n, d are constants.

This result, therefore, puts a certain restriction over the choice of the angular frequency parameter μ for obtaining solutions of the Prandtl's boundary layer equations which also simultaneously satisfy the Navier-Stokes equations. An obvious conclusion is that the frequency parameter should be large such that its lower bound is given by the estimate (41). Also, as pointed out by Stuart [7, p. 393], that the boundary layer theory is not directly applicable, even at large values of $R_\mu = \mu d^2/\varepsilon^2$ because of the modification of pressure, can now be formalized. On the basis of the results obtained in this paper it can be concluded that the solutions of the Prandtl's boundary layer equations are the solutions of the Navier-Stokes equations for R sufficiently large and $R_\mu > \frac{3b}{nd} R$ provided that the modification of pressures due to fluctuations are such that

$$|\{p_1(x,0)\}_x - \{\overline{p}_1(x)\}_x| \le MR_\mu^{-\gamma_1} .$$

CONCLUSIONS

The purpose of this paper has been to investigate the effects of superposed fluctuating flows on the solutions of Prandtl's and Navier-Stokes equations. Necessary mathematical criteria have been obtained for the solutions of the two widely used viscous flow models to approach one another. It has been shown that if $R_\mu > \frac{3b}{nd} R$, then the solutions of the boundary layer equations are valid solutions of the full viscous equations. Besides, it has also been shown that the boundary layer equations can be used for $R_\mu \gg 1$ provided that the modified pressure due to the fluctuations satisfies the inequality

$$|\{p_1(x,0)\}_x - \{\overline{p}_1(x)\}_x| \le MR_\mu^{-\gamma_1}$$

ACKNOWLEDGEMENT

The research reported in this paper has been supported in part by the Army Research Office - Durham.

REFERENCES

1. Nickel, K., "Die Prandtlschen Grenzschichtdifferentialgleichungen als Grenzfall der Navier-Stokesschen und der Eulerschen Differentialgleichungen," Archive for Rational Mechanics and Analysis, Vol. 13, 1 (1963).

2. Oleinik, O. A., "Stability of Solutions of a System of Boundary Layer Equations for a Non-Stationary Flow of Incompressible Fluid," Journal of Applied Mathematics and Mechanics, (PMM), Vol. 30, No. 3, 505 (1966).

3. Fife, P. C., "Considerations Regarding the Mathematical Basis for Prandtl's Boundary Layer Theory," Archive of Rational Mechanics and Analysis, Vol. 28, 184 (1968).

4. Serrin, J., "On the Mathematical Basis of Prandtl's Boundary Layer Theory-an Example," Ibid, 217 (1968).

5. Brzychczy, S., "A Comparison of Solutions of Prandtl's and Navier-Stokes System of Equations at Low Viscosity," Bulletin L'Academi Polonaise Series Des Sciences, Mathematique, Astronomie et. Physique, Vol. 16, No. 3, 175 (1968).

6. Lighthill, M. J., "The Response of Laminar Skin Friction and Heat Transfer to Fluctuations in the Stream Velocity," Proceeding Royal Society (London), Series A, Vol. 224, 1 (1954).

7. Stuart, J. T., Article on Unsteady Boundary Layers, in Laminar Boundary Layers, Ed. L. Rosenhead, Oxford, at the Clarendon Press (1963).

ON THE INTRINSIC REPRESENTATION OF FLOWS WITH LAMB SURFACES

S. L. Passman
United States Naval Academy

ABSTRACT

The basic equations for the representation of flows in terms of "intrinsic coordinates", i.e., a field of unit vectors consisting of the tangents, principal normals, and binormals to the streamlines, have been developed by a number of authors. These equations can be thought of as divided into two types. The purely kinematical equations depend solely on the magnitudes and vector line patterns of the velocity, vorticity, and acceleration fields, while the dynamical-constitutive equations depend on Euler's equations of motion and/or constitutive assumptions for the particular fluid considered.

In this paper some of the kinematical theory of intrinsic representation of flows on surfaces developed by Marris and Passman is extended and applied to the case of flows with Lamb surfaces. Some special properties of the surfaces are pointed out, and particular attention is given to the geometry of the stream and vortex lines in relation to the Lamb surfaces. "Flat flows" and flows of solenoidal vector-line rotation are shown to have some interesting special properties. Permanence is studied, and some special properties of complex-lamellar flows and flows with complex-lamellar vorticity are considered.

It is shown that a number of theorems which are known in the context of the flows of fluids with relatively restricted constitutive equations, for example the case of a steady circulation-preserving flow of an inviscid Prim gas with no heat flux, hold for the case of the motion of a general continuum. The clarity of the arguments and the simplicity and generality of the conclusions when couched in kinematical terms are emphasized.

INTRODUCTION

In his classic treatise [1], C. Truesdell emphasizes that many of the theorems of fluid dynamics are, in fact, kinematical in nature and therefore can be derived without reference to specific constitutive equations.

I here use the technique of resolving the components of kinematical vector fields associated with the motion of a fluid[1] along the tangent, principal normal and binormal to the streamlines. This method involves certain difficulties of a mathematical nature which are relatively unusual in continuum mechanics. However, many of the kinematical quantities of central importance in fluid dynamics assume particularly simple and elegant forms in terms of these so-called "intrinsic coordinates."

Some of the results presented by Marris and Passman [2] concerning the kinematics of "flat flows" are generalized, and their relation to flows with Lamb surfaces are discussed. It is shown that some results recently presented in the context of relatively restricted constitutive assumptions, in particular by Suryanarayan for the case of steady flow of a linearly viscous incompressible fluid [3] and an inviscid Prim gas with no heat flux [4] are in fact either kinematical in nature or are direct consequences of more general kinematical theorems, and are thus independent of constitutive equations.

Mathematical Preliminaries

Let $\underset{\sim}{x}$ be the coordinates of a point in absolute physical space, and let $\underset{\sim}{\phi}$ (,) be a function of four variables which is twice continuously differentiable in each of the variables. We adopt the convention that the values of $\underset{\sim}{\phi}$ (,) are given by $\underset{\sim}{\phi}$ (x,t), where t is a scalar variable interpreted as the time. We say $\underset{\sim}{\phi}$ is steady if t does not appear explicitly as an argument in $\underset{\sim}{\phi}$ ( ):

$$\frac{\partial \underset{\sim}{\phi}}{\partial t} = 0 \tag{1}$$

In order to simplify notation, we ignore the essential difference between a function and its values.

---

1. Of course as long as we discuss kinematics only, all results are equally applicable to motion of any continuum. However, since this method has both origins and important applications in the motion of fluids, I use the terminology of fluid mechanics.

By a theorem of calculus[2] there exist, at least locally, a set of scalar functions α, β, γ called the Monge potentials for $\underset{\sim}{\phi}$ such that

$$\underset{\sim}{\phi} = \alpha \text{ grad } \beta + \text{grad } \gamma \tag{2}$$

where "grad" denotes the vector gradient with respect to $\underset{\sim}{x}$. If it is possible to write $\underset{\sim}{\phi}$ in the form

$$\underset{\sim}{\phi} = \alpha \text{ grad } \beta \tag{3}$$

then $\underset{\sim}{\phi}$ is said to be complex-lamellar. Equivalent to (3) is the condition

$$\underset{\sim}{\phi} \cdot \text{curl } \underset{\sim}{\phi} = 0 \tag{4}$$

A complex-lamellar field is the most general field for which normal surfaces exist.

Let $\underset{\sim}{v}$ be the nonvanishing velocity field of a fluid, and assume that $\underset{\sim}{v}$ enjoys the same smoothness properties as $\underset{\sim}{\phi}$. We can always write

$$\underset{\sim}{v} = v\underset{\sim}{s} \tag{5}$$

where $v = |\underset{\sim}{v}|$ is the magnitude of $\underset{\sim}{v}$, and $\underset{\sim}{s}$ is a unit vector in the direction of $\underset{\sim}{v}$. If $\underset{\sim}{n}$ is the principal normal and $\underset{\sim}{b}$ the binormal to $\underset{\sim}{v}$, then we define the intrinsic derivatives

$$\begin{aligned} \frac{\delta}{\delta s} &= \underset{\sim}{s} \cdot \text{grad} \\ \frac{\delta}{\delta n} &= \underset{\sim}{n} \cdot \text{grad} \\ \frac{\delta}{\delta b} &= \underset{\sim}{b} \cdot \text{grad} \end{aligned} \tag{6}$$

We have the well-known Frenet-Serret formulae

$$\begin{aligned} \frac{\delta \underset{\sim}{s}}{\delta s} &= \kappa \underset{\sim}{n} \\ \frac{\delta \underset{\sim}{n}}{\delta s} &= -\kappa \underset{\sim}{s} + \tau \underset{\sim}{b} \\ \frac{\delta \underset{\sim}{b}}{\delta s} &= -\tau \underset{\sim}{n} \end{aligned} \tag{7}$$

2. See, e.g., [5], Para. 105.

where κ is the curvature of the s-lines, and τ is the torsion of the s-lines. In this work, we always assume $\kappa \neq 0$.

The relations (7) have been generalized. It was shown by Bjørgum [6] that

$$\begin{aligned} \text{grad } \underset{\sim}{s} = & + \underset{\sim\sim}{sn}\,\kappa \\ & + \underset{\sim\sim}{nn}\,\theta_{ns} + \underset{\sim\sim}{nb}\,\tfrac{1}{2}(\psi_s + \Omega_s) \\ & + \underset{\sim\sim}{bn}\,\tfrac{1}{2}(\psi_s - \Omega_s) + \underset{\sim\sim}{bb}\,\theta_{bs} \end{aligned} \tag{8}$$

and by Marris and Passman [2] that

$$\begin{aligned} \text{grad } \underset{\sim}{n} = & - \underset{\sim\sim}{ss}\,\kappa + \underset{\sim\sim}{sb}\,\tau \\ & - \underset{\sim\sim}{ns}\,\theta_{ns} - \underset{\sim\sim}{nb}\,\text{div } \underset{\sim}{b} \\ & - \underset{\sim\sim}{bs}\,\tfrac{1}{2}(\psi_s - \Omega_s) + \underset{\sim\sim}{bb}\,(\kappa + \text{div } \underset{\sim}{n}) \end{aligned} \tag{9}$$

and

$$\begin{aligned} \text{grad } \underset{\sim}{b} = & - \underset{\sim\sim}{sn}\,\kappa \\ & - \underset{\sim\sim}{ns}\,\tfrac{1}{2}(\psi_s + \Omega_s) + \underset{\sim\sim}{nn}\,\text{div } \underset{\sim}{b} \\ & - \underset{\sim\sim}{bs}\,\theta_{bs} - \underset{\sim\sim}{bn}\,(\kappa + \text{div } \underset{\sim}{n}) \end{aligned} \tag{10}$$

The system of anholonomic coordinates defined by the field of unit vectors $\underset{\sim}{s}$, $\underset{\sim}{n}$, $\underset{\sim}{b}$ has the property that if F be any function, the second order mixed intrinsic derivatives do not commute. In fact, it was shown in [2] that[3]

$$\frac{\delta^2 F}{\delta b \delta n} - \frac{\delta^2 F}{\delta n \delta b} = \Omega_s \frac{\delta F}{\delta s} - \text{div } \underset{\sim}{b} \frac{\delta F}{\delta n} + (\kappa + \text{div } \underset{\sim}{n}) \frac{\delta F}{\delta b} \tag{11}$$

$$\frac{\delta^2 F}{\delta s \delta b} - \frac{\delta^2 F}{\delta b \delta s} = \Omega_n \frac{\delta F}{\delta n} - \theta_{bs} \frac{\delta F}{\delta b} \tag{12}$$

$$\frac{\delta^2 F}{\delta n \delta s} - \frac{\delta^2 F}{\delta s \delta n} = \kappa + \theta_{ns} \frac{\delta F}{\delta n} + \Omega_b \frac{\delta F}{\delta b} \tag{13}$$

---

3. Here $\dfrac{\delta^2 F}{\delta b \delta n} = \dfrac{\delta}{\delta b}\left(\dfrac{\delta F}{\delta n}\right)$.

The axial-vectors of (8)-(10) are

$$\operatorname{curl} \underset{\sim}{s} = \Omega_s \underset{\sim}{s} + \kappa \underset{\sim}{b} \qquad (14)$$

$$\operatorname{curl} \underset{\sim}{n} = (-\operatorname{div} \underset{\sim}{b})\underset{\sim}{s} - \left(\tau + \frac{1}{2}(\psi_s - \Omega_s)\right)\underset{\sim}{n} + \theta_{ns} \underset{\sim}{b} \qquad (15)$$

$$\operatorname{curl} \underset{\sim}{b} = (\kappa + \operatorname{div} \underset{\sim}{n})\underset{\sim}{s} - \theta_{bs} \underset{\sim}{n} - \left(\tau - \frac{1}{2}(\psi_s + \Omega_s)\right)\underset{\sim}{b} \qquad (16)$$

The geometrical interpretations of κ and τ are well-known. Geometrical interpretations for the remaining scalar parameters in (8)-(10) have been given in [2] and [6]. Of particular importance is the abnormality Ω_s of the s-lines. The curl of (5) is

$$\operatorname{curl} \underset{\sim}{v} = v \operatorname{curl} \underset{\sim}{s} + \operatorname{grad} v \times \underset{\sim}{s} \qquad (17)$$

so that

$$\underset{\sim}{v} \cdot \operatorname{curl} \underset{\sim}{v} = v^2 \underset{\sim}{s} \cdot \operatorname{curl} \underset{\sim}{s} + v\underset{\sim}{s} \cdot (\operatorname{grad} v \times \underset{\sim}{s})$$

thus

$$\underset{\sim}{s} \cdot \operatorname{curl} \underset{\sim}{s} = \frac{\underset{\sim}{v} \cdot \operatorname{curl} \underset{\sim}{v}}{v^2} \qquad (18)$$

and $\underset{\sim}{s} \cdot \operatorname{curl} \underset{\sim}{s} = 0$ if and only if $\underset{\sim}{v} \cdot \operatorname{curl} \underset{\sim}{v} = 0$. By (14) we have

$$\Omega_s = \underset{\sim}{s} \cdot \operatorname{curl} \underset{\sim}{s} \qquad (19)$$

Assume that $\underset{\sim}{v}$ is complex-lamellar, that is, let there exist a nonzero function A and a nonconstant function B such that[4]

$$\underset{\sim}{v} = A \operatorname{grad} B \qquad (20)$$

By (5)

$$v\underset{\sim}{s} = A \operatorname{grad} B \qquad (21)$$

Taking the curl of (21) gives

$$v \operatorname{curl} \underset{\sim}{s} + \operatorname{grad} v \times \underset{\sim}{s} = \operatorname{grad} A \times \operatorname{grad} B$$

which by (14) and (19) is

$$v(\Omega_s \underset{\sim}{s} + \kappa \underset{\sim}{b}) + \operatorname{grad} v \times \underset{\sim}{s} = \operatorname{grad} A \times \frac{v}{A} \underset{\sim}{s} \qquad (22)$$

---

4. Henceforth, whenever $\underset{\sim}{v}$ is complex-lamellar, the symbols A and B will be used as in (20).

Forming the dot product of (22) with $\underset{\sim}{s}$, we have

$$\Omega_s = 0 \tag{23}$$

that is, the abnormality of a complex-lamellar field is zero. In fact the converse of this statement holds also, so that a field is complex-lamellar if and only if its abnormality vanishes.

An explicit intrinsic form for the vorticity

$$\underset{\sim}{w} = \text{curl } \underset{\sim}{v} \tag{24}$$

is easily derived from (14), (17) and the intrinsic form of the gradient operator

$$\text{grad} = \underset{\sim}{s} \frac{\delta}{\delta s} + \underset{\sim}{n} \frac{\delta}{\delta n} + \underset{\sim}{b} \frac{\delta}{\delta b} \tag{25}$$

It is

$$\underset{\sim}{w} = \Omega_s \, v \, \underset{\sim}{s} + \frac{\delta v}{\delta b} \underset{\sim}{n} + \left(\kappa v - \frac{\delta v}{\delta n} \right) \underset{\sim}{b} \qquad (26)^5$$

A Beltrami flow (screw motion) is one which satisfies

$$\underset{\sim}{w} \times \underset{\sim}{v} = 0 \tag{27}$$

For any rotational flow which is not a Beltrami flow, the Lamb vector is defined by

$$\underset{\sim}{\lambda} = \underset{\sim}{w} \times \underset{\sim}{v} \tag{28}$$

By (5), (26), and the fact that the ordered triple ($\underset{\sim}{s}$, $\underset{\sim}{n}$, $\underset{\sim}{b}$) constitutes a right-handed orthogonal triad of unit vectors, the intrinsic form of (28) is

$$\underset{\sim}{\lambda} = v \left[- \frac{\delta v}{\delta b} \underset{\sim}{b} + \left(\kappa v - \frac{\delta v}{\delta n} \right) \underset{\sim}{n} \right] \tag{29}$$

If and only if the Lamb vector is complex-lamellar, there is a nonzero function C and a nonconstant function D such that[6]

$$\underset{\sim}{\lambda} = C \text{ grad } D \tag{30}$$

---

5. This equation was discovered by Masotti [7].

6. Whenever the Lamb vector is complex-lamellar, the symbols C and D are used as in (30).

The surfaces D = constant are called Lamb surfaces. Lamb surfaces always contain the vortex lines and the streamlines.

It is emphasized that Lamb surfaces do not always exist. In a subsequent section we note some nontrivial sufficient conditions for their existence.

Kinematical Theorems

We now assume that Lamb surfaces exist, so that

$$\underset{\sim}{\lambda} = C \text{ grad } D \tag{30}$$

and derive some kinematical theorems. Since

$$\underset{\sim}{\lambda} = v \left[- \frac{\delta v}{\delta b} \underset{\sim}{b} + \left(\kappa v - \frac{\delta v}{\delta n} \right) \underset{\sim}{n} \right] \tag{29}$$

the normal to the streamline coincides with the normal to the Lamb surface if and only if $\frac{\delta v}{\delta b} = 0$, thus by a well-known result from differential geometry we have

Theorem 1.[7] The streamlines are geodesics on the Lamb surfaces if and only if

$$\frac{\delta v}{\delta b} = 0 \tag{31}$$

i.e., the speed is constant along the b-lines.

By a theorem of Marris and Passman[8], there exists a family of surfaces such that the streamlines are geodesics on this family if and only if

$$\Omega_n = \underset{\sim}{n} \cdot \text{curl } \underset{\sim}{n} = 0 \qquad (32)^9$$

---

7. Suryanarayan [4] has proved that a vortex line is a geodesic on a Lamb surface in a steady circulation-preserving motion of an inviscid Prim gas with no heat flux if and only if the component of the velocity vector along the principal normal to the vortex line vanishes. It is relatively easy to recast this theorem in kinematical form, so that it is, in a sense, complementary to Theorem 1.

8. [2], Theorem 3.1.

9. By (15) is it obvious that

$$\Omega_n = - \left[\tau + \frac{1}{2} (\psi_s - \Omega_s) \right].$$

However, the connection between the conditions (31) and (32) is relatively subtle. We rewrite (29) as

$$\underset{\sim}{\lambda} = -\frac{\delta}{\delta b}\left(\frac{v^2}{2}\right)\underset{\sim}{b} + \left[\kappa v^2 - \frac{\delta}{\delta n}\left(\frac{v^2}{2}\right)\right]\underset{\sim}{n} \tag{33}$$

We have

$$\text{curl}\,\underset{\sim}{\lambda} = \left[\kappa v^2 - \frac{\delta}{\delta n}\left(\frac{v^2}{2}\right)\right]\text{curl}\,\underset{\sim}{n} - \left[\frac{\delta}{\delta b}\left(\frac{v^2}{2}\right)\right]\text{curl}\,\underset{\sim}{b}$$
$$+ \text{grad}\left[\kappa v^2 - \frac{\delta}{\delta n}\left(\frac{v^2}{2}\right)\right]\times\underset{\sim}{n} - \text{grad}\left[\frac{\delta}{\delta b}\left(\frac{v^2}{2}\right)\right]\times\underset{\sim}{b} \tag{34}$$

By (32), (33), (34), and some familiar properties of orthogonal vectors

$$\underset{\sim}{\lambda}\cdot\text{curl}\,\underset{\sim}{\lambda} = \left[\kappa v^2 - \frac{\delta}{\delta n}\left(\frac{v^2}{2}\right)\right]^2\Omega_n - \left[\kappa v^2 - \frac{\delta}{\delta n}\left(\frac{v^2}{2}\right)\right]\left[\frac{\delta}{\delta b}\left(\frac{v^2}{2}\right)\right]\underset{\sim}{n}\cdot\text{curl}\,\underset{\sim}{b}$$
$$- \left[\kappa v^2 - \frac{\delta}{\delta n}\left(\frac{v^2}{2}\right)\right]\text{grad}\left[\frac{\delta}{\delta b}\left(\frac{v^2}{2}\right)\right]\times\underset{\sim}{b}\cdot\underset{\sim}{n}$$
$$- \frac{\delta}{\delta b}\left(\frac{v^2}{2}\right)\left[\kappa v^2 - \frac{\delta}{\delta n}\left(\frac{v^2}{2}\right)\right]\underset{\sim}{b}\cdot\text{curl}\,\underset{\sim}{n} + \left[\frac{\delta}{\delta b}\left(\frac{v^2}{2}\right)\right]^2\underset{\sim}{b}\cdot\text{curl}\,\underset{\sim}{b}$$
$$- \frac{\delta}{\delta b}\left(\frac{v^2}{2}\right)\text{grad}\left[\kappa v^2 - \frac{\delta}{\delta n}\left(\frac{v^2}{2}\right)\right]\times\underset{\sim}{n}\cdot\underset{\sim}{b} \tag{35}$$

It is seen that all of the terms in (35) with the exception of the first vanish when $\frac{\delta v}{\delta b}$ vanishes in a neighborhood. Thus we have

<u>Theorem 2</u>. For a flow which is not a Beltrami flow, if $\frac{\delta v}{\delta b} = 0$, then

$$\underset{\sim}{\lambda}\cdot\text{curl}\,\underset{\sim}{\lambda} = 0$$

if and only if

$$\Omega_n = 0$$

Combining Theorem 1 with Theorem 2, we obtain

<u>Theorem 3</u>. For a flow in which the component of the vorticity normal to the streamline vanishes, Lamb surfaces exist if and only if either of the conditions

$$\underset{\sim}{\lambda}\cdot\text{curl}\,\underset{\sim}{\lambda} = 0$$

or

$$\Omega_n = 0$$

are satisfied. Furthermore, the streamlines are geodesics on the Lamb surfaces.

Even though in a flow which satisfies the hypotheses of Theorem 3, the streamlines are geodesics on the Lamb surfaces, and the vortex lines and b-lines (vector lines of $\underset{\sim}{b}$) are contained in the Lamb surfaces, in general there is still considerable freedom in the behavior of both the vortex lines and the b-lines.

By known theorems of geometry[10], if

$$\theta_{bs} = \underset{\sim}{n} \cdot \text{curl } \underset{\sim}{b} = 0 \tag{36}$$

then the Lamb surfaces are developable. A flow which satisfies (32) and (36) is called a flat flow. In this case the b-lines, as well as the stream lines, are geodesics on the Lamb surfaces. We have

Theorem 4. For a flat flow which satisfies the condition $\frac{\delta v}{\delta b} = 0$, Lamb surfaces exist, and the streamlines and b-lines constitute a net of orthogonal geodesics on the Lamb surfaces.

Let $\underset{\sim}{v}$ be a complex-lamellar flow, so that

$$\underset{\sim}{v} = A \text{ grad } B \tag{20}$$

and let the Lamb vector be complex-lamellar

$$\underset{\sim}{\lambda} = C \text{ grad } D \tag{30}$$

By (28) we have

$$\underset{\sim}{v} \cdot \underset{\sim}{\lambda} = AC \text{ grad } B \cdot \text{grad } D = 0 \tag{37}$$

Hence follows

Theorem 5. In a complex-lamellar flow with complex-lamellar Lamb vector, the Lamb surfaces and the surfaces orthogonal to the streamlines intersect orthogonally along the vortex lines.

A direct application of a theorem of Joachimsthal[11] yields the

Corollary. In a complex-lamellar motion with Lamb surfaces, a necessary and sufficient condition that a vortex line be a line of curvature

---

10. [2], page 45.

11. [5], page 305. The application of this theorem in the context of fluid mechanics was pointed out by Suryanarayan [4].

on a Lamb surface is that it be a line of curvature on a surface orthogonal to the streamlines.

Theorem 5 has another interesting corollary. Lagrange's acceleration formula is

$$\underset{\sim}{a} = \frac{\partial \underset{\sim}{v}}{\partial t} + \underset{\sim}{w} \times \underset{\sim}{v} + \text{grad}\ \frac{v^2}{2} \tag{38}$$

Circulation-preserving flows are of particular interest in fluid mechanics. It is well-known that a flow is circulation-preserving if and only if

$$\text{curl}\ \underset{\sim}{a} = 0 \tag{39}$$

Thus,

$$\text{curl}\ \underset{\sim}{a} = \frac{\partial \underset{\sim}{w}}{\partial t} + \text{curl}\ (\underset{\sim}{w} \times \underset{\sim}{v}) \tag{40}$$

In a circulation-preserving flow with steady vorticity, Lamb surfaces exist. Thus we obtain the

Corollary. In a complex-lamellar circulation-preserving flow, the Lamb surfaces and the surfaces orthogonal to the streamlines intersect orthogonally along the vortex lines.

By (20) and Theorems 3 and 5, we obtain

Theorem 6. In a complex-lamellar flow with Lamb surfaces[12], if $\frac{\delta v}{\delta b} = 0$, then the b-lines coincide with the vortex lines. Furthermore, the streamlines are geodesics on the Lamb surfaces.

Theorems 4 and 6 give

Theorem 7. For a flat complex-lamellar flow which satisfies the condition $\frac{\delta v}{\delta b} = 0$, Lamb surfaces exist, and the streamlines and vortex lines constitute a net of orthogonal geodesics on the Lamb surfaces.

Let the vorticity vector be complex-lamellar

$$\underset{\sim}{w} = E\ \text{grad}\ F \tag{41}$$

By a theorem of Bjørgum[13] the magnitude of the vorticity vector is constant if and only if the divergence of the unit tangent to the

12. And, therefore, in a complex-lamellar circulation-preserving flow with steady vorticity, ...

13. [6], page 35.

vortex line vanishes. This quantity is recognized[14] as the mean curvature of the surfaces normal to the vorticity. Thus we obtain

Theorem 8. In any flow with complex-lamellar vorticity, the magnitude of the vorticity is constant if and only if the surfaces F = constant are minimal surfaces.

A trivial calculation gives the (known) result that in a complex-lamellar flow with complex-lamellar vorticity and Lamb surfaces, the Lamb surfaces, the surfaces orthogonal to the streamlines, and the surfaces orthogonal to the vortex lines are mutually orthogonal.

In his elegant works [9, 10] A. W. Marris introduced flows of solenoidal vector-line rotation. A flow is of solenoidal vector-line rotation if the curvature κ and abnormality Ω_s of its s-lines are both finite and nonvanishing, and if

$$\operatorname{div}\,(\Omega_s \underset{\sim}{v}) = 0 \tag{42}$$

It is obvious that all Beltrami flows are of solenoidal vector-line rotation. However, examples have been given of solenoidal vector-line rotation flows which are not Beltrami flows. It is these flows that we consider here.

Equations (15), (16) and (34) yield

$$\begin{aligned}\operatorname{curl} \underset{\sim}{\lambda} = v\left[\operatorname{div}(\Omega_s \underset{\sim}{v}) - 2\kappa \frac{\delta v}{\delta b}\right] \underset{\sim}{s} + \left[\frac{\delta^2}{\delta b \delta s}\left(\frac{v^2}{2}\right) + \kappa\, \Omega_n\, v^2\right] \underset{\sim}{n} \\ + \left[\left(\kappa \frac{\delta}{\delta s}\left(\frac{v^2}{2}\right) + \operatorname{div}(\kappa\, v^2 \underset{\sim}{s})\right) - \left(\frac{\delta^2}{\delta n \delta s}\left(\frac{v^2}{2}\right) + \kappa\, v^2\, \theta_{bs}\right)\right] \underset{\sim}{b}\end{aligned} \tag{43}$$

therefore

$$\underset{\sim}{s} \cdot \operatorname{curl} \underset{\sim}{\lambda} = v \operatorname{div}(\Omega_s \underset{\sim}{v}) - 2\,\kappa \frac{\delta v}{\delta b} \tag{44}$$

and

$$\underset{\sim}{n} \cdot \operatorname{curl} \underset{\sim}{\lambda} = \frac{\delta^2}{\delta b \delta s}\left(\frac{v^2}{2}\right) + \kappa\, \Omega_n\, v^2 \tag{45}$$

Equation (45) may be written in a more useful form. Choosing $F = \frac{v^2}{2}$ in (12), we obtain from (45)

---

14. See, e.g., [8], page 3.

$$\underset{\sim}{n} \cdot \text{curl } \underset{\sim}{\lambda} = \frac{\delta^2}{\delta s \delta b}\left(\frac{v^2}{2}\right) - \Omega_n \frac{\delta}{\delta n}\left(\frac{v^2}{2}\right) + \theta_{bs} \frac{\delta}{\delta b}\left(\frac{v^2}{2}\right) \tag{46}$$

A flow is said to be of constrained solenoidal vector-line rotation if it is of solenoidal vector-line rotation and $\frac{\delta v}{\delta b} = 0$. Direct application of a theorem of Marris[15] to (44) and (46) gives

Theorem 9. A steady flat flow of constrained solenoidal vector-line rotation which is not complex-lamellar, and in which $\frac{\delta v}{\delta n} \neq 0$, is a flow of permanent solenoidal vector-line rotation.

In other words, sufficient conditions that a material region of solenoidal vector-line rotation remain a material region of solenoidal vector-line rotation in a steady flow are

$$\Omega_n = 0, \quad \theta_{bs} = 0, \quad \frac{\delta v}{\delta b} = 0 \tag{47}$$

We let $\underset{\sim}{w}_{\parallel}$ be the vector component of the vorticity parallel to the velocity vector, and $\underset{\sim}{w}_{\perp}$ be the vector component of the vorticity perpendicular to the velocity vector, so that

$$\underset{\sim}{w} = \underset{\sim}{w}_{\parallel} + \underset{\sim}{w}_{\perp} \tag{48}$$

where, by (5) and (26)

$$\underset{\sim}{w}_{\parallel} = \Omega_s \underset{\sim}{v} \tag{49}$$

and

$$\underset{\sim}{w}_{\perp} = \frac{\delta v}{\delta b} \underset{\sim}{n} + \left(\kappa v - \frac{\delta v}{\delta n}\right) \underset{\sim}{b} \tag{50}$$

Through an intricate line of reasoning involving the Helmholtz-Zorawski criterion[16], Marris[17] has proved that the only steady flows of solenoidal vector-line rotation for which the vector-tubes of both $\underset{\sim}{w}_{\parallel}$ and $\underset{\sim}{w}_{\perp}$ are material tubes are either circulation-preserving flows or flows in which $\underset{\sim}{w}_{\perp}$ and curl $(\underset{\sim}{w} \times \underset{\sim}{v})$ each point along $\underset{\sim}{b}$. By (43), (46), (50) and Theorem 4 we obtain

Theorem 10. In a steady flat flow of constrained solenoidal vector-line rotation

---

15. [10], Theorem 3.1.
16. [1], Para. 28.
17. [10], Theorem 3.4.

a) The vector tubes of both $\underset{\sim}{w}_{\parallel}$ and $\underset{\sim}{w}_{\perp}$ are permanent.
b) Lamb surfaces exist, and the streamlines and b-lines constitute a set of orthogonal geodesics on the Lamb surfaces.

Some Sufficient Conditions for the Existence of Lamb Surfaces

In the preceding sections we have examined some properties of Lamb surfaces and some consequences of their existence. In this section we note some special flows and special materials in which these surfaces always exist. Many of the results presented are already known[18].

A flow is said to be isochoric if it satisfies the condition

$$\operatorname{div} \underset{\sim}{v} = 0 \tag{51}$$

By the equation of continuity for a continuum, an equivalent condition is

$$\rho = \text{constant} \tag{52}$$

where ρ is the density of the continuum. All flows of incompressible materials are isochoric.

Kinematical Conditions / Marris[19] has proven the following theorem: Let $\underset{\sim}{v}$ be an isochoric flow of solenoidal vector-line rotation, and let $\Omega_s \underset{\sim}{v}$ be a Beltrami flow. Then

$$\underset{\sim}{w} \times \underset{\sim}{v} = - v^2 \operatorname{grad} \log \Omega_s \tag{53}$$

In this case the abnormality is constant on the Lamb surfaces.

By (4), the necessary and sufficient condition for the existence of Lamb surfaces

$$\underset{\sim}{\lambda} = C \operatorname{grad} D \tag{30}$$

is equivalent to

$$\underset{\sim}{\lambda} \cdot \operatorname{curl} \underset{\sim}{\lambda} = 0 \tag{31}$$

By (28) and (38)

$$\underset{\sim}{\lambda} = \underset{\sim}{a} - \frac{\partial \underset{\sim}{v}}{\partial t} - \operatorname{grad} \frac{v^2}{2} \tag{54}$$

so by (24)

18. See [1].
19. [9], Theorem 3.6.

$$\lambda \cdot \operatorname{curl} \lambda = \lambda \cdot \left(\operatorname{curl} a - \frac{\partial w}{\partial t}\right) \tag{55}$$

and a necessary and sufficient condition for the existence of Lamb surfaces is

$$\lambda \cdot \left(\operatorname{curl} a - \frac{\partial w}{\partial t}\right) = 0 \tag{56}$$

By (39) and (56), in a circulation-preserving flow of steady vorticity, Lamb surfaces exist.

Inviscid Fluids / For an inviscid fluid with conservative body force, if p is the pressure and ν the body force potential

$$a = - \operatorname{grad} \nu - \frac{1}{\rho} \operatorname{grad} p \tag{57}$$

Two easy cases arise. For an incompressible fluid

$$a = - \operatorname{grad} (\nu + \frac{p}{\rho}) \tag{58}$$

so that by (28) and (38)

$$\lambda = - \operatorname{grad} \left(\nu + \frac{p}{\rho} + \frac{v^2}{2}\right) - \frac{\partial v}{\partial t} \tag{59}$$

Thus, in a flow with steady vorticity[20] of an incompressible inviscid fluid with conservative body force, Lamb surfaces exist.

For a compressible fluid

$$\operatorname{curl} a = \operatorname{grad} p \times \operatorname{grad} \frac{1}{\rho} \tag{60}$$

If the flow is barotropic, that is, if a relation of the form

$$f(p,\rho,t) = 0 \tag{61}$$

exists, then by (60), curl $a = 0$, and we have Lamb surfaces exist in a barotropic flow with steady vorticity of an inviscid fluid subject to conservative body forces.

Linearly Viscous Fluids / For a linearly viscous fluid subject to conservative body force

---

20. And thus in a steady flow.

$$\rho \underset{\sim}{a} = - \rho \text{ grad } \nu - \text{grad } [p + (\lambda+2\mu) \text{ div } \underset{\sim}{v}] - \mu \text{ curl } \underset{\sim}{w} \quad (62)$$

where λ and μ are the viscosities, assumed uniform.

By (38)

$$\rho \underset{\sim}{\lambda} = - \rho \frac{\partial \underset{\sim}{v}}{\partial t} - \rho \text{ grad}\left(\frac{v^2}{2}\right) - \text{grad}[p + (\lambda+2\mu) \text{ div } \underset{\sim}{v}] - \mu \text{ curl } \underset{\sim}{w} \quad (63)$$

If

$$\text{curl curl } \underset{\sim}{w} = 0 \quad (64)$$

then there exists a scalar σ called the flexion potential[21] such that

$$\text{curl } \underset{\sim}{w} = \text{grad } \sigma \quad (65)$$

In this case, (63) becomes

$$\rho \underset{\sim}{\lambda} = - \rho \frac{\partial \underset{\sim}{v}}{\partial t} - \rho \text{ grad}\left(\frac{v^2}{2} + \nu\right) - \text{grad}[p + (\lambda+2\mu) \text{ div } \underset{\sim}{v} + \mu\sigma] \quad (66)$$

Two results are readily apparent from (66). First, in a flow of steady vorticity of an incompressible linearly viscous fluid of uniform viscosities subject to a conservative body force, if a flexion potential exists, Lamb surfaces exist. Second, in a steady flow of a linearly viscous fluid of uniform viscosities subject to no body force, if a flexion potential exists, and if the speed is constant[22], Lamb surfaces exist.

ACKNOWLEDGEMENT

A number of the theorems in this work are based on special cases discovered by Professor E. R. Suryanarayan. I wish to thank my friend and teacher, Regents' Professor A. W. Marris, whose writings inspired this work.

REFERENCES

1. Truesdell, C. A., The Kinematics of Vorticity, Indiana University Press, Bloomington, 1954.[23]

---

21. Flexion potentials exist for at least some viscometric flows. See [1] and [11].

22. The case where the speed is constant has been studied. See [12] and [13].

23. This work is, unfortunately, out of print. Much of the material contained in it appears in [14].

2. Marris, A. W. and Passman, S. L., "Vector Fields and Flows on Developable Surfaces," Archive for Rational Mechanics and Analysis, Volume 32, Number 1, 1969, pp. 29-86.

3. Suryanarayan, E. R., "Intrinsic Equations Governing the Flow of a Steady, Incompressible, Viscous Fluid," Zeitschrift für angewandte Mathematik und Mechanik, Volume 48, Number 6, 1968, pp. 377-384.

4. Suryanarayan, E. R., "Intrinsic Equations of Rotational Gas Flows," Israel Journal of Mathematics, Volume 5, 1967, pp. 118-126.

5. Brand, L., Vector and Tensor Analysis, John Wiley, New York, 1947.

6. Bjørgum, O., "On Beltrami Vector Fields and Flows, Part 1, A Comparative Study of Some Basic Types of Vector Fields," Universitetet I Bergen, Årbok 1951, Naturvitenskapelig Rekke nr. 1.

7. Masotti, A., "Decomposizione Intrinseca del Vortice e sue Applicazione," Rendiconti dell'Istituto Lombardo di Scienze e Lettre, Series 2, Volume 60, 1927, pp. 869-874.

8. Weatherburn, C. E., Differential Geometry of Three Dimensions, Volume II, Cambridge University Press, Cambridge, 1930.

9. Marris, A. W., "Vector Fields of Solenoidal Vector-Line Rotation," Archive for Rational Mechanics and Analysis, Volume 27, Number 3, 1967, pp. 195-232.

10. Marris, A. W., "Addendum to 'Vector Fields of Solenoidal Vector-Line Rotation': A class of Permanent Flows of Solenoidal Vector-Line Rotation," Archive for Rational Mechanics and Analysis, Volume 32, Number 2, 1969, pp. 154-168.

11. Coleman, B. D., Markovitz, H. and Noll, W., Viscometric Flows of Non-Newtonian Fluids, Springer-Verlag, New York, 1966.

12. Hamel, G., "Potentialströmungen mit konstanter Geschwindigkeit," Sitzungsberichte der Preußischen Akademie der Wissenschaften, Sitzung der physikalischemathematischen Klasse, 1937, pp. 5-20.

13. Howard, L. N., Constant Speed Flows, MS Thesis, Princeton University, 1953.

14. Truesdell, C. A. and Toupin, R. A., "The Classical Field Theories," Handbuch der Physik, Volume III/1, Springer-Verlag, Berlin, 1960, pp. 226-790.

M A T E R I A L   B E H A V I O R

EFFECT OF FIBER END, FIBER ORIENTATION AND SPACING IN COMPOSITE MATERIALS

Hui Pih
University of Tennessee

David R. Sutliff
University of Tennessee

ABSTRACT

A photoelastic investigation was made on the effect of different parameters on the stresses in the matrix of composite materials. The parameters considered are fiber end-geometry, fiber orientation, and fiber spacing or volume ratio. The end-geometry investigated included the square end, the semi-circular end, vee ends and wedge ends. The fiber orientation included 0°, 30°, and 45°, orientation angles. The fiber spacings used corresponded to fiber volumes of 15% and 60%. The investigation of fiber orientation effect and fiber volume effect was carried out on the same set of multiple fiber models each with fibers orientated at different angles to the loading direction. Models were fabricated using Epon 815 epoxy as matrix, cast around aluminum fibers.

The matrix maximum shear-stress concentration factor was determined for each case. The data showed that the maximum shear-stress concentration factor was as high as 12 in some wedge end models. The volume ratio tests indicated that the stress concentration factor could be reduced by increasing the percentage of fibers. The stress concentration factor was also seen to decrease as the fiber orientation angle increased from 0° to 45° with respect to the load axis. Examination of the variation of the matrix shear stress along the fiber boundary indicated that the critical aspect ratio for discontinuous fibers could vary from 2 to 16.

LIST OF NOTATIONS

A	Total cross-sectional area
D	Fiber width
E_f/E_m	Ratio of modulus of elasticity of fiber to modulus of elasticity of matrix
K_L	Maximum shear-stress concentration factor on lower corner of discontinuous-fiber tip in orientation-volume ratio specimens (see sketch in Table III)
K_U	Maximum shear-stress concentration factor on upper corner of discontinuous fiber tip in orientation-volume ratio specimens (see sketch in Table III)
P	Applied tensile load
V_f	Fiber volume ratio
X	Distance along the fiber length
τ	Shear-stress
τ_{avg}	P/2A
$\overline{\tau}$	Maximum shear-stress in specimen matrix at matrix-fiber interface, located at a distance from the fiber tip such that the shear-stress has dropped off to a more-or-less constant value

INTRODUCTION

In recent years considerable research effort has been devoted to fiber reinforced metals. Such composites, somewhat similar in principle to the well-known glass-fiber-reinforced plastics, are usually used where high strength-to-weight ratios are required, where high temperature strength is desired, and where special material properties are needed. Various materials have been used in fiber reinforced metals. Some examples are aluminum reinforced with either stainless steel, sapphire whiskers, or boron fibers. The fibers are usually discontinuous in such metal composites. In designing with fiber reinforced metals some basic knowledge regarding the stress field in the matrix is needed. Such information would include the effects of the fiber end geometry, the fiber orientation with respect to the load, and the fiber spacing or fiber to matrix volume ratio. There have been many investigations made on some aspects of these problems by other researchers [1-6]. This paper presents a portion of a comprehensive investigation of the stress in the matrix as effected by different parameters using the photoelastic method. Only the results from two-dimensional models are included in this paper. Investigations with three-dimensional models will be published later. Since the matrix materials concerned are usually ductile, only the maximum shear stresses are considered.

Experimental Procedure

The prototype for this investigation is a three-dimensional composite consisting of discontinuous elastic fibers of circular cross-section embedded in an elastic matrix. The ratio of the elastic moduli of fiber and matrix E_f/E_m for the composite under consideration is 23. The two-dimensional models used in this investigation simulate an enlarged slice through a typical fiber, with the slice representing a plane parallel to the fiber axis and cutting through the center of the fiber. The resin used was shell Epon 815 with triethylene tetramine hardener mixed in the proportion of nine to one by weight. All two-dimensional models were made by molding the resin around 1/8-inch thick aluminum fibers using two glass plates separated by three plexiglas side spacers as the mold. In order to provide sealing and to prevent the resin from adhering to the spacers, Dow 7 Compound silicone mold release agent was applied to the spacers prior to the assembling of the mold by clamps. The inner surface of each of the glass plates was lined with a sheet of Post Polytex 126 drafting film to allow easy removal of the cured specimen from the mold and to give smooth surfaces.

The fiber spacings for the orientation-volume ratio specimens were computed based on a hypothetical composite containing regularly spaced fibers distributed such that a typical group forms a hexagonal pattern. Spacings corresponding to fiber volume ratios of 15 percent and 60 percent were utilized. Fiber orientations of 0°, 30° and 45° were investigated. Figure 1 shows a typical specimen for fiber end geometry effects, the loading arrangement, and the various types of end geometries investigated. A sample specimen for fiber orientation and volume ratio effect investigation is shown in Figure 2.

The determination of isoclinics and fringe orders were made in a 10-inch field transmitted-light polariscope with the aid of a microphotometer. The loading frame was mounted on a milling machine base which provided the motion of the model in two orthogonal directions; hence any point of the focused image could be brought to the aperture of the photometer search unit. Since the matrix-fiber bonding strength and

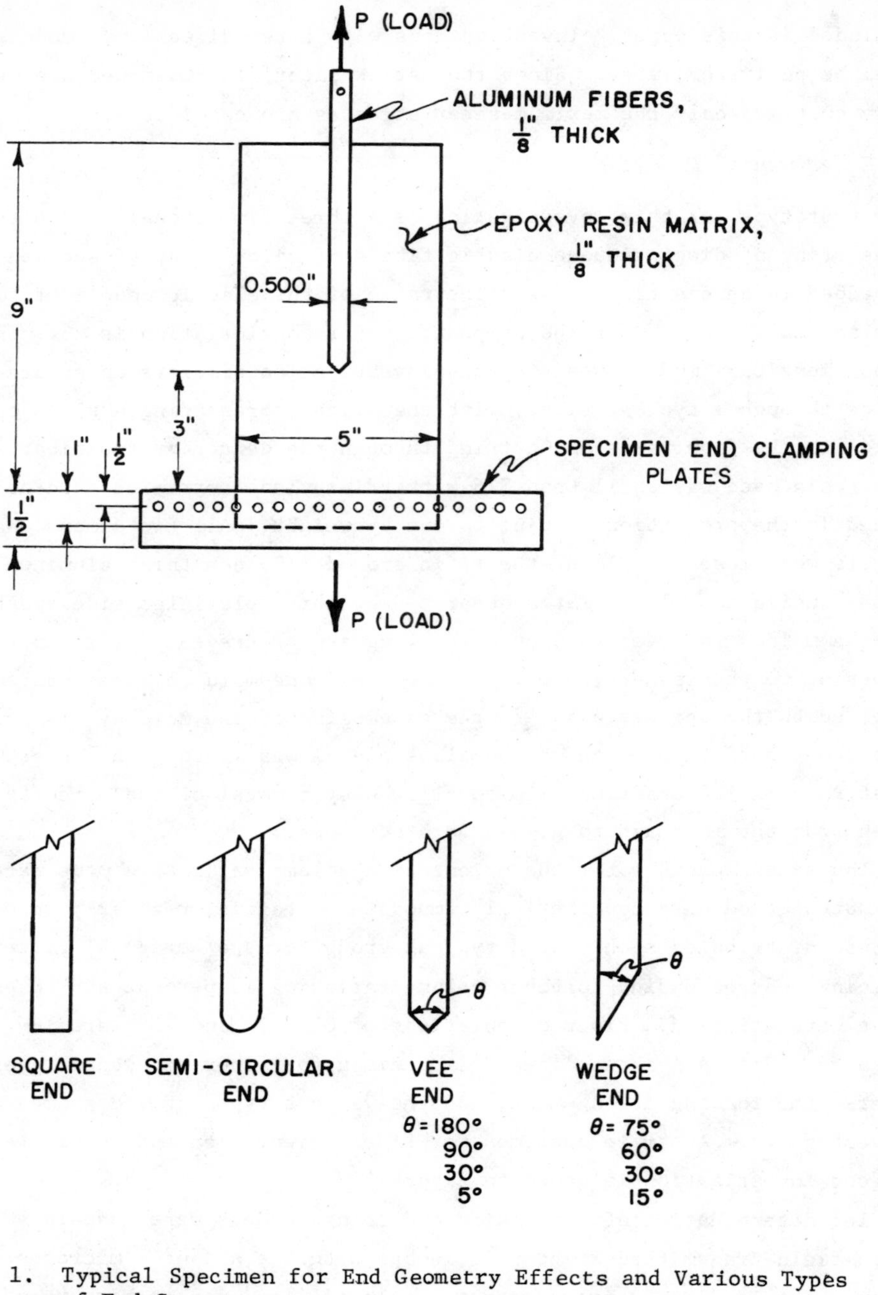

Fig. 1. Typical Specimen for End Geometry Effects and Various Types of End Geometry.

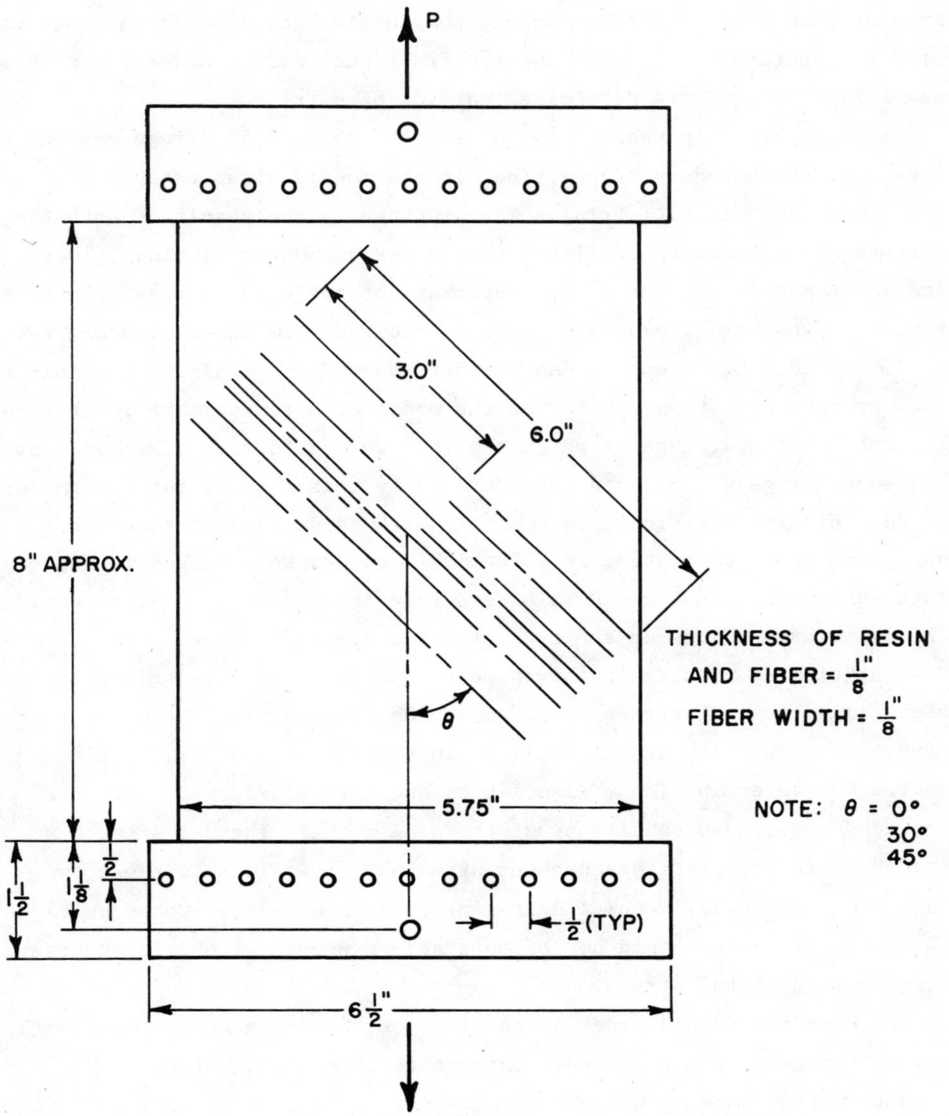

Fig. 2. Typical Specimen for Orientation and Volume Ratio Effects.

the yield point of the matrix would not allow a fringe order much greater than four, a Babinet-Soleil compensator was used in combination with the photometer to determine the fractional fringe orders. In this way fringe orders were determined to 0.01 of a fringe.

Residual birefringence of the order of 0.25 to 0.50 fringe was observed at the boundary of the fiber in the models after removal from the mold. Such initial fringes were apparently the result of both the differing coefficients of linear thermal expansion of aluminum fiber and epoxy matrix and the slight shrinkage of the epoxy during polymerization. The thermal expansion effect resulted from the exothermic reaction of the curing epoxy. An attempt was made to minimize the initial or residual fringe by curing the model at a temperature lower than the ambient temperature at which the test was performed. The apparent residual fringe was reduced considerably by this method, but the amount of reduction was difficult to control. It was decided to test all specimens at a temperature of 75°F(±1°F) and devise a method to separate analytically the residual stress from the observed total stress. The calculated values or the true stresses due to loads are used in the presentation of results in this paper. The analytical technique of separating residual stress is based on the transformation equations of stress in elasticity and is outlined in the appendix of [7]. It requires the determination of isoclinics and fringe orders in both the unloaded and loaded conditions of the same model. The use of such a procedure is necessary because the principal directions in these two conditions are usually quite different from each other. Consequently the residual stress could not be obtained by simple algebraic subtraction from the total stress.

The boundary fringe order at the edge of the fiber was determined by taking fringe readings at small increments of distance along a chosen path from the boundary using the compensator, and extrapolating to the edge. In some cases points as close as 0.005" apart were used in the determination of the fiber-matrix boundary fringe orders.

In working with specimens with multiple fibers closely spaced, such as those used in fiber volume and fiber orientation studies, the slight shrinkage of the epoxy matrix caused a small continuous variation of the matrix thickness between two adjacent fibers. This caused a lens effect and resulted in the image becoming somewhat obscure when projected on the photometer screen, which made determination of the fringe order very difficult. For this reason, all multiple fiber specimens were ground flat and polished before being used in tests.

Results and Discussion

Figures 3 through 6 show sample fringe patterns of the specimens used for studying fiber-end geometry effects. Typical fringe patterns from specimens for the fiber orientation and spacing investigation are shown in Figure 7 through 9. All fringe patterns presented were taken with the polariscope set for light field. Representative graphs of normalized maximum shear-stress distribution at the fiber-matrix interface for the end-geometry effect specimen are shown in Figures 10 through 13. Results from the fiber orientation effect specimens are presented in Figures 14 through 19. In these figures the effect of the two volume ratios are also indicated. The primary basis for normalizing the stress distribution curves shown in Figures 10 through 16 was the average maximum shear-stress $\overline{\tau}$ at a distance from the fiber end where the stress leveled off to a more-or-less constant value. For convenience in comparing the authors' results with the results of other investigators, a secondary scale is also included in Figures 10 through 13. The basis for normalization used in computing the secondary scale is the average maximum shear stress $\tau_{avg} = P/2A$. Figures 17 through 19 are graphs representing the same data as shown in Figures 14 through 16, but using the secondary normalizing basis τ_{avg}. However, the maximum shear stress concentration factors presented in Tables I through IV are computed using $\overline{\tau}$.

Maximum shear-stress concentration factors in the matrix for specimens with symmetrical fiber ends are summarized in Table I. As the central angle of the vee-end specimens decreased from 180° (square end) to 5°, the stress concentration factor first decreased and then increased. The stress concentration factor for the square-end specimen appeared at the corners and had the value of 6.5. The highest shear-stress concentration factor for vee-end specimens was 7.2, occurring at the apex of the 5° angle. The maximum stress concentration factor for the semicircular fiber-end specimen occurred 67.5° from the axis of the fiber and had a value of 4.0. Table II gives the summary of the maximum stress concentration factors for wedge-end fiber specimens, those

Fig. 3. Fringe Pattern for Square End Specimen (Light Field).

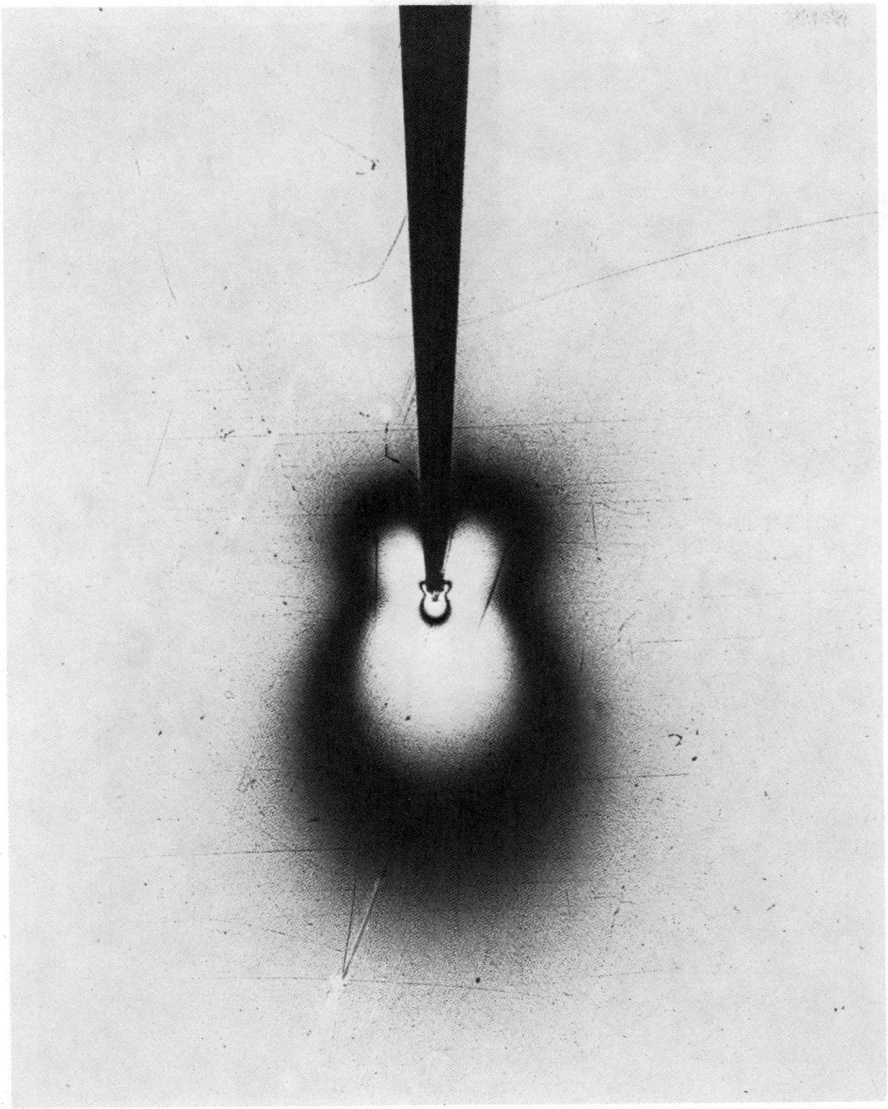

Fig. 4. Fringe Pattern for 5° Vee-End Specimen (Light Field).

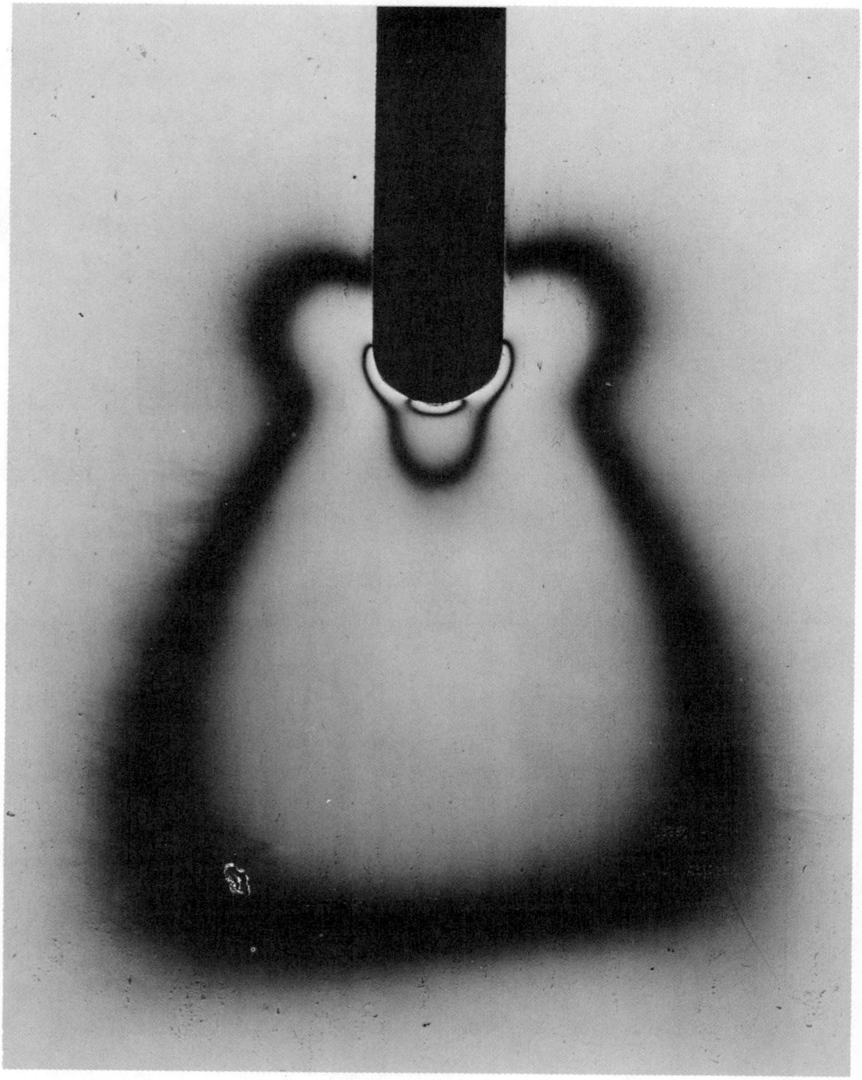

Fig. 5. Fringe Pattern for Semi-Circular End Specimen (Light Field).

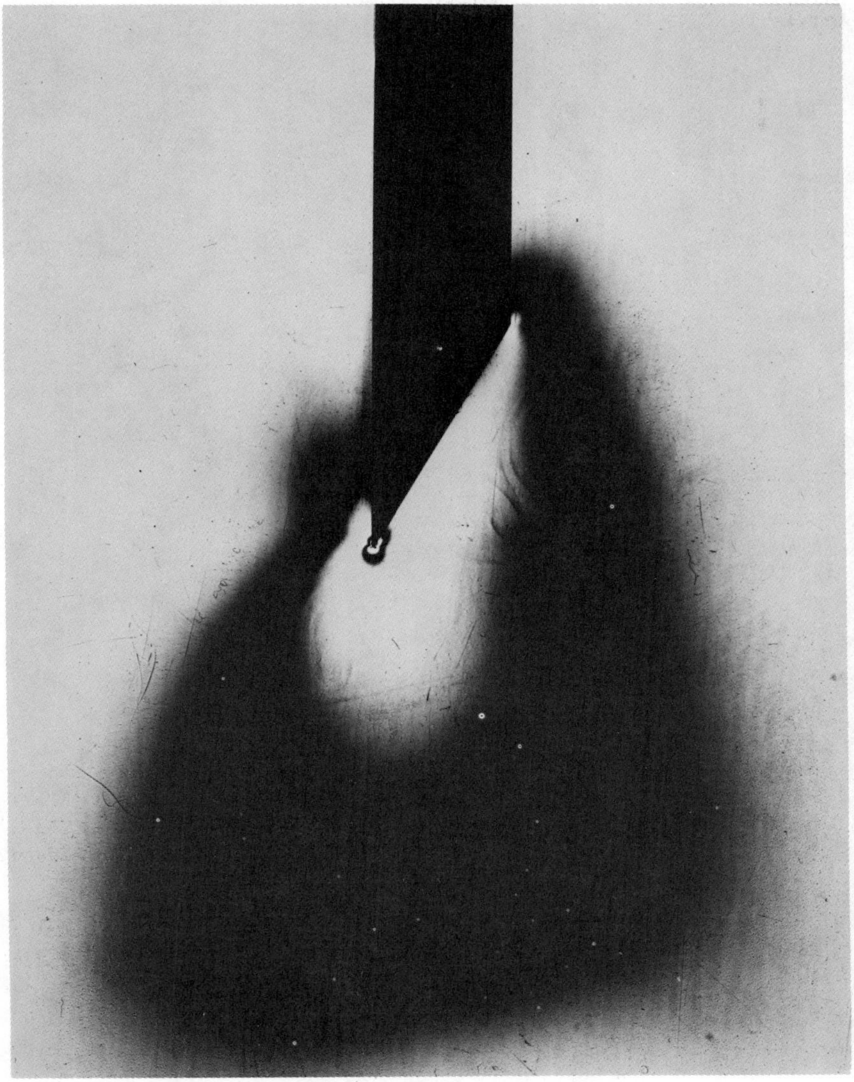

Fig. 6. Fringe Pattern for 30° Wedge-End Specimen (Light Field).

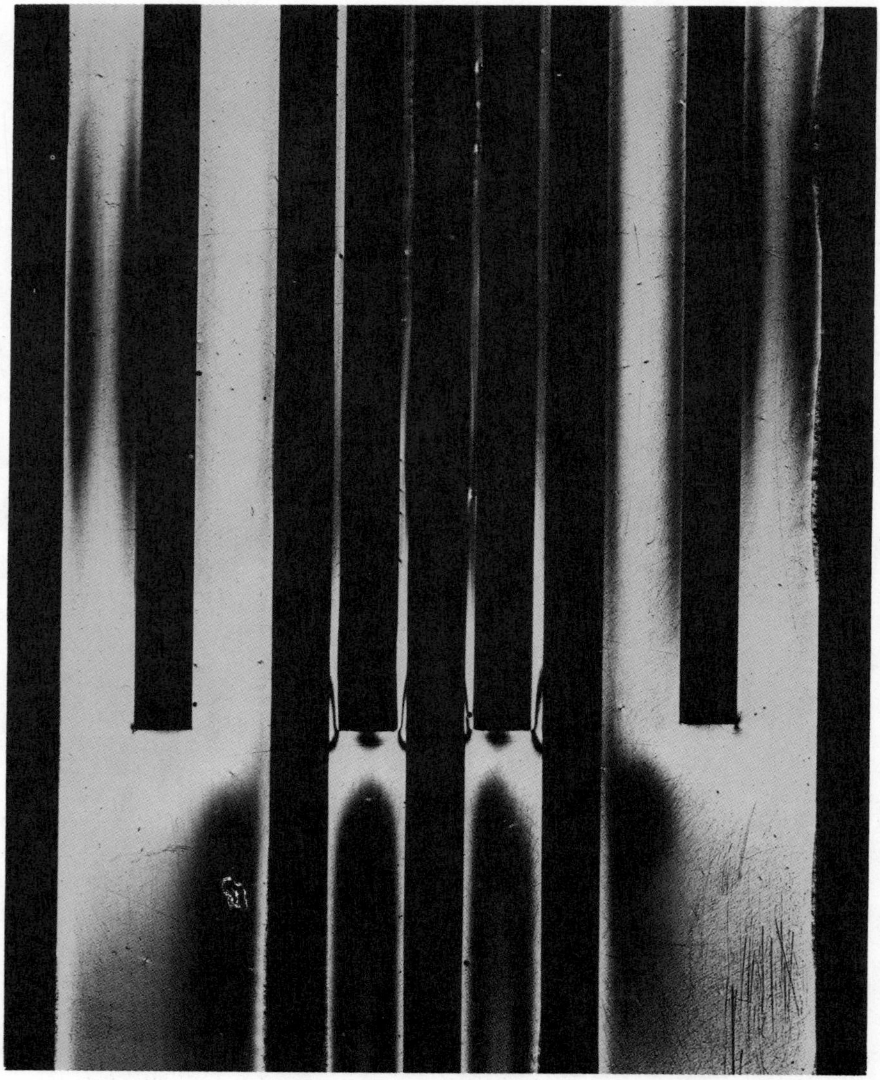

Fig. 7. Fringe Pattern for 0° Orientation Specimen (Light Field).

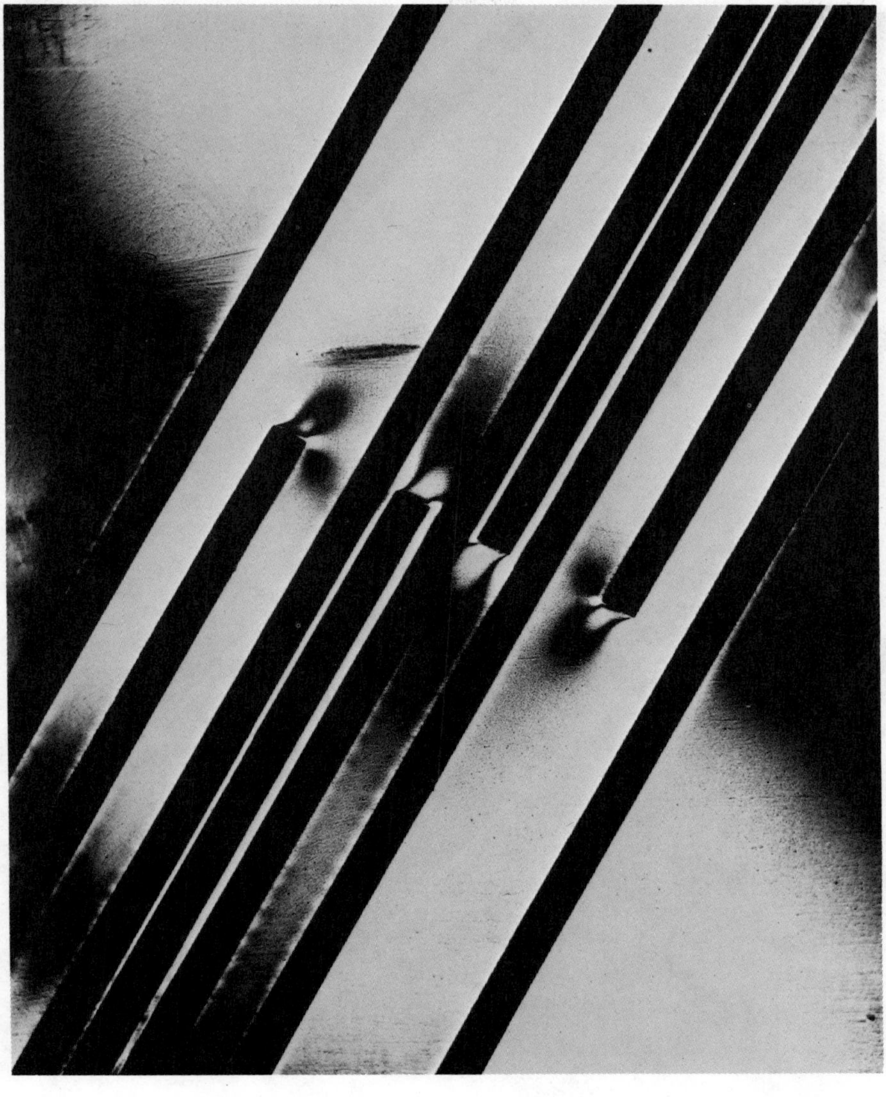

Fig. 8. Fringe Pattern for 30° Orientation Specimen (Light Field).

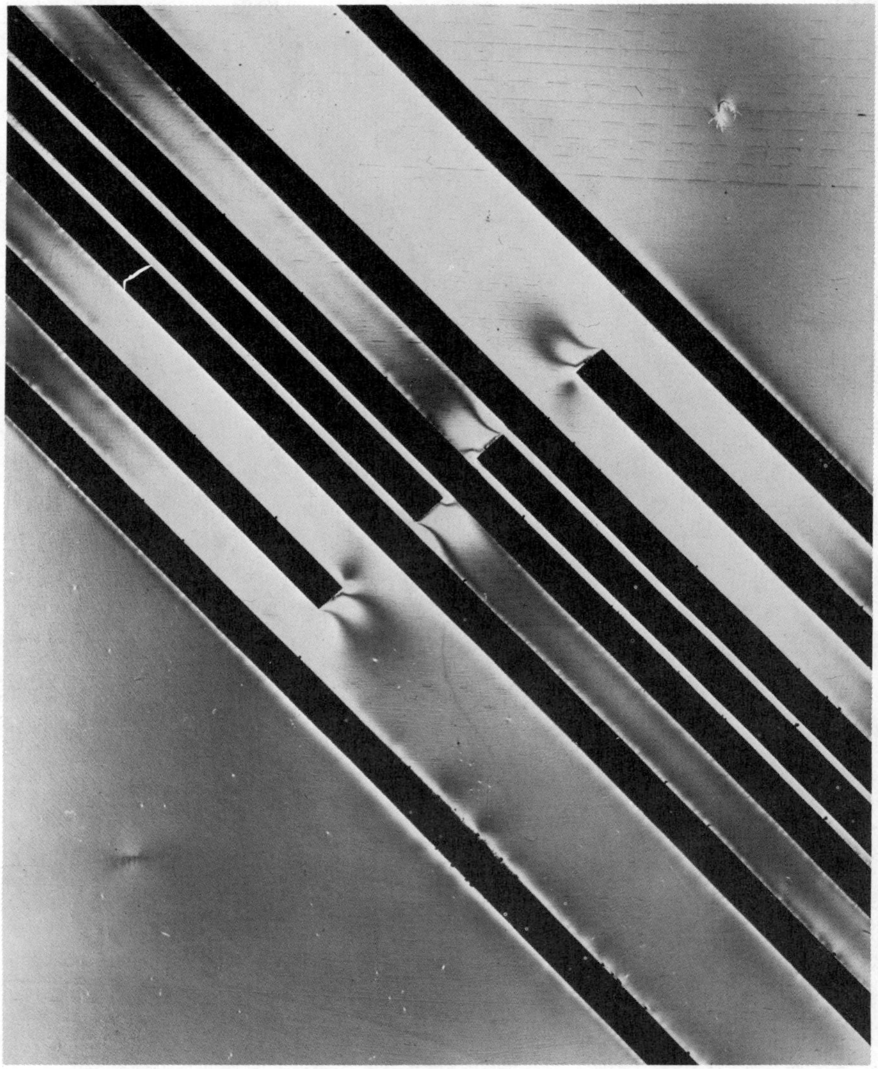

Fig. 9. Fringe Pattern for 45° Orientation Specimen (Light Field).

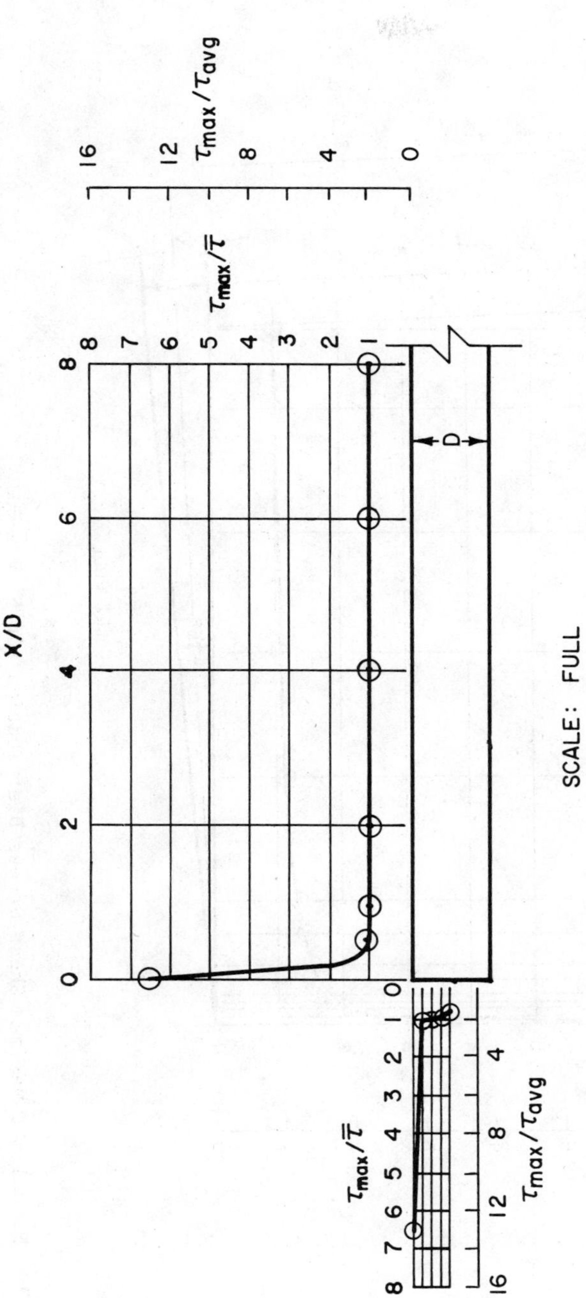

Fig. 10. Normalized Maximum Shear Stress Distribution for Square-End Specimen.

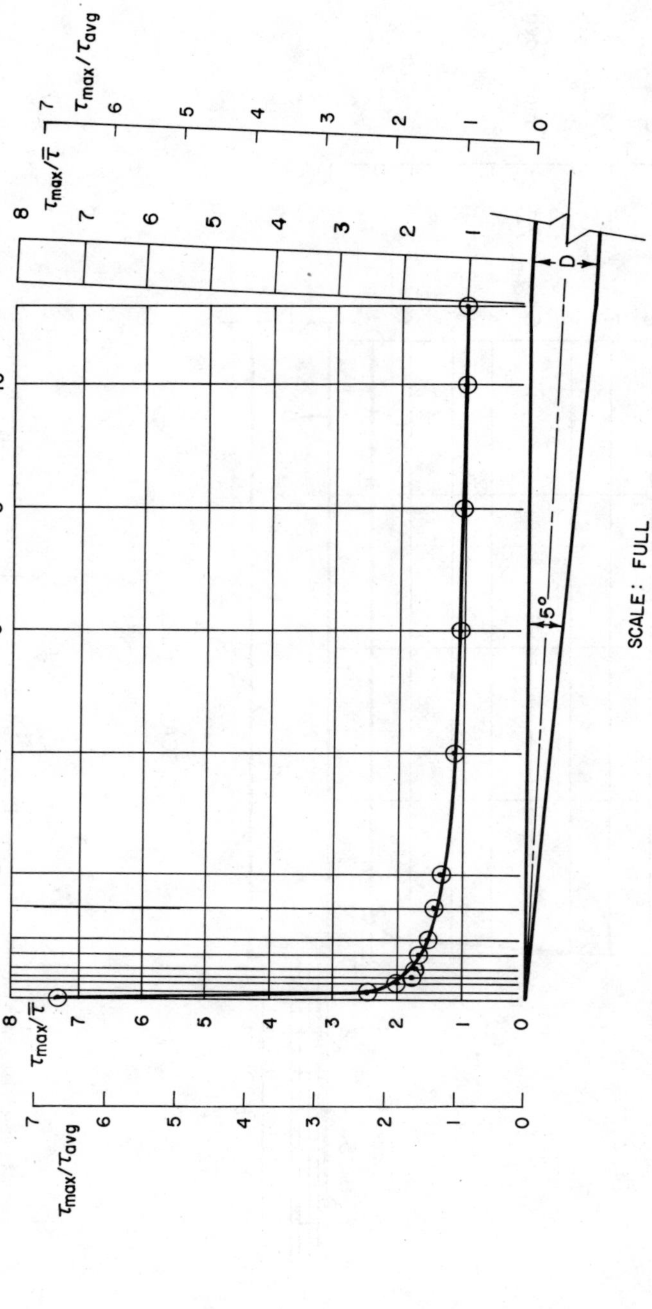

Fig. 11. Normalized Maximum Shear Stress Distribution for 5° Vee-End.

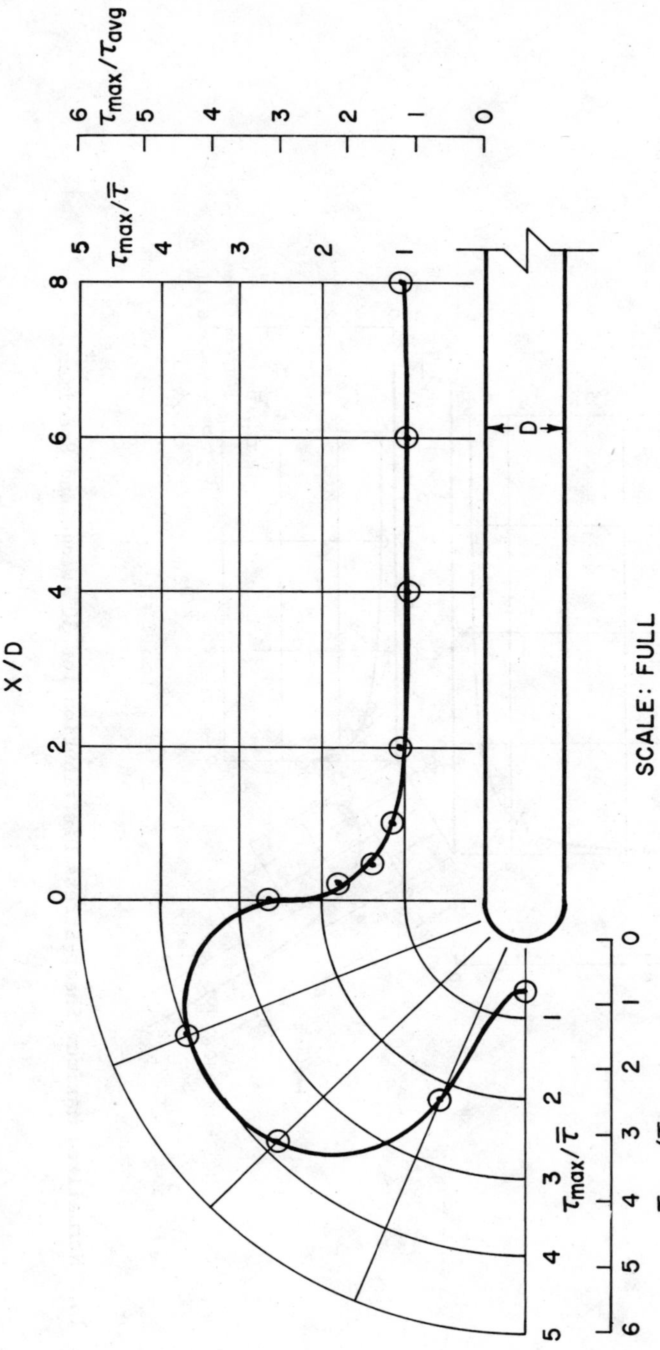

Fig. 12. Normalized Maximum Shear Stress Distribution for Semi-Circular End Specimen.

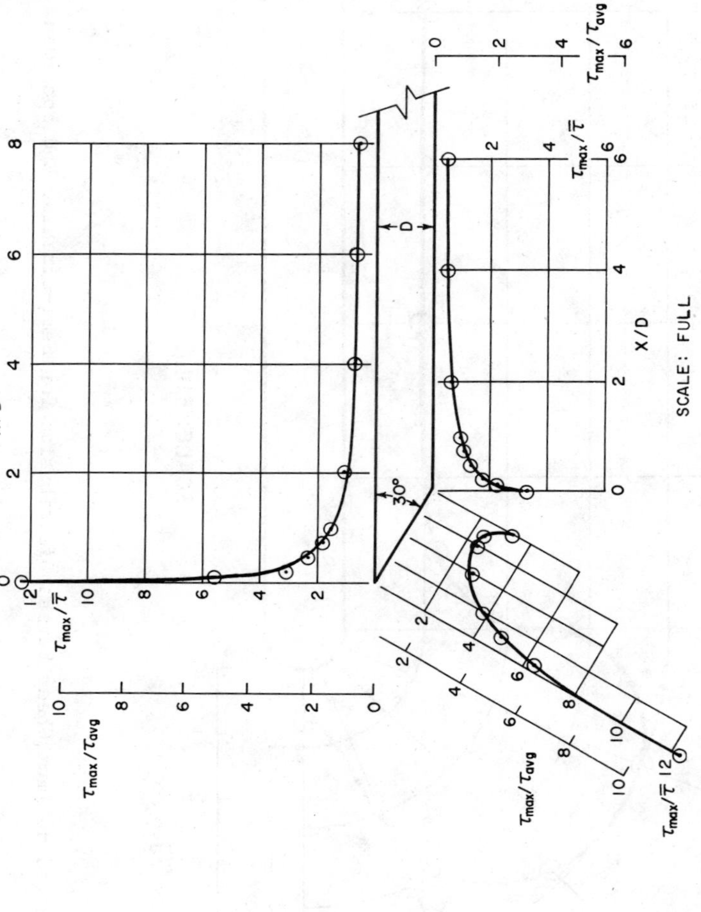

Fig. 13. Normalized Maximum Shear-Stress Distribution for 30° Wedge End Specimen.

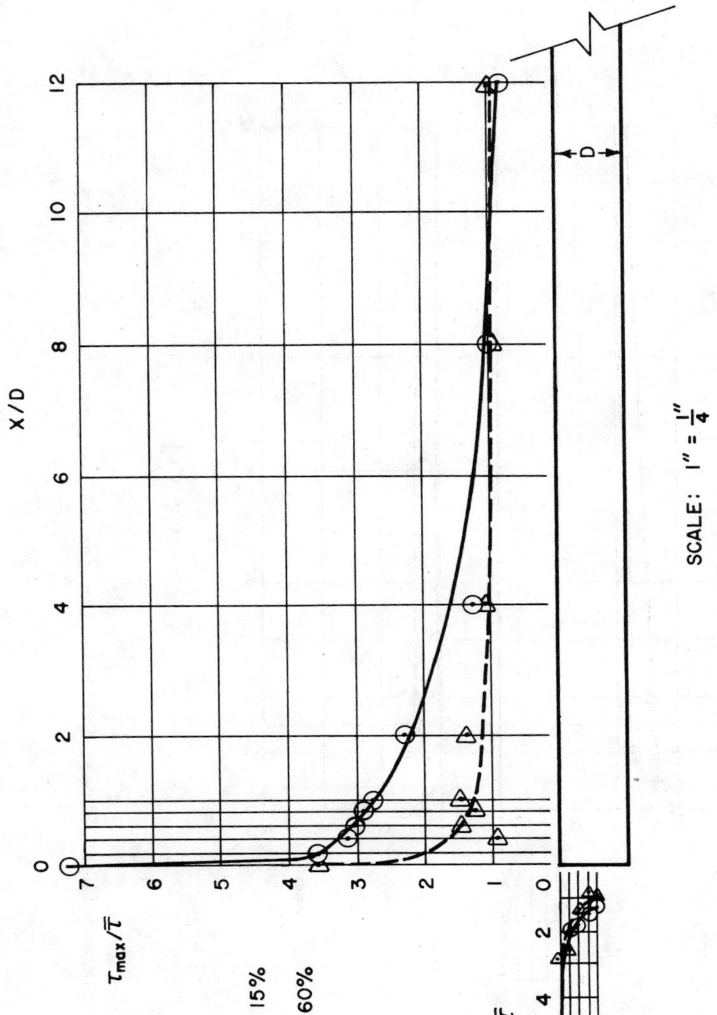

Fig. 14. Normalized Maximum Shear Stress Distribution for 0° Orientation Specimen Based on $\bar{\tau}$.

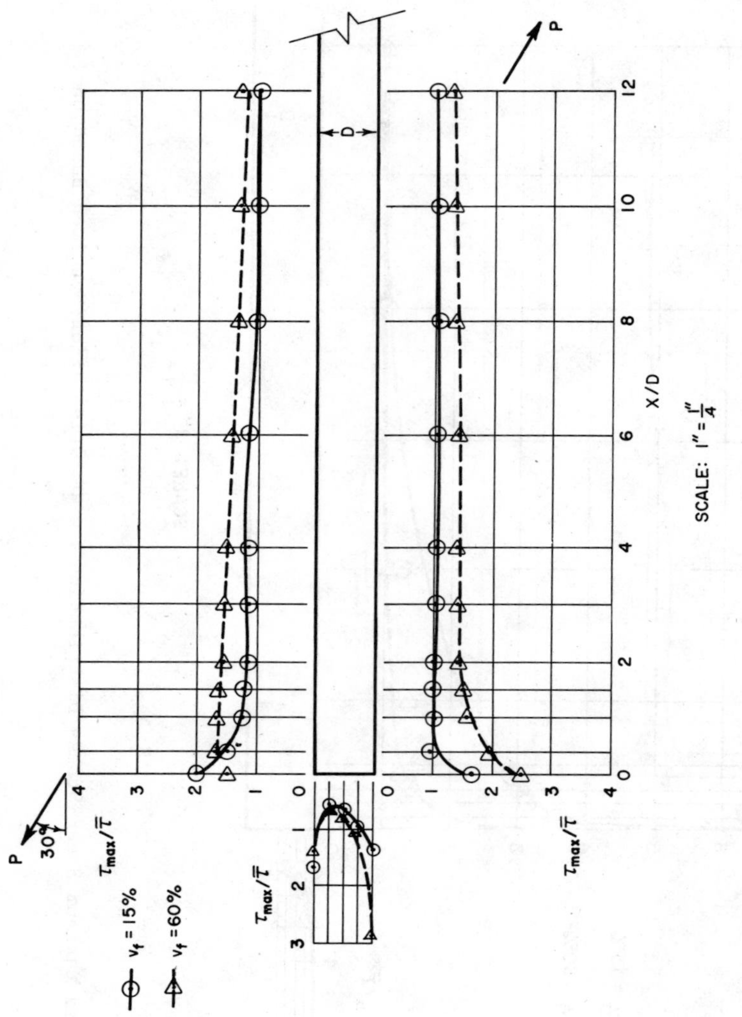

Fig. 15. Normalized Maximum Shear Stress Distribution for 30° Orientation Specimen Based on $\bar{\tau}$.

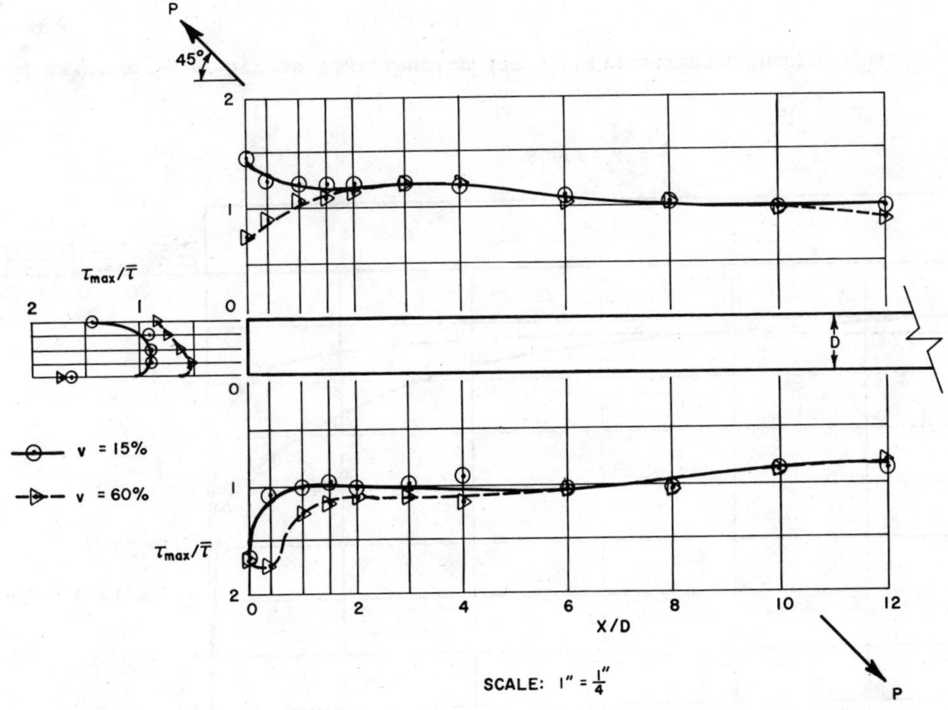

Fig. 16. Normalized Maximum Shear Stress Distribution for 45° Orientation Specimen Based on $\bar{\tau}$.

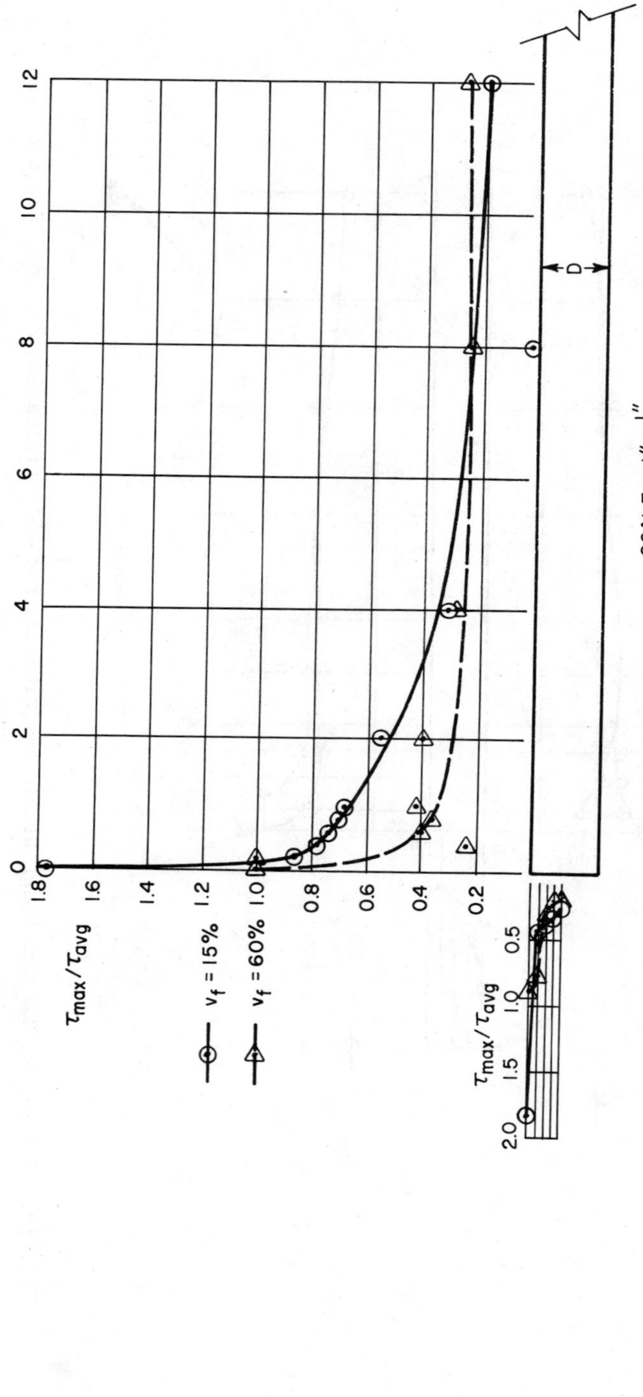

Fig. 17. Normalized Maximum Shear-Stress Distribution for 0° Orientation Specimen Based on τ_{avg}.

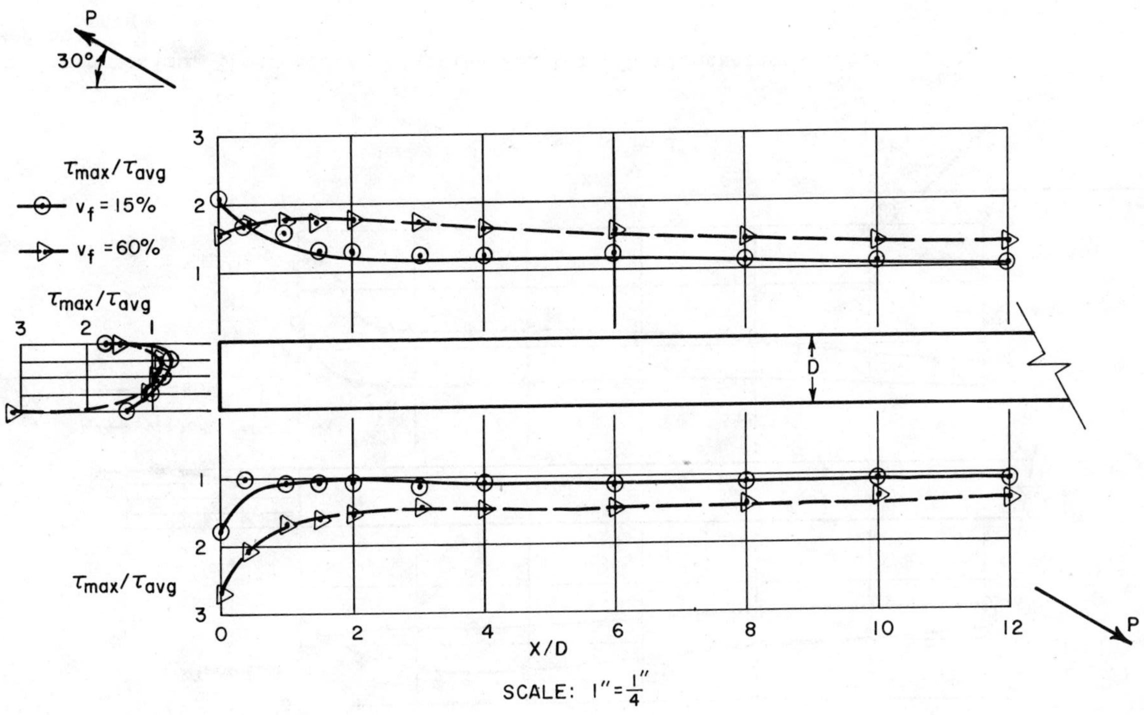

Fig. 18. Normalized Maximum Shear-Stress Distribution for 30° Orientation Specimen Based on τ_{avg}.

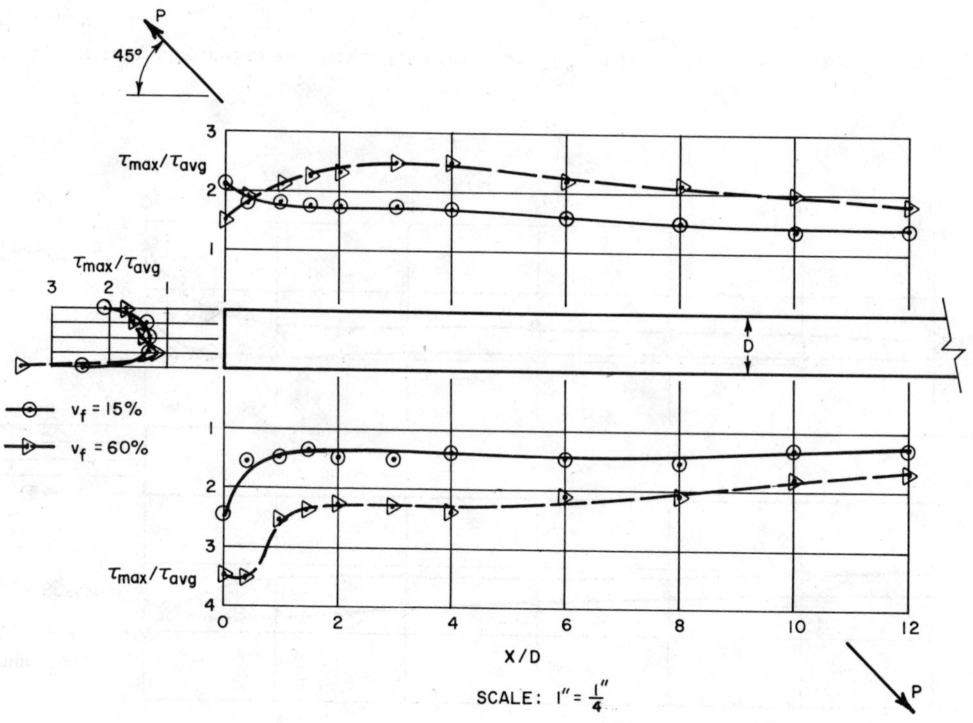

Fig. 19. Normalized Maximum Shear-Stress Distribution for 45° Orientation Specimen Based on τ_{avg}.

TABLE I. MAXIMUM SHEAR-STRESS CONCENTRATION FACTORS FOR SPECIMENS WITH SYMMETRICAL END GEOMETRY

End Geometry	Stress Concentration Factor		Critical Aspect Ratio
	Location		
	Side	Tip	
Square End	6.5	---	2
90° Vee	4.3	4.3	4
60° Vee	2.2	3.4	4
30° Vee	1.2	3.8	4
5° Vee	1.0	7.2	16
	67 1/2° From Axis of Fiber		
Semicircular	4		4

TABLE II. MAXIMUM SHEAR-STRESS CONCENTRATION FACTORS FOR SPECIMENS WITH NON-SYMMETRICAL END GEOMETRY

End Geometry	Shear-Stress Concentration Factor		Critical Aspect Ratio
	Location		
	Side	Tip	
60° Wedge	5.2	4.0	2
45° Wedge	3.2	3.3	4
30° Wedge	2.8	12.1	8
15° Wedge	2.0	9.0	8

values ranging from 2.0 to 12.1. The location of the maximum stress concentration effect varied in wedge-end specimens. For the 60° wedge specimen the maximum shear stress concentration factor of 5.2 appeared at the side corners of the fiber end, whereas with the specimens with wedge angles of 45°, 30°, and 15°, maximum stress concentration occurred at the fiber tip. As the wedge angle decreased, the maximum matrix shear-stress concentration at the fiber-side corner decreased gradually, whereas that at the fiber tip did not follow a regular pattern. The maximum stress concentration factor obtained at the tip of the fiber of 30° wedge angle was 12.1.

Twice the distance measured in number of fiber diameters (width) from the fiber tip necessary for the maximum shear-stress to drop to a constant value is called the critical aspect ratio. The factor of two results from the fact that half of the fiber length was considered in this analysis. In the real case both ends of the discontinuous fiber contribute to the maximum shear stress distribution along the length of the fiber. The values of the critical aspect ratio for the cases summarized in Table I varied from two to sixteen. The values for the cases presented in Table II varied between two and eight.

The specimens used to study the effects of the fiber orientation were made such that the fiber spacings represented two different fiber to matrix volume ratios, 15 percent and 60 percent. Thus the effects of both fiber orientation and volume ratio on the matrix maximum shear stress concentration could be observed in the same model. The end geometry chosen for the discontinuous fibers was the square end. This configuration was chosen because from previous tests it was known to yield a fairly high stress concentration. Table III shows the stress concentrations resulting from these specimens. The values K_L and K_U referred to the stress concentration factors of the lower and upper corners at the end of a discontinuous fiber. The high values of K_L and K_U occurred in the 0° orientation specimen, whereas the low values occurred in the 45° orientation model. It should also be observed from Table III that in the 0° orientation model, as the fiber to matrix volume ratio V_f changed from 15 percent to 60 percent, the value $K(K_L=K_U)$ changed from 7.2 to 3.8. For both the 30° and 45° orientation specimens, K_L decreased as V_f changed from 15 percent to 60 percent. K_U increased for the 30° specimen, but remained constant for the 45° model, as V_f increased. The stress concentration factors for these two fiber orientations were considerably less than those for the 0° orientations. The critical aspect ratios in these specimens were about the same as in models for fiber end effects, ranging from six to sixteen.

The results of this investigation will be compared with some results obtained by other researchers. MacLaughlin [2,3] carried out a variety of two-dimensional photoelastic experiments on composite materials. In his earlier tests [2], a steel fiber-epoxy matrix system was used, with

TABLE III. MAXIMUM SHEAR-STRESS CONCENTRATION FACTORS FOR ORIENTATION-VOLUME RATIO SPECIMENS

Angle	Fiber Volume (V_f) = 15%			Fiber Volume (V_f) = 60%		
θ	K_L	K_U	Critical Aspect Ratio	K_L	K_U	Critical Aspect Ratio
0°	7.2	7.2	16	3.8	3.8	10
30°	2.0	1.7	8	1.4	2.5	6
45°	1.5	1.7	16	0.7	1.7	16

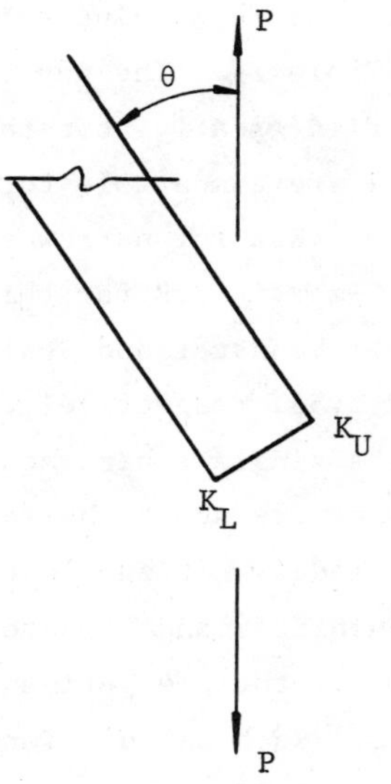

an elastic modulus ratio E_f/E_m of 3000. His second series of tests [3] utilized two epoxy resins of different elastic moduli as fiber and matrix materials, resulting in an elastic modulus ratio E_f/E_m of 40. The results of the latter tests are used to compare with those of the present investigation in which the elastic modulus ratio is 23. Tyson and Davies [4] performed two-dimensional photoelastic experiments on models with single square-end fibers using Araldite CT200 as the matrix and dural as the fiber. The elastic modulus ratio E_f/E_m for this combination is 21. In their first series of experiments, Schuster and Scala [5] embedded a single sapphire whisker in a Budd Company epoxy matrix, yielding an elastic modulus ratio E_f/E_m of 140. In their second series of tests, [6], they used boron as fibers embedded in the Budd Company type L-08 epoxy resin, resulting in an E_f/E_m of about 125. Cases of a single short fiber and two overlaping fibers with various spacings were investigated. A comparison of maximum shear-stress concentration factors for square end fibers from the present investigation with those from the various sources mentioned above is presented in Table IV. It can be observed that the results from the various investigations differ considerably. The most significant variations occur when comparing the stress concentrations of the narrow gap multiple fiber specimens at 0° orientation of this paper with the results of MacLaughlin [3] and Schuster and Scala [6]. The elastic modulus ratios of the three cases differ, as can be seen from Table IV. The physical sizes of the fibers used in these three tests varied greatly, but the ratios of fiber spacing to fiber diameter (width) are comparable for both the narrow and wide spacings. It can be seen that for narrow gaps, the maximum shear stress concentration factor K-max is 3.8 for this paper, 9.5 from MacLaughlin [3], and 5.05 from Schuster and Scala [6]. For wide gaps, the values are 7.2, 7.1, and 2.83, respectively. It is interesting to note that the results from the single fiber, square-end specimen and wide-gap specimen of this paper are about the same as that reported by MacLaughlin for his wide gap model. It should be mentioned that the values quoted as being MacLaughlin's and Schuster and Scala's results are obtained by calculation from their experimental curves in the same manner as used by the authors. Such calculations were necessary since MacLaughlin, Schuster and Scala used $\tau_{avg} = P/2A$ as the basis for their curve normalization. As a check on the authors' results, the experiment with the narrow fiber gap was repeated with a different specimen. This specimen had only three fibers instead of the original design of nine and the gap width corresponded to a fiber volume ratio of 60 %. The data from this test resulted in a value of K-max close to that obtained previously. This would seem to substantiate the results of the previous test of this paper for the narrow gap, 0° orientation model. A possible explanation for the variation of K-max values for multiple fiber specimens may be offered by the considerable differences between the modulus ratios of the three investigations mentioned above. It may be seen in Table IV that as the fiber to matrix elastic modulus ratio

TABLE IV. COMPARISON OF MAXIMUM SHEAR-STRESS CONCENTRATION FACTORS FROM VARIOUS SOURCES WITH SQUARE-ENDED FIBER SPECIMENS

Source	$\frac{E_f}{E_m}$	Single Fiber Square End	Multi-Fiber Wide Gap Square End	Multi-Fiber Narrow Gap Square End
Pih & Sutliff	23	6.5	7.2 (V_f = 15%)	3.8 (V_f = 60%)
MacLaughlin [2]	3000	2.5	---	---
MacLaughlin [3]	40	---	7.1 (V_f = 16%)	9.5 (V_f = 45%)
Tyson & Davis [4]	21	10	---	---
Schuster & Scala [5]	140	2.5	---	---
Schuster & Scala [6]	125	---	2.83 (0.004" spacing)	5.05 (0.002" spacing)

increases, K-max for wide gap cases decreases whereas that for the narrow gap cases shows no regularity. This point needs further experimental verification.

CONCLUSIONS

Considering the end-geometry results, it was seen that the highest maximum shear-stress concentration factor reached a value of 12.1. This particular value was obtained in the 30° wedge-end specimen. The lowest maximum shear-stress concentration factor was obtained in the 45° wedge-end test. These fiber-end configurations are quite likely to be encountered in an actual reinforcing whisker (although they may not be as regularly formed as those used in this investigation). It may be concluded, therefore, that if matrix yielding must be avoided, the possibility of such high stress concentration values should be considered in the design of the composite. Matrix yielding does not necessarily infer complete failure of the composite, but, as noted by Dow [1], yielding increases the fiber length necessary for effective reinforcement.

The fiber-orientation tests showed that the maximum shear-stress concentration effects for the 15 percent fiber volume-ratio dropped by more than half, as the fiber orientation angle (measured with respect to the applied stress direction) increased from 0° to 45°. A similar decrease, not as great, was noted for the 60 percent volume ratio. If the direction of applied stress could be closely controlled, advantage might be taken of this decrease in stress concentration effects.

The results of the volume-ratio experiments show that for composites with axially loaded fibers, a decreasing maximum shear-stress concentration effect may be expected as the fiber content increases. However, for the case when fibers are at a large angle with respect to the applied stress direction, the percentage volume-ratio has less effect on stress concentration than for small orientation angles.

The results of all the experiments performed in this investigation indicated that the distance measured in the number of fiber diameters away from the tip necessary for the maximum shear-stress to drop off to a constant level is lower than reported by MacLaughlin [2], [3]. X/D ratios of 1 to 8 were obtained which correspond to critical aspect ratios of from 2 to 16, whereas MacLaughlin [3] reported values from about 40 to 80.

ACKNOWLEDGEMENTS

The authors would like to express their appreciation for the support of the Air Force Materials Laboratory, Wright-Patterson Air Force Base, Ohio, under contract No. F33615-67-1679.

REFERENCES

1. Dow, N. F., "Study of Stresses Near a Discontinuity in a Filament-Reinforced Composite Metal," Report No. R63SD61, G. E. Space Sciences Laboratory, August, 1965.

2. MacLaughlin, T. F., "Effect of Fiber Geometry on Stress in Fiber-Reinforced Composite Materials," Experimental Mechanics, Vol. 6, No. 10, 1966, pp. 481-492.

3. MacLaughlin, T. F., "A Photoelastic Analysis of Fiber Discontinuities in Composite Materials," Journal of Composite Materials, Vol. II, No. 1, 1968, pp. 44-55.

4. Tyson, W. R. and Davis, G. J., "A Photoelastic Study of the Shear Stresses Associated with the Transfer of Stress during Fiber Reinforcement," British Journal of Applied Physics, Vol. 16, 1965, pp. 199-205.

5. Schuster, D. M. and Scala, E., "The Mechanical Interaction of Sapphire Whiskers and a Birefringent Matrix," Transactions of the Metallurgical Society of the American Institute of Metallurgical Engineers, Vol. 230, December, 1964, pp. 1635-1640.

6. Schuster, D. M. and Scala, E., "Single and Multifiber Interactions in Discontinuously Reinforced Composites," Journal of American Institute of Aeronatuics and Astronautics, Vol. 6, No. 3, March, 1968, pp. 527-532.

7. Pih, H. and Sutliff, D. R., "Photoelastic Analyses of Reinforced Composites," AFML-TR-68-380, Air Force Materials Laboratory, Air Force Systems Command, Wright-Patterson Air Force Base, Ohio, November, 1968.

ON STRAIN ENERGY AND CONSTITUTIVE RELATIONS FOR ALKALI METALS

J. Eftis
The George Washington University

G. M. Arkilic
The George Washington University

D. E. MacDonald
The George Washington University

ABSTRACT

An expression for the strain energy as a continuous differentiable function of the Green-Cauchy deformation tensor is obtained for the Alkali metals at absolute zero temperature. The development is based on well established quantum and classical calculations of the various contributions to the crystal energy. Stress-deformation relations are next obtained. As a check on the accuracy of the strain energy, theoretical calculations of the values of the second-order elastic coefficients are obtained and compared to known experimental data. The predicted values are shown to compare quite well with the experimental values.

LIST OF NOTATIONS

E_o, E_f, E_{ex}	Various contributions to the crystal energy
N	Number of atoms per unit volume
V	Crystal volume
$\vec{R}_n$, $\vec{K}_m$	Direct and reciprocal lattice vectors
Ω_{DL}	Volume of a unit cell of the direct lattice
r_s	Radius of the atomic sphere
η	Positive but otherwise arbitrary number

Δ	Crystal lattice spacing at absolute zero
r_c	Effective ion core radius
α	Valence electron effective mass ratio
r_o	Atomic radius at the electron ground state energy minimum
μ, $\tilde{C}$, $\tilde{D}$	Constants where $\tilde{D} = \tilde{C}\, e^{2r_c/\mu}$
n_α, m_α	Positive and negative integers
X_α	Rectangular coordinates specifying the undeformed configuration
$\vec{e}_\alpha$	Orthonormal base vectors of the X_α coordinate system
$\vec{a}_\alpha$, $\vec{b}^\alpha$	Unit cell edge vector of the direct and reciprocal lattices respectively
$u_{\alpha\beta}$	Deformation parameter
$a_{\alpha\beta}$	Rectangular components of $\vec{a}_\alpha$
δ^α_β, $\delta_{\alpha\beta}$	Kronecker delta
$G_{\alpha\beta}$, $G^{\alpha\beta}$	Covariant and contravarient components of the metric tensor referred to the cooridnates X_α
$E_{\alpha\beta}$	Lagrangian strain tensor
$C_{\alpha\beta}$, $\bar{C}^{1}_{\alpha\beta}$	Green-Cauchy deformation tensor and its associated inverse
A, U, C, E, I	Matrix representations of the tensors $a_{\alpha\beta}$, $u_{\alpha\beta}$, $C_{\alpha\beta}$, $E_{\alpha\beta}$ and the Kronecker delta
U^T	Transpose of U
I_3	Third principal invariant of $C_{\alpha\beta}$
Σ	Strain energy density
$\beta_1, \ldots\ldots, \beta_{12}$	Numerical coefficients
$T_{\kappa\lambda}$	Kirchhoff-Piola stress tensor
$C_{\kappa\lambda\mu\nu}$	Second-order elastic coefficients
C_{1111}, C_{1122}, C_{2323}	Independent non-vanishing second-order elastic coefficients
$\tilde{B}$	Bulk modulus
$\Phi(m)$, $\Gamma(n)$, $\Psi(n)$, $\Omega(n)$	Lattice sum functions
$\sum'_n$, $\sum'_m$	Lattice sums where $\sum'_n \equiv \sum_{n_1} \sum_{n_2} \sum_{n_3}$ $\sum'_m \equiv \sum_{m_1} \sum_{m_2} \sum_{m_3}$

INTRODUCTION

In the general elastic theory material response is characterized either by a strain energy function, sometimes referred to as an elastic potential, or by elastic response functions, depending on whether one refers to the Green hyperelastic theory or to the Cauchy theory. In either case, the problem of explicitly determining such functions for any solid remains a formidable one, whether contemplated theoretically or experimentally.

While there has been considerable investigation of what the general arguments for a strain energy function should be, with the exception of rubber like materials, very little of specific nature is known for other kinds of solids. For certain metals however, a direct recourse to physical theory for determination of a strain energy density is possible, as is shown in this investigation. What is basically required for each metal, or class of metals having the same atomic and lattice structures, is a sufficiently accurate calculation of the various contributions to the total energy of the solid. The importance or dominance of any one or more of these contributions will depend upon the atomic and lattice structures of the particular metal in question. We note that in this way the inherent microstructure of a solid shapes the explicit form of its associated strain energy and, thereby, the general nature of its elastic response.

The essence of the approach shown here lies in the ability to express analytically the total energy of an arbitrarily deformed crystal as a continuous differentiable function of some measure of the deformability of the solid, which can be considered to be the strain energy. With such a form in hand, it then becomes a straight forward matter, in principle, to calculate all quantities which characterize elastic response corresponding to arbitrary deformations, e.g., constitutive relations, various elastic coefficients in the natural as well as in initially deformed states, the acoustical tensor and wave propagation speeds, etc. In this paper we show only two such calculations, one of which allows for direct comparisons with known experimental data.

Another point of general theoretical interest to continuum mechanics might appropriately be mentioned here. In classical elasticity theory it has become almost traditional to infer the existence of a strain energy function strictly on the basis of classical thermodynamic argument, whereas in our work the strain energy is adopted directly from theories of solid state physics.

Crystal Energy

For monovalent small ion core crystals, e.g., the Alkali metals, the crystal energy at zero temperature can be well approximated by the following contributions [1], [2],

$$E = E_o + E_f + E_{ex} + E_{co} + E_{es} + E_{nc} + E_{bs} . \tag{1}$$

The first four terms are due to the presence of a valence electron gas and are, respectively, the electron ground state, the mean kinetic, the exchange and the correlation energies [3], [4], [5]. Inherent in the quantum calculation of these contributions are the well known adiabatic, one-electron and free electron approximations. The last three terms appearing on the right side of Eq. (1) are the lattice electrostatic energy [6], and the energies due to the core-core non-Coulomb interactions and the band structure [7], [8]. The latter represents a second-order perturbation correction to the free electron approximation calculated by means of pseudopotential formalism. Omitted from Eq. (1) are several very small contributions arising from ion core oscillations at zero temperature, electron-core and core-core polarization (Van der Waals) effects.

In calculation of mechanical properties which involve derivatives of the crystal energy up to order two, the band structure contribution has been shown to be negligibly small for Alkali metals [1], consequently in what follows it will be omitted. However, for calculations involving third and higher order derivatives, e.g., third-order elastic coefficients, the band structure energy is known to be significant and must be retained [2]. Accordingly the analytical representation of Eq. (1), in the absence of the band structure contribution, can be written in atomic units as

$$E = N \left[\frac{r_o^2}{r_s^3} + \alpha \frac{2.210}{r_s^2} - \frac{0.916}{r_s} + 0.031 \text{ Ln } r_s - 0.115 - \frac{2\pi}{\eta^2 \Omega_{DL}} - \frac{2\eta}{\sqrt{\pi}} \right.$$

$$\left. + \frac{2\pi}{\Omega_{DL}} \sum_m{}' \frac{e^{-K_m/\eta^2}}{K_m^2} + \sum_n{}' \frac{\text{erfc}\{\eta R_n\}}{R_n} + \frac{\tilde{D}}{2} \sum_n{}' e^{-R_n/\mu} \right] \tag{2}$$

In this expression N is the number of ions in a crystal volume V, r_s is the radius of an atomic sphere of volume $\Omega = 4/3\ r_s^3 = V/N = \Omega_{DL}/2$, R_n

and K_m are the magnitudes of the direct and reciprocal lattice vectors respectively and Ω_{DL} is the volume of an orthogonal unit cell of the direct body-centered cubic lattice. The summation signs $\sum'_m \sum'_n$ represent $\sum_{m_1} \sum_{m_2} \sum_{m_3}$ and $\sum_{n_1} \sum_{n_2} \sum_{n_3}$ where m_1, m_2, m_3, n_1, n_2, n_3 are positive and negative integers which must satisfy certain restrictions in order to properly incorporate the anisotropy inherent in the lattice structure. Erfc represents the complimentary error function, while η is a positive but otherwise arbitrary number which is chosen so as to effect rapid simultaneous convergence of the lattice sums in which it appears. The crystal energy can be shown to be invariant with respect to the choice of η. The quantities r_o, α, μ and $\tilde{D}$ where $\tilde{D}$ includes the effective ion core radius r_c, are known and can be considered as constants whose values are shown in Table 1. A detailed survey of the development of Eq. (2) can be found in [9].

TABLE 1. ATOMIC AND LATTICE CONSTANTS

Element	Δ (bu)	r_o (bu) [10]	α [11]	r_c (bu) [12]	μ (bu) [13]	$\tilde{C}$ ergs $\times 10^{12}$ [13]	$\tilde{D}$ ryd
Lithium	7.249	2.84	0.730	0.90	0.652	2.00	1.4
Sodium	8.138	3.00	1.009	1.65	0.652	1.25	9.2
Potassium	9.791	3.78	1.066	2.24	0.652	1.25	56.8
Rubidium	10.278	3.94	1.148	2.49	0.652	1.25	121.9
Cesium	11.029	4.27	1.206	2.75	0.652	1.25	267.0

Strain Energy Density

At absolute zero temperature the crystal energy corresponding to any deformed configuration of the lattice can be considered as a strain energy. For homogeneous deformations, which preserve the original periodicity of the lattice, one can calculate the deformed crystal energy directly from Eq. (2). This energy will have the same value at each lattice site of the crystal, assuming the crystal to be free of all internal defects. Any non-homogeneous deformation can be considered to be locally (microscopically) homogeneous at any point provided the neighborhood of that point be sufficiently small, for example, a few lattice spacings. Under these circumstances, the deformed crystal energy can be viewed as a continuous function of position across each such neighborhood which, macroscopically speaking, represents a point. Thus we can interpret the deformed crystal energy, calculated in this manner, as the strain energy corresponding to any arbitrary deformation, wherein the strain energy is a continuous point function in the usual continuum mechanics sense.

Denoting deformed quantities by primes, we next look to express the variables R'_n, K'_m, Ω'_{DL} and r'_s in terms of some suitable measure of the deformability of the crystal. The undeformed unit cell of a body-centered cubic direct lattice is most conveniently defined as follows: let $\vec{e}_\alpha$, ($\alpha = 1,2,3$), represent the orthonormal base vectors of the rectangular coordinate system X_α, which serves to specify the undeformed configuration or undeformed state, and let $\vec{a}_\alpha$ denote the unit cell edge vectors and Δ the lattice spacing at absolute zero temperature. Then the position vector to any lattice site of the direct lattice is

$$\vec{R}_n = \frac{1}{2} n_\alpha \vec{a}_\alpha = \frac{\Delta}{2} n_\alpha \vec{e}_\alpha \tag{3}$$

provided the n_α take on only those positive and negative integral values (including zero) such that the ordered triplets (n_1, n_2, n_3) are either all even or all odd integers. The summation convention or repeated indices is here implied. The corresponding reciprocal lattice, which is face-centered cubic, is specified by the unit cell whose edge vectors $\vec{b}^\alpha$ are defined by the set of relations

$$\vec{a}_\alpha . \vec{b}^\beta = 2\pi \ \delta^\beta_\alpha, \qquad \vec{b}^\alpha = \frac{2\pi}{\Delta} \vec{e}_\alpha \ . \tag{4}$$

The position vector to any lattice site of the reciprocal lattice is therefore

$$\vec{K}_m = \frac{1}{2} m_\alpha \vec{b}^\alpha = \frac{\pi}{\Delta} m_\alpha \vec{e}_\alpha \ . \tag{5}$$

Here the m_α take on only those positive and negative integral values (including zero) for which the sum ($m_1 + m_2 + m_3$) is always even. Introducing the notation $\vec{R}_n = \vec{R}(n)$, $\vec{K}_m = \vec{K}(m)$, we can then write for the component form of these vectors

$$R_\alpha(n) = \frac{\Delta}{2} n_\alpha, \qquad K_\alpha(m) = \frac{\pi}{\Delta} m_\alpha \ . \tag{6}$$

Consider a homogeneous deformation where each ion core of the lattice, originally located by $\vec{R}(n)$ is displaced to a new position

$$\vec{R}'(n) = \vec{R}(n) + \delta\,\vec{R}(n)\ . \tag{7}$$

Introducing the constant deformation parameters $u_{\alpha\beta}$ associated with the homogeneous deformation, where

$$u_{\alpha\beta} = u_{\beta\alpha}, \qquad \det|u_{\alpha\beta}| \neq 0, \qquad (\alpha,\beta = 1,2,3) \tag{8}$$

then

$$R'_\alpha(n) = R_\alpha(n) + u_{\alpha\beta}\,R_\beta(n) \tag{9}$$

and

$$\delta\vec{R}'(n) = u_{\alpha\beta}\,R_\beta(n)\,\vec{e}_\alpha\ . \tag{10}$$

The symmetry condition on the $u_{\alpha\beta}$ is imposed to account for the fact that the crystal energy is invariant with respect to orthogonal transformations of the coordinate frame or, equivalently, with respect to rigid body rotations. From equations (6), (7) and (10) it follows that

$$R'(n) = \frac{\Delta}{2}\left\{n_\alpha n_\alpha + n_\alpha n_\beta[2u_{\alpha\beta} + u_{\alpha\gamma}u_{\gamma\beta}]\right\}^{1/2}\ . \tag{11}$$

In terms of the linearly independent set of unit cell edge vectors $\vec{a}_\alpha$ we can define the metric tensor relative to the cooridnates X_α by

$$G_{\alpha\beta} = \vec{a}_\alpha . \vec{a}_\beta = \Delta^2\ \delta_{\alpha\beta} \tag{12}$$

where in component form

$$\vec{a}_\alpha = a_{\alpha\beta}\vec{e}_\beta = \Delta\delta_{\alpha\beta}\ \vec{e}_\beta\ . \tag{13}$$

The deformation takes the set $\vec{a}_\alpha$ into the deformed set $\vec{a}'_\alpha$ with components

$$a'_{\alpha\beta} = a_{\alpha\beta} + u_{\beta\gamma}a_{\gamma\alpha}\ . \tag{14}$$

Consequently relative to the coordinates of the deformed state

$$G'_{\alpha\beta} = \vec{a}'_\alpha . \vec{a}'_\beta = (a_{\alpha\gamma} + u_{\gamma\delta}a_{\alpha\delta})(a_{\beta\gamma} + u_{\gamma\mu}a_{\beta\mu}) \tag{15}$$

where the right hand representation is in terms of the coordinates X_α. The deformation measure is then

$$G'_{\alpha\beta} - G_{\alpha\beta} = \Delta^2(u_{\alpha\beta} + u_{\beta\alpha} + u_{\alpha\gamma}u_{\gamma\beta}) = 2\Delta^2 E_{\alpha\beta} = 2\Delta^2 E_{\beta\alpha} \quad (16)$$

with $E_{\alpha\beta}$ the components of the Lagrangian strain tensor. Combining equations (12) and (16)

$$G'_{\alpha\beta} = \Delta^2(2E_{\alpha\beta} + \delta_{\alpha\beta}) = \Delta^2 C_{\alpha\beta} = \Delta^2 C_{\beta\alpha} \quad (17)$$

where $C_{\alpha\beta}$ are the components of the Green-Cauchy deformation tensor referred to the coordinates of the undeformed state. In view of equations (16) and (17)

$$R'(n) = \frac{\Delta}{2}\left\{n_\alpha n_\beta C_{\alpha\beta}\right\}^{1/2} \quad . \quad (18)$$

Similarly one can show that

$$K'^2(m) = \left(\frac{\pi}{\Delta}\right)^2 m_\alpha m_\beta \overset{-1}{C}_{\alpha\beta} \quad . \quad (19)$$

Here

$$\overset{-1}{C}_{\alpha\beta} = \frac{\text{cofactor } C_{\alpha\beta}}{\det|C_{\alpha\beta}|} = \overset{-1}{C}_{\beta\alpha} \quad (20)$$

defines the inverse Green-Cauchy deformation tensor.

Introducing the matrix representations A, U, C, E for the associated tensors $a_{\alpha\beta}$, $u_{\alpha\beta}$, $C_{\alpha\beta}$, $E_{\alpha\beta}$, and noting that for the undeformed crystal $\Omega_{DL} = \Delta^3$ we have from Eq. (13)

$$\det|A| = \det|\Delta\delta_{\alpha\beta}| = \Omega_{DL} \quad . \quad (21)$$

Hence for the deformed crystal, using Eq. (14)

$$\det|A'| = \Omega'_{DL} = \det|I + U|\Delta^3 \quad (22)$$

where I is the identity matrix. From equations (16), (17) and the symmetry of the matrix U follows the identity

$$[I + U][I + U^T] = I + U + U^T + UU^T = I + 2E = C \quad (23)$$

from which

$$\det|C| = [\det|I + U|]^2 = I_3 \tag{24}$$

where I_3 denotes the third principal invariant of the deformation tensor $C_{\alpha\beta}$. With $\Omega'_{DL} = (8/3)\pi r_s'^3$, we have from equations (22) and (24)

$$\Omega'_{DL} = \Delta^3 I_3^{1/2} \tag{25}$$

$$r_s'^3 = \frac{3}{\pi}\left(\frac{\Delta}{2}\right)^3 I_3^{1/2} . \tag{26}$$

The strain energy density per unit volume of the undeformed crystal is

$$\Sigma = \frac{E'}{V} = \frac{2E'}{N\Omega_{DL}} = \frac{2}{\Delta^3}\frac{E'}{N} \tag{27}$$

where the deformed crystal energy E' is obtained from Eq. (2) by replacing R_n, K_m, Ω_{DL} and r_s by their deformed counterparts as expressed by equations (18), (21), (27) and (28). Dropping all irrelevant constant terms, the above substitution will then yield for the strain energy density at zero temperature, in atomic units,

$$\Sigma = \left\{\beta_1 - \frac{1}{\eta^2}\beta_2\right\} I_3^{-1/2} + \beta_3 I_3^{-1/3} - \beta_4 I_3^{-1/6} + \beta_5 \mathrm{Ln}\left\{\beta_6 I_3^{1/6}\right\}$$

$$+ \beta_7 I_3^{-1/2} \sum_m{}' \frac{e^{-\frac{\beta_8}{\eta^2}(m_\alpha m_\beta C^{-1}_{\alpha\beta})}}{m_\gamma m_\delta \bar{C}^{1}_{\gamma\delta}} + \beta_9 \sum_n{}' \frac{\mathrm{erfc}\left\{\eta\beta_{10}(n_\alpha n_\beta C_{\alpha\beta})^{1/2}\right\}}{(n_\gamma n_\delta C_{\gamma\delta})^{1/2}}$$

$$+ \beta_{11} \sum_n{}' e^{-\beta_{12}(n_\alpha n_\beta C_{\alpha\beta})^{1/2}} \tag{28}$$

where

$$\beta_1 = \frac{16\pi}{3}\frac{r_o^2}{\Delta^6} \qquad \beta_4 = \left(\frac{\pi}{3}\right)^{1/3}\frac{3.644}{\Delta^4} \qquad \beta_7 = \frac{4}{\pi\Delta^4}$$

$$\beta_2 = \frac{4\pi}{\Delta^6} \qquad \beta_5 = \frac{0.062}{\Delta^3} \qquad \beta_8 = \frac{\pi^2}{\Delta^2}$$

$$\beta_3 = \left(\frac{\pi}{3}\right)^{2/3}\frac{17.680\alpha}{\Delta^5} \qquad \beta_6 = \left(\frac{3}{\pi}\right)^{1/3}\frac{\Delta}{2} \qquad \beta_9 = \frac{4}{\Delta^4}$$

$$\beta_{10} = \frac{\Delta}{2} \qquad \beta_{11} = \frac{\tilde{D}}{\Delta^3} \qquad \beta_{12} = \frac{\Delta}{2\mu} .$$

Several observations of general interest can be made concerning the functional form $\Sigma = \Sigma(C_{\alpha\beta}, n_\alpha, m_\alpha, \{\beta_{(k)}\})$ which represents Eq. (28) at absolute zero temperature. This form, with $C_{\alpha\beta}$ as argument, is properly invariant both with respect to allowable coordinate transformations and with respect to changes of frame of reference, i.e., time dependent orthogonal transformation of coordinates. The anisotropy of the underlying crystal lattice is directly accounted for by the allowed values of the integers n_α, m_α taken along the crystallographic axes of the direct and reciprocal lattices in the lattice sums. The set of constants $\beta_1, \ldots, \beta_{12}$ which include Δ, α, r_o and $\tilde{D} = \tilde{C}\, e^{2r_c/\mu}$ characterize to some extent both the atomic and lattice structure of the solid since Δ is the crystal lattice spacing at zero degrees, r_o is the value of the atomic radius for which the valence electron ground state energy is minimum, α is the effective valence electron mass ratio near the bottom of the conduction band and is a measure of the "freeness" of the valence electrons, while r_c is the effective ion core radius. The constants $\tilde{C}$ and μ, which appear in the Born-Mayer central force potential used to approximate the non-Coulomb core-core repulsion, are obtained from Alkali Halide crystal data where the ion-ion interactions are basically of this form.

Having the strain energy as an explicit continuous differentiable function of the deformation tensor allows for general and concise calculations of quantities which characterize elastic response corresponding to arbitrary crystal deformations. The development shown above is a modified version of work included in one of the authors' doctoral dissertation [9], completed in 1967.

Previous calculations of this kind, for example theoretical calculations of elastic coefficients, starting with the original calculation by Fuchs [7], in 1935, up to the most recent work of Suzuki, Granato and Thomas [2], in 1968, have been restricted to special deformations and therefore, from a mechanics point of view, lacking in generality of approach.

Constitutive Relations

Constitutive relations for hyperelastic solids, that is, for solids for which a strain energy density is known or assumed, can have one of several equivalent forms. The one most convenient for our purposes relates the Kirchhoff-Piola stress tensor to the deformation tensor by the relations

$$T_{\kappa\lambda} = 2\,\frac{\partial \Sigma}{\partial C_{\kappa\lambda}}\,, \qquad \kappa,\lambda = 1,2,3\,. \tag{29}$$

From the symmetry of the $C_{\alpha\beta}$ in Eq. (28) follows symmetry of the stress tensor $T_{\kappa\lambda} = T_{\lambda\kappa}$, which classifies the Alkali metals as non-polar solids. Physically speaking, this result is of course a direct consequence of the fact that polarization contributions to the crystal energy are comparatively small. Calculation of the stress-deformation relations from equations (28) and (29) gives

$$\begin{aligned}
T_{\kappa\lambda} = {} & \left\{-\left(\beta_1 - \frac{1}{\eta^2}\beta_2\right)I_3^{-1/2} - \frac{2}{3}\beta_3 I_3^{-1/3} + \frac{1}{3}\beta_4 I_3^{-1/6} + \frac{1}{3}\beta_5\right\} \overset{-1}{C}_{\kappa\lambda} \\
& + \beta_7 I_3^{-1/2} \sum_m{}' \frac{m_\rho m_\sigma (\overset{-1}{C}_{\rho\kappa}\overset{-1}{C}_{\lambda\sigma} + \overset{-1}{C}_{\sigma\kappa}\overset{-1}{C}_{\lambda\rho})}{m_\gamma m_\delta \overset{-1}{C}_{\gamma\delta}}\, e^{-\frac{\beta_8}{\eta^2}(m_\alpha m_\beta \overset{-1}{C}_{\alpha\beta})} \\
& + \frac{\beta_7\beta_8}{\eta^2} I_3^{-1/2} \sum_m{}' \frac{m_\rho m_\sigma (\overset{-1}{C}_{\rho\kappa}\overset{-1}{C}_{\lambda\sigma} + \overset{-1}{C}_{\sigma\kappa}\overset{-1}{C}_{\lambda\rho})}{(m_\gamma m_\delta \overset{-1}{C}_{\gamma\delta})^2}\, e^{-\frac{\beta_8}{\eta^2}(m_\alpha m_\beta \overset{-1}{C}_{\alpha\beta})} \\
& - \beta_7 I_3^{-1/2} \overset{-1}{C}_{\kappa\lambda} \sum_m{}' \frac{e^{-\frac{\beta_8}{\eta^2}(m_\alpha m_\beta \overset{-1}{C}_{\alpha\beta})}}{m_\gamma m_\delta \overset{-1}{C}_{\gamma\delta}} - \frac{2\eta\beta_9\beta_{10}}{\sqrt{\pi}}\,\cdot \\
& \cdot \sum_n{}' \frac{n_\kappa n_\lambda}{n_\gamma n_\delta C_{\gamma\delta}}\, e^{-\eta^2\beta_{10}^2 (n_\alpha n_\beta C_{\alpha\beta})} \\
& - \beta_9 \sum_n{}' \frac{n_\kappa n_\lambda}{(n_\gamma n_\delta C_{\gamma\delta})^{3/2}}\, \mathrm{erfc}\{\eta\beta_{10}(n_\alpha n_\beta C_{\alpha\beta})^{1/2}\} \\
& - \beta_{11}\beta_{12} \sum_n{}' \frac{n_\kappa n_\lambda}{(n_\gamma n_\delta C_{\gamma\delta})^{1/2}}\, e^{-\beta_{12}(n_\alpha n_\beta C_{\alpha\beta})^{1/2}}
\end{aligned} \tag{30}$$

where use has been made of the following relations:

$$\frac{\partial I_3^{(p)}}{\partial C_{\kappa\lambda}} = p\, I_3^{(p)} \overset{-1}{C}_{\kappa\lambda}$$

$$\frac{\partial \overset{-1}{C}_{\alpha\beta}}{\partial C_{\kappa\lambda}} = -\frac{1}{2}(\overset{-1}{C}_{\alpha\kappa}\overset{-1}{C}_{\lambda\beta} + \overset{-1}{C}_{\beta\kappa}\overset{-1}{C}_{\lambda\alpha})$$

$$\frac{\partial}{\partial C_{\kappa\lambda}}\left\{\mathrm{erfc}[\eta\beta_{10}(n_\alpha n_\beta C_{\alpha\beta})^{1/2}]\right\} = -\frac{\eta\beta_{10}}{\sqrt{\pi}}\frac{n_\kappa n_\lambda}{(n_\gamma n_\delta C_{\gamma\delta})^{1/2}} e^{-\eta^2\beta_{10}^2(n_\alpha n_\beta C_{\alpha\beta})}$$

In the undeformed state C = I, assuming a perfect crystal, the stress must everywhere vanish or, equivalently, the energy density is at a minimum. Setting $C_{\kappa\lambda} = \overset{-1}{C}_{\kappa\lambda} = \delta_{\kappa\lambda}$ and $I_3 = 1$, Eq. (30) reduces to

$$\begin{aligned}
T_{\kappa\lambda}(C = I) = &\left\{-\beta_1 + \frac{1}{\eta^2}\beta_2 - \frac{2}{3}\beta_3 + \frac{1}{3}\beta_4 + \frac{1}{3}\beta_5\right\}\delta_{\kappa\lambda} \\
&- \beta_7\delta_{\kappa\lambda}\sum_m{}' \frac{e^{-\frac{\beta_8}{\eta^2}(m_\alpha m_\alpha)}}{m_\gamma m_\gamma} + \frac{2\beta_7\beta_8}{\eta^2}\sum_m{}' m_\kappa m_\lambda \frac{e^{-\frac{\beta_8}{\eta^2}(m_\alpha m_\alpha)}}{m_\gamma m_\gamma} \\
&+ 2\beta_7\sum_m{}' m_\kappa m_\lambda \frac{e^{-\frac{\beta_8}{\eta^2}(m_\alpha m_\alpha)}}{(m_\gamma m_\gamma)^2} - \frac{2\eta\beta_9\beta_{10}}{\sqrt{\pi}}\sum_n{}' n_\kappa n_\lambda \frac{e^{-\eta^2\beta_{10}^2(n_\alpha n_\alpha)}}{n_\gamma n_\gamma} \\
&- \beta_9\sum_n{}' n_\kappa n_\lambda \frac{\mathrm{erfc}\{\eta\beta_{10}(n_\alpha n_\alpha)^{1/2}\}}{(n_\gamma n_\gamma)^{3/2}} - \beta_{11}\beta_{12}\sum_n{}' n_\kappa n_\lambda \frac{e^{-\beta_{12}(n_\alpha n_\alpha)^{1/2}}}{(n_\gamma n_\gamma)^{1/2}} .
\end{aligned} \tag{31}$$

On the basis of crystal symmetry arguments it can be shown that for $\kappa \neq \lambda$ the right side of Eq. (31) vanishes identically. Thus

$$T_{\kappa\lambda}(C = I)_{\kappa\neq\lambda} = 0 . \tag{32}$$

With $\kappa = \lambda$

$$\frac{1}{3} T_{\kappa\kappa}(C = I) = - \beta_1 + \frac{1}{\eta^2} \beta_2 - \frac{2}{3} \beta_3 + \frac{1}{3} \beta_4 + \frac{1}{3} \beta_5$$

$$- \frac{1}{3} \beta_7 \sum_m{}' \frac{e^{-\frac{\beta_8}{\eta^2}(m_\alpha m_\alpha)}}{m_\gamma m_\gamma} + \frac{2}{3} \frac{\beta_7 \beta_8}{\eta^2} \sum_m{}' e^{-\frac{\beta_8}{\eta^2}(m_\alpha m_\alpha)}$$

$$- \frac{2\eta\beta_9\beta_{10}}{3\sqrt{\pi}} \sum_m{}' e^{-\eta^2\beta_{10}^2(n_\alpha n_\alpha)} - \frac{1}{3} \beta_9 \sum_n{}' \frac{\operatorname{erfc}\{\eta\beta_{10}(n_\alpha n_\alpha)^{1/2}\}}{(n_\gamma n_\gamma)^{1/2}}$$

$$- \frac{1}{3} \beta_{11}\beta_{12} \sum_n{}' \frac{e^{-\beta_{12}(n_\alpha n_\alpha)^{1/2}}}{(n_\gamma n_\gamma)^{-1/2}} + \frac{2}{3} \beta_7 \sum_m{}' \frac{e^{-\frac{\beta_8}{\eta^2}(m_\alpha m_\alpha)}}{(m\ m)} \qquad (33)$$

The right side of Eq. (33) representing the pressure $\frac{1}{3}(T_{11} + T_{22} + T_{33})$ will not be exactly zero because of the approximations inherent in the calculation of the crystal energy. Consequently we can choose the lattice spacing such that Eq. (33) sums to zero. These values, corresponding to an accuracy of approximately one atmosphere pressure, are listed in Table 1.

The wealth of experimental data available for values of the second-order elastic coefficients for Alkali metals provides an opportunity for at least one specific check on the accuracy of the crystal energy given by Eq. (2). Second-order elastic coefficients are formally defined by the relations

$$C_{\kappa\lambda\mu\nu} = \left\{4 \frac{\partial^2 \Sigma}{\partial C_{\kappa\lambda} \partial C_{\mu\nu}}\right\}_{C=I} . \qquad (34)$$

Since the strain energy density is continuous and differentiable to any order with respect to the symmetric deformation tensor

$$C_{\kappa\lambda\mu\nu} = C_{\lambda\kappa\mu\nu} = C_{\kappa\lambda\nu\mu}$$

and

$$C_{\kappa\lambda\mu\nu} = C_{\mu\nu\kappa\lambda} .$$

This pair of symmetry relations reduces the number of independent coefficients to twenty-one. For the case of cubic symmetry the number of non-vanishing independent coefficients are furthermore reduced to three, these being

$$C_{1111} = C_{2222} = C_{3333}, \quad C_{2323} = C_{1313} = C_{1212},$$

$$C_{1122} = C_{1133} = C_{2233} \,. \tag{35}$$

As is well known, the principal minors of the matrix $(C_{\kappa\lambda\mu\nu})$ will be positive if

$$C_{2323} > 0, \; C_{1122} > 0, \; C_{1111} - C_{1122} > 0 \,. \tag{36}$$

Direct substitution of Eq. (28) into Eq. (34) with C=I gives

$$\begin{aligned}
C_{\kappa\lambda\mu\nu} &= \left(\beta_1 - \frac{1}{\eta^2}\beta_2 + \frac{4}{9}\beta_3 - \frac{1}{9}\beta_4\right)\delta_{\kappa\lambda}\delta_{\mu\nu} \\
&+ \left(\beta_1 - \frac{1}{\eta^2}\beta_2 + \frac{2}{3}\beta_3 - \frac{1}{3}\beta_4 - \frac{1}{3}\beta_5\right)\left(\delta_{\kappa\mu}\delta_{\nu\lambda} + \delta_{\lambda\mu}\delta_{\nu\kappa}\right) \\
&+ \beta_7 \sum_m{}' (\delta_{\kappa\lambda}\delta_{\mu\nu} + \delta_{\kappa\mu}\delta_{\nu\lambda} + \delta_{\lambda\mu}\delta_{\nu\kappa})\, \Phi_{(1)}(m) \\
&- 2\beta_7 \sum_m{}' (m_\kappa m_\lambda \delta_{\mu\nu} + m_\mu m_\nu \delta_{\kappa\lambda} + m_\lambda m_\mu \delta_{\nu\kappa} + m_\nu m_\lambda \delta_{\kappa\mu} + m_\kappa m_\nu \delta_{\lambda\mu} \\
&\qquad + m_\kappa m_\mu \delta_{\nu\lambda})\, \Phi_{(2)}(m) \\
&- \frac{2\beta_7\beta_8}{\eta^2} \sum_m{}' (m_\kappa m_\lambda \delta_{\mu\nu} + m_\mu m_\nu \delta_{\kappa\lambda} + m_\lambda m_\mu \delta_{\nu\kappa} + m_\nu m_\lambda \delta_{\kappa\mu} + m_\kappa m_\nu \delta_{\lambda\mu} \\
&\qquad + m_\kappa m_\mu \delta_{\nu\lambda})\, \Phi_{(1)}(m) \\
&- \frac{8\beta_7\beta_8}{\eta^2} \sum_m{}' m_\kappa m_\lambda m_\mu m_\nu \, \Phi_{(2)}(m) + 8\beta_7 \sum_m{}' m_\kappa m_\lambda m_\mu m_\nu \, \Phi_{(3)}(m) \\
&+ \frac{4\beta_7\beta_8^2}{\eta^2} \sum_m{}' m_\kappa m_\lambda m_\mu m_\nu \, \Phi_{(1)}(m) + 3\beta_9 \sum_n{}' n_\kappa n_\lambda n_\mu n_\nu \, \Gamma_{(5/2)}(n) \\
&+ \frac{4\eta^3\beta_9\beta_{10}^3}{\sqrt{\pi}} \sum_n{}' n_\kappa n_\lambda n_\mu n_\nu \, \Psi_{(1)}(n) + \frac{6\eta\beta_9\beta_{10}}{\sqrt{\pi}} \sum_n{}' n_\kappa n_\lambda n_\mu n_\nu \, \Psi_{(2)}(n) \\
&+ \beta_{11}\beta_{12}^2 \sum_n{}' n_\kappa n_\lambda n_\mu n_\nu \, \Omega_{(1)}(n) + \beta_{11}\beta_{12} \sum_n{}' n_\kappa n_\lambda n_\mu n_\nu \, \Omega_{(3/2)}(n)
\end{aligned} \tag{37}$$

where

$$\Phi_{(0)}(m) = e^{-\frac{\beta_8}{\eta^2}(m_\alpha m_\alpha)} \qquad \Psi_{(0)}(n) = e^{-\eta^2\beta_{10}^2(n_\alpha n_\alpha)}$$

$$\Phi_{(1)}(m) = \frac{\Phi_{(0)}(m)}{m_\alpha m_\alpha} \qquad \Psi_{(1)}(n) = \frac{\Psi_{(0)}(n)}{(n_\alpha n_\alpha)}$$

$$\Phi_{(2)}(m) = \frac{\Phi_{(0)}(m)}{(m_\alpha m_\alpha)^2} \qquad \Psi_{(2)}(n) = \frac{\Psi_{(0)}(n)}{(n_\alpha n_\alpha)^2}$$

$$\Phi_{(3)}(m) = \frac{\Phi_{(0)}(m)}{(m_\alpha m_\alpha)^3} \qquad \Omega_{(0)}(n) = e^{-\beta_{12}(n_\alpha n_\alpha)^{1/2}}$$

$$\Gamma_{(0)}(n) = \mathrm{erfc}\{\eta\beta_{10}(n_\alpha n_\alpha)^{1/2}\} \qquad \Omega_{(1)}(n) = \frac{\Omega_{(0)}(n)}{(n_\alpha n_\alpha)}$$

$$\Gamma_{(5/2)}(n) = \frac{\Gamma_{(0)}(n)}{(n_\alpha n_\alpha)^{5/2}} \qquad \Omega_{(3/2)}(n) = \frac{\Omega_{(0)}(n)}{(n_\alpha n_\alpha)^{3/2}}$$

Again by crystal symmetry arguments one can show that the $C_{\kappa\lambda\mu\nu}$ calculated by Eq. (37) satisfy the requirements of Eq. (35) identically. The non-vanishing coefficients C_{1111}, C_{1122} and C_{2323} are obtainable from Eq. (37) directly and are as follows:

$$C_{1111} = [3(\beta_1 - \frac{1}{\eta^2}\beta_2) + \frac{16}{9}\beta_3 - \frac{7}{9}\beta_4 - \frac{2}{3}\beta_5] + 3\beta_7 \sum_m{}' \Phi_{(1)}(m)$$

$$- 12\beta_7 \sum_m{}' m_1^2 \Phi_{(2)}(m)$$

$$- \frac{12\beta_7\beta_8}{\eta^2} \sum_m{}' m_1^2 \Phi_{(1)}(m) + 8\beta_7 \sum_m{}' m_1^4 \Phi_{(3)}(m) + \frac{8\beta_7\beta_8}{\eta^2} \sum_m{}' m_1^4 \Phi_{(2)}(m)$$

$$+ \frac{4\beta_7\beta_8{}^2}{\eta^2} \sum_m{}' m_1^4 \Phi_{(1)}(m) + 3\beta_9 \sum_n{}' n_1^4 \Gamma_{(5/2)}(n) + \frac{4\eta^3\beta_9\beta_{10}^3}{\sqrt{\pi}} \sum_n{}' n_1^4 \Psi_{(1)}(n)$$

$$+ \frac{6\eta\beta_9\beta_{10}}{\sqrt{\pi}} \sum_n{}' n_1^4 \Psi_{(2)}(n) + \beta_{11}\beta_{12}^2 \sum_n{}' n_1^4 \Omega_{(1)}(n)$$

$$+ \beta_{11}\beta_{12} \sum_n{}' n_1^4 \Omega_{(3/2)}(n) \ . \qquad (38)$$

$$C_{1122} = (\beta_1 - \frac{1}{\eta^2}\beta_2 + \frac{4}{9}\beta_3 - \frac{1}{9}\beta_4) + \beta_7 \sum_m{}' \Phi_{(1)}(m) - 4\beta_7 \sum_m{}' m_1^2\, \Phi_{(2)}(m)$$

$$- \frac{4\beta_7\beta_8}{\eta^2} \sum_m{}' m_1^2\, \Phi_{(1)}(m) + 8\beta_7 \sum_m{}' m_1^2 m_2^2\, \Phi_{(3)}(m) + \frac{8\beta_7\beta_8}{\eta^2} \sum_m{}' m_1^2 m_2^2\, \Phi_{(2)}(m)$$

$$+ \frac{4\beta_7\beta_8^2}{\eta^4} \sum_m{}' m_1^2 m_2^2\, \Phi_{(1)}(m) + 3\beta_9 \sum_n{}' n_1^2 n_2^2\, \Gamma_{(5/2)}(n)$$

$$+ \frac{4\eta^3\beta_9\beta_{10}^3}{\sqrt{\pi}} \sum_n{}' n_1^2 n_2^2\, \Psi_{(1)}(n)$$

$$+ \frac{6\eta\beta_9\beta_{10}}{\sqrt{\pi}} \sum_n{}' n_1^2 n_2^2\, \Psi_{(2)}(n) + \beta_{11}\beta_{12}^2 \sum_n{}' n_1^2 n_2^2\, \Omega_{(1)}(n)$$

$$+ \beta_{11}\beta_{12} \sum_n{}' n_1^2 n_2^2\, \Omega_{(3/2)}(n) \;. \qquad (39)$$

$$C_{2323} = (\beta_1 - \frac{1}{\eta^2}\beta_2 + \frac{2}{3}\beta_3 - \frac{1}{3}\beta_4 - \frac{1}{3}\beta_5) + \beta_7 \sum_m{}' \Phi_{(1)}(m)$$

$$- 4\beta_7 \sum_m{}' m_2^2\, \Phi_{(2)}(m)$$

$$- \frac{4\beta_7\beta_8}{\eta^2} \sum_m{}' m_2^2\, \Phi_{(1)}(m) + 8\beta_7 \sum_m{}' m_2^2 m_3^2\, \Phi_{(3)}(m) + \frac{8\beta_7\beta_8}{\eta^2} \sum_m{}' m_2^2 m_3^2\, \Phi_{(2)}(m)$$

$$+ \frac{4\beta_7\beta_8^2}{\eta^4} \sum_m{}' m_2^2 m_3^2\, \Phi_{(1)}(m) + 3\beta_9 \sum_n{}' n_2^2 n_3^2\, \Gamma_{(5/2)}(n)$$

$$+ \frac{4\eta^3\beta_9\beta_{10}^3}{\sqrt{\pi}} \sum_n{}' n_2^2 n_3^2\, \Psi_{(1)}(n)$$

$$- \frac{6\eta\beta_9\beta_{10}}{\sqrt{\pi}} \sum_n{}' n_2^2 n_3^2\, \Psi_{(2)}(n) + \beta_{11}\beta_{12}^2 \sum_n{}' n_2^2 n_3^2\, \Omega_{(1)}(n)$$

$$+ \beta_{11}\beta_{12} \sum_n{}' n_2^2 n_3^2\, \Omega_{(3/2)}(n) \qquad (40)$$

Numerical calculation of C_{1111}, C_{1122}, C_{2323} and the bulk modulus $\tilde{B} = \frac{1}{3}(C_{1111} + 2C_{1122})$, based on these equations, are shown in Table 2, together with the most recent published experimental values. The values of Δ, α, r_o, μ and $\tilde{D}$ used in these calculations are those listed in Table 1. The calculated values of the coefficients show good agreement with the experimental values and satisfy the requirements of Eq. (36) as well.

TABLE 2. SECOND-ORDER ELASTIC COEFFICIENTS IN UNITS OF 10^{11} DYNES/CM^2

Element	C_{1111}	C_{1122}	C_{2323}	$\tilde{B}$	Remarks
Lithium	1.44	1.21	1.09	1.29	Experimental at 78°K, [14]
	1.33	1.12	0.81	1.19	Calculated
Sodium	0.88	0.73	0.62	0.78	Experimental at 0°K, [15]
	0.84	0.70	0.54	0.75	Calculated
Potassium	0.42	0.34	0.29	0.37	Experimental at 4°K, [16]
	0.42	0.36	0.26	0.38	Calculated
Rubidium	0.34	0.29	0.22	0.31	Experimental at 0°K, [17]
	0.35	0.30	0.22	0.32	Calculated
Cesium	0.25	0.21	0.17	0.22	Experimental at 0°K, [18]
	0.27	0.23	0.17	0.24	Calculated

Error in experimental values is estimated to be of the order $\pm 0.01 \times 10^{11}$ dynes/cm^2.

ACKNOWLEDGEMENT

The authors wish to acknowledge the partial support of the research extended by the NASA-Langley Research Center under NASA Grant NGR 09-010-053. The authors also appreciate the valuable comments of Pat Klaus and the computer time provided by The George Washington University Computer Center.

REFERENCES

1. Wallace, D. C., "Pseudopotential Calculation of the Thermal Expansion Coefficient of Sodium and Potassium," Physical Review, Vol. 176, 1968, pp. 832-837.

2. Suzuki, T., Granato, A. V. and Thomas, J. F., "Second and Third Order Elastic Coefficients of Alkali Metals," Physical Review, Vol. 175, 1968, pp. 766-781.

3. Bardeen, J., "An Improved Calculation of the Energies of Lithium and Sodium," Journal of Chemical Physics, Vol. 6, 1938, pp. 367-371.

4. Raimes, S., The Wave Mechanics of Electrons in Metals, North Holland, Amsterdam, 1961.

5. Pines, D., "Electron Interactions in Metals," Solid State Physics, Vol. 1, Edited by F. Seitz and D. Turnbull, Academic Press, New York, 1955, pp. 368-450.

6. Fuchs, K., "A Quantum Mechanical Investigation of the Cohesive Forces of Metallic Copper," Proceedings of The Royal Society, Vol. 151, Series A, 1935, pp. 585-601.

7. Fuchs, K., "A Quantum Mechanical Calculation of the Elastic Constants of Monovalent Metals," Proceedings of The Royal Society, Vol. 153, Series A, 1936, pp. 622-639.

8. Harrison, W. A., Pseudopotentials in the Theory of Metals, W. A. Benjamin, New York, 1966.

9. Eftis, J., "A Non Linear Continuum Theory of Alkali Metals Based on Quantum Mechanics," D.Sc. Dissertation, The George Washington University, Washington, D.C., 1967.

10. Kuhn, T. S., "An Application of the W.K.B. Method to the Cohesive Energy of Monovalent Metals," Physical Review, Vol. 79, 1950, pp. 515-519.

11. Brooks, H., "Binding in the Alkali Metals," Theory of Alloy Phases, American Society for Metals, Cleveland, 1956, pp. 100-219.

12. Seitz, F., Modern Theory of Solids, McGraw-Hill, New York, 1940.

13. Mott, N. F. and Jones, H., The Theory and Properties of Metals and Alloys, Dover Pub., New York, 1936.

14. Slotwinski, T. and Trivisonno, J., "Temperature Dependence of the Elastic Constants of Single Crystal Lithium," Journal of Physics and Chemistry of Solids, Vol. 30, 1969, pp. 1276-1279.

15. Diederich, M. E. and Trivisonno, J., "Temperature Dependence of the Elastic Constants of Sodium," Journal of Physics and Chemistry of Solids, Vol. 27, 1966, pp. 637-642.

16. Marquardt, W. R. and Trivisonno, J., "Low Temperature Elastic Constants of Potassium," Journal of Physics and Chemistry of Solids, Vol. 26, 1965, pp. 273-278.

17. Gutman, E. J. and Trivisonno, J., "Temperature Dependence of the Elastic Constants of Rubidium," Journal of Physics and Chemistry of Solids, Vol. 28, 1967, pp. 805-809.

18. Kollarits, F. J. and Trivisonno, J., "Single-Crystal Elastic Constants of Cesium," Journal of Physics and Chemistry of Solids, Vol. 29, 1968, pp. 2133-2139.

VISCOELASTIC ANALYSIS OF GRAPHITE UNDER NEUTRON IRRADIATION AND TEMPERATURE DISTRIBUTION[1]

Shih-Jung Chang
Oak Ridge National Laboratory

C. E. Pugh
Oak Ridge National Laboratory

S. E. Moore
Oak Ridge National Laboratory

ABSTRACT

Graphite under neutron irradiation exhibits significant creep and dimensional change, both of which are dependent on the accumulated neutron exposure (dose) and temperature. The theory of linear viscoelasticity for a thermo-rheologically simple material is adapted to the stress analysis of irradiated graphite in the presence of temperature gradients. For steady neutron flux, the accumulated neutron exposure, which is in general nonuniform throughout a body, is identified as the "reduced time." Temperature is included as an additional parameter with no direct influence on the reduced time.

Generalized plane-strain conditions for a body with an arbitrary two-dimensional cross section and a uniform neutron flux across the section are formulated for applied temperature distributions, neutron-induced dimensional changes, and boundary loadings. The viscoelastic solution for this general problem is shown to be the sum of the solutions for four associated elastic problems, when each is multiplied by an appropriate function of neutron exposure. Numerical results are obtained for various thick-walled cylinders which represent graphite core components in a Molten-Salt Breeder Reactor (MSBR) design study. An

---

1. Research sponsored by the U.S. Atomic Energy Commission under contract with the Union Carbide Corporation.

asymptotic expression for the axial stress components is derived for large values of neutron exposure.

LIST OF NOTATIONS

A_o	Material property constant
D	Accumulated neutron exposure
E	Young's modulus
G	Relaxation function
H	Heat transfer coefficient
J_x	Creep function in the transverse plane
J_z	Creep function in the axial direction
J_{zx}	Creep function in shear
J_p	Primary creep
J_s	Secondary creep
K	Creep coefficient
L	Length of the cylinder
R	Hydraulic radius
T	Temperature
T_x	Boundary traction, x-component
T_y	Boundary traction, y-component
$T_{a,b}$	Surface temperatures
Z	Coordinate in the axial direction
α	Coefficient of thermal expansion
ε,γ	Strain
Θ	Neutron flux
κ_a	Thermal conductivity
μ	Poisson's ratio
σ,τ	Stress
ϕ	Stress function
ψ	Dimension change function

INTRODUCTION

Graphite structural members in the core of a nuclear reactor experience an internal heat generation, exhibit creep and tend to change dimensions as functions of neutron exposure. At temperature levels of 500 to 1000°C currently being considered for the design of a molten salt breeder reactor (MSBR), the graphite initially contracts, reaches a minimum volume and then expands, as discussed by Kasten et al. [1]. The original volume is regained and the graphite continues to expand at an increasing rate for fast neutron dose values above about 3×10^{22} nvt (E > 50 kev)[2] until the structural integrity is destroyed. A reasonable design criteria would be to limit the operating life of the graphite structural elements by the fast neutron exposure (fluence), or time, required for the graphite to return to its original volume, provided that the stresses induced by differential dimensional changes within the structure remain low.

A viscoelastic analysis of the mechanical behavior of irradiated graphite is developed in order to permit the evaluation of such design criteria and to provide a method of stress analysis. This analysis is based upon the experimental results reported by Kennedy [2] which show that graphite under irradiation can be represented by a linear viscoelastic model if the accumulated neutron exposure (dose) is identified as a "reduced time" variable.

The constitutive equations for describing this material behavior are first developed analogous to those for a thermo-rheologically simple material in the presence of non-uniform temperature distributions. The equations are initially expressed in a form to characterize a transversely isotropic material, since many nuclear grade graphites exhibit this type of material symmetry as a result of fabrication processes. Simplifications are then made consistent with the assumptions of generalized plane strain conditions. Upon assuming a uniform neutron flux distribution across an arbitrarily shaped cross section, the viscoelastic solution is obtained for applied boundary tractions, temperature distribution and neutron-induced dimensional change in terms of associated elastic solutions for isotropic graphites.

---

2. Neutron dose is a measure of accumulated exposure to neutrons whose energy levels are greater than a certain threshold level, in this case 50×10^3 electron-volts (E > 50 kev). The unit "nvt" is an acronym for the product of "n", the neutron density (neutrons/cm^3), times "v", the average neutron velocity (cm/sec), times "t" the exposure time (sec). The unit "nvt" thus has dimensions of neutrons/cm^2.

The formulation is then applied to the analysis of various concentric circular cylinders subjected to radial temperature distributions and to temperature-dependent neutron-induced dimensional changes. The components of stress and strain are calculated as functions of neutron exposure, and an asymptotic solution is developed for determining axial stress values for neutron exposures greater than 10^{22} nvt (E > 50 kev). Design lifetimes for these graphite cylinders are also computed.

Constitutive Equations

Experiments [2] have shown that the uniaxial creep curve for irradiated graphite approximates the linear superposition principle in such a way that the creep strain shown in Fig. 1 at neutron dose D_2 can be represented by a linear combination of the creep due to the stress σ_1 at zero dose and that due to an additional stress $-\sigma_2$ at D_1 as given by the following relation:

$$\varepsilon(D_2) = \sigma_1 J(D_2) - \sigma_2 J(D_2 - D_1) \tag{1}$$

where J(D) is a dose-dependent creep function. Hence, for a continuously changing stress σ, the strain ε for an arbitrary accumulated dose D can be represented by the integral relation

$$\varepsilon(D) = \int_0^D J(D - D') \frac{d\sigma}{dD'} dD' \tag{2}$$

where D' is an integration variable ranging over the history of the loading program. This equation, analogous to that of linear viscoelasticity [3,4], provides a basic constitutive equation, in which the stress and the strain are linearly related.

Many nuclear grades of graphite exhibit mechanical behaviors which are to various degrees transversely isotropic in nature. Therefore, it is convenient to generalize Eq. (2) to the following multiaxial constitutive equations which are valid for that type of material symmetry:

$$\varepsilon_x = J_x * (d\sigma_x - \mu_x d\sigma_y) - \mu_z J_z * d\sigma_z + \alpha_x T + \psi_x(T,D) \tag{3}$$

$$\varepsilon_y = J_x * (d\sigma_y - \mu_x d\sigma_x) - \mu_z J_z * d\sigma_z + \alpha_x T + \psi_x(T,D) \tag{4}$$

$$\varepsilon_z = J_z * (d\sigma_z - \mu_z d\sigma_x - \mu_z d\sigma_y) + \alpha_z T + \psi_z(T,D) \tag{5}$$

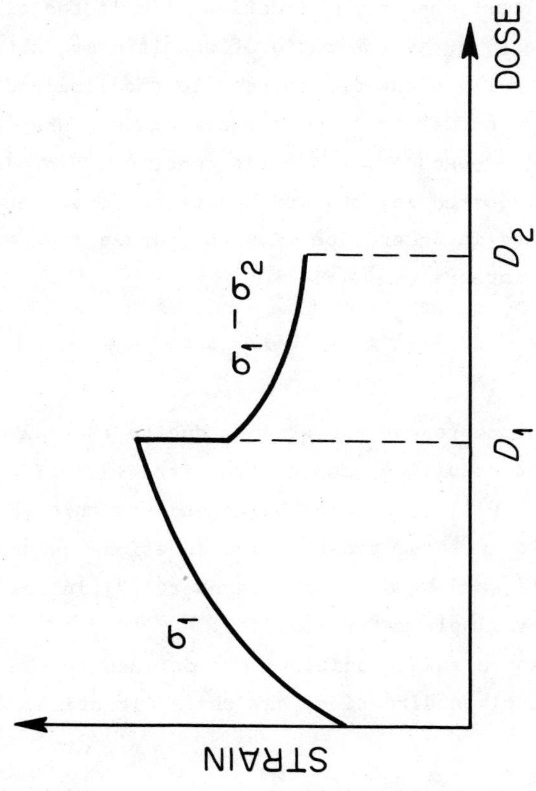

Fig. 1. Linear Superposition for a Viscoelastic Material.

$$\gamma_{xy} = 2(1 + \mu_x)\, J_x * d\tau_{xy} \tag{6}$$

$$\gamma_{yz} = J_{zx} * d\tau_{yz} \tag{7}$$

$$\gamma_{zx} = J_{zx} * d\tau_{zx} \tag{8}$$

where the z axis is assumed to be the axis of material symmetry and both Poisson ratios μ_x and μ_z to be constants.[3] The Poisson ratio μ_x is defined as the ratio of induced lateral strain to longitudinal strain for a uniaxial test when both directions lie in the plane of isotropy (x,y). Whereas, μ_z is the ratio of the lateral strain induced in a direction in the plane of isotropy to the longitudinal strain in the direction normal to the isotropic plane. When these Poisson ratios are dose-dependent, two creep functions, in addition to J_x, J_z, and J_{zx}, are required for the stress-strain representation. The notation (*) is used in accordance with the convention for representing a convolution integral,

$$J * d\sigma = \int_0^D J(D - D')\, \frac{\partial\sigma}{\partial D'}\, dD' \tag{9}$$

The terms αT and $\psi(T,D)$ represent the strains due to thermal expansion and dimensional changes resulting from neutron irradiation, respectively. The neutron dose D will in general be nonuniform throughout a body and plays the same role in these constitutive equations as does the "reduced time" variable used by Muki and Sternberg [7] in the analysis of thermo-rheologically simple materials.

The generalized plane-strain conditions are defined by the case when the normal strain in a given direction, say the z direction, assumes a

---

3. Experimental measurements of the strain ratio variables μ_x and μ_z have not been made for graphites during irradiation. However, experimental evidence which tends to support the above assumption has been obtained by Simmons [5]. Strain ratio measurements were made on a number of isotropic reactor grade graphites at room temperature before and after irradiation with no observable change. Experimental strain ratio measurements [6] have also been made at room temperature on a number of anisotropic reactor grade graphites in which a significant amount of plastic deformation occurs. In these experiments the strain ratio values remained reasonably constant over the entire loading range.

constant value ε_o, all derivatives with respect to z vanish, and the net resultant force in the z direction vanishes. Under these conditions, Eqs. (7) and (8) identically vanish and Eq. (5) reduces to:

$$J_z * d\sigma_z = \mu_z J_z * (d\sigma_x + d\sigma_y) - \alpha_z T - \psi_z(T,D) + \varepsilon_o \tag{10}$$

Through the use of Eq. (10), the two-dimensional constitutive equations which characterize these generalized plane-strain conditions can be expressed by Eqs. (3), (4), and (6) in the form

$$\varepsilon_x = (J_x - \mu_z^2 J_z) * d\sigma_x - (\mu_x J_x + \mu_z^2 J_z) * d\sigma_y + (\alpha_x + \mu_z \alpha_z)T + \psi_x + \mu_z \psi_z - \mu_z \varepsilon_o \tag{11}$$

$$\varepsilon_y = (J_x - \mu_z^2 J_z) * d\sigma_y - (\mu_x J_x + \mu_z^2 J_z) * d\sigma_x + (\alpha_x + \mu_z \alpha_z)T + \psi_x + \mu_z \psi_z - \mu_z \varepsilon_o \tag{12}$$

$$\gamma_{xy} = 2(1 + \mu_x)\, J_x * d\tau_{xy} \tag{13}$$

Thus, for this type of transversely isotropic material, two creep functions J_x and J_z, along with two Poisson ratios μ_x and μ_z, are required for the viscoelastic stress analysis under generalized plane-strain conditions when the isotropic plane coincides with the cross section of the specimen.

For an isotropic graphite, the following simplifications can be made in the generalized plane-strain formulation:

$$\mu_z = \mu_x = \mu$$

$$J_x = J_z = J$$

$$\alpha_x = \alpha_z = \alpha$$

$$\psi_x = \psi_z = \psi$$

and it follows that

$$\varepsilon_x = (1 - \mu^2)J * \left(d\sigma_x - \frac{\mu}{1 - \mu}\, d\sigma_y\right) + (1 + \mu)(\alpha T + \psi) - \mu\varepsilon_o \tag{14}$$

$$\varepsilon_y = (1 - \mu^2)J * \left[d\sigma_y - \frac{\mu}{1 - \mu} d\sigma_x\right] + (1 + \mu)(\alpha T + \psi) - \mu\varepsilon_o \quad (15)$$

$$\gamma_{xy} = 2(1 + \mu)J * d\tau_{xy} \quad (16)$$

It is seen from Eqs. (14), (15), and (16) that the viscoelastic stress analysis of an isotropic graphite under these conditions requires the determination of only one creep function J(D), and one Poisson ratio μ. Experimental results [2] show that the creep function can be considered as the sum of an elastic contribution, a primary creep term, and a secondary creep term. The primary creep is expressed in terms of the accumulated neutron exposure by

$$J_p(D) = \frac{1}{2E}\left[1 - e^{-A_oD}\right] \quad (17)$$

and the secondary creep is linearly dependent upon the dose, thus

$$J_s(D) = K(T)D \quad (18)$$

The secondary creep coefficient K(T) is dependent upon the temperature [1], whereas A_o and E in the primary creep term are constants. The constant A_o is large in the sense that the second term in the primary creep expression $J_p(D)$ becomes negligible for neutron exposures less than typical current design doses.[4] In the subsequent analysis, it is assumed that K(T) has a constant value which in practice would correspond to some mean temperature. This assumption is necessary to obtain the governing Eq. (24), given in the next section. The overall creep function, including the elastic part, is then

$$J(D) = \frac{1}{E} + K(T)D + \frac{1}{2E}\left[1 - e^{-A_oD}\right] \quad (19)$$

This form of the creep function for graphite under irradiation can be represented analogously by a model of springs and dashpots with the spring constants and viscous coefficients shown in Fig. 2. If A_o is

---

4. Typical design doses for the type of reactors considered later in this paper range up to 3×10^{22} nvt.

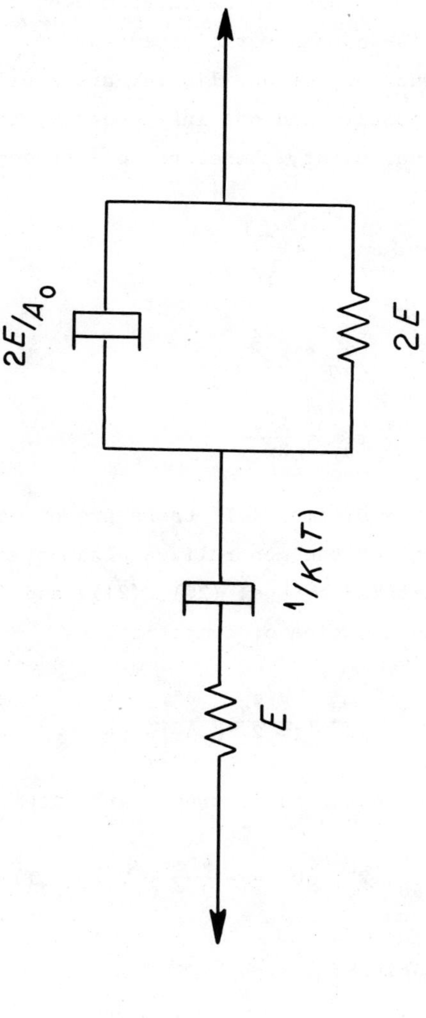

Fig. 2. Viscoelastic Model Representation for Irradiated Graphite.

large, the right dashpot can be removed, leaving two springs and a dashpot connected in series.

Formulation and Solution

In this section the intent is to illustrate the relation between the thermal stress problem in an elastic material and that in a viscoelastic material. Consider an arbitrary two-dimensional cross section where the neutron flux is assumed to be uniform over the entire section and the creep function is independent of temperature. As discussed by Sokolnikoff [8], the equations of equilibrium are expressed only in terms of the stress components and not influenced by the constitutive equations; it will be convenient, therefore to introduce the Airy stress function ϕ such that

$$\sigma_x = \frac{\partial^2 \phi}{\partial y^2} \tag{20}$$

$$\sigma_y = \frac{\partial^2 \phi}{\partial x^2} \tag{21}$$

$$\tau_{xy} = \frac{\partial^2 \phi}{\partial x \partial y} \tag{22}$$

where $\phi = \phi(x,y,D)$ and $D = D(\text{time})$. If there are no body forces, the equations of equilibrium for the generalized plane-strain formulation will be identically satisfied by Eqs. (20), (21), and (22). After substituting these into the equation of compatibility

$$\frac{\partial^2 \varepsilon_y}{\partial x^2} + \frac{\partial^2 \varepsilon_x}{\partial y^2} = \frac{\partial^2 \gamma_{xy}}{\partial x \partial y} \tag{23}$$

the governing equation of ϕ for an isotropic graphite is

$$\int_0^D J(D - D') \frac{\partial}{\partial D'} \nabla^4 \phi \, dD' = - \frac{1}{1 - \mu} \nabla^2 [\psi(D,T) + \alpha T] \tag{24}$$

After inversion, ϕ satisfies

$$\nabla^4 \phi = - \frac{1}{1 - \mu} \int_0^D G(D - D') \frac{\partial}{\partial D'} \left\{ \nabla^2 [\psi(D,T) + \alpha T] \right\} dD' \tag{25}$$

where the relaxation function G is related to the creep function J by

$$\int_0^D G(D - D') \frac{\partial}{\partial D'} J(D')dD' = H(D) \tag{26}$$

and H(D) is the unit step function. Specifically, the relaxation function which corresponds to the creep function given by Eq. (19) is

$$G(D) = \frac{E}{\sqrt{(EK + 1.5A_o)^2 - 4EKA_o}} \left[(k_1 + A_o)e^{k_1 D} - (k_2 + A_o)e^{k_2 D} \right] \tag{27}$$

where

$$k_1 = -0.5(EK + 1.5A_o) + 0.5\sqrt{(EK + 1.5A_o)^2 - 4EKA_o} \tag{28}$$

$$k_2 = -0.5(EK + 1.5A_o) - 0.5\sqrt{(EK + 1.5A_o)^2 - 4EKA_o} \tag{29}$$

and where k_1 and k_2 are seen to be negative. For prescribed boundary traction, the boundary conditions are

$$\frac{\partial\phi}{\partial y} = \int_C T_x \, ds \tag{30}$$

and

$$\frac{\partial\phi}{\partial x} = -\int_C T_y \, ds \tag{31}$$

where T_x and T_y are the x- and y-components of the boundary traction acting on the boundary C of the cross section of the body.

It will be established that if the temperature field is independent of time and if the temperature-dependent neutron-induced dimensional change is given by

$$\psi(D,T) = A_2(T)D^2 + A_1(T)D \tag{32}$$

then the stress function ϕ is expressed by

$$\phi(x,y,D) = \phi^a(x,y) + \phi^b(x,y)\frac{G(D)}{G(o)} + \phi^c(x,y)\, F_1(D) + \phi^d(x,y)\, F_2(D) \tag{33}$$

where ϕ^a, ϕ^b, ϕ^c, and ϕ^d are elastic solutions, corresponding to boundary tractions, thermal expansion, dimensional change $A_1(T)$, and dimensional change $A_2(T)$, respectively, and

$$F_1(D) = \frac{1}{G(o)} \int_o^D G(D - D')dD' \qquad (34)$$

and

$$F_2(D) = \frac{1}{G(o)} \int_o^D G(D - D')2D'dD' \qquad (35)$$

In the elastic solutions for the ϕ's, $E = G(o)$. From this consideration, therefore, the viscoelastic solution for an arbitrary plane-strain problem can be found immediately, provided a nonhomogeneous biharmonic solution is available for calculation of the elastic plane-strain problems with the indicated loadings. In the event that an analytical solution is not available a numerical method could be used.

The above correspondence can be seen from an examination of the solution of Eq. (25) and the boundary conditions Eqs. (30) and (31). The solution for ϕ can be divided into two parts, say ϕ_h and ϕ_p, where the particular solution

$$\phi_p(x,y,D) = - \frac{1}{2\pi(1-\mu)} \int_o^D G(D - D') \frac{\partial}{\partial D'} \left\{ \iint [\psi(D,T) + \alpha T] \log r' \, d\xi d\eta \right\} dD' \qquad (36)$$

in which

$$r' = [(x - \xi)^2 + (y - \eta)^2]^{1/2}$$

and where ξ and η are integration variables ranging over the cross section of the body. Consequently, ϕ_h satisfies

$$\nabla^4 \phi_h = 0 \qquad (37)$$

subject to the boundary conditions

$$\frac{\partial \phi_h}{\partial y} = \int T_x \, ds - \frac{\partial \phi_p}{\partial y} \qquad (38)$$

and

$$\frac{\partial \phi_h}{\partial x} = - \int T_y \, ds - \frac{\partial \phi_p}{\partial x} \qquad (39)$$

By substituting the expression given in Eq. (32) for $\psi(D,T)$ into Eq. (36), ϕ_p can be separated as

$$\phi_p(x,y,D) = \frac{G(D)}{G(o)} \phi_p^b(x,y) + F_1(D)\ \phi_p^c(x,y) + F_2(D)\ \phi_p^d(x,y) \qquad (40)$$

where

$$\phi_p^b(x,y) = -\frac{G(o)}{2\pi(1-\mu)} \iint \alpha T \log r' \, d\xi d\eta \qquad (41)$$

$$\phi_p^c(x,y) = -\frac{G(o)}{2\pi(1-\mu)} \iint A_1(T) \log r' \, d\xi d\eta \qquad (42)$$

$$\phi_p^d(x,y) = -\frac{G(o)}{2\pi(1-\mu)} \iint A_2(T) \log r' \, d\xi d\eta \qquad (43)$$

Moreover, the homogeneous solution ϕ_h is obtained from Eq. (37) and the boundary conditions Eqs. (38) and (39) which are of the same form as for the elastic problem.

The stress function is related to the boundary traction by Eqs. (38) and (39). Hence, the homogeneous solution can be written as

$$\phi_h(x,y,D) = \phi_h^a(x,y) + \frac{G(D)}{G(o)} \phi_h^b(x,y) + F_1(D)\ \phi_h^c(x,y) + F_2(D)\ \phi_h^d(x,y) \qquad (44)$$

where $\phi_h^a(x,y)$ is due to the boundary traction; and $F_1(D)$ and $F_2(D)$ are the same functions used in Eq. (40). Therefore, combining Eqs. (40) and (44) gives

$$\phi(x,y,D) = \phi^a(x,y) + \frac{G(D)}{G(o)} \phi^b(x,y) + F_1(D)\ \phi^c(x,y) + F_2(D)\ \phi^d(x,y) \qquad (45)$$

where $\phi(x,y) = \phi_h(x,y) + \phi_p(x,y)$.

Thus, four elastic solutions ϕ^a, ϕ^b, ϕ^c, and ϕ^d will be enough to describe the thermo-viscoelastic solution for a plane-strain problem with boundary tractions, thermal gradients, and neutron-induced dimensional changes of the form given by Eq. (32) provided that the accumulated neutron dose D is a function only of time and not of position. For problems such as the design studies presented below, in which the variation of dose across the cross section is small relative to the average, assuming a uniform dose distribution equal to the average yields results which are satisfactory for design purposes.

Application to MSBR Core Design Studies

As a specific example for application of the viscoelastic representation of graphite behavior under fast neutron exposure, a design study was conducted for graphite elements in the core of a molten salt breeder reactor [1]. Typically, these elements are long rods with a central hole and are constructed of a graphite that is essentially isotropic. The exact shape of the cross section has not been specified, but can be represented as circular for purposes of preliminary studies. Molten salt passes through the central hole and along the outer surface. The thickness of the wall is minimal so that any given cross section of the element will experience a nearly uniform fast neutron flux. The flux distribution along the length of the rod varies approximately as $\sin(\pi Z/L)$, where L is the length of the rod. The internal heat generation within the graphite is roughly uniform and is conducted radially to the molten salt. The analysis of these elements considers the graphite to be isotropic.

The specific problems solved are concentric circular cylinders with inner radius a, outer radius b, length L, and b/a ratio of 6.667. To illustrate the influence of the geometric size of the elements on their lifetimes, several values of b ranging from 4 cm to 6 cm were chosen. As shown in [1] these cylinders are surrounded by molten salt whose temperature is

$$T_s(°C) = 625 - 75 \cos\left(\pi \frac{Z}{L} \right) \tag{46}$$

The temperature-dependent thermal conductivity of the graphite is given by

$$\kappa_a = 0.358 \left[\frac{T(°K)}{773}\right]^{-0.7} \text{watts/cm-°C} \tag{47}$$

as shown in Fig. 3. The heat transfer coefficient of the hydraulic film is of the form

$$H = a^{-0.2} \, [1.444 \times 10^{-3} \, T(°C) - 0.228] \text{ watts-cm}^{0.2}/\text{cm}^2\text{-°C} \tag{48}$$

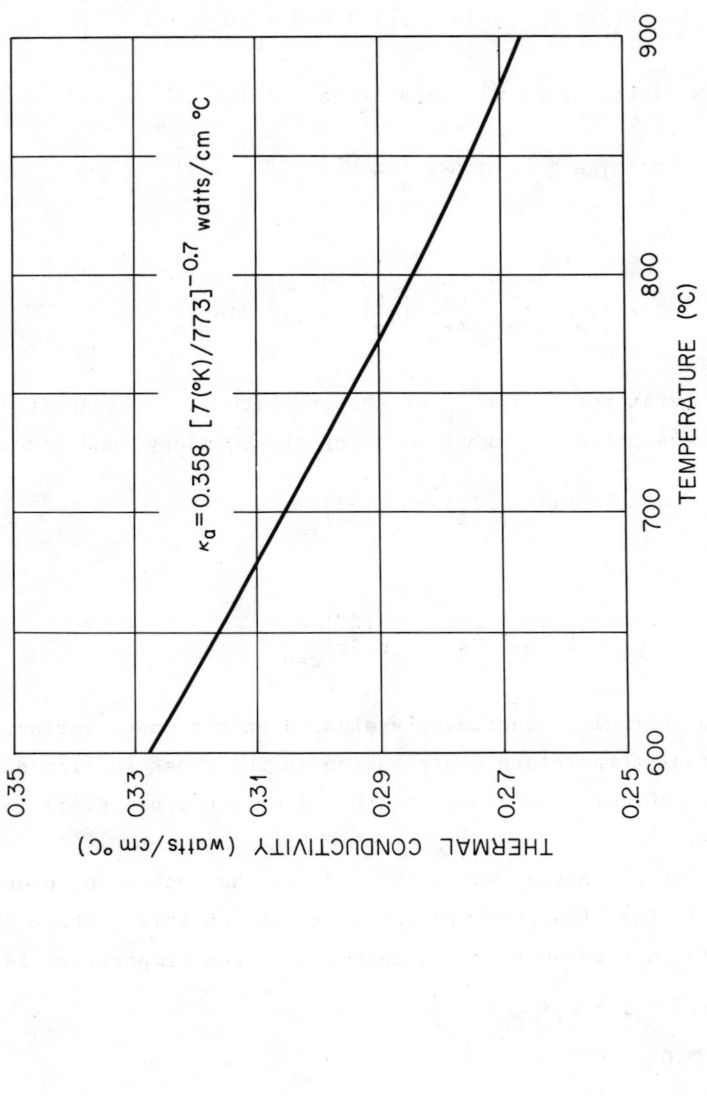

Fig. 3. Thermal Conductivity as a Function of Temperature.

The internal heat generation rate resulting from both prompt and delayed γ rays is given by

$$Q = 1.2 + 9.0 \sin\left(\pi \frac{Z}{L}\right) \text{ watts/cm}^3 \tag{49}$$

The axial distribution of the fast neutron flux is

$$\Theta(E > 50 \text{ kev}) = \Theta_{max} \sin\left(\pi \frac{Z}{L}\right) = 4.5 \times 10^{14} \sin\left(\pi \frac{Z}{L}\right) \tag{50}$$

The temperature distribution within a cross section of the cylinder is

$$T(°C) = T_a - C \log \frac{r}{a} - \frac{Qa^2}{4\kappa_a}\left[\left(\frac{r}{a}\right)^2 - 1\right] \tag{51}$$

where

$$C = \left\{T_a - T_b - \frac{Qa^2}{4\kappa_a}\left[\left(\frac{b}{a}\right)^2 - 1\right]\right\} / \log \frac{b}{a} \tag{52}$$

The surface temperatures T_a and T_b of the graphite at the graphite-salt interfaces are evaluated through the use of the boundary conditions:

$$H(T_a - T_s) = \kappa_a \left(\frac{dT}{dr}\right)_{r=a} \tag{53}$$

and

$$H(T_b - T_s) = \kappa_a \left(\frac{dT}{dr}\right)_{r=b} \tag{54}$$

where κ_a is the thermal conductivity evaluated at the inner surface (r=a). The radial temperature distribution in the cross section defined by Z/L = 0.60 for a cylinder with b = 5 cm and b/a = 6.667 is shown in Fig. 4.

The coefficient of thermal expansion and all the mechanical properties appearing in Eqs. (14) through (19), except the steady-state creep coefficient K(T), are taken to be independent of the temperature level.

$$E = 1.7 \times 10^6 \text{ psi}$$

$$A_o = 2.0 \times 10^{-22} \text{ neut}^{-1}\text{-cm}^2$$

$$\mu = 0.27$$

$$K(T) = (5.3 - 1.45 \times 10^{-2}T + 1.4 \times 10^{-5}T^2) \times 10^{-5}$$
$$\text{for } 550°C < T < 800°C$$

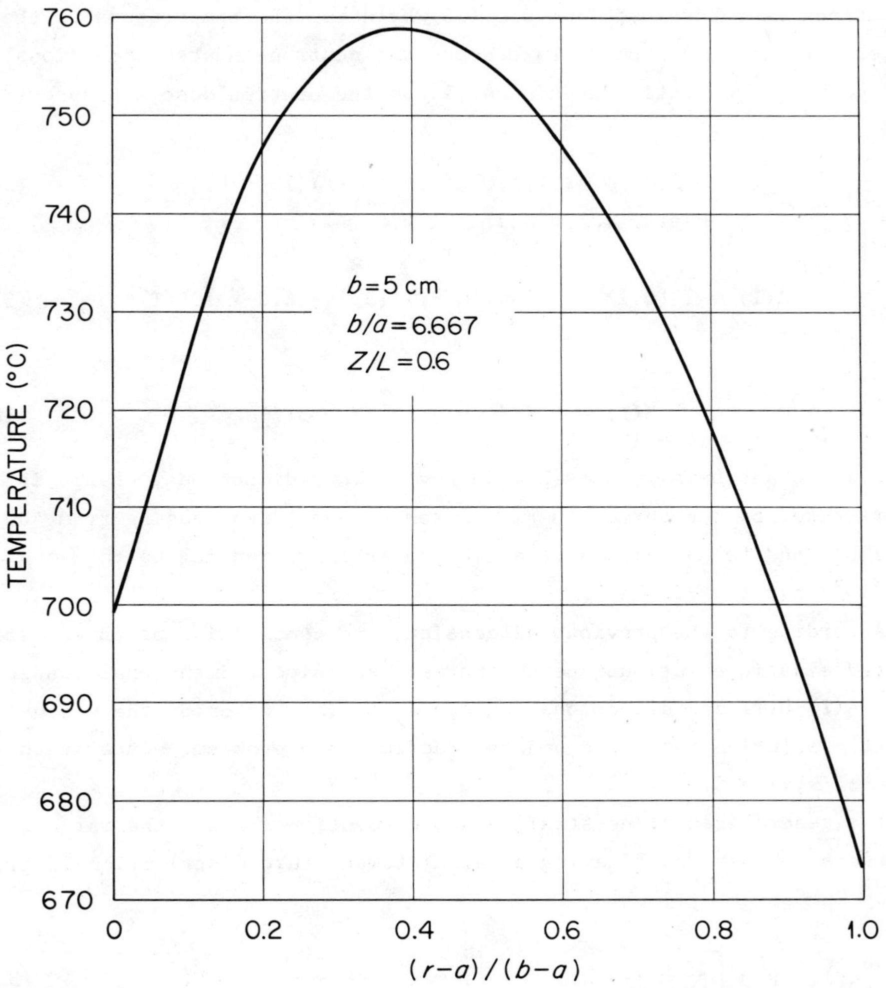

Fig. 4. Radial Temperature Profile.

$$\alpha = 6.20 \times 10^{-6}\ {}^\circ C^{-1} \tag{55}$$

The value of the steady-state creep coefficient used in subsequent calculations is determined from Eq. (55) by using the temperature of the inner surface. The temperature-dependent neutron-induced dimensional change has a quadratic dependence [1] on the neutron dose as expressed by

$$\psi(D,T) = A(T)[(10^{-22}D)^2 + B(T)(10^{-22}D)] \tag{56}$$

where

$$A(T) = \frac{1}{3}(0.11 - 7.0 \times 10^{-5}T)/(5.7 - 6.0 \times 10^{-3}T)^2 \tag{57}$$

and

$$B(T) = 2 \times (6.0 \times 10^{-3}T - 5.7) \tag{58}$$

T is in °C and D is in nvt (E > 50 kev). This dimensional change is represented by the curves in Fig. 5 for temperatures ranging from 400 to 750°C and for an accumulated neutron exposure ranging up to 3×10^{22} nvt (E > 50 kev).

According to the previous discussion, the combination of three associated elastic solutions due to thermal expansion, dimensional change $A_1 = A(T)\cdot B(T)$ and dimensional change $A_2 = A(T)$, describe the viscoelastic solution for the boundary traction free problem, since in this case $\phi^a(x,y) = 0$.

The generalized plane-strain elastic solution for the thermal stresses in a cylinder having a radial temperature distribution is given by Timoshenko [9] as

$$\sigma_r^b(r) = \frac{E}{1-\mu}\left[\frac{1}{b^2 - a^2}\left(1 - \frac{a^2}{r^2}\right)\cdot\int_a^b \alpha T(\xi)\xi d\xi - \frac{1}{r^2}\int_a^r \alpha T(\xi)\xi d\xi\right] \tag{59}$$

$$\sigma_\theta^b(r) = \frac{E}{1-\mu}\left[\frac{1}{b^2 - a^2}\left(1 + \frac{a^2}{r^2}\right)\int_a^b \alpha T(\xi)\xi d\xi + \frac{1}{r^2}\int_a^r \alpha T(\xi)\xi d\xi - \alpha T\right] \tag{60}$$

$$\sigma_z^b(r) = \frac{E}{1-\mu}\left[\frac{2}{b^2 - a^2}\int_a^b \alpha T(\xi)\xi d\xi - \alpha T\right] \tag{61}$$

where the superscript b is used to denote the elastic thermal stress as used before. Similarly, superscripts c and d are used to designate the

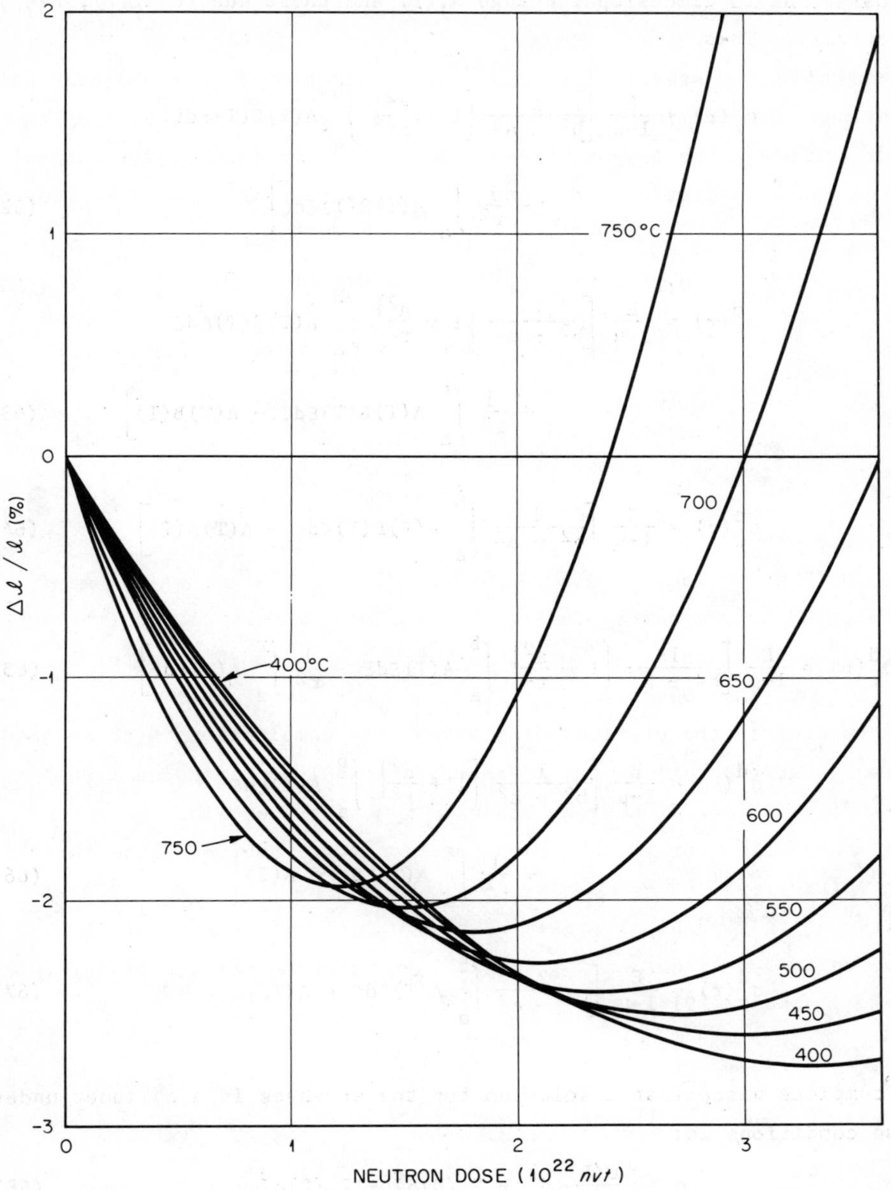

Fig. 5. Neutron-Induced Dimensional Changes in Graphite at Various Temperatures.

stresses due to dimensional change $A_1(T)$ and those due to $A_2(T)$, respectively. Thus

$$\sigma_r^c(r) = \frac{E}{1-\mu}\left[\frac{1}{b^2 - a^2}\left(1 - \frac{a^2}{r^2}\right)\int_a^b A(T)B(T)\xi d\xi - \frac{1}{r^2}\int_a^r A(T)B(T)\xi d\xi\right] \quad (62)$$

$$\sigma_\theta^c(r) = \frac{E}{1-\mu}\left[\frac{1}{b^2 - a^2}\left(1 + \frac{a^2}{r^2}\right)\int_a^b A(T)B(T)\xi d\xi + \frac{1}{r^2}\int_a^r A(T)B(T)\xi d\xi - A(T)B(T)\right] \quad (63)$$

$$\sigma_z^c(r) = \frac{E}{1-\mu}\left[\frac{2}{b^2 - a^2}\int_a^b A(T)B(T)\xi d\xi - A(T)B(T)\right] \quad (64)$$

and

$$\sigma_r^d(r) = \frac{E}{1-\mu}\left[\frac{1}{b^2 - a^2}\left(1 - \frac{a^2}{r^2}\right)\int_a^b A(T)\xi d\xi - \frac{1}{r^2}\int_a^r A(T)\xi d\xi\right] \quad (65)$$

$$\sigma_\theta^d(r) = \frac{E}{1-\mu}\left[\frac{1}{b^2 - a^2}\left(1 + \frac{a^2}{r^2}\right)\int_a^b A(T)\xi d\xi + \frac{1}{r^2}\int_a^r A(T)\xi d\xi - A(T)\right] \quad (66)$$

$$\sigma_z^d(r) = \frac{E}{1-\mu}\left[\frac{2}{b^2 - a^2}\int_a^b A(T)\xi d\xi - A(T)\right] \quad (67)$$

The complete viscoelastic solution for the stresses in a cylinder under these conditions is:

$$\sigma_r = \frac{G(D)}{G(o)}\sigma_r^b + F_1(D)\sigma_r^c + F_2(D)\sigma_r^d \quad (68)$$

$$\sigma_\theta = \frac{G(D)}{G(o)}\sigma_\theta^b + F_1(D)\sigma_\theta^c + F_2(D)\sigma_\theta^d \quad (69)$$

$$\sigma_z = \frac{G(D)}{G(o)}\sigma_z^b + F_1(D)\sigma_z^c + F_2(D)\sigma_z^d \quad (70)$$

where $F_1(D)$ and $F_2(D)$ are defined by Eqs. (34) and (35). Since the displacements in an elastic material are independent of the elastic modulus, the viscoelastic radial displacement is the same as that given by the elastic solution [9], that is,

$$u_r(r,D) = \frac{1+\mu}{1-\mu}\left\{\frac{1}{r}\int_a^r [\psi(D,T) + \alpha T]\xi d\xi\right.$$

$$\left. + \left[\frac{1-3\mu}{1+\mu}\frac{r}{b^2-a^2} + \frac{1}{b^2-a^2}\frac{a^2}{r}\right]\int_a^b [\psi(D,T) + \alpha T]\xi d\xi\right\}. \quad (71)$$

Stress Solution for Large Dose

It is shown below that, for small EK/A_o, as the neutron dose becomes large

$$F_1(D) \to \text{constant} \quad (72)$$

and

$$F_2(D) \to \frac{2}{EK\left(1 + \frac{1}{3}\frac{EK}{1.5A_o}\right)} D \quad (73)$$

Then by using Eqs. (72) and (73) with Eq. (70), the rate of change of σ_z is seen to approach a constant value as D becomes large. This asymptotic value is given by

$$\frac{\partial\sigma_z}{\partial D} \simeq \frac{2}{EK\left(1 + \frac{1}{3}\frac{EK}{1.5A_o}\right)}\frac{E}{1-\mu}\left[\frac{2}{b^2-a^2}\int_a^b A(T)\xi d\xi - A(T)\right] \quad (74)$$

These results can be shown by observing from Eqs. (27) and (34) that $F_1(D)$ tends to a constant as D goes to ∞, and by using the following integral in Eq. (35),

$$\int_0^D e^{k_1(D-D')} D'dD' = -\frac{1}{k_1}\left[D - \int_0^D e^{k_1(D-D')} dD'\right] \quad (75)$$

The second term on the right-hand side of Eq. (75) tends to a constant as $D \to \infty$ by the same reasoning as used for $F_1(D)$. Therefore we obtain, for large D,

$$F_2(D) \simeq \frac{2}{\sqrt{(EK + 1.5A_o)^2 - 4EKA_o}} \left[-\left(1 + \frac{A_o}{k_1}\right) + \left(1 + \frac{A_o}{k_2}\right)\right] D$$

which is simplified by using Eqs. (28) and (29) to give

$$F_2(D) = \frac{2A_o}{k_1 k_2} D \tag{76}$$

But for small EK/A_o, expanding the square root,

$$k_1 = -0.5 \times 1.5A_o \left\{1 + \frac{EK}{1.5A_o} + \left[\left(1 + \frac{EK}{1.5A_o}\right)^2 - \frac{4EK}{(1.5)^2A_o}\right]^{1/2}\right\}$$

$$\simeq -0.5 \times 1.5A_o \left[1 + \frac{EK}{1.5A_o} - \left(1 - \frac{1}{2}\frac{EK}{(1.5)^2A_o}\right)\right]$$

or

$$k_1 = -0.5 \times 1.5A_o \left(\frac{4}{3}\frac{EK}{1.5A_o}\right) \tag{77}$$

and

$$k_2 = -0.5 \times 1.5A_o \times 2\left(1 + \frac{1}{3}\frac{EK}{1.5A_o}\right) \tag{78}$$

Therefore Eq. (73) follows, and the desired result Eq. (74) is obtained.

Numerical Results

The stresses and strains were determined from the generalized plane-strain solutions for cylinders subject to the conditions which exist on the cross sections defined by Z/L ranging from 0.20 to 0.80 in increments of 0.10. As will be shown later, the conditions which exist on cross sections near Z/L = 0.60 give rise to the minimum lifetime in the cylinder. Therefore, many of the numerical results displayed subsequently in this paper correspond to the conditions which exist on the cross section defined by Z/L = 0.60.

The strains in each cylinder are identical to those of the elastic solution which corresponds to the prescribed temperature distribution and neutron-induced dimensional changes. The value of the circumferential strain ε_θ at the outer boundary is the same as that of the longitudinal strain ε_z, and the variation of this value with accumulated dose up to 3×10^{22} nvt (E > 50 kev) is shown in Fig. 6.

The stresses were calculated with the aid of a digital computer by evaluating Eqs. (68) through (70). For the conditions investigated the axial stress σ_z at the surface r=b initially changes very rapidly, but before a dose of 10^{22} nvt is reached (about 3×10^{21} nvt) this stress has developed a linear dependence on dose. Figure 7 shows a typical plot of σ_z as a function of dose and specifically corresponds to r = b = 5.0 cm, Z/L = 0.60, and b/a = 6.667. Figure 8 shows the stress σ_z existing at the outer surfaces of the three cylinders studied as functions of Z/L when D = 10^{22} nvt. The constant stress rates $d\sigma_z/dD$ which exist for D > 10^{22} nvt, are shown in Fig. 9 for these cylinders, also as functions of axial position. Thus, the axial stress present for a dose greater than 10^{22} nvt can be calculated from Figs. 8 and 9 by using the following relation:

$$\sigma_z = \sigma_z\Big]_{D = 10^{22}} + \frac{d\sigma_z}{dD}(D - 10^{22}) \tag{79}$$

This procedure also gives the corresponding value of σ_θ, since $\sigma_\theta = \sigma_z$ on the surface r = b.

Lifetime Conditions

The design lifetimes of the cylinders studied were evaluated in terms of each of two criteria defined for design purposes. The first criterion is called the volumetric distortion criterion and determines the dose and consequently the time required for the volumetric dilatation, $\varepsilon_r + \varepsilon_\theta + \varepsilon_z$, when integrated over the cross section, to return to zero. The second criterion is called the axial strain criterion and closely approximates the first by determining the dose required for the axial strain ε_z to return to zero on the surface r = b. The second criterion has additional physical significance when a thin layer of pyrolytic carbon coating is applied to the outer surface of the cylinder, since small cracks will develop in the coating when ε_z becomes greater than zero. Since the neutron flux varies with axial position, each criterion gives lifetime predictions which also vary with axial position.

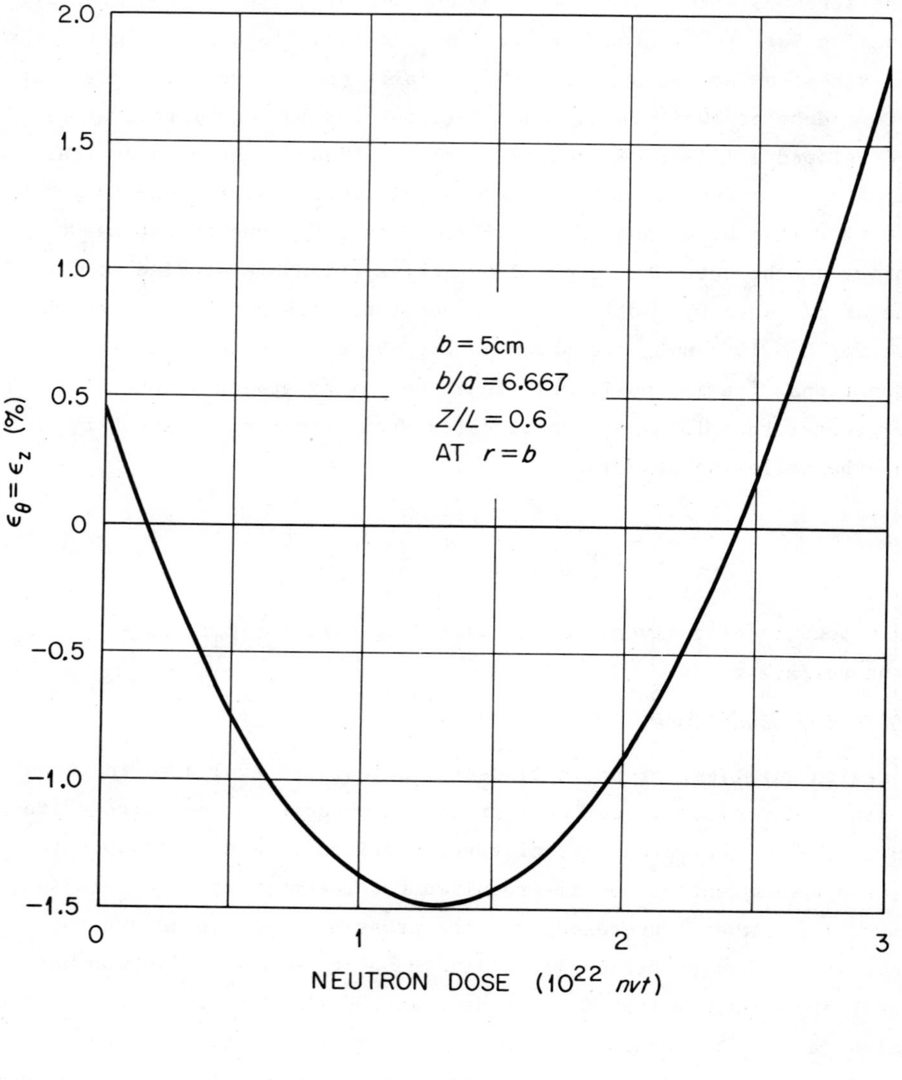

Fig. 6. Circumferential Strain at Outside Surface as a Function of Fluence Level.

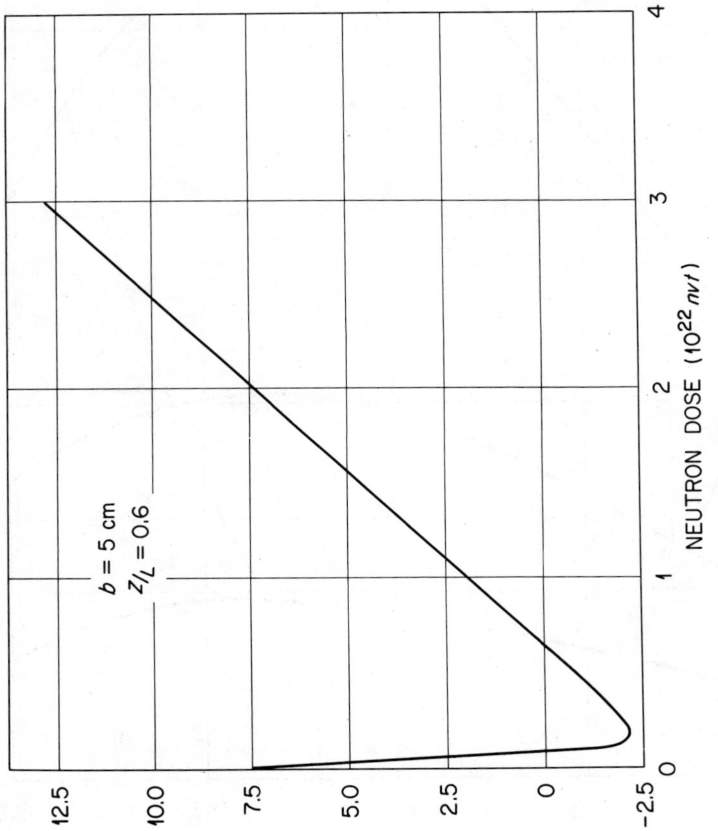

Fig. 7. Axial Stress at the Outer Surface as a Function of Fluence Level.

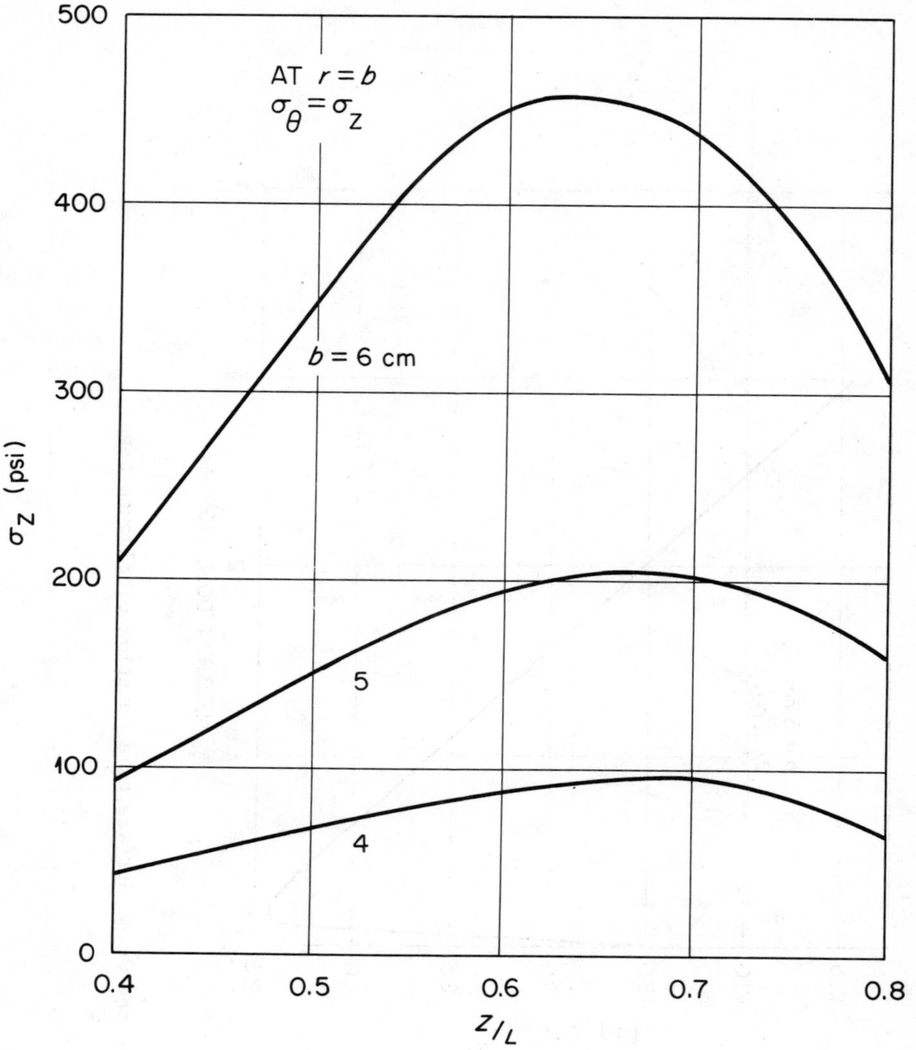

Fig. 8. Axial Stress at the Outer Surface as a Function of Axial Position for a Fluence of D = 10^{22} nvt (E > 50 kev).

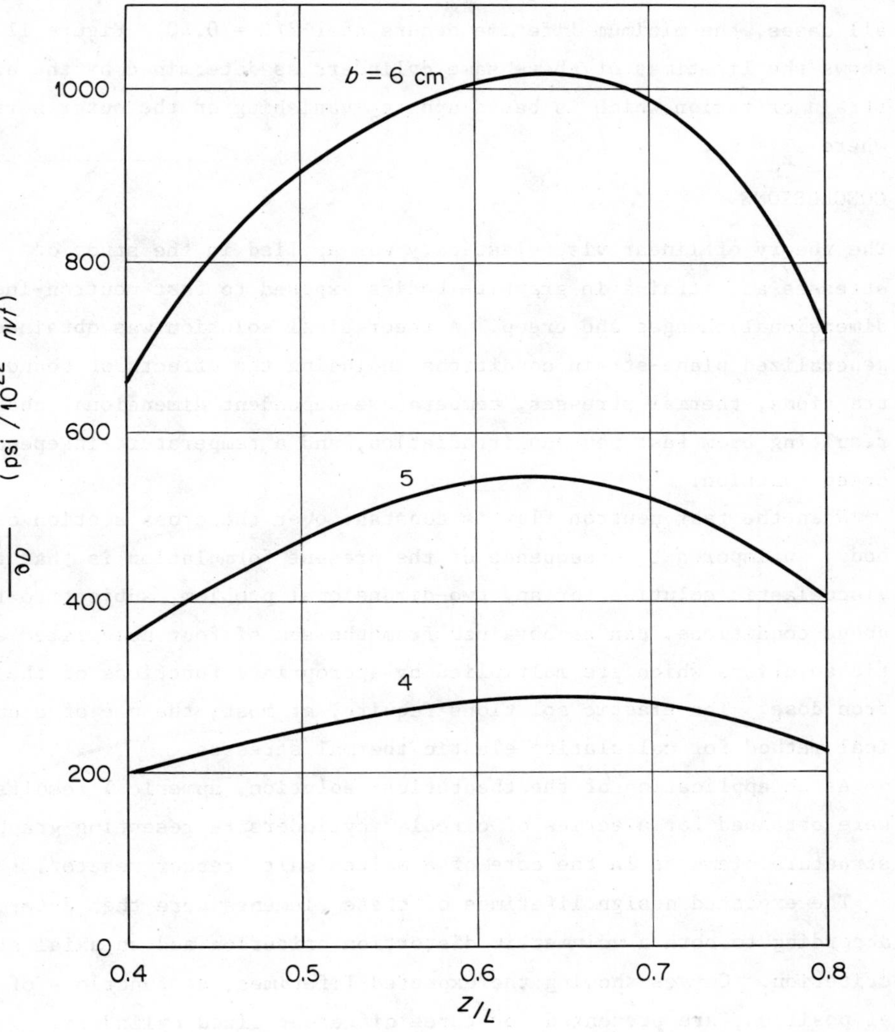

Fig. 9. Constant Axial Stress Rate as a Function of Axial Position for Fluence Levels Above D = 10^{22} nvt (E > 50 kev).

Figure 10 shows the lifetimes, in months, at various axial positions calculated on the basis of the volumetric distortion criterion for cylinders of outer radii 4, 5, and 6 cm and a (b/a) ratio of 6.667. In all cases, the minimum lifetime occurs near Z/L = 0.60. Figure 11 shows the lifetimes of these same cylinders as determined by the axial strain criterion which is based upon ε_z vanishing on the outer surface, where $\varepsilon_z = \varepsilon_\theta$.

CONCLUSIONS

The theory of linear viscoelasticity was applied in the study of stresses and strains in graphite bodies exposed to fast neutron-induced dimensional changes and creep. A theoretical solution was obtained for generalized plane-strain conditions including the effects of boundary tractions, thermal stresses, temperature-dependent dimensional changes resulting from fast neutron irradiation, and a temperature-independent creep function.

When the fast neutron flux is constant over the cross section of the body, an important consequence of the present formulation is that the viscoelastic solution for any two-dimensional problem, subject to the above conditions, can be obtained from the sum of four associated elastic solutions which are multiplied by appropriate functions of the neutron dose. The elastic solutions require, at most, the use of a numerical method for calculating elastic thermal stresses.

As an application of the theoretical solution, numerical results were obtained for a series of circular cylinders representing graphite structure elements in the core of a molten salt breeder reactor.

The expected design lifetimes of these elements were then determined according to both a volumetric distortion criterion and an axial strain criterion. Curves showing the expected lifetimes, as functions of axial position, are presented for three different sized cylinders.

ACKNOWLEDGEMENTS

The authors express their appreciation to B. L. Greenstreet for his supervision of this work and for many helpful suggestions and discussions. Appreciation is also extended to W. P. Eatherly for supplying the technical liaison between this work and the Oak Ridge National Laboratory Molten Salt Breeder Reactor Program.

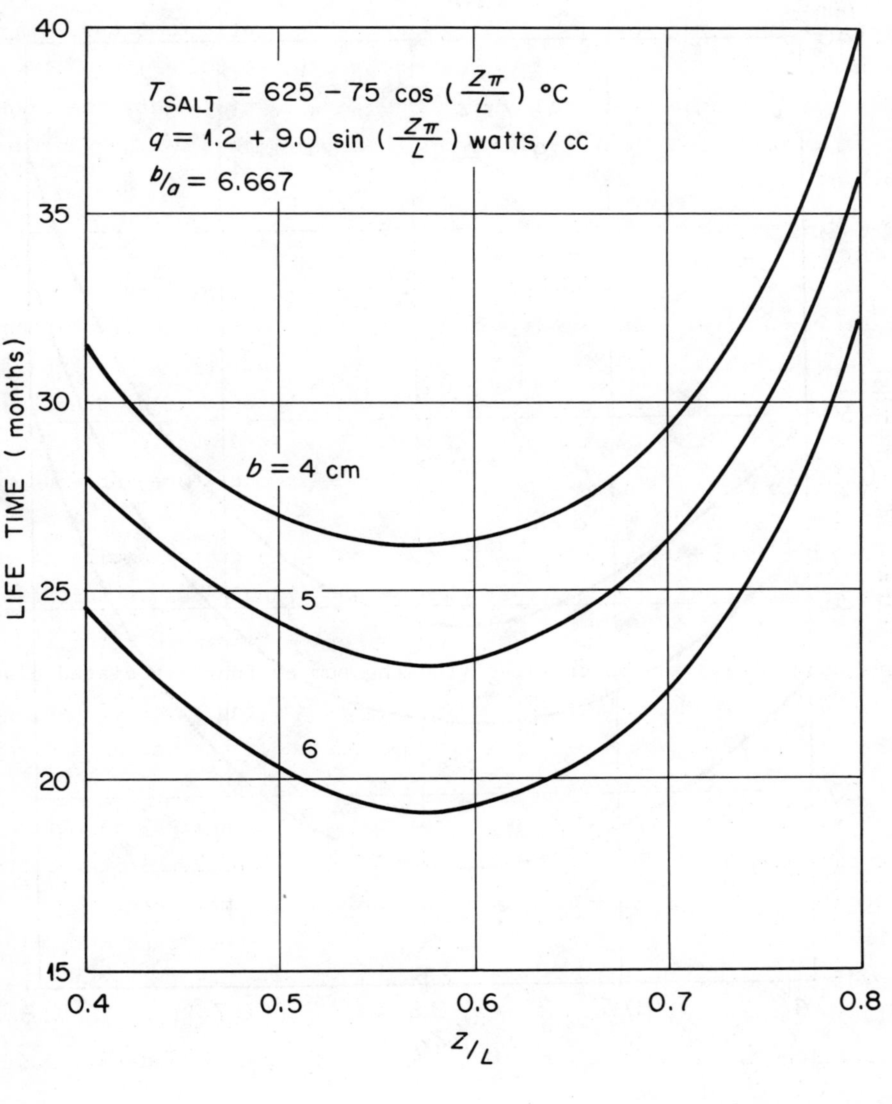

Fig. 10. Lifetimes as Functions of Axial Position According to the Volumetric Distortion Criterion.

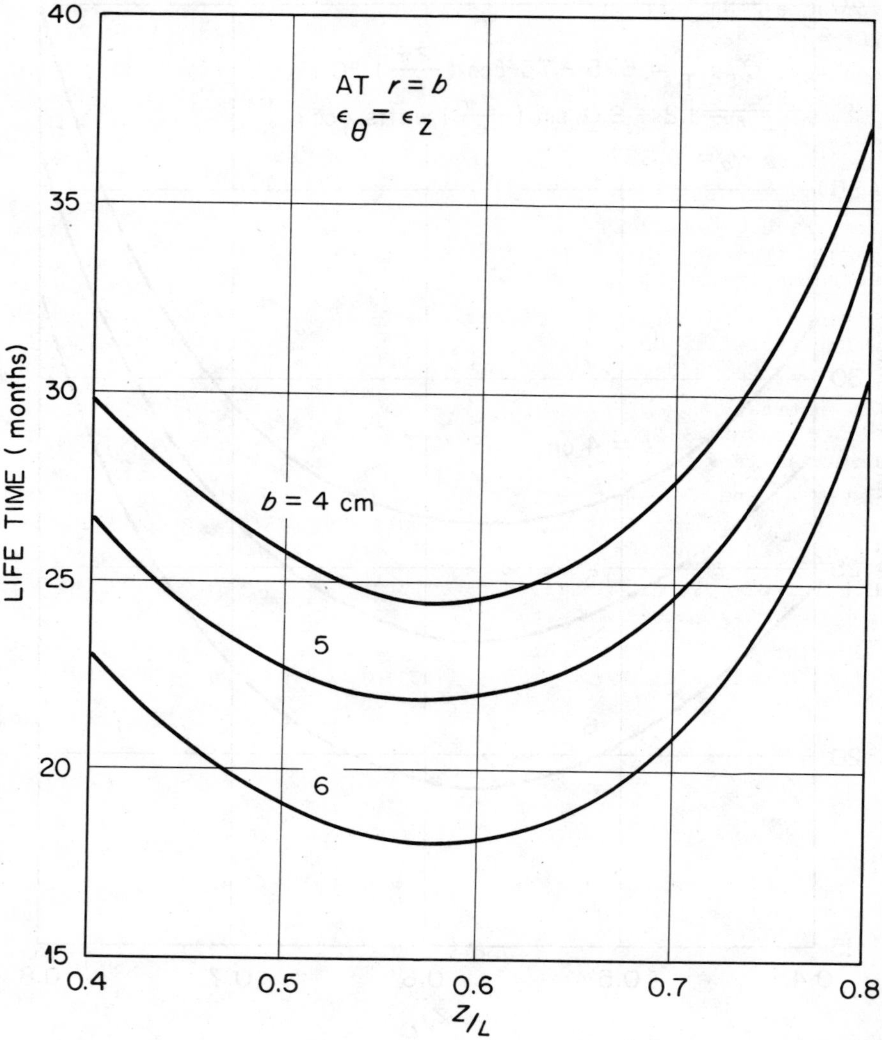

Fig. 11. Lifetimes as Functions of Axial Position According to the Axial Strain Criterion.

REFERENCES

1. Kastens, et al., "Graphite Behavior and Its Effects on MSBR Performance," Nuclear Engineering and Design, Vol. 9, No. 2, 1969, pp. 157-195.

2. Kennedy, C. R., "Creep of Graphite Under Irradiation," GCRP Semiannual Progress Report for Period Ending Sept. 30, 1965, USAEC Report ORNL-3885, Oak Ridge National Laboratory, 1965, pp. 198-203.

3. Lee, E. H., "Stress Analysis in Viscoelastic Bodies," Quarterly of Applied Mathematics, Vol. 13, 1955, pp. 183-190.

4. Lee, E. H., "Viscoelastic Stress Analysis," First Symposium on Naval Structural Mechanics, Edited by J. N. Goodier and N. J. Hoff, Pergamon Press, Ltd., New York, 1960, pp. 456-482.

5. Simmons, J. H. W., Atomic Energy Research Establishment, Research Group, Harwell, United Kingdom, personal communication to C. R. Kennedy, Oak Ridge National Laboratory, 1969.

6. Greenstreet, W. L., Smith, J. E., Yahr, G. T. and Valachovic, R. S., "The Mechanical Behavior of Artificial Graphites as Portrayed by Uniaxial Tests," Carbon, 8 (1970) (to be published).

7. Muki, R. and Sternberg, Eli, "On Transient Thermal Stress in Viscoelastic Materials with Temperature-dependent Properties," Journal of Applied Mechanics, Vol. 28, 1961, pp. 193-207.

8. Sokolnikoff, I. S., Mathematical Theory of Elasticity, McGraw-Hill Book Company, New York, 1956.

9. Timoshenko, S. and Goodier, J. N., Theory of Elasticity, 2nd edition, McGraw-Hill Book Company, New York, 1951, pp. 433-437.

S H E L L S

ON THE TRANSIENT RESPONSE OF A CLOSED SPHERICAL SHELL TO A LOCAL RADIAL IMPULSE

Ali E. Engin
The University of Michigan

ABSTRACT

This investigation is concerned with determination of the transient response of a closed spherical shell subjected to a local, radial and axisymmetric impulse. Prior to application of the impulse the shell is assumed to be at rest with respect to an inertial coordinate system. Analysis is based on linear shell theory which includes both membrane and bending effects of the shell for the proper description of the wave propagation. Midsurface normal stresses, stress and moment resultants are plotted as a function of the polar angle at various times. The paper is concluded with a discussion of the locations of the shell susceptible to severe damage on the basis of numerical results obtained from a data suitable for a theoretical model representing the human skull.

LIST OF NOTATIONS

A_o, A_{nm}	Arbitrary constants
D	Flexural rigidity, $Eh^3/12(1-\nu^2)$
E	Young's modulus
K	Extensional rigidity, $Eh/(1-\nu^2)$
M_ϕ, M_θ	Moment resultants
M_z	Linear momentum along polar axis
N_ϕ, N_θ	Stress resultants
$P_n(\cos\phi)$	Legendre polynomials of the first kind
$P_n'(\cos\theta)$	Associated Legendre polynomials of the first kind and first order

V_z	Velocity imparted to the center of mass
a	Radius of spherical shell
a_n	Coefficients of Legendre polynomial expansion of ζ
b_n	Coefficients of associated Legendre polynomial expansion of Ψ
c_s	Wave speed, $[E/\rho_s(1-\nu^2)]^{1/2}$
h	Shell thickness
r,ϕ,θ	Spherical coordinates
t	Time
u,w	Meridional and radial displacement components of the shell midsurface
α^2	Thickness parameter, $h^2/12a^2$
α_{nm}	Phase angles
δ_{nm}	Amplitude ratios
$\varepsilon_\phi,\varepsilon_\theta$	Midsurface strains
$\varepsilon_\phi^{(z)}\varepsilon_\theta^{(z)}$	z-surface strains
ζ,Ψ	Nondimensional radial and meridional displacement components of the shell midsurface
$\kappa_\phi,\kappa_\theta$	Midsurface curvatures
λ_n	$n(n+1)$
ν	Poisson's ratio
ρ_s	Mass density of shell material
$\sigma_\phi,\sigma_\theta$	Normal stresses for the midsurface
$\sigma_\phi^{(z)},\sigma_\theta^{(z)}$	Normal stresses for the z-surface
τ	Nondimensional time, c_st/a
Ω	Nondimensional frequency, $\omega a/c_s$
ω	Angular frequency

INTRODUCTION

The problem being considered is that of the transient response characteristics of a closed spherical shell subjected to a local, radial and impulsive load. Two considerations led to the analysis of such a problem. First, the complete determination of the transient response of a closed spherical shell subjected to local impulsive load is a point of interest in theoretical mechanics due to the transient nature of the problem. Secondly, it is hoped that a closed spherical shell will serve as a simple theoretical model representing the human skull when subjected to impulsive external loads.

Studies on the dynamic analysis of various elastic shells are numerous, but only a few representative ones will be mentioned here. Dynamic analysis of shells dates back as early as 1882 when Lamb [1] used an extensional formulation in the study of closed spherical shells. A few years later a famous dispute took place between Rayleigh [2] and Love [3] in an endeavor to construct a theory for the vibration of bells. Rayleigh's treatment was inextensional, i.e. he assumed that no stretching of the midsurface of the shell takes place during deformation, whereas Love [4] included both flexural and extensional effects. Love's formulation of the problem has become the classical bending theory of shells now known as Love's first approximation. Based on the extensional theory of Love, Silbiger [5] studied free and forced oscillations of spherical shells and Baker [6] obtained some numerical results. Naghdi and Kalnins [7], using classical bending theory, investigated axisymmetric as well as asymmetric vibrations of thin spherical shells and obtained some numerical results for the natural frequencies and for mode shapes. Kalnins [8], using linear bending theory, made vibration analyses of spherical shells closed at one pole and open at other and determined natural frequencies and mode shapes for opening angles ranging from shallow to closed shells. He also explained certain paradoxical situations which occurred at the lower branch of Love's frequency spectrum in terms of the effects of bending. Klein [9] applied the finite element approach to the dynamic analysis of multilayer shells with special emphasis on the computational aspects and obtained a solution for a shallow spherical cap under a time dependent axisymmetric pressure load. Medick [10], within the framework of modified shell theory, obtained the initial response of a restricted class of thin shells which are essentially spherical and shallow in the neighborhood of loading. Based on the linear classical shell theory Long [11] investigated the effect of radial preload on the natural frequencies of thin closed spherical shells and found that pure radial and torsional modes are virtually independent of the radial preload. Recently, McIvor and Sonstegard [12] studied the axisymmetric response of a closed spherical shell to a nearly uniform radial impulse and the associated stability problem of the breathing mode.

For the present investigation the material of the closed spherical shell is considered to be homogenous and isotropic. The loading pattern is taken to be local, radial, impulsive and axisymmetric. Since the load is applied locally, linear shell theory which includes membrane and bending effects of the shell is used for the proper description of the wave propagation. The problem is treated as an initial value problem and appropriate initial conditions are discussed in detail. The solutions thus obtained are in the form of infinite series.

Equations of Motion and their Solutions

The equations of motion of a closed spherical shell in vacuo can be derived by use of Hamilton's principle as it was done in [13] for the closed fluid-filled spherical shell. The nondimensionalized form of these equations for small and axisymmetric oscillations in the absence of fluid are:

$$\alpha^2 \left[\frac{\partial^2\Psi}{\partial\phi^2} + \cot\phi \frac{\partial\Psi}{\partial\phi} - (\nu+\cot^2\phi)\Psi - \frac{\partial^3\zeta}{\partial\phi^3} - \cot\phi \frac{\partial^2\zeta}{\partial\phi^2} + (\nu+\cot^2\phi) \frac{\partial\zeta}{\partial\phi} \right]$$

$$+ \frac{\partial^2\Psi}{\partial\phi^2} + \cot\phi \frac{\partial\Psi}{\partial\phi} - (\nu+\cot^2\phi)\Psi + (1+\nu) \frac{\partial\zeta}{\partial\phi} - \frac{\partial^2\Psi}{\partial\tau^2} = 0 \tag{1}$$

and

$$\alpha^2 \left[\frac{\partial^3\Psi}{\partial\phi^3} + 2\cot\phi \frac{\partial^2\Psi}{\partial\phi^2} - (1+\nu+\cot^2\phi) \frac{\partial\Psi}{\partial\phi} + (\cot^2\phi-\nu+2)\Psi\cot\phi \right.$$

$$\left. - \frac{\partial^4\zeta}{\partial\phi^4} - 2\cot\phi \frac{\partial^3\zeta}{\partial\phi^3} + (1+\nu+\cot^2\phi) \frac{\partial^2\zeta}{\partial\phi^2} - (2-\nu+\cot^2\phi)\cot\phi \frac{\partial\zeta}{\partial\phi} \right]$$

$$- (1+\nu) \left(\frac{\partial\Psi}{\partial\phi} + \Psi\cot\phi + 2\zeta\right) - \frac{\partial^2\zeta}{\partial\tau^2} = 0 \tag{2}$$

In Eqs. (1) and (2), the nondimensional parameters are defined as

$$\Psi = u/a, \quad \zeta = w/a, \quad \tau = (c_s/a)t, \quad \alpha^2 = h^2/12a^2$$

where u and w are the meridional and the radial displacements of the shell midsurface respectively, and $c_s = [E/\rho_s(1-\nu^2)]^{1/2}$ is the apparent wave speed[1] around the shell; α^2 is a thickness parameter for the

1. The wave speed c_s corresponds to the speed of compressional waves in an infinite plate for the limiting case of symmetrical waves of long wavelength.

shell and if it is set equal to zero in Eqs. (1) and (2), equations of motion reduce to those obtainable by the membrane theory alone.

Consider the following series expansions for the nondimensional radial and the meridional displacements of the shell midsurface:

$$\zeta(\phi,\tau) = \sum_{n=0}^{\infty} a_n(\tau)\ P_n(\cos\phi) \tag{3a}$$

and

$$\Psi(\phi,\tau) = \sum_{n=1}^{\infty} b_n(\tau)\ P_n'(\cos\phi) \tag{3b}$$

where $P_n(\cos\phi)$ are Legendre polynomials of the first kind and $P_n'(\cos\phi)$ are associated Legendre polynomials of the first order, first kind. Since the second solutions of the Legendre equations are singular at the poles they are not included in the expansions of ζ and Ψ.

It can be shown that substitution of Eqs. (3a) and (3b) into Eqs. (1) and (2) and the repeated utilization of the differential equations satisfied by P_n and P_n', yields the following system of equations for the determination of $a_n(\tau)$ and $b_n(\tau)$:

for n = 0 $$\frac{d^2a_o}{d\tau^2} + 2(1+\nu)a_o = 0 \tag{4}$$

for $n \geq 1$:

$$\frac{d^2b_n(\tau)}{d\tau^2} + (1-\nu-\lambda_n)\ (1+\alpha^2)b_n(\tau) - [1+\nu-\alpha^2(1-\nu-\lambda_n)]a_n(\tau) = 0, \tag{5}$$

and

$$\frac{d^2a_n(\tau)}{d\tau^2} + \left\{2(1+\nu) + \alpha^2[\lambda_n^2-\lambda_n(1-\nu)]\right\} a_n(\tau)$$
$$- \left\{(1+\nu)\lambda_n + \alpha^2[\lambda_n^2-\lambda_n(1-\nu)]\right\} b_n(\tau) = 0\ . \tag{6}$$

where $\lambda_n = n(n+1)$. Equations (4), (5) and (6) are linear differential equations with constant coefficients and they are analogous to the equations of motion of linear two degree of freedom system whose solutions are well known. Thus, the solutions of Eqs. (4), (5) and (6) are generally in the following form:

$$a_o = A_o \sin(\Omega_o\tau + \alpha_o), \tag{7}$$

$$a_n = \sum_{m=1}^{2} A_{nm} \sin(\Omega_{nm}\tau + \alpha_{nm}) \quad , \tag{8}$$

and

$$b_n = \sum_{m=1}^{2} \delta_{nm} A_{nm} \sin(\Omega_{nm}\tau + \alpha_{nm}) \quad , \tag{9}$$

where A_o, A_{nm}, δ_{nm} and α_{nm} are arbitrary constants, and Ω_{nm} are the positive real roots of the following frequency equation which can be obtained by usual methods:

$$\Omega^4 + \left\{(1-\nu-\lambda_n)(1+\alpha^2) - 2(1+\nu) - \alpha^2[\lambda_n^2-\lambda_n(1-\nu)]\right\} \Omega^2$$

$$- (1+\nu)\left\{2(1-\nu-\lambda_n)(1+\alpha^2) + \lambda_n[1+\nu-\alpha^2(1-\nu-\lambda_n)]\right\}$$

$$- \alpha^2(2-\lambda_n)[\lambda_n^2-\lambda_n(1-\nu)] = 0 \tag{10}$$

One of the steps in the derivation of Eq. (10) also yields the following expression for δ_{nm}:

$$\delta_{nm} = \frac{1+\nu-\alpha^2[1-\nu-\lambda_n]}{\Omega_{nm}^2+(1+\alpha^2)[1-\nu-\lambda_n]} \qquad \begin{matrix} m = 1,2 \\ n = 1,2,3,\cdots \end{matrix} \tag{11}$$

Substitution of Eqs. (7), (8) and (9) into Eqs. (3a) and (3b) formally gives the solutions of Eqs. (1) and (2):

$$\zeta(\phi,\tau) = A_o \sin(\Omega_o\tau+\alpha_o) + \sum_{n=1}^{\infty}\sum_{m=1}^{2} A_{nm} \sin(\Omega_{nm}\tau + \alpha_{nm}) P_n(\cos\phi) \tag{12a}$$

$$\Psi(\phi,\tau) = \sum_{n=1}^{\infty}\sum_{m=1}^{2} \delta_{nm} A_{nm} \sin(\Omega_{nm}\tau + \alpha_{nm}) P_n'(\cos\phi) \tag{12b}$$

where A_o, A_{nm}, α_o and α_{nm} will be determined by appropriate initial conditions of the problem.

Transient Response

In this section the transient response of the closed spherical shell subjected to a local, radial, and axisymmetric impulsive load will be determined. The shell is assumed to be at rest with respect to an inertial coordinate system prior to the application of the load. The impulsive nature of the external load will be represented as a velocity input applied at one of the poles of the shell as shown in Fig. 1. Thus, transient response will be the complete determination of the solutions, given formally in Eqs. (12a) and (12b), with appropriate initial conditions.

Two quite obvious initial conditions on the displacement components of the shell midsurface are:

$$\zeta(\phi,o) = 0 \qquad \Psi(\phi,o) = 0 \tag{13}$$

The initial conditions on the first time derivative of ζ and Ψ are not obvious and their determination involves following several steps:

(1) We first expand the function

$$g(\phi) = \begin{cases} V(\phi) & 0<\phi<\phi_0 \\ 0 & \phi_0<\phi<\pi \end{cases}$$

in a series of Legendre polynomials of the form

$$g(\phi) = \sum_{n=0}^{\infty} V_n P_n(\cos\phi) \tag{14}$$

In particular, if $V(\phi) = V$ constant, then, the coefficients V_n are found, in view of the orthogonality of the Legendre polynomials in the interval [-1,1], to be

$$V_n = \frac{1}{2} V[P_{n-1}(\cos\phi_o) - P_{n+1}(\cos\phi_o)] \quad n=1,2,\cdots \tag{15}$$

it being realized, of course, that $P_{-1}(\cos\phi_o) \equiv 1$.

(2) The linear momentum, M_z, along the polar axis PP', is the component of the radial momentum due to initial radial velocity V on the polar cap defined by $0<\phi<\phi_o$. The linear momentum along the polar axis is:

$$M_z = \int_{p.s.v.} \rho_s h\, V \cos\phi dA$$

where $dA = 2\Pi a^2 \sin\phi d\phi$

p.s.v. = partial shell volume.

Or in view of Eq. (14)

$$M_z = 2\Pi a^2 \rho_s h \int_0^{\phi_o} \sum_{n=o}^{\infty} V_n P_n(\cos\phi) \sin\phi \cos\phi \, d\phi \tag{16}$$

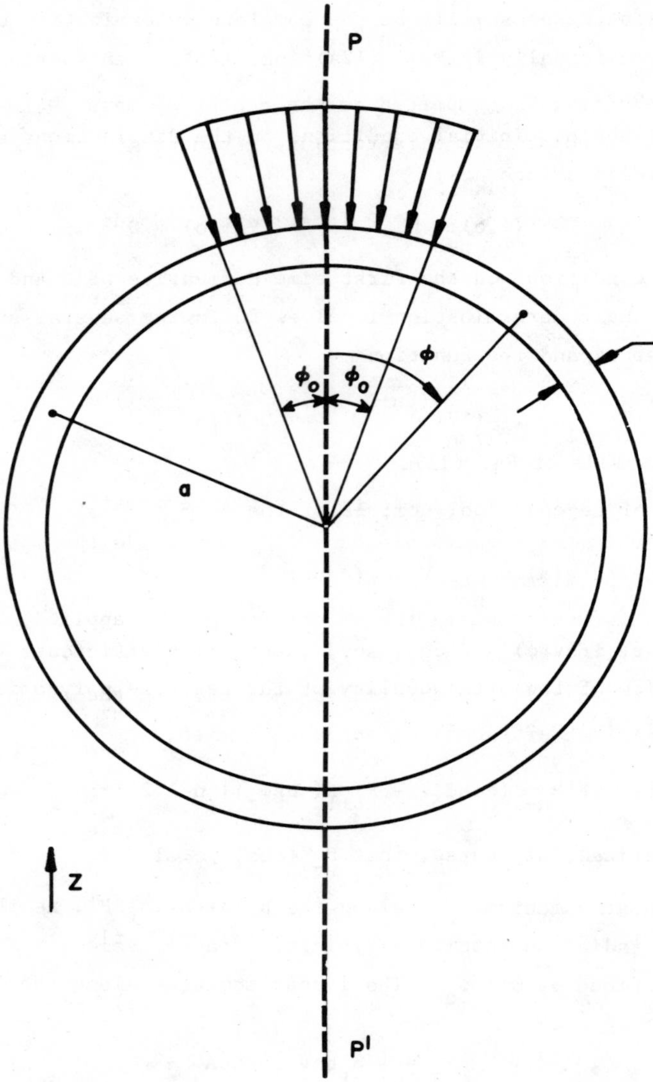

Fig. 1. Axisymmetric Impulsive Load Application.

The mass of the shell consistent with thin shell theory is:

$$m_s = \frac{4}{3}\rho_s \Pi(3ha^2 + \frac{h^3}{4}) \simeq 4\Pi\rho_s a^2 h$$

Hence, the velocity, V_z, imparted to the center of mass of the shell (in the negative polar axis direction) is given by

$$V_z = \frac{1}{2}\int_0^{\phi_0} \sum_{n=0}^{\infty} V_n P_n(\cos\phi) \sin\phi \cos\phi \, d\phi \tag{17}$$

Using the transformation $x = \cos\phi$, one can show after some manipulation that

$$V_z = \frac{1}{8} V_0(1-\cos 2\phi_0) + \sum_{n=1}^{\infty} \frac{V_n}{(2n+1)V} [V_n \cos\phi_0 + \frac{V_{n-1}}{(2n-1)} - \frac{V_{n+1}}{(2n+3)}] \tag{18}$$

where use was made of Eq. (15).

(3) To find the relative distribution of the deformation velocity with respect to the center of mass of the shell, we divide the spherical shell into two portions:

(A) $0<\phi<\phi_0$ (Region where the velocity input is applied)

(B) $\phi_0<\phi<\Pi$ (Outside of region (A)).

For region (A), we call the deformation velocity in the radial direction $\frac{\partial\overline{w}}{\partial t}$ and in the meridional direction $\frac{\partial\overline{u}}{\partial t}$; then,

$$\frac{\partial\overline{w}}{\partial t} = V - V_z \cos\phi$$

$$\frac{\partial\overline{u}}{\partial t} = 0 - V_z \sin\phi \tag{19}$$

or using Eq. (14) we can write Eq. (19) more explicitly

$$\frac{\partial\overline{w}}{\partial t} = V_0 + (V_1 - V_z)\cos\phi + \sum_{n=2}^{\infty} V_n P_n(\cos\phi)$$

and

$$\frac{\partial\overline{u}}{\partial t} = V_z P_1'(\cos\phi)$$

where V_n's are determined from Eq. (15) and V_z from Eq. (18). Initially, at region (B) the shell suffers only the velocity which is imparted to the center of mass of the shell in the negative polar-axis direction. As time increases, the propagation of bending wave from the pole of velocity input to the opposite pole introduces deformation velocities at region (B). This will be seen very clearly in the next section where the numerical results are given. The initial conditions thus obtained on the time derivatives of ζ and Ψ are:

$$\frac{\partial\zeta(\phi,o)}{\partial\tau} = \frac{1}{c_s}\frac{\partial\overline{w}}{\partial t}$$

and

$$\frac{\partial\Psi(\phi,o)}{\partial\tau} = \frac{1}{c_s}\frac{\partial\overline{u}}{\partial t} \tag{20}$$

This completes the determination of all the necessary initial conditions of the problem.

Application of the initial conditions, Eqs. (13) and (20) into solutions, Eqs. (12a) and (12b), leads to $\alpha_o = \alpha_{nm} = 0$ for all n and m. Hence, from Eqs. (12a) and (12b):

$$\frac{\partial\zeta(\phi,o)}{\partial\tau} = A_o\Omega_o + \sum_{n=1}^{\infty}\sum_{m=1}^{2} A_{nm}\Omega_{nm} P_n(\cos\phi) = \frac{1}{c_s}\frac{\partial\overline{w}}{\partial t} \tag{21a}$$

and

$$\frac{\partial\Psi(\phi,o)}{\partial\tau} = \sum_{n=1}^{\infty}\sum_{m=1}^{2} \delta_{nm}A_{nm}\Omega_{nm} P_n'(\cos\phi) = \frac{1}{c_s}\frac{\partial\overline{u}}{\partial t} \tag{21b}$$

Comparison of coefficients of Legendre polynomials on both sides of Eqs. (21a) and (21b) yields the following relationships for the determination of constants A_{nm}:

for n = 0: $$A_o = \frac{V_o}{c_s\Omega_o}$$

for n = 1:
$$A_{11}\Omega_{11} + A_{12}\Omega_{12} = \frac{1}{c_s}(V_1 - V_z)$$
$$\delta_{11}A_{11}\Omega_{11} + \delta_{12}A_{12}\Omega_{12} = \frac{1}{c_s}V_z \tag{22a}$$

for $n \geq 2$:
$$A_{n1}\Omega_{n1} + A_{n2}\Omega_{n2} = \frac{1}{c_s}V_n$$
$$\delta_{n1}A_{n1}\Omega_{n1} + \delta_{n2}A_{n2}\Omega_{n2} = 0 \tag{22b}$$

Consequently, from Eq. (22a)

$$A_{11} = \frac{\delta_{12}V_1 + V_z(1-\delta_{12})}{c_s\Omega_{11}\ (\delta_{12}-\delta_{11})} \quad \text{and} \quad A_{12} = \frac{\delta_{11}V_1 + V_z(1-\delta_{11})}{c_s\Omega_{11}\ (\delta_{11}-\delta_{12})}$$

Similarly, from Eq. (22b), for $n \geq 2$

$$A_{n1} = \frac{\delta_{n2} V_n}{\Omega_{n1} c_s (\delta_{n2} - \delta_{n1})} \quad \text{and} \quad A_{n2} = \frac{\delta_{n1} V_n}{\Omega_{n2} c_s (\delta_{n1} - \delta_{n2})}$$

Since all the values of A_{nm}, δ_{nm} and Ω_{nm} are known for each n ($n=0,1,2,\cdots$) and m ($m=1,2$), the nondimensional displacement components of the shell midsurface for the transient response are completely determinate and the final form of Eqs. (12a) and (12b) is:

$$\zeta(\phi,\tau) = \frac{V_o}{c_s \Omega_o} \sin(\Omega_o \tau) + \frac{\delta_{12} V_1 + V_z(1-\delta_{12})}{c_s \Omega_{11}(\delta_{12}-\delta_{11})} \sin(\Omega_{11}\tau) \cos\phi$$

$$+ \sum_{n=2}^{\infty} \frac{V_n}{c_s} \left[\frac{\delta_{n1}}{\Omega_{n2}(\delta_{n1}-\delta_{n2})} \sin(\Omega_{n2}\tau) + \frac{\delta_{n2}}{\Omega_{n1}(\delta_{n2}-\delta_{n1})} \sin(\Omega_{n1}\tau) \right] P_n(\cos\phi) \tag{23a}$$

$$\Psi(\phi,\tau) = -\delta_{11} \frac{\delta_{12} V_1 + V_z(1-\delta_{12})}{c_s \Omega_{11}(\delta_{12}-\delta_{11})} \sin(\Omega_{11}\tau) \sin\phi$$

$$+ \sum_{n=2}^{\infty} \frac{V_n \delta_{n1} \delta_{n2}}{c_s} \left[\frac{\sin(\Omega_{n2}\tau)}{\Omega_{n2}(\delta_{n1}-\delta_{n2})} + \frac{\sin(\Omega_{n1}\tau)}{\Omega_{n1}(\delta_{n2}-\delta_{n1})} \right] \left[\frac{n\cos\phi \, P_n(\cos\phi) - n \, P_{n-1}(\cos\phi)}{\sin\phi} \right] \tag{23b}$$

where the value of the term in the second bracket in Eq. (23b) is equal to zero at the poles ($\phi=0°$ and $\phi=180°$); this confirms the physical situation that the meridional displacements at the poles should vanish for the response to axisymmetric external loads.

Having determined the midsurface displacement components ζ and Ψ, we obtain the midsurface strains for axisymmetric torsionless motion of the shell from the following expressions:

$$\varepsilon_\phi = \frac{\partial\Psi}{\partial\phi} + \zeta \qquad \kappa_\phi = \frac{1}{a}\left(\frac{\partial^2\zeta}{\partial\phi^2} + \frac{\partial\Psi}{\partial\phi}\right)$$

$$\varepsilon_\theta = \Psi\cot\phi + \zeta \qquad \kappa_\theta = \frac{\cot\phi}{a}\left(-\frac{\partial\zeta}{\partial\phi} + \Psi\right) \tag{24}$$

In Eq. (24) ε_ϕ and ε_θ are the tangential strains; whereas κ_ϕ and κ_θ are the bending strains and they can be viewed as the variations of the curvature of the midsurface of the shell during deformation. It can be shown (i.e. see Novozhilov [14]) that the z-surface[2] strains are related to those of the midsurface in the following manner:

$$\varepsilon_\phi^{(z)} = \frac{1}{1+z/a}(\varepsilon_\phi + z\kappa_\phi)$$

$$\varepsilon_\theta^{(z)} = \frac{1}{1+z/a}(\varepsilon_\theta + z\kappa_\theta) \tag{25}$$

For isotropic and homogeneous shell material Hooke's law and the hypothesis of Kirchoff yield the biaxial stress-strain relations:

$$\sigma_\phi^{(z)} = \frac{E}{1-\nu^2}(\varepsilon_\phi^{(z)} + \nu\varepsilon_\theta^{(z)})$$

$$\sigma_\theta^{(z)} = \frac{E}{1-\nu^2}(\varepsilon_\theta^{(z)} + \nu\varepsilon_\phi^{(z)}) \tag{26}$$

where E is Young's modulus and ν is Poisson's ratio. Thus, the stress distribution in the shell is found at any given time by substituting Eqs. (23a) and (23b) into Eqs. (24), (25) and (26).

Numerical Results and Conclusions

Since this investigation received its stimulus from the consideration that a spherical shell can serve as a simple theoretical model representing the human head subjected to impulsive loads, we use the following data for the numerical computations:

---

2. Any surface which is equidistant from the midsurface is called z-surface; for the midsurface z=0. The possible values of z are $-h/2 \leq z \leq h/2$, where h is the shell thickness.

$$\begin{aligned} \rho_s &= 0.0772 \text{ lbm/in}^3 \\ E &= 2 \times 10^6 \text{ lbf/in}^2 \\ \nu &= .25 \\ a &= 3 \text{ in} \\ h &= .15 \text{ in} \end{aligned} \qquad (27)$$

From the shell data we note that a/h is within the justifiable thin shell theory limits; also the calculated value for c_s is 103,200 in/sec which is in close agreement with the wave speed of 106,000 in/sec through the skull mentioned by Goldsmith in [15]. The axisymmetric velocity input is considered to be applied on the shell with a constant magnitude of 528 in/sec on a polar cap of 15° angle. Thus, the addition of V = 528 in/sec and ϕ_o = 15° to the above completes the necessary data. Using the data in Eqs. (23) through (26) we obtain shell midsurface displacement components ζ, Ψ, midsurface and z-surface strain quantities ε_ϕ, ε_θ, $\varepsilon_\phi^{(z)}$, $\varepsilon_\theta^{(z)}$ and stresses $\sigma_\phi^{(z)}$ and $\sigma_\theta^{(z)}$. Sufficient convergence for the series representing the solutions was achieved by taking summations up to 50 terms.

On the figures, the encircled numbers designate the multiples of the time increment. The time increment chosen represents 1/10 of the calculated time which the stress wave on the shell takes to arrive at the opposite pole. Thus, ① refers to actual time of $t = 9.125 \times 10^{-6}$ sec or nondimensional time $\tau = 0.3141$ and ⑩ refers to actual time of $t = 9.125 \times 10^{-5}$ sec or nondimensional time $\tau = 3.141$. On Figs. 4 and 5 the circle of radius r_1 represents the zero magnitude of stress; the outward direction is used for the compressive and the inward direction for the tensile stresses.

In Fig. 2 the nondimensional radial shell displacement at the pole of velocity input is plotted as a function of the polar angle for various time increments. Fig. 3 shows the same displacement quantity plotted against the nondimensional time; this figure also contains the plot of the radial displacement at the opposite pole. Normal stresses σ_ϕ and σ_θ acting on the midsurface of the shell (z=0) are illustrated by polar plots in Figs. 4 and 5. From these plots as well as from the others one can easily see the propagation of the stress wave around the shell.

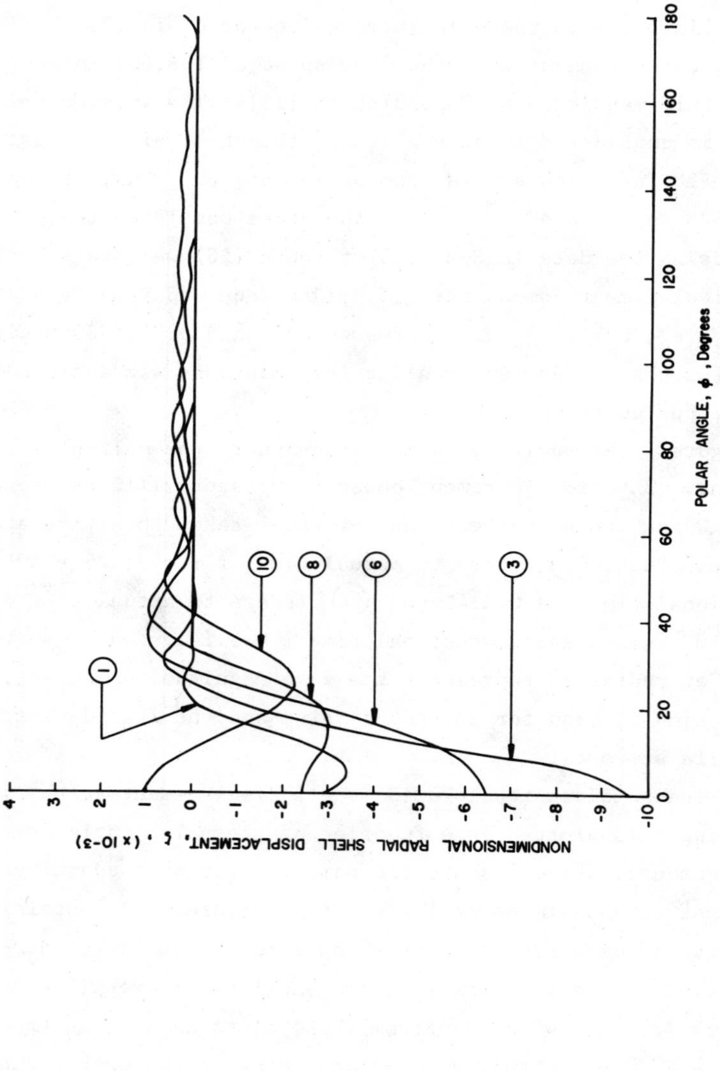

Fig. 2. Nondimensional Radial Shell Displacement Versus Polar Angle ϕ.

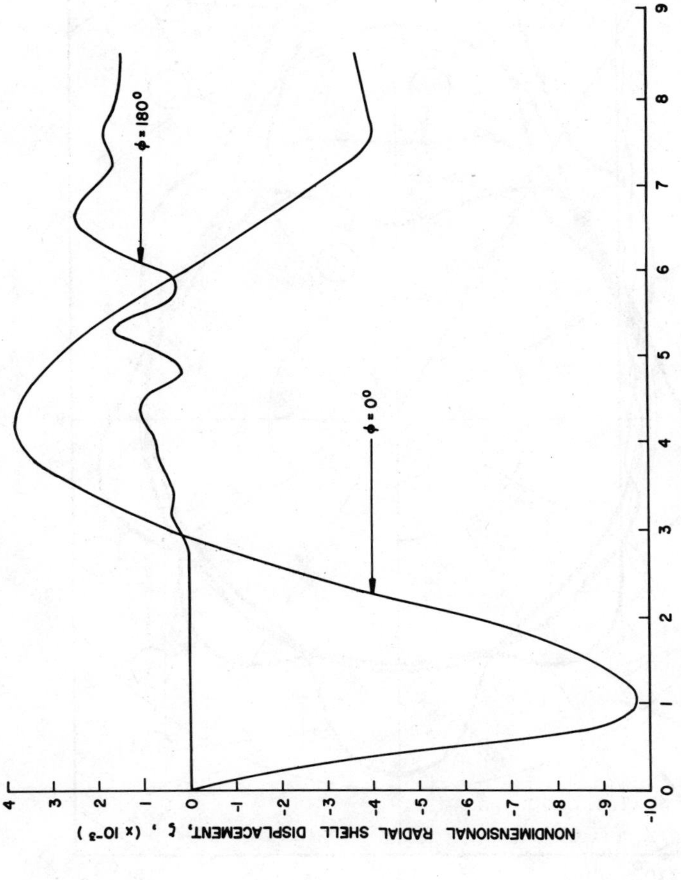

Fig. 3. Nondimensional Radial Shell Displacement Versus Nondimensional Time at the Poles $\phi = 0°$ and $\phi = 180°$.

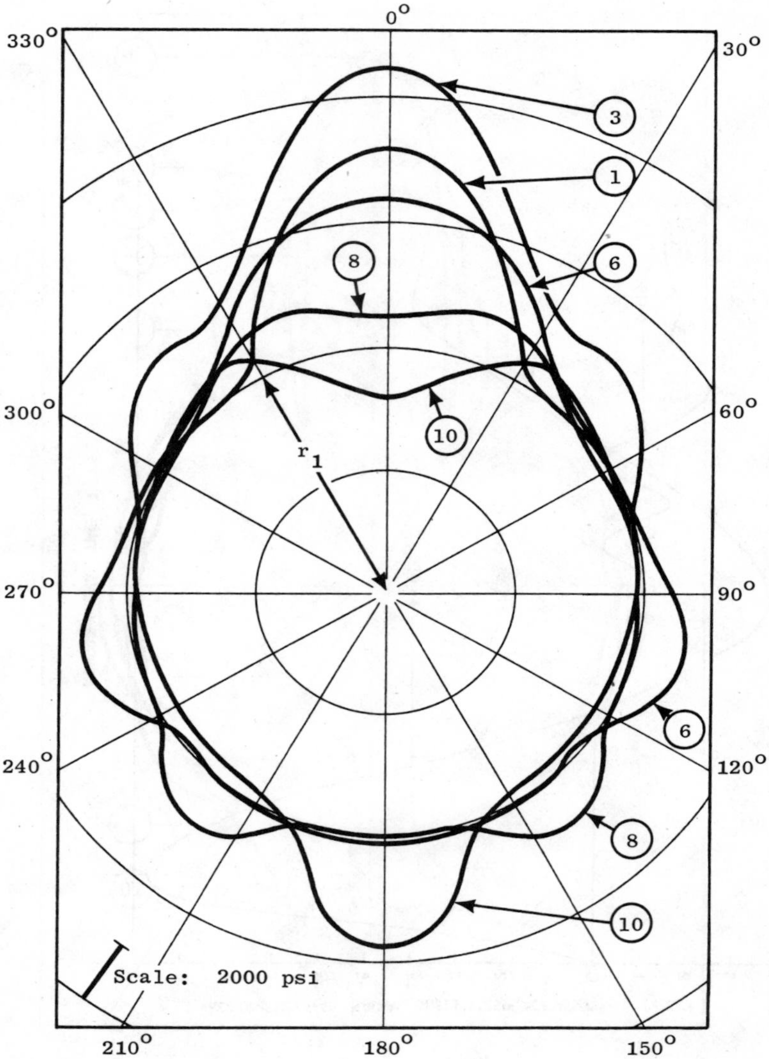

Fig. 4. Normal Stress in the ϕ-Direction as a Function of the Polar Angle ϕ at Various Times, z=0.

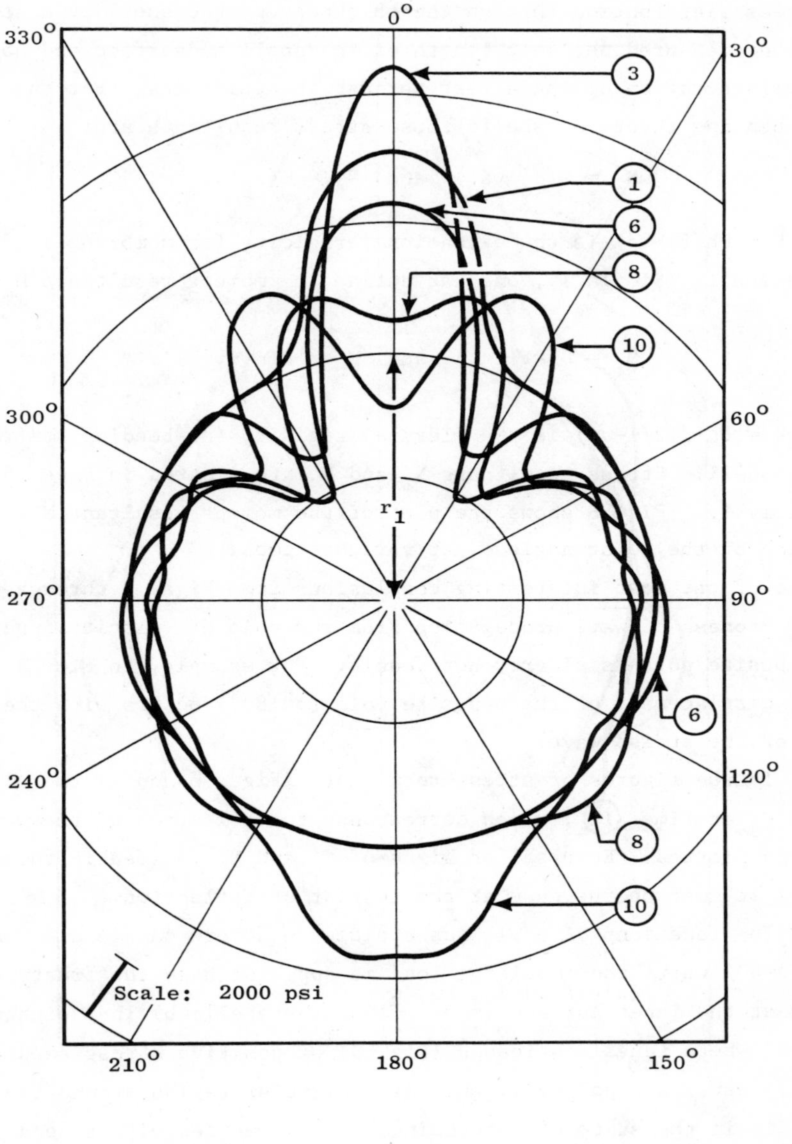

Fig. 5. Normal Stress in the θ-Direction as a Function of the Polar Angle ϕ at Various Times, z=0.

The usual practice in the shell theory is to express the resultant of stress distribution through the thickness of the shell by a stress resultant measured per unit length of the shell midsurface and obtained by the integration of the stress through the thickness. For the classical bending theory of shells these stress resultants are:

$$N_\phi = K(\varepsilon_\phi + \nu\varepsilon_\theta) \quad \text{and} \quad N_\theta = K(\varepsilon_\theta + \nu\varepsilon_\phi) \tag{28}$$

where $K = Eh/(1-\nu^2)$ is the extensional rigidity (or membrane stiffness) of the shell. Similarly, one can define the moment resultants M_ϕ and M_θ:

$$M_\phi = D(\kappa_\phi + \nu\kappa_\theta) \quad \text{and} \quad M_\theta = D(\kappa_\theta + \nu\kappa_\phi) \tag{29}$$

where $D = Eh^3/12(1-\nu^2)$ is the flexural rigidity (or bending stiffness) of the shell. Stress resultants N_ϕ and N_θ are plotted in Figs. 6 and 7 respectively. Fig. 8 shows the plot of the moment resultant M_ϕ, as a function of the polar angle ϕ, at various times.

Some of the most interesting conclusions from Figs. 2 through 8 are:

1) Process of wave propagation from the pole of velocity input to the opposite pole is clearly noticeable. For example, in Fig. 3 the radial displacement of the opposite pole (ϕ=180°) occurs with the arrival of the stress wave.

2) In the figures of stress resultants (Figs. 6 and 7) the plots of N_ϕ and N_θ at time (11), which corresponds to reflection of the wave, are also plotted. Reversal of signs of N_ϕ and N_θ is seen in these figures as it must be the case at the instant of reflection.

3) The locations of shell susceptible to severe damage are: a) The pole (ϕ=0°) where the impulsive load is applied; here the fracture starts at the inner surface ($z = -\frac{h}{2}$) of the shell; b) The neighborhood of ϕ=35° where tensile stresses (Fig. 5) or positive stress resultants (Fig. 7) develop repeatedly; this is a circular region around the pole and it is in the state of outbending. In connection with a head injury model, Evans [16] discusses these locations on the basis of experiments conducted by E. S. Gurdjian, H. R. Lissner, and J. E. Webster.

In conclusion, the immediate extension of this analysis for different pulse shapes is possible by proper utilization of the convolution integrals on the solutions given in the paper.

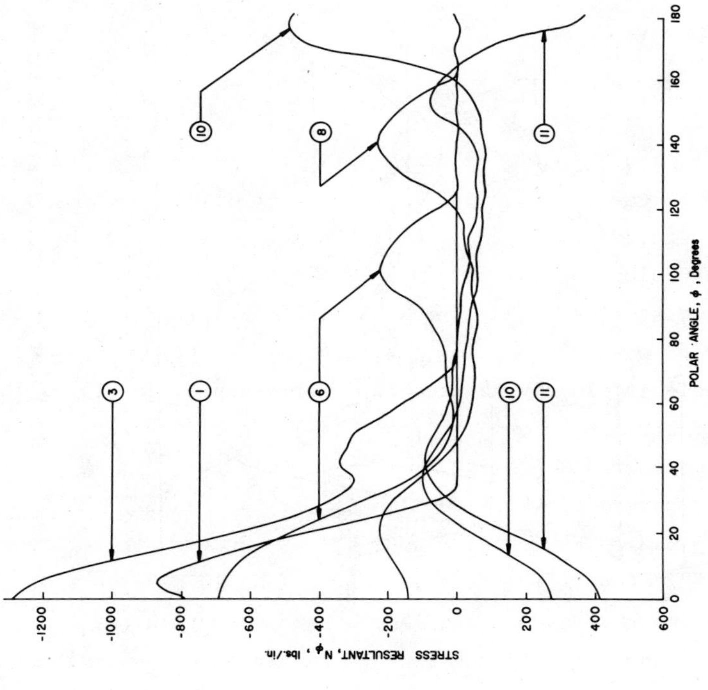

Fig. 6. Stress Resultant N_ϕ as a Function of the Polar Angle ϕ at Various Times.

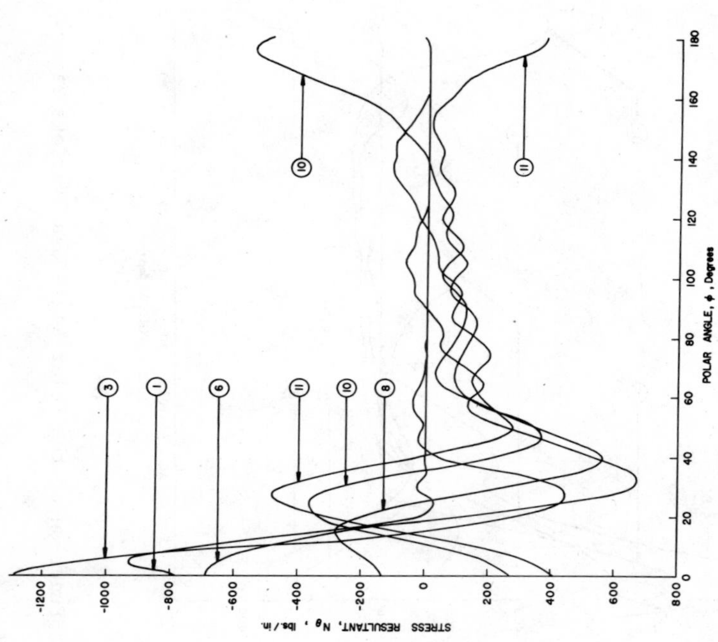

Fig. 7. Stress Resultant N_θ as a Function of the Polar Angle ϕ at Various Times.

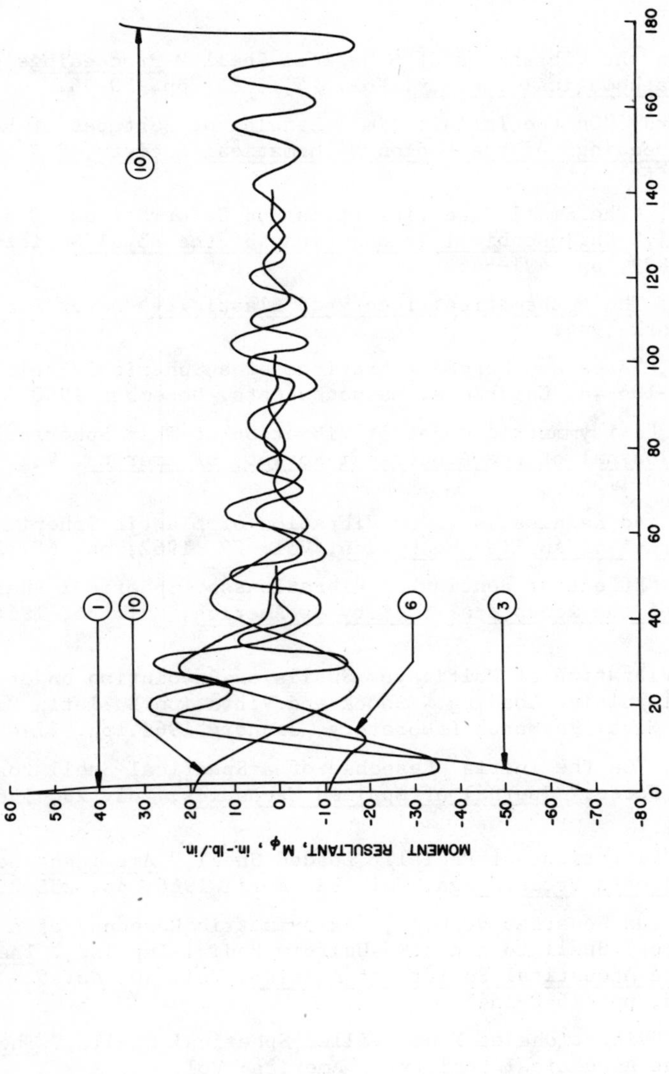

Fig. 8. Moment Resultant M_ϕ as a Function of the Polar Angle ϕ at Various Times.

ACKNOWLEDGMENT

This investigation was supported by the Biomechanics Department of the Highway Safety Research Institute of The University of Michigan under contract No. PH-43-67-1136 sponsored by the National Institute for Neurological Diseases and Stroke.

REFERENCES

1. Lamb, H., "On the Vibrations of Spherical Shell," Proceedings of the London Mathematical Society, Vol. 14, 1883, pp. 50-56.
2. Rayleigh, Lord, "On the Infinitesimal Bending of Surfaces of Revolution," Proceedings of the London Mathematical Society, Vol. 13, 1882, pp. 4-ff.
3. Love, A.E.H., "The Small Free Vibrations and Deformations of a Thin Elastic Shell," Philosophical Transactions of the Royal Society, Vol. 179A, 1889, pp. 491-546.
4. Love, A.E.H., The Mathematical Theory of Elasticity, Dover Publications, New York 1944.
5. Silbiger, A., "Free and Forced Vibrations of a Spherical Shell," ONR Report U-106-48, Cambridge, Massachusetts, December 1960.
6. Baker, W.E., "Axisymmetric Modes of Vibration of Thin Spherical Shell," The Journal of the Acoustical Society of America, Vol. 33, 1961, pp. 1749-1758.
7. Naghdi, P.M. and Kalnins, A., "On Vibration of Elastic Spherical Shells," Journal of Applied Mechanics, Vol. 29, 1962, pp. 65-72.
8. Kalnins, A., "Effect of Bending on Vibrations of Spherical Shells," The Journal of the Acoustical Society of America, Vol. 36, 1964, pp. 74-81.
9. Klein, S., "Vibration of Multilayer Shells of Revolution under Dynamic and Impulsive Loading," Shock and Vibration Bulletin No. 35 part 3, U.S. Naval Research Laboratory, January 1966, pp. 27-45.
10. Medick, M.A., "On the Initial Response of a Spherical Shell to a Concentrated Force," Journal of Applied Mechanics, Vol. 29, 1962, pp. 689-695.
11. Long, C.F., "Vibrations of Radially Loaded Shell," American Society of Civil Engineers Proceedings, Vol. 92, April 1966, pp. 235-250.
12. McIvor, I.K. and Sonstegard, D.A., "Axisymmetric Response of a Closed Spherical Shell to a nearly Uniform Radial Impulse," The Journal of the Acoustical Society of America, Vol. 40, No. 6, December 1966, pp. 1540-1547.
13. Engin, A.E., "Vibrations of Fluid-Filled Spherical Shells," The Journal of the Acoustical Society of America, Vol. 46, No. 1 (part 2), July 1969, pp. 186-190.
14. Novozhilov, V.V., Thin Shell Theory, Second Edition, Noordhoff Ltd. Groninger, Holland, 1964.

15. Goldsmith, W., "The Physical Processes Producing Head Injury," Proceedings of the Head Injury Conference, J. P. Lippincott Co., 1966, pp. 350-382.

16. Evans, F.G., Stress and Strain in Bones, Thomas, Springfield, Ill. pp. 34-53, 1957.

ON THE ACCURACY AND APPLICATION OF THE POINT MATCHING METHOD FOR SHALLOW SHELLS

Arthur W. Leissa
Ohio State University

Adel S. Kadi
Ohio State University

ABSTRACT

The main purpose of this paper is to provide some understanding of the accuracy of the point matching method when used on shell problems. Although the point matching method has been used extensively on boundary value and eigenvalue problems governed by differential equations of lower order, little has been done with the method on the eighth order equations of shell theory. For this purpose a test problem is chosen which, not only has practical application, but has an exact solution -- the uniformly loaded, shallow spherical shell supported along a square boundary by shear diaphragms. This problem has an exact solution which is a generalization of the Navier solution used for the bending of simply-supported rectangular plates. For the point matching method, solutions to the governing differential equations are also taken in polar coordinates as suggested by Reissner for use with circular boundaries. After proper transformations these solutions are expressed in a general form for boundaries having arbitrary normal and tangential directions for use with a general-purpose computer program. Residual edge displacements, bending moments, and membrane forces are computed for various degrees of sophistication of point matching solutions, and the effect of these residuals upon internal deflections, bending moments, and membrane forces is established by comparison with the exact, Navier-type solution.

It is found that due to the rapid, oscillatory decay of some of the functions used, certain boundary residuals can be quite large without significantly affecting the stresses and deflections within the major portion of the shell. As a matter of additional information, previously unavailable results for the uniformly loaded, spherical shell having an equilateral, triangular planform supported by shear diaphragms are also given.

INTRODUCTION

The point matching method has long been known to be a useful technique for the solution of boundary value and eigenvalue problems. The method depends upon finding exact solutions to the governing differential equation (s) of the region, with boundary conditions being matched either exactly or in the least squares sense at a finite number of boundary points. The technique has been used extensively on various problems governed by second order and fourth order differential equations (cf., Refs. 1 - 8) and to a very limited extent on shell problems [9, 10], which are represented by eighth order differential systems.

In spite of the relative complexity of systems of shell equations, some exact solutions are available, particularly in rectangular and polar coordinates. Correspondingly, these solutions can be forced to satisfy some sets of boundary conditions for rectangular and circular boundaries, respectively. However, for other sets of edge conditions (in particular, mixed boundary conditions) or for irregular (i.e., general) boundary shapes the prospects of satisfying the boundary conditions in the usual, classical, exact ways are indeed remote.

The point matching method would appear to be an excellent approach to handle arbitrary boundary shapes and edge conditions for shell problems. Indeed, as it was pointed out earlier, the technique has already achieved some success in this use. Conway and Leissa [9] demonstrated the method for two problems involving shallow spherical shells: (1) one having a fully-fixed, square boundary and loaded by uniform pressure and (2) a rigid, elliptical insert which is loaded normal to a shell of unlimited extent. Clausen and Leissa [10] used the technique with multiple poles to study the effects of coupling between two closely located holes in a spherical shell upon the local stresses and deflections.

However, approximate methods are only of value if an estimate of accuracy can be made. In the case of the point matching method an evaluation must be made of the residuals along the boundary and their effects within the region. In previous work using the point matching method on lower order differential systems these effects have been studied (cf., Refs. 11 and 12). For a thin shell the problem is more complicated for, as it will be shown later in the present paper, due to the rapid, oscillatory decay of some of the functions used, certain boundary residuals can be quite large without significantly affecting the stresses and deflections within the major portion of the shell.

The main objective of this paper is to provide some understanding of the accuracy of the point matching technique when used on shell problems. For this purpose a test problem is chosen which, not only has practical application, but has an exact solution -- the uniformly loaded, shallow spherical shell supported along a square boundary by shear diaphragms. This mathematical model is a good representation of a roof dome supporting its own weight and covering a building having a square planform. The problem has an exact solution which is a generalization of the Navier solution used for the bending of simply-supported rectangular plates. For the point matching method, solutions to the governing differential equations are also taken in polar coordinates as suggested by Reissner [13,14] for use with circular boundaries. After proper transformations these solutions are expressed in a general form for boundaries having arbitrary normal and tangential directions for use with a general-purpose computer program. Residual edge displacements, bending moments, and membrane forces are computed for various degrees of sophistication of point matching solutions, and the effect of these residuals upon internal deflections, bending moments, and membrane forces is established by comparison with the exact, Navier-type solution.

Finally, the method is applied to a problem having no previously published solution -- the uniformly loaded, shallow spherical shell having an equilateral, triangular planform and supported along its edges by shear diaphragms. Useful design results for deflections, bending moments, and membrane forces are given.

A Navier-Type Solution

Consider a shallow, spherical shell whose planform dimensions are a x b, having a spherical radius R. In this case the general equations for a shallow, isotropic shell (cf., Ref. 15, Eqs. 10 and 11) the governing system of differential equations reduces to

$$\nabla^4\Phi - \frac{Eh}{R}\nabla^2 w = -(1-\nu)\nabla^2\Omega$$
$$\nabla^4 w + \frac{1}{RD}\nabla^2\Phi = \frac{q}{D} - 2\frac{\Omega}{RD} \tag{1}$$

where w is the transverse deflection, Φ is an Airy stress function, R is the spherical radius, D is the flexural rigidity $Eh^3/12(1-\nu^2)$, E is Young's modulus, h is the shell thickness, ν is Poisson's ratio, ∇^2 is the two-dimensional Laplacian operator, q is the normal loading intensity, and Ω is a suitable potential function which, when differentiated, gives the tangential components of loading.

A Navier-type solution assumes that all edges are supported by "shear diaphragms", i.e., the following boundary conditions are satisfied:

$$w = M_n = N_n = u_t = 0 \tag{2}$$

where M_n and N_n are the normal bending moment and membrane force, respectively, and u_t is the displacement tangent to both the middle surface of the shell and the boundary curve. The boundary conditions are satisfied exactly by choosing

$$w = \sum_m \sum_n A_{mn} \sin \alpha x \sin \beta y$$
$$\Phi = \sum_m \sum_n B_{mn} \sin \alpha x \sin \beta y \tag{3}$$

provided that the loading functions are also represented by compatible double sine series; i.e.,

$$q = \sum_m \sum_n a_{mn} \sin \alpha x \sin \beta y$$
$$\Omega = \sum_m \sum_n b_{mn} \sin \alpha x \sin \beta y \tag{4}$$

where

$$\alpha = \frac{m\pi}{a} \quad (m = 1,2,\cdots)$$
$$\beta = \frac{n\pi}{b} \quad (n = 1,2,\cdots) \tag{5}$$

Substituting Eqs. (3) and (4) into Eqs. (1) gives

$$A_{mn} = \frac{\frac{1}{D}\left[a_{mn} - \frac{1}{R}(1 + \nu)\, b_{mn}\right]}{\left[\frac{Eh}{R^2D} + (\alpha^2 + \beta^2)^2\right]}$$

$$B_{mn} = \frac{b_{mn}\left[(1-\nu)(\alpha^2 + \beta^2)^2 + \frac{2Eh}{R^2D}\right] - \frac{Eh}{RD}\, a_{mn}}{(\alpha^2 + \beta^2)\left[\frac{Eh}{R^2D} + (\alpha^2 + \beta^2)^2\right]} \qquad (6)$$

For the particular case of loading consisting solely of uniform normal pressure, the Fourier load coefficients become

$$a_{mn} = \frac{4}{ab}\int_0^a \int_0^b q_o \sin \alpha x \sin \beta y \, dxdy$$

$$= \frac{16q_o}{\pi^2 mn} \qquad \begin{matrix}(m = 1,3,\cdots) \\ (n = 1,3,\cdots)\end{matrix} \qquad (7)$$

$$b_{mn} = 0$$

The solution given by Eqs. (3) and (6) may be evaluated for the useful physical quantities of slope, bending moment, transverse shear, and membrane force in the usual manner (cf., Ref. 15).

Although the solution is "exact", nevertheless, infinite series must be summed, and the number of terms to be kept becomes a matter of practical consideration. A study was conducted to determine the number of terms to be used for the production of acceptable results. The following values were assigned for the constants

$$E = 30 \times 10^6$$

$$R/h = 50$$

$$R/a = 1.932$$

$$a/b = 1$$

$$\nu = 0.3$$

Table I shows the number of terms and the corresponding deflection evaluated at the center and the transverse shear evaluated at the midpoint ($x = 1.0$, $y = 0.5$). The transverse shear, which requires third derivatives of w, clearly will have a slower rate of convergence.

TABLE I. CONVERGENCE OF THE NAVIER-TYPE SOLUTION

No. of Terms	$\frac{w}{q_o}$ (x = 0.5, y = 0.5)	$\frac{Q_x}{q_o}$ (x = 1.0, y = 0.5)
1	$0.43545389 \times 10^{-5}$	$-0.42795316 \times 10^{-1}$
25	$0.38486531 \times 10^{-5}$	$-0.97275573 \times 10^{-1}$
64	$0.38478501 \times 10^{-5}$	$-1.03458060 \times 10^{-1}$
169	$0.38479280 \times 10^{-5}$	$-1.08853860 \times 10^{-1}$
625	$0.38479084 \times 10^{-5}$	$-1.12482890 \times 10^{-1}$
1444	$0.38478848 \times 10^{-5}$	$-1.13810580 \times 10^{-1}$

From the results shown in Table I and a comparison of the execution times, it was decided that 25 terms in each direction is sufficient, making the total number of terms retained $(25)^2 = 625$. The approximation to the loading was also investigated; using 625 terms in the series, it was found, as shown in Fig. 1, that the series only had difficulty in approximating the uniform pressure in the vicinity of the boundaries. Obviously, exactly at the boundaries the series for q sums identically to zero. The loading requires fourth derivatives of the solution functions and, hence, shows the greatest deviation.

Solution in Polar Coördinates

Expressing the Laplacian operator in polar coordinates in Eq. (1), and dividing the solutions into the complementary and particular parts,

$$w = w_p + w_c$$
$$\Phi = \Phi_p + \Phi_c \tag{8}$$

it can be shown [13 - 15] that for a simply connected region containing the coordinate origin the complementary solution is

$$w_c = C_{o1} + C_{o3}\text{ber } X + c_{o4}\text{bei } X + \sum_{n=1}^{\infty} (C_{n1}X^n + C_{n3}\text{ber}_n X + C_{n4}\text{bei}_n X) \cos n\theta$$
$$+ \sum_{n=1}^{\infty} (\overline{C}_{n1} X^n + \overline{C}_{n3}\text{ber}_n X + \overline{C}_{n4}\text{bei}_n X) \sin n\theta \tag{9}$$

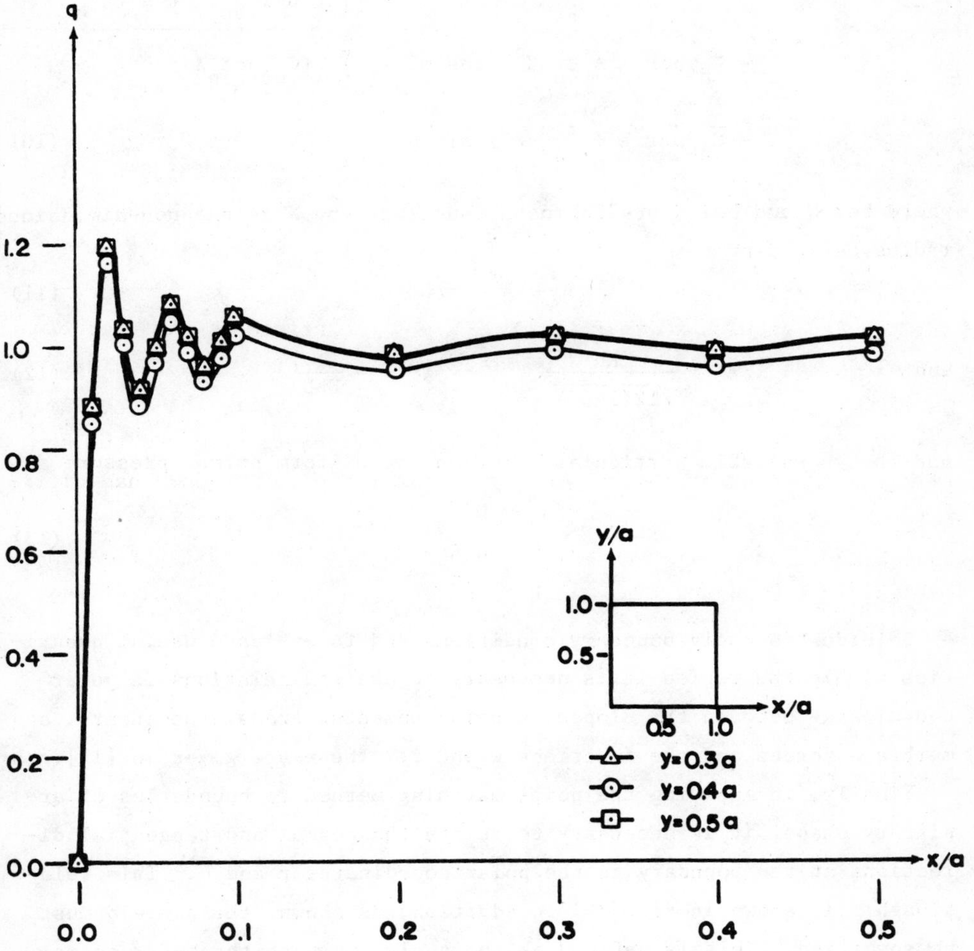

Fig. 1. Load Variation Along Lines Parallel to the x-Axis.

$$|\lambda|\Phi_c = c_{o3}\text{bei } X - C_{o4}\text{ber } X + C_{19}(X\theta \sin\theta - X \ln X \cos\theta)$$

$$+ \overline{C}_{19}\ (X\theta \cos\theta + X \ln X \sin\theta) + \sum_{n=1}^{\infty} (C_{n3}\text{bei } X$$

$$- C_{n4}\text{ber } X + C_{n7}X^n) \cos n\theta + \sum_{n=1}^{\infty} (\overline{C}_{n3}\text{bei}_n X$$

$$- \overline{C}_{n4}\text{ber } X + \overline{C}_{n7}\ X^n) \sin n\theta \qquad (10)$$

where ber X and bei X are Thompson functions and X is the non-dimensional radius defined by

$$X = r/\ell \qquad (11)$$

and

$$\ell^2 = \frac{Rh}{\sqrt{12(1-\nu^2)}}, \qquad \lambda^2 = -\frac{1}{EhD} \qquad (12)$$

and that a suitable particular solution for uniform normal pressure is

$$w_p = 0$$
$$\phi_p = \frac{q_o R}{4} r^2 \qquad (13)$$

In order to apply boundary conditions and to evaluate useful quantities within the region it is necessary to use the relations in polar coordinates between the slopes, bending moments, transverse shears, and membrane forces and the functions w and ϕ. These are given in [15].

Finally, in applying the point matching method to boundaries of arbitrary shape, it is necessary to relate the normal and tangential directions at the boundary to the polar coordinates r and θ. This relationship is shown in Fig. 2. In addition, as shown, the angle ϕ must be specified. This is defined as the angle by which the outer normal <u>leads</u> the radial direction (i.e., shown positive in Fig. 2).

The following equations relate useful quantities in the arbitrary directions n and t to the polar coordinates.

A. Slope in the normal direction:

$$\frac{\partial w}{\partial n} = \frac{\partial w}{\partial r} \cos\phi + \frac{1}{r}\frac{\partial w}{\partial \theta} \sin\phi \qquad (14)$$

B. Slope in the tangential direction:

Obtainable from Eq. (14) by replacing ϕ by $(\phi + \pi/2)$.

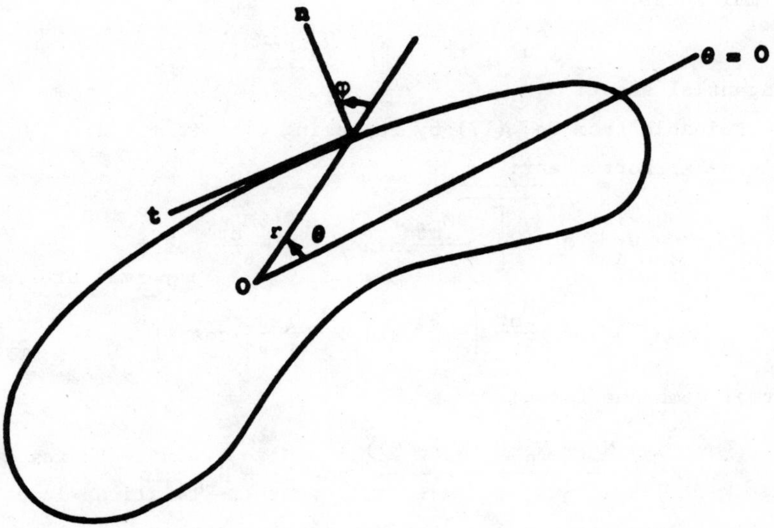

Fig. 2. Normal and Tangential Coordinates on an Arbitrary Shape.

C. Moment in the normal direction:

$$M_n = \frac{1}{2}(M_r + M_\theta) + \frac{1}{2}(M_r - M_\theta) \cos 2\phi + M_{r\theta} \sin 2\phi \tag{15}$$

D. Moment in the tangential direction:

Obtainable from Eq. (15) by replacing ϕ by $(\phi + \pi/2)$.

E. Twisting moment:

$$M_{nt} = -\frac{1}{2}(M_r - M_\theta) \sin 2\phi + M_{r\theta} \cos 2\phi \tag{16}$$

F. Normal shear:

$$Q_n = Q_r \cos \phi + Q_\theta \sin \phi \tag{17}$$

G. Tangential shear:

Obtainable from Eq. (17) by replacing ϕ by $(\phi + \pi/2)$.

H. Kelvin-Kirchoff shear:

$$V_n = Q_n + \left[-\frac{\partial M_{nt}}{\partial r} \sin \phi + \frac{1}{r}\frac{\partial M_{nt}}{\partial \theta} \cos \phi + \frac{\partial M_{nt}}{\partial \phi}\left(-\frac{\partial \phi}{\partial r} \sin \phi + \frac{1}{r}\frac{\partial \phi}{\partial \theta} \cos \phi\right)\right]. \tag{18}$$

I. Normal membrane force:

$$N_n = \frac{N_r + N_\theta}{2} + \frac{(N_r - N_\theta)}{2} \cos 2\phi + N_{r\theta} \sin 2\phi \tag{19}$$

J. Tangential membrane force:

Obtainable from Eq. (19) by replacing ϕ by $(\phi + \pi/2)$.

K. Shearing membrane force:

$$N_{nt} = -\frac{1}{2}(N_r - N_\theta) \sin 2\phi + N_{r\theta} \cos 2\phi \tag{20}$$

L. Normal displacement:

$$u_n = u \cos \phi + v \sin \phi \tag{21}$$

M. Tangential displacement:

Obtainable from Eq. (21) by replacing ϕ by $(\phi + \pi/2)$.

To obtain explicit expressions for useful quantities in the normal and tangential directions in terms of r, θ, and ϕ, it is now necessary to substitute Eqs. (8) through (13) into Eqs. (14) through (21), using the expressions for N_r, N_θ, $N_{r\theta}$, M_r, M_θ, $M_{r\theta}$, Q_r, Q_θ, u and v given on pp. 54 and 55 of [15]. The expanded, explicit expressions have been derived and incorporated into a computer program, but giving them would require an Appendix of length longer than this entire paper. They can be found in [16].

Application of the Point Matching Method to the Test Problem

The square planform of the spherical shell supported by a shear diaphragm is shown in Fig. 3, where x' and y' are related to the x and y coordinates of the previously given exact, Navier-type solution by

$$\begin{aligned} x &= x' + a/2 \\ y &= y' + b/2 \end{aligned} \tag{22}$$

and the polar coordinates used in Eqs. (9) through (11) are related to x' and y' by

$$\begin{aligned} x' &= r \cos \theta \\ y' &= r \sin \theta \end{aligned} \tag{23}$$

For uniform pressure loading, the problem has four-fold symmetry; consequently, odd functions of θ can be discarded from Eqs. (9) and (10), and the remaining terms in the series can be taken as n = 4,8,... The unknown constants C_{o1}, C_{o3}, C_{o4}, C_{n1}, C_{n3}, C_{n4} and C_{n7} can be determined by satisfying the boundary conditions at discrete points, where the number of boundary condition equations obtained from these discrete points is equal to the number of unknown constants. In the present case the four boundary conditions given by Eq. (2) were applied at each point, except at x' = a/2, y' = 0, where $u_t = 0$ is identically satisfied by symmetry. Because of symmetry, only 1/8 of the boundary is required. Symmetry duplicates the boundary conditions at corresponding points along the remaining 7/8 of the boundary. The number of boundary condition equations is

$$k = 3 + 4(I - 1)$$

where k = number of boundary equations, and I = number of points chosen along the boundary segment. The cases having 3, 4, 5, and 6 equally spaced points (Fig. 4) on the segment were considered.

Table II shows the residuals obtained for a typical solution. The maximum value of the residual for each case is compared with the maximum value of the parameter under consideration within the shell in Table III, for the four separate solutions having 3, 4, 5, and 6 points matched. These ratios provide a meaningful interpretation of the <u>scale</u>

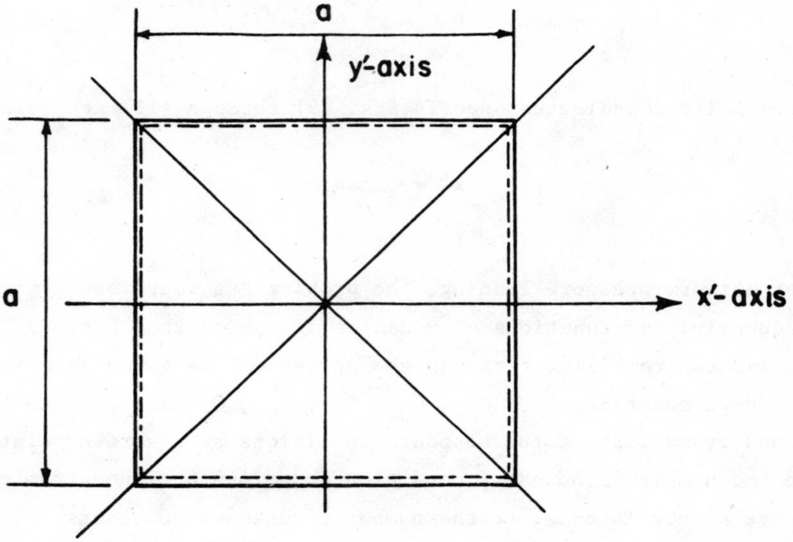

Fig. 3. Coordinates for Shallow Shell Having Square Planform.

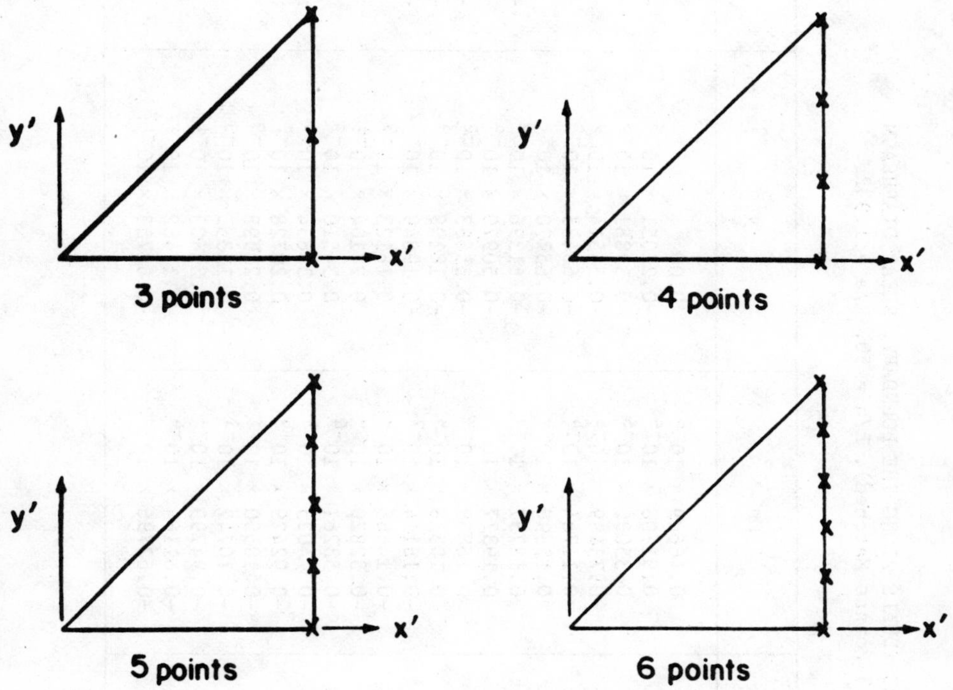

Fig. 4. Boundary Points Used with Point Matching Method.

TABLE II. RESIDUALS ALONG THE BOUNDARY, SHEAR DIAPHRAGM
(3 Points Matched), R/h = 50, R/a = 1.932

y'/a	w	Mn	v	Nn
0.000*	-0.37403×10^{-12}	0.46609×10^{-8}	0.00	-0.21830×10^{-5}
0.025	-0.35745×10^{-9}	0.91708×10^{-6}	-0.21051×10^{-9}	-0.20095×10^{-3}
0.050	-0.13672×10^{-8}	0.35090×10^{-5}	-0.39881×10^{-9}	-0.76190×10^{-3}
0.075	-0.28528×10^{-8}	0.73489×10^{-5}	-0.54514×10^{-9}	-0.15831×10^{-2}
0.100	-0.45385×10^{-8}	0.11764×10^{-4}	-0.63435×10^{-9}	-0.25073×10^{-2}
0.125	-0.60798×10^{-8}	0.15890×10^{-4}	-0.65770×10^{-9}	-0.33403×10^{-2}
0.150	-0.71008×10^{-8}	0.18757×10^{-4}	-0.61396×10^{-9}	-0.38746×10^{-2}
0.175	-0.72402×10^{-8}	0.19377×10^{-4}	-0.50970×10^{-9}	-0.39174×10^{-2}
0.200	-0.61997×10^{-8}	0.16859×10^{-4}	-0.35883×10^{-9}	-0.33204×10^{-2}
0.225	-0.37945×10^{-8}	0.10516×10^{-4}	-0.18109×10^{-9}	-0.20080×10^{-2}
0.250*	0.12013×10^{-11}	-0.16114×10^{-7}	0.19849×10^{-12}	-0.23320×10^{-5}
0.275	0.50172×10^{-8}	-0.14668×10^{-4}	0.16123×10^{-9}	0.25595×10^{-2}
0.300	0.10865×10^{-7}	-0.32829×10^{-4}	0.28104×10^{-9}	0.54203×10^{-2}
0.325	0.16937×10^{-7}	-0.53261×10^{-4}	0.34510×10^{-9}	0.82125×10^{-2}
0.350	0.22433×10^{-7}	-0.74025×10^{-4}	0.34834×10^{-9}	0.10490×10^{-1}
0.375	0.26422×10^{-7}	-0.92429×10^{-4}	0.20728×10^{-9}	0.11786×10^{-1}
0.400	0.27948×10^{-7}	-0.10500×10^{-3}	0.20998×10^{-9}	0.11698×10^{-1}
0.425	0.26188×10^{-7}	-0.10747×10^{-3}	0.11355×10^{-9}	0.10017×10^{-1}
0.450	0.20669×10^{-7}	-0.94799×10^{-4}	0.37403×10^{-10}	0.68901×10^{-2}
0.475	0.11555×10^{-7}	-0.61164×10^{-4}	0.17482×10^{-11}	0.30348×10^{-3}
0.500*	0.37090×10^{-11}	-0.67796×10^{-8}	-0.62753×10^{-12}	0.24661×10^{-5}

*Points on the boundary matched.

TABLE III. RATIO OF MAXIMUM BOUNDARY RESIDUALS TO MAXIMUM VALUES OF PHYSICAL PARAMETERS IN THE SHELL INTERIOR

No. of Points Matched	$\left(\frac{\text{Res. } w}{w}\right)$ max.	$\left(\frac{\text{Res. } M_n}{M_n}\right)$ max.	$\left(\frac{\text{Res. } v}{v}\right)$ max.	$\left(\frac{\text{Res. } N_n}{N_n}\right)$ max.
3	0.73%	1.42%	0.16%	1.07%
4	1.64%	12.25%	3.35%	4.88%
5	0.05%	1.12%	0.01%	0.04%
6	0.02%	1.00%	0.002%	0.01%

of the maximum boundary residuals. Finally, numerical results for the various point matching solutions for the different physical parameters evaluated within the shell are compared with these given by the Navier (exact) solution in Figures 5, 6, and 7. The values given at each point correspond, from top to bottom, to the point matching results using 3, 4, 5 and 6 points, sequentially. The exact results are given in parentheses.

The residuals shown in Tables II and III are low, with the exception of the particular case when four equally spaced boundary points are used. The propagation of the error in satisfying boundary conditions when four boundary points are used is evidenced in Figs. 5, 6, and 7. However, it should be noted that the resulting errors in normal deflection, bending moment, and membrane force are all less than one percent within most of the interior. This effect was observed even more vividly in the course of solving other problems with the digital computer program. That is, large boundary residuals can exist in shell problems without significantly affecting the interior of the region.

Results for a Triangular Planform

The problem of the shallow, spherical shell loaded by uniform pressure and supported along an equilateral triangular planform by shear diaphragms has no known solution in the literature. Using the five equally-spaced boundary points shown in Fig. 8, a very accurate solution was obtained, as can be seen from Table IV. In Table IV the dimension "a" is the radius from the origin (located at the centroid) to the corner point (or 2/3 of the altitude).

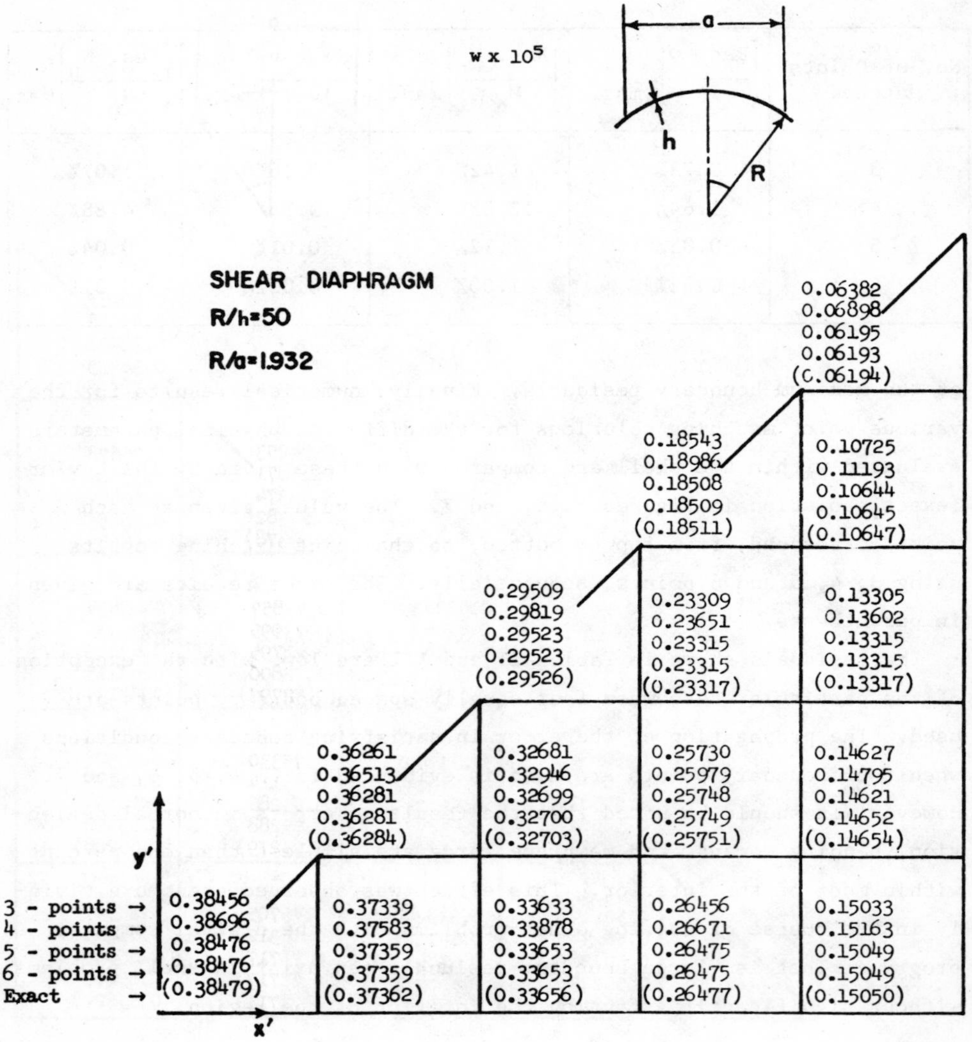

Fig. 5. Values of the Deflection at Interior Points.

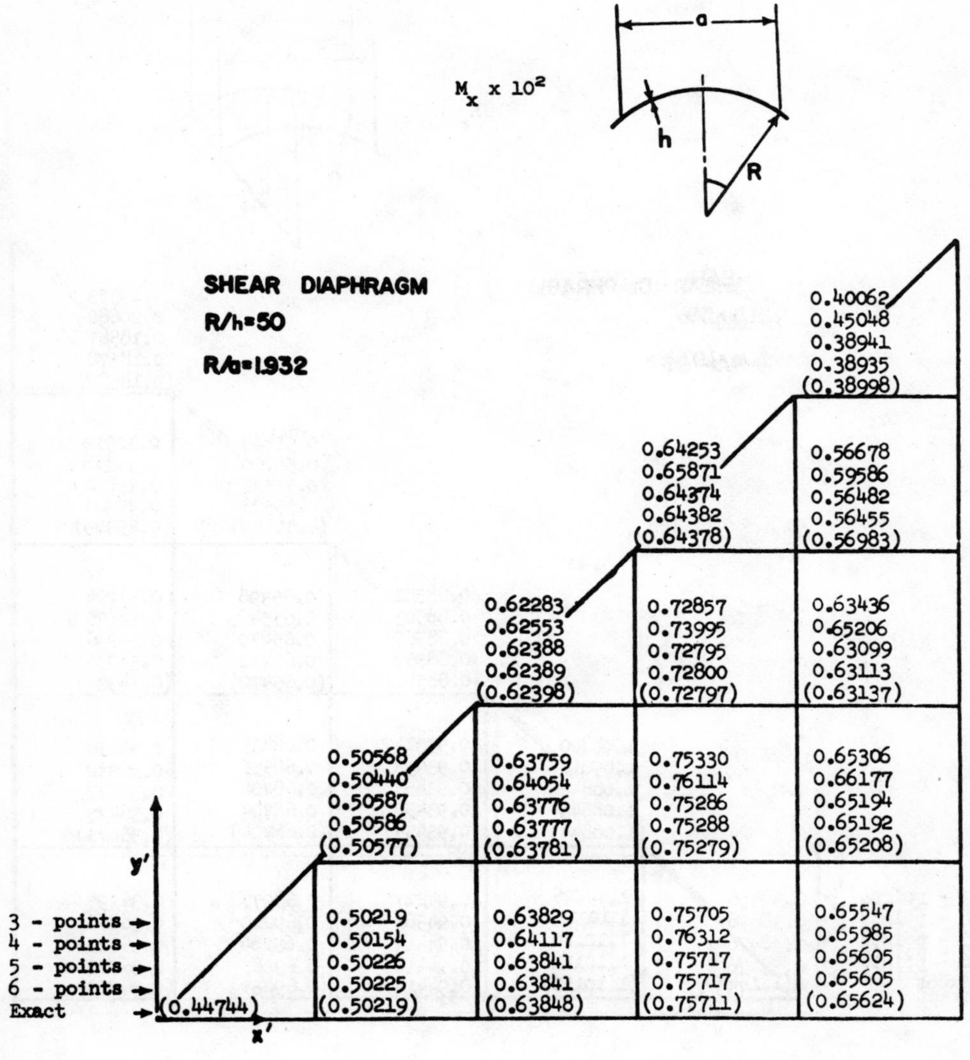

Fig. 6. Bending Moment at Interior Points.

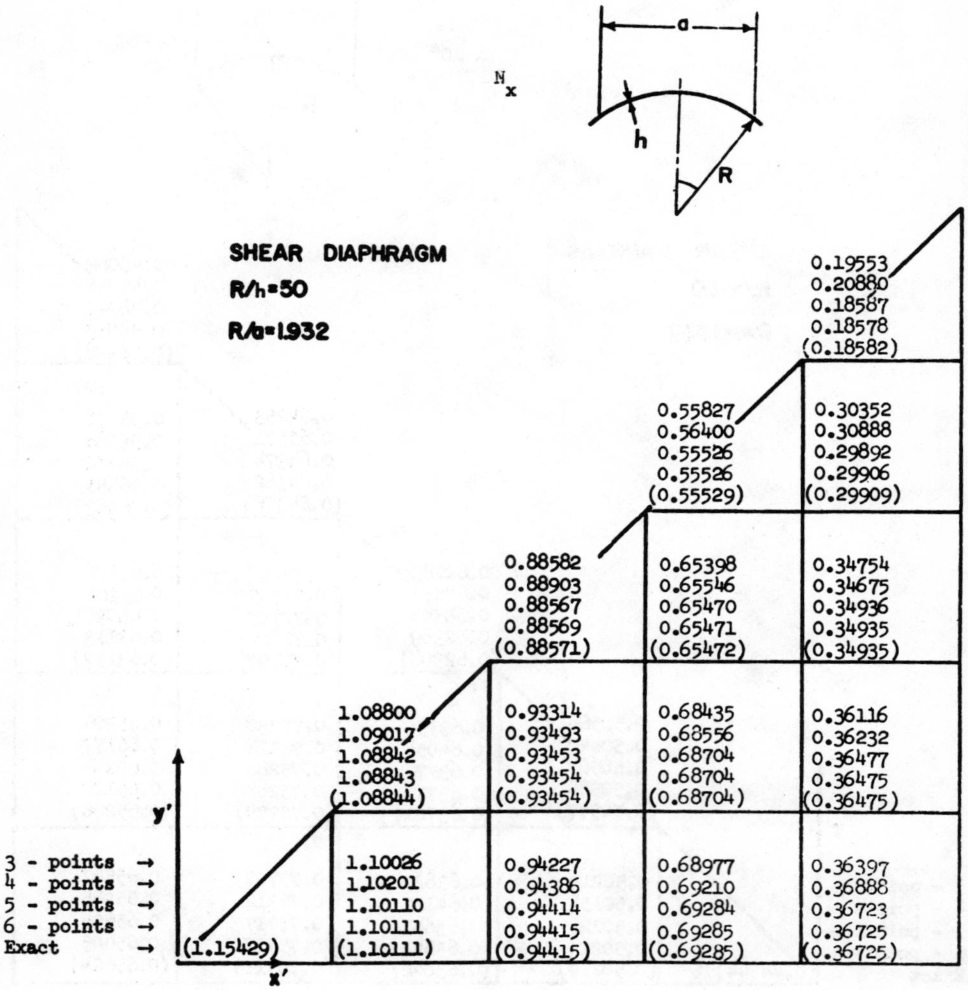

Fig. 7. Membrane Force at Interior Points.

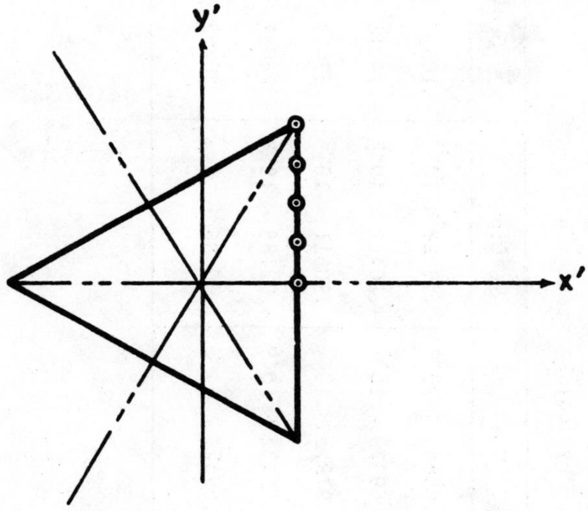

Fig. 8. Shallow Shell with Equilateral, Triangular Planform, Showing Boundary Points Matched.

TABLE IV. SPHERICAL SHELL SUPPORTED AT THE BOUNDARY BY SHEAR DIAPHRAGM TRIANGULAR PLANFORM OBTAINED BY POINT MATCHING
($R/h = 50$, $R = 1.932$, $a = 1/\sqrt{2}$, $b = a \cos \pi/3$)

a. Values of the Physical Parameters along $\theta=0$

x'/b	0.0	0.2	0.4	0.6	0.8	1.0
w	$.30354 \times 10^{-5}$	$.29241 \times 10^{-5}$	$.25664 \times 10^{-5}$	$.19328 \times 10^{-5}$	$.10577 \times 10^{-5}$	$-.11337 \times 10^{-12}$
$\frac{\partial w}{\partial n}$	.0	$-.32384 \times 10^{-5}$	$-.69373 \times 10^{-5}$	$-.10761 \times 10^{-4}$	$-.14011 \times 10^{-4}$	$-.15472 \times 10^{-4}$
M_n		$.94380 \times 10^{-2}$	$.97975 \times 10^{-2}$	$.90611 \times 10^{-2}$	$.62413 \times 10^{-2}$	$.13223 \times 10^{-7}$
u_n	.0	$-.76022 \times 10^{-7}$	$-.15352 \times 10^{-6}$	$-.22188 \times 10^{-6}$	$-.26967 \times 10^{-6}$	$-.28702 \times 10^{-6}$
N_n		.76597	.59627	.40786	.20702	$-.23916 \times 10^{-5}$

b. Residuals along the Boundary

y'/a	w	M_n	u_t	N_n
.0000*	$-.25381 \times 10^{-12}$	$.12376 \times 10^{-7}$	$.00000 \times 10^{-39}$	$-.24140 \times 10^{-5}$
.0765	$.94195 \times 10^{-12}$	$.48486 \times 10^{-8}$	$.14135 \times 10^{-11}$	$-.21756 \times 10^{-5}$
.1531*	$.42942 \times 10^{-12}$	$-.70529 \times 10^{-9}$	$.22513 \times 10^{-11}$	$-.23693 \times 10^{-5}$
.2296	$-.67536 \times 10^{-11}$	$.91259 \times 10^{-8}$	$.23975 \times 10^{-11}$	$-.31590 \times 10^{-5}$
.3062*	$-.15881 \times 10^{-10}$	$-.11645 \times 10^{-7}$	$.21843 \times 10^{-11}$	$-.25257 \times 10^{-5}$
.3827	$-.17412 \times 10^{-10}$	$-.86784 \times 10^{-7}$	$.20033 \times 10^{-11}$	$-.14379 \times 10^{-5}$
.4593*	$-.15996 \times 10^{-10}$	$-.13238 \times 10^{-7}$	$.23776 \times 10^{-11}$	$-.83745 \times 10^{-5}$
.5358	$-.26169 \times 10^{-10}$	$.45932 \times 10^{-6}$	$.37939 \times 10^{-11}$	$-.20787 \times 10^{-4}$
.6124*	$-.41424 \times 10^{-11}$	$-.22676 \times 10^{-6}$	$.48992 \times 10^{-11}$	$-.35837 \times 10^{-5}$

*Points matched on the boundary

c. Ratios of Maximum Residuals to Maximum Values of Physical Parameter within the Shell

	w	M_n	u_t	N_n
Maximum residual along the boundary	26169×10^{-10}	$.45932 \times 10^{-6}$	$.48992 \times 10^{-11}$	$.20787 \times 10^{-4}$
Maximum value of the parameter within the shell	30354×10^{-5}	$.97975 \times 10^{-2}$	$.28702 \times 10^{-6}$	.96600
Percentage of maximum residual to maximum value	0.0009%	0.0047%	0.0017%	0.0021%

REFERENCES

1. Slater, J. C., "Electron Energy Bands in Metals," Physical Review, Vol. 45, 1934, pp. 794-801.

2. Barta, J., "On the Numerical Solution of a Two Dimensional Elasticity Problem," Zeitschrift fur Angewandte Mathematik und Mechanik, Vol. 7, No. 3, 1937, pp. 184-185.

3. Conway, H. D., "The Approximate Analysis of Certain Boundary Value Problems," Journal of Applied Mechanics, Vol. 27, 1960, pp. 275-277.

4. Conway, H. D. and Leissa, A. W., "A Method for Investigating Buckling of Plates and Certain Other Eigenvalue Problems," Journal of Applied Mechanics, Vol. 27, 1960, pp. 557-558.

5. Niedenfuhr, F. W. and Leissa, A. W., "The Torsion of Prismatic Bars of Regular Polygonal Cross Section," Journal of the Aero/Space Sciences, Vol. 29, 1961, pp. 424-426.

6. Leissa, A. W. and Niedenfuhr, F. W., "A Study of the Cantilevered Square Plate Subjected to a Uniform Loading," Journal of the Aero/Space Sciences, Vol. 29, 1962, pp. 162-169.

7. Hulbert, L. E., "The Numerical Solution of Two Dimensional Problems of the Theory of Elasticity," Ph.D. Dissertation, The Ohio State Univ., 1963.

8. Leissa, A. W. and Clausen, W. E., "Application of Point Matching to Problems in Micromechanics," Fundamental Aspects of Fiber Reinforced Plastic Composites, edited by Schwartz and Schwartz, John Wiley and Sons, 1968, pp. 29-44.

9. Conway, H. D. and Leissa, A. W., "Application of the Point Matching Method to Shallow Spherical Shell Theory," Journal of Applied Mechanics, Vol. 29, 1962, pp. 745-747.

10. Clausen, W. E. and Leissa, A. W., "Stress Coupling Between Holes in Shallow Spherical Shells," Proceedings, Symposium of the International Association for Shell Structures, Leningrad, 1966.

11. Leissa, A. W. and Brann, J. H., "On the Torsion of Bars Having Symmetry Axis," International Journal of Mechanical Sciences, 1964, pp. 45-50.

12. Leissa, A. W., Hulbert, L. E., Hopper, A. T., and Clausen, W. E., "A Comparison of Approximate Methods for the Solution of Plate Bending Problems," Proceedings of the AIAA/ASME Ninth Structures, Structural Dynamics and Materials Conference, Palm Springs, Cal., April 1-3, 1968.

13. Reissner, E., "Stresses and Displacements of Shallow Spherical Shells," Journal of Mathematics and Physics, Part I, Vol. 25, 1946, pp. 80-85, Part II, Vol. 26, 1947, pp. 279-300.

14. Reissner, E., "On the Determination of Stresses and Displacements for Unsymmetrical Deformations of Shallow Spherical Shells, Journal of Mathematics and Physics, Vol. 38, 1959, pp. 16-35.

15. Niedenfuhr, F. W., Leissa, A. W., and Gaitens, M. J., "A Method of Analysis for Shallow Shells of Revolution Supported Elastically on Concentric Rings," Developments in Theoretical and Applied Mechanics, Proceedings of the Second Southeastern Conference on Theoretical and Applied Mechanics.

16. Leissa, A. W. and Kadi, A. S., "Utilization of the Point Matching Technique for Structural Shell Analysis," Final Report, Air Force Flight Dynamics Laboratory, Contract No. F 33615-67-C-1177, May, 1969.

A PROOF OF THE ACCURACY OF A SET OF SIMPLIFIED BUCKLING EQUATIONS FOR CIRCULAR CYLINDRICAL ELASTIC SHELLS[1]

D. A. Danielson
University of Virginia

J. G. Simmonds
University of Virginia

ABSTRACT

It is shown that the simplified buckling equations (derived earlier by the authors using order of magnitude arguments) for circular cylindrical elastic shells under axial compression can be derived exactly from a modified expression for the second variation of the potential energy. As a consequence, it is rigorously shown that the buckling load predicted by the simplified equations will differ from the buckling load predicted by any first approximation shell theory by a negligible amount.

INTRODUCTION

A classical problem in shell theory is to compute the axial buckling load of a circular cylindrical elastic shell subject to prescribed end conditions. Indeed, this may well be called the classical problem in shell buckling in view of the inordinate attention it has received in the literature. This high interest is easy to explain: cylindrical shells have widespread practical use, they are easy to fabricate and easy to test experimentally and, because of their simple geometry, they are the easiest of all shells to analyze mathematically.

---

1. This research was supported by the National Science Foundation under Grant Nos. GK-4629 and GP-15333.

Theoretical analyses of shell buckling are roughly of two types:

(1) Those which assume that the undeformed shell is geometrically and elastically perfect and that the pre-buckling state is adequately described by linear membrane theory (classical buckling theory).
(2) Those which attempt to include shell imperfections or nonlinear effects to account for the large discrepancies often observed between the experimental and classical buckling loads.

Here, two comments should be made in defense of classical theory. First, several recent experiments on carefully manufactured circular cylindrical shells have shown that, if initial geometric imperfections are truly small, classical theory, used with the right boundary conditions, is entirely adequate. A convincing discussion of this point is given in an excellent review article by Stein [1]. Second, the exact mathematical description of various nonclassical effects is extremely complicated; but, since small disturbances are involved, singular perturbation techniques are often applicable. In such analyses, the classical linear equations play a key role as "first approximation outer equations" or "base equations."

In the present paper, which falls into category (1), we give a rigorous derivation of a set of simple linear differential equations and boundary conditions governing the bifurcation buckling of a perfect circular cylindrical elastic shell under an axial dead load. The final equations are only slightly more complicated than the popular Donnell equations [2, 3], yet, as will be shown, they are as accurate as any that embody the assumptions of classical, first approximation shell theory [4]. (Thus, for example, our simplified equations are as accurate as the far more elaborate Flügge equations [5]). In the original derivation of these simplified equations [6, 7], order of magnitude arguments were used to justify the addition of various small terms to the stress-strain relations. The results of the present paper show that, for circular cylindrical shells, such arguments are completely valid and this, in turn, increases our confidence in their use in the analysis of shells of arbitrary geometry.

To render the derivation of the buckling equations more transparent, we first derive in Section 2 a set of simplified <u>linear</u>, <u>static</u> equations for edge loaded circular cylindrical shells. These are obtained exactly by standard variational procedures, starting from the principle of minimum potential energy. However, in place of the usual (dimensionless) uncoupled strain energy density V_ℓ of Love [8], we use the (dimensionless) modified energy density V_k of Koiter [9], which differs from Love's by terms of relative order h/R, the ratio of the shell thickness to the midsurface radius. Within the framework of first approximation shell theory, the energy densities V_ℓ and V_k are completely equivalent.

Using the results of Section 2 as a guide, we derive in Section 3 a set of simplified buckling equations exactly, starting from a modified expression for the second variation of the standard potential energy functional for dead loaded shells. The modifications consist of using an expression, V_s, for the strain energy density which differs from V_k by terms of order λ. Here λ, the dimensionless axial load, is of the order of the prebuckling strain.

In the final section, we prove rigorously that the critical buckling load λ_s^c predicted by our simplified equations differs from the critical buckling load λ_ℓ^c predicted by the unsimplified equations by terms of relative order $(h/R, \lambda_\ell^c)$.

Simplified Linear Equations

The principle of minimum potential energy states that the (dimensionless) potential functional

$$Q[\underset{\sim}{u}] = \iint_A V[\underset{\sim}{u}]dA - \int_{\partial A_s} W[\underset{\sim}{u}]ds \tag{1}$$

is an absolute minimum if and only if the midsurface displacement vector $R\underset{\sim}{u}$ satisfies the equilibrium equations over the midsurface A and all boundary conditions along the edge curve ∂A. In Eq. (1), EhV is the strain energy density, E is Young's modulus, R^2dA is the differential element of surface area, Rds is the differential element of arc along the edge, ∂A_s is that portion of the edge over which the stresses are prescribed, and EhRW is the work (per unit length) of the edge loads. Surface loads have been omitted for brevity.

Koiter [9] has shown that the simplest possible set of equations in terms of displacement components is obtained if one takes $V = V_k$, where

$$V_k = V_\ell + \varepsilon^2[-(1-\nu)\gamma_x\rho_\theta + \gamma_\theta(\rho_x+\rho_\theta) + \gamma_\theta{}^2/2$$

$$+ (1-\nu)\gamma_{x\theta}\rho_{x\theta} - 3(1-\nu)\gamma_{x\theta}^2/4] \tag{2}$$

and

$$2V_\ell = [\gamma_x^2 + \gamma_\theta^2 + 2\nu\gamma_x\gamma_\theta + 2(1-\nu)\gamma_{x\theta}^2]/(1-\nu^2)$$

$$+ \varepsilon^2[\rho_x^2 + \rho_\theta^2 + 2\nu\rho_x\rho_\theta + 2(1-\nu)\rho_{x\theta}^2] \tag{3}$$

Here

$$\varepsilon = \frac{h}{\sqrt{12(1-\nu^2)}R} \tag{4}$$

ν is Poisson's ratio, γ_x, γ_θ, and $\gamma_{x\theta}$ are extensional strains, and ρ_x/R, ρ_θ/R, and $\rho_{x\theta}/R$ are bending strains.

By solving the linear, algebraic eigenvalue problem which arises from maximizing the ratio of the second term in Eq. (2) to the first, we find that

$$|V_k-V_\ell| \le \varepsilon K V_\ell \tag{5}$$

where

$$K = \sqrt{\frac{3 - 2\nu + \sqrt{5 - 4\nu}}{2}} + \varepsilon$$

$$< 2 + \varepsilon \tag{6}$$

Koiter's modified strain energy density V_k may be expressed in terms of $\underset{\sim}{u}$ (and its derivatives) by use of the following strain-displacement relations [9, 10]:

$$\gamma_x = u', \ \gamma_\theta = v^{\cdot} + w, \ \gamma_{x\theta} = (u^{\cdot} + v')/2 \tag{7}$$

$$\rho_x = w'', \ \rho_\theta = w^{\cdot\cdot} - v^{\cdot}, \ \rho_{x\theta} = w'^{\cdot} + u^{\cdot}/4 - 3v'^{\cdot}/4 \tag{8}$$

In these equations, u, v, and w are the components of $\underset{\sim}{u}$ in the axial, circumferential, and outward radial directions, respectively. Primes and dots denote, respectively, differentiation with respect to x and θ, where Rx is axial distance and θ is angular position. With the right hand side of Eq. (1) expressed solely in terms of displacement components, the standard procedures of variational calculus may be used to obtain three equilibrium equations in terms of the displacement components.

However, with the aim of producing a functional whose Euler differential equations lead directly to the simplified equations in [6, 7], we consider the following new function $V_k^*[\underset{\sim}{\ell}, \underset{\sim}{\gamma}, \underset{\sim}{u}]$, obtained from $V_k[\underset{\sim}{u}]$ by reintroducing the extensional strains by means of Lagrange multipliers[2] ℓ_x, ℓ_θ, $\ell_{x\theta}$:

$$V_k^*[\underset{\sim}{\ell}, \underset{\sim}{\gamma}, \underset{\sim}{u}] = V_k[\underset{\sim}{u}] + \ell_x(u'-\gamma_x) + \ell_{x\theta}(u^{\cdot} + v' - 2\gamma_{x\theta})$$

$$+ \ell_\theta(v^{\cdot} + w - \gamma_\theta) \qquad (9)$$

If we now make use of the relations (7) and (8), the modified strain energy density becomes

$$V_k^*[\underset{\sim}{\ell}, \underset{\sim}{\gamma}, \underset{\sim}{u}] = (1/2)[\gamma_x^2 + \gamma_\theta^2 + 2\nu\gamma_x\gamma_\theta + 2(1-\nu)\gamma_{x\theta}^2]/(1-\nu^2)$$

$$+ (\varepsilon^2/2)(\Delta w + w)^2 + \ell_x(u'-\gamma_x) + \ell_{x\theta}(u^{\cdot} + v' - 2\gamma_{x\theta})$$

$$+ \ell_\theta(v^{\cdot} + w - \gamma_\theta) + (1-\nu)\ \varepsilon^2[(-w'w^{\cdot\cdot} - u^{\cdot}v + u^{\cdot}w^{\cdot} + v^{\cdot}w')'$$

$$+ (w'w'^{\cdot} + u'v - u'w^{\cdot} - v'w')^{\cdot}] \qquad (10)$$

where $\Delta w = w'' + w^{\cdot\cdot}$. With the use of the divergence theorem, the term in the last set of brackets, integrated over A, may be transformed into a line integral over ∂A; therefore this term will not affect the Euler differential equations of our variational problem.

The modified potential Q_k^* corresponding to $V_k^*[\underset{\sim}{\ell}, \underset{\sim}{\gamma}, \underset{\sim}{u}]$ is now a functional of the three functions $\underset{\sim}{\ell}$, $\underset{\sim}{\gamma}$, and $\underset{\sim}{u}$. It is a standard result from the calculus of variations that

$$\delta Q_k[\underset{\sim}{u}] = 0 \Longleftrightarrow \delta Q_k^*[\underset{\sim}{\ell}, \underset{\sim}{\gamma}, \underset{\sim}{u}] = 0 \qquad (11)$$

The Euler equations implied by $\delta Q_k^* = 0$ are the strain-displacement relations (7), the "stress"-strain relations

$$(1-\nu^2)\ell_x = \gamma_x + \nu\gamma_\theta,\quad (1-\nu^2)\ell_\theta = \gamma_\theta + \nu\gamma_x,\quad (1+\nu)\ell_{x\theta} = \gamma_{x\theta} \qquad (12)$$

---

2. ℓ_x, ℓ_θ, and $\ell_{x\theta}$ may be thought of as "pseudo" membrane stresses.

the equilibrium equations

$$\ell_x' + \ell_{x\theta}^{\cdot} = 0 \tag{13}$$

$$\ell_{x\theta}' + \ell_\theta^{\cdot} = 0 \tag{14}$$

$$\varepsilon^2(\Delta + 1)^2 w + \ell_\theta = 0 \tag{15}$$

and the boundary conditions, which we omit for brevity.

The general solution of Eq. (13) and Eq. (14) is

$$\ell_x = \phi^{\cdot\cdot}, \ \ell_{x\theta} = -\phi'^{\cdot}, \ \ell_\theta = \phi'' \tag{16}$$

where ϕ is an arbitrary stress function. Now observe that with the use of equations (7) and (16), the equations (12) become

$$(1-\nu^2)\phi^{\cdot\cdot} = u' + \nu(v^{\cdot} + w) \tag{17}$$

$$(1-\nu^2)\phi'' = v^{\cdot} + w + \nu u' \tag{18}$$

$$2(1+\nu)\phi'^{\cdot} = -(u^{\cdot} + v') \tag{19}$$

Eq. (19) may be written as

$$[u + (1+\nu)\phi']^{\cdot} + [v + (1+\nu)\phi^{\cdot}]' = 0 \tag{20}$$

which implies that there exists a function Ω (not necessarily single-valued) such that

$$u + (1+\nu)\phi' = -\Omega', \ v + (1+\nu)\phi^{\cdot} = \Omega^{\cdot} \tag{21}$$

Physically, $\Omega'^{\cdot}$ is the rotation about the shell midsurface normal.

In our earlier papers [6, 7], we have worked with the curvature function ζ defined by

$$\zeta = w - \Omega \tag{22}$$

With the use of Eq. (21), the displacement components u and v may be expressed in terms of the basic unknowns ϕ, ζ, and w:

$$u = [-w + \zeta - (1+\nu)\phi]'$$

$$v = [w - \zeta - (1+\nu)\phi]^{\cdot} \tag{23}$$

We note in passing that, in view of Eq. (23), any boundary conditions can be expressed in terms of the basic unknowns ϕ, ζ, and w. However, only in certain special cases (such as simple support) is it possible to express the boundary conditions in terms of less than three real unknowns.

The basic equations relating ϕ, ζ, and w are now easily obtained. Elimination of u and v from the equations (17)-(19) results in

$$w' = \Delta^2\phi$$

Substitution of Eq. (23) into Eq. (17) and Eq. (18) and rearrangement yields

$$w^{\cdot\cdot} + w = \zeta^{\cdot\cdot} + \Delta\phi \quad \text{and} \quad w'' = \zeta'' - \Delta\phi$$

Combining these results, and using Eq. (15), we obtain our final equations

$$\varepsilon^2\Delta(\Delta+1)\zeta + \phi'' = 0 \tag{24}$$

$$\Delta(\Delta+1)\phi - \zeta'' = 0 \tag{25}$$

$$w'' = \zeta'' - \Delta\phi, \quad w^{\cdot\cdot} + w = \zeta^{\cdot\cdot} + \Delta\phi \tag{26}$$

There are three essential simplifications contained in and implied by these equations. First, Poisson's ratio ν nowhere appears explicitly (it does appear in the parameter ε, but only in combination with h/R). Second, the equations (24) and (25) can be combined into the single equation

$$\varepsilon\Delta(\Delta+1)g + ig'' = 0 \tag{27}$$

for the complex-valued function

$$g = \phi + i\varepsilon\zeta \tag{28}$$

This step effectively halves the order of the governing equations. (If we introduce the stress function f, which is the static-geometric analogue of w, and use Eq. (26), we can obtain an equation identical in form to Eq. (27) for the variable $\Psi = w + i\varepsilon^{-1}f$. Such an equation was first derived in [10] with the aid of order of magnitude arguments.) And third, with ϕ, ζ, and w in hand, explicit expressions for u and v follow from Eq. (23). If one works exclusively with displacement components, the best one can do is to obtain expressions for $\Delta^2 u$ and $\Delta^2 v$ in terms of w.

In complex form, our equations resemble those derived by Sanders [11]. In fact, if small terms are neglected, our equations can be made to agree with his. By prodigous calculation, Sanders shows how his equations can be derived from a complicated expression for the strain energy density. However, in order to obtain his final simplified equations, Sanders must omit many small terms. On the other hand, we have shown that our equations follow directly and exactly from Koiter's relatively uncomplicated strain energy density.

The Simplified Buckling Equations

The equations of neutral equilibrium, or buckling equations, are obtained from the condition that the second variation $EhR^2P[\underset{\sim}{u}]$ of the potential energy[3] attains a minimum value of zero for a nonvanishing displacement field $\underset{\sim}{u}$. The vector $R\underset{\sim}{u}$ now represents the additional displacement measured from the prebuckling equilibrium state. For a circular cylindrical shell of length R under a uniform axial end load $2\pi EhR\lambda$ (positive in compression) applied at the two ends, Koiter [12] has shown that

$$P[\underset{\sim}{u}] = \int_0^{2\pi}\int_0^{\ell} \{V[\underset{\sim}{u}] - \lambda \underset{\sim}{u}'\cdot\underset{\sim}{u}'/2\}dxd\theta \tag{29}$$

The buckling equations in terms of the displacement components may be obtained by variational principles from the equation

$$\delta P[\underset{\sim}{u}] = 0 \tag{30}$$

Associated with the resulting buckling equations are many eigenvalues λ; the smallest of these is called the (dimensionless) critical buckling load λ^c.

The usual buckling equations are obtained by taking the strain energy density $V = V_\ell$ in Eq. (29). However, to obtain the simplified buckling equations presented in [6, 7], we take $V = V_s{}^*$, where $V_s{}^*$ is obtained by adding terms of order λ to the function $V_k{}^*$ as follows:

$$V_s{}^*[\underset{\sim}{\ell}, \underset{\sim}{\gamma}, \underset{\sim}{u};\lambda] = V_k{}^*[\underset{\sim}{\ell}, \underset{\sim}{\gamma}, \underset{\sim}{u}] + \lambda\left[\frac{A(\gamma_x + \nu\gamma_\theta)^2}{2(1-\nu^2)} + \frac{B\gamma_{x\theta}{}^2}{1+\nu} + \frac{(u')^2}{2}\right] \tag{31}$$

3. We have dropped the customary subscript 2 on P.

In Eq. (31)

$$A = \frac{2 + (1 - \nu)\lambda}{1 - \nu - 2\nu\lambda} \quad \text{and} \quad B = \frac{3 + \nu + 2\lambda}{2 + (1 - \nu)\lambda} \tag{32}$$

(The choice of these constants involves a considerable amount of tedious algebra with which we shall not belabor the reader.)

The Euler equations implied by

$$\delta P_s*[\underset{\sim}{\ell}, \underset{\sim}{\gamma}, \underset{\sim}{u};\lambda] = 0 \tag{33}$$

are the strain-displacement relations (7), the "stress"-strain relations

$$(1 - \nu^2)\ell_x = (1 + \lambda A)(\gamma_x + \nu\gamma_\theta), \; (1 - \nu^2)\ell_\theta = (1 + \nu^2\lambda A)\gamma_\theta$$

$$+ \nu(1 + \lambda A)\gamma_x, \; (1 + \nu)\ell_{x\theta} = (1 + \lambda B)\gamma_{x\theta} \tag{34}$$

the equilibrium equations

$$\ell_x' + \dot{\ell}_{x\theta} = 0 \tag{35}$$

$$\ell_{x\theta}' + \dot{\ell}_\theta - \lambda v'' = 0 \tag{36}$$

$$\varepsilon^2(\Delta + 1)^2 w + \ell_\theta + \lambda w'' = 0 \tag{37}$$

and the following boundary conditions on the edges x = 0, ℓ:

$$\ell_x + \varepsilon^2(1 - \nu)(\dot{v} - \ddot{w}) = 0 \quad \text{or } u = 0$$

$$\ell_{x\theta} - \varepsilon^2(1 - \nu)(\dot{u} + \dot{w}') - \lambda v' = 0 \quad \text{or } v = 0$$

$$\varepsilon^2(\Delta + 1)w' + \varepsilon^2(1 - \nu)(\ddot{u} + \ddot{w}') + \lambda w' = 0 \quad \text{or } w = 0 \tag{38}$$

$$(\Delta + 1)w + (1 - \nu)(\dot{v} - \ddot{w}) = 0 \quad \text{or } w' = 0$$

With the use of Eq. (7) and Eq. (34), it can be shown that

$$v'' = \frac{2(1 + \nu)}{1 + \lambda B}\,\ell'_{x\theta} - \frac{1 + \nu^2\lambda A}{1 + \lambda A}\,\dot{\ell}_x + \nu\dot{\ell}_\theta \tag{39}$$

In view of Eq. (39), the solution of Eq. (35) and Eq. (36) can be verified to be

$$\ell_x = (1 + \lambda C)\ddot{\phi}, \; \ell_\theta = \phi'' - \lambda\ddot{\phi}, \; \ell_{x\theta} = -(1 + \lambda C)\dot{\phi}' \tag{40}$$

where

$$C = \frac{2 + \nu + \lambda}{1 - \nu\lambda} \tag{41}$$

Now observe that with the use of Eq. (7) and Eq. (40), the relations (34) become

$$(1 - \nu^2)(1 + \lambda C)\phi^{\cdot\cdot} = (1 + \lambda A)[u' + \nu(v^{\cdot} + w)] \tag{42}$$

$$(1 - \nu^2)(\phi'' - \lambda\phi^{\cdot\cdot}) = (1 + \nu^2\lambda A)(v^{\cdot} + w) + \nu(1 + \lambda A)u' \tag{43}$$

$$2(1 + \nu)(1 + \lambda C)\phi'^{\cdot} = -(1 + \lambda B)(u^{\cdot} + v') \tag{44}$$

Rewriting Eq. (44) we obtain

$$[u + (1 + \nu)\phi']^{\cdot} + [v + (1 + \nu)(1 + \lambda D)\phi^{\cdot}]' = 0 \tag{45}$$

where

$$D = \frac{1 + \nu}{1 - \nu\lambda} \tag{46}$$

Eq. (45) implies that there exists a function Ω (not necessarily single-valued) such that

$$u + (1 + \nu)\phi' = -\Omega', \quad v + (1 + \nu)(1 + \lambda D)\phi^{\cdot} = \Omega^{\cdot} \tag{47}$$

As in Section 2, we work with the curvature function ζ, defined by Eq. (22). This leads to the following expressions for u and v in terms of the basic unknowns ϕ, ζ, and w:

$$\begin{aligned} u &= [-w + \zeta - (1 + \nu)\phi]' \\ v &= [w - \zeta - (1 + \nu)(1 + \lambda D)\phi]^{\cdot} \end{aligned} \tag{48}$$

The basic equations relating ϕ, ζ, and w may now be obtained. If u and v are eliminated from the equations (42)-(44), there results

$$w'' = \Delta^2\phi$$

Substitution of Eq. (48) into Eq. (42) and Eq. (43) and rearrangement yields

$$w^{\cdot\cdot} + w = \zeta^{\cdot\cdot} + \Delta\phi \text{ and } w'' = \zeta'' - \Delta\phi$$

Combining these results, and using Eq. (37), we obtain our final simplified buckling equations

$$\varepsilon^2\Delta(\Delta + 1)\zeta + \phi'' + \lambda(\Delta^2\phi - \phi^{\cdot\cdot}) = 0$$

$$\Delta(\Delta + 1)\phi - \zeta'' = 0$$

$$w'' = \zeta'' - \Delta\phi \tag{49}$$

$$w^{\cdot\cdot} + w = \zeta^{\cdot\cdot} + \Delta\phi$$

The buckling equations (49) are precisely those used in [7].

With the use of Eq. (40) and Eq. (48) the boundary conditions (38) may be written in terms of ϕ, ζ, and w. Since it can be shown in specific cases (see [7], for example) that small terms in the boundary conditions do not affect the buckling load significantly, we reproduce below only the dominant terms in the resulting boundary conditions at $x = 0, \ell$:

$$\phi^{\cdot\cdot} - (1 - \nu)\varepsilon^2\zeta^{\cdot\cdot} = 0 \quad \text{or} \quad w' - \zeta' + (1 + \nu)\phi' = 0$$

$$\phi'^{\cdot} + (1 - \nu)\varepsilon^2\zeta'^{\cdot} + \lambda(w'^{\cdot} - \zeta'^{\cdot}) = 0 \quad \text{or} \quad w^{\cdot} - \zeta^{\cdot} - (1 + \nu)\phi^{\cdot} = 0$$

$$\varepsilon^2[\zeta'' + (2 - \nu)(w^{\cdot\cdot} + w)]' + \lambda w' = 0 \quad \text{or} \quad w = 0 \tag{50}$$

$$\zeta'' + \nu(w^{\cdot\cdot} + w) = 0 \quad \text{or} \quad w' = 0$$

The boundary conditions (50) are the same as were used in [7].

We have shown that the simplified buckling equations can be derived exactly from the variational problem (33). The associated critical buckling load λ_s^c is shown in the next section to be related to the critical buckling load λ_ℓ^c associated with the use of Love's uncoupled energy density by $\lambda_s^c = \lambda_\ell^c[1 + O(h/R, \lambda_\ell^c)]$.

Accuracy of the Simplified, Critical Buckling Load, λ_s^c

To establish the relative accuracy of λ_s^c compared to λ_ℓ^c, we need upper and lower bounds on V_s in terms of V_ℓ.

From the definition (3) of V_ℓ, note that

$$V_\ell \geq \frac{(\gamma_x + \nu\gamma_\theta)^2}{2(1 - \nu^2)} + \frac{\gamma_\theta^2}{2} + \frac{\gamma_{x\theta}^2}{1 + \nu} = \frac{\gamma_x^2}{2} + \frac{(\gamma_\theta + \nu\gamma_x)^2}{2(1 - \nu^2)} + \frac{\gamma_{x\theta}^2}{1 + \nu} \tag{51}$$

Since λ is equal to the prebuckling axial strain there is no loss of generality if we assume $\lambda \leq 1/4$. Furthermore $0 \leq \nu \leq 1/2$; hence it follows from Eq. (32) that

$$A \leq 9, \quad B < A \tag{52}$$

With Eq. (51) and Eq. (52), it now follows from Eq. (31) that

$$|V_s - V_k| \leq 10\lambda V_\ell \tag{53}$$

that is

$$V_k - 10\lambda V_\ell \leq V_s \leq V_k + 10\lambda V_\ell \tag{54}$$

But from Eq. (5)

$$(1 - \varepsilon K)V_\ell \leq V_k \leq (1 + \varepsilon K)V_\ell \tag{55}$$

Since the shell is thin, we may certainly assume $\varepsilon \leq 1$; hence, by Eq. (6), $K < 3$. It now follows from Eq. (54) and Eq. (55) that

$$(1 - 3\varepsilon - 10\lambda)V_\ell \leq V_s \leq (1 + 3\varepsilon + 10\lambda)V_\ell \tag{56}$$

Thus, since V_ℓ is positive definite, we are guaranteed that V_s is positive definite so long as

$$|3\varepsilon + 10\lambda| < 1 \tag{57}$$

a condition which, necessarily, must be true for thin shell theory to be applicable.

The critical buckling loads λ_ℓ^c and λ_s^c are characterized by the conditions

$$\lambda_\ell^c = \min \iint V_\ell[\underset{\sim}{u}]dA \tag{58}$$

and

$$\lambda_s^c = \min \iint V_s[\underset{\sim}{u};\lambda_s^c]dA \tag{59}$$

where the minimum is taken over all sufficiently smooth displacement fields $\underset{\sim}{u}$ satisfying the kinematic boundary conditions and the normalization condition

$$(1/2)\iint \underset{\sim}{u}'\cdot\underset{\sim}{u}'dA = 1 \tag{60}$$

(The occurrence of the initial buckling load λ_s^c on the right hand side of Eq. (59) may, at first, appear strange to the reader accustomed to the conventional form of the Rayleigh quotient. However, the moral of the present paper is that if one wishes to proceed analytically then, at the expense of starting with a somewhat complicated strain energy density $V_s[\underset{\sim}{u};\lambda]$ one may obtain an uncomplicated set of reduced equations.)

Let $\underset{\sim}{u}_\ell$ and $\underset{\sim}{u}_s$ denote displacement fields satisfying, respectively, Eq. (58) and Eq. (59). Then, with the aid of Eq. (56), we have

$$\lambda_\ell^c \le \iint V_\ell[\underset{\sim}{u}_s]dA \le \frac{\iint V_s[\underset{\sim}{u}_s;\lambda_s^c]dA}{1 - 3\varepsilon - 10\lambda_s^c} \le \frac{\lambda_s^c}{1 - 3\varepsilon - 10\lambda_s^c} \tag{61}$$

and

$$\lambda_s^c \le \iint V_s[\underset{\sim}{u}_\ell;\lambda_s^c]dA \le (1 + 3\varepsilon + 10\lambda_s^c)\iint V_\ell[\underset{\sim}{u}_\ell]dA \le (1 + 3\varepsilon + 10\lambda_s^c)\lambda_\ell^c \tag{62}$$

Hence

$$(1 - 3\varepsilon - 10\lambda_s^c)\lambda_\ell^c \le \lambda_s^c \le (1 + 3\varepsilon + 10\lambda_s^c)\lambda_\ell^c \tag{63}$$

or, with the use of Eq. (57),

$$\lambda_s^c = \lambda_\ell^c[1 + O(h/R,\ \lambda_\ell^c)] \tag{64}$$

REFERENCES

1. Stein, Manuel, "Some Recent Advances in the Investigation of Shell Buckling," American Institute of Aeronautics and Astronautics Journal, Vol. 6, No. 12, 1968, pp. 2339-2345.

2. Donnell, L. H., "Stability of Thin-Walled Tubes Under Torsion," NACA Report No. 479, 1933.

3. Donnell, L. H., "A New Theory for the Buckling of Thin Cylinders Under Axial Compression and Bending," Transactions American Society of Mechanical Engineers, Vol. 56, 1934, pp. 795-806.

4. Koiter, W. T., "A Consistent First Approximation in the General Theory of Thin Elastic Shells," Proceedings, Symposium on the Theory of Thin Elastic Shells, Delft, 1959, edited by W. T. Koiter, North Holland Publishing Co., 1960, pp. 12-33.

5. Flügge, W., Stresses in Shells, Springer-Verlag, 1960, Chapter 7.

6. Danielson, D. A. and Simmonds, J. G., "Accurate Buckling Equations for Arbitrary and Cylindrical Elastic Shells," International Journal of Engineering Science, Vol. 7, 1969, pp. 459-468.

7. Simmonds, J. G. and Danielson, D. A., "New Results for Buckling Loads of Axially Compressed Cylindrical Shells Subject to Relaxed Boundary Conditions," to be published in the Journal of Applied Mechanics.

8. Love, A. E. H., A Treatise on the Mathematical Theory of Elasticity, Cambridge University Press, 1893, p. 236.

9. Koiter, W. T., "Summary of Equations for Modified, Simplest Possible Accurate Linear Theory of Thin Circular Cylindrical Shells," (unpublished notes).

10. Simmonds, J. G., "A Set of Simple, Accurate Equations for Circular Cylindrical Elastic Shells," International Journal of Solids and Structures, Vol. 2, 1966, pp. 525-541.

11. Sanders, J. L., "On the Novozhilov Circular Cylinder Theory," Division of Engineering and Applied Physics Report SM-32, Harvard University, April, 1969.

12. Koiter, W. T., "General Equations of Elastic Stability for Thin Shells," Proceedings Symposium on the Theory of Thin Shells, to Honor L. H. Donnell, University of Houston, Houston, Texas, 1967, pp. 187-228.